ELEMENTS OF INTERNAL CONTROL (ch 4)

Control environment
Risk assessment
Control activities
Information & communication
Monitoring

PRINCIPLES OF CASH MANAGEMENT (ch 4)

Keep inventory levels low
Timing of payment of liabilities
Speed up collection of receivables
Invest idle cash

BANK RECONCILIATION (ch 4)

Cash Balance (Bank Statement)	Cash Balance (Company Records)
Add: Deposits in transit	Add: Bank credits on bank statement
Less: Outstanding checks	Less: Bank debits on bank statement
Adjusted Cash Balance	Adjusted Cash Balance

Adjusted Cash Balance should be equal

CALCULATION OF INTEREST (ch 4, 8) (REVENUE OR EXPENSE)

Interest = Face value × Interest rate × Fraction of one year

OPERATING ASSETS - Depreciation (ch 7)

Depreciation Expense	xxx	
Accumulated Depreciation		xxx

Methods to calculate periodic depreciation expense:

Straight-line	$\dfrac{\text{Cost} - \text{Residual Value}}{\text{Expected Useful Life}}$
Declining-balance	Declining balance rate × book value
Units-of-Production	$\dfrac{\text{Actual Usage of Asset}}{\text{Expected Usage of Asset}} \times$ Depreciable Cost

DISPOSAL OF ASSETS (ch 7)

Proceeds from sale
Less: Book value of asset
Gain (Loss) on sale of asset

BONDS

Bonds Sold at	Yield Compared to Stated Rate	Interest Over the Life of the Bonds
Premium (above Par)	Yield < Stated Rate	Interest Expense < Interest Paid
Par	Yield = Stated Rate	Interest Expense = Interest Paid
Discount (below Par)	Yield > Stated Rate	Interest Expense > Interest Paid

Bond interest paid = Face amount of bonds × Stated interest rate

Bond interest expense = Interest paid + Discount amortization

OR Interest paid − Premium amortization

Premium amortization calculations:

Straight-line method	$\dfrac{\text{Bond discount (premium)}}{\text{Number of interest periods}}$
Effective interest method	Carrying value × effective interest rate × fraction of year

INSTALLMENT NOTES: INTEREST CALCULATION (ch 9)

Note Payable Balance at the Beginning of the Period x Interest Rate x Fraction of year

NET ACCOUNTS RECEIVABLE (ch 5)

Bad debt expense must be estimated to be recorded in the period of the sale. This results in an allowance for doubtful accounts balance until specific uncollectible accounts can be identified and removed from accounts receivable.

Percentage of credit sales method:
Estimate bad debt expense as a percentage of net credit sales. Also known as the income statement approach because the amount for the income statement account is determined first.

Aging method:
Analyze accounts receivable to determine the value of net accounts receivable. Adjust allowance for doubtful accounts accordingly. Also known as the balance sheet approach because the amount for the balance sheet account is determined first.

Adusting entry under either method:
Bad Debt Expense   xxx
    Allowance for Doubtful Accounts   xxx

STOCKHOLDERS' EQUITY (ch 10)

Capital stock { Common stock; Add'l PIC on common stock
Preferred stock; Add'l PIC on preferred stock

+ Retained earnings
− Treasury stock
Total stockholders' equity

STATEMENT OF CASH FLOWS (ch 11)

Operating activities
Net income
Add: Amortization, depreciation, losses on asset disposal, decreases in current assets, increases in current liabilities
Deduct: Gains on disposal of assets increases in current assets, decreases in current liabilities

Investing activities
Financing Activities
Net change in cash
Cash balance, beginning of year
Cash balance, end of year

NET SALES (ch 5)

Sales
− Sales discounts
− Sales returns & allowances
Net sales

COST OF GOODS SOLD MODEL (ch 6)

Beginning inventory
+ Net purchases
Cost of goods available for sale
− Ending inventory
Cost of goods sold

FINANCIAL STATEMENT ANALYSIS (ch 12)

Cross-sectional, Time-series analysis
Horizontal analysis, Vertical analysis

Ratio analysis { Liquidity ratios
Debt management ratios
Asset efficiency ratios
Profitability ratios
Stockholder ratios

DuPont analysis

INVENTORY COSTING METHODS (ch 6)

Allocates of cost of goods available for sale to ending inventory and cost of goods sold

Method	Costs in ending inventory	Cost of goods sold
Specific ID	Actual units in inventory	Actual units sold
FIFO	Most recent purchases	Earliest purchases
LIFO	Earliest purchases	Most recent purchases
Avg. cost	Weighted average of goods available	Weighted average of goods available

Cornerstones Videos

Each "Cornerstone" in the book is accompanied by a short video clip that students may view online or download onto portable video players. The clips provide clear, step-by-step examples that are consistently presented for today's visual learners. They walk students through each step of every "Cornerstone."

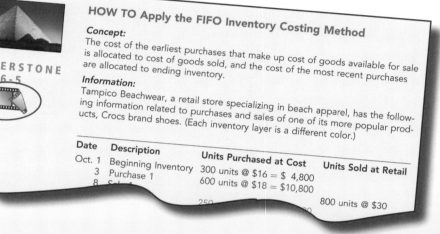

HOW TO Apply the FIFO Inventory Costing Method

Concept:
The cost of the earliest purchases that make up cost of goods available for sale is allocated to cost of goods sold, and the cost of the most recent purchases are allocated to ending inventory.

Information:
Tampico Beachwear, a retail store specializing in beach apparel, has the following information related to purchases and sales of one of its more popular products, Crocs brand shoes. (Each inventory layer is a different color.)

Date	Description	Units Purchased at Cost	Units Sold at Retail
Oct. 1	Beginning Inventory	300 units @ $16 = $ 4,800	
3	Purchase 1	600 units @ $18 = $10,800	
8		250	800 units @ $30

80% of students surveyed wanted access to video presentations to help explain the concepts.

70% of instructors who reviewed these videos indicated they would recommend or require students to use them.

"The video is excellent for students who prefer a visual presentation of the example and the concepts. It is also useful for students who missed class or don't remember class. I like this feature very much."

—Professor Michael E. Yampuler, University of Houston

"I think this series of videos will be a wonderful addition to the text. Today's generation of students appears to put much more emphasis on a 'visual' approach to learning, and this will help respond to that style."

—Professor Douglas Larson, Salem State University

To view these videos, visit the *Cornerstones* Website:
www.cengage.com/accounting/rich/videos
Password: richfinancial

CORNERSTONES

of
Financial Accounting

Current Trends Update

Jay S. Rich

Illinois State University

▲

Jefferson P. Jones

Auburn University

▲

Maryanne M. Mowen

Oklahoma State University

▲

Don R. Hansen

Oklahoma State University

SOUTH-WESTERN
CENGAGE Learning™

Australia • Brazil • Japan • Korea • Mexico • Singapore • Spain • United Kingdom • United States

SOUTH-WESTERN
CENGAGE Learning™

**Cornerstones of Financial Accounting—
Current Trends Update**

**Jay S. Rich, Jefferson P. Jones,
Maryanne M. Mowen, Don R. Hansen**

Vice President of Editorial, Business: Jack
W. Calhoun

Editor-in-Chief: Rob Dewey

Senior Acquisitions Editor: Matthew Filimonov

Supervising Development Editor:
Aaron Arnsparger

Marketing Manager: Kristen Hurd

Marketing Coordinator: Gretchen Swann

Senior Content Project Manager: Tim Bailey

Production Technology Analyst: Emily Gross

Director of Program Management:
John Barans

Senior Media Editor: Scott Fidler

Senior Manufacturing Buyer: Doug Wilke

Production Service: LEAP Publishing Services,
Inc.

Compositor: Knowledgeworks Global, Limited

Art Director: Stacy Jenkins Shirley

Cover and Internal Designer: Joe DeVine,
Red Hangar Design

Cover Image: ® Corbis/Roger Ressmeyer

For product information and technology assistance, contact us at
Cengage Learning Customer & Sales Support, 1-800-354-9706

For permission to use material from this text or product,
submit all requests online at **www.cengage.com/permissions**
Further permissions questions can be emailed to
permissionrequest@cengage.com

Exam*View*® is a registered trademark of eInstruction Corp. Windows and
PowerPoint presentation software are registered trademarks of the Microsoft
Corporation used herein under license.

Library of Congress Control Number: 2009927874

Student Edition:
ISBN-13: 978-0-538-75128-5
ISBN-10: 0-538-75128-2

South-Western Cengage Learning
5191 Natorp Boulevard
Mason, OH 45040
USA

Cengage Learning products are represented in Canada by
Nelson Education, Ltd.

For your course and learning solutions, visit **www.cengage.com**
Purchase any of our products at your local college store or at
our preferred online store **www.ichapters.com**

Printed in Canada
1 2 3 4 5 6 7 13 12 11 10 09

"This book is dedicated to our students—past, present, and future—who are at the heart of our passion for teaching."

Brief Contents

HOW TO USE **"CORNERSTONES"**— YOUR NEW **PERFECT** FOUNDATION FOR SUCCESSFUL LEARNING

Carefully crafted from the ground up, the "Cornerstones" in the text help you set up and solve fundamental calculations or procedures. And the "Cornerstones" go beyond simple preparation by focusing on the underlying accounting principle. There is a "Cornerstone" for every major concept in the book, serving as a "How To" guide. When you are able to master the foundations of financial accounting, it is easier to understand how accounting is used for decision-making in the business world.

Each "Cornerstone" has four parts: **Concept, Information, Required**, and **Solution**. Here, you can see the full process to better understand the source of each number.

The **Concept** section links the "Cornerstone" to fundamental underlying accounting concepts such as the matching principle here.

The **Information** portion of each "Cornerstone" provides the necessary data to arrive at a solution.

The **Required** section of each exhibit provides you with each step that must be solved.

The **Solution** ends each "Cornerstone," showing the calculations for each of the required steps in the problem. This helps you understand the necessary concepts.

HOW TO Compute Depreciation Expense Using the Declining Balance Method

CORNERSTONE 7-3

Concept:
As the service potential of a fixed asset declines, the cost of the asset is allocated as an expense among the accounting periods in which the asset is used and benefits are received (the matching principle).

Information:
On January 1, 2009, Morgan, Inc. acquired a machine for $50,000. Morgan expects the machine to be worth $5,000 at the end of its five-year useful life. Morgan uses the double-declining-balance method of depreciation.

Required:
1. Compute the double-declining-balance rate of depreciation for the machine.
2. Prepare a depreciation schedule that shows the amount of depreciation expense for each year of the machine's life.
3. Prepare the journal entry required to record depreciation expense in 2009.

Solution:
1. The double-declining-balance rate of depreciation (40 percent) equals twice the straight-line rate of depreciation and is calculated as follows:

$$\frac{1}{\text{Useful Life}} \times 2 = \frac{1}{5} \times 2 = \frac{2}{5} \text{ or } 40\%$$

...reciation sc...

Each "Cornerstone" has an online video offering a step-by-step presentation of the **Concept, Information, Required**, and **Solution** sections.

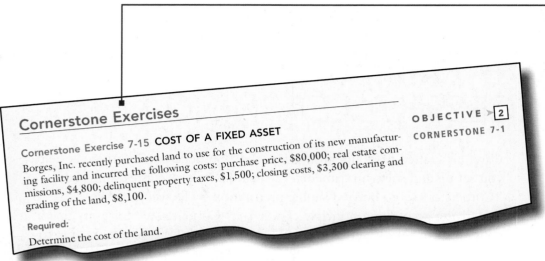

End-of-Chapter **Cornerstone Exercises** are often linked to specific "Cornerstone" features, providing a valuable reference as you complete homework. Because the Cornerstone Exercises are so closely linked to the in-chapter "Cornerstones," you quickly become an independent learner!

Cornerstone Exercises

Cornerstone Exercise 7-15 **COST OF A FIXED ASSET**

Borges, Inc. recently purchased land to use for the construction of its new manufacturing facility and incurred the following costs: purchase price, $80,000; real estate commissions, $4,800; delinquent property taxes, $1,500; closing costs, $3,300 clearing and grading of the land, $8,100.

Required:
Determine the cost of the land.

OBJECTIVE ▶ 2
CORNERSTONE 7-1

Beginning in 2006, South-Western began researching how accounting students use and read their textbooks. We personally interviewed hundreds of students.

Our **Conclusions**

- The primary driver of success in accounting is **homework**.
- Students believe a textbook helps them succeed, but they are using books differently than the previous generation.
- Students use books as a **source of examples** and descriptions to help them complete homework. They may "skim" the text before or after class, but very few read the text from beginning to end.

As a result of this research, *Cornerstones* was fine-tuned to provide you with greater efficiency and more relevance, promising better results. *Cornerstones* provides you with the confidence to be more independent, allowing you more time to learn additional concepts.

"I have recently tried the problems in *Cornerstones* and found that the step-by-step examples that are placed within the text helped extremely...I compared the chapters in *Cornerstones* to our textbook and felt that *Cornerstones* was much easier to understand by just reading the chapter."

—Katie Hogan, Student at University of Cincinnati

The *Cornerstones Learning System* is based on how students learn accounting today. This system incorporates the following key features:

- The actual "Cornerstones" within the chapters – unique to this family of texts!
- The "Cornerstones" references within the end-of-chapter Cornerstones Exercises.
- The summary of "Cornerstones" at the end of each chapter with page references.
- Online reinforcement of "Cornerstones" concepts with videos and demonstrations.

Cornerstones Videos

Each "Cornerstone" in the book is accompanied by a short video clip that you may view online or download onto your portable video player. The clips provide clear, step-by-step examples that are consistently presented for today's visual learners. They walk you through each step of every "Cornerstone."

70% of instructors who reviewed these videos indicated they would recommend or require students to use them.

80% of students surveyed wanted access to video presentations to help explain the concepts.

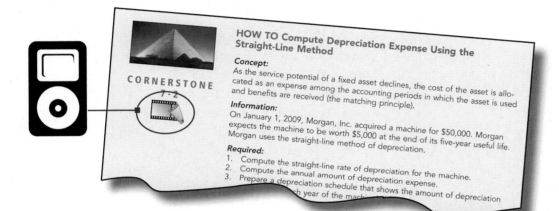

CORNERSTONE
7-2

HOW TO Compute Depreciation Expense Using the Straight-Line Method

Concept:
As the service potential of a fixed asset declines, the cost of the asset is allocated as an expense among the accounting periods in which the asset is used and benefits are received (the matching principle).

Information:
On January 1, 2009, Morgan, Inc. acquired a machine for $50,000. Morgan expects the machine to be worth $5,000 at the end of its five-year useful life. Morgan uses the straight-line method of depreciation.

Required:
1. Compute the straight-line rate of depreciation for the machine.
2. Compute the annual amount of depreciation expense.
3. Prepare a depreciation schedule that shows the amount of depreciation

To view the Cornerstone Videos, visit the *Cornerstones* Companion Website at

www.cengage.com/accounting/rich/videos

and enter the following password: **richfinancial**

"The video is excellent for students who prefer a visual presentation of the example and the concepts. It is also useful for students who missed class or don't remember class. I like this feature very much."

—Professor Ron Lazer, University of Houston

Text Website
www.cengage.com/accounting/rich

Ensure understanding and success with this comprehensive, resource-rich support site. It's everything you need to ensure positive outcomes. The interactive student study center provides interactive quizzes and online tools that encourage learning.

ACKNOWLEDGMENTS
AND
THANKS

We would like to thank the following reviewers and focus group participants who helped shape *Cornerstones of Financial Accounting*:

Gilda Agacer, Monmouth University

Markus Ahrens, St. Louis Community College—Meramec

Sheryl J. Alley, Ball State University

Felix E. Amenkhienan, Radford University

Janice Ammons, Quinnipiac University

Keith Atkinson, University of Central Arkansas

Don Babbitt, St. Louis Community College—Florissant Valley

Monica Banyi, Oregon State University

Rick Barnhart, Grand Rapids Community College

Progyan Basu, University of Maryland

D'Arcy Becker, University of Wisconsin—Eau Claire

Mark Bezik, Idaho State University

Swati Bhandarkar, The University of Georgia

L. Charles Bokemeier, Michigan State University

Anna Marie Boulware, St. Charles Community College

Linda Bressler, University of Houston—Downtown

Daniel R. Brickner, Eastern Michigan University

Robert Bromley, Central Michigan University

Molly Brown, James Madison University

Philip Brown, Harding University

Laurie Burney, Mississippi State University

Marci L. Butterfield, University of Utah

Sharon N. Campbell, University of North Alabama

Eugene Cardamone, Hudson Valley Community College

Joseph M. Catalina, Hudson Valley Community College

Gayle Chaky, Dutchess Community College

Barbara Chaney, University of Montana

Chak-Tong Chau, University of Houston—Downtown

Alan Cherry, Loyola Marymount University

Robert Churchman, Harding University

Scott Colvin, Naugatuck Valley Community College

Joan Cook, Milwaukee Area Tech College

John M. Coulter, Western New England College

Sue Counte, St. Louis Community College

John Crawford, Tarrant County College—South

Patricia E. Creech, Northeastern Oklahoma A&M

Marcia A. Croteau, University of Maryland—Baltimore County

Jefferson T. Davis, Weber State University

Araya Debessay, University of Delaware

Donna Dietz, North Dakota State University

Cathy Duffy, Carthage College

Dave Eichelberger, Athens State University

Susan W. Eldridge, University of Nebraska—Omaha

Caroline Falconetti, Nassau Community College

Janice Feingold, Moorpark College

Linda Flaming, Monmouth University

Michael Foland, Southwestern Illinois College

Diana R. Franz, University of Toledo

Mary Ella Gainor, Bryant University

Lisa Gillespie, Loyola University of Chicago

Alan Glazer, Florida A&M University

Carol M. Graham, University of San Francisco

Rita Grant, Grand Valley State University

Anthony Greig, Purdue University

Harriette O. Griffin, North Carolina State University

Gretchen Guenther, College of St. Rose

Michael J. Gurevitz, Montgomery College

Umit Gurun, University of Texas—Dallas

Jack O. Hall, Jr., Western Kentucky University

Cynthia Jackson, Northeastern University

Robert C. Jinkens, University of Hawaii

William Johnstone, Montgomery College

David Juriga, St. Louis Community College

Catherine Katagiri, College of St. Rose

Anthony Craig Keller, Missouri State University

Ann Galligan Kelley, Providence College

D. Donald Kent, Jr., The College at Brockport

J. Edward Ketz, The Pennsylvania University

John M. Killoran, University of Missouri—St. Louis

Mehmet Kocakulah, University of Southern Indiana

John Koeplin, University of San Francisco

Emil Koren, St. Leo University

Robert Kravet, Fairfield University

Tim Krumwiede, Bryant University

Marie Kulesza, University of Hartford

Cathy Xanthaky Larson, Middlesex Community College

Douglas A. Larson, Salem State College

Janice E. Lawrence, University of Nebraska—Lincoln

Ron Lazer, University of Houston

Natasha Librizzi, Milwaukee Area Tech College

William Link, University of Missouri—St. Louis

James M. Lukawitz, University of Memphis

Maria Mari, Miami Dade College

Dawn W. Massey, Fairfield University

Lynn Mazzola, Nassau Community College

Debra McGilsky, Central Michigan University

Yaw M. Mensah, Rutgers University

Paul H. Mihalek, Central Connecticut State University

Jeanne Miller, Cypress College

Julian Lowell Mooney, Georgia Southern University

Arabian Morgan, Orange Coast College

Barbara Nyden, Missouri State University

Judy Peterson, Monmouth College

Ray Pfeiffer, University of Massachusetts

Catherine Plante, University of New Hampshire

Kathy S. Pollock, Indiana University-Purdue University—Ft. Wayne

K. K. Raman, University of North Texas

Robert Rambo, Providence College

Aaron L. Reeves Jr., St. Louis Community College—Forest Park

Dolores Rinke, Purdue University—Calumet

Anwar Salimi, California State Polytechnic University—Pomona

Gary Schader, Kean University

Joann Segovia, Minnesota State University—Moorhead

Randy Serrett, University of Houston—Downtown

Lewis Shaw, Suffolk University

J. Riley Shaw, The University of Mississippi

Robbie Sheffy, Tarrant County College

Lynn Shuster, Central Pennsylvania College

Kathleen Simons, Bryant University

Gerald Smith, University of Northern Iowa

Sheldon R. Smith, Utah Valley State College

Nancy Snow, University of Toledo

Joanie Sompayrac, University of Tennessee—Chattanooga

John Stancil, Florida Southern College

Vic Stanton, Stanford University

William Talbot, Montgomery College

Suzanne Traylor, University at Albany—SUNY

Nancy Uddin, Monmouth University

Joan Van Hise, Fairfield University

John Varga, Orange Coast College

Andrea B. Weickgenannt, Northern Kentucky University

Anne R. Wessely, St. Louis Community College—Meramec

Catherine H. West, University of Massachusetts

Scott White, Lindenwood University

Marvin Williams, University of Houston—Downtown

Satina V. Williams, Marist College

Jeffrey Wong, University of Nevada—Reno

Christian Wurst, Temple University

Donald E. Wygal, Rider University

Dr. Michael Yampuler, University of Houston

Kathryn Yarbrough, University of North Carolina—Charlotte

Special thanks to hundreds of students at the following schools for their valuable feedback:

Austin Community College

Arizona State University

California Polytechnic University—Pomona

Central Connecticut State University

Dalton State University

Eastern Illinois University

Glendale Community College

Miracosta College

Northeastern Illinois University

Northern Kentucky University

Purdue University

Richard J. Daley College

Sinclair Community College

St. Norbert College

SUNY College at Oneonta

University of Cincinnati

University of Georgia

University of Massachusetts—Amherst

University of Massachusetts—Boston

University of Missouri—St. Louis

University of Wisconsin—LaCrosse

Western Oregon University

Xavier University

Contents

About the **Authors**

Dr. Jay S. Rich is an Associate Professor of Accounting at Illinois State University. He received his B.S., M.S., and Ph.D. from the University of Illinois. Prior to entering the Ph.D. program, he worked as an auditor at Price Waterhouse & Co. in Chicago and earned his CPA in 1985. He has published articles in *The Accounting Review, Auditing: A Journal of Practice & Theory, Accounting Horizons, Organizational Behavior and Human Decision Processes, Accounting Organizations and Society,* among others and served on the editorial board of *Auditing: A Journal of Practice & Theory*. He has been awarded both the Outstanding Dissertation Award and Notable Contribution to the Literature Award by the Audit Section of the American Accounting Association. His primary teaching interest is financial accounting and he has taught numerous courses at the undergraduate, masters, and doctoral levels. His outside interests include his family, travel, reading, and watching sports.

Dr. Jefferson P. Jones is the PricewaterhouseCoopers Associate Professor of Accounting in the School of Accountancy at Auburn University. He received his Bachelor's and Master of Accountancy degrees from Auburn University and his Ph.D. from Florida State University. Professor Jones has received numerous teaching awards: he is the recipient of the 2004 Auburn University College of Business McCartney Teaching Award, the 2008, 2007, 2006, 2005, 2003, and 2001 Beta Alpha Psi Outstanding Teaching Award, and the 2000 Auburn University School of Accountancy Teaching Award. He has also been recognized in *Who's Who Among America's Teachers* (2002 and 2004). Professor Jones holds a CPA certificate in the state of Alabama and previously worked for Deloitte & Touche. Professor Jones is a coauthor of *Intermediate Accounting*. He has also published articles in professional journals, including *Advances in Accounting, Review of Quantitative Finance and Accounting, Issues in Accounting Education, International Journal of Forecasting, The CPA Journal, Managerial Finance, Journal of Accounting and Finance Research,* and *The Journal of Corporate Accounting and Finance*. Professor Jones has made numerous presentations around the country on research and pedagogical issues. He is a member of the American Accounting Association, the American Institute of Certified Public Accountants (AICPA), and the Alabama Society of CPAs (ASCPA). Professor Jones is married, has two children, and enjoys playing golf.

Dr. Dan L. Heitger is Associate Professor of Accounting and Co-Director of the Center for Business Excellence at Miami University. He received his Ph.D. from Michigan State University and his undergraduate degree in accounting from Indiana University. He actively works with executives and students of all levels in developing and teaching courses in managerial and cost accounting, risk management and business reporting. He co-founded an organization that provides executive education for large international organizations. His interactions with business professionals, through executive education and the Center, allow him to bring a current and real-world perspective to his writing. His published research focuses on managerial accounting and risk management issues and has appeared in *Harvard Business Review, Behavioral Research in Accounting, Issues in Accounting Education, Journal of Accountancy, and Management Accounting Quarterly*. His outside interests include hiking with his family in the National Park system.

Dr. Maryanne M. Mowen is Associate Professor of Accounting at Oklahoma State University. She received her Ph.D. from Arizona State University. She brings an interdisciplinary perspective to teaching and writing in cost and management accounting, with degrees in history and economics. She also teaches classes in ethics and the impact of the Sarbanes-Oxley Act on accountants. Her scholarly research is in the areas of management accounting, behavioral decision theory, and compliance with the Sarbanes-Oxley Act. She has published articles in journals such as *Decision Science, The Journal of Economics and Psychology,* and *The Journal of Management Accounting Research*. Dr. Mowen has served as a consultant to mid-sized and Fortune 100 companies, and works with corporate controllers on management accounting issues. Outside the classroom, she enjoys hiking, traveling, reading mysteries, and working crossword puzzles.

Dr. Don R. Hansen is the Head of the School of Accounting and Kerr McGee Chair at Oklahoma State University. He received his Ph.D. from the University of Arizona in 1977. He has an undergraduate degree in mathematics from Brigham Young University. His research interests include activity-based costing and mathematical modeling. He has published articles in both accounting and engineering journals including *The Accounting Review, The Journal of Management Accounting Research, Accounting Horizons,* and *IIE Transactions*. He has served on the editorial board of *The Accounting Review*. His outside interests include family, church activities, reading, movies, and watching sports.

1

Accounting and the Financial Statements

After studying Chapter 1, you should be able to:

1. Explain the nature of accounting.

2. Identify the forms of business organizations and the types of business activities.

3. Describe the relationships shown by the fundamental accounting equation.

4. Prepare a classified balance sheet and understand the information it communicates.

5. Prepare an income statement and understand the information it communicates.

6. Prepare the statement of retained earnings and understand the information it communicates.

7. Understand the information communicated by the statement of cash flows.

8. Describe the relationships among the financial statements.

9. Describe other information contained in the annual report and the importance of ethics in accounting.

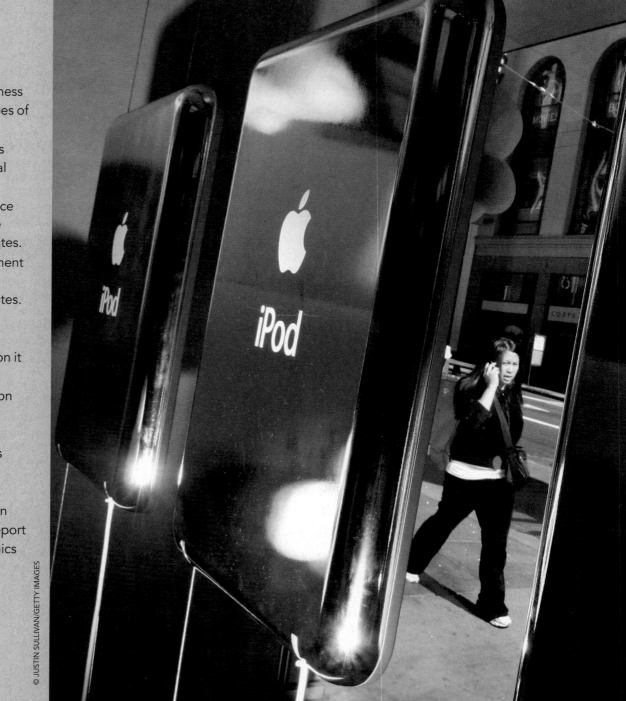

© JUSTIN SULLIVAN/GETTY IMAGES

Experience Financial Accounting
with Apple

In 1976, Steve Jobs and Steve Wozniak, the founders of **Apple Computer, Inc.**[1] began building personal computers in the garage of Jobs' parents. By 1984, Apple had become a leader in the personal computing industry, and its Macintosh computer is regarded by many as a key contributor to the development of the desktop publishing market. Apple appeared invincible. However, the development of Microsoft's Windows operating system and several product failures led many to predict the end of one of the computer industry's most prominent companies. How could a company with such a bright future experience failure? And, perhaps more remarkable, how could a company on the verge of extinction, experience the kind of success that Apple has recently experienced? With the introduction of the iMac, the iPod, and the iTunes Store, Apple's stock price increased from approximately $7 per share in June 1998 to more than $120 in June 2007 as shown in the chart below.

What type of information can help someone predict the successes of a company like Apple? A good place to start is with the financial information contained in a company's annual report. This financial information is provided in the form of financial statements—a summary of the results of a company's operations. A study of a company's financial statements will give you insights into a company that will aid you in your investment decisions. It will help you determine how successful a company has been in the past as well as its prospects for the future. While this information is easily accessible and free of charge, your final judgment on a company's future prospects will be influenced by how well you understand the information contained in its financial statements.

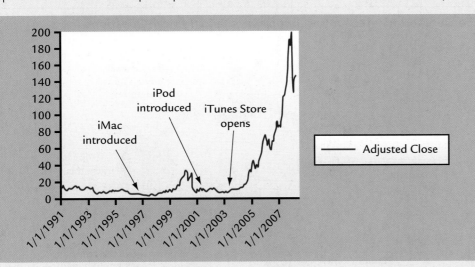

iPod introduced

iMac introduced

iTunes Store opens

Adjusted Close

[1] In February 2007, Apple Computer Inc. changed its name to Apple Inc. to reflect that the future of Apple lies beyond simply the personal computer.

OBJECTIVE ▶ 1

Explain the nature of accounting.

What Is Accounting?

Our economy is comprised of many different businesses. Some companies, such as Apple Inc., focus on providing goods, which for Apple take the form of Macintosh computers, iPod portable digital music players, iPhone cellular phones, or downloadable music. Other companies are primarily concerned with providing services. For example, **Walt Disney** offers a variety of entertainment services from theme parks to motion pictures. While most entities, like Apple and Disney, exist in order to earn a profit, some are organized to achieve some other benefit to society (e.g., school districts exist to meet the educational needs of a community). Regardless of their objective, all entities use accounting to plan future operations, make decisions, and evaluate performance.

Accounting is the process of identifying, measuring, recording, and communicating financial information about a company's activities so decision makers can make informed decisions. Accounting information is useful because it helps people answer questions and make better decisions.

The demand for accounting information comes from both inside and outside the business. Inside the business, managers use accounting information to help them plan and make decisions about the company. For example, they can use accounting information to predict the consequences of their future actions and to help decide which actions to take. They also use accounting information to control the operations of the company and evaluate the effectiveness of their past decisions. Employees use accounting information to help them judge the future prospects of their company, which should translate into future promotion opportunities. Outside the business, investors use accounting information to evaluate the future prospects of a company and decide where to invest their money. Creditors use accounting information to evaluate whether to loan money to a company. Even governments use accounting information to determine taxes owed by companies, to implement regulatory objectives, and to make policy decisions. This demand for accounting information is summarized by Exhibit 1-1.

Accounting is more than the process of recording information and maintaining accounting records—activities that are frequently called bookkeeping. Accounting is the "language of business". That is, accounting can be viewed as an information system that communicates the economic activities of a company to interested parties. The focus of this book is on providing information that satisfies the needs of external decision-makers (outside demand) and is termed **financial accounting**. The objectives of financial accounting involve providing decision-makers with information that assists them in assessing the amounts, timing, and uncertainties of a company's future

---

Exhibit 1-1

The Demand for Accounting Information and Typical Questions

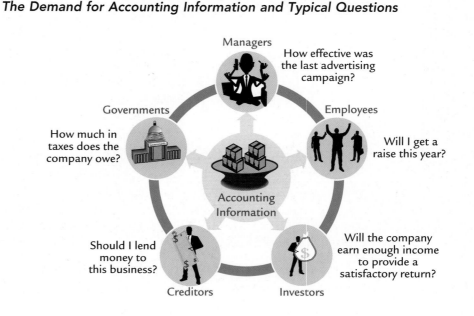

cash flows. This information is provided through four basic financial statements: the balance sheet, the income statement, the statement of retained earnings, and the statement of cash flows.

In this chapter, we will discuss the basic functioning of the accounting system within a business. We will address the following questions:

- What forms do businesses take?
- What are the basic activities in which businesses engage?
- How does the accounting system report these activities?
- How can decision-makers use the information provided by the accounting system?

Regardless of your major or future plans, knowledge of accounting and the ability to use accounting information will be critical to your success in business.

CONCEPT Q&A

How will accounting affect my life?

Possible Answer:

The business that sells us goods or services uses accounting to keep track of how much money it received as well as the cost of operating the business. Calculating the amount of tax that is due to the government requires accounting. When we invest our money, we should use accounting to understand a company's business and its prospects for the future. Plans that we make for the future often involve accounting to determine how much money we will need. Accounting will impact many aspects of our daily lives.

Businesses: Forms and Activities

OBJECTIVE ▶ 2
Identify the forms of business organizations and the types of business activities.

Accounting identifies, measures, records, and communicates financial information about an accounting entity. An accounting entity is a company that has an identity separate from that of its owners and managers and for which accounting records are kept. This text emphasizes accounting for entities which take one of three different forms: sole proprietorship, partnership, or corporation.

Forms of Business Organization

A **sole proprietorship** is a business owned by one person. Sole proprietorships, which account for more than 70 percent of all businesses, are usually small, local businesses such as restaurants, photography studios, retail stores, or website providers. This organizational form is popular due to the simplicity and low cost of formation. While a sole proprietorship is an accounting entity separate from its owner, the owner is personally responsible for the debt of the business. Sole proprietorships can be formed or dissolved at the wishes of the owner.

A **partnership** is a business owned jointly by two or more individuals. Small businesses and many professional practices of physicians, lawyers, and accountants, are often organized as partnerships. Relative to sole proprietorships, partnerships provide increased access to financial resources as well as access to the individual skills of each of the partners. Similar to sole proprietorships, partnerships are accounting entities separate from the owner-partners; however, the owner-partners are jointly responsible for all the debt of the partnership.[2] Finally, the partnership is automatically dissolved when any partner leaves the partnership; of course, the remaining partners may form a new partnership and continue to operate.

A **corporation** is a business organized under the laws of a particular state. A corporation, such as Apple, is owned by one or more persons called *stockholders,* whose ownership interests are represented by shares of stock. A primary advantage of the corporate form is the ability to raise large amounts of money (capital) by issuing shares of stock. Unlike a sole proprietorship or a partnership, a corporation is an "artificial person" and the stockholders' legal responsibility for the debt of the business is limited to the amount they invested in the business. In addition, shares of stock can be easily transferred from one owner to another through capital markets without affecting the corporation that originally issued the stock. The ability to raise capital by selling new shares, the limited legal liability of owners, and the transferability of the shares give the corporation an advantage over other forms of business

---

[2] Many professional partnerships—including the largest public accounting firms—have been reorganized as *limited liability partnerships* (LLPs), which protect the personal assets of the partner from being used to pay partnership debts.

organization. However, corporate shareholders generally pay more taxes than owners of sole proprietorships or partnerships. Exhibit 1-2 illustrates the advantages and disadvantages of each form of organization.

While the combined number of sole proprietorships and partnerships greatly exceeds that of corporations, the majority of business in the United States is conducted by corporations. Therefore, this book emphasizes the corporate form of organization.

Exhibit 1-2

Forms of Business Organization

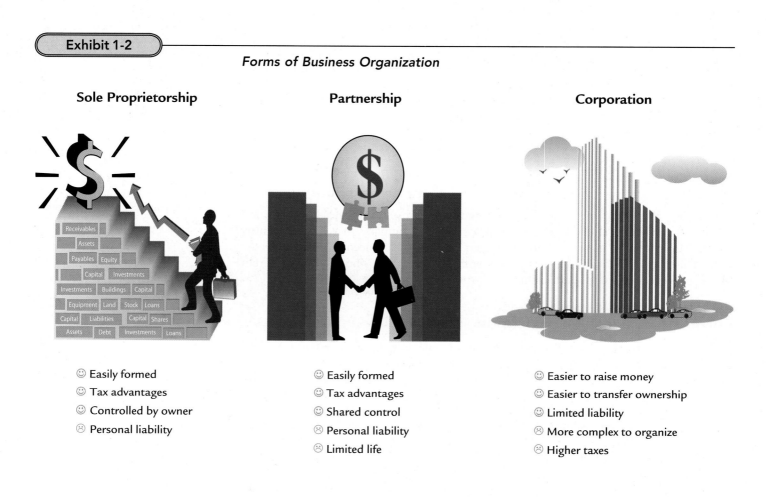

Sole Proprietorship	Partnership	Corporation
☺ Easily formed	☺ Easily formed	☺ Easier to raise money
☺ Tax advantages	☺ Tax advantages	☺ Easier to transfer ownership
☺ Controlled by owner	☺ Shared control	☺ Limited liability
☹ Personal liability	☹ Personal liability	☹ More complex to organize
	☹ Limited life	☹ Higher taxes

DECISION-MAKING & ANALYSIS

Choice of Organizational Form

Joe Brooks, who is starting a campus-area bookstore, is in the process of choosing among three organizational forms—sole proprietorship, partnership, or corporation. Brooks has enough personal wealth to finance 40 percent of the business, but he must get the remaining 60 percent from other sources. The following are questions that Brooks must consider before deciding which form of entity to establish:

1. *How does organizational form impact Brooks' ability to obtain the needed funds?*

   Whichever type of organizational form Brooks chooses, the additional 60 percent of the funds needed could be borrowed from a bank. However, if it proves difficult to get banks to support a new business, partnerships and corporations offer advantages over sole proprietorships. The advantage resides in the ability to obtain funds from a partner or through the issuance of stock.

2. *What is the impact of organizational form on control of the business?*

   A sole proprietorship would offer Brooks the most control over the operations of the business. A partnership would transfer a 60 percent controlling interest to one or more partners who would join Brooks. Similarly, a corporation would transfer a 60 percent controlling interest to other stockholders. However, if the stock were widely dispersed among many investors, Brooks might retain effective control of operations with a 40 percent interest.

Business Activities

Regardless of the form of a business, all businesses engage in a multitude of activities that can be categorized as financing, investing, or operating activities. These activities are illustrated in Exhibit 1-3. Because a major function of accounting is to identify, measure, record, and communicate information about these activities to interested parties, we will take a closer look at these activities.

Financing Activities

A company's financing activities include obtaining the funds necessary to begin and operate a business. These funds come from either issuing stock or borrowing money. Most companies use both types of financing to obtain funds.

When a corporation borrows money from another entity such as a bank, it must repay the amount borrowed. The person to whom the corporation owes money is called a **creditor**. This obligation to repay a creditor is termed a **liability** and can take many forms. A common way for a corporation to obtain cash is to borrow money with the promise to repay the amount borrowed plus interest at a future date. Such borrowings are commonly referred to as *notes payable*. A special form of note payable that is used by corporations to obtain large amounts of money is called a *bond payable*.

In addition to borrowing money from creditors, a corporation may issue shares of stock to investors in exchange for cash. The dollar amount paid to a corporation for these shares is termed *common stock* and represents the basic ownership interest in a corporation. As of September 29, 2007, Apple had issued 872,328,972 shares of common stock. The corporation is not obligated to repay the stockholder the amount invested; however, many corporations distribute a portion of their earnings to stockholders on a regular basis. These distributions are called *dividends*.

Creditors and stockholders have a claim on the **assets**, or economic resources, of a corporation. However, the claims on these resources differ. In the case of financial difficulty or distress, the claims of the creditors (called liabilities) must be paid prior to the claims of the stockholders (called **stockholders' equity**). The stockholders' claims are considered a residual interest in the assets of a corporation that remain after deducting its liabilities.

Investing Activities

Once a corporation has obtained funds through its financing activities, it buys assets that enable a corporation to operate. For example, Apple has bought approximately $1.8 billion in land, buildings, machinery, and equipment

Exhibit 1-3

Business Activities

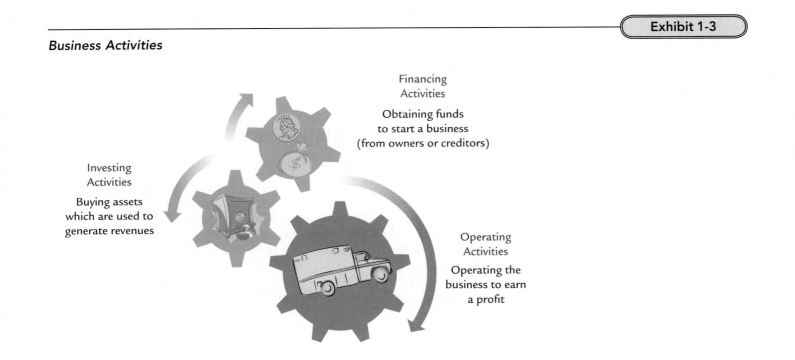

Financing
Activities

Obtaining funds
to start a business
(from owners or creditors)

Investing
Activities

Buying assets
which are used to
generate revenues

Operating
Activities

Operating the
business to earn
a profit

that it uses in its operations. The corporation may also obtain intangible assets that lack physical substance, such as copyrights and patents. Apple reported $337 million of intangible assets related to technology and trademarks that it uses in its operations. The purchase (and sale) of the assets that are used in operations (commonly referred to as property, plant, and equipment) are a corporation's investing activities.

Regardless of its form, assets are future economic benefits that a corporation controls. The assets purchased by a corporation vary depending on the type of business that the corporation engages in, and the composition of these assets is likely to vary across different companies and different industries. For example, in 2007, property, plant, and equipment made up approximately 7 percent of Apple's total assets. This is typical of many technology companies. In contrast, property, plant, and equipment made up 66 percent of the total assets of Southwest Airlines, a company that relies heavily on airplanes to produce revenue.

Operating Activities   Once a corporation has acquired the assets that it needs, it can begin to operate. While different businesses have different purposes, they all want to generate revenue. **Revenue** is the increase in assets that results from the sale of products or services. For example, Apple reported revenue of approximately $24.6 billion in 2007. In addition to revenue, assets such as *cash, accounts receivable* (the right to collect an amount due from customers), *supplies,* and *inventory* (products held for resale) often result from operating activities.

To earn revenue, a corporation will incur various costs or expenses. **Expenses** are the cost of assets used, or the liabilities created, in the operation of the business. Apple reported expenses of $15.852 billion related to the cost of iPods and other products sold in 2007.

The liabilities that arise from operating activities can be of different types. For example, if a corporation purchases goods on credit from a supplier, the obligation to repay the supplier is called an *account payable.* As of September 29, 2007, Apple reported approximately $4.9 billion of accounts payable. Other examples of liabilities created by operating activities include *wages payable* (amounts owed to employees for work performed) and *income taxes payable* (taxes owed to the government).

The results of a company's operating activities can be determined by comparing revenues to expenses. If revenues are greater than expenses, a corporation has earned **net income**. If expenses are greater than revenues, a corporation has incurred a **net loss**.

OBJECTIVE ▶ 3
Describe the relationships shown by the fundamental accounting equation.

Communication of Accounting Information

The financing, investing, and operating activities of a company are recorded by accounting systems in the form of detailed transactions. To effectively communicate a company's activities to decision-makers, these detailed transactions are summarized and reported in a set of standardized reports called **financial statements**. The role of financial statements is to provide information that will help investors, creditors, and others make judgments and predictions that serve as the basis for the various decisions they make. Financial statements help to answer questions such as those shown in Exhibit 1-4.

The Four Basic Financial Statements

Companies prepare four basic financial statements:

- The **balance sheet** reports the resources (assets) owned by a company and the claims against those resources (liabilities and stockholders' equity) at a specific point in time.
- The **income statement** reports how well a company has performed its operations (revenues, expenses, and income) over a period of time.
- The **statement of retained earnings** reports how much of the company's income was retained in the business and how much was distributed to owners for a period of time.[3]
- The **statement of cash flows** reports the sources of a company's cash inflow and the uses of a company's cash over a period of time.

[3] Information contained in the statement of retained earnings is often included in a more comprehensive statement of changes in stockholders' equity, which describes changes in all components of stockholders' equity.

Exhibit 1-4

Questions Answered by Financial Statements

How much better off is the
company at the end of the
year than it was at the
beginning of the year?

What are the economic
resources of the company
and the claims against those
resources?

From what sources did a
company's cash come and for
what did the company
use cash during the year?

While financial statements can be prepared for any point or period of time (e.g., monthly, quarterly, or annually), most companies prepare financial statements at the end of each month, quarter, and year. Note that the balance sheet is a point-in-time description, whereas the other financial statements are period-of-time descriptions that explain the business activities between balance sheet dates as shown in Exhibit 1-5.

These four statements are prepared and issued at the end of the year, and frequently companies issue statements monthly or quarterly to satisfy the users' needs for timely information. The annual statements usually are accompanied by supporting information and explanatory material called the notes to the financial statements.

While these financial statements provide the kind of information users want and need, the financial statements do not interpret this information. The financial statement user must use his or her general knowledge of business and accounting to interpret the financial statements as a basis for decision-making. One of the main objectives of this text is help you develop an ability to interpret and analyze real financial statements.

The Fundamental Accounting Equation

To understand financial statements, it is necessary that you understand how the accounting system records, classifies, and reports information about business activities. The **fundamental accounting equation** illustrates the foundation of the accounting system.

Exhibit 1-5

Financial Statement Time Periods

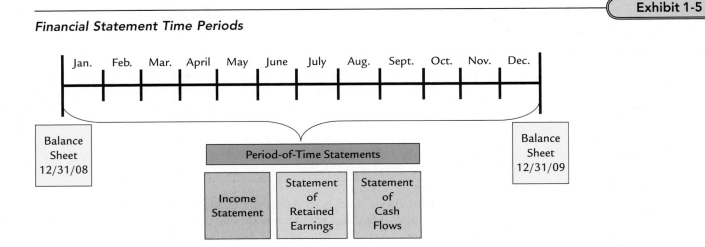

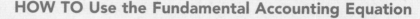

$$Assets = Liabilities + Stockholders'\ Equity$$

The fundamental accounting equation captures two basic features of any company. The left side of the accounting equation shows the assets, or economic resources of a company. The right side of the accounting equation indicates who has a claim on the company's assets. These claims may be the claims of creditors (liabilities) or they may be the claims of owners (stockholders' equity).

The implication of the fundamental accounting equation is that what a company owns (its assets) must always be equal to what it owes (its liabilities and stockholders' equity). Cornerstone 1-1 illustrates this key relationship implied by the fundamental accounting equation.

**CORNERSTONE
1-1**

HOW TO Use the Fundamental Accounting Equation

Concept:
A company's resources (its assets) must always equal the claims on those resources (its liabilities and stockholders' equity).

Information:
On January 1, 2009, Gundrum Company reported assets of $125,000 and liabilities of $75,000. During 2009, assets increased by $44,000 and stockholders' equity increased by $15,000.

Required:
1. What is the amount reported for stockholders' equity on January 1, 2009?
2. What is the amount reported for liabilities on December 31, 2009?

Solution:
1. Stockholders' equity on January 1, 2009, is $50,000. This amount is calculated by rearranging the fundamental accounting equation as follows:

$$Assets = Liabilities + Stockholders'\ Equity$$
$$\$125,000 = \$75,000 + Stockholders'\ Equity$$
$$Stockholders\ equity = \$125,000 - \$75,000 = \underline{\mathbf{\$50,000}}$$

2. At December 31, 2009, liabilities are $104,000. This amount is computed by adding the change to the appropriate balance sheet elements and then rearranging the fundamental accounting equation as follows:

$$Assets = Liabilities + Stockholders'\ Equity$$
$$(\$125,000 + \$44,000) = Liabilities + (\$50,000 + 15,000)$$
$$Liabilities = (\$125,000 + \$44,000) - (\$50,000 + 15,000)$$
$$= \$169,000 - \$65,000 = \underline{\mathbf{\$104,000}}$$

The fundamental accounting equation will be used to capture all of the economic activities recorded by an accounting system. In Chapter 2, this equation will be expanded and used to analyze specific transactions and events.

OBJECTIVE ▶ 4

Prepare a classified balance sheet and understand the information it communicates.

The Classified Balance Sheet

The purpose of the balance sheet is to report the financial position of a company (its assets, liabilities, and stockholders' equity) at a specific point in time. The relationship between the elements of the balance sheet is given by the fundamental accounting equation (Assets = Liabilities + Stockholders' Equity). Note that the balance sheet gets its name because the economic resources of a company (assets) must always equal, or be in balance with, the claims against those resources (liabilities and stockholders' equity).

The balance sheet is organized, or classified, to help users identify the fundamental economic similarities and differences between the various items within the balance sheet. These classifications help users answer questions such as (1) how a company obtained its resources and (2) whether a company will be able to pay its obligations when they become due. While companies often use different classifications and different levels of detail on their balance sheets, some common classifications are shown in Exhibit 1-6.

Let's examine the balance sheet classifications in more detail by looking at Apple's balance sheet shown in Exhibit 1-7. With regard to the heading of the financial statement, several items are of interest. First, the company for which the accounting information is collected and reported is clearly defined. Second, the title of the financial statement follows the name of the company. Third, the specific date of the statement is listed. Apple operates on a fiscal year that ends in September. A **fiscal year** is an accounting period that runs for one year. While many companies adopt a fiscal year that corresponds to the calendar year, others adopt a fiscal year that more closely corresponds with their business cycle. Finally, Apple reports its financial results rounded to the nearest millions of dollars. Large companies often round the amounts presented to make for a more clear presentation. For Apple, the reported cash amount of $9,352 is actually $9,352,000,000.

Current Assets

The basic classification of a company's assets is between current and noncurrent items. In a typical company, it is reasonable to designate one year as the dividing line between current and noncurrent items. However, if the operating cycle of a company is longer than one year, it may be necessary to extend this dividing line beyond one year so that it corresponds to the length of the operating cycle. The **operating cycle** of a company is the average time that it takes a company to purchase goods, resell the goods, and collect the cash from customers. In other words, **current assets** consist of cash and other assets that are reasonably expected to be converted into cash within one year or one operating cycle, whichever is longer. Because most companies

Exhibit 1-6

Common Balance Sheet Classifications

How did the company get it?

What does the company have?

ASSETS:
Current assets (e.g., cash, accounts receivable, inventories)
Long-term investments
Property, plant, and equipment, (e.g., land, equipment)
Intangible assets (e.g., patents, copyrights)

LIABILITIES:
Current liabilities (e.g., accounts payable, salaries payable)
Long-term liabilities (e.g., notes payable, bonds payable)

STOCKHOLDERS' EQUITY:
Contributed capital (e.g., common stock)
Retained earnings

Exhibit 1-7

Classified Balance Sheet of Apple Inc.

Apple Inc.
Balance Sheet*
September 29, 2007
(in millions of dollars)

ASSETS

Current assets:		
Cash	$ 9,352	
Short-term investments	6,034	
Accounts receivable	1,637	
Inventories	346	
Other current assets	4,587	
Total current assets		$21,956
Property, plant, and equipment:		
Land and buildings	$ 762	
Machinery and equipment	2,079	
Less: accumulated depreciation	(1,009)	
Total property, plant, and equipment		1,832
Intangible assets		337
Other assets		1,222
Total assets		$25,347

LIABILITIES AND STOCKHOLDERS' EQUITY

Current liabilities:		
Accounts payable	$4,970	
Salaries payable	254	
Unearned revenue	1,410	
Other current liabilities	2,665	
Total current liabilities		$ 9,299
Long-term liabilities:		1,516
Total liabilities		$10,815
Stockholders' equity:		
Contributed capital	$5,368	
Retained earnings	9,101	
Other equity**	63	
Total stockholders' equity		14,532
Total liabilities and stockholders' equity		$25,347

*The balance sheet information was taken from the annual report of Apple Inc. and has been summarized and reformatted by the authors.
**The $63 million of other equity reported by Apple represents accumulated other comprehensive income. The accounting for accumulated other comprehensive income is beyond the scope of this text and is not discussed.

have operating cycles less than one year, we will use the one-year dividing line to distinguish between current and noncurrent items. Common types of current assets are:

• Cash
• Short-term investments or marketable securities—investments in the stocks and bonds of other companies as well as government securities
• Accounts receivable—the right to collect an amount due from customers
• Inventories—goods or products held for resale to customers
• Other current assets—a "catch-all" category that includes items such as prepaid expenses (advance payments for rent, insurance, and other services) and supplies

Current assets are listed on the balance sheet in order of liquidity or nearness to cash. That is, the items are reported in the order in which the company expects to convert them into cash.

Noncurrent Assets

Assets that are not classified as current are classified as long-term or noncurrent assets. These include (1) long-term investments, (2) property, plant, and equipment, (3) intangible assets, and (4) other noncurrent assets.

Long-term investments are similar to short-term investments, except that the company expects to hold the investment for longer than one year. This category also includes land or buildings that a company is not currently using in operations. Apple does not currently report any long-term investments, but if it did, they would be reported immediately before property, plant, and equipment.

Property, plant, and equipment represents the tangible, long-lived, productive assets used by a company in its operations to produce revenue. This category includes land, buildings, machinery, manufacturing equipment, office equipment, and furniture. Apple reported property, plant, and equipment of $1,832 million, representing 7.2 percent ($1,832 ÷ $25,347) of its total assets. Because property, plant, and equipment helps to produce revenue over a number of years, companies assign, or allocate, a portion of the asset's cost as an expense in each period in which the asset is used. This process is called *depreciation*. The *accumulated depreciation* shown on Apple's balance sheet represents the total amount of depreciation that the company has expensed over the life of its assets. Because accumulated depreciation is subtracted from the cost of an asset, it is called a *contra-asset*.

Intangible assets are similar to property, plant, and equipment in that they provide a benefit to a company over a number of years; however, these assets lack physical substance. Examples of intangible assets include patents, copyrights, trademarks, and goodwill. *Other noncurrent assets* is a catch-all category that includes items such as deferred charges (long-term prepaid expenses) and other miscellaneous noncurrent assets.

> ## CONCEPT Q&A
>
> There are many classifications on the balance sheet that are essentially subtotals. Is it really important to place accounts within the right category or is it enough to simply understand if they are assets, liabilities, or stockholders' equity?
>
> ---
>
> **Possible Answer:**
> It is critical that you be able to identify accounts as assets, liabilities, or stockholders' equity accounts. However, the classifications are also important. Financial accounting is concerned with communicating useful information to decision-makers. These classifications provide decision-makers with critical information about the structure of assets, liabilities, and stockholders' equity that assists them in understanding a company's financial position.

Current Liabilities

Current liabilities are closely related to current assets. **Current liabilities** consist of obligations that will be satisfied within one year or the operating cycle, whichever is longer. These liabilities can be satisfied through the payment of cash or by providing goods or services. **Current liabilities are typically listed in the order in which they will be paid** and include:

- Accounts payable—an obligation to repay a vendor or supplier for merchandise supplied to the company
- Salaries payable—an obligation to pay an employee for services performed
- Unearned revenue—an obligation to deliver goods or perform a service for which a company has already been paid
- Interest payable—an obligation to pay interest on money that a company has borrowed
- Taxes payable—an obligation to pay taxes on a company's income

Long-Term Liabilities and Stockholders' Equity

Long-term liabilities are the obligations of the company that will require payment beyond one year or the operating cycle, whichever is longer. Common examples are:

- Notes payable—an obligation to repay cash borrowed at a future date
- Bonds payable—a form of an interest-bearing note payable issued by corporations in an effort to attract a large amount of investors

Stockholders' equity is the final major classification on a company's balance sheet. Stockholder's equity arises from two sources:

- Contributed capital—the owners' contributions of cash and other assets to the company (includes the common stock of a company)
- Retained earnings—the accumulated net income of a company that has not been distributed to owners in the form of dividends

If a firm has been profitable for many years, and if its stockholders have been willing to forgo large dividends, retained earnings may be a large segment of equity. Apple reported approximately $9.1 billion of retained earnings at September 29, 2007 which represents over 62 percent of its total stockholders' equity.

Together, a company's liabilities and equity make up the **capital** of a business. Apple has debt capital, capital raised from creditors, of approximately $10.8 billion (total liabilities). Of this, approximately $9.3 billion comes from current creditors, while approximately $1.5 billion comes from long-term creditors. Apple's equity capital, which is the capital raised from stockholders, is approximately $14.5 billion (total stockholders' equity).

Using the fundamental accounting equation and the common classifications of balance sheet items, a company will prepare its balance sheet. Cornerstone 1-2 illustrates the steps in the preparation of a classified balance sheet.

CORNERSTONE 1-2

HOW TO Prepare a Classified Balance Sheet

Concept:
The balance sheet reports the financial position of a company (its assets, liabilities, and stockholders' equity) at a specific point in time.

Information:
Hightower Inc. reported the following account balances at December 31, 2009:

Inventories	$ 2,300	Accounts receivable	$ 4,200	Accounts payable	$ 3,750
Land	12,100	Cash	2,500	Common stock	14,450
Salaries payable	1,200	Equipment	21,000	Patents	2,500
Retained earnings	11,300	Accumulated depreciation	5,800	Notes payable	8,100

Required:
Prepare Hightower Inc.'s balance sheet at December 31, 2009.

Solution:
The preparation of a classified balance sheet involves five steps:

1. Prepare a heading that includes the name of the company, the title of the financial statement, and the time period covered.
2. List the assets of the company in order of their liquidity or nearness to cash. Use appropriate classifications. Add the assets and double underline the total.
3. List the liabilities of the company in order of their time to maturity. Use appropriate classifications.
4. List the stockholders' equity balances with appropriate classifications.
5. Add the liabilities and stockholders' equity and double underline the total.

In general, only the first items in a column as well as any subtotals or totals have dollar signs. Also when multiple items exist within a classification, these items are grouped together in a separate column (to the left of the main column) and their total is placed in the main column.

Hightower Inc.
Balance Sheet
December 31, 2009

} Step 1

ASSETS

Current assets:		
Cash	$ 2,500	
Accounts receivable	4,200	
Inventories	2,300	
Total current assets		$ 9,000
Property, plant, and equipment:		
Land	$12,100	
Equipment	21,000	
Less: accumulated depreciation	(5,800)	
Total property, plant, and equipment		27,300
Intangible assets:		
Patents		2,500
Total assets		$38,800

Step 2

LIABILITIES AND STOCKHOLDERS' EQUITY

Current liabilities:		
Accounts payable	$ 3,750	
Salaries payable	1,200	
Total current liabilities		$ 4,950
Long-term liabilities:		
Notes payable		8,100
Total liabilities		$13,050
Stockholders' equity:		
Common stock	$14,450	
Retained earnings	11,300	
Total stockholders' equity		25,750
Total liabilities and stockholders' equity		$38,800

Step 3 / Step 4 / Step 5

Using Balance Sheet Information

The balance sheet conveys important information about the structure of assets, liabilities, and stockholders' equity to users of financial statements. For example, the relationship between current assets and current liabilities gives users insights into a company's **liquidity**—a company's ability to pay obligations as they become due. Two useful measures of liquidity are **working capital** (current assets − current liabilities) and the **current ratio** (current assets ÷ current liabilities). Working capital and current ratios for a company are helpful to an investor when these numbers are compared to those of other companies in the same industry. It is even more helpful to look at the trend of these measures over several years.

Because current liabilities will be settled with current assets, Apple's working capital of $12,657 million ($21,956 million − $9,299 million) signals that it has adequate funds with which to pay its current obligations. Because working capital is expressed in a dollar amount, the information it can convey is limited. For example, comparing Apple's working capital of $12,657 million to **Dell**'s working capital of $2,148 million would be misleading since Apple is more than three times as large (in

DECISION-MAKING & ANALYSIS

Assessing the Creditworthiness of a Prospective Customer

Thin Inc., a newly organized health club in Des Moines, Iowa, has approached the regional office of NordicTrack to purchase $50,000 worth of exercise equipment. Thin Inc. offers to pay the full amount in six months plus 9 percent interest. John Peterson, the regional credit manager for NordicTrack has asked you, a member of his staff, to evaluate the creditworthiness of Thin Inc. and make a recommendation. At your request, Thin Inc. provides the following figures from its balance sheet:

Current Assets		Current Liabilities	
Cash	$10,000	Accounts payable	$25,000
Accounts receivable	50,000	Notes payable	30,000
Supplies	4,000	Current portion of mortgage payable	18,000
Total	$64,000	Total	$73,000

Allowing a company to purchase assets on credit requires evaluating the debtor's ability to repay the loan out of current assets. You raise the following questions to determine Thin's ability to repay the short-term loan:

1. *What is the present relationship between Thin's current assets and current liabilities?*

   Thin's current liabilities exceed current assets by $9,000 ($64,000 − $73,000) resulting in negative working capital. In addition, its current ratio is 0.88 ($64,000 ÷ $73,000).

2. *Is there likely to be any change in the relationship between current assets and current liabilities during the period of the loan?*

   There is no evidence that Thin's liquidity problem will improve. Actually, it appears that Thin will have difficulty in paying its current liabilities as they come due. Thus it seems unrealistic for Thin to take on additional current liabilities at this time.

3. *Would you allow Thin Inc. to purchase the exercise equipment on credit?*

   You recommend that, unless Thin can demonstrate how it will pay its current short-term obligations as well as the additional funds that would be owed to NordicTrack, short-term credit should not be extended.

terms of net assets). The current ratio is an alternative measure of liquidity that allows comparisons to be made between different companies. For example, Apple's current ratio of 2.36 ($21,956 million ÷ $9,299 million) can be compared with its competitors (e.g., Dell's current ratio is 1.12).[4] Apple's current ratio tells us that for every dollar of current liabilities, Apple has $2.36 of current assets. When compared to Dell, Apple is much more liquid.

OBJECTIVE ▶ 5
Prepare an income statement and understand the information it communicates.

The Income Statement

The income statement reports the results of a company's operations—the sale of goods and services and the associated cost of operating the company—for a given period. The long-term survival of a company depends on its ability to produce net income by earning revenues in excess of expenses. Income enables a company to pay for the capital it uses (dividends to stockholders and interest to creditors) and attract new capital necessary for continued existence and growth. Investors buy and sell stock and creditors loan money based on their beliefs about a company's future performance. The past income reported on a company's income statement provides investors with information about a company's ability to earn future income.

[4] Information for Dell was obtained from Dell's fiscal year 2007 annual report that ended on February 2, 2007.

Elements of the Income Statement

The income statement consists of two major items: revenues and expenses. An income statement for Apple is presented in Exhibit 1-8.

Examining the heading of the income statement, you should notice that it follows the same general format as the balance sheet—it indicates the name of the company, the title of the financial statement, and the time period covered by the statement. However, the income statement differs from the balance sheet in that it covers a period of time instead of a specific date.

Revenues are the increase in assets that result from the sale of products or services. Revenues can arise from different sources and have different names depending on the source of the revenue. *Sales revenue* arises from the principal activity of the business. For Apple, its sales revenue comes from sales of hardware (e.g., iPod, Macintosh computers, iPhone), software (operating systems), peripheral products and accessories, digital content (e.g., iTunes store sales) and service and support. Apple, like most other companies, generally recognizes sales revenue in the period that a sale occurs. Revenues also can be generated from activities other than the company's principal operations (e.g., nonoperating activities). For example, in addition to sales of its products, Apple also earns *interest income* from investments.

Expenses are the cost of resources used to earn revenues during a period. Expenses have different names depending on their function. Apple's income statement in Exhibit 1-8 reports five different expenses. *Cost of sales* (often called *cost of goods sold*) is the cost to the seller of all goods sold during the accounting period.[5] *Selling, general, and administrative expenses* are the expenses that a company incurs in selling goods, providing services, or managing the company that are not directly related to production. These expenses include advertising expenses, salaries paid to salespersons or managers, depreciation on administrative buildings and expenses related to insurance, utilities, property taxes, and repairs. *Research and development expense* represents the cost of developing new products. *Other expense* is a catch-all category used to capture other miscellaneous expenses incurred by the company. *Income tax expense* represents the income taxes paid on the company's pretax income.

Net income, or net earnings, is the difference between total revenues and expenses. Apple reported net income of $3,496 million ($24,653 million − $21,157 million). If total expenses are greater than total revenues, the company would report a net loss. Cornerstone 1-3 shows how to prepare an income statement.

Exhibit 1-8

Income Statement

Apple Inc.
Income Statement*
For the fiscal year ended September 29, 2007
(in millions of dollars)

Revenues:		
Net sales	$24,006	
Interest income	647	$24,653
Expenses:		
Cost of sales	$15,852	
Selling, general, and administrative expenses	2,963	
Research and development expense	782	
Other expenses	48	
Income tax expense	1,512	21,157
Net income		$ 3,496

*The income statement information was taken from the annual report of Apple Inc. and has been summarized and reformatted by the authors.

[5] We will discuss procedures for calculating cost of sales in a later chapter.

CORNERSTONE
1-3

HOW TO Prepare an Income Statement

Concept:
The income statement reports the results of a company's operations (revenues less expenses) for a given period of time.

Information:
Hightower Inc. reported the following account balances for the year ending December 31, 2009:

Cost of sales	$31,300	Interest expense	$ 540
Salaries expense	8,800	Sales revenue	50,600
Insurance expense	700	Depreciation expense	1,500
Interest revenue	1,200	Rent expense	2,100
Income tax expense	2,000		

Required:
Prepare Hightower Inc.'s income statement for the year ending December 31, 2009.

Solution:
The preparation of an income statement involves four steps:

1. Prepare a heading that includes the name of the company, the title of the financial statement, and the time period covered.
2. List the revenues of the company, starting with sales revenue (or service revenue) and then listing other revenue items. Add the revenues to get total revenue.
3. List the expenses of the company, usually starting with cost of sales (if it exists). Add the expenses to get total expenses.
4. Subtract the expenses from the revenues to get net income (or net loss if expenses exceed revenues). Double-underline net income.

In general, only the first items in a column as well as any subtotals or totals have dollar signs. Also when multiple items exist within a classification, these items are grouped together in a separate column (to the left of the main column) and their total is placed in the main column.

Hightower Inc.
Income Statement
For the Year Ended December 31, 2009

$\left.\right\}$ Step 1

Revenues:		
Sales revenue	$50,600	
Interest revenue	1,200	
Total revenues		$51,800

$\left.\right\}$ Step 2

Expenses:		
Cost of sales	$31,300	
Salaries expense	8,800	
Rent expense	2,100	
Depreciation expense	1,500	
Insurance expense	700	
Interest expense	540	
Income tax expense	2,000	
Total expenses		46,940
Net income		$ 4,860

$\left.\right\}$ Step 3

$\left.\right\}$ Step 4

Income Statement Formats

Companies prepare their income statements in one of two different formats. The format that we illustrated in Cornerstone 1-3 is called a *single-step income statement*. In a single-step income statement, there are only two categories: total revenues and total expenses. Total expenses are subtracted from total revenues in a *single step* to arrive at net income. The advantage of a single-step income statement is its simplicity.

A second income statement format is the *multiple-step income statement*. The multiple-step income statement provides classifications of revenues and expenses that financial statement users find useful. A multiple-step income statement contains three important subtotals:

1. **Gross margin (gross profit)**—the difference between net sales and cost of sales (or cost of goods sold)
2. **Income from operations**—the difference between gross margin and operating expenses
3. **Net income**—the difference between income from operations and any nonoperating revenues and expenses

A multiple-step income statement for Apple is shown in Exhibit 1-9.

Let's examine these three classifications, First, the difference between net sales and cost of goods sold is reported as a company's *gross margin* or *gross profit*. Gross margin represents the initial profit made from selling a product, but it is *not* a measure of total profit because other operating expenses have not yet been subtracted. However, gross margin is closely watched by managers and other financial statement users. A change in a company's gross margin can give insights into a company's current pricing and purchasing policies, thereby providing insight into the company's future performance.

Second, *income from operations* is computed by subtracting operating expenses from gross margin. Operating expenses are the expenses the business incurs in selling goods or providing services and managing the company. Operating expenses typically include research and development expenses, selling expenses, and general and administrative expenses. Income from operations indicates the level of profit produced by the principle activities of the company. Apple can increase its income from operations by either increasing its gross margin or decreasing its operating expenses.

Exhibit 1-9

Multiple-Step Income Statement

Apple Inc.
Income Statement*
For the fiscal year ended September 29, 2007
(in millions of dollars)

Net sales	$24,006	
Cost of sales	15,852	
Gross margin		$8,154
Operating expenses:		
Research and development expense	$ 782	
Selling, general, and administrative expenses	2,963	
Total operating expenses		3,745
Income from operations		$4,409
Other income and expense:		
Interest income	$ 647	
Other expenses	(48)	599
Income before income taxes		$5,008
Income tax expense		1,512
Net income		$3,496

*The income statement information was taken from the annual report of Apple Inc. and has been summarized and reformatted by the authors.

Exhibit 1-10

Typical Nonoperating Items

Other Revenues and Gains

Interest revenue on investments

Dividend revenue from investments
    in stock of other companies

Rent revenue

Gains on sale of property, plant,
    and equipment

Other Expenses and Losses

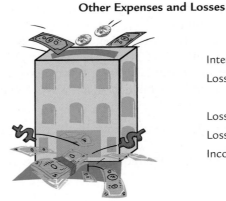

Interest expense from loans

Losses from sale of property,
    plant, and equipment

Losses from accidents or vandalism

Losses from employee strikes

Income tax expense

Finally, a multiple-step income statement reports nonoperating activities in a section which is frequently called *other income and expenses*. *Nonoperating activities* are revenues and expenses from activities other than the company's principle operations. They include gains and losses from the sale of equipment and other items that were not acquired for resale. For many companies, the most important nonoperating item is interest. Exhibit 1-10 lists some common nonoperating items.

These nonoperating items are subtracted from income from operations to obtain income before taxes. Income tax expense is then subtracted to obtain net income.

Regardless of the format used, notice that there is no difference in the amount of the revenue or expense items reported. That is, net income is the same under either the single-step or the multiple-step format. The only difference is how the revenues and expenses are classified.

Using Income Statement Information

The income statement provides information about the future profitability and growth of a company. **Earnings per share**, which measures the net income earned for each share of common stock is probably one of the most frequently cited ratios in financial analysis.[6] Examining earnings per share ratios (and other financial information) for a company over time, investors can gain insight into the earnings performance and profitability of a company.

For example, assume that you want to invest in one of two companies, either Growth, Inc., or Stagnation Company. Your first step is to examine some key elements from the current income statements of each company:

Growth, Inc.		Stagnation Company	
Sales revenue	$1,000,000	Sales revenue	$1,000,000
Gross margin	$400,000	Gross margin	$400,000
Net income	$50,000	Net income	$50,000
Number of shares	20,000 shares	Number of shares	10,000 shares
Earnings per share	$2.50	Earnings per share	$5.00

Next, examine a five–year summary of sales revenue and net income for the two firms in order to detect trends for each company over time.

Growth, Inc.

	2006	2007	2008	2009	2010
Sales revenue	$625,000	$700,000	$750,000	$875,000	$1,000,000
Net income	$30,000	$36,000	$40,000	$42,000	$50,000
Earnings per share	$1.50	$1.80	$2.00	$2.10	$2.50

[6] Earnings per share will be discussed in more depth in Chapter 10.

Stagnation Company

	2006	2007	2008	2009	2010
Sales revenue	$1,025,000	$975,000	$997,000	$950,000	$1,000,000
Net income	$51,000	$48,000	$46,000	$49,000	$50,000
Earnings per share	$5.10	$4.80	$4.60	$4.90	$5.00

As an investor, you seek those investments that will provide the largest return at the lowest risk. One factor considered to be associated with large returns is growth, and accounting information can help you judge a company's growth potential. In assessing the growth potential for our two hypothetical companies, you note that, over the last five years, Growth's sales and net income have steadily increased while Stagnation's sales and net income have remained, on average, stable. Additionally, Growth exhibits a clear upward trend in its earnings per share ratio while Stagnation's earnings per share ratio has, on average, declined. Therefore, while the future never can be predicted with certainty, the past five years' data suggest that, if Growth continues to grow more rapidly than Stagnation, an investment in Growth would probably yield the larger return.

Statement of Retained Earnings

OBJECTIVE ▶ 6

Prepare the statement of retained earnings and understand the information it communicates.

The owners of a company contribute capital in one of two ways:

1. directly, though purchases of common stock from the company, and
2. indirectly, by the company retaining some or all of the net income earned each year rather than paying it out in dividends.

As noted earlier, the income earned by the company but not paid out in the form of dividends is called retained earnings. A company may choose to retain a portion of its earnings in order to provide profit to be used for future growth. The statement of retained earnings summarizes and explains the changes in retained earnings during the accounting period.[7] Exhibit 1-11 shows the statement of retained earnings for Apple.

Exhibit 1-11

Statement of Retained Earnings

Apple Inc.
Statement of Retained Earnings*
For the fiscal year ended September 29, 2007
(in millions of dollars)

Retained earnings, Sept. 30, 2006	$5,607
Add: Net income	3,496
	$9,103
Less: Dividends	0
Other**	(2)
Retained earnings, Sept. 29, 2007	$9,101

*The statement of retained earnings was created by the authors from information contained in Apple Inc.'s 2007 annual report.
**The other item deducted in Apple's statement of retained earnings is related to common stock issued under Apple's stock plans. This is an unusual item and beyond the scope of this text and is not discussed.

[7] Some companies may choose to report a statement of changes in stockholders' equity, which explains the changes in all of the stockholders' equity accounts, rather than a statement of retained earnings.

Notice the heading is similar to the heading for the income statement in that it covers a period of time (the fiscal year ended September 29, 2007). In addition, Apple declared no dividends for 2007 but chose to keep the net income earned within the company. The preparation of a statement of retained earnings is detailed in Cornerstone 1-4.

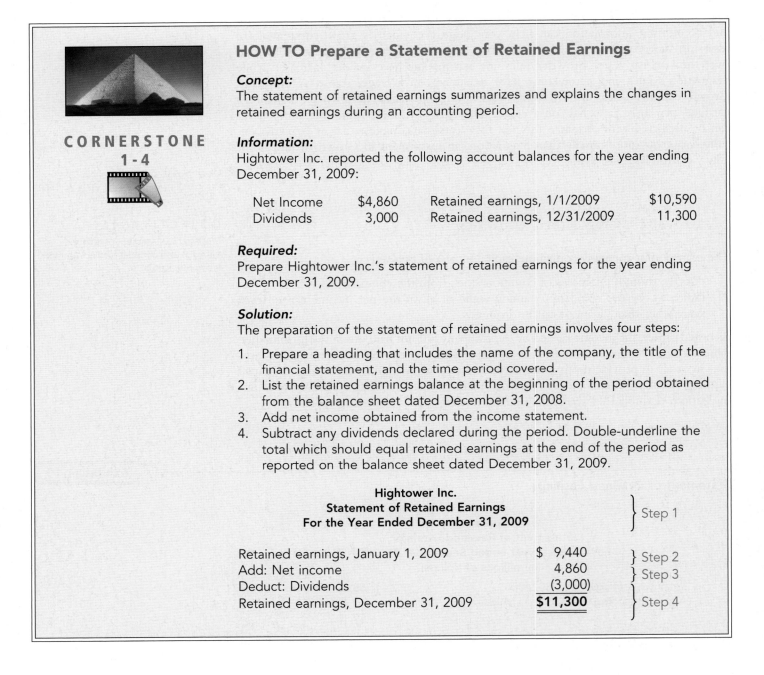

CORNERSTONE 1-4

HOW TO Prepare a Statement of Retained Earnings

Concept:
The statement of retained earnings summarizes and explains the changes in retained earnings during an accounting period.

Information:
Hightower Inc. reported the following account balances for the year ending December 31, 2009:

Net Income	$4,860	Retained earnings, 1/1/2009	$10,590
Dividends	3,000	Retained earnings, 12/31/2009	11,300

Required:
Prepare Hightower Inc.'s statement of retained earnings for the year ending December 31, 2009.

Solution:
The preparation of the statement of retained earnings involves four steps:

1. Prepare a heading that includes the name of the company, the title of the financial statement, and the time period covered.
2. List the retained earnings balance at the beginning of the period obtained from the balance sheet dated December 31, 2008.
3. Add net income obtained from the income statement.
4. Subtract any dividends declared during the period. Double-underline the total which should equal retained earnings at the end of the period as reported on the balance sheet dated December 31, 2009.

Hightower Inc.
Statement of Retained Earnings
For the Year Ended December 31, 2009   } Step 1

Retained earnings, January 1, 2009	$ 9,440	} Step 2
Add: Net income	4,860	} Step 3
Deduct: Dividends	(3,000)	
Retained earnings, December 31, 2009	**$11,300**	} Step 4

Use of the Statement of Retained Earnings

The statement of retained earnings is used to monitor a company's dividend payouts to its shareholders. For example, some older investors seek out companies with high dividend payouts so that they will receive cash during the year. Also, creditors are interested in a company's dividend payouts. If a company pays out too much in dividends, the company may not have enough cash on hand to repay its debt when it becomes due.

Statement of Cash Flows

OBJECTIVE ▶7
Understand the information communicated by the statement of cash flows.

The last of the major financial statements, the statement of cash flows, describes the company's cash receipts (cash inflows) and cash payments (cash outflows) for a period of time. The statement of cash flows for Apple is shown in Exhibit 1-12. Cash flows are classified into one of three categories:

- **Cash flows from operating activities**—any cash flows directly related to earning income. This category includes cash sales and collections of accounts receivable as well as cash payments for goods, services, salaries, and interest.
- **Cash flows from investing activities**—any cash flow related to the acquisition or sale of investments and long-term assets such as property, plant, and equipment.
- **Cash flows from financing activities**—any cash flow related to obtaining capital of the company. This category includes the issuance and repayment of debt, common stock transactions, and the payment of dividends.

The preparation of the statement of cash flows will be discussed in Chapter 11.

Use of the Statement of Cash Flows

The statement of cash flows is used by creditors who wish to assess the creditworthiness of a company. A company with healthy cash flow—particularly if it comes from operating activities—is in a good position to repay debts as they come due and is usually a low-risk borrower. Stockholders are also interested in the adequacy of cash flows as an indicator of the company's ability to pay dividends and to expand its business. The statement of cash flows is covered in more detail in Chapter 11.

Relationships Among the Statements

OBJECTIVE ▶8
Describe the relationships among the financial statements.

At this point, it is important to notice the natural relationships of the four basic financial statements and the natural progression from one financial statement to another. Normally, we begin an accounting period with a balance sheet. During the year, the company earns net income from operating its business. Net income from the income statement increases retained earnings on the statement of retained earnings. Ending retained earnings from the statement of retained earnings is reported in the stockholders' equity section of the balance sheet at the end of the accounting period. Finally, the statement of cash flow explains the change in cash on the balance sheets at the beginning and end of the accounting period. These relationships are shown in Exhibit 1-13.

Exhibit 1-12

Statement of Cash Flows

Apple Inc.
Statement of Cash Flows*
For the fiscal year ended September 29, 2007
(in millions of dollars)

Net cash provided from operating activities	$ 5,470
Net cash used by investing activities	(3,249)
Net cash provided from financing activities	739
Net change in cash	$ 2,960
Cash at the beginning of the year	6,392
Cash at the end of the year	$ 9,352

*The statement of cash flow information was taken from the annual report of Apple Inc. and has been summarized and reformatted by the authors.

Exhibit 1-13

Relationships Among the Financial Statements

Beginning of the Period →→→ End of the Period

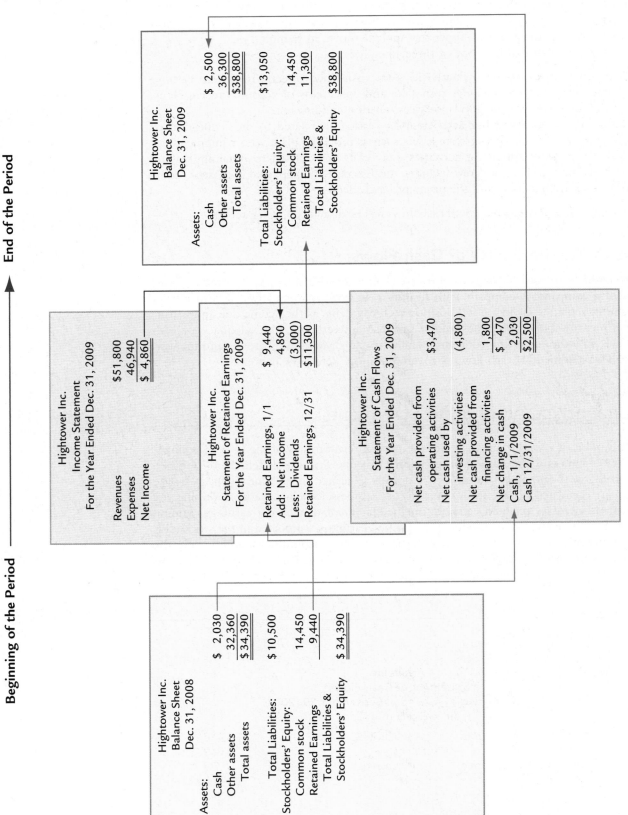

Hightower Inc.
Income Statement
For the Year Ended Dec. 31, 2009

Revenues	$51,800
Expenses	46,940
Net Income	$ 4,860

Hightower Inc.
Statement of Retained Earnings
For the Year Ended Dec. 31, 2009

Retained Earnings, 1/1	$ 9,440
Add: Net income	4,860
Less: Dividends	(3,000)
Retained Earnings, 12/31	$11,300

Hightower Inc.
Statement of Cash Flows
For the Year Ended Dec. 31, 2009

Net cash provided from operating activities	$3,470
Net cash used by investing activities	(4,800)
Net cash provided from financing activities	1,800
Net change in cash	$ 470
Cash, 1/1/2009	2,030
Cash 12/31/2009	$2,500

Hightower Inc.
Balance Sheet
Dec. 31, 2008

Assets:	
Cash	$ 2,030
Other assets	32,360
Total assets	$34,390
Total Liabilities:	$10,500
Stockholders' Equity:	
Common stock	14,450
Retained Earnings	9,440
Total Liabilities & Stockholders' Equity	$34,390

Hightower Inc.
Balance Sheet
Dec. 31, 2009

Assets:	
Cash	$ 2,500
Other assets	36,300
Total assets	$38,800
Total Liabilities:	$13,050
Stockholders' Equity:	
Common stock	14,450
Retained Earnings	11,300
Total Liabilities & Stockholders' Equity	$38,800

Other Items in the Annual Report and Professional Ethics

O B J E C T I V E ➤ 9

Describe other information contained in the annual report and the importance of ethics in accounting.

The financial statements discussed in the previous section were reported to users in an *annual report*. The annual report includes the financial statements of a company and other important information such as the notes to the financial statements, management's discussion and analysis of the condition of the company, and the auditor's report. For publicly-traded companies that are required to file reports with the Securities and Exchange Commission, the annual report is contained within the company's 10-K filing.

Notes to the Financial Statements

The **notes to the financial statements (or footnotes)** clarify and expand upon the information presented in the financial statements. The notes are an integral part of the financial statements and help to fulfill the accountant's responsibility for full disclosure of all relevant information. Without the information contained in the notes, the financial statements are incomplete and could not be adequately understood by users. The information contained in the notes can be either quantitative (numerical) or qualitative (nonnumerical).

Generally, the first note contains a summary of significant accounting policies. For example, the following is an excerpt from Apple's notes to the financial statements concerning its accounting for revenues:

CONCEPT Q&A

Is there a single equation or financial statement which captures the business activities (operating, investing, and financing) that all companies engage in?

Possible Answer:

The fundamental accounting equation captures the business activities of companies and encompasses all of the major financial statements. While certain statements provide more information on certain business activities (e.g., the income statement provides information about a company's operating activities), information is also contained in other statements as well (e.g., current assets and current liabilities provide insight into a company's operations). Therefore, all financial statements and the notes to the financial statements must be examined as an integrated whole.

> **Revenue Recognition**
>
> The Company recognizes revenue when persuasive evidence of an arrangement exists, delivery has occurred, the sales price is fixed or determinable, and collection is probable. Product is considered delivered to the customer once it has been shipped and title and risk of loss have been transferred. For most of the Company's product sales, these criteria are met at the time the product is shipped.

Other footnotes provide additional detail on line items presented in the financial statements. For example, while Apple only reports a single number on the balance sheet for property, plant, and equipment, the company provides a detailed breakdown of the components of property, plant, and equipment (land, building, machinery, equipment, and furniture) in the notes. Other notes provide disclosures about items not reported in the financial statements. For instance, Apple provides detailed explanations of its stock option activity over the last three years—an activity not directly reported on the financial statements yet of significant interest to users.

Management's Discussion and Analysis

The annual report also includes a section entitled "**Management's Discussion and Analysis**." In this section, management provides a discussion and explanation of various items reported in the financial statements. Additionally, management uses this opportunity to highlight favorable and unfavorable trends and significant risks facing the company. For example, in explaining the increase in sales from the previous years, Apple disclosed the following:

Net sales of iPods increased $629 million or 8% during 2007 compared to 2006. Unit sales of iPods increased 31% compared to 2006. The iPod growth was primarily driven by increased sales of the iPod shuffle and iPod nano particularly in international markets. iPod unit sales growth was significantly greater than iPod net sales due to a shift in overall iPod product mix, as well as due to lower selling prices for the iPod classic, iPod nano and iPod shuffle in 2007 compared to 2006.

Report of Independent Accountants

An independent accountant (or auditor) is an accounting professional who conducts an examination of a company's financial statements. The objective of this examination is to gather evidence that will enable the auditor to form an opinion as to whether the financial statements fairly present the financial position and result of operations of the company. The auditor's opinion of the financial statements is presented in the form of an **audit report**. Exhibit 1-14 shows an excerpt from the audit report for Apple.

Because financial statement users cannot directly observe the company's accounting practices, companies hire auditors to give the users of the financial statements assurance or confidence that the financial statements are a fair presentation of the company's financial health. In performing an audit, it is impractical for an auditor to retrace every transaction of the company for the entire accounting period. Instead, the auditor performs procedures (e.g., sampling of transactions) that enable an opinion to be expressed on the financial statement as a whole.

Exhibit 1-14

Auditor's Report

Report of Independent Registered Public Accounting Firm (partial)

The Board of Directors and Shareholders
Apple, Inc.:

We have audited the accompanying consolidated balance sheets of Apple Inc. and subsidiaries (the Company) as of September 29, 2007 and September 30, 2006, and the related consolidated statements of operations, shareholders' equity, and cash flows for each of the years in the three-year period ended September 29, 2007. These consolidated financial statements are the responsibility of the Company's management. Our responsibility is to express an opinion on these consolidated financial statements based on our audits.

We conducted our audits in accordance with the standards of the Public Company Accounting Oversight Board (United States). Those standards require that we plan and perform the audit to obtain reasonable assurance about whether the financial statements are free of material misstatement. An audit includes examining, on a test basis, evidence supporting the amounts and disclosures in the financial statements. An audit also includes assessing the accounting principles used and significant estimates made by management, as well as evaluating the overall financial statement presentation. We believe that our audits provide a reasonable basis for our opinion.

In our opinion, the consolidated financial statements referred to above present fairly, in all material respects, the financial position of Apple Inc. and subsidiaries as of September 29, 2007 and September 30, 2006, and the results of their operations and their cash flows for each of the years in the three-year period ended September 29, 2007, in conformity with U.S. generally accepted accounting principles.

We also have audited, in accordance with the standards of the Public Company Accounting Oversight Board (United States), Apple Inc.'s internal control over financial reporting as of September 29, 2007, based on criteria established in *Internal Control—Integrated Framework* issued by the Committee of Sponsoring Organizations of the Treadway Commission (COSO), and our report dated November 15, 2007 expressed an unqualified opinion on the effectiveness of the Company's internal control over financial reporting.

/s/ KPMG LLP
Mountain View, California
November 15, 2007

DECISION-MAKING & ANALYSIS

Career Analysis

Virtually every organization must have an accounting system; thus, accountants are employed in a wide range of businesses. Accounting knowledge and experience can also open doors to other areas of business.

1. *What skills and character traits are required for accountants?*

Accountants must have well-developed analytical skills and must be effective communicators, both verbally and in writing. Most accounting assignments—whether in business, government, or public accounting—are team assignments in which team members must be able to communicate effectively and work quickly and cooperatively to a solution. As a profession, accounting is subject to professional competence requirements and requires a high level of academic study. In addition, accountants must have personal integrity and behave ethically.

2. *What credentials are useful for a career in accounting?*

Most members of public accounting firms, and many management accountants and consultants, are (or are in the process of becoming) Certified Public Accountants (CPAs). The CPA designation is awarded under state law in each of the 50 states to ensure that accountants who offer their services to the public are properly qualified. The CPA is earned by meeting education and experience requirements and by passing a professional examination. The examination is administered nationally by the American Institute of Certified Public Accountants (AICPA). Other valuable professional certifications are the Certified Management Accountant (CMA) designation, which is awarded by the Institute of Management Accountants, and the Certified Internal Auditor (CIA) designation, which is awarded by the Institute of Internal Auditors. Some accountants have obtained the Certified Fraud Examiner (CFE) designation awarded by the Association of Certified Fraud Examiners.

3. *What are the career paths of accountants?*

Accountants work for many types of organizations, including private companies, public accounting firms, governments, and banks. An accounting graduate who begins in public accounting enters as a staff accountant and from there progresses to senior accountant, to manager, and finally to partner. Public accountants perform financial statement audits, provide tax services to their clients, and/or offer management consulting services (e.g., the design and installation of accounting systems). Some accounting graduates choose to begin employment with either profit or nonprofit organizations. In such organizations, an accountant may perform duties that include general accounting, internal auditing, budgeting, and cost accounting. With the knowledge and experience gained through accounting, many accountants have the opportunity to advance within the organization to the corporate executive level. As you can see, the career opportunities for accountants are virtually boundless.

Professional Ethics

Confidence that standards of ethical behavior will be maintained—even when individuals have incentives to violate those standards—is essential to the conduct of any business activity. Owners of businesses must trust their managers, managers must trust each other and their employees, and the investing public must trust its auditors to behave according to accepted ethical standards, which may or may not be reflected in formal written codes. The violation of ethical standards may bring clear and direct penalties but more often bring subtle and long-lasting negative consequences for individuals and companies.

For the economy to function effectively and efficiently, users must have faith that the information reported in financial statements is accurate and dependable. This can only be accomplished through ethical behavior. The American Institute of Certified Public Accountants (AICPA), recognizing that its members have an obligation of self-discipline above and beyond the requirements of generally accepted accounting principles, has adopted a code of professional conduct which provides ethical guidelines for accountants in the performance of their duties. These ethical principles require accountants to serve the public interest with integrity. For example, auditors should fulfill their duties with objectivity, independence, and due professional care. In no situation should an auditor yield to pressure from management to report positively on financial statements that overstate the company's performance or prospects. Violation of these ethical standards can result in severe penalties, including revocation of an accountant's license to practice as a certified public accountant.

In recent years, there have been an increasing number of news reports about unethical behavior involving accounting practices. Acting ethically is not always easy. However, because of the important role of accounting in society, accountants are expected to maintain the highest level of ethical behavior. Throughout this book, you will be exposed to ethical dilemmas that we urge you to consider.

Summary of Learning Objectives

LO1. Explain the nature of accounting.
- Accounting is the process of identifying, measuring, recording and communicating financial information.
- This information is used both inside and outside of the business to make better decisions.
- Accounting is also called the language of business.
- Financial accounting focuses on the needs of external decision-makers.

LO2. Identify the forms of business organizations and the types of business activities.
- The three forms of business organizations are a sole proprietorship (owned by one person), a partnership (jointly owned by two or more individuals), and a corporation (separate legal entity organized under the laws of a particular state).
- Regardless of the form of business, all businesses are involved in three activities. Financing activities include obtaining funds necessary to begin and operate a business. Investing activities involve buying the assets that enable a business to operate. Operating activities are the activities of a business that generate a profit.

LO3. Describe the relationships shown by the fundamental accounting equation.
- The fundamental accounting equation captures all of the economic activities recorded by an accounting system.
- The left side of the accounting equation shows the assets, or economic resources of a company.
- The right side of the accounting equation shows the claims on the company's assets (liabilities or stockholders' equity).

LO4. Prepare a classified balance sheet and understand the information it communicates.
- A balance sheet reports the resources (assets) owned by a company and the claims against those resources (liabilities and stockholders' equity) at a specific point in time.
- These elements are related by the fundamental accounting equation: Assets = Liabilities + Stockholders Equity.
- In order to help users identify the fundamental economic similarities and differences between the various items on the balance sheet, assets and liabilities are classified as either current or noncurrent (long-term). Stockholders' equity is classified as either contributed capital or retained earnings.

LO5. Prepare an income statement and understand the information it communicates.
- The income statement reports how well a company has performed its operations over a period of time and provides information about the future profitability and growth of a company.

- The income statement includes the revenues and expenses of a company which can be reported in either a single-step or multiple-step format.

LO6.   Prepare the statement of retained earnings and understand the information it communicates.

- The statement of retained earnings reports how much of a company's income was retained in the business and how much was distributed to owners for a period of time.
- The statement of retained earnings provides users with insights into a company's dividend payouts.

LO7.   Understand the information communicated by the statement of cash flows.

- The statement of cash flows reports the sources of a company's cash inflow and the uses of a company's cash over time.
- The statement of cash flows can be used to assess the creditworthiness of a company.

LO8.   Describe the relationships among the financial statements.

- There is a natural relationship among the four basic financial statements so that financial statements are prepared in a particular order.
- Starting with the balance sheet at the beginning of the accounting period, financial statements are generally prepared in the following order: income statement, the statement of retained earnings, and the balance sheet at the end of the accounting period.
- The statement of cash flow explains the change in cash on the balance sheets at the beginning and end of the accounting period.

LO9.   Describe other information contained in the annual report and the importance of ethics in accounting.

- The notes to the financial statements clarify and expand upon the information presented in the financial statements, and are considered an integral part of a company's financial statements.
- Management's discussion and analysis provides a discussion and explanation of various items reported in the financial statements.
- The auditor's report gives the auditor's opinion as to whether the financial statements fairly present the financial condition and results of operations of the company.
- Maintenance of standards of ethical behavior is essential to the conduct of any business activity. Violation of these standards often brings significant short- and long-term negative consequences for individuals and companies.
- The maintenance of a high ethical standard is necessary for users to have faith in the accuracy of the financial statements, which is a key factor in the effective and efficient functioning of the economy.

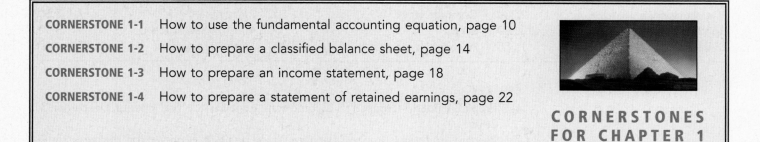

CORNERSTONE 1-1   How to use the fundamental accounting equation, page 10

CORNERSTONE 1-2   How to prepare a classified balance sheet, page 14

CORNERSTONE 1-3   How to prepare an income statement, page 18

CORNERSTONE 1-4   How to prepare a statement of retained earnings, page 22

**CORNERSTONES
FOR CHAPTER 1**

Key Terms

Accounting, 4	Income statement, 8
Assets, 7	Intangible assets, 13
Audit report, 26	Liability, 7
Balance sheet, 8	Liquidity, 15
Capital, 14	Long-term investments, 13
Cash flows from financing activities, 23	Long-term liabilities, 13
Cash flows from investing activities, 23	Management's Discussion and Analysis, 25
Cash flows from operating activities, 23	
Corporation, 5	Net income, 19
Creditor, 7	Net loss, 8
Current assets, 11	Notes to the financial statements (or footnotes), 25
Current liabilities, 13	
Current ratio, 15	Operating cycle, 11
Earnings per share, 20	Partnership, 5
Expenses, 8	Property, plant, and equipment, 13
Financial accounting, 4	Revenue, 8
Financial statements, 8	Sole proprietorship, 5
Fiscal year, 11	Statement of cash flows, 8
Fundamental accounting equation, 9	Statement of retained earnings, 8
Gross margin (gross profit), 19	Stockholders' equity, 7
Income from operations, 19	Working capital, 15

Review Problem

I. Preparing Financial Statements

Concept:

A company's business activities are summarized and reported in its financial statements. The balance sheet reports the company's financial position (assets, liabilities, and stockholders' equity) at a specific point in time. The income statement reports the results of a company's operations (revenues less expenses) for a given period of time. The statement of retained earnings summarizes and explains the changes in retained earnings during the accounting period.

Information:

Enderle Company reported the following account balances at December 31, 2009:

Equipment	$19,800	Sales revenue	$82,500	Interest expense	$ 1,150
Retained earnings, 12/31/2009	15,450	Accumulated depreciation	5,450	Retained earnings, 1/1/2009	10,300
Copyright	1,200	Cash	1,900	Depreciation expense	3,500
Accounts payable	5,500	Salaries expense	18,100	Cost of sales	52,000
Interest revenue	2,300	Common stock	11,500	Inventories	5,600
Bonds payable	10,000	Land	15,000	Income tax expense	3,000
Dividends	1,850	Accounts receivable	3,700	Interest payable	300

Required:

1. Prepare Enderle Company's income statement for the year ending December 31, 2009.
2. Prepare Enderle Company's statement of retained earnings for the year ending December 31, 2009.
3. Prepare Enderle Company's balance sheet at December 31, 2009.

Solution:

1.

Enderle Company
Income Statement
For the Year Ended December 31, 2009

Revenues:		
Sales revenue	$82,500	
Interest revenue	2,300	
Total revenues		$84,800
Expenses:		
Cost of sales	$52,000	
Salaries expense	18,100	
Depreciation expense	3,500	
Interest expense	1,200	
Income tax expense	3,000	
Total expenses		77,800
Net income		$ 7,000

2.

Enderle Company
Statement of Retained Earnings
For the Year Ended December 31, 2009

Retained earnings, January 1, 2009	$ 10,300
Add: Net income	7,000
Deduct: Dividends	(1,850)
Retained earnings, December 31, 2009	**$15,450**

3.

Enderle Company
Balance Sheet
December 31, 2009

ASSETS		
Current assets:		
Cash	$ 2,900	
Accounts receivable	3,700	
Inventories	5,600	
Total current assets		$12,200
Property, plant, and equipment:		
Land	$15,000	
Equipment	19,800	
Less: accumulated depreciation	(5,450)	
Total property, plant, and equipment		29,350
Intangible assets:		
Copyright		1,200
Total assets		$42,750

LIABILITIES AND STOCKHOLDERS' EQUITY		
Current liabilities:		
Accounts payable	$ 5,500	
Interest payable	300	
Total current liabilities		$ 5,800
Long-term liabilities:		
Bonds payable		10,000
Total liabilities		$15,800
Stockholders' equity:		
Common stock	$11,500	
Retained earnings	15,450	
Total stockholders' equity		26,950
Total liabilities and stockholders' equity		$42,750

Discussion Questions

1. Define *accounting*. How does accounting differ from *bookkeeping*?
2. Why is there a demand for accounting information? Name five groups that create demand for accounting information about businesses, and describe how each group uses accounting information.
3. What is an accounting entity?
4. Name and describe three different forms of business organization.
5. Name and describe the three main types of business activities.
6. Define the words *assets, liabilities,* and *stockholders' equity.* How are the three words related?
7. Define the words *revenue* and *expense.*
8. Name and briefly describe the purpose of the four financial statements.
9. What types of questions are answered by the financial statements?
10. What is point–in–time measurement? How does it differ from period-of-time measurement?
11. Write the fundamental accounting equation. What is its significance?
12. What information is included in the heading of each of the four financial statements?
13. Define current assets and current liabilities. Why are current assets and current liabilities separated from noncurrent assets and long-term liabilities on the balance sheet?
14. Describe how items are ordered within the current assets and current liabilities sections on a balance sheet.
15. Name the two main components of stockholders' equity. Describe the main sources of change in each component.
16. What equation describes the income statement?
17. How does the multiple-step income statement differ from the single-step income statement?
18. Explain the items reported on a statement of retained earnings.
19. Name and describe the three categories of the statement of cash flows.
20. How is the statement of changes in retained earnings related to the balance sheet? How is the income statement related to the statement of changes in retained earnings?
21. Describe the items (other than the financial statements) found in the annual report.
22. Give an example of unethical behavior by a public accountant and describe its consequences.

Multiple-Choice Exercises

1-1 Which of the following statements is *false* concerning forms of business organization?

a. A sole proprietorship is an easy type of business to form.
b. It is easier for a corporation to raise large sums of money than it is for a sole proprietorship or partnership.
c. A corporation has tax advantages over the other forms of business organization.
d. Owners of sole proprietorships and partnerships have personal liability for the debts of the business while owners of corporations have limited legal liability.

1-2 Which of the following statements regarding business activities is *true*?

a. Operating activities involve buying the assets that enable a company to generate revenue.
b. Investing activities center around earning interest on a company's investments.
c. Companies spend a relatively small amount of time on operating activities.
d. Financing activities include obtaining the funds necessary to begin and operate a business.

1-3 At December 31, Pitt Inc. has assets of $8,500 and liabilities of $6,300. What is the stockholders' equity for Pitt at December 31?

a. $14,700
b. $10,700
c. $ 8,500
d. $ 2,200

1-4 Which of the following is *not* one of the four basic financial statements?

a. auditor's report
b. income statement
c. balance sheet
d. statement of cash flows

1-5 What type of questions do the financial statements help to answer?

a. Is the company better off at the end of the year than at the beginning of the year?
b. What resources does the company have?
c. What did a company use its cash for during the year?
d. All of the above.

1-6 Which of the following is *not* shown in the heading of a financial statement?

a. The title of the financial statement
b. The name of the auditor
c. The name of the company
d. The time period covered by the financial statement

1-7 At December 31, Marker reported the following items: cash, $12,200; inventory, $2,500; accounts payable, $4,300, accounts receivable, $3,500; common stock, $5,900; property, plant, and equipment, $10,000; interest payable, $1,400; retained earnings, $16,600. What is the total of Marker's current assets?

a. $28,200
b. $18,400
c. $18,200
d. $13,900

1-8 Using the information in Multiple-Choice Exercise 1-7, what is Marker's stockholders' equity?

a. $22,500
b. $18,200
c. $12,500
d. $5,700

1-9 Which of the following statements regarding the income statement is *true*?

a. The income statement shows the results of a company's operations at a specific point in time.
b. The income statement consists of assets, expenses, liabilities, and revenues.
c. The income statement provides information about the future profitability and growth of a company.
d. Typical income statement accounts include Sales revenue, Unearned revenue, and Cost of sales.

1-10 For the most recent year, Grant Company reported revenues of $150,000, cost of goods sold of $84,000, inventory of $5,000, salaries expense of $40,000, rent expense of $15,000, and cash of $20,000. What was Grant's net income?

a. $66,000
b. $11,000
c. $26,000
d. $95,000

1-11 Which of the following statements concerning retained earnings is *true*?

a. Retained earnings is the difference between revenues and expenses.
b. Retained earnings is increased by dividends and decreased by net income.
c. Retained earnings is reported as a liability on the balance sheet.
d. Retained earnings represents the income that has not been distributed as dividends.

1-12 Which of the following sentences regarding the statement of cash flows is *false*?

a. The statement of cash flows describes the company's cash receipts and cash payments for a period of time.
b. The ending cash balance on the statement of cash flows equals the change in cash shown on the balance sheet.
c. The statement of cash flows reports cash flows in three categories: cash flows from operating activities, cash flows from investing activities, and cash flows from financing activities.
d. The statement of cash flows may be used by creditors to assess the creditworthiness of a company.

1-13 Which of the following statements is *true*?

a. The auditor's opinion is typically included in the notes to the financial statements.
b. The notes to the financial statements are an integral part of the financial statements that clarify and expand on the information presented in the financial statements.
c. The management's discussion and analysis section does not convey any information that cannot be found in the financial statements themselves.
d. The annual report is required to be filed with the New York Stock Exchange.

Cornerstone Exercises

Cornerstone Exercise 1-14 FORMS OF BUSINESS ORGANIZATION

Consider the forms of business organization discussed in the chapter.

Required:

What are the three different forms of business organization? List the advantages and disadvantages of each form.

Cornerstone Exercise 1-15 BUSINESS ACTIVITIES

Listed below are various activities that companies engage in during a period.

a. The sale of goods or services
b. The purchase of equipment
c. The payment of a dividend
d. The purchase of supplies
e. Contribution of cash by owners
f. The sale of equipment
g. Borrowed money from a bank

Required:

For each of the activities listed above, classify the activity as operating (O), investing (I), or financing (F).

Cornerstone Exercise 1-16 USING THE ACCOUNTING EQUATION

OBJECTIVE 3
CORNERSTONE 1-1

Listed below are three independent scenarios.

Scenario	Assets	Liabilities	Equity
1	(a)	$39,000	$40,000
2	$125,000	(b)	75,000
3	$ 23,000	$12,000	(c)

Required:

Use the fundamental accounting equation to find the missing amounts.

Cornerstone Exercise 1-17 USING THE ACCOUNTING EQUATION

OBJECTIVE 3
CORNERSTONE 1-1

At the beginning of the year, Morgan Company had total assets of $325,000 and total liabilities of $225,000.

Required:

Use the fundamental accounting equation to answer the following independent questions:

a. What is total stockholders' equity at the beginning of the year?
b. If, during the year, total assets increased by $100,000 and total liabilities increased by $25,000, what is the amount of total stockholders' equity at the end of the year?
c. If, during the year, total assets decreased by $50,000 and total stockholders' equity increased by $25,000, what is the amount of total liabilities at the end of the year?
d. If, during the year, total liabilities increased by $110,000 and total stockholders' equity decreased by $50,000, what is the amount of total assets at the end of the year?

Cornerstone Exercise 1-18 FINANCIAL STATEMENTS

CORNERSTONE 1-2
CORNERSTONE 1-3
CORNERSTONE 1-4

Listed below are elements of the financial statements.

a. Revenue
b. Assets

c. Dividends
d. Net change in cash
e. Expenses
f. Cash flow from operating activities
g. Liabilities
h. Stockholders' equity

Required:

Match each financial statement item with its financial statement: balance sheet (B), income statement (I), statement of retained earnings (RE), or statement of cash flows (CF).

OBJECTIVE ▶ 4
CORNERSTONE 1-2

Cornerstone Exercise 1-19 **BALANCE SHEET**

Listed below are items that may appear on a balance sheet.

Item		Classification	
1.	Accounts payable	a.	Current assets
2.	Machinery	b.	Property, plant, and equipment
3.	Inventory	c.	Intangible assets
4.	Common stock	d.	Current liabilities
5.	Notes payable	e.	Long-term liabilities
6.	Cash	f.	Contributed capital
7.	Copyright	g.	Retained earnings
8.	Net income less dividends		
9.	Accumulated depreciation		
10.	Accounts receivable		

Required:

Match each item with its appropriate classification on the balance sheet.

OBJECTIVE ▶ 4
CORNERSTONE 1-2

Cornerstone Exercise 1-20 **BALANCE SHEET**

An analysis of the transactions of Cavernous Homes, Inc., yields the following totals at December 31, 2009: cash, $2,200; accounts receivable, $5,100; notes payable, $4,000; supplies, $8,500; common stock, $10,000; and retained earnings, $1,800.

Required:

Prepare a balance sheet for Cavernous Homes, Inc., at December 31, 2009.

OBJECTIVE ▶ 5
CORNERSTONE 1-3

Cornerstone Exercise 1-21 **INCOME STATEMENT**

An analysis of the transactions of Canary Cola, Inc., for the year 2009 yields the following information: revenue, $70,000; supplies expense, $30,900; rent expense, $24,000; and dividends, $7,000.

Required:

What is the amount of net income reported by Canary Cola for 2009?

OBJECTIVE ▶ 6
CORNERSTONE 1-4

Cornerstone Exercise 1-22 **STATEMENT OF RETAINED EARNINGS**

Parker Company has a balance of $25,000 in retained earnings on January 1, 2009. During 2009, Parker reported revenues of $60,000 and expenses of $47,000. Parker also paid a dividend of $8,000.

Required:

What is the amount of retained earnings on December 31, 2009?

Exercises

Exercise 1-23 DECISIONS BASED ON ACCOUNTING INFORMATION

OBJECTIVE ▶ 1

Decision-makers use accounting information in a wide variety of decisions including the following:

1. Deciding whether or not to invest in a business
2. Deciding whether or not to lend money to a business
3. Deciding whether or not an individual has paid enough in taxes
4. Deciding whether or not to place merchandise on sale in order to reduce inventory
5. Deciding whether or not to demand additional benefits for employees

Required:

Identify each decision with one of the following decision-makers who is primarily responsible for the decision: a government (G), an investor (I), a labor union (U), business managers (M), or a bank (B).

Exercise 1-24 FORMS OF BUSINESS ORGANIZATIONS

OBJECTIVE ▶ 2

Listed below are the three types of business entities and definitions, examples, or descriptions.

Entity	Definition, Example, or Description
Sole proprietorship	1. Can sell goods (merchandising)
Partnership	2. Owned by one person and legally not separate from the owner
Corporation	3. Can make and sell goods (manufacturing)
	4. Jointly owned by two or more persons and legally not separate from the owners
	5. Owned by one or more persons and legally separate from the owner(s)
	6. Can provide and sell services
	7. The Coca-Cola Company
	8. A law firm owned by some of the employees, who are each liable for the financial obligations of the entity

Required:

For each of the three types of business entities, select as many of the definitions, examples, or descriptions as apply to that type of entity.

Exercise 1-25 BUSINESS ACTIVITIES

OBJECTIVE ▶ 2

Bill and Steve recently formed a company that manufactures and sells high-end kitchen appliances. The following are a list of activities that occurred during the year.

a. Bill and Steve each contributed cash in exchange for common stock in the company.
b. Land and a building to be used as a factory to make the appliances were purchased for cash.
c. Machines used to make the appliances were purchased for cash.
d. Various materials used in the production of the appliances were purchased for cash.
e. Three employees were paid cash to operate the machines and make the appliances.
f. Running low on money, the company borrowed money from a local bank.
g. The money from the bank loan was used to buy advertising on local radio and television stations.
h. The company sold the appliances to local homeowners for cash.
i. Due to extremely high popularity of its products, Bill and Steve built another factory building on its land for cash.
j. The company paid a cash dividend to Bill and Steve.

Required:

Classify each of the business activities listed as either an operating activity (O), an investing activity (I), or a financing activity (F).

OBJECTIVE  Exercise 1-26 **ACCOUNTING CONCEPTS**

A list of accounting concepts and related definitions are presented below.

Concept	Definition
1. Revenue	a. Owner's claim on the resources of a company
2. Expense	b. The difference between revenues and expenses
3. Dividend	c. Increase in assets from the sale of goods or services
4. Asset	d. Economic resources of a company
5. Stockholders' equity	e. Cost of assets consumed in the operation of a business
6. Net income (loss)	f. Creditors' claims on the resources of a company
7. Liability	g. Distribution of earnings to stockholders

Required:

Match each of the concepts with its corresponding definition.

OBJECTIVE ▶ 3 Exercise 1-27 **THE FUNDAMENTAL ACCOUNTING EQUATION**

Financial information for three independent cases is given below.

	Assets	Liabilities	Equity
a.	$107,000	$?	$51,000
b.	275,000	150,000	?
c.	?	15,000	65,000

Required:

Compute the missing numbers in each of the three independent cases described above.

OBJECTIVE ▶ 4 Exercise 1-28 **BALANCE SHEET STRUCTURE**

The following accounts exist in the ledger of Higgins Company: Accounts payable, Accounts receivable, Accumulated depreciation on building, Accumulated depreciation on equipment, Bonds payable, Building, Common stock, Cash, Equipment, Taxes payable, Inventory, Notes payable, Prepaid insurance, Retained earnings, Trademarks, Wages payable.

Required:

Organize the above items into a properly prepared classified balance sheet.

OBJECTIVE ▶ 4 Exercise 1-29 **IDENTIFYING CURRENT ASSETS AND LIABILITIES**

Dunn Sporting Goods sells athletic clothing and footwear to retail customers. Dunn's accountant indicates that the firm's operating cycle averages six months. At December 31, 2009, Dunn has the following assets and liabilities:

a. Prepaid rent in the amount of $16,000. Dunn's rent is $500 per month.
b. A $9,100 account payable due in 45 days.
c. Inventory in the amount of $44,230. Dunn expects to sell $38,000 of the inventory within three months. The remainder will be placed in storage until September 2010. The items placed in storage should be sold by November 2010.
d. An investment in marketable securities in the amount of $1,900. Dunn expects to sell $700 of the marketable securities in six months. The remainder are not expected to be sold until 2012.
e. Cash in the amount of $350.
f. An equipment loan in the amount of $60,000 of which $10,000 is due in three months. The next $10,000 payment is due in March 2011. Interest of $6,000 is also due with the $10,000 payment due in three months.
g. An account receivable from a local university in the amount of $2,850. The university has promised to pay the full amount in three months.
h. Store equipment at a cost of $8,500. Accumulated depreciation has been recorded on the store equipment in the amount of $1,250.

Required:

1. Prepare the current asset and current liability portions of Dunn's December 31, 2009 balance sheet.
2. Compute Dunn's working capital and current ratio at December 31, 2009. What do these ratios tell us about Dunn's liquidity?

Exercise 1-30 CURRENT ASSETS AND CURRENT LIABILITIES

OBJECTIVE ➤ 4

Hanson Construction has an operating cycle of nine months. On December 31, 2009, Hanson has the following assets and liabilities:

a. A note receivable in the amount of $1,000 to be collected in six months.
b. Cash totaling $600.
c. Accounts payable totaling $1,800, all of which will be paid within two months.
d. Accounts receivable totaling $12,000, including an account for $8,000 that will be paid in two months and an account for $4,000 that will be paid in 18 months.
e. Construction supplies costing $9,200, all of which will be used in construction within the next 12 months.
f. Construction equipment costing $60,000, on which depreciation of $22,400 has accumulated.
g. A note payable to the bank in the amount of $40,000, of which $7,000 is to be paid within the next year and the remainder in subsequent years.

Required:

1. Calculate the amounts of current assets and current liabilities reported on Hanson's balance sheet at December 31, 2009.
2. Comment on Hanson's liquidity.

Exercise 1-31 DEPRECIATION

OBJECTIVE ➤ 4 5

Swanson Products was organized as a new business on January 1, 2009. On that date, Swanson acquired equipment at a cost of $400,000, which is depreciated at a rate of $40,000 per year.

Required:

Describe how the equipment and its related depreciation will be reported on the balance sheet at December 31, 2009, and on the 2009 income statement.

Exercise 1-32 STOCKHOLDERS' EQUITY

OBJECTIVE ➤ 4

On January 1, 2009, Mulcahy Manufacturing, Inc., a newly formed corporation, issued 1,000 shares of common stock in exchange for $150,000 cash. No other shares were issued during 2009, and no shares were repurchased by the corporation. On November 1, 2009, the corporation's major stockholder sold 300 shares to another stockholder for $60,000. The corporation reported net income of $22,300 for 2009.

Required:

Prepare the stockholders' equity section of the corporation's balance sheet at December 31, 2009.

Exercise 1-33 CLASSIFIED BALANCE SHEET

OBJECTIVE ➤ 4

College Spirit sells sportswear with logos of major universities. At the end of 2009, the following balance sheet account balances were available.

Accounts payable	$106,300
Accounts receivable	6,700
Accumulated depreciation on furniture and fixtures	21,700
Bonds payable	180,000
Cash	14,200
Common stock	300,000
Furniture and fixtures	88,000
Income taxes payable	11,400
Inventory, sportswear	479,400

Long-term investment in equity securities	$110,000
Note payable, short-term	50,000
Prepaid rent, building (current)	54,000
Retained earnings, 12/31/2009	82,900

Required:

1. Prepare a classified balance sheet for College Spirit at December 31, 2009.
2. Compute College Spirit's working capital and current ratio at December 31, 2009. Comment on College Spirit's liquidity.

OBJECTIVE ▶ 4   Exercise 1-34 **CLASSIFIED BALANCE SHEET**

Jerrison Company operates a wholesale hardware business. The following balance sheet accounts and balances are available for Jerrison at December 31, 2009.

Accounts payable	$ 62,100
Accounts receivable	96,300
Accumulated depreciation on data processing equipment	172,400
Accumulated depreciation on warehouse	216,800
Accumulated depreciation on warehouse operations equipment	31,200
Bonds payable (due 2013)	200,000
Building, warehouse	419,500
Cash	8,400
Common stock	250,000
Equipment, data processing	309,000
Equipment, warehouse operations	106,100
Income taxes payable	21,600
Interest payable	12,200
Inventory (merchandise)	187,900
Land	41,000
Long-term investments in equity securities	31,900
Notes payable (due June 1, 2010)	50,000
Prepaid insurance (for 4 months)	5,700
Retained earnings, 12/31/2009	?
Salaries payable	14,400
Short-term investments in marketable securities	21,000

Required:

1. Prepare a classified balance sheet for Jerrison Company at December 31, 2009.
2. Compute Jerrison's working capital and current ratio at December 31, 2009. Comment on Jerrison's liquidity.

OBJECTIVE ▶ 5   Exercise 1-35 **INCOME STATEMENT STRUCTURE**

The following accounts exist in the ledger of Butler Company: administrative salaries expense, advertising expense, cost of goods sold, depreciation expense on office equipment, interest expense, income tax expense, sales revenue, and salesperson salaries expense.

Required:

Organize the above items into a properly prepared single-step income statement.

OBJECTIVE ▶ 5   Exercise 1-36 **INCOME STATEMENT**

ERS, Inc., maintains and repairs office equipment. ERS had an average of 10,000 shares of common stock outstanding for the year. The following income statement account balances are available for ERS at the end of 2009.

Advertising expense	$ 24,200
Depreciation expense on service van	17,500
Income taxes expense (30% of income before taxes)	15,150
Interest expense	10,900

Rent expense on building	$ 58,400
Rent expense on office equipment	11,900
Salaries expense for administrative personnel	202,100
Service revenue	928,800
Supplies expense	66,400
Wages expense for service support staff	38,600
Wages expense for service technicians	448,300

Required:

1. Prepare a single-step income statement for ERS for 2009.
2. Compute earnings per share for ERS. Comment on ERS's profitability.

Exercise 1-37 **MULTIPLE-STEP INCOME STATEMENT**   OBJECTIVE ➤ 5

The following information is available for Bergin Pastry Shop.

Gross margin	$30,700
Income from operations	9,200
Income taxes expense (15% of income before taxes)	?
Interest expense	1,800
Net sales	80,300

Required:

Prepare a multiple-step income statement for Bergin.

Exercise 1-38 **INCOME STATEMENT**   OBJECTIVE ➤ 5

The following information is available for Wright Auto Supply at December 31, 2009.

Cost of goods sold	$277,000
Depreciation expense on building	29,000
Income taxes expense (30% of income before taxes)	37,260
Interest expense	2,700
Rent expense on equipment	18,000
Salaries, administrative	32,000
Sales revenue	571,900
Wages expense, salespeople	89,000

Required:

1. Prepare a single-step income statement for the year ended December 31, 2009.
2. Prepare a multiple-step income statement for the year ended December 31, 2009.
3. Comment on the differences between the single-step and the multiple-step income statements.

Exercise 1-39 **STATEMENT OF RETAINED EARNINGS**   OBJECTIVE ➤ 6

At the end of 2008, Sherwood Company had retained earnings of $21,240. During 2009, Sherwood had revenues of $831,400 and expenses of $792,100, and paid cash dividends in the amount of $31,500.

Required:

1. Determine the amount of Sherwood's retained earnings at December 31, 2009.
2. Comment on Sherwood's dividend policy.

Exercise 1-40 **STATEMENT OF CASH FLOWS**   OBJECTIVE ➤ 7

Walters, Inc. began operations on January 1, 2009. The following information relates to Walters' cash flows during 2009.

Cash received from owners	$200,000
Cash paid for purchase of land and building	129,000
Cash paid for advertising	21,000
Cash received from customers	131,000

Cash paid to purchase machine	$ 32,000
Cash paid to employees for salaries	47,000
Cash paid for dividends to stockholders	5,000
Cash paid for supplies	23,000

Required:

1. Calculate the cash provided/used for each cash flow category.
2. Comment on the creditworthiness of Walters, Inc.

OBJECTIVE ▶ 8   **Exercise 1-41 RELATIONSHIPS AMONG THE FINANCIAL STATEMENTS**

Zachary Corporation's December 31, 2008 balance sheet included the following amounts:

Cash	$ 23,400
Retained earnings	107,600

Zachary's accountant provided the following data for 2009:

Revenues	$ 673,900
Expenses	582,100
Dividends	34,200
Cash inflow from operating activities	875,300
Cash outflow for investing activities	(994,500)
Cash inflow from financing activities	156,600

Required:

Calculate the amount of cash and retained earnings at the end of 2009.

OBJECTIVE ▶ 8   **Exercise 1-42 RELATIONSHIPS AMONG THE FINANCIAL STATEMENTS**

The following information is available at the end of 2009.

Total assets on 12/31/2008	$70,000
Total assets on 12/31/2009	78,000
Total liabilities on 12/31/2008	-0-
Total liabilities on 12/31/2009	-0-
Common stock on 12/31/2008	50,000
Common stock on 12/31/2009	50,000
Net income for 2009	12,000

Required:

Calculate the amount of dividends reported on the statement of retained earnings for 2009.

OBJECTIVE ▶ 8   **Exercise 1-43 RELATIONSHIPS AMONG THE FINANCIAL STATEMENTS**

During 2009, Moore Corporation paid $16,000 of dividends. Moore's assets, liabilities, and common stock at the end of 2008 and 2009 were:

	12/31/2008	12/31/2009
Total assets	$149,200	$188,100
Total liabilities	54,600	56,700
Common stock	60,000	60,000

Required:

Using the information provided, compute Moore's net income for 2009.

OBJECTIVE ▶ 9   **Exercise 1-44 ANNUAL REPORT ITEMS**

A company's annual report includes the following items:

Financial statements
Notes to the financial statements
Management's discussion and analysis
Report of independent accountants

Required:

For each of the following items, where would you most likely find the information in the annual report?

a. Detailed information on the outstanding debt of a company, including the interest rate being charged and the maturity date of the debt.
b. A description of the risks associated with operating the company in an international market.
c. The total resources and claims to the resources of a company.
d. A description of the accounting methods used by the company.
e. An opinion as to whether the financial statements are a fair presentation of the company's financial position and results of operations.
f. A discussion of the sales trends of the company's most profitable products.
g. The amount of dividends paid to common stockholders.

Exercise 1-45 PROFESSIONAL ETHICS

OBJECTIVE ▶ 9

Ethical behavior is essential to the conduct of business activity. Consider each of the following business behaviors:

1. A manager prepares financial statements that grossly overstate the performance of the business.
2. A CPA resigns from an audit engagement rather than allow a business client to violate an accounting standard.
3. An internal auditor decides against confronting an employee of the business with minor violations of business policy. The employee is a former college classmate of the auditor.
4. An accountant advises his client on ways to legally minimize tax payments to the government.
5. A manager legally reduces the price of a product to secure a larger share of the market.
6. Managers of several large companies secretly meet to plan price reductions designed to drive up-and-coming competitors out of the market.
7. An accountant keeps confidential details of her employers' legal operations that would be of interest to the public.
8. A recently dismissed accountant tells competitors details about her former employer's operations as she seeks a new job.

Required:

Identify each behavior as ethical (E) or unethical (U).

Problem Set A

Problem 1-46A APPLYING THE FUNDAMENTAL ACCOUNTING EQUATION

OBJECTIVE ▶ 3

At the beginning of 2009, Huffer Corporation had total assets of $226,800, total liabilities of $84,200, common stock of $80,000, and retained earnings of $62,600. During 2009, Huffer had net income of $31,500, paid dividends of $11,900, and sold additional common stock for $12,000. Huffer's total assets at the end of 2009 were $278,200.

Required:

Calculate the amount of liabilities that Huffer must have at the end of 2009 in order for the balance sheet equation to balance.

Problem 1-47A ACCOUNTING RELATIONSHIPS

OBJECTIVE ▶ 4 5 6 8

Information for Beethoven Music Company is given below.

Total assets at the beginning of the year	$150,000
Total assets at the end of the year	(a)
Total liabilities at the beginning of the year	90,000
Total liabilities at the end of the year	130,000

Equity at the beginning of the year	$ (b)
Equity at the end of the year	102,000
Dividends paid during the year	(c)
Net income for the year	80,000
Revenues	550,000
Expenses	(d)

Required:

Use the relationships in the balance sheet, income statement, and statement of retained earnings to determine the missing values.

OBJECTIVE ➤ 5 **Problem 1-48A ARRANGEMENT OF THE INCOME STATEMENT**

Powers Wrecking Service demolishes old buildings and other structures and sells the salvaged materials. During 2009, Powers had $400,000 of revenue from demolition services and $137,000 of revenue from salvage sales. Powers also had $1,500 of interest revenue from investments. Powers incurred $240,000 of wages expense, $24,000 of depreciation expense, $50,000 of fuel expense, $84,000 of rent expense, $17,000 of miscellaneous expense, and $25,000 of income tax expense.

Required:

Prepare a single-step income statement for Powers Wrecking Service for 2009.

OBJECTIVE ➤ 4 5 6 8 **Problem 1-49A INCOME STATEMENT AND BALANCE SHEET RELATIONSHIPS**

Each column presents financial information taken from one of four different companies, with one or more items of data missing.

	Company			
Financial Statement Item	A	B	C	D
Total revenue	$100	$ 700	(e)	$2,900
Total expense	75	(c)	50	(g)
Net income (net loss)	(a)	150	15	(600)
Total assets	900	2,000	(f)	8,000
Total liabilities	400	(d)	120	2,000
Total equity	(b)	800	80	(h)

Required:

Use your understanding of the relationships among financial statements and financial statement items to find the missing values (a–h).

OBJECTIVE ➤ 4 5 **Problem 1-50A INCOME STATEMENT AND BALANCE SHEET**

The following information for Rogers Enterprises is available at December 31, 2009, and includes all of Rogers' financial statement amounts except retained earnings:

Accounts receivable	$ 72,000
Cash	15,000
Common stock (10,000 shares)	70,000
Income tax expense	6,000
Income tax payable	4,000
Interest expense	16,000
Notes payable (due in 10 years)	25,000
Prepaid rent, building	30,000
Property, plant, and equipment	90,000
Rent expense	135,000
Retained earnings	?
Salaries expense	235,000
Salaries payable	15,000

Service revenue	$460,000
Supplies	42,000
Supplies expense	36,000

Required:

Prepare a single-step income statement and a classified balance sheet for the year ending December 31, 2009, for Rogers Enterprises.

Problem 1-51A STATEMENT OF RETAINED EARNINGS

Dittman Expositions has the following data available:

Dividends, 2009	$ 8,500
Dividends, 2010	9,900
Expenses, 2009	386,500
Expenses, 2010	410,600
Retained earnings, 12/31/2008	16,900
Revenues, 2009	409,700
Revenues, 2010	438,400

Required:

Prepare statements of retained earnings for 2009 and 2010.

Problem 1-52A RETAINED EARNINGS STATEMENTS

The table below presents the statements of retained earnings for Bass Corporation for three successive years. Certain numbers are missing.

	2008	2009	2010
Retained earnings, beginning	$21,500	$ (b)	$33,600
Add: Net income	9,200	10,100	(f)
	30,700	(c)	(g)
Less: Dividends	(a)	(d)	3,900
Retained earnings, ending	$27,200	$ (e)	$41,200

Required:

Use your understanding of the relationship between successive statements of retained earnings to calculate the missing values (a–g).

Problem 1-53A INCOME STATEMENT, STATEMENT OF RETAINED EARNINGS, AND BALANCE SHEET

The following information relates to Ashton Appliances for 2009.

Accounts payable	$ 18,000
Accounts receivable	70,000
Accumulated depreciation, building	100,000
Accumulated depreciation, fixtures	30,000
Bonds payable (due in 7 years)	192,000
Building	300,000
Cash	41,000
Common stock	245,000
Cost of goods sold	510,000
Depreciation expense, building	10,000
Depreciation expense, fixtures	12,000
Furniture and fixtures	130,000
Income tax expense	14,000
Income tax payable	12,000
Insurance expense	36,000
Interest expense	21,000

Inventory	$ 60,000
Other assets	93,000
Rent expense, store equipment	79,000
Retained earnings, 12/31/2008	54,000
Salaries expense, administrative	101,000
Salaries payable	7,000
Sales revenue	946,000
Wages expense, store	127,000

Required:

1. Prepare a single-step income statement for 2009, a statement of retained earnings for 2009, and a properly classified balance sheet as of December 31, 2009.
2. How would a multiple-step income statement be different from the single-step income statement you prepared for Ashton Appliances?

OBJECTIVE ▸ 8

Problem 1-54A STOCKHOLDERS' EQUITY RELATIONSHIPS

Data from the financial statements of four different companies are presented in separate columns in the table below. Each column has one or more data items missing.

	Company			
Financial Statement Item	V	W	X	Y
Equity, 12/31/2008				
Common stock	$50,000	$35,000	(i)	$15,000
Retained earnings	12,100	(e)	26,400	21,900
Total equity	(a)	$44,300	$66,400	$36,900
Net income (loss) for 2009	$ 7,000	$ (1,800)	$ 6,000	(m)
Dividends during 2009	$ 2,000	$ -0-	(j)	$ 1,400
Equity, 12/31/2009				
Common stock	$50,000	$35,000	$55,000	$15,000
Retained earnings	(b)	(f)	(k)	27,600
Total equity	(c)	(g)	$84,500	(n)
Total assets, 12/31/2009	$92,500	(h)	$99,200	(o)
Total liabilities, 12/31/2009	(d)	$14,800	(l)	$10,700

Required:

Use your understanding of the relationships among the financial statement items to determine the missing values (a–o).

OBJECTIVE ▸ 3 8

Problem 1-55A RELATIONSHIPS AMONG FINANCIAL STATEMENTS

Carson Corporation reported the following amounts for assets and liabilities at the beginning and end of a recent year.

	Beginning of Year	End of Year
Assets	$390,000	$420,000
Liabilities	130,000	145,000

Required:

Calculate Carson's net income or net loss for the year in each of the following independent situations:

1. Carson declared no dividends, and its common stock remained unchanged.
2. Carson declared no dividends and issued additional common stock for $33,000 cash.
3. Carson declared dividends totaling $11,000, and its common stock remained unchanged.
4. Carson declared dividends totaling $17,000 and issued additional common stock for $29,000.

Problem Set B

Problem 1-46B **APPLYING THE FUNDAMENTAL ACCOUNTING EQUATION**

OBJECTIVE ▶ 3

At the beginning of 2009, KJ Corporation had total assets of $553,700, total liabilities of $261,800, common stock of $139,000, and retained earnings of $152,900. During 2009, KJ had net income of $256,200, paid dividends of $71,100, and sold additional common stock for $94,000. KJ's total assets at the end of 2009 were $721,800.

Required:

Calculate the amount of liabilities that KJ must have at the end of 2009 in order for the balance sheet equation to balance.

Problem 1-47B **THE FUNDAMENTAL ACCOUNTING EQUATION**

OBJECTIVE ▶ 4 5 6 8

Information for TTL, Inc., is given below.

Total assets at the beginning of the year	$ (a)
Total assets at the end of the year	730,000
Total liabilities at the beginning of the year	300,000
Total liabilities at the end of the year	(b)
Equity at the beginning of the year	250,000
Equity at the end of the year	(c)
Dividends paid during the year	35,000
Net income for the year	(d)
Revenues	950,000
Expenses	825,000

Required:

Use the relationships in the balance sheet, income statement, and statement of retained earnings to determine the missing values.

Problem 1-48B **ARRANGEMENT OF THE INCOME STATEMENT**

OBJECTIVE ▶ 5

Parker Renovation Inc. renovates historical buildings for commercial use. During 2009, Parker had $762,000 of revenue from renovation services and $5,000 of interest revenue from miscellaneous investments. Parker incurred $227,000 of wages expense, $135,000 of depreciation expense, $75,000 of insurance expense, $114,000 of utilities expense, $31,000 of miscellaneous expense, and $57,000 of income tax expense.

Required:

Prepare a single-step income statement for Parker Renovation Inc. for 2009.

Problem 1-49B **INCOME STATEMENT AND BALANCE SHEET RELATIONSHIPS**

OBJECTIVE ▶ 4 5 6 8

Each column presents financial information taken from one of four different companies, with one or more items of data missing.

Financial Statement Item	Company			
	A	B	C	D
Total revenue	$900	$ 500	(e)	$1,200
Total expense	820	(c)	350	(g)
Net income (net loss)	(a)	250	115	(400)
Total assets	700	1,800	(f)	3,150
Total liabilities	300	(d)	420	2,400
Total equity	(b)	900	50	(h)

Required:

Use your understanding of the relationships among financial statements and financial statement items to find the missing values (a–h).

OBJECTIVE > 4 5

Problem 1-50B INCOME STATEMENT AND BALANCE SHEET

Ross Airport Auto Service provides parking and minor repair service at the local airport while customers are away on business or pleasure trips. The following account balances (except for retained earnings) are available for Ross Airport Auto Service at December 31, 2009.

Accounts payable	$ 16,700
Accounts receivable	39,200
Accumulated depreciation, equipment	38,800
Cash	6,700
Common stock (20,000 shares)	100,000
Depreciation expense, equipment	14,300
Dividends	6,300
Equipment	269,500
Income tax expense	2,700
Income tax payable	1,100
Interest expense	18,300
Interest payable	1,800
Interest revenue, long-term investments	4,100
Inventory, repair parts	4,900
Long-term investments in debt securities	35,000
Notes payable (due May 2, 2016)	160,000
Prepaid rent (3 months)	27,300
Rent expense	103,500
Retained earnings, 12/31/2009	51,700
Service revenue, parking	224,600
Service revenue, repair	208,100
Supplies expense, repair parts	36,900
Wages expense	246,100
Wages payable	12,500

Required:

Prepare a single-step income statement and a classified balance sheet for Ross Airport Auto Service for the year ended December 31, 2009.

OBJECTIVE > 6

Problem 1-51B STATEMENT OF RETAINED EARNINGS

Magical Experiences Vacation Company has the following data available:

Dividends, 2009	$ 12,200
Dividends, 2010	18,900
Expenses, 2009	185,300
Expenses, 2010	310,600
Retained earnings, 12/31/2008	47,100
Revenues, 2009	242,900
Revenues, 2010	391,400

Required:

Prepare statements of retained earnings for 2009 and 2010.

OBJECTIVE > 6

Problem 1-52B RETAINED EARNINGS STATEMENTS

The table below presents the statements of retained earnings for Dillsboro Corporation for three successive years. Certain numbers are missing.

	2008	2009	2010
Retained earnings, beginning	$ (a)	$19,500	$26,700
Add: Net income	11,100	(c)	9,500
	26,900	(d)	(f)
Less: Dividends	7,400	5,200	(g)
Retained earnings, ending	$ (b)	$ (e)	$34,100

Required:

Use your understanding of the relationship between successive statements of retained earnings to calculate the missing values (a–g).

Problem 1-53B INCOME STATEMENT, STATEMENT OF RETAINED EARNINGS, AND BALANCE SHEET

OBJECTIVE ➤ 4 5 6

McDonald Marina provides docking and cleaning services for pleasure boats at its marina in southern Florida. The following account balances are available:

Accounts payable	$ 26,400
Accounts receivable	268,700
Accumulated depreciation, building	64,500
Accumulated depreciation, docks	950,400
Bonds payable (due 2014)	2,000,000
Building	197,300
Cash	22,300
Common stock (40,000 shares)	600,000
Depreciation expense, building	21,500
Depreciation expense, docks	246,300
Dividends	25,300
Equipment, docks	2,490,000
Income taxes expense	21,700
Interest expense	236,000
Interest payable	18,000
Land	875,000
Rent expense, office equipment	14,600
Rent payable, office equipment	2,400
Retained earnings, 12/31/2008	128,600
Service revenue, cleaning	472,300
Service revenue, docking	1,460,000
Supplies expense	89,100
Supplies inventory	9,800
Utilities expense	239,400
Wages expense	987,200
Wages payable	21,600

Required:

Prepare a single-step income statement, a statement of changes in retained earnings, and a classified balance sheet for McDonald Marina for the year ended December 31, 2009.

Problem 1-54B STOCKHOLDERS' EQUITY RELATIONSHIPS

OBJECTIVE ➤ 8

Data from the financial statements of four different companies are presented in separate columns in the table below. Each column has one or more data items missing.

Financial Statement Item	Company			
	A	B	C	D
Equity, 12/31/2008				
Common stock	$45,000	$39,000	$ 80,000	$25,000
Retained earnings	18,800	15,300	6,900	(k)
Total equity	$63,800	(d)	$ 86,900	$38,900
Net income (loss) for 2009	(a)	$ 7,100	$ 9,700	$ (4,500)
Dividends during 2009	$ 2,100	$ 800	(h)	$ -0-
Equity, 12/31/2009				
Common stock	$45,000	$39,000	$ 80,000	$25,000
Retained earnings	21,700	(e)	(i)	(l)
Total equity	(b)	(f)	$ 95,300	(m)
Total assets, 12/31/2009	(c)	$88,200	$113,400	(n)
Total liabilities, 12/31/2009	$14,400	(g)	(j)	$15,700

Required:

Use your understanding of the relationships among the financial statement items to determine the missing values (a–n).

OBJECTIVE ▶ 3 8 ### Problem 1-55B RELATIONSHIPS AMONG FINANCIAL STATEMENTS

Leno Corporation reported the following amounts for assets and liabilities at the beginning and end of a recent year.

	Beginning of Year	End of Year
Assets	$278,000	$320,000
Liabilities	90,000	105,000

Required:

Calculate Leno's net income or net loss for the year in each of the following independent situations:

1. Leno declared no dividends, and its common stock remained unchanged.
2. Leno declared no dividends and issued additional common stock for $12,000 cash.
3. Leno declared dividends totaling $8,000, and its common stock remained unchanged.
4. Carson declared dividends totaling $11,000 and issued additional common stock for $15,000.

Cases

Case 1-56 USING ACCOUNTING INFORMATION

James Hadden is a freshman at Major State University. His earnings from a summer job, combined with a small scholarship and a fixed amount per term from his parents, are his only sources of income. He has a new MasterCard that was issued to him the week he began classes. It is spring term, and Jim finds that his credit card is "maxed out" and that he does not have enough money to carry him to the end of the term. Jim confesses that irresistible opportunities for spring term entertainment have caused him to overspend his resources.

Required:

Describe how accounting information could have helped Jim avoid this difficult situation.

Case 1-57 ANALYSIS OF ACCOUNTING PERIODICALS

The accounting profession is organized into three major groups: (1) accountants who work in nonbusiness entities, (2) accountants who work in business entities, and (3) accountants in public practice. The periodical literature of accounting includes monthly or quarterly journals that are written primarily for accountants within each of these groups.

Required:

1. Use your library and identify one journal published for each of the three professional groups. Identify the publisher of each journal and describe its primary audience.
2. Choose two of the three audiences you have just described. Briefly explain how members of one audience would benefit by reading a journal published primarily for members of the other audience.

Case 1-58 CAREER PLANNING

A successful career requires us to take advantage of opportunities that are difficult to foresee. Success is also aided by having a plan or strategy by which to choose among career alternatives as they arise.

Required:

1. How do you want to be employed in five years, and what must you do to get there?
2. How do you want to be employed in ten years, and what must you do to get there?

Case 1-59 FINANCIAL STATEMENT ANALYSIS

Agency Rent-A-Car, Inc., rents cars to customers whose vehicles are unavailable due to accident, theft, or repair ("Wheels while your car heals"). The company has a fleet of more than 40,000 cars located at 700 offices throughout the United States and Canada. Its balance sheets at January 31, 2009 and January 31, 2008, contain the following information (all dollar amounts are stated in thousands of dollars):

	1/31/2009	1/31/2008
Assets		
Cash	$ 4,400	$ 3,308
Accounts receivable	27,409	30,889
Supplies	6,864	7,440
Property and equipment	279,189	287,456
Other assets	15,666	14,441
	$333,528	$343,534
Liabilities and Stockholders' Equity		
Accounts payable	$ 18,152	$ 33,184
Other noncurrent liabilities	157,861	163,062
Stockholders' equity	157,515	147,288
	$333,528	$343,534

Required:

1. What is the dollar amount of current assets and current liabilities at January 31, 2009? At January 31, 2008? What does this information tell you about the company's liquidity?
2. Assume that stockholders were paid dividends of $1,200 during 2009 and that there were no other changes in stockholders' equity except for net income. How much net income did the business earn during the year?

Case 1-60 FINANCIAL STATEMENT ANALYSIS

Reproduced on the following page are portions of the president's letter to shareholders and selected income statement and balance sheet data for the Wright Brothers Aviation Company. Wright Brothers is a national airline that provides both passenger service and package delivery service.

Required:

1. What trends do you detect in revenues, operating income, and net income for the period 2005–2009?
2. What happened to the difference between current assets and current liabilities over the 2005–2009 period? To what do you attribute this result?
3. The price of Wright Brothers stock declined steadily throughout the 2005–2009 period. Do you consider this decline to be a reasonable reaction to the financial results reported? Why or why not?

To Our Stockholders:

In 2009, the airline industry began to show some life. As fuel prices leveled and travelers showed an increased willingness to fly domestically, it was generally perceived that a gradual recovery was in place. The worldwide increase in the demand for air travel throughout the year translated into improved demand for the Company's services. In fact, revenues for both the passenger and package segments improved in every quarter of 2009. Most importantly, the Company started generating cash from operations in the last half of the year, and the passenger segments returned to generating profits in the third quarter. . . .

With improved operating performance as the basis for negotiating a financial restructuring, the next critical step for the Company is to satisfactorily restructure its obligations in order to insure that the Company can operate effectively in the future. With that in mind, a strategic decision, albeit a difficult one, was made in February 2009—the Company filed for reorganization under Chapter 11 of the U.S. Bankruptcy Code. . . .

	2009	2008	2007	2006	2005
Revenues:					
Passenger services	$ 141,343	$ 136,057	$ 354,246	$ 390,080	$ 337,871
Package services	35,199	60,968	145,940	203,675	202,615
Total revenues	176,542	197,025	500,186	593,755	540,486
Operating income	(54,584)	(92,613)	(16,663)	52,137	39,527
Net income (loss)	(182,647)	(340,516)	(67,269)	(14,553)	(22,461)
Current assets	123,553	134,009	183,268	193,943	209,944
Total assets	542,523	678,846	1,068,509	1,180,484	1,263,922
Current liabilities	698,583	641,645	542,640	129,369	120,960
Long-term debt	—	—	144,297	576,446	655,383
Stockholders' equity	(272,632)	(82,280)	265,686	335,088	357,155

Case 1-61 RESEARCH AND ANALYSIS USING THE ANNUAL REPORT

Obtain Apple, Inc.'s 2007 annual report either through the "Investor Relations" portion of their website (do a web search for Apple investor relations) or go to http://www.sec.gov and click "Search for company filings" under "Filings & Forms (EDGAR)."

Required:

Answer the following questions:

1. On what date did Apple's fiscal year end? Was this date different from the previous year? If so, why?
2. How many years of balance sheet and income statement information does Apple present?
3. With regard to the balance sheet:
   a. What amounts did Apple report as assets, liabilities, and stockholders' equity for 2007?
   b. Did the amounts reported as assets, liabilities, and stockholders' equity change over the last year? If so, by how much?
   c. What amounts were reported as current assets and current liabilities for the years presented?
   d. Provide an assessment of Apple's liquidity based on the information obtained in part (b).
4. With regard to the income statement:
   a. What amounts did Apple report as revenues, expenses, and net income for 2007?
   b. Do you detect any trends with regard to revenues, expenses, or net income?
5. With regard to the statement of cash flows:
   a. What amounts did the company report for cash flow from operating activities, cash flow from investing activities, and cash flow from financing activities for 2007?
   b. How much cash did the company spend on purchasing PP&E in 2007?

6. With regard to management's discussion and analysis:
   a. What accounting policies and estimates does Apple consider critical? Where would these policies and estimates be described?
   b. Does management believe that the company performed well during the current year? On what do you base this assessment?
7. Are the financial statements audited? If so, by whom?

Case 1-62 COMPARATIVE ANALYSIS: ABERCROMBIE & FITCH vs. AEROPOSTALE

Refer to the financial statements of **Abercrombie & Fitch** and **Aeropostale** that are supplied with this text.

Required:

Answer the following questions:

1. What is the fiscal year-end of Abercrombie & Fitch? Of Aeropostale? Why would you expect these to be the same?
2. With regard to the balance sheet:
   a. What amounts did each company report for assets, liabilities, and stockholders' equity for the year ended February 3, 2007?
   b. What amounts were reported as current assets and current liabilities for the year ended February 3, 2007?
   c. Assess the liquidity of each company.
   d. Describe any other similarities and differences that you noticed between the two companies.
3. With regard to the income statement:
   a. What amounts did Abercrombie & Fitch report as revenues, expenses, and net income for the year ended February 3, 2007 (fiscal 2006)? What amounts did Aeropostale report as revenues, expenses, and net income for the fiscal year ended February 3, 2007?
   b. Compare any trends that you detect with regard to revenues, expenses, and net income?
   c. What are the earnings per share of each company? What insights does this give you with regard to future profitability and growth?
4. What were the major sources and uses of cash for each company?
5. What is management's assessment of each company's past performance and future prospects? Where did you find this information?

Case 1-63 PROFESSIONAL ETHICS

Professional ethics guide public accountants in their work with financial statements.

Required:

1. Why is ethical behavior by public accountants important to society?
2. Describe the incentives that public accountants have to behave *unethically*.
3. Describe the incentives that public accountants have to behave *ethically*.

Case 1-64 ETHICAL ISSUES

Lola, the CEO of JB Inc., and Frank, the accountant for JB Inc., were recently having a meeting to discuss the upcoming release of the company's financial statements. Following is an excerpt of their conversation:

Lola: These financial statements don't show the hours of hard work that we've put in to restore this company to financial health. In fact, these results may actually prevent us from obtaining loans that are critical to our future.

Frank: Accounting does allow for judgment. Tell me your primary concerns and let's see if we can work something out.

Lola: My first concern is that the company doesn't appear very liquid. As you can see, our current assets are only slightly more than current liabilities. The company has always paid its bills—even when cash was tight. It's not really fair that the financial statements don't reflect this.

Frank: Well, we could reclassify some of the long-term investments as current assets instead of noncurrent assets. Our expectation is that we will hold these investments for several years, but we could sell them at any time; therefore, it's fair to count these as current assets. We could also reclassify some of the accounts payable as noncurrent. Even though we expect to pay them within the next year, no one will ever look close enough to see what we've done. Together these two changes should make us appear more liquid and properly reflect the hard work we've done.

Lola: I agree. However, if we make these changes, our long-term assets will be smaller and our long-term debt will be larger. Many analysts may view this as a sign of financial trouble. Isn't there something we can do?

Frank: Our long-term assets are undervalued. Many were purchased years ago and recorded at historical cost. However, companies that bought similar assets are allowed to record them at an amount closer to their current market values. I've always thought this was misleading. If we increase the value of these long-term assets to their market value, this should provide the users of the financial statements with more relevant information and solve our problem, too.

Lola: Brilliant! Let's implement these actions quickly and get back to work.

Required:

Describe any ethical issues that have arisen as the result of Lola and Frank's conversation.

2

The Accounting Information System

After studying Chapter 2, you should be able to:

1. Describe the assumptions and principles that underlie accounting.
2. Explain the relationships among economic events, transactions, and the expanded accounting equation.
3. Analyze the effect of business transactions on the accounting equation.
4. Discuss the role of accounts and how debits and credits are used in the double-entry accounting system.
5. Prepare journal entries for transactions.
6. Explain why transactions are posted to the general ledger.
7. Prepare a trial balance and explain its purpose.

Experience Financial Accounting
with General Electric

Tracing its roots back to Thomas Edison, the **General Electric Company (GE)** has become one of the largest and most diversified companies in the world, with customers in over 100 countries and more than 300,000 employees worldwide. GE is comprised of four businesses:

- NBC-Universal—one of the world's leading media and entertainment companies that provides network television services, produces television programs and movies, and operates theme parks.

- Technology Infrastructure—provides essential technologies in the aviation, transportation, enterprise solutions, and healthcare markets. Products in this business include aircraft engines, locomotives, power generation systems, oil and gas compressors and turbines, energy technologies (e.g., solar and nuclear), water treatment facilities, and medical technologies such as x-rays, MRIs, and patient-monitoring systems.

- Energy Infrastructure—focuses on the development, implementation, and improvement of products and technologies that harness energy resources.

- GE Capital—provides financial products and services to consumers and commercial businesses around the world. Products include business loans and leases, as well as home and personal loans, credit cards, and insurance to over 130 million consumers.

With so many different activities throughout the world, GE faces a difficult task in measuring and reporting its many business activities.

Companies like GE rely on comprehensive accounting systems to capture, record, and report their various business activities. The type of system depends on many factors, including the company's size, the volume of transactions it processes, and the information needs of its users. Larger companies like GE will use computerized accounting systems in order to efficiently provide reliable information that is needed by the users of its financial statements. In fact, GE takes this responsibility very seriously. In its annual report, GE states that "great companies are built on a foundation of reliable financial information." While GE invests heavily in its accounting system, it recognizes that no system is foolproof. Therefore, GE bases its financial accounting system on several key principles, including rigorous oversight by management and dedication to a system of internal controls that are designed to ensure the accuracy and reliability of its accounting records, transparent financial disclosures, and protection of its assets. With such an emphasis on its accounting system, users of GE's financial statements can feel confident that GE's business activities were recorded and reported properly. In short, it is GE's accounting system that brings "light" to GE's varied business activities.

Fundamental Accounting Concepts

In the previous chapter, we described the typical business activities in which companies engage and how accounting systems report these activities through the financial statements. In this chapter, we will discuss the underlying concepts behind any accounting system. We will also begin a discussion of the procedures that companies use to record information about business activities and how this information ultimately is transformed into financial statements. That is, you will see where the numbers on the financial statements actually come from. An understanding of these procedures is essential if you are to be an effective user of financial statements. As you review the financial statements, you are assessing a company's performance, cash flows, and financial position. To make those assessments, you need to be able to infer the actions of a company from what you see in the financial statements. That inference depends on your understanding of how companies transform the results of their activities into financial statements.

These transforming procedures are called the **accounting cycle**. We will begin the discussion of the accounting cycle in this chapter and will extend it into the next chapter. The accounting cycle is a simple and orderly process, based on a series of steps and conventions. If the financial statements are to present fairly the effects of the company's activities, proper operation of the accounting cycle is essential. For example, if General Electric failed to properly apply accounting procedures, it is likely that many of its business activities would be improperly recorded (if they were even recorded at all) and its financial statements would be seriously misstated.

In this chapter, we will discuss the basic concepts and procedures that underlie accounting systems and how the completion of each accounting procedure moves the accounting system toward its end product—the financial statements. We will address the following questions:

- What concepts and assumptions underlie accounting information?
- How do companies record business activities?
- What procedures are involved in transforming information about business activities into financial statements?
- How do business activities affect the financial statements?

The Conceptual Framework

In order to make it easier to use financial statements over time and across companies, a common set of rules and conventions has been developed to guide the preparation of financial statements. These rules and conventions, called **generally accepted accounting principles (GAAP)**, were developed by several different organizations over a number of years. In the United States, the **Securities and Exchange Commission (SEC)** has the power to set accounting rules for publicly-traded companies. However, the SEC has delegated this authority to the **Financial Accounting Standards Board (FASB)**. While the FASB is the primary standard-setter in the United States, the FASB has been working closely with the **International Accounting Standards Board (IASB)** in an attempt to reduce the differences in accounting standards around the world. Currently the SEC accepts financial statements of foreign companies that are prepared under the rules of the IASB.[1]

Generally accepted accounting principles rest on a conceptual framework of accounting. This framework derives from the fundamental objective of financial reporting: to provide information that is useful in making business and economic decisions. The conceptual framework is designed to support the development of accounting standards and provide a consistent body of thought for financial reporting. An understanding of the conceptual framework should help you in understanding complex accounting standards by providing a logical structure to financial

---

[1] The SEC is also considering allowing U.S. companies to prepare their financial statements using either the standards of the FASB or the IASB. If this is allowed, there is a real possibility that the IASB may replace the FASB as the primary standard-setter in the United States.

accounting; in other words, the concepts help to explain "why" accountants adopt certain practices. Exhibit 2-1 summarizes the characteristics of useful information as well as the underlying assumptions and principles that make up the conceptual framework and serve as the foundation of GAAP.

Qualitative Characteristics of Useful Information

Given the overall objective of providing useful information, the FASB has developed four qualitative characteristics that useful information should possess: relevance, reliability, comparability, and consistency.

Accounting information is **relevant** if it is capable of making a difference in a business decision by helping users predict future events or if it provides feedback about prior expectations. In addition, information is only relevant if it is provided in a timely manner. If information is not provided when it is needed, it lacks relevance. Users can depend on **reliable** information. To be reliable, information should be verifiable (independent parties agree that the information is free from error or bias), representationally faithful (the information accurately portrays what it is intended to portray), and neutral (free from bias). Information is comparable if it allows comparisons to be made between companies. **Comparability** is normally achieved when different companies use the same accounting methods. **Consistency** refers to the application of the same accounting principles by a single company over time. Consistent application of accounting principles helps users identify financial trends of a company.[2]

It should be noted that trade-offs are often necessary in evaluating these criteria. For example, the most relevant information may not be able to be measured reliably. Similarly, changing economic situations may require a change in the accounting principle used. Such a change may decrease the consistency of the information presented. In these situations, the accountant must exercise judgment in determining the accounting principles that would produce the most useful information for the decision-maker. In all situations, accountants should follow a **full disclosure** policy. That is, any information that would make a difference to financial statement users should be revealed.

Exhibit 2-1

The Conceptual Framework

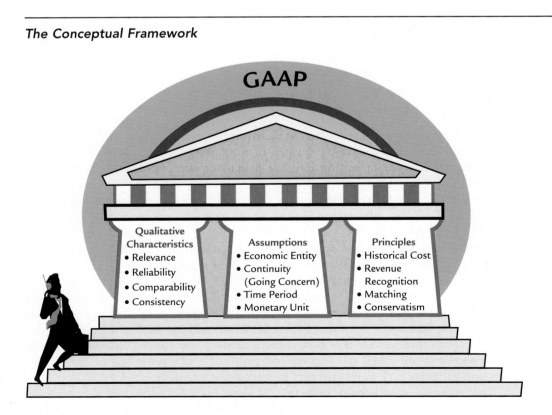

[2] A current proposal seeks to replace these four qualitative characteristics with two fundamental qualitative characteristics (relevance and faithful representation) and four enhancing qualitative characteristics (comparability, verifiability, timeliness, and understandability). For more information, visit this text's Web site.

Two constraints to the qualitative characteristics described above help to further clarify what accounting information should be disclosed in the financial statements. First, the benefit received from accounting information should be greater than the costs of providing the information (**cost vs. benefit**). Second, useful information should be **material**; that is, the information should be capable of influencing a decision. If an item is judged to be immaterial (e.g., the size of the item is so small that the user's decision would not be influenced), the company does not have to follow GAAP in the reporting of this information.

Assumptions

The four basic assumptions that underlie accounting are: the economic entity assumption, the continuity assumption, the time-period assumption, and the monetary unit assumption.

In Chapter 1 we discussed different forms of business organizations. Under the **economic entity assumption**, each company is accounted for separately from its owners. A GE shareholder's personal transactions, for instance, are not recorded in GE's financial statements. The **continuity (or going-concern) assumption** assumes that a company will continue to operate long enough to carry out its existing commitments. Without this assumption, many of our accounting procedures could not be followed. For example, if GE were expected to go bankrupt in the near future, its assets and liabilities would be reported on the balance sheet at an amount the company expects to receive if sold (less any costs of disposal). The **time-period assumption** allows the life of a company to be divided into artificial time periods so net income can be measured for a specific period of time (e.g., monthly, quarterly, annually). Without this assumption, a company's income could only be reported at the end of its life. The **monetary unit assumption** requires that a company account for and report its financial results in monetary terms (e.g., U.S. dollar, euro, Japanese yen). This assumption implies that certain nonmonetary items (e.g., brand loyalty, customer satisfaction) are not reported in a company's financial statements.

CONCEPT Q&A

Companies assume they are going concerns. Wouldn't the valuation of a company's assets be more relevant if this assumption was relaxed and the net assets valued at their current selling costs?

Possible Answer:

Current selling costs are only relevant if the company intends to sell the assets in the near term. However, many assets (e.g., machinery, buildings) are used over long periods of time, and in these situations, the use of current selling prices would be of little value to financial statement users. In addition, the cost of obtaining current values for these assets would greatly outweigh the benefits received.

Principles

Principles are general approaches that are used in the measurement and recording of business activities. The four basic principles of accounting are: the historical cost principle, the revenue recognition principle, the matching principle, and the conservatism principle.

The **historical cost principle** requires that the activities of a company are initially measured at their cost—the exchange price at the time the activity occurs. For example, when GE buys equipment used in manufacturing its products, it initially records the equipment at the cost paid to acquire the equipment. Further, the historical cost principle requires that the equipment continue to be reported at its historical cost in future periods until the equipment is disposed of. Accountants use historical cost because it provides a reliable measure of the activity. However, the historical cost principle has been criticized as being a less relevant measure than alternatives such as market values. The FASB is aware of these criticisms and has been attempting to develop standards that provide the most relevant amount that can be reliably measured. In recent years, the FASB has allowed increasing use of market values for certain assets and liabilities such as investments in marketable securities.

The **revenue recognition principle** is used to determine when revenue is recorded and reported. Under this principle, revenue is to be recognized or recorded in the period in which it is earned and the collection of cash is reasonably assured. The **matching principle** requires that an expense be recorded and reported in the same period as the revenue that it helped generate. Together, the application of the revenue recognition and matching principles determine a company's net income. These two principles will be discussed in more detail in Chapter 3.

The **conservatism principle** states that accountants should take care to avoid overstating assets or income when they prepare financial statements. The idea behind this principle is that conservatism is a prudent reaction to uncertainty and offsets management's natural optimism about the company's future prospects. However, conservatism should never be used to justify the deliberate understatement of assets or income.

Given this conceptual foundation, we will now turn our attention to the process of recording information about business activities in the accounting system.

The Accounting Cycle

OBJECTIVE ▶ 2
Explain the relationships among economic events, transactions, and the expanded accounting equation.

The sequence of procedures used by companies to transform the effects of business activities into financial statements is called the accounting cycle. The accounting cycle is shown in Exhibit 2-2.

The steps in the accounting cycle are performed each period and then repeated. Steps 1 through 4 are performed regularly each period as business activities occur. We will discuss these four steps in this chapter. Steps 5 through 7 are performed at the end of a period and are discussed in Chapter 3.

Economic Events

As we discussed in Chapter 1, a company engages in a multitude of activities that can be categorized as financing, investing, or operating activities. Each of these activities consists of many different **events** that affect the company. Some of these events are *external* and result from exchanges between the company and another entity outside of the company. For example, when GE issues common stock to investors, purchases equipment used to make an aircraft engine, sells a home appliance at a local retail store, or pays its employees a salary, it is engaging in an exchange with another entity. Other events are *internal* and result from the company's own actions. When GE uses

Exhibit 2-2

The Accounting Cycle

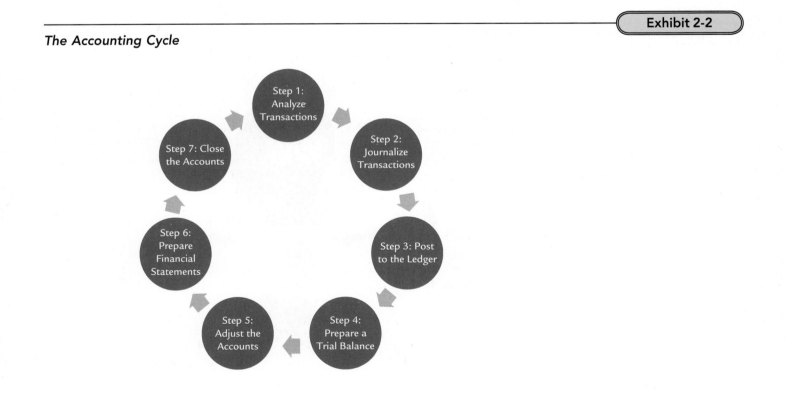

equipment to make its products, no other entity is involved; however, the event still has an impact on the company.

An objective of accounting is to measure the effects of events that influence a company and incorporate these events into the accounting system and, ultimately, the financial statements. However, not every event that affects a company is recorded in the accounting records. In order for an event to be recorded, or recognized, in the accounting system, the items making up the event must impact a financial statement element (asset, liability, stockholders' equity, revenue, or expense) and be measurable with sufficient reliability.

The first requirement usually is met when at least one party to a contract performs its responsibility according to the contract. For example, assume a buyer and seller agree upon the delivery of an asset and sign a contract. The signing of the contract usually is not recorded in the accounting system because neither party has performed its responsibility. Instead, recognition typically will occur once the buyer receives the asset or pays the seller, whichever comes first.

Even if the event impacts a financial statement element, it must be possible to reliably measure the event if it is to be recorded. A sudden increase in the price of oil or natural gas, for instance, may have an effect on GE's ability to sell its oil and natural gas compressors and turbines. However, the effects of this price increase cannot be measured reliably and will not be recognized in the financial statements. Providing a reliable measurement that is free from error or bias is important in accounting because unreliable information can mislead users of financial statements. A decision-maker would find it extremely difficult, if not impossible, to use financial statements that include unreliable numbers that failed to faithfully represent what has actually occurred. It is very important to pay attention to the recognition criteria as you consider an event for inclusion in the accounting system.

An accounting transaction results from an economic event that causes one of the elements of the financial statements (assets, liabilities, stockholders' equity, revenues, or expenses) to change and that can be measured reliably. We will use the term **transaction** to refer to any event, external or internal, that is recognized in the financial statements. The process of identifying events to be recorded in the financial statements is illustrated in Exhibit 2-3.

Exhibit 2-3

Transaction Identification

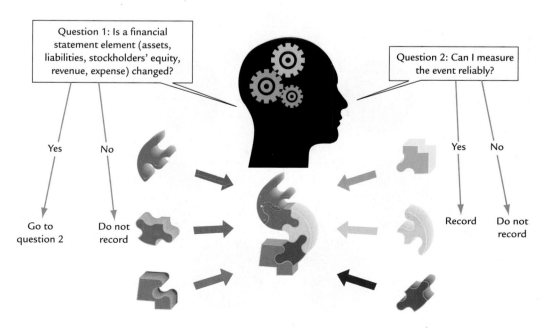

The Expanded Accounting Equation

Because accounting is concerned with the measurement of transactions and their effect on the financial statements, a starting point in the measurement and recording process is the fundamental accounting equation. Recall that this equation (Assets = Liabilities + Stockholders' Equity) expresses a company's resources and claims against these resources.

The two sides of the accounting equation change in response to business activities; however, the two sides must always be equal or "in balance" as a business moves through time. Accounting systems record business activities in a way that maintains this equality. As a consequence, every transaction has a two-part, or double-entry, effect on the equation.

In addition, recall that the balance sheet and the income statement are related through retained earnings. Specifically, net income (revenues minus expenses) increases retained earnings. Given this relationship, the fundamental accounting equation can be rewritten to show the elements that make up stockholders' equity.

With the expanded accounting equation shown in Exhibit 2-4, we are now ready to analyze how transactions affect a company's financial statements.

Exhibit 2-4

The Expanded Accounting Equation

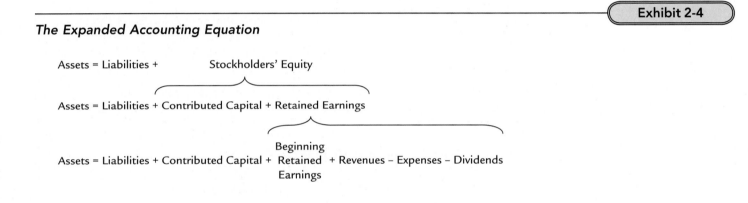

Step 1: Analyze Transactions

OBJECTIVE ▶ 3
Analyze the effect of business transactions on the accounting equation.

Transaction analysis is the process of determining the economic effects of a transaction on the elements of the accounting equation. Transaction analysis usually begins with the gathering of *source documents* that describe business activities. Source documents can be internally or externally prepared and include items such as purchase orders, cash register tapes, and invoices. In many accounting systems, source documents may be stored electronically on computer hard drives or other storage media. Source documents will describe the transaction and monetary amounts involved. These documents are the beginning of a "trail" of visible evidence that a transaction was processed by the accounting system.

After gathering the source documents, accountants must analyze these business activities to determine which transactions meet the criteria for recognition in the accounting records. Remember, not all transactions get recognized in the accounting system. For a transaction to be recorded in the accounting records, its effects must be reliably measured and it must affect a financial statement element (asset, liability, equity, revenue, or expense). Once it is determined that a transaction should be recorded in the accounting system, the transaction must be analyzed to determine how it will affect the accounting equation. In performing transaction analysis, it is important to remember that the accounting equation must always remain in balance. Therefore, each transaction will have at least two effects on the accounting equation. Cornerstone 2-1 illustrates the basic process of transaction analysis.

**CORNERSTONE
2-1**

HOW TO Perform Transaction Analysis

Concept:
The economic effect of a transaction will have a two-part, or dual, effect on the accounting equation that results in the equation remaining in balance.

Information:
Luigi, Inc., purchases a $3,000 computer from WorstBuy Electronics on credit, with payment due in 60 days.

Required:
Determine the effect of the transaction on the elements of the financial statements. Use the accounting equation with the following captions: assets, liabilities, contributed capital, and retained earnings.

Solution:
Transaction analysis involves the following three steps:

Step 1: Write down the accounting equation. We use an expanded version of the accounting equation because it provides more information in the analysis. However, the basic accounting equation could also be used if you desire.

Step 2: Identify the financial statement elements that are affected by the transaction. A computer is an economic resource, or asset, that will be used by Luigi in its business. This purchase created an obligation, or liability, for Luigi that is expected to be settled within 60 days.

Step 3: Determine whether the element increased or decreased. The receipt of the computer increased assets. The creation of the obligation caused Luigi's liabilities to increase.

These three steps are illustrated below:

Assets	=	Liabilities	+	Stockholders' Equity	
				Contributed Capital	Retained Earnings
+$3,000		+$3,000			

Note that the transaction analysis in Cornerstone 2-1 conformed to the two underlying principles of transaction analysis:

- There was a dual effect on the accounting equation.
- The accounting equation remained in balance (assets equaled liabilities plus stockholders' equity after the transaction).

All transactions can be analyzed using the process described above.

To provide a further illustration of the effect of transactions on the accounting equation, consider the case of HiTech Communications, Inc. HiTech is a newly formed corporation that operates an advertising agency that specializes in promoting computer-related products in the Cincinnati area. We show the effects of thirteen transactions on HiTech's financial position during its first month of operations, March 2009.

Transaction 1: Issuing Common Stock

On March 1, HiTech sold 1,000 shares of common stock to several investors for cash of $12,000. The effect of this transaction on the accounting equation is:

Assets	=	Liabilities	+	Stockholders' Equity	
				Contributed Capital	Retained Earnings
+$12,000				+$12,000	

The sale of stock increases assets, specifically cash, and also increases shareholders' equity (contributed capital or common stock). Notice that there is a dual effect, and although both assets and equity change, the equality of the equation is maintained.

Transaction 2: Borrowing Cash

On March 2, HiTech raised additional funds by borrowing $3,000 from First Third Bank of Cincinnati. HiTech promised to pay the amount borrowed plus 8 percent interest to First Third Bank in one year. The financial effect of this transaction is:

Assets	=	Liabilities	+	Stockholders' Equity	
				Contributed Capital	Retained Earnings
+$3,000		+$3,000			

This borrowing has two effects: the asset cash is increased and a liability is created. HiTech has an obligation to repay the cash borrowed according to the terms of the borrowing. Such a liability is termed a note payable. Because transactions *1* and *2* are concerned with obtaining funds to begin and operate a business, they are classified as financing activities.

Transaction 3: Purchase of Equipment for Cash

On March 3, HiTech purchased office equipment (e.g., computer equipment) from MicroCenter, Inc., for $4,500 in cash. The effect of this transaction on the accounting equation is:

Assets	=	Liabilities	+	Stockholders' Equity	
				Contributed Capital	Retained Earnings
+$4,500					
−$4,500					

There is a reduction in cash (an asset) as it is spent and a corresponding increase in another asset, equipment. The purchased equipment is an asset because HiTech will use it to generate future revenue. Notice that this transaction merely converts one asset (cash) into another (equipment). Total assets remain unchanged and the accounting equation remains in balance. Because transaction *3* is concerned with buying long-term assets that enable HiTech to operate, it is considered an investing activity.

Transaction 4: Purchasing Insurance

On March 4, HiTech purchased a six-month insurance policy for $1,200 cash. The effect of this transaction on the accounting equation is:

Assets	=	Liabilities	+	Stockholders' Equity	
				Contributed Capital	Retained Earnings
+$1,200					
−$1,200					

There is a reduction in cash (an asset) as it is spent and a corresponding increase in another asset, prepaid insurance. The purchased insurance is an asset because the insurance will benefit more than one accounting period. This type of asset is often referred to as a prepaid asset. Notice that like transaction 3, this transaction merely converts one asset (cash) into another (prepaid insurance). Total assets remain unchanged and the accounting equation remains in balance. Because transaction 4 is concerned with the operations of the company, it is classified as an operating activity.

Transaction 5: Purchase of Supplies on Credit

On March 6, HiTech purchased office supplies from Hamilton Office Supply for $6,500. Hamilton Office Supply agreed to accept full payment in 30 days. As a result of this transaction, HiTech received an asset (supplies) but also incurred a liability to pay for these supplies in 30 days. The financial effect of this transaction is:

Assets	=	Liabilities	+	Stockholders' Equity	
				Contributed Capital	Retained Earnings
+$6,500		+$6,500			

A transaction where goods are purchased on credit is often referred to as a purchase "on account" and the liability that is created is referred to as an Accounts Payable. Because transaction 5 is concerned with the operations of the company, it is classified as an operating activity.

Transaction 6: Sale of Services for Cash

On March 10, HiTech sold advertising services to Miami Valley Products in exchange for $8,800 in cash. Remember from Chapter 1 that revenue is defined as an increase in assets resulting from the sale of products or services. As an advertising company, the sale of advertising services is HiTech's primary revenue-producing activity. Therefore, this transaction results in an increase in assets (cash) and an increase in revenue.

Assets	=	Liabilities	+	Stockholders' Equity	
				Contributed Capital	Retained Earnings
+$8,800					+$8,800

As shown in the expanded accounting equation discussed earlier, *revenues increase retained earnings*. The dual effects (the increase in assets and the increase in retained earnings) maintain the balance of the accounting equation. Because transaction 6 is concerned with the operations of the company, it is classified as an operating activity.

Transaction 7: Sale of Services for Credit

On March 15, HiTech sold advertising services to the *Cincinnati Enquirer* for $3,300. HiTech agreed to accept full payment in 30 days. When a company performs services for which they will be paid at a later date, this is often referred to as a sale "on account." Instead of receiving cash, HiTech received a promise to pay from the *Cincinnati Enquirer*. This right to collect amounts due from customers creates an asset called an Accounts Receivable. Similar to the cash sale in transaction 6, the credit sale represents revenue for HiTech because assets (accounts receivable) were increased as a result of the sale of the advertising service. The financial effect of this transaction is:

Assets	=	Liabilities	+	Stockholders' Equity	
				Contributed Capital	Retained Earnings
+$3,300					+$3,300

Consistent with the revenue recognition principle discussed earlier in this chapter, *revenue is recorded when earned* (e.g., the service is provided), regardless of whether cash was received. Because transaction *7* is concerned with the operations of the company, it is classified as an operating activity.

Transaction 8: Receipt of Cash in Advance

On March 19, HiTech received $9,000 from the *OA News* for advertising services to be completed in the next three months. Similar to transaction *6,* HiTech received cash for services. However, due to the revenue recognition principle, HiTech cannot recognize revenue until it has performed the advertising service. Therefore, the receipt of cash creates a liability for HiTech for the work that is due in the future. The effect of this transaction on the accounting equation is:

Assets	=	Liabilities	+	Stockholders' Equity	
				Contributed Capital	Retained Earnings
+$9,000		+$9,000			

The liability that is created by the receipt of cash in advance of performing the revenue-generating activities is called an unearned revenue. Because transaction *8* is concerned with the operations of the company, it is classified as an operating activity.

Transaction 9: Payment of a Liability

On March 23, HiTech pays $6,000 cash for the supplies previously purchased from Hamilton Office Supply on credit (transaction *5*). The payment results in a reduction of an asset (cash) and the settlement of HiTech's obligation (liability) to Hamilton Office Supply. The financial effect of this transaction is:

Assets	=	Liabilities	+	Stockholders' Equity	
				Contributed Capital	Retained Earnings
−$6,000		−$6,000			

As a result of this cash payment, the liability "Accounts Payable" is reduced to $500 ($6,500 − $6,000). This means that HiTech still owes Hamilton Office Supply $500. Notice that the payment of cash did not result in an expense. The expense related to supplies will be recorded as supplies are used. Because Transaction *9* is concerned with the operations of the company, it is classified as an operating activity.

Transaction 10: Payment of Salaries

On March 26 (a Friday), HiTech paid weekly employee salaries of $1,800. Remember from Chapter 1 that an expense is the cost of an asset consumed in the operation of the business. Because an asset (cash) is consumed as part of HiTech's normal operations, salaries are an expense. As shown in the expanded accounting equation discussed earlier, *expenses decrease retained earnings.* The effect of this transaction on the accounting equation is:

Assets	=	Liabilities	+	Stockholders' Equity	
				Contributed Capital	Retained Earnings
−$1,800					−$1,800

Consistent with the matching principle discussed earlier in this chapter, *expenses are recorded in the same period as the revenue that it helped generate.* Because transaction *10* is concerned with the operations of the company, it is classified as an operating activity.

Transaction 11: Collection of a Receivable

On March 29, HiTech collected $3,000 cash from the *Cincinnati Enquirer* for services sold earlier on credit (transaction *7*). The collection of cash increases assets. In addition, the accounts receivable (an asset) from the *Cincinnati Enquirer* is also reduced. The financial effect of this transaction is:

Assets	=	Liabilities	+	Stockholders' Equity	
				Contributed Capital	Retained Earnings
+$3,000 −$3,000					

As a result of this cash payment, the *Cincinnati Enquirer* still owes HiTech $300. Notice that the cash collection did not result in the recognition of a revenue. The revenue was recognized as the service was performed (transaction *7*). Because transaction *11* is concerned with the operations of the company, it is classified as an operating activity.

Transaction 12: Payment of Utilities

On March 30, HiTech paid its utility bill of $5,200 for March. Because an asset (cash) is consumed as HiTech performs its advertising services, the cost of utilities used during the month is an expense. The effect of this transaction on the accounting equation is:

Assets	=	Liabilities	+	Stockholders' Equity	
				Contributed Capital	Retained Earnings
−$5,200					−$5,200

Similar to the payment of salaries, utility expense is recorded as a decrease in retained earnings in the same period that it helped to generate revenue. Because transaction *12* is concerned with the operations of the company, it is classified as an operating activity.

Transaction 13: Payment of a Dividend

On March 31, HiTech declared and paid a cash dividend of $500 to its stockholders. Dividends are not an expense. Dividends are a distribution of net income and are recorded as a direct reduction of retained earnings. The effect of this transaction on the accounting equation is:

Assets	=	Liabilities	+	Stockholders' Equity	
				Contributed Capital	Retained Earnings
−$500					−$500

The payment of a dividend is classified as a financing activity.

Exhibit 2-5 summarizes the transactions of HiTech Communications, Inc., in order to show their cumulative effect on the accounting equation. The transaction number is shown in the first column on the left. Revenue and expense items are identified on the right. Notice that this summary reinforces the two key principles discussed earlier:

- Each transaction has a dual effect on the elements of the accounting equation.
- The accounting equation always remains in balance—the total change in assets ($29,100) equals the change in liabilities plus stockholders' equity ($29,100).

Exhibit 2-5

Summary of Transactions

	Assets	=	Liabilities +	Stockholders' Equity	
				Contributed Capital	Retained Earnings
(1)	+ $12,000			+ $12,000	
(2)	+ $3,000		+ $3,000		
(3)	+ $4,500				
	− $4,500				
(4)	+ $1,200				
	− $1,200				
(5)	+ $6,500		+ $6,500		
(6)	+ $8,800				+ $8,800 } Revenue
(7)	+ $3,300				+ $3,300
(8)	+ $9,000		+ $9,000		
(9)	− $6,000		− $6,000		
(10)	− $1,800				− $1,800
(11)	+ $3,000				Expense
	− $3,000				
(12)	− $5,200				− $5,200
(13)	− $500				− $500 Dividend
	$29,100		$12,500	$12,000	$4,600

$29,100   = $29,100

Transaction analysis can be used to answer many important questions about a company and its activities. Using the information in Exhibit 2-5, we can answer the following questions:

* *What are the amounts of total assets, total liabilities, and total equity at the end of March?* At the end of March, HiTech has total assets of $29,100, total liabilities of $12,500 and total equity of $16,600 ($12,000 of contributed capital plus $4,600 of retained earnings). These amounts for assets, liabilities, and stockholders' equity at the end of March would be carried over as the beginning amounts for April.
* *What is net income for the month?* Net income is $5,100 which represents the excess of revenues of $12,100 ($8,800 + $3,300) over expenses of $7,000 ($5,200 + $1,800). Notice that dividends are not included in income; instead they are included on the statement of retained earnings.
* *How much cash was received during the month? How much was spent? How much cash does HiTech have at the end of the month?* During March HiTech received a total of $35,800 in cash ($12,000 + $3,000 + $8,800 + $9,000 + $3,000) and spent a total of $19,200 ($4,500 + $1,200 + $6,000 + $1,800 + $5,200 + $500). At the end of the month, HiTech had cash on hand of $16,600 ($35,800 − $19,200).

The summary in Exhibit 2-5 can become quite cumbersome. For example, in order to determine the amount of cash that HiTech has at the end of the month, you may find it necessary to refer back to the actual transactions to determine which ones involved cash and which did not. In addition, what if an investor or creditor wanted to know not only net income but also the types of expenses that HiTech incurred? (e.g., What was the dollar amount spent for salaries?). Clearly, to answer these questions, more information is needed than the transaction summary presents. For a company like GE, a spreadsheet such as the preceding one would prove inadequate to convey its financial information to investors and creditors. A better way to record and track information that is consistent with the preceding model is necessary. The solution is double-entry accounting.

Double-Entry Accounting

Double-entry accounting describes the system used by companies to record the effects of transactions on the accounting equation. The effects of transactions are recorded in accounts. Under double-entry accounting, each transaction affects at least two accounts. In this section, we will explore accounts and the process by which transactions get reflected in specific accounts.

Accounts

To aid in the recording of transactions, an organizational system consisting of accounts has been developed. An **account** is a record of increases and decreases in each of the basic elements of the financial statements. Each financial statement element is composed of a variety of accounts. All changes in assets, liabilities, stockholders' equity, revenues, or expenses are then recorded in the appropriate account. The list of accounts used by the company is termed a **chart of accounts**. A typical list of accounts is shown in Exhibit 2-6. These accounts were all discussed in Chapter 1.

Exhibit 2-6

Typical Accounts

Assets	Liabilities	Stockholders' Equity	Revenue	Expense
Cash	Accounts Payable	Common Stock	Sales	Cost of Goods Sold
Short-term Investments	Salaries Payable	Retained Earnings	Interest Revenue	Salary Expense
Accounts Receivable	Unearned Revenue		Rent Revenue	Rent Expense
Inventory	Interest Payable			Insurance Expense
Long-term Investments	Taxes Payable			Depreciation Expense
Land	Notes Payable			Advertising Expense
Building	Bonds Payable			Utility Expense
Equipment				Repair Expense
Intangibles				Property Tax Expense

Every company will have a different chart of accounts depending on the nature of its business activities. However, once a company selects which accounts will be used, all transactions must be recorded into these accounts. As the company engages in transactions, the transaction will either increase or decrease an account. The amount in an account at any time is called the *balance* of the account. For example, the purchase of equipment will increase the balance in the equipment account, whereas the disposal of equipment will decrease the balance of the equipment account. For financial reporting purposes, the balances of related accounts typically are combined and reported as a single amount. For example, GE reports a combined, or net, amount of property, plant, and equipment on its balance sheet. However, in its footnotes, GE discloses the amounts of individual accounts such as land, buildings, and machinery.

Although an account can be shown in a variety of ways, transactions are frequently analyzed using a **T-account**. The T-account gets its name because it resembles the capital letter T (see Exhibit 2-7). A T-account is a two-column record that consists of an account

Exhibit 2-7

Form of a T-Account

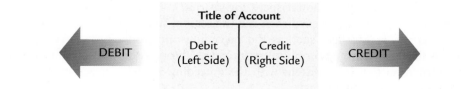

title and two sides divided by a vertical line—the left and the right side. The left side is referred to as the **debit** side and the right side is referred to as the **credit** side.

Note that the terms debit and credit simply refer to the left and the right side of an account. The left is always the debit side and the right is always the credit side. *Debit and credit do not represent increases or decreases.* (Increases or decreases to accounts are discussed in the next section.) Instead, debit and credit simply refer to *where* an entry is made in an account. The terms debit and credit will also be used to refer to the act of entering dollar amounts into an account. For example, entering an amount on the left side of an account will be called debiting the account. Entering an amount on the right side of an account is called crediting the account.

You may be tempted to associate the terms credit and debit with positive or negative events. For example, assume you returned an item that you purchased with a credit card to the local store and the store credited your card. This is generally viewed as a positive event since you now owe less money than you previously owed. Or, if you receive a notice that your bank had debited your account to pay for service charges that you owe, this is viewed negatively because you now have less money in your account. You should try to resist this temptation. In accounting, *debit means the left side of an account and credit means the right side of an account.*

Debit and Credit Procedures

Using the accounting equation, we can incorporate debits and credits in order to determine how balance sheet accounts increase or decrease. This procedure is shown in Cornerstone 2-2.

HOW TO Determine Increases or Decreases to a Balance Sheet Account

Concept:
Increases or decreases to an account are based on the normal balance of the account.

Information:
In your introductory accounting course, you are confronted with the three balance sheet accounts—assets, liabilities, and stockholders' equity.

Required:
Determine how each of the three balance sheet accounts increases or decreases.

Solution:
Our analysis begins with a T-account depiction of each balance sheet account and consists of three steps:

Step 1: Draw a T-account and label each side of the t-account as either debit or credit. Note that debit is always written on the left side of each account, and credit is always written on the right side.

Step 2: Determine the normal balance of an account. All accounts have a **normal balance**. Because assets are located on the left side of the accounting equation, their normal balance is a debit. Because liabilities and stockholders' equity are on the right side of the accounting equation, their normal balance is a credit. While individual transactions will increase and decrease an account, it would be unusual for an account to have a nonnormal balance.

CORNERSTONE 2-2

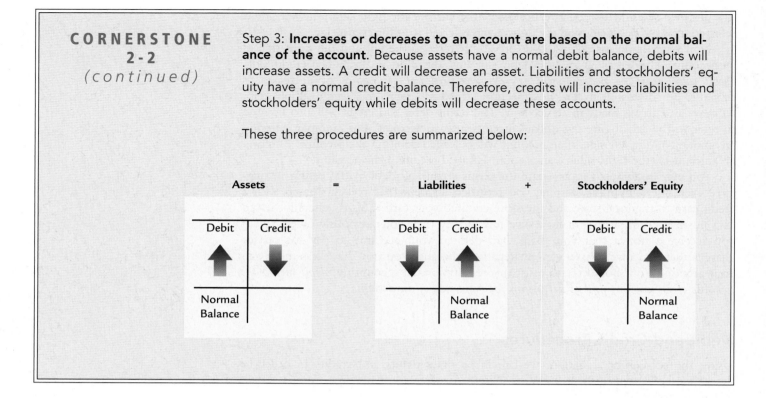

CORNERSTONE 2-2 *(continued)*

Step 3: Increases or decreases to an account are based on the normal balance of the account. Because assets have a normal debit balance, debits will increase assets. A credit will decrease an asset. Liabilities and stockholders' equity have a normal credit balance. Therefore, credits will increase liabilities and stockholders' equity while debits will decrease these accounts.

These three procedures are summarized below:

As we illustrated earlier in the chapter, every transaction will increase or decrease the elements of the accounting equation—assets, liabilities, and stockholders' equity. The direction of these increases and decreases must be such that the accounting equation stays in balance—the left side must equal the right side. In other words, *debits must equal credits*. This equality of debits and credits provides the foundation of **double-entry accounting** in which the two-sided effect of a transaction is recorded in the accounting system.

A similar procedure can be used to determine how increases and decreases are recorded for other financial statement elements. From the expanded accounting equation shown in Exhibit 2-4, we can see that stockholders' equity consists of both contributed capital (e.g., common stock) and retained earnings. As stockholder equity accounts, both contributed capital and retained earnings have normal credit balances as shown in Exhibit 2-8. Because these accounts have normal credit balances, they are increased by credits and decreased by debits.

 Exhibit 2-8

Normal Balances of Contributed Capital and Retained Earnings

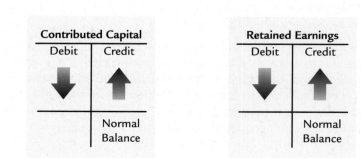

Retained earnings represent a company's accumulated net income (revenues minus expenses) minus any dividends. As we saw from the transaction analysis presented earlier in the chapter:

- Revenues increase retained earnings
- Expenses decrease retained earnings
- Dividends decrease retained earnings

Using these relationships, Cornerstone 2-3 demonstrates how increases and decreases in these accounts are recorded.

HOW TO Determine Increases or Decreases to Revenues, Expenses and Dividends

CORNERSTONE 2-3

Concept:
Increases or decreases to an account are based on the normal balance of the account.

Information:
In your introductory accounting course, you are confronted with the three accounts—revenues, expenses, and dividends.

Required:
Determine how each of these three accounts increases or decreases.

Solution:
Our analysis begins with a T-account depiction of each account and consists of three steps:

Step 1: Label each side of the t-account as either debit or credit.

Step 2: Determine the normal balance of an account.

- Revenues increase stockholders' equity through retained earnings. Therefore, revenues have a normal credit balance.
- Expenses decrease stockholders' equity through retained earnings. Therefore, expenses have a normal debit balance.
- Dividends are defined as a distribution of retained earnings. Because dividends reduce retained earnings and stockholders' equity, dividends have a normal debit balance.

Step 3: Increases or decreases to an account are based on the normal balance of the account.

- Because revenues have a normal credit balance, credits will increase revenues. Debits will decrease revenues.
- Expenses and dividends have a normal debit balances. Therefore, debits will increase expenses and dividends while credits will decrease these accounts.

These procedures are summarized below.

CONCEPT Q&A

On a bank statement, a credit to a person's account means the account has increased. Similarly, a debit means the account has decreased. Why don't credit and debit always mean "add" and "subtract"?

Possible Answer:

From the bank's perspective, a person's account is a liability since the bank must pay cash on demand. Because liabilities have normal credit balances, a credit will increase the account and a debit will decrease the account. However, from an individual's perspective, cash is an asset which has a normal debit balance. Therefore, debits increase cash and credits decrease cash. It is critical to always look at the normal balance of an account before determining if a transaction increases or decreases an account.

From Cornerstone 2-3, you should notice several items. First, revenues and expenses have opposite effects on retained earnings; therefore, revenues and expenses have opposite normal balances. Second, any change (increase or decrease) in revenue, expense, or dividends effects the balance of stockholders' equity. Specifically, an increase in revenue increases stockholders' equity and a decrease in revenue decreases stockholders' equity. An increase in expense or dividends decreases stockholders' equity. A decrease in expense or dividends increases stockholders' equity. Finally, when revenues exceed expenses, a company has reported net income which increases stockholders' equity. When revenues are less than expenses, a company has reported a net loss, which reduces stockholders' equity.

These debit and credit procedures are summarized in Exhibit 2-9.

Exhibit 2-9

Summary of Debit and Credit Procedures

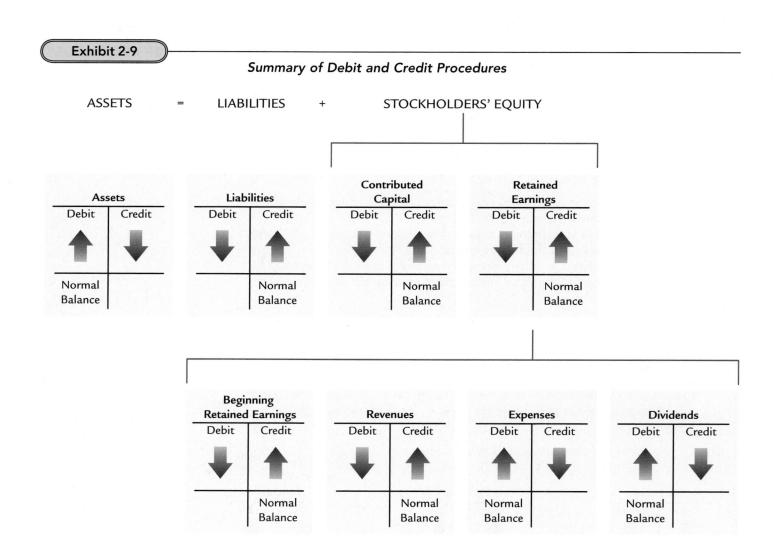

The important point from this analysis is that while debits are always on the left and credits are always on the right, the effect of a debit or credit on an account balance depends upon the normal balance of that account.

Step 2: Journalize Transactions

OBJECTIVE ▶ 5
Prepare journal entries for transactions.

While it would be possible to record transactions directly into accounts in a manner similar to that illustrated earlier in the chapter, most companies enter the effects of the transaction in a journal using the debit and credit procedures described in the previous section. A **journal** is a chronological record showing the debit and credit effects of transactions on a company. Each transaction is represented by a **journal entry** so that the entire effect of a transaction is contained in one place. The process of making a journal entry is often referred to as *journalizing* a transaction. Because a transaction first enters the accounting records through journal entries, the journal is often referred to as the *book of original entry.*

A journal entry consists of three parts: (1) the date of the transaction, (2) the accounts and amounts to be increased or decreased, and (3) a brief explanation of the transaction. Each journal entry shows the debit and credit effects of a transaction on specific accounts. In preparing a journal entry, almost every company follows the process illustrated in Cornerstone 2-4.

HOW TO Make a Journal Entry

Concept:
A journal entry records the effects of a transaction on accounts using debits and credits.

Information:
On January 1, Luigi, Inc., purchases a $3,000 computer from WorstBuy Electronics on credit, with payment due in 60 days.

Required:
Prepare a journal entry to record this transaction.

Solution:
Preparing a journal entry involves three basic steps.

Step 1: Analyze the transaction using the procedures described in Cornerstone 2-1. The result of this analysis is shown below.

Assets	=	Liabilities	+	Stockholders' Equity	
				Contributed Capital	Retained Earnings
+$3,000		+$3,000			

Step 2: Determine which accounts are affected. The purchase of a computer has increased the asset account "Equipment." In addition, the liability that was created is called "Accounts Payable."

Step 3: Prepare the journal entry using the debit and credit procedures in Cornerstones 2-2 and 2-3. For the asset "Equipment," the increase is recorded with a debit. For the liability "Accounts Payable," the increase is recorded with a credit.

Date	Account and Explanation	Debit	Credit
Jan. 1	Equipment	3,000	
	Accounts Payable		3,000
	(Purchased office equipment on credit)		

**CORNERSTONE
2-4**

From Step 3 of Cornerstone 2-4, notice several items. First, the date of the transaction is entered in the date column. Second, for each entry in the journal, the debit (the account and amount) is entered first and flush to the left. If there were more than one debit, it would be entered directly underneath the first debit on the next line. The credit (the account and the amount) is written below the debits and indented to the right. The purpose of this standard format is to make it possible for anyone using the journal to identify debits and credits quickly and correctly. Third, *total debits must equal total credits.* Finally, an explanation may appear beneath the credit.

In some instances, more than two accounts may be affected by an economic event. For example, assume that Luigi, Inc., purchases a $3,000 computer from WorstBuy Electronics by paying $1,000 cash with the remainder due in 60 days. The purchase of this equipment increased the asset "Equipment," decreased the asset "Cash," and increased the liability "Accounts Payable" as shown in the analysis below:

Assets	=	Liabilities	+	Stockholders' Equity	
				Contributed Capital	Retained Earnings
+$3,000		+$2,000			
−$1,000					

Luigi would make the following journal entry

Date	Account and Explanation	Debit	Credit
Jan. 1	Equipment	3,000	
	Cash		1,000
	Accounts Payable		2,000
	(Purchased office equipment for cash and on credit)		

This type of entry is called a *compound journal entry* because more than two accounts were affected.

The use of a journal helps prevent the introduction of errors in the transformation of business activities into financial statement amounts. Because all parts of the transaction appear together, it is easy to see whether equal debits and credits have been entered. If debits equal credits for *each* journal entry, then debits equal credits for *all* journal entries. At the end of the period, this fact leads to a useful check on the accuracy of journal entries. However, if the wrong amounts or the wrong accounts are used, debits can still equal credits, yet the journal entries will be incorrect. Additionally, each entry can be examined to see if the accounts that appear together are logically appropriate.

DECISION-MAKING & ANALYSIS

Detecting Journal Entry Errors

You have been asked to inspect a delivery company's journal. Upon doing so, you find the following entry:

Date	Account and Explanation	Debit	Credit
June 29	Equipment, Delivery Truck	11,000	
	Prepaid Rent		11,000
	(Purchased delivery truck)		

You know that delivery trucks are not exchanged for prepaid rent, so you conclude that an error was made in preparing this journal entry. Had the same data been entered directly into the accounts, the error would have been much more difficult to detect and correct.

ETHICS When an error is discovered in a journal entry, the accountant has an ethical responsibility to correct the error (subject to materiality constraints), even if others would never be able to tell that the error had occurred! For example, if an accountant accidentally records a sale of merchandise by crediting Interest Revenue instead of Sales Revenue, total revenue would be unaffected. However, this error could significantly affect summary performance measures such as gross margin (sales minus cost of goods sold) that are important to many investors. When material errors are discovered, they should be corrected, even if this means embarrassment to the accountant.◆

To provide a further illustration of recording transactions using journal entries, consider the case of HiTech Communications, Inc. that was presented earlier in the chapter. For the remainder of the book, we will analyze each transaction and report its effects on the accounting equation in the margin next to the journal entry. Next, we identify the accounts that were affected by incorporating account titles into the transaction analysis model. Finally, we prepare the journal entry based on the analysis. You should always perform these steps as you prepare journal entries.

CONCEPT Q&A

If all journal entries have equal debits and credits, how can mistakes or errors occur?

Possible Answer:

Mistakes or errors could still occur when entire transactions are not recorded, transactions are recorded at the wrong amounts or in the wrong accounts, or transactions are not recorded in the proper accounting period. In addition, an accountant may post incorrect amounts or post the correct amount to an incorrect account. While journal entries provide a safeguard against errors and mistakes, it will not prevent them all.

Transaction 1: Issuing Common Stock

On March 1, HiTech sold 1,000 shares of common stock to several investors for cash of $12,000.

Date	Account and Explanation	Debit	Credit
March 1	Cash	12,000	
	Common Stock		12,000
	(Issued common stock)		

		Stockholders'
Assets =	Liabilities +	Equity
+12,000		+12,000

Transaction 2: Borrowing Cash

On March 2, HiTech raised additional funds by borrowing $3,000 on a one-year, 8 percent note payable to First Third Bank of Cincinnati.

Date	Account and Explanation	Debit	Credit
March 2	Cash	3,000	
	Notes Payable		3,000
	(Borrowed cash from bank)		

		Stockholders'
Assets =	Liabilities +	Equity
+3,000	+3,000	

Transaction 3: Purchase of Equipment for Cash

On March 3, HiTech purchased office equipment (e.g., computer equipment) from MicroCenter, Inc., for $4,500 in cash.

Date	Account and Explanation	Debit	Credit
March 3	Equipment	4,500	
	Cash		4,500
	(Purchased equipment)		

		Stockholders'
Assets =	Liabilities +	Equity
+4,500		
−4,500		

Transaction 4: Purchasing Insurance

On March 4, HiTech purchased a six-month insurance policy for $1,200 in cash.

Date	Account and Explanation	Debit	Credit
March 4	Prepaid Insurance	1,200	
	Cash		1,200
	(Purchased insurance in advance)		

		Stockholders'
Assets =	Liabilities +	Equity
+1,200		
−1,200		

Transaction 5: Purchase of Supplies on Credit

On March 6, HiTech purchased office supplies from Hamilton Office Supply for $6,500. Hamilton Office Supply agreed to accept full payment in 30 days.

		Stockholders'
Assets =	**Liabilities** +	**Equity**
+6,500	+6,500	

Date	Account and Explanation	Debit	Credit
March 6	Supplies	6,500	
	Accounts Payable		6,500
	(Purchased supplies on account)		

Transaction 6: Sale of Services for Cash

On March 10, HiTech sold advertising services to Miami Valley Products in exchange for $8,800 in cash.

		Stockholders'
Assets =	**Liabilities** +	**Equity**
+8,800		+8,800

Date	Account and Explanation	Debit	Credit
March 10	Cash	8,800	
	Service Revenue		8,800
	(Sold advertising services)		

Transaction 7: Sale of Services for Credit

On March 15, HiTech sold advertising services to the *Cincinnati Enquirer* for $3,300. HiTech agreed to accept full payment in 30 days.

		Stockholders'
Assets =	**Liabilities** +	**Equity**
+3,300		+3,300

Date	Account and Explanation	Debit	Credit
March 15	Accounts Receivable	3,300	
	Service Revenue		3,300
	(Sold advertising services)		

Transaction 8: Receipt of Cash in Advance

On March 19, HiTech received $9,000 in advance for advertising services to be completed in the next three months.

		Stockholders'
Assets =	**Liabilities** +	**Equity**
+9,000	+9,000	

Date	Account and Explanation	Debit	Credit
March 19	Cash	9,000	
	Unearned Revenue		9,000
	(Sold advertising services in advance)		

Transaction 9: Payment of a Liability

On March 23, HiTech pays $6,000 cash for the supplies previously purchased from Hamilton Office Supply (transaction 5).

		Stockholders'
Assets =	**Liabilities** +	**Equity**
−6,000	−6,000	

Date	Account and Explanation	Debit	Credit
March 23	Accounts Payable	6,000	
	Cash		6,000
	(Paid accounts payable)		

Transaction 10: Payment of Salaries

On March 26, HiTech paid employees their weekly salary of $1,800 cash.

		Stockholders'
Assets =	**Liabilities** +	**Equity**
−1,800		−1,800

Date	Account and Explanation	Debit	Credit
March 26	Salaries Expense	1,800	
	Cash		1,800
	(Paid employee salaries)		

Transaction 11: Collection of a Receivable

On March 29, HiTech collected $3,000 cash from the *Cincinnati Enquirer* for services sold earlier on credit (transaction 7).

Date	Account and Explanation	Debit	Credit
March 29	Cash	3,000	
	Accounts Receivable		3,000
	(Collected accounts receivable)		

Assets	= Liabilities +	Stockholders' Equity
+3,000		
−3,000		

Transaction 12: Payment of Utilities

On March 30, HiTech paid its utility bill of $5,200 for March.

Date	Account and Explanation	Debit	Credit
March 30	Utilities Expense	5,200	
	Cash		5,200
	(Paid for utilities used)		

Assets	= Liabilities +	Stockholders' Equity
−5,200		−5,200

Transaction 13: Payment of a Dividend

On March 31, HiTech declared and paid a cash dividend of $500 to its stockholders.

Date	Account and Explanation	Debit	Credit
March 31	Dividends	500	
	Cash		500
	(Declared and paid a cash dividend)		

Assets	= Liabilities +	Stockholders' Equity
−500		−500

Step 3: Post to the Ledger

OBJECTIVE ▶ 6

Explain why transactions are posted to the general ledger.

Because the journal lists each transaction in chronological order, it can be quite difficult to use the journal to determine the balance in any specific account. For example, refer to the journal entries shown earlier for HiTech Communications. What is the balance in cash at the end of the month? This relatively simple question is difficult to answer with the use of the journal.

To overcome this difficulty, companies will use a general ledger to keep track of the balances of specific accounts. A **general ledger** is simply a collection of all the individual financial statement accounts that a company uses.[3] In a manual accounting system, a ledger could be as a simple as a notebook with a separate page for each account. Ledger accounts are often shown using the T-account format introduced earlier or the column-balance format. We will describe the column-balance format next.

The process of transferring the information from the journalized transaction to the general ledger is called **posting**. Posting is essentially copying the information from the journal into the ledger. Debits in the journal are posted as debits to the specific ledger account, and credits in the journal are posted as credits in the specific ledger account. To facilitate this process, most journals and ledgers have a column titled "Posting Reference." As the information is copied into the ledger, the number assigned to the account is placed in the "Posting Reference" column of the journal and the journal page number is placed in the "Posting Reference" column of the ledger. This column provides a link between the ledger and journal that (1) helps to prevent errors in the posting process and (2) allows you to trace the effects of a transaction through the accounting system. The posting process is illustrated in Exhibit 2-10 which shows an illustration of a journal page and a ledger page for HiTech Communications.

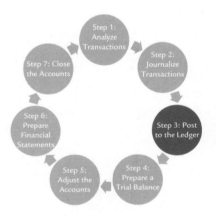

---

[3] Most companies supplement the general ledger with subsidiary ledgers that record "subaccounts" that make up the larger general ledger account. For example, most companies have an account called Accounts Receivable in the general ledger. However, the accounts receivable for individual customers are usually contained in a subsidiary ledger. The general ledger account will equal the total balance of all the accounts in the subsidiary ledger for that account.

Exhibit 2-10

The Posting Process

GENERAL JOURNAL				
				Page: 2
Date	Account and Explanation	Post. Ref.	Debit	Credit
Mar. 31	Dividends	1100	500	
	Cash	1000		500
	(Declared and paid cash dividend)			

GENERAL LEDGER					
Account: CASH				Account Number: 1000	
Date	Explanation	Post. Ref.	Debit	Credit	Balance
Mar. 1	Issued stock	1	12,000		12,000
2	Borrowed from bank	1	3,000		15,000
3	Purchased equipment	1		4,500	10,500
4	Purchased insurance	1		1,200	9,300
10	Sold advertising services	1	8,800		18,100
19	Sold advertising services in advance	1	9,000		27,100
23	Paid accounts payable	1		6,000	21,100
28	Paid salaries	1		1,800	19,300
29	Collected receivable	2	3,000		22,300
30	Paid utilities	2		5,200	17,100
31	Paid dividend	2		500	16,600

The ledger for HiTech Communications is shown using T-accounts in Exhibit 2-11. The number in parentheses corresponds to the transaction number.

OBJECTIVE ▶ 7

Prepare a trial balance and explain its purpose.

Step 4: Prepare a Trial Balance

To aid in the preparation of financial statements, some companies will prepare a trial balance before they prepare financial statements. The **trial balance** is a list of all active accounts and each account's debit or credit balance. The accounts are listed in the order they appear in the ledger—assets first, then liabilities, stockholders' equity, revenues, and expenses. By organizing accounts in this manner, the trial balance serves as a useful tool in preparing the financial statements. The trial balance for HiTech Communications is shown in Exhibit 2-12.

In addition, the trial balance is used to *prove the equality of debits and credits*. If debits did not equal credits, the accountant would quickly know that an error had been made. The error could have been in the journalizing of the transaction, the posting of the transaction, or in the computation of the balance in the ledger. However, *a word of caution is necessary* here: A trial balance whose debits equal credits does *not* mean that all transactions were recorded correctly. A trial balance will not detect errors of analysis or amounts. Sometimes the wrong account is selected for a journal entry or an incorrect amount is recorded for a transaction. In other cases, a journal entry is omitted or entered twice. As long as both the debit and credit portions of the journal entry or posting reflect the incorrect information, the debit and credit totals in a trial balance will be equal.

Exhibit 2-11

General Ledger of HiTech Communications

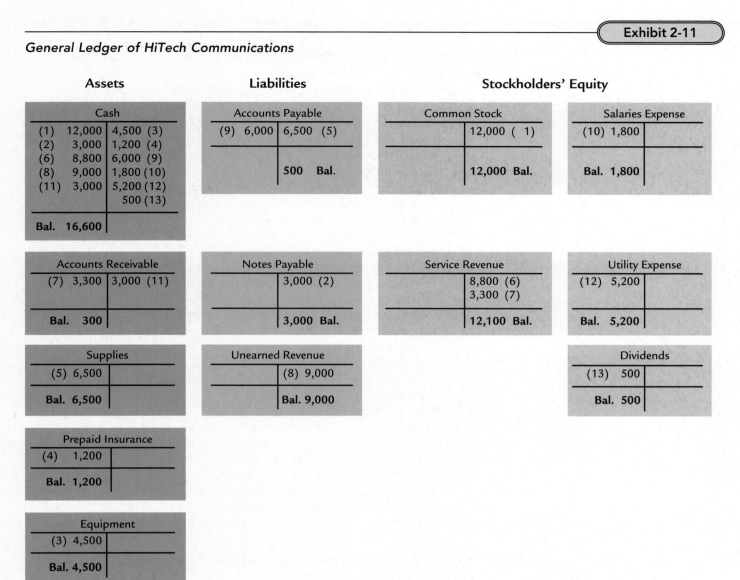

| | Assets | | Liabilities | | Stockholders' Equity | |

Assets

Cash

(1)	12,000	4,500	(3)
(2)	3,000	1,200	(4)
(6)	8,800	6,000	(9)
(8)	9,000	1,800	(10)
(11)	3,000	5,200	(12)
		500	(13)
Bal.	**16,600**		

Accounts Receivable

| (7) | 3,300 | 3,000 | (11) |
| **Bal.** | **300** | | |

Supplies

| (5) | 6,500 | |
| **Bal.** | **6,500** | |

Prepaid Insurance

| (4) | 1,200 | |
| **Bal.** | **1,200** | |

Equipment

| (3) | 4,500 | |
| **Bal.** | **4,500** | |

Liabilities

Accounts Payable

| (9) | 6,000 | 6,500 | (5) |
| | | 500 | **Bal.** |

Notes Payable

| | | 3,000 | (2) |
| | | 3,000 | **Bal.** |

Unearned Revenue

| | | 9,000 | (8) |
| | | **9,000** | **Bal.** |

Stockholders' Equity

Common Stock

| | | 12,000 | (1) |
| | | 12,000 | **Bal.** |

Service Revenue

		8,800	(6)
		3,300	(7)
		12,100	**Bal.**

Salaries Expense

| (10) | 1,800 | |
| **Bal.** | **1,800** | |

Utility Expense

| (12) | 5,200 | |
| **Bal.** | **5,200** | |

Dividends

| (13) | 500 | |
| **Bal.** | **500** | |

Exhibit 2-12

Trial Balance

HiTech Communications, Inc. Trial Balance March 31, 2009		
Account	**Debit**	**Credit**
Cash	$16,600	
Accounts Receivable	300	
Supplies	6,500	
Prepaid Insurance	1,200	
Equipment	4,500	
Accounts Payable		$ 500
Unearned Revenue		9,000
Notes Payable		3,000
Common Stock		12,000
Dividends	500	
Service Revenue		12,100
Salaries Expense	1,800	
Utility Expense	5,200	
	$36,600	$36,600

Summary of Learning Objectives

LO1. Describe the assumptions and principles that underlie accounting.

- The qualitative characteristics of accounting information are:
  1. Relevance—refers to whether information is capable of making a difference in the decision-making process. Relevant information is provided in a timely manner and either helps to predict the future or provides feedback about prior expectations.
  2. Reliability—information that can be depended upon by users. Reliable information should be verifiable, representationally faithful, and neutral.
  3. Comparability—allows comparisons to be made between companies.
  4. Consistency—refers to the application of the same accounting principle by a single company over time.
- The four assumptions are:
  1. Economic entity—each company is accounted for separately from its owners
  2. Continuity (going-concern)—assumption that a company will continue to operate long enough to carry out its commitments
  3. Time-period—allows the life of a company to be divided into artificial time periods
  4. Monetary unit—requires financial information to be reported in monetary terms
- The four principles are:
  1. Historical cost—requires a business activity to be recorded at the exchange price at the time the activity occurs
  2. Revenue recognition—requires revenue to be recognized when it is realized and earned
  3. Matching principle—requires that expenses be recognized in the same period as the revenue that it helped generate
  4. Conservatism—requires care to be taken to avoid overstating assets or income.

LO2. Explain the relationships among economic events, transactions, and the expanded accounting equation.

- A company's business activities (operating, investing, and financing) consist of many different economic events that are both external to the company as well as internal to the company. Accounting attempts to measure the economic effect of these events. However, not all events are recognized, or recorded, in the accounting system.
- A transaction is an economic event that is recognized in the financial statements. An accounting transaction causes the elements of the accounting equation (assets, liabilities, contributed capital, retained earnings, revenues, expenses, or dividends) to change in a way that maintains the equality of their relationship.

LO3. Analyze the effect of business transactions on the accounting equation.

- This is Step 1 of the accounting cycle.
- Transaction analysis is the process of determining the economic effects of a transaction on the elements of the accounting equation.
- Transaction analysis involves three steps:
  Step 1: Write down the accounting equation (basic or expanded version).
  Step 2: Identify the financial statement elements that are affected by the transaction.
  Step 3: Determine whether the element increased or decreased. Each transaction will have a dual-effect on the accounting equation, and the accounting equation will remain in balance after the effects of the transaction are recorded.

LO4. Discuss the role of accounts and how debits and credits are used in the double-entry accounting system.

- An account is a record of increases and decreases in each of the basic elements of the financial statements.
- Each financial statement element is made up of a number of different accounts.
- All transactions are recorded into accounts.
- The final account balance, after all changes are recorded, is used in the preparation of the financial statements.
- The left side of an account is referred to as a debit. The right side of an account is referred to as a credit.
- All accounts have a normal balance which is a positive account balance. Assets, expenses, and dividends have a normal debit balance. Liabilities, stockholders' equity, and revenues have a normal credit balance.
- Increases or decreases to an account are based on the normal balance of an account. Normal debit balance accounts (assets, expenses, and dividends) are increased with debits and decreased with credits. Normal credit balance accounts (liabilities, equity, and stockholders' equity) are increased with credits and decreased with debits.

LO5. Prepare journal entries for transactions.

- This is Step 2 of the accounting cycle.
- A journal entry represents the debit and credit effects of a transaction in the accounting records.
- A journal entry is prepared by following three steps:
  Step 1: Analyzing the transaction.
  Step 2: Determining which accounts are affected.
  Step 3: Using the debit and credit procedures to record the effects of the transaction.
- A journal entry is recorded in chronological order and consists of the date of the transaction, the accounts affected, the amount of the transaction, and a brief explanation.

LO6. Explain why transactions are posted to the general ledger.

- This is Step 3 of the accounting cycle.
- To overcome the difficulty of determining account balances listed chronologically in the journal, information in the journal is transferred to the general ledger in a process called posting.
- As result of posting, the general ledger accumulates the effects of transactions in individual financial statement accounts.

LO7. Prepare a trial balance and explain its purpose.

- This is Step 4 of the accounting cycle.
- The trial balance is a list of all active accounts, in the order they appear in the ledger, and each account's debit or credit balance.
- The trial balance is used to prove the equality of debits and credits and helps to uncover errors in journalizing or posting transactions.
- The trial balance serves as a useful tool in preparing the financial statements.

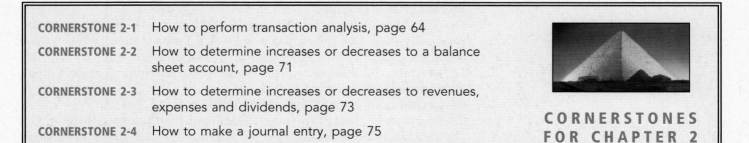

CORNERSTONE 2-1	How to perform transaction analysis, page 64
CORNERSTONE 2-2	How to determine increases or decreases to a balance sheet account, page 71
CORNERSTONE 2-3	How to determine increases or decreases to revenues, expenses and dividends, page 73
CORNERSTONE 2-4	How to make a journal entry, page 75

**CORNERSTONES
FOR CHAPTER 2**

Key Terms

Account, 70

Accounting cycle, 58

Chart of accounts, 70

Comparability, 59

Conservatism principle, 61

Consistency, 59

Continuity (or going-concern) assumption, 60

Cost vs. benefit, 60

Credit, 71

Debit, 71

Double-entry accounting, 72

Economic entity assumption, 60

Events, 61

Financial Accounting Standards Board (FASB), 58

Full disclosure, 59

General ledger, 79

Generally accepted accounting principles (GAAP), 58

Historical cost principle, 60

International Accounting Standards Board (IASB), 58

Journal, 75

Journal entry, 75

Matching principle, 60

Material, 60

Monetary unit assumption, 60

Normal balance, 71

Posting, 79

Relevant, 59

Reliable, 59

Revenue recognition principle, 60

Securities and Exchange Commission (SEC), 58

T-account, 70

Time-period assumption, 60

Transaction, 62

Transaction analysis, 63

Trial balance, 80

Review Problem

I. The Accounting Cycle

Concept:

Economic events are recorded in the accounting system through a process of analyzing transactions, journalizing these transactions in a journal, and posting them to the ledger. These activities are the initial steps in the accounting cycle.

Information:

Boonville Delivery Service was recently formed to fill a need for speedy delivery of small packages. In December 2009, its first month of operations, the following transactions occurred.

a. On December 1, Boonville sells common stock to several investors for $32,000.

b. On December 2, Boonville borrows $20,000 on a one-year note payable from Warrick National Bank, to be repaid with 8 percent interest on December 7, 2010.

c. On December 2, Boonville pays rent of $8,000 on its package sorting building for the month of December.

d. On December 6, Boonville purchases $7,000 worth of office furniture by paying $1,400 in cash and signing a one-year, 12 percent note payable for the balance.

e. On December 20, Boonville completes a delivery contract for Tornado Corporation and bills its customer $15,000.

f. On December 24, Boonville makes a rush delivery for $5,300 cash.

g. On December 28, Tornado pays the $15,000 owed from transaction *e*.

h. On December 28, Boonville signs an agreement with BigTime Computers to accept and deliver approximately 400 packages per business day during the next 12 months. Boonville expects to receive $400,000 of revenue for this contract, but the exact amount will depend on the number of packages delivered.

i.   On December 29, Boonville receives a $1,500 bill from Mac's Catering for catering services performed at a Christmas party Boonville held for its clients. (No previous entry has been made for this activity.)

j.   On December 31, Boonville pays $2,600 cash in salaries to its secretarial staff for work performed in December.

k.   On December 31, Boonville declares and pays dividends of $5,000 on its common stock.

Required:

1.   Analyze and journalize the transactions *a* through *k*.
2.   Post the transactions to the general ledger.
3.   Prepare the December 31, 2009 trial balance for Boonville.

Solution:

1.   **Analyzing and Journalizing Transactions**

Transaction a: Issuing Common Stock.

Assets	=	Liabilities	+	Stockholders' Equity	
				Contributed Capital	Retained Earnings
Cash				Common Stock	
+$32,000				+$32,000	

Date	Account and Explanation	Debit	Credit
Dec. 1	Cash	32,000	
	Common Stock		32,000
	(Issued common stock)		

Transaction b: Borrowing Cash

Assets	=	Liabilities	+	Stockholders' Equity	
				Contributed Capital	Retained Earnings
Cash		Note Payable			
+$20,000		+$20,000			

Date	Account and Explanation	Debit	Credit
Dec. 2	Cash	20,000	
	Note Payable		20,000
	(Borrowed cash from bank)		

Transaction c: Paying Rent

Assets	=	Liabilities	+	Stockholders' Equity	
				Contributed Capital	Retained Earnings
Cash					Rent Expense
−$8,000					−$8,000

Date	Account and Explanation	Debit	Credit
Dec. 2	Rent Expense	8,000	
	Cash		8,000
	(Paid rent for December)		

Transaction d: *Purchasing Asset with Cash and Credit*

Assets	=	Liabilities	+	Stockholders' Equity	
				Contributed Capital	Retained Earnings
Cash −$1,400		Notes Payable +$5,600			
Office Furniture +$7,000					

Date	Account and Explanation	Debit	Credit
Dec. 6	Office Furniture	7,000	
	Cash		1,400
	Notes Payable		5,600
	(Purchased office furniture)		

Transaction e: *Performing Services for Credit*

Assets	=	Liabilities	+	Stockholders' Equity	
				Contributed Capital	Retained Earnings
Accounts Receivable +$15,000					Service Revenue +$15,000

Date	Account and Explanation	Debit	Credit
Dec. 20	Accounts Receivable	15,000	
	Service Revenue		15,000
	(Performed delivery services)		

Transaction f: *Performing Services for Cash*

Assets	=	Liabilities	+	Stockholders' Equity	
				Contributed Capital	Retained Earnings
Cash +$5,300					Service Revenue +$5,300

Date	Account and Explanation	Debit	Credit
Dec. 24	Cash	5,300	
	Service Revenue		5,300
	(Performed delivery services)		

Transaction g: *Collecting an Accounts Receivable*

Assets	=	Liabilities	+	Stockholders' Equity	
				Contributed Capital	Retained Earnings
Cash +$15,000					
Accounts Receivable −$15,000					

Date	Account and Explanation	Debit	Credit
Dec. 28	Cash	15,000	
	Accounts Receivable		15,000
	(Collected accounts receivable)		

Transaction h: *Signing of an Agreement to Provide Service*

This is an example of an important event that does not produce a journal entry at the time it occurs. There will be no recording of the transaction until either party performs on their parts of the contract (e.g., until Boonville provides the delivery service or BigTime Computers makes a payment to Boonville).

Transaction i: *Using Services*

Assets	=	Liabilities	+	Stockholders' Equity	
				Contributed Capital	Retained Earnings
		Accounts Payable +$1,500			Miscellaneous Expense +$1,500

Date	Account and Explanation	Debit	Credit
Dec. 29	Miscellaneous Expense	1,500	
	Accounts Payable		1,500
	(Used catering service)		

Transaction j: *Payment of Salaries*

Assets	=	Liabilities	+	Stockholders' Equity	
				Contributed Capital	Retained Earnings
Cash −$2,600					Salaries Expense −$2,600

Date	Account and Explanation	Debit	Credit
Dec. 31	Salaries Expense	2,600	
	Cash		2,600
	(Paid secretarial staff salaries)		

Transaction k: *Declaring and Paying a Cash Dividend*

Assets	=	Liabilities	+	Stockholders' Equity	
				Contributed Capital	Retained Earnings
Cash −$5,000					Dividends −$5,000

Date	Account and Explanation	Debit	Credit
Dec. 31	Dividends	5,000	
	Cash		5,000
	(Declared and paid a cash dividend)		

2. Posting of Transactions to the Ledger

General Ledger of Boonville Delivery Service

Assets	Liabilities	Stockholders' Equity

Cash

(a)	32,000	8,000	(c)
(b)	20,000	1,400	(d)
(f)	5,300	2,600	(j)
(g)	15,000	5,000	(k)
Bal.	**55,300**		

Accounts Payable

		1,500	(i)
		1,500	Bal.

Common Stock

		32,000	(a)
		32,000	Bal.

Salaries Expense

(j)	2,600	
Bal.	**2,600**	

Accounts Receivable

(e)	15,000	15,000	(g)
Bal.	**0**		

Notes Payable

		20,000	(b)
		5,600	(d)
		25,600	Bal.

Service Revenue

		15,000	(e)
		5,300	(f)
		20,300	Bal.

Miscellaneous Expense

(i)	1,500	
Bal.	**1,500**	

Office Furniture

(d)	7,000	
Bal.	**7,000**	

Rent Expense

(c)	8,000	
Bal.	**8,000**	

Dividends

(k)	5,000	
Bal.	**5,000**	

3. Preparing a Trial Balance

Boonville Delivery Service
Trial Balance
December 31, 2009

Account	Debit	Credit
Cash	$55,300	
Accounts Receivable	0	
Office Furniture	7,000	
Accounts Payable		$ 1,500
Notes Payable		25,600
Common Stock		32,000
Dividends	5,000	
Service Revenue		20,300
Rent Expense	8,000	
Salaries Expense	2,600	
Miscellaneous Expense	1,500	
	$79,400	$79,400

Discussion Questions

1. What is the conceptual framework of accounting? What is its objective?
2. Identify the characteristics of useful information.
3. Discuss the trade-offs between relevant and reliable information.
4. Distinguish between comparability and consistency.
5. Describe the two constraints on providing useful information.
6. Identify the four assumptions that underlie accounting.

7. Discuss the four principles that are used to measure and record business transactions.
8. How are the financial statements related to generally accepted accounting principles?
9. Of all the events that occur each day, how would you describe those that are recorded in a firm's accounting records?
10. In order for a transaction to be recorded in a business' accounting records, the effects of the transaction must be reliably measurable in dollars. What is reliable measurement and why is it important?
11. What is the basic process used in transaction analysis?
12. In analyzing a transaction, can a transaction only affect one side of the accounting equation? If so, give an example.
13. How do revenues and expenses affect the accounting equation?
14. What is a T-account? Describe the basic components of any account.
15. Do you agree with the statement that "debits mean increase and credits mean decrease"? If not, what do debit and credit mean?
16. The words *debit* and *credit* are used in two ways in accounting: "e.g., to debit an account" and "a debit balance." Explain both usages of the terms *debit* and *credit*.
17. All accounts have normal balances. What is the normal balance of each of these accounts?

    a. cash
    b. sales
    c. notes payable
    d. inventory
    e. retained earnings
    f. salary expense
    g. equipment
    h. unearned revenue

18. When a journal entry is made, what must be equal? Why?
19. Can accounting transactions be directly recorded in the general ledger? If so, why do most companies initially record transactions in the journal?
20. Why is the term *double-entry* an appropriate expression for describing an accounting system?
21. What are the initial steps in the accounting cycle and what happens in each step?
22. What kinds of errors will a trial balance detect? What kinds of errors will not be detectable by a trial balance?

Multiple-Choice Exercises

2-1 What organization is the primary standard-setter in the United States?

a. Securities and Exchange Commission
b. Financial Accounting Standards Board
c. International Accounting Standards Board
d. American Institute of Certified Public Accountants

2-2 Which of the following is *not* a characteristic of useful information?

a. Relevance
b. Reliability
c. Conservatism
d. Comparability

2-3 Information that provides feedback about prior expectations is:

	Relevant	Reliable
a.	Yes	Yes
b.	Yes	No
c.	No	Yes
d.	No	No

2-4 Information that is representationally faithful is considered to be:

	Relevant	Reliable
a.	Yes	Yes
b.	Yes	No
c.	No	Yes
d.	No	No

2-5 Which of the following is *not* an assumption that underlies accounting?

a. Economic entity
b. Time-period
c. Continuity (going concern)
d. Historical cost

2-6 Which principle requires that expenses be recorded and reported in the same period as the revenue that it helped generate?

a. Matching
b. Historical cost
c. Revenue recognition
d. Conservatism

2-7 Taylor Company recently purchased a piece of equipment for $2,000 which would be paid within 30 days after delivery. At what point would the event be recorded in Taylor's accounting system?

a. When Taylor signs the agreement with the seller.
b. When Taylor receives the asset from the seller.
c. When Taylor receives an invoice (a bill) from the seller.
d. When Taylor pays $2,000 cash to the seller.

2-8 The effects of purchasing inventory on credit are to:

a. increase assets and increase stockholders' equity.
b. increase assets and increase liabilities.
c. decrease assets and decrease stockholders' equity.
d. decrease assets and decrease liabilities.

2-9 The effects of paying salaries for the current period are to:

a. increase assets and increase stockholders' equity
b. increase assets and increase liabilities
c. decrease assets and decrease stockholders' equity
d. decrease assets and decrease liabilities

2-10 Which of the following statements is *false*?

a. The amount in an account at any time is called the balance of the account.
b. Transactions are frequently analyzed using a T-account.
c. All T-accounts have both a debit and a credit side.
d. The left side of a T-account is called the credit side.

2-11 Which of the following statements are *true*?

I. Debits represent decreases and credits represent increases.
II. Debits must always equal credits.
III. Assets have normal debit balances while liabilities and stockholders' equity have normal credit balances.

a. I
b. II and III
c. I and II
d. All of the above are true.

2-12 Debits will:

a. increase assets, liabilities, revenues, expenses, and dividends
b. decrease assets, liabilities, revenues, expenses, and dividends
c. increase assets, expenses, and dividends
d. decrease liabilities, revenues, and dividends

2-13 Which of the following statements are *true*?

  I.   A journal provides a chronological record of a transaction.
 II.   A journal entry contains the complete effect of a transaction.
III.   The first step in preparing a journal entry involves analyzing the transaction.

a. I and II
b. II and III
c. I and III
d. All of the above are true.

2-14 Posting:

a. is an optional step in the accounting cycle.
b. involves transferring the information in journal entries to the general ledger.
c. is performed after a trial balance is prepared.
d. involves transferring information to the trial balance.

2-15 A trial balance:

a. lists all accounts and their balances.
b. lists only revenue and expense accounts.
c. will help detect omitted journal entries.
d. detects all errors that could be made during the journalizing or posting steps of the accounting cycle.

Cornerstone Exercises

Cornerstone Exercise 2-16 QUALITATIVE CHARACTERISTICS

OBJECTIVE ➤ 1

Three statements are given below.

a. A company uses the same depreciation method from period to period.
b. A trash can that is purchased for $10 is expensed even though it will be used for many years.
c. When several accountants agree that the financial information is free from error or bias, the information is said to possess this characteristic.

Required:

Give the qualitative characteristic or constraint that is most applicable to each of the following statements.

Cornerstone Exercise 2-17 QUALITATIVE CHARACTERISTICS

OBJECTIVE ➤ 1

Three statements are given below.

a. A quality of information that enables an analyst to evaluate the financial performance of two different companies in the same industry.

b. Timely information that is used to predict future events or provide feedback about prior events is said to possess this characteristic.

c. A financial item that may be useful to investors is not required to be reported because the cost of measuring and reporting this information is judged to be too great.

Required:

Give the qualitative characteristic or constraint that is most applicable to each of the following statements.

OBJECTIVE ▸ 1

Cornerstone Exercise 2-18 ACCOUNTING ASSUMPTIONS

Four statements are given below.

a. The accounting records of a company are kept separate from its owners.

b. The accountant assigns revenues and expenses to specific years before preparing the financial statements.

c. A company values its inventory reported in the financial statements in terms of dollars instead of units.

d. Property, plant, and equipment is recorded at cost (less any accumulated depreciation) instead of liquidation value.

Required:

Give the accounting assumption that is most applicable to each of the following statements.

OBJECTIVE ▸ 1

Cornerstone Exercise 2-19 ACCOUNTING PRINCIPLES

Four statements are given below.

a. A company recognizes revenue when the goods are delivered to a customer, even though cash will not be collected from the customer for 30 days.

b. Land, located in a desirable location, is reported at the original acquisition price, even though its value has increased by over 100 percent since it was purchased.

c. The cost paid for a delivery truck is recorded as an asset and expensed over the next five years as it is used to help generate revenue.

d. Inventory, which was recently damaged by a flood, is reported at the lower of its cost or market value.

Required:

Give the accounting principle that is most applicable to each of the following statements.

OBJECTIVE ▸ 2

Cornerstone Exercise 2-20 EVENTS AND TRANSACTIONS

Several events are listed below.

a. Common stock is issued to investors.

b. An agreement is signed with a janitorial service to provide cleaning services over the next 12 months.

c. Inventory is purchased.

d. A two-year insurance policy is purchased.

e. Inventory is sold to customers.

f. Two investors sell their common stock to another investor.

Required:

For each of the events, identify which ones qualify for recognition in the financial statements. For events that do not qualify for recognition, explain your reasoning.

OBJECTIVE ▸ 3

CORNERSTONE 2-1

Cornerstone Exercise 2-21 TRANSACTION ANALYSIS

Four transactions are listed below.

a. Purchased supplies on account.

b. Used supplies in operations of the business.

c.   Sold goods to customers on credit.

d.   Collected amounts due from customers.

Required:

Prepare three columns labeled assets, liabilities, and stockholders' equity. For each of the transactions, indicate whether the transaction increased (+), decreased (−) or had no effect (NE) on assets, liabilities, or stockholders' equity.

Cornerstone Exercise 2-22 **TRANSACTION ANALYSIS**

OBJECTIVE ➤ 3

CORNERSTONE 2-1

Morgan, Inc., entered into the following transactions.

a.   Sold common stock to investors in exchange for $45,000 cash.

b.   Borrowed $4,000 cash from First State Bank.

c.   Purchased $9,000 of supplies on credit.

d.   Paid for the purchase in *c*.

Required:

Show the effect of each transaction using the following model.

Assets	=	Liabilities	+	Stockholders' Equity	
				Contributed Capital	Retained Earnings

Cornerstone Exercise 2-23 **TRANSACTION ANALYSIS**

OBJECTIVE ➤ 3

CORNERSTONE 2-1

The Mendholm Company entered into the following transactions.

a.   Performed services on account, $14,000

b.   Collected $5,000 from client related to services performed in *a*

c.   Paid salaries of $3,500 for the current month

d.   Paid $1,500 dividend to stockholders

Required:

Show the effect of each transaction using the following model:

Assets	=	Liabilities	+	Stockholders' Equity	
				Contributed Capital	Retained Earnings

Cornerstone Exercise 2-24 **DEBIT AND CREDIT PROCEDURES**

OBJECTIVE ➤ 4

CORNERSTONE 2-2
CORNERSTONE 2-3

Refer to the accounts listed below.

a.   Accounts Receivable

b.   Retained Earnings

c.   Sales

d.   Accounts Payable

e.   Repair Expense

f.   Equipment

g.   Common Stock

h.   Salary Expense

Required:

For each of the accounts, complete the following table by entering the normal balance of the account (debit or credit) and the word increase or decrease in the debit and credit columns.

Account	Normal Balance	Debit	Credit

OBJECTIVE ▶ 5
CORNERSTONE 2-4

Cornerstone Exercise 2-25 JOURNALIZE TRANSACTIONS

Four transactions are listed below.

a. Issued common stock to several investors for $71,000
b. Purchased equipment for $7,800 cash
c. Made cash sales of $12,400 to customers
d. Issued a $3,200 dividend to stockholders

Required:

Prepare journal entries for the transactions.

OBJECTIVE ▶ 5
CORNERSTONE 2-4

Cornerstone Exercise 2-26 JOURNALIZE TRANSACTIONS

Four transactions are listed below.

a. Borrowed cash of $8,000 from Middle State Bank
b. Made cash sales of $7,500 to customers
c. Paid salaries of $9,800 to employees for services performed
d. Purchased and used $4,100 of supplies in operations of the business

Required:

Prepare journal entries for the transactions.

OBJECTIVE ▶ 6

Cornerstone Exercise 2-27 POSTING JOURNAL ENTRIES

Listed below are selected T-accounts and their beginning balances for Lee Corporation.

Cash	Supplies	Notes Payable
12,000	6,300	0

Sales	Salary Expense	Supplies Expense
19,500	9,200	1,350

Required:

Post the transactions in Cornerstone Exercise 2-26 to these accounts and compute an ending balance.

OBJECTIVE ▶ 7

Cornerstone Exercise 2-28 PREPARING A TRIAL BALANCE

Listed below are the ledger accounts for Borges, Inc., at December 31, 2009. All accounts have normal balances.

Service Revenue	$21,630	Dividends	$ 1,250
Cash	15,600	Salary Expense	4,300
Accounts Payable	4,600	Equipment	11,600
Common Stock	15,000	Accounts Receivable	4,900
Rent Expense	2,080	Advertising Expense	1,500

Required:

Prepare a trial balance for Borges, Inc.

Exercises

OBJECTIVE ▶ 1

Exercise 2-29 QUALITATIVE CHARACTERISTICS

Listed below are the four qualitative characteristics that make accounting information useful.

Relevance
Reliability
Comparability
Consistency

Required:

Match the appropriate qualitative characteristic with the statements below.

a. When users can depend on the quality of information provided, the accounting information possesses this characteristic.
b. The characteristic that allows a user to compare the financial results of a company from one accounting period to another accounting period.
c. If information confirms prior expectations, it possesses this characteristic.
d. Freedom from bias reflects this characteristic.
e. When several companies in the same industry use the same accounting methods, this qualitative characteristic exists.
f. Information that accurately portrays an economic event satisfies this characteristic.
g. Providing information on a timely basis enhances this characteristic.
h. When several accountants can agree on the measurement of an activity, the information possesses this characteristic.
i. If information helps to predict future events, it possesses this characteristic.

Exercise 2-30 ASSUMPTIONS AND PRINCIPLES

OBJECTIVE ➤ 1

Presented below are the four assumptions and four principles used in measuring and reporting accounting information.

Assumptions	Principles
Economic entity	Historical cost
Continuity (going-concern)	Revenue recognition
Time-period	Matching
Monetary unit	Conservatism

Required:

Identify the assumption or principle that best describes each situation below.

a. Specifies that revenue should only be recognized when earned and realized
b. Requires that an activity be recorded at the exchange price at the time the activity occurred
c. Allows a company to report financial activities separate from the activities of the owners
d. Implies that items such as customer satisfaction cannot be reported in the financial statements
e. Requires that expenses be recorded and reported in the same period as the revenue that it helped generate
f. Justifies why some assets and liabilities are not reported at their value if sold
g. Allows the life of a company to be divided into artificial time periods so accounting reports can be provided on a timely basis
h. Is a prudent reaction to uncertainty

Exercise 2-31 EVENTS AND TRANSACTIONS

OBJECTIVE ➤ 2

The following economic events that were related to K&B Grocery Store occurred during 2009.

a. On February 15, K&B placed an order for a new cash register with NCR, for which $700 would be paid after delivery.
b. On February 17, K&B received a bill from Indianapolis Power and Light indicating that it had used electric power during January 2009 at a cost of $120; the bill need not be paid until February 25, 2009.
c. On February 20, the K&B store manager purchased a new passenger car for $15,000 in cash. The car is entirely for personal use and was paid for from the manager's personal assets.
d. On February 21, the cash register ordered on February 15 was delivered. Payment was not due until March.
e. On February 23, K&B paid $120 to Indianapolis Power and Light.
f. On February 26, K&B signed a two-year extension of the lease on the store building occupied by the store. The new lease was effective on April 1, 2009, and required an increase in the monthly rental from $5,750 to $5,900.
g. On March 1, K&B paid $5,750 to its landlord for March rent on the store building.

Required:

1. Using the words "qualify" and "does not qualify," indicate whether each of the above events would qualify as a transaction and be recognized and recorded in the accounting system on the date indicated.
2. For any events that did not qualify as a transaction to be recognized and recorded, explain why it does not qualify.

OBJECTIVE ▶ 3

Exercise 2-32 **TRANSACTION ANALYSIS**

The following events occurred for Parker Company.

a. Paid $5,000 cash for land
b. Performed consulting services for a client in exchange for $1,200 cash
c. Performed consulting services for a client on account, $700
d. Stockholders invested $12,000 cash in the business
e. Purchased office supplies on account, $300
f. Collected $500 from client in transaction *c*
g. Paid $250 on account for supplies purchased in transaction *e*
h. Paid $200 cash for the current month's rent
i. Paid a $1,000 cash dividend to stockholders

Required:

1. Analyze the effect of each transaction on the accounting equation. For example, for transaction *a*, the answer is "Increase assets (land) $5,000 and decrease assets (cash) $5,000."
2. For *e*, what accounting principle did you use to determine the amount to be recorded for supplies?

OBJECTIVE ▶ 3

Exercise 2-33 **TRANSACTION ANALYSIS**

Amanda Webb opened a home health care business under the name Home Care, Inc. During its first month of operations, the business had the following transactions:

a. Sold common stock to Ms. Webb and other stockholders in exchange for $25,000 cash
b. Paid $15,000 cash for a parcel of land on which the business will eventually build an office building
c. Purchased supplies for $2,900 on credit
d. Paid rent for the month on office space and equipment, $600 cash
e. Performed services for clients in exchange for $3,400
f. Paid salaries for the month, $1,200
g. Purchased and used $950 of supplies
h. Paid $2,100 on account for supplies purchased in transaction *c*
i. Performed services for clients on credit in the amount of $770
j. Paid a $500 dividend to stockholders

Required:

Prepare an analysis of the effects of these transactions on the accounting equation of the business. Use the format below.

Assets	=	Liabilities	+	Stockholders' Equity	
				Contributed Capital	Retained Earnings

OBJECTIVE ▶ 3

Exercise 2-34 **TRANSACTION ANALYSIS AND BUSINESS ACTIVITIES**

The accountant for Compton Inc. has collected the following information:

a. Compton purchased a tract of land from Jacobsen Real Estate for $860,000 to be used in its operations.
b. Compton issued 2,000 shares of its common stock to George Micros in exchange for $120,000 cash.

c. Compton purchased a John Deere backhoe for $42,000 on credit.
d. Michael Rotunno paid Compton $8,000 cash for services performed. The services had been performed by Compton several months ago for a total price of $10,000 of which Rotunno had previously paid $2,000.
e. Compton paid its monthly payroll by issuing checks totaling $38,000.
f. Compton declared and paid its annual dividend of $10,000 cash.

Required:

1. Prepare an analysis of the effects of these transactions on the accounting equation of the business. Use the format below.

Assets	=	Liabilities	+	Stockholders' Equity	
				Contributed Capital	Retained Earnings

2. Indicate whether the transaction is a financing, investing, or operating activity.

Exercise 2-35 INFERRING TRANSACTIONS FROM BALANCE SHEET CHANGES

OBJECTIVE ▸ 3

Each of the following balance sheet changes is associated with a particular transaction:

a. Cash increases by $100,000 and capital stock increases by $100,000.
b. Cash decreases by $22,000 and land increases by $22,000.
c. Cash decreases by $9,000 and retained earnings decreases by $9,000.
d. Cash increases by $15,000 and notes payable increases by $15,000.

Required:

Describe each transaction listed above.

Exercise 2-36 TRANSACTION ANALYSIS

OBJECTIVE ▸ 3

Goal Systems, a business consulting firm, engaged in the following transactions:

a. Sold capital stock for $50,000 cash
b. Borrowed $20,000 from a bank
c. Purchased equipment for $7,000 cash
d. Prepaid rent on office space for six months in the amount of $6,600
e. Performed consulting services in exchange for $4,300 cash
f. Performed consulting services on credit in the amount of $16,000
g. Incurred and paid wage expense of $7,500
h. Collected $7,200 of the receivable arising from transaction f
i. Purchased supplies for $1,100 on credit
j. Used $800 of the supplies purchased in transaction i
k. Paid for all of the supplies purchased in transaction i

Required:

For each transaction described above, indicate the effects on assets, liabilities, and stockholders' equity using the format below.

Assets	=	Liabilities	+	Stockholders' Equity	
				Contributed Capital	Retained Earnings

Exercise 2-37 TRANSACTION ANALYSIS

OBJECTIVE ▸ 3

During December, Cynthiana Refrigeration Service engaged in the following transactions:

a. On December 3, Cynthiana sold a one-year service contract to Cub Foods for $8,000 cash.
b. On December 10, Cynthiana repaired equipment of the A&W Root Beer Drive-In. A&W paid $800 in cash for the service call.

c. On December 10, Cynthiana purchased a new GMC truck for business use. The truck cost $16,500. Cynthiana paid $2,500 down and signed a one-year note for the balance.

d. Cynthiana received an $8,000 order of repair parts from Carrier Corporation on December 19. Carrier is expected to submit a bill for $8,000 in early January.

e. On December 23, Cynthiana purchased 20 turkeys from Cub Foods for $280 cash. Cynthiana gave the turkeys to its employees as a Christmas gift.

Required:

For each transaction described above, indicate the effects on assets, liabilities, and stockholders' equity using the format below.

Assets	=	Liabilities	+	Stockholders' Equity	
				Contributed Capital	Retained Earnings

OBJECTIVE ▶ 4

Exercise 2-38 NORMAL BALANCES AND FINANCIAL STATEMENTS

The following accounts are available for Haubstadt Shoe Works:

Accounts Payable
Accounts Receivable
Accumulated Depreciation, Building
Accumulated Depreciation, Equipment
Building
Cash
Common Stock
Cost of Goods Sold
Depreciation Expense, Building
Depreciation Expense, Equipment
Equipment
General and Administrative Expense
Interest Expense
Inventory
Long-Term Notes Payable
Retained Earnings
Sales Revenue
Selling Expense

Required:

Using a table like the one below, indicate whether each account normally has a debit or credit balance and indicate on which of the financial statements (income statement, statement of retained earnings, or balance sheet) each account appears.

Account	Debit	Credit	Financial Statement

OBJECTIVE ▶ 4

Exercise 2-39 DEBIT AND CREDIT EFFECTS OF TRANSACTIONS

Lincoln Corporation was involved in the following transactions during the current year:

a. The owners invested cash in the business in exchange for common stock.
b. Lincoln borrowed cash from the local bank on a note payable.
c. Lincoln purchased operating assets on credit.
d. Lincoln purchased supplies inventory on credit.
e. Lincoln provided services in exchange for cash from the customer.
f. A customer secured services from Lincoln on credit.
g. The payable from transaction *d* was paid in full.
h. The receivable from transaction *f* was collected in full.
i. Lincoln paid wages in cash.

j.   Lincoln used a portion of the supplies purchased in transaction *d*.
k.   Lincoln paid dividends in cash.

Required:

Prepare a table like the one shown below and indicate the effect on assets, liabilities, and stockholders' equity. Be sure to enter debits and credits in the appropriate columns for each of the transactions. Transaction *a* is entered as an example:

Assets	=	Liabilities	+	Stockholders' Equity	
				Contributed Capital	Retained Earnings
a. Increase (Debit)				Increase (Credit)	

Exercise 2-40 DEBIT AND CREDIT EFFECT ON TRANSACTIONS

OBJECTIVE ▶ 4

Jefferson Framers engaged in the following transactions:

a.   Purchased land for $15,200 cash
b.   Purchased equipment for $23,600 in exchange for a one-year, 11 percent note payable
c.   Purchased office supplies on credit for $1,200 from Office Depot
d.   Paid the $10,000 principal plus $700 interest on a note payable
e.   Paid an account payable in the amount of $2,600
f.   Provided $62,100 of services on credit
g.   Provided $11,400 of services for cash
h.   Collected $29,800 of accounts receivable
i.   Paid $13,300 of wages in cash
j.   Sold common stock for $21,000 cash

Required:

Using a table like the one below, enter the necessary information for each transaction. Transaction *a* is entered as an example.

Transaction	Account	Increase/Decrease	Debit/Credit	Amount
(a)	Land	Increase	Debit	$15,200
	Cash	Decrease	Credit	$15,200

Exercise 2-41 JOURNALIZING TRANSACTIONS

OBJECTIVE ▶ 5

Kauai Adventures rents surfboards and snorkeling and scuba equipment. During March 2009, Kauai engaged in the following transactions:

March 2   Received $34,200 cash from customers for rental
3   Purchased on credit five new surfboards for $110 each
6   Paid wages to employees in the amount of $11,500
9   Paid office rent for the month in the amount of $3,300
12   Purchased a new Ford truck for $17,800; paid $1,000 down in cash and secured a loan from Princeville Bank for the $16,800 balance
13   Collected a $650 account receivable
16   Paid an account payable in the amount of $790
23   Borrowed $10,000 on a six-month, 12 percent note payable
27   Paid the monthly telephone bill of $345
30   Paid a monthly advertising bill of $1,960

Required:

Prepare a journal entry for each of these transactions.

OBJECTIVE ▶ 5

Exercise 2-42 JOURNALIZING TRANSACTIONS

Remington Communications has been providing cellular phone service for several years. During November and December 2009, the following transactions occurred:

Nov. 2   Remington received $1,200 for November phone service from Enrico Company.
      6   Remington purchased $5,800 of supplies from Technology Associates on account.
     10   Remington paid $4,250 to its hourly employees for their weekly wages.
     15   Remington paid $5,800 to Technology Associates in full settlement of their account payable.
     18   Remington purchased and used supplies of $2,150.
     21   Remington received a bill from Monticello Construction for $900 for repairs made to Remington's loading dock on November 15. Remington plans to pay the bill in early December, when it is due.
Dec. 4   Remington paid the $900 to Monticello Construction.

Required:

1. Prepare a journal entry for each of these transactions.
2. What accounting principle did you apply in recording the November 10 transaction?

OBJECTIVE ▶ 5

Exercise 2-43 TRANSACTION ANALYSIS AND JOURNAL ENTRIES

Pasta House, Inc., was organized in January 2009. During the year, the following transactions occurred:

a. On January 14, Pasta House, Inc., sold Martin Halter, the firm's founder and sole owner, 10,000 shares of its common stock for $7 per share.
b. On the same day, Bank One loaned Pasta House $30,000 on a 10-year note payable.
c. On February 22, Pasta House purchased a building and the land on which it stands from Frank Jakubek for $14,000 cash and a 5-year, $36,000 note payable. The land and building had appraised values of $10,000 and $40,000, respectively.
d. On March 1, Pasta House signed an $18,000 contract with Cosby Renovations to remodel the inside of the building. Pasta House paid $6,000 down and agreed to pay the remainder when Cosby completed its work.
e. On May 3, Cosby completed its work and submitted a bill to Pasta House for the remaining $12,000.
f. On May 20, Pasta House paid $12,000 to Cosby Renovations.
g. On June 4, Pasta House purchased restaurant supplies from Glidden Supply for $950 cash.

Required:

Prepare a journal entry for each of these transactions.

OBJECTIVE ▶ 4 5 6 7

Exercise 2-44 ACCOUNTING CYCLE

Rosenthal Decorating, Inc., is a commercial painting and decorating contractor that began operations in January 2009. The following transactions occurred during the year:

a. On January 15, Rosenthal sold 500 shares of its common stock to William Hensley for $10,000.
b. On January 24, Rosenthal purchased $720 of painting supplies from Westwood Builders' Supply on account.
c. On February 20, Rosenthal paid $720 cash to Westwood Builders' Supply for the painting supplies purchased on January 24.
d. On April 25, Rosenthal billed Bultman Condominiums $12,500 for painting and decorating services performed in April.
e. On May 12, Rosenthal received $12,500 from Bultman Condominiums for the painting and decorating work billed in April.

f. On June 5, Rosenthal sent Arlington Builders a $9,500 bill for a painting job completed on that day.
g. On June 24, Rosenthal paid wages for work performed during the preceding week in the amount of $6,700.

Required:

1. Prepare a journal entry for each of the transactions listed above.
2. Post the transactions to T-accounts.
3. Prepare a trial balance at June 30, 2009.

Exercise 2-45 PREPARING A TRIAL BALANCE PREPARATION

OBJECTIVE ➤ 7

The following accounts and account balances are available for Badger Auto Parts at December 31, 2009:

Accounts Payable	$ 9,200
Accounts Receivable	41,100
Accumulated Depreciation, Furniture and Fixtures	47,300
Cash	3,700
Common Stock	100,000
Cost of Goods Sold	189,000
Depreciation Expense, Furniture and Fixtures	10,400
Furniture and Fixtures	128,000
General and Administrative Expense	9,700
Income Taxes Expense	3,700
Income Taxes Payable	3,600
Interest Expense	7,200
Interest Payable	1,800
Inventory	60,500
Long-Term Notes Payable	50,000
Prepaid Rent	15,000
Retained Earnings, 12/31/2008	15,900
Sales Revenue	268,000
Selling Expense	27,500

Required:

Prepare a trial balance. Assume that all accounts have normal balances.

Exercise 2-46 EFFECT OF ERRORS ON A TRIAL BALANCE

OBJECTIVE ➤ 7

The bookkeeper for Riley, Inc., made the following errors:

a. A cash purchase of supplies of $357 was recorded as a debit to Supplies for $375 and a credit to Cash of $375.
b. A cash sale of $3,154 was recorded as a debit to Cash of $3,154 and a credit to Sales of $3,145.
c. A purchase of equipment was recorded once in the journal and posted twice to the ledger.
d. Cash paid for salaries of $4,100 was recorded as a debit to Salaries Expense of $4,100 and a credit to Accounts Payable of $4,100.
e. A credit sale of $8,300 was recorded correctly. However, the debit posting to Accounts Receivable was omitted.

Required:

Indicate whether or not the trial balance will balance after the error. If the trial balance will not balance, indicate the direction of the misstatement for any effected account (e.g., cash will be overstated by $50).

Problem Set A

OBJECTIVE ▶ 3   **Problem 2-47A EVENTS AND TRANSACTIONS**

The accountant for Boatsman Products, Inc., received the following information:

a. Boatsman sent its customers a new price list. Prices were increased an average of 3 percent on all items.

b. Boatsman accepted an offer of $150,000 for land that it had purchased two years ago for $130,000. Cash and the deed for the property are to be exchanged in five days.

c. Boatsman accepted $150,000 cash and gave the purchaser the deed for the property described in item *b*.

d. Boatsman's president purchased 600 shares of the firm's common stock from another stockholder. The president paid $15 per share. The former shareholder had purchased the stock from Boatsman for $4 per share.

e. Boatsman leases its delivery trucks from a local dealer. The dealer also performs maintenance on the trucks for Boatsman. Boatsman received a $1,254 bill for maintenance from the dealer.

Required:

Indicate whether or not each item qualifies as a transaction and should be recorded in the accounting system. Explain your reasoning.

OBJECTIVE ▶ 3 7   **Problem 2-48A ANALYZING TRANSACTIONS**

Luis Madero, after working for several years with a large public accounting firm, decided to open his own accounting service. The business is operated as a corporation under the name Madero Accounting Services. The following captions and amounts summarize Madero's balance sheet at July 31, 2009.

	Assets		=	Liabilities		+	Equity	
Cash	Accounts Receivable	Supplies	=	Accounts Payable	Notes Payable	+	Capital Stock	Retained Earnings
8,000	+ 15,900	+ 4,100	=	2,500	+ 4,000	+	12,000	+ 9,500

The following events occurred during August 2009.

a. Sold common stock to Ms. Garriz in exchange for $20,000 cash
b. Paid $700 for first month's rent on office space
c. Purchased supplies of $2,100 on credit
d. Borrowed $5,000 from the bank
e. Paid $1,200 on account for supplies purchased earlier on credit
f. Paid secretary's salary for August of $1,850
g. Performed accounting services for clients who paid cash upon completion of the service in the total amount of $2,700
h. Performed accounting services for clients on credit in the total amount of $1,500
i. Purchased and used $500 in supplies
j. Collected $690 cash from clients for whom services were performed on credit
k. Paid $300 dividend to stockholders

Required:

1. Record the effects of the transactions listed above on the accounting equation. Use format given in the problem, starting with the totals at July 31, 2009.
2. Prepare the trial balance at August 31, 2009.

OBJECTIVE ▶ 3 4 7   **Problem 2-49A INFERRING TRANSACTIONS FROM T-ACCOUNTS**

The following T-accounts summarize the operations of Chen Construction Company for July 2009.

Cash			
7/1	200		
7/2	1,000	150	7/5
7/7	2,500	700	7/9
7/11	150	750	7/14

Accounts Receivable			
7/1	1,400	150	7/11

Supplies			
7/1	750		
7/4	250		

Land			
7/1	3,000		
7/9	700		

Accounts Payable			
		1,100	7/1
7/5	150	250	7/4

Common Stock			
		4,000	7/1
		1,000	7/2

Retained Earnings			
		250	7/1
7/14	750	2,500	7/7

Required:

1. Assuming that only one transaction occurred on each day (beginning on July 2) and that no dividends were paid, describe the transaction that most likely took place.
2. Prepare a trial balance at July 31, 2009.

Problem 2-50A DEBIT AND CREDIT PROCEDURES

OBJECTIVE ➤ 4

A list of accounts for Montgomery, Inc., appears below.

Accounts Payable
Accounts Receivable
Accumulated Depreciation
Cash
Common Stock
Depreciation Expense
Equipment
Income Tax Expense
Interest Expense
Land
Notes Payable
Prepaid Rent
Retained Earnings
Salaries Expense
Service Revenue
Supplies Inventory

Required:

Complete the table below for these accounts. The information for the first account has been entered as an example.

Account	Type of Account	Normal Balance	Increase	Decrease
Accounts Payable	Liability	Credit	Credit	Debit

Problem 2-51A JOURNALIZING TRANSACTIONS

OBJECTIVE ➤ 5

Monroe Company rents electronic equipment. During September 2009, Monroe engaged in the transactions described below.

Sept.	5	Purchased a Chevrolet truck for $32,000 cash
	8	Purchased Sony amplifiers for $2,500 on account
	10	Purchased $1,750 of office supplies on credit
	11	Rented sound equipment to a traveling stage play for $15,000. The producer of the play paid for the service at the time it was provided.
	12	Rented sound equipment and lights to a local student organization for a school dance for $5,100. The student organization will pay for services within 30 days.

Sept.	18	Paid employee wages of $4,300 that have been earned during September
	22	Collected the receivable from the September 12 transaction
	23	Borrowed $12,800 cash from a Citibank on a three-year note payable
	28	Sold common stock to new stockholders for $35,750
	30	Paid a $3,850 cash dividend to stockholders

Required:

Prepare a journal entry for each transaction.

OBJECTIVE ➤ 5 6

Problem 2-52A JOURNALIZING AND POSTING TRANSACTIONS

Cincinnati Painting Service, Inc., specializes in painting houses. During the month of June, Cincinnati Painting engaged in the following transactions:

June	3	Purchased painting supplies from River City Supply for $750 on credit
	8	Purchased a used van from Hamilton Used Car Sales for $6,500, paying $2,000 down and agreeing to pay the balance in six months
	14	Paid $3,200 to hourly employees for work performed in June
	22	Billed various customers a total of $8,700 for June painting jobs
	26	Received $5,100 cash from James Eaton for a house painting job completed and billed in May
	29	Collected $300 from Albert Montgomery on completion of a one-day painting job. This amount is not included in the June 22 bills.

Required:

1. Prepare a journal entry for each transaction.
2. Post the journal entries to Cincinnati Painting's ledger accounts.

OBJECTIVE ➤ 2 3 4
5 6 7

Problem 2-53A THE ACCOUNTING CYCLE

Karleen's Catering Service provides catered meals to individuals and businesses. Karleen's purchases its food ready to serve from Mel's Restaurant. In order to prepare a realistic trial balance, the events described below are aggregations of many individual events during 2009.

a.   During the year, Karleen's paid office rent of $11,500.
b.   Telephone expenses incurred and paid were $950.
c.   Wages of $67,400 were earned by employees and paid during the year.
d.   During the year, Karleen's provided catering services:

| On credit | $142,100 |
| For cash | 21,700 |

e.   Karleen's paid $62,100 for food and beverage supplies purchased.
f.   Karleen's paid dividends in the amount of $4,000.
g.   Karleen's collected accounts receivable in the amount of $134,200.

Required:

1. Analyze the events for their effect on the accounting equation.
2. Prepare journal entries (ignore the date since these events are aggregations of individual events).
3. Post the journal entries to ledger accounts.
4. Prepare a trial balance. Assume that all beginning account balances at January 1, 2009, are zero.

OBJECTIVE ➤ 2 3 4
5 6 7

Problem 2-54A COMPREHENSIVE PROBLEM

Western Sound Studios records and masters audio tapes of popular artists in live concerts. The performers use the tapes to prepare "live" albums, CDs, and MP3s. The following account balances were available at the beginning of 2009:

Accounts Payable	$ 11,900
Accounts Receivable	384,000
Cash	16,300
Common Stock	165,000
Interest Payable	11,200
Long-Term Notes Payable	100,000
Rent Payable, Building	4,000
Rent Payable, Recording Equipment	7,000
Retained Earnings, 12/31/2008	101,200

During 2009, the following transactions occurred (the events described below are aggregations of many individual events):

a. Taping services in the amount of $994,000 were billed.
b. The accounts receivable at the beginning of the year were collected.
c. In addition, cash for $983,000 of the services billed in transaction *a* was collected.
d. The rent payable for the building was paid. In addition, $48,000 of building rental costs was paid in cash. There was no rent payable or prepaid at year-end.
e. The equipment rent payable on January 1 was paid. In addition, $84,000 of equipment rental costs was paid in cash. There was no rent payable or prepaid at year-end.
f. Utilities expense of $56,000 was incurred and paid in 2009.
g. Salaries expense for the year was $702,000. All $702,000 was paid in 2009.
h. The interest payable at January 1 was paid. During the year, an additional $11,000 of interest was paid. At year-end no interest was payable.
i. Income taxes for 2009 in the amount of $19,700 were incurred and paid.

Required:

1. Establish a ledger for the accounts listed above and enter the beginning balances. Use a chart of accounts to order the ledger accounts.
2. Analyze each transaction. Journalize as appropriate. (Ignore the date since these events are aggregations of individual events.)
3. Post your journal entries to the ledger accounts. Add additional ledger accounts when needed.
4. Use the ending balances in the ledger accounts to prepare a trial balance.

Problem Set B

Problem 2-47B EVENTS AND TRANSACTIONS

OBJECTIVE ▶ 3

The following list contains events that occurred during January 2009 at the local Ford dealer, Malcom Motors:

a. California Central University (CCU) signed a contract to purchase a fleet of Ford Crown Victoria vehicles from Malcom Motors at a total price of $200,000, payable to Malcom in two equal amounts—one on August 1, 2009, and one on September 1, 2009. The cars will be delivered to CCU during August 2009.
b. The principal stockholder in Malcom Motors sold 10 percent of her stock in the company to John Lewis, the president of Malcom Motors, in exchange for $100,000 in cash.
c. Malcom Motors issued new stock to John Lewis in exchange for $50,000 in cash.
d. Malcom Motors owns the building it occupies; the company occupied the building during the entire month of January.
e. Malcom Motors owns land used for the storage of cars awaiting sale; the land was used by the company during the entire month of January.
f. Malcom Motors paid its lawyer $1,000 for services rendered in connection with the purchase agreement signed with California Central University.
g. Maintenance Management Company performed cleaning services for Malcom Motors during January under a contract that does not require payment for those services until March 1, 2009.

Required:

Indicate whether each item qualifies as a transaction and should be recorded in the accounting system. Explain your reasoning.

OBJECTIVE ▶ 3 7   **Problem 2-48B ANALYZING TRANSACTIONS**

Several years ago, Mary Emerson founded Emerson Consulting, Inc., a consulting business specializing in financial planning for young professionals. The following captions and amounts summarize Emerson Consulting's balance sheet at December 31, 2008, the beginning of the current year:

	Assets		=	Liabilities		+	Equity	
Cash	Accounts Receivable	Supplies	=	Accounts Payable	Notes Payable	+	Capital Stock	Retained Earnings
3,000	+ 6,600	+ 4,800	=	500	+ 1,000	+	10,000	+ 2,900

During January 2009, the following transactions occurred:

a. Sold common stock to a new stockholder in exchange for $2,000 cash
b. Performed advisory services for a client for $1,550 and received the full amount in cash
c. Received $750 on account from a client for whom services had been performed on credit
d. Purchased supplies for $650 on credit
e. Paid $500 on accounts payable
f. Performed advisory services for $2,700 on credit
g. Paid cash of $1,200 for secretarial services during January
h. Paid cash of $800 for January's office rent
i. Paid rent for January 2009 in the amount of $900
j. Paid a dividend of $400

Required:

1. Record the effects of the transactions listed above on the accounting equation for the business. Use the format given in the problem, starting with the totals at December 31, 2008.
2. Prepare the trial balance at January 31, 2009.

OBJECTIVE ▶ 3 4 7   **Problem 2-49B INFERRING TRANSACTIONS FROM T-ACCOUNTS**

The following T-accounts summarize the operations of Brilliant Minds, Inc., a tutoring service, for April 2009.

Cash				Accounts Receivable				Supplies	
4/1	500	700	4/8	4/1	700	375	4/24	4/1	900
4/3	2,000	325	4/9					4/15	150
4/18	1,500	140	4/11						
4/24	375	150	4/15						

Equipment		Accounts Payable				Notes Payable		
4/1	1,200	4/9	325	625	4/1		2,000	4/3
4/8	700							

Common Stock		Retained Earnings			
	2,000 4/1	4/11	140	675	4/1
				1,500	4/18

Required:

1. Assuming that only one transaction occurred on each day (beginning on April 3) and that no dividends were paid, describe the transaction that most likely took place.
2. Prepare a trial balance at April 30, 2009.

Problem 2-50B DEBIT AND CREDIT PROCEDURES

OBJECTIVE ▶ 4

A list of accounts for Montgomery, Inc., appears below.

Accounts Payable
Accounts Receivable
Bonds Payable
Building
Cash
Common Stock
Cost of Goods Sold
Depreciation Expense
Income Taxes Payable
Insurance Expense
Intangibles
Interest Expense
Inventory
Long-Term Investments
Retained Earnings
Sales
Unearned Revenue
Utility Expense

Required:

Complete the table below for these accounts. The information for the first account has been entered as an example.

Account	Type of Account	Normal Balance	Increase	Decrease
Accounts Receivable	Asset	Debit	Debit	Credit

Problem 2-51B JOURNALIZING TRANSACTIONS

OBJECTIVE ▶ 5

Monilast Chemicals engaged in the following transactions during December 2009:

Dec. 2 Prepaid rent on office furniture for six months, $9,000
    3 Borrowed $25,000 on a nine-month, 12 percent note
    7 Provided services on credit, $35,000
  10 Purchased supplies on credit, $12,000
  13 Collected accounts receivable, $29,000
  19 Sold common stock, $40,000
  22 Paid employee wages for December, $8,000
  23 Paid accounts payable, $10,000
  25 Provided services for cash, $11,000
  30 Paid utility bills for December, $2,000

Required:

Prepare a journal entry for each transaction.

Problem 2-52B JOURNALIZING AND POSTING TRANSACTIONS

OBJECTIVE ▶ 5 6

Findlay Testing, Inc., provides water testing and maintenance services for owners of hot tubs and swimming pools. During September the following transactions occurred:

Sept. 1 Purchased chemical supplies for $1,750 cash
    5 Paid office rent for September, October, and November; the rent is $800 per month
    8 Purchased $710 of office supplies on account
  13 Received $600 from Simon Kenton in response to a bill sent in August for testing his hot tub water

Sept. 18 Received $7,500 from Alexander Blanchard upon completion of overhaul of his swimming pool water circulation system. Since the job was completed and collected for on the same day, no bill was sent to Blanchard.

25 Billed the city of Bellefontaine $4,200 for testing the water in the city's outdoor pools during September

30 Recorded and paid September salaries of $3,720

Required:

1. Prepare a journal entry for each transaction.
2. Post the journal entries to Findley Testing's ledger accounts.

OBJECTIVE

Problem 2-53B THE ACCOUNTING CYCLE

Sweetwater Temporary Clerical Help Service opened for business in June 2009. From the opening until the end of the year, Sweetwater engaged in the activities described below. So that a realistic trial balance can be prepared, the events described below are aggregations of many individual events.

a. Sold 10,000 shares of common stock for $3.50 per share
b. Purchased office equipment from OfficeMax for $14,200 cash
c. Received $121,800 from clients for services provided
d. Paid wages of $84,900
e. Borrowed $15,000 from the Bank of America on a three-year note payable
f. Paid office rent of $17,500
g. Purchased office supplies on credit for $1,300 from OfficeMax
h. Paid $1,000 toward the payable established in transaction *g*
i. Paid telephone charges incurred during the year of $910

Required:

1. Analyze the events for their effect on the accounting equation.
2. Prepare journal entries (ignore the date since these events are aggregations of individual events).
3. Post the journal entries to ledger accounts.
4. Prepare a trial balance.

OBJECTIVE

Problem 2-54B COMPREHENSIVE PROBLEM

Mulberry Services sells electronic data processing services to firms too small to own their own computing equipment. Mulberry had the following accounts and account balances as of January 1, 2009:

Accounts Payable	$ 14,000
Accounts Receivable	130,000
Common Stock	114,000
Cash	6,000
Interest Payable	8,000
Long-Term Notes Payable	80,000
Prepaid Rent, Computing Equipment (Short-Term)	96,000
Retained Earnings, 12/31/2008	16,000

During 2009, the following transactions occurred (the events described below are aggregations of many individual events):

a. During 2009, Mulberry sold $690,000 of computing services, all on credit.
b. Mulberry collected $570,000 from the credit sales in transaction *a* and an additional $129,000 from the accounts receivable outstanding at the beginning of the year.
c. Mulberry paid the interest payable of $8,000.
d. Wages of $379,000 were paid in cash.
e. Administrative expenses of $90,000 were incurred and paid.
f. The prepaid rent at the beginning of the year was used in 2009. In addition, $28,000 of computer rental costs were incurred and paid. There is no prepaid rent or rent payable at year-end.

g. Mulberry purchased computer paper for $13,000 cash in late December.
h. None of the paper was used by year-end.
i. Advertising expense of $26,000 was incurred and paid.
j. Income tax of $10,300 was incurred and paid in 2009.
k. $10,000 of interest was paid on the long-term loan.

Required:

1. Establish a ledger for the accounts listed above and enter the beginning balances. Use a chart of accounts to order the ledger accounts.
2. Analyze each transaction. Journalize as appropriate. (Ignore the date since these events are aggregations of individual events.)
3. Post your journal entries to the ledger accounts. Add additional ledger accounts when needed.
4. Use the ending balances in the ledger accounts to prepare a trial balance.

Cases

Case 2-55 ANALYSIS OF THE ACCOUNTING CYCLE

Susan Eel wants to sell you her wholesale fish store. She shows you a balance sheet with total assets of $150,000 and total liabilities of $20,000. According to the income statement, last year's net income was $40,000.

When examining the accounting records, you notice that several accounts receivable in the $10,000 to $15,000 range are not supported by source documents. You also notice that there is no source documentation to support the $30,000 balance in the building account and the $10,000 balance in the equipment account. Susan tells you that she gave the building and refrigeration equipment to the business in exchange for stock. She also says that she has not had time to set up and monitor any paperwork for accounts receivable or accounts payable.

Required:

1. What requirements for transaction recognition appear to have been ignored when the accounts receivable, building, and equipment were recorded?
2. What would be the effect on the financial statements if the values appearing in the balance sheet for accounts receivable, building, and equipment were overstated? What would be the effect if the accounts payable were understated?
3. Assuming that you would like to purchase the company, what would you do to establish a reasonable purchase price?

Case 2-56 ANALYSIS OF THE EFFECTS OF CURRENT ASSET AND CURRENT LIABILITY CHANGES ON CASH FLOWS

You have the following data for Cable Company's accounts receivable and accounts payable for 2009:

Accounts receivable, 1/1/2009	$ 5,900
2009 sales on credit	97,400
Accounts receivable, 12/31/2009	7,200
Wages payable, 1/1/2009	4,600
2009 wage expense	38,100
Wages payable, 12/31/2009	5,300

Required:

1. How much cash did Cable collect from customers during 2009?
2. How would you classify cash collected from customers on the statement of cash flows?
3. How much cash did Cable pay for wages during 2009?
4. How would you classify the cash paid for wages on the statement of cash flows?

Case 2-57 ETHICAL ISSUES

Kathryn Goldsmith is the chief accountant for Clean Sweep, a national carpet-cleaning service with a December fiscal year-end. As Kathryn was preparing the 2009 financial statements for Clean Sweep, she noticed several odd transactions in the general ledger for December. For example, rent for January 2010, which was paid in December 2009, was recorded by debiting rent expense instead of prepaid rent. In another transaction, Kathryn noticed that the use of supplies was recorded with a debit to insurance expense instead of supplies expense. Upon further investigation, Kathryn discovered that the December ledger contained numerous such mistakes. Even with the mistakes, the trial balance still balanced.

Kathryn traced all of the mistakes back to a recently hired bookkeeper, Ben Goldsmith, Kathryn's son. Kathryn had hired Ben tohelp out in the accounting department over Christmas break so that he could earn some extra money for school. After discussing the situation with Ben, Kathryn determined that Ben's mistakes were all unintentional.

Required:

1. What ethical issues are involved?
2. What are Kathryn's alternatives? Which would be the most ethical alternative to choose?

Case 2-58 RESEARCH AND ANALYSIS USING THE ANNUAL REPORT

Obtain General Electric's 2008 annual report either through the "Investor Relations" portion of its Web site (do a web search for GE investor relations) or go to http://www.sec.gov and click "Search for company filings" under "Filings and Forms (EDGAR)."

Required:

Answer the following questions:
1. Determine the amounts in the accounting equation for the most recent year. Does it balance?
2. What is the normal balance for the following accounts?
   a. Current Receivables
   b. Short-Term Borrowings
   c. Sales of Services
   d. Property, Plant, and Equipment—Net
   e. Cost of Goods Sold
   f. Inventories
   g. Provision for Income Taxes
3. Identify the additional account that is most likely involved when:
   a. Accounts Payable is decreased.
   b. Accounts Receivables is increased.
   c. Common Stock is increased.
   d. Short-Term Borrowings is increased.

Case 2-59 COMPARATIVE ANALYSIS: ABERCROMBIE & FITCH vs. AEROPOSTALE

Refer to the financial statements of **Abercrombie & Fitch** and **Aeropostale** that are supplied with this text.

Required:

Answer the following questions:
1. Determine the amounts in the accounting equation for the year ending February 3, 2007 for each company. Does the accounting equation balance?
2. Set up a T-account for Abercrombie & Fitch's accounts receivable account and include the beginning and ending balances. Complete the T-account to reflect the sales and cash collections for the year. Assume all sales are on account.
3. Provide the journal entry to record the following two events and post the amount to the T-account. For simplicity, assume the event was recorded in a single journal entry.
   a. What journal entry is necessary to record Abercrombie & Fitch's net sales for the year ending February 3, 2007? Assume that all sales were made on account.

b. What journal entry is necessary to record Abercrombie & Fitch's cash collections from customers during the year ending February 3, 2007?

4. Where does Abercrombie & Fitch and Aeropostale report credit card receivables? (Hint: You may want to refer to the Summary of Significant Accounting Policies in the Notes to the Financial Statements.)

5. Provide the journal entry to record the amount of selling, general, and administrative expenses incurred during the year ending February 3, 2007 (fiscal 2006). Assume all expenses incurred during the year were paid during the year. Why are Aeropostale's selling, general, and administrative expenses smaller than Abercrombie & Fitch's selling, general, and administrative expenses?

Case 2-60 ACCOUNTING FOR PARTIALLY COMPLETED EVENTS: A PRELUDE TO CHAPTER 3

Ehrlich Smith, the owner of The Shoe Box, has asked you to help him understand the proper way to account for certain accounting items as he prepares his 2009 financial statements. Smith has provided the following information and observations:

a. A three-year fire insurance policy was purchased on May 1, 2009, for $1,800. Smith believes that a part of the cost of the insurance policy should be allocated to each period that benefits from its coverage.

b. The store building was purchased for $60,000 in January 2001. Smith expected then (as he does now) that the building will be serviceable as a shoe store for 20 years from the date of purchase. In 2001, Smith estimated that he could sell the property for $6,000 at the end of its serviceable life. He feels that each period should bear some portion of the cost of this long-lived asset that is slowly being consumed.

c. The Shoe Box borrowed $20,000 on a one-year, 11 percent note that is due on September 1 next year. Smith notes that $22,200 cash will be required to repay the note at maturity. The $2,200 difference is, he feels, a cost of using the loaned funds and should be spread over the periods that benefit from the use of the loan funds.

Required:

1. Explain what Smith is trying to accomplish with the three preceding items. Are his objectives supported by the concepts that underlie accounting?

2. Describe how each of the three items should be reflected in the 2009 income statement and the December 31, 2009 balance sheet to accomplish Smith's objectives.

3

Accrual Accounting

Experience Financial Accounting
with FedEx

FedEx Corporation began operations in 1973 with 14 jets that connected 25 U.S. cities. Some employees even used their own cars to deliver packages! As a pioneer of the hub and spoke model for overnight package delivery, FedEx is now the world's largest express transportation company with operations in over 220 countries. During this time, FedEx claims many industry "firsts"— including being the first to offer next-day delivery by 10:30 a.m. and the first to offer Saturday delivery. With more than 143,000 employees, 669 aircraft, and 53,000 vehicles and trailers,[1] FedEx has the ability to "absolutely, positively" get a package delivered overnight.

While companies conduct business throughout the year, the accounting for business activities does not stop at the end of the year. The end of the fiscal year, or accounting period, is a busy time as companies make adjustments to the accounting information. These adjustments are necessary because a company's business activities often occur over several accounting periods. These adjustments are often quite significant. In its 2007 annual report as shown in

Exhibit 3-1

Excerpt from FedEx's Financial Statements

FedEx Corporation
Consolidated Income Statement (partial)
For the Year Ended May 31, 2007

(in millions)	
Revenues	$ 35,214
Operating expenses	(31,938)
Other income (expense)	(61)
Income before income taxes	$ 3,215
Income taxes	(1,199)
Net income	$ 2,016

Sample of expenses resulting from adjustment:

Salaries and compensated absences	$ 755
Employee benefits	599
Insurance	548
Taxes other than income taxes	310
Depreciation and amortization	1,742
Other	561
Total (14% of Operating expenses)	$4,515

[1] Information obtained from FedEx's 2007 Annual Report.

Exhibit 3-1, FedEx's financial statements include many expenses that would not have been recognized without adjustments.

This sample of expenses, which doesn't include all the adjustments made, represents over 14 percent of the total expenses that FedEx reported on its 2007 income statement. When FedEx recognized these expenses (except for depreciation and amortization), it also recorded a liability for them. These liabilities represented 51% of FedEx's current liabilities. The adjustment to recognize depreciation and amortization expense resulted in a decrease in assets of $1.742 million. Clearly, the failure to adjust for these expenses would significantly affect FedEx's financial statements.

OBJECTIVE ➤ 1
Explain the difference between cash-basis and accrual-basis accounting.

Completing the Accounting Cycle

In the previous chapter, we examined how companies use the double-entry accounting system to record business activities that occur during the accounting period. However, accountants also make numerous adjustments at the end of accounting periods for business activities that occur over several accounting periods—activities like the performance of services for customers, the renting of office space, and the use of equipment. As shown in the opening scenario of this chapter, these adjustments can be significant.

Why are so many business activities recognized in the accounts through adjustments rather than through the normal journal entries recorded within the accounting period that we described in Chapter 2? The illustrations used in Chapter 2 excluded activities that were still underway at the end of the accounting period. Accrual accounting requires that any incomplete activities be recognized in the financial statements. This often requires estimates and judgments about the timing of revenue and expense recognition. The end result is that accountants must adjust the accounts to properly reflect these partially-completed business activities.

In this chapter, we will review the concepts that form the basis for adjustments—the time-period assumption, the revenue recognition principle, and the matching principle. We will then complete the accounting cycle that was introduced in Chapter 2 by exploring the preparation and effects of adjusting journal entries, preparing financial statements from the adjusted accounts, and closing the accounts in order to prepare for the next accounting period. We will address the following questions:

- What is the difference between the cash basis and the accrual basis of accounting?
- What is the purpose of adjusting entries?
- What types of transactions require adjustment and how are the adjustments recorded in the accounting system?
- Which accounts are closed at the end of the period and why is this necessary?

The recognition of business activities in financial accounting uses the accrual basis of accounting. In the following section, we will examine the differences between accrual-basis and cash-basis accounting. In addition, we will look at the three key concepts—the time-period assumption, the revenue recognition principle, and the matching principle—that underlie the accrual basis of accounting.

Accrual Versus Cash Basis of Accounting

If you were asked how much your income for the month was, what would you do? Most likely, you would go online and look at your bank activity for the month. You would then list the total of the deposits as revenue and the total of the withdrawals as expenses. The difference would be your income. This method of accounting is called **cash-basis accounting**. Under cash-basis accounting, revenue is recorded when cash is received, regardless of when it is actually earned. Similarly, an expense is recorded when cash is paid, regardless of when it is actually incurred. Therefore, cash-basis accounting does not tie recognition of revenues and expenses to the actual business activity but rather the exchange of cash. In addition, by recording only the cash effect of transactions, cash-basis financial statements may not reflect all of the assets and liabilities of a company at a particular date. For this reason, most companies, except for the smallest, do not use cash-basis accounting.

    Accrual-basis accounting (also called accrual accounting) is an alternative to cash-basis accounting that is required by generally accepted accounting principles. Under accrual accounting, transactions are recorded when they occur. Accrual accounting is superior to cash-basis because it ties income measurement to selling, the principle activity of the company. That is, revenue is recognized as it is earned and expenses are recognized when they are incurred. In contrast to cash-basis accounting, accrual accounting is a more complex system that records both *cash and noncash* transactions.

Key Elements of Accrual Accounting

OBJECTIVE ▶ 2
Explain how the time-period assumption, revenue recognition, and matching principles affect the determination of income.

As shown in Exhibit 3-2, an accrual accounting system rests on three elements of the conceptual framework that were introduced in Chapter 2—the time-period assumption, the revenue recognition principle, and the matching principle.

Time-Period Assumption

Investors, creditors and other financial statement users demand timely information from companies. For that reason, it is necessary for companies to report their financial results for specific periods of time—a month, a quarter, or a year. The **time-period assumption** allows companies to artificially divide their operations into time periods so that they can satisfy users' demands for information.

    If all transactions occurred at a single point in time, the creation of financial reports for specific time periods would not be a problem. However, companies

Exhibit 3-2

Key Elements of Accrual Accounting

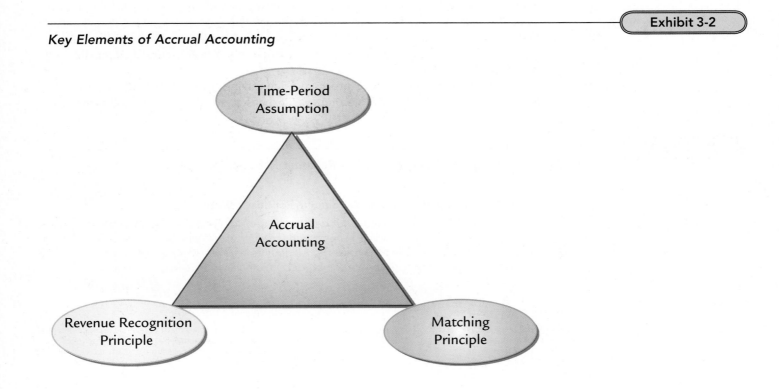

frequently engage in activities that continue for some period of time and affect more than one time period. For example, the aircraft and vehicles used by FedEx are purchased at a single point in time but are used over many years. In addition, FedEx often receives cash from a company to deliver products in one time period, although the actual delivery does not occur until a different time period. To properly record the use of these aircraft and the providing of its service, accrual accounting requires that FedEx assign the revenue and expenses to the proper time period. This is quite often a difficult task and is guided by the revenue recognition and matching principles.

The Revenue Recognition Principle

The **revenue recognition principle** is used to determine when revenue is recorded and reported. Under this principle, revenue is to be recognized or recorded in the period in which both of the following conditions are met:

* The revenue has been earned
* The collection of cash is reasonably assured.

These requirements are usually met when goods have been delivered to a customer or when services have been performed for a customer. At this point, the risks and rewards of ownership usually have been transferred from the seller to the buyer.[2] **Notice that revenue is recorded when these two conditions are met, regardless of when cash is received**.

To illustrate revenue recognition, assume that on March 31, FedEx picks up a computer from **Apple**'s distribution center and receives a cash payment of $30 to ship the computer to a customer. FedEx delivers the computer on April 2. Even though cash was received on March 31, FedEx will recognize the $30 of revenue on April 2, the date the computer is delivered to the customer. Notice that revenue is not recognized until it is earned by FedEx (delivery of the computer), and that the receipt of cash prior to the delivery does not affect when revenue is recognized. Exhibit 3-3 shows an excerpt of FedEx's revenue recognition policy that is disclosed in the notes to its financial statements.

The Matching Principle

Companies incur expenses for a variety of reasons. Sometimes expenses are incurred when an asset is used. In other instances, expenses are incurred when a liability is created. For example, FedEx incurs fuel expense as it uses fuel to delivers its packages. FedEx also incurs salary expense when its employees work but are not paid immediately. The key idea is that **an expense is recorded when it is incurred, regardless of when cash is paid**.

Expense recognition is the process of identifying an expense with a particular time period. Under accrual accounting, expenses are recognized following the

---

Exhibit 3-3

Annual Report Excerpt: FedEx's Revenue Recognition Policy

Note 1: Summary of Significant Accounting Policies (in part)

REVENUE RECOGNITION. We recognize revenue upon delivery of shipments for our transportation businesses and upon completion of services for our business services, logistics and trade services businesses. For shipments in transit, revenue is recorded based on the percentage of service completed at the balance sheet date.

---

[2] The Securities and Exchange Commission expanded upon this principle and stated that the revenue recognition criteria are normally met when (1) delivery has occurred or services have been rendered, (2) persuasive evidence of an arrangement exists, (3) the selling price is fixed or determinable, and (4) the collection of cash is reasonably assured.

matching principle, which requires that expenses be recorded and reported in the same period as the revenue that it helped to generate. Expenses for an accounting period should *include* only those costs used to earn revenue that was recognized in the accounting period. Expenses for an accounting period should *exclude* those costs used to earn revenue in an earlier period and those costs that will be used to earn revenue in a later period. Thus, the key to expense recognition is matching the expense with revenue.

ETHICS The revenue recognition and matching principles can and have been abused in recent years. As companies strive to meet or exceed Wall Street expectations, management may be tempted to recognize revenue that has not yet been earned or to hide expenses that should be recognized. In recent years, the Securities and Exchange Commission (SEC) has conducted numerous investigations involving the abuse of both revenue and expense recognition. Some notable cases are listed in Exhibit 3-4.

Exhibit 3-4

Instances of Accounting Abuses

Company	Action
Regina Vacuum	Backdated sales invoices, improperly recorded revenue on consignment sales that had not been earned, and hid unpaid bills in a filing cabinet to reduce expenses. Chairman, CEO, and president Donald Sheelen pleaded guilty to fraud, fined $25,000, and sentenced to one year in a work release program in Florida.
Miniscribe	Improperly recognized revenue through a variety of means, including packaging and shipping bricks as finished products. Chief executive Q.T. Wiles fined $250 million.
Sunbeam	Used a variety of techniques to improperly recognize revenue (e.g, bill and hold transactions, channel stuffing). CEO Al Dunlap fined $500,000 and barred from ever serving as an officer or director of a public company.
WorldCom	Improperly reduced operating expenses, which inflated income, by reversing (releasing) accrued liabilities and improperly classifying certain expenses as assets. Chief executive Bernie Ebbers was sentenced to 25 years in jail.

While the above actions were fraudulent and led to severe fines or jail time for many of the company executives, other innocent parties were also affected by these unethical actions. Stockholders, many of whom who had bought the stock at an inflated price, saw a significant drop in the stock's value after these actions were made public. In addition, innocent employees lost their jobs as the companies struggled to deal with the fraud that occurred. When faced with an ethical dilemma to manipulate the recognition of revenue or expense, make the decision that best portrays the economic reality of your company. It will be a decision that will let you sleep at night.◆

Applying the Principles

If you want to use the financial statements, it is important for you to understand how the revenue recognition and matching principles affect the amounts reported on the financial statements. To illustrate the effect of these principles, Cornerstone 3-1 compares how the application of these principles results in accrual-basis income that differs from cash-basis income.

Notice that accrual accounting follows the revenue recognition and matching principles. That is, revenue is recognized when it is earned and expenses are matched with

CONCEPT Q&A

Cash-basis accounting seems straightforward. Why do we complicate matters by introducing accrual accounting?

Possible Answer:

The fundamental objective of financial reporting is to provide information that is useful in making business and economic decisions. Most of these decisions involve predicting a company's future cash flows. The use of accrual accounting through the application of the revenue recognition and matching principles ties income recognition to the principal activity of the company, selling goods and services. Therefore, accrual accounting provides a better estimate of future cash flows than cash-basis accounting.

CORNERSTONE 3-1

HOW TO Apply the Revenue Recognition and Matching Principles

Concept:
Under accrual accounting, revenue is recognized when it is earned and the collection of cash is reasonably assured. Expenses are recognized in the same period as the revenue they helped generate.

Information:
The state of Georgia hired Conservation Inc., a consulting company specializing in the conservation of natural resources, to explore the state's options for providing water resources to the Atlanta metropolitan area. In November 2009, Conservation Inc. incurred $60,000 of expenditures, on account, investigating the water shortage facing the state. Conservation Inc. also delivered its recommendations to the state and billed the state $100,000 for its work.
In December 2009, Conservation Inc. paid the $60,000 of expenses.
In January 2010, Conservation Inc. received the state's check for $100,000.

Required:
1. Calculate income for November 2009, December 2009, and January 2010 using the cash-basis of accounting.
2. Calculate income for November 2009, December 2009, and January 2010 using the accrual-basis of accounting.

Solution:
1. Cash-basis income is computed as follows:

November 2009		December 2009		January 2010	
Revenue	$0	Revenue	$ 0	Revenue	$100,000
Expense	0	Expense	60,000	Expense	0
Net Income	$0	Net Income	$(60,000)	Net Income	$100,000

➡ Performed Service ➡ Paid Expenses ➡ Received Payment

2. Accrual-basis income is computed as follows:

November 2009		December 2009		January 2010	
Revenue	$100,000	Revenue	$0	Revenue	$0
Expense	60,000	Expense	0	Expense	0
Net Income	$ 40,000	Net Income	$0	Net Income	$0

➡ Performed Service ➡ Paid Expenses ➡ Received Payment

revenues. Even though Conservation Inc. did not receive the payment from the state of Georgia until January 2010, Conservation Inc. had performed services in November 2009 and appropriately recognized the revenue as the service was performed. The $60,000 of expenses were matched with revenues and also recognized in November 2009. If cash-basis accounting would have been used, the expenses, $40,000, would have been recognized in December 2009 (when the cash was paid), and revenue, $100,000, would have been recognized in January 2010 (when the cash was received). By following the revenue recognition and matching principles, net income was properly recognized in the period that the business activity occurred. In short, the difference between cash-basis and accrual-basis accounting is a matter of timing.

DECISION-MAKING & ANALYSIS

Recognition of a Security Service Contract

Secure Entry Inc., a security company, has a two-year contract with the Metropolis Stadium Authority to provide security services at its stadium gates. The contract was signed in April 2008 and is effective for calendar years 2009 and 2010. Under the terms of the contract, Metropolis Stadium Authority agrees to make 24 equal monthly payments to Secure Entry beginning in October 2008. Security services will begin to be performed in January 2009.

1. *When would Secure Entry Inc. record the contract?*

Secure Entry would record the contract in October 2008, when Metropolis makes the first payment. At that time, Secure Entry would record an increase in cash for the amount of the payment received and an equal increase in a liability (Unearned Revenue) to recognize that future services are owed. Note that Secure Entry would not record the contract in its accounting system in April 2008 because the event does meet the recognition criteria discussed in Chapter 2.

2. *When would Secure Entry recognize revenue related to the contract?*

Consistent with the revenue recognition principle, Secure Entry would begin recognizing revenue related to the contract in 2009, when services are performed.

3. *When would Secure Entry recognize the salary expense related to the security services provided at Metropolis Stadiums?*

According to the matching principle, expenses related to the performance of security services should be matched against revenue from providing the security services. Because the revenue will be recognized monthly beginning in January 2009, the matching principle requires that the salary expense related to providing security services be recognized monthly beginning in 2009, as the security services are performed.

Accrual Accounting and Adjusting Entries

OBJECTIVE ▸ 3

Identify the kinds of transactions that may require adjustments at the end of an accounting period.

A company accounts for its activities using accrual accounting in order to produce financial statements that include the effects of the activities when they occur, regardless of when cash was received or paid. Accrual accounting requires that revenues be recognized when earned and expenses be recognized when incurred. In this section, we will examine the adjustments required to implement accrual accounting.

Which Transactions Require Adjustment?

If all accounting transactions occurred at a point in time, the application of accrual accounting would, like cash-basis accounting, be relatively straightforward. However, many activities continue for some period of time. Obvious examples include the use of rented facilities or interest on borrowed money.[3] Because entries in the accounting system are made at particular points in time rather than continuously, adjustments are needed at the end of an accounting period to record these partially complete activities. **Adjusting entries** are journal entries made at the end of an accounting period to record the completed portion of these partially completed transactions. Adjusting entries are necessary to apply the revenue recognition and matching principles and ensure that a company's financial statements include the proper amount for revenues, expenses, assets, liabilities, and stockholders' equity.

---

[3] The distinction between business activities requiring adjustment and those that do not depends to some extent on our ability and willingness to keep track of activities. Some activities may occur so frequently or are so difficult to measure individually that no record of individual activities is maintained. In such cases, the sequence of individual activities becomes, for all intents and purposes, a continuous activity. For example, the use of office supplies is often treated as a continuous business activity because it is too costly to maintain a record of each time supplies are used.

In Cornerstone 3-2, three representative transactions are described and the implications of the "length" of these transactions for recognition in the accounting system and for adjustment is discussed.

**CORNERSTONE
3-2**

HOW TO Determine Which Transactions Require Adjustment

Concept:
Adjusting journal entries are required for continuous transactions that are partially complete at the end of an accounting period.

Information:
Computer Town sells computer equipment as well as providing computer repair service. Sales are typically made in cash or on account. Repair service is provided under service contracts. Customers purchase a service contract for a specified period of time (two, three, or five years) and pay for this contract up-front. The customer pays nothing when the computer is brought in for repair.

Required:
1. How should Computer Town account for cash and credit sales of equipment?
2. How should Computer Town account for repair services provided under service contracts?
3. How should Computer Town account for the use of office supplies?

Solution:
1. Cash sales should be recorded as they occur and the equipment is delivered, often at a cash register that tracks total sales for the day. When orders are received from customers who want to purchase equipment on credit, the sale should be recorded when the equipment is delivered to the customer. In both situations, the sale is complete at a single point in time (the delivery of the equipment) and no adjusting entry is needed.
2. In contrast to both cash and credit sales of equipment, repair service contracts are continuous activities. At the end of the accounting period, a portion of the revenue associated with incomplete service contracts should be recognized as an adjustment. Revenue is earned as time passes under the service contract and should be recorded in proportion to the period of time that has passed since the contract became effective. The unexpired portion of the service contract should be recorded as a liability (unearned revenue) until earned. Any expenses associated with the repair services should be recognized as the repair service revenue is recognized (the matching principle).
3. The use of supplies can be viewed as a sequence of individual activities. However, the preparation of documents required to keep track of each activity individually would be too costly. Instead the use of supplies will be treated as a continuous transaction and recognized through an adjusting entry. Any supplies used will be reported as an expense while the unused portion of supplies is reported as an asset.

Notice that in the second and third situations, the continuous activities cannot be properly recorded by the normal journal entries made within the accounting period as described in Chapter 2. For these continuous transactions, the preparation of adjusting entries is necessary to get the account balances properly stated and up-to-date. These end-of-period adjustments can have significant effects on a company's financial statements, as we illustrated for FedEx at the beginning of this chapter.

Step 5: Adjusting the Accounts

Under accrual accounting, revenue is recognized when it is earned and the collection of cash is reasonably assured. Expenses are recognized in the same period as the revenue they helped generate. Adjustments are often necessary because timing differences exist between when a revenue or expense is recognized and cash is received or paid. These timing differences give rise to two categories of adjusting entries—accruals and deferrals. As shown in Exhibit 3-5, each category has two subcategories, which gives rise to four possible types of adjustments.

The purpose of all adjustments is to make sure that revenues and expenses get recorded in the proper time period. As the revenue and expense balances are adjusted, asset and liability balances will be adjusted also. Therefore, **all adjusting entries will affect at least one income statement account and one balance sheet account**. **Note that cash is never affected by adjustments.**

Exhibit 3-5

Types of Adjusting Entries

Accruals:
1. **Accrued revenues:** Previously unrecorded revenues that have been earned but for which no cash has yet been received
2. **Accrued expenses:** Previously unrecorded expenses that have been incurred but not yet paid in cash

Deferrals:
1. **Deferred (unearned) revenues:** Liability arising from the receipt of cash for which revenue has not yet been earned
2. **Deferred (prepaid) expenses:** Asset arising from the payment of cash which has not been used or consumed by the end of the period

To assist you in making adjusting journal entries, a three-step procedure can be followed.

Step 1: Identify pairs of income statement and balance sheet accounts that require adjustment.

Step 2: Calculate the amount of the adjustment based on the amount of revenue that was earned or the amount of expense that was incurred during the accounting period.

Step 3: Record the adjusting journal entry.

Cornerstones 3-3 through 3-6, shown in the following sections, explain how to make each of the four types of adjustments that are necessary at the end of an accounting period.

CONCEPT Q&A

Why don't adjusting entries involve cash?

Possible Answer:
Cash receipts and cash payments occur at a specific point in time and are recorded through normal, within-period journal entries. Adjusting entries, on the other hand, record partially completed transactions. Adjusting entries are concerned with applying the revenue recognition and matching principles to these continuous activities. Because revenue and expense recognition does not depend on cash receipt or cash payment, adjusting entries for continuous revenue and expense activities will not involve cash.

Accrued Revenues

It is common for a company to engage in revenue-producing activities, yet not be paid until after the activity is complete. For example, FedEx recognizes revenue when it delivers a package, even though the customer may not be billed and will not pay for the service until later. In addition, some packages are in transit at the end of an accounting period, meaning that FedEx has only partially completed its service. These transactions for which FedEx has earned revenue but not received the cash are called **accrued revenues**. Other examples of accrued revenues include interest earned, but not yet received, on a loan that is made. While interest is earned as time passes, the company only receives the cash related to interest periodically (e.g., monthly, semiannually, or annually). Therefore, an adjustment is necessary to record the amount of interest earned but not yet received.

For accrued revenues, an adjustment is necessary to record the revenue and the associated increase in a company's assets, usually an account receivable. Exhibit 3-6 demonstrates the process necessary to record accrued revenues. Note that the accrual of revenue is necessary because the revenue was earned prior to the receipt of cash.

Exhibit 3-6

Accrued Revenues

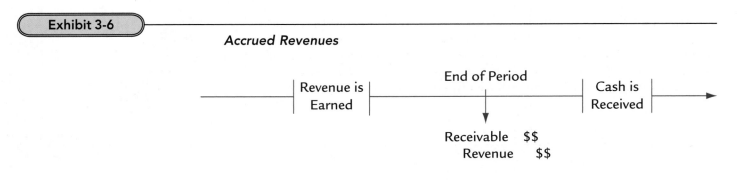

The adjusting entry required to record accrued revenues is shown in Cornerstone 3-3.

**CORNERSTONE
3-3**

HOW TO Record Accrued Revenues

Concept:
Revenue is recognized when it is earned, regardless of when cash is received. The adjusting entry for an accrued revenue will result in an increase to a revenue account and an increase to an asset account.

Information:
Assume that Porter Properties, Inc., a calendar-year company, rented office space to the Tiger Travel Agency on November 1, 2009, for $5,000 per month to be occupied immediately. Porter Properties requires Tiger Travel to make a rental payment at the end of every three months. No payment was made on November 1.

Required:
1. Prepare the adjusting journal entry necessary on December 31, 2009, for Porter Properties.
2. Prepare the entry necessary on January 31, 2010, to record the receipt of cash.

Solution:
1. At the end of the accounting period, Porter Properties will perform the following three steps to prepare the adjusting entry:

    Step 1: Identify the accounts that require adjustment. Rent Revenue needs to be increased because Porter Properties has earned revenue from providing the office space. The revenue recognition principle requires revenue to be recognized when it is earned, regardless of when cash is collected. Because no payment was received, Porter Properties would need to increase Rent Receivable to reflect their right to receive payment from Tiger Travel.
    Step 2: Calculate the amount of the adjustment. The amount of the adjustment would be $10,000, calculated as $5,000 per month times the two months that the office space was occupied by Tiger Travel.

Step 3: Record the adjusting journal entry. The adjusting journal entry at December 31, 2009, would be:

**C O R N E R S T O N E
3 - 3**
(continued)

Date	Account and Explanation	Debit	Credit
Dec. 31, 2009	Rent Receivable	10,000	
	Rent Revenue		10,000
	(To record rent revenue earned in 2009 but not received)		

Assets =	Liabilities +	Stockholders' Equity
+10,000		+10,000

2. When the cash is received, Porter Properties will make the following entry:

Date	Account and Explanation	Debit	Credit
Jan. 31, 2010	Cash	15,000	
	Rent Revenue		5,000
	Rent Receivable		10,000
	(To record revenue earned in 2010 and the receipt of cash)		

Assets =	Liabilities +	Stockholders' Equity
+15,000		+5,000
−10,000		

The amount of cash received, $15,000, is calculated as $5,000 per month times the three months that the office space was rented. The $5,000 of Rent Revenue represents the one month earned in 2010.

If the adjusting entry on December 31, 2009, was not made, assets, stockholders' equity, revenues, and income would be understated. The adjusting journal entry recognizes two months of revenue (November and December 2009) in the accounting period in which it was earned and updates the corresponding balance in rent receivable. The revenue has been earned because Porter Properties has provided a service to Tiger Travel. Later, when cash is received, the remaining portion of the revenue that was earned in January 2010 is recognized and the receivable is reduced to reflect that it was paid. Consistent with the revenue recognition principle, revenue is recorded in the period that it is earned.

Accrued Expenses

Similar to the situation with accrued revenues, many companies will incur expenses in the current accounting period but not pay cash for these expenses until a later period. For example, in Exhibit 3-1, we showed you that FedEx reported $283 million of salary expense related to services performed by FedEx employees but not paid as of the end of the year. This situation is quite common for several operating costs such as payroll, taxes, utilities, rent, and interest. **Accrued expenses** are previously unrecorded expenses that have been incurred but not yet paid in cash.

For accrued expenses, an adjustment is necessary to record the expense and the associated increase in a company's liabilities, usually a payable. Exhibit 3-7 demonstrates the process necessary to record accrued expenses.

Exhibit 3-7

Accrued Expenses

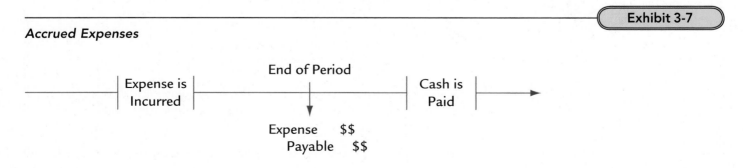

Note that the accrual of the expense is necessary because the expense was incurred prior to the payment of cash. The adjusting entry required to record accrued expenses is shown in Cornerstone 3-4.

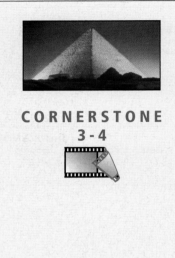

CORNERSTONE 3-4

HOW TO Record Accrued Expenses

Concept:
Expenses are recorded as they are incurred, regardless of when cash is paid. The adjusting entry for an accrued expense will result in an increase to an expense account and an increase to a liability account.

Information:
Assume that Porter Properties, Inc., a calendar-year company, paid its clerical employees every two weeks. Employees work five days a week for a total of 10 work days every two weeks. Also assume that December 31 is four days into a 10-day pay period for which these employees will collectively earn $50,000 every two weeks.

Required:
1. Prepare the adjusting journal entry necessary on December 31, 2009, for Porter Properties.
2. Prepare the entry necessary on January 10, 2010, to record the payment of salaries.

Solution:
1. At the end of the accounting period, Porter Properties will perform the following three steps to prepare the adjusting entry:

   Step 1: Identify the accounts that require adjustment. Salaries Expense needs to be increased because Porter Properties has incurred an expense related to its employees working for four days in December that needs to be matched against December revenues (an application of the matching principle). Because no payment to the employees was made, Porter Properties would need to increase Salaries Payable to reflect its obligation to pay its employees.
   Step 2: Calculate the amount of the adjustment. The amount of the adjustment would be $20,000, calculated as 4/10 of the $50,000 bi-weekly salaries.
   Step 3: Record the adjusting entry. The adjusting journal entry at December 31, 2009, would be:

Date	Account and Explanation	Debit	Credit
Dec. 31, 2009	Salaries Expense	20,000	
	Salaries Payable		20,000
	(To record expenses incurred not paid)		

Assets = Liabilities +	Stockholders' Equity
+20,000	−20,000

2. When the cash is paid, Porter Properties will make the following entry:

Date	Account and Explanation	Debit	Credit
Jan 10, 2010	Salaries Expense	30,000	
	Salaries Payable	20,000	
	Cash		50,000
	(To record expense incurred in 2010 and the payment of cash)		

Assets = Liabilities +	Stockholders' Equity
−50,000 −20,000	−30,000

The amount of the salaries expense for the current year, $30,000, would be calculated as 6/10 of the $50,000 bi-weekly salaries. This would represent the six days worked in January.

If the adjusting journal entry on December 31, 2009, were not made, liabilities and expenses would be understated while income and stockholders' equity would be overstated. The adjusting journal entry recognizes the expense that was incurred during the accounting period and updates the balance in the corresponding liability. Later, when the cash is paid to the employees, the portion of the expense that was incurred in January 2010 is recognized and the previously created liability is reduced. Consistent with the matching principle, expenses are recorded in the period that they were incurred.

Deferred (Unearned) Revenues

A business may collect payment for goods or services that it sells before it delivers those goods or services. For example, FedEx often collects cash for a package delivery prior to the actual performance of the delivery service. When the cash is collected, the revenue recognition is deferred, or delayed, until the service is performed. Transactions for which a company has received cash but has not yet earned the revenue are called **deferred revenues**. Other examples of deferred revenues include rent received in advance, magazine or newspaper subscriptions received in advance, and tickets (e.g., for airlines, sporting events, concerts) sold in advance. In all of these situations, the receipt of cash creates a liability (called an **unearned revenue**) for the company to deliver goods or perform services in the future. The unearned revenue account delays, or defers, the recognition of revenue by recording the revenue as a liability until it is earned.

As the goods are delivered or the service is performed, an adjustment is necessary to reduce the previously recorded liability and to recognize the portion of the revenue that has been earned. The portion of revenue that has not been earned remains in the liability account, unearned revenue, until it is earned. Therefore, revenue recognition is delayed, or deferred, until the revenue is earned. Exhibit 3-8 demonstrates the process necessary to record deferred revenues.

Exhibit 3-8

Deferred Revenues

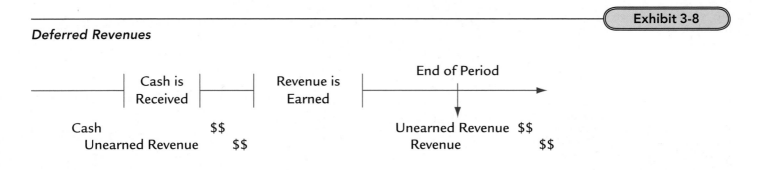

Note that the deferral of revenue is necessary because the revenue was not earned at the time of cash receipt. The adjusting entry recognizes the amount of revenue that has been earned from the time of cash receipt until the end of the accounting period. The adjusting entry required to adjust deferred revenues is shown in Cornerstone 3-5.

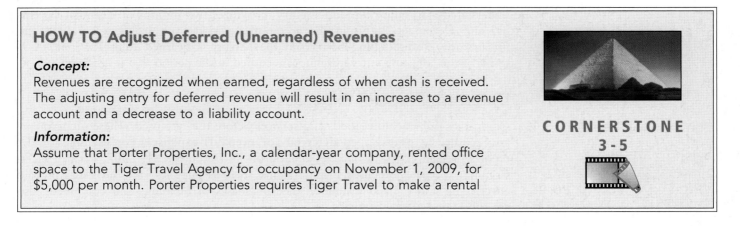

HOW TO Adjust Deferred (Unearned) Revenues

Concept:
Revenues are recognized when earned, regardless of when cash is received. The adjusting entry for deferred revenue will result in an increase to a revenue account and a decrease to a liability account.

Information:
Assume that Porter Properties, Inc., a calendar-year company, rented office space to the Tiger Travel Agency for occupancy on November 1, 2009, for $5,000 per month. Porter Properties requires Tiger Travel to make a rental

CORNERSTONE
3-5

**CORNERSTONE
3-5
(continued)**

payment every three months. If Tiger Travel pays its entire three-month rental in advance, Porter Properties has agreed to reduce the monthly rental to $4,500. Tiger Travel agrees and pays Porter Properties $13,500 for three months rental.

Required:
1. Prepare the entry on November 1, 2009, to record the receipt of cash.
2. Prepare the adjusting journal entry necessary on December 31, 2009, for Porter Properties.

Solution:
1. When the cash is received, Porter Properties will make the following entry to defer the revenue:

Assets = Liabilities +	Stockholders' Equity
+13,500 +13,500	

Date	Account and Explanation	Debit	Credit
Nov. 1, 2009	Cash	13,500	
	Unearned Rent Revenue		13,500
	(To record receipt of cash for three months rent)		

2. At the end of the accounting period, Porter Properties will perform the following three steps to prepare the adjusting entry:

Step 1: Identify the accounts that require adjustment. Rent Revenue needs to be increased because Porter Properties has earned revenue from providing the office space. Because a liability was previously recorded, Porter Properties would need to decrease the liability, Unearned Rent Revenue, to reflect the decrease in their obligation to perform the service.
Step 2: Calculate the amount of the adjustment. The amount of the adjustment would be $9,000, calculated as $4,500 per month times the two months that the office space was rented.
Step 3: Record the adjusting entry. The adjusting journal entry at December 31, 2009, would be:

Assets = Liabilities +	Stockholders' Equity
−9,000	+9,000

Date	Account and Explanation	Debit	Credit
Dec. 31, 2009	Unearned Rent Revenue	9,000	
	Rent Revenue		9,000
	(To record rent revenue earned in 2009)		

If the adjusting entry on December 31, 2009, was not made, liabilities (Unearned Rent Revenue) would be overstated while stockholders' equity and revenue would be understated. The adjusting journal entry recognizes two months of revenue (November and December 2009) in the accounting period in which it was earned and updates the corresponding balance in the liability, Unearned Rent Revenue. As a result of the adjusting entry, revenue is recorded in the period that it is earned.

Deferred (Prepaid) Expenses

Companies often acquire goods and services before they are used. These prepayments are recorded as assets called **deferred (or prepaid) expenses**. For example, FedEx reports prepaid expenses of $244 million on its December 31, 2007, balance sheet. Common prepaid expenses include items such as supplies, prepaid rent, prepaid advertising, and prepaid insurance. The purchases of buildings and equipment also are considered prepayments.

As the prepaid asset is used to generate revenue, an adjustment is necessary to reduce the previously recorded prepaid asset and recognize the related expense. The portion of the prepaid asset that has not been used represents the unexpired benefits from the prepayment and remains in the asset account until it is used. Therefore, expense recognition is delayed, or deferred, until the expense is incurred. Exhibit 3-9 demonstrates the process necessary to record deferred expenses.

Exhibit 3-9

Deferred (Prepaid) Expenses

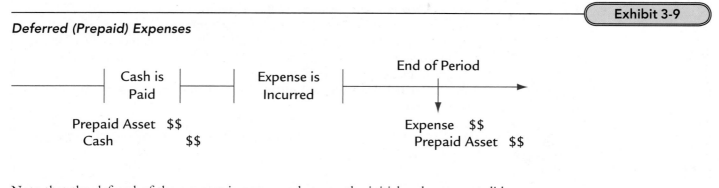

Note that the deferral of the expense is necessary because the initial cash payment did not result in an expense. Instead, an asset that provides future economic benefit was created. The adjusting entry recognizes the amount of expense that has been incurred from the time of the cash payment until the end of the accounting period. The adjusting entry required to adjust deferred expenses is shown in Cornerstone 3-6.

HOW TO Adjust Deferred (Prepaid) Expenses

Concept:
Expenses are recognized when incurred, regardless of when cash is paid. The adjusting entry for deferred expenses will result in an increase to an expense account and a decrease to an asset account.

CORNERSTONE
3-6

Information:
Assume that Porter Properties, Inc., a calendar-year company, had $4,581 of office supplies on hand at the beginning of November. On November 10, Porter Properties purchased office supplies totaling $12,365. The amount of the purchase was added to the Office Supplies account. At the end of the year, the balance in Office Supplies was $16,946 ($4,581 + $12,365) but a count of office supplies on hand indicated that $3,263 of supplies remained on hand.

Required:
1. Prepare the entry on November 10, 2009, to record the purchase of supplies.
2. Prepare the adjusting journal entry necessary on December 31, 2009, for Porter Properties.

Solution:
1. When the supplies are purchased, Porter Properties will make the following entry to defer the expense:

Date	Account and Explanation	Debit	Credit
Nov. 10, 2009	Office Supplies	12,365	
	Cash		12,365
	(To record purchase of office supplies)		

Assets =	Liabilities +	Stockholders' Equity
+12,365		
−12,365		

**CORNERSTONE
3-6**
(continued)

2. At the end of the accounting period, Porter Properties will perform the following three steps to prepare the adjusting entry:

    Step 1: Identify the accounts that require adjustment. Office Supplies Expense needs to be increased because Porter Properties has used office supplies during November and December of 2009. The use of the supplies would also decrease the asset, Office Supplies.

    Step 2: Calculate the amount of the adjustment. The amount of the adjustment would be $13,683. This amount represents the cost of supplies used during November and December 2009. It is calculated as $16,946 of supplies available to be used minus $3,263 of supplies on hand (and, therefore, unused) at the end of the year.

    Step 3: Record the adjusting entry. The adjusting journal entry at December 31, 2009, would be:

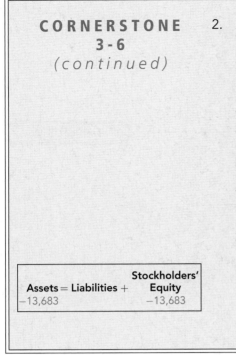

Date	Account and Explanation	Debit	Credit
Dec. 31, 2009	Office Supplies Expense	13,683	
	Office Supplies		13,683
	(To record the use of office supplies during 2009)		

Assets = Liabilities + Stockholders' Equity
−13,683   −13,683

If the adjusting entry on December 31, 2009, was not made, assets, stockholders' equity, and net income would be overstated and expenses would be understated. The adjusting journal entry recognizes the expense incurred during November and December 2009 and updates the corresponding balance in the asset, Office Supplies. As a result of the adjusting entry, the expense is recorded in the period that it is incurred.

Depreciation   While most deferred (prepaid) expenses are accounted for in a manner similar to that illustrated in Cornerstone 3-6, the purchase of long-lived assets such as buildings and equipment presents a unique situation. Recall from Chapter 1, that these types of assets are classified as property, plant, and equipment on the balance sheet. Because property, plant, and equipment helps to produce revenue over a number of years (instead of just one period), the matching principle requires companies to systematically assign, or allocate, the asset's cost as an expense in each period in which the asset is used. This process is called **depreciation**. This concept and the methods used to compute depreciation expense are discussed in Chapter 7.

The depreciation process requires an adjustment to recognize the expense incurred during the period and reduce the long-lived asset. The unused portion of the asset is reported as a component of property, plant, and equipment on the balance sheet. Therefore, the purchase of a long-lived asset is essentially a long-term prepayment for the service that the asset will provide.

Assume that Porter Properties purchased an office building on January 1, 2007, for $450,000. The depreciation expense on this building is $15,000 per year. Because depreciation is a continuous activity, Porter Properties would need to make the following adjustment at the end of 2009.

Assets = Liabilities + Stockholders' Equity
−15,000   −15,000

Date	Account and Explanation	Debit	Credit
Dec. 31, 2009	Depreciation Expense	15,000	
	Accumulated Depreciation		15,000
	(To record depreciation for 2009)		

Depreciation expense represents the portion of the cost of the long-lived asset that is matched against the revenues that the asset helped to generate. In addition, the depreciation process reduces the asset. Accountants normally use a contra-account to reduce the amount of a long-lived asset. **Contra accounts** are accounts that have a

Exhibit 3-10

Financial Statement Presentation of Accumulated Depreciation

Porter Properties Inc. Balance Sheet December 31, 2009		Sample of accumulated depreciation presentation:	
Assets:		Building	$ 450,000
Current assets	$ 370,000	Less: Accumulated depreciation	(45,000)
Property, plant,		Building (net)	$ 405,000
and equipment (net)	1,450,000		
Other assets	80,000		
Total assets	$ 1,900,000		
Liabilities	$ 825,000		
Equity	1,075,000		
Total liabilities and equity	$ 1,900,000		

balance that is opposite of the balance in a related account. In this case, Accumulated Depreciation is a contra account to the building. Therefore, while the asset has a normal debit balance, the contra account has a normal credit balance. Contra accounts are deducted from the balance of the related asset account in the financial statements, and the resulting difference is known as the *book value* of the asset. Therefore, by increasing the contra account, the above journal entry reduces the book value of the asset. Exhibit 3-10 shows the financial statement presentation of the accumulated depreciation account.

Notice that accumulated depreciation shows the total amount of depreciation taken in all years of the asset's life ($15,000 per year for 2007, 2008, and 2009). Therefore, the balance in the accumulated depreciation account will increase over the asset's life. The use of the contra account provides more information to users of the financial statements because it preserves both the original cost of the asset and the total cost that has expired to date.

Summary of Financial Statement Effects of Adjusting Entries

The effects of the adjustment process are summarized in Exhibit 3-11.

Exhibit 3-11

Effects of Adjusting Entries on the Financial Statements

Type of Adjustment	Asset	Liability	Stockholders' Equity	Revenue	Expense
Accrued Revenue	↑		↑	↑	
Accrued Expense		↑	↓		↑
Deferred Revenue	↓		↑	↑	
Deferred Expense	↓		↓		↑

CONCEPT Q&A

What is the relationship between the cash receipt or payment and the recognition of accruals or deferrals?

Possible Answer:

*Adjusting entries can be classified as accruals or deferrals depending on the timing of the cash flow relative to when the revenue is earned or the expense is incurred. When the revenue is earned or the expense is incurred **before** the associated cash flow occurs, an accrual adjusting entry is necessary. When the revenue is earned or the expense is incurred **after** the associated cash flow occurs, a deferral adjusting entry is necessary.*

Adjusting entries are internal events that do not involve another company. The purpose of all adjustments is to make sure that revenues and expenses get recorded in the proper time period. As the revenue and expense balances are adjusted, asset and liability balances will be adjusted also. Therefore, note that *all adjusting entries will affect at least one income statement account and one balance sheet account.* Remember that *the cash account is never used in an adjusting entry.*

Comprehensive Example

To provide a comprehensive example of the adjusting process, consider the trial balance of HiTech Communications that was introduced in Chapter 2. This trial balance is reproduced in Exhibit 3-12 for your convenience.

Exhibit 3-12

Trial Balance

HiTech Communications, Inc.
Trial Balance
March 31, 2009

Account	Debit	Credit
Cash	$16,600	
Accounts Receivable	300	
Supplies	6,500	
Prepaid Insurance	1,200	
Equipment	4,500	
Accounts Payable		$ 500
Unearned Revenue		9,000
Notes Payable		3,000
Common Stock		12,000
Dividends	500	
Service Revenue		12,100
Salaries Expense	1,800	
Utility Expense	5,200	
	$36,600	$36,600

Upon review of the trial balance, the accountant for HiTech noted that several accounts needed to be adjusted. Specifically, the following adjustments were needed.

Adjustment 1: Accrued Revenue   HiTech's accountant noted that HiTech had performed $1,500 of advertising services for which it had not yet billed the customer. Because the services had not yet been billed, no entry was made in the accounting system. However, HiTech must record the revenue that was earned during the accounting period, even though the cash flow will not occur until later. The adjusting entry to record this accrued revenue is:

Assets = Liabilities +	Stockholders' Equity
+1,500	+1,500

Date	Account and Explanation	Debit	Credit
March 31	Accounts Receivable	1,500	
	Service Revenue		1,500
	(To recognize services earned)		

Adjustment 2: Accrual of Interest   The note payable for $3,000 that HiTech signed on March 2 required it to pay interest at an annual rate of 8 percent. The formula for computing interest is:

$$\text{Interest} = \text{Principal} \times \text{Interest Rate} \times \text{Time}$$

The principal amount of the loan is usually the face value of the note. The interest rate is stated as an annual rate, and the time period is the fraction of a year that the note is outstanding. For HiTech, interest expense for March 2009 is computed as:

$$Interest = \$3,000 \times 8\% \times 1/12 = \$20$$

Because interest expense has been incurred but the cash payment for interest will not occur until a later date, interest is an accrued expense that requires an increase to an expense account and an increase to a liability account. The adjusting entry to recognize accrued interest is:

Date	Account and Explanation	Debit	Credit
March 31	Interest Expense	20	
	Interest Payable		20
	(To recognize accrued interest)		

Assets	= Liabilities +	Stockholders' Equity
	+20	−20

Adjustment 3: Accrual of Salaries

HiTech paid its weekly salaries on March 26, a Friday, and properly recorded an expense (Transaction 10 from Chapter 2). Salaries for a five-day work week are $1,800, or $360 per day. HiTech will not pay salaries again until April 2. However, employees worked on March 29, March 30, and March 31. Because employees have worked but will not be paid until a later date, an adjustment is necessary to record the salaries incurred in March. Accrued salaries are $1,080 (3 days × $360 per day). The adjusting entry to recognize accrued salaries is:

Date	Account and Explanation	Debit	Credit
March 31	Salaries Expense	1,080	
	Salaries Payable		1,080
	(To recognize accrued salaries)		

Assets	= Liabilities +	Stockholders' Equity
	+1,080	−1,080

Adjustment 4: Deferred (Unearned) Revenue

HiTech's trial balance shows that a customer paid $9,000 in advance for services to be performed at a later date. This amount was originally recorded as a liability, Unearned Revenue. As HiTech performs services, the liability will be reduced and revenue will be recognized. Based on HiTech's analysis of work performed during March, it is determined that $3,300 of revenue has been earned. The adjusting entry to record this previously unearned revenue is:

Date	Account and Explanation	Debit	Credit
March 31	Unearned Revenue	$3,300	
	Service Revenue		$3,300
	(To recognize service revenue earned)		

Assets	= Liabilities +	Stockholders' Equity
	−3,300	+3,300

Adjustment 5: Prepaid Expense—Supplies

HiTech's trial balance shows a balance of $6,500 in the Supplies account. However, an inventory count at the close of business on March 31 determined that supplies on hand were $1,200. Because it was not efficient to record supplies expense during the period, HiTech must make an adjustment at the end of the period to record the supplies used during the period. It was determined that HiTech used $5,300 ($6,500 available to be used minus $1,200 not used) of supplies. The adjustment necessary to record the supplies used during March is:

Date	Account and Explanation	Debit	Credit
March 31	Supplies Expense	5,300	
	Supplies		5,300
	(To recognize supplies used)		

Assets	= Liabilities +	Stockholders' Equity
−5,300		−5,300

Adjustment 6: Prepaid Expense—Insurance

HiTech's trial balance shows a balance of $1,200 in the Prepaid Insurance account related to a six-month insurance policy purchased at the beginning of March. Because time has passed since the purchase of the insurance policy, the asset, Prepaid Insurance, has partially expired and an expense needs to be recognized. The expired portion of the insurance is $200 ($1,200 × 1/6). The adjustment necessary to record insurance expense is:

	Stockholders'
Assets = Liabilities +	**Equity**
−200	−200

Date	Account and Explanation	Debit	Credit
March 31	Insurance Expense	200	
	Prepaid Insurance		200
	(To recognize insurance used)		

Adjustment 7: Depreciation HiTech's trial balance shows that $4,500 of equipment was purchased. As this equipment is used to generate revenue, a portion of the cost of the equipment must be allocated to expense. For HiTech, assume that depreciation expense is $125 per month. The adjustment necessary to record depreciation expense is:

	Stockholders'
Assets = Liabilities +	**Equity**
−125	−125

Date	Account and Explanation	Debit	Credit
March 31	Depreciation Expense	125	
	Accumulated Depreciation—		
	Equipment		125
	(To recognize depreciation on equipment)		

The ledger for HiTech Communications, after posting of the adjusting journal entries, is shown in Exhibit 3-13.

Exhibit 3-13

General Ledger of HiTech Communications

Assets

Cash
Bal. 16,600	
Bal. 16,600	

Accounts Receivable
Bal. 300	
(A1) 1,500	
Bal. 1,800	

Supplies
Bal. 6,500	
	5,300 (A5)
Bal. 1,200	

Prepaid Insurance
Bal. 1,200	
	200 (A6)
Bal. 1,000	

Equipment
| Bal. 4,500 | |
| Bal. 4,500 | |

Accumulated Depreciation
| | 125 (A7) |
| | 125 Bal. |

Liabilities

Accounts Payable
| | 500 Bal. |
| | 500 Bal. |

Notes Payable
| | 3,000 Bal. |
| | 3,000 Bal. |

Unearned Revenue
	9,000 Bal.
(A4) 3,300	
	5,700 Bal.

Interest Payable
| | 20 (A2) |
| | 20 Bal. |

Salaries Payable
| | 1,080 (A3) |
| | 1,080 Bal. |

Stockholders' Equity

Common Stock
| | 12,000 Bal. |
| | 12,000 Bal. |

Service Revenue
	12,100 Bal.
	1,500 (A1)
	3,300 (A4)
	16,900 Bal.

Salaries Expense
Bal. 1,800	
(A3) 1,080	
Bal. 2,880	

Utility Expense
| Bal. 5,200 | |
| Bal. 5,200 | |

Depreciation Expense
| (A7) 125 | |
| Bal. 125 | |

Interest Expense
| (A2) 20 | |
| Bal. 20 | |

Insurance Expense
| (A6) 200 | |
| Bal. 200 | |

Supplies Expense
| (A5) 5,300 | |
| Bal. 5,300 | |

Dividends
| Bal. 500 | |
| Bal. 500 | |

Two major items should be apparent. First, adjusting entries affect one balance sheet account and one income statement account. Without adjusting entries, the balances reported on both the balance sheet and the income statement would have been incorrect. If the adjustments were not recorded, HiTech would have understated revenue by $4,800 and understated expenses by $6,725. Second, notice that adjusting entries do not affect cash.

Step 6: Preparing the Financial Statements

OBJECTIVE ▶ 5
Prepare financial statements from an adjusted trial balance.

After a company has journalized and posted all of the adjusting entries, it updates the trial balance to reflect the adjustments that have been made. This trial balance is called an **adjusted trial balance**. Similar to the trial balance, the adjusted trial balance lists all of the active accounts and proves the equality of debits and credits. In addition, the adjusted trial balance is the primary source of information needed to prepare the financial statements. The adjusted trial balance for HiTech Communications is shown in Exhibit 3-14.

The financial statements can now be prepared using the balances obtained from the adjusted trial balance. As discussed in Chapter 1, the financial statements are interrelated. That is, there is a natural progression from one financial statement to another as the numbers in one financial statement flow into another financial statement. Because of this natural progression, financial statements are prepared in a particular order. First, the income statement is prepared from the revenue and expense accounts. Next, net income is used as a component of the retained earnings statements. Finally, retained earnings is presented on the balance sheet as a component of equity. The financial statements and their interrelationship are shown in Exhibits 3-15 through 3-17.

Exhibit 3-14

Adjusted Trial Balance

HiTech Communications, Inc.
Trial Balance
March 31, 2009

Account		Debit	Credit
Cash		$16,600	
Accounts receivable		1,800	
Supplies		1,200	
Prepaid insurance		1,000	
Equipment		4,500	
Accumulated depreciation—equipment	Balance Sheet Accounts		$ 125
Accounts payable			500
Unearned revenue			5,700
Interest payable			20
Salaries payable			1,080
Notes payable			3,000
Common stock			12,000
Dividends		500	
Service revenue			16,900
Salaries expense		2,880	
Utility expense	Income Statement Accounts	5,200	
Depreciation expense		125	
Interest expense		20	
Insurance expense		200	
Supplies expense		5,300	
		$39,325	$39,325

Exhibit 3-15

Income Statement

HiTech Communications, Inc. Income Statement For the Month Ended March 31, 2009		
Service revenue		$16,900
Expenses:		
Salaries expense	$ 2,880	
Utility expense	5,200	
Depreciation expense	125	
Interest expense	20	
Insurance expense	200	
Supplies expense	5,300	13,725
Net income		$ 3,175

Exhibit 3-16

Statement of Retained Earnings

HiTech Communications, Inc. Statement of Retained Earnings For the Month Ended March 31, 2009	
Retained earnings, March 1, 2009	$ 0
Add: Net income	3,175
	$3,175
Less: Dividends	(500)
Retained earnings, March 31, 2009	$2,675

Exhibit 3-17

Balance Sheet

HiTech Communications, Inc. Balance Sheet March 31, 2009					
ASSETS			**LIABILITIES AND STOCKHOLDERS' EQUITY**		
Current assets:			Current liabilities:		
Cash	$16,600		Accounts payable	$ 500	
Accounts receivable	1,800		Unearned revenue	5,700	
Supplies	1,200		Interest payable	20	
Prepaid insurance	1,000		Salaries payable	1,080	
Total current assets		$20,600	Total current liabilities		$ 7,300
Property, plant, and equipment:			Long-term liabilities:		
Equipment	$ 4,500		Notes payable		3,000
Less: Accumulated depreciation	(125)		Total liabilities		$10,300
Total property, plant, & equipment		4,375	Stockholders' equity:		
			Common stock	$12,000	
			Retained earnings	2,675	
			Total stockholders' equity		14,675
Total assets		$ 24,975	Total liabilities & stockholders' equity		$24,975

Step 7: Closing the Accounts

When we introduced the fundamental accounting equation in Chapter 1, we identified three kinds of balance sheet accounts: assets, liabilities, and stockholders' equity. These accounts are **permanent accounts** in that their balances are carried forward from the current accounting period to future accounting periods. We also identified three other accounts: revenues, expenses and dividends. These accounts are used to collect the activities of only one period, so they are considered **temporary accounts**. The final step of the accounting cycle, closing the accounts, is done to:

1. Transfer the effects of revenues, expenses, and dividends (the temporary accounts) to the permanent stockholders' equity account, Retained Earnings.
2. Clear the revenue, expenses, and dividends (reduce their balances to zero) so they are ready to accumulate the business activities of the next accounting period. Without closing entries, these accounts would accumulate the business activities of *all* accounting periods, not just the current time period.

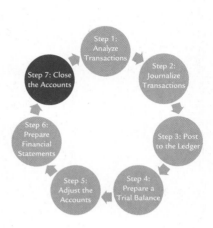

The closing process is accomplished through a series of journal entries that are dated as of the last day of the accounting period. Often, another temporary account, called income summary, is used to aid the closing process. The use of the income summary account allows the company to easily identify the net income (or net loss) for the period. The closing process can be completed in a four-step procedure:

Step 1: Close revenues to income summary.

Step 2: Close expenses to income summary. At this point, the balance in the income summary account should be equal to net income.

Step 3: Close income summary to retained earnings.

Step 4: Close dividends to retained earnings.

The closing process is illustrated in Cornerstone 3-7.

HOW TO Close the Accounts

**CORNERSTONE
3-7**

Concept:
The closing process is designed to transfer the balances in the temporary accounts to retained earnings and to prepare the temporary accounts for the next accounting period.

Information:
For 2009, Porter Properties' general ledger shows the following balances: Rental Revenue $2,174,000; Salaries Expense $1,300,000; Supplies Expense $150,000; Interest Expense $15,000; Insurance Expense $20,000; Retained Earnings at the beginning of the year, $1,135,000; and Dividends $5,000.

Required:
Prepare the closing entries for Porter Properties at December 31, 2009.

Solution:
The closing process involves four steps:

Step 1: Close revenues to Income Summary.

Date	Account and Explanation	Debit	Credit
Dec. 31	Service Revenue	2,174,000	
	Income Summary		2,174,000
	(To close revenues accounts)		

**CORNERSTONE
3-7
(continued)**

Step 2: Close expenses to Income Summary.

Date	Account and Explanation	Debit	Credit
Dec. 31	Income Summary	1,485,000	
	Salaries Expense		1,300,000
	Supplies Expense		150,000
	Interest Expense		15,000
	Insurance Expense		20,000
	(To close expense accounts)		

Step 3: Close Income Summary to Retained Earnings.

Date	Account and Explanation	Debit	Credit
Dec. 31	Income Summary	689,000	
	Retained Earnings		689,000
	(To close Income Summary)		

Step 4: Close Dividends to Retained Earnings.

Date	Account and Explanation	Debit	Credit
Dec. 31	Retained Earnings	5,000	
	Dividends		5,000
	(To close Dividends)		

CONCEPT Q&A

What would happen if we didn't make closing entries?

Possible Answer:

The closing process transfers temporary account balances (revenues, expenses, and dividends) to retained earnings. If the accounts were not closed, these amounts would not get properly reflected in stockholders' equity and the accounting equation wouldn't balance. In addition, the temporary accounts would accumulate amounts from different accounting periods, making it extremely difficult to determine the effect of business activities for a specific accounting period.

Notice that revenues, which have a normal credit balance, are closed by debiting the revenue account. Similarly, expenses, which normally have a debit balance are closed by crediting the expense accounts. Also, after the first two journal entries, the balance in the income summary account is $689,000 ($2,174,000 − $1,485,000), which is the amount of income for the period. This amount is then transferred to retained earnings. Finally, the dividends account is not closed to income summary (because dividends are not part of income) but closed directly to retained earnings. The ending retained earnings account will have a balance of $1,819,000 ($1,135,000 + 689,000 − 5,000). The closing process for Porter Properties is illustrated in Exhibit 3-18.

OBJECTIVE ▶ 7
Understand the steps in the accounting cycle.

Summary of the Accounting Cycle

In Chapter 2, we introduced the accounting cycle as a sequence of procedures that transforms business activities into financial statements. The accounting cycle is shown in Exhibit 3-19.

Notice that the accounting cycle begins with the analysis of transactions to determine which business activities are recognized in the accounting records and their effect on the fundamental accounting equation. Those criteria that met the recognition criteria are journalized and posted to the ledger. These three steps are repeated many times during an accounting period. The remaining steps of the accounting cycle are performed only at the end of the accounting period. For those transactions still underway at the end of the accounting period, the portion that has been completed

Exhibit 3-18

The Closing Process

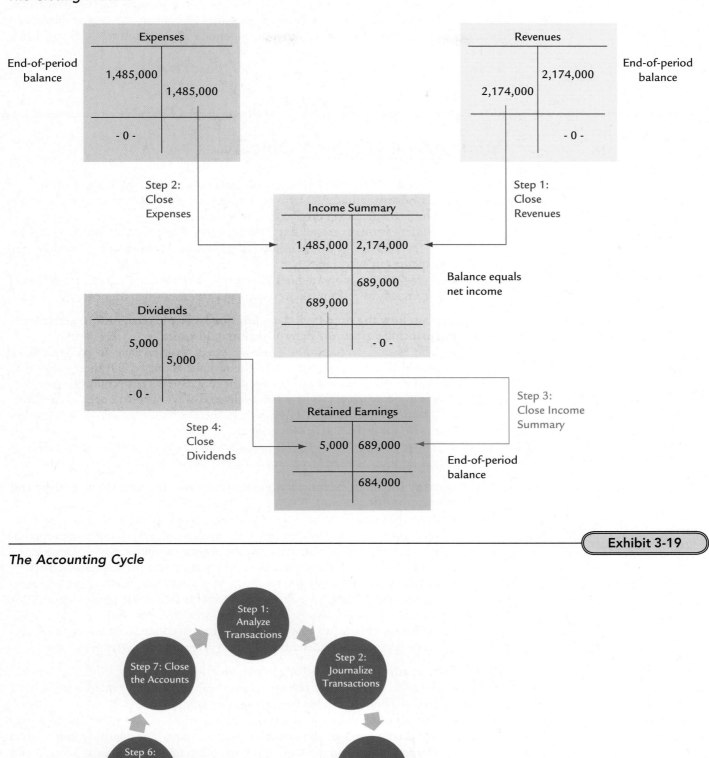

Exhibit 3-19

The Accounting Cycle

is recognized with adjustments. Next, the financial statements are prepared. Finally, the temporary accounts—revenues, expenses, and dividends—are closed and their balances transferred to retained earnings. At this point, the income statement accounts have zero balances, and the balance sheet accounts all contain the correct beginning balances for the start of the next accounting period. The accounting cycle can begin again.

Summary of Learning Objectives

LO1. Explain the difference between cash-basis and accrual-basis accounting.
- Cash-basis and accrual-basis accounting are two alternatives for recording business activities in the accounting records.
- Under cash-basis accounting, revenues and expenses are recorded when cash is received or paid, regardless of when the revenues are earned or the expenses are incurred.
- Accrual-basis accounting ties income measurement to the selling activities of a company by recognizing revenues and expenses when they occur.

LO2. Explain how the time-period assumption, revenue recognition, and matching principles affect the determination of income.
- The revenue recognition principle states that revenue is recognized or recorded in the period in which the revenue is earned and the collection of cash is reasonably assured (realized or realizable). These conditions are normally met when goods have been delivered or services have been performed.
- The matching principle requires that expenses be recognized in the same period as the revenue it helped generate.
- The application of these two principles results in income being measured as the business activity occurs, regardless of when cash is received or paid.

LO3. Identify the kinds of transactions that may require adjustments at the end of an accounting period.
- Many business activities do not occur at a single point in time but continuously over time. Because entries in the accounting system are made at particular points in time, adjustments are needed at the end of an accounting period to record the completed portion of any partially completed activities.
- Adjusting entries apply the revenue recognition and matching principles to ensure that a company's financial statements reflect the proper amount for revenues, expenses, assets, liabilities, and stockholders' equity.
- Adjusting entries are categorized as either accruals (accrued revenues and accrued expenses) or deferrals (deferred revenues and deferred expenses).

LO4. Prepare adjusting entries for accruals and deferrals.
- Accruals occur when revenues have been earned or expenses have been incurred but no cash has been received or paid.
- The adjusting entry for an accrued revenue will result in an increase to a revenue account and an increase to an asset account. The adjusting entry for an accrued expense account will result in an increase to an expense account and an increase to a liability account.
- Deferrals (prepayments) occur when cash has been received or paid prior to revenue being earned or the expense being incurred.
- The adjusting entry for a deferred revenue will result in an increase to a revenue account and a decrease to a liability account. The adjusting entry for a deferred expense will result in an increase to an expense account and a decrease to an asset account.

LO5. Prepare financial statements from an adjusted trial balance.

- An adjusted trial balance lists all of the active accounts and updates the trial balance to reflect the adjustments that have been made.
- The adjusted trial balance is the primary source of information needed to prepare the financial statements.
- Due to the interrelation between the financial statements, the income statement is prepared first, followed by the statement of retained earnings, and finally, the balance sheet.

LO6. Explain why and how companies prepare closing entries.

- Closing entries (a) transfer the effects of revenues, expenses, and dividends to the stockholders' equity account, Retained Earnings, and (b) clear the balances in revenues expenses, and dividends (reduce their balances to zero) so that they are ready to accumulate the business activities of the next accounting period.
- To close the accounts, companies make a series of journal entries, dated as of the last day of the accounting period.

LO7. Understand the steps in the accounting cycle.

- During the accounting period, transactions are analyzed to determine their effect on the accounting equation.
- Transactions that meet the recognition criteria are then journalized and posted to the general ledger.
- A trial balance is prepared to summarize the effects of these transactions.
- At the end of the accounting period, adjusting entries are prepared to recognize the completed portion of any partially completed business activities.
- The financial statements are then prepared from the adjusted trial balance and the temporary accounts are closed.
- The accounting cycle then repeats for the next accounting period.

CORNERSTONE 3-1 How to apply the revenue recognition and matching principles, page 118

CORNERSTONE 3-2 How to determine which transactions require adjustment, page 120

CORNERSTONE 3-3 How to record accrued revenues, page 122

CORNERSTONE 3-4 How to record accrued expenses, page 124

CORNERSTONE 3-5 How to adjust deferred (unearned) revenues, page 125

CORNERSTONE 3-6 How to adjust deferred (prepaid) expenses, page 127

CORNERSTONE 3-7 How to close the accounts, page 135

CORNERSTONES FOR CHAPTER 3

Key Terms

Accrual-basis accounting, 115

Accrued expenses, 123

Accrued revenues, 121

Adjusted trial balance, 133

Adjusting entries, 119

Cash-basis accounting, 115

Contra accounts, 128

Deferred (or prepaid) expenses, 126

Deferred revenues, 125

Depreciation, 128

Matching principle, 117

Permanent accounts, 135

Revenue recognition principle, 116

Temporary accounts, 135

Time-period assumption, 115

Unearned revenue, 125

Appendix: Using a Worksheet to Prepare Financial Statements

The discussion of closing completes our presentation of the essential procedures that make up the accounting cycle. Accountants often use an informal schedule called a **worksheet** to assist them in organizing and preparing the information necessary to perform the end-of-period steps in the accounting cycle—namely the preparation of adjusting entries, financial statements, and closing entries. The worksheet is not a financial statement but simply an organizational tool that summarizes the information generated by the accounting system and enables the accountant to check the information for completeness and consistency. While worksheets can be completed manually, most worksheets today are created in computer spreadsheets.

A typical worksheet is shown in Exhibit 3-20. This exhibit uses the information for HiTech Communications that was presented in Chapter 2 and earlier in Chapter 3. The completion of the worksheet requires the following steps:

- **Step 1: Unadjusted Trial Balance.** The worksheet starts with the unadjusted trial balance. The first column contains the listing of accounts used during the period in the same order as the accounts appear in the trial balance—the balance sheet accounts first followed by the income statement accounts. Note that a retained earnings account was added. Because this is the first month of operations, this account has a zero balance. The next two columns contain the unadjusted balances of these accounts and are totaled to ensure the equality of debits and credits.
- **Step 2: Adjusting Entry Columns.** The next two columns contain the adjustments made to record the completed portion of business activities that remain underway at the end of the accounting period. Rather than take the time to make formal adjusting journal entries, the accountant typically enters the adjustments directly into the worksheet and then makes the formal journal entries after the worksheet has been completed. Two items should be noted. First, adjustments often require the addition of accounts not included in the unadjusted trial balance. These additional accounts can be added, in no particular order, beneath the previous listing of accounts. Second, letters are typically used on a worksheet to identify the adjusting entries and to allow the accountant to easily match the debit and credit sides of each adjusting entry. The letters (a) through (g) correspond to the adjusting entries (1) through (7) shown earlier in the chapter. The two columns are totaled to ensure the equality of debits and credits.
- **Step 3: Adjusted Trial Balance.** The next two columns represent an adjusted trial balance. The adjustments in columns entered in columns D and E are added to or subtracted from the unadjusted balances in columns B and C. The two columns are totaled to ensure the equality of debits and credits. The adjusted trial balance is the basis for preparing the financial statements.
- **Step 4: Income Statement.** The income statement balances are transferred to the income statement columns of the worksheet and the columns are totaled. The difference between the two columns is the net income or loss of the period. In Exhibit 3-20, HiTech reports its net income of $3,175 in the debit column of the income statement and the credit column of the statement of retained earnings. This entry is made (1) to balance the two income statement columns and (2) to transfer net income to retained earnings.
- **Step 5: Statement of Retained Earnings**. The amounts for beginning retained earnings and dividends are transferred from the adjusted trial balance columns (columns F and G) to the statement of retained earnings columns (columns J and K). The columns are totaled and the difference is the amount of ending retained earnings. This amount is entered in the debit column of the statement of retained earnings (to balance the two columns) and transferred to the credit column of the balance sheet as shown by letter (i).
- **Step 6**: **Balance Sheet.** The final portion of the worksheet is completed by transferring all the balance sheet account balances from the adjusted trial balance columns (columns F and G) to the balance sheet columns (columns L and M).

At this point, the worksheet provides all the necessary information to prepare the financial statements. The completed financial statements were shown in Exhibits 3-15, 3-16, and 3-17.

Exhibit 3-20

Worksheet

HiTech Communications, Inc.
Work Sheet
For the Month Ended March 31, 2010

Account Titles	Unadjusted Trial Balance Debit	Unadjusted Trial Balance Credit	Adjusting Entries Debit	Adjusting Entries Credit	Adjusted Trial Balance Debit	Adjusted Trial Balance Credit	Income Statement Debit	Income Statement Credit	Statement of Retained Earnings Debit	Statement of Retained Earnings Credit	Balance Sheet Debit	Balance Sheet Credit
Cash	16,600				16,600						16,600	
Accounts Receivable	300		(a) 1,500		1,800						1,800	
Supplies	6,500			(e) 5,300	1,200						1,200	
Prepaid Insurance	1,200			(f) 200	1,000						1,000	
Equipment	4,500				4,500						4,500	
Accounts Payable		500				500						500
Unearned Revenue		9,000	(d) 3,300			5,700						5,700
Notes Payable		3,000				3,000						3,000
Common Stock		12,000				12,000						12,000
Retained Earnings, 3/1/2010	500	0				0				0		
Dividends	500				500				500			
Service Revenue		12,100		(a) 1,500 (d) 3,300		16,900		16,900				
Salaries Expense	1,800		(c) 1,080		2,880		2,880					
Utility Expense	5,200				5,200		5,200					
	36,600	36,600										
Interest Expense			(b) 20		20		20					
Interest Payable				(b) 20		20						20
Salaries Payable				(c) 1,080		1,080						1,080
Supplies Expense			(e) 5,300		5,300		5,300					
Insurance Expense			(f) 200		200		200					
Depreciation Expense			(g) 125		125		125					
Accumulated Depreciation — Equipment				(g) 125		125						125
			11,525	11,525	39,325	39,325	13,725	16,900				
Net Income							(h) 3,175			(h) 3,175		
							16,900	16,900	500	3,175		
Retained Earnings, 3/31/2010									(i) 2,675			(i) 2,675
									3,175	3,175	25,100	25,100

Appendix: Summary of Learning Objectives

LO8. Understand how to use a worksheet to prepare financial statements.
- A worksheet is an informal schedule that assists accountants in organizing and preparing the information necessary to perform the end-of-period steps in the accounting cycle.
- The worksheet begins with a trial balance and includes columns for adjusting entries, the adjusted trial balance, the income statement, the statement of retained earnings, and the balance sheet.

Key Terms

Worksheet, 140

Review Problem

The Adjustment Process

Concept:

Adjusting journal entries are required for continuous transactions that are partially complete at the end of an accounting period. This often requires estimates and judgments about the timing of revenue and expense recognition. Once the adjustments are made, financial statements can be prepared and the accounts are closed so that the accounts are ready to accumulate business activities in the next accounting period.

Information:

Kenny's Laundry has one laundry plant and uses five rented storefronts on the west side of Indianapolis as its retail locations. At the end of 2009, Kenny's Laundry had the following balances in its accounts before adjustment:

Cash	Accounts Receivable	Supplies Inventory
4,800	26,000	128,000

Land	Building	Accumulated Depreciation, Building
124,400	249,000	36,000

Equipment	Accumulated Depreciation, Equipment	Other Assets
122,000	24,000	16,000

Accounts Payable	Notes Payable (due 2015)	Unearned Service Revenue
8,000	120,000	12,000

Common Stock	Retained Earnings, 12/31/2008	Service Revenue
240,000	69,000	874,200

Rent Expense	Wages Expense	Insurance Expense
168,000	431,000	14,000

Salaries Expense	Interest Expense
92,000	8,000

An examination identified the following items that require adjustment:

a. Kenny's launders shirts for the service staff of a local car dealer. At the end of 2009, the car dealer owes Kenny's $1,040 for laundry services that have been performed but will not be billed until early in 2010.
b. Kenny's supplies inventory on hand at 12/31 was $21,400.
c. Kenny's launders uniforms for a nearby McDonalds franchise. The franchisee pays Kenny's in advance for the laundry service once each three months. After examining the records, Kenny's accountant determines that the Laundry has earned $8,400 of the $12,000 of unearned revenue.
d. Salaries in the amount of $1,500 are owed but unpaid and unrecorded.
e. Two months' interest at 8 percent on the note payable (due in 2015) is owed but unpaid and unrecorded.
f. Depreciation expense for the building is $12,000
g. Depreciation expense for the equipment is $24,000.
h. Income taxes expense of $5,200 is owed but unpaid and unrecorded.

Required:

1. Determine the adjusting entries at 12/31/2009 for Kenny's Laundry.
2. Record and post the effects of the adjustments to the before adjustment account balances.
3. Prepare an income statement, statement of changes in retained earnings, and a balance sheet for Kenny's Laundry using the adjusted account balances.
4. Close the necessary accounts.

Solution:

1. The adjustments for Kenny's Laundry are as follows:

a. The adjustment to record accrued revenue for services already provided is:

Date	Account and Explanation	Debit	Credit
Dec. 31	Accounts Receivable	1,040	
	Service Revenue		1,040
	(To recognize revenue for services performed but not billed)		

	Stockholders'
Assets = Liabilities +	**Equity**
+1,040	+1,040

b. The before adjustment balance in supplies inventory is $128,000. Supplies actually on hand are $21,400. Supplies expense (used) is $106,600 ($128,000 − $21,400):

Date	Account and Explanation	Debit	Credit
Dec. 31	Supplies Expense	106,600	
	Supplies		106,600
	(To recognize supplies used)		

	Stockholders'
Assets = Liabilities +	**Equity**
−106,600	−106,600

c. The adjustment to record the amount of deferred revenue earned in 2009 is:

Date	Account and Explanation	Debit	Credit
Dec. 31	Unearned Service Revenue	8,400	
	Service Revenue		8,400
	(To recognize revenue earned)		

	Stockholders'
Assets = Liabilities +	**Equity**
−8,400	+8,400

d. The entry to record the accrual of salaries is:

Date	Account and Explanation	Debit	Credit
Dec. 31	Salaries Expense	1,500	
	Salaries Payable		1,500
	(To recognize salary expense incurred but not paid)		

	Stockholders'
Assets = Liabilities +	**Equity**
+1,500	−1,500

e. Interest expense is $1,600 ($120,000 × 8% × 2/12). The entry to accrue interest expense is:

Date	Account and Explanation	Debit	Credit
Dec. 31	Interest Expense	1,600	
	Interest Payable		1,600
	(To recognize interest expense incurred but not paid)		

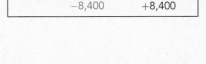

	Stockholders'
Assets = Liabilities +	**Equity**
+1,600	−1,600

f. The entry to record depreciation expense for the building is:

	Assets = Liabilities +	Stockholders' Equity
	−12,000	−12,000

Date	Account and Explanation	Debit	Credit
Dec. 31	Depreciation Expense	12,000	
	Accumulated Depreciation, Building		12,000
	(To record depreciation expense)		

g. The entry to record depreciation expense for the equipment is:

	Assets = Liabilities +	Stockholders' Equity
	−24,000	−24,000

Date	Account and Explanation	Debit	Credit
Dec. 31	Depreciation Expense	24,000	
	Accumulated Depreciation, Equipment		24,000
	(To record depreciation expense)		

h. The adjustment for income taxes expense is:

	Assets = Liabilities +	Stockholders' Equity
	+5,200	−5,200

Date	Account and Explanation	Debit	Credit
Dec. 31	Income Tax Expense	5,200	
	Income Taxes Payable		5,200
	(To record accrual of income taxes)		

2. The adjusted account balances for Kenny's Laundry are shown in Exhibit 3-21.

Exhibit 3-21

Kenny's Laundry Adjusted Account Balances

Cash	
4,800	

Accounts Receivable	
26,000	
(a) 1,040	
27,040	

Supplies Inventory	
128,000	106,600 (b)
21,400	

Land	
124,400	

Building	
249,000	

Accumulated Depreciation, Building	
	36,000
	12,000 (f)
	48,000

Equipment	
122,000	

Accumulated Depreciation, Equipment	
	24,000
	24,000 (g)
	48,000

Other Assets	
16,000	

Accounts Payable	
	8,000

Notes Payable (due 2015)	
	120,000

Interest Payable	
	- 0 -
	1,600 (e)
	1,600

Salaries Payable	
	- 0 -
	1,500 (d)
	1,500

Income Taxes Payable	
	- 0 -
	5,200 (h)
	5,200

Unearned Service Revenue	
	12,000
	8,400 (c)
	3,600

(Continued)

Common Stock	
	240,000

Retained Earnings, 12/31/2008	
	69,000

Service Revenue	
	874,200
	1,040 (a)
	8,400 (c)
	883,640

Rent Expense	
168,000	

Wages Expense	
431,000	

Insurance Expense	
14,000	

Salaries Expense	
92,000	
(d) 1,500	
93,500	

Interest Expense	
8,000	
(e) 1,600	
9,600	

Supplies Expense	
-0-	
(b) 106,600	
106,600	

Depreciation Expense, Building	
-0-	
(f) 12,000	
12,000	

Depreciation Expense, Equipment	
-0-	
(g) 24,000	
24,000	

Income Taxes Expense	
-0-	
(h) 5,200	
5,200	

3. The income statement, statement of changes in retained earnings, and balance sheet for Kenny's Laundry are prepared from the adjusted account balances and appear in Exhibit 3-22 below.

Exhibit 3-22

Financial Statements for Kenny's Laundry

Kenny's Laundry
Income Statement
For the Year Ended December 31, 2009

Service revenue		$883,640
Less expenses:		
Rent	$168,000	
Wages	431,000	
Insurance	14,000	
Salaries	93,500	
Supplies	106,600	
Depreciation, building	12,000	
Depreciation, equipment	24,000	849,100
Income from operations		$ 34,540
Interest expense		9,600
Income before income taxes		$ 24,940
Income taxes expense		5,200
Net income		$ 19,740

Kenny's Laundry
Statement of Changes in Retained Earnings
For the Year Ended December 31, 2009

Retained earnings, 12/31/2008	$69,000
Add: Net income	19,740
	$88,740
Less: Dividends	-0-
Retained earnings, 12/31/2009	$88,740

(Continued)

Kenny's Laundry
Balance Sheet
December 31, 2009

ASSETS			

Current assets:			
Cash		$ 4,800	
Accounts receivable		27,040	
Supplies		21,400	
Total current assets			$ 53,240
Property, plant, and equipment:			
Land		$124,400	
Building	$249,000		
Less: Accumulated depreciation	48,000	201,000	
Equipment	$122,000		
Less: Accumulated depreciation	48,000	74,000	
Total property, plant, and equipment			399,400
Other assets			16,000
Total assets			$468,640

LIABILITIES AND STOCKHOLDERS' EQUITY			

Current liabilities:			
Accounts payable		$ 8,000	
Salaries payable		1,500	
Interest payable		1,600	
Income taxes payable		5,200	
Unearned service revenue		3,600	
Total current liabilities			$ 19,900
Long-term liabilities:			
Notes payable (due 2015)			120,000
Total liabilities			$139,900
Stockholders' equity:			
Common stock		$240,000	
Retained earnings		88,740	
Total stockholders' equity			328,740
Total liabilities and stockholders' equity			$468,640

4. The entries to close the accounts are:

Date	Account and Explanation	Debit	Credit
Dec. 31	Service Revenue	883,640	
	Income Summary		883,640
	(To close revenues)		
	Income Summary	863,900	
	Rent Expense		168,000
	Wages Expense		431,000
	Insurance Expense		14,000
	Salaries Expense		93,500
	Supplies Expense		106,600
	Depreciation Expense, Building		12,000
	Depreciation Expense, Equipment		24,000
	Interest Expense		9,600
	Income Tax Expense		5,200
	(To close expenses)		
31	Income Summary	19,740	
	Retained Earnings		19,740
	(To close Income Summary)		

Discussion Questions

1. How does accrual-basis net income differ from cash-basis net income?
2. Explain when revenue may be recognized in the accounting records.
3. What happens during the accounting cycle?
4. Provide two examples of transactions that begin and end at a particular point-in-time and two examples of continuous transactions.
5. Why are adjusting entries needed?
6. What accounting concepts require that adjusting entries be employed?
7. Describe the recording of transactions that begin and end at a particular point-in-time and continuous transactions. In your answer, be sure to refer to within-period journal entries and adjusting entries.
8. For each of the four categories of adjusting entries, describe the business activity that produces circumstances requiring adjustment.
9. What is the difference between an *accrual* and a *deferral*?
10. Which type of adjustment will (a) increase both assets and revenues, (b) increase revenues and decrease liabilities, (c) increase expenses and decrease assets, and (d) increase both expenses and liabilities?
11. How is the amount for an interest expense (or interest revenue) adjustment determined?
12. Describe the effect on the financial statements when an adjustment is prepared that records (a) unrecorded revenue and (b) unrecorded expense.
13. On the basis of what you have learned about adjustments, why do you think that adjusting entries are made on the last day of the accounting period rather than at several earlier times during the accounting period?
14. What is the purpose of closing entries?
15. Describe the four steps in the closing process.
16. Identify each of the following categories of accounts as temporary or permanent: assets, liabilities, equity, revenues, expenses, dividends. How is the distinction between temporary and permanent accounts related to the closing process?
17. Why are only the balance sheet accounts permanent?
18. List the seven steps in the accounting cycle in the order in which they occur.
19. (Appendix) What is the relationship between the accounting cycle and the work-sheet?
20. (Appendix) Describe the structure of the worksheet and the accounting information it contains.

Multiple-Choice Exercises

3-1 Which of the following statements is *true*?

a. Under cash-basis accounting, revenues are recorded when earned and expenses are recorded when incurred.
b. Generally accepted accounting principles require companies to use cash-basis accounting.
c. The key elements of accrual-basis accounting are the revenue recognition principle, the matching principle, and the historical cost principle.
d. Accrual-basis accounting records both cash and noncash transactions when they occur.

3-2 In December 2009, Swanstrom, Inc., receives a cash payment of $3,000 for services performed in December 2009 and a cash payment of $10,000 for services to be performed in January 2010. Swanstrom also receives the December utility bill for $800. For December 2009, under the accrual basis of accounting, Swanstrom would recognize:

a. $13,000 of revenue and $800 of expense
b. $13,000 of revenue and $0 of expense
c. $3,000 of revenue and $800 of expense
d. $3,000 of revenue and $0 of expense

3-3 Which transaction would require adjustment at December 31?

a. The sale of merchandise for cash on December 30.
b. A one-year insurance policy (which is immediately effective) was purchased on December 1.
c. Common stock was issued on November 30.
d. Salaries were paid to employees on December 31 for work performed in December.

3-4 Which of the following statements is *not* true?

a. The cash account will always be affected by adjusting journal entries.
b. Adjusting entries are necessary because timing differences exist between when a revenue or expense is recognized and cash is received or paid.
c. Adjusting entries always affect one revenue or expense account and one asset or liability account.
d. Adjusting entries can be classified as either accruals or deferrals.

3-5 Dallas Company loaned $10,000 to Ewing Company on December 1, 2009. Ewing will pay Dallas $600 of interest ($50 per month) on November 30, 2010. Dallas's adjusting entry at December 31, 2009 is:

a. Interest Expense   50
    Cash   50
b. Interest Receivable   50
    Interest Revenue   50
c. Cash   50
    Interest Revenue   50
d. No adjusting entry is required.

3-6 Ron's Diner received the following bills for December 2009 utilities:

- Electricity: $400 on December 29, 2009
- Telephone: $150 on January 5, 2010

Both bills were paid on January 10, 2010. On the December 31, 2009 balance sheet, Ron's Diner will report accrued expenses of:

a. $550
b. $400
c. $150
d. $ 0

3-7 In September 2009, GolfWorld Magazine obtained $12,000 of subscriptions for one year of magazines and credited Unearned Subscription Revenue. The magazines will begin to be delivered in October 2009. At December 31, 2009, GolfWorld should make the following adjustment:

a. Debit Subscription Revenue by $3,000 and credit Unearned Subscription Revenue by $3,000.
b. Debit Subscription Revenue by $9,000 and credit Unearned Subscription Revenue by $9,000.
c. Debit Unearned Subscription Revenue by $3,000 and credit Subscription Revenue by $3,000.
d. Debit Unearned Subscription Revenue by $9,000 and credit Subscription Revenue by $9,000.

3-8 Hurd, Inc., prepays rent every three months on March 1, June 1, September 1, and December 1. Rent for the three months totals $2,700. On December 31, 2009, Hurd, Inc., will report:

a. Prepaid Rent of $2,700
b. Prepaid Rent of $1,800
c. Prepaid Rent of $ 900
d. Prepaid Rent of $ 0

3-9 Which of the following statements is incorrect regarding preparing financial statements?

a. The adjusted trial balance is the primary source of information needed to prepare the financial statements.
b. The financial statements are prepared in the following order: (1) the income statement; (2) the statement of retained earnings; (3) the balance sheet.
c. The adjusted trial balance lists only the balance sheet accounts in a "debit" and "credit" format.
d. The income statement and the balance sheet are related through the retained earnings account.

3-10 Reinhardt Company reported revenues of $110,000 and expenses of $75,000 on its 2009 income statement. In addition, Reinhardt paid $4,000 of dividends during the 2009. On December 31, 2009, Reinhardt prepared closing entries. The net effect of the closing entries on retained earnings was a(n):

a. Decrease of $ 4,000
b. Decrease of $79,000
c. Increase of $35,000
d. Increase of $31,000

3-11 Which of the following is *true* regarding the accounting cycle?

a. The temporary accounts are closed after the financial statements are prepared.
b. The accounts are adjusted after preparing the financial statements.
c. Journal entries are made prior to the transaction being analyzed.
d. A trial balance is usually prepared after the accounts are closed.

Cornerstone Exercises

Cornerstone Exercise 3-12 ACCRUAL- AND CASH-BASIS REVENUE

OBJECTIVE ▶ 1
CORNERSTONE 3-1

McDonald Music sells used CDs for $2.00 each. During the month of April, McDonald Music sold 21,200 CDs for cash and 7,300 CDs on credit. McDonald's cash collections in April included the $42,400 for the 21,200 CDs sold for cash, $11,800 for CDs sold on credit during the previous month, and $8,100 for CDs sold on credit during April.

Required:

Calculate the amount of revenue recognized in April under (a) the cash-basis of accounting and (b) the accrual-basis of accounting.

Cornerstone Exercise 3-13 ACCRUAL- AND CASH-BASIS EXPENSES

OBJECTIVE ▶ 1
CORNERSTONE 3-1

Speedy Delivery Company provides next-day delivery across the southeastern United States. During May, Speedy incurred $120,000 in fuel costs. Speedy paid $90,000 of the fuel cost in May, with the remainder paid in June. In addition, Speedy paid $15,000 in May to another fuel supplier in an effort to build up its supply of fuel.

Required:

Calculate the amount of expense recognized in May under (a) the cash-basis of accounting and (b) the accrual-basis of accounting.

Cornerstone Exercise 3-14 REVENUE AND THE RECOGNITION PRINCIPLE

OBJECTIVE ▶ 2
CORNERSTONE 3-1

Heartstrings Gift Shoppe sells an assortment of gifts for any occasion. During October, Heartstrings started a Gift-of-the-Month program. Under the terms of this program, Heartstrings would select and deliver a random gift each month, over the next 12 months, to the person the customer selects as a recipient. During October, Heartstrings sold 20 of these packages for a total of $8,400 in cash.

Required:

For the month of October, calculate the amount of revenue that Heartstrings will recognize.

OBJECTIVE ▶ 2
CORNERSTONE 3-1

Cornerstone Exercise 3-15 EXPENSES AND THE MATCHING PRINCIPLE

The following information describes transactions for Morgenstern Advertising Company during July:

a. On July 5, Morgenstern purchased and received $21,500 of supplies on credit from Drexel Supply Inc. Morgenstern paid $18,500 cash to Drexel and used $16,200 of the supplies during July.
b. Morgenstern paid $9,600 to salespeople for salaries earned during July. An additional $1,610 was owed to salespeople at July 31 for salary earned during the month.
c. Paid $1,900 to the local utility company for electric service. Electric service in July was $1,650 of the $1,900 total bill.

Required:

Calculate the amount of expense recognized in July under (a) the cash-basis of accounting and (b) the accrual-basis of accounting.

OBJECTIVE ▶ 3
CORNERSTONE 3-2

Cornerstone Exercise 3-16 IDENTIFICATION OF ADJUSTING ENTRIES

Singleton, Inc., had the following transactions during the year.

a. Merchandise was sold to customers on credit.
b. Purchased equipment to be used in the operation of its business.
c. A two-year insurance contract was purchased.
d. Received cash for services to be performed over the next year.
e. Paid monthly employee salaries.
f. Borrowed money from First Bank by signing a note payable due in five years.

Required:

Identify and explain why each transaction may or may not require adjustment.

OBJECTIVE ▶ 4
CORNERSTONE 3-3

Cornerstone Exercise 3-17 ACCRUED REVENUE ADJUSTING ENTRIES

Powers Rental Service had the following items that require adjustment at year-end.

a. Earned $6,420 of revenue from the rental of equipment for which the customer had not yet paid.
b. Interest of $400 on a note receivable has been earned but not yet received.

Required:

1. Prepare the adjusting entries needed at December 31.
2. What is the effect on the financial statements if these adjusting entries are not made?

OBJECTIVE ▶ 4
CORNERSTONE 3-4

Cornerstone Exercise 3-18 ACCRUED EXPENSE ADJUSTING ENTRIES

Manning Manufacturing Inc. had the following items that require adjustment at year-end.

a. Salaries of $3,180 which were earned in December are unrecorded and unpaid.
b. Used $2,598 of utilities in December which are unrecorded and unpaid.
c. Interest of $1,200 on a note payable has not been recorded or paid.

Required:

1. Prepare the adjusting entries needed at December 31.
2. What is the effect on the financial statements if these adjusting entries are not made?

OBJECTIVE ▶ 4
CORNERSTONE 3-5

Cornerstone Exercise 3-19 DEFERRED REVENUE ADJUSTING ENTRIES

Olney Cleaning Company had the following items that require adjustment at year-end.

a. For one cleaning contract, $14,000 cash was received in advance. The cash was credited to unearned revenue upon receipt. At year-end, $3,750 of the service revenue was still unearned.

b. For another cleaning contract, $9,500 cash was received in advance and credited to unearned revenue upon receipt. At year-end, $4,300 of the services had been provided.

Required:

1. Prepare the adjusting journal entries needed at December 31.
2. What is the effect on the financial statements if these adjusting entries are not made?
3. What is the balance in unearned revenue at December 31 related to the two cleaning contracts?

Cornerstone Exercise 3-20 DEFERRED EXPENSE ADJUSTING ENTRIES

OBJECTIVE 4
CORNERSTONE 3-6

Best Company had the following items that require adjustment at year-end.

a. Cash for equipment rental in the amount of $4,200 was paid in advance. The $4,200 was debited to prepaid equipment rent when paid. At year-end, $3,150 of the prepaid rent had been used.

b. Cash for insurance in the amount of $6,500 was paid in advance. The $6,500 was debited to prepaid insurance when paid. At year-end, $1,300 of the prepaid insurance was still unused.

Required:

1. Prepare the adjusting journal entries needed at December 31.
2. What is the effect on the financial statements if these adjusting entries are not made?
3. What is the balance in prepaid equipment rent and insurance expense at December 31?

Cornerstone Exercise 3-21 ADJUSTMENT FOR SUPPLIES

OBJECTIVE 4
CORNERSTONE 3-6

Pain-Free Dental Group, Inc., purchased dental supplies of $15,500 during the year. At the end of the year, a physical count of supplies showed $2,300 of supplies on hand.

Required:

1. Prepare the adjusting entry needed at the end of year.
2. What is the amount of supplies reported on Pain-Free's balance sheet at the end of the year and supplies expense reported on the income statement?

Cornerstone Exercise 3-22 ADJUSTMENT FOR DEPRECIATION

OBJECTIVE 4
CORNERSTONE 3-6

LaGarde Company has a machine that it purchased for $125,000 on January 1. Annual depreciation on the machine is estimated to be $11,400.

Required:

1. Prepare the adjusting entry needed at the end of the year.
2. What is the book value of the machine reported on LaGarde's balance sheet at the end of the year?

Cornerstone Exercise 3-23 FINANCIAL STATEMENT EFFECTS OF ADJUSTING ENTRIES

OBJECTIVE 4
CORNERSTONE 3-3
CORNERSTONE 3-4
CORNERSTONE 3-5
CORNERSTONE 3-6

When adjusting entries were made at the end of the year, the accountant for Parker Company did not make the following adjustments.

a. $2,900 of wages had been earned but were unpaid
b. $3,750 of revenue had been earned but was uncollected and unrecorded.
c. $2,400 of revenue had been earned. The customer had prepaid for this service and the amount was originally recorded in the Unearned Revenue account.
d. $1,200 of insurance coverage had expired. Insurance had been initially recorded in the Prepaid Insurance account.

Required:

Identify the effect on the financial statements of the adjusting entries that were omitted.

OBJECTIVE ➤ 5

Cornerstone Exercise 3-24 PREPARING AN INCOME STATEMENT

Sparrow Company had the following adjusted trial balance at December 31, 2009.

	Debit	Credit
Cash	$ 3,300	
Accounts Receivable	5,240	
Prepaid Insurance	4,400	
Equipment	40,000	
Accumulated Depreciation, Equipment		$ 24,000
Accounts Payable		3,100
Salaries Payable		4,400
Unearned Revenue		3,750
Common Stock		8,000
Retained Earnings		2,130
Dividends	10,500	
Service Revenue		95,000
Salaries Expense	48,000	
Rent Expense	15,000	
Insurance Expense	2,200	
Depreciation Expense	4,000	
Income Tax Expense	7,740	
Total	$140,380	$ 140,380

Required:

Prepare a single-step income statement for Sparrow Company for 2009.

OBJECTIVE ➤ 5

Cornerstone Exercise 3-25 PREPARING A STATEMENT OF RETAINED EARNINGS

Refer to the adjusted trial balance in **Cornerstone Exercise 3-24**.

Required:

Prepare a statement of retained earnings for Sparrow Company for 2009.

OBJECTIVE ➤ 5

Cornerstone Exercise 3-26 PREPARING A BALANCE SHEET

Refer to the adjusted trial balance in **Cornerstone Exercise 3-24**.

Required:

Prepare a classified balance sheet for Sparrow Company at December 31, 2009.

OBJECTIVE ➤ 6
CORNERSTONE 3-7

Cornerstone Exercise 3-27 PREPARING AND ANALYZING CLOSING ENTRIES

Refer to the adjusted trial balance in **Cornerstone Exercise 3-24**.

Required:

1. Prepare the closing entries for Sparrow Company at December 31, 2009.
2. How does the closing process affect retained earnings?

OBJECTIVE ➤ 7

Cornerstone Exercise 3-28 THE ACCOUNTING CYCLE

The following is a list of steps in the accounting cycle.

a. Post to the ledger
b. Close the accounts
c. Analyze transactions
d. Adjust the accounts
e. Prepare financial statements
f. Journalize transactions
g. Prepare a trial balance

Required:

1. Arrange the steps of the accounting cycle in proper order.
2. Explain what occurs at each step of the accounting cycle.

Exercises

Exercise 3-29 ACCRUAL- AND CASH-BASIS EXPENSE RECOGNITION

OBJECTIVE ➤ 1

The following information is taken from the accrual accounting records of Kroger Sales Company:

a. During January, Kroger paid $8,500 for supplies to be used in sales to customers during the next two months (February and March). The supplies will be used evenly over the next two months.
b. Kroger pays its employees at the end of each month for salaries earned during that month. Salaries paid at the end of February and March amounted to $4,750 and $5,100, respectively.
c. Kroger placed an advertisement in the local newspaper during March at a cost of $700. The ad promoted the pre-Spring sale during the last week in March. Kroger did not pay for the newspaper ad until mid-April.

Required:

1. Under cash-basis accounting, how much expense should Kroger report for February and March?
2. Under accrual-basis accounting, how much expense should Kroger report for February and March?
3. Which basis of accounting provides the most useful information for decision-makers? Why?

Exercise 3-30 REVENUE RECOGNITION

OBJECTIVE ➤ 2

Each of the following situations relates to the recognition of revenue:

a. A store sells a gift card in December which will be given as a Christmas present. The card is not redeemed until January.
b. A furniture store sells furniture in June with no payments and no interest for six months.
c. An airline sells an airline ticket in February (and collects the fare in February) for a flight in March to a spring break destination.
d. A theme park sells a season pass which allows entrance into the park for an entire year.
e. A package delivery service delivers a package in October but doesn't bill the customer and receive payment until November.

Required:

For each situation, indicate when the company should recognize revenue.

Exercise 3-31 REVENUE AND EXPENSE RECOGNITION

OBJECTIVE ➤ 2

Electronic Repair Company repaired a high-definition television for Sarah Merrifield in December 2009. Sarah paid $50 at the time of the repair and agreed to pay Electronic Repair Company $50 each month for five months beginning on January 15, 2010. Electronic Repair Company used $80 of supplies, which were purchased in November 2009, to repair the television.

Required:

1. In what month or months should revenue from this service be recorded by Electronic Repair Company?
2. In what month or months should the expense related to the repair of the television be recorded by Electronic Repair Company?
3. Describe the accounting principles used to answer the above questions.

Exercise 3-32 CASH-BASIS AND ACCRUAL-BASIS ACCOUNTING

OBJECTIVE ➤ 1 2

The records of Summers Building Company reveal the following information for 2009.

a. Cash receipts during 2009 (including $50,000 paid by stockholders in exchange for common stock) were $220,000.
b. Cash payments during 2009 (including $8,000 of dividends paid to stockholders) were $132,000.

c. Total selling price of services billed to customers during 2009 was $183,000.
d. Salaries earned by employees during 2009 was $107,000.
e. Cost of supplies used during 2009 in operation of the business was $42,000.

Required:

1. Calculate Summers Building Company's net income for 2009 on an accrual basis.
2. Calculate Summers Building Company's net income for 2009 on a cash-basis.
3. Explain how the cash-basis of accounting allows for the management of income.

OBJECTIVE ▶ 2

Exercise 3-33 REVENUE RECOGNITION AND MATCHING

Omega Transportation Inc., headquartered in Atlanta, Georgia, engaged in the following transactions:

- billed customers $2,387,000 for transportation services
- collected cash from customers in the amount of $1,364,000
- purchased fuel supplies for $1,262,000 cash
- used fuel supplies that cost $1,253,000
- employees earned salaries of $256,000
- paid employees $25,000 cash for salaries

Required:

Determine the amount of sales revenue and total expenses for Omega's income statement.

OBJECTIVE ▶ 2

Exercise 3-34 RECOGNIZING EXPENSES

Treadway Dental Services gives each of its patients a toothbrush with the name and phone number of the dentist office and a logo imprinted on the brush. Treadway purchased 15,000 of the toothbrushes in October 2009 for $3,000. The toothbrushes were delivered in November and paid for in December 2009. Treadway began to give the patients the toothbrushes in February 2010. By the end of 2010, 5,000 of the toothbrushes remained in the supplies account.

Required:

1. How much expense should be recorded for the 15,000 toothbrushes in 2009 and 2010 to properly match expenses with revenues?
2. Describe how the 5,000 toothbrushes that remain in the supplies account will be handled in 2011.

OBJECTIVE ▶ 1 2

Exercise 3-35 REVENUE RECOGNITION AND MATCHING

Carrico Advertising Inc. performs advertising services for several Fortune 500 companies. The following information describes Carrico's activities during 2009.

a. At the beginning of 2009, customers owed Carrico $43,700 for advertising services performed during 2008. During 2009, Carrico performed an additional $692,400 of advertising services on account. Carrico collected $708,700 cash from customers during 2009.
b. At the beginning of 2009, Carrico had $15,000 of supplies on hand for which it owed suppliers $8,150. During 2009, Carrico purchased an additional $12,000 of supplies on credit. Carrico also paid $19,300 cash owed to suppliers for goods previously purchased on credit. Carrico had $2,800 of supplies on hand at the end of 2009.
c. Carrico's 2009 operating and interest expenses were $428,000 and $137,000, respectively.

Required:

1. Calculate Carrico's 2009 income before taxes.
2. Calculate the amount of Carrico's accounts receivable, supplies, and accounts payable at December 31, 2009. Explain the underlying principles behind why these three accounts exist.

OBJECTIVE ▶ 3

Exercise 3-36 IDENTIFICATION OF ADJUSTING ENTRIES

Conklin Services prepares financial statements only once per year using an annual accounting period ending on December 31. Each of the following statements describes an entry made by Conklin on December 31 of a recent year.

a. On December 31, Conklin completed a service agreement for Pizza Planet and recorded the related revenue. The job started in August.

b. Conklin provides weekly service visits to the local C.J. Nickel department store to check and maintain various pieces of computer printing equipment. On December 31, Conklin recorded revenue for the visits completed during December. The cash will not be received until January.

c. Conklin's salaried employees are paid on the last day of every month. On December 31, Conklin recorded the payment of December salaries.

d. Conklin's hourly wage employees are paid every Friday. On December 31, Conklin recorded as payable the wages for the first three working days of the week in which the year ended.

e. On December 31, Conklin recorded the receipt of a shipment of office supplies from Office Supplies, Inc. to be paid for in January.

f. On December 31, Conklin recorded the estimated use of supplies for the year. The supplies were purchased for cash earlier in the year.

g. Early in December, Conklin was paid in advance by Parker Enterprises for two months of weekly service visits. Conklin recorded the advance payment as a liability. On December 31, Conklin recorded revenue for the service visits to Parker Enterprises that were completed during December.

h. On December 31, Conklin recorded depreciation expense on office equipment for the year.

Required:

Indicate whether each entry is an *adjusting entry* or a *regular journal entry*, and if it is an adjusting entry, identify it as one of the following types: (1) revenue recognized before collection, (2) expense recognized before payment, (3) revenue recognized after collection, or (4) expense recognized after payment.

Exercise 3-37 IDENTIFICATION AND ANALYSIS OF ADJUSTING ENTRIES

OBJECTIVE ➤ 3

Medina Motor Service is preparing adjusting entries for the year ended December 31, 2009. The following items describe Medina's continuous transactions during 2009:

a. Medina's salaried employees are paid on the last day of every month.

b. Medina's hourly employees are paid every other Friday for the preceding two weeks' work. The next payday falls on January 5, 2010.

c. In November 2009, Medina borrowed $600,000 from Bank One giving a 7.6 percent note payable with interest due in January 2010. The note was properly recorded.

d. Medina rents a portion of its parking lot to the neighboring business under a long-term lease agreement that requires payment of rent six months in advance on April 1 and October 1 of each year. The October 1, 2009, payment was made and recorded as prepaid rent.

e. Medina's service department recognizes the entire revenue on every auto service job when the job is complete. At December 31, several service jobs are in process.

f. Medina recognizes depreciation on shop equipment annually at the end of each year.

g. Medina purchases all of its office supplies from Office Supplies Inc. All purchases are recorded in the office supplies inventory account. Supplies expense is calculated and recorded annually at the end of each year.

Required:

Indicate whether or not each item requires an adjusting entry at December 31, 2009. If an item requires an adjusting entry, indicate which accounts are increased by the adjustment and which are decreased.

Exercise 3-38 REVENUE ADJUSTMENTS

OBJECTIVE ➤ 4

Sentry Transport, Inc., of Atlanta provides in-town parcel delivery services in addition to a full range of passenger services. Sentry engaged in the following activities during the current year:

a. Sentry received $1,200 cash in advance from Rich's Department Store for an estimated 200 deliveries during December 2009 and January and February of 2010.

The entire amount was recorded as unearned revenue when received. During December 2009, 60 deliveries were made for Rich's.

b. Sentry operates several small buses that take commuters from suburban communities to the central downtown area of Atlanta. The commuters purchase, in advance, tickets for 50 one-way trips. Each 50-ride ticket costs $180. At the time of purchase, Sentry credits the cash received to unearned revenue. At year-end, Sentry estimates that revenue from 1,800 one-way rides has been earned.

c. Sentry operates several buses that provide transportation for the clients of a social service agency in Atlanta. Sentry bills the agency quarterly at the end of January, April, July, and October for the service performed that quarter. The contract price is $900 per quarter. Sentry follows the practice of recognizing revenue from this contract in the period in which the service is performed.

d. On December 23, Delta Airlines chartered a bus to transport its marketing group to a meeting at a resort in West Virginia. The meeting will be held during the last week in January 2010, and Delta agrees to pay for the entire trip on the day the bus departs. At year-end, none of these arrangements have been recorded by Sentry.

Required:

1. Prepare adjusting entries at December 31 for these four activities.
2. What would be the effect on revenue if the adjusting entries were not made?

OBJECTIVE ▶ 4

Exercise 3-39 EXPENSE ADJUSTMENTS

Faraday Electronic Service repairs stereos and DVD players. During a recent year, Faraday engaged in the following activities:

a. On September 1, Faraday paid Wausau Insurance $1,860 for its liability insurance for the next 12 months. The full amount of the prepayment was debited to prepaid insurance.

b. At December 31, Faraday estimates that $830 of utility costs are unrecorded and unpaid.

c. Faraday rents its testing equipment from JVC. Equipment rent in the amount of $1,440 is unpaid and unrecorded at December 31.

d. In late October, Faraday agreed to become the sponsor for the sports segment of the evening news program on a local television station. The station billed Faraday $3,300 for three months' sponsorship—November 2009, December 2009, and January 2010—in advance. When these payments were made, Faraday debited prepaid advertising expense. At December 31, two months' advertising expense has been used and one month remains unused.

Required:

1. Prepare adjusting entries at December 31 for these four activities.
2. What would be the effect on expenses if the adjusting entries were not made?

OBJECTIVE ▶ 4

Exercise 3-40 PREPAYMENTS, COLLECTIONS IN ADVANCE

Greensboro Properties, Inc., owns a building in which it leases office space to small businesses and professionals. During 2009, Greensboro Properties engaged in the following transactions:

a. On March 1, Greensboro Properties paid $14,400 in advance to Patterson Account Services for billing services for the entire year beginning March 1, 2009. The full amount of the prepayment was debited to prepaid rent.

b. On May 1, Greensboro Properties received $24,000 for one year's rent from Angela Cottrell, a lawyer and new tenant. Greensboro Properties credited unearned rental revenue for the full amount collected from Cottrell.

c. On July 31, Greensboro Properties received $480,000 for six months' rent on an office building that is occupied by Newnan and Calhoun, a regional accounting firm. The rental period begins on August 1, 2009. The full amount received was credited to unearned rental revenue.

d. On November 1, Greensboro Properties paid $3,300 to Pinkerton Security for three months' security services beginning on that date. The entire amount was debited to prepaid professional services.

Required:

1. Prepare the journal entry to record the receipt or payment of cash for each of the transactions.
2. Prepare the adjusting entries you would make at December 31, 2009, for each of these items.
3. What would be the effect on the income statement and balance sheet if these entries were not recorded?

Exercise 3-41 **PREPAYMENT OF EXPENSES**

OBJECTIVE ➤ 4

JDM, Inc., made the following prepayments for expense items during 2009:

a. Prepaid building rent for one year on April 1. JDM paid $6,300, debiting prepaid rent for the amount paid.
b. Prepaid six months' insurance on October 1 by paying $870. Prepaid insurance was debited.
c. Purchased $3,750 of office supplies on October 15, debiting office supplies inventory for the full amount. Office supplies costing $385 remain unused at Dec. 31, 2009.
d. Paid $2,880 for a 12-month service contract for maintenance on a computer. The contract begins November 1. The full amount of the payment was debited to prepaid maintenance.

Required:

1. Prepare journal entries to record the payment of cash for each transaction.
2. Prepare adjusting entries for the prepayments at December 31, 2009.
3. For all of the above items, assume that the accountant failed to make the adjusting entries. What would be the effect on net income?

Exercise 3-42 **ADJUSTMENT FOR SUPPLIES**

OBJECTIVE ➤ 4

The downtown Chicago Nieman Marcus store purchases large quantities of supplies, including plastic garment bags and paper bags and boxes. At December 31, 2009, the following information is available concerning these supplies:

Supplies inventory, 1/1/2009	$ 4,150
Supplies inventory, 12/31/2009	5,220
Supplies purchased for cash during 2009	15,700

All purchases of supplies during the year are debited to the supplies inventory.

Required:

1. What is the expense reported on the income statement associated with the use of supplies during 2009?
2. What is the proper adjusting entry at December 31, 2009?
3. By how much would assets and income be overstated or understated if the adjusting entry were not recorded?

Exercise 3-43 **ADJUSTING ENTRIES**

OBJECTIVE ➤ 4

Allentown Services, Inc., is preparing adjusting entries for the year ending December 31, 2009. The following data are available:

a. Interest is owed at December 31, 2009, on a six-month, 9 percent note. Allentown borrowed $100,000 from NBD on September 1, 2009.
b. Allentown provides daily building maintenance services to Mack Trucks for a quarterly fee of $2,400, payable on the fifteenth of the month following the end of each quarter. No entries have been made for the services provided to Mack Trucks during the quarter ended December 31, and the related bill will not be sent until January 15, 2010.

c. At the beginning of 2009, the cost of office supplies on hand was $1,220. During 2009, office supplies with a total cost of $6,480 were purchased from Office Depot and debited to office supplies inventory. On December 31, 2009, Allentown determined the cost of office supplies on hand to be $970.

d. On September 23, 2009, Allentown received a $6,300 payment from Bethlehem Steel for nine months of maintenance services beginning on October 1, 2009. The entire amount was credited to unearned revenue when received.

Required:

1. Prepare the appropriate adjusting entries at December 31, 2009.
2. What would be the effect on the balance sheet and the income statement if the accountant failed to make the above adjusting entries?

OBJECTIVE ➤ 4

Exercise 3-44 ADJUSTING ENTRIES

Reynolds Computer Service offers data processing services to retail clothing stores. The following data have been collected to aid in the preparation of adjusting entries for Reynolds Computer Service for 2009:

a. Computer equipment was purchased from IBM in 2006 at a cost of $540,000. Annual depreciation is $72,500.

b. A fire insurance policy for a two-year period beginning September 1, 2009, was purchased from Good Hands Insurance Company for $10,320 cash. The entire amount of the prepayment was debited to prepaid insurance. (Assume that the beginning balance of prepaid insurance was $0 and that there were no other debits or credits to that account during 2009.)

c. Reynolds has a contract to perform the payroll accounting for Dayton's Department Stores. At the end of 2009, $8,400 of services have been performed under this contract but are unbilled.

d. Reynolds rents 12 computer terminals for $40 per month per terminal from Extreme Terminals Inc. At December 31, 2009, Reynolds owes Extreme Terminals for half a month's rent on each terminal. The amount owed is unrecorded.

e. Perry's Tax Service prepays rent for time on Reynolds' computer. When payments are received from Perry's Tax Service, Reynolds credits unearned revenue. At December 31, 2009, Reynolds has earned $1,430 for computer time used by Perry's Tax Service during December 2009.

Required:

1. Prepare adjusting entries for each of the transactions.
2. What would be the effect on the balance sheet and the income statement if the accountant failed to make the above adjusting entries?

OBJECTIVE ➤ 4

Exercise 3-45 EFFECT OF ADJUSTMENTS ON THE FINANCIAL STATEMENTS

VanBrush Enterprises, a painting contractor, prepared the following adjusting entries at year-end:

a.	Wages Expense	3,700	
	Wages Payable		3,700
b.	Accounts Receivable	6,500	
	Service Revenue		6,500
c.	Unearned Revenue	5,245	
	Service Revenue,		
	Advertising		5,245
d.	Rent Expense	3,820	
	Prepaid Rent		3,820

Required:

Show the effect of these adjustments on (1) assets, liabilities, and equity and (2) revenues, expenses, and net income.

Exercise 3-46 **PREPARATION OF CLOSING ENTRIES**

Grand Rapids Consulting, Inc., began 2009 with a retained earnings balance of $38,100 and has the following accounts and balances at year-end:

Sales Revenue	$155,000
Salaries Expense	83,000
Rent Expense	15,000
Utilities Expense	7,900
Office Supplies Expense	4,200
Income Taxes Expense	12,300
Dividends (declared and paid)	16,400

Required:

1. Prepare the closing entries made by Grand Rapids Consulting at the end of 2009.
2. Prepare Grand Rapids Consulting's statement of retained earnings for 2009.

Exercise 3-47 **PREPARATION OF CLOSING ENTRIES**

James and Susan Morley recently converted a large turn-of-the-century house into a hotel and incorporated the business as Saginaw Enterprises. Their accountant is inexperienced and has made the following closing entries at the end of Saginaw's first year of operations:

Income Summary	210,000	
Service Revenue		177,000
Accumulated Depreciation		33,000
Depreciation Expense	33,000	
Income Taxes Expense	8,200	
Utilities Expense	12,700	
Wages Expense	66,000	
Supplies Expense	31,000	
Accounts Payable	4,500	
Income Summary		155,400
Income Summary	54,600	
Retained Earnings		54,600
Dividends	3,200	
Income Summary		3,200

Required:

1. Indicate what is wrong with the closing entries above.
2. Prepare the correct closing entries. Assume that all necessary accounts are presented above and that the amounts given are correct.
3. Explain why closing entries are necessary.

Exercise 3-48 **PREPARATION OF A WORKSHEET**

Unadjusted account balances at December 31, 2009, for Rapisarda Company at the top of the next page.

The following data are not yet recorded:

a. Depreciation on the equipment is $25,000.
b. Unrecorded wages owed at December 31, 2009: $2,000.
c. Prepaid rent at December 31, 2009: $10,000.
d. Income tax rate: 30 percent.

Required:

Prepare a completed worksheet for Rapisarda Company.

Account Titles	Debit	Credit
Cash	$ 2,000	
Accounts Receivable	33,000	
Prepaid Rent	26,000	
Equipment	211,000	
Accumulated Depreciation, Equipment		$ 75,000
Other Assets	24,000	
Accounts Payable		12,000
Note Payable (due in 10 years)		40,000
Common Stock		100,000
Retained Earnings, 12/31/2008		11,000
Service Revenue		243,000
Rent Expense	84,000	
Wages Expense	97,000	
Interest Expense	4,000	
Totals	$481,000	$481,000

Problem Set A

OBJECTIVE ▶ 1

Problem 3-49A CASH-BASIS AND ACCRUAL-BASIS INCOME

George Hathaway, an electrician, entered into an agreement with a real estate management company to perform all maintenance of basic electrical systems and air-conditioning equipment in the apartment buildings under the company's management. The agreement, which is subject to annual renewal, provides for the payment of a fixed fee of $6,000 on January 1 of each year plus amounts for parts and materials billed separately at the end of each month. Amounts billed at the end of one month are collected in the next month. During the first three months of 2009, George makes the following additional billings and cash collections:

	Billings for Parts and Materials	Cash Collected	Cash Paid for Parts and Materials	Cost of Parts and Materials Used
January	$420	$6,110*	$310	$320
February	0	420	290	250
March	330	0	300	300

*Includes $110 for parts and materials billed in December 2008.

Required:

1. Calculate the amount of cash-basis income reported for each of the first three months.
2. Calculate the amount of accrual-basis income reported for each of the first three months.
3. Why do decision-makers prefer the accrual basis of accounting?

OBJECTIVE ▶ 2

Problem 3-50A REVENUE RECOGNITION AND MATCHING

Security Specialists performs security services for local businesses. During 2009, Security Specialists performed $900,000 of security services and collected $930,000 cash from customers. Security Specialist's employees earned salaries of $42,000 per month. During 2009, Security Services paid salaries of $495,000 cash for work performed. At the beginning of 2009, Security Specialists had $3,000 of supplies on hand. Supplies of $80,000 were purchased during the year, and $11,000 of supplies were on hand at the end of the year. Other general and administrative expenses incurred during the year were $31,000.

Required:

1. Calculate revenue for 2009.
2. Calculate expenses for 2009.

3. Prepare the 2009 income statement.
4. Describe the accounting principles used to prepare the income statement.

Problem 3-51A IDENTIFICATION AND PREPARATION OF ADJUSTING ENTRIES

Kuepper's Day Care is a large day-care center in South Orange, New Jersey. The day-care center serves several nearby businesses, as well as a number of individual families. The businesses pay $6,180 per child per year for day-care services for their employees' children. The businesses pay in advance on a quarterly basis. For individual families, day-care services are provided monthly and billed at the beginning of the next month. The following transactions describe Kuepper's activities during December 2009:

a. Day-care service in the amount of $12,450 was provided to individual families during December 2009. These families will not be billed until January 2010.
b. At December 1, 2009, the balance in unearned revenue was $43,775. At December 31, 2009, Kuepper determined that $3,090 of this revenue was still unearned.
c. On December 31, the day-care center collected $131,325 from businesses for services to be provided in 2010.
d. On December 31, 2009, the center recorded depreciation of $2,675 on a bus that it uses for field trips.
e. The day-care center had prepaid insurance at December 1, 2009, of $4,200. An examination of the insurance policies indicates that prepaid insurance at December 31, 2009, is $2,200.
f. On December 1, Kuepper borrowed $60,000 by issuing a five-year, $60,000, 9 percent note payable.
g. Interest on the $60,000 note payable is unpaid and unrecorded at December 31.
h. Salaries of $25,320 are owed but unpaid on December 31.
i. The inventory of disposable diapers, on December 1 is $4,400. At December 31, the cost of diapers in inventory is $890.

Required:

1. Identify whether each entry is an adjusting entry or a regular journal entry. If the entry is an adjusting entry, identify it as an accrued revenue, accrued expense, deferred revenue, or deferred expense.
2. Prepare the entries necessary to record the above transactions.

Problem 3-52A PREPARATION OF ADJUSTING ENTRIES

Bartow Photographic Services takes wedding and graduation photographs. At December 31, the end of Bartow's accounting period, the following information is available:

a. All wedding photographs are paid for in advance, and all cash collected for them is credited to unearned revenue. Except for a year-end adjusting entry, no other entries are made for revenue from wedding photographs. During the year, Bartow received $42,600 for wedding photographs. At year-end, $33,900 of the $42,600 had been earned. The beginning-of-the-year balance of unearned revenue was zero.
b. During December, Bartow photographed 60 members of the next year's graduating class of Shaw High School. The school has asked Bartow to print one copy of a photograph of each student for the school files; Bartow delivers these photographs on December 28 and will bill the school $5.00 per student in January of next year. Revenue from photographs ordered by students will be recorded as the orders are received during the early months of next year.
c. Developing and printing equipment rent of $18,000 for one year beginning on August 1 was paid on August 1 to Nikon. When made, the payment was debited to prepaid rent.
d. Depreciation on the firm's building for the current year is $14,400.
e. Wages of $4,170 are owed but unpaid and unrecorded at January 31.
f. Supplies inventory at the beginning of the year was $3,200. During the year, supplies costing $19,600 were purchased from Kodak. When the purchases were made, their cost was debited to supplies inventory. At year-end a physical inventory indicated that supplies costing $4,100 were on hand.

Required:

1. Prepare the adjusting entries for each of these items.
2. By how much would net income be overstated or understated if the accountant failed to make the adjusting entries?

OBJECTIVE ➤ 4

Problem 3-53A EFFECTS OF ADJUSTING ENTRIES ON THE ACCOUNTING EQUATION

Four adjusting entries are shown below.

a.	Wages Expense	2,490	
	Wages Payable		2,490
b.	Accounts Receivable	3,350	
	Service Revenue		3,350
c.	Rent Expense	1,760	
	Prepaid Rent		1,760
d.	Unearned Service Revenue	4,130	
	Service Revenue		4,130

Required:

Analyze the adjusting entries and identify their effects on the financial statement accounts. (Ignore any income tax effects.) Use the following format for your answer:

Transaction	Assets	Liabilities	Beginning Common Stock	Retained Earnings	Revenues	Expenses

OBJECTIVE ➤ 4 5

Problem 3-54A ADJUSTING ENTRIES AND FINANCIAL STATEMENTS

You have the following unadjusted trial balance for Rogers Corporation at December 31, 2009:

Rogers Corporation
Unadjusted Trial Balance
December 31, 2009

Account	Debit	Credit
Cash	$ 3,100	
Accounts Receivable	15,900	
Office Supplies Inventory	4,200	
Prepaid Rent	9,500	
Equipment	625,000	
Accumulated Depreciation, Equipment		$ 104,000
Other Assets	60,900	
Accounts Payable		9,400
Unearned Revenue		11,200
Note Payable (due 2012)		50,000
Common Stock		279,500
Retained Earnings, 12/31/2008		37,000
Service Revenue		598,000
Wages Expense	137,000	
Rent Expense	229,000	
Interest Expense	4,500	
Total	$1,089,100	$1,089,100

At year-end, you have the following data for adjustments:

a. An analysis indicates that prepaid rent on December 31 should be $7,900.
b. A physical inventory shows that $1,100 of office supplies is on hand.

c. Depreciation for 2009 is $85,000.
d. An analysis indicates that unearned revenue should be $8,400.
e. Wages in the amount of $2,800 are owed but unpaid and unrecorded at year-end.
f. Six months' interest at 9 percent on the note was paid on September 30. Interest for the period from October 1 to December 31 is unpaid and unrecorded.
g. Income taxes at 30 percent are owed but unrecorded and unpaid.

Required:

1. Prepare the adjusting entries.
2. Prepare an income statement, a statement of changes in retained earnings, and a balance sheet using adjusted account balances.
3. Why would you not want to prepare financial statements until after the adjusting entries are made?

Problem 3-55A INFERRING ADJUSTING ENTRIES FROM ACCOUNT BALANCE CHANGES

OBJECTIVE ▸ 4

The following schedule shows all the accounts of Fresno Travel Agency that received year-end adjusting entries:

Account	Unadjusted Account Balance	Adjusted Account Balance
Prepaid Insurance	$ 23,270	$ 4,550
Prepaid Rent	3,600	4,800
Accumulated Depreciation	156,000	(a)
Wages Payable	0	3,770
Unearned Revenue, service	3,620	(b)
Service Revenue	71,600	73,920
Insurance Expense	0	(c)
Rent Expense	29,700	(d)
Depreciation Expense	0	16,000
Wages Expense	44,200	(e)

Required:

1. Calculate the missing amounts identified by the numbers (a) through (e).
2. Prepare the five adjusting entries that must have been made to cause the account changes as indicated.

Problem 3-56A PREPARATION OF CLOSING ENTRIES AND AN INCOME STATEMENT

OBJECTIVE ▸  5 6

Round Grove Alarm Company provides security services to homes in northwestern Indiana. At year-end 2009, after adjusting entries have been made, the following list of account balances is prepared:

Accounts Receivable	$ 37,000
Accounts Payable	23,000
Accumulated Depreciation, Equipment	124,000
Common Stock	150,000
Depreciation Expense, Equipment	42,000
Dividends	6,000
Equipment	409,500
Income Tax Expense	24,300
Income Taxes Payable	24,300
Interest Expense	4,800
Notes Payable (due in 2012)	34,000
Other Assets	7,700
Prepaid Rent	5,000
Rent Expense	30,000
Retained Earnings, 12/31/2008	29,400
Salaries Payable	12,600

(Continued)

Salaries Expense	$144,000
Service Revenue	605,500
Supplies Expense	51,900
Supplies Inventory	12,700
Utilities Expense	48,800
Wages Expense	186,500
Wages Payable	7,400

Required:

1. Prepare closing entries for Round Grove Alarm Company.
2. Prepare an income statement for Round Grove Alarm Company.

OBJECTIVE ▸ 4 5 6 7   **Problem 3-57A COMPREHENSIVE PROBLEM: REVIEWING THE ACCOUNTING CYCLE**

Tarkington Freight Service provides delivery of merchandise to retail grocery stores in the Northeast. At the beginning of 2009, the following account balances were available:

Cash	$ 92,100
Accounts Receivable	361,500
Supplies	24,600
Prepaid Advertising	2,000
Building, Warehouse	2,190,000
Accumulated Depreciation, Warehouse	280,000
Equipment	795,000
Accumulated Depreciation, Equipment	580,000
Land	304,975
Accounts Payable	17,600
Wages Payable	30,200
Notes Payable (due in 2013)	1,000,000
Common Stock	1,400,000
Retained Earnings, 12/31/2008	462,375

During 2009 the following transactions occurred:

a. Tarkington delivered merchandise to customers, all on credit, for $2,256,700. Tarkington also made cash deliveries of merchandise for $686,838.
b. There remains $286,172 of accounts receivable to be collected at December 31, 2009.
c. Tarkington purchased advertising of $138,100 during 2009 and debited the amount to prepaid advertising.
d. Supplies of $27,200 were purchased on credit and debited to the supplies account.
e. Accounts payable at the beginning of 2009 were paid early in 2009. There remains $5,600 of accounts payable unpaid at year-end.
f. Wages payable at the beginning of 2009 were paid early in 2009. Wages were earned and paid during 2009 in the amount of $666,142.
g. During the year, Trish Hurd, a principle stockholder, purchased an automobile costing $42,000 for her personal use.
h. One-half year's interest at 6 percent was paid on the note payable on July 1, 2009.
i. Property taxes were paid on the land and buildings in the amount of $170,000.
j. Dividends were declared and paid in the amount of $25,000.

The following data are available for adjusting entries:

- Supplies in the amount of $13,685 remained unused at year-end.
- Annual depreciation on the warehouse building is $70,000.
- Annual depreciation on the warehouse equipment is $145,000.
- Wages of $60,558 were unrecorded and unpaid at year-end.
- Interest for six months at 6 percent per year on the note is unpaid and unrecorded at year-end.
- Advertising of $14,874 remained unused at the end of 2009.
- The income tax rate is 30 percent.

Required:

1. Post the 2009 beginning balances to T-accounts. Prepare journal entries for transactions *a* through *k* and post the journal entries to T-accounts adding any new T-accounts you need.
2. Prepare the adjustments and post the adjustments to the T-accounts adding any new T-accounts you need.
3. Prepare an income statement.
4. Prepare a statement of changes in retained earnings.
5. Prepare a classified balance sheet
6. Prepare closing entries.
7. Did you include transaction *g* among Tarkington's 2009 journal entries? Why or why not?

Problem 3-58A   PREPARING A WORKSHEET

OBJECTIVE ➤ 4 5 6 7 8

Marsteller Properties, Inc., owns apartments that it rents to university students. At December 31, 2009, the following unadjusted account balances were available:

Cash	$ 4,600
Rent Receivable	32,500
Supplies	4,700
Prepaid Insurance	60,000
Buildings	4,560,000
Accumulated Depreciation, Buildings	1,015,000
Land	274,000
Other Assets	26,100
Accounts Payable	57,300
Mortgage Payable (due in 2011)	2,000,000
Common Stock	1,500,000
Retained Earnings, 12/31/2008	39,200
Rent Revenue	660,000
Maintenance Expense	73,200
Rent Expense	58,700
Wages Expense	84,300
Utilities Expense	3,400
Interest Expense	90,000

The following information is available for adjusting entries:

a. An analysis of apartment rental contracts indicates that $3,800 of apartment rent is unbilled and unrecorded at year-end.
b. A physical count of supplies reveals that $1,400 of supplies are on hand at December 31, 2009.
c. Annual depreciation on the buildings is $204,250
d. An examination of insurance policies indicates that $12,000 of the prepaid insurance applies to coverage for 2009.
e. Six months' interest at 9 percent is unrecorded and unpaid on the mortgage payable.
f. Wages in the amount of $6,100 are unpaid and unrecorded at December 31.
g. Utilities costs of $300 are unrecorded and unpaid at December 31.
h. Income taxes, 15 percent of income before taxes, is unrecorded and unpaid at December 31.

Required:

1. Prepare a worksheet for Marsteller Properties, Inc.
2. Prepare an income statement, a statement of changes in retained earnings, and a classified balance sheet for Marsteller Properties, Inc.
3. Prepare the closing entries.

Problem Set B

OBJECTIVE ▶ 1   ### Problem 3-49B CASH-BASIS AND ACCRUAL-BASIS INCOME

Martin Sharp, who repairs lawn mowers, collects cash from his customers when the repair services are completed. He maintains an inventory of repair parts that are purchased from a wholesale supplier. Martin's records show the following information for the first three months of 2009.

	Cash Collected for Repair Work	Cost of Repair Parts Purchased	Cash Payments to Supplier	Cost of Parts Used in Repairs
January	$2,100	$820	$710	$605
February	1,500	0	440	275
March	1,950	675	0	390

Required:

1. Ignoring expenses other than repair parts, calculate net income for each of the three months on a cash basis.
2. Ignoring expenses other than repair parts, calculate net income for each of the three months on an accrual basis.
3. Why do decision-makers prefer the accrual basis of accounting?

OBJECTIVE ▶ 2   ### Problem 3-50B REVENUE RECOGNITION AND MATCHING

Aunt Bea's Catering Service provides catering service for special occasions. During 2009, Aunt Bea performed $125,000 of catering services and collected $118,500 of cash from customers. Salaries earned by Aunt Bea's employees during 2009 were $38,500. Aunt Bea paid employees $35,000 during 2009. Aunt Bea had $1,200 of supplies on hand at the beginning of the year and purchased an additional $8,000 of supplies during the year. Supplies on hand at the end of 2009 were $1,800. Other selling and administrative expenses incurred during 2009 were $5,800.

Required:

1. Calculate revenue for 2009.
2. Calculate expenses for 2009.
3. Prepare the 2009 income statement.
4. Describe the accounting principles used to prepare the income statement.

OBJECTIVE ▶ 3 4   ### Problem 3-51B IDENTIFICATION AND PREPARATION OF ADJUSTING ENTRIES

Morgan Dance Inc. provides ballet, tap, and jazz dancing instruction to promising young dancers. Morgan began operations in January 2010 and is preparing its monthly financial statements for January 2010. The following items describe Morgan's transactions in January 2010:

a. Morgan requires that dance instruction be paid in advance—either monthly or quarterly. On January 1, Morgan received $2,500 for dance instruction to be provided during 2010.
b. On January 31, 2010, Morgan noted that $400 of dance instruction revenue is still unearned.
c. Morgan's hourly employees were paid $1,200 for work performed in January.
d. Morgan's insurance policy requires semi-annual premium payments. Morgan paid the $6,000 insurance policy which covered the first half of 2010 in December 2009.
e. When there are no scheduled dance classes, Morgan rents its dance studio for birthday parties for $80 per two hour party. Three birthday parties were held during January. Morgan will not bill the parents until February.
f. Morgan purchased $250 of office supplies on January 10.
g. On January 31, Morgan determined that office supplies of $140 were unused.

h. Morgan received a January utility bill for $320. The bill will not be paid until it is due in February.

Required:

1. Identify whether each entry is an adjusting entry or a regular journal entry. If the entry is an adjusting entry, identify it as an accrued revenue, accrued expense, deferred revenue, or deferred expense.
2. Prepare the entries necessary to record the above transactions.

Problem 3-52B PREPARATION OF ADJUSTING ENTRIES

OBJECTIVE ▶ 4

West Beach Resort operates a resort complex that specializes in hosting small business and professional meetings. West Beach closes its fiscal year on January 31, a time when it has few meetings under way. At January 31, 2010, the following data are available:

a. A training meeting is under way for 16 individuals from Fashion Design. Fashion Design paid $2,500 in advance for each person attending the 10-day training session. The meeting began on January 27 and will end on February 5.
b. Twenty-one people from Northern Publishing are attending a sales meeting. The daily fee for each person attending the meeting is $180 (charged for each night a person stays at the resort). The meeting began on January 29, and guests will depart on February 2. Northern will be billed at the end of the meeting.
c. Depreciation on the golf carts used to transport the guests' luggage to and from their rooms is $13,000 for the year. West Beach records depreciation yearly.
d. At January 31, Friedrich Catering is owed $1,795 for food provided for guests through that date. This amount of food service expense is unrecorded.
e. An examination indicates that the cost of office supplies on hand at January 31, 2010 is $189. During the year, $698 of office supplies was purchased from Supply Depot. The cost of supplies purchased was debited to office supplies inventory. No office supplies were on hand on January 31, 2009.

Required:

1. Prepare adjusting entries at January 31 for each of these items.
2. By how much would net income be overstated or understated if the accountant failed to make the adjusting entries?

Problem 3-53B EFFECTS OF ADJUSTING ENTRIES ON THE ACCOUNTING EQUATION

OBJECTIVE ▶ 4

Four adjusting entries are shown below:

a. Interest Expense   1,458
    Interest Payable   1,458
b. Interest Receivable   839
    Interest Revenue   839
c. Insurance Expense   3,160
    Prepaid Insurance   3,160
d. Unearned Rent Revenue   5,721
    Rent Revenue   5,721

Required:

Analyze the adjusting entries and identify their effects on the financial statement accounts. (Ignore any income tax effects.) Use the following format for your answer:

Transaction	Assets	Liabilities	Beginning Common Stock	Retained Earnings	Revenues	Expenses

OBJECTIVE ▸ 4 5

Problem 3-54B ADJUSTING ENTRIES AND FINANCIAL STATEMENTS

The unadjusted trial balance for Mitchell Pharmacy appears below.

Mitchell Pharmacy
Unadjusted Trial Balance
December 31, 2009

Account	Debit	Credit
Cash	$ 3,400	
Accounts Receivable	64,820	
Inventory	583,400	
Prepaid Insurance	11,200	
Building	230,000	
Accumulated Depreciation, Building		$ 44,000
Land	31,200	
Other Assets	25,990	
Accounts Payable		47,810
Notes Payable (due 2011)		150,000
Common Stock		600,000
Retained Earnings, 12/31/2008		41,200
Service Revenue		950,420
Wages Expense	871,420	
Interest Expense	12,000	
Total	$1,833,430	$1,833,430

The following information is available at year-end for adjustments:

a. An analysis of insurance policies indicates that $1,400 of the prepaid insurance is coverage for 2010.
b. Depreciation expense for 2009 is $8,800.
c. Four months' interest at 8 percent is owed but unrecorded and unpaid on the note payable.
d. Wages of $4,410 are owed but unpaid and unrecorded at December 31.
e. Income taxes expense, computed at 30 percent of income before taxes, is owed but unrecorded and unpaid at December 31.

Required:

1. Prepare the adjusting entries.
2. Prepare an income statement, a statement of changes in retained earnings, and a balance sheet using adjusted account balances.
3. Why would you not want to prepare financial statements until after the adjusting entries are made?

OBJECTIVE ▸ 4

Problem 3-55B INFERRING ADJUSTING ENTRIES FROM ACCOUNT BALANCE CHANGES

The following schedule shows all the accounts of Eagle Imports that received year-end adjusting entries:

Account	Unadjusted Account Balance	Adjusted Account Balance
Prepaid Insurance	$ 15,390	$ (a)
Accumulated Depreciation	80,000	103,000
Interest Payable	0	(b)
Wages Payable	0	(c)
Unearned Revenue, Service	8,250	2,620
Service Revenue	122,500	(d)
Insurance Expense	0	12,746

(Continued)

Account	Unadjusted Account Balance	Adjusted Account Balance
Interest Expense	$ 3,500	$ 5,300
Depreciation Expense	0	(e)
Wages Expense	38,200	41,800

Required:

1. Calculate the missing amounts identified by the numbers (a) through (e).
2. Prepare the five adjusting entries that must have been made to cause the account changes as indicated.

Problem 3-56B PREPARATION OF CLOSING ENTRIES AND AN INCOME STATEMENT

OBJECTIVE ➤ 5 6

Port Austin Boat Repair Inc. has entered and posted its adjusting entries for 2009. The following are the adjusted account balances:

Sales Revenue	$578,500
Interest Revenue	8,100
Accounts Payable	8,330
Wages Expense	405,300
Accounts Receivable, 12/31/2009	65,000
Supplies Expense	65,000
Supplies, 12/31/2009	179,000
Prepaid Rent	7,200
Rent Expense	28,800
Unearned Revenue	12,200
Insurance Expense	94,300
Wages Payable	11,700
Utilities Expense	14,000
Interest Expense	9,500
Depreciation Expense, Equipment	20,000
Accumulated Depreciation, Equipment	75,000
Income Tax Expense	12,300
Income Tax Payable	8,300
Dividends	7,800

Required:

1. Using the accounts and balances above, prepare the closing entries for 2009.
2. Prepare an income statement for Port Austin Boat Repair Inc.

Problem 3-57B COMPREHENSIVE PROBLEM: REVIEWING THE ACCOUNTING CYCLE

OBJECTIVE ➤ 4 5 6 7

Wilburton Riding Stables provides stables, care for animals, and grounds for riding and showing horses. The account balances at the beginning of 2009 were:

Cash	$ 2,200
Accounts Receivable	4,400
Supplies, Feed	24,100
Supplies, Straw	3,700
Land	167,000
Buildings	115,000
Accumulated Depreciation, Buildings	36,000
Equipment	57,000
Accumulated Depreciation, Equipment	16,500
Accounts Payable	23,700
Income Taxes Payable	15,100
Interest Payable	2,700
Wages Payable	14,200

(Continued)

Notes Payable (due in 2013)	$ 60,000
Common Stock	150,000
Retained Earnings	55,200

During 2009, the following transactions occurred:

a. Wilburton provided animal care services, all on credit, for $210,300. Wilburton rented stables to customers who cared for their own animals and paid cash of $20,500. Wilburton rented its grounds to individual riders, groups, and show organizations for $41,800 cash.
b. There remains $15,600 of accounts receivable to be collected at December 31, 2009.
c. Feed in the amount of $62,900 was purchased on credit and debited to the supplies, feed account.
d. Straw was purchased for $7,400 cash and debited to the supplies, straw account.
e. Wages payable at the beginning of 2009 were paid early in 2009. Wages were earned and paid during 2009 in the amount of $112,000.
f. The income taxes payable at the beginning of 2009 were paid early in 2009. The accounts payable at the beginning of the year were also paid during the year. There remains $13,600 of accounts payable unpaid at year-end.
g. One year's interest at 9 percent was paid on the note payable on July 1, 2009.
h. During 2009, Jon Wilburton, a principal stockholder, purchased a horse for his wife Jennifer to ride. The horse cost $7,000, and Wilburton used his personal credit to purchase it. The horse is stabled at the Wilburtons' home rather than at the riding stables.
i. Property taxes were paid on the land and buildings in the amount of $17,000.
j. Dividends were declared and paid in the amount of $7,200.

The following data are available for adjusting entries:

- Feed in the amount of $26,000 remained unused at year-end. Straw in the amount of $4,400 remained unused at year-end.
- Annual depreciation on the buildings is $6,000.
- Annual depreciation on the equipment is $5,500.
- Wages of $4,000 were unrecorded and unpaid at year-end.
- Interest for six months at 9 percent per year on the note is unpaid and unrecorded at year-end.
- The income tax rate is 30 percent.

Required:

1. Post the 2009 beginning balances to T-accounts. Prepare journal entries for transactions *a* through *j* and post the journal entries to T-accounts adding any new T-accounts you need.
2. Prepare the adjustments and post the adjustments to the T-accounts adding any new T-accounts you need.
3. Prepare an income statement.
4. Prepare a statement of changes in retained earnings.
5. Prepare a classified balance sheet.
6. Prepare closing entries.
7. Did you include transaction *h* among Wilburton's 2009 journal entries? Why or why not?

OBJECTIVE ▶ 4 5 6 7 8

Problem 3-58B PREPARING A WORKSHEET

Flint, Inc., operates a cable television system. At December 31, 2009, the following unadjusted account balances were available:

Cash	$ 2,000
Accounts Receivable	89,000
Office Supplies	5,000

(Continued)

Land	$ 37,000
Building	209,000
Accumulated Depreciation, Building	40,000
Equipment	794,000
Accumulated Depreciation, Equipment	262,000
Other Assets	19,700
Accounts Payable	29,500
Notes Payable (due in 2013)	250,000
Common Stock	300,000
Retained Earnings, 12/31/2008	14,700
Dividends	28,000
Service Revenue	985,000
Subscription Expense	398,000
Telephone Expense	10,500
Utilities Expense	34,000
Wages Expense	196,000
Miscellaneous Expense	44,000
Interest Expense	15,000

The following data are available for adjusting entries:

a. At year-end $1,500 of office supplies remain unused.
b. Annual depreciation on the building is $20,000.
c. Annual depreciation on the equipment is $150,000.
d. The interest rate on the note is 8 percent. Four months' interest is unpaid and unrecorded at December 31, 2009.
e. At December 31, 2009, service revenue of $94,000 has been earned but is unbilled and unrecorded.
f. Utility bills of $2,800 are unpaid and unrecorded at December 31, 2009.
g. The income tax rate is 25 percent.

Required:

1. Prepare a worksheet for Flint.
2. Prepare an income statement, a statement of changes in retained earnings, and a classified balance sheet for Flint.
3. Prepare the closing entries.

Cases

Case 3-59 CASH- OR ACCRUAL-BASIS ACCOUNTING

Katie Vote owns a small business that rents computers to students at the local university. Katie's typical rental contract requires the student to pay the year's rent of $900 ($100 per month) in advance. When Katie prepares financial statements at the end of December, her accountant requires that Katie spread the $900 over the nine months that the computer is rented. Therefore, Katie can recognize only $400 of revenue (four months) from each computer rental contract in the year the cash is collected and must defer (delay) recognition of the remaining $500 (five months) to the next year. Katie argues that getting students to agree to rent the computer is the most difficult part of the activity so she ought to be able to recognize all $900 as revenue when the cash is received from a student.

Required:

Why do you believe that generally accepted accounting principles require the use of accrual accounting rather than cash-basis accounting for transactions like the one described here? (Hint: You might find it helpful to read paragraphs 42–48 of *FASB Statement of Financial Accounting Concepts No. 1*, which can be found at http://www.fasb.org, as you formulate your answer).

Case 3-60 RECOGNITION OF SERVICE CONTRACT REVENUE

Jackson Dunlap is president of New Miami Maintenance Inc. which provides building maintenance services. On October 15, 2009, Mr. Dunlap signed a service contract with Western College. Under the contract, New Miami will provide maintenance services for all of Western's buildings for a period of two years, beginning on January 1, 2010, and Western will pay New Miami on a monthly basis, beginning on January 31, 2010. Although the same amount of maintenance services will be rendered in every month, the contract provides for higher monthly payments in the first year.

Initially, Mr. Dunlap proposed that some portion of the revenue from the contract should be recognized in 2009; however his accountant, Rita McGonigle, convinced him that this would be inappropriate. Then Mr. Dunlap proposed that the revenue should be recognized in an amount equal to the cash collected under the contract in 2009. Again, Ms. McGonigle argued against his proposal, saying that generally accepted accounting principles required recognition of an equal amount of contract revenue each month.

Required:

1. Give a reason that might explain Mr. Dunlap's desire to recognize contract revenue earlier rather than later.
2. Put yourself in the position of Rita McGonigle. How would you convince Mr. Dunlap that his two proposals are unacceptable and that an equal amount of revenue should be recognized every month?
3. If Ms. McGonigle's proposal is adopted, how would the contract be reflected in the balance sheets at the end of 2009 and at the end of 2010?

Case 3-61 REVENUE RECOGNITION

Beth Rader purchased North Shore Health Club in June 2009. Beth wanted to increase the size of the business by selling five-year memberships for $5,000, payable at the beginning of the membership period. The normal yearly membership fee is $1,500. Since few prospective members were expected to want to spend $5,000 at the beginning of the membership period, Beth arranged for a local bank to provide a $1,000 installment loan to prospective members. By the end of 2009, 250 customers had purchased the five-year memberships using the loan provided by the bank.

Beth prepared her income statement for 2009 and included $1,250,000 ($5,000 × 250 members) as revenue because the Club had collected the entire amount in cash. Beth's accountant objected to the inclusion of the entire $1,250,000. The accountant argued that the $1,250,000 should be recognized as revenue as the Club provides services for these members during the membership period. Beth countered with a quotation from generally accepted accounting principles:

Profit is deemed to be realized when a sale in the ordinary course of business is effected, unless the circumstances are such that collection of the sale price is not reasonably assured.

Beth notes that memberships have been sold and the collection of the selling price has occurred. Therefore, she argues that all $1,250,000 is revenue in 2009.

Required:

1. Write a short statement supporting either Beth or the accountant in this dispute.
2. Would your answer change if the $5,000 fee were nonrefundable? Why or why not?

Case 3-62 APPLYING THE MATCHING CONCEPT

Newman Properties Inc. completed construction of a new shopping center in July 2009. During the first six months of 2009, Newman spent $750,000 for salaries, preparation of documents, travel, and other similar activities associated with securing tenants for the center. Newman was successful (Nordstrom, Best Buy, and Office Depot will be tenants) and the center will open on August 1 with all its stores rented on four-year leases. The rental revenue that Newman expects to receive from the current tenants is $8,500,000 per year for four years. The leases will be renegotiated at the end of the fourth year. The accountant for Newman wonders whether the $750,000 should be expensed in 2009 or whether it should be initially recorded as an asset and matched against revenues over the four-year lease term.

Required:

Write a short statement indicating why you support expensing the $750,000 in the current period or spreading the expense over the four-year lease term.

Case 3-63 ADJUSTING ENTRIES FOR REFUND COUPONS

Cal-Lite Products, Inc., manufactures a line of food products that appeals to persons interested in weight loss. To stimulate sales, Cal-Lite includes cash refund coupons in many of its products. Cal-Lite issues the purchaser a check when the coupon is returned to the company, which may be many months after the product is sold to stores and distributors. In addition, a significant number of coupons issued to customers are never returned. As cash distributions are made to customers, they are recorded in an expense account.

Required:

1. Explain the conceptual basis for the determination of refund expense in each year. Describe the information and calculations required to estimate the amount of expense for each year.
2. Describe the year-end adjusting entry required at the end of the first year of the program's existence.
3. Describe the adjusting entry at the end of the second year of the program's existence.

Case 3-64 ADJUSTING ENTRIES FOR MOTION PICTURE REVENUES

Link Pictures, Inc., sells (licenses) the rights to exhibit motion pictures to theaters. Under the sales contract, the theater promises to pay a license fee equal to the larger of a guaranteed minimum or a percentage of the box office receipts. In addition, the contract requires the guaranteed minimum to be paid in advance. Consider the following contracts entered by Link during 2009:

a. Contract **A** authorizes a group of theaters in Buffalo, New York, to exhibit a film called Garage for two weeks ending January 7, 2010. Box office statistics indicate that first-week attendance has already generated licensing fees well in excess of the guaranteed minimum.
b. Contract **B** authorizes a chain of theaters in Miami, Florida, to exhibit a film called Blue Denim for a period of two weeks ending January 20, 2010. In most first-run cities, the film has attracted large crowds, and the percentage of box office receipts has far exceeded the minimum.
c. Contract **C** authorizes a chain of theaters in San Francisco to exhibit a film called Toast Points for a period of two weeks ending on January 5, 2010. The film is a "dog" and the theaters stopped showing it after the first few days. All prints of the film were returned by December 31, 2009.

The guaranteed minimum has been paid on all three contracts and recorded as unearned revenue. No other amounts have been received, and no revenue has been recorded for any of the contracts. Adjusting entries for 2009 are just about to be made.

Required:

Describe the adjusting entry you would make at December 31, 2009, to record each contract. (Hint: You may want to refer to FASB Statement No. 53, Financial Reporting by Producers and Distributors of Motion Picture Films.)

Case 3-65 THE EFFECT OF ADJUSTING ENTRIES ON THE FINANCIAL STATEMENTS (A CONCEPTUAL APPROACH)

Don Berthrong, the manager of the local Books-A-Million, is wondering whether adjusting entries will affect his financial statements. Don's business has grown steadily for several years, and Don expects it to continue to grow for the next several years at a rate of 5 to 10 percent per year. Nearly all Don's sales are for cash. Other than cost of goods sold, which is not affected by adjusting entries, most of Don's expenses are for items that require cash outflows (e.g., rent on the building, wages, utilities, insurance).

Required:

1. Would Don's financial statement be affected significantly by adjusting entries?
2. Consider all businesses. What kinds of transactions would require adjustments that would have a significant effect on the financial statements? What kinds of businesses would be likely to require these kinds of adjustments?

Case 3-66 INTERPRETING CLOSING ENTRIES

Barnes Building Systems made the following closing entries at the end of a recent year:

a.	Income Summary	384,300	
	Retained Earnings		384,300
b.	Retained Earnings	35,000	
	Dividends		35,000
c.	Sales Revenue	425,700	
	Income Summary		425,700
d.	Income Summary	104,100	
	Interest Expense		104,100

Required:

1. What was Barnes's net income?
2. By how much did Barnes's retained earnings change?
3. If the sales revenue identified in entry *c* was Barnes's only revenue, what was the total amount of Barnes's expenses?

Case 3-67 RESEARCH AND ANALYSIS USING THE ANNUAL REPORT

Obtain **FedEx Corporation**'s 2007 annual report either through the "Investor Relations" portion of their website (do a web search for FedEx investor relations) or go to http://www.sec.gov and click "Search for company filings" under "Filings & Forms (EDGAR)."

Required:

Answer the following questions:

1. How does FedEx apply the revenue recognition principle?
2. With regard to the balance sheet and the income statement, what accounts may have required adjusting entries? Would these accounts require accruals or deferrals?
3. How much did FedEx owe its employees for services performed at the end of the 2007 fiscal year?
4. How much would FedEx credit to Income Summary for 2007? How much would be debited to Income Summary for 2007?
5. How much did FedEx report as income tax expense for 2007? How much did FedEx report as cash paid for taxes for 2007? Why are the amounts different and where does this difference get reported on FedEx's financial statements?

Case 3-68 COMPARATIVE ANALYSIS: ABERCROMBIE & FITCH vs. AEROPOSTALE

Refer to the financial statements of **Abercrombie & Fitch** and **Aeropostale** that are supplied with this text.

Required:

Answer the following questions:

1. Does each company apply the revenue recognition principle to sales to customers and to gift cards in the same manner?
2. Which accounts on the balance sheet and income statement of each company may require adjusting entries? Would these accounts require accruals or deferrals?
3. How much would Abercrombie & Fitch credit to Income Summary for the year ending February 3, 2007 (fiscal 2006)? How much would Aeropostale credit to Income Summary for the fiscal year ending February 3, 2007? How much would Abercrombie & Fitch debit to Income Summary for the year ending February 3, 2007 (fiscal 2006)? How much would Aeropostale debit to Income Summary for the fiscal year ending February 3, 2007?
4. How much did each company report as an accrued expense for gift cards for the most recent year? Explain why this amount is reported as a liability.
5. Compare how much each company reported as income tax expense and as cash paid for taxes for the most recent year. Why are the amounts different and where would this difference be reported on the financial statements?

4

Internal Control and Cash

After studying Chapter 4, you should be able to:

1 Discuss the role of internal controls in managing a business.

2 Discuss the five elements of internal control.

3 Describe how businesses control cash.

4 Describe how businesses account and report cash.

5 Describe the cyclical nature of business activity.

6 Explain the principles of cash management.

7 (Appendix 4A) Describe the classification and accounting for investments.

© Kevin Phillips/Digital Vision/Getty Images

Experience Financial Accounting
with Initech

Peter Gibbons is a software engineer at Initech. He has an awful commute, an annoying boss, and a girlfriend he's pretty sure is cheating on him. Of course, Peter is the fictional star of the 1999 film *Office Space*. So, what do Peter and Initech have to do with accounting? In the movie, Initech is going through a downsizing and Peter finds out his best friends, Samir and (the unfortunately named) Michael Bolton, are about to be fired. To get back at Initech, the three friends decide to alter the company's software to take the fractions of a penny that are rounded off when calculating interest and deposit them into their personal account. Such schemes are real and go by various names such as "penny shaving" or "salami slicing." They believe their scheme is undetectable because nobody will notice the gradual theft of these miniscule amounts. However, over time the sheer number of transactions will accumulate to a large sum.

The morning after altering Initech's software, Peter checks the account balance and finds it contains over $300,000. In a panic Peter calls his friends and Michael Bolton concedes he made a "small" mistake. In the movie the three friends attempt to repay the money and are "saved" by a fire that burns Initech's offices. You may think that this could never happen, but a mention of such a scheme appears over 30 years ago in Thomas Whiteside's 1978 book, *Computer Capers: Tales of Electronic Thievery, Embezzlement and Fraud*. In this book, Whiteside documents how a programmer diverted money from the rounded down sales commissions for three years before he was caught.

In a somewhat related scheme, a hacker noticed that when opening online brokering accounts (such as through **Google** checkout, **PayPal**, and many brokerage houses), it is common practice for the companies to send a confirming payment of a few cents to ensure you have access to the bank account or credit card. He then wrote an automated program (known as a "bot") to open almost 60,000 such accounts, collecting many thousands of these small payments into a few personal bank accounts. This isn't obviously illegal; however, he did run afoul of mail and bank fraud laws because he used false names, addresses, and Social Security numbers when opening the accounts.

In this chapter we discuss the policies and procedures companies put in place to prevent unintentional error, theft, and fraud. These policies and procedures are referred to as the internal control system. For example, a commonly seen control that is designed to prevent use of bots to sign up or log in to web functions is a security check where the user must type in the distorted letters seen in a box (e.g., **Ticketmaster** does this to thwart scalpers).

OBJECTIVE ▶ 1
Discuss the role of internal controls in managing a business.

Role of Internal Control

Except in very small businesses, top management delegates responsibility for engaging in business activities and recording their effects in the accounting system to other managers and employees. Management wants to make sure that these employees: (1) operate within the scope of their assigned responsibility and (2) act for the good of the business. To control subordinates' activities, management puts in place procedures that collectively are called the **internal control system**.

Internal control systems include all the policies and procedures established by top management and the board of directors to provide reasonable assurance that the company's objectives are being met in three areas: (1) effectiveness and efficiency of operations, (2) reliability of financial reporting, and (3) compliance with applicable laws and regulations (The Committee of Sponsoring Organizations of the Treadway Commission [COSO], *Internal Control—Integrated Framework*, 1992). As such, internal control systems include many elements only indirectly related to our primary concern—the accounting system and financial statements. For example, policies and procedures concerning the extent and nature of research and development or advertising activities may have an important effect on the achievement of an entity's objectives but only indirectly affect its accounting system and financial statements.

Under the Sarbanes-Oxley Act of 2002, top management of publicly-traded corporations has an increased responsibility for a system of internal controls that ensures the reliability of the financial statements (#2 in the previous paragraph). For example, Section 404 of the Act requires management to produce an internal control report. This report must acknowledge that management is responsible for establishing and maintaining an adequate internal control system and procedures for financial reporting and also assess the effectiveness of these controls. Further, Section 302 of the Act requires the principal executive and financial officers to certify that they are responsible for establishing and maintaining the system of internal control over financial reporting (see Exhibit 4-1). This certification was designed to prevent top management from denying knowledge or understanding of deceptive financial reporting as was tried in court by executives of **WorldCom**, among others.

In this chapter, we will examine the elements of internal controls and demonstrate controls over cash, a company's most vulnerable asset. We will address the following questions:

- What are the five elements of internal control?
- How are those controls applied to cash?
- How do financing and operating cycles affect cash?
- Why is cash management so important to a company?

OBJECTIVE ▶ 2
Discuss the five elements of internal control.

Elements of Internal Control

The Committee of Sponsoring Organizations of the Treadway Commission (COSO) identified five elements of an internal control system (see Exhibit 4-2). Each element is crucial to the (1) effectiveness and efficiency of operations, (2) reliability of financial reporting, and (3) compliance with applicable laws and regulations. We will now discuss each of these five elements in turn.

Control Environment and Ethical Behavior

The foundation of the internal control system is the **control environment**—the collection of environmental factors that influence the effectiveness of control procedures. The control environment includes the philosophy and operating style of management, the personnel policies and practices of the business, and the overall integrity, attitude, awareness, and actions of everyone in the business concerning the importance of control and is more commonly called the *tone at the top*.

An important feature of the control environment is recognizing that an individual employee's goals may differ from the goals of other individuals and the goals of the

Exhibit 4-1

Section 302 Certification by Steven P. Jobs (CEO of Apple) Taken from SEC Filings for the Year Ended September 29, 2007

I, Steven P. Jobs, certify that:

1. I have reviewed this annual report on Form 10-K of Apple Inc.;

2. Based on my knowledge, this report does not contain any untrue statement of a material fact or omit to state a material fact necessary to make the statements made, in light of the circumstances under which such statements were made, not misleading with respect to the period covered by this report;

3. Based on my knowledge, the financial statements, and other financial information included in this report, fairly present in all material respects the financial condition, results of operations and cash flows of the registrant as of, and for, the periods presented in this report;

4. The registrant's other certifying officer(s) and I are responsible for establishing and maintaining disclosure controls and procedures (as defined in Exchange Act Rules 13a-15(e) and 15d-15(e)) and internal control over financial reporting (as defined in Exchange Act Rules 13a-15(f) and 15d-15(f)) for the registrant and have:

(a) Designed such disclosure controls and procedures, or caused such disclosure controls and procedures to be designed under our supervision, to ensure that material information relating to the registrant, including its consolidated subsidiaries, is made known to us by others within those entities, particularly during the period in which this report is being prepared;

(b) Designed such internal control over financial reporting, or caused such internal control over financial reporting to be designed under our supervision, to provide reasonable assurance regarding the reliability of financial reporting and the preparation of financial statements for external purposes in accordance with generally accepted accounting principles;

(c) Evaluated the effectiveness of the registrant's disclosure controls and procedures and presented in this report our conclusions about the effectiveness of the disclosure controls and procedures, as of the end of the period covered by this report based on such evaluation; and

(d) Disclosed in this report any change in the registrant's internal control over financial reporting that occurred during the registrant's most recent fiscal quarter (the registrant's fourth fiscal quarter in the case of an annual report) that has materially affected, or is reasonably likely to materially affect, the registrant's internal control over financial reporting; and

5. The registrant's other certifying officer(s) and I have disclosed, based on our most recent evaluation of internal control over financial reporting, to the registrant's auditors and the audit committee of the registrant's board of directors (or persons performing the equivalent functions):

(a) All significant deficiencies and material weaknesses in the design or operation of internal control over financial reporting which are reasonably likely to adversely affect the registrant's ability to record, process, summarize, and report financial information; and

(b) Any fraud, whether or not material, that involves management or other employees who have a significant role in the registrant's internal control over financial reporting.

Date: November 15, 2007

By:

Steven P. Jobs
Chief Executive Officer

Exhibit 4-2

Elements of Internal Control

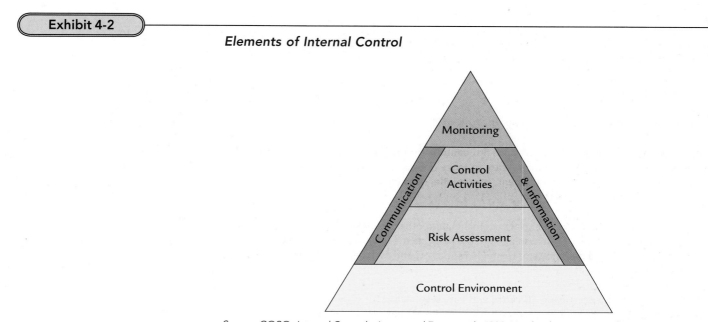

Source: COSO, *Internal Control—Integrated Framework*, 1992. Used with permission of COSO.

business. For example, managers may receive a bonus based on certain accounting numbers such as sales. In this case, managers have been known to ship a large quantity of merchandise to customers right before year end—even if the merchandise was not ordered (e.g., **Bausch and Lomb, IBM,** etc.). Although much of the merchandise was returned in the following year, sales targets for the current year were met and bonuses were paid. This practice was so prevalent that a term—channel stuffing—was coined to describe the practice. Of course, control procedures assume particular importance in the presence of conflicting goals, but they are not sufficient to prevent individuals from taking actions that are bad for the business.

Resolving these conflicting incentives in an ethical manner that promotes organizational objectives is highly dependent on the tone at the top. Studies suggest that a vast majority of U.S. accounting frauds, approximately 84 percent between 1987 and 1997, involve top management. Of course, top management can put mechanisms in place to promote ethical behavior. For example, hiring and firing practices that put zero tolerance on unethical behavior are increasingly common. Additionally, the Sarbanes-Oxley Act requires publicly-traded corporations to establish formal procedures to receive, retain, and address any information that may affect the company's accounting or auditing. To comply with this requirement companies have created ethics hotlines that allow employees to anonymously report unethical behavior. This was an important step in empowering subordinates to report unethical behavior by their superiors. However, hotlines only address procedures to receive the information. Additionally, companies must have procedures in place to make sure such information is never destroyed and that it is communicated to those with the power to resolve any issues, such as the board of directors and upper management.

ETHICS Donna Jones has just been hired as an accounting clerk at a large manufacturing company. One of her jobs is to summarize invoices presented for payment by various creditors. Once the summary has been inspected by Carmen Adams, the assistant controller to whom Donna reports, Donna presents the summary to the controller for approval. The controller's approval requires a simple signature on the summary form. Dick Stewart, of the controller's staff, then prepares and mails the checks.

During Donna's second week on the job, Carmen Adams tells her that City Consulting Services, Inc., will make trouble for the company unless paid immediately and that Donna shouldn't bother to secure the controller's authorization for the day's invoices, in order to speed payment. "Dick Stewart, who prepares the checks, is rarely at his desk and never looks at signatures anyway. It would cost us at least another day to get the controller's signature. Just put the unsigned summary on Stewart's desk, and the check will be in the mail by the end of the day," says Carmen.

Donna knows that Carmen Adams will give her a low performance rating if she refuses to follow these instructions, and she wants to do well on her first job. Further, she is quite sure that Dick Stewart will not notice the omitted control procedure, particularly if he doesn't see Donna leave the summary on his desk. On the other hand, Donna knows that the controller's approval is viewed as an important control procedure. Consider two possible endings for this story:

1. *Donna decides to go along with Carmen.* Every month, Carmen tells Donna the same story about City Consulting Services, and Donna places the unauthorized summary on Dick Stewart's unoccupied desk. All goes well until the internal auditor runs a routine check on the credit ratings of the various entities with which the company does business and discovers that City Consulting Services is nothing more than a bank account established by Carmen Adams. Carmen is charged with fraud, and Donna's role in the fraud is exposed in the public trial that follows. Donna is not charged in the case, but she loses her job and has great difficulty finding another comparable position.

2. *Donna refuses to go along with Carmen.* Donna receives a negative review from Adams and is asked to leave the company. During an exit interview, Donna tells the controller why she believes Carmen gave her a negative review. The controller instructs the internal audit department to follow up on City Consulting Services at which time it is discovered to be nothing more than a bank account established by Carmen Adams. Carmen is charged with fraud. The controller contacts Donna saying, "Although I wasn't very encouraging during your exit interview, your comments led me to ask internal auditing to investigate Carmen Adams' activities. As a result, we have uncovered her scheme to defraud the company, and would like you to return to the company."

Like Donna Jones, most people in business face difficult ethical dilemmas from time to time. The "right thing to do" is an individual decision that must be approached thoughtfully and after careful consideration of the possible long-term as well as short-term consequences. The effectiveness of internal control systems depends on the ethical tone set by management and the ethical awareness of all company personnel.◆

Risk Assessment

Risk assessment procedures (also called Enterprise Risk Management or ERM) are designed to identify, analyze, and manage **strategic risks** and **business process risks**.

Strategic Risks
Strategic risks are possible threats to the organization's success in accomplishing its objectives and are *external* to the organization. These risks are often classified around industry forces such as competitors, customers, substitute products or services, suppliers, and threat of new competitors (these are known as Porter's Five Forces) or macro factors such as Political, Economic, Social, and Technological (also known as PEST factors).

Although entire courses are devoted to management of these strategic risks, the general idea is simple to illustrate. Consider an industry that is affected by changes in lifestyles (this is a Social factor in PEST) such as restaurants. If a company in the restaurant industry fails to adequately identify and analyze, for example, dietary preferences such as low-saturated fats, the organization's objectives may be severely compromised. A more specific example can be made using **Barnes & Noble**'s response to **Amazon**. When Amazon was formed in 1995, Barnes & Noble was in the midst of high growth and rollout of their cafes and music shops within supersized bookstores. Barnes & Noble was so deeply rooted in its "bricks-and-mortar" that it failed to respond to a technological factor: the Internet's transformation of the industry. In fact, top management so feared that a web presence would harm sales at their stores, that it was more than two years before the rollout of Barnesandnoble.com. Near the time of the rollout Steve Riggio, creator of Barnesandnoble.com and brother of Barnes & Noble founder Len Riggio, said, "It's better to cannibalize yourself than to be cannibalized." Unfortunately for Barnes & Noble, the two year delay allowed Amazon to secure the leading web presence for booksellers—a lead that Barnes & Noble has been unable to erode.

Business Process Risks   Business processes are the *internal* processes of the company—specifically, how the company allocates its resources to meet its objectives. There are many business processes, but some of the more common ones are materials acquisition, production, logistics and distribution, branding and marketing, and human resources. The nature and relative importance of the business processes will vary from company to company based on their specific objectives. For example, **Dell** has adopted a low-cost provider objective. As such, it has concentrated on achieving operating efficiencies in order processing, production, and distribution. **Apple**, on the other hand, has adopted a product differentiation objective. This objective has led to an emphasis on product quality and continual research to develop better products with more features. As such, the risk assessment controls for these two companies will differ. Dell will be focused on monitoring inventory levels and production times, while Apple will focus on quality control and product development.

Control Activities

Control activities are the policies and procedures top management establishes to help insure that its objectives are met. The control activities most directly related to the accounting system and financial statements vary widely from one business to another, but generally can be identified with one of the following five categories:

Clearly Defined Authority and Responsibility

The *authority* to perform important duties is delegated to specific individuals, and those individuals should be held *responsible* for the performance of those duties in the evaluation of their performance. Among the designated duties of an individual may be the authority to perform specified types of activities for the business or to authorize others to execute such transactions. The clear delegation of authority and responsibility motivates individuals to perform well because they know they are accountable for their actions. For example, when a cash register is short of money, the cashier signed into the register is clearly responsible for the error. If any cashier could use any cash register at any time, we would have no idea which cashier was responsible for the discrepancy.

Segregation of Duties

Accounting record keeping responsibilities should be segregated from the duties of administering operations, engaging in operating activities, or overseeing assets. In other words, accounting and administrative duties should be performed by different individuals, so that no one person prepares all the documents and records for an activity. This **segregation of duties** (also called separation of duties) reduces the likelihood that records could be used to conceal *irregularities* (intentional misstatements, theft, or fraud) and increases the likelihood that irregularities will be discovered. Segregation of duties also reduces the likelihood that unintentional record-keeping errors will remain undiscovered. Although segregation of duties cannot eliminate the possibility of fraud, it does require people to work together. For example, if the same person was responsible for collecting the cash and admitting the customer at a movie theatre, this person could pocket the cash and let the customer in without issuing a ticket. In this case, the number of tickets issued would match up with the cash collected because no ticket was issued and the cash was pocketed. Instead, movie theatres have one person collect the cash and issue the ticket and a second person admits the customer only with a ticket. Obviously, cash paid by customers can still be pocketed, but the segregation of duties will require both employees to engage in the fraudulent scheme (we call this collusion) or the cash collected will not match the tickets collected.

Perhaps the most important aspect of segregation of duties is separating the record-keeping responsibility from the physical control of the assets. For example, if a customer pays $1,000, the employee who collects the $1,000 could easily steal some or all of the money if (s)he has access to the accounting records. In this case the employee could record that the money was paid and hide the fact that the money was not in the company or record that some or all of the money was not paid and the debt was "bad."

Adequate Documents and Records Accounting records are the basis for the financial statements and other reports prepared for managers, owners, and others both inside and outside the business. Summary records and their underlying documentation must provide information about specific activities and help in the evaluation of individual performance. For example, prenumbered shipping documents provide a basis for monitoring shipments of goods to customers. When warehouse employees receive a shipping document, they ship the goods. If the shipping documents were not prenumbered, a shipping document could be sent to the warehouse and later destroyed. Without the missing number in the sequence to signal a missing document, nobody would realize that the document was missing.

Safeguards over Assets and Records Both assets and records must be secured against theft and destruction. **Safeguarding** requires physical protection of the assets through, for example, fireproof vaults, locked storage facilities, keycard access, and anti-theft tags on merchandise. An increasingly important part of safeguarding assets and records is access controls for computers. Not that long ago, access passwords were quite simple (e.g., spouse's name), often written down, and never changed. Now access controls often mandate use of both alpha and numeric characters and require password changes every few months. Safeguards must be provided for computer programs and data files, which are more fragile and susceptible to unauthorized access than manual record-keeping systems.

Checks on Recorded Amounts Recorded amounts should be checked by an independent person to determine that amounts are correct and that they correspond to properly authorized activities. These procedures include clerical checks, reconciliations, comparisons of asset inspection reports with recorded amounts, computer-programmed controls, and management review of reports. For example, as discussed in the Segregation of Duties section, physical access to cash (e.g., writing checks and depositing cash at the end of the day) should be separated from maintaining the accounting records for cash. In this case, the accounting records should also be checked (or reconciled) to the bank statement with any discrepancies resolved immediately. Bank reconciliations are illustrated later in the chapter.

Such controls are effective at mitigating unintentional error, theft, and fraud. One of the elements typically cited in discussions of theft and fraud is opportunity. That is, persons committing theft or fraud believe they have the opportunity to "get away with it." Control activities are designed to prevent and detect theft and fraud by reducing employees' opportunity to conceal their actions. Yet, every year billions of dollars are lost to employee theft and fraud because effectively designed control activities are not followed.

Information and Communication

An internal control system will be unable to help a company achieve its objective unless adequate information is identified and gathered on a timely basis. Further, this information must be communicated to the appropriate employees in the organization. For example, consider a company like **Mercedes** that has a strategy of providing high-quality products. This company may gather information on the percentage of production that is rejected by quality control. If that percentage rises, it signals the possibility of problems in production (e.g., inferior material being used, poor training of new personnel, etc.). If such information is gathered and communicated, these problems can be addressed before the company's reputation for high quality is harmed; if, on the other hand, such information is not gathered and communicated, then management may not become aware of the problem until returns and complaints are made by dissatisfied customers. At this time, it may be too late to avoid damage to their reputation.

Monitoring

Monitoring is the process of tracking potential and actual problems in the internal control system. Monitoring is accomplished through normal supervising activities such as when a manager asks a subordinate how things are going. However, best practices for larger organizations suggest that an internal audit group help monitor the effectiveness of the internal control system. Monitoring the system of internal controls allows the organization to identify potential and actual weaknesses that could, if uncorrected, produce problems.

In fact, the Sarbanes-Oxley Act also requires all publicly-traded corporations to have an internal audit function that reports to the audit committee of the board of directors. The Act allows companies to outsource internal audit, but precludes the business that provides the (external) financial-statement audit from performing internal audit services because it may impair the independence of the financial-statement audit.

Relationship Between Control Activities and the Accounting System

The **accounting system** consists of the methods and records used to identify, measure, record, and communicate financial information about a business. Although we distinguish between the accounting system and the internal control system, the two are really one integrated system designed to meet the needs of a particular business. It is difficult to generalize about the relationship between internal control activities and accounting systems, because it directly depends on the objectives of a particular business. Consequently, the relationship is best explored through an example.

For our illustration we will consider Hendrickson Theaters, Inc. Hendrickson operates 10 movie theaters in a single city. All the theaters are rented, as are the projection equipment and concession facilities. Hendrickson's administrative offices, furnishings, and office equipment are also rented. The following chart of accounts indicates the general structure of Hendrickson's simple accounting system:

Chart of Accounts for Hendrickson Theaters, Inc.

Assets	*Revenues*
Cash	Admissions revenue
Concessions inventory	Concessions revenue
Prepaid rent	*Expenses*
Liabilities	Salaries expense
Accounts payable	Wages expense
Salaries payable	Cost of concessions sold
Wages payable	Rent expense, movie
Equity	Rent expense, theater
Capital stock	Rent expense, equipment
Retained earnings	Rent expense, office
	Utilities expense
	Advertising expense
	Office supplies expense

Hendrickson's accountant makes journal entries daily for revenues, biweekly for wages, and monthly for the other expenses using general purpose accounting software. Because Hendrickson has a relatively small number of accounts, its accounting system is quite simple, still a complete description would require many pages. Furthermore, a complete description is unnecessary to demonstrate the basic relationship between system elements and control procedures. The portion of Hendrickson's accounting system related to revenues and the associated control activities are described in Exhibit 4-3.

Internal controls are designed to protect all assets. But the more liquid an asset (the more "liquid" an asset, the more easily it is converted into cash), the more likely it is to be stolen. Therefore, the controls over cash (the most liquid asset) must be designed with special care. We now turn our attention to cash controls.

> **Exhibit 4-3**

Relationship Between the Accounting System and Control Procedures

HENDRICKSON THEATERS, INC.
Illustrations from the Internal Control Structure for Revenue and Cash

Accounting System	Control Procedures
Entries: Admissions and concessions revenues are recorded daily by increasing both cash and the appropriate revenue accounts.	*Authority and responsibility:* Each theater manager is responsible for the control of cash in his or her theater, but the central office accountant makes all general ledger entries related to cash.
Documentation: The electronic cash register at each ticket booth and concession stand prepares a detailed list of cash transactions and a daily cash summary report. The daily summary reports from the 10 theaters are electronically transferred to the central office each night and are automatically summarized upon receipt. Each morning, the accountant generates a paper report and makes revenue entries in the computerized general ledger.	*Segregation of duties:* Maintenance of the general ledger is segregated from responsibility for local cash control. Ticket sellers and concession operators may assist in preparation of daily cash deposits, but the manager must check and sign deposit documents.
	Documentation: Prenumbered admission tickets are dispensed by machine at each theater. The machine also prepares a report of the tickets issued each day, which is used by the theater manager to reconcile cash collected with the number of tickets sold.
Reports: A variety of revenue analyses can be prepared on the computer system, including analyses by theater, movie, day of the week, and month.	*Safeguards:* The cash accumulates in each theater until the end of each day. When cash drawers reach a specified level, however, the cash register signals that a fixed amount of cash should be removed by the manager and placed in the theater's safe.
	Checks: On an unannounced schedule, Hendrickson's accountant visits each theater and verifies cash receipts reported against the number of tickets issued. On these same visits, the accountant checks concession revenues against the amounts reported by inventorying concession supplies.

Cash Controls

> **OBJECTIVE ▸ 3**
> Describe how businesses control cash.

When controls over cash are poorly designed or are not being followed, employees are more likely to believe that they can steal cash without getting caught (i.e., they have the opportunity). The *Association of Certified Fraud Examiners'* 2002 fraud study suggested that 80 percent of all workplace frauds involved employee theft of company assets (i.e., embezzlement) and 90 percent of these thefts involved cash.[1] For example, casinos take in huge amounts of cash. At one casino in Connecticut, employees who counted cash were required to wear jumpsuits with no pockets while counting the cash. Further, supervisors observed the counters through one-way mirrors. That sounds good; however, one employee shoved over $200,000 under the elastic wristband of his jumpsuit over the course of a few months. He would take the

---

[1] The other 20 percent includes such things as fraudulent financial statements.

money out of his sleeve and put it in his pockets during bathroom breaks. Now the casino uses clear jumpsuits for its cash counters.

Of course, casinos operate in a particularly difficult environment to control cash. But all companies must use the internal control activities described in the previous section to effectively control cash. For example, the authority to collect, hold, and pay cash must be clearly assigned to specific individuals. As discussed earlier, whenever feasible, cash-handling activities and cash record-keeping activities should be assigned to *different* individuals. Moreover, cash records should be examined often by an objective party as a basis for evaluating the performance of cash-handling activities. These controls should be supported by an appropriately designed record-keeping system. Additionally, cash should be safeguarded in vaults and banks. The following Decision-Making & Analysis illustrates these activities in a student organization where segregation of duties is often difficult.

DECISION-MAKING & ANALYSIS

Internal Control over Cash in a Student Organization

Internal control is frequently a problem for student organizations (clubs, fraternities, sororities, etc.). Internal control over cash is likely to be weak in such organizations. Usually one individual, the treasurer, is given the responsibility for collecting dues, depositing cash in the bank, writing all checks, maintaining accounting records, and preparing bank reconciliations and financial statements. This is a clear violation of segregation of duties. Although some members may recognize the internal control advantages of segregation of duties, student organizations frequently face the reality that segregation of duties is not nearly as important as simply finding someone willing to perform the treasurer's tasks.

What steps can be taken by a typical student organization to strengthen its internal control system? The following list contains seven questions that should be answered by the leaders of a student organization. A "no" answer to any question indicates a potential internal control weakness.

1. *Is supporting documentation obtained from vendors whenever cash is paid or a liability is incurred?*

   The use of appropriate documentation assures the proper payment of bills and facilitates the appropriate accrual of liabilities on the year end balance sheet.

2. *Is every vendor invoice and all supporting documentation cancelled (e.g., by writing "Paid by check number 841 on November 29, 2009") at the time the check is written?*

   This action helps assure that duplicate payments are not made.

3. *Does the organization's faculty advisor initial all checks written for amounts greater than some specified minimum (say $500)?*

   This control reduces the possibility of unauthorized payments.

4. *Are receipts of members' fees and dues deposited promptly (at least once a week)?*

   Prompt deposits help avoid misplacing receipts.

5. *Does the organization have procedures to assist in the collection of membership dues?*

   Despite the mutual trust and friendship that are a part of most student organizations, uncollectible accounts can be a serious problem. The treasurer may need the assistance of formal procedures in collecting overdue accounts (e.g., placing sanctions on members who fail to pay).

6. *Does the organization have an accounting policies and procedures manual?*

   Such a manual may be needed to prepare the year-end financial report in conformity with university and/or national governing body requirements.

7. *Are complete minutes of all officers' meetings maintained?*

   The minutes should include (a) a listing of all changes in membership and officers, including the names of new members, (b) a schedule of dues that documents all financial obligations of members, (c) approval of payments, and (d) authorization of check signers. Including this information, along with descriptions of important decisions of the organization's governing body, documents all the important activities of the organization.

Although many of the cash controls with which you are most familiar (e.g., cash registers) might appear to be outside the accounting system, we will highlight three important areas where the accounting system interacts with the internal control system to strengthen cash controls: (1) bank reconciliations, (2) cash over and short, and (3) petty cash.

Reconciliation of Accounting Records to Bank Statement

The use of a bank is one of the most important controls over cash. The bank duplicates the company's accounting by keeping their own accounting records of your account. Unfortunately, the bank's accounting records and company's accounting records rarely agree because the transactions are not recorded at the same time (e.g., a company writes a check on January 18 and credits cash immediately; however, the bank will not debit your account until the check is presented to the bank—typically many days later). Therefore, to ensure that the accounting records are consistent with the bank's accounting records, any differences must be "reconciled." This process is called the **bank reconciliation**.

Periodically—usually once a month—the bank returns all checks processed during the period, together with a detailed record of the activity of the account. The document is a *bank statement*, which shows the beginning and ending account balance and the individual deposits and withdrawals recorded by the bank during the period. Basically, the bank statement is a copy of the bank's accounting records showing each customer the increases and decreases in their balances (see Exhibit 4-4). Remember, a checking account is a liability for the bank (i.e., the bank owes you the balance). Therefore, deposits and other events that increase your bank account balance are labeled "credits" on the bank statement (because they increase the bank's liability to you), and withdrawals and other events that decrease your bank account balance are labeled "debits" (because they decrease the bank's liability to you).

Reconciliation of these separately maintained records serves two purposes: First, it serves a control function by identifying errors and providing an inspection of detailed records that deters theft. Second, reconciliation serves a transaction detection function by identifying transactions performed by the bank, so the business can make the necessary entries in its records.

Sources of Differences Between Cash Account and Bank Statement Balance

In general, differences between the cash account balance (see Exhibit 4-5) and the bank statement balance develop from three sources: (1) transactions recorded by the business, but not recorded by the bank in time to appear on the current bank statement, (2) transactions recorded by the bank, but not yet recorded by the business, and (3) errors in recording transactions on either set of records. Let us consider examples of each source of difference.

Transactions Recorded by the Business but Not Recorded by the Bank in Time to Appear on the Current Bank Statement

One type of transaction in this category is an **outstanding check**. This is a check issued and recorded by the business that has not been "cashed" by the recipient of the check. The business has (properly) recorded the check as lowering its cash balance and the bank has (properly) not recorded the check as lowering the business' account balance because it has not been cashed. For example, when a check is written during December, but not cashed until January, the business' December 31 cash balance will be lower than its account balance on the December 31 bank statement.

Another transaction in this category is a **deposit in transit**, which is an amount received and recorded by the business, but which has not been recorded by the bank in time to appear on the current bank statement. Deposits in transit cause the bank balance to be smaller than the business's cash account balance. Deposits in transit arise because many banks post any deposit received after 2:00 or 3:00 P.M. into their

Exhibit 4-4

Bank Statement

THIRD NATIONAL BANK
123 W. Main Street
Batavia, OH 45103

Member FDIC

Account Statement

Statement Date:
August 31, 2009

OHIO ENTERPRISES, INC.
519 MAIN STREET
BATAVIA, OH 45103

Account Number:
40056

Previous Balance	Checks and Debits	Deposits and Credits	Current Balance
$7,675.20	$10,685.26	$7,175.10	$4,165.04

Checks and Debits			Deposits and Credits		Daily Balance	
Date	No.	Amount	Date	Amount	Date	Amount
8/3/09	1883	182.00			8/3/09	7,493.20
8/4/09	1884	217.26	8/4/08	2,673.10	8/4/09	9,949.04
8/6/09	1885	1,075.00			8/6/09	8,874.04
8/7/09	1886	37.50	8/7/08	4,500.00	8/7/09	13,336.54
8/10/09	1887	826.00			8/10/09	12,510.54
8/11/09	1888	50.00			8/11/09	12,460.54
8/12/09	1889	2,670.00				
8/12/09	1890	67.90			8/12/09	9,722.64
8/13/09	1891	890.00			8/13/09	8,832.64
8/14/09	1892	27.50			8/14/09	8,805.14
8/17/09	1893	111.00			8/17/09	8,694.14
8/18/09	DM	380.00			8/18/09	8,314.14
8/19/09	1894	60.00				
8/19/09	1895	510.00			8/19/09	7,744.14
8/20/09	1896	30.00			8/20/09	7,714.14
8/21/09	1897	1,600.00			8/21/09	6,114.14
8/24/09	1898	78.00			8/24/09	6,036.14
8/25/09	NSF	200.00			8/25/09	5,836.14
8/26/09	1899	208.80			8/26/09	5,627.34
8/27/09	1900	1,250.00			8/27/09	4,377.34
8/28/09	1902	175.00			8/28/09	4,202.34
8/31/09	1903	25.30	8/31/08 INT	2.00		
8/31/09	SC	14.00			8/31/09	4,165.04

Symbols:	CM Credit Memo	EC Error Correction	NSF Non-sufficient funds
	DM Debit Memo	INT Interest Earned	SC Service Charge

Reconcile your account immediately

records on the next business day and because businesses often make deposits on weekends or holidays when the bank is not open for business, which could cause the deposit to appear on the next bank statement.

Transactions Recorded by Bank, but Not Yet Recorded by the Business
Several types of transactions fall within this category. Bank **service charges** are fees charged by the bank for checking account services. The amount of the fee is not known to the business (and therefore cannot be recorded) until the bank statement is received. Bank service charges unrecorded by the business at the end of a month cause the bank balance to be smaller than the business's cash account balance.

Exhibit 4-5

T-Account for Cash, Prior to Reconciliation

OHIO ENTERPRISES, INC.

Cash

| Balance, 7/31/09 | $6,200.94 | | | | |

Date	Amount Deposited	Check Number	Check Amount	Check Number	Check Amount
8/1	$2,673.10	1886	$ 37.50	1896	$ 30.00
8/5	4,500.00	1887	826.00	1897	1,600.00
8/31	300.00	1888	50.00	1898	87.00
Total deposits	$7,473.10	1889	2,670.00	1899	208.80
		1890	67.90	1900	1,250.00
		1891	890.00	1901	93.00
		1892	27.50	1902	175.00
		1893	111.00	1903	25.30
		1894	60.00	1904	72.50
		1895	510.00	1905	891.00
				Total disbursements	$9,682.50

| Balance, 8/31/09 | $3,991.54 | | | | |

A **Non-Sufficient Funds (NSF) check** is a check that has been returned to the depositor because funds in the issuer's account are not sufficient to pay the check (also called a "bounced" check). The amount of the check was added to the depositor's account when the check was deposited; however, since the check cannot be paid, the bank deducts the amount of the NSF check from the account. This deduction is recorded by the bank before it is recorded by the business. NSF, then, checks cause the bank balance to be smaller than the cash account balance.

Debit and credit memos are also recorded by the bank before they are recorded by the business. A debit memo might result, for example, if the bank makes a prearranged deduction from the business' account to pay a utility bill. Debit memos recorded by the bank but not yet recorded by the business cause the bank balance to be smaller than the cash account balance. A credit memo could result if the bank collected a note receivable for the business and deposited the funds in the business's account. Credit memos recorded by the bank, but not recorded by the business, cause the bank balance to be larger than the cash account balance.

After the reconciliation process, the business must make adjusting journal entries to record all the transactions that have been recorded by the bank but not yet recorded in the business's ledger cash account.

Errors The previous differences between the accounting records and bank account balances are the result of time lags between the recording of a transaction by the business and its recording by the bank. Errors in recording transactions represent yet another source of difference between a business' cash account balance and the bank balance. For example, a $76.00 check may be erroneously entered into the business' cash account for $67.00. Such errors are inevitable in any

CONCEPT Q&A

If a debit increases an asset and decreases a liability and a credit decreases an asset and increases a liability, why does the bank "credit" your account when you make a deposit and "debit" your account when you make a withdrawal?

Possible Answer:
Because the "credit" and "debit" are from the bank's point of view. When you make a deposit, it actually increases the bank's liability to you—the bank now owes you more. When you make a withdrawal, it decreases the bank's liability to you.

accounting system and should be corrected as soon as discovered. In addition, an effort should be made to determine the cause of any error as a basis for corrective action. Obviously, an intentional error designed to hide misappropriation of funds calls for quite different corrective action than does an error resulting from human fatigue or machine failure.

To begin the reconciliation you start with the "cash balance from the bank statement" and the "cash balance from company records." These two balances are then adjusted as necessary to produce identical "adjusted cash balance" by following these steps:

1. Compare the deposits on the bank statement to the deposits debited to the cash account. Any deposits debited to the cash account, but not on the bank statement are likely deposits in transit. However, you should look at a deposit slip to ensure that these amounts were actually deposited. Deposits in transit should be added to the "cash balance from the bank statement."

2. Compare the paid (often called "cancelled") checks returned with the bank statement to the amounts credited to the cash account and the list of outstanding checks from prior months. Any checks credited to the cash account, but not on the bank statement are likely outstanding checks. These amounts should be subtracted from the "cash balance from the bank statement."

3. Look for items on the bank statement that have not been debited or credited to the cash account. These include items such as bank service charges, interest payments, NSF checks, automatic payments (debit memos), and bank collections on behalf of the company (credit memos). Bank debits to our account should be subtracted from the "cash balance from company records," while bank credits should be added to the "cash balance from company records." Of course, all these amounts should be verified as correctly applied to your account.

4. If at this time the "adjusted cash balances" are not the same, you must search for errors. The most common error is a "transposition" error in which, for example, a check is written for $823, but recorded as $283 (the 8 and 2 are transposed). In this case, the accounting records will show a $283 credit to the cash account, but the bank will show a $823 debit to the company's account. All errors made by the company must be added or subtracted from the "cash balance from company records." All errors made by the bank must be added or subtracted from the "cash balance from the bank statement."

The process is illustrated in Cornerstone 4-1.

Once the bank reconciliation is completed, some adjustments to the accounting records may be necessary. No adjustments are necessary for outstanding checks or deposits in transit because the accounting records have correctly recorded these amounts. However, adjustments are necessary for any company errors or items such as bank charges or interest that the company does not find out about until receiving the bank statement.

CORNERSTONE 4-1

HOW TO Perform a Bank Reconciliation

Concept:

The sources of difference between the cash account and bank account balances are determined by a comparison of the accounting records and the bank statement. In general, this procedure has three parts: (1) compare balances, (2) compare credits to the cash account to debits on the bank statement (you are looking for differences such as outstanding checks and debit memos), and (3) compare debits to the cash account to credits on the bank statement (you are looking for differences such as deposits in transit and credit memos).

Information:

Use the bank statement in Exhibit 4-4 and the cash account in Exhibit 4-5. Recognize that the beginning balance was reconciled at the end of last month (July). Assume that this was performed correctly and all outstanding checks (numbers 1883, 1884, and 1885) and deposits in transit from July cleared during August.

Required:

1. Determine the adjustments needed by comparing the bank statement to the cash account.
2. Using the following form, complete the bank reconciliation.

Cash balance from bank statement
Add:
Less:
Adjusted cash balance

Cash balance from company records
Add:
Less:
Adjusted cash balance

Solution:

1. The August 31 deposit debited to the cash account does not appear on the bank statement. It is still in transit. Comparison of the bank statement and the cash account reveals that checks 1901, 1904, and 1905 are outstanding. Also note that the amount posted to the cash account for check 1898 does not equal the amount cleared on the bank statement. By examining the cancelled check, you find that the error is on the company's records. The check was written for $78.00, not $87.00.

2.

Cash balance from bank statement		$ 4,165.04
Add: Deposit in transit (8/31)		300.00
Less: Outstanding checks		
1901	$ 93.00	
1904	72.50	
1905	891.00	(1,056.50)
Adjusted cash balance		**$3,408.54**
Cash balance from company records		$ 3,991.54
Add:		
Error in recording check 1898 (we recorded as $87, should be $78)	$ 9.00	
Interest	2.00	11.00
Less:		
Service charge	$ 14.00	
NSF check	200.00	
Electric bill (Debit Memo)	380.00	(594.00)
Adjusted cash balance		**$3,408.54**

**CORNERSTONE
4 - 1**
(continued)

The bank reconciliation typically produces adjusting entries like those shown in Cornerstone 4-2. However, there are additional benefits when the reconciliation is performed by someone with no other responsibilities related to cash (the duties of reconciling cash and cash record keeping should be segregated). Specifically, if the person who writes the checks also performs the reconciliation, then it is easier for them to cover up theft and fraud.

HOW TO Make Adjusting Entries as a Result of the Bank Reconciliation

CORNERSTONE 4-2

Concept:
Adjusting journal entries are required for all transactions correctly recorded by the bank that have not yet been included in the accounting records.

Information:
Refer to the Bank Reconciliation performed in Cornerstone 4-1.

Required:
Provide the necessary adjusting journal entries.

Solution:
To correct error in recording check 1898:

Assets = Liabilities +	Stockholders' Equity
+9 +9	

Date	Account and Explanation	Debit	Credit
	Cash	9	
	Accounts Payable		9

To record interest:

Assets = Liabilities +	Stockholders' Equity
+2	+2

Date	Account and Explanation	Debit	Credit
	Cash	2	
	Interest Income		2

To record bank service charge:

Assets = Liabilities +	Stockholders' Equity
−14	−14

Date	Account and Explanation	Debit	Credit
	Bank Service Charge Expense	14	
	Cash		14

To record NSF check:

Assets = Liabilities +	Stockholders' Equity
+200 −200	

Date	Account and Explanation	Debit	Credit
	Accounts Receivable	200	
	Cash		200

To record debit memo for payment of electric bill:

Assets = Liabilities +	Stockholders' Equity
−380	−380

Date	Account and Explanation	Debit	Credit
	Utilities Expense	380	
	Cash		380

Cash Over and Short

Another important control activity requires that cash receipts be deposited in a bank daily. At the end of each day, the amount of cash received during the day is debited to the cash accounts to which it has been deposited. The amount deposited should equal the total of cash register tapes. If it does not (and differences will occasionally occur even when cash-handling procedures are carefully designed and executed), the discrepancy is recorded in an account called **cash over and short**.

To illustrate the use of the cash over and short account, suppose that on a certain day a business has prepared for a deposit total of $20,671.12. However, the total of cash register tapes and other documents supporting the receipt of cash on that day is $20,685.14, including collections of accounts receivable of $6,760.50. The $14.02 difference is the amount of cash short, and the following journal entry records this amount along with the day's receipts:

Date	Account and Explanation	Debit	Credit
	Cash	20,671.12	
	Cash Over and Short	14.02	
	Sales Revenue ($20,685.14 − $6,760.50)		13,924.64
	Accounts Receivable		6,760.50

Assets = Liabilities +	Stock-holders' Equity
+20,671.12	−14.02
−6,760.50	+13,924.64

Observe that a cash *overage* requires a credit to cash over and short, whereas a cash *shortage* would require a debit.

One common source of cash over and short is errors in making change for cash sales. Significant amounts of cash over and short signal the need for a careful investigation of the causes and appropriate corrective action. Cash over and short is usually treated as an income statement account and is reported as a part of other expenses or other revenues.

Petty Cash

Cash controls are more effective when companies pay with a check. For example, only certain people have the authority to sign the check. Further, these people do not keep the accounting records and they will only sign the check with the proper documentation supporting the payment (e.g., evidence that the goods being paid for were properly ordered and received). Additionally, upon signing the check the supporting documents are marked paid to avoid duplicate payment. Finally, checks are prenumbered, which makes it easy to identify any missing checks.

However, issuing checks to pay small amounts is usually more costly than paying cash.[2] To reduce such costs, a company may establish a **petty cash** fund to pay for small dollar amount items such as stamps or a cake for an employee birthday party. The petty cash fund is formed by giving a small amount of cash to a petty cash custodian. The custodian will then pay for small dollar amounts directly out of the fund. Also, employees will often use their own money to pay for an item, then bring the receipt to the custodian. The custodian will reimburse the employee for the amount shown on the receipt from the petty cash fund and keep the receipt. At the end of the month the custodian submits all the receipts (and any other supporting documentation) to the company. After ensuring the appropriateness of all the receipts, the custodian is given the total amount to replenish the petty cash fund. It is only at this time that the company records the amounts spent in the accounting records. However, because the custodian replenishes petty cash at the end of the month, the accounting records are appropriately updated each month. This process is illustrated in Cornerstone 4-3.

HOW TO Account for Petty Cash

Concept:
A petty cash fund account is debited for the entire amount given to the custodian when the fund is established. When the custodian replenishes the fund at the end of the month the appropriate expenses are recorded. The petty cash fund account is not adjusted unless the total amount of the fund is changed.

Information:
On January 1, Oregon Industries establishes a petty cash fund of $500. The petty cash custodian has been with the company for many years and has demonstrated an ability to maintain careful records. On January 31, the custodian

CORNERSTONE
4 - 3

---

[2] Checks are costly to use. They cost money to print. They cost money to mail. They cost money to process. Some estimate the cost of processing a check to be over $1. Therefore, banks have developed ways for businesses to transfer money without the use of paper checks. For example, most employees do not see an actual paycheck any longer; instead, the money is automatically deposited into their bank account. These are called electronic fund transfers (EFT). Use of EFTs is quite common and over the last 10 to 15 years has become commonplace at the individual level through the use of debit cards.

CORNERSTONE 4-3
(continued)

presents the following records of the month's transactions, together with related documents, and requests reimbursement:

Jan. 12	Hansen's Grocery (coffee)	$ 30
15	U.S. Post Office (postage)	70
17	Northwest Messenger (package delivery)	25
19	Office Depot (Office supplies)	175
25	Mr. Strand, Controller (food for lunch meeting)	63
	Total	**$363**

Company personnel (other than the petty cash custodian) examine the documents to determine that they are authentic and that each transaction is supported by appropriate documentation. The company then issues a check to the custodian for $363.00 to replenish the fund.

Required:

1. Make the necessary journal entry to establish the petty cash fund on January 1.
2. Make the necessary journal entry to record the replenishment of the fund on January 31.
3. Make the necessary journal entry to record the replenishment of the fund on January 31 assuming that Oregon Industries also decided to increase the fund balance to $600.

Solution:

1. *Establishment of petty cash fund on January 1:*

Assets = Liabilities +	Stockholders' Equity
+500	
−500	

Date	Account and Explanation	Debit	Credit
	Petty Cash Fund	500.00	
	Cash		500.00

2. *Replenishment of petty cash fund and recognition of expense on January 31:*

Assets = Liabilities +	Stockholders' Equity
−363	−175
	−70
	−25
	−93

Date	Account and Explanation	Debit	Credit
	Office Supplies Expense	175.00	
	Postage Expense	70.00	
	Delivery Expense	25.00	
	Miscellaneous Expense	93.00	
	Cash		363.00

Although the expenditures of petty cash require entries in the records maintained by the custodian, they are not recorded in Oregon Industries' accounting records until the fund is replenished. Also note that replenishment does not alter the balance of the petty cash fund on Oregon's records; the balance remains $500.00.

3. *Replenishment of petty cash fund and recognition of expense on January 31 with an increase of the fund balance to $600:*

Assets = Liabilities +	Stockholders' Equity
−463	−175
+100	−70
	−25
	−93

Date	Account and Explanation	Debit	Credit
	Petty Cash Fund	100.00	
	Office Supplies Expense	175.00	
	Postage Expense	70.00	
	Delivery Expense	25.00	
	Miscellaneous Expense	93.00	
	Cash		463.00

Replenishment of petty cash may also occur during the month if the amount of petty cash available gets too low. At that time, the same steps described in Cornerstone 4-3 would be followed. However, to assure that all expenses are recorded in the appropriate accounting period, replenishment should occur at the end of the month or accounting period. As an additional control measure, a company should periodically verify its petty cash balances by counting the cash in the hands of custodians. The amount of cash held by each custodian should equal the balance shown in the custodian's petty cash record.

We have spent considerable time discussing internal controls both in general, and over cash, in particular, for two reasons. First, internal controls are an integral part of the accounting system and business. Second, the accounting and reporting of cash is not that difficult. Now, we will turn to accounting and reporting for cash.

Accounting and Reporting Cash

Describe how businesses account and report cash.

When cash is received, a cash account is increased by a debit; and when cash is paid out, a cash account is decreased by a credit. As discussed in the bank reconciliation section, receipt and payment of cash are frequently accomplished by a check sent through the mail, a process that may require several days, and additional time may pass between receipt of the check and its deposit in the bank by the payee. Despite the fact that there may be a time lag between the issuance of a check and the actual transfer of funds, the accounting system treats payment by check in exactly the same way that it treats the transfer of currency. The receipt of either a check or currency is recorded by a debit to cash. Conversely, either the issue of a check or the payment of currency is recorded by a credit to cash.

Cash is reported on both the balance sheet and the statement of cash flows. The balance sheet reports the amount of cash available at the balance sheet date. The statement of cash flows shows the sources and uses of cash during the year. The statement of cash flows will be discussed in more detail in Chapter 11. As shown in Exhibit 4-6, the balance sheet typically reports cash and cash equivalents.

As explained in the notes to Abercrombie & Fitch's financial statements, **cash equivalents** "include amounts on deposit with financial institutions and investments, primarily held in money market accounts, with original maturities of less than 90 days." This is a standard definition and indicates that cash equivalents are (1) easily convertible into known amounts of cash and (2) close enough to maturity that they are relatively insensitive to changes in interest rates.

But why do companies bother to invest their cash in such short-term investments? The answer is that such investments earn a greater rate of return than cash sitting in a bank account. Refer to Exhibit 4-6 and you'll see that Abercrombie & Fitch had almost $82,000,000 in cash and equivalents at February 3, 2007. If their investment strategy earns a mere 1 percent more than a bank account, they would earn an

Exhibit 4-6

Balance Sheet Reporting of Cash for Abercrombie & Fitch

Abercrombie & Fitch, Inc.
Consolidated Balance Sheet
(in thousands)

	Feb. 3, 2007	Jan. 28, 2006
ASSETS		
Current assets:		
Cash and Equivalents	$81,959	$50,687

extra $820,000 in interest for the year. We will consider cash management strategies, but first we discuss the financing and operating cycles because these affect the amount of cash needed.

Financing and Operating Cycles

Business transactions form sequences of connected and regularly repeated patterns of activity. Although these patterns or cycles vary somewhat from one business to another, most are composed of the following activities:

1. **Receiving assets** (mainly cash) from owners (stockholders) and creditors (bankers and bondholders).
2. **Purchasing assets** from outside suppliers, including merchandise for resale or materials to produce salable goods or services.
3. **Selling goods or services** to customers.
4. **Collecting cash from customers** for goods and services sold.
5. **Repaying owners and creditors** the assets they invested plus appropriate compensation.

Exhibit 4-7 shows how these five activities are arranged in the *financing and operating cycles* of a typical business selling goods to its customers. The business receives financial resources from owners and creditors. These resources are used to purchase various assets, including goods that will be held in inventory until sold to customers. The business sells all goods on credit, creating accounts receivable, and cash is not replenished until the receivables are collected, which completes the operating cycle. At regular intervals, dividends are paid to stockholders (owners) and interest is paid to creditors, which completes the financing cycle. Ultimately, of course, the amount originally received from stockholders and creditors is repaid, although in the case of stockholders, it may not be repaid until the business is dissolved.

Financing Cycle

The **financing cycle** is the elapsed time between the receipt of financial resources from owners and creditors and the repayment of the original amounts received. The length of the financing cycle varies with the type of financing used by the enterprise. Some borrowings may pass through the financing cycle in a year or less, whereas others may require 5 to 10 years or even longer. As noted above, the financing cycle for cash received from stockholders may be the entire lifetime of the business enterprise. Thus, the overall financing cycle for most businesses is likely to be many years.

Exhibit 4-7

The Financing and Operating Cycles

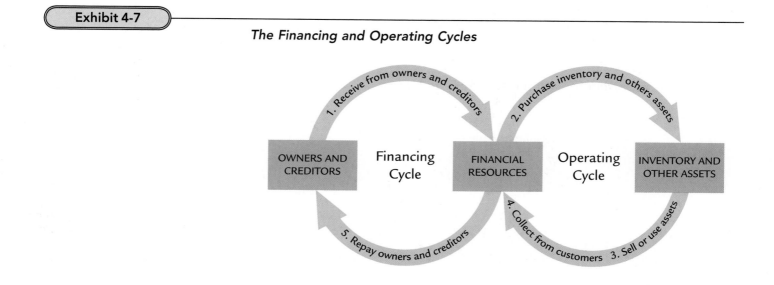

Operating Cycle

The **operating cycle** is the elapsed time between the purchase of goods for resale (or the purchase of materials to produce salable goods or services) and the collection of cash from customers (presumably a larger amount of cash than was invested in the goods sold). Although typically a year or less, the operating cycle can be as short as a few days for perishable goods, or as long as many years for the production and sale of products such as timber or wine.

Let us illustrate the determination of an operating cycle. **H. H. Gregg** of Indianapolis is a large appliance retailer that provides long–term financing for customers. Appliances remain in inventory for an average of three months before being sold. Most are sold on credit, and it takes an average of 12 months to collect the full amount of a sale. Thus, Gregg's operating cycle is 15 months, representing the average purchase-to-collection interval (three months to sell plus 12 months to collect).

A business's operating cycle is usually much shorter than its financing cycle. Indeed, it is the opportunity to use outside resources to finance multiple operating cycles that enables a business to generate profit and to pay interest and dividends. *The length of the operating cycle influences the classification of assets and liabilities on balance sheets.* In addition, the operating cycle plays an important role in the measurement of income. The length of the operating cycle also affects the amount of capital a business needs and the policies that govern its sales of goods and services, as the Decision-Making & Analysis demonstrates.

DECISION-MAKING & ANALYSIS

Operating Cycle and Capital Requirements

Consider two companies named Long and Short that are engaged in selling the same product, called a Gismo. Each company sells, on credit, 1,000 Gismos per month (12,000 per year) to similar customers at $10 per unit. Each company has in inventory of 200 Gismos that were purchased at a cost of $6 per unit (a total inventory of $1,200). Each company has $1,000 in cash and no assets other than accounts receivable and inventory. Short collects its accounts receivable within one month, so that at any point in time one month's sales, or $10,000, are in Short's accounts receivable. Long, on the other hand, collects its accounts receivable three months after a sale and therefore at any given time has three months' sales, or $30,000, in accounts receivable. At present, the two companies have the following balance sheets:

Short			Long		
ASSETS			ASSETS		
Cash		$ 1,000	Cash		$ 1,000
Inventory		1,200	Inventory		1,200
Accounts receivable		10,000	Accounts receivable		30,000
Total		$12,200	Total		$32,200
LIABILITIES AND EQUITY			LIABILITIES AND EQUITY		
Equity		$12,200	Loans payable		$20,000
Total		$12,200	Equity		12,200
			Total		$32,200

1. *What is the effect of the difference in operating cycle on the capital requirements of Long and Short, respectively?*

   A comparison of the two balance sheets shows that Long needs $20,000 more capital than Short, because of Long's longer operating cycle. The $20,000 needed is the difference between Short's $12,200 in assets and Long's $32,200 in assets.

2. *What is the effect of the differences in the capital requirements of the two companies on their sales price?*

   Long's expenses will be higher than Short's expenses because the additional borrowing results in additional interest expense. Presumably, Long would not allow its customers to take three months to pay unless compensated for doing so. Thus, Long will probably charge a higher price because of the extended payment terms, making Long's revenue higher than Short's.

With an understanding of the financing and operating cycles, we now turn our attention to cash management strategies.

OBJECTIVE ➤ 6

Explain the principles of cash management.

Cash Management

As discussed in the previous section, the activities of the operating cycle transform cash into goods and services and then back, through sales, into cash. This sequence of activities includes a continual process of paying and receiving cash. A company can significantly increase its net income through its cash management policies. At a high level, cash management principles entail a delay in paying suppliers (so a company can earn as much interest on their cash as possible), speeding up collection from customers (in order to invest the cash sooner), and earning the greatest return on any excess cash. We can follow these principles through the operating cycle.

The first stage of the operating cycle is buying inventory. We have long recognized that money that is tied up in inventory sitting on the shelves is not earning any return. As such, an important aspect of cash management is to keep inventory levels low. This decreases the need for cash. Companies have made great strides in inventory management over the last few decades. In fact, many manufacturers have no more than a couple of days' sales in inventory.

The second stage of the operating cycle is paying for the inventory. As with all payments, a good cash management principle is to delay payments as long as possible while maintaining a good relationship with the payee. Keeping the cash in our hands for the longest time possible allows us to collect more interest on the money. This may seem trivial, but consider a company like **Microsoft**. Its 2007 SEC filings reveal approximately $3.2 billion in accounts payable. If Microsoft can earn 5 percent on this money, it will earn close to $450,000 per day in interest. You may practice this in your own lives if you wait until April 15 to pay any income taxes owed or pay your tuition on the last possible day.

The third stage is selling the inventory, which often produces receivables. As good cash management suggests delaying payments, it conversely suggests increasing the speed of receivable collections. This is an area that has become increasingly sophisticated over the last 20 years. In fact, many companies sell their receivables rather than wait for their customers to pay. Of course, they sell the receivables for less than they will receive (which represents interest and return for the buyer), but it also allows the company to receive the cash sooner and avoid hiring employees to service the receivables.

Beyond delaying payments and speeding up collections, businesses try to keep their bank cash balances to a minimum because most bank accounts earn relatively small amounts of interest. Accordingly, short-term investments are purchased with temporary cash surpluses. The value and composition of short-term investment portfolios change continually in response to seasonal factors and other shifts in the business environment. As for the accounting for short-term investments, this is discussed in the appendix.

These investments will usually be liquidated (i.e., converted to cash through selling or maturity) before the business undertakes any significant short-term borrowing because the interest expense on short-term borrowings usually exceeds the return on short-term investments. Nonetheless, temporary shortages can result from the day-to-day ups and downs in the inflows and outflows of cash, as well as unforeseen needs for cash. A business with a good credit rating can borrow funds to resolve a temporary cash shortage. Such borrowings frequently are made under a line of credit, an agreement between the company and its bank in which the bank promises to lend the company funds up to a specified limit and at specified interest rates. The use of short-term investments as part of cash management is illustrated in the following Decision-Making & Analysis.

DECISION-MAKING & ANALYSIS

Cash Management by Ohio Wire

Ohio Wire is a medium-size manufacturer of cable and wire used in the construction of bridges and buildings. Since most basic construction is seasonal, Ohio Wire tends to have surplus cash in the early months of each year. The company treasurer constructs a cash budget at the beginning of each year in an effort to determine, in advance, the periods in which cash will be available for short-term investment and the periods in which such investments will have to be liquidated. The budget shows that the treasurer anticipates the expenditure of cash at a steady rate of $300,000 per quarter. Budgeted cash receipts vary, however, according to the following schedule:

First quarter 2010	$452,000
Second quarter 2010	320,000
Third quarter 2010	155,000
Fourth quarter 2010	325,000
First quarter 2011	527,000

Ohio Wire begins the year with a cash balance of $50,000, no short-term investments, and no short-term debt. The business operates under the policy that the end-of-quarter cash balance should equal $50,000 plus the expected excess of disbursements over receipts, if any, during the next quarter. If receipts are expected to exceed disbursements during the next quarter, then the end-of-quarter balance should equal $50,000. The following questions might be asked concerning Ohio Wire's cash management policy:

1. *What addition to, or liquidation of, short-term investments should be made during each quarter in 2010? Will short-term borrowing be necessary?*

   Consider the calculation to be made at the beginning of the first quarter of 2010. The cash balance on January 1 is $50,000, expected receipts for the first quarter are $452,000, and expected expenditures are $300,000, which will produce an end-of-first-quarter cash balance of $202,000 ($50,000 + $452,000 − $300,000). Since receipts are expected to exceed expenditures during the second quarter, the end-of-first-quarter cash balance should equal $50,000. To reduce the cash balance to the desired level of $50,000, investments of $152,000 ($202,000 − $50,000) must be made during the first quarter. At the beginning of each quarter, the required investment, borrowing, or liquidation for the ensuing quarter is calculated in a similar way, as shown in the following schedule:

	First Quarter 2010	Second Quarter 2010	Third Quarter 2010	Fourth Quarter 2010
Calculation of Ending Balance Before Adjustment for Investments, Borrowing, or Liquidations				
Cash receipts	$452,000	$ 320,000	$ 155,000	$325,000
Cash disbursements	300,000	300,000	300,000	300,000
Excess (deficiency) of cash receipts	$152,000	$ 20,000	$(145,000)	$ 25,000
Beginning cash balance	50,000	50,000	195,000	50,000
Ending cash balance before adjustment	$202,000	$ 70,000	$ 50,000	$ 75,000
Calculation of Required Ending Balance				
Next quarter's deficiency of cash receipts	$ 0	$ 145,000	$ 0	$ 0
Minimum cash balance	50,000	50,000	50,000	50,000
Required ending balance	$ 50,000	$ 195,000	$ 50,000	$ 50,000
Short-Term Adjustment				
Amount to invest (borrow or liquidate)	$152,000	$(125,000)	$ 0	$ 25,000

   In sum, the business should plan to invest $152,000 in short-term securities during the first quarter, liquidate securities in the amount of $125,000 during the second quarter; neither buy nor sell securities during the third quarter, and invest $25,000 in securities during the fourth quarter. No short-term borrowing is necessary.

2. *How did Ohio Wire determine its minimum cash balance to be $50,000?*

   Formal decision-making techniques and models are available to assist in making such judgments. But it is also possible that Ohio Wire simply established the $50,000 minimum as a result of trial and error with a variety of cash management policies. Arrangements with banks also influence cash management policies. Banks sometimes require depositors to maintain a minimum balance.

Effective cash management ultimately requires some understanding of future cash flows. For example, if the company is planning to expand or pay off a loan, it must make sure it has the necessary cash on hand. If a company receives most of its cash for the year around the holidays, it must effectively manage the excess until the time it is needed. These projections are made as part of the budgeting process and are an integral part of managerial accounting courses.

Summary of Learning Objectives

LO1.   Discuss the role of internal controls in managing a business.
- Internal control systems provide reasonable assurance that the company's objectives are being met in three areas:
  - effectiveness and efficiency of operations
  - reliability of financial reporting
  - compliance with applicable laws and regulations

LO2.   Discuss the five elements of internal control.
- The internal control system includes:
  - the control environment
  - risk assessment
  - control activities
  - information & communication
  - monitoring
- Although we distinguish between the accounting system and the internal controls system, the two are really one integrated system designed to meet the needs of a particular business.

LO3.   Describe how businesses control cash.
- Keeping control over cash is extremely difficult.
- It is important to:
  - safeguard cash
  - adequately segregate the custody of cash from the authorization of payments and the accounting records.
- Cash accounts include:
  - Cash in bank
  - Change funds
  - Petty cash
- Controls over these cash accounts include:
  - Bank reconciliations
  - Daily deposits and recording cash over and short amounts
  - Accounting procedures for petty cash funds

LO4.   Describe how businesses account and report cash.
- A cash account is debited when cash is received and credited when cash is paid out.
- Cash is reported on the balance sheet as the amount of cash and cash equivalents available on the balance sheet date.
- The statement of cash flows shows the sources and uses of cash during the accounting period.
- Cash equivalents are amounts that are easily convertible into known amounts of cash and investments that are close to maturity.

LO5.   Describe the cyclical nature of business activity.
- The financing and operating cycles of the business starts when the business receives financial resources from owners and creditors.
- These resources are used to purchase various assets, including goods that will be held in inventory until sold to customers.

- When a business sells goods on credit, creating accounts receivable, cash is not replenished until the receivables are collected, which completes the operating cycle.
- At regular intervals, dividends are paid to stockholders (owners) and interest is paid to creditors, which completes the financing cycle.
- Ultimately, the amount originally received from stockholders and creditors is repaid, although in the case of stockholders, it may not be repaid until the business is dissolved.

LO6. Explain the principles of cash management.
- Cash management is an important function at all companies because business is really a continuous cycle of paying and receiving cash.
- Although aspects of cash management have become extremely sophisticated, basic strategies are:
  - keeping inventory levels low
  - delaying payment of liabilities as long as possible
  - speeding up collection of receivables
  - investing idle cash to earn the greatest possible return while still being available when needed

---

CORNERSTONE 4-1   How to perform a bank reconciliation, page 190

CORNERSTONE 4-2   How to make adjusting entries as a result of the bank reconciliation, page 192

CORNERSTONE 4-3   How to account for petty cash, page 193

CORNERSTONES FOR CHAPTER 4

Key Terms

Accounting system, 184
Bank reconciliation, 187
Business process risks, 181
Cash equivalents, 195
Cash over and short, 192
Control activities, 182
Control environment, 178
Deposit in transit, 187
Financing cycle, 196
Internal control system, 178

Non-Sufficient Funds (NSF) check, 189
Operating cycle, 197
Outstanding check, 187
Petty cash, 193
Safeguarding, 183
Segregation of duties, 182
Service charges, 188
Strategic risks, 181

Appendix: Classification and Accounting for Investments

OBJECTIVE ▶ 7
Describe the classification and accounting for investments.

Although companies can invest excess cash in virtually any asset (e.g., land), in this section we will concentrate on the most common investments—buying equity or debt securities. An equity security represents an ownership interest in a corporation. Although most equity securities are common stock, preferred stock is also an equity security. A debt security exists when another entity owes the security holder some combination of interest and principal. Debt securities include corporate bonds, U.S. treasury securities, municipal bonds, etc.

Accounting for investments in equity securities differs depending upon the amount of common stock owned. The difference exists because of the nature of the ownership interest. If we own less than 20 percent of the common stock, the investment is generally considered to be "passive"; that is, we are not attempting to exert influence over the operating and financial policies of the corporation. In this case, the fair value method is used. This is discussed in more detail below.

If we own between 20 percent and 50 percent of the outstanding common stock, then we are assumed to possess "significant influence" over the operating and financial policies of the corporation. In this case, the equity method is used to account for the investment. The equity method is discussed in more advanced accounting courses.

Finally, if we own over 50 percent of the common stock, then we are assumed to "control" the operating and financial policies of the corporation (we are the parent and they are our subsidiary). In this case the subsidiary's financial statements are "consolidated" with ours. Consolidation will also be discussed in more advanced accounting courses.

When we own less than 20 percent of the outstanding common stock of a corporation, the equity securities are classified as either (1) **trading securities** or (2) **available-for-sale securities**. Debt securities are also classified as trading or available-for-sale, but debt securities may also be classified in a third category—**held-to-maturity**. The distinction between these classifications is as follows:

1. **Trading securities** are equity or debt investments that management intends to sell in the near term. Trading securities are bought and sold frequently and typically are owned for under one month. Trading securities are always classified as current assets on the balance sheet.
2. **Available-for-sale securities** are equity and debt investments that management intends to sell in the future, but not necessarily in the near term. In reality, they are all investments that don't warrant inclusion as trading securities or held-to-maturity securities. On the balance sheet, available-for-sale securities are classified as current or noncurrent assets depending on whether they will be sold within one year or one operating cycle, whichever is longer.
3. **Held-to-maturity securities** are debt investments (not equity, because stock does not mature) that management intends to hold until the debt contract requires the borrower to repay the debt in its entirety. On the balance sheet, held-to-maturity securities are classified as noncurrent assets unless the date of maturity is within one year or one operating cycle, whichever is longer.

Debt securities that are classified as "held-to-maturity" are valued at an amortized cost basis. This method is discussed in Chapter 9. Securities (both debt and equity) that are classified as "trading" or "available-for-sale" are valued at fair market value. An overview of the accounting for investments in debt and equity securities is shown in Exhibit 4-8.

Accounting for Trading and Available-for-Sale Securities

Like other assets, trading and available-for-sale securities are recorded at cost, which is also fair value on the date of purchase. To illustrate, on August 1, Redbird Corporation made the following purchases of securities:

Security	Type	Classification	Amount
Illinois Enterprises	Equity	Trading	$ 10,000
Metzler Design	Debt	Trading	6,000
IMG	Equity	Trading	4,100
Total Trading Securities			**$20,100**
Alabama Co.	Debt	AFS	$ 8,100
Mutare, Inc.	Debt	AFS	6,300
ABC	Equity	AFS	12,000
Total Available-for-Sale Securities			**$26,400**

Exhibit 4-8

Accounting for Investments in Debt and Equity Securities

Investments in Equity Securities	Method	Reporting of Dividends	Reporting of Unrealized Gains and Losses	Where Discussed
1. Passive Investment—Own <20% of the Stock				
a. Trading	Fair Value	Net Income	Net Income	In this appendix
b. Available-for-sale	Fair Value	Net Income	Other Comprehensive Income	In this appendix
2. Significant Influence—Own 20% to 50% of the Stock	Equity	Reduces Investment Account	Not Recognized	Intermediate
3. Control—Own >50% of the Stock	Consolidation	Eliminated	Not Recognized	Advanced
Investments in Debt Securities		**Reporting of Interest Income**		
1. Trading	Fair Value	Net Income	Net Income	In this appendix
2. Available-for-sale	Fair Value	Net Income	Other Comprehensive Income	In this appendix
3. Held-to-maturity	Amortized Cost	Net Income	Not recognized	Chapter 9

The acquisitions are recorded by the following entry:

Date	Account and Explanation	Debit	Credit
	Investments—Trading Securities	20,100	
	Investments—Available-for-Sale Securities	26,400	
	Cash		46,500

Assets = Liabilities +	Stockholders' Equity
+20,100	
+26,400	
−46,500	

On September 30, Redbird Corporation received cash dividends of $300 from IMG and $200 from ABC, which are recorded by the following entry:[3]

Date	Account and Explanation	Debit	Credit
	Cash	500	
	Dividend Income		500

Assets = Liabilities +	Stockholders' Equity
+500	+500

On December 20, the market price of IMG stock had climbed to $4,900, and Redbird decided to sell its entire holding. The following entry records the sale:

Date	Account and Explanation	Debit	Credit
	Cash	4,900	
	Investments—Trading Securities		4,100
	Gain on Sale of Investments		800

Assets = Liabilities +	Stockholders' Equity
+4,900	+800
−4,100	

The $800 gain will be included in Redbird Corporation's year-end net income, as will the $300 dividend received on September 30. In summary, this investment yielded two forms of income—dividends ($300) and a gain on sale ($800)—giving Redbird Corporation additional net income of $1,100.

---

[3] Dividend income should be recognized by investors at the dividend declaration date rather than the dividend payment date. When a cash dividend is declared in one year and paid in the following year, the investor should record the dividend declaration at year-end by a debit to dividends receivable and a credit to dividend income. In the following year, when the related cash is received, the investor should debit cash and credit dividends receivable.

Exhibit 4-9

Investment Portfolio Data

**Redbird Corporation
Investment Portfolio
December 31, 2009**

Security	Classification	Acquisition Cost	Market Value at 12/31
Illinois Enterprises	Trading	$ 10,000	$ 8,800
Metzler Design	Trading	6,000	6,400
Total Trading Securities		**$16,000**	**$15,200**
Alabama Co.	AFS	$ 8,100	$ 8,600
Mutare, Inc.	AFS	6,300	6,500
ABC	AFS	12,000	13,500
Total Available-for-Sale Securities		**$26,400**	**$28,600**

In addition, Mutare, Metzler Design, and Alabama Co. (the three debt securities) pay interest totaling $1,500 on December 31, which is recorded with the following entry:

	Stockholders'
Assets = Liabilities +	Equity
+1,500	+1,500

Date	Account and Explanation	Debit	Credit
	Cash	1,500	
	Interest Income		1,500

On the balance sheet, both trading and available-for-sale securities are recorded at fair value. Use of the fair value method results in "unrealized holding gains and losses" because the value of the securities must be written up or down to fair market value at the balance sheet date (this is often called "marking to market"). For example, consider the following securities shown in Exhibit 4-9.

On December 31, Redbird Corporation would make the following entries to "mark the investments to market":

	Stockholders'
Assets = Liabilities +	Equity
+2,200	+2,200

Date	Account and Explanation	Debit	Credit
	Allowance to Adjust Available-for-Sales Securities to Market	2,200	
	Unrealized Gain on Available-for-Sale Securities		2,200*

*Recognize that for Available-for-sale securities any unrealized Gain or loss goes to the "other comprehensive income" portion of stockholders' equity—not to the income statement.

	Stockholders'
Assets = Liabilities +	Equity
−800	−800

Date	Account and Explanation	Debit	Credit
	Unrealized Loss on Trading Securities	800*	
	Allowance to Adjust Trading Securities to Market		800

*Recognize that for trading securities any unrealized gain or loss goes to the income statement.

The allowance accounts (both Available-for-Sale and Trading) are valuation accounts containing the unrealized gains and losses on the short-term investment portfolio (Available-for-Sale and Trading, respectively). Valuation accounts are used to record changes in the fair values of the investments so that the investment accounts (both Available-for-Sale and Trading) reflect the original cost. At the balance sheet date, the allowance accounts are adjusted to reflect the current amount of unrealized gain or loss in the investment portfolio. On the balance sheet, the allowance accounts are netted with the respective investment accounts (i.e., added if the allowance has a debit balance and subtracted if it has a credit balance) to report the investments at fair value as follows:

Redbird Corporation
Partial Balance Sheet
December 31, 2009

Current Assets:		
Trading securities, at cost	$16,000	
Less: Allowance to adjust trading securities to market	800	
Trading securities, at market		$15,200*
Noncurrent Assets:		
Available-for-sale securities, at cost	$26,400	
Add: Allowance to adjust available-for-sale securities to market	2,200	
Available-for-sale securities, at market		$28,600*

*While trading securities will always be classified as current assets, available-for-sale securities are classified as current or noncurrent assets depending on whether they will be sold within one year or one operating cycle, whichever is longer.

To summarize, the debits and credits for trading securities and available-for-sale securities are identical. The only difference is that unrealized gains and losses affect the financial statements differently. Specifically, unrealized gains and losses for trading securities are included on the income statement and, thus, flow into retained earnings. Unrealized gains and losses for available-for-sale securities, on the other hand, are *not* included on the income statement; instead, they are included as part of "other comprehensive income" a separate account in stockholders' equity.

Summary of Appendix Learning Objectives

LO7.   Describe the classification and accounting for investments.
- Investments in equity securities are classified as:
    - trading securities
    - available-for-sale securities
- Investments in debt securities are classified as:
    - trading securities
    - available-for-sale securities
    - held-to-maturity (equity securities cannot be classified as held-to-maturity because equity does not have a maturity date)
- Held-to-maturity securities are accounted for at amortized cost, but this is discussed in Chapter 9.
- The debits and credits for trading and available-for-sale securities are identical.
- Both trading and available-for-sale securities are valued at fair market value on the balance sheet, which results in "unrealized gains and losses" (these are differences between the purchase price and fair market value at the balance sheet date).
- The only difference is that any unrealized gains or losses for trading securities go to the income statement while available-for-sale securities bypass the income statement and go to "other comprehensive income"—a separate category in stockholders' equity.

Appendix Key Terms

Available-for-sale securities, 202   Trading securities, 202
Held-to-maturity, 202

Review Problem

Bank Reconciliation

Fugazi Enterprises has the following information in its accounting records for their primary checking account:

Balance at April 30	$ 18,350
Checks written during May	114,700
Deposits during May	112,200

Fugazi's May bank statement contained the following information:

Balance per bank at April 30		$ 19,800
Credits during May:		
Deposits		109,600
Debits during May:		
Checks paid	$107,400	
Debit memo (May utilities)	8,000	
Bank service charge	80	115,480
Balance per bank at May 31		$ 13,920

The April bank reconciliation had deposits in transit of $850 and outstanding checks of $2,300. All these items cleared during May. These were the only reconciling items in April.

Required:

1. Prepare a bank reconciliation at May 31.
2. Prepare any adjusting entries necessary because of the bank reconciliation.

Solution:

1.

Cash Balance from Bank Statement		$13,920
Add: Deposits in Transit	$112,200 − ($109,600 − $850)*	3,450
Less: Outstanding Checks	$114,700 − ($107,400 − $2,300)**	(9,600)
Adjusted Cash Balance		**$ 7,770**
Cash Balance from Company Records	($18,350 + $112,200 − $114,700)	$15,850
Add:		
Less:		
Debit Memo (utilities)	$8,000	
Service Charge	80	(8,080)
Adjusted Cash Balance		**$ 7,770**

*$112,200 were deposited during May, but the account was only credited for $109,600 during May. However, this $109,600 included $850 that was in transit at April 30, so only $108,750 ($109,600 − $850) of the May deposits were credited to our account.
**$114,700 in checks were written in May and $107,400 in checks cleared the bank during May. However, this $107,400 included $2,300 in checks that were outstanding from April, so only $105,100 ($107,400 − $2,300) in checks cleared that were written in May.

2.

Date	Account and Explanation	Debit	Credit
May 31	Utilities Expense	8,000	
	Bank Service Charge Expense	80	
	Cash		8,080

Assets = Liabilities +	Stockholders' Equity
−8,080	−8,000
	−80

Discussion Questions

1. What is the purpose of an internal control system?
2. Internal control systems include policies and procedures to do what?

3. Section 404 of the Sarbanes-Oxley Act increased top management's responsibility for what?
4. What are the five elements of internal control?
5. What is meant by "tone at the top"? Why is it so important to an effective system of internal controls?
6. What are strategic risks?
7. What are business process risks?
8. What are the five categories of control activities?
9. How do these control activities help protect a company against error, theft, and fraud?
10. How do control activities relate to the accounting system?
11. Why does a company give particular attention to internal controls for cash?
12. Why is it important to segregate the duties for handling cash from the duties for keeping the accounting records for cash?
13. Describe two advantages of performing reconciliations of the cash account to the balances on the bank statements.
14. Describe the potential sources of difference between a cash account and its associated bank statement balance.
15. What kinds of bank reconciliation items require the firm to make adjusting entries?
16. Describe how cash over and short can be used for internal control purposes.
17. Why do most companies have petty cash funds?
18. What are cash equivalents?
19. Why do companies invest their cash in short-term investments?
20. What is the difference between the financing and operating cycles?
21. Describe the basic cash management principles.
22. Why do companies hold short-term investments?
23. How do available-for-sale securities differ from trading securities?
24. What is the allowance to adjust short-term investments to market and why is it used?

Multiple-Choice Exercises

4-1 What is the primary role of internal controls in managing a business?

a. To ensure that no cash is stolen.
b. To ensure that the financial statements are presented in such a manner as to provide relevant and reliable information for financial statement users and the company's creditors.
c. To encourage theft and to ensure that segregation of duties does not take place.
d. To constrain subordinates' activities in order to ensure that employees do not deviate from the scope of their responsibilities and that they act in the best interest of the business.

4-2 Which of the following is *not* one of the three areas for which internal control systems are intended to provide reasonable assurance?

a. Effectiveness and efficiency of operations
b. Certification that the financial statements are without error
c. Reliability of financial reporting
d. Compliance with applicable laws and regulations

4-3 Which of the following is *not* one of the five elements of internal control?

a. Analysis of control procedures
b. Control environment
c. Risk assessment
d. Information and communication

4-4 Which of the following is *not* one of the five categories of control activities?

a. Segregation of duties
b. Clearly defined authority and responsibility
c. Defalcation and financial reporting
d. Checks on recorded amounts

4-5 The internal audit function is part of what element of the internal control system?

a. Control Activities
b. Risk Assessment
c. Control Environment
d. Monitoring

4-6 Which of the following is *not* generally an internal control activity?

a. Establishing clear lines of authority to carry out specific tasks
b. Physically counting inventory in a perpetual inventory system
c. Reducing the cost of hiring seasonal employees
d. Limiting access to computerized accounting records

4-7 Allowing only certain employees to order goods and services for the company is an example of what internal control procedure?

a. Segregation of duties
b. Safeguarding of assets and records
c. Independent verifications
d. Proper authorizations

4-8 Deposits made by a company but not yet reflected in a bank statement are called

a. Deposits in transit
b. Credit memoranda
c. Debit memoranda
d. None of the above

4-9 Which one of the following would *not* appear on a bank statement for a checking account?

a. Service charges
b. Interest earned
c. Outstanding checks
d. Deposits

4-10 Which one of the following is *not* a cash equivalent?

a. 30-day certificate of deposit
b. 60-day corporate commercial paper
c. 90-day U.S. Treasury bill
d. 180-day note issued by a local or state government

4-11 Business activity is best described as:

a. predictable
b. lacking deviation
c. cyclical
d. noncyclical

4-12 The five primary activities of a business generally consist of:

a. receiving assets, selling assets, issuing financial statements, collecting cash, and making cash disbursements
b. receiving assets, purchasing assets, selling goods or services, collecting cash from customers, and repaying owners and creditors
c. receiving cash, disbursing cash, buying assets, issuing dividends, and paying off liabilities
d. making a profit, issuing financial statements, repaying debts, issuing dividends to shareholders, and complying with laws and regulations

4-13 Effective cash management and control includes all of the following *except*:

a. The use of a petty cash fund
b. Bank reconciliations
c. Short-term investments of excess cash
d. Purchase of stocks and bonds

4-14 Cash management principles do *not* include:

a. paying suppliers promptly
b. delaying payment of suppliers
c. speeding up collection from customers
d. earning the greatest return possible on excess cash

4-15 Which one of the following statements is *true*?

a. Good cash management practices dictate that a company should maintain as large a balance as possible in its cash account.
b. Sound internal control practice dictates that cash disbursements should be made by check, unless the disbursement is very small.
c. The person handling the cash should also prepare the bank reconciliation.
d. Petty cash can be substituted for a checking account to expedite the payment of all disbursements.

4-16 (Appendix) Investments in equity securities are deemed to be "passive" if:

a. 100 percent of the firm's stock is owned
b. between 50 percent and 100 percent of the firm's stock is owned
c. between 20 percent and 50 percent of the firm's stock is owned
d. less than 20 percent of the firm's stock is owned

4-17 (Appendix) Equity and debt investments that management intends to sell in the future, but not necessarily in the near term, are called:

a. Trading securities
b. Available-for-sale securities
c. Debt securities
d. Stock securities

4-18 (Appendix) When the market value of a company's available-for-sale securities is lower than its cost, the difference should be:

a. shown as a liability
b. shown as a valuation allowance subtracted from the historical cost of the investments
c. shown as a valuation allowance added to the historical cost of the investments
d. no entry is made, the securities are shown at historical cost

Cornerstone Exercises

OBJECTIVE ▶ 1

Cornerstone Exercise 4-19 ROLE OF INTERNAL CONTROL

Internal controls play a crucial role in a business.

Required:

Discuss why internal controls are important. What are the potential consequences of an internal control failure?

OBJECTIVE ▶ 2

Cornerstone Exercise 4-20 ELEMENTS OF INTERNAL CONTROL

The Committee of Sponsoring Organizations of the Treadway Commission (COSO) discussed five elements of internal control.

Required:

Define and discuss these five elements of internal control.

OBJECTIVE ▶ 3

CORNERSTONE 4-1

Cornerstone Exercise 4-21 BANK RECONCILIATION

Firebird Corp. prepares monthly bank reconciliations of its checking account balance. The bank statement for May 2009 indicated the following:

Balance, May 31, 2009	$29,700
Service charge for May	80
Interest earned during May	120
NSF check from Valerie Corp. (deposited by Firebird)	230
Note ($4,000) and interest ($100) collected for	
Firebird from a customer of Firebird's	4,100

An analysis of canceled checks and deposits and the records of Firebird Corp. revealed the following items:

Checking account balance per Firebird's books	$26,040
Outstanding checks as of May 31	2,950
Deposit in transit at May 31	3,110
Error in recording check #4456 issued by Firebird	90

The correct amount of check #4456 is $760. It was recorded as a cash disbursement of $670 by mistake. The check was issued to pay for merchandise purchases. The check appeared on the bank statement correctly.

Required:

Prepare a bank reconciliation schedule at May 31, 2009, in proper form.

OBJECTIVE ▶ 3

CORNERSTONE 4-2

Cornerstone Exercise 4-22 ADJUSTING ENTRY FROM BANK RECONCILIATION

A customer paid for merchandise with a check that has been erroneously entered into Mutare's cash account for $48 (it actually has been issued and paid for $84).

Required:

Record the appropriate journal entry to correct the error.

OBJECTIVE ▶ 3

CORNERSTONE 4-2

Cornerstone Exercise 4-23 ADJUSTING ENTRY FROM BANK RECONCILIATION

Pyramid Corporation is assessed a $25 fee as the result of a $62 NSF check. Neither the fee nor the NSF check has been accounted for on Pyramid's books.

Required:

Record the appropriate journal entry to update Pyramid's books.

Cornerstone Exercise 4-24 **BANK RECONCILIATION**

OBJECTIVE ▶ 3
CORNERSTONE 4-1

The accountant for Bellows Corp. was preparing a bank reconciliation as of April 30, 2009. The following items were identified:

Bellows' book balance	$46,200
Outstanding checks	1,100
Interest earned on checking account	50
Customer's NSF check returned by the bank	500

In addition, Bellows made an error in recording a customer's check; the amount was recorded in cash receipts as $150; the bank recorded the amount correctly as $510.

Required:

What amount will Bellows report as its adjusted cash balance at April 30, 2009?

Cornerstone Exercise 4-25 **BANK RECONCILIATION**

OBJECTIVE ▶ 3
CORNERSTONE 4-1
CORNERSTONE 4-2

Tiny Corp. prepares monthly bank reconciliations of its checking account balance. The bank statement for October 2009 indicated the following:

Balance, October 31, 2009	$7,920
Service charge for October	20
Interest earned during October	30
NSF check from Green Corp. (deposited by Tiny)	32
Note ($1,000) and interest ($40) collected for Tiny	
from a customer	1,040

An analysis of canceled checks and deposits and the records of Tiny revealed the following items:

Checking account balance per Tiny's books	$7,170
Outstanding checks as of October 31	952
Deposit in transit at October 31	1,310
Error in recording a check issued by Tiny. (Correct amount of the check is $450, but was recorded as a cash disbursement of $540. The check was issued to pay for merchandise originally purchased on account.)	90

Required:

1. Prepare a bank reconciliation at October 31, 2009, in proper form.
2. Record any necessary adjusting journal entries.

Cornerstone Exercise 4-26 **CASH OVER AND SHORT**

OBJECTIVE ▶ 3

On a recent day, Pence Company obtained the following data from its cash registers:

	Cash Sales per Register Tape	Cash in Register after Removing Opening Change
Register 1	$12,656.12	$12,649.81
Register 2	11,429.57	11,432.16
Register 3	11,591.18	11,590.18

Pence deposits its cash receipts in its bank account daily.

Required:

Prepare a journal entry to record these cash sales.

OBJECTIVE ▶ 3

Cornerstone Exercise 4-27 CASH OVER AND SHORT

Walker Department Store has one cash register. On a recent day, the cash register tape reported sales in the amount of $2,247.63. Actual cash in the register (after deducting and removing the opening change amount of $50) was $2,238.48, which was deposited in the firm's bank account.

Required:

Prepare a journal entry to record these cash collections.

OBJECTIVE ▶ 3
CORNERSTONE 4-3

Cornerstone Exercise 4-28 PETTY CASH FUND

Murphy, Inc., maintains a balance of $1,000 in its petty cash fund. On December 31, 2009, Murphy's petty cash account has a balance of $425. Murphy replenishes the petty cash account to bring it back up to $1,000.

Required:

What entry is made to record the replenishment of the petty cash fund?

OBJECTIVE ▶ 3
CORNERSTONE 4-3

Cornerstone Exercise 4-29 PETTY CASH WITH CHANGE IN FUND BALANCE

Basque, Inc., maintains a petty cash fund with a balance of $500. On December 31, 2009, Basque's petty cash account has a balance of $275. Murphy replenishes the petty cash account, as it does at the end of every month, but also decides to increase the balance to $750.

Required:

What entry is made to record this activity?

OBJECTIVE ▶ 4

Cornerstone Exercise 4-30 CASH REPORTING

Brown Industries has the following items:

Currency	$20,000
Customer checks that have not been deposited	500
Cash in saving and checking accounts	80,000
Certificates of deposits that originally matured in 18 months	25,000
U.S. government bonds that originally matured in 3 months	12,000
U.S. government bonds that originally matured in 12 months	18,000

Required:

How much should Brown report as cash and equivalents on its balance sheet?

OBJECTIVE ▶ 5

Cornerstone Exercise 4-31 FINANCING AND OPERATING CYCLES

Business activity is often described as being cyclical in nature.

Required:

Describe the cyclical nature of business activity. Make sure to discuss the operating and financing cycle.

OBJECTIVE ▶ 5

Cornerstone Exercise 4-32 OPERATING CYCLE

Businesses must decide whether to issue credit to customers.

Required:

Describe how selling to customers on credit affects the operating cycle.

OBJECTIVE ▶ 6

Cornerstone Exercise 4-33 CASH MANAGEMENT

Effective cash management is very important to the operating performance of a business.

Required:

Explain the principles of cash management. Why might it be advantageous to delay paying suppliers?

Cornerstone Exercise 4-34 (APPENDIX) TRADING SECURITIES

OBJECTIVE ➤ 7

Franzen Finance began operations in 2009 and invests in securities classified as trading securities. During 2009, it entered into the following trading security transactions:

Purchased 20,000 shares of ABC common stock at $38 per share
Purchased 32,000 shares of XYZ common stock at $17 per share

At December 31, 2009, ABC common stock was trading at $39.50 per share and XYZ common stock was trading at $16.50 per share.

Required:

1. Provide the necessary adjusting entry to value the available-for-sale securities at fair market value.
2. What is the income statement effect of this adjusting entry?

Cornerstone Exercise 4-35 (APPENDIX) AVAILABLE-FOR-SALE SECURITIES

OBJECTIVE ➤ 7

Tolland Financial began operations in 2010 and invests in securities classified as available for sale. During 2010, it entered into the following available-for-sale security transactions:

Purchased 10,000 shares of DTR common stock at $50 per share
Purchased 44,000 shares of MJO common stock at $22 per share

At December 31, 2010, DTR common stock was trading at $62 per share and MJO common stock was trading at $21 per share.

Required:

1. Provide the necessary adjusting entry to value the available-for-sale securities at fair market value.
2. What is the income statement effect of this adjusting entry?

Exercises

Exercise 4-36 INTERNAL CONTROL SYSTEM

OBJECTIVE ➤ 1 2

Required:

A list of terms and another list of definitions and examples are presented below. Make a list numbered 1 through 5 and match the letter of the most directly related definition or example with the number of each term.

Term	Definition or Example
1. Control environment	a. The internal audit group is testing the operating effectiveness of various internal control activities.
2. Strategic risk	
3. Business process risk	b. A member of upper management was fired for violating the company's code of conduct.
4. Monitoring	
5. Information and communication	c. Reports documenting problems with production are forwarded to management.
	d. Competitors begin offering extended warranty coverage on products.
	e. Problems with our suppliers have resulted in lost sales because our stores were out of stock.

Exercise 4-37 INTERNAL CONTROL TERMINOLOGY

OBJECTIVE ➤ 1 2

Required:

A list of terms and another list of definitions and examples are presented below. Make a list numbered 1 through 7 and match the letter of the most directly related definition or example with the number of each term.

Term	Definition or Example
1. Internal control structure	a. Company policy prevents accountants from handling cash.
2. Accounting controls	b. Company policy requires receiving reports to be made for all deliveries by suppliers.
3. Segregation of duties	c. Cash deposits are reconciled with cash register records at the end of every day.
4. Adequate documents and records	d. This includes the accounting system, all policies and procedures of the business, and the environment in which they operate.
5. Safeguards over assets and records	e. Every evening, a jewelry store removes all items of merchandise valued at over $100 from its display cases.
6. Checks on recorded amounts	f. These are policies and procedures that govern the identification, measurement, recording, and communication of economic information.
7. Effective personnel policies	g. Every new employee is required to spend two days in training courses to learn company policies.

OBJECTIVE ▶ 2   Exercise 4-38 **CLASSIFYING INTERNAL CONTROL PROCEDURES**

Required:

Match each of the control procedures listed below with the most closely related control procedures type. Your answer should pair each of the numbers 1 through 10 with the appropriate letter.

Control Procedure Types
A. Clearly defined authority and responsibility
B. Segregation of duties
C. Adequate documents and records
D. Safeguards over assets and records
E. Checks on recorded amounts

Control Procedures
1. The controller is required to sign the daily summary of expenditures to authorize payment.
2. Division managers are evaluated annually on the basis of their division's profitability.
3. Invoices received from outside suppliers are filed with purchase orders.
4. Employees with access to the accounting records are not permitted to open the mail, because it contains many payments by check from customers.
5. The extent of access to the many segments of the company's computer system is tightly controlled by individual identification cards and passwords that change at regular intervals.
6. Each shipment to customers from inventory is recorded on a specially printed form bearing a sequential number; these forms are the basis for entries into the computer system, which makes entries to inventory records and produces periodic reports of sales and shipments.
7. At regular intervals, internal audit reviews a sample of expenditure transactions to determine that payment has been made to a bona fide supplier and that the related goods or services were received and appropriately used.
8. A construction company stores large steel girders in an open yard surrounded by a 5-foot fence and stores welding supplies in a controlled-access, tightly secured concrete building.
9. Cash registers display the price of each item purchased to the customer as it is recorded and produce a customer receipt that describes each item and gives its price.

10. The person in the controller's office who prepares and mails checks to suppliers cannot make entries in the general ledger system.

Exercise 4-39 INTERNAL CONTROL OF CASH

OBJECTIVE ➤ 2 3

Edward Thompson, a longtime employee of a small grocery wholesaler, is responsible for maintaining the company's cash records and for opening the daily mail, through which the company receives about 40 percent of its daily cash receipts. Virtually all cash received by mail is in the form of checks made payable to the company. Thompson is also responsible for preparing deposits of currency and checks for the bank at the end of each day.

Required:

1. Explain briefly how Thompson might be able to steal some of the company's cash receipts.
2. What internal control procedures would you recommend to prevent this theft?

Exercise 4-40 CASH OVER AND SHORT

OBJECTIVE ➤ 3

Miller Enterprises deposits the cash received during each day at the end of the day. Miller deposited $12,730 on October 3 and $15,610 on October 4. Cash register records and other documents supporting the deposits are summarized as follows:

	10/3	10/4
Cash sales	$ 4,072	$ 5,405
Collections on account	8,650	10,212
Total receipts	$12,722	$15,617

Required:

1. Calculate the amount of cash over or cash short for each day.
2. Prepare the journal entry to record the receipt and deposit of cash on October 3.
3. Prepare the journal entry to record the receipt and deposit of cash on October 4.

Exercise 4-41 BANK RECONCILIATION

OBJECTIVE ➤ 3

Johnson Corporation's bank statement for October reports an ending balance of $6,248, whereas Johnson's cash account shows a balance of $5,680 on October 31. The following additional information is available:

a. A $165 deposit made on October 31 was not recorded by the bank until November.
b. At the end of October, outstanding checks total $792.
c. The bank statement shows bank service charges of $20 not yet recorded by the company.
d. The company erroneously recorded for $397 a check actually written and paid by the bank for $379.
e. A $57 check from a customer, deposited by the company on October 29, was returned with the bank statement for lack of funds.

Required:

Prepare the October bank reconciliation for Johnson Corporation.

Exercise 4-42 BANK RECONCILIATION

OBJECTIVE ➤ 3

The cash account for Fleming Company contains the following information for April:

Cash balance, 3/31	$ 3,500
Cash received during April	21,400
	$24,900

Cash disbursements during April:

Check 7164	$11,000	
Check 7165	1,800	
Check 7166	3,900	
Check 7167	6,100	22,800
Cash balance, 4/30		$ 2,100

The bank statement for April contains the following information:

Bank balance, 3/31		$11,800
Add: Deposits during April		21,400
		$33,200
Less: Checks paid during April:		
Check 7162	$ 5,200	
Check 7163	3,100	
Check 7164	11,000	
Check 7165	1,800	21,100
Bank balance, 4/30		$12,100

Required:
1. Identify the outstanding checks at April 30.
2. Prepare the reconciliation of the bank and cash account balances at April 30.
3. Identify the outstanding checks at March 31.
4. Prepare the reconciliation of the bank and cash account balances at March 31.

OBJECTIVE ⟩ 3   Exercise 4-43 **BANK RECONCILIATION**

Valentine Investigations has the following information for its cash account:

Balance, 1/31	$ 5,030
Deposits during February	93,160
Checks written during February	92,270

Valentine's bank statement for February contained the following information:

Balance per bank, 1/31		$ 6,730
Add: February deposits		90,190
		$96,920
Less: Checks paid in February	$89,790	
Bank service charge	80	
Debit memo (electric bill)	630	90,500
Balance per bank, 2/28		$ 6,420

A comparison of company records with the bank statement provided the following data:

	At 1/31	At 2/28
Deposits in transit	$ 510	$3,480
Outstanding checks	2,210	4,690

Required:
1. Prepare a bank reconciliation.
2. Prepare adjusting entries for Valentine based on the information developed in the bank reconciliation.

Exercise 4-44 ADJUSTING ENTRIES FROM A BANK RECONCILIATION

OBJECTIVE ➤ 3

Cooper Advisory Services identified the following items on its October reconciliation that may require adjusting entries:

a. A deposit of $260 was recorded in Cooper's accounting records, but not on the October 31 bank statement.
b. A check for $6,430 was outstanding at October 31.
c. Included with the bank statement was a check for $250 written by Hooper Advertising Services. The bank had, in error, deducted this check from Cooper's account.
d. Bank service charges were $120.
e. An NSF check written by one of Cooper's customers in the amount of $1,290 was returned by the bank with Cooper's bank statement.

Required:

For each of these five items, prepare an adjusting entry for Cooper's journal, if any is required.

Exercise 4-45 RECORDING PETTY CASH ACCOUNT TRANSACTIONS

OBJECTIVE ➤ 3

During March, Anderson Company engaged in the following transactions involving its petty cash fund:

a. On March 1, Anderson Company established the petty cash fund by issuing a check for $400 to the fund custodian.
b. On March 4, the custodian paid $176 out of petty cash for freight charges on new furniture.
c. On March 12, the custodian paid $87 out of petty cash for office supplies.
d. On March 22, the custodian paid $22 out of petty cash for express mail services for reports sent to the Environmental Protection Agency.
e. On March 25, the custodian filed a claim for reimbursement of petty cash expenditures during the month totaling $285.
f. On March 31, Anderson issued a check for $285 to the custodian, replenishing the fund for expenditures during the month.

Required:

Prepare the journal entries required to record the petty cash account transactions that occurred during the month of March.

Exercise 4-46 COMPONENTS OF CASH

OBJECTIVE ➤ 4

The office manager for Bullock Products had accumulated the following information at the end of a recent year:

Item	Amount
Accounts receivable	$16,450
Change for cash registers (currency and coin)	2,500
Amount on deposit in checking account	9,280
Amount on deposit in savings account	25,000
Balance in petty cash	300
Checks received from customers, but not yet deposited in bank	430
Checks sent by Bullock to suppliers, but not yet presented at bank for payment	670
Deposits in transit	1,240
IOU from Gerry Bullock, company president	1,000
Notes receivable	10,000
NSF check written by Johnson Company	320
Prepaid postage	250

Required:

Calculate the amount for cash in Bullock's balance sheet.

OBJECTIVE ▶ 5

Exercise 4-47 OPERATING CYCLE

A list of businesses is presented below:

Business	Operating-Cycle Description
1. Appliance store 2. Clothing store 3. Electric utility 4. Tree nursery 5. Fast food restaurant	a. Very short—customers typically pay cash, and inventory is often held less than one day. b. A few months—merchandise is typically on hand for several weeks, and some customers may use credit. c. More than one year—merchandise may be in inventory for several months, and most customers will pay for purchases after one or two years. d. Several years—a number of years are required to prepare merchandise for sale. Customers probably pay cash for most items. e. A few months—customers pay monthly. The current assets used to provide customer services are consumed within a few months.

Required:

Match each business with a description of the operating cycle for that business.

OBJECTIVE ▶ 5

Exercise 4-48 FINANCING AND OPERATING CYCLES

Which of the following activities belong to the operating cycle, and which belong to the financial cycle?

a. Collection of cash from customers
b. Payment of dividends to stockholders
c. Acquisition of goods for resale
d. Borrowing of cash from a bank
e. Receipt of cash from owners in exchange for capital stock
f. Performance of services for customers
g. Acquisition of raw materials for manufacture of salable products
h. Repayment to a lender of an amount borrowed
i. Delivery of goods to customers

OBJECTIVE ▶ 5

Exercise 4-49 OPERATING CYCLE AND CURRENT RECEIVABLES

For each of the businesses described below, indicate the length of the operating cycle and the duration of the longest receivable that can be classified as current on the business's balance sheet.

a. Dither and Sly are attorneys-at-law who specialize in federal income tax law. They complete their typical case in six months or less and collect from the typical client within one additional month.
b. Johnston's Market specializes in fresh meat and fish. All merchandise must be sold within one week of purchase. Most sales are for cash, and any receivables are generally paid by the end of the following month.
c. Mortondo's is a women's clothing store specializing in high-style merchandise. Merchandise spends an average of seven months on the rack following purchase. Most sales are on credit, and the typical customer pays within one month of sale.
d. Trees, Inc., grows Christmas trees and sells them to various Christmas tree lots. Most receivables are paid within a month of delivery of the trees. It takes six years to grow a tree.

OBJECTIVE ▶ 7

Exercise 4-50 (APPENDIX) ALLOWANCE FOR AVAILABLE-FOR-SALE SECURITIES

McCarthy Corporation's allowance to reduce available-for-sale securities to market is $7,200 on December 31 (i.e., it is a credit balance), before the lower-of-cost-or-market adjustment. The cost and market value of the available-for-sale portfolio at December 31 are $120,000 and $117,000, respectively.

Required:

Prepare the adjusting entry, if any, to adjust the allowance at year-end.

Exercise 4-51 (APPENDIX) ADJUSTING THE ALLOWANCE TO ADJUST TRADING SECURITIES TO MARKET

OBJECTIVE ➤ 7

Perry Corporation has the following information for its portfolio of trading securities at the end of the past four years:

Date	Portfolio Cost	Portfolio Market Value
12/31/06	$162,300	$153,800
12/31/07	109,600	106,200
12/31/08	148,900	151,300
12/31/09	139,000	138,700

Required:

1. Prepare the journal entries, if necessary, to adjust the allowance account at the end of 2007, 2008, and 2009.
2. What is the income statement effect of the 2009 entry?
3. How would your answer to 2 change if this was an available-for-sale portfolio?

Exercise 4-52 (APPENDIX) INVESTMENTS IN AVAILABLE-FOR-SALE SECURITIES

OBJECTIVE ➤ 7

Williams Corporation acquired the following equity securities during 2009:

200 shares of Southwestern Company capital stock	$14,600
500 shares of Montgomery Products capital stock	14,500

Williams's investment in both of these companies is passive and Williams classifies these securities as available-for-sale. During 2009, Southwestern paid a dividend of $1.20 per share, and Montgomery paid a dividend of $1.80 per share. At December 31, 2009, the Southwestern stock has a market value of $75 per share, and the Montgomery stock has a market value of $25 per share.

Required:

1. Prepare entries for Williams's journal to record these two investments and the receipt of the dividends.
2. Calculate the market value of Williams's investment portfolio at December 31, 2009.
3. Provide the necessary adjusting entry at December 31, 2009.
4. How would these securities be disclosed on the December 31, 2009, balance sheet?

Problem Set A

Problem 4-53A ROLE OF INTERNAL CONTROL

OBJECTIVE ➤ 1 2

Internal control systems include policies and procedures designed to provide reasonable assurance that the corporation's objectives are being met in three areas:

a. effectiveness and efficiency of operations
b. reliability of financial reporting
c. compliance with applicable laws and regulations

Like any other business, a grocery store uses internal control activities to meet their objectives in these three areas.

Required:

Attempt to name a control for each area and describe how the control helps accomplish the store's objectives in these areas.

OBJECTIVE ▶ 2 3   ### Problem 4-54A INTERNAL CONTROL PROCEDURES FOR CASH RECEIPTS

Corey and Dee Post are planning to open and operate a 24-hour convenience store near a university campus. Corey and Dee are concerned that part of the cash that customers pay for merchandise might be kept by some of the store's employees.

Required:

Identify some internal control procedures that could help ensure that all cash paid by customers is remitted to the business.

OBJECTIVE ▶ 2 3   ### Problem 4-55A INTERNAL CONTROL FOR CASH

After comparing cash register tapes with inventory records, the accountant for Benning Convenience Stores is concerned that someone at one of the stores is not recording some of that store's cash sales and is stealing the cash from the unreported sales.

Required:

1. Explain why a comparison of sales and inventory records would reveal a situation in which cash sales are not being recorded and cash from those sales is being stolen.
2. Describe how an employee might be able to steal cash from sales.
3. What internal control procedure would you recommend be employed to make the theft you described in 2 more difficult?

OBJECTIVE ▶ 3   ### Problem 4-56A BANK RECONCILIATION

Shortly after July 31, Morse Corporation received a bank statement containing the following information:

Date		Checks			Deposits	Balance
6/30	Beg. balance					$ 7,958
7/1					$ 1,200	9,158
7/2		$ 620	$ 550	$ 344	12,500	20,144
7/3		35	8,100			12,009
7/5		311	97	4,000	9,100	16,701
7/9		4,500	790	286		11,125
7/12		34	7,100			3,991
7/15		634	1,880		7,000	8,477
7/19		3,780	414			4,283
7/24		1,492	649			2,142
7/29		350	677*		4,620	5,735
7/31		575	18**			5,142

*NSF check
**Bank service charge

December cash transactions and balances on Morse's records are shown in the following T-account:

Cash

Balance, 6/60	**$7,609**				
Date	Amount Deposited	Check Number	Check Amount	Check Number	Check Amount
7/1	$12,500	176	$8,100	186	$ 1,880
7/5	9,100	177	97	187	634
7/15	7,000	178	4,000	188	3,780
7/29	4,620	179	311	189	649
7/30	2,050	180	7,100	190	1,492
Total deposits	$35,270	181	4,500	191	37
		182	790	192	350
		183	34	193	575
		184	286	194	227
		185	414	195	1,123
				Total disbursements	$36,379
Balance, 7/31	**$ 6,500**				

Required:

1. Prepare a bank reconciliation for July.
2. Prepare the adjusting entries made by Morse Corporation as a result of this reconciliation process.
3. What amount is reported as cash on the balance sheet at July 31?

Problem 4-57A **BANK RECONCILIATION**

OBJECTIVE ➤ 3

Raymond Corporation received the following bank statement for the month of October 2009:

Date		Checks			Deposits	Balance
9/30 Beg. balance						$ 4,831.50
10/2	$1,204.50				$2,970.18	6,597.18
10/4	43.80	$ 321.70				6,231.68
10/8	905.36					5,326.32
10/10	100.20		60.00	$38.11		5,128.01
10/13					4,000.00	9,128.01
10/14	290.45*					8,837.56
10/17	516.11	309.24				8,012.21
10/19	106.39	431.15	21.72		2,850.63	10,303.58
10/21	3,108.42					7,195.16
10/23	63.89					7,131.27
10/25	290.00**	111.90				6,729.37
10/27	88.90					6,640.47
10/31	20.00***	1,308.77				5,311.70

*NSF check
**Debit memo
***Service charge

The Cash in Bank account of Raymond Corporation provides the following information:

Date	Item	Debit	Credit	Balance
10/1	Balance from 9/30			$ 6,553.38
10/2	Check #1908		$ 321.70	6,231.68
10/5	Check #1909		905.36	5,326.32
10/6	Check #1910		100.20	5,226.12
10/6	Check #1911		60.00	5,166.12
10/7	Check #1912		38.11	5,128.01
10/12	Deposit #411	$4,000.00		9,128.01
10/15	Check #1913		516.11	8,611.90
10/16	Check #1914		309.24	8,302.66
10/17	Check #1915		431.15	7,871.51
10/17	Check #1916		21.72	7,849.79
10/18	Deposit #412	2,850.63		10,700.42
10/18	Check #1917		106.39	10,594.03
10/20	Check #1918		63.89	10,530.14
10/20	Check #1919		3,108.42	7,421.72
10/23	Check #1920		111.90	7,309.82
10/25	Check #1921		88.90	7,220.92
10/29	Check #1922		1,803.77	5,417.15
10/30	Check #1923		284.77	5,132.38
10/31	Check #1924		628.32	4,504.06
10/31	Deposit #413	3,408.20		7,912.26

The items on the bank statement are correct. The debit memo is for the payment by the bank of Raymond's office furniture rent for October.

Required:

1. Prepare a bank reconciliation. (Hint: There is one transposition error in the cash account.)
2. Prepare adjusting entries based on the bank reconciliation.
3. What amount is reported for cash in bank in the balance sheet at October 31?

OBJECTIVE ▸ 3 ## Problem 4-58A BANK RECONCILIATION

The cash account of Dixon Products reveals the following information:

Cash

Balance, 4/30	11,800		
Deposits during May	37,600	Checks written during May	41,620

The bank statement for May contains the following information:

Bank balance, 4/30		$11,750
Add: Deposits during May		37,250
		$49,000
Less: Checks paid during May	$40,230	
NSF check from Frolin, Inc.	190	
Bank service charges	40	40,460
Bank balance, 5/31		$ 8,540

A comparison of detailed company records with the bank statement indicates the following information:

	At 4/30	At 5/31
Deposit in transit	$800	$1,150
Outstanding checks	750	2,140

The bank amounts are determined to be correct.

Required:

1. Prepare a bank reconciliation for May.
2. Prepare the adjusting entries made by Dixon as a result of the reconciliation process.
3. What amount is reported for cash on the balance sheet at May 31?

OBJECTIVE ▸ 3 ## Problem 4-59A RECORDING PETTY CASH TRANSACTIONS

SCB, Inc., had a balance of $600 in cash in its petty cash fund at the beginning of September. The following transactions took place in September:

a. On September 4, the custodian paid $34 out of petty cash for new stationery on which the company president's name appeared prominently.
b. On September 11, the custodian paid $167 out of petty cash for maintenance manuals for the firm's new jet aircraft.
c. On September 15, the custodian paid $37 out of petty cash for transportation-in.
d. On September 23, the custodian paid $46 out of petty cash to have documents delivered to the lawyers who were defending the firm in a lawsuit.
e. On September 27, the custodian paid $231 out of petty cash to reimburse the president for costs he had incurred when bad weather prevented the company jet from landing to pick him up after a meeting.
f. On September 30, the custodian submitted receipts for the above expenditures and a check was drawn for the amount to replenish the fund.

Required:

Prepare the journal entries made by the corporation to record these transactions.

Problem 4-60A (APPENDIX) RECORDING AVAILABLE-FOR-SALE SECURITIES TRANSACTIONS INCLUDING A SALE AFTER ADJUSTMENT TO THE ALLOWANCE ACCOUNT

OBJECTIVE

Morton Products had no investment in available-for-sale securities at January 1, 2009. During 2009, Morton engaged in the following marketable security transactions:

a.   Purchased 400 shares of Sterling Company stock for $24 per share.
b.   Purchased 600 shares of Burt Corporation stock for $32 per share.
c.   Received a $2-per-share dividend on the Sterling stock.
d.   Sold 250 shares of the Sterling stock for $27 per share.

At the end of 2009, the Sterling stock had a market value of $26 per share, and the Burt stock had a market value of $29 per share.

Required:

1.   Prepare journal entries for each of the four transactions assuming they are classified as available-for-sale securities.
2.   If necessary, prepare a journal entry to recognize the December 31, 2009, market values. What is the income statement effect of this entry?
3.   How would these investments be reported on the December 31, 2009, balance sheet?

Problem 4-61A (APPENDIX) INVESTMENTS IN TRADING SECURITIES

OBJECTIVE

Maxwell Company engaged in the following transactions involving short-term investments:

a.   Purchased 200 shares of Bartco stock for $12,800.
b.   Received a $1.60-per-share dividend on the Bartco stock.
c.   Sold 40 shares of the Bartco stock for $61 per share.
d.   Purchased 380 shares of Newton stock for $20,900.
e.   Received a dividend of $1.00 per share on the Newton stock.

At December 31, the Bartco stock has a market value of $60 per share, and the Newton stock has a market value of $59 per share.

Required:

1.   Prepare entries for Maxwell's journal to record these transactions assuming they are trading securities.
2.   Calculate the market value of Maxwell's short-term investment portfolio at December 31.
3.   Provide the necessary adjusting entry at December 31.
4.   What is the income statement effect of the adjusting entry?
5.   How would these investments be reported on the December 31 balance sheet?

Problem Set B

Problem 4-53B ROLE OF INTERNAL CONTROL

OBJECTIVE

Internal control systems include policies and procedures designed to provide reasonable assurance that the corporation's objectives are being met in three areas:

a.   effectiveness and efficiency of operations
b.   reliability of financial reporting
c.   compliance with applicable laws and regulations

Like any other business, a bookstore uses internal control activities to meet its objectives in these three areas.

Required:

Attempt to name a control for each area and describe how the control helps accomplish the store's objectives in these areas.

OBJECTIVE ⟩ 2 3

Problem 4-54B **INTERNAL CONTROL PROCEDURES FOR CASH RECEIPTS**

Sean and Liz Kinsella are planning to open and operate a coffee shop on a university campus. Sean and Liz are concerned that part of the cash that customers pay for food might be kept by some of the store's employees.

Required:

Identify some internal control procedures that could help ensure that all cash paid by customers is remitted to the business.

OBJECTIVE ⟩ 2 3

Problem 4-55B **INTERNAL CONTROL FOR CASH**

After comparing cash register tapes with inventory records, the accountant for Good Times Music store is concerned that someone at one of the stores is not recording some of that store's cash sales and is stealing the cash from the unreported sales.

Required:

1. Explain why a comparison of sales and inventory records would reveal a situation in which cash sales are not being recorded and cash from those sales is being stolen.
2. Describe how an employee might be able to steal cash from sales.
3. What internal control procedure would you recommend be employed to make the theft you described in 2 more difficult?

OBJECTIVE ⟩ 3

Problem 4-56B **BANK RECONCILIATION**

Shortly after July 31, Towanda Corporation received a bank statement containing the following information:

Date		Checks			Deposits	Balance
6/30 Beg. balance						$ 6,500
7/1					$ 300	6,800
7/2	$ 270	$ 150	$ 330		4,500	10,550
7/3	25	7,025				3,500
7/5	150	450	1,400		10,000	11,500
7/9	1,500	25	325			9,650
7/12	500	100				9,050
7/15	1,600	2,700			3,500	8,250
7/19	75	425				7,750
7/24	650	550				6,550
7/29	275	525*				5,750
7/31	475	25**				5,250

*NSF check
**Bank service charge

     December cash transactions and balances on Towanda's records are shown in the following T-account:

Cash

Balance, 6/30		$5,550					
Date		Amount Deposited	Check Number	Check Amount	Check Number	Check Amount	
7/1		$ 300	176	$ 270	186	$ 25	
7/5		4,500	177	150	187	100	
7/15		10,000	178	330	188	500	
7/29		3,500	179	25	189	2,700	
7/30		950	180	7,025	190	1,600	
Total deposits		$19,250	181	150	191	75	
			182	450	192	425	
			183	1,400	193	550	
			184	1,500	194	650	
			185	325	195	275	
					Total disbursements	$18,525	
Balance, 7/31		**$ 6,275**					

Required:

1. Prepare a bank reconciliation for July.
2. Prepare the adjusting entries made by Towanda Corporation as a result of this reconciliation process.
3. What amount is reported as cash on the balance sheet at July 31?

Problem 4-57B BANK RECONCILIATION

OBJECTIVE ▶ 3

Donald Corporation received the bank statement shown below for the month of October 2009:

Date		Checks			Deposits	Balance
9/30 Beg. balance						$ 5,205
10/2	$1,200				$2,950	6,955
10/4	50	$ 300				6,605
10/8	900					5,705
10/10	100	60	$35			5,510
10/13					4,000	9,510
10/14	300*					9,210
10/17	525	325				8,360
10/19	105	430	20		2,850	10,655
10/21	3,110					7,545
10/23	65					7,480
10/25	250**	110				7,120
10/27	90					7,030
10/31	25***	1,305				5,700

*NSF check
**Debit memo
***Service charge

The Cash in Bank account of Donald Corporation provides the following information:

Date	Item	Debit	Credit	Balance
10/1	Balance from 9/30			$ 6,905.00
10/2	Check #1908		$ 300.00	6,605.00
10/5	Check #1909		900.00	5,705.00
10/6	Check #1910		100.00	5,605.00
10/6	Check #1911		60.00	5,545.00
10/7	Check #1912		35.00	5,510.00

Date	Item	Debit	Credit	Balance
10/12	Deposit #411	$4,000.00		$ 9,510.00
10/15	Check #1913		$ 525.00	8,985.00
10/16	Check #1914		325.00	8,660.00
10/17	Check #1915		430.00	8,230.00
10/17	Check #1916		20.00	8,210.00
10/18	Deposit #412	2,850.00		11,060.00
10/18	Check #1917		105.00	10,955.00
10/20	Check #1918		65.00	10,890.00
10/20	Check #1919		3,110.00	7,780.00
10/23	Check #1920		110.00	7,670.00
10/25	Check #1921		90.00	7,580.00
10/29	Check #1922		1,350.00	6,230.00
10/30	Check #1923		250.00	5,980.00
10/31	Check #1924		650.00	5,330.00
10/31	Deposit #413	3,300.00		8,630.00

The items on the bank statement are correct. The debit memo is for the payment by the bank of Donald's office furniture rent for October.

Required:

1. Prepare a bank reconciliation. (Hint: There is one transposition error in the cash account.)
2. Prepare adjusting entries based on the bank reconciliation.
3. What amount is reported for cash in bank on the balance sheet at October 31?

OBJECTIVE ▶ 3   **Problem 4-58B BANK RECONCILIATION**

The cash account of Mason Products reveals the following information:

Cash			
Balance, 4/30	10,100		
Deposits during May	39,600	Checks written during May	40,000

The bank statement for May contains the following information:

Bank balance, 4/30			$10,100
Add: Deposits during May			37,400
			$47,500
Less: Checks paid during May		$38,500	
NSF check from Higgins, Inc.		140	
Bank service charges		60	38,700
Bank balance, 5/31			$ 8,800

A comparison of detailed company records with the bank statement indicates the following information:

	At 4/30	At 5/31
Deposit in transit	$900	$2,200
Outstanding checks	550	1,500

The bank amounts are determined to be correct.

Required:

1. Prepare a bank reconciliation for May.
2. Prepare the adjusting entries made by Mason Products as a result of the reconciliation process.
3. What amount is reported for cash on the balance sheet at May 31?

Problem 4-59B RECORDING PETTY CASH TRANSACTIONS

OBJECTIVE ▶ 3

Chicago, Inc., had a balance of $1,200 in cash in its petty cash fund at the beginning of September. The following transactions took place in September:

a. On September 4, the custodian paid $75 out of petty cash for new stationery on which the company president's name appeared prominently.
b. On September 11, the custodian paid $350 out of petty cash for maintenance manuals for the firm's new jet aircraft.
c. On September 15, the custodian paid $25 out of petty cash for transportation-in.
d. On September 23, the custodian paid $50 out of petty cash to have documents delivered to the lawyers who were defending the firm in a lawsuit.
e. On September 27, the custodian paid $175 out of petty cash to reimburse the president for costs he had incurred when bad weather prevented the company jet from landing to pick him up after a meeting.
f. On September 30, the custodian submitted receipts for the above expenditures and a check was drawn for the amount to replenish the fund.

Required:

Prepare the journal entries made by the corporation to record these transactions.

Problem 4-60B (APPENDIX) RECORDING AVAILABLE-FOR-SALE SECURITIES TRANSACTIONS INCLUDING A SALE AFTER ADJUSTMENT TO THE ALLOWANCE ACCOUNT

OBJECTIVE ▶ 7

TommyBoy Products had no investment in available-for-sale securities at January 1, 2010. During 2010, TommyBoy engaged in the following marketable security transactions:

a. Purchased 200 shares of Silver Company stock for $12 per share.
b. Purchased 300 shares of Gold Corporation stock for $16 per share.
c. Received a $1-per-share dividend on the Silver stock.
d. Sold 125 shares of the Silver stock for $13.50 per share.

At the end of 2010, the Silver stock had a market value of $13 per share, and the Gold stock had a market value of $14.50 per share.

Required:

1. Prepare journal entries for each of the four transactions assuming they are classified as available-for-sale securities.
2. If necessary, prepare a journal entry to recognize the December 31, 2010, market values. What is the income statement effect of this entry?
3. How would these investments be reported on the December 31, 2009, balance sheet?

Problem 4-61B (APPENDIX) SHORT-TERM INVESTMENTS

OBJECTIVE ▶ 7

Margie's Company engaged in the following transactions involving short-term investments:

a. Purchased 200 shares of Softco stock for $25,600.
b. Received a $3.20-per-share dividend on the Softco stock.
c. Sold 80 shares of the Softco stock for $122 per share.
d. Purchased 380 shares of Kepler stock for $41,800.
e. Received a dividend of $2.00 per share on the Kepler stock.

At December 31, the Softco stock has a market value of $120 per share, and the Kepler stock has a market value of $118 per share.

Required:

1. Prepare entries for Margie's journal to record these transactions assuming they are trading securities.
2. Calculate the market value of Margie's short-term investment portfolio at December 31.
3. Provide the necessary adjusting entry at December 31.
4. What is the income statement effect of the adjusting entry?
5. How would these investments be reported on the December 31 balance sheet?

Cases

Case 4-62 ETHICS AND CASH CONTROLS

Suppose that you have just been hired as a part-time clerk in a large department store. Each week you work three evenings and all day Saturday. Without the income provided by this job, you would be unable to stay in college. Charles Riley, the manager in the clothing department to which you are assigned, has worked for the store for many years. Managers receive both a salary and a commission on their sales.

Late one afternoon, just as you begin work, Mr. Riley is ringing up a purchase. You observe that the purchase consists of two expensive suits, a coat, and several pairs of trousers and that the customer declines Mr. Riley's offer to have the store's tailor do the alterations. After the customer departs with his merchandise and as Mr. Riley is departing for the evening, you say, "See you tomorrow." Mr. Riley gives a brief, barely audible response and departs for the evening.

As you return to the sales counter, you glance at the paper tape displayed through a small opening in the cash register that records all sales on an item-by-item basis. You have just completed the store course in register operation, so you are quite familiar with the register and the tape it produces. To your surprise, you note that the last sale consisted of just a single pair of trousers.

Required:

1. What do you conclude about this transaction?
2. What are the possible consequences for the store, for Mr. Riley, and for you personally of reporting your observations to Mr. Riley's superiors?
3. What are the possible consequences for the store, for Mr. Riley, and for you personally of *not* reporting your observations to Mr. Riley's superiors?
4. What would your decision be?

Case 4-63 THE OPERATING CYCLE

There are two retail stores in Millersburgh. One is a full-service store that typically sells on credit to its customers; the other is a discount store that usually sells for cash. Full-service stores typically charge higher prices than do discount stores for identical items.

Required:

1. Does the operating cycle suggest some economic reason for a portion of this price difference? Explain your answer.
2. Can you think of other reasons why a full-service store might charge more than a discount store for the same merchandise?

Case 4-64 INTERNAL CONTROLS FOR CASH DISBURSEMENTS

Campus Supply Store purchases merchandise on credit from a large number of suppliers. During the past five years, Campus's annual sales have grown from $100,000 to $1,500,000. A recent article in the local newspaper disclosed that an employee of another firm had been arrested for embezzling funds from his employer by diverting payments for purchases to his own bank account. Because of that article, the accountant for Campus has decided to examine Campus's procedures for purchases and payables.

Currently three different employees are authorized to order merchandise for the store. These employees normally complete paperwork provided by the suppliers' sales representatives, keeping a copy for their records. When the ordered merchandise arrives, whomever the delivery person can locate signs for the package. Bills are sent to the store by suppliers and are paid by Campus's accountant when due.

Required:

1. Indicate which general principles of internal control are violated by Campus's procedures for purchases and payables.
2. Recommend procedures that would incorporate the five general categories of internal control where possible.

Case 4-65 INTERNAL CONTROLS FOR COLLECTION OF RECEIVABLES

Carolyn Furniture Galleries sells traditional furniture from two stores in St. Louis. Carolyn's credit terms allow customers to pay for purchases over three months with no finance charges. Carolyn's accountant has been responsible for approving customers for credit, recording cash received from customers in the accounting records, depositing cash collections in the bank, and following up on customers who are behind in their payments. Each month the accountant has prepared a report for Carolyn's president, indicating the cash collected, outstanding receivables, and uncollectible accounts.

Carolyn's president has been concerned about a significant increase in uncollectible accounts that began about two years ago, shortly after the current accountant was hired. Recently, a personal friend of Carolyn's president called. The caller had moved from St. Louis to Denver about six months ago. A month ago, the caller's new bank had refused a loan because a credit rating bureau in St. Louis had indicated that the caller had left bills unpaid at Carolyn Furniture. Carolyn's president knew that the caller had paid his account before leaving the community.

Carolyn's president called a detective agency and arranged for an investigation. Two weeks later, Carolyn's president was informed that the accountant had been spending much more money than his salary would warrant. Carolyn then called its auditor and arranged to have the accounting records for receivables and uncollectible accounts examined. This examination indicated that about $400,000 of cash had been stolen from the firm by the accountant. The accountant had identified customers who had moved and had recorded cash sales to continuing customers as credit sales in the accounts of the relocated customers. Carolyn's accountant had kept the cash received from the cash sales and had eventually written off the fictitious credit sales as uncollectible accounts. Without the accountant's knowledge, one of Carolyn's new employees had sent the names of the customers who had apparently defaulted on their accounts to the credit bureau.

Required:

Identify the internal control weaknesses that permitted the accountant to steal the $400,000. Suggest internal control procedures that would make it difficult for someone else to repeat this theft.

Case 4-66 CASH MANAGEMENT

Hollis Corporation has the following budgeted schedule for expected cash receipts and cash disbursement.

Month	Expected Cash Receipts	Expected Cash Disbursements
July	$210,000	$200,000
August	280,000	210,000
September	230,000	190,000
October	160,000	180,000

Hollis begins July with a cash balance of $20,000, $15,000 of short-term debt, and no short-term investments. Hollis uses the following cash management policy:

a. End-of-month cash should equal $20,000 plus the excess of disbursements over receipts for the next month.
b. If receipts are expected to exceed disbursements in the next month, the current month ending cash balance should be $20,000.
c. Excess cash should be invested in short-term investments unless there is short-term debt, in which case excess cash should first be used to reduce the debt.
d. Cash deficiencies are met first by selling short-term investments and second by incurring short-term debt.

Required:

1. Calculate the expected buying and selling of short-term investments and the incurrence and repayment of short-term debt at the end of July, August, and September.
2. Discuss the general considerations that help accountants develop a cash management policy.

Case 4-67 CASH AND INTERNAL CONTROLS

Identify a business with which you are familiar.

Required:

1. Describe the ways in which it prevents theft of cash.
2. Can you think of a way in which dishonest employees could circumvent the internal controls and steal cash?

Case 4-68 RESEARCHING AND ANALYSIS USING THE ANNUAL REPORT

Obtain **Microsoft**'s 2007 10-K through the "Investor Relations" portion of their website (do a search for Microsoft investor relations) or go to http://www.sec.gov and click "Search for company filings" under "Filings & Forms (EDGAR)."

Required:

1. How much cash and equivalents and short-term investments did Microsoft hold as a percentage of total assets in 2006 and 2007?
2. What is Microsoft's definition of a cash equivalent (see Note 1)? Does this appear consistent with other companies' definitions?
3. Look at Note 3 and specify how much of Microsoft's cash and equivalent balance is actually cash. What is their largest (in dollar terms) cash equivalent?
4. Look at Note 3 and list Microsoft's three largest short-term investment categories for 2007.
5. Look at Microsoft's corporate notes and bonds at June 30, 2007, from Note 3. What is the amount of unrealized gains and unrealized losses for these holdings? How much is considered cash equivalents? How much is considered short-term investments? Why are some classified as cash equivalents and some as short-term investments?
6. Locate the certifications required by the CEO and CFO under Section 302 of the Sarbanes-Oxley Act. (Hint: It is in the exhibits at the end of the 10-K.) Who signed these certifications?

Case 4-69 COMPARATIVE ANALYSIS: ABERCROMBIE & FITCH vs. AEROPOSTALE

Refer to the financial statements of **Abercrombie & Fitch** and **Aeropostale** that are supplied with this text.

Required:

1. How much cash and equivalents and short-term investments (or marketable securities) did Aeropostale and Abercrombie & Fitch hold as a percentage of total assets at February 3, 2007, and January 28, 2006?

2. Speculate as to differences in cash management policies between the two companies.
3. Describe the change in the mix of cash and equivalents and marketable securities for Abercrombie & Fitch between 2006 and 2007. Speculate as to why this may have happened.
4. Locate the Audit Opinion and describe the criteria by which Abercrombie & Fitch's and Aeropostale's internal control systems were evaluated.

5

Sales and Receivables

After studying this chapter, you should be able to:

1. Explain the criteria for revenue recognition.
2. Measure net sales revenue.
3. Describe internal control procedures for merchandise sales.
4. Describe the principal types of receivables.
5. Measure and interpret bad debt expense and the allowance for doubtful accounts.
6. Describe the cash flow implications of accounts receivable.
7. Account for notes receivable from inception to maturity.
8. Analyze profitability and asset management using sales and receivables.

Experience Financial Accounting
with Mitsubishi

Mitsubishi's U.S. sales increased from 191,000 cars in 1998 to 322,000 cars in 2001. This 68.5% sales growth made it the fastest growing auto brand in the U.S. Marketed toward Gen Y, Mitsubishi developed an "edgy" image with cross promotions such as Universal Film's *2 Fast 2 Furious*. They also offered a "0-0-0" finance offer—0 percent down, 0 percent interest, and $0 monthly payments for 12 months.

Unfortunately, the economic downturn at the turn of the century hurt Mitsubishi's Gen Y target buyer particularly hard. Consequently, many buyers in the 0-0-0 financing program never made a single payment (some reports put this number as high as 50 percent or 60 percent of the buyers in this program), leaving Mitsubishi with a year-old used car. This resulted in Mitsubishi taking a loss on bad debts of $454 million during the first half of 2003. Since Mitsubishi operates on a fiscal year of April 1–March 31, this loss was reported in fiscal year 2002.

As you will learn in this chapter, net realizable value is the amount that a company expects to collect from its outstanding accounts receivable. Notice in the graph below, the drop in net realizable value in 2002, due to the loss on bad debts. A loss on bad debts is reported on the income statement, but as you can see here, the loss also impacts the balance sheet. This illustrates an important lesson. You have to be careful to whom you give credit.

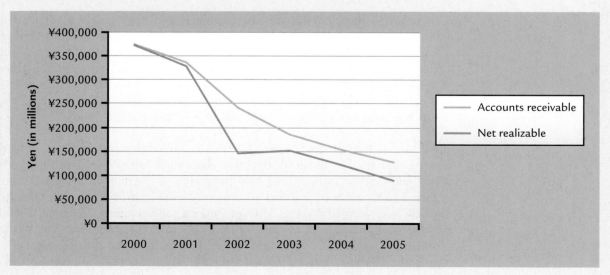

Sales Revenue

There are two primary questions in revenue recognition. First, in which period (e.g., 2009 or 2010) should the revenue be recognized? Second, what amount of revenue should be recorded?

OBJECTIVE ➤ 1

Explain the criteria for revenue recognition.

Timing of Revenue Recognition

While cash-basis accounting recognizes revenue in the period payment is received (as on your tax return), accrual-basis accounting recognizes revenue when it is (1) **realized** or **realizable** and (2) **earned**. The term "realized" means that non-cash resources (i.e., inventory) have been exchanged for cash or near cash (e.g., accounts receivable). Obviously, this describes the typical sales transaction where a store exchanges, for example, a pair of shoes (its inventory and a non-cash resource) for cash or an account receivable. "Realizable" describes a situation where non-cash resources (i.e., inventory) are readily convertible into known amounts of cash. For example, after a gold mine extracts the gold, the gold (a non-cash resource) is readily convertible into cash because there is an active market for gold. Other examples of non-cash resources readily convertible to cash include wheat, corn, and soybeans.

As for the second criterion, revenues are considered "earned" when the earnings process is substantially complete. For most retail sales this occurs at the point of sale. That is, the store fulfills its obligation to you when it lets you walk out of the store with the pair of shoes you just bought. For service organizations, the earnings process is substantially complete when the service is performed. For example, if you pay $1,200 for a year-long membership to a health club, the health club should recognize $100 per month. Or, when you pay for a plane ticket in January to fly to Mexico during spring break, the airline will recognize the revenue after you fly.

Because sales transactions can be extremely complicated and businesses frequently attempt to recognize revenue too soon, the Securities and Exchange Commission (SEC) has issued further guidance on revenue recognition. Specifically, the SEC maintains that revenue is realized or realizable and earned when the following criteria are met [Staff Accounting Bulletin (SAB) 104]:

1. Persuasive evidence of an arrangement exists (e.g., a contract or other proof of the details of the exchange).
2. Delivery has occurred or services have been provided.
3. The seller's price to the buyer is fixed and determinable.
4. Collectability is reasonably assured.

Although these criteria are easy to understand, they can be difficult to apply to complicated sales contracts. Such complicated transactions are best left to more advanced accounting courses. For now, recognize that the vast majority of sales transactions are straightforward and simple—service companies (e.g., airlines, accountants, lawyers, health clubs, lawn services, etc.) recognize revenue in the period they provide the services to the customer and sellers of goods recognize revenue in the period when title passes (e.g., the customer takes possession of the goods).

ETHICS Publicly-traded corporations are under tremendous pressure to meet analyst targets for key financial-statement data, such as sales (and earnings per share). Many corporations, when faced with the reality of sales not meeting analysts' targets, resorted to a variety of practices to avoid such shortfalls. For example, **Bristol-Myers Squibb** was accused by the SEC of, among other things, "channel stuffing." In channel stuffing companies ship more goods to a customer than the customer ordered near the end of a period. However, because sales are recognized at the time of shipment, all these sales are recorded in the current period. Of course, this practice will result in lower sales in the subsequent period when the customer returns the unwanted goods.◆

Amount of Revenue Recognized

The appropriate amount of revenue to recognize is generally the cash received or the cash equivalent of the receivable. However, companies often induce customers to buy by modifying the terms of the sale. In this section, we discuss three changes to sales revenues: discounts, returns, and allowances. Sales discounts are offered at the time of a sale to encourage the purchaser to pay promptly. Returns and allowances take place after the time of a sale. Let us begin our examination of these three changes to revenue by discussing sales discounts.

Sales Discounts

To encourage prompt payment, businesses may offer a **sales discount**. This discount is a reduction of the normal selling price and is attractive to both the seller and the buyer. For the buyer, it is a reduction to the cost of the goods and services. For the seller, the cash is more quickly available and collection costs are reduced. For example, when cash is not available quickly, the seller may need to borrow money in order to pay its suppliers, employees, etc. The interest expense associated with borrowing money has a negative effect on net income.

Sales invoices use a standard notation to state discount and credit terms. For example, the invoice of a seller who expects payment in 30 days and offers a 2 percent discount if payment is made within 10 days would bear the notation 2/10, n/30 (which is read "2/10, net 30"). The notation n/30 indicates that the gross amount of the invoice (the full pre-discount amount) must be paid in 30 days. The notation 2/10 indicates that, if payment is made within the 10-day discount period, the amount owed is 2 percent less than the gross (pre-discount) amount of the invoice. Of course, if payment is made within the 20 days following the end of the discount period, then the amount owed is equal to the gross (pre-discount) amount of the invoice.

Most companies record the sale and the associated receivable at the gross (pre-discount) amount of the invoice. This is called the "gross method."[1] If payment is received after the discount period, the cash received equals the associated receivable so no adjustment is needed. But when a discount is taken, the amount of the discount is recorded in a contra-revenue account (i.e., it reduces Gross Sales Revenue to Net Sales Revenue) called *sales discounts*, which balances the entry. This method is illustrated in Cornerstone 5-1.

HOW TO Record Receivables using the Gross Method

Concept:
Some businesses offer discounts off the full price for paying cash promptly. When the gross method is used, the receivable is recorded at the gross (pre-discount) amount of the invoice. Under the gross method, if the discount is taken, a debit is made to "Sales Discounts" at the time of payment.

Information:
On May 5, 2009, Bolt Manufacturing Company sold merchandise with a gross price of $15,000 to Richardson's Wholesale Hardware. Bolt offered terms of 2/10, n/30.

C O R N E R S T O N E
5 - 1

---

[1] GAAP also allows the "net method" of accounting for receivables with sales discounts. This method is demonstrated in intermediate accounting courses.

**CORNERSTONE
5-1
(continued)**

Required:
1. Prepare the journal entry to record the sale using the gross method.
2. Prepare the journal entry assuming the payment is received on May 15, 2009 (within the discount period).
3. Prepare the journal entry assuming the payment is received on May 25, 2009 (after the discount period).
4. How would Sales Revenues be disclosed on the Income Statement assuming the payment is made within 10 days?

Solution:

1. Entry on May 5, 2009:

Date	Account and Explanation	Debit	Credit
May 5, 2009	Accounts Receivable	15,000	
	Sales Revenue		15,000
	(Record sale of merchandise)		

Assets	=	Liabilities +	Stockholders' Equity
+15,000			+15,000

2. Entry on May 15, 2009:

Date	Account and Explanation	Debit	Credit
May 15, 2009	Cash (15,000 × 98%)	14,700	
	Sales Discounts	300	
	Accounts Receivable		15,000
	(Record collection within the discount period)		

Assets	=	Liabilities +	Stockholders' Equity
+14,700			−300
−15,000			

3. Entry on May 25, 2009:

Date	Account and Explanation	Debit	Credit
May 25, 2009	Cash	15,000	
	Accounts Receivable		15,000
	(Record collection after the discount period)		

Assets	=	Liabilities +	Stockholders' Equity
+15,000			
−15,000			

4. Partial income statement:

Sales revenue	$15,000
Less: Sales discounts	300
Net sales	$14,700

It is also important to monitor changes in how customers use sales discounts. For example, customers who stop taking sales discounts may be experiencing cash flow problems and therefore are potential credit risks. On the other hand, failure of a large number of customers to take discounts may indicate that an increase in the discount percentage is needed.

Finally, sales discounts must be distinguished from both trade and quantity discounts. A *trade discount* is a reduction in the selling price granted by the seller to a particular class of customers, for example, to customers who purchase goods for resale rather than for use. A *quantity discount* is a reduction in the selling price granted by the seller because selling costs per unit are less when larger quantities are ordered. This is why, for example, a 32-ounce soft drink does not cost double what a 16-ounce one costs at a restaurant. For accounting purposes, the selling or invoice price is usually assumed to be the price after adjustment for the trade or quantity discounts; accordingly, trade and quantity discounts are not recorded separately in the accounting records.

Sales Returns and Allowances

Occasionally, a customer will return goods as unsatisfactory. In other cases, a customer may agree to keep goods with minor defects if the seller is willing to make an "allowance" by reducing the selling price. The accounting for sales returns and allowances, which is described in the paragraphs that follow, has the effect of reversing all or part of a previously recorded sale.

Merchandise or goods returned by the customer to the seller are **sales returns**. A contra-revenue account called *sales returns and allowances* (allowances are discussed next) is used to record the selling price of returned goods. For example, on August 31, 2009, Bolt Manufacturing sold $12,000 of house paint to Charlie's Hardware. On October 15, 2009, Charlie's returned $4,000 of the paint because it had arrived after the painting season, as a result of a trucking strike. Bolt made the following entries to record these events:

Date	Account and Explanation	Debit	Credit
August 31, 2009	Accounts Receivable	12,000	
	Sales Revenue		12,000
	(Record sale of merchandise)		
October 15, 2009	Sales Returns & Allowances	4,000	
	Accounts Receivable		4,000
	(Record return of merchandise)		

Assets =	Liabilities +	Stockholders' Equity
+12,000		+12,000

Assets =	Liabilities +	Stockholders' Equity
−4,000		−4,000

In an example such as the preceding one, if the customer has already paid the account receivable, the seller might refund the purchase price and record a credit to cash. However, if the customer regularly purchases from the firm, the return can simply be applied as a credit to accounts receivable in anticipation of the customer's next purchase.

When goods are only slightly defective, are shipped late, or in some other way are rendered less valuable, a customer may be induced to keep the goods if a price reduction, called a **sales allowance**, is offered by the seller. Companies also record these price reductions in *sales returns and allowances*. For example, on November 1, 2009, Bolt Manufacturing sold several snowblowers for $9,800 to Johnson Home and Garden Store. The blowers shipped were larger than those Johnson had ordered and were therefore more difficult to sell. On November 15, Bolt offered, and Johnson accepted, a $1,600 reduction in the total selling price as an allowance for the size difference. Bolt made the following accounting entries to record these events:

Date	Account and Explanation	Debit	Credit
November 1, 2009	Accounts Receivable	9,800	
	Sales Revenue		9,800
	(Record sale of merchandise)		
November 15, 2009	Sales Returns & Allowances	1,600	
	Accounts Receivable		1,600
	(Record allowance for incorrect merchandise)		

Assets =	Liabilities +	Stockholders' Equity
+9,800		+9,800

Assets =	Liabilities +	Stockholders' Equity
−1,600		−1,600

If the bill has already been paid, the firm can either refund a portion of the purchase price and record a credit to cash or apply the allowance against future purchases by the customer by recording a credit to accounts receivable.

On the income statement, as indicated in Chapter 2, sales returns and allowances, like sales discounts, are subtracted from gross sales revenue to produce **net sales revenue**, as shown here:

Sales revenue	$752,000
Less: Sales returns and allowances	5,600
Net sales	$746,400

In other words, sales returns and allowances is a contra-revenue account. Presenting both gross sales revenue and sales returns and allowances, rather than net sales revenue alone, permits financial-statement users to respond to unusual

DECISION-MAKING & ANALYSIS

Sales Returns and Allowances

Interplains, Inc., sells gears to heavy equipment manufacturers. Data for the past four years for sales revenue, sales returns and allowances, and net income are shown below.

	2007	2008	2009	2010
Sales revenue	$624,000	$653,000	$671,000	$887,000
Sales returns and allowances	6,100	6,400	6,300	14,800
Net income	30,000	29,000	31,500	12,200

The following questions raise issues that might provide some insight into the significant change in the relationship between sales revenue and sales returns and allowances in 2010:

1. *Have there been any significant changes in the quality of production?*

   Sales revenue, which had been relatively stable, increased by 32 percent in 2010. Often, significant growth in output is accompanied by quality assurance problems, as might be indicated by the 135 percent growth in sales returns and allowances. A check of production data might reveal the use of less highly trained workers or supervisors, or might indicate that the current workforce is being worked heavily on overtime.

2. *Have there been any significant changes in the economic environment of the firm?*

   Notice the significant decrease in net income despite the large increase in sales revenue. When this happens, you must attempt to discover why. For example, when a firm becomes significantly more or less profitable, the attitude of the employees toward their work can change, causing changes in the quality of output. Some key employees may leave a firm with declining profitability, thus causing quality difficulties.

behavior in either account. Careful users of financial statements look for unusual behavior in both sales revenue and sales returns and allowances in the income statement. Often, significant changes in these accounts help to explain other changes in income statement or balance sheet accounts, as we illustrate in the Decision-Making & Analysis above.

OBJECTIVE ▶ 3
Describe internal control procedures for merchandise sales.

Internal Control for Sales

Since sales revenues have a significant effect on a company's net income, internal control procedures must be established to ensure that the amounts reported for these items are correct. For sales revenues, these controls normally involve the following documents and procedures:

1. Accounting for a sale begins with the receipt of a purchase order or some similar document from a customer. The order document is necessary for the buyer to be obligated to accept and pay for the ordered goods.
2. Shipping and billing documents are prepared based on the order document. Billing documents are usually called *invoices.*
3. A sale and its associated receivable are recorded only when the order, shipping, and billing documents are all present.

As illustrated in Exhibit 5-1, sales revenue should be recorded only when these three control documents are completed. When any of these three internal controls is not present, it is possible for valid sales to be unrecorded and for invalid sales to be recorded.

For sales returns and allowances, internal control procedures must be established that identify the conditions and documentation required before a sales return or a sales allowance can be recorded. These controls protect the firm from unwarranted reductions in revenues and receivables.

Exhibit 5-1

Internal Controls Recording Sales Revenue

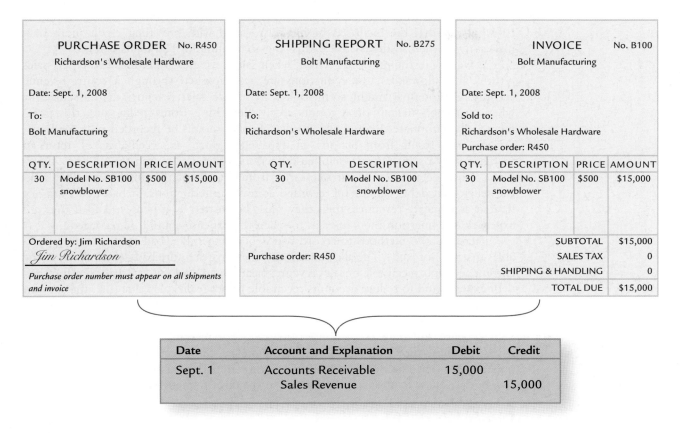

	PURCHASE ORDER	No. R450

Richardson's Wholesale Hardware

Date: Sept. 1, 2008

To:

Bolt Manufacturing

QTY.	DESCRIPTION	PRICE	AMOUNT
30	Model No. SB100 snowblower	$500	$15,000

Ordered by: Jim Richardson

Jim Richardson

Purchase order number must appear on all shipments and invoice

	SHIPPING REPORT	No. B275

Bolt Manufacturing

Date: Sept. 1, 2008

To:

Richardson's Wholesale Hardware

QTY.	DESCRIPTION
30	Model No. SB100 snowblower

Purchase order: R450

	INVOICE	No. B100

Bolt Manufacturing

Date: Sept. 1, 2008

Sold to:

Richardson's Wholesale Hardware

Purchase order: R450

QTY.	DESCRIPTION	PRICE	AMOUNT
30	Model No. SB100 snowblower	$500	$15,000

SUBTOTAL	$15,000
SALES TAX	0
SHIPPING & HANDLING	0
TOTAL DUE	$15,000

Date	Account and Explanation	Debit	Credit
Sept. 1	Accounts Receivable	15,000	
	Sales Revenue		15,000

Types of Receivables

OBJECTIVE ▶ 4
Describe the principal types of receivables.

A receivable is money due from another business or individual. Receivables are typically categorized along three different dimensions. First, a distinction is made between "accounts" receivable and "notes" receivable. A "note" is a legal document given by a borrower to a lender stating the timing of repayment and the amount (principal and/or interest) to be repaid. We discuss notes receivable later in the chapter. **Accounts receivable**, on the other hand, do not have a formal note. For example, while you likely signed a formal agreement to rent your apartment, you probably did not sign a formal agreement for your utilities. Another dimension on which receivables are distinguished is whether they are current or noncurrent. Although in practice both accounts and notes receivable are typically classified as current, we should note that accounts receivable are typically due in 30 to 60 days and do not have interest while notes receivable have interest and typically are due in anywhere from three to 12 months. Of course, if the due date is over one year, the note receivable typically will be classified as noncurrent. Finally, receivables are also distinguished by whether they are trade or nontrade receivables. **Trade receivables** are due from customers purchasing inventory in the ordinary course of business while **nontrade receivables** arise from transactions not involving inventory (e.g., interest receivable or cash advances to employees).

Accounting for Bad Debts

OBJECTIVE ▶ 5
Measure and interpret bad debt expense and the allowance for doubtful accounts.

We discussed the recognition of accounts receivable in the sales section, but an equally important concept is ensuring that the proper amount for accounts receivable is shown on the balance sheet. GAAP requires accounts receivable to be shown at their "net realizable value," which is the amount of cash the company expects to collect. Unfortunately, the amount of cash collected will almost never equal the total amount recognized in accounts receivable because some customers will not pay (e.g., a customer declares bankruptcy and ceases operations). When customers do not pay their accounts receivable, bad debts result (also called uncollectible accounts). Although efforts are made to control bad debts, it is an expense of providing credit to customers (the hope is that the increased business associated with providing credit more than makes up for the bad debts). We discuss the accounting for bad debts below.

As we saw in the previous section, when sales revenues are reduced to reflect sales returns and allowances, the reductions are accomplished through a contra-revenue account. Although it might seem logical to reduce sales revenues in the same way when customers default on accounts receivable arising from credit sales, this treatment is inappropriate. Reductions in sales revenue should be recorded only for transactions that result from actions of the seller, such as acceptance of returned merchandise (a sales return) or price reductions offered to purchasers (a sales allowance). Since defaults on credit sales arise from actions of the purchaser rather than the seller, bad debts cannot be recorded as revenue reductions. If bad debts are not treated as negative revenues, then they must be treated as expenses. And if they are expenses, the question then arises as to when the expense should be recorded.

There are two methods to record bad debts (remember, bad debts are the receivables that are not paid). The allowance method estimates future bad debts related to the current accounts receivable or sales revenue balance and uses this estimate to record bad debt expense and to reduce accounts receivable to net realizable value (i.e., the amount of cash expected to be collected from these receivables). The direct write-off method, on the other hand, waits until a customer defaults on a payment and then records a bad debt expense and reduces accounts receivable. For reasons discussed in more detail below, the allowance method is GAAP. Nonetheless, the direct write-off method is frequently used when accounts receivable are not material because it is easier. We will discuss both of these methods, but we'll look at the direct write-off method first.

Direct Write-Off Method

The simplest method is to record the expense in the period of default. This is called the direct write-off method. Under this method **bad debt expense** is increased and accounts receivable is decreased only at the time an account is determined to be uncollectible. For example, suppose ABC, Inc., owes Hawthorne Company $10,000 on account. On March 20, 2009, Hawthorne learns that ABC has gone out of business. Hawthorne would make the following entry:

Date	Account and Explanation	Debit	Credit
March 20, 2009	Bad Debt Expense	10,000	
	Accounts Receivable		10,000
	(Record write-off of ABC, Inc., account)		

		Stockholders'
Assets =	Liabilities +	Equity
−10,000		−10,000

As you remember, the matching concept requires that expenses be matched with the related revenues in the period in which the revenues are recognized on the income statement. Therefore, bad debt expense is properly matched with revenues only if it is recorded in the period of sale. Since accounts are often determined to be uncollectible in accounting periods subsequent to the sale period, the direct write-off method is inconsistent with the matching concept and can only be used if bad debts are immaterial. Further, the accounts receivable balance is shown on the balance sheet as the total amount owed by customers, rather than the net realizable value of amounts owed by customers.

Allowance Method

To be consistent with the matching principle, bad debt expense must be recorded in the period of the related sale. But most likely it is unknown that a specific account will become uncollectible (default) until after the period of the sale. Therefore, bad debt expense related to the sales for the period must be estimated in order to record it in the period of the sale.

The result is that bad debt expense is recognized before the actual default. Because defaults for the current period's sales have not actually occurred, the specific accounts receivable are not lowered; instead, an account is established to "store" the estimate until specific accounts are identified as uncollectible. This account is called **Allowance for Doubtful Accounts**. For example, assume at the end of the first year of operations Hawthorne has an accounts receivable balance of $1,000,000. Although no customers have defaulted, Hawthorne estimates that $25,000 of that balance is uncollectible. At the end of the first year Hawthorne would make the following adjusting entry:

Date	Account and Explanation	Debit	Credit
December 31, 2008	Bad Debt Expense	25,000	
	Allowance for Doubtful Accounts		25,000
	(Record estimate of uncollectible accounts)		

Assets =	Liabilities +	Stockholders' Equity
−25,000		−25,000

Admittedly, this entry looks very similar to the entry shown in the direct write-off method section. The major difference is the timing of the entry. The direct write-off method makes the entry in the period the customer defaults, while the allowance method makes the entry in the period of sale. Hawthorne's balance sheet would report accounts receivable on the balance sheet as follows:

Accounts Receivable	$1,000,000
Less: Allowance for Doubtful Accounts	25,000
Accounts Receivable (net)	$ 975,000

However, it is important to recognize that Hawthorne's balance sheet would report the full $1,000,000 as accounts receivable under the direct write-off method at the end of the first year.

When a specific account is ultimately determined to be uncollectible under the allowance method, it is *written off* by a debit to the allowance account and a credit to accounts receivable. This write-off removes the defaulted balance from the accounts receivable balance and also removes it from the estimate "storage" account.

Under the allowance procedure, two methods commonly used to estimate bad debt expense are the *percentage of credit sales method* and the *aging method*.

CONCEPT Q&A

Why is the direct write-off method not GAAP?

Possible Answer:

Because the direct write-off method fails to "match" the bad debt expense to the sales revenue that it helped generate and does not show accounts receivable at net realizable value on the balance sheet.

Percentage of Credit Sales Method

The simpler of the two methods for determining bad debt expense is the **credit sales method**. Using past experience and management's views of how the future may differ from the past (e.g., if credit policies change), it is possible to estimate the percentage of the current period's credit sales that will eventually become uncollectible. This percentage is multiplied by the total credit sales for the period to calculate the estimated bad debt expense for the period. The adjusting entry is then prepared to recognize the bad debt expense as shown in Cornerstone 5-2.

HOW TO Estimate Bad Debt Expense with the Percentage of Credit Sales Method

Concept:
Bad debt expense should be recorded in the period of the sale to match the expense with the revenue. The bad debt expense amount can be calculated as a percentage of credit sales. The percentage is determined from past experience with credit sales. The adjusting entry records bad debt expense and adjusts the balance in allowance for doubtful accounts.

Information:
Crimson Company has credit sales of $620,000 during 2009 and estimates at the end of 2009 that 1.43 percent of these credit sales will eventually default. Also,

CORNERSTONE
5-2

**CORNERSTONE
5-2**
(continued)

during 2009 a customer defaults on a $524 balance related to goods purchased in 2008. Prior to the adjusting entries, Crimson's accounts receivable and allowance for doubtful accounts balances were $304,000 and $134 (credit), respectively.

Required:
1. Estimate the bad debt expense for the period.
2. Prepare the journal entry to record the write off of the defaulted $524 balance.
3. Prepare the adjusting entry to record the bad debt expense for 2009.
4. What is the net accounts receivable balance at the end of the year? How would this balance have changed if Crimson had not written off the $524 balance during 2009?

Solution:
1. $620,000 \times 0.0143 = \$8,866$
2.

Date	Account and Explanation	Debit	Credit
December 31, 2009	Allowance for Doubtful Accounts	524	
	Accounts Receivable		524
	(Record write-off of defaulted account)		

		Stockholders'
Assets = **Liabilities** +		**Equity**
+524		
−524		

3. The calculation in part 1 estimated the *ending* balance of bad debt expense. This amount is also the adjustment because the balance before the adjustment is zero. Of course, this is usually the case for income statement accounts because they were closed at the end of the prior year.

Date	Account and Explanation	Debit	Credit
December 31, 2009	Bad Debt Expense	8,866	
	Allowance for Doubtful Accounts		8,866
	(Record adjusting entry for bad debt expense estimate)		

		Stockholders'
Assets = **Liabilities** +		**Equity**
−8,866		−8,866

Bad Debt Expense

Preadjustment Balance, 12/31/09	0	
Adjustment	**8,866**	
Ending Balance	8,866	

Allowance for Doubtful Accounts

		134	Beginning Balance
Write-offs during 2009	524		
Preadjustment Balance, 12/31/09	390		
		8,866	**Adjustment**
		8,476	Ending Balance

4.

	Year End	Assuming No Write-Off
Accounts receivable	$303,476	$304,000
Less: Allowance for doubtful accounts	8,476*	9,000**
Net accounts receivable	$295,000	$295,000

*See T-account in part 3.
**T-account from part 3 without the $524 debit for the write-off.

Part 4 illustrates that under the allowance method the write-off of a specific account does not affect net accounts receivable.

Occasionally, accounts receivable that are written off are later partially or entirely collected. Suppose on February 5, 2010, Crimson receives $25 of the $524 that was written off at the end of the previous year (see Part 2 of Cornerstone 5-2). Crimson would make the following entries:

Date	Account and Explanation	Debit	Credit
February 5, 2010	Accounts Receivable	25	
	Allowance for Doubtful Accounts		25
	(Reverse portion of write-off)		
	Cash	25	
	Accounts Receivable		25
	(Record collection of account receivable)		

		Stockholders'
Assets =	Liabilities +	Equity
+25		
−25		
+25		
−25		

Crimson's first entry reverses the appropriate portion of the write-off; it restores the appropriate portion of the accounts receivable and allowance for doubtful accounts balances. The second entry records the cash collection in the typical manner.

The credit sales method takes an income statement approach. That is, it uses an income statement number (credit sales) to estimate the ending balance of an income statement account (bad debt expense). This method is primarily concerned with reflecting the estimate of bad debt expense appropriately on the income statement. Because of the focus on the expense account, any existing balance in the allowance account is ignored when determining the amount of the adjusting entry. This is the underlying difference between the percentage of credit sales method and the aging method.

Aging Method   Under the **aging method**, bad debt expense is estimated by determining the collectability of the accounts receivable rather than by taking a percentage of total credit sales. At the end of each accounting period, the individual accounts receivable are categorized by age. Then an estimate is made of the amount expected to default in each age category based on past experience and expectations about how the future may differ from the past. As you may expect, the overdue accounts are more likely to default than the currently due accounts, as shown in the example below:

Accounts Receivable Age	Amount	Proportion Expected to Default	Amount Expected to Default
Less than 15 days	$190,000	0.01	$1,900
16–30 days	40,000	0.04	1,600
31–60 days	10,000	0.10	1,000
Over 61 days	9,000	0.30	2,700
	$249,000		$7,200

The total amount expected to default on year-end accounts receivable, $7,200 in the above example, is the amount that should be the ending balance in the allowance for doubtful accounts. Since the objective of the aging method is to estimate the ending balance in the allowance for doubtful accounts, any existing balance in the allowance account must be considered when determining the amount of the adjusting entry as shown in Cornerstone 5-3.

HOW TO Estimate the Allowance for Doubtful Accounts with the Aging Method

Concept:
An aging of the accounts receivable balance will determine the appropriate value of net accounts receivable to be presented on the balance sheet. This results in an estimate of the appropriate balance for the allowance for doubtful accounts. The adjusting entry brings allowance for doubtful accounts to the appropriate balance and records bad debt expense.

CORNERSTONE
5-3

**CORNERSTONE
5-3**
(continued)

Information:

On January 1, 2009, Sullivan, Inc., has the following balances for accounts receivable and allowance for doubtful accounts:

Accounts receivable	$224,000 (debit)
Allowance for doubtful accounts	6,700 (credit)

During 2009, Sullivan had $3,100,000 of credit sales, collected $3,015,000 of accounts receivable, and wrote off $60,000 of accounts receivable as uncollectible.

Required:

1. What is Sullivan's preadjustment balance in accounts receivable on December 31, 2009?
2. What is Sullivan's preadjustment balance in allowance for doubtful accounts on December 31, 2009?
3. Assuming Sullivan's analysis of the accounts receivable balance indicates that $7,200 of the current accounts receivable balance is uncollectible, by what amount will the allowance for doubtful accounts need to be adjusted?
4. What will be the ending balance in bad debt expense?
5. Prepare the necessary adjusting entry for 2009.

Solution:

1.

Accounts Receivable			
Beginning Balance	224,000		
Sales	3,100,000	3,015,000	Collections
		60,000	Write-offs
Preadjustment Balance	249,000		

2.

Allowance for Doubtful Accounts			
		6,700	Beginning Balance
Write-offs	60,000		
Preadjustment Balance	53,300		

3.

Allowance for Doubtful Accounts			
Preadjustment Balance, 12/31/09	53,300		
		60,500*	**Adjusting Entry**
		7,200**	Adjusted Balance

*Necessary adjustment to end up with an ending balance of $7,200.
**Estimate of ending balance determined by analyzing the receivables aging. This information was given in part 3 of the "Required" section.

4.

Bad Debt Expense		
Preadjustment Balance, 12/31/09	0	
Adjustment	**60,500**	
Ending Balance	60,500	

5.

Date	Account and Explanation	Debit	Credit
Dec. 31, 2009	Bad Debt Expense	60,500	
	Allowance for Doubtful Accounts		60,500
	(Record adjusting entry for bad debt expense estimate)		

Assets = Liabilities +	Stockholders' Equity
−60,500	−60,500

In summary, GAAP requires companies to show accounts receivable at net realizable value on the balance sheet and match bad debt expense to the period of sale (i.e., the allowance method) rather than waiting until specific accounts are written off to record the bad debt expense (i.e., the direct write-off method), unless accounts receivable are immaterial. Under the allowance method there are two approaches for estimating bad debt expense. Percentage of credit sales is an income statement approach that focuses on estimating the proper bad debt expense to match with that period's credit sales on the income statement. The aging method, on the other hand, is a balance sheet approach that analyzes the accounts receivable to estimate its net realizable value. This estimate provides the necessary ending allowance for doubtful accounts balance to report net accounts receivable at net realizable value.

Although bad debts result from actions of the purchaser (nonpayment), the amount of bad debt expense is influenced by the credit policies of the seller, as the following analysis illustrates.

CONCEPT Q&A

What are the conceptual and practical differences between the credit sales and aging methods?

Possible Answer:

The credit sales method estimates the amount to be shown as bad debt expense on the income statement. The aging method estimates the amount to be shown as the allowance for doubtful accounts on the balance sheet. The preadjustment balance in these accounts must be adjusted so that the ending balance equals the respective estimates. However, because bad debt expense is an income statement account that is closed to retained earnings at the end of every period, its preadjustment balance should be zero. As such, the adjustment is equal to the estimate of the ending balance. The allowance for doubtful accounts, on the other hand, is a balance sheet account and will typically have an existing balance.

DECISION-MAKING & ANALYSIS

Are Bad Debts Always Bad?

"In God we trust. All others pay cash." Thus reads a sign prominently situated on the counter of the Mt. Sterling Drug Company. For many years, Andy Forsythe, the owner of Mt. Sterling Drug, has been a pharmaceutical wholesaler. An outgoing and friendly individual who believes that the "personal touch" is an important ingredient in any successful business, Andy has always been very popular among pharmacists in the local community. However, recently Mt. Sterling Drug hasn't grown as much as Andy had hoped. He observes that the amount of sales to a group of longtime, loyal, and reliable customers has been steadily dwindling.

Andy has steadfastly maintained his "cash only" sales terms. "A bad debt is like money down the drain," he says. "Short of costly legal action, there's nothing you can do to recover your money. I refuse to have my company's future jeopardized by getting involved in bad debts."

Some of Andy's competitors, affiliates of large corporate conglomerates, have been attempting to lure business away from smaller wholesalers like Mt. Sterling by offering retail pharmacies various incentives. Among these are credit terms whereby a customer typically has 30 to 60 days to pay for a purchase and receives a 1 to 2 percent discount for prompt payment (usually within 10 days of sale). Although he is concerned about losing business to these larger companies, Andy fears bad debts even more.

Is Andy correct? Should bad debts be avoided at all costs?

There is no question that the inability to collect an account receivable is a serious problem. However, most wholesalers have come to accept bad debts as just another business expense. Certainly no company would grant credit knowing that the specific customer will not pay for the goods purchased. Nonetheless, granting credit is a "necessary evil"—something that must be done to generate repeat business and maintain a competitive position.

Andy's friendship with the local pharmacists does not guarantee that he will receive their business, especially if they can get a better deal elsewhere. Further, prudent screening of each customer's credit history should enable him to identify at least some of those who may have difficulty paying their accounts. Placing such restrictions as relatively low credit limits on these risky accounts or, in some cases, denying credit altogether should help Andy keep bad debts to a minimum. Suppose Mt. Sterling's gross margin is 30 percent of sales and that, as a result of the more liberal credit policy, sales increase by $100,000 and bad debts are limited to 3 percent of the new credit sales. Then Mt. Sterling's income from operations should increase by $27,000 (increased gross margin of $30,000 less bad debt expense of $3,000), rather than decreasing as Andy fears.

We now will focus on the cash management principles associated with accounts receivable.

OBJECTIVE ➤ 6
Describe the cash flow implications of accounts receivable.

Cash Management Principles Related to Accounts Receivable

In Chapter 4 we mentioned that a principle of cash management is increasing the speed of cash collection for receivables. An increasingly common practice is to **factor**, or sell, receivables. When receivables are factored, the seller receives an immediate cash payment reduced by the factor's fees. The factor, the buyer of the receivables, acquires the right to collect the receivables and the risk of uncollectibility. In a typical factoring arrangement, the sellers of the receivables have no continuing responsibility for their collection.

Factoring arrangements vary widely, but typically the factor charges a fee ranging from 1 percent to 3 percent. This fee compensates the factor for the time value of money (i.e., interest), the risk of uncollectability, and the tasks of billing and collection. For example, if Bolt Manufacturing factors $1,000,000 of receivables with a 1 percent fee, they would make the following entry:

Account and Explanation	Debit	Credit
Cash	990,000	
Factoring Fee Expense	10,000	
Accounts Receivable		1,000,000
(Record factoring of receivables)		

Assets	= Liabilities +	Stock-holders' Equity
+990,000		−10,000
−1,000,000		

Large businesses and financial institutions frequently package factored receivables as financial instruments or securities and sell them to investors. This process is known as **securitization**. For example, **General Motors Acceptance Corporation (GMAC)** sells car loans to special financial institutions set up by investment banks. The financial institutions pay GMAC with funds raised from the sale of securities or notes, called certificates for automobile receivables (CARs). Banks use similar arrangements to package their credit card receivables into securities called certificates for amortizing revolving debts (CARDs).

Credit and Debit Cards

Bank **credit cards**, such as **Visa** and **MasterCard**, are really just a special form of factoring. The issuer of the credit card (i.e., the bank) pays the seller the amount of each sale less a service charge (on the date of purchase) and then collects the full amount of the sale from the buyer (at some later date).[2] For example, if a retail customer uses a **Citibank** Visa Card to purchase $100 of merchandise from Bolt Manufacturing, Bolt would make the following entry assuming Citibank charges a 1.55 percent service charge:

Account and Explanation	Debit	Credit
Cash	98.45	
Service Charge Expense	1.55	
Sales Revenue		100.00
(Record sales)		

Assets	= Liabilities +	Stockholders' Equity
+98.45		−1.55
		+100.00

Although a 1.55 percent service charge may seem expensive, credit card sales provide sellers with a number of advantages over supplying credit directly to customers. First, sellers receive the money immediately. Second, they avoid bad debts because as long as the credit card verification procedures are followed, the credit card company absorbs the cost of customers who do not pay. Third, recordkeeping costs lessen because employees are not needed to manage these accounts. Fourth, sellers believe that by accepting credit cards, their sales will increase. For example, how many of you have ever driven away from a gas station that does not accept credit cards or even one that merely does not allow you to pay at the pump?

---

[2] The bank may also pay the full amount of the sale to the seller and then bill the service charge at the end of the period.

Of course, many large retailers are willing to take on these costs to avoid the credit card service charge. For example, **Sears**, **Kohls**, **Target**, **Macy's**, and most other large retailers have internal credit cards. When these cards are used the seller records it like any other accounts receivable and no service charge expense is incurred; however, they are accepting the risk of uncollectible accounts and the cost of servicing these accounts.

Non-bank credit cards, such as **American Express**, also result in a receivable for the seller because the issuer of the credit card (e.g., American Express) does not immediately pay the cash to the seller. American Express also charges a higher service charge to the seller. Consequently, sellers find American Express to be more costly than bank cards, such as Visa or MasterCard, which explains why many businesses do not accept American Express.

A **debit card** authorizes a bank to make an immediate electronic withdrawal (debit) from the holder's bank account. The debit card is used like a credit card except that a bank electronically reduces (debits) the holder's bank account and increases (credits) the merchant's bank account for the amount of a sale made on a debit card.

Debit cards appear to be somewhat disadvantageous to the card holder as transactions cannot be rescinded by stopping payment. Further, a purchase using a debit card causes an immediate reduction in a bank account balance, while a check written at the same time will require at least one or two days to clear, allowing the depositor to benefit from the additional money in the account until the check is presented at the bank for payment. However, debit cards offer significant advantages to banks and merchants in reduced transaction-processing costs. Thus, banks and merchants have incentive to design debit cards that minimize or eliminate the disadvantages and costs to card users.

Notes Receivable

OBJECTIVE ➤ 7

Account for notes receivable from inception to maturity.

Notes receivable are receivables that generally specify an interest rate and a maturity date at which any interest and principal must be repaid. Our discussion here is limited to simple notes that specify the repayment of interest and principal in a single payment on a given day (more complicated notes are described in Chapter 10).

The excess of the total amount of money paid to a lender over the amount borrowed is called **interest**. The amount borrowed is the **principal**. In other words, the total amount paid to the lender equals the sum of the interest and the principal for the note.

Interest can be considered compensation paid to the lender for giving up the use of resources for the period of a note (i.e., the time value of money). The interest rate specified in the note is an annual rate. Therefore, when calculating interest, you must consider the duration of the note using the following formula:

$$\text{Interest} = \text{Principal} \times \text{Annual interest rate} \times \text{Fraction of one year}$$

Further, you will recall from Chapter 2 that the matching concept and the revenue recognition concept require that expenses and revenues be identified with specific accounting periods. If only one month of interest has been incurred by year-end, an adjusting entry is required to recognize interest revenue and a corresponding interest receivable. Any remaining interest is recognized in subsequent periods.[3]

---

[3] Interest is, in fact, often computed in terms of days rather than months. Suppose, for example, that the three-month note runs for 92 days (two 31-day months and one 30-day month). The total interest on the 92-day note would be $302.47 [($10,000)(0.12)(92/365)], and the first 31-day month's interest would be $101.92 [($10,000)(0.12)(31/365)]. Observe that daily interest complicates the arithmetic associated with interest calculations but does not alter the basic form of the calculations. To simplify interest computations, we will use monthly interest throughout this chapter. The accounting for notes receivable is demonstrated in Cornerstone 5-4.

CORNERSTONE
5-4

HOW TO Account for Notes Receivable

Concept:
Notes receivable are recognized for the amount of cash loaned or goods/services sold. This is the principal amount of the note receivable. Any excess of the amount received over principal is recognized as interest revenue in the period the interest was earned.

Information:
Schleswig, Inc., an equipment dealer, sells a $50,000 truck to Dover Electric Company on January 1, 2008, in exchange for a note bearing 10 percent interest.

Required:
1. Prepare the journal entry to record the sale on January 1, 2008.
2. How much interest will be paid if Dover Electric repays the note on July 1, 2008?
3. Prepare Schleswig's journal entry to record the cash received to pay off the note and interest on July 1, 2008.
4. How much interest will be paid if Dover Electric repays the note on December 31, 2008?
5. Prepare Schleswig's journal entry to record the cash received to pay off the note and interest on December 31, 2008.
6. How much interest will be paid if Dover Electric repays the note on March 31, 2009?
7. Prepare Schleswig's journal entries to accrue for interest on December 31, 2008 and record the cash received to pay off the note and interest on March 31, 2009.

Solution:
1.

Date	Account and Explanation	Debit	Credit
January 1, 2008	Notes Receivable	50,000	
	Sales Revenue		50,000
	(Record sale)		

Assets =	Liabilities +	Stockholders' Equity
+50,000		+50,000

2. Interest = Principal × Annual Interest Rate × Fraction of One Year
   = $50,000 × 10% × (6/12)
   = $2,500

3.

Date	Account and Explanation	Debit	Credit
July 1, 2008	Cash	52,500	
	Notes Receivable		50,000
	Interest Revenue		2,500
	(Record collection of note receivable)		

Assets =	Liabilities +	Stockholders' Equity
+52,500		+2,500
−50,000		

4. Interest = Principal × Annual Interest Rate × Fraction of One Year
   = $50,000 × 10% × (12/12)
   = $5,000

5.

Date	Account and Explanation	Debit	Credit
December 31, 2008	Cash	55,000	
	Notes Receivable		50,000
	Interest Revenue		5,000
	(Record collection of note receivable)		

Assets =	Liabilities +	Stockholders' Equity
+55,000		+5,000
−50,000		

6.   Interest = Principal × Annual Interest Rate × Fraction of One Year

$$= \$50,000 \times 10\% \times (15/12)$$

$$= \$6,250$$

CORNERSTONE
5 - 4
(continued)

7.

Date	Account and Explanation	Debit	Credit
December 31, 2008	Interest Receivable	5,000	
	Interest Revenue		5,000
	(Record accrual of interest)		

	Stockholders'
Assets = Liabilities +	Equity
+5,000	+5,000

Date	Account and Explanation	Debit	Credit
March 31, 2009	Cash	56,250	
	Notes Receivable		50,000
	Interest Receivable		5,000
	Interest Revenue		1,250
	(Record collection of note receivable)		

	Stockholders'
Assets = Liabilities +	Equity
+56,250	+1,250
−5,000	
−50,000	

Analyzing Sales and Receivables

Analysts of the financial statements are extremely concerned with both sales and receivables.

OBJECTIVE ➤ 8
Analyze profitability and asset management using sales and receivables.

Sales

Because sales revenue is such a key component of a company's success, analysts are interested in a large number of ratios that incorporate sales. Many of these ratios attempt to measure the return the company is earning on sales. These are called profitability ratios. For example, the ratio of income statement subtotals such as gross margin, operating income, and net income to sales are examined, but really any income statement subtotal deemed important can be of interest. The three most common ratios are the gross profit ratio (gross profit ÷ net sales), the operating margin ratio (operating income ÷ net sales), and the net profit margin ratio (net income ÷ net sales).

Each of these ratios reveals information about a company's strategy and the competition it faces. For example, consider two large players in the retail industry— **Wal-Mart** and Macy's. Information available indicates that these two stores possess the following five-year averages for these ratios:

	Wal-Mart	Macy's	Industry
Gross Margin Ratio	23.14%	40.51%	26.16%
Operating Margin Percentage	3.59%	8.69%	6.05%
Net Profit Margin	3.49%	4.56%	3.62%

Macy's higher gross margin percentage suggests that Macy's is able to charge a premium on its merchandise. That is, Macy's follows a product differentiation strategy in which it tries to convince customers that its products are superior, distinctive, etc. Wal-Mart, on the other hand, is a low-cost provider, who attempts to convince customers that it offers the lowest prices.

Analysts also like to look at the operating margin percentage and net profit margin to see how much is left from a sales dollar after paying for the product and all its operations. For these ratios Macy's still retains a larger percentage of each sales dollar than Wal-Mart. How is it, then, that Wal-Mart makes so much money? It has a lot of sales dollars—its total revenue of almost $375 billion in 2008 is approximately 14 times greater than Macy's $27 billion.

Receivables

Analysts are also concerned with asset management. Asset management refers to how efficiently a company is using the resources at its disposal. One of the most widely-used asset management ratios is accounts receivable turnover, which is net sales ÷ average net accounts receivable.

This ratio provides a measure of how many times average trade receivables are collected during the period. In theory, net credit sales would be a much better numerator, but that figure is not normally disclosed. A higher number is better because it indicates that the company is more quickly collecting cash (through sales) from its inventory. As discussed in Chapter 4's section on cash management, this holds down borrowing costs and allows for a greater investment. Changes in this ratio over time are also very important. For example, a significant reduction in receivables turnover may indicate that management is extending credit to customers who are not paying.

Accounts receivable turnover for Wal-Mart and Macy's are:

	Wal-Mart	Macy's	Industry
Accounts Receivable Turnover	115.35	53.70	29.11

As expected, Wal-Mart is extremely efficient with its asset management because effective cash management is necessary for low cost providers. Of course, it is difficult to compare Macy's to Wal-Mart because they likely engage in different financing practices. For example, a greater proportion of Wal-Mart sales are made using cash or external credit cards (e.g., Visa), while Macy's has a larger proportion of sales using internal credit cards (i.e., a Macy's card). The internal credit cards result in lower accounts receivable turnover. Cornerstone 5-5 illustrates the calculation of these ratios for Wal-Mart.

**CORNERSTONE
5-5**

HOW TO Calculate the Gross Profit, Operating Margin, Net Profit Margin, and Accounts Receivable Turnover Ratios

Concept:
The gross profit, operating margin, and net profit margin ratios provide measures of the return the company is earning on sales. The accounts receivable turnover ratio provides a measure of how many times average accounts receivables are collected during the period.

Information:
The following information (in millions) is available for Wal-Mart for its fiscal year ending January 31, 2008:

Net Sales	$374,526	Accounts Receivable, 1/31/08	$3,654
Gross Profit	88,011	Accounts Receivable, 1/31/07	2,840
Operating Income	12,884		
Net Income	12,731		

Required:
1. Compute the gross profit ratio for Wal-Mart for 2008.
2. Compute the operating margin ratio for Wal-Mart for 2008.
3. Compute the net profit margin ratio for Wal-Mart for 2008.
4. Compute the accounts receivable turnover for Wal-Mart for 2008.

Solution:
1. Wal-Mart's gross profit ratio is:

$$\text{Gross Profit Ratio} = \frac{\text{Gross Profit}}{\text{Net Sales}}$$

$$= \frac{\$88,011}{\$374,526} = 0.235, \text{ or } 23.50\%$$

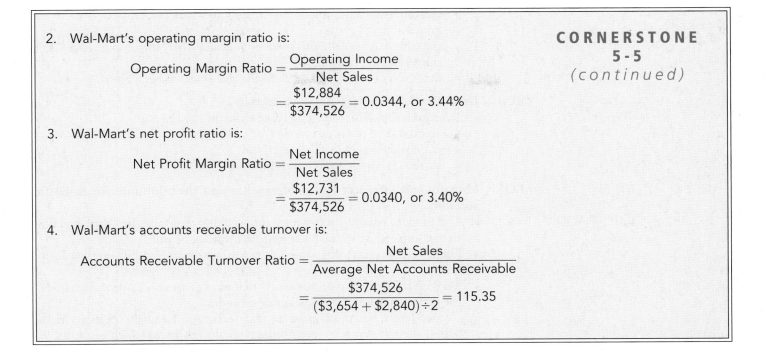

2. Wal-Mart's operating margin ratio is:

$$\text{Operating Margin Ratio} = \frac{\text{Operating Income}}{\text{Net Sales}}$$

$$= \frac{\$12,884}{\$374,526} = 0.0344, \text{ or } 3.44\%$$

3. Wal-Mart's net profit ratio is:

$$\text{Net Profit Margin Ratio} = \frac{\text{Net Income}}{\text{Net Sales}}$$

$$= \frac{\$12,731}{\$374,526} = 0.0340, \text{ or } 3.40\%$$

4. Wal-Mart's accounts receivable turnover is:

$$\text{Accounts Receivable Turnover Ratio} = \frac{\text{Net Sales}}{\text{Average Net Accounts Receivable}}$$

$$= \frac{\$374,526}{(\$3,654 + \$2,840) \div 2} = 115.35$$

**CORNERSTONE
5-5**
(continued)

Summary of Learning Objectives

LO1. Explain the criteria for revenue recognition.
- Revenue is recognized when it is:
  - realized or realizable
  - earned
- The terms "realized" and "realizable" mean that the selling price is fixed and determinable and collectibility is reasonably assured.
- Revenue is considered earned when delivery has occurred or services have been provided.

LO2. Measure net sales revenue.
- The appropriate amount of revenue to recognize is generally the cash received or the cash equivalent of accounts receivable.
- However, companies often induce customers to buy by offering:
  - sales discounts
  - sales returns
  - sales allowances
- Sales discounts are reductions of the normal selling price to encourage prompt payment.
- Sales returns occur when a customer returns goods as unsatisfactory.
- Sales allowances occur when a customer agrees to keep goods with minor defects if the seller reduces the selling price.
- These events are recorded in contra-revenue accounts that reduce gross sales to net sales.

LO3. Describe internal control procedures for merchandise sales.
- Since sales revenues have a significant effect on a company's net income, internal control procedures must be established to ensure that the amounts reported are correct.
- Typically sales are not recorded until a three-way match is performed between the:

- customer purchase order (which indicates that the customer wants the goods)
- the shipping document (which indicates that the goods have been shipped to the customer)
- the invoice (which indicates that the customer has been billed

LO4.   Describe the principal types of receivables.
- Receivables are classified along three different dimensions:
  - accounts and notes receivable
  - trade and non-trade receivables
  - current and noncurrent receivables

LO5.   Measure and interpret bad debt expense and the allowance for doubtful accounts.
- The primary issues in accounting for accounts receivable are when and how to measure bad debts (i.e., accounts that will not be paid).
- GAAP requires receivables to be shown at net realizable value on the balance sheet.
- Further, the matching principle says that an expense should be recognized in the period in which it helps generate revenues.
- Consequently, we must estimate and recognize bad debt expense in the period the sale is made—even though we do not know which accounts will be uncollectible.
- The estimate is made by using either:
  - the credit sales method or
  - the aging method
- The credit sales method estimates the bad debt expense directly.
- The aging method estimates the ending balance needed in the allowance for doubtful accounts, and bad debt expense follows.

LO6.   Describe the cash flow implications of accounts receivable.
- Companies can increase the speed of cash collection on receivables by factoring, or selling, their receivables.
- The buyer of the receivables will charge a fee to compensate themselves for the time value of money, the risk of uncollectability, and the tasks of billing and collection.
- Receivables may also be packaged as financial instruments or securities and sold to investors. This is referred to as securitization.
- A special case of selling receivables is accepting credit cards like MasterCard and Visa.

LO7.   Account for notes receivable from inception to maturity.
- Notes receivable are recognized for the amount of cash borrowed or goods/services purchased.
- This is the principal amount of the note receivable.
- Any excess of amount repaid over principal is recognized as interest revenue in the period the interest was earned.

LO8.   Analyze profitability and asset management using sales and receivables.
- Because sales revenue is such a key component of a company's success, analysts are interested in a large number of ratios that incorporate sales.
- Many of these ratios attempt to measure how much the company is making on sales. These are called profitability ratios.
  - Gross profit percentage
  - Operating margin percentage
  - Net profit margin
- Analysts are also concerned with asset management. Asset management refers to how efficiently a company is using the resources at its disposal.
- One of the most widely-used asset management ratios is accounts receivable turnover.

CORNERSTONE 5-1	How to record receivables using the gross method, page 235
CORNERSTONE 5-2	How to estimate bad debt expense with the percentage of credit sales method, page 241
CORNERSTONE 5-3	How to estimate the allowance for doubtful accounts with the aging method, page 243
CORNERSTONE 5-4	How to account for notes receivable, page 248
CORNERSTONE 5-5	How to calculate the gross profit, operating margin, net profit margin, and accounts receivable turnover ratios, page 250

CORNERSTONES FOR CHAPTER 5

Key Terms

Review Problem

Recording Sales and Receivables

Qwurk Productions performs graphic design services including designing and maintaining websites. The following activities occurred during 2009 and 2010:

11/1/09	Qwurk delivers a new logo to GDC Advisors and submits a bill for $2,000 with terms 2/10, n/30.
11/15/09	Qwurk delivers an overall web concept to Mutare, which Mutare approves. Qwurk submits a bill for $1,000 with terms 2/10, n/30.
11/20/09	Qwurk delivers paper and envelopes incorporating the new logo to GDC Advisors and submits a bill for $200.
11/22/09	Mutare pays for the 11/15 bill related to a new overall web concept.
11/25/09	GDC complains that the printing on much of the paper and envelopes is unacceptable. Qwurk offers to reduce the bill from $200 to $75. GDC accepts.
11/29/09	GDC pays for the 11/1 bill for a new logo and $75 for the 11/20 bill for paper and envelopes.
12/1/09	Qwurk installs a new website incorporating order fulfillment applications for Redbird Enterprises. Redbird signs a note to pay $20,000 plus 6 percent interest due on 7/1/19.
12/15/09	Qwurk writes off a $600 account receivable.
12/31/09	After performing an aging of its accounts receivable, Qwurk estimates that $2,000 of its accounts receivable will be uncollectible on a total balance of $600,000. The allowance for doubtful accounts has a credit balance of $300 prior to adjustment.

| 7/1/10 | Redbird pays the note and interest in full. |
| 12/31/10 | For the year ended December 31, 2010, Qwurk has sales of $6,000,000; sales discounts of $15,000; sales returns and allowances of $20,000. |

Required:

1. Provide the journal entry for November 1, 2009 assuming Qwurk uses the gross method of recording receivables.
2. Provide the journal entry for November 15, 2009 assuming Qwurk uses the gross method of recording receivables.
3. Provide the journal entry for November 20, 2009 assuming Qwurk uses the gross method of recording receivables.
4. Calculate how much Mutare paid and provide the journal entry for November 22, 2009.
5. Provide the journal entry for November 25, 2009.
6. Calculate how much GDC paid and provide the journal entry for November 29, 2009.
7. Provide the journal entry for December 1, 2009.
8. Provide the journal entry for December 15, 2009.
9. Provide the necessary adjusting entries for December 31, 2009.
10. What is the net realizable value of Qwurk's accounts receivable at December 31, 2009?
11. Calculate how much interest Redbird paid and provide the journal entry for July 1, 2010.
12. Provide the income statement presentation of Qwurk's 2010 Sales.

Solution:

1.

Assets = Liabilities +	Stockholders' Equity
+2,000	+2,000

Date	Account and Explanation	Debit	Credit
Nov. 1, 2009	Accounts Receivable	2,000	
	Sales		2,000

2.

Assets = Liabilities +	Stockholders' Equity
+1,000	+1,000

Date	Account and Explanation	Debit	Credit
Nov. 15, 2009	Accounts Receivable	1,000	
	Sales		1,000

3.

Assets = Liabilities +	Stockholders' Equity
+200	+200

Date	Account and Explanation	Debit	Credit
Nov. 20, 2009	Accounts Receivable	200	
	Sales		200

4.

Assets = Liabilities +	Stockholders' Equity
+980	−20
−1,000	

Date	Account and Explanation	Debit	Credit
Nov. 22, 2009	Cash	980*	
	Sales Discounts	20	
	Accounts Receivable		1,000

*Gross amount	$1,000
Less: Discount ($1,000 × 2%)	20
Total paid	$ 980

5.

Assets = Liabilities +	Stockholders' Equity
−125	−125

Date	Account and Explanation	Debit	Credit
Nov. 25, 2009	Sales Returns & Allowances	125	
	Accounts Receivable		125

6.

Date	Account and Explanation	Debit	Credit
Nov. 29, 2009	Cash [$2,000 (from 11/1) + $75 (from 11/20 and 11/25)]	2,075	
	Accounts Receivable		2,075

Assets = Liabilities +		**Stockholders' Equity**
+2,075		
−2,075		

*Gross amount	$2,000
Less: Discount (not allowed; paid after 10 days)	0
Total paid	$2,000

7.

Date	Account and Explanation	Debit	Credit
Dec. 1, 2009	Notes Receivable	20,000	
	Sales		20,000

Assets = Liabilities +		**Stockholders' Equity**
+20,000		+20,000

8.

Date	Account and Explanation	Debit	Credit
Dec. 15, 2009	Allowance for Doubtful Accounts	600	
	Accounts Receivable		600

Assets = Liabilities +		**Stockholders' Equity**
+600		
−600		

9.   *To record one month's interest on the December 1, 2009 note receivable:*

Date	Account and Explanation	Debit	Credit
Dec. 31, 2009	Interest Receivable (20,000 × 6% × 1/12)	100	
	Interest Income		100

Assets = Liabilities +		**Stockholders' Equity**
+100		+100
−1,700		−1,700

To adjust the allowance for doubtful accounts to reflect Qwurk's estimate:

Bad Debt Expense	1,700	
Allowance for Doubtful Accounts		1,700*

*Qwurk's estimate warrants a $2,000 credit balance. Because the account already has a $300 credit balance, a $1,700 credit is needed.

10.

December 31, 2009	Accounts receivable	$600,000
	Less: Allowance for doubtful	
	accounts	2,000
	Net accounts receivable	$598,000

Net Accounts Receivable are shown at net realizable value.

11.   July 1, 2010:

$$\text{Interest paid} = \$20,000 \times 6\% \times 7/12$$
$$= \$700$$

However, interest income recognized for Qwurk is for the period January 1, 2010 through July 1, 2010. The interest for December 2009 was recognized in 2009 (see journal entry in *8*).

Assets = Liabilities +		**Stockholders' Equity**
+20,700		+600
−100		
−20,000		

Cash	20,700	
Interest Income		600
Interest Receivable (from *8*)		100
Notes Receivable		20,000

12.

Gross sales revenue	$6,000,000
Less: Sales discounts	15,000
Less: Sales returns and allowances	20,000
Net sales revenue	$5,965,000

Discussion Questions

1. When is revenue recognized?
2. Explain the criteria for revenue recognition.
3. When is revenue generally considered earned?
4. What four criteria has the SEC issued as further guidance for revenue recognition?
5. How is net sales revenue calculated?
6. Why might users of financial statements prefer the separate disclosure of gross sales revenue and sales returns and allowances to the disclosure of a single net sales revenue amount?
7. Why are sales discounts offered?
8. What are sales returns?
9. What are sales allowances? How do sales allowances differ from sales discounts?
10. What are trade discounts and quantity discounts? From an accounting viewpoint, how does the effect of trade and quantity discounts on selling (or invoice) price differ from the effect of sales discounts?
11. What documents must be present to trigger the recording of a sale (and associated receivable) in the accounting records?
12. Describe the documents that underlie the typical accounting system for sales. Give an example of a failure of internal control that might occur if these documents were not properly prepared.
13. What are the principal types of receivables?
14. Under the allowance method, why do we make an entry to record bad debt expense in the period of sale rather than in the period in which an account is determined to be uncollectible?
15. Why is the direct write-off method not GAAP?
16. What is the conceptual difference between the (1) percentage of credit sales and (2) aging methods of estimating bad debts?
17. What kind of account is *allowance for doubtful accounts*? What does it represent?
18. Why do companies issue credit when their past experience indicates that some customers will not pay?
19. How much interest will be due at maturity for each of the following interest-bearing notes?

	Principal	Months to Maturity	Annual Interest Rate
a.	$10,000	2	12%
b.	42,000	5	14
c.	18,000	4	13
d.	37,000	6	11

20. A business borrows $1,000, giving a note that requires repayment of the amount borrowed in two payments of $600 each, one at the end of each of the next two six-month periods. Calculate the total interest on the note. What is the principal amount of the note?
21. A business borrows $1,000, giving a note that requires an interest rate of 12 percent per year and repayment of principal plus interest in a single payment at the end of one year. Calculate the total interest on the note. What is the amount of the single payment?
22. Describe what happens when receivables are factored.
23. Accepting major credit cards requires the seller to pay a service charge. What advantages does the seller obtain by accepting major credit cards?
24. Why is interest typically charged on notes receivable, but not on accounts receivable?

25. How may analyzing sales and receivables provide information about a firm's profitability?
26. How may analyzing sales and receivables provide information about a firm's asset management?

Multiple-Choice Exercises

5-1 Which of the following is *not* one of the criteria for revenue recognition?

a. Delivery has occurred or services have been provided.
b. The seller's price to the buyer is fixed and determinable.
c. Collectability is certain.
d. Persuasive evidence of an arrangement exists.

5-2 Food To Go is a local catering service. Conceptually, when should Food To Go recognize revenue from its catering service?

a. at the date the customer places the order
b. at the date the meals are served
c. at the date the invoice is mailed to the customer
d. at the date the customer's payment is received

5-3 When is revenue from the sale of merchandise normally recognized?

a. when the customer takes possession of the merchandise
b. when the customer pays for the merchandise
c. either on the date the customer takes possession of the merchandise or the date on which the customer pays
d. when the customer takes possession of the merchandise, if sold for cash, or when payment is received, if sold on credit

5-4 What does the phrase, "Revenue is recognized at the point of sale" mean?

a. Revenue is recorded in the accounting records when the cash is received from a customer, and reported on the income statement when sold to the customer.
b. Revenue is recorded in the accounting records and reported on the income statement when the cash is received from the customer.
c. Revenue is recorded in the accounting records when the goods are sold to a customer, and reported on the income statement when the cash payment is received from the customer.
d. Revenue is recorded in the accounting records and reported on the income statement when goods are sold and delivered to a customer.

5-5 On August 31, 2009, Montana Corporation signed a four-year contract to provide services for Minefield Company at $30,000 per year. Minefield will pay for each year of services on the first day of each service year, starting with September 1, 2009. Using the accrual basis of accounting, when should Montana Corporation recognize revenue?

a. on the first day of each year when the cash is received
b. on the last day of each year after the services have been provided
c. equally throughout the year as services are earned
d. only at the end of the entire contract

5-6 Under the gross method, the seller records discounts taken by the buyer

a. at the end of the period in question
b. never; discounts are irrelevant under the gross method
c. after the receivable is collected
d. in a contra-revenue account

5-7 On April 20, McLean Company sells merchandise on account to Tazwell Corporation for $3,000 with terms 1/10, n/30. On April 28, Tazwell pays for half of the merchandise and on May 19 it pays for the other half. What is the total amount of cash McLean received?

a. $3,000
b. $2,985
c. $2,970
d. $2,700

5-8 Which of the following statements concerning internal control procedures for merchandise sales is *not* correct?

a. A sale and its associated receivable are recorded only when the order, shipping, and billing documents are all present.
b. Shipping and billing documents are prepared based on the order document.
c. The order document is not necessary for the buyer to be obligated to accept and pay for the ordered goods.
d. Accounting for a sale begins with the receipt of a purchase order or some similar document from a customer.

5-9 All of the following are ways in which receivables are distinguished except:

a. accounts or notes receivable
b. collectible or uncollectible
c. trade or nontrade receivable
d. current or noncurrent

5-10 Which one of the following best describes the allowance for doubtful accounts?

a. contra account
b. liability account
c. income statement account
d. cash flow account

5-11 If a company uses the direct write-off method of accounting for bad debts,

a. it is applying the matching principle.
b. it will record bad debt expense only when an account is determined to be uncollectible.
c. it will reduce the accounts receivable account at the end of the accounting period for estimated uncollectible accounts.
d. it will report accounts receivable in the balance sheet at their net realizable value.

5-12 Which of the following best describes the objective of estimating bad debt expense with the credit sales method?

a. to determine the amount of actual bad debt during a given period
b. to estimate the amount of bad debt expense based on an aging of accounts receivable
c. to estimate bad debt expense based on a percentage of credit sales made during the period
d. to facilitate the use of the direct write-off method

5-13 Which of the following best describes the concept of the aging method of receivables?

a. An accurate estimate of bad debt expense may be arrived at by multiplying historical bad debt rates by the amount of credit sales made during a period.
b. The precise amount of bad debt expense may be arrived at by multiplying historical bad debt rates by the amount of credit sales made during a period.
c. Accounts receivable should be directly written off when the due date arrives and the customers have not paid the bill.
d. Estimating the appropriate balance for the allowance for doubtful accounts results in the appropriate value for net accounts receivable on the balance sheet.

5-14 The aging method is closely related to the:

a. income statement
b. balance sheet
c. statement of cash flows
d. statement of retained earnings

5-15 The credit sales approach is closely related to the:

a. income statement
b. balance sheet
c. statement of cash flows
d. statement of retained earnings

5-16 The process by which firms package factored receivables as financial instruments or securities and sell them to investors is known as:

a. credit extension
b. aging of accounts receivable
c. bundling
d. securitization

5-17 Which one of the following statements is true if a company's collection period for accounts receivable is unacceptably long?

a. The company may need to borrow to acquire operating cash.
b. The company may offer trade discounts to lengthen the collection period.
c. Cash flows from operations may be higher than expected for the company's sales.
d. The company should expand operations with its excess cash.

5-18 Zenephia Corp. accepted a nine-month note receivable from a customer on October 1, 2008. If Zenephia has an accounting period which ends on December 31, 2008, when would it most likely recognize interest revenue from the note?

a. on December 31, 2008 only
b. on July 1, 2009 only
c. on December 31, 2008 and June 30, 2009
d. on October 1, 2008

5-19 The "principal" of a note receivable refers to:

a. the amount of interest due
b. the present value of the note
c. the financing company that is lending the money
d. the amount of cash borrowed

5-20 Net profit margin percentage is calculated by:

a. dividing net income by (net) sales
b. dividing operating income by (net) sales
c. subtracting operating income from (net) sales
d. subtracting net income from (net) sales

Cornerstone Exercises

OBJECTIVE ➤ 1

Cornerstone Exercise 5-21 SERVICE REVENUE

Kibitz Fitness received $12,000 from customers on September 30, 2009. These payments were advance payments of yearly membership dues.

Required:

At December 31, 2009, calculate what the balances in the Unearned Service Revenue and Service Revenue accounts will be.

OBJECTIVE ➤ 1

Cornerstone Exercise 5-22 SERVICE REVENUE

Softball Magazine Company received advance payments of $5,000 from customers during 2009. At December 31, 2009, $1,200 of the advance payments still had not been earned.

Required:

After the adjustments are recorded and posted at December 31, 2009, calculate what the balances will be in the Unearned Magazine Revenue and Magazine Revenue accounts?

OBJECTIVE ➤ 2
CORNERSTONE 5-1

Cornerstone Exercise 5-23 SALES DISCOUNTS TAKEN

Bolton Garage Doors Corporation sold merchandise with a price of $22,500 to Sammy's Wholesale Company. Bolton offered terms of 2/10, n/30.

Required:

Prepare the journal entry to record the sale using the gross method. Also, prepare the journal entry assuming the payment is made within 10 days (within the discount period).

OBJECTIVE ➤ 2
CORNERSTONE 5-1

Cornerstone Exercise 5-24 SALES DISCOUNTS NOT TAKEN

Bolton Garage Doors Corporation sold merchandise with a gross price of $22,500 to Sammy's Wholesale Company. Bolton offered terms of 2/10, n/30 and uses the gross method.

Required:

Prepare the journal entry assuming the payment is made after 10 days (after the discount period).

OBJECTIVE ➤ 2
CORNERSTONE 5-1

Cornerstone Exercise 5-25 SALES DISCOUNTS

Ramsden Manufacturing sold merchandise with a gross price of $25,000 to Garner's Hardware Store. Ramsden offered terms of 3/10, n/30.

Required:

Prepare the necessary journal entries to record the sale under the gross method.

OBJECTIVE ➤ 5
CORNERSTONE 5-2

Cornerstone Exercise 5-26 PERCENTAGE OF CREDIT SALES

Clarissa Company has credit sales of $400,000 during 2010 and estimates at the end of 2010 that 2 percent of these credit sales will eventually default. Also, during 2010 a customer defaults on a $775 balance related to goods purchased in 2009. Prior to the write off for the $775 default, Clarissa's accounts receivable and allowance for doubtful accounts balances were $402,000 and $129 (credit), respectively.

Required:

Estimate the appropriate balance for bad debt expense and prepare the adjusting entry to record the bad debt expense for 2010.

Cornerstone Exercise 5-27 WRITE-OFF OF UNCOLLECTIBLE ACCOUNTS

OBJECTIVE ➤ 5
CORNERSTONE 5-2

The Rock has credit sales of $650,000 during 2010 and estimates at the end of 2010 that 3 percent of these credit sales will eventually default. Also, during 2010 a customer defaults on a $1,225 balance related to goods purchased in 2009.

Required:

Prepare the journal entry to record the write-off of the defaulted $1,225 balance.

Cornerstone Exercise 5-28 AGING METHOD

OBJECTIVE ➤ 5
CORNERSTONE 5-3

On January 1, 2009, Hungryman, Inc., has the following balances for accounts receivable and allowance for doubtful accounts:

Accounts Receivable	$363,000
Allowance for Doubtful Accounts (a credit balance)	44,000

During 2009, Hungryman had $3,100,000 of credit sales, collected $2,915,000 of accounts receivable, and wrote off $50,000 of accounts receivable as uncollectible. At year end, Hungryman performs an aging of its accounts receivable balance and estimates that $15,000 will be uncollectible.

Required:

1. Calculate Hungryman's preadjustment balance in accounts receivable on December 31, 2009.
2. Calculate Hungryman's preadjustment balance in allowance for doubtful accounts on December 31, 2009.
3. Prepare the necessary adjusting entry for 2009.

Cornerstone Exercise 5-29 AGING METHOD

OBJECTIVE ➤ 5
CORNERSTONE 5-3

On January 1, 2010, Smith, Inc., has the following balances for accounts receivable and allowance for doubtful accounts:

Accounts Receivable	$273,000
Allowance for Doubtful Accounts (a credit balance)	4,600

During 2010, Smith had $2,175,000 of credit sales, collected $2,235,000 of accounts receivable, and wrote off $4,000 of accounts receivable as uncollectible. At year end, Smith performs an aging of its accounts receivable balance and estimates that $4,500 will be uncollectible.

Required:

1. Calculate Smith's preadjustment balance in accounts receivable on December 31, 2010.
2. Calculate Smith's preadjustment balance in allowance for doubtful accounts on December 31, 2010.
3. Prepare the necessary adjusting entry for 2010.

Cornerstone Exercise 5-30 PERCENTAGE OF CREDIT SALES METHOD

OBJECTIVE ➤ 5
CORNERSTONE 5-2

At December 31, 2009, Garner has a $1,000 credit balance in its allowance for doubtful accounts. Garner estimates that 1.5 percent of its 2010 credit sales will eventually default. During 2010, Garner had credit sales of $575,000.

Required:

Estimate the bad debt expense under the percentage of credit sales method.

Cornerstone Exercise 5-31 COLLECTION OF AMOUNTS PREVIOUSLY WRITTEN OFF

OBJECTIVE ➤ 5

Customer A owes XYZ Corp. $524. XYZ determines that the total amount is uncollectible and writes off all of Customer A's debt. Customer A later pays $260 to XYZ Corp.

Required:

Make the appropriate journal entries (if any) to record the receipt of the $260 by XYZ Corp. assuming XYZ uses the allowance method.

OBJECTIVE ➤ 6

Cornerstone Exercise 5-32 FACTORING RECEIVABLES

On July 1, Wilson, Inc., factors $200,000 of accounts receivable. The factor charges a 1.5 percent fee.

Required:

Prepare the journal entry to record the factoring of the accounts receivable on July 1.

OBJECTIVE ➤ 6
CORNERSTONE 5-3

Cornerstone Exercise 5-33 ACCOUNTS RECEIVABLE BALANCE

Beginning accounts receivable were $10,000. All sales were on account and totaled $700,000. Cash collected from customers totaled $650,000.

Required:

Calculate the ending accounts receivable balance.

OBJECTIVE ➤ 5
CORNERSTONE 5-3

Cornerstone Exercise 5-34 ACCOUNTS RECEIVABLE BALANCE

Beginning accounts receivable were $50,000 and ending accounts receivable were $70,000. $300,000 cash was collected from customers' credit sales.

Required:

Calculate the amount of sales on account during the period.

OBJECTIVE ➤ 6
CORNERSTONE 5-3

Cornerstone Exercise 5-35 ACCOUNTS RECEIVABLE BALANCE

Beginning accounts receivable were $11,000 and ending accounts receivable were $14,000. All sales were on credit and totaled $559,000.

Required:

Determine how much cash was collected from customers.

OBJECTIVE ➤ 6

Cornerstone Exercise 5-36 ACCOUNTING FOR CREDIT CARD SALES

Judy's College Shirts sells sweatshirts with imprinted college logos in Honey Creek Mall. At the end of a recent day, Judy's cash register included credit card documents for the following sales amounts:

MasterCard	$493.56
Visa	371.93

The merchant's charges are 2.3 percent for MasterCard and 2.8 percent for Visa. Judy's also had cash sales of $2,390.41 and $1,300.50 of sales on credit to Rampdan Services, a local business.

Required:

Prepare a journal entry to record these sales.

OBJECTIVE ➤ 7
CORNERSTONE 5-4

Cornerstone Exercise 5-37 NOTES RECEIVABLE

Portuguese, Inc., a truck dealership, sells a truck costing $18,000 to Undervalued Company on January 1, 2009, in exchange for a $40,000 note bearing 9 percent interest.

Required:

1. Prepare the journal entry to record the sale on January 1, 2009.
2. Determine how much interest Portuguese will receive if the note is repaid on July 1, 2009.
3. Provide Portuguese's journal entry to record the cash received to pay off the note and interest on July 1, 2009.

OBJECTIVE ➤ 7
CORNERSTONE 5-4

Cornerstone Exercise 5-38 NOTES RECEIVABLE

Frenchie, Inc., a truck dealership, sells a truck costing $15,000 to Overvalued Company on January 1, 2009, in exchange for a $30,000 note bearing 12 percent interest.

Required:

1. Prepare the journal entry to record the sale on January 1, 2009.
2. Determine how much interest Frenchie will receive if the note is repaid on December 31, 2009.
3. Prepare Frenchie's journal entry to record the cash received to pay off the note and interest on December 31, 2009.

Cornerstone Exercise 5-39 **RATIO ANALYSIS**

OBJECTIVE ➤ 8

CORNERSTONE 5-5

The following information pertains to Cobb Corporation's financial results for the past year.

Net sales	$100,000
CGS	35,000
Other expenses	12,000
Net income	53,000

Required:

1. Calculate Cobb's gross profit ratio.
2. Calculate Cobb's net profit margin ratio.

Cornerstone Exercise 5-40 **RATIO ANALYSIS**

OBJECTIVE ➤ 8

CORNERSTONE 5-5

ABC Corporation's 2008 net sales and average net trade accounts receivable were $4,300,000 and $975,000, respectively.

Required:

Calculate ABC's accounts receivable turnover.

Cornerstone Exercise 5-41 **RATIO ANALYSIS**

OBJECTIVE ➤ 8

CORNERSTONE 5-5

Bo Sports' 2008 net sales, average net trade accounts receivable, and net income were $7,300,000, $1,655,000, and $745,000, respectively.

Required:

Calculate Bo's:

1. accounts receivable turnover
2. net profit margin ratio

Exercises

Exercise 5-42 **CALCULATION OF REVENUE**

OBJECTIVE ➤ 1

Wallace Motors, which began business on December 31, 2009, buys and sells used cars. All its sales are to other car dealers. Four cars were purchased during January and none were purchased during February. The cars were sold under the following terms:

a. Three of the four cars were sold to Russell Auto Sale for a total of $75,000; the cars were delivered to Russell on January 18. Russell paid Wallace $20,000 on January 18 and the remaining $55,000 on February 12.
b. The fourth car purchased during January was sold to Hastings Classics for $28,000. The car was delivered to Hastings on January 25. Hastings paid Wallace on January 30.

Required:

Calculate the monthly revenue for Wallace Motors for January and February 2010.

Exercise 5-43 **REVENUE RECOGNITION**

OBJECTIVE ➤ 1

Volume Electronics sold a television to Sarah Merrifield on December 15, 2009. Sarah paid $100 at the time of the purchase and agreed to pay $100 each month for five months beginning January 15, 2010. The television had been purchased by Volume Electronics at a cost of $450 in June 2009. Volume had paid the $450 in August 2009.

Required:

Determine in what month or months revenue from this sale should be recorded by Volume Electronics to ensure proper application of accrual accounting.

OBJECTIVE ▸ 1   **Exercise 5-44 CALCULATION OF REVENUE FROM CASH COLLECTION**

Anderson Lawn Service provides mowing, weed control, and pest management services for a flat fee of $60 per lawn per month. During July, Anderson collected $4,980 in cash from customers, which included $420 for lawn care provided in June. At the end of July, Anderson had not collected from 11 customers who had promised to pay in August when they returned from vacation.

Required:

Calculate the amount of Anderson's revenue for July.

OBJECTIVE ▸ 2   **Exercise 5-45 EFFECTS OF SALES DISCOUNTS**

Citron Mechanical Systems makes all sales on credit, with terms 2/10, n/30. During 2009, the list price (prediscount) of goods sold was $498,500. Customers paid $350,000 (list price) of these sales within the discount period and the remaining $148,500 (list price) after the discount period. Citron uses the gross method of recording sales.

Required:

1. Compute the amount of sales that Citron recorded for 2009.
2. Compute the amount of cash that Citron collected from these sales.
3. Prepare a summary journal entry to record these sales and a second summary entry to record the cash collected.

OBJECTIVE ▸ 2   **Exercise 5-46 SALES DISCOUNT RECORDED AT GROSS**

Nevada Company sold merchandise with a list price of $12,500 to Small Enterprises with terms 3/15, n/30. Nevada records sales at gross.

Required:

1. Prepare the entries to record this sale in Nevada's journal.
2. Prepare the entry for Nevada's journal to record receipt of cash in payment for the sale *within* the discount period.
3. Prepare the entry for Nevada's journal to record receipt of cash in payment for the sale *after* the discount period.

OBJECTIVE ▸ 2   **Exercise 5-47 SALES, SALES RETURNS, AND SALES ALLOWANCES**

Rubin Enterprises had the following sales-related transactions on a recent day:

a. List price of goods sold on credit was $14,700; terms 3/15, n/45.
b. Cash sales were $1,150.
c. Goods with a list price of $1,200 were returned. The goods had been sold last week on credit with terms 3/15, n/45, and the customer had not yet paid for the merchandise.
d. Rubin provided an allowance of $250 to a customer because the goods were delivered after the promised date. The customer had paid cash at the time of the sale, so Rubin paid the $250 allowance in cash.

Required:

Prepare a journal entry for each of these transactions assuming Rubin uses the gross method.

OBJECTIVE ▸ 2   **Exercise 5-48 SALES RETURNS**

Swan and Bloom, Inc., is a wholesaler of novelty items to small stores. All sales are on credit with no discount offered. During March, Swan and Bloom accepted the following sales returns:

a. Johnson Company returned merchandise with a list price of $600. Johnson had not yet paid for the returned merchandise.
b. Becker Bargains returned merchandise with a list price of $750. Becker had paid for the merchandise.

c.   Fifth Avenue Market returned merchandise with a list price of $200. The bill for the returned merchandise had been paid.

d.   Thorn Catering returned merchandise with a list price of $600. Thorn had paid for the merchandise.

Required:

1.   Record the returns, assuming that cash refunds are paid to customers who had paid for their purchases.
2.   Record the returns, assuming that Swan and Bloom makes a credit to accounts receivable for all customers.
3.   Determine under what circumstances Swan and Bloom might credit accounts receivable even though the customer has paid for the merchandise.

Exercise 5-49 INTERNAL CONTROL FOR SALES

Arrow Products is a mail-order computer software sales outlet. Most of Arrow's customers call on its toll-free phone line and order software, paying with a credit card.

Required:

Explain why the shipping and billing documents are important internal controls for Arrow.

Exercise 5-50 AVERAGE UNCOLLECTIBLE ACCOUNT LOSSES AND BAD DEBT EXPENSE

The accountant for Porile Company prepared the following data for sales and losses from uncollectible accounts:

Year	Credit Sales	Losses from Uncollectible Accounts*
2005	$514,000	$ 7,710
2006	582,000	9,312
2007	670,000	10,385
2008	772,000	11,966

*Losses from uncollectible accounts are the actual losses related to sales of that year (rather than write-offs of that year).

Required:

1.   Calculate the average percentage of losses from uncollectible accounts for 2005 through 2008.
2.   Assume that the credit sales for 2009 are $874,000 and that the weighted average percentage calculated in (1) is used as an estimate of losses from uncollectible accounts for 2009 credit sales. Determine the bad debt expense for 2009 using the credit sales method.

Exercise 5-51 BAD DEBT EXPENSE: PERCENTAGE OF CREDIT SALES METHOD

Gilmore Electronics had the following data for a recent year:

Cash sales	$ 26,700
Credit sales	428,600
Accounts receivable determined to be uncollectible	6,300

Gilmore uses the allowance procedure to record bad debt expense. The firm's estimated rate for bad debts is 2.15 percent of credit sales.

Required:

1.   Prepare the journal entry to write off the uncollectible accounts.
2.   Prepare the journal entry to record bad debt expense.

OBJECTIVE ▸ 5   **Exercise 5-52 BAD DEBT EXPENSE: PERCENTAGE OF CREDIT SALES METHOD**

Bradford Plumbing had the following data for a recent year:

Credit sales	$289,000
Allowance for doubtful accounts, 1/1 (a credit balance)	4,120
Accounts receivable, 1/1	38,700
Collections on account receivable	291,000
Accounts receivable written off	4,620

Bradford estimates that 2.2 percent of credit sales will eventually default.

Required:

1. Compute bad debt expense for the year.
2. Determine the ending balances in accounts receivable and allowance for doubtful accounts.

OBJECTIVE ▸ 5   **Exercise 5-53 BAD DEBT EXPENSE: AGING METHOD**

Glencoe Supply had the following accounts receivable aging schedule at the end of a recent year.

Accounts Receivable Age	Amount	Proportion Expected to Default	Allowance Required
Current	$310,500	0.004	$ 1,242
1–30 days past due	47,500	0.02	950
31–45 days past due	25,000	0.08	2,000
46–90 days past due	12,800	0.20	2,560
91–135 days past due	6,100	0.25	1,525
Over 135 days past due	4,200	0.60	2,520
			$10,797

The balance in Glencoe's allowance for doubtful accounts at the beginning of the year was $49,620 (credit). During the year, accounts in the total amount of $51,232 were written off.

Required:

1. Determine bad debt expense.
2. Prepare the journal entry to record bad debt expense.

OBJECTIVE ▸ 5   **Exercise 5-54 AGING RECEIVABLES AND BAD DEBT EXPENSE**

Perkinson Corporation sells paper products to a large number of retailers. Perkinson's accountant has prepared the following aging schedule for its accounts receivable at the end of the year.

Accounts Receivable Category	Amount	Proportion Expected to Default
Within discount period	$384,500	0.004
1–30 days past discount period	187,600	0.015
31–60 days past discount period	41,800	0.085
Over 60 days past discount period	21,400	0.200

Before adjusting entries are entered, the balance in the allowance for doubtful accounts is a *debit* of $7,213.

Required:

1. Calculate the desired postadjustment balance in Perkinson's allowance for doubtful accounts.
2. Determine bad debt expense for the year.

Exercise 5-55 ALLOWANCE FOR DOUBTFUL ACCOUNTS

At the beginning of the year, Kullerud Manufacturing had a credit balance in its allowance for doubtful accounts of $6,307. During the year Kullerud made credit sales of $890,000, collected receivables in the amount of $812,000, wrote off receivables in the amount of $31,425, and recorded bad debt expense of $33,750.

Required:

Compute the ending balance in Kullerud's allowance for doubtful accounts.

Exercise 5-56 CORRECTING AN ERRONEOUS WRITE-OFF

The new bookkeeper at Karlin Construction Company was asked to write off two accounts totaling $1,710 that had been determined to be uncollectible. Accordingly, he debited accounts receivable for $1,710 and credited bad debt expense for the same amount.

Required:

1. Determine what was wrong with the bookkeeper's entry assuming Karlin uses the allowance method.
2. Give both the entry he should have made and the entry required to correct his error.

Exercise 5-57 FACTORING ACCOUNTS RECEIVABLE

On February 1, Anderson, Inc., factors $1,200,000 of accounts receivable. The factor charges a 2 percent fee.

Required:

Prepare the journal entry to record the factoring of the accounts receivable on February 1.

Exercise 5-58 ACCOUNTING FOR NOTES RECEIVABLE

Tucker Products sold inventory costing $20,000 to Thomas, Inc., in exchange for a five-month, $50,000, 12 percent note receivable. Thomas, Inc., paid Tucker the full amount of interest and principal on April 30, 2010.

Required:

Prepare the necessary entries for Tucker to record the transaction described above.

Exercise 5-59 RECORDING NOTES RECEIVABLE: ISSUANCE, PAYMENT, AND DEFAULT

Marydale Products permits its customers to defer payment by giving personal notes instead of cash. All the notes bear interest and require the customer to pay the entire note in a single payment six months after issuance. Consider the following transactions, which describe Marydale's experience with two such notes:

a. On October 31, Marydale accepts a six-month, 12 percent note from customer A in lieu of a $3,600 cash payment for merchandise delivered on that day.
b. On February 28, Marydale accepts a six-month, $2,400, 12 percent note from customer B in lieu of a $2,400 cash payment for merchandise delivered on that day.
c. On April 30, customer A pays the entire note plus interest in cash.
d. On August 31, customer B pays the entire note plus interest in cash.

Required:

Prepare the necessary journal and adjusting entries required to record transactions *a* through *d* in Marydale's records.

Exercise 5-60 RATIO ANALYSIS

The following information was taken from Nash, Inc.'s trial balances as of December 31, 2008, and December 31, 2009.

	12/31/2009	12/31/2008
Accounts receivable	$ 32,000	$ 39,000
Accounts payable	47,000	36,000
Sales	219,000	128,000
Sales returns	4,000	2,300
Retained earnings	47,000	16,000
Dividends	5,000	1,000
Net income	36,000	9,000

Required:

Calculate the net profit margin and accounts receivable turnover for 2009.

OBJECTIVE ➤ 8

Exercise 5-61 RATIO ANALYSIS

The following information was taken from Logsden Manufacturing's trial balances as of December 31, 2008, and December 31, 2009.

	12/31/2009	12/31/2008
Accounts receivable	$ 13,000	$ 17,000
Accounts payable	22,000	15,000
CGS	140,000	119,000
Sales	274,000	239,000
Sales returns	12,000	11,000
Retained earnings	47,000	16,000
Dividends	5,000	1,000
Income from operations	25,000	16,000
Net income	21,000	18,000

Required:

Calculate the gross profit ratio and operating margin ratio for 2009.

Problem Set A

OBJECTIVE ➤ 1

Problem 5-62A REVENUE RECOGNITION

Katie Vote owns a small business that rents computers to students at the local university for the nine month school year. Katie's typical rental contract requires the student to pay the year's rent of $900 ($100 per month) in advance. When Katie prepares financial statements at the end of December, her accountant requires that Katie spread the $900 over the nine months that a computer is rented. Therefore, Katie can recognize only $400 revenue (four months) from each computer rental contract in the year the cash is collected and must defer recognition of the remaining $500 (five months) to next year. Katie argues that getting students to agree to rent the computer is the most difficult part of the activity so she ought to be able to recognize all $900 as revenue when the cash is received from a student.

Required:

Explain why you believe that generally accepted accounting principles require the use of accrual accounting rather than cash-basis accounting for transactions like the one described here.

OBJECTIVE ➤ 2

Problem 5-63A DISCOUNT POLICY AND GROSS MARGIN

Compton Audio sells MP3 players. During 2008, Compton sold 1,000 units at an average of $300 per unit. Each unit cost Compton $180. At present, Compton offers no sales discounts. Compton's controller suggests that a generous sales discount policy would increase annual sales to 1,400 units and also improve cash flow. She proposes 7/10, n/30 and believes that 80 percent of the customers will take advantage of the discount.

Required:

1. If the controller is correct, determine how much the new sales discount policy would add to net sales.
2. Explain why the sales discount policy might improve cash flow.

Problem 5-64A EFFECTS OF DISCOUNTS ON SALES AND PURCHASES

Helmkamp Products sells golf clubs and accessories to pro shops. Gross sales in 2009 were $1,150,200 (Helmkamp's list price) on terms 3/15, n/45. Customers paid for $822,800 (Helmkamp's list price) of the merchandise within the discount period and the remaining $327,400 after the end of the discount period. Helmkamp records purchases and sales using the gross method to account for sales discounts.

Required:

1. Compute the amount of net sales.
2. Determine how much cash was collected from sales.

Problem 5-65A SALES DISCOUNTS

Sims Company regularly sells merchandise to Lauber Supply on terms 3/15, n/20 and records sales at gross. During a recent month, the two firms engaged in the following transactions:

a. Sims sold merchandise with a list price of $33,000.
b. Sims sold merchandise with a list price of $48,000.
c. Lauber paid for the purchase in transaction *a* within the discount period.
d. Lauber paid for the purchase in transaction *b* after the discount period.

Required:

1. Provide the journal entries for Sims to record the sales in *a* and *b*.
2. Provide the journal entry to record Lauber's payment in *c*.
3. Provide the journal entry to record Lauber's payment in *d*.

Problem 5-66A RECORDING SALES

Sullivan Company sells industrial cleaning supplies and equipment to other businesses. During the first quarter of 2009, the following transactions occurred:

a. On January 10, Sullivan sold on credit 50 cases of paper towels to the WMT Manufacturing Company at a list price of $800 for the entire lot of 50 cases.
b. On January 14, West Side Mall Corporation purchased on credit from Sullivan two floor polishers at a list price of $150 each and 10 cases of nonskid wax at a list price of $50 per case.
c. On January 16, West Side Mall returned to Sullivan four cases of the wax purchased on January 14.
d. On January 24, WMT paid Sullivan for its purchase of January 10.
e. Tom's Cleaning Service purchased on credit from Sullivan three cases of carpet shampoo at a list price of $64 per case on January 31.
f. On February 3, West Side Mall paid Sullivan for its purchase less the wax returned on January 16.
g. Tom's Cleaning Service paid Sullivan for its purchase of January 31 on February 10.
h. WMT returned to Sullivan a case of oversize paper towels on February 16. Sullivan credited WMT's account.

Required:

Prepare Sullivan's journal entries to record each of these transactions.

Problem 5-67A SALES AND SALES RETURNS WITH DISCOUNTS

Fuente Office Supply sells all merchandise on credit with terms 2/10, n/30 using the gross method to record sales. Fuente engaged in the following transactions:

a. May 1: Fuente sold 50 staplers to Aaron Enterprises at a list price of $12 per stapler.
b. May 5: Fuente accepted four staplers returned by Aaron Enterprises.
c. May 10: Aaron paid for the 46 staplers they kept.

d. May 11: Fuente sold 25 filing cabinets to Buckles Corporation at a list price of $70 per cabinet.

e. May 23: Buckles returned five filing cabinets that it did not need.

f. June 4: Buckles paid for the 20 filing cabinets they kept.

Required:

Prepare journal entries for each of these transactions assuming Fuente records sales using the gross method.

OBJECTIVE ▶ 3   **Problem 5-68A INTERNAL CONTROL FOR SALES**

Yancy's Hardware has three stores. Each store manager is paid a salary plus a bonus on the sales made by his or her store. On January 5, 2010, Bill Slick, manager of one of the stores, resigned. Bill's store had doubled its expected December 2009 sales, producing a bonus for Bill of $8,000 in December alone. Charles Brook, an assistant manager at another store, was assigned as manager of Bill Slick's store. Upon examination of the store's accounting records, Charles reports to Yancy that the store's records indicated sales returns and allowances of $110,000 in the first four days of January 2010, an amount equal to about half of December 2009 sales.

Required:

1. Explain what the large amount of sales returns and allowances suggest that Bill Slick might have done.
2. Determine how Yancy could protect itself from a manager who behaved as Bill Slick did.

OBJECTIVE ▶ 5   **Problem 5-69A BAD DEBT EXPENSE: PERCENTAGE OF CREDIT SALES METHOD**

The Glass House, a glass and china store, sells nearly half its merchandise on credit. During the past four years, the following data were developed for credit sales and losses from uncollectible accounts:

Year of Sales	Credit Sales	Losses from Uncollectible Accounts*
2006	$197,000	$12,608
2007	202,000	13,299
2008	212,000	13,285
2009	273,000	22,274
Total	$884,000	$61,466

*Losses from uncollectible accounts are the actual losses related to sales of that year (rather than write-offs of that year).

In 2010, The Glass House expanded its line significantly and began to sell to new kinds of customers.

Required:

1. Calculate the loss rate for each year from 2006 through 2009.
2. Determine whether there appears to be a significant change in the loss rate over time.
3. If credit sales for 2010 are $392,000, determine what loss rate you would recommend to estimate bad debts.
4. Using the rate you recommend, record bad debt expense for 2010.

OBJECTIVE ▶ 5   **Problem 5-70A AGING METHOD BAD DEBT EXPENSE**

Cindy Bagnal, the manager of Cayce Printing Service, has provided you with the following aging schedule for Cayce's accounts receivable:

Accounts Receivable Category	Amount	Proportion Expected to Default
0–20 days	$ 88,200	0.02
21–40 days	21,500	0.08
41–60 days	11,700	0.15
Over 60 days	5,300	0.30
	$126,700	

Cindy indicates that the $126,700 of accounts receivable identified in the table does not include $8,900 of receivables that should be written off.

Required:

1. Journalize the $8,900 write-off.
2. Determine the desired postadjustment balance in allowance for doubtful accounts.
3. If the balance in allowance for doubtful accounts before the $8,900 write-off was a debit of $450, compute bad debt expense.

Problem 5-71A DETERMINING BAD DEBT EXPENSE USING THE AGING METHOD

OBJECTIVE ➤ 5

At the beginning of the year, Tennyson Auto Parts had an accounts receivable balance of $31,800 and a balance in the allowance for doubtful accounts of $2,980 (credit). During the year Tennyson had credit sales of $624,300, collected accounts receivable in the amount of $602,700, wrote off $18,600 of accounts receivable, and had the following data for accounts receivable at the end of the period:

Accounts Receivable Age	Amount	Proportion Expected to Default
Current	$20,400	0.01
1–15 days past due	5,300	0.02
16–45 days past due	3,100	0.08
46–90 days past due	3,600	0.15
Over 90 days past due	2,400	0.30
	$34,800	

Required:

1. Determine the desired postadjustment balance in allowance for doubtful accounts.
2. Determine the balance in allowance for doubtful accounts before the bad debt expense adjusting entry is posted.
3. Compute bad debt expense.
4. Prepare the adjusting entry to record bad debt expense.

Problem 5-72A ACCOUNTING FOR NOTES RECEIVABLE

OBJECTIVE ➤ 7

Yarnell Electronics sells computer systems to small businesses. During 2009, Yarnell engaged in the following activities involving notes receivable:

a. On November 1, Yarnell sold a $5,000 system to Ross Company. Ross gave Yarnell a six-month, 11 percent note as payment.
b. On December 1, Yarnell sold an $8,000 system to Searfoss, Inc. Searfoss gave Yarnell a nine-month, 10 percent note as payment.
c. On April 30, 2010, Ross paid the amount due on its note.
d. On August 31, 2010, Searfoss paid the amount due on its note.

Required:

Prepare entries for Yarnell Electronics to record these transactions.

Problem 5-73A RATIO ANALYSIS

OBJECTIVE ➤ 8

Selected information from Bigg Company's financial statements follows.

	Fiscal Year Ended December 31		
	2010	2009	2008
		(in thousands)	
Gross sales	$2,004,719	$1,937,021	$1,835,987
Less: Sales discounts	4,811	4,649	4,406
Less: Sales returns and allowances	2,406	2,324	2,203
Net sales	$1,997,502	$1,930,048	$1,829,378
Cost of goods sold	621,463	619,847	660,955
Gross profit	$1,376,039	$1,310,201	$1,168,423
Operating expenses	577,369	595,226	583,555
Operating income	$ 798,670	$ 714,975	$ 584,868
Other income (expenses)	15,973	(5,720)	(8,773)
Net income	$ 814,643	$ 709,255	$ 576,095

	At December 31		
	2010	2009	2008
		(in thousands)	
Accounts receivable	$201,290	$195,427	$182,642
Less: Allowance for doubtful accounts	2,516	2,736	2,192
Net accounts receivable	$198,774	$192,691	$180,450

Required:

1. Calculate the following ratios for 2009 and 2010:
   a. gross profit ratio
   b. operating margin ratio
   c. net profit margin ratio
   d. accounts receivable turnover
2. For each of the first three ratios listed above, provide a plausible explanation for any differences that exist (e.g., Why is the net profit margin higher or lower than it was the previous year?, etc.).
3. Explain what each ratio attempts to measure. Make an assessment about Bigg Company based upon the ratios you have calculated. Are operations improving or worsening?

Problem Set B

OBJECTIVE ▶ 1 Problem 5-62B **REVENUE RECOGNITION**

Mary Wade owns a small business that rents parking spaces to students at the local university. Mary's typical rental contract requires the student to pay the year's rent of $720 ($60 per month) in advance. When Mary prepares financial statements at the end of December, her accountant requires that Mary spread the $720 over the 12 months that a parking space is rented. Therefore, Mary can recognize only $240 revenue (four months) from each contract in the year the cash is collected and must defer recognition of the remaining $480 (eight months) to next year. Mary argues that getting students to agree to rent the parking space is the most difficult part of the activity so she ought to be able to recognize all $720 as revenue when the cash is received from a student.

Required:

Explain why you believe that generally accepted accounting principles require the use of accrual accounting rather than cash-basis accounting for transactions like the one described here.

Problem 5-63B DISCOUNT POLICY AND GROSS MARGIN

Parker Electronics sells cell phones. During 2008, Parker sold 1,500 units at an average of $250 per unit. Each unit cost Parker $120. At present, Parker offers no sales discounts. Parker's controller suggests that a generous sales discount policy would increase annual sales to 2,000 units and also improve cash flow. She proposes 6/15, n/20 and believes that 75 percent of the customers will take advantage of the discount.

Required:

1. If the controller is correct, determine how much the new sales discount policy would add to net sales.
2. Explain why the sales discount policy might improve cash flow.

Problem 5-64B EFFECTS OF DISCOUNTS ON SALES AND PURCHASES

Smithson Products sells shoes and accessories to retail stores. Gross sales in 2009 were $1,500,250 (Smithson's list price) on terms 2/10, n/30. Customers paid for $925,500 (Smithson's list price) of the merchandise within the discount period and the remaining $574,750 after the end of the discount period. Smithson records purchases and sales using the gross method to account for sales discounts.

Required:

1. Compute the amount of net sales.
2. Determine how much cash was collected from sales.

Problem 5-65B SALES DISCOUNTS

OBJECTIVE ▶ 2

Spartan, Inc., regularly sells chemicals to Grieder Supply on terms 4/10, n/30 and records sales at gross. During a recent month, the two firms engaged in the following transactions:

a. Spartan sold merchandise with a list price of $37,000.
b. Spartan sold merchandise with a list price of $52,000.
c. Grieder paid for the purchase in transaction *a* within the discount period.
d. Grieder paid for the purchase in transaction *b* after the discount period.

Required:

1. Provide the journal entries for Spartan to record the sales in *a* and *b*.
2. Provide the journal entry to record Grieder's payment in *c*.
3. Provide the journal entry to record Grieder's payment in *d*.

Problem 5-66B RECORDING SALES

Marvel Company sells industrial cleaning supplies and equipment to other businesses. During the first quarter of 2009, the following transactions occurred:

a. On January 10, Marvel sold on credit 25 cases of paper towels to the Ramsden Manufacturing Company at a list price of $1,000 for the entire lot of 25 cases.
b. On January 14, Jackson Corporation purchased on credit, two floor polishers at a list price of $200 each and 15 cases of nonskid wax at a list price of $40 per case.
c. On January 16, Jackson returned three cases of the wax purchased on January 14.
d. On January 24, Ramsden paid for its purchase on January 10.
e. Stella's Cleaning Company purchased on credit, four cases of carpet shampoo at a list price of $75 per case on January 31.
f. On February 3, Jackson paid for its purchase less the wax returned on January 16.
g. Stella's Cleaning Company paid for its purchase of January 31 on February 10.
h. Ramsden returned a case of oversize paper towels on February 16. Marvel credited Ramsden's account.

Required:

Prepare journal entries to record each of these transactions.

OBJECTIVE ▶ 1 2   **Problem 5-67B SALES AND SALES RETURNS WITH DISCOUNTS**

Callaway Supply sells all merchandise on credit with terms 3/15, n/30. Callaway engaged in the following transactions:

a.   May 1: Callaway sold 40 staplers to Logsdon Enterprises at a list price of $15 per stapler.
b.   May 5: Callaway accepted six staplers returned by Logsdon Enterprises.
c.   May 10: Logsdon paid for the 34 staplers they kept.
d.   May 11: Callaway sold 32 filing cabinets to Jett, Inc., at a list price of $55 per cabinet.
e.   May 23: Jett returned five filing cabinets that it did not need.
f.   June 4: Jett paid for the 27 filing cabinets they kept.

Required:

Prepare journal entries for each of these transactions assuming Callaway records sales using the gross method.

OBJECTIVE ▶ 3   **Problem 5-68B INTERNAL CONTROL FOR SALES**

Johnson Tires has three stores. Each store manager is paid a salary plus a bonus on the sales made by his or her store. On January 5, 2010, Kevin Sampson, manager of one of the stores, resigned. Kevin's store had doubled its expected December 2009 sales, producing a bonus for Kevin of $7,000 in December alone. Jason Jones, an assistant manager at another store, was assigned as manager of Kevin Sampson's store. Upon examination of the store's accounting records, Jason reports to Johnson that the store's records indicated sales returns and allowances of $124,000 in the first four days of January 2010, an amount equal to about half of December 2009 sales.

Required:

1.   Explain what the large amount of sales returns and allowances suggest that Kevin Sampson might have done.
2.   Determine how Johnson could protect itself from a manager who behaved as Kevin Sampson did.

OBJECTIVE ▶ 5   **Problem 5-69B BAD DEBT EXPENSE: PERCENTAGE OF CREDIT SALES METHOD**

Kelly's Collectibles sells nearly half its merchandise on credit. During the past four years, the following data were developed for credit sales and losses from uncollectible accounts:

Year of Sales	Credit Sales	Losses from Uncollectible Accounts*
2006	$205,000	$15,527
2007	185,000	11,692
2008	209,000	14,184
2009	253,000	21,933
Total	$852,000	$63,336

*Losses from uncollectible accounts are the actual losses related to sales of that year (rather than write-offs of that year).

In 2010, Kelly's Collectibles expanded its line significantly and began to sell to new kinds of customers.

Required:

1.   Calculate the loss rate for each year from 2006 through 2009.
2.   Determine if there appears to be a significant change in the loss rate over time.
3.   If credit sales for 2010 are $373,000, explain what loss rate you would recommend to estimate bad debts.
4.   Using the rate you recommend, record bad debt expense for 2010.

Problem 5-70B AGING METHOD BAD DEBT EXPENSE

OBJECTIVE ▸ 5

Carol Simon, the manager of Handy Plumbing has provided you with the following aging schedule for Handy's accounts receivable:

Accounts Receivable Category	Amount	Proportion Expected to Default
0–20 days	$ 92,600	0.03
21–40 days	12,700	0.09
41–60 days	17,800	0.14
Over 60 days	2,100	0.30
	$125,200	

Carol indicates that the $125,200 of accounts receivable identified in the table does not include $9,400 of receivables that should be written off.

Required:

1. Journalize the $9,400 write-off.
2. Determine the desired postadjustment balance in allowance for doubtful accounts.
3. If the balance in allowance for doubtful accounts before the $9,400 write-off was a debit of $550, compute bad debt expense.

Problem 5-71B DETERMINING BAD DEBT EXPENSE USING THE AGING METHOD

OBJECTIVE ▸ 5

At the beginning of the year, Lennon Electronics had an accounts receivable balance of $29,800 and a balance in the allowance for doubtful accounts of $2,425 (credit). During the year, Lennon had credit sales of $752,693, collected accounts receivable in the amount of $653,800, wrote off $20,400 of accounts receivable, and had the following data for accounts receivable at the end of the period:

Accounts Receivable Age	Amount	Proportion Expected to Default
Current	$22,700	0.01
1–15 days past due	8,600	0.04
16–45 days past due	4,900	0.09
46–90 days past due	3,200	0.17
Over 90 days past due	2,100	0.30
	$41,500	

Required:

1. Determine the desired postadjustment balance in allowance for doubtful accounts.
2. Determine the balance in allowance for doubtful accounts before the bad debt expense adjusting entry is posted.
3. Compute bad debt expense.
4. Prepare the adjusting entry to record bad debt expense.

Problem 5-72B ACCOUNTING FOR NOTES RECEIVABLE

OBJECTIVE ▸ 7

Sloan Systems sells voice mail systems to small businesses. During 2009, Sloan engaged in the following activities involving notes receivable:

a. On November 1, Sloan sold an $8,000 system to Majors Company. Majors gave Sloan a six-month, 9 percent note as payment.
b. On December 1, Sloan sold a $6,000 system to Hadley, Inc. Hadley gave Sloan a nine-month, 12 percent note as payment.
c. On April 30, 2010, Majors paid the amount due on its note.
d. On August 31, 2010, Hadley paid the amount due on its note.

Required:

Prepare entries for Sloan Systems to record these transactions.

OBJECTIVE ▶ 8   **Problem 5-73B** RATIO ANALYSIS

Selected information from Small Company's financial statements follows.

	Fiscal Year Ended December 31		
	2010	2009	2008
	(in thousands)		
Gross sales	$1,663,917	$1,697,195	$1,714,167
Less: Sales discounts	2,995	3,055	3,086
Less: Sales returns and allowances	2,496	2,546	2,571
Net sales	$1,658,426	$1,691,594	$1,708,510
Cost of goods sold	881,876	891,027	860,512
Gross profit	$ 776,550	$ 800,567	$ 847,998
Operating expenses	482,050	496,958	487,214
Operating income	$ 294,500	$ 303,609	$ 360,784
Other income (expenses)	3,534	(3,036)	(1,804)
Net income	$ 298,034	$ 300,573	$ 358,980

	At December 31		
	2010	2009	2008
	(in thousands)		
Accounts receivable	$376,062	$365,109	$341,223
Less: Allowance for doubtful accounts	8,461	71,926	5,971
Net accounts receivable	$367,601	$293,183	$335,252

Required:

1. Calculate the following ratios for 2009 and 2010:
   a. gross profit ratio
   b. operating margin ratio
   c. net profit margin ratio
   d. accounts receivable turnover
2. For each of the first three ratios listed above provide a plausible explanation for any differences that exist (e.g., Why is the net profit margin higher or lower than it was the previous year? etc.).
3. Explain what each ratio attempts to measure. Make an assessment about Small Company based upon the ratios you have calculated. Are operations improving or worsening?

Cases

Case 5-74 ETHICS AND REVENUE RECOGNITION

Alan Dunlap is CEO of a large appliance wholesaler. Alan is under pressure from Wall Street Analysts to meet his aggressive sales revenue growth projections. Unfortunately, near the end of the year he realizes that sales must dramatically improve if his projections are going to be met. To accomplish this objective he orders his sales force to contact their largest customers and offer them price discounts if they buy by the end of the year. Mr. Dunlap also offered to deliver the merchandise to a third-party warehouse with whom the customers could arrange delivery when the merchandise was needed.

Required:

1. Do you believe that revenue from these sales should be recognized in the current year? Why or why not?
2. What are the probable consequences of this behavior for the company in future periods?
3. What are the probable consequences of this behavior for investors analyzing the current year financial statements?

Case 5-75 RECOGNITION OF SERVICE CONTRACT REVENUES

Jackson Dunlap is president of New Miami Maintenance, Inc., which provides building maintenance services. On October 15, 2008, Mr. Dunlap signed a service contract with Western College. Under the contract, New Miami will provide maintenance services for all Western's buildings for a period of two years, beginning on January 1, 2009, and Western will pay New Miami on a monthly basis, beginning on January 31, 2009. Although the same amount of maintenance services will be rendered in every month, the contract provides for higher monthly payments in the first year.

Initially, Mr. Dunlap proposed that some portion of the revenue from the contract should be recognized in 2008; however, his accountant, Rita McGonigle, convinced him that this would be inappropriate. Then Mr. Dunlap proposed that the revenue should be recognized in an amount equal to the cash collected under the contract in 2008. Again, Ms. McGonigle argued against his proposal, saying that generally accepted accounting principles required recognition of an equal amount of contract revenue each month.

Required:

1. Give a reason that might explain Mr. Dunlap's desire to recognize contract revenue earlier rather than later.
2. Put yourself in the position of Rita McGonigle. How would you convince Mr. Dunlap that his two proposals are unacceptable and that an equal amount of revenue should be recognized every month?
3. If Ms. McGonigle's proposal is adopted, how would the contract be reflected in the balance sheets at the end of 2008 and at the end of 2009?

Case 5-76 REVENUE RECOGNITION

Beth Rader purchased North Shore Health Club in June 2009. Beth wanted to increase the size of the business by selling five-year memberships for $2,000, payable at the beginning of the membership period. The normal yearly membership fee is $500. Since few prospective members were expected to have $2,000, Beth arranged for a local bank to provide a $2,000 installment loan to prospective members. By the end of 2009, 250 customers had purchased the five-year memberships using the loan provided by the bank.

Beth prepared her income statement for 2009 and included $250,000 as revenue because the Club had collected the entire amount in cash. Beth's accountant objected to the inclusion of the entire $250,000. The accountant argued that the $250,000 should be recognized as revenue as the Club provides services for these members during the membership period. Beth countered with a quotation from a part of "Generally Accepted Accounting Principles," *Accounting Research Bulletin 43, Chapter 1, Section A, No. 1:*

> "Profit is deemed to be realized when a sale in the ordinary course of business is effected, unless the circumstances are such that collection of the sale price is not reasonably assured."

Beth notes that the memberships have been sold and that collection of the selling price has occurred. Therefore, she argues that all $250,000 is revenue in 2009.

Required:

Write a short statement supporting either Beth or the accountant in this dispute.

Case 5-77 SALES DISCOUNT POLICIES

Consider three businesses, all of which offer price reductions to their customers. The first is an independently owned gas station located at a busy intersection in Cincinnati, Ohio, that offers a 3 percent discount for cash purchases of gasoline. The second is a large home improvement store located near an interstate exit in suburban Cleveland that offers building contractors terms of 3/10, n/45. And third is a clothing manufacturer and catalog retailer located in Columbus. Several times during each year, a catalog is distributed in which men's dress shirts are heavily discounted if purchased in lots of four or more.

Required:

1. What are the main objectives of the discount policies in each of the three businesses?
2. How does accounting information assist each business in achieving its discount policy objectives?

Case 5-78 FINANCIAL ANALYSIS OF RECEIVABLES

A chain of retail stores located in Kansas and Nebraska has requested a loan from the bank at which you work. The balance sheet of the retail chain shows significant accounts receivable related to its in-house credit card. You have been assigned to evaluate these receivables.

Required:

1. What questions concerning the quality of these receivables can you answer by analyzing the retailer's financial statements?
2. What additional questions would you raise, and what information would you request from the retailer to answer these questions?

Case 5-79 INCOME EFFECTS OF UNCOLLECTIBLE ACCOUNTS

The credit manager and the accountant for Goldsmith Company are attempting to assess the effect on net income of writing off $100,000 of receivables. Goldsmith uses the aging method of determining bad debt expense and has the following aging schedule for its accounts receivable at December 31, 2009:

Accounts Receivable Category	Amount	Proportion Expected to Default
Current	$2,980,400	0.004
1–30 days past due	722,600	0.035
31–60 days past due	418,500	0.095
Over 60 days past due	322,800	0.250
	$4,444,300	

The receivables being considered for write-off are all over 60 days past due.

Required:

1. Assume that the tax rate is 30 percent. What will be the effect on net income if the $100,000 is written off?
2. What data would you examine to provide some assurance that a company was not holding uncollectible accounts in its accounts receivable rather than writing them off when they are determined to be uncollectible?

Case 5-80 RESEARCH AND ANALYSIS USING THE ANNUAL REPORT

Obtain **Under Armour**'s 2007 10-K through the "Investor Relations" portion of their website. (Using a search engine, search for: Under Armour investor relations.) Once at the Investor Relations section of the website, look for "SEC Filings." When you see the list of all the filings either filter for the "Annual Filings" or search for "10-K." Another option is to go to http://www.sec.gov and click "Search for company filings" under "Filings & Forms (EDGAR)."

Required:

1. What was Under Armour's allowance for doubtful accounts in 2006 and 2007?
2. Look at under the "Accounts Receivable" heading to Note 2 (Summary of Significant Accounting Policies). Does Under Armour use the percentage of credit sales method or the aging method to estimate bad debt expense?
3. Was a larger percentage of the gross accounts receivable considered uncollectible at December 31, 2006 or 2007?
4. Calculate Under Armour's receivables turnover for 2006 and 2007 (Accounts Receivable, net, was $53,132 at December 31, 2005). If the industry average for receivables turnover is 9.81, how do you evaluate their efficiency with receivables?
5. Calculate Under Armour's gross profit ratio, operating margin ratio, and net profit margin ratio for 2006 and 2007.
6. If the industry average for gross profit ratio is 24.88 percent, what sort of strategy do you think Under Armour is pursuing?
7. Evaluate the trend of Under Armour's operating margin ratio and net profit margin ratio and relate the trend to the industry averages of 7.65 percent and 5.99 percent, respectively.

Case 5-81 COMPARATIVE ANALYSIS: ABERCROMBIE & FITCH vs. AEROPOSTALE

Refer to the financial statements of **Abercrombie & Fitch** and **Aeropostale** that are supplied with this text.

Required:

1. Look at Abercrombie & Fitch's Note 2 (Summary of Significant Accounting Policies) under the headings (1) Credit Card Receivables and (2) Fair Value of Financial Instruments. Based on these disclosures, describe the nature of A&F's receivables reported on the balance sheet. What is the balance in their allowance for doubtful accounts?
2. Look at Aeropostale's Note 1 (Summary of Significant Accounting Policies) under the headings (1) Cash Equivalents and (2) Fair Value of Financial Instruments. Based on these disclosures how does Aeropostale's receivables differ from Abercrombie & Fitch's receivables? Why isn't there a receivables balance on Aeropostale's balance sheet?
3. Using the balances reported on the balance sheets, what is Abercrombie & Fitch's receivables turnover for the year ended February 3, 2007?
4. Calculate Abercrombie & Fitch's and Aeropostale's gross profit ratio for the years ended February 3, 2007 and January 28, 2006. What can you infer about the strategy pursued by these two companies based on these measures assuming the industry average is around 38 percent?
5. Calculate Abercrombie & Fitch's and Aeropostale's operating margin ratio for the years ended February 3, 2007 and January 28, 2006. Comment on these measures assuming the industry average is around 10 percent.
6. Calculate Abercrombie & Fitch's and Aeropostale's net profit margin ratio for the years ended February 3, 2007 and January 28, 2006. Comment on these measures assuming the industry average is around 6.5 percent.

6

Cost of Goods Sold and Inventory

After studying Chapter 6, you should be able to:

1 Describe the types of inventories held by merchandisers and manufacturers, and understand how inventory costs flow through a company.

2 Explain how to record purchases and sales of inventory using a perpetual inventory system.

3 Apply the four inventory costing methods to compute ending inventory and cost of goods sold under a perpetual inventory system.

4 Analyze the financial reporting and tax effects of the various inventory costing methods.

5 Apply the lower of cost or market rule to the valuation of inventory.

6 Evaluate inventory management using the gross profit and inventory turnover ratios.

7 Describe how errors in ending inventory affect income statements and balance sheets.

8 (Appendix 6A) Explain how to record purchases of inventory using a periodic inventory system.

9 (Appendix 6B) Compute ending inventory and cost of goods sold under a periodic inventory system.

© TIM BOYLE/GETTY IMAGES

Experience Financial Accounting

with Wal-Mart

Wal-Mart Stores Inc., based in Bentonville, Arkansas, is the world's largest public corporation with $345 billion in sales for their 2007 fiscal year. With over 127 million customers visiting over 4,000 Wal-Mart stores per week, Wal-Mart is the largest grocery retailer and toy seller in the United States. In addition, Wal-Mart operates over 2,800 facilities in 12 different countries. Given the large volume of merchandise that is sold, Wal-Mart's profits depend heavily on the control and management of its inventory. After all, inventory does make up 72 percent of Wal-Mart's current assets!

For many companies, inventory is at the heart of the operating cycle and must be carefully managed and controlled. Managing and controlling inventory involves keeping enough inventory on the shelves to meet the customers' demands while minimizing the cost of carrying inventory. If a company doesn't have enough inventory on its shelves, it will lose sales. On the other hand, too much inventory will increase carrying costs such as storage and interest costs as well as increase the risk of obsolescence. Wal-Mart has long been recognized as a

---

Exhibit 6-1

Composition of Wal-Mart's Current Assets

Wal-Mart Stores, Inc.
Consolidated Balance Sheets (partial)
January 31, 2007

(in millions)	2007
ASSETS:	
Current assets:	
Cash and cash equivalents	$ 7,373
Receivables	2,840
Inventories	33,685
Prepaid expenses and other	2,690
Total current assets	$46,588

Pie chart:
- Cash — 16%
- Receivables — 6%
- Inventories — 72%
- Prepaid expenses and other — 6%

world leader in its effective use of technology to manage and control its inventory and distribution.

As you will see in this chapter, even though inventory is an asset, it can have a major impact on net income. That is because all inventory accounting systems allocate the cost of inventory between ending inventory and cost of goods sold. Therefore, the valuation of inventory affects cost of goods sold, which in turn, affects net income. By managing and controlling its inventory, Wal-Mart has been able to tie up less of its money in inventory than its competitors, resulting in greater profits. This focus on inventory allows Wal-Mart to sell its merchandise at "always low prices. Always."

OBJECTIVE ▶ 1
Describe the types of inventories held by merchandisers and manufacturers, and understand how inventory costs flow through a company.

Nature of Inventory and Cost of Goods Sold

Inventory represents products held for resale and is classified as a current asset on the balance sheet. The inventories of large companies like **General Electric, Procter and Gamble**, and Wal-Mart are composed of thousands of different products or materials and millions of individual units that are stored in hundreds of different locations. For other companies, inventories are a much less significant portion of their total assets. Exhibit 6-2 shows the relative composition of inventory for Wal-Mart and **Microsoft**.

For companies like Wal-Mart, these vast and varied inventories are at the heart of company operations and must be carefully controlled and accounted for. For example, one of Wal-Mart's key performance measures is the comparison of inventory growth to sales growth. For its 2007 fiscal year, Wal-Mart's inventory growth was 5.6 percent while sales growth was up 11.7 percent—an indication that Wal-Mart is efficiently using its inventory to generate sales.

When companies like Wal-Mart sell their inventory to customers, the cost of the inventory becomes an expense called cost of goods sold. **Cost of goods sold**, or cost of sales, represents the outflow of resources caused by the sale of inventory and is the most important expense on the income statement of companies that sell goods instead of services. Note that **gross margin** (also called **gross profit**), a key performance measure, is defined as sales revenue less cost of goods sold. Thus, gross

---

Exhibit 6-2

Relative Composition of Inventory for Different Companies

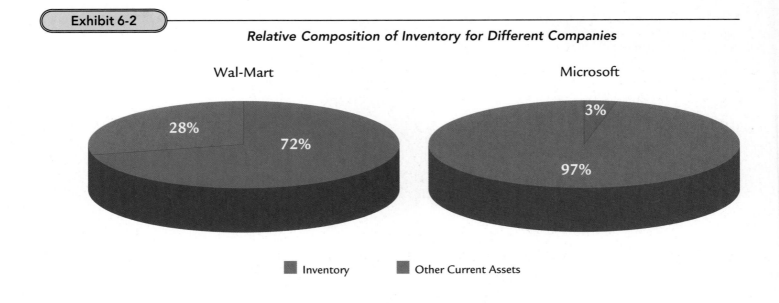

Wal-Mart   Microsoft

28%   72%   3%   97%

■ Inventory   ■ Other Current Assets

margin indicates the extent to which the resources generated by sales can be used to pay operating expenses (selling and administrative expenses) and provide for net income. For 2007, Wal-Mart reported a gross margin of $80,840 million (net sales of $344,992 million less cost of sales of $264,152 million) or 23.4 percent of net sales.

The cost of inventory has a direct effect on cost of goods sold and gross margin. Therefore, to correctly interpret and analyze financial statements, one must understand inventory accounting. Accounting for inventories requires a matching of costs with revenues based on an appropriate inventory costing method. As you will see in this chapter, management is allowed considerable latitude in determining the cost of inventory and may choose among several different costing methods. In addition, certain departures from cost are allowed by GAAP. These choices that managers make affect the balance sheet valuation of inventory, the amount of reported net income, and the income taxes payable from year to year.

In this chapter, we will examine the process of accounting for inventory and cost of goods sold. We will address the following questions:

* What are the different types of inventory?
* What costs should be included in inventory?
* Which inventory system (perpetual or periodic) should be employed?
* How are inventory transactions recorded?
* How is cost of goods sold computed?
* What are the financial effects of the four alternative inventory costing methods?
* How does the application of the lower-of-cost-or-market rule affect inventory valuation?

An understanding of inventory accounting will help in the analysis of financial statements as well as in managing a business.

Types of Inventory and Flow of Costs

In previous chapters, we generally have illustrated companies that sell services such as advertising agencies, delivery companies, repair companies, and accounting firms. For these companies, inventory plays a much smaller role. For example, in 2007, **Google** didn't even report an amount for inventory! Our focus in this chapter will be on companies that sell inventory. These companies are often referred to as either merchandisers or manufacturers.

Merchandisers are companies that purchase inventory in a finished condition and hold it for resale without further processing. *Retailers* like Wal-Mart, **Sears**, and **Target** are merchandisers that sell directly to consumers, while *wholesalers* are merchandisers that sell to other retailers. The inventory held by merchandisers is termed **merchandise inventory**. Merchandise inventory is an asset. When that asset is sold to a customer, it becomes an expense called cost of goods sold which appears on the income statement. Wal-Mart's inventory disclosure, shown earlier in Exhibit 6-1, is an example of a typical disclosure made by a merchandising company.

Manufacturers are companies that buy and transform raw materials into a finished product which is then sold. **Sony**, **Toyota**, and **Eastman Kodak** are all manufacturing companies. Manufacturing companies classify inventory into three categories: raw materials, work-in-process, and finished goods. *Raw materials inventory* are the basic ingredients used to make a product. When these raw materials are purchased, Raw Materials Inventory is increased. As raw materials are used to manufacture a product, they become part of work-in-process inventory. *Work-in-process inventory* consists of the raw materials that are used in production as well as other production costs such as labor and utilities. These costs stay in this account until the product is complete. Once the production process is complete, these costs are moved to the finished goods inventory account. The *finished goods inventory* account represents the cost of the final product that is available for sale. When the finished goods inventory is sold to a customer, it becomes an expense called cost of goods sold which appears on the income statement.

The inventory disclosure of Eastman Kodak, shown in Exhibit 6-3, is an example of a typical disclosure made by a manufacturing company.

While inventories of manufacturers present some accounting measurement problems that are beyond the scope of this text, the accounting concepts discussed in this chapter apply to inventories of both merchandisers and manufacturers. The relationship between the various inventory accounts and cost of goods sold is shown in Exhibit 6-4.

Exhibit 6-3

Inventory Disclosure of Eastman Kodak

(in millions)	2007	2006
Current Assets	December 31,	
Cash and cash equivalents	$2,947	$1,469
Receivables, net	1,939	2,072
Inventories, net	943	1,001
Other current assets	224	1,015
Total current assets	$6,053	$5,557

Note 3: Inventories, net

(in millions)	December 31,	
	2007	2006
Finished goods	$537	$ 606
Work-in-process	235	192
Raw materials	171	203
Total inventories, net	$943	$1,001

Exhibit 6-4

Flow of Inventory Costs

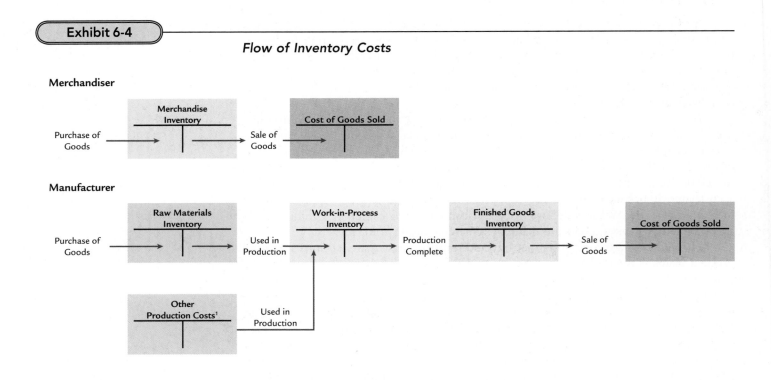

[1] Work-in-Process Inventory consists of raw materials used in production (also known as direct materials) as well as other production costs. These other production costs are called direct labor and factory overhead. The process by which these costs are converted to a final cost of a product is beyond the scope of this text and is covered in managerial accounting.

The concepts involved in accounting for inventories of manufacturers and merchandisers are similar. However, due to the additional complexities of accounting for manufacturing inventory, the remainder of this chapter will focus on merchandising companies.

The Cost of Goods Sold Model

As shown in Exhibit 6-4, cost of goods sold is the cost of the outflow from inventory to customers. That is, cost of goods sold is the cost to the seller of all goods sold during the accounting period. Recall that the *matching principle* requires that any costs used to generate revenue should be recognized in the same period that the revenue is recognized. Because revenue is recognized as goods are sold, cost of goods sold is an expense.

The relationship between cost of goods sold and inventory is given by the cost of goods sold model:

> Beginning inventory
> \+ Purchases
> = Cost of goods available for sale
> − Ending inventory
> = Cost of goods sold

Except in the case of a new company, merchandisers and manufacturers will start the year with an amount of inventory on hand called *beginning inventory*. During the year, any *purchases* of inventory are added to the inventory account. The sum of beginning inventory and purchases represents the **cost of goods available for sale**. The portion of the cost of goods available for sale that remains unsold at the end of the year is the company's *ending inventory* (the ending inventory for one period becomes the beginning inventory of the next period). The portion of the cost of goods available for sale that is sold becomes *cost of goods sold*. The cost of goods sold model is illustrated in Exhibit 6-5.

Note that the determination of cost of goods sold requires an allocation of the cost of goods available for sale between ending inventory and cost of goods sold. An application of the cost of goods sold model is illustrated in Cornerstone 6-1.

Exhibit 6-5

The Cost of Goods Sold Model

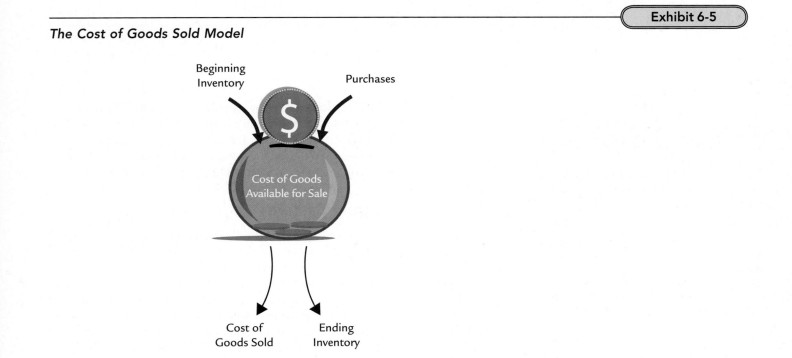

**CORNERSTONE
6-1**

HOW TO Apply the Cost of Goods Sold Model

Concept:
The determination of cost of goods sold requires an allocation of the cost of goods available for sale between ending inventory and cost of goods sold.

Information:
Bargain Shops, a retail clothing store, had a beginning inventory of $26,000 on January 1, 2009. During 2009, the company purchased goods from a supplier costing $411,000. At the end of 2009, the cost of the unsold inventory was $38,000.

Required:
Compute cost of goods sold at December 31, 2009.

Solution:
Cost of goods sold of $399,000 is computed by using the cost of goods sold model as follows:

Beginning inventory	$ 26,000
+ Purchases	411,000
= Cost of goods available for sale	$437,000
− Ending inventory	38,000
= Cost of goods sold	$399,000

Note that the general structure of the cost of goods sold model can be rearranged to solve for any missing amount if the other three amounts are known. For example, if Bargain Shops did not know the cost of ending inventory but knew the cost of goods sold was $399,000, the company could determine ending inventory by rearranging the model as follows:

Beginning inventory	$ 26,000
+ Purchases	411,000
= Cost of goods available for sale	$437,000
− Cost of goods sold	399,000
= Ending inventory	$ 38,000

CONCEPT Q&A

Because all inventories ultimately get expensed as cost of goods sold, why not just record all costs as cost of goods sold when they are incurred?

Possible Answer:

Costs related to inventories are initially recorded in an inventory account to help a company achieve a proper matching of expenses with revenues. By recording costs in an inventory account, a company can delay the recognition of the expense until the goods are sold. If all inventory related costs were expensed when incurred, users of financial statements would see a distorted picture of the profitability of a company.

This reinforces the concept that the computation of cost of goods sold or ending inventory is simply an allocation of the cost of goods available for sale. An understanding of this cost of goods sold model should enhance your understanding of how the matching concept is applied to cost of goods sold.

Inventory Systems

Because inventory is at the heart of the operating cycle for most wholesalers and retailers, the inventory accounting systems that record purchases and sales and track the level of inventory are particularly important in such companies. These systems provide the information needed to determine cost of goods sold and perform financial statement analysis. In addition, these systems signal the need to purchase additional inventory or the need to make special efforts to sell existing inventory. They also provide information necessary to safeguard the inventory from misappropriation or theft. In short, these systems provide the information that managers need to manage and control inventory.

Companies use one of two types of inventory accounting systems—a perpetual inventory system or a periodic inventory system.

Perpetual Inventory System In a **perpetual inventory system**, balances for inventory and cost of goods sold are continually (perpetually) updated with each sale or purchase of inventory. This type of system requires that detailed records be maintained on a transaction-by-transaction basis for each purchase and sale of inventory. For example, every time that Wal-Mart purchases inventory from a supplier, it records this purchase directly in its inventory records. Similarly, when Wal-Mart makes a sale to a customer, it will not only record the sale (as illustrated in Chapter 5) but will also update its inventory and cost of goods sold balances by decreasing inventory and increasing cost of goods sold. In other words, a perpetual inventory system records both the *revenue* and *cost* side of sales transactions. The journal entries for a perpetual system are shown later in this chapter.

With the volume of transactions that Wal-Mart has on a daily basis, this task may appear quite daunting. However, with the advent of "point of sale" cash register systems and optical bar code scanners, the implementation of a perpetual inventory system has become quite common. Some companies, like Wal-Mart, are taking this idea a step further and using radio frequency identification technology (RFID) to track inventory. By attaching RFID tags to its inventory, Wal-Mart is able to more easily track inventory from its suppliers to the final customer, with the promise of dramatic reductions in inventory losses.

In a perpetual inventory system, the accounting system keeps an up-to-date record of both ending inventory and cost of goods sold at any point in time. However, a company that uses a perpetual system should still take a physical count of inventory at least once a year to confirm the balance in the inventory account. Any difference between the physical count of inventory and the inventory balance provided by the accounting system could be the result of errors, waste, breakage, or theft.

Periodic Inventory System A **periodic inventory system** does not require companies to keep detailed, up-to-date inventory records. Instead, a periodic system records the cost of purchases as they occur (in an account separate from the inventory account), takes a physical count of inventory at the end of the period, and applies the cost of goods sold model to determine the balances of ending inventory and cost of goods sold. Thus, a periodic system only produces balances for ending inventory and cost of goods sold at the end of each accounting period (periodically). If a company using the periodic system needs to know the balance of inventory or cost of goods sold during a period, it must either (1) perform a physical count of inventory or (2) use inventory estimation techniques (which are covered in intermediate accounting courses).[2]

Comparison of Perpetual and Periodic Inventory Systems Perpetual and periodic systems offer distinct benefits and any choice between the two inventory systems must weigh the system's advantages against its operating costs. The principle advantage of a periodic system is that it is relatively inexpensive to operate. Because perpetual systems require entering and maintaining more data than periodic systems, the additional costs can be quite substantial for a company with thousands of different items in inventory. However, with technological advances, this advantage is rapidly disappearing. The perpetual system has the obvious advantage of making the balances of inventory and cost of goods sold continuously available. This provides management with greater control over inventory than they would have under a periodic inventory system. Providing managers with more timely information that gives them greater

---

[2] More information on the periodic inventory system is provided in Appendixes 6A and 6B at the end of this chapter.

DECISION-MAKING & ANALYSIS

Just-in-Time Inventory Management

Inventory managers must balance the costs of carrying inventory against the costs of being caught short, largely the cost of lost sales. If suppliers can be relied upon to deliver needed inventory on very short notice and in ready-to-use forms, then very low inventory levels are consistent with both minimum carrying costs and minimum "out-of-stock" costs. This approach to inventory management, which requires attention to detail and very "tight" relationships with suppliers, is called just-in-time inventory management.

1. *What information is necessary to maintain a just-in-time inventory policy?*

To synchronize the arrival of new inventory with the selling of the old inventory, inventory managers need detailed information about order-to-delivery times, receiving-to-ready-for-sale times, and inventory quantities. Delivery and make-ready times are used to control and minimize time lags between shipment of goods by suppliers and delivery to customers. In some retail stores, for example, merchandise arrives tagged, stacked, and ready for placement on the sales floor while in other retail stores several days may be required to get the merchandise ready for sale. Information on inventory quantities is used to calculate the inventory level at which to reorder an item.

2. *Does just-in-time inventory management require a perpetual inventory system?*

No. While many companies do use a perpetual inventory system for just-in-time inventory management, a quantities-only perpetual system is sufficient to signal the need to reorder. To reduce costs, many companies use a quantities-only perpetual system combined with a periodic inventory system to determine inventory costs.

control over inventory can be a significant and extremely valuable advantage in a competitive business environment. For example, much of Wal-Mart's success has been attributed to its sophisticated inventory management and control system.

We will illustrate a perpetual inventory system in this chapter because of its growth and popularity in many different types of companies.

OBJECTIVE ➤ 2

Explain how to record purchases and sales of inventory using a perpetual inventory system.

Recording Inventory Transactions—Perpetual System

The *historical cost principle* requires that the activities of a company are initially measured at their cost—the exchange price at the time the activity occurs. Applied to inventory, this principle implies that *inventory cost includes the purchase price of the merchandise plus any cost of bringing the goods to a salable condition and location.*[3] This definition of inventory costs means that in addition to the purchase price, inventory cost will include other "incidental" costs such as freight charges to deliver the merchandise to the company's warehouse, insurance cost on the inventory while it is in transit, and various taxes. In general, a company should stop accumulating costs as a part of inventory once the inventory is ready for sale.[4] In this section, we will explore the accounting for purchases and sales of inventory for a merchandiser under a perpetual inventory system.

Accounting for Purchases of Inventory

Let's first take a look at how a merchandising company would account for goods purchased for resale. In a perpetual inventory system, the merchandise inventory account is used to record the costs associated with acquiring goods.

---

[3] *Accounting Research Bulletin No. 43*, "Inventory Pricing" (New York: American Institute of Certified Public Accountants, June 1953), Chapter 4, Statement 3.

[4] For a manufacturing company, costs should be accumulated as raw materials inventory until the goods are ready for use in the manufacturing process.

Purchases   **Purchases** refers to the cost of merchandise acquired for resale during the accounting period. The purchase of inventory is recorded by increasing the merchandise inventory account. All purchases should be supported by a *source document* such as an *invoice* that provides written evidence of the transaction and provides all relevant details of the purchase. A typical invoice is shown in Exhibit 6-6. Note the various details on the invoice such as the names of the seller and the purchaser, the invoice date, the credit terms, the freight terms, a description of the goods purchased, and the total invoice amount.

Relying on the historical cost principle, the cost of purchases must include the effects of purchase discounts, purchase returns, and transportation charges.

Purchase Discounts   As noted in Chapter 5, it is common for companies that sell goods on credit to offer their customers sales discounts to encourage prompt payment. From the viewpoint of the customer or purchaser, such price reductions are called **purchase discounts**. The credit terms specify the amount and timing of payments from the purchaser to the seller. For example, credit terms of "2/10, n/30" mean that a 2 percent discount may be taken on the invoice price if payment is made within 10 days of the invoice date. This reduced payment period is known as the **discount period**. Otherwise, full payment is due within 30 days of the invoice date. If a purchase discount is taken, the purchaser reduces the Merchandise Inventory account for the amount of the

---

Exhibit 6-6

Sample Invoice

Shoes Unlimited					INVOICE

We Care About Your Feet

301 College Street
Irvine, California 92612
Phone 800-555-2389 Fax 949-555-2300

INVOICE #100
DATE: Sept. 1, 2008

TO:

J. Parker Jones, Purchasing Manager
Brandon Shoes
879 University Blvd.
Auburn, Alabama 36830

SALESPERSON	P.O. NUMBER	REQUISITIONER	SHIPPED VIA	F.O.B. POINT	TERMS
E. Higgins	4895721	J. Parker Jones	UPS	Destination	2/10, n/30

QUANTITY	DESCRIPTION	UNIT PRICE	TOTAL
100	Model No. 754 Athletic Running Shoe	$100	$10,000
		SUBTOTAL	$10,000
		SALES TAX	800
		SHIPPING & HANDLING	150
		TOTAL DUE	$10,950

discount taken. The result of recording the purchase discount is that the merchandise inventory account reflects the net cost of the inventory purchased.

Generally, merchandisers should take all available discounts. Failure to pay within the discount period is equivalent to paying interest for the use of money and can be quite expensive. For example, failure to take advantage of the 2 percent discount for credit terms of "2/10, n/30" is equivalent to an annual interest rate of 36.5 percent.[5] Clearly, paying within the discount period is a good cash management policy.

Purchase Returns and Allowances   Merchandise is inspected when received and may be tested in various ways before it becomes available for sale. Perhaps the wrong merchandise was delivered, the merchandise did not conform to specification, the merchandise was damaged or defective, or it arrived too late at its destination. If the purchaser is dissatisfied with the merchandise, it is frequently returned to the seller for credit or for a cash refund. The cost of merchandise returned to suppliers is called **purchase returns**. In some instances, the purchaser may choose to keep the merchandise if the seller is willing to grant a deduction (allowance) from the purchase price. This situation is called a **purchase allowance**. Increases in purchase returns and allowances may signal deteriorating supplier relationships; thus purchase returns are monitored very closely by purchasing managers. Because Merchandise Inventory was increased when the purchase was initially made, a purchase return or allowance is recorded by decreasing merchandise inventory.

Transportation Costs   Transportation, or freight, costs are expenditures made to move the inventory from the seller's location to the purchaser's location. The proper recording of transportation costs depends upon whether the buyer or the seller pays for the transportation. Effectively, this question is the same as asking at what point the ownership of the inventory transfers from the seller to the buyer. The point at which ownership, or title, of the inventory changes hands depends on the shipping terms of the contract. The shipping terms can be either F.O.B. (free on board) shipping point or F.O.B. destination. Exhibit 6-7 illustrates the following points:

- If the shipping terms are **F.O.B. shipping point**, ownership of the inventory passes from the seller to the buyer at the shipping point. Under F.O.B. shipping point terms, the buyer normally pays the transportation costs, commonly termed

---

| Exhibit 6-7 | |

Shipping Terms

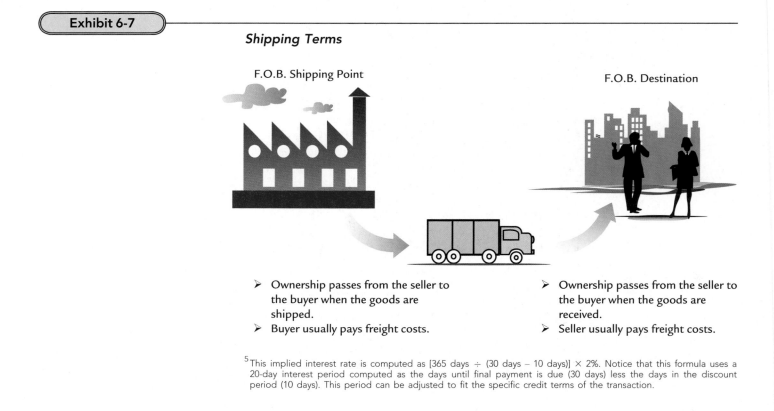

F.O.B. Shipping Point

F.O.B. Destination

➤ Ownership passes from the seller to the buyer when the goods are shipped.
➤ Buyer usually pays freight costs.

➤ Ownership passes from the seller to the buyer when the goods are received.
➤ Seller usually pays freight costs.

[5] This implied interest rate is computed as [365 days ÷ (30 days − 10 days)] × 2%. Notice that this formula uses a 20-day interest period computed as the days until final payment is due (30 days) less the days in the discount period (10 days). This period can be adjusted to fit the specific credit terms of the transaction.

freight-in. These costs are considered part of the total cost of purchases and the Merchandise Inventory account is increased.

- When the shipping terms are **F.O.B. destination**, ownership of the inventory passes when the goods are delivered to the buyer. Under F.O.B. destination shipping terms, the seller is usually responsible for paying the transportation costs, commonly termed **freight-out**. In this case, the transportation costs are not considered part of inventory; instead, the seller will expense these costs as a selling expense on the income statement.

Recording Purchase Transactions   To summarize, the purchase price of inventory includes any cost of bringing the goods to a salable condition and location. Therefore, the merchandise inventory account is increased for the invoice price of a purchase as well as any transportation costs paid for by the buyer. Any purchase discounts, returns, or allowances reduce the merchandise inventory account. Cornerstone 6-2 illustrates the journal entries required to record purchases of merchandise inventory.

HOW TO Record Purchase Transactions in a Perpetual Inventory System

**CORNERSTONE
6-2**

Concept:
The cost of inventory includes the purchase price of the merchandise plus any cost of bringing the goods to a salable condition and location.

Information:
On September 1, 2009, Brandon Shoes purchased 50 pairs of hiking boots for $3,750 cash and paid $150 of transportation costs. Also, on September 1, Brandon purchased 100 pairs of running shoes for $10,000; however the seller paid the transportation costs of $300. The running shoes were purchased on credit with credit terms of 2/10, n/30. Brandon paid for one-half ($5,000) of the running shoes on September 10, within the discount period. The remaining shoes were paid for on September 30. After inspection, Brandon determined that 10 pairs of the hiking boots were defective and returned them on September 30.

Required:
1. Prepare journal entries to record the purchase of the hiking boots.
2. Prepare the journal entry to record the purchase of the running shoes.
3. Prepare the journal entries to record the payment for the running shoes on September 10 and September 30.
4. Prepare the journal entry to record the return of the defective hiking boots on September 30.

Solution:
1. The cash purchase of the hiking boots includes the $3,750 invoice price plus the $150 of transportation costs (freight-in):

Date	Account and Explanation	Debit	Credit
Sept. 1	Merchandise Inventory	3,750	
	Cash		3,750
	(Purchased inventory for cash)		
1	Merchandise Inventory	150	
	Cash		150
	(To record the payment of freight costs)		

Assets = Liabilities +	Stockholders' Equity
+3,750	
−3,750	

Assets = Liabilities +	Stockholders' Equity
+150	
−150	

**CORNERSTONE
6-2
(continued)**

Assets = Liabilities +	Stockholders' Equity
+10,000	+10,000

2. The credit purchase of the running shoes includes only the $10,000 invoice price:

Date	Account and Explanation	Debit	Credit
Sept. 1	Merchandise Inventory	10,000	
	Accounts Payable		10,000
	(Purchased inventory on credit)		

Note: The costs of the freight is not recorded because it was paid by the seller (F.O.B. destination or freight-out). The seller would record a selling expense and credit Cash to record the freight charges.

3. Brandon paid for $5,000 of the running shoes purchase less a discount of $100 ($5,000 × 2%). The journal entry is:

Assets = Liabilities +	Stockholders' Equity
−4,900 −5,000	
−100	

Date	Account and Explanation	Debit	Credit
Sept. 10	Accounts Payable	5,000	
	Cash		4,900
	Merchandise Inventory		100
	(Paid for one-half the running shoes purchase)		

The journal entry to record the payment *outside* of the discount period is:

Assets = Liabilities +	Stockholders' Equity
−5,000 −5,000	

Date	Account and Explanation	Debit	Credit
Sept. 30	Accounts Payable	5,000	
	Cash		5,000
	(Paid for one-half the running shoes purchase)		

4. The journal entry required to return the $750 of defective hiking boots (calculated as $3,750 ÷ 50 pairs = $75 per pair × 10 pairs) is:

Assets = Liabilities +	Stockholders' Equity
+750	
−750	

Date	Account and Explanation	Debit	Credit
Sept. 30	Cash	750	
	Merchandise Inventory		750
	(Returned defective hiking boots)		

These journal entries illustrate that under a perpetual inventory system, inventory is constantly updated with each purchase so that the net effect of purchases is reflected in the inventory account. The computation of net purchases for Brandon Shoes is summarized in Exhibit 6-8. Although the original invoice price was $13,750, the consideration of purchase discounts, returns and transportation charges resulted in a much different value in the merchandise inventory account.

Exhibit 6-8

Calculation of Net Purchases

Invoice price of purchase	$13,750
Less: Purchase discounts	(100)
Purchase returns and allowances	(750)
Add: Transportation costs (freight-in)	150
Net cost of purchases	$13,050

Accounting for Sales of Inventory

In addition to purchase transactions, merchandising companies must also account for the inventory effects of sales and sales returns. Because a perpetual inventory system is being used, the merchandise inventory account is also affected.

Sales   As discussed in Chapter 5, companies recognize sales revenue when it is earned and the collection of cash is reasonably assured. The recording of sales revenue involves two journal entries. In the first journal entry (discussed in Chapter 5), sales revenue is recognized. The second journal recognizes, consistent with the matching principle, the cost of the goods that are sold. It also reduces the merchandise inventory account so that the perpetual inventory system will reflect an up-to-date balance for inventory.

Sales Returns   If a customer returns an item for some reason, the company will make an adjustment to sales as shown in Chapter 5. In addition, the company must make a second entry to adjust cost of goods sold and to increase inventory to reflect the return of the merchandise.

Recording Inventory Effects of Sales Transactions   The use of a perpetual inventory system requires that two journal entries be made for both sales and sales return transactions. These journal entries are illustrated in Cornerstone 6-3.

CORNERSTONE 6-3

HOW TO Record Sales Transactions in a Perpetual Inventory System

Concept:
The sale or return of inventory in a perpetual system requires two journal entries—one to record the revenue portion of the transaction and one to record the expense (and inventory) portion of the transaction.

Information:
On August 1, Brandon Shoes sold 100 pairs of football cleats to the local college football team for $12,000 cash (each pair of cleats was sold for $120 per pair). Brandon paid $10,000 (or $100 per pair) for the cleats from its supplier. On August 15, the local college football team returned 10 pairs of cleats for a cash refund of $1,200.

Required:
1. Prepare the journal entries to record the sale of the football cleats.
2. Prepare the journal entries to record the return of the football cleats.

Solution:
1.

Date	Account and Explanation	Debit	Credit
Aug. 1	Cash	12,000	
	Sales Revenue		12,000
	(To record sale to customer)		
1	Cost of Goods Sold	10,000	
	Merchandise Inventory		10,000
	(To record the cost of merchandise sold)		

Assets =	Liabilities +	Stockholders' Equity
+12,000		+12,000

Assets =	Liabilities +	Stockholders' Equity
−10,000		−10,000

| | | CORNERSTONE 6-3 *(continued)* | | | |

CORNERSTONE
6-3
(continued)

	Stockholders'
Assets = Liabilities +	Equity
−1,200	−1,200

	Stockholders'
Assets = Liabilities +	Equity
+1,000	+1,000

2.

Date	Account and Explanation	Debit	Credit
Aug. 15	Sales Returns and Allowances	1,200	
	Cash		1,200
	(To record return of merchandise)		
15	Merchandise Inventory	1,000	
	Cost of Goods Sold		1,000
	(To record the cost of merchandise returned)		

In each of the transactions in Cornerstone 6-3, the external selling price of $120 was recorded as Sales Revenue. The cost of goods sold (or inventory) portion of the transaction was recorded at the cost to Brandon Shoes of $100. Therefore, for each pair of shoes sold, Brandon Shoes made a gross margin of $20 ($120 − $100). The total cost of goods sold recognized by Brandon Shoes is $9,000 ($10,000 − $1,000). *In dealing with sales to customers, it is important to remember to record revenues at the selling price and to record expenses (and inventory) at cost.*

Costing Inventory

A key feature of the cost of goods sold model illustrated in Cornerstone 6-1 is that the determination of cost of goods sold requires an allocation of the cost of goods available for sale between ending inventory and cost of goods sold. If the prices paid for goods are constant over time, this allocation is easy to compute—just multiply the cost per unit times the number of units on hand at year-end (to determine the cost of ending inventory) or times the number of units sold (to determine the cost of goods sold). The ending inventory and cost of goods sold have the same cost whether it is composed of the oldest units available for sale, the newest units available for sale, or some mixture of the old and new units. For example, if Speigel Company began operations by purchasing 1,000 units of a single product available for $24 each, total goods available for sale would be $24,000 (1,000 units × $24). If 800 units were sold during the period, the cost of the remaining 200-unit ending inventory is $4,800 ($24 × 200 units). Cost of goods sold is $19,200 (800 units sold × $24, or $24,000 − $4,800). It makes no difference which of the 1,000 units remain in ending inventory.

On the other hand, if the price paid for a good changes over time, the cost of goods available for sale may include units with different costs per unit. In such cases, the question arises: Which prices should be assigned to the units sold and which assigned to the units in ending inventory? For example, assume that Speigel Company purchased the same total of 1,000 units during a period at different prices as follows:

Jan. 3	300 units purchased at $22 per unit	=	$ 6,600
Jan. 15	400 units purchased at $24 per unit	=	9,600
Jan. 24	300 units purchased at $26 per unit	=	7,800
	Cost of goods available for sale		$24,000

While the cost of goods available for sale is the same ($24,000), the cost of the 200-unit ending inventory depends on which goods remain in ending inventory. If the ending inventory is made up of the $22 per unit goods:

• The cost of ending inventory is $4,400 (200 × $22); and
• The cost of goods sold is $19,600 ($24,000 − $4,400).

If the ending inventory is made up of the $26 per unit goods,

• The cost of ending inventory is $5,200 (200 × $26); and
• The cost of goods sold is $18,800 ($24,000 − $5,200).

The determination of which units are sold and which units remain in ending inventory depend on the selection of the cost allocation method.

One way to resolve this problem is to specifically identify the units sold and their respective costs. If units have serial numbers or some other unique identifier and are relatively few in number, such a procedure is feasible. In most cases, however, specific identification is not a practical means of determining cost of goods sold and ending inventory. Instead of tracking the specific units sold and in inventory, companies usually make simple assumptions about cost flow.

Inventory Costing Methods

OBJECTIVE ▶ 3
Apply the four inventory costing methods to compute ending inventory and cost of goods sold under a perpetual inventory system.

The inventory system (perpetual or periodic) determines *when* cost of goods sold is calculated—for every sales transaction or at the end of the period. An *inventory costing method* determines how costs are allocated to cost of goods sold and ending inventory. Although the assumption about the composition of ending inventory and cost of goods sold could take many different forms—each leading to a different inventory costing method—accountants typically use one of four inventory costing methods[6]:

1. Specific identification
2. First-in, first-out (FIFO)
3. Last-in, first-out (LIFO)
4. Average cost

Each of these four costing methods represents a different procedure for allocating the cost of goods available for sale between ending inventory and cost of goods sold. Only the specific identification method allocates the cost of purchases according to the *physical flow* of specific units through inventory. That is, specific identification is based on a *flow of goods* principle. In contrast, the other three methods—FIFO, LIFO, and average cost—are based on a *flow of cost* principle. When the FIFO, LIFO, or average cost methods are used, the physical flow of goods into inventory and out to the customers is generally unrelated to the flow of unit costs. We make this point here so that you will not be confused in thinking that a cost flow assumption describes the physical flow of goods in a company. *Generally accepted accounting principles do not require that the cost flow assumption be consistent with the physical flow of goods.*

Companies disclose their choice of inventory methods in a note to the financial statements. The 2007 annual report of Wal-Mart includes the following statement:

Notes to Consolidated Financial Statements

1. Summary of Significant Accounting Policies
Inventories.
The company values inventories at the lower of cost or market as determined primarily by the retail method of accounting, using the last-in, first-out ("LIFO") method for substantially all of the Wal-Mart stores segment's merchandise inventories. Sam's Club merchandise and merchandise in our distribution warehouses are valued based on the weighted average cost using the LIFO method. Inventories of foreign operations are primarily valued by the retail method of accounting, using the first-in, first-out ("FIFO") method. At January 31, 2007 and 2006, our inventories valued at LIFO approximate those inventories as if they were valued at FIFO.

Like many companies, Wal-Mart uses more than one method in determining the total cost of inventory. In general, LIFO and FIFO are the most widely used methods. Exhibit 6-9 shows the percentage of companies using each inventory costing method.

[6] The following sections on inventory costing methods use the perpetual inventory system. Appendix 6B uses the periodic inventory system.

Exhibit 6-9

Use of Inventory Costing Methods

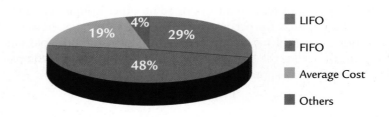

- LIFO
- FIFO
- Average Cost
- Others

Source: AICPA, Accounting Trends & Techniques, 61st edition, 2007, par. 2.63, p. 146.

With the exception of specific identification, the inventory costing methods allocate cost of goods available for sale between ending inventory and cost of goods sold using the following process.

Step 1: Calculate the cost of goods available for sale *immediately prior* to any sale transaction.

Step 2: Apply the inventory costing method to determine ending inventory and cost of goods sold.

Step 3: Repeat steps 1 and 2 for all inventory transactions during the period. The sum of the cost of goods sold computed in step 2 is the cost of goods sold for the period. Ending inventory is the amount computed during the final application of step 2 for the period.

To understand how the inventory costing systems allocate costs (step 2), it is useful to think of inventory as if it were a stack of separate layers, separated by the purchase price. Each time a purchase is made at a unit cost different from that of a previous purchase, a new layer of inventory cost is added to the top of the stack. As inventory is sold it is removed from the stack according to the cost flow assumption used.

Specific Identification

The **specific identification method** determines the cost of ending inventory and the cost of goods sold based on the identification of the *actual* units sold and in inventory. This method does not require an assumption about the flow of costs but actually assigns cost based on the specific flow of inventory. It requires that detailed records be kept of each purchase and sale be maintained so that a company knows exactly which items were sold and the cost of those items. Historically, this method was practical only for situations in which very few, high-cost items were purchased and sold—for example, a car dealership. With the introduction of bar coding, electronic scanners, and radio frequency identification, this method has become easier to implement, but its application is still relatively rare. The specific identification method is illustrated in Cornerstone 6-4.

CORNERSTONE
6-4

HOW TO Apply the Specific Identification Method

Concept:
Cost of goods sold and ending inventory are determined based on the identification of the actual units sold and in inventory.

Information:
Tampico Beachwear, a retail store specializing in beach apparel, has the following information related to purchases and sales of one of its more popular products, Crocs brand shoes. (Each inventory layer is a different color.)

CORNERSTONE
6-4
(continued)

Date	Description	Units Purchased at Cost	Units Sold at Retail
Oct. 1	Beginning Inventory	300 units @ $16 = $ 4,800	
3	Purchase 1	600 units @ $18 = $10,800	
8	Sale 1		800 units @ $30
15	Purchase 2	250 units @ $20 = $ 5,000	
20	Purchase 3	150 units @ $22 = $ 3,300	
25	Sale 2		300 units @ $30
	Goods available for sale: 1,300 units = $23,900		Sales: 1,100 units = $33,000

A review of purchase and sales invoices reveals that the following units remain in ending inventory at the end of the month:

Description	Units Sold	Units in Ending Inventory
Beginning Inventory	300	—
Purchase 1	550	50
Purchase 2	170	80
Purchase 3	80	70
Total	1,100	200

Required:

1. Compute the cost of ending inventory at October 31 under the specific identification method.
2. Compute the cost of goods sold at October 31 under the specific identification method.

Solution:

1. Ending inventory at October 31 is $4,040, computed as:

50 units @ $18	$ 900
80 units @ $20	1,600
70 units @ $22	1,540
200 units	$4,040

2. Cost of goods sold is $19,860, computed as:

300 units @ $16	$ 4,800
550 units @ $18	9,900
170 units @ $20	3,400
80 units @ $22	1,760
1,100 units	$19,860

Three items are of interest. First, the sum of ending inventory ($4,040) and cost of goods sold ($19,860) equals cost of goods available for sale ($23,900). The specific identification method, like all inventory costing methods, allocates the cost of goods available for sale between ending inventory and cost of goods sold. Second, because there are usually far fewer units in ending inventory than in cost of goods sold, it is often easier to compute the cost of ending inventory and then find the cost of goods sold by subtracting ending inventory from cost of goods available for sale ($23,900 − $4,040 = $19,860). Finally, the determination of inventory cost affects both the balance sheet and the income statement. The amount assigned to ending inventory will appear on the balance sheet. The amount assigned to cost of goods sold appears on the income statement and is used in the calculation of a company's gross margin.

First-In, First-Out (FIFO)

The **first-in, first-out (FIFO) method** is based on the assumption that costs move through inventory in an unbroken stream, with the costs entering and leaving the inventory in the same order. In other words, *the earliest (oldest) purchases (the first in) are assumed to be the first sold (the first out) and the more recent purchases are in ending inventory.* Every time that inventory is sold, the cost of the earliest (oldest) purchases that make up cost of goods available for sale is allocated to the cost of goods sold, and the cost of the most recent purchases are allocated to ending inventory. In many instances, this cost flow assumption is an accurate representation of the physical flow of goods. Cornerstone 6-5 illustrates the application of the FIFO method.

**CORNERSTONE
6-5**

HOW TO Apply the FIFO Inventory Costing Method

Concept:
The cost of the earliest purchases that make up cost of goods available for sale is allocated to cost of goods sold, and the cost of the most recent purchases are allocated to ending inventory.

Information:
Tampico Beachwear, a retail store specializing in beach apparel, has the following information related to purchases and sales of one of its more popular products, Crocs brand shoes. (Each inventory layer is a different color.)

Date	Description	Units Purchased at Cost	Units Sold at Retail
Oct. 1	Beginning Inventory	300 units @ $16 = $ 4,800	
3	Purchase 1	600 units @ $18 = $10,800	
8	Sale 1		800 units @ $30
15	Purchase 2	250 units @ $20 = $ 5,000	
20	Purchase 3	150 units @ $22 = $ 3,300	
25	Sale 2		300 units @ $30
		Goods available for sale: 1,300 units = $23,900	Sales: 1,100 units = $33,000

Required:
Compute the cost of ending inventory and the cost of goods sold at October 31 using the FIFO method.

Solution:
To compute the cost of ending inventory and cost of goods sold, follow these three steps:

Step 1: Compute the cost of goods available for sale immediately *prior* to the first sale. This produces an inventory balance of $15,600. Notice that this inventory balance is made up of two layers—a $16 layer and an $18 layer.

Step 2: Apply FIFO to determine ending inventory and cost of goods sold. Under FIFO, you must allocate the cost of goods available for sale between inventory (the most recent purchases) and cost of goods sold (the earliest purchases).

Date	Description	Inventory Balance		Cost of Goods Sold	
Oct. 1	Beginning inventory	300 × $16	= $ 4,800		
3	Purchase 1 (600 @ $18)	300 × $16 = $ 4,800 ⎱ 600 × $18 = $10,800 ⎰ = $15,600			
8	Sale 1 (800 @ $30)	100 × $18	= $ 1,800	300 × $16 = $4,800 ⎱ 500 × $18 = $9,000 ⎰ = $13,800	

Step 3: Repeat Steps 1 and 2 for the remaining inventory transactions during the period.

Date	Description	Inventory Balance		Cost of Goods Sold	
Oct. 8	Inventory on hand	100 × $18	= $ 1,800		
15	Purchase 2 (250 @ $20)	100 × $18 = $1,800 ⎱ 250 × $20 = $5,000 ⎰ = $ 6,800			
20	Purchase 3 (150 @ $22)	100 × $18 = $1,800 ⎱ 250 × $20 = $5,000 ⎰ 150 × $22 = $3,300 ⎰ = $10,100			
25	Sale 2 (300 @ $30)	50 × $20 = $1,000 ⎱ 150 × $22 = $3,300 ⎰ = $ 4,300		100 × $18 = $1,800 ⎱ 200 × $20 = $4,000 ⎰ = $5,800	

Ending inventory reported on the balance sheet is $4,300. Cost of goods sold reported on the income statement is $19,600, the sum of cost of goods sold during the period ($13,800 + $5,800). Because the sum of ending inventory and cost of goods sold ($4,300 + $19,600) equals cost of goods available for sale ($23,900), Tampico could have also calculated cost of goods as the difference between cost of goods available for sale and ending inventory ($23,900 – $4,300).

Last-In, First-Out (LIFO)

The **last-in, first-out (LIFO) method** allocates the cost of goods available for sale between ending inventory and cost of goods sold based on the assumption that the most recent purchases (the last in) are the first to be sold (the first out). Under the LIFO method, *the most recent purchases (newest costs) are allocated to the cost of goods sold and the earliest purchases (oldest costs) are allocated to inventory.* Except for companies that stockpile inventory (e.g., piles of coal, stacks of hay, stacks of rock), this cost flow assumption rarely coincides with the actual physical flow of inventory. Cornerstone 6-6 illustrates the application of the LIFO method.

Ending inventory reported on the balance sheet is $3,600. Cost of goods sold reported on the income statement is $20,300, the sum of cost of goods sold during the period ($14,000 + $6,300). Because the sum of ending inventory and cost of goods sold ($3,600 + $20,300) equals cost of goods available for sale ($23,900), Tampico could have also calculated cost of goods as the difference between cost of goods available for sale and ending inventory ($23,900 – $3,600).

Average Cost

The **average cost method** allocates the cost of goods available for sale between ending inventory and cost of goods sold based on a weighted average cost per unit. This

CORNERSTONE
6-6

HOW TO Apply the LIFO Inventory Costing Method

Concept:
The cost of the most recent purchases that make up cost of goods available for sale is allocated to cost of goods sold, and the cost of the earliest (oldest) purchases are allocated to ending inventory.

Information:
Tampico Beachwear, a retail store specializing in beach apparel, has the following information related to purchases and sales of one of its more popular products, Crocs brand shoes. (Each inventory layer is a different color.)

Date	Description	Units Purchased at Cost	Units Sold at Retail
Oct. 1	Beginning Inventory	300 units @ $16 = $ 4,800	
3	Purchase 1	600 units @ $18 = $10,800	
8	Sale 1		800 units @ $30
15	Purchase 2	250 units @ $20 = $ 5,000	
20	Purchase 3	150 units @ $22 = $ 3,300	
25	Sale 2		300 units @ $30
		Goods available for sale: 1,300 units = $23,900	Sales: 1,100 units = $33,000

Required:
Compute the cost of ending inventory and the cost of goods sold at October 31 using the LIFO method.

Solution:
To compute the cost of ending inventory and cost of goods sold, follow these three steps:

Step 1: Compute the cost of goods available for sale immediately *prior* to the first sale. This produces an inventory balance of $15,600. Notice that this inventory balance is made up of two layers—a $16 layer and an $18 layer.

Step 2: Apply LIFO to determine ending inventory and cost of goods sold. Under LIFO, you must allocate the cost of goods available for sale between inventory (the earliest purchases) and cost of goods sold (the most recent purchases).

Date	Description	Inventory Balance	Cost of Goods Sold
Oct. 1	Beginning inventory	300 × $16 = $ 4,800	
3	Purchase 1 (600 @ $18)	300 × $16 = $ 4,800 ⎱ = $15,600 600 × $18 = $10,800 ⎰	
8	Sale 1 (800 @ $30)	100 × $16 = $ 1,600	600 × $18 = $10,800 ⎱ = **$14,000** 200 × $16 = $ 3,200 ⎰

Step 3: Repeat Steps 1 and 2 for the remaining inventory transactions during the period.

Date	Description	Inventory Balance	Cost of Goods Sold
Oct. 8	Inventory on hand	100 × $16 = $ 1,600	
15	Purchase 2 (250 @ $20)	100 × $16 = $1,600 ⎱ = $ 6,600 250 × $20 = $5,000 ⎰	
20	Purchase 3 (150 @ $22)	100 × $16 = $1,600 ⎱ 250 × $20 = $5,000 ⎰ = $ 9,900 150 × $22 = $3,300	
25	Sale 2 (300 @ $30)	100 × $16 = $1,600 ⎱ = **$3,600** 100 × $20 = $2,000 ⎰	150 × $22 = $3,300 ⎱ = **$6,300** 150 × $20 = $3,000 ⎰

weighted average cost per unit is calculated after each purchase of inventory as follows:

$$\text{Weighted Average Cost per Unit} = \frac{\text{Cost of Goods Available for Sale}}{\text{Units Available for Sale}}$$

Because a new average is computed after each purchase, this method is often called the moving-average method. This weighted average cost per unit is then multiplied by (1) the number of units sold to determine cost of goods sold and (2) the units on hand to determine ending inventory. Cornerstone 6-7 illustrates the application of the average cost method.

HOW TO Apply the Average Cost Inventory Costing Method

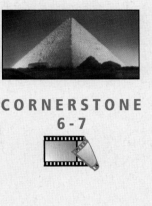

**CORNERSTONE
6-7**

Concept:
The cost of goods available for sale is allocated between ending inventory and cost of goods sold based on a weighted average cost of the goods available for sale.

Information:
Tampico Beachwear, a retail store specializing in beach apparel, has the following information related to purchases and sales of one of its more popular products, Crocs brand shoes. (Each inventory layer is a different color.)

Date	Description	Units Purchased at Cost	Units Sold at Retail
Oct. 1	Beginning Inventory	300 units @ $16 = $ 4,800	
3	Purchase 1	600 units @ $18 = $10,800	
8	Sale 1		800 units @ $30
15	Purchase 2	250 units @ $20 = $ 5,000	
20	Purchase 3	150 units @ $22 = $ 3,300	
25	Sale 2		300 units @ $30
		Goods available for sale: 1,300 units = $23,900	Sales: 1,100 units = $33,000

Required:
Compute the cost of ending inventory and the cost of goods sold at October 31 using the average cost method.

Solution:
To compute the cost of ending inventory and cost of goods sold, follow these three steps:

Step 1: Compute the cost of goods available for sale immediately *prior* to the first sale. This produces an inventory balance of $15,600.

Step 2: Apply the average cost method to determine ending inventory and cost of goods sold. Under the average cost method, you must allocate the cost of goods available for sale between inventory and cost of goods sold using a weighted average cost per unit. The weighted average cost is computed by taking the goods available for sale and dividing it by the number of units available for sale. This produces a weighted average cost prior to the October 8 sale of $17.333 per unit ($15,600 ÷ 900 units).

Date	Description	Inventory Balance		Cost of Goods Sold
Oct. 1	Beginning inventory	300 × $16	= $ 4,800	($16 /unit)
3	Purchase 1 (600 @ $18)	300 × $16 = 4,800 600 × $18 = 10,800 } = $15,600		($17.3333/unit)[a]
8	Sale 1 (800 @ $30)	100 × $17.3333	= $ 1,733	800 × 17.3333 = **$13,867**

[a] $15,600 ÷ 900 units = $17.3333/unit

CORNERSTONE 6-7 (continued)

Step 3: Repeat Steps 1 and 2 for the remaining inventory transactions during the period.

Date	Description	Inventory Balance		Cost of Goods Sold
Oct. 8	Inventory on hand	100 × $17.3333	= $ 1,733	(17.3333/unit)
15	Purchase 2 (250 @ $20)	100 × $17.3333 = 1,733 250 × $20.00 = 5,000 }	= $ 6,733	(19.2371/unit)[b]
20	Purchase 3 (150 @ $22)	350 × $19.2371 = 6,733 150 × $22.00 = 3,300 }	= $10,033	(20.0660/unit)[c]
25	Sale 2 (300 @ $30)	200 × $20.0660	= $ 4,013	300 × 20.0660 = **$6,020**

[b] $6,733 ÷ 350 units = $19.2371/unit
[c] $10,033 ÷ 500 units = $20.0660/unit

Ending inventory reported on the balance sheet is $4,013. Cost of goods sold reported on the income statement is $19,887, the sum of cost of goods sold during the period ($13,867 + $6,020). Because the sum of ending inventory and cost of goods sold ($4,013 + $19,887) equals cost of goods available for sale ($23,900), Tampico could have also calculated cost of goods as the difference between cost of goods available for sale and ending inventory ($23,900 − $4,013).

The average cost method results in an allocation to ending inventory and cost of goods sold that is somewhere between the allocation produced by FIFO and the allocation produced by LIFO.

OBJECTIVE ▶ 4
Analyze the financial reporting and tax effects of the various inventory costing methods.

Analysis of Inventory Costing Methods

Accounting policy decisions concerning inventory can have major effects on the financial statements. Proper management of these decisions, within the bounds of generally accepted accounting principles and good business ethics, can also affect the timing of income tax payments and the judgments of creditors, stockholders, and others involved in the company's affairs. Thus, it is important to understand the consequences of these accounting choices.

CONCEPT Q&A

Why doesn't the FASB simply mandate the most conceptually correct inventory costing method instead of giving companies a choice between alternative methods?

Possible Answer:

All inventory costing methods provide an allocation of the total dollar amount of goods available for sale between ending inventory and cost of goods sold. No one cost method is conceptually superior to any other. For example, LIFO actually achieves a better matching of current costs with current revenues on the income statement; however, the resulting balance sheet valuation can be quite misleading about the current market value of inventory on the balance sheet. Companies make the choice between inventory methods for a variety of reasons unique to their own situation. Some companies will adopt LIFO for the tax benefits, while others will adopt FIFO because they want to report higher profits or simply because FIFO is less expensive to implement.

Financial Statement Effects of Alternative Costing Methods

Although companies cannot readily change from one inventory costing method to another, financial statement analysts frequently ask the hypothetical question, "How much would inventory and income have been if a different costing method had been used?" If the prices paid for purchased inventory are stable, all inventory costing methods will yield the same amounts for ending inventory and cost of goods sold. However, when purchase prices vary, FIFO, LIFO and the average cost methods will produce different amounts for ending inventory, cost of goods sold and, therefore, income. To properly analyze financial statements, it is necessary to understand the impact of changing prices on inventories and income.

To illustrate, consider the inventory data for Tampico Beachwear, which had revenues for the period of $33,000 (1,100 units sold × $30 per unit) and operating expenses of $4,000 (assumed amount). This information and the related

Exhibit 6-10

Financial Statement Effects of Alternative Inventory Costing Methods

	Tampico Beachwear Condensed Income Statements For the month ending October 31					
	FIFO		LIFO		Average Cost	
Sales		$33,000		$33,000		$33,000
Beginning inventory	$ 4,800		$ 4,800		$ 4,800	
Add: Purchases	19,100		19,100		19,100	
Cost of goods available for sale	$23,900		$23,900		$23,900	
Less: Ending inventory	4,300		3,600		4,013	
Cost of goods sold		19,600		20,300		19,887
Gross margin		$13,400		$12,700		$13,113
Operating expenses		4,000		4,000		4,000
Income before taxes		$ 9,400		$ 8,700		$ 9,113
Income tax expense (30%)		2,820		2,610		2,734
Net income		$ 6,580		$ 6,090		$ 6,379

FIFO, LIFO, and average cost inventory calculations in Cornerstones 6-5 through 6-7 produced the income statement amounts shown in Exhibit 6-10.

Notice that sales, purchases, and cost of goods available for sale are the same for each company. However the changing purchase prices of each inventory layer result in different amounts for cost of goods sold, gross margin, and net income.

When purchase prices are rising, as they are in our example (remember that shoes went from $16 to $18 to $20 to $22), the FIFO method produces the highest cost for ending inventory, the lowest cost of goods sold, and, therefore, the highest gross margin (and net income) of the three methods. In contrast, the LIFO method produced the lowest cost for ending inventory, the highest cost of goods sold, and, therefore, the lowest gross margin (and net income) of the three methods. The average cost method produced amounts for inventory, cost of goods sold and net income that fell between the FIFO and LIFO extremes. When purchase prices are *falling,* the situation is reversed. Exhibit 6-11 summarizes these relationships.

Exhibit 6-11

Financial Statement Effects of Alternative Inventory Costing Methods

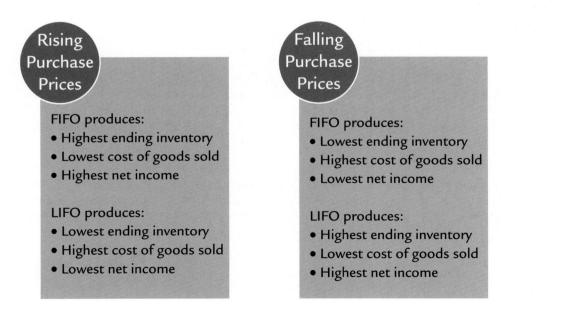

Rising Purchase Prices

FIFO produces:
- Highest ending inventory
- Lowest cost of goods sold
- Highest net income

LIFO produces:
- Lowest ending inventory
- Highest cost of goods sold
- Lowest net income

Falling Purchase Prices

FIFO produces:
- Lowest ending inventory
- Highest cost of goods sold
- Lowest net income

LIFO produces:
- Highest ending inventory
- Lowest cost of goods sold
- Highest net income

Thus, during periods of rising prices, we expect LIFO companies to report lower amounts for inventory cost and higher amounts for cost of goods sold than comparable FIFO companies. And during periods of falling prices, we expect LIFO companies to report higher amounts of inventory cost and lower amounts for cost of goods sold than comparable FIFO companies.[7] Due to these effects, it can be argued that:

- LIFO results in the more realistic amount for income because it matches the most current costs, which are closer to the current market value, against revenue.
- FIFO results in the more realistic amount for inventory because it reports the most current costs, which are closer to the current market value, on the balance sheet.

To assist in comparisons between companies that prepare their financial statements under different inventory costing methods, companies that use LIFO are required to report the amount that inventory would increase (or decrease) if the company had used FIFO. This amount is referred to as the **LIFO reserve**. For example, **General Mills'** disclosure of its LIFO reserve for 2007 is shown in Exhibit 6-12.

This disclosure shows that inventories would have been $78 million higher under FIFO for the 2007 fiscal year. Analysts can adjust the inventory amount by substituting in the FIFO inventory values ($1,252 million and $1,117 million for 2007 and 2006, respectively) for the LIFO values reported on the balance sheet. In addition, income would have been higher under FIFO by $16 million ($78 million – $62 million)—the difference between the LIFO reserve for 2007 and 2006.

Exhibit 6-12

LIFO Reserve Disclosure

General Mills Inc.
Notes to Consolidated Financial Statements
Note 17: Supplemental Information (in part):

(in millions)	May 27, 2007	May 28, 2006
Inventories:		
..... (components) at FIFO	$1,252	$1,117
Excess of FIFO or weighted average cost over LIFO	(78)	(62)
Inventories, at LIFO	$1,174	$1,055

DECISION-MAKING & ANALYSIS

LIFO Liquidations

Tomlinson Health Management is an aggressively managed new business that provides pharmacy services to retirement communities, nursing homes, and small hospitals in a three-state area. In order to secure tax benefits, Tomlinson uses LIFO for most of its inventories. Tomlinson's business has become increasingly competitive in recent years and the current year's income has taken a significant step down. Avery Tomlinson, the principal stockholder and CEO, has instructed the purchasing department to hold year-end inventories to the absolute minimum.

1. *What is the structure of the LIFO inventory?*

Tomlinson's inventory has grown over a period of years. The LIFO inventory is composed of layers, each one representing a year's contribution to the inventory at the earliest purchase prices of that year. During a period of rising prices, the LIFO inventory will be made up of the relatively older costs trapped in the LIFO layers. If the quantity of inventory falls, some of these older costs, with

---

[7] An exception to the relationships described in Exhibit 6-12 occurs when the quantity of inventory drops, releasing old LIFO layers to cost of goods sold. If inventory drops when prices have been rising, LIFO results in higher net income than FIFO, as explained in the "LIFO reserve" analysis section. On the other hand, if inventory drops when prices have been falling, LIFO results in lower net income than FIFO.

relatively low unit prices, will be released to cost of goods sold. This produces a lower cost of goods sold, and higher income, than one computed at current FIFO prices.

2. *What motivates Mr. Tomlinson to reduce inventories?*

Mr. Tomlinson may be engaging in the questionable practice of "earnings management." Reducing inventories releases old, low-priced LIFO layers to the income statement, lowering cost of goods sold and raising net income. Of course, Tomlinson's act may also raise current income taxes and impair business operations due to insufficient quantities of inventory.

Income Tax Effects of Alternative Costing Methods

We have seen that in periods of rising prices, LIFO allocates the newest—and therefore highest—inventory purchase prices to cost of goods sold. Higher cost of goods sold produces lower gross margin and lower income. Thus, in periods of rising prices, businesses tend to choose LIFO for computing taxable income, because it produces the lowest current taxable income and the lowest current income tax payment. In Exhibit 6-10, LIFO produced income tax expense of $2,610 compared to income tax expense of $2,820 if FIFO had been used.

Of course, in the long-run, all inventory costs will find their way to cost of goods sold and, therefore, the income statement. When inventory levels fall, old (low-price) LIFO layers become part of cost of goods sold, taxable income rises, and higher taxes are paid. Thus, choosing LIFO to minimize current taxes does not avoid the payment of taxes; it merely postpones it, temporarily reducing the company's capital requirements for a period of time. The federal income tax code requires businesses that use LIFO for tax purposes to use LIFO for financial reporting purposes as well. This is known as the LIFO conformity rule.

Consistency in Application

Although each of the four inventory costing methods is acceptable, once a business adopts a particular costing method for an item, it must continue to use it consistently over time.[8] The consistent application of an accounting principle over time discourages changes in accounting methods from one period to another, even if acceptable alternative methods exist. This enhances the comparability and usefulness of accounting information. A change in accounting method may still be made; however, the effects of the change must be fully disclosed. The consistent application of accounting methods and the required disclosures of any accounting changes permit readers of financial statements to assume that accounting methods do not change over time unless specifically indicated.

Lower of Cost or Market Rule

OBJECTIVE ▶ 5
Apply the lower of cost or market rule to the valuation of inventory.

The inventory accounting procedures described to this point have followed the historical cost principle—inventory is recorded in the firm's records at its historical purchase price (or cost). The price for which inventory items can be sold (that is, in their market value) may decline because the goods have become obsolete, damaged, or have otherwise diminished in value. For example, clothes that have gone out of style due to changing fashions or seasons have declined in value. Similarly, technology companies experience rapid obsolescence due to rapidly changing technologies. In cases where the market value of inventory has dropped below its original cost, generally accepted accounting principles permit a departure from the historical cost concept.

This departure from the historical cost principle is called the **lower of cost or market (LCM) rule**. Under LCM, if the market value of a company's inventory is

---

[8] All items of inventory need not be accounted for by the same costing method. Many companies use LIFO for a portion of inventory for which prices are expected to rise and FIFO or average cost for the portion of inventory for which prices are not expected to rise.

lower than its cost, the company reduces the amount recorded for inventory to its market value. To apply LCM, a company must first determine the cost of its inventory using one of the inventory costing methods discussed earlier in the chapter (specific identification, FIFO, LIFO, or average cost). Next, the company will establish the market value of the inventory. Under LCM, market value is defined as current *replacement cost*, the current purchase price for identical goods.[9] Finally, the market value is compared with historical cost (usually on an item-by-item basis), and the lower of market value or historical cost is used as the cost for the inventory on the financial statements.

Cornerstone 6-8 illustrates the application of the LCM rule.

**CORNERSTONE
6 - 8**

HOW TO Value Inventory at Lower of Cost or Market

Concept:
Inventory should be conservatively valued at the lower of its cost or market value.

Information:
MacKenzie Electronics prepared the following analysis of its inventory at December 31:

Product	Quantity	Historical Cost per Item	Replacement Cost (Market Value) per Item
42″ LCD HDTV	12	$1,000	$1,100
50″ Plasma HDTV	7	1,300	1,000
DVD Recorders	20	120	100

Required:
1. Determine the lower of cost or market value for each item of inventory.
2. Prepare the journal entry needed on December 31 to value the inventory at LCM.

Solution:
1. The LCM amounts are shown in the last column of the analysis below:

Product	Cost	Market Value	Lower of Cost or Market
42″ LCD HDTV	$12,000 (12 × $1,000)	$13,200 (12 × $1,100)	$12,000
50″ Plasma HDTV	9,100 (7 × $1,300)	7,000 (7 × $1,000)	7,000
DVD Recorders	2,400 (20 × $ 120)	2,000 (20 × $ 100)	2,000
	$23,500	$22,200	$21,000

2. To apply LCM, the inventory must be reduced by $2,500 ($23,500 − $21,000) as follows:

Date	Account and Explanation	Debit	Credit
Dec. 31	Cost of Goods Sold	2,500	
	Merchandise Inventory		2,500
	(To reduce the inventory to market value)		

Assets =	Liabilities +	Stockholders' Equity
−2,500		−2,500

[9] In determining the replacement cost (market value) of inventory, a company is subject to two constraints. First, the replacement cost cannot be more than the net realizable value (selling price less costs to sell) of the inventory. Second, replacement cost cannot be less than the net realizable value less a normal profit margin (markup). This concept is discussed more fully in intermediate accounting texts.

Note that the market value of the LCD HDTVs is greater than its historical cost; however, for the other two products, historical cost is greater than market value. Thus only the plasma HDTVs and the DVD recorders are reduced to market; the LCD HDTVs remain at historical cost. The journal entry reduces inventory to its market value, and the loss is recorded as an increase to cost of goods sold in the period that the market value of the item dropped.

The LCM rule is an application of the conservatism principle. The *conservatism principle* leads accountants to select the accounting methods or procedures that produce the lowest (most conservative) net income and net assets in the current period. Thus, accountants tend to recognize expenses and losses as early as possible and to recognize gains and revenues as late as possible. By conservatively valuing inventory, the LCM rule is designed to avoid overstating the current earnings and financial strength of a company. Of course, accelerating the recognition of expenses or losses and delaying recognition of revenues or gains moves them to a future period. Consequently, to the extent that conservatism produces understatements of net income and net assets in the current period, it also produces equal overstatements of net income and net assets in one or more later periods.

DECISION-MAKING & ANALYSIS

LCM and the Overvaluation of Inventory

PC Location, Inc. operates six computer stores in the Chicago area. Several months before year-end, PC Location took delivery on 500 laptop computers purchased from Dell at $800 per unit. By the end of the year, the computers have reached the stores, where they have been offered at a price of $1,000; but few have sold. In mid-December, Dell announces a new, much improved laptop model with a suggested retail price of $1,500.

As controller of PC Location, you are required to prepare the year-end financial statements for review by the external auditor. You know that PC Location is currently negotiating with Second Chicago Bank to increase its long-term loan as a basis for further expansion of its stores. Second Chicago has said it wants an early look at PC Location's financial statements for the current year. You also know that the 450 Dell laptops remaining in inventory are obsolete and are likely to sell for about $400 each—which should be treated as their market value for financial reporting purposes.

You tell the chief executive officer (CEO) that operating income for the year has taken a $180,000 hit [450 laptops × ($800 − $400)] as a result of the ill-considered laptop purchase and resulting inventory write-down. But she asks you to put off recognizing the write-down until Second Chicago has seen the preliminary financial statements. "Let the auditors write down the inventory when they show up in February," she says. "That's what we pay them for."

1. *What are the personal consequences for you, if you do as the CEO asks? If you refuse?*

    If you agree to ignore the required lower of cost or market adjustment, Second Chicago may decide to grant the loan on the basis of the misleading financial statements. But when they receive the audited financial statements several months later, an investigation will no doubt be launched, and you are likely to take the blame. Of course, if you refuse to go along with the CEO, you may find yourself unemployed.

2. *What are the consequences for PC Location?*

    Playing games with unaudited financial statements in order to mislead a lender can permanently damage the business' access to capital. The truth will eventually be told in the audited financial statements. It's rarely, if ever, worth the risk.

3. *What should you do in this situation?*

    You should be prepared to support your adjustment and to argue the disastrous consequences of trying to mislead Second Chicago. You should also be prepared to present alternatives to proceeding with the new loan at this time. Perhaps the expansion can be deferred until the business can demonstrate that its earnings have recovered from the misguided purchase. Of course, the CEO may be adamant, and you may pay a personal price.

OBJECTIVE ▸ 6

Evaluate inventory management using the gross profit and inventory turnover ratios.

Analyzing Inventory

As noted at the first of the chapter, inventories are at the heart of many companies' operations and must be carefully controlled and accounted for. Two measures of how successful a company is at managing and controlling its inventory are the gross profit ratio and inventory turnover.

Key Performance Measures

The **gross profit ratio**, gross profit ÷ net sales, is carefully watched by managers, investors, and analysts as a key indicator of a company's ability to sell inventory at a profit. In short, the gross profit ratio tells us how many cents of every dollar are available to cover expenses other than cost of goods sold and to earn a profit. An increasing gross profit ratio could signal that a company is able to charge more for its products due to high demand or has effectively controlled the cost of its inventory. A decrease in this ratio could signal trouble. For example, a company may have reduced its selling price due to increased competition or it is paying more for its inventory.

The **inventory turnover ratio**, cost of goods sold ÷ average inventory, describes how quickly inventory is purchased (or produced) and sold. Companies want to satisfy the conflicting goals of having enough inventory on hand to meet customer demand while minimizing the cost of holding inventory (e.g., storage costs, obsolescence). Inventory turnover provides an indicator of how much of the company's funds is tied up in inventory. High inventory turnover ratios indicate that a company is rapidly selling its inventory, thus reducing inventory costs. Low inventory turnover reflects that the company may be holding too much inventory, thereby incurring avoidable costs or signaling that demand for a company's products has fallen. By dividing inventory turnover by 365 days, financial statement users can compute the **average days to sell inventory**. Cornerstone 6-9 illustrates the analysis of these performance measures for Wal-Mart.

CORNERSTONE
6-9

HOW TO Calculate the Gross Profit and Inventory Turnover Ratios

Concept:
The gross profit and inventory turnover ratios provide measures of how successful a company is at managing and controlling its inventory.

Information:
The following information (in millions) is available for Wal-Mart for its fiscal year ending January 31, 2007:

Net sales	$344,992	Inventory, 1/31/2006	$31,910
Cost of goods sold	264,152	Inventory, 1/31/2007	33,685

Required:
1. Compute the gross profit ratio for Wal-Mart for 2007.
2. Compute the inventory turnover ratio and the average days to sell inventory for Wal-Mart for 2007.

Solution:
1. Wal-Mart's gross profit (margin) is $80,840 ($344,992 net sales − $264,152 cost of sales). Using this gross margin, Wal-Mart's gross profit ratio is:

$$\text{Gross Profit Ratio} = \frac{\text{Gross Profit}}{\text{Net Sales}}$$
$$= \frac{\$80,840}{\$344,992}$$
$$= 0.234 \text{ or } 23.4\%$$

2. Inventory turnover and average days to sell inventory are:

CORNERSTONE
6-9
(continued)

$$\text{Inventory Turnover Ratio} = \frac{\text{Cost of Goods Sold}}{\text{Average Inventory}}$$

$$= \frac{\$264,152}{(\$31,910 + \$33,685) \div 2} = 8.054$$

$$\text{Average Days to Sell Inventory} = \frac{365 \text{ days}}{\text{Inventory Turnover}} = \frac{365}{8.054} = 45.319 \text{ days}$$

Wal-Mart's gross profit ratio of 23.4 percent, while smaller than the industry average of 27.10 percent[10], was still up 0.2 percent from the previous year. In its MD&A, Wal-Mart attributed this increase to improved margins in its general merchandise and food areas. Additionally, Wal-Mart notes that the lower than industry average gross margin was driven by the increasing percentage of its business in lower-margin food areas. Wal-Mart's inventory turnover of 8.054 times is greater than the industry average of 6.59. It takes Wal-Mart, on average, approximately 45 days to sell its inventory. While its margin is lower than the industry average, the higher inventory turnover suggests that Wal-Mart is efficiently managing its inventory, which is good news for Wal-Mart's profitability.

Effects of Inventory Errors

OBJECTIVE ▶ 7
Describe how errors in ending inventory affect income statements and balance sheets.

The cost of goods sold model, illustrated in Cornerstone 6-1, describes the relationship between inventory and cost of goods sold. This relationship implies that the measurement of inventory affects both the balance sheet and the income statement. Even with recent technological advances, it is easy to make errors in determining the cost of the hundreds of items in a typical ending inventory. Incorrect counts, mistakes in costing, or errors in identifying items are common. Because the ending inventory of one period is the beginning inventory of the next period, errors in the measurement of ending inventory affect two accounting periods.

To illustrate the effect of an error in valuing ending inventory on the financial statements, consider the information in Exhibit 6-13. The "Correct" column shows the financial statements for 2009 and 2010 as they would appear if no error were made. The "Erroneous" column shows the financial statements for the two years as they would appear if the firm understated its inventory at December 31, 2009, as a result of miscounting or in some other way undervaluing inventory by $15,000. The "Error" column describes the effect of the error on each line of the statements.

The understatement of the 2009 ending inventory causes an overstatement of 2009 cost of goods sold. Thus, gross margin for 2009 is understated by $15,000. Ignoring income taxes, this error would then flow into both net income and retained earnings for 2009. However, the effect is not limited to 2009. Because the ending inventory for 2009 is the beginning inventory for 2010, the beginning inventory for 2010 is understated by $15,000. Assuming no other errors are made, this would lead to an understatement of cost of goods sold and an overstatement of gross margin (and net income) by $15,000. However, notice that when this flows into retained earnings, the understatement in 2009 is offset by the overstatement in 2010 so that

[10] Industry average ratios were obtained from Reuters.

Exhibit 6-13

Effects of an Inventory Error

(amounts in thousands)		Correct		Erroneous	Error*
Income Statement (partial)					
Sales			$500	$500	
Cost of goods sold:					
Beginning inventory	$ 50			$ 50	
Purchases	250			250	
Cost of goods available for sale	$300			$300	
Less: Ending inventory	60			45	−$15
Cost of goods sold		240		255	+$15
Gross margin		$260		$245	−$15
Balance Sheet (partial)					
Inventory			$ 60	$ 45	−$15
Retained earnings			$100	$ 85	−$15
Income Statement (partial)					
Sales			$600	$600	
Cost of goods sold:					
Beginning inventory	$ 60			$ 45	−$15
Purchases	290			290	
Cost of goods available for sale	$350			$335	−$15
Less: Ending inventory	50			50	
Cost of goods sold		300		285	−$15
Gross margin		$300		$315	+$15
Balance Sheet (partial)					
Inventory			$ 50	$ 50	
Retained earnings			180	180	

Left column labels: "2009 Financial Statements" (top section) and "2010 Financial Statements" (bottom section)

* A minus sign (−) indicates an understatement and a plus sign (+) indicates an overstatement.

retained earnings is correctly stated by the end of 2010. This illustrates the self-correcting nature of inventory errors.

Cornerstone 6-10 illustrates the analysis of inventory errors.

**CORNERSTONE
6-10**

HOW TO Analyze Inventory Errors

Concept:
Errors in the measurement of ending inventory will affect both the current and subsequent period balance sheet as well as the current period income statement.

Information:
Dunn Corporation reported net income of $75,000 for 2009. Early in 2010, Dunn discovers that the December 31, 2009 ending inventory was overstated by $6,000.

Required:
Determine the financial statement effects of the inventory errors for 2009 and 2010.

Solution:
For 2009, assets (ending inventory) are overstated by $6,000. Using the cost of goods sold model, cost of goods sold is equal to cost of goods available for sale less ending inventory. The overstatement of ending inventory causes an understatement of cost of goods sold (an expense) by $6,000. This error flows through to income and retained earnings (equity). Because the ending inventory for 2009 is the beginning inventory for 2010, the error has the opposite

effects on income for 2010. Assuming no other errors are made, the inventory error self-corrects and the 2010 balance sheet is correctly stated. These effects are summarized below.

CORNERSTONE
6 - 10
(continued)

	Assets	Liabilities	Equity	Revenues	Expenses	Income
2009	$6,000 overstated	No effect	$6,000 overstated	No effect	$6,000 understated	$6,000 overstated
2010	No effect	No effect	No effect	No effect	$6,000 overstated	$6,000 understated

Even though inventory errors are self-correcting over two periods, it is still necessary to correct them in order to produce properly stated financial information. If the error is not corrected, both income statements and the 2009 balance sheet will be incorrect. The correction of errors is covered in intermediate accounting.

Summary of Learning Objectives

LO1.   Describe the types of inventories held by merchandisers and manufacturers, and understand how inventory costs flow through a company.

- Merchandising companies hold one type of inventory termed merchandise inventory.
- Manufacturing companies have three types of inventory—raw materials, work-in-process, and finished goods.
- When goods are purchased, the cost of the purchase is recorded in merchandise inventory (for merchandisers) or raw materials inventory (for manufacturers). During the production process, manufacturers record the cost (raw materials, labor, and overhead) in work-in-process and then transfer the cost to finished goods inventory when the product is complete.
- Once the product is sold, the cost is transferred out of the inventory account (either Merchandise Inventory or Finished Goods) and into Cost of Goods Sold to match it with sales revenue.
- The relationship between inventory and cost of goods sold is described by the cost of goods sold model.

LO2.   Explain how to record purchases and sales of inventory using a perpetual inventory system.

- In a perpetual inventory system, purchases of inventory are recorded by increasing the inventory account.
- If a purchase discount exists, inventory is reduced by the amount of the discount taken.
- When a purchased item is returned (purchase return) or a price reduction is granted by the seller (purchase allowance), the inventory item is reduced by the amount of the purchase return or allowance given.
- If transportation costs exist and the shipping terms are F.O.B shipping point, the transportation costs are considered part of the total cost of purchases and the inventory account is increased.
- If transportation costs exist and the shipping terms are F.O.B. destination, the seller pays these costs and records them as a selling expense on the income statement.
- In a perpetual inventory system, sales are recorded through two journal entries: (1) record the sales revenue, and (2) increase Cost of Goods Sold and decrease the inventory account.

- If an item is later returned, two entries must also be made: (1) increase Sales Returns and Allowances (a contra-revenue account), and (2) increase the inventory account and decrease Cost of Goods Sold.

LO3. Apply the four inventory costing methods to compute ending inventory and cost of goods sold under a perpetual inventory system.

- The four inventory costing methods are: specific identification; first-in, first-out (FIFO); last-in, first-out (LIFO); and average cost.
- The specific identification method determines the cost of ending inventory and the cost of goods sold based on the identification of the actual units sold and in inventory.
- The other three inventory costing methods allocate cost of goods available for sale between ending inventory and cost of goods sold using the following process.

  Step 1: Calculate the cost of goods available for sale *immediately prior* to any sale transaction.

  Step 2: Apply the inventory costing method to determine ending inventory and cost of goods sold.

  Step 3: Repeat steps 1 and 2 for all inventory transactions during the period. The sum of the cost of goods sold computed in step 2 is the cost of goods sold for the period. Ending inventory is the amount computed during the final application of step 2 for the period.

LO4. Analyze the financial reporting and tax effects of the various inventory costing methods.

- If the prices paid for purchased inventory are stable, all inventory costing methods will yield the same amounts for ending inventory and cost of goods sold.
- When purchase prices vary, FIFO, LIFO and the average cost methods will produce different amounts for ending inventory, cost of goods sold and, therefore, income.
- When prices are rising, the FIFO method produces the highest cost for ending inventory, the lowest cost of goods sold, and the highest gross margin (and net income).
- In contrast, the LIFO method produced the lowest cost for ending inventory, the highest cost of goods sold, and, therefore, the lowest gross margin (and net income) of the three methods. Because LIFO results in lower income, it results in the lowest income taxes.
- When purchase prices are *falling,* the situation is reversed.
- The average cost method produced amounts for inventory, cost of goods sold, and net income that fell between the FIFO and LIFO extremes.

LO5. Apply the lower of cost or market rule to the valuation of inventory.

- If the market value of inventory has dropped below its original cost, generally accepted accounting principles permit a departure from the historical cost concept.
- A company is allowed to reduce the amount recorded for inventory to its market value, where market value is defined as the current replacement cost.
- This lower of cost or market rule is an application of the conservatism principle.

LO6. Evaluate inventory management using the gross profit and inventory turnover ratios.

- Two useful measures of how successful a company is at managing and controlling its inventory are the gross profit ratio (gross profit ÷ net sales) and the inventory turnover ratio (cost of goods sold ÷ average inventory).
- The gross profit ratio indicates how many cents of every dollar are available to cover expenses other than cost of goods sold and to earn a profit.
- The inventory turnover ratio describes how quickly inventory is purchased (or produced) and sold.

LO7. **Describe how errors in ending inventory affect income statements and balance sheets.**

- Inventory errors can arise for a number of reasons, including incorrect counts of inventory, mistakes in costing, or errors in identifying items.
- Because the ending inventory of one period is the beginning inventory of the next period, an error in the measurement of ending inventory will affect the cost of goods sold and net income of two consecutive periods.
- Inventory errors are self-correcting, therefore, the assets and stockholders' equity of only the first period are misstated (assuming no other errors are made).

CORNERSTONE 6-1	How to apply the cost of goods sold model, page 286	
CORNERSTONE 6-2	How to record purchase transactions in a perpetual inventory system, page 291	
CORNERSTONE 6-3	How to record sales transactions in a perpetual inventory system, page 293	
CORNERSTONE 6-4	How to apply the specific identification method, page 296	**CORNERSTONES FOR CHAPTER 6**
CORNERSTONE 6-5	How to apply the FIFO inventory costing method, page 298	
CORNERSTONE 6-6	How to apply the LIFO inventory costing method, page 300	
CORNERSTONE 6-7	How to apply the average cost inventory costing method, page 301	
CORNERSTONE 6-8	How to value inventory at lower of cost or market, page 306	
CORNERSTONE 6-9	How to calculate the gross profit and inventory turnover ratios, page 308	
CORNERSTONE 6-10	How to analyze inventory errors, page 310	

Key Terms

Average cost method, 299

Average days to sell inventory, 308

Cost of goods available for sale, 285

Cost of goods sold, 282

Discount period, 289

First-in, first-out (FIFO) method, 298

F.O.B. destination, 291

F.O.B. shipping point, 290

Freight-in, 291

Freight-out, 291

Gross margin (gross profit), 282

Gross profit ratio, 308

Inventory, 282

Inventory turnover ratio, 308

Last-in, first-out (LIFO) method, 299

LIFO reserve, 304

Lower of cost or market (LCM) rule, 305

Merchandise inventory, 283

Periodic inventory system, 287

Perpetual inventory system, 287

Purchase allowance, 290

Purchase discounts, 289

Purchase returns, 290

Purchases, 289

Specific identification method, 296

Appendix 6A: Periodic Inventory System

In a periodic inventory system, the inventory records are not kept continually, or perpetually, up-to-date. Instead, under a periodic inventory system, the inventory account is updated at the end of the period based on a physical count of the inventory on hand. The balance in the Merchandise inventory account remains unchanged during the period. As purchase transactions occur, they are recorded in one of four temporary accounts: Purchases, Purchase Discounts, Purchase Returns and Allowances, or Transportation-In.

- The purchases account accumulates the cost of the inventory acquired during the period.
- The purchase discounts account accumulates the amount of discounts on purchases taken during the period.
- The purchase returns and allowances account accumulates the cost of any merchandise returned to the supplier or any reductions (allowances) in the purchase price granted by the seller.
- The transportation-in account accumulates the cost paid by the purchaser to transport inventory from suppliers.

The balances in these temporary accounts, along with the beginning and ending inventory balances obtained from the physical count of inventory, are used to compute cost of goods sold using the cost of goods sold model illustrated in Cornerstone 6-1.

Cornerstone 6-11 illustrates how to record purchase transactions in a periodic inventory system.

CORNERSTONE 6-11

HOW TO Record Purchase Transactions in a Periodic Inventory System

Concept:
The cost of inventory includes the purchase price of the merchandise plus any cost of bringing the goods to a salable condition and location.

Information:
Assume that on September 1, 2009, Brandon Shoes purchased 50 pairs of hiking boots for $3,750 cash and paid $150 of transportation costs. Also, on September 1, Brandon purchased 100 pairs of running shoes for $10,000; however the seller paid the transportation costs of $300. The running shoes were purchased on credit with credit terms of 2/10, n/30. Brandon paid for one-half ($5,000) of the running shoes on September 10, within the discount period. The remaining shoes were paid for on September 30. After inspection, Brandon determined that 10 pairs of the hiking boots were defective and returned them on September 5.

Required:
1. Prepare journal entries to record the purchase of the hiking boots.
2. Prepare the journal entry to record the purchase of the running shoes.
3. Prepare the journal entries to record the payment for the running shoes on September 10 and September 30.
4. Prepare the journal entry to record the return of the defective hiking boots.

Solution:
1. The journal entry to record the purchase of the hiking boots and the related transportation charges is:

Date	Account and Explanation	Debit	Credit
Sept. 1	Purchases	3,750	
	Cash		3,750
	(Purchase of inventory for cash)		
1	Transportation-In	150	
	Cash		150
	(Payment of freight costs)		

CORNERSTONE 6-11 *(continued)*

Assets	= Liabilities +	Stockholders' Equity
−3,750		−3,750

2. The journal entry to record the credit purchase of the running shoes is:

Date	Account and Explanation	Debit	Credit
Sept. 1	Purchases	10,000	
	Accounts Payable		10,000
	(To record the purchase of inventory on credit)		

Assets	= Liabilities +	Stockholders' Equity
−150		−150

Assets	= Liabilities +	Stockholders' Equity
	+10,000	−10,000

Note: The cost of the freight is not recorded because it was paid by the seller (FOB destination or freight-out).

3. Brandon paid for $5,000 of the running shoes purchase less a discount of $100 ($5,000 2%). The journal entry is:

Date	Account and Explanation	Debit	Credit
Sept. 10	Accounts Payable	5,000	
	Cash		4,900
	Purchase Discount		100
	(To record payment within the discount period)		

Assets	= Liabilities +	Stockholders' Equity
−4,900	−5,000	+100

The journal entry to record the payment *outside* of the discount period is:

Date	Account and Explanation	Debit	Credit
Sept. 30	Accounts Payable	5,000	
	Cash		5,000
	(To record payment outside of the discount period)		

Assets	= Liabilities +	Stockholders' Equity
−5,000	−5,000	

4. The journal entry required to return the $750 of defective hiking boots (calculated as $3,750 ÷ 50 pairs = $75 per pair; $75 × 10 pairs) is:

Date	Account and Explanation	Debit	Credit
Sept. 5	Cash	750	
	Purchase Returns and Allowances		750
	(Returned 10 defective hiking boots)		

Assets	= Liabilities +	Stockholders' Equity
+750		+750

Under either the periodic or the perpetual inventory system, the net cost of purchases (shown below) is the same.

Purchases	$13,750
Less: Purchase discounts	(100)
Purchase returns and allowances	(750)
Add: Transportation costs (freight-in)	150
Net cost of purchases	$13,050

Additionally, for sales transactions, there is no need to make a second journal entry to record the expense (and inventory) portion of a transaction. Instead, only the revenue portion is recorded as shown earlier in the text.

The differences between a periodic and perpetual inventory system are summarized in Exhibit 6-14.

Exhibit 6-14

Perpetual vs. Periodic Inventory Systems

Activity	Perpetual System	Periodic System
Purchase	Inventory purchases are recorded in *the merchandise inventory account.*	The costs of inventory purchases are recorded in *the purchases account.*
Sale	When a sale is made, an entry is made to record the amount of sales revenue. *A second entry is made that increases the cost of goods sold account and decreases the merchandise inventory account.*	When a sale is made, an entry is made to record the amount of sales revenue only. *No entry is made to cost of goods sold or inventory.*
Costing ending inventory	At the end of the period, *the cost of ending inventory is the balance in the inventory account* (which is verified by a physical count of inventory).	*The amount of ending inventory is determined at the end of the accounting by taking a physical count of inventory,* a procedure by which all items of inventory on a given date are identified and counted.
Determining cost of goods sold	Cost of goods sold for the period is the *balance in the cost of goods sold account* at the end of the period.	Cost of goods sold is determined only at the end of the period by *applying the cost of goods sold model.*

Appendix 6A: Summary of Learning Objectives

LO8. Explain how to record purchases of inventory using a periodic inventory system.

- In a periodic inventory system, purchases of inventory are recorded by increasing the purchases account.
- If a purchase discount exists, the purchases discount account is increased by the amount of the discount taken.
- When a purchased item is returned (purchase return) or a price reduction is granted by the seller (purchase allowance), the purchase returns and allowances account is increased by the amount of the purchase return or allowance given.
- If transportation costs exist and the shipping terms are F.O.B shipping point, the transportation costs are considered part of the total cost of purchases and the purchases account is increased.
- If transportation costs exist and the shipping terms are F.O.B. destination, the seller pays these costs and records them as a selling expense on the income statement.

CORNERSTONE 6-11 How to record purchase transactions in a periodic inventory system, page 314

CORNERSTONES FOR APPENDIX 6A

OBJECTIVE ▶ 9
Compute ending inventory and cost of goods sold under a periodic inventory system.

Appendix 6B: Inventory Costing Methods and the Periodic Inventory System

Regardless of whether a company uses a perpetual inventory system or a periodic inventory system, inventory costing methods are designed to allocate the cost of goods available for sale between ending inventory and cost of goods sold. Under a periodic inventory system, the inventory costing methods are applied as if all purchases during an accounting period take place prior to any sales of the period. While this is not a realistic assumption, it does simplify the computation of the ending inventory and cost of goods sold since only one allocation needs to be made, regardless of the number of purchases and sales. Given this assumption, you will then apply the following steps to determine ending inventory and cost of goods sold:

Step 1: Calculate the cost of goods available for sale for the period.

Step 2: Apply the inventory costing method to determine ending inventory and cost of goods sold.

First-In, First-Out (FIFO)

Under the FIFO method, *the earliest purchases (the first in) are assumed to be the first sold (the first out) and the more recent purchases are in ending inventory.* Cornerstone 6-12 illustrates the application of the FIFO method. Notice that this is the same information used to illustrate the inventory costing methods applied to a perpetual inventory system (Cornerstones 6-5 through 6-7). However, the information on purchases is listed first and the sales can be combined because all purchases are assumed to occur prior to any sales. A periodic FIFO inventory costing method is shown in Cornerstone 6-12.

HOW TO Apply the FIFO Inventory Costing Method in a Periodic Inventory System

**CORNERSTONE
6-12**

Concept:
The cost of the earliest purchases that make up cost of goods available for sale is allocated to cost of goods sold, and the cost of the most recent purchases are allocated to ending inventory.

Information:
Tampico Beachwear, a retail store specializing in beach apparel, has the following information related to purchases and sales of one of its more popular products, Crocs brand shoes. Ending inventory is made up of 200 units (1,300 units available for sale – 1,100 units sold). (Each inventory layer is a different color.)

Date	Description	Units Purchased at Cost	Units Sold at Retail
Oct. 1	Beginning Inventory	300 units @ $16 = $ 4,800	
3	Purchase 1	600 units @ $18 = $10,800	
8	Sale 1		800 units @ $30
15	Purchase 2	250 units @ $20 = $ 5,000	
20	Purchase 3	150 units @ $22 = $ 3,300	
25	Sale 2		300 units @ $30
	Goods available for sale: 1,300 units = $23,900		Sales: 1,100 units = $33,000

Required:
Compute the cost of ending inventory and the cost of goods sold at October 31 using the FIFO method.

Solution:
Step 1: Compute the cost of goods available for sale for the period ($23,900).

**CORNERSTONE
6-12**
(continued)

Step 2: Apply FIFO to determine ending inventory and cost of goods sold. This cost of goods available for sale is allocated between inventory (the most recent purchases) and cost of goods sold (the oldest purchases) as follows:

Ending Inventory	Cost of Goods Sold
150 units × $22 = $3,300	300 units × $16 = $ 4,800
50 units × $20 = 1,000	600 units × $18 = 10,800
200 units $4,300	200 units × $20 = 4,000
	1,100 unit $19,600

Last-In, First-Out (LIFO)

Under the LIFO method, *the most recent purchases (newest costs) are allocated to the cost of goods sold and the earliest purchases (oldest costs) are allocated to ending inventory.* Cornerstone 6-13 illustrates the application of the LIFO method.

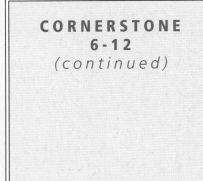

**CORNERSTONE
6-13**

HOW TO Apply the LIFO Inventory Costing Method in a Periodic Inventory System

Concept:
The cost of the most recent purchases that make up cost of goods available for sale is allocated to cost of goods sold, and the cost of the earliest (oldest) purchases are allocated to ending inventory.

Information:
Tampico Beachwear, a retail store specializing in beach apparel, has the following information related to purchases and sales of one of its more popular products, Crocs brand shoes. Ending inventory is made up of 200 units (1,300 units available for sale – 1,100 units sold). (Each inventory layer is a different color.)

Date	Description	Units Purchased at Cost	Units Sold at Retail
Oct. 1	Beginning Inventory	300 units @ $16 = $ 4,800	
3	Purchase 1	600 units @ $18 = 10,800	
8	Sale 1		800 units @ $30
15	Purchase 2	250 units @ $20 = 5,000	
20	Purchase 3	150 units @ $22 = 3,300	
25	Sale 2		300 units @ $30
	Goods available for sale: 1,300 units = $23,900		Sales: 1,100 units = $33,000

Required:
Compute the cost of ending inventory and the cost of goods sold at October 31 using the LIFO method.

Solution:
Step 1: Compute the cost of goods available for sale for the period ($23,900).
Step 2: Apply LIFO to determine ending inventory and cost of goods sold.
This cost of goods available for sale is allocated between inventory (the oldest purchases) and cost of goods sold (the most recent purchases) as follows:

Ending Inventory	Cost of Goods Sold	
200 units × $16 = $3,200	100 units × $16 = $ 1,600	
	600 units × $18 = 10,800	
	250 units × $20 = 5,000	
	150 units × $22 = 3,300	
	1,100 units	**$20,700**

Average Cost

Under the average cost method, the weighted average cost per unit is multiplied by the number of units in ending inventory to produce the cost of ending inventory and by the number of units sold to produce cost of goods sold. In contrast to the perpetual inventory system, the weighted average cost per unit is not continually calculated. Rather it is calculated based on the total cost of goods available for sale and the total units available for sale. This method is commonly referred to as the weighted-average method. Cornerstone 6-14 illustrates the application of the average cost method.

HOW TO Apply the Average Cost Inventory Costing Method in a Periodic Inventory System

**CORNERSTONE
6-14**

Concept:
The cost of goods available for sale is allocated between ending inventory and cost of goods sold based on a weighted average cost of the goods available for sale.

Information:
Tampico Beachwear, a retail store specializing in beach apparel, has the following information related to purchases and sales of one of its more popular products, Crocs brand shoes. Ending inventory is made up of 200 units (1,300 units available for sale − 1,100 units sold). (Each inventory layer is a different color.)

Date	Description	Units Purchased at Cost	Units Sold at Retail
Oct. 1	Beginning Inventory	300 units @ $16 = $ 4,800	
3	Purchase 1	600 units @ $18 = $10,800	
8	Sale 1		800 units @ $30
15	Purchase 2	250 units @ $20 = $ 5,000	
20	Purchase 3	150 units @ $22 = $ 3,300	
25	Sale 2		300 units @ $30
	Goods available for sale: 1,300 units = $23,900		Sales: 1,100 units = $33,000

Required:
Compute the cost of ending inventory and the cost of goods sold at October 31 using the average cost method.

Solution:
Step 1: Compute the cost of goods available for sale for the period ($23,900).

**CORNERSTONE
6-14**
(continued)

Step 2: Apply the average cost method to determine ending inventory and cost of goods sold. This method requires you to compute a weighted average cost of the goods available for sale:

$$\text{Weighted Average Cost per Unit} = \frac{\text{Cost of Goods Available for Sale}}{\text{Units Available for Sale}}$$

$$= \frac{\$23,900}{1,300 \text{ units}} = \mathbf{\$18.3846}$$

The cost of goods available for sale ($23,900) is allocated between inventory and cost of goods sold using the average cost of the inventory as follows:

Ending Inventory	Cost of Goods Sold
200 units × $18.3846 = **$3,677**	1,100 units × $18.3846 = **$20,223**

Note that under all inventory costing methods, periodic inventory systems allocate the cost of purchased goods between cost of goods sold and ending inventory only at the end of the period. In contrast, the perpetual inventory system performs this allocation each time a sale is made. Because of this difference in the timing of cost allocations, the two systems nearly always yield different amounts for the cost of goods sold and ending inventory under both the LIFO and average cost assumptions. FIFO amounts, however, are always the same under both periodic and perpetual inventory systems.[11]

Appendix 6B: Summary of Learning Objectives

LO9. **Compute ending inventory and cost of goods sold under a periodic inventory system.**
- Under a periodic inventory system, the inventory costing methods are applied as if all purchases during an accounting period take place prior to any sales of the period. Given this assumption, you will then apply the following steps:
  Step 1: Calculate the cost of goods available for sale for the period.
  Step 2: Apply the inventory costing method to determine ending inventory and cost of goods sold.

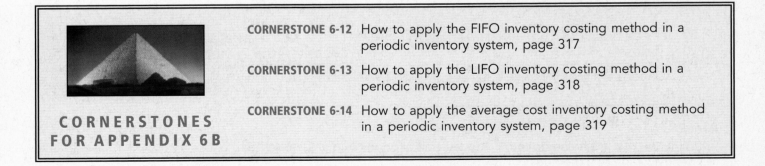

**CORNERSTONES
FOR APPENDIX 6B**

CORNERSTONE 6-12 How to apply the FIFO inventory costing method in a periodic inventory system, page 317

CORNERSTONE 6-13 How to apply the LIFO inventory costing method in a periodic inventory system, page 318

CORNERSTONE 6-14 How to apply the average cost inventory costing method in a periodic inventory system, page 319

[11] This occurs because FIFO always allocates the earliest items purchased to cost of goods sold, resulting in ending inventory being the latest items purchased. Under both the perpetual and periodic inventory systems, these are the same units of inventory at the same cost. Therefore, the timing of the cost allocation is irrelevant under FIFO.

Review Problem

I. Accounting for Inventory

Concept:

The cost of goods available for sale is allocated between ending inventory and cost of goods sold based on a costing method chosen by company management. Under a perpetual inventory system, the accounting records are continually (perpetually) updated each sale or purchase of inventory.

Information:

Sagamore Supplies, an office supply wholesale store, uses a perpetual inventory system. Sagamore recorded the following activity for one of its inventory accounts:

Date	Activity	# of Units	Cost per Unit
Oct. 1	Beginning inventory	2,500	$16
15	Purchase	5,100	$17
Nov. 3	Sale	5,900	
20	Purchase	4,800	$18
Dec. 10	Sale	5,300	

Additional information on the purchases and sales is as follows:

- All purchases were cash purchases.
- All sales were cash sales and all inventory items were sold for $25 per unit.

Required:

1. Compute the cost of ending inventory and the cost of goods sold using the FIFO, LIFO, and average cost methods.
2. Assume that Sagamore uses the FIFO inventory costing method. Prepare the journal entries to record the purchases and sales of inventory.

Solution:

1.

a. Under FIFO, the cost of ending inventory is $21,600 and cost of goods sold is $191,500 ($97,800 + $93,700).

Date	Description	Inventory Balance		Cost of Goods Sold	
Oct. 1	Beginning inventory	2,500 × $16	= $ 40,000		
15	Purchase (5,100 @ $17)	2,500 × $16 = $40,000 ⎱ 5,100 × $17 = $86,700 ⎰ = $126,700			
Nov. 3	Sale (5,900 @ $25)	1,700 × $17	= $ 28,900	2,500 × $16 = $40,000 ⎱ 3,400 × $17 = $57,800 ⎰	= **$97,800**

This is an interim calculation. Because the period is not over, these steps need to be repeated until the end of the accounting period.

Date	Description	Inventory Balance		Cost of Goods Sold	
Nov. 3	Inventory on hand	1,700 × $17	= $ 28,900		
20	Purchase (4,800 @ $18)	1,700 × $17 = $28,900 ⎱ 4,800 × $18 = $86,400 ⎰ = $115,300		1,700 × $17 = $28,900 ⎱ 3,600 × $18 = $64,800 ⎰	= **$93,700**
Dec. 10	Sale (5,300 @ $25)	1,200 × $18	= $ 21,600		

b. Under LIFO, the cost of ending inventory is $19,200 and cost of goods sold is $193,900 ($99,500 + $94,400).

Date	Description	Inventory Balance		Cost of Goods Sold	
Oct. 1	Beginning inventory	2,500 × $16	= $ 40,000		
15	Purchase (5,100 @ $17)	2,500 × $16 = $40,000 ⎱ 5,100 × $17 = $86,700 ⎰ = $126,700			
Nov. 3	Sale (5,900 @ $25)	1,700 × $16	= $ 27,200	5,100 × $17 = $86,700 ⎱ 800 × $16 = $12,800 ⎰	= **$99,500**

This is an interim calculation. Because the period is not over, these steps need to be repeated until the end of the accounting period.

Date		Description	Inventory Balance		Cost of Goods Sold
Nov.	3	Inventory on hand	1,700 × $16	= $ 27,200	
	20	Purchase (4,800 @ $18)	1,700 × $16 = $27,200 ⎫ 4,800 × $18 = $86,400 ⎭= $113,600		
Dec.	10	Sale (5,300 @ $25)	1,200 × $16	= $ 19,200	4,800 × $18 = $86,400 ⎫ 500 × $16 = $8,000 ⎭= **$94,400**

    c.   Under average cost, the cost of ending inventory is $21,183 and cost of goods sold is $191,917 ($98,359 + $93,558).

Date		Description	Inventory Balance		Cost of Goods Sold
Oct.	1	Beginning inventory	2,500 × $16	= $ 40,000 ($16 /unit)	
	15	Purchase (5,100 @ $17)	2,500 × $16 = $40,000 ⎫ 5,100 × $17 = $86,700 ⎭= $126,700 ($16.671/unit)[a]		
Nov.	3	Sale (5,900 @ $25)	1,700 × $16.671	= $ 28,341	5,900 × $16.671 = **$98,359**

[a] $126,700 ÷ 7,600 units = $16.671/unit

This is an interim calculation. Because the period is not over, these steps need to be repeated until the end of the accounting period.

Date		Description	Inventory Balance		Cost of Goods Sold
Nov.	3	Inventory on hand	1,700 × $16.671	= $ 28,341	
	20	Purchase (4,800 @ $18)	1,700 × $16.671 = $28,341 ⎫ 4,800 × $18 = $86,400 ⎭= $114,741 ($17.6525/unit)[1]		
Dec.	10	Sale 2 (5,300 @ $25)	1,200 × $17.6525	= $ 21,183	5,300 × $17.6525 = **$93,558**

[1] $114,741 ÷ 6,500 units = $17.6525/unit

2.   The journal entries required to record the inventory transactions (assuming FIFO) are:

Date	Account and Explanation	Debit	Credit
Oct. 15	Merchandise Inventory	40,000	
	Cash		40,000
	(Purchased inventory for cash)		
Nov. 3	Cash	147,500	
	Sales Revenue		147,500
	(Sold 5,900 units @ $25 per unit)		
3	Cost of Goods Sold	97,800	
	Merchandise Inventory		97,800
	(Cost of sale of 5,900 units)		
20	Merchandise Inventory	86,400	
	Cash		86,400
	(Purchased inventory for cash)		
Dec. 10	Cash	132,500	
	Sales Revenue		132,500
	(Sold 5,300 units @ $25 per unit)		
10	Cost of Goods Sold	93,700	
	Merchandise Inventory		93,700
	(Cost of sale of 5,300 units)		

Assets = Liabilities + Stockholders' Equity
+40,000
−40,000

Assets = Liabilities + Stockholders' Equity
+147,500   +147,500

Assets = Liabilities + Stockholders' Equity
−97,800   −97,800

Assets = Liabilities + Stockholders' Equity
+86,400
−86,400

Assets = Liabilities + Stockholders' Equity
+132,500   +132,500

Assets = Liabilities + Stockholders' Equity
−93,700   −93,700

Discussion Questions

1. What are the differences between merchandisers and manufacturers?
2. Describe the types of inventories used by manufacturers and merchandisers.
3. Compare the flow of inventory costs between merchandisers and manufacturers.
4. What are components of cost of goods available for sale and cost of goods sold?
5. How is cost of goods sold determined?
6. How do the perpetual and periodic inventory accounting systems differ from each other?
7. Why are perpetual inventory systems more expensive to operate than periodic inventory systems? What conditions justify the additional cost of a perpetual inventory system?
8. Why are adjustments made to the invoice price of goods when determining the cost of inventory?
9. Identify the accounting items for which adjustments are made to the invoice price of goods when determining the net cost of purchases.
10. Describe the difference between F.O.B. shipping point and F.O.B. destination.
11. Why do sales transactions under a perpetual inventory system require two journal entries?
12. Why do the four inventory costing methods produce different amounts for the cost of ending inventory and cost of goods sold when purchase prices are changing?
13. The costs of which units of inventory are allocated to ending inventory or cost of goods sold using the FIFO, LIFO, and average cost methods?
14. If inventory prices are rising, which inventory costing method should produce the smallest payment for taxes?
15. How would reported income differ if LIFO rather than FIFO were used when purchase prices are rising? When purchase prices are falling?
16. How would the balance sheet accounts be affected if LIFO rather than FIFO were used when purchase prices are rising? When purchase prices are falling?
17. What is the LIFO reserve and when is it used?
18. Why are inventories written down to the lower of cost or market?
19. What is the effect on the current period income statement and the balance sheet when inventories are written down using the lower of cost or market method? What is the effect on future period income statement and balance sheets?
20. What does the gross profit ratio and the inventory turnover ratio tell company management about inventory?
21. How does an understatement of ending inventory affect the financial statements of two periods? How does an overstatement of ending inventory affect the financial statements of two periods?
22. (Appendix 6A) What accounts are used to record inventory purchase transactions under the periodic inventory system? Why aren't these accounts used in a perpetual inventory system?
23. (Appendix 6B) "For each inventory costing method, perpetual and periodic systems yield the same amounts for ending inventory and cost of goods sold." Do you agree or disagree with this statement? Explain.

Multiple-Choice Exercises

6-1 If beginning inventory is $50,000, purchases is $260,000, and ending inventory is $35,000, what is cost of goods sold as determined by the cost of goods sold model?

a. $175,000
b. $245,000
c. $275,000
d. $345,000

6-2 Which of the following transactions would *not* result in an entry to the merchandise inventory account in the buyer's accounting records under a perpetual inventory system?

a. The purchase of merchandise on credit.
b. The payment of freight by the seller for goods received from a supplier.
c. The return of merchandise to the supplier.
d. The payment of a credit purchase of merchandise within the discount period.

6-3 Briggs Company purchased $10,000 of inventory on credit with credit terms of 2/10, n/30. Briggs paid for the purchase within the discount period. How much did Briggs pay for the inventory?

a. $9,000
b. $9,800
c. $10,000
d. $10,200

6-4 Which of the following transactions would *not* result in an adjustment to the Merchandise Inventory account under a perpetual inventory system?

a. The sale of merchandise for cash.
b. The sale of merchandise on credit.
c. The return of merchandise by a customer.
d. The receipt of payment from a customer within the discount period.

6-5 U-Save Automotive Group purchased 10 vehicles during the current month. Two trucks were purchased for $18,000, two SUVs were purchased for $22,000, and six hybrid cars were purchased for $31,000. A review of the sales invoices revealed that five of the hybrid cars were sold and both trucks were sold. What is the cost of U-Save's ending inventory if it uses the specific identification method?

a. $75,000
b. $89,100
c. $93,000
d. $222,000

The following information is used for Multiple-Choice Exercises 6-6 through 6-8:

Morgan Inc. has the following units and costs for the month of April:

	Units Purchased at Cost	Units Sold at Retail
Beginning Inventory, April 1	1,000 units at $20	
Purchase 1, April 9	1,200 units at $23	
Sale 1, April 12		1,800 units at $40
Purchase 2, April 22	800 units at $25	

6-6 If Morgan uses a perpetual inventory system, what is the cost of ending inventory under FIFO at April 30?

a. $24,600
b. $29,200
c. $38,400
d. $43,000

6-7 If Morgan uses a perpetual inventory system, what is the cost of goods sold under LIFO at April 30?

a. $28,000
b. $29,200

c. $38,400
d. $39,600

6-8 If Morgan uses a perpetual inventory system, what is the cost of ending inventory under average cost at April 30? (Use four decimal places for per unit calculations and round all other numbers to the nearest dollar.)

a. $27,040
b. $28,655
c. $38,945
d. $40,560

6-9 When purchase prices are rising, which of the following statements is *true*?

a. LIFO produces a higher cost for ending inventory than FIFO.
b. FIFO produces a lower amount for net income than LIFO.
c. LIFO produces a higher cost of goods sold than FIFO.
d. Average cost produces a higher net income than FIFO or LIFO.

6-10 Which method results in a more realistic amount for income because it matches the most current costs against revenue?

a. FIFO
b. LIFO
c. Average cost
d. Specific identification

6-11 Which of the following statements regarding the lower of cost or market (LCM) rule is *true*?

a. The LCM rule is an application of the historical cost principle.
b. If a company uses the LCM rule, there is no need to use a cost flow assumption such as FIFO, LIFO, or average cost.
c. When the market value of inventory is above the historical cost of inventory, an adjustment is made to increase inventory to its market value and increase income.
d. When the replacement cost of inventory drops below the historical cost of inventory, an adjustment is made to decrease inventory to its market value and decrease income.

6-12 Which of the following statements is *true* with regard to the gross profit ratio?

1. An increase in the gross profit rate may indicate that a company is efficiently managing its inventory.
2. An increase in cost of goods sold would increase the gross profit rate (assuming sales remain constant).
3. An increase in selling expenses would lower the gross profit rate.

a. 1
b. 2
c. 1 and 2
d. 1 and 3

6-13 An increasing inventory turnover ratio indicates that:

a. a company is having trouble selling its inventory.
b. a company may be holding too much inventory.
c. a company has reduced the time it takes to sell inventory.
d. a company has sold inventory at a higher profit.

6-14 Ignoring taxes, if a company understates its ending inventory by $10,000 in the current year:

a. assets for the current year will be overstated by $10,000.
b. cost of goods sold for the current year will be understated by $10,000.
c. retained earnings for the current year will be unaffected.
d. net income for the subsequent year will be overstated by $10,000.

6-15 (Appendix 6A) Which of the following statements is true for a company that uses a periodic inventory system?

a. The purchase of inventory requires a debit to Merchandise Inventory.
b. The payment of a purchase within the discount period requires a credit to Purchase Discount.
c. The return of defective inventory requires a debit to Purchase Returns and Allowances.
d. Any amounts paid for freight are debited to Merchandise Inventory.

The following information is used for Multiple-Choice Exercises 6-16 through 6-18:

Morgan Inc. has the following units and costs for the month of April:

	Units Purchased at Cost	Units Sold at Retail
Beginning Inventory, April 1	1,000 units at $20	
Purchase 1, April 9	1,200 units at $23	
Sale 1, April 12		1,800 units at $40
Purchase 2, April 22	800 units at $25	

6-16 (Appendix 6B) If Morgan uses a periodic inventory system, what is the cost of goods sold under FIFO at April 30?

a. $24,600
b. $29,200
c. $38,400
d. $43,000

6-17 (Appendix 6B) If Morgan uses a periodic inventory system, what is the cost of ending inventory under LIFO at April 30?

a. $24,600
b. $29,200
c. $38,400
d. $43,000

6-18 (Appendix 6B) If Morgan uses a periodic inventory system, what is the cost of ending inventory under average cost at April 30? (Use four decimal places for per unit calculations and round all other numbers to the nearest dollar.)

a. $27,040
b. $28,655
c. $38,945
d. $40,560

Cornerstone Exercises

OBJECTIVE ▶ 1
CORNERSTONE 6-1

Cornerstone Exercise 6-19 APPLYING THE COST OF GOODS SOLD MODEL

Hempstead Company has the following data for 2009:

Item	Units	Cost
Inventory, 12/31/2008	990	$10,890
Purchases	4,510	49,610
Inventory, 12/31/2009	720	7,920

Required:

1. How many units were sold?
2. Using the cost of goods sold model, determine the cost of goods sold.

Cornerstone Exercise 6-20 RECORDING PURCHASE TRANSACTIONS

Mathis Company and Reece Company use the perpetual inventory system. The following transactions occurred during the month of April:

a. On April 1, Mathis Company purchased merchandise on account from Reece Company with credit terms of 2/10, n/30. The selling price of the merchandise was $3,500 and the cost of the merchandise sold was $2,450.
b. On April 1, Mathis paid freight charges of $100 cash to have the goods delivered to its warehouse.
c. On April 8, Mathis returned $1,000 of the merchandise. The cost of the merchandise returned was $700.
d. On April 10, Mathis paid Reece the balance due.

Required:

1. Prepare the journal entry to record the April 1 purchase (ignore any freight charges) of merchandise by Mathis Company.
2. Prepare the journal entry to record the payment of freight on April 1.
3. Prepare the journal entry to record the April 8 return of merchandise.
4. Prepare the journal entry to record the April 10 payment to Reece Company.

Cornerstone Exercise 6-21 RECORDING SALES TRANSACTIONS

OBJECTIVE > 2
CORNERSTONE 6-3

Refer to the information in **Cornerstone Exercise 6-20**.

Required:

Prepare the journal entries to record these transactions on the books of Reece Company.

The following information is used for Cornerstone Exercises 6-22 through 6-25.

Filimonov Inc. has the following information related to purchases and sales of one of its inventory items:

Date	Description	Units Purchased at Cost	Units Sold at Retail
June 1	Beginning Inventory	150 units @ $10 = $1,500	
9	Purchase 1	200 units @ $12 = $2,400	
14	Sale 1		300 units @ $25
22	Purchase 2	250 units @ $14 = $3,500	
29	Sale 2		225 units @ $25

Cornerstone Exercise 6-22 INVENTORY COSTING: FIFO

OBJECTIVE > 3
CORNERSTONE 6-5

Refer to the information for Filimonov Inc. in the box above. Assume that Filimonov uses a perpetual inventory system.

Required:

Calculate the cost of goods sold and the cost of ending inventory using the FIFO inventory costing method.

Cornerstone Exercise 6-23 INVENTORY COSTING: LIFO

OBJECTIVE > 3
CORNERSTONE 6-6

Refer to the information for Filimonov Inc. in the box above. Assume that Filimonov uses a perpetual inventory system.

Required:

Calculate the cost of goods sold and the cost of ending inventory using the LIFO inventory costing method.

Cornerstone Exercise 6-24 INVENTORY COSTING: AVERAGE COST

OBJECTIVE > 3
CORNERSTONE 6-7

Refer to the information for Filimonov Inc. in the box above. Assume that Filimonov uses a perpetual inventory system.

Required:

Calculate the cost of goods sold and the cost of ending inventory using the average cost method. (Use four decimal places for per unit calculations and round all other numbers to the nearest dollar.)

OBJECTIVE ▶ 4

CORNERSTONE 6-5
CORNERSTONE 6-6
CORNERSTONE 6-7

Cornerstone Exercise 6-25 EFFECTS OF INVENTORY COSTING METHODS

Refer to your answers for Filimonov Inc. in **Cornerstone Exercises 6-22** through **6-24**.

Required:

1. In a period of rising prices, which inventory costing method produces the highest amount for ending inventory?
2. In a period of rising prices, which inventory costing method produces the highest net income?
3. In a period of rising prices, which inventory costing method produces the lowest payment for income taxes?
4. In a period of rising prices, which inventory method generally produces the most realistic amount for cost of goods sold? For inventory? Would your answer change if inventory prices were decreasing during the period?

OBJECTIVE ▶ 5

CORNERSTONE 6-8

Cornerstone Exercise 6-26 LOWER OF COST OR MARKET

The accountant for Murphy Company prepared the following analysis of its inventory at year-end:

Item	Units	Cost per Unit	Market Value
RSK-89013	500	$38	$44
LKW-91247	329	49	45
QEC-57429	462	25	33

Required:

Compute the carrying value of the ending inventory using the lower of cost or market method applied on an item-by-item basis.

OBJECTIVE ▶ 6

CORNERSTONE 6-9

Cornerstone Exercise 6-27 INVENTORY ANALYSIS

Singleton Inc. reported the following information for the current year:

Net sales	$650,000	Inventory, 1/1	$21,250
Cost of goods sold	474,500	Inventory, 12/31	$24,850
Gross profit	$175,500		

Required:

Compute Singleton's (a) gross profit ratio, (b) inventory turnover ratio, and (c) average days to sell inventory.

OBJECTIVE ▶ 7

CORNERSTONE 6-10

Cornerstone Exercise 6-28 INVENTORY ERRORS

McLelland Inc. reported net income of $150,000 for 2009 and $165,000 for 2010. Early in 2010, McLelland discovers that the December 31, 2009 ending inventory was overstated by $8,000. For simplicity, ignore taxes.

Required:

1. What is the correct net income for 2009? For 2010?
2. Assuming the error was not corrected, what is the effect on the balance sheet at December 31, 2009? At December 31, 2010?

OBJECTIVE ▶ 8

CORNERSTONE 6-11

Cornerstone Exercise 6-29 (APPENDIX 6A) RECORDING PURCHASE TRANSACTIONS

Refer to the information for **Cornerstone Exercise 6-20**. Assume that Mathis uses a periodic inventory system.

Required:

1. Prepare the journal entry to record the April 1 purchase (ignore any freight charges) of merchandise by Mathis Company.

2. Prepare the journal entry to record the payment of freight on April 1.
3. Prepare the journal entry to record the April 8 return of merchandise.
4. Prepare the journal entry to record the April 10 payment to Reece Company.

Cornerstone Exercise 6-30 (APPENDIX 6B) INVENTORY COSTING METHODS: PERIODIC FIFO

Refer to the information for Filimonov Inc. given earlier (see **Cornerstone Exercise 6-22**). Assume that Filimonov uses a periodic inventory system.

Required:

Calculate the cost of goods sold and the cost of ending inventory using the FIFO inventory costing method.

Cornerstone Exercise 6-31 (APPENDIX 6B) INVENTORY COSTING METHODS: PERIODIC LIFO

Refer to the information for Filimonov Inc. given earlier (see **Cornerstone Exercise 6-23**). Assume that Filimonov uses a periodic inventory system.

Required:

Calculate the cost of goods sold and the cost of ending inventory using the LIFO inventory costing method.

Cornerstone Exercise 6-32 (APPENDIX 6B) INVENTORY COSTING METHODS: PERIODIC AVERAGE COST

Refer to the information for Filimonov Inc. given earlier (see **Cornerstone Exercise 6-24**). Assume that Filimonov uses a periodic inventory system.

Required:

Calculate the cost of goods sold and the cost of ending inventory using the average cost method. (Use four decimal places for per unit calculations and round all other numbers to the nearest dollar.)

Exercises

Exercise 6-33 APPLYING THE COST OF GOODS SOLD MODEL

Wilson Company sells a single product. At the beginning of the year, Wilson had 120 units in stock at a cost of $8 each. During the year Wilson purchased 850 more units at a cost of $8 each and sold 210 units at $13 each, 250 units at $15 each, and 360 units at $14 each.

Required:

1. Using the cost of goods sold model, what is the amount of ending inventory and cost of goods sold?
2. What is Wilson's gross margin for the year?

Exercise 6-34 PERPETUAL AND PERIODIC INVENTORY SYSTEMS

Below is a list of inventory systems options:

a. Perpetual inventory system
b. Periodic inventory system
c. Both perpetual and periodic inventory systems

Required:

Match each option with one of the following:

1. Inventory purchases are recorded in a purchases account.
2. Inventory purchases are recorded in an inventory account.
3. Only revenue is recorded as sales are made during the period; the cost of goods sold is recorded at the end of the period.

4. Both revenue and cost of goods sold are recorded during the period as sales are made.
5. Cost of goods sold is determined as each sale is made.
6. Cost of goods sold is determined only at the end of the period by subtracting the cost of ending inventory from the cost of goods available for sale.
7. The inventory is verified by a physical count.

OBJECTIVE ▶ 2

Exercise 6-35 RECORDING PURCHASES

Compass Inc., purchased 1,000 bags of insulation from Glassco, Inc. The bags of insulation cost $4.25 each. Compass paid Turner Trucking $260 to have all 1,000 bags of insulation shipped to its warehouse. Compass returned 50 bags that were defective and paid for the remainder. Assume that Compass uses the perpetual inventory system and that Glassco, Inc. did not offer a purchase discount.

Required:

1. Prepare a journal entry to record the purchase of the 1,000 bags of insulation.
2. Prepare the entry to record the payment for shipping.
3. Prepare the entry for the return of the 50 defective bags.
4. Prepare the entry to record the payment for the 950 bags kept by Compass.
5. What is the total cost of this purchase?

OBJECTIVE ▶ 2

Exercise 6-36 RECORDING PURCHASES

Dawson Enterprises uses the perpetual system to record inventory transactions. In a recent month, Dawson engaged in the following transactions:

a. On April 1, Dawson purchased merchandise on credit for $21,900 with terms 2/10, n/30.
b. On April 2, Dawson purchased merchandise on credit for $24,600 on terms 3/15, n/25.
c. On April 9, Dawson paid for the purchase made on April 1.
d. On April 25, Dawson paid for the merchandise purchased on April 2.

Required:

Prepare journal entries for these four transactions.

OBJECTIVE ▶ 2

Exercise 6-37 RECORDING PURCHASES AND SHIPPING TERMS

On May 12, Digital Distributors received three shipments of merchandise. The first was shipped F.O.B. shipping point, had a total invoice price of $150,000, and was delivered by a trucking company that collected an additional $12,000 for transportation charges from Digital Distributors. The second was shipped F.O.B. shipping point and had a total invoice price of $89,000, including transportation charges of $6,200 that were prepaid by the seller. The third shipment was shipped F.O.B. destination and had an invoice price of $22,000, excluding transportation charges of $1,200 paid by the seller. Digital uses a perpetual inventory system.

Required:

Prepare journal entries to record these purchases.

OBJECTIVE ▶ 2

Exercise 6-38 RECORDING PURCHASES AND SALES

Printer Supply Company sells computer printers and printer supplies. One of its products is a toner cartridge for laser printers. At the beginning of 2009, there were 200 cartridges on hand at a cost of $60 each. During 2009, Printer Supply Company purchased 1,400 cartridges at $60 each. After inspection, Printer determined that 10 cartridges were defective and returned them to the supplier. Printer also sold 800 cartridges at $95 each and sold an additional 750 cartridges at $102 each after a midyear selling price increase. Customers returned 15 of the cartridges that were purchased at $102 to Printer for miscellaneous reasons. Assume that Printer Supply Company uses a perpetual inventory system.

Required:

1. Prepare summary journal entries to record the purchases and sales of inventory. Assume that all purchases and sales are on credit but no discounts were offered.
2. What is the cost of inventory, cost of goods sold, and gross profit for 2009?

Exercise 6-39 INVENTORY COSTING METHODS

OBJECTIVE ➤ 3 4

Crandall Distributors uses a perpetual inventory system and has the following data available for inventory, purchases, and sales for a recent year.

Activity	Units	Purchase Price (per unit)	Sale Price (per unit)
Beginning inventory	120	$5.90	
Purchase 1, Jan 18	550	6.00	
Sale	330		$8.80
Sale	280		9.00
Purchase 2, March 10	650	6.20	
Sale	270		9.00
Sale	290		9.50
Purchase 3, Sept. 30	250	6.30	
Sale	240		9.90

Required:

1. Compute the cost of ending inventory and the cost of goods sold using the specific identification method. Assume the ending inventory is made up of 50 units from beginning inventory, 40 units from purchase 1, 40 units from purchase 2, and 30 units from purchase 3.
2. Compute the cost of ending inventory and cost of goods sold using the FIFO inventory costing method.
3. Compute the cost of ending inventory and cost of goods sold using the LIFO inventory costing method.
4. Compute the cost of ending inventory and cost of goods sold using the average cost inventory costing method. (Use four decimal places for per unit calculations and round all other numbers to the nearest dollar.)
5. Compare the ending inventory and cost of goods sold computed under all four methods. What can you conclude about the effects of the inventory costing methods on the balance sheet and the income statement?

Exercise 6-40 INVENTORY COSTING METHODS

OBJECTIVE ➤ 3 4 6

Welding Products Company purchased 1,000 cases of welding rods at a cost of $95 per case on April 17. On August 19, the company purchased another 1,000 cases at a cost of $112 per case. (Assume that there was no beginning inventory.) Sales data for the welding rods are as follows:

Date	Cases Sold
May 2	200
June 29	600
July 2	50
Sept. 4	500
Oct. 31	420

Welding Products uses a perpetual inventory system and the sales price of the welding rods was $130 per case.

Required:

1. Compute the cost of ending inventory and cost of goods sold using the FIFO method.
2. Compute the cost of ending inventory and cost of goods sold using the LIFO method.
3. Compute the cost of ending inventory and cost of goods sold using the average cost method. (Use four decimal places for per unit calculations and round all other numbers to the nearest dollar.)

4. Assume that operating expenses are $22,500 and Welding Products has a 30% tax rate. How much will the cash paid for income taxes differ among the three inventory methods?

5. Compute Welding Product's gross profit ratio and inventory turnover ratio under each of the three inventory costing methods. How would the choice of inventory costing method affect these ratios?

OBJECTIVE ▸4

Exercise 6-41 FINANCIAL STATEMENT EFFECTS OF FIFO AND LIFO

The chart below lists financial statement items that may be affected by the use of either the FIFO or LIFO inventory costing methods:

	FIFO	LIFO
Ending inventory		
Cost of goods sold		
Gross margin		
Income before taxes		
Payments for income taxes		
Net income		

Required:

Assuming that prices are rising, complete the chart by indicating whether the specified item is (a) higher or (b) lower under FIFO and LIFO.

OBJECTIVE ▸4

Exercise 6-42 EFFECTS OF INVENTORY COSTING METHODS

Jefferson Enterprises has the following income statement data available for 2009:

Sales revenue	$737,200
Operating expenses	243,700
Interest expense	39,500
Income tax rate	34%

Jefferson uses a perpetual inventory accounting system and the average cost method. Jefferson is considering adopting the FIFO or LIFO method for costing inventory. Jefferson's accountant prepared the following data:

	If Average Cost Used	If FIFO Used	If LIFO Used
Ending inventory	$ 56,400	$ 73,200	$ 41,700
Cost of goods sold	401,600	384,800	416,300

Required:

1. Compute income before taxes, income tax expense, and net income for each of the three inventory costing methods (rounded to the nearest dollar).

2. Why are the cost of goods sold and ending inventory amounts different for each of the three methods? What do these amounts tell us about the purchase price of inventory during the year?

3. Which method produces the most realistic amount for net income? For inventory? Explain your answer.

OBJECTIVE ▸3 4

Exercise 6-43 INVENTORY COSTING METHODS

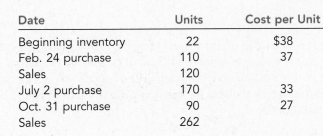

Neyman, Inc. has the following data for purchases and sales of inventory:

Date	Units	Cost per Unit
Beginning inventory	22	$38
Feb. 24 purchase	110	37
Sales	120	
July 2 purchase	170	33
Oct. 31 purchase	90	27
Sales	262	

All sales were made at a sales price of $45 per unit. Assume that Neyman uses a perpetual inventory system.

Required:

1. Compute the cost of goods sold and the cost of ending inventory using the FIFO, LIFO, and average cost methods. (Use four decimal places for per unit calculations and round all other numbers to the nearest dollar.)
2. Why is the cost of goods sold lower with LIFO than with FIFO?

Exercise 6-44 EFFECTS OF FIFO AND LIFO

OBJECTIVE ➤ 3 4

Sheepskin Company sells to colleges and universities a special paper that is used for diplomas. Sheepskin typically makes one purchase of the special paper each year on January 1. Assume that Sheepskin uses a perpetual inventory system. You have the following data for the three years ending in 2009.

2007

Beginning Inventory	0 pages
Purchases	10,000 pages at $1.60 per page
Sales	8,500 pages

2008

Beginning Inventory	1,500 pages
Purchases	16,200 pages at $2.00 per page
Sales	15,000 pages

2009

Beginning Inventory	2,700 pages
Purchases	18,000 pages at $2.50 per page
Sales	20,100 pages

Required:

1. What would the ending inventory and cost of goods sold be for each year if FIFO is used?
2. What would the ending inventory and cost of goods sold be for each year if LIFO is used?
3. For each year, explain the cause of the differences in cost of goods sold under FIFO and LIFO.

Exercise 6-45 LOWER OF COST OR MARKET

OBJECTIVE ➤ 5

Meredith's Appliance Store has the following data for the items in its inventory at the end of the accounting period.

Item	Number of Units	Historical Cost per Unit	Market Value per Unit
Window air conditioner	15	$194	$110
Dishwasher	34	240	380
Refrigerator	27	382	605
Microwave	19	215	180
Washer (clothing)	36	195	290
Dryer (clothing)	21	168	245

Required:

Compute the carrying value of Meredith's ending inventory using the lower of cost or market rule applied on an item-by-item basis.

Exercise 6-46 LOWER OF COST OR MARKET

OBJECTIVE ➤ 5

Shaw Systems sells a limited line of specially made products, using television advertising campaigns in large cities. At year-end, Shaw has the following data for its inventory:

Item	Number of Units	Historical Cost per Unit	Market Value per Unit
Phone	600	$ 24	$ 20
Stereo	180	177	190
Electric shaver	220	30	35
MP3 alarm clock	430	26	25
Handheld game system	570	40	19

Required:

Compute the carrying value of the ending inventory using the lower of cost or market rule applied on an item-by-item basis.

OBJECTIVE ➤ 6

Exercise 6-47 ANALYZING INVENTORY

Examining the recent financial statements of McLelland Clothing, Inc., you note the following:

Sales	$754,693
Cost of goods sold	528,600
Average inventory	76,900

Required:

Calculate McLelland's gross profit ratio, inventory turnover ratio, and assuming a 365-day year, the average days to sell inventory. Be sure to explain what each ratio means.

OBJECTIVE ➤ 7

Exercise 6-48 EFFECTS OF AN ERROR IN ENDING INVENTORY

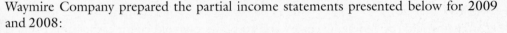

Waymire Company prepared the partial income statements presented below for 2009 and 2008:

	2009		2008	
Sales revenue		$538,200		$483,700
Cost of goods sold:				
Beginning inventory	$ 39,300		$ 32,100	
Purchases	343,200		292,700	
Cost of goods available for sale	$382,500		$324,800	
Ending inventory	46,800	335,700	39,300	285,500
Gross margin		$202,500		$198,200
Operating expenses		167,200		151,600
Income before taxes		$ 35,300		$ 46,600

During 2010, Waymire's accountant discovered that ending inventory for 2008 had been overstated by $7,900.

Required:

1. Prepare corrected income statements for 2009 and 2008.
2. Prepare a schedule showing each financial statement item affected by the error and the amount of the error for that item. Indicate whether each error is an overstatement (+) or an understatement (−).

OBJECTIVE ➤ 8

Exercise 6-49 (APPENDIX 6A) RECORDING PURCHASES

Compass, Inc., purchased 1,000 bags of insulation from Glassco, Inc. The bags of insulation cost $4.25 each. Compass paid Turner Trucking $260 to have all 1,000 bags of insulation shipped to its warehouse. Compass returned 50 bags that were defective and paid for the remainder. Assume that Compass uses the periodic inventory system.

Required:

1. Prepare a journal entry to record the purchase of the 1,000 bags of insulation.
2. Prepare the entry to record the payment for shipping.
3. Prepare the entry for the return of the 50 defective bags.
4. Prepare the entry to record the payment for the 950 bags kept by Compass.
5. What is the total cost of this purchase?
6. If you have previously worked Exercise 6-35, compare your answers. What are the differences? Be sure to explain why the differences occurred.

Exercise 6-50 (APPENDICES 6A AND B) RECORDING PURCHASES AND SALES   OBJECTIVE ▶ 8 9

Printer Supply Company sells computer printers and printer supplies. One of its products is a toner cartridge for laser printers. At the beginning of 2009, there were 200 cartridges on hand at a cost of $60 each. During 2009, Printer Supply Company purchased 1,400 cartridges at $60 each, sold 800 cartridges at $95 each, and sold an additional 750 cartridges at $102 each after a midyear selling price increase. Printer returned 10 defective cartridges to the supplier. In addition, customers returned 15 cartridges that were purchased at $102 to printer for various reasons. Assume that Printer Supply Company uses a periodic inventory system.

Required:

1. Prepare journal entries to record the purchases and sales of inventory. Assume that all purchases and sales are on credit but no discounts were offered.
2. What is the cost of inventory, cost of goods sold, and gross profit for 2009?
3. If you have previously worked Exercise 6-38, compare your answers. What are the differences? Be sure to explain why the differences occurred.

Exercise 6-51 (APPENDIX 6B) INVENTORY COSTING METHODS: PERIODIC   OBJECTIVE ▶ 9
INVENTORY SYSTEM

Jackson Company had 200 units in beginning inventory at a cost of $24 each. Jackson's 2009 purchases were:

Date	Purchases
Feb. 21	6,200 units at $28 each
July 15	5,500 units at $32 each
Sept. 30	8,100 units at $34 each

Jackson uses a periodic inventory system and sold 19,600 units at $45 each during 2009.

Required:

1. Calculate the cost of ending inventory and the cost of goods sold using the FIFO, LIFO and average cost methods. (Use four decimal places for per unit calculations and round all other numbers to the nearest dollar.)
2. Prepare income statements through gross margin using each of the costing methods in (1). What is the effect of each method on income?

Exercise 6-52 (APPENDIX 6B) INVENTORY COSTING METHODS: PERIODIC   OBJECTIVE ▶ 9
INVENTORY SYSTEM

The inventory accounting records for Lee Enterprises contained the following data:

Beginning inventory	400 units at $12 each
Purchase 1, Feb. 26	2,300 units at $14 each
Sale, March 9	2,500 units at $27 each
Purchase 2, June 14	2,200 units at $15 each
Sale, Sept. 22	2,100 units at $29 each

Required:

1. Calculate the cost of ending inventory and the cost of goods sold using the FIFO, LIFO, and average cost methods. (Use four decimal places for per unit calculations and round all other numbers to the nearest dollar.)
2. Compare the ending inventory and cost of goods sold computed under all three methods. What can you conclude about the effects of the inventory costing methods on the balance sheet and the income statement?

OBJECTIVE ▶ 9 ### Exercise 6-53 (APPENDIX 6B) INVENTORY COSTING METHODS: PERIODIC SYSTEM

Harrington Company had the following data for inventory during a recent year:

	Units	Cost per Unit		Total Cost
Beginning inventory		500	$ 9.00		$ 4,500
Purchase 1, 1/28	1,600	9.60	$15,360	
Purchase 2, 5/2	1,200	10.30	12,360	
Purchase 3, 8/13	1,400	10.80	15,120	
Purchase 4, 11/9	1,100	11.10	12,210	
Total purchases	5,300			55,050
Goods available for sale	5,800			$59,550
Less: Sales	5,240			
Ending inventory	560			

Assume that Harrington uses a periodic inventory accounting system.

Required:

1. Using the FIFO, LIFO, and average cost methods, compute the ending inventory and cost of goods sold. (Use four decimal places for per unit calculations and round all other numbers to the nearest dollar.)
2. Which method will produce the most realistic amount for income? For inventory?
3. Which method will produce the lowest amount paid for taxes?

Problem Set A

OBJECTIVE ▶ 2 ### Problem 6-54A RECORDING SALE AND PURCHASE TRANSACTIONS

Alpharack Company sells a line of tennis equipment to retailers. Alpharack uses the perpetual inventory system and engaged in the following transactions during April 2009, its first month of operations:

a. On April 2, Alpharack purchased, on credit, 320 Wilbur T-100 tennis rackets with credit terms of 2/10, n/30. The rackets were purchased at a cost of $30 each. Alpharack paid Barker Trucking $150 to transport the tennis rackets from the manufacturer to Alpharack's warehouse, shipping terms were F.O.B. shipping point, and the items were shipped on April 2.

b. On April 3, Alpharack purchased, for cash, 150 packs of tennis balls for $10 per pack.

c. On April 4, Alpharack purchased tennis clothing, on credit, from Designer Tennis Wear. The cost of the clothing was $8,000. Credit terms were 2/10, n/25.

d. On April 10, Alpharack paid for the purchase of the tennis rackets in (a).

e. On April 15, Alpharack determined that $500 of the tennis clothing was defective. Alpharack returned the defective merchandise to Designer Tennis Wear.

f. On April 20, Alpharack sold 100 tennis rackets at $90 each, 100 packs of tennis balls at $12 per pack, and $4,000 of tennis clothing. All sales were for cash. The cost of the merchandise sold was $5,450.

g. On April 23, customers returned $575 of the merchandise purchased on April 20. The cost of the merchandise returned was $300.

h. On April 25, Alpharack sold another 50 tennis rackets, on credit, for $90 each and 25 packs of tennis balls at $12 per pack, for cash. The cost of the merchandise sold was $2,000.

i. On April 29, Alpharack paid Designer Tennis Wear for the clothing purchased on April 4 less the return on April 15.

j. On April 30, Alpharack purchased 20 tennis bags, on credit, from Bag Designs for $320. The bags were shipped F.O.B. destination and arrived at Alpharack on May 3.

Required:

1. Prepare the journal entries to record the sale and purchase transactions for Alpharack during April 2009.
2. Assuming operating expenses of $8,500, prepare Alpharack's income statement for April 2009. (Ignore income tax expense.)

Problem 6-55A INVENTORY COSTING METHODS

OBJECTIVE ➤ 2 3 4

Anderson's Department Store has the following data for inventory, purchases and sales of merchandise for December:

Activity	Units	Purchase Price (per unit)	Sale Price (per unit)
Beginning Inventory	5	$6.00	
Purchase, Dec. 2	16	6.40	
Purchase, Dec. 5	20	7.00	
Sale, Dec. 7	13		$12.00
Sale, Dec. 10	15		12.00
Purchase Dec. 12	8	7.50	
Sale, Dec. 14	18		12.00

Anderson uses a perpetual inventory system. All purchases and sales were for cash.

Required:

1. Compute cost of goods sold and the cost of ending inventory using FIFO. (Use two decimal places for all calculations and answers.)
2. Compute cost of goods sold and the cost of ending inventory using LIFO. (Use two decimal places for all calculations and answers.)
3. Compute cost of goods sold and the cost of ending inventory using the average cost method. (Use four decimal places for per unit calculations and round all other numbers to two decimal places.)
4. Prepare the journal entries to record these transactions assuming Anderson chooses to use the FIFO method.
5. Which method would result in the lowest amount paid for taxes?

Problem 6-56A INVENTORY COSTING METHODS

OBJECTIVE ➤ 3 4

Gavin Products uses a perpetual inventory system. For 2008 and 2009, Gavin has the following data:

Activity	Units	Purchase Price (per unit)	Sale Price (per unit)
2008			
Beginning Inventory	200	$ 9.00	
Purchase, 2/15/2008	300	11.00	
Sale, 3/10/2008	320		$25.00
Purchase, 9/15/2008	500	12.00	
Sale, 11/3/2008	550		25.00
Purchase 12/20/2008	150	13.00	
2009			
Sale, 4/4/2009	200		25.00
Purchase, 6/25/2009	200	14.00	
Sale, 12/18/2009	150		25.00

Required:

1. For each year, compute cost of goods sold, the cost of ending inventory, and gross margin using FIFO.
2. For each year, compute cost of goods sold, the cost of ending inventory, and gross margin using LIFO.
3. For each year, compute cost of goods sold, the cost of ending inventory, and gross margin using the average cost method. (Use four decimal places for per unit calculations and round all other numbers to the nearest dollar.)
4. Which method would result in the lowest amount paid for taxes?
5. Which method produces the most realistic amount for income? For inventory? Explain your answer.
6. Compute Gavin's gross profit ratio and inventory turnover ratio under each of the three inventory costing methods. How would the choice of inventory costing method affect these ratios?

OBJECTIVE ▶ 5

Problem 6-57A **LOWER OF COST OR MARKET**

Sue Stone, the president of Tippecanoe Home Products has prepared the following information for the company's television inventory at the end of 2009:

Model	Quantity	Cost per Unit	Market Value per Unit
T-260	11	$250	$445
S-256	24	325	300
R-193	18	210	230
Z-376	12	285	250

Required:

Determine the carrying amount of the inventory using lower of cost or market applied on an item-by-item basis.

OBJECTIVE ▶ 3 5

Problem 6-58A **INVENTORY COSTING AND LCM**

Ortman Enterprises sell a chemical used in various manufacturing processes. On January 1, 2009, Ortman had 5,000,000 gallons on hand, for which it had paid $0.50 per gallon. During 2009, Ortman made the following purchases:

Date	Gallons	Cost per Gallon	Total Cost
2/20	10,000,000	$0.52	$ 5,200,000
5/15	25,000,000	0.56	14,000,000
9/12	32,000,000	0.60	19,200,000

During 2009, Ortman sold 65,000,000 gallons at $0.75 per gallon (35,000,000 gallons were sold on 6/29 and 30,000,000 gallons were sold on 11/22), leaving an ending inventory of 7,000,000 gallons. Assume that Ortman uses a perpetual inventory system. Ortman uses the lower of cost or market for its inventories, as required by generally accepted accounting principles.

Required:

1. Assume that the market value of the chemical is $0.76 per gallon on December 31, 2009. Compute the cost of ending inventory using the FIFO, LIFO, and average cost methods. (Use four decimal places for per unit calculations and round all other numbers to the nearest dollar.)
2. Assume that the market value of the chemical is $0.58 per gallon on December 31, 2009. Compute the cost of ending inventory using the FIFO, LIFO, and average cost methods. (Use four decimal places for per unit calculations and round all other numbers to the nearest dollar.)

OBJECTIVE ▶ 7

Problem 6-59A **EFFECTS OF AN INVENTORY ERROR**

The income statements for Graul Corporation for the three years ending in 2009 appear below:

	2009	2008	2007
Sales revenue	$4,643,200	$4,287,500	$3,647,900
Cost of goods sold	2,475,100	2,181,600	2,006,100
Gross margin	$2,168,100	$2,105,900	$1,641,800
Operating expense	1,548,600	1,428,400	1,152,800
Income from operations	$ 619,500	$ 677,500	$ 489,000
Other expenses	137,300	123,600	112,900
Income before taxes	$ 482,200	$ 553,900	$ 376,100
Income tax expense (34%)	163,948	188,326	127,874
Net income	$ 318,252	$ 365,574	$ 248,226

During 2009, Graul discovered that the 2007 ending inventory had been misstated due to the following two transactions being recorded incorrectly:

a. A purchase return of inventory costing $63,000 was recorded twice.
b. A credit purchase of inventory made on 12/20 for $22,000 was not recorded. The goods were shipped F.O.B. shipping point and were shipped on 12/22/2007.

Required:

1. Was ending inventory for 2007 overstated or understated? By how much?
2. Prepare correct income statements for all three years.
3. Did the error in 2007 affect cumulative net income for the three-year period? Explain your response.
4. Why was the 2009 net income unaffected?

Problem 6-60A (APPENDICES 6A AND 6B) INVENTORY COSTING METHODS   OBJECTIVE ▶ 8 9

Anderson's Department Store has the following data for inventory, purchases, and sales of merchandise for December:

Activity	Units	Purchase Price (per unit)	Sale Price (per unit)
Beginning Inventory	5	$6.00	
Purchase, Dec. 2	16	6.40	
Purchase, Dec. 5	20	7.00	
Sale, Dec. 7	13		$12.00
Sale, Dec. 10	15		12.00
Purchase Dec. 12	8	7.50	
Sale, Dec. 14	18		12.00

Anderson uses a periodic inventory system. All purchases and sales are for cash.

Required:

1. Compute cost of goods sold and the cost of ending inventory using FIFO (round all answers to two decimal places).
2. Compute cost of goods sold and the cost of ending inventory using LIFO (round all answers to two decimal places).
3. Compute cost of goods sold and the cost of ending inventory using the average cost method. (Use four decimal places for per unit calculations and round all other numbers to two decimal places.)
4. Prepare the journal entries to record these transactions assuming Anderson chooses to use the FIFO method.
5. Which method would result in the lowest amount paid for taxes?
6. If you worked Problem 6-55A, compare your results. What are the differences? Be sure to explain why the differences occurred.

Problem 6-61A (APPENDIX 6B) INVENTORY COSTING METHODS   OBJECTIVE ▶ 9

Gavin Products uses a periodic inventory system. For 2008 and 2009, Gavin has the following data:

Activity	Units	Purchase Price (per unit)	Sale Price (per unit)
2008			
Beginning Inventory	200	$ 9.00	
Purchase, 2/15/2008	300	11.00	
Sale, 3/10/2008	320		$25.00
Purchase, 9/15/2008	500	12.00	
Sale, 11/3/2008	550		25.00
Purchase 12/20/2008	150	13.00	
2009			
Sale, 4/4/2009	200		25.00
Purchase, 6/25/2009	200	14.00	
Sale, 12/18/2009	150		25.00

All purchases and sales are for cash.

Required:

1. Compute cost of goods sold, the cost of ending inventory, and gross margin for each year using FIFO.
2. Compute cost of goods sold, the cost of ending inventory, and gross margin for each year using LIFO.
3. Compute cost of goods sold, the cost of ending inventory, and gross margin for each year using the average cost method. (Use four decimal places for per unit calculations and round all other numbers to the nearest dollar.)
4. Which method would result in the lowest amount paid for taxes?
5. Which method produces the most realistic amount for income? For inventory? Explain your answer.
6. What is the effect of purchases made later in the year on the gross margin when LIFO is employed? When FIFO is employed? Be sure to explain why any differences occur.
7. If you worked Problem 6-56A, compare your answers. What are the differences? Be sure to explain why any differences occurred.

Problem Set B

OBJECTIVE ➤ 2

Problem 6-54B RECORDING SALE AND PURCHASE TRANSACTIONS

Jordan Footwear sells athletic shoes and uses the perpetual inventory system. During June, Jordan engaged in the following transactions its first month of operations:

a. On June 1, Jordan purchased, on credit, 100 pairs of basketball shoes and 210 pairs of running shoes with credit terms of 2/10, n/30. The basketball shoes were purchased at a cost of $75 per pair, and the running shoes were purchased at a cost of $55 per pair. Jordan paid Mole Trucking $250 cash to transport the shoes from the manufacturer to Jordan's warehouse, shipping terms were F.O.B. shipping point, and the items were shipped on June 1 and arrived on June 4.
b. On June 2, Jordan purchased 80 pairs of cross-training shoes for cash. The shoes cost Jordan $60 per pair.
c. On June 6, Jordan purchased 120 pairs of tennis shoes on credit. Credit terms were 2/10, n/25. The shoes were purchased at a cost of $40 per pair.
d. On June 10, Jordan paid for the purchase of the basketball shoes and the running shoes in (a).
e. On June 12, Jordan determined that $480 of the tennis shoes were defective. Jordan returned the defective merchandise to the manufacturer.
f. On June 18, Jordan sold 50 pairs of basketball shoes at $110 per pair, 100 pairs of running shoes for $85 per pair, 18 pairs of cross-training shoes for $100 per pair, and 35 pairs of tennis shoes for $65 per pair. All sales were for cash. The cost of the merchandise sold was $11,850.
g. On June 21, customers returned 10 pairs of the basketball shoes purchased on June 18. The cost of the merchandise returned was $750.
h. On June 23, Jordan sold another 20 pairs of basketball shoes, on credit, for $110 per pair and 15 pairs of cross-training shoes for $100 cash per pair. The cost of the merchandise sold was $2,400.
i. On June 30, Jordan paid for the June 6 purchase of tennis shoes less the return on June 12.
j. On June 30, Jordan purchased 60 pairs of basketball shoes, on credit, for $75 each. The shoes were shipped F.O.B. destination and arrived at Jordan on July 3.

Required:

1. Prepare the journal entries to record the sale and purchase transactions for Jordan during June 2009.
2. Assuming operating expenses of $5,300, prepare Jordan's income statement for June 2009. (Ignore income tax expense.)

Problem 6-55B INVENTORY COSTING METHODS

OBJECTIVE ➤ 2 3 4

Edward's Company began operations in February 2009. Edward's accounting records provide the following data for the remainder of 2009 for one of the items the company sells:

Activity	Units	Purchase Price (per unit)	Sale Price (per unit)
Beginning Inventory	9	$ 90	
Purchase, Feb. 15	6	100	
Purchase, March 22	8	110	
Sale, April 9	10		$180
Purchase, May 29	9	120	
Sale, July 10	15		180
Purchase, Sept. 10	8	130	
Sale, Oct. 15	12		180

Edward's uses a perpetual inventory system. All purchases and sales were for cash.

Required:

1. Compute cost of goods sold and the cost of ending inventory using FIFO.
2. Compute cost of goods sold and the cost of ending inventory using LIFO.
3. Compute cost of goods sold and the cost of ending inventory using the average cost method. (Use four decimal places for per unit calculations and round all other numbers to two decimal places.)
4. Prepare the journal entries to record these transactions assuming Edward's chooses to use the FIFO method.
5. Which method would result in the lowest amount paid for taxes?

Problem 6-56B INVENTORY COSTING METHODS

OBJECTIVE ➤ 3 4

Hartwell Products Company uses a perpetual inventory system. For 2008 and 2009, Hartwell has the following data:

Activity	Units	Purchase Price (per unit)	Sale Price (per unit)
2008			
Beginning Inventory	100	$45	
Purchase, 2/25/2008	700	52	
Sale, 4/15/2008	600		$90
Purchase, 8/30/2008	500	56	
Sale, 11/13/2008	600		90
Purchase, 12/20/2008	400	58	
2009			
Sale, 3/8/2009	400		90
Purchase, 6/28/2009	900	62	
Sale, 12/18/2009	800		90

Required:

1. For each year, compute cost of goods sold, the cost of ending inventory, and gross margin using FIFO.
2. For each year, compute cost of goods sold, the cost of ending inventory, and gross margin using LIFO.
3. For each year, compute cost of goods sold, the cost of ending inventory, and gross margin using the average cost method. (Use four decimal places for per unit calculations and round all other numbers to the nearest dollar.)
4. Which method would result in the lowest amount paid for taxes?
5. Which method produces the most realistic amount for income? For inventory? Explain your answer.
6. Compute Hartwell's gross profit ratio and inventory turnover ratio under each of the three inventory costing methods. How would the choice of inventory costing method affect these ratios?

OBJECTIVE ➤ 5

Problem 6-57B LOWER OF COST OR MARKET

Kevin Spears, the accountant of Tyler Electronics Inc., has prepared the following information for the company's inventory at the end of 2009:

Model	Quantity	Cost per Unit	Market Value per Unit
RSQ535	30	$100	$180
JKY942	12	75	125
LLM112	54	85	80
KZG428	23	115	140

Required:

Determine the carrying amount of the inventory using lower of cost or market applied on an item-by-item basis.

OBJECTIVE ➤ 3 5

Problem 6-58B INVENTORY COSTING AND LCM

J&J Enterprises sells paper cups to fast-food franchises. On January 1, 2009, J&J had 5,000 cups on hand, for which it had paid $0.10 per cup. During 2009, J&J made the following purchases and sales:

Date	Units	Cost per Unit	Total Cost
2/20	100,000	$0.12	$12,000
5/15	57,000	0.14	7,980
9/12	85,000	0.15	12,750

During 2009, J&J sold 240,000 cups at $0.35 per cup (80,000 cups were sold on 4/2 and 160,000 cups were sold on 10/20), leaving an ending inventory of 7,000 cups. J&J uses the lower of cost or market for its inventories, as required by generally accepted accounting principles.

Required:

1. Assume that the market value of the cups is $0.38 per gallon on December 31, 2009. Compute the cost of ending inventory using the FIFO, LIFO, and average cost methods. (Use four decimal places for per unit calculations and round all other numbers to the nearest dollar.)
2. Assume that the market value of the chemical is $0.12 per cup on December 31, 2009. Compute the cost of ending inventory using the FIFO, LIFO, and average cost methods. (Use four decimal places for per unit calculations and round all other numbers to the nearest dollar.)

OBJECTIVE ➤ 7

Problem 6-59B EFFECTS OF AN INVENTORY ERROR

The income statements for Picard Company for the three years ending in 2009 appear below:

	2009	2008	2007
Sales revenue	$1,168,500	$998,400	$975,300
Cost of goods sold	785,800	675,450	659,800
Gross margin	$ 382,700	$322,950	$315,500
Operating expense	162,500	142,800	155,300
Income from operations	$ 220,200	$180,150	$160,200
Other expenses	73,500	58,150	54,500
Income before taxes	$ 146,700	$122,000	$105,700
Income tax expense (34%)	49,878	41,480	35,938
Net income	$ 96,822	$ 80,520	$ 69,762

During 2009, Picard discovered that the 2007 ending inventory had been misstated due to the following two transactions being recorded incorrectly:

a. Inventory costing $25,000 that was returned to the manufacturer (a purchase return) was not recorded and included in ending inventory.

b. A credit purchase of inventory made on 8/30/2007 for $15,000 was recorded twice. The goods were shipped F.O.B. shipping point and were shipped on 9/5/2007.

Required:

1. Was ending inventory for 2007 overstated or understated? By how much?
2. Prepare correct income statements for all three years.
3. Did the error in 2007 affect cumulative net income for the three-year period? Explain your response.
4. Why was the 2009 net income unaffected?

Problem 6-60B (APPENDICES 6A AND 6B) INVENTORY COSTING METHODS   OBJECTIVE ➤ 8 9

Edward's Company began operations in February 2009. Edward's accounting records provide the following data for the remainder of 2009 for one of the items the company sells:

Activity	Units	Purchase Price (per unit)	Sale Price (per unit)
Beginning Inventory	9	$ 90	
Purchase, Feb. 15	6	100	
Purchase, March 22	8	110	
Sale, April 9	10		$180
Purchase, May 29	9	120	
Sale, July 10	15		180
Purchase, Sept. 10	8	130	
Sale, Oct. 15	12		180

Edward's uses a periodic inventory system. All purchases and sales were for cash.

Required:

1. Compute cost of goods sold and the cost of ending inventory using FIFO.
2. Compute cost of goods sold and the cost of ending inventory using LIFO.
3. Compute cost of goods sold and the cost of ending inventory using the average cost method. (Use four decimal places for per unit calculations and round all other numbers to the nearest dollar.)
4. Prepare the journal entries to record these transactions assuming Edward's chooses to use the FIFO method.
5. Which method would result in the lowest amount paid for taxes?
6. If you worked Problem 6-55B, compare your results. What are the differences? Be sure to explain why the differences occurred.

Problem 6-61B (APPENDIX 6B) INVENTORY COSTING METHODS   OBJECTIVE ➤ 9

Hartwell Products Company uses a periodic inventory system. For 2008 and 2009, Hartwell has the following data (assume all purchases and sales are for cash):

Activity	Units	Purchase Price (per unit)	Sale Price (per unit)
2008			
Beginning Inventory	100	$45	
Purchase, 2/25/2008	700	52	
Sale, 4/15/2008	600		$90
Purchase, 8/30/2008	500	56	
Sale, 11/13/2008	600		90
Purchase, 12/20/2008	400	58	
2009			
Sale, 3/8/2009	400		90
Purchase, 6/28/2009	900	62	
Sale, 12/18/2009	800		90

Required:

1. Compute cost of goods sold, the cost of ending inventory, and gross margin for each year using FIFO.

2. Compute cost of goods sold, the cost of ending inventory, and gross margin for each year using LIFO.
3. Compute cost of goods sold, the cost of ending inventory, and gross margin for each year using the average cost method. (Use four decimal places for per unit calculations and round all other numbers to the nearest dollar.)
4. Which method would result in the lowest amount paid for taxes?
5. Which method produces the most realistic amount for income? For inventory? Explain your answer.
6. What is the effect of purchases made later in the year on the gross margin when LIFO is employed? When FIFO is employed? Be sure to explain why any differences occur.
7. If you worked 6-56B, compare your answers. What are the differences? Be sure to explain why any differences occurred.

Cases

Case 6-62 INVENTORY VALUATION AND ETHICS

Mary Cravens is an accountant for City Appliance Corporation. One of Mary's responsibilities is developing the ending inventory amount for the calculation of cost of goods sold each month. At the end of September, Mary noticed that the ending inventory for a new brand of televisions was much larger than she had expected. In fact, there had been hardly any change since the end of the previous month when the shipments of televisions arrived. Mary knew that the firm's advertising had featured the new brand's products, so she had expected that a substantial portion of the televisions would have been sold.

Because of these concerns, Mary went to the warehouse to make sure the numbers were correct. While at the warehouse, Mary noticed that 30 of the televisions in question were on the loading dock for delivery to customers and another, larger group, perhaps 200 sets, were in an area set aside for sales returns. Mary asked Barry Tompkins, the returns supervisor, why so many of the televisions had been returned. Barry said that the manufacturer had used a cheap circuit board that failed on many of the sets after they had been in service for a week or two. Mary then asked how the defective televisions had been treated when the inventory was taken at the end of September. Barry said that the warehouse staff had been told to include in the ending inventory any item in the warehouse that was not marked for shipment to customers. Therefore, all returned merchandise was considered part of ending inventory.

Mary asked Barry what would be done with the defective sets. Barry said that they would probably have to be sold to a liquidator at a few cents on the dollar. Mary knew from her examination of the inventory data that all the returned sets had been included in the September inventory at their original cost.

Mary returned to the office and prepared a revised estimate of ending inventory using the information Barry Tompkins had given her to revalue the ending inventory of the television sets. She submitted the revision along with an explanatory note to her boss, Susan Grant. A few days later, Susan stopped by Mary's office to report on a conversation with the chief financial officer, Herb Cobb. Herb told her that the original ending inventory amount would not be revised. Herb said that the television sets in question had been purchased by the owner's brother and that no one was prepared to challenge the owner's brother.

Required:

1. What would happen to cost of goods sold, gross margin, income from operations, and net income if the cost of the returned inventory had been reduced to its liquidation price as Mary had proposed?
2. What should Mary do now?

Case 6-63 EFFECTS OF PRICE AND QUANTITY ON INVENTORY COSTING DATA

Quicksilver, Inc., is considering its choice of inventory costing for one of the items in its merchandise inventory. Quicksilver's accountant has prepared the following data for that item:

	FIFO	LIFO	Average Cost
Beginning inventory	$ 50,400	$ 50,400	$ 50,400
Purchases	460,300	460,300	460,300
Cost of goods available for sale	$510,700	$510,700	$510,700
Ending inventory	(72,600)	(54,200)	(60,900)
Cost of goods sold	$438,100	$456,500	$449,800

Required:

1. What does this data imply about the number of items in beginning and ending inventory?
2. Can you infer from this data whether the prices at which Quicksilver purchased the items increased or decreased? Explain your answer.

Case 6-64 INVENTORY COSTING WHEN INVENTORY QUANTITIES ARE SMALL

A number of companies have adopted a just-in-time procedure for acquiring inventory. These companies have arrangements with their suppliers that require the supplier to deliver inventory just as the company needs the goods. As a result, just-in-time companies keep very little inventory on hand.

Required:

1. Should the inventory costing method (FIFO or LIFO) have a material effect on cost of goods sold when a company adopts the just-in-time procedure and reduces inventory significantly?
2. Once a company has switched to the just-in-time procedure and has little inventory, should the inventory costing method (LIFO or FIFO) affect cost of goods sold?

Case 6-65 INVENTORY PURCHASE PRICE VOLATILITY

In 2009, Steel Technologies, Inc., changed from the LIFO to the FIFO method for its inventory costing. Steel Technologies' annual report indicated that this change had been instituted because the price at which the firm purchased steel was highly volatile.

Required:

Explain how FIFO cost of goods sold and ending inventory would be different from LIFO when prices are volatile.

Case 6-66 THE EFFECT OF REDUCTIONS IN INVENTORY QUANTITIES

Hill Motor Company, one of the country's largest automobile manufacturers, disclosed the following information about its inventory in the notes to its financial statements:

Inventories are stated generally at cost, which is not in excess of market value. The cost of inventory is determined by the last-in, first-out (LIFO) method. If the first-in, first-out (FIFO) method of inventory valuation had been used, inventory would have been about $2,519 million higher at December 31, 2009 and $2,668 million higher at December 31, 2008. As a result of decreases in inventory, certain inventory quantities carried at lower LIFO costs prevailing in prior years, as compared with costs of current purchases, were liquidated in 2009 and 2008. These inventory adjustments improved pre-tax operating results by approximately $134 million in 2009, $294 million in 2008.

Required:

1. Explain why the reduction in inventory quantities increased Hill Motor Company's net income.
2. If Hill Motor Company had used the FIFO inventory costing method, would the reduction in ending inventory quantities have increased net income?

Case 6-67 ERRORS IN ENDING INVENTORY

From time to time, business news will report that the management of a company has misstated its profits by knowingly establishing an incorrect amount for its ending inventory.

Required:

1. Explain how a misstatement of ending inventory can affect profit.
2. Why would a manager intent on misstating profits choose ending inventory to achieve the desired effect?

Case 6-68 ETHICS AND INVENTORY

An electronics store has a large number of computers in its inventory that use outdated technology. These computers are reported at their cost. Shortly after the December 31 year-end, the store manager insists that the computers can be sold for well over their cost. But the store's accountant has been told by the sales staff that it will be difficult to sell these computers for more than half of their inventory cost.

Required:

1. Why is the store manager reluctant to admit that these computers have little sales value?
2. What are the consequences for the business of failing to recognize the decline in value?
3. What are the consequences for the accountant of participating in a misrepresentation of the inventory's value?

Case 6-69 RESEARCH AND ANALYSIS USING THE ANNUAL REPORT

Obtain Wal-Mart's 2008 annual report either through the "Investor Relations" portion of its website (do a web search for Wal-Mart investor relations) or go to http://www.sec.gov and click "Search for company filings" under "Filings and Forms (EDGAR)."

Required:

1. What amount did Wal-Mart report for inventories in its consolidated balance sheets at January 31, 2008? At January 31, 2007?
2. What inventory valuation method does Wal-Mart use to determine the cost of its inventories? (Hint: You may need to refer to the notes to the consolidated financial statements.)
3. What amount did Wal-Mart report for cost of goods sold for 2008, 2007, and 2006?
4. Compute the gross profit and inventory turnover ratios for 2008. What do these ratios tell you?
5. Does Wal-Mart use the lower of cost or market method to account for its inventory? Does it appear that Wal-Mart will write down its inventory to market value?
6. What would be the effect on the financial statements if Wal-Mart were to overstate its inventory by 1 percent?

Case 6-70 COMPARATIVE ANALYSIS: ABERCROMBIE & FITCH vs. AEROPOSTALE

Refer to the financial statements of **Abercrombie & Fitch** and **Aeropostale** that are supplied with this text.

Required:

1. What amounts do Abercrombie & Fitch and Aeropostale report for inventories in its Consolidated Balance Sheets at February 3, 2007 and January 28, 2006?

2. Do Abercrombie & Fitch and Aeropostale use the same method to value its inventories?

3. What amount does Abercrombie & Fitch report for cost of goods sold for the years ending February 3, 2007, January 28, 2006, and January 29, 2005 (fiscal 2006, 2005, and 2004)? What amount does Aeropostale report for cost of goods sold for the years ending February 3, 2007, January 28, 2006, and January 29, 2005?

4. Compute the gross profit and inventory turnover ratios for fiscal year ending February 3, 2007, for each company? What do these ratios tell you about the success of each company in managing and controlling its inventory?

5. Do Abercrombie & Fitch and Aeropostale use the lower of cost market method to account for their inventories? By what amount have they written inventories down in the fiscal year ending February 3, 2007?

7

Operating Assets

Experience Financial Accounting
with Verizon

With revenues in excess of $93 billion, **Verizon Communications, Inc.** is one of the world's leading providers of telecommunications services. Verizon boasts over 8.2 million broadband customers as well as almost 66 million subscribers to its wireless voice and data communication services. With users demanding enhanced data-carrying capabilities, higher transmission speeds, increased multimedia capabilities, and other features, Verizon must constantly expand and upgrade its network. One concern for Verizon management is that their network will enable them to provide sufficient capacity so that their customers will enjoy superior coverage and reliability. Recognizing that its network is a key factor in differentiating itself from its competitors, Verizon has spent more than any other telecommunications company in America (over $100 billion since 2000) on its technology infrastructure. This amount includes more than $30 billion to maintain, upgrade, and expand its wireless network. The results of these investments have led Verizon to claim that it operates the most reliable wireless network in the country, which has led to impressive growth in the number of subscribers to its wireless services.

For a company like Verizon, effective management of its long-term operating assets (e.g., its wireless network) is essential for the generation of revenue and profit.

Verizon's strategy for success rests on two key premises which relate to its network. First, the network must

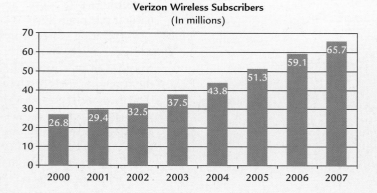

Verizon Wireless Subscribers
(In millions)

provide reliable access to every location that its customers need to access. For a simple call home or in crisis situations, customers must be able to count on Verizon's network to function effectively. Second, Verizon is committed to investing in new technology in order to maintain a high level of customer satisfaction and remain competitive in the telecommunications industry. Without continual investment, Verizon knows it will lose customers. Consistent with these goals, Verizon spent $17.5 billion in 2007 related to the build-up, expansion, and upgrade of its network. These expenditures represent an asset on Verizon's balance sheet that it hopes will provide a future benefit in terms of growth in market share and profitability.

By closely analyzing a company's expenditures on productive assets, you will be able to better assess the company's long-term productivity, profitability, and ability to generate cash flow.

OBJECTIVE **1**

Define, classify, and describe the accounting for operating assets.

Understanding Operating Assets

In this chapter, we will examine the measurement and reporting issues related to **operating assets**, which are the long-lived assets that are used by the company in the normal course of operations. Unlike the goods and services that a company sells, operating assets are not transferred to customers. Instead, operating assets are used by a company in the normal course of operations to generate revenue. They are usually held by a company until they are no longer of service to the company or, in other words, until their *service potential* has been exhausted. The typical operating asset is used for a period of 4 to 10 years, although some are held for only 2 or 3 years and others for as long as 30 or 40 years. Operating assets are divided into three categories:

1. Property, plant, and equipment (often called *fixed assets* or *plant assets*)
2. Intangibles
3. Natural resources

Property, plant, and equipment (PP&E) are *tangible operating assets* that can be seen and touched. They include, among other things, land, buildings, machines, and automobiles. *Intangible assets*, which generally result from legal and contractual rights, do not have physical substance. They include patents, copyrights, trademarks, licenses, and goodwill. *Natural resources* are tangible operating assets to which special accounting procedures apply. Natural resources include timberlands and deposits of natural resources such as coal, oil, and gravel.

Operating assets represent future economic benefits, or service potential, that will be used in the normal course of operations. At acquisition, an operating asset is recorded at its cost, including the cost of acquiring the asset and the cost of preparing the asset for use (cost concept). These costs are said to be *capitalized*, which means that they are reported as long-term assets with a service potential of greater than one year. As the service potential of an operating asset declines, the cost of the asset is allocated as an expense among the accounting periods in which the asset is used and benefits are received (the matching principle). This allocation is called *depreciation* for plant assets, *amortization* for intangible assets, and *depletion* for natural resources.

Operating assets are often the most costly of the various types of assets acquired by an entity. For manufacturing companies, property, plant, and equipment frequently represents a major percentage of a manufacturing company's total assets. However in other industries, such as computer software, operating assets may be a relatively insignificant portion of a company's assets. For many companies, depreciation, amortization, and depletion are also among the largest items of periodic expense. Exhibit 7-1 shows the percentages of operating assets in relation to total assets for various companies.

Exhibit 7-1

Percentages of Operating Assets in Relation to Total Assets

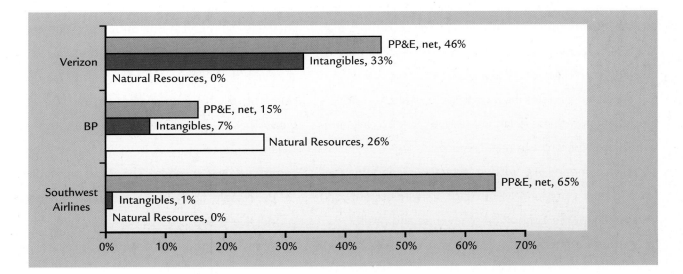

For Verizon, operating assets (property, plant, and equipment plus intangible assets) comprise approximately 79 percent of its total assets. Fixed assets include the expenditures required to build, upgrade, and expand its wireless network. However, Verizon has significant investments in intangible operating assets, primarily licenses that provide Verizon with the exclusive right to use certain radio frequencies to provide wireless services. In contrast, companies such as **BP** (one of the largest oil companies in the world) have relatively more natural resources (oil and natural gas properties), while **Southwest Airlines'** operating assets are made up primarily of its airplanes. This information about a company's operating assets gives financial statement users insights into a company's ability to satisfy customer demands (productive capacity) and the effectiveness of management in using the company's assets to generate revenue. While the relative mix of operating assets may vary among companies, it is clear that the management of operating assets is critical to a company's long-term success.

In this chapter, we will discuss the measurement and reporting issues related to the initial acquisition, use, and disposition of operating assets. We will address the following questions:

- What is included in the cost of an operating asset?
- How should an operating asset's cost be allocated to expense?
- How should expenditures subsequent to acquisition be treated?
- How is the retirement of an operating asset recorded?

Acquisition of Property, Plant, and Equipment

OBJECTIVE ➤ 2
Explain how the cost principle applies to recording the cost of a fixed asset.

Property, plant, and equipment are the tangible operating assets used in the normal operations of a company. These assets are tangible in the sense that they have a visible, physical presence in the company. Property, plant, and equipment includes:

- Land—the site of a manufacturing facility or office building[1]
- Buildings—structures used in operations (e.g., factory, office, warehouse)
- Equipment—assets used in operations (machinery, furniture, automobiles)

In this chapter, we will examine how to determine the cost for these assets, calculate their depreciation expense, and record their retirement from service.

Measuring the Cost of a Fixed Asset

The cost of a fixed asset is any expenditure necessary to acquire the asset and to prepare the asset for use. For example, the cost of a machine would be its purchase price (less any discount offered) plus sales taxes, freight, installation costs, and the cost of labor and materials for trial runs that check its performance. Expenditures that are included as part of the cost of the asset are said to be *capitalized*. Exhibit 7-2 shows expenditures that are typically included as part of the cost of property, plant, and equipment.

Expenditures that are *not* included as part of the cost of the asset are expensed immediately. Generally, recurring costs that benefit a period of time, not the asset's life, are expensed instead of capitalized.

ETHICS The distinction between whether an expenditure should be capitalized or expensed can have dramatic consequences for a company's financial statements. It was **WorldCom's** handling of this issue that triggered one of the largest financial restatements in U.S. history. By improperly capitalizing $3.8 billion that should have been expensed immediately, WorldCom was able to increase its income and its operating cash flow, thereby concealing large losses.◆

---

[1] Land purchased for future use or as an investment is not considered part of property, plant, and equipment.

Exhibit 7-2

Typical Costs of Acquiring Property, Plant, and Equipment

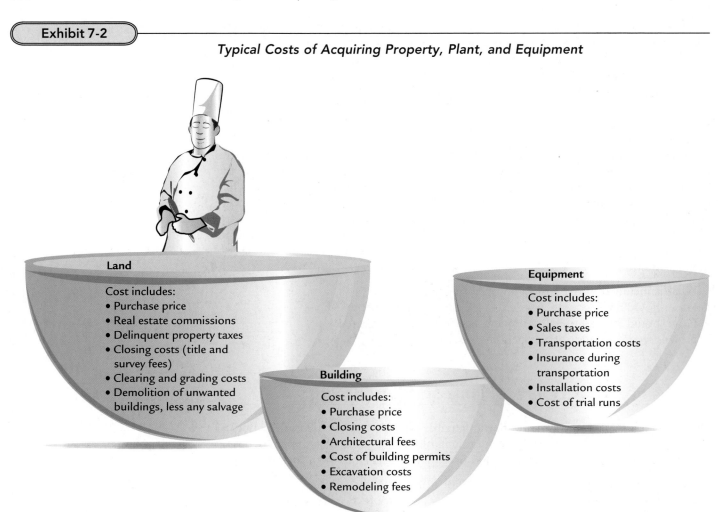

Recording the Cost of a Fixed Asset

The cost principle requires that a company record its fixed assets at historical cost. When cash is paid in exchange for an asset, the amount of cash given, plus any other expenditure necessary to prepare the asset for use, becomes part of the historical cost of the acquired asset. However, when its purchase price is large, a fixed asset may be purchased by issuing debt. One might think that the interest paid on the debt should be added to the purchase price. However, interest generally is viewed as resulting from a financing decision rather than from the decision to acquire the asset. Therefore, interest on borrowed funds normally is not added to the purchase price of an asset.[2]

When noncash consideration, such as land or other noncash assets, is given in exchange for an asset, the purchase price of the acquired asset is the fair value of the asset given up or the fair value of the asset received, whichever is more clearly determinable. The fair value (or fair market value) of an asset is the estimated amount of cash that would be required to acquire the asset. This cash equivalent cost can be inferred from information about similar assets in comparable transactions.

Cornerstone 7-1 illustrates the accounting procedures for the measurement and recording of the cost of an operating asset. It shows that all costs necessary to acquire the machine and prepare it for use—freight ($2,900) and installation costs ($5,300 + $800 + $1,500)—are included in the machine's historical cost. Interest on the note

[2] Financial Accounting Standards Board, *Statement of Financial Accounting Standards No. 34. "Capitalization of Interest,"* permits the addition of interest to the cost of assets requiring a long period of preparation for use, such as ships, large plants, or buildings.

HOW TO Measure and Record the Cost of a Fixed Asset

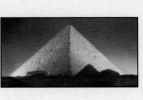

CORNERSTONE
7-1

Concept:
The cost of a fixed asset is any expenditure necessary to acquire the asset and to prepare it for use.

Information:
On June 29, 2009, Drew Company acquired a new automatic milling machine from Dayton, Inc. Drew paid $20,000 in cash and signed a one-year, 10 percent note for $80,000. Following the purchase, Drew incurred freight charges, on account, of $2,900 to ship the machine from Dayton's factory to Drew's plant. After the machine arrived, Drew paid J. B. Contractors $5,300 for installation. Drew also used $800 of materials and $1,500 of labor on trial runs.

Required:
1. Determine the cost of the machine.
2. Prepare the journal entry necessary to record the purchase of the machine.

Solution:
1. The cost of the machine is $110,500. The acquisition consists of the cash payment ($20,000), the amount of debt needed to finance the purchase ($80,000), freight charges on account ($2,900), installation costs ($5,300), and materials ($800) and labor ($1,500) for trial runs.
2. Drew would record the purchase of the machine as follows:

Date	Account and Explanation	Debit	Credit
June 29, 2009	Equipment	110,500	
	Cash ($20,000 + $5,300)		25,300
	Notes Payable		80,000
	Accounts Payable (for freight charges)		2,900
	Inventory, Materials		800
	Wages Payable		1,500
	(Record purchase of machine)		

Assets	=	Liabilities	+	Stockholders' Equity
+110,500		+80,000		
−25,300		+2,900		
−800		+1,500		

payable, however, is excluded from the machine's cost and is added to interest expense when it accrues. Finally, note that the cost is capitalized (recorded as an asset), and there is no effect on the income statement.

Had Drew given 1,600 shares of its own stock, which was selling for $50 per share, instead of the 10 percent note, the acquisition would have been recorded as follows:

Date	Account and Explanation	Debit	Credit
June 29, 2009	Equipment	110,500	
	Cash ($20,000 + $5,300)		25,300
	Common Stock		80,000
	Accounts Payable (for freight charges)		2,900
	Inventory, Materials		800
	Wages Payable		1,500
	(Record purchase of machine)		

Assets	=	Liabilities	+	Stockholders' Equity
+110,500		+2,900		+80,000
−25,300		+1,500		
−800				

Since the fair value of the stock [$50 × 1,600 = $80,000] equals the amount of the note, the cost is the same in both entries.

OBJECTIVE ➤ 3
Understand the concept of depreciation.

Depreciation

We observed earlier that the cost of a fixed asset represents the cost of future benefits or service potential to a company. With the exception of land, this service potential declines over the life of each asset as the asset is used in the operations of the company. **Depreciation** is the process of allocating, in a systematic and rational manner, the cost of a tangible fixed asset (other than land) to expense over the asset's useful life. The matching principle provides the conceptual basis for measuring and recognizing depreciation and requires that the cost of a fixed asset be allocated as an expense among the accounting periods in which the asset is used and revenues are generated by its use.

The amount of depreciation expense is recorded each period by making the following adjusting journal entry:

Depreciation Expense	xxx	
Accumulated Depreciation		xxx

The amount of depreciation recorded each period, or **depreciation expense**, is reported on the income statement. **Accumulated depreciation**, which represents the total amount of depreciation expense that has been recorded for an asset since the asset was acquired, is reported on the balance sheet as a contra-asset. That is, accumulated depreciation is deducted from the cost of the asset to get the asset's **book value** (or **carrying value**). Exhibit 7-3 shows the disclosures relating to property, plant, and equipment and depreciation made by Verizon in its 2007 Annual Report.

Before continuing, two points are critical to understand. First, depreciation is a *cost allocation process*. It is *not* an attempt to measure the fair value of the asset or obtain some other measure of the asset's value. In fact, the book value (cost less accumulated depreciation) of an asset that is reported on a company's balance sheet is often quite different from the market value of the asset. Second, depreciation is *not* an attempt to accumulate cash for the replacement of an asset. Depreciation is a cost allocation process that does not involve cash.

CONCEPT Q&A

If a company did not record all of the costs necessary to acquire an asset and prepare it for use, what would be the effect on the financial statements?

Possible Answer:

If costs were not recorded as an asset, these costs would be immediately expensed which would lower income in the current period. By recording these costs as assets, the company delays the recognition of expense until the service potential of the asset is used.

Exhibit 7-3

Excerpt from Verizon's 2006 Annual Report

Notes to Consolidated Financial Statements

NOTE 5 Property, Plant, and Equipment, Net:

Land	$ 839
Buildings and equipment	19,734
Network equipment	173,654
Furniture, office, and data processing equipment	11,912
Work in progress	1,988
Leasehold improvements	3,612
Other	2,255
	$ 213,994
Less: Accumulated depreciation	128,700
Property, plant, and equipment, net	$ 85,294

DECISION-MAKING & ANALYSIS

Future Asset Replacement

The examination of companies' balance sheets can provide useful insights into when a company's fixed assets may need to be replaced and how much cash may be required for that purpose. Assume that you are considering a major investment in one of two long-haul trucking companies. The two companies are about the same size, travel competitive routes, and have similar net incomes. However, your inspection of the balance sheets of both companies reveals a significant difference in the accumulated depreciation for the trucks, as shown below.

	Company 1	Company 2
Trucks	$600,000	$550,000
Less: Accumulated depreciation	138,000	477,000
Book value	$462,000	$ 73,000

The following are questions that you might raise while investigating the significance of this difference in accumulated depreciation:

1. *Does the difference suggest that the timing of future cash outflows needed to replace fully depreciated trucks will be different for the two companies?*

   Company 2's trucks are close to being fully depreciated. That is, the accumulated depreciation is almost equal to the historical cost of the asset. Assuming that estimates of useful life are consistent with economic life, it would appear that Company 2 will have to spend more cash in the near future than Company 1 for truck replacement.

2. *Do these expected differences in future cash outflows for asset replacement have any implications for you as an investor?*

   Company 2 may have to find more cash in the near future than Company 1. To do so, Company 2 might cut dividends to provide the cash internally. It might obtain the cash by issuing debt. However, the interest on the debt would reduce earnings, and debt would also make Company 2 a more risky investment. Company 2 might sell equity to raise the extra cash, but additional equity would reduce the present owners' claim on earnings and assets. Company 2 might also sell some other assets to obtain the cash; however, the amount and pattern of net income likely would be changed by a sale of assets.

Although more information is needed about Company 2 in order to know the precise impact of the impending replacement, the comparison of the two accumulated depreciation amounts helps us gain insights into the companies and leads us to ask some important questions concerning future cash flows. Although the recording of depreciation expense does not alter cash flow, accumulated depreciation signals the approaching future time for replacement of fixed assets, which usually does require cash.

Information Required for Measuring Depreciation

Three items of information are necessary in order to measure depreciation: (1) the cost of the fixed asset, (2) the residual value (salvage value) of the fixed asset, and (3) the useful life (or expected life) of the fixed asset.

Cost   As discussed earlier in the chapter, the cost of a fixed asset is any expenditure necessary to acquire the asset and to prepare the asset for use. In addition to cost, we also need to examine two other items—useful life and estimates of residual value—to measure depreciation. Exhibit 7-4 shows the relationship among the factors used to compute depreciation expense.

Useful Life   The **useful life** of an asset is the period of time over which the company anticipates deriving benefit from the use of the asset.[3] The useful life of any fixed asset reflects both the physical capacities of the asset and the company's plans for its use. Many companies plan to dispose of assets before their entire service potential is exhausted. For example, major automobile rental companies typically use an automobile

---

[3] The useful life can be estimated in *service units* as well as in *units of time*. For example, an airline may choose to measure the useful life of its aircraft in hours of use rather than years.

Exhibit 7-4

Components of Depreciation Expense

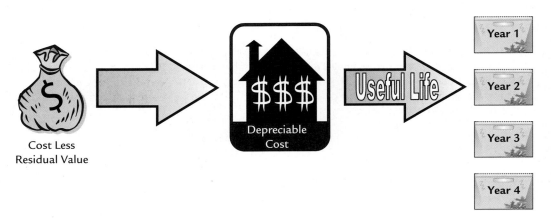

for only a part of its entire economic life before disposing of it. The useful life also is influenced by technological change. Many assets lose their service potential through obsolescence long before the assets are physically inoperable. Verizon uses an estimated useful life of 3 to 40 years for its fixed assets.

Residual Value   **Residual value** (also called **salvage value**) is the amount of cash or trade-in consideration that the company expects to receive when the asset is retired from service. Accordingly, the residual value reflects the company's plans for the asset and its expectations about the value of the asset to others once its expected life with the company is over. A truck used for 2 years may have a substantial residual value, whereas the same truck used for 10 years may have minimal residual value. Residual value is based on projections of some of the same future events that are used to estimate an asset's useful life. Since depreciation expense depends on estimates of both useful life and residual value, depreciation expense itself is an estimate.

The cost of the asset less its residual value gives an asset's **depreciable cost**. The depreciable cost of the asset is the amount that will be depreciated (expensed) over the asset's useful life.

OBJECTIVE ➤ 4
Compute depreciation expense using various depreciation methods.

Depreciation Methods

The service potential of a fixed asset is assumed to decline with each period of use, but the pattern of decline is not the same for all assets. Some assets decline at a constant rate each year while others decline sharply in the early years of use and then more gradually as time goes on. For other assets, the pattern of decline depends on how much the asset is used in each period. *Depreciation methods* are the standardized calculations required to determine periodic depreciation expense. In the following section, we will discuss three of the most common depreciation methods:

1. straight-line
2. declining balance
3. units-of-production

For any of these depreciation methods, the total amount of depreciation expense that has been recorded (accumulated depreciation) over the life of the asset will never exceed the depreciable cost (cost less residual value) of the asset.

Exhibit 7-5 shows the methods most commonly used by 600 of the largest U.S. companies.

Exhibit 7-5

The Relative Use of Depreciation Methods

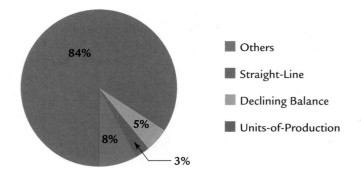

- Others
- Straight-Line
- Declining Balance
- Units-of-Production

Verizon reported the following in its notes to the financial statements:

> We record plant, property and equipment at cost ... Plant, property and equipment ... is generally depreciated on a straight-line basis over the following estimated useful lives: buildings, 8 to 40 years; plant equipment, 3 to 15 years; and other equipment, 3 to 5 years.

Straight-Line Method

As its name implies, the **straight-line depreciation** method allocates an equal amount of an asset's cost to depreciation expense for each year of the asset's useful life. It is appropriate to apply this method to those assets for which an equal amount of service potential is considered to be used each period. The straight-line method is the most widely used method because it is simple to apply and is based on a pattern of service potential decline that is reasonable for many plant assets.

The computation of straight-line depreciation expense is based on an asset's depreciable cost, which is the excess of the asset's cost over its residual value. Straight-line depreciation expense for each period is calculated by dividing the depreciable cost of an asset by the asset's useful life:

$$\text{Straight-Line Depreciation} = \frac{(\text{Cost} - \text{Residual Value})}{\text{Expected Useful Life}}$$

Alternatively, some companies will calculate an annual rate at which the asset should be depreciated. The fraction, (1/Useful Life), is called the *straight-line rate*. Using the straight-line rate, a company would compute depreciation expense by multiplying the straight-line rate by the asset's depreciable cost. Cornerstone 7-2 illustrates the computation of depreciation expense using the straight-line method.

CONCEPT Q&A

Why does the FASB allow companies to use different depreciation methods instead of requiring the use of a single depreciation method that would improve comparability?

Possible Answer:
The depreciation method chosen by a company should capture the declining service potential of an operating asset. Because assets are used differently, alternative methods are allowed so that the use of the asset can be better matched with the revenue it helped generate.

HOW TO Compute Depreciation Expense Using the Straight-Line Method

Concept:
As the service potential of a fixed asset declines, the cost of the asset is allocated as an expense among the accounting periods in which the asset is used and benefits are received (the matching principle).

Information:
On January 1, 2009, Morgan, Inc., acquired a machine for $50,000. Morgan expects the machine to be worth $5,000 at the end of its five-year useful life. Morgan uses the straight-line method of depreciation.

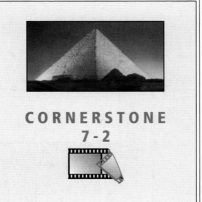

CORNERSTONE 7-2

**CORNERSTONE
7-2
(continued)**

Required:

1. Compute the straight-line rate of depreciation for the machine.
2. Compute the annual amount of depreciation expense.
3. Prepare a depreciation schedule that shows the amount of depreciation expense for each year of the machine's life.
4. Prepare the journal entry required to record depreciation expense in 2009.

Solution:

1. The straight-line rate of 20 percent is found as follows:

$$\text{Straight-Line Rate} = \frac{1}{\text{Useful Life}} = \frac{1}{5 \text{ years}} = 20\%$$

2. The annual amount of depreciation expense is $9,000 per year. This amount is calculated as:

$$\text{Straight-Line Depreciation Expense} = \frac{\$50,000 - \$5,000}{5 \text{ years}}$$

$$= \$9,000 \text{ per year}$$

   Alternatively, depreciation expense may be found by multiplying the straight-line rate (20 percent) by the asset's depreciable cost ($45,000).

3. The depreciation schedule is shown below:

End of Year	Depreciation Expense	Accumulated Depreciation	Book Value
			$50,000
2009	$ 9,000	$ 9,000	41,000
2010	9,000	18,000	32,000
2011	9,000	27,000	23,000
2012	9,000	36,000	14,000
2013	9,000	45,000	5,000
	$45,000		

4. The journal entry required at the end of 2009 is:

Date	Account and Explanation	Debit	Credit
Dec. 31, 2009	Depreciation Expense	9,000	
	Accumulated Depreciation		9,000
	(Record straight-line depreciation expense)		

Assets =	Liabilities +	Stockholders' Equity
−9,000		−9,000

Exhibit 7-6

Straight-Line Pattern of Depreciation

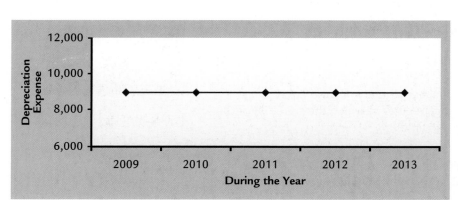

As illustrated in Cornerstone 7-2, Morgan, Inc., will record the same amount of depreciation expense ($9,000) each year. Exhibit 7-6 shows the depreciation pattern over the asset's five-year life.

The contra-asset account, accumulated depreciation, increases at a constant rate of $9,000 per year until it equals the depreciable cost ($45,000). The book value of the machine (cost less accumulated depreciation) decreases by $9,000 per year, until it equals the residual value ($5,000) at the end of the asset's useful life.

Declining Balance Method

The **declining balance depreciation method** is an accelerated depreciation method that produces a declining amount of depreciation expense each period by multiplying the declining book value of an asset by a constant depreciation rate. It is called an accelerated method because it results in a larger amount of depreciation expense in the early years of an asset's life relative to the straight-line method. However, because the total amount of depreciation expense (the depreciable cost) must be the same under any depreciation method, accelerated methods result in a smaller amount of depreciation expense in the later years of an asset's life. The declining balance method is appropriate for assets that are subject to a rapid decline in service potential due to factors such as rapid obsolescence.

The declining balance depreciation rate is some multiple (m) of the straight-line rate:

$$\text{Declining Balance Rate} = (m) \times \text{Straight-Line Rate}$$

The multiple (m) is often 2, in which case the declining balance method is called the *double-declining-balance method*. (In this text, a multiple of 2 is used for the declining balance method unless otherwise noted.) The declining balance rate also can be computed by using a more complicated formula that is described in later accounting courses.

Declining balance depreciation expense for each period of an asset's useful life equals the declining balance rate times the asset's book value (cost less accumulated depreciation) at the beginning of the period. Thus declining balance depreciation expense for each period is computed by using the following equation:

$$\text{Declining Balance Depreciation Expense} = \text{Declining Balance Rate} \times \text{Book Value}$$

The calculation of declining balance depreciation expense differs in two important ways from the calculation of straight-line depreciation expense. First, the straight-line method multiplies a depreciation rate by the *depreciable cost* of the asset, but the declining balance method multiplies a depreciation rate by the *book value* of the asset. Because the book value declines as depreciation expense is recorded, this produces a declining pattern of depreciation expense over time. Second, the straight-line method records an equal amount of depreciation expense *each period* of the asset's life. However, it is likely that the computation of depreciation expense under the declining balance method would cause the asset's book value to fall below its residual value. Because an asset's book value cannot be depreciated below its residual value, a lower amount of depreciation expense (relative to what is calculated under the declining balance method) must be recorded so that depreciation stops once the residual value is reached. Cornerstone 7-3 illustrates the computation of depreciation expense using the declining balance method.

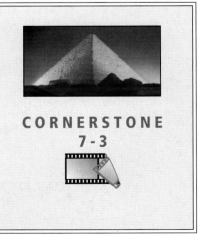

HOW TO Compute Depreciation Expense Using the Declining Balance Method

Concept:
As the service potential of a fixed asset declines, the cost of the asset is allocated as an expense among the accounting periods in which the asset is used and benefits are received (the matching principle).

Information:
On January 1, 2009, Morgan, Inc., acquired a machine for $50,000. Morgan expects the machine to be worth $5,000 at the end of its five-year useful life. Morgan uses the double-declining-balance method of depreciation.

CORNERSTONE
7-3

**CORNERSTONE
7-3
(continued)**

Required:

1. Compute the double-declining-balance rate of depreciation for the machine.
2. Prepare a depreciation schedule that shows the amount of depreciation expense for each year of the machine's life.
3. Prepare the journal entry required to record depreciation expense in 2009.

Solution:

1. The double-declining-balance rate of depreciation (40 percent) equals twice the straight-line rate of depreciation and is calculated as follows:

$$\frac{1}{\text{Useful Life}} \times 2 = \frac{1}{5} \times 2 = \frac{2}{5} \text{ or } 40\%$$

2. The depreciation schedule is shown below:

End of Year	Depreciation Expense (Rate × Book Value)	Accumulated Depreciation	Book Value
			$50,000
2009	40% × $50,000 = $20,000	$20,000	30,000
2010	40% × $30,000 = 12,000	32,000	18,000
2011	40% × $18,000 = 7,200	39,200	10,800
2012	40% × $10,800 = 4,320	43,520	6,480
2013	1,480*	45,000	5,000
	$45,000		

* The computed amount of $2,592 (40% × $6,480) would cause book value to be lower than residual value. Therefore, depreciation expense of $1,480 is taken in 2013 so that the book value equals the residual value.

3. The journal entry required at the end of 2009 is:

Date	Account and Explanation	Debit	Credit
Dec. 31, 2009	Depreciation Expense	20,000	
	Accumulated Depreciation		20,000
	(Record declining balance depreciation expense)		

Assets = Liabilities +	Stockholders' Equity
−20,000	−20,000

Exhibit 7-7

Declining Balance Pattern of Depreciation

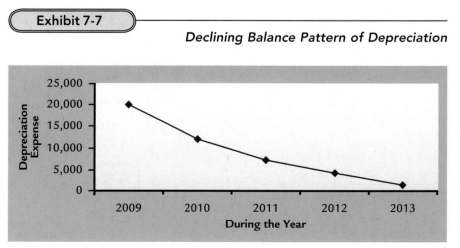

Relative to the straight-line method, Morgan, Inc.'s use of the double-declining-balance method of depreciation resulted in the recognition of higher depreciation expense in the early years of the asset's life and lower depreciation expense in the later years of the asset's life. This depreciation pattern is shown in Exhibit 7-7.

This pattern of expense is consistent with an asset whose service potential is used more rapidly (and its contribution to revenue is greater) in the early years of the asset's life. For this reason, the declining balance method is often used by companies in industries that experience rapid obsolescence.

Units-of-Production Method

The two previous depreciation methods resulted in a pattern of expense that was related to the passage of time. However, when the decline in an asset's service potential is proportional to the usage of the asset and asset usage can be measured, depreciation expense can be computed using the **units-of-production method**. Usage is typically gauged by a measure of productive capacity (e.g., units produced, hours worked, or miles driven). An automobile is an example of an asset whose service potential usually declines with use, where usage is measured by the number of miles traveled.

Under the units-of-production method, depreciation expense is computed by multiplying an asset's depreciable cost by a usage ratio, as shown in the following equation:

$$\text{Units-of-Production} \atop \text{Depreciation Expense} = \underbrace{\frac{\text{Actual Usage of Asset}}{\text{Expected Usage of Asset}}}_{\text{(Usage Ratio)}} \times \text{Depreciable Cost}$$

The usage ratio is the *actual* usage of the asset in the depreciation period divided by the total *expected* usage of the asset. For example, if a company replaces its executive jet every 5,000 flight hours, the usage ratio for a year in which the jet was used for 1,000 hours would be 0.20 [1,000/5,000]. An example of depreciation expense computed by the units-of-production method is shown in Cornerstone 7-4. Depending on the use of the asset during the year, the units-of-production depreciation method can result in a pattern of depreciation expense that may appear accelerated, straight-line, decelerated, or erratic.

HOW TO Compute Depreciation Expense Using the Units-of-Production Method

CORNERSTONE
7-4

Concept:
As the service potential of a fixed asset declines (as measured by usage), the cost of the asset is allocated as an expense among the accounting periods in which the asset is used and benefits are received (the matching principle).

Information:
On January 1, 2009, Morgan, Inc., acquired a machine for $50,000. Morgan expects the machine to be worth $5,000 at the end of its five-year useful life. Morgan expects the machine to run for 30,000 machine hours. The actual machine hours are given below:

	Actual Usage
Year	(in machine hours)
2009	3,000
2010	9,000
2011	7,500
2012	4,500
2013	6,000

Morgan uses the units-of-production method of depreciation.

Required:
1. Prepare a depreciation schedule that shows the amount of depreciation expense for each year of the machine's life.
2. Prepare the journal entry required to record depreciation expense in 2009.

**CORNERSTONE
7-4**
(continued)

Solution:

1. The depreciation schedule is shown below.

End of Year	Usage Ratio* ×	Depreciable Cost =	Depreciation Expense	Accumulated Depreciation	Book Value
					$50,000
2009	3,000 ÷ 30,000	$45,000	$ 4,500	$ 4,500	45,500
2010	9,000 ÷ 30,000	45,000	13,500	18,000	32,000
2011	7,500 ÷ 30,000	45,000	11,250	29,250	20,750
2012	4,500 ÷ 30,000	45,000	6,750	36,000	14,000
2013	6,000 ÷ 30,000	45,000	9,000	45,000	5,000
			$45,000		

* Actual Usage ÷ Total Expected Usage

2. The journal entry required at the end of 2009 is:

Date	Account and Explanation	Debit	Credit
Dec. 31, 2009	Depreciation Expense	4,500	
	Accumulated Depreciation		4,500
	(Record units-of-production depreciation expense)		

Assets =	Liabilities +	Stockholders' Equity
−4,500		−4,500

Exhibit 7-8

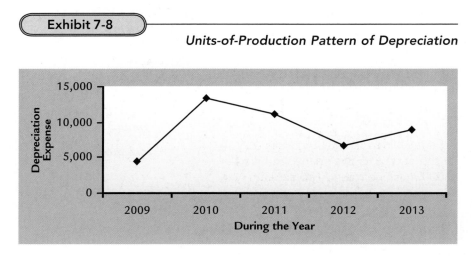

Units-of-Production Pattern of Depreciation

Note that when production varies widely and irregularly from period to period, the units-of-production method will result in an erratic pattern of depreciation expense. This depreciation pattern is illustrated in Exhibit 7-8.

Relative to the prior year, Morgan reported an increase in depreciation expense in 2010 and 2013; depreciation expense decreased in all other years. Thus, the units-of-production method does not produce a predictable pattern of depreciation expense. While this method does an excellent job of applying the matching concept, it is difficult to apply because it requires estimation of expected usage (which is a more difficult task than simply estimating useful life in years) and is used less widely than the other two depreciation methods.

Comparison of Depreciation Methods

Now that all three depreciation methods have been introduced, let us summarize their features:

*   The straight-line depreciation method produces a constant amount of depreciation expense in each period of the asset's life and is consistent with a constant rate of decline in service potential.
*   The declining balance depreciation method accelerates the assignment of an asset's cost to depreciation expense by allocating a larger amount of cost to the early years

Exhibit 7-9

Depreciation Patterns over Time

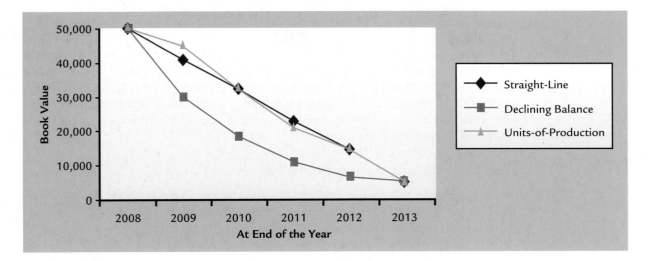

of an asset's life. This is consistent with a decreasing rate of decline in service potential and a decreasing amount for depreciation expense.

- The units-of-production depreciation method is based on a measure of the asset's use in each period, and the periodic depreciation expense rises and falls with the asset's use. In this sense, the units-of-production depreciation method is based not on a standardized pattern of declining service potential but on a pattern tailored to the individual asset and its use.

Exhibit 7-9 shows how the book value of Morgan's fixed asset changes over time due to the use of the straight-line, declining balance, and units-of-production depreciation methods.

Note that the total amount of depreciation expense ($45,000) recognized by Morgan, Inc., was the same under all three methods. This resulted in the asset having a book value of $5,000 at the end of 2013. At this point, book value is equal to residual value. While the total depreciation expense for each method was the same, the yearly amounts of depreciation expense recognized were different. Because each method is acceptable under GAAP, management should select the method that best matches the pattern of decline in service potential of the asset. This should result in a matching of the expense to the period in which the asset helped to generate revenue. Once a company chooses a method, that method should be consistently applied over time to enhance the comparability of the financial information.

ETHICS The use of estimates in depreciation calculations presents an ethical issue for the accountant. If an estimate is biased upward or downward, it can have significant financial statement impacts. For example, the accountant may face pressures to increase the useful life of an asset beyond what is reasonable. This upwardly biased estimate of useful life has the effect of decreasing the amount of depreciation expense recorded and increasing the company's net income. The accountant must resist these pressures and provide an unbiased estimate that faithfully portrays the service potential of the asset.◆

Depreciation for Partial Years

If an asset that is subject to depreciation is acquired on the first day of the accounting period, then the years of the asset's life coincide with the annual accounting periods. Under this condition, depreciation expense for each year of the asset's life

CONCEPT Q&A

If all depreciation methods result in the same amount being recorded as an expense over the life of the operating asset, why would a financial statement user be concerned with the depreciation method chosen?

Possible Answer:

The choice of depreciation method affects the amount recognized as an expense during each year of the operating asset's life. Therefore, the company's reported income each year would be different based on the depreciation method chosen.

equals the depreciation expense for the corresponding accounting period. If, however, a depreciable asset is acquired during the accounting period (instead of at the beginning of the period), the years of the asset's life do not coincide with the annual accounting period. Under this condition, the matching concept requires that depreciation expense for each year of the asset's life be divided between two accounting periods. To illustrate, consider an asset purchased on April 1, 2009, which is being depreciated using the straight-line method. Depreciation for a full year (12 months) is $20,000.[4] The asset would contribute depreciation expense of $15,000 to the partial year of 2009 [($20,000)(9/12)] and depreciation expense of $20,000 to the full year of 2010 [($20,000)(3/12) + ($20,000)(9/12)]. For the sake of simplicity, most examples, exercises, and problems in this book assume that asset acquisitions occur at the beginning of the accounting period.

Depreciation and Income Taxes

While a company will choose between the three depreciation methods discussed earlier as it prepares its financial statements, the depreciation method used in preparing its tax return need not be the same. The depreciation method used by a company to prepare its tax return is specified by the Internal Revenue Code. Tax depreciation rules are designed to stimulate investment in operating assets and, therefore, are not guided by the matching concept. Tax depreciation rules provide for the rapid

DECISION-MAKING & ANALYSIS

Impact of Depreciation Policy on Income

The measurement of periodic depreciation expense in a company that owns hundreds of depreciable assets in dozens of different categories calls for the exercise of careful judgment. Most large companies establish policies for depreciable assets that specify the measurement of cost, the estimation of useful lives and residual values, and the choice of depreciation methods. Since depreciation expense is a significant expense for many companies, net income may be quite sensitive to changes in depreciation policies and to differences in policies from one company to another. The following analysis demonstrates the importance of such changes to a bank loan officer.

Assume that you are a loan officer of the Prairie State Bank. The president of a ready-mix concrete company from a neighboring community, Concrete Transit Company, has applied for a five-year, $150,000 loan to finance his company's expansion. You have examined Concrete's financial statements for the past three years and have summarized the following data:

	2009	2008	2007
Sales revenue	$649,000	$613,000	$584,000
Cost of goods sold	317,000	304,000	287,000
Gross margin	$332,000	$309,000	$297,000
Operating expenses	288,000	263,000	249,000
Income from operations	$ 44,000	$ 46,000	$ 48,000
Miscellaneous expenses	25,000	23,000	20,000
Income before taxes	$ 19,000	$ 23,000	$ 28,000
Tax expense	4,000	6,000	7,000
Net income	$ 15,000	$ 17,000	$ 21,000
Depreciation expense*	$ 15,000	$ 15,000	$ 15,000
Plant assets	$470,000	$470,000	$470,000
Less: Accumulated depreciation	110,000	95,000	80,000
Book value	$360,000	$375,000	$390,000

* Included in operating expenses.

[4] Although acquisitions may occur *during* a month, for purposes of simplifying depreciation calculations, many companies follow the policy of substituting the date of the nearer first of the month for the actual transaction date. Thus, acquisitions on March 25 or April 9 would be treated as acquisitions on April 1 for purposes of calculating depreciation expense.

Your analysis of the financial statements indicates that the statement amounts and the relationships among them are as you expect, except for depreciation expense. Because you have another loan customer who is in the same business, you expected depreciation expense to be about 15 percent of the cost of the plant assets. Following are some questions you might ask in attempting to determine why the company's annual depreciation expense is so much less than you expected:

1. *What variables can cause depreciation expense to differ from what is expected?*

   Depreciation expense can be different from the expected amount because different methods are used from those expected or because estimates of expected life or residual value differ from those expected.

2. *You determine that Concrete Transit Company uses the straight-line depreciation method and that depreciation expense is, in fact, less than might be expected. In what direction do you think Concrete Transit has changed its estimate of expected life and residual value?*

   Concrete Transit must be using much higher estimates of residual value or of expected life than do other companies in similar businesses.

3. *If you alter the company's depreciation expense to 15 percent of the cost of the plant assets, what happens to net income for the years 2007 through 2009?*

   Depreciation expense increases from $15,000 to $70,500 for each year. Net income is affected by the increase in depreciation expense as follows:

	Reported	**Adjusted**
2007	$21,000	($27,500)*
2008	17,000	(32,500)
2009	15,000	(36,500)

   * In 2007 operating expenses increase by $55,500 to $304,500. Income (loss) from operations is then ($7,500). Income (loss) before taxes becomes ($27,500). Since there are no taxes when income before taxes is negative, the adjusted net income for 2005 is a net loss of $27,500. The amounts for 2008 and 2009 are determined similarly.

4. *Should your bank make the loan?*

   The adjusted net income amounts suggest that the company has been increasingly unprofitable. Since the principal and interest for the five-year loan would have to be repaid from cash provided by operations, the absence of profit suggests that the loan should not be made.

(accelerated) expensing of depreciable assets which lowers taxes. By bringing forward the bulk of depreciation expense, tax depreciation rules enable companies to save cash by delaying the payment of taxes. Most companies use the Modified Accelerated Cost Recovery System (MACRS) to compute depreciation expense for their tax returns, which is similar to the declining balance method. MACRS is not acceptable for financial reporting purposes.

Expenditures After Acquisition

OBJECTIVE ▶ 5
Distinguish between capital and revenue expenditures.

In addition to expenditures made when property, plant, and equipment is acquired, companies will incur costs over the life of the asset that range from ordinary repairs and maintenance to major overhauls, additions, and improvements. Companies must decide whether these expenditures should be capitalized (added to an asset account) or expensed (reported in total on the income statement).

Expenditures that do not increase the future economic benefits of the asset are called **revenue expenditures** and are expensed in the same period the expenditure is made. Verizon's policy with regard to revenue expenditures, as disclosed in the notes to the financial statements, is shown below:

We charge the cost of maintenance and repairs, including the cost of replacing minor items not constituting substantial betterments, principally to Cost of Services and Sales as these costs are incurred.

These expenditures maintain the level of benefits provided by the asset, relate only to the current period, occur frequently, and typically involve relatively small dollar amounts. An example of a revenue expenditure is the normal repair and maintenance of an asset and includes items such as an oil change for a truck, painting of a building, and the replacement of a minor part of a machine.

Expenditures that extend the life of the asset, expand the productive capacity, increase efficiency, or improve the quality of the product, are called **capital expenditures**. Because these expenditures provide benefits to the company in both current and future periods, capital expenditures are added to an asset account and are subject to depreciation. These expenditures typically involve relatively large dollar amounts. Examples of capital expenditures include major repairs (e.g., a transmission rebuild), additions, remodeling of buildings, and improvements. For example, Verizon reported capital expenditures of approximately $17.5 billion related to the build-out, upgrade, and expansion of both its wired and wireless network capacity and the introduction of new technology.

When a capital expenditure is made, it is necessary for a company to change its estimate of depreciation expense. In making this change in estimate, the company does not change previously recorded amounts related to depreciation. Instead, any revision of depreciation expense is accounted for in current and future periods.

To illustrate how a company would revise its estimate of depreciation expense, assume that Parker Publishing Company owned a printing press with a cost of $300,000, a residual value of $50,000, and a useful life of 10 years. Parker had been depreciating this asset using the straight-line method at a rate of $25,000 per year [($300,000 − $50,000)/10 years). On January 1, Parker Publishing Company paid $90,000 to add a digital typesetting component to an existing printing press. After the addition, the printing press is expected to have a remaining useful life of six years and a residual value of $10,000. To compute the revised depreciation expense, Parker will perform the following steps:

Step 1: Obtain the book value of the asset at the date of the capital expenditure. On the date of the capital expenditure, the printing press had a book value of $100,000 (cost of $300,000 less accumulated depreciation of $200,000).

Step 2: Add the cost of the expenditure to the book value. Adding the cost of the addition ($90,000) to the book value of the asset ($100,000) results in a revised book value of $190,000.

Step 3: Compute depreciation expense using the information for the asset after the capital expenditure. Using the updated information for the asset, straight-line depreciation expense is $30,000 per year [($190,000 − $10,000) ÷ 6 years]. Note that Parker uses the revised residual value and useful life in computing depreciation expense after the date of the capital expenditure.

OBJECTIVE ▶ 6
Describe the process of recording an impairment of a fixed asset.

Impairment of Property, Plant, and Equipment

As noted earlier, depreciation is a cost allocation process and does not attempt to measure the fair value of the asset. As a result, the book value of an asset and the fair value of an asset may be quite different. When the fair value of the asset falls significantly below the book value of the asset, it is possible that the asset may be impaired. An **impairment** is a permanent decline in the future benefit or service potential of an asset. The impairment may be due to numerous factors, including too little depreciation expense being recorded in previous years or obsolescence of the asset. A company is required to review an asset for impairment if events or circumstances lead the company to believe that an asset may be impaired.

The impairment test consists of two steps:

1. Existence: An impairment exists if the future cash flows expected to be generated by the asset are less than the asset's book value.
2. Measurement: If an impairment exists, the impairment loss is measured as the difference between the book value and the fair value of the asset.

Cornerstone 7-5 illustrates the accounting for an impairment.

HOW TO Record an Impairment of Property, Plant, and Equipment

**CORNERSTONE
7-5**

Concept:
If there is a permanent decline in the service potential of an operating asset, the asset's book value should be reduced to reflect this reduction in service potential.

Information:
Tabor Company acquired a machine on January 1, 2002, for $150,000. On January 3, 2009, when the machine has a book value of $60,000, Tabor believes that recent technological innovations may have led to an impairment in the value of the machine. Tabor estimates the machine will generate future cash flows of $50,000 and its current fair value is $42,000.

Required:
1. Determine if the machine is impaired as of January 2009.
2. If the machine is impaired, compute the loss from impairment.
3. Prepare the journal entry to record the impairment.

Solution:
1. The machine is impaired because the estimated future cash flows expected to be generated by the machine ($50,000) are less than the book value of the machine ($60,000).
2. The loss from impairment is $18,000, computed as the fair value ($42,000) less the book value ($60,000) of the machine.
3. The journal entry to record the impairment is:

Date	Account and Explanation	Debit	Credit
Jan. 3, 2009	Loss from Impairment	18,000	
	Equipment – Machine		18,000
	(To record impairment)		

Assets = Liabilities +	Stockholders' Equity
−18,000	−18,000

Note that this journal entry has the effect of writing an impaired asset down to its fair value which is consistent with the convention of conservatism.

Disposal of Fixed Assets

OBJECTIVE ▸ 7
Describe the process of recording the disposal of a fixed asset.

Although companies usually dispose of fixed assets voluntarily, disposition may also be forced. **Voluntary disposal** occurs when the company determines that the asset is no longer useful. The disposal may occur at the end of the asset's useful life or at some other time. For example, obsolescence due to unforeseen technological developments may lead to an earlier than expected disposition of the asset. **Involuntary disposal** occurs when assets are lost or destroyed through theft, acts of nature, or by accident.

Rarely do disposals occur on the first or last day of an accounting period. Therefore, the disposal of property, plant, and equipment usually requires two journal entries:

1. An entry to record depreciation expense up to the date of disposal.
2. An entry to:

   • Remove the asset's book value (the cost of the asset **and** the related accumulated depreciation)

- Record a gain or loss on disposition of the asset, which is computed as the difference between the proceeds from the sale and the book value of the asset.

Gains and losses on the disposition of property, plant, and equipment are normally reported as "other revenues or gains" or "other expenses and losses," respectively, and appear immediately after income from operations on a multiple-step income statement.

Verizon's policy for recording disposals, as shown in the notes to its 2007 financial statements is shown below.

When the depreciable assets ... are retired or otherwise disposed of, the related cost and accumulated depreciation are deducted from the plant accounts, and any gains or losses on disposition are recognized in income.

Cornerstone 7-6 illustrates the accounting for the disposition of property, plant, and equipment.

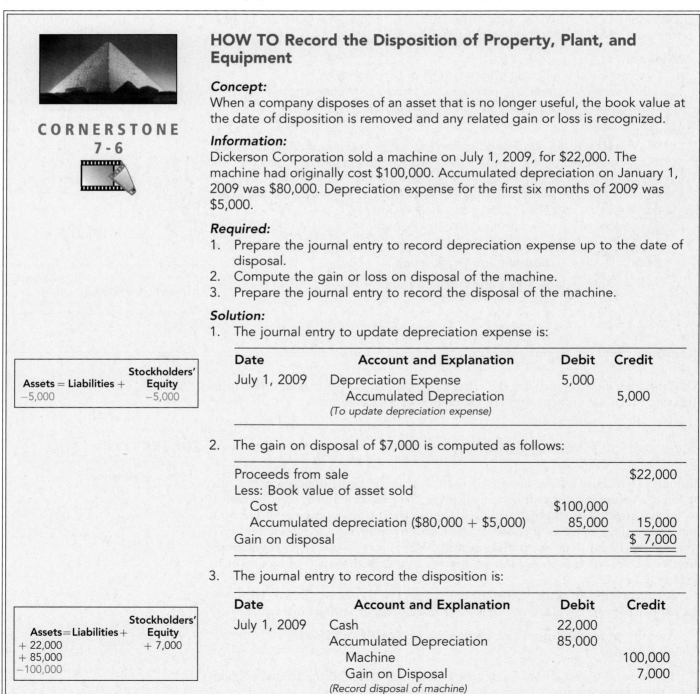

CORNERSTONE
7-6

HOW TO Record the Disposition of Property, Plant, and Equipment

Concept:
When a company disposes of an asset that is no longer useful, the book value at the date of disposition is removed and any related gain or loss is recognized.

Information:
Dickerson Corporation sold a machine on July 1, 2009, for $22,000. The machine had originally cost $100,000. Accumulated depreciation on January 1, 2009 was $80,000. Depreciation expense for the first six months of 2009 was $5,000.

Required:
1. Prepare the journal entry to record depreciation expense up to the date of disposal.
2. Compute the gain or loss on disposal of the machine.
3. Prepare the journal entry to record the disposal of the machine.

Solution:
1. The journal entry to update depreciation expense is:

Date	Account and Explanation	Debit	Credit
July 1, 2009	Depreciation Expense	5,000	
	Accumulated Depreciation		5,000
	(To update depreciation expense)		

Assets = Liabilities +	Stockholders' Equity
−5,000	−5,000

2. The gain on disposal of $7,000 is computed as follows:

Proceeds from sale		$22,000
Less: Book value of asset sold		
Cost	$100,000	
Accumulated depreciation ($80,000 + $5,000)	85,000	15,000
Gain on disposal		$ 7,000

3. The journal entry to record the disposition is:

Date	Account and Explanation	Debit	Credit
July 1, 2009	Cash	22,000	
	Accumulated Depreciation	85,000	
	Machine		100,000
	Gain on Disposal		7,000
	(Record disposal of machine)		

Assets = Liabilities +	Stockholders' Equity
+ 22,000	+ 7,000
+ 85,000	
−100,000	

Note that Dickerson recorded depreciation expense up to the date of disposal. Once this journal entry is made, the book value is updated to reflect the increased accumulated depreciation. This revised book value is then used to compute the Gain on Disposal which appears in the "other revenues and gains" section of the income statement.

If Dickerson had received $12,000 for the asset, the following computation would be made:

Proceeds from sale		$12,000
Less: Book value of asset sold		
Cost	$100,000	
Accumulated depreciation ($80,000 + $5,000)	(85,000)	15,000
Loss on disposal		$ (3,000)

Because the proceeds from the sale were less than the book value, Dickerson would record a loss as follows:

Date	Account and Explanation	Debit	Credit
July 1, 2009	Cash	12,000	
	Accumulated Depreciation	85,000	
	Loss on Disposal	3,000	
	Machine		100,000
	(Record disposal of machine)		

Assets =	Liabilities +	Stockholders' Equity
+ 12,000		−3,000
+ 85,000		
−100,000		

Dickerson would report the loss in the "other expenses and losses" section of the income statement.

Analyzing Fixed Assets

OBJECTIVE ▸ 8
Evaluate the use of fixed assets.

Because fixed assets are a major productive asset of most companies, it is useful to understand if the company is using these assets efficiently. In other words, how well is the company using its fixed assets to generate revenue? One measure of how efficiently a company is using its fixed assets is the **fixed asset turnover ratio**. It is calculated by dividing net sales by average fixed assets. The more efficient a company uses its fixed assets, the higher the ratio will be.

In addition to examining the efficiency of the use of fixed assets, investors are also concerned with the condition of a company's fixed assets. Because older assets tend to be less efficient than newer assets, the age of a company's fixed assets can provide useful insights for financial statement users. The age of a company's fixed assets also can provide an indication of a company's capital replacement policy and assist managers in estimating future capital expenditures. A rough estimate of the **average age of fixed assets** can be computed by dividing accumulated depreciation by depreciation expense. Cornerstone 7-7 illustrates the calculation of the fixed asset turnover ratio and the average age of fixed assets.

The fixed asset ratio tells us that for each dollar invested in fixed assets, Brandon Company generates sales of $1.56. In addition, Brandon Company's assets are, on average, 3.74 years old. Whether this is good or bad requires a comparison of these ratios to prior years' fixed asset turnover ratios and fixed asset turnover ratios of other companies in the industry. These ratios can provide a relative assessment of how efficiently fixed assets are being used as well as the condition of the assets.

Intangible Assets

OBJECTIVE ▸ 9
Understand the measurement and reporting of intangible assets.

Intangible operating assets, like tangible assets, represent future economic benefit to the company, but unlike tangible assets, they lack physical substance. Patents,

**CORNERSTONE
7-7**

HOW TO Calculate Fixed Asset Ratios

Concept:
The analysis of fixed assets can provide useful information as to how efficient the assets have been used as well as the condition of the assets.

Information:
The following information was obtained from the December 31, 2009, financial statements of Brandon Company:

Property, plant, and equipment, 1/1/2009	$2,145,000
Accumulated depreciation, 1/1/2009	1,162,000
Net property, plant, and equipment, 1/1/2009	$ 983,000
Property, plant, and equipment, 12/31/2009	$2,494,000
Accumulated depreciation, 12/31/2009	1,481,000
Net property, plant, and equipment, 12/31/2009	$1,013,000
Net sales	$1,553,000
Depreciation expense	$ 396,000

Required:
1. Compute the fixed asset turnover ratio for Brandon Company.
2. Compute the average age of Brandon Company's fixed assets, as of 12/31/2009.

Solution:
1. The fixed asset turnover ratio for Brandon Company is computed as:

$$\text{Fixed Asset Turnover} = \text{Net Sales} \div \text{Average Fixed Assets}$$
$$= 1,553,000 \div [(983,000 + 1,013,000) \div 2]$$
$$= 1.56 \text{ times}$$

2. The average age of Brandon Company's fixed assets at 12/31/2009 is:

$$\text{Average Age} = \text{Accumulated Depreciation} \div \text{Depreciation Expense}$$
$$= 1,481,000 \div 396,000$$
$$= 3.74 \text{ years}$$

copyrights, trademarks, leaseholds, organization costs, franchises, and goodwill are all examples of intangible assets. The economic benefits associated with most intangible assets are in the form of legal rights and privileges conferred on the owner of the asset. Thus the economic value of a patent, for example, is the legal right to restrict, control, or charge for the use of the idea or process covered by the patent.

Because intangible assets lack physical substance, it is often easy to overlook their importance to the overall value of a company. Recent research suggests that between 60 percent and 80 percent of a company's market value may be tied to intangible assets. Thus, for many companies, intangible assets may be the most important asset that a company has. A pharmaceutical company such as **Merck** could easily argue that the true value of the company lies with its intellectual capital and patents, not its tangible property, plant, and equipment. However, due to unique issues with intangibles (e.g., the highly uncertain nature of future benefits, the possibility of wide fluctuations in value), the value of many intangible assets is not adequately captured by current accounting standards. For example, Merck's intangible assets only make up approximately 4 percent of its total assets. Clearly, the value of Merck's intangible assets is understated. As the value of intangible assets continues to be a key driver of company value, the measurement and evaluation of intangibles will certainly be a crucial issue.

Accounting for Intangible Assets

Intangible assets are recorded at cost. Similar to fixed assets, the cost of an intangible asset is any expenditure necessary to acquire the asset and to prepare the asset for use. For intangible assets purchased from outside the company, the primary element of the cost is the purchase price. Costs such as registration, filing, and legal fees are considered a necessary cost and are capitalized as part of the intangible asset.

For internally developed intangible assets, the cost of developing the asset is expensed as incurred and normally recorded as **research and development (R&D) expense**. While expenditures for R&D may lead to intangible assets such as patents and copyrights, R&D is not an intangible asset. While many disagree with this position, current accounting standards require that all R&D be recorded as an expense. Exhibit 7-10 provides a listing of some typical intangible assets.

Companies also incur significant costs such as legal fees, stock issue costs, accounting fees, and promotional fees when they are formed. It can be argued that these **organizational costs** are an intangible asset that provides a benefit to a company indefinitely. However, current accounting standards treat organizational costs as an expense in the period the cost is incurred.

CONCEPT Q&A

If intangible assets represent a major amount of many companies' value, wouldn't any estimate of the intangible asset's value be better than not recording the asset at all?

Possible Answer:
While intangible assets are certainly relevant to financial statement users, information must be reliably measured to be recorded in the financial statements. For many intangibles, the inability to measure the intangible asset reliably results in the inability to record the intangible asset. This trade-off between the relevance and reliability of information is often a matter of judgment.

Exhibit 7-10

Common Types of Intangible Assets

Intangible Asset	Description	Cost Includes	Amortization
Patent	Right to manufacture, sell, or use product. The legal life is 20 years from the date of grant.	Purchase price, registration fees, legal costs	Shorter of the economic life or legal life
Copyright	Right to publish, sell, or control a literary or artistic work. The legal life is life of author plus 70 years.	Purchase price, registration fees, legal costs	Shorter of the economic life or legal life
Trademark	Right to the exclusive use of a distinctive name, phrase, or symbol. The legal life is 20 years but it can be renewed indefinitely.	Purchase price, registration fees, legal costs	Not amortized since it has an indefinite life; reviewed at least annually for impairment
Franchise	Exclusive right to conduct a certain type of business in some particular geographic area. Life of the franchise depends on specific terms of the franchise contract.	Initial cost paid to acquire the franchise	Shorter of the economic life or legal life
Goodwill	Unidentifiable intangible asset that arises from factors such as customer satisfaction, quality products, skilled employees, and business location. Goodwill is only recognized in business combinations.	The excess of the purchase price over the fair value of the identifiable net assets acquired in a business combination.	Not amortized since it has an indefinite life; reviewed at least annually for impairment

Once an intangible asset is recorded, companies must determine if the asset has a finite life or an indefinite life. The cost of an intangible asset with a finite life, like the cost of a tangible asset, is allocated to accounting periods over the life of the asset to reflect the decline in service potential. This process is referred to as **amortization**. Most companies will amortize the cost of an intangible asset on a straight-line basis over the shorter of the economic or legal life of the asset.[5] For example, a patent has a legal life of 20 years from the date it is granted. However, the economic advantage offered by a patent often expires before the end of its legal life as a result of other technological developments. Therefore, the shorter economic life should be used to amortize the cost of the patent. If an intangible asset is determined to have an indefinite life, it is *not* amortized but is reviewed at least annually for impairment. Cornerstone 7-8 illustrates the accounting for the acquisition and amortization of intangible assets.

Several items are of note: First, most intangible assets do not have a residual value. Therefore, the cost that is being amortized is usually the entire cost of the

CORNERSTONE 7-8

HOW TO Account for Intangible Assets

Concept:
Intangible assets are recorded at the cost necessary to acquire the asset and to prepare the asset for use. The cost of the asset is allocated as an expense among the accounting periods in which the asset is used and benefits are received (the matching principle).

Information:
On January 1, 2009, King Company acquired a patent from Queen, Inc., for $40,000. The patent was originally granted on January 1, 2002, and had 14 years of its legal life remaining. However, due to technological advancements, King estimates the patent will only provide benefits for 10 years. In addition, King also purchased a trademark from Queen for $60,000.

Required:
1. Prepare any journal entries necessary to record the acquisition of the patent and the trademark.
2. Compute the amortization expense for the patent and the trademark.
3. Prepare any adjusting journal entries necessary to record the amortization expense.

Solution:
1. The patent and trademark are recorded at their historical cost as follows:

Date	Account and Explanation	Debit	Credit
Jan. 1, 2009	Patent	40,000	
	Trademark	60,000	
	Cash		100,000
	(To purchase patent and trademark)		

Assets=Liabilities +	Stockholders' Equity
+ 40,000	
+ 60,000	
−100,000	

2. The amortization expense related to the patent ($4,000) is computed as:

$$\frac{\text{Cost} - \text{Residual Value}}{\text{Useful Life}} = \frac{\$40,000 - \$0}{10 \text{ years}} = \$4,000$$

---

[5] While the straight-line method of amortization is commonly used, any systematic and rational amortization method is acceptable under GAAP.

CORNERSTONE
7-8
(continued)

Because the trademark has an indefinite life, no amortization is necessary.
3. The journal entry to record the amortization expense for the patent is:

Date	Account and Explanation	Debit	Credit
Dec. 31, 2009	Amortization Expense	4,000	
	Patent		4,000
	(To record amortization of patent)		

Assets =	Liabilities +	Stockholders' Equity
−4,000		−4,000

intangible asset. Second, King amortized the patent over the shorter of its remaining legal life (14 years) or its economic life (10 years). This is consistent with recognizing amortization expense over the period that the intangible asset is expected to provide benefits. Third, King recorded the amortization expense by directly crediting the intangible asset, Patent. After the amortization expense is recorded, the book value of the patent is $36,000 ($40,000 − $4,000). Finally, amortization expense is reported as operating expense on the income statement.

DECISION-MAKING & ANALYSIS

Measuring and Estimating the Dimensions of a Patent

Marietta Corporation is a research-intensive company engaged in the design and sale of ceramic products. For the past year, half of Marietta's research staff has been engaged in designing a process for coating iron and steel with a ceramic material for use in high-temperature areas of automobile engines. The company has secured a patent for its process and is about to begin marketing equipment that uses the patented process. Accordingly, the company's controller must establish the cost of developing the patent and formulate a procedure to amortize the patent.

1. *What considerations arise in measuring the cost of the patent?*

   The cost of the patent should include lawyers' fees and other similar costs incurred in securing the patent. In addition, the controller believes that half the year's cost of research activities should be assigned to the patent, including salaries paid to researchers and the costs of facilities and supplies used. However, accounting standards require that research and development expenditures be included in expense in the year in which they are incurred. Therefore the research activities should be expensed when incurred and not assigned to the patent, as the controller believes.

2. *What considerations arise in formulating an amortization procedure for the patent?*

   Although the patent lasts for 20 years, Marietta expects the patented equipment to be a viable product for only five years. Moreover, 80 percent of the sales are expected to occur in the first two years following the introduction of the equipment. The company expects to introduce an improved version of the equipment, which will be covered by another patent, within about four years. One of the assistant controllers argues, therefore, that the cost of this patent should be spread over the life of both the current equipment and its successor, with most of the cost amortized in the first two years following introduction of the current equipment. However, given the uncertainty of the projections on which the argument rests, the controller decides to amortize the entire cost of the patent over a five-year period, with 80 percent of the cost divided equally between years 1 and 2 and the remaining 20 percent divided equally among years 3 through 5. Of course, amortization will not begin until the equipment actually reaches the market. Until then, the cost of the patent is carried as an intangible asset on the balance sheet.

Natural Resources

OBJECTIVE ▶ 10
Understand the measurement and reporting of natural resources.

Natural resources, such as coal deposits, oil reserves, and mineral deposits, make up an important part of the operating assets for many companies. For example, BP has oil and gas properties of over $118 billion, representing approximately 26 percent of its total assets. Like intangible operating assets, natural resources present formidable estimation and measurement problems. However, natural resources differ from other operating assets in two important ways. First, unlike fixed assets, natural resources are physically consumed as they are used by a company. Second, natural resources can generally be replaced or restored only by an act of nature. (Timberlands are renewed by replanting and growth, but coal deposits and most mineral deposits are not subject to renewal.)

The accounting for natural resources is quite similar to the accounting for intangible assets and fixed assets. At acquisition, all the costs necessary to ready the natural resource for separation from the earth are capitalized. At the time a company acquires the property on which a natural resource is located (or the property rights to the natural resource itself), only a small portion of the costs necessary to ready the asset for removal are likely to have been incurred. Costs such as sinking a shaft to an underground coal deposit, drilling a well to an oil reserve, or removing the earth over a mineral deposit can be several times greater than the cost of acquiring the property.

As a natural resource is removed from the earth, the cost of the natural resource is allocated to each unit of natural resource removed. This process of allocating the cost of the natural resource to each period in which the resource is used is called **depletion**. Depletion is computed by using a procedure similar to that for the units-of-production method of depreciation. First, a depletion rate is computed as follows:

$$\text{Depletion Rate} = \frac{\text{Cost} - \text{Residual Value}}{\text{Recoverable Units}}$$

Second, depletion is calculated by multiplying the depletion rate by the number of units of the natural resource recovered during the period:

$$\text{Depletion} = \text{Depletion Rate} \times \text{Units Recovered}$$

As the natural resource is extracted, the intangible asset is reduced and the amount of depletion computed is added to inventory. As the inventory is sold, the company will recognize an expense (cost of goods sold) related to the natural resource. Cornerstone 7-9 illustrates how to account for depletion of a natural resource.

Two items are of particular importance. First, notice that Miller records depletion in an inventory account. As the coal is sold, inventory will be reduced and cost of goods

**CORNERSTONE
7-9**

HOW TO Account for Depletion of a Natural Resource

Concept:
All costs necessary to acquire the natural resource and prepare it for use are capitalized as part of the natural resource. The depletion of the natural resource is added to inventory as the resource is depleted.

Information:
In 2008 the Miller Mining Company purchased a 4,000-acre tract of land in southern Indiana for $12,000,000, on which it developed an underground coal mine. Miller spent $26,000,000 to sink shafts to the coal seams and otherwise prepare the mine for operation. Miller estimates that there are 10,000,000 tons of recoverable coal and that the mine will be fully depleted eight years after mining begins in early 2009. The land has a residual value of $500,000. During 2009, 800,000 tons of coal was mined.

Required:
1. Compute the cost of the natural resource
2. Compute the depletion rate.
3. How much depletion is taken in 2009?
4. Prepare the journal entry necessary to record depletion.

Solution:
1. The cost of the natural resource ($38,000,000) includes all costs necessary to get the mine ready for use and is computed as:

**CORNERSTONE
7-9**
(continued)

Cost	$12,000,000
Development/preparation costs	26,000,000
Cost	$38,000,000

2. The depletion rate, $3.75 per ton, is computed as:

Depletion Rate = $38,000,000 − $500,000 ÷ 10,000,000 tons = $3.75 per ton

3. If Miller mines 800,000 tons of coal in 2009, then depletion for the year is:

Depletion = $3.75 × 800,000 = $3,000,000

4. The following entry is necessary to record depletion for 2009:

Date	Account and Explanation	Debit	Credit
Dec. 31, 2009	Inventory, Coal	3,000,000	
	Accumulated Depletion, Coal Mine		3,000,000
	(To record depletion of coal mine)		

	Stockholders'
Assets = Liabilities +	**Equity**
+3,000,000	
−3,000,000	

Assuming all of the coal is sold in 2009, the following entry should be made:

Cost of Goods Sold	3,000,000	
Inventory, Coal		3,000,000

sold will be recognized. Thus, the expense related to depletion will be matched with the revenue that is generated from the sale of the natural resource. Second, Miller recorded depletion in an accumulated depletion account.[6] At December 31, 2009, Miller could present the coal mine among its assets in the balance sheet as shown in Exhibit 7-11:

Exhibit 7-11

Disclosure of Natural Resource

Property, Plant, and Equipment:	
Land	$ 2,200,000
Equipment and machinery	19,800,000
Coal mine (cost of $38,000,000 less accumulated depletion of $3,000,000)	35,000,000
Total property, plant, and equipment	$57,000,000

Summary of Learning Objectives

LO1. Define, classify, and describe the accounting for operating assets.
- Operating assets are the long-lived assets used by the company in the normal course of operations to generate revenue.
- Operating assets consist of three categories: property, plant, and equipment, intangibles and natural resources.
- Generally, operating assets are recorded at cost.
- As the service potential of the asset is used, the asset's cost is allocated as an expense (called depreciation, amortization or depletion).

LO2. Explain how the cost principle applies to recording the cost of a fixed asset.
- The cost is any expenditure necessary to acquire the asset and to prepare the asset for use.
- This amount is generally the cash paid.
- If noncash consideration is involved, cost is the fair value of the asset received or the fair value of the asset given up, whichever is more clearly determinable.

[6] An alternative practice allowed by GAAP is to credit depletion directly to the asset account.

LO3.   Understand the concept of depreciation.
- Depreciation is the process of allocating the cost of a tangible fixed asset to expense over the asset's useful life.
- Depreciation is not an attempt to measure fair value.
- Instead, depreciation is designed to capture the declining service potential of a fixed asset.
- Three factors are necessary to compute depreciation expense: cost, residual value, and useful life.

LO4.   Compute depreciation expense using various depreciation methods.
- The straight-line method allocates an equal amount of the asset's cost to each year of the asset's useful life by dividing the asset's depreciable cost (cost less residual value) by the asset's useful life.
- The declining balance method is an accelerated method of depreciation that produces a declining amount of depreciation expense each period by multiplying the declining book value of an asset by a constant depreciation rate (computed as some multiple of the straight-line rate of depreciation).
- The units-of-production method recognizes depreciation expense based on the actual usage of the asset. A usage ratio (actual usage divided by total expected usage) is multiplied by the depreciable cost of the asset to get depreciation expense for each period.

LO5.   Distinguish between capital and revenue expenditures.
- Revenue expenditures are expenditures that do not increase the future benefit of an asset and are expensed as incurred.
- Capital expenditures extend the life of the asset, expand productive capacity, increase efficiency or improve the quality of the product.
- Capital expenditures are added to the asset account and are subject to depreciation.

LO6.   Describe the process of recording an impairment of a fixed asset.
- Impairment exists when the future cash flows expected to be generated by an asset are less than the book value of the asset.
- In this situation, an impairment loss (the difference between the book value and fair value of the asset) is recognized and the asset is reduced.

LO7.   Describe the process of recording the disposal of a fixed asset.
- When a fixed asset is disposed of (either voluntarily or involuntarily), a gain or loss is recognized.
- The gain or loss is the difference between the proceeds from the sale and the book value of the asset.
- The gain or loss is reported on the income statement as "other revenues or gains" or "other expenses and losses," respectively.

LO8.   Evaluate the use of fixed assets.
- The efficiency with which a company uses its fixed assets to generate can be analyzed by using the fixed asset turnover ratio (net sales divided by average fixed assets).
- The condition of a company's assets and insights into the company's capital replacement policy can be examined by computing the **average age of fixed assets** (accumulated depreciation divided by depreciation expense).

LO9.   Understand the measurement and reporting of intangible assets.
- Intangible assets are recorded at cost, which is any expenditure necessary to acquire the asset and prepare it for use.
- If the intangible asset has a finite life, it is amortized over the shorter of the economic or legal life of the asset.
- If the intangible asset has an indefinite life, it is not amortized but is reviewed at least annually for impairment.

LO10. Understand the measurement and reporting of natural resources.
- The cost of natural resources is any cost necessary to acquire and prepare the resource for separation from the earth.
- As the natural resource is removed, the cost is allocated to each unit of the natural resource that is removed and recorded in an inventory account. This process is called depletion.
- Depletion is calculated using a procedure similar to the units-of-production depreciation method.

CORNERSTONE 7-1	How to measure and record the cost of a fixed asset, page 353
CORNERSTONE 7-2	How to compute depreciation expense using the straight-line method, page 357
CORNERSTONE 7-3	How to compute depreciation expense using the declining balance method, page 359
CORNERSTONE 7-4	How to compute depreciation expense using the units-of-production method, page 361
CORNERSTONE 7-5	How to record an impairment of property, plant, and equipment, page 367
CORNERSTONE 7-6	How to record the disposition of property, plant, and equipment, page 368
CORNERSTONE 7-7	How to calculate fixed asset ratios, page 370
CORNERSTONE 7-8	How to account for intangible assets, page 372
CORNERSTONE 7-9	How to account for depletion of a natural resource, page 374

CORNERSTONES FOR CHAPTER 7

Key Terms

Accumulated depreciation, 354

Amortization, 372

Average age of fixed assets, 369

Book value (carrying value), 354

Capital expenditures, 366

Copyright, 371

Declining balance depreciation method, 359

Depletion, 374

Depreciable cost, 356

Depreciation, 354

Depreciation expense, 354

Fixed asset turnover ratio, 369

Franchise, 371

Goodwill, 371

Impairment, 366

Intangible operating assets, 369

Involuntary disposal, 367

Natural resources, 373

Operating assets, 350

Organizational costs, 371

Patent, 371

Property, plant, and equipment, 351

Research and development (R&D) expense, 371

Residual value (salvage value), 356

Revenue expenditures, 365

Straight-line depreciation, 357

Trademark, 371

Units-of-production method, 361

Useful life, 355

Voluntary disposal, 367

Review Problem

I. Accounting for Operating Assets

Concept:

At acquisition, operating assets are capitalized at their historical cost. As the service potential of an operating asset declines, the cost of the asset is allocated as an expense among the accounting periods in which the asset is used and benefits are received.

Information:

The Carroll Company manufactures a line of cranes, shovels, and hoists, all of which are electronically controlled. During 2009, the following transactions occurred:

a. On January 2, 2009, Carroll purchased a building by signing a note payable for $702,900. The building is expected to have a useful life of 30 years and a residual value of $3,900.
b. On January 3, Carroll purchased a delivery truck for $34,650 cash. The delivery truck is expected to have a useful life of five years and a $5,000 residual value.
c. Immediately after the acquisition, Carroll spent $5,350 on a new engine for the truck. After installing the engine, Carroll estimated that this expenditure increased the useful life of the truck to eight years. The residual value is still expected to be $5,000.
d. In order to assure a coal supply for its heating plant, Carroll acquired a small operating coal mine for $1,980,000. Carroll estimated that the recoverable coal reserves at acquisition were 495,000 tons. Carroll's mine produced 40,000 tons of coal during 2009.
e. Carroll owns a patent that it purchased in 2008 for $100,000. The patent has 12 years remaining on its legal life but Carroll estimates its economic life to be 10 years. Carroll uses the straight-line amortization method.

Required:

1. Record the acquisition of the building and the delivery truck.
2. Compute and record a full year's depreciation expense for 2009 on the building (use the straight-line depreciation method) and on the truck (use the double-declining-balance depreciation method).
3. Compute and record 2009 depletion for the coal mine.
4. Compute and record the amortization expense on the patent for 2009 on a straight-line basis.

Solution:

1. The cost of the building is $702,900 and is recorded as:

Date	Account and Explanation	Debit	Credit
Jan. 2, 2009	Building	702,900	
	Note Payable		702,900
	(Purchased building by issuing note payable)		

		Stockholders'
Assets =	**Liabilities** +	**Equity**
+702,900	+702,900	

The cost of the truck is $40,000 ($34,650 acquisition price + $5,350 from the overhaul of the engine). The purchase of the truck is recorded as:

Date	Account and Explanation	Debit	Credit
Jan. 3, 2009	Truck	40,000	
	Cash		40,000
	(Purchase of truck for cash)		

		Stockholders'
Assets =	**Liabilities** +	**Equity**
−40,000		
+40,000		

2. Depreciation on the items of property, plant, and equipment in the basket purchase:

STRAIGHT-LINE DEPRECIATION ON THE BUILDING

$$\text{Straight-Line Depreciation Expense} = \frac{\text{Cost} - \text{Residual Value}}{\text{Expected Life}}$$

$$= \frac{\$702,900 - \$3,900}{30 \text{ years}} = \$23,300 \text{ per year}$$

Date	Account and Explanation	Debit	Credit
Dec. 31, 2009	Depreciation Expense, Building	23,300	
	Accumulated Depreciation, Building		23,300
	(To record depreciation on building)		

Assets	= Liabilities +	Stockholders' Equity
−23,300		−23,300

DOUBLE-DECLINING-BALANCE DEPRECIATION FOR THE TRUCK

$$\frac{\text{Declining Balance}}{\text{Depreciation Expense}} = \text{Declining Balance Rate} \times \text{Book Value}$$

Declining Balance Rate $= (1/\text{Useful Life}) \times 2 = (1/8) \times 2 = 2/8$, or 25%

Cost $= \$34,650$ (from transaction *b*) $+ \$5,350$ overhaul (from transaction *c*)
$= \$40,000$

End of Year	Depreciation Expense	Accumulated Depreciation	Book Value
			$40,000
2009	25% × $40,000 = $10,000	$10,000	30,000
2010	25% × $30,000 = 7,500	17,500	22,500
2011	25% × $22,500 = 5,625	23,125	16,875
2012	25% × $16,875 = 4,219	27,344	12,656
2013	25% × $12,656 = 3,164	30,508	9,492
2014	25% × $9,492 = 2,373	32,881	7,119
2015	25% × $7,119 = 1,780	34,661	5,339
2016	339*	35,000	5,000
	$35,000		

* The amount needed to achieve a $5,000 book value.

Date	Account and Explanation	Debit	Credit
Dec. 31, 2009	Depreciation Expense, Truck	10,000	
	Accumulated Depreciation, Truck		10,000
	(To record depreciation on truck)		

Assets	= Liabilities +	Stockholders' Equity
−10,000		−10,000

3. Depletion on the coal mine:

DEPLETION

$$\text{Depletion Rate} = \frac{\text{Cost} - \text{Residual Value}}{\text{Recoverable Units}}$$

$$= \frac{\$1,980,000}{495,000} = \$4.00 \text{ per ton}$$

Depletion = Depletion Rate × Units Recovered
$= \$4.00 \times 40,000 = \$160,000$

Date	Account and Explanation	Debit	Credit
Dec. 31, 2009	Inventory, Coal	160,000	
	Accumulate Depletion, Coal Mine		160,000
	(To record depletion)		

Assets	= Liabilities +	Stockholders' Equity
+160,000		
−160,000		

4. Amortization of the patent:

$$\text{Straight-Line Amortization Expense} = \frac{\text{Cost} - \text{Residual Value}}{\text{Expected Life}}$$

$$= \frac{\$100,000 - \$0}{8 \text{ years}}$$

$$= \$12,500 \text{ per year}$$

	Stockholders'	
Assets = Liabilities +	**Equity**	
−12,500	−12,500	

Date	Account and Explanation	Debit	Credit
Dec. 31, 2009	Amortization Expense	12,500	
	Patent		12,500
	(To record amortization of patent)		

Discussion Questions

1. How do operating assets differ from nonoperating assets? What benefits do operating assets provide to the company?
2. What are the classifications of operating assets? How do they differ from one another?
3. How does the cost concept affect accounting for operating assets? Under this concept, what is included in the cost of a fixed asset?
4. How is the cost of a fixed asset measured in a cash transaction? In a noncash transaction?
5. How does the matching concept affect accounting for fixed assets?
6. What factors must be known or estimated in order to compute depreciation expense?
7. How do the accelerated and straight-line depreciation methods differ?
8. What objective should guide the selection of a depreciation method for financial reporting purposes?
9. What objective should be of primary importance in the selection of a depreciation method for income tax reporting?
10. What accounting concepts should be considered when evaluating the accounting for expenditures that are made for fixed assets subsequent to acquisition? Be sure to distinguish between revenue and capital expenditures.
11. What is an impairment of a fixed asset?
12. How is the sale of equipment at an amount greater than its book value recorded? How would your answer change if the equipment is sold at an amount less than its book value?
13. Describe the benefits that intangible assets provide to an enterprise.
14. What factors should be considered when selecting the amortization period for an intangible asset?
15. What basis underlies the computation of depletion?

Multiple-Choice Exercises

7-1 Anniston Company purchased equipment and incurred the following costs:

Purchase price	$40,000
Cost of trial runs	800
Installation costs	200
Sales tax	2,000

What is the cost of the equipment?

a. $40,000
b. $42,000
c. $42,900
d. $43,000

7-2 The cost principle requires that companies record fixed assets at

a. Historical cost
b. Fair value
c. Book value
d. Market value

7-3 When depreciation expense is recorded each period, what account is debited?

a. Accumulated Depreciation
b. Cash
c. Depreciation Expense
d. The fixed asset account involved

Use the following information for Multiple-Choice Exercises 7-4 through 7-6:

Cox Inc. acquired a machine for $800,000 on January 1, 2009. The machine has a salvage value of $10,000 and a five-year useful life. Cox expects the machine to run for 15,000 machine hours. The machine was actually used for 4,500 hours in 2009 and 3,000 hours in 2010.

7-4 What amount would Cox record as accumulated depreciation at December 31, 2010, if the straight-line depreciation method were used?

a. $284,400
b. $316,000
c. $320,000
d. $324,000

7-5 What amount would Cox record as depreciation expense at December 31, 2010, if the double-declining-balance method were used?

a. $192,000
b. $193,600
c. $316,000
d. $320,000

7-6 What amount would Cox record as depreciation expense for 2009 if the units-of-production method were used (round your answer to the nearest dollar)?

a. $200,000
b. $237,000

c. $240,000
d. $268,000

7-7 Which of the following statements is *true* regarding depreciation methods?

a. The use of a declining-balance method of depreciation will produce lower depreciation charges in the early years of an asset's life compared to the straight-line depreciation method.
b. Over the life of an asset, a declining-balance depreciation method will recognize more depreciation expense relative to the straight-line method.
c. The use of a higher estimated life and a higher residual value will lower the annual amount of depreciation expense recognized under the straight-line method.
d. The use of a declining-balance method instead of the straight-line method will produce higher book values for an asset in the early years of the asset's life.

7-8 Normal repair and maintenance of an asset is an example of what?

a. Revenue expenditure
b. Capital expenditure
c. An expenditure that will be depreciated
d. An expenditure that should be avoided

7-9 Murnane Company purchased a machine on February 1, 2005, for $100,000. In January 2009, when the book value of the machine is $70,000, Murnane believes the machine is impaired due to recent technological advances. Murnane expects the machine to generate future cash flow of $10,000 and has estimated the fair value of the machine to be $55,000. What is the loss from impairment?

a. $5,000
b. $15,000
c. $30,000
d. $45,000

7-10 Jerabek Inc. decided to sell one of its fixed assets that had a cost of $50,000 and accumulated depreciation of $35,000 on July 1, 2009. On that date, Jerabek sold the fixed asset for $20,000. What was the resulting gain or loss from the sale of the asset?

a. $5,000 loss
b. $5,000 gain
c. $15,000 loss
d. $15,000 gain

7-11 Which of the following statements is *true*?

a. The average age of the fixed assets is computed by dividing accumulated depreciation by depreciation expense.
b. The fixed asset turnover ratio assists managers in determining the estimated future capital expenditures that are needed.
c. If net sales increases, the fixed asset turnover ratio will decrease.
d. A relatively low fixed asset turnover ratio signals that a company is efficiently using its assets.

7-12 Which of the following is *not* an intangible asset?

a. Patent
b. Research & development
c. Trademark
d. Goodwill

7-13 Heston Company acquired a patent on January 1, 2009, for $60,000. The patent has a remaining legal life of 15 years, but Heston expects to receive benefits from the patent for only five years. What amount of amortization expense does Heston record in 2009 related to the patent?

a. $4,000
b. $6,000
c. $12,000
d. None of the above—patents are not amortized.

7-14 Howton Paper Company purchased $1,200,000 of timberland in 2008 for its paper operations. Howton estimates that there are 10,000 acres of timberland and it cut 2,000 acres in 2009. The land is expected to have a residual value of $200,000 once all the timber is cut. Which of the following is *true* with regard to depletion?

a. Howton will record depletion expense of $240,000 in 2009.
b. Howton's depletion rate is $120 per acre of timber.
c. Howton should deplete the timber at a rate of 20% (2,000 acres ÷ 10,000 acres) per year.
d. Depletion will cause Howton's timber inventory to increase.

Cornerstone Exercises

Cornerstone Exercise 7-15 **COST OF A FIXED ASSET**

Borges, Inc., recently purchased land to use for the construction of its new manufacturing facility and incurred the following costs: purchase price, $80,000; real estate commissions, $4,800; delinquent property taxes, $1,500; closing costs, $3,300 clearing and grading of the land, $8,100.

Required:

Determine the cost of the land.

Cornerstone Exercise 7-16 **ACQUISITION COST**

Cox Company recently purchased a machine by paying $10,000 cash and signing a six month, 10% note for $10,000. In addition to the purchase price, Cox incurred the following costs related to the machine: freight charges $800; interest charges $500; special foundation for machine $400; installation costs $1,100.

Required:

Determine the cost of the machine.

Cornerstone Exercise 7-17 **STRAIGHT-LINE DEPRECIATION**

OBJECTIVE ➤ 3 4
CORNERSTONE 7-2

Irons Delivery, Inc., purchased a new delivery truck for $42,000 on January 1, 2009. The truck is expected to have a $2,000 residual value at the end of its five-year useful life. Irons uses the straight-line method of depreciation.

Required:

Prepare the journal entry to record depreciation expense for 2009 and 2010.

Cornerstone Exercise 7-18 **DECLINING BALANCE DEPRECIATION**

OBJECTIVE ➤ 3 4
CORNERSTONE 7-3

Use the same information in **Cornerstone Exercise 7-17**, except that Irons uses the double-declining-balance method of depreciation.

Required:

Prepare the journal entry to record depreciation expense for 2009 and 2010.

Cornerstone Exercise 7-19 **UNITS-OF-PRODUCTION DEPRECIATION**

OBJECTIVE ➤ 3 4
CORNERSTONE 7-4

Use the same information in **Cornerstone Exercise 7-17**, except that Irons uses the units-of-production method of depreciation. Irons expects the truck to run for 150,000 miles. The actual miles driven in 2009 and 2010 were 40,000 and 36,000, respectively.

Required:

Prepare the journal entry to record depreciation expense for 2009 and 2010.

Cornerstone Exercise 7-20 **IMPAIRMENT**

Brown Industries had two machines that it believes may be impaired. Information on the machines is shown below.

	Book Value	Estimated Future Cash Flows	Fair Value
Machine 1	$42,000	$50,000	$40,000
Machine 2	55,000	40,000	32,000

Required:

For each machine, determine if the machine is impaired. If so, calculate the amount of the impairment loss.

OBJECTIVE ▶ 7
CORNERSTONE 7-6

Cornerstone Exercise 7-21 DISPOSAL OF AN OPERATING ASSET

On August 30, Williams Manufacturing Company decided to sell one of its fabricating machines that was 15 years old for $4,000. The machine, which originally cost $100,000, had accumulated depreciation of $97,500.

Required:

Prepare the journal entry to record the disposal of the machine.

OBJECTIVE ▶ 8
CORNERSTONE 7-7

Cornerstone Exercise 7-22 ANALYZE FIXED ASSETS

At December 31, 2009, Clark Corporation reported beginning net fixed assets of $84,365, ending net fixed assets of $103,548, accumulated depreciation of $48,753, net sales of $212,722, and depreciation expense of $12,315.

Required:

Compute Clark Corporation's fixed asset turnover ratio and the average age of its fixed assets.

OBJECTIVE ▶ 9
CORNERSTONE 7-8

Cornerstone Exercise 7-23 COST OF INTANGIBLE ASSETS

Advanced Technological Devices, Inc., acquired a patent for $130,000. It spent an additional $20,000 defending the patent in legal proceedings.

Required:

Determine the cost of the patent.

OBJECTIVE ▶ 9
CORNERSTONE 7-8

Cornerstone Exercise 7-24 AMORTIZATION OF INTANGIBLE ASSETS

Using the same information in **Cornerstone Exercise 7-23**, assume that Advanced Technological Devices amortizes the patent on a straight-line basis over its remaining economic life of 12 years.

Required:

Prepare the journal entry to record the amortization expense related to the patent.

OBJECTIVE ▶ 10
CORNERSTONE 7-9

Cornerstone Exercise 7-25 DEPLETION OF NATURAL RESOURCES

Brandon Oil Company recently purchased oil and natural gas reserves in a remote part of Alaska for $800,000. Brandon spent $10,000,000 preparing the oil for extraction from the ground. Brandon estimates that 120,000,000 barrels of oil will be extracted from the ground. The land has a residual value of $20,000. During 2009, 15,000,000 barrels are extracted from the ground.

Required:

Calculate the amount of depletion taken in 2009.

Exercises

OBJECTIVE ▶ 1

Exercise 7-26 BALANCE SHEET PRESENTATION

Listed below are items that may appear on a classified balance sheet.

1. Land
2. Amounts due from customers
3. Office building
4. Truck
5. Goods held for resale
6. Amounts owed to others
7. Patent
8. Timberland
9. Land held as investment
10. Goodwill

Required:

Indicate whether each item is included as an operating asset on a classified balance sheet. If not included as an operating asset, indicate the proper balance sheet classification.

Exercise 7-27 BALANCE SHEET CLASSIFICATION

Flying High Airlines, a small commuter airline, has the following items on its balance sheet—airplane, fuel truck, trademark, baggage handling machine, building, airplane fuel.

Required:

Indicate the proper balance sheet classification of each item.

Exercise 7-28 ACQUISITION COST

Listed below are items that may relate to property, plant, and equipment.

1. Purchase price of a machine
2. Delinquent property taxes
3. Interest on debt used to purchase equipment
4. Sales taxes paid on purchase of equipment
5. Costs to install a machine
6. Ordinary repairs to equipment
7. Cost to remodel a building
8. Architectural fees paid for design of a building
9. Cost of training employees to run equipment
10. Transportation costs to have furniture delivered

Required:

Determine whether each item is included as part of the cost of property, plant, and equipment. For any item excluded from the cost of property, plant, and equipment, explain why the item was excluded.

Exercise 7-29 COST OF A FIXED ASSET

Laurel Cleaners purchased an automatic dry cleaning machine for $135,000 from TGF Corporation on April 1, 2009. Laurel paid $35,000 in cash and signed a five-year, 10 percent note for $100,000. Laurel will pay interest on the note each year on March 31, beginning in 2010. Transportation charges of $3,500 for the machine were paid by Laurel. Laurel also paid $2,400 for the living expenses of the TGF installation crew. Solvent, necessary to operate the machine, was acquired for $1,000. Of this amount, $500 of the solvent was used to test and adjust the machine.

Required:

1. Compute the cost of the new dry cleaning machine.
2. Explain why you excluded any expenditures from the cost of the dry cleaning machine.

Exercise 7-30 COST OF A FIXED ASSET

OBJECTIVE 2

Colson Photography Service purchased a new digital imaging machine on April 15 for $13,400. During installation Colson incurred and paid in cash the following costs:

Rental of drill	$150
Electrical contractor	400
Plumbing contractor	190

Colson also paid $160 to replace a bracket on the digital imager that was damaged when one of Colson's employees dropped a box on it while it was being installed.

Required:

1. Determine the cost of the digital imaging machine.
2. Explain why you included or excluded the $160 bracket replacement cost.

OBJECTIVE ▸ 2

Exercise 7-31 COST OF FIXED ASSETS

Mooney Sounds, a local stereo retailer, needed a new store because it had outgrown the leased space it had used for several years. Mooney acquired and remodeled a former grocery store. As a part of the acquisition, Mooney incurred the following costs:

Cost of grocery store	$350,000
Cost of land (on which the grocery store is located)	65,000
New roof for building	74,000
Lumber used for remodeling	23,200
Paint	515
Wire and electrical supplies	4,290
New doors	6,400
New windows	3,850
Wages paid to workers for remodeling	12,500
Additional inventory purchased for grand opening sale	45,300

Required:

Determine the cost of the land and the building.

OBJECTIVE ▸ 2 4

Exercise 7-32 COST AND DEPRECIATION

On January 1, 2009, Quick Stop, a convenience store, purchased a new soft-drink cooler. Quick Stop paid $23,000 cash for the cooler. Quick Stop also paid $730 to have the cooler shipped to its location. After the new cooler arrived, Quick Stop paid $2,410 to have the old cooler dismantled and removed. Quick Stop also paid $820 to a contractor to have new wiring and drains installed for the new cooler. Quick Stop estimated that the cooler would have a useful life of six years and a residual value of $200. Quick Stop uses the straight-line method of depreciation.

Required:

1. Prepare any necessary journal entries to record the cost of the cooler.
2. Prepare the adjusting entry to record 2009 depreciation expense on the new cooler.
3. What is the book value of the cooler at the end of 2009?

OBJECTIVE ▸ 3

Exercise 7-33 CHARACTERISTICS OF DEPRECIATION METHODS

Below is a common list of depreciation methods and characteristics related to depreciation.

DEPRECIATION METHODS
a. Straight-line depreciation method
b. Declining-balance depreciation method
c. Units-of-production depreciation method when actual units produced increases over the life of the asset.

CHARACTERISTICS
1. Allocates the same amount of cost to each period of a depreciable asset's life.
2. Results in depreciation expense that decreases over the life of the asset.
3. Results in depreciation expense that increases over the life of the asset.
4. Consistent with the matching concept.
5. Calculated by multiplying a *constant* depreciation rate by depreciable cost.
6. Calculated by applying a *constant* depreciation rate to the asset's book value at the beginning of the period.
7. Results in lowest income taxes in early years of the asset's life.

Required:

Match one or more of the depreciation methods with each characteristic.

OBJECTIVE ▸ 3 4

Exercise 7-34 DEPRECIATION METHODS

Berkshire Corporation purchased a copying machine for $9,800 on January 1, 2009. The machine's residual value was $1,175 and its expected life was five years or 2,000,000 copies. Actual usage was 480,000 copies the first year and 440,000 the second year.

Required:

1. Compute depreciation expense for 2009 and 2010 using the:
    a. straight-line method
    b. double-declining-balance method
    c. units-of-production method
2. For each depreciation method, what is the book value of the machine at the end 2009? At the end of the 2010?
3. Assume that Berkshire Corporation decided to use the double-declining-balance method of depreciation. What is the effect on assets and income relative to if Berkshire had used the straight-line method of depreciation?

Exercise 7-35 **DEPRECIATION METHODS**

 OBJECTIVE ➤ 3 4

Clearcopy, a printing company, acquired a new press on January 1, 2009. The press cost $171,600 and had an expected life of eight years or 4,500,000 pages and an expected residual value of $15,000. Clearcopy printed 675,000 pages in 2009.

Required:

1. Compute 2009 depreciation expense using the:
    a. straight-line method
    b. double-declining-balance method
    c. units-of-production method
2. What is the book value of the machine at the end of 2009?

Exercise 7-36 **DEPRECIATION METHODS**

 OBJECTIVE ➤ 3 4

Quick-as-Lightning, a delivery service, purchased a new delivery truck for $40,000 on January 1, 2009. The truck is expected to have a useful life of ten years or 150,000 miles and an expected residual value of $3,000. The truck was driven 15,000 miles in 2009 and 13,000 miles in 2010.

Required:

1. Compute depreciation expense for 2009 and 2010 using the:
    a. straight-line method
    b. double-declining-balance method
    c. units-of-production method
2. For each method, what is the book value of the machine at the end 2009? At the end of 2010?

Exercise 7-37 **CHOICE AMONG DEPRECIATION METHODS**

 OBJECTIVE ➤ 3 4

Walnut Ridge Production, Inc., purchased a new computerized video editing machine at a cost of $370,000. The system has a residual value of $55,000 and an expected life of five years.

Required:

1. Compute depreciation expense, accumulated depreciation, and book value for the first three years of the machine's life using:
    a. the straight-line method
    b. the double-declining-balance method
2. Which method would produce the largest income in the first, second, and third year, respectively, of the asset's life?
3. Why might the controller of Walnut Ridge Production be interested in the effect of choosing a depreciation method? Evaluate the legitimacy of these interests.

Exercise 7-38 **REVISION OF DEPRECIATION**

 OBJECTIVE ➤ 3 4

On January 1, 2007, Blizzards-R-Us purchased a snow-blowing machine for $85,000. The machine was expected to have a residual value of $5,000 at the end of its five-year useful life. On January 1, 2009, Blizzards-R-Us concluded that the machine would have a remaining useful life of six years with a residual value of $800.

Required:

Determine the revised annual depreciation expense for 2009.

OBJECTIVE ➤ 5

Exercise 7-39 CAPITAL VERSUS REVENUE EXPENDITURE

Warrick Water Company, a privately owned business, supplies water to several communities. Warrick has just performed an extensive overhaul on one of its water pumps. The overhaul is expected to extend the life of the pump by 10 years. The residual value of the pump is unchanged. You have been asked to determine which of the following costs should be capitalized as a part of this overhaul. Those costs not capitalized should be expensed.

Element of Cost	Classification and Explanation
New pump motor	
Repacking of bearings (performed monthly)	
New impeller	
Painting of pump housing (performed annually)	
Replacement of pump foundation	
New wiring (needed every five years)	
Installation labor, motor	
Installation labor, impeller	
Installation labor, wiring	
Paint labor	
Placement of fence around pump*	

* A requirement of the Occupational Safety and Health Administration that will add to maintenance costs over the remaining life of the pump.

Required:

Classify each cost as part of the overhaul or as an expense. Be sure to explain your reasoning for each classification.

OBJECTIVE ➤ 5

Exercise 7-40 EXPENDITURES AFTER ACQUISITION

The following expenditures were incurred during the year:

1. Paid $4,000 for an overhaul of an automobile engine.
2. Paid $20,000 to add capacity to a cellular phone company's wireless network.
3. Paid $200 for routine maintenance of a manufacturing machine.
4. Paid $10,000 to remodel an office building.
5. Paid $300 for ordinary repairs

Required:

Classify the following expenditures as either capital or revenue expenditures.

OBJECTIVE ➤ 5

Exercise 7-41 EXPENDITURES AFTER ACQUISITION

Roanoke Manufacturing placed a robotic arm on a large assembly machine on January 1, 2009. The assembly machine was acquired on January 1, 2002 and was expected to last another three years. The following information is available concerning the assembly machine.

Cost, assembly machine	$750,000
Accumulated depreciation, 1/1/2009	480,000

The robotic arm cost $210,000 and was expected to extend the useful life of the machine by three years. Therefore, the useful life of the assembly machine, after the arm replacement, is six years. The assembly machine is expected to have a residual value of $120,000 at the end of its useful life.

Required:

1. Prepare the journal entry necessary to record the addition of the robotic arm.
2. Compute 2009 depreciation expense for the machine and prepare the necessary journal entry.
3. What is the book value of the machine at the end of 2009?
4. What would have been the effect on the financial statements if Roanoke Manufacturing had expensed the addition of the robotic arm?

Exercise 7-42 **EXPENDITURES AFTER ACQUISITION AND DEPRECIATION**

Eastern National Bank installed a wireless encryption device in January 2005. The device cost $120,000. At the time the device was installed, Eastern estimated that it would have an expected life of eight years and a residual value of $10,000. By 2008 the bank's business had expanded and modifications to the device were necessary. At the end of 2008, Eastern spent $45,000 on modifications for the device. The modified device was entered into service on the first business day of 2009. Eastern estimates that the expected life of the device from January 2009 is six years and the new residual value is $5,000. Eastern uses the straight-line method of depreciation. Had Eastern not modified the device, it estimates that processing delays would have caused the bank to lose business that will provide a profit of at least $100,000 per year.

Required:

1. Compute the accumulated depreciation for the device at the time the modifications were made (four years after acquisition).
2. What is the book value of the device before and after the modification?
3. What will be annual straight-line depreciation expense for the device after the modification?
4. The bank's president notes, "Since the after-modification depreciation expense exceeds the before-modification depreciation expense, this modification was a poor idea." Comment on the president's assertion.

Exercise 7-43 **IMPAIRMENT**

On January 1, 2002, the Key West Company acquired a pie-making machine for $50,000. The machine was expected to have a useful life of 10 years with no residual value. Key West uses the straight-line depreciation method. On January 1, 2009, due to technological changes in the bakery industry, Key West believed that the asset might be impaired. Key West estimates the machine will generate net cash flows of $12,000 and has a current fair value of $5,000.

Required:

1. What is the book value of the machine on January 1, 2009?
2. Compute the loss related to the impairment.
3. Prepare the journal entry necessary to record the impairment of the machine.

Exercise 7-44 **SALE OF PLANT ASSET**

Perfect Auto Rentals sold one of its cars on January 1, 2009. Perfect had acquired the car on January 1, 2007, for $13,500. At acquisition Perfect assumed that the car would have an estimated life of three years and a residual value of $3,000. Assume that Perfect has recorded straight-line depreciation expense for 2007 and 2008.

Required:

1. Prepare the journal entry to record the sale of the car assuming the car sold for:
   a. $6,500 cash
   b. $4,000 cash
   c. $7,000 cash
2. How should the gain or loss on the disposition (if any) be reported on the income statement?

Exercise 7-45 **SALE OF PLANT ASSET**

Pacifica Manufacturing retired a computerized metal stamping machine on December 31, 2009. Pacifica sold the machine to another company and did not replace it. The following data are available for the machine:

Cost (installed), 1/1/2004	$920,000
Residual value expected on 1/1/2004	160,000
Expected life, 1/1/2004	8 years

The machine was sold for $188,000 cash. Pacifica uses the straight-line method of depreciation.

Required:

1. Prepare the journal entry to record depreciation expense for 2009.
2. Compute accumulated depreciation at December 31, 2009.
3. Prepare the journal entry to record the sale of the machine.
4. Explain how the gain or loss on the sale would be reported on the 2009 income statement.

OBJECTIVE ▶ 8

Exercise 7-46 ANALYZE FIXED ASSETS

Tabor Industries is a technology company that operates in a highly competitive environment. In 2006, management had significantly curtailed its capital expenditures due to cash flow problems. Tabor reported the following information for 2009:

- Net fixed assets (beginning of year) $489,000
- Net fixed assets (end of year) 505,000
- Net sales 1,065,000
- Accumulated depreciation (end of year) 543,000
- Depreciation expense 116,000

An analyst reviewing Tabor's financial history noted that Tabor had previously reported fixed asset turnover ratios and average age of its assets as follows:

	2004	2005	2006	2007	2008
Fixed asset turnover	2.48	2.45	2.74	2.57	2.33
Average age of assets (years)	1.81	1.79	1.94	2.81	3.74

During this time frame, the industry average fixed asset turnover ratio is 2.46 and the industry average age of assets is 1.79 years.

Required:

1. Compute Tabor's fixed asset turnover ratio.
2. Compute the average age of Tabor's fixed assets.
3. Comment on Tabor's fixed asset turnover ratios and the average age of the fixed assets.

OBJECTIVE ▶ 9

Exercise 7-47 ACQUISITION AND AMORTIZATION OF INTANGIBLE ASSETS

TLM Technologies had these transactions related to intangible assets during 2009.

Jan. 2 Purchased a patent from Luna Industries for $200,000. The remaining legal life of the patent is 15 years and TLM expects the patent to be useful for 8 years.

5 Paid legal fees in a successful legal defense of the patent of $80,000.

June 29 Registered a trademark with the federal government. Registration costs were $12,000. TLM expects to use the trademark indefinitely.

Sept. 2 Paid research and development costs of $500,000.

Required:

1. Prepare the journal entries necessary to record the transactions.
2. Prepare the entries necessary to record amortization expense for the intangible assets.
3. What is the balance of the intangible assets at the end of 2009?

OBJECTIVE ▶ 9

Exercise 7-48 AMORTIZATION OF INTANGIBLES

On January 1, 2009, Boulder Investments, Inc., acquired a franchise to operate a Burger Doodle restaurant. Boulder paid $160,000 for a 10-year franchise and incurred organization costs of $12,000.

Required:

1. Prepare the journal entry to record the cash payment for the franchise fee and the organization costs.
2. Prepare the journal entry to record the annual amortization expense at the end of the first year.

Exercise 7-49 **DEPLETION RATE**

OBJECTIVE ▸ 10

Oxford Quarries purchased 45 acres of land for $225,000. The land contained stone that Oxford will remove from the ground, finish, and then sell as facing material for buildings. Oxford spent $435,000 preparing the quarry for operation. Oxford estimates that the quarry contains 55,000 tons of usable stone and that it will require six years to remove all the usable stone once quarrying begins. Upon completion of quarrying, Oxford estimates that the land will have a residual value of $11,000. During the current year, Oxford extracted 8,500 tons of stone.

Required:

1. Compute the depletion rate per ton.
2. Prepare the journal entry to record the extraction of the stone.

Exercise 7-50 **DEPLETION OF TIMBER**

OBJECTIVE ▸ 10

Bedford Ridge Development purchased a 5,000-acre tract of forested land in southern Georgia. The tract contained about 1,500,000 pine trees that, when mature, can be used for utility poles. Bedford paid $900 per acre for the timberland. The land has a residual value of $180 per acre when all the trees are harvested. During 2009, Bedford harvested 150,000 trees.

Required:

1. Compute the depletion per tree.
2. Prepare the journal entry to record the harvesting of the trees for 2009.

Exercise 7-51 **BALANCE SHEET PRESENTATION**

OBJECTIVE ▸ 1 3 4 8

The following information relates to the assets of Westfield Semiconductor as of December 31, 2009. Westfield uses the straight-line method for depreciation and amortization.

Asset	Acquisition Cost	Expected Life	Residual Value	Time Used
Land	$104,300	Infinite	$100,000	10 years
Building	430,000	25 years	30,000	10 years
Machine	285,000	5 years	10,000	2 years
Patent	80,000	10 years	0	3 years
Truck	21,000	100,000 miles	3,000	44,000 miles

Required:

Use the information above to prepare the property, plant, and equipment and intangible assets portions of a classified balance sheet for Westfield Semiconductors.

Problem Set A

Problem 7-52A **FINANCIAL STATEMENT PRESENTATION OF OPERATING ASSETS**

OBJECTIVE ▸ 1

Olympic Acquisitions, Inc., prepared the following post-closing trial balance at December 31, 2009:

	Debit	Credit
Cash	$ 6,400	
Accounts receivable	15,000	
Supplies	26,000	
Land	42,000	
Buildings	155,000	
Equipment	279,000	

(Continued)

	Debit	Credit
Truck	32,000	
Franchise	49,600	
Goodwill	313,500	
Accounts payable		$ 4,100
Accumulated depreciation, buildings		112,000
Accumulated depreciation, equipment		153,000
Accumulated depreciation, truck		16,300
Wages payable		7,000
Interest payable		7,300
Income taxes payable		12,000
Notes payable (due in 8 years)		190,000
Common stock		300,000
Retained earnings		116,800
Totals	$918,500	$918,500

Required:

Prepare a classified balance sheet for Olympic Acquisitions at December 31, 2009. Olympic reports the three categories of operating assets in separate subsections of assets.

OBJECTIVE ▸ 2   Problem 7-53A **COST OF A FIXED ASSET**

Mist City Car Wash purchased a new brushless car-washing machine for one of its bays. The machine cost $31,800. Mist City borrowed the purchase price from its bank on a one-year, 12 percent note payable. Mist City paid $500 to have the machine transported to its place of business and an additional $200 in shipping insurance. Mist City incurred the following costs as a part of the installation:

Plumbing	$2,700
Electrical	1,640
Water (for testing the machine)	35
Soap (for testing the machine)	18

During the testing process, one of the motors became defective when soap and water entered the motor because its cover had not been installed properly by Mist City's employees. The motor was replaced at a cost of $450.

Required:

Compute the cost of the car-washing machine.

OBJECTIVE ▸ 3 4   Problem 7-54A **DEPRECIATION METHODS**

Hansen Supermarkets purchased a radio frequency identification (RFID) system for one of its stores at a cost of $150,000. Hansen determined that the system had an expected life of seven years (or 50,000,000 items scanned) and an expected residual value of $7,200.

Required:

1. Determine the amount of depreciation expense for the first and second years of the system's life using the (a) straight-line and (b) double-declining-balance depreciation methods.
2. If the number of items scanned the first and second years were 7,200,000 and 8,150,000, respectively, compute the amount of depreciation expense for the first and second years of the system's life using the units-of-production depreciation method.
3. Compute the book values for all three depreciation methods as of the end of the first and second years of the system's life.

Problem 7-55A DEPRECIATION SCHEDULES

OBJECTIVE ▶ 3 4

Wendt Corporation acquired a new depreciable asset for $80,000. The asset has a four-year expected life and a residual value of zero.

Required:

1. Prepare a depreciation schedule for all four years of the asset's expected life using the straight-line depreciation method.
2. Prepare a depreciation schedule for all four years of the asset's expected life using the double-declining-balance depreciation method.
3. What questions should be asked about this asset to decide which depreciation method to use?

Problem 7-56A EXPENDITURES AFTER ACQUISITION

OBJECTIVE ▶ 3 4 5

Pasta, a restaurant specializing in fresh pasta, installed a pasta cooker in early 2007 at a cost of $11,800. The cooker had an expected life of five years and a residual value of $600 when installed. As the restaurant's business increased, it became apparent that renovations would be necessary so the cooker's output could be increased. In January 2010, Pasta spent $8,200 to install new heating equipment and $4,100 to add pressure-cooking capability. After these renovations, Pasta estimated that the remaining useful life of the cooker was 10 years and that the residual value was now $1,500.

Required:

1. Compute one year's straight-line depreciation expense on the cooker before the renovations.
2. Assume that three full years of straight-line depreciation expense had been recorded on the cooker before the renovations were made. Compute the book value of the cooker after the renovations were made.
3. Compute one year's straight-line depreciation expense on the renovated cooker.

Problem 7-57A REPAIR DECISION

OBJECTIVE ▶ 5

Clermont Transit operates a summer ferry service to islands in the Ohio River. Farmers use the ferry to move farming equipment to and from the islands. Clermont's ferry is in need of repair. A new engine and steering assembly must be installed, or the Coast Guard will not permit the ferry to be used. Because of competition, Clermont will not be able to raise its rates for ferry service if these repairs are made. Costs of providing the ferry service will not be decreased if the repairs are made.

Required:

1. Identify the factors that Clermont should consider when evaluating whether or not to make the repairs.
2. Since the revenue rate cannot be increased and costs will not be decreased if the repairs are made, can the cost of the repairs be capitalized? Why or why not?

Problem 7-58A DISPOSITION OF OPERATING ASSETS

OBJECTIVE ▶ 7

In order to provide capital for new hotel construction in other locations, Wilton Hotel Corporation has decided to sell its hotel in Pierre, South Dakota. Wilton auctions the hotel and its contents on October 1, 2009, with the following results:

Land	$600,000
Building	300,000
Furniture and fixtures	120,000

Wilton's accounting records reveal the following information about the assets sold:

Asset	Acquisition Cost	Accumulated Depreciation
Land	$ 15,000	
Building	350,000	$295,000
Furniture and fixtures	298,000	133,000

Required:

Prepare a separate journal entry to record the disposition of each of these assets.

OBJECTIVE ➤ 9 10   **Problem 7-59A** NATURAL RESOURCE AND INTANGIBLE ACCOUNTING

McLeansboro Oil Company acquired an operating oil well during a recent year. The following assets were acquired for $1,350,000 cash.

Asset	Fair Value	Expected Life
Oil well	$1,100,000	55,000 barrels
Land	85,000	Indefinite
Pump	65,000	550,000 barrels

Required:

1. Write the entry to record this acquisition in McLeansboro's journal. (Hint: Record the cost in excess of fair value as goodwill.)
2. If McLeansboro pumps and sells 11,000 barrels of oil in one year, compute the amount of depletion.
3. Prepare journal entries to record depletion for the 11,000 barrels of oil pumped and sold.
4. Is the goodwill amortized? Explain your reasoning.
5. Why are the land and the pump capitalized separately from the oil well?

OBJECTIVE ➤ 9   **Problem 7-60A** ACCOUNTING FOR INTANGIBLE ASSETS

On January 1, 2003, Technocraft, Inc., acquired a patent that was used for manufacturing semiconductor-based electronic circuitry. The patent was originally recorded in Technocraft's ledger at its cost of $1,796,000. Technocraft has been amortizing the patent over an expected economic life of 10 years. Residual value was assumed to be zero. Technocraft sued another company for infringing on its patent. On January 1, 2010, Technocraft spent $180,000 on this suit and won a judgment to recover the $180,000 plus damages of $500,000. The sued company paid the $680,000.

Required:

1. Compute and record amortization expense on the patent for 2009 (prior to the lawsuit).
2. Prepare the necessary journal entry on January 1, 2010, to record the expenditure of $180,000 to defend the patent.
3. Prepare the journal entry to record the award of $680,000 on January 1, 2010.
4. Indicate the entry you would have made had Technocraft lost the suit. (Assume that the patent would be valueless if Technocraft had lost the suit.)

Problem Set B

OBJECTIVE ➤ 1   **Problem 7-52B** FINANCIAL STATEMENT PRESENTATION OF OPERATING ASSETS

Athens, Inc., prepared the following post-closing trial balance at December 31, 2009:

	Debit	Credit
Cash	$ 3,100	
Accounts receivable	28,000	
Prepaid insurance	8,500	
Land	21,200	
Buildings	308,000	
Equipment	124,000	
Patent	9,800	
Goodwill	42,400	
Accounts payable		$ 7,600

	Debit	Credit
Accumulated depreciation, buildings		102,000
Accumulated depreciation, equipment		48,000
Unearned revenue		9,700
Interest payable		3,800
Income taxes payable		17,100
Notes payable (due in 10 years)		170,000
Common stock		125,000
Retained earnings		61,800
Totals	$545,000	$545,000

Required:

Prepare a classified balance sheet for Athens Inc. at December 31, 2009. Athens reports the three categories of operating assets in separate subsections of assets.

Problem 7-53B COST OF A FIXED ASSET

Metropolis Country Club purchased a new tractor to be used for golf course maintenance. The machine cost $53,200. Metropolis borrowed the purchase price from its bank on a one-year, 10 percent note payable. Metropolis incurred the following costs:

Shipping costs	$300
Shipping insurance	150
Calibration of cutting height	83

Required:

Compute the cost of the lawnmower.

Problem 7-54B DEPRECIATION METHODS

Graphic Design Inc. purchased a state-of-the-art laser engraving machine for $90,000. Parker determined that the system had an expected life of 10 years (or 2,000,000 items engraved) and an expected residual value of $5,400.

Required:

1. Determine the amount of depreciation expense for the first and second years of the machine's life using the (a) straight-line and (b) double-declining-balance depreciation methods.
2. If the number of items engraved the first and second years was 205,000 and 187,000 respectively, compute the amount of depreciation expense for the first and second years of the machine's life using the units-of-production depreciation method.
3. Compute the book values for all three depreciation methods as of the end of the first and second years of the system's life.

Problem 7-55B DEPRECIATION SCHEDULES

Dunn Corporation acquired a new depreciable asset for $150,000. The asset has a five-year expected life and a residual value of zero.

Required:

1. Prepare a depreciation schedule for all five years of the asset's expected life using the straight-line depreciation method.
2. Prepare a depreciation schedule for all five years of the asset's expected life using the double-declining-balance depreciation method.
3. What questions should be asked about this asset to decide which depreciation method to use?

Problem 7-56B EXPENDITURES AFTER ACQUISITION

Murray's Fish Market, a store that specializes in providing fresh fish to the Nashville, Tennessee area, installed a new refrigeration unit in early 2007 at a cost of $21,500. The refrigeration unit has an expected life of eight years and a residual value of $500 when installed. As the fish market's business increased, it became apparent that renovations were necessary so that the capacity of the refrigeration unit could be increased. In January 2010, Pasta spent $18,800 to install an additional refrigerated display unit (that was connected to the original unit) and replace the refrigeration coils. After this addition and renovation, Murray's Fish Market estimated that the remaining useful life of the original refrigeration unit was 12 years and that the residual value was now $1,000.

Required:

1. Compute one year's straight-line depreciation expense on the refrigeration unit before the addition and renovations.
2. Assume that three full years of straight-line depreciation expense were recorded on the refrigeration unit before the addition and renovations were made. Compute the book value of the refrigeration unit after the renovations were made.
3. Compute one year's straight-line depreciation expense on the renovated refrigeration unit.

OBJECTIVE ➤ 5

Problem 7-57B REMODELING DECISION

Ferinni Company operates a travel agency out of a historic building in Smalltown. Ferinni's CEO believes that the building needs to be remodeled in order to reach a wider customer base. The CEO proposes building a new entry that would be adjacent to Main Street in order to attract more foot traffic. The current entry faces a parking deck at the rear of the building and is easily overlooked by customers. The new entry will require the rearrangement of several offices inside the building. Because of competition from Internet travel sites, Ferinni will not be able to raise rates for its travel service after the remodeling is made.

Required:

1. Identify the factors that Ferinni should consider when evaluating whether to remodel the building.
2. Since the revenue rate cannot be increased, can the cost of the remodeling be capitalized? Why or why not?

OBJECTIVE ➤ 7

Problem 7-58B DISPOSITION OF OPERATING ASSETS

Salva Pest Control disposed of four assets recently. Salva's accounting records provided the following information about the assets at the time of their disposal:

Asset	Cost	Accumulated Depreciation
Pump	$ 5,900	$ 4,800
Truck	18,600	17,500
Office equipment	4,200	4,000
Chemical testing apparatus	7,300	4,000

The truck was sold for $2,000 cash, and the chemical testing apparatus was donated to the local high school. Because the pump was contaminated with pesticides, $500 in cash was paid to a chemical disposal company to decontaminate the pump and dispose of it safely. The office equipment was taken to the local landfill.

Required:

Prepare a separate journal entry to record the disposition of each of these assets.

OBJECTIVE ➤ 9 10

Problem 7-59B NATURAL RESOURCE AND INTANGIBLE ACCOUNTING

In 2002, the Mudcat Gas Company purchased a natural gas field in Oklahoma for $158,000,000. The fair value of the land was $1,500,000 and the fair value of the natural gas reserves was $156,217,500. At that time, estimated recoverable gas was 104,145,000 cubic feet.

Required:

1. Write the entry to record this acquisition in Mudcat's journal. (Hint: Record the cost in excess of fair value as goodwill.)
2. If Mudcat recovers and sells 2,500,000 cubic feet in one year, compute the depletion.
3. Prepare journal entries to record depletion for the 2,500,000 cubic feet of natural gas recovered and sold.
4. Is the goodwill amortized? Explain your reasoning.
5. Why is the land capitalized separately from the natural gas reserves?

Problem 7-60B ACCOUNTING FOR INTANGIBLE ASSETS

OBJECTIVE ▶ 9

Blackford and Medford Publishing Company own the copyright on many top authors. In 2010, Blackford and Medford acquired the copyright on the literary works of Susan Monroe, an underground novelist in the 1960s, for $800,000 cash. Due to a recent resurgence of interest in the 1960s, the copyright has an estimated economic life of eight years. The residual value is estimated to be zero.

Required:

1. Prepare a journal entry to record the acquisition of the copyright.
2. Compute and record the 2010 amortization expense for the copyright.

Cases

Case 7-61 ETHICS, INTERNAL CONTROLS, AND THE CAPITALIZATION DECISION

James Sage, an assistant controller in a large company, has a friend and former classmate, Henry Cactus, who sells computers. Sage agrees to help Cactus get part of the business that has been going to a large national computer manufacturer for many years. Sage knows that the controller would not approve a shift away from the national supplier but believes that he can authorize a number of small orders for equipment that will escape the controller's notice. Company policy requires that all capital expenditures be approved by a management committee; however, expenditures under $2,000 are all expenses and are subject to much less scrutiny. The assistant controller orders four computers to be used in a distant branch office. In order to keep the size of the order down, he makes four separate orders over a period of several months.

Required:

1. What are the probable consequences of this behavior for the company? For the assistant controller?
2. Describe internal control procedures that would be effective in discouraging and detecting this kind of behavior.

Case 7-62 MANAGEMENT'S DEPRECIATION DECISION

Great Basin Enterprises, a large holding company, acquired North Spruce Manufacturing, a medium-sized manufacturing business, from its founder, who wishes to retire. Despite great potential for development, North Spruce's income has been dropping in recent years. Great Basin installs a new management group (including a new controller) at North Spruce and gives the group six years to expand and revitalize the operations; management compensation includes a bonus based on net income generated by the North Spruce operations. If North Spruce does not show considerable improvement by the end of the sixth year, Great Basin will consider selling it. The new management immediately makes significant investments in new equipment but finds that new revenues develop slowly. Most of the new equipment will be replaced in 8 to 10 years. To defer income taxes to the maximum extent, the controller uses accelerated depreciation methods and the minimum allowable "expected lives" for the new equipment, which average 5 years. In preparing financial statements, the controller uses the straight-line depreciation method and expected lives that average 12 years for the new equipment.

Required:

1. Why did the controller compute depreciation expense on the financial statements as he or she did?
2. What are the possible consequences of the controller's decision on the amount of depreciation expense shown on the financial statements if this decision goes unchallenged?

Case 7-63 THE EFFECT OF ESTIMATES OF LIFE AND RESIDUAL VALUE ON DEPRECIATION EXPENSE

Hattiesburg Manufacturing purchased a new computer-integrated system to manufacture a group of fabricated metal and plastic products. The equipment was purchased from Bessemer Systems at a cost of $630,000. As a basis for determining annual depreciation expense, Hattiesburg's controller requests estimates of the expected life and residual value for the new equipment. The engineering and production departments submit the following divergent estimates:

	Engineering Department Estimates	Production Department Estimates
Expected life	9 years	7 years
Residual value	$90,000	0

Before considering depreciation expense for the new equipment, Hattiesburg Manufacturing has net income in the amount of $250,000. Hattiesburg uses the straight-line method of depreciation.

Required:

1. Compute a full year's depreciation expense for the new equipment, using each of the two sets of estimates.
2. Ignoring income taxes, what will be the effect on net income of including a full year's depreciation expense based on the engineering estimates? Based on the production estimates?
3. If a business has a significant investment in depreciable assets, the expected life and residual value estimates can materially affect depreciation expense and therefore net income. What might motivate management to use the highest or lowest estimates? How would cash outflows for income taxes be affected by the estimates?

Case 7-64 RESEARCH & ANALYSIS USING THE ANNUAL REPORT

Obtain Verizon Communications, Inc.'s most current annual report either through the "Investor Relations" portion of their website (do a web search for Verizon Communications investor relations) or go to http://www.sec.gov and click "search for company filings" under "Filings & Forms (EDGAR)."

Required:

1. What method of depreciation does Verizon use? What are the typical useful lives of Verizon's operating assets?
2. What is the cost of Verizon's property, plant, and equipment? List the major components of Verizon's property, plant, and equipment.
3. What amount of accumulated depreciation is associated with property, plant, and equipment?
4. Refer to the statement of cash flows:
   a. What is the amount of depreciation expense reported for each of the last three years?
   b. How much did Verizon spend on the acquisition of operating assets (capital expenditures) in each of the last three years?

   c. How much property, plant, and equipment was disposed of in the last year?

   d. Is the change in depreciation expense consistent with the pattern of capital expenditures observed? Why or why not?

5. What is the change in accumulated depreciation for the most recent year? Is this change explained by the depreciation expense reported? If not, what other items might cause accumulated depreciation to change?

6. Describe Verizon's capital expenditure plans for the future.

7. Explain Verizon's accounting policy with regard to intangible assets.

8. List the types of intangible assets that Verizon possesses. What is Verizon's largest intangible asset?

Case 7-65 COMPARATIVE ANALYSIS: ABERCROMBIE & FITCH vs. AEROPOSTALE

Refer to the financial statements of **Abercrombie & Fitch** and **Aeropostale** that are supplied with this text.

Required:

1. With regard to depreciation methods:

   a. What depreciation method does Abercrombie & Fitch use? What depreciation method does Aeropostale use?

   b. What are the typical useful lives of each company's operating assets?

   c. What effect will the useful lives have on the company's financial statements?

2. Refer to the statement of cash flows:

   a. What is the amount of depreciation and amortization expense that each company reported for the three years presented?

   b. How much did each company spend on the acquisition of operating assets (capital expenditures) in each of the last three years?

   c. Is the change in depreciation and amortization expense consistent with the pattern of capital expenditures observed? Why or why not?

3. Compute the fixed asset turnover and the average age of fixed assets for each company. What conclusions can you draw from these ratios?

8

Current and Contingent Liabilities

After studying Chapter 8, you should be able to:

1. Explain liability recognition and measurement criteria.
2. Identify and record the kinds of activities that produce current liabilities.
3. Describe contingent liabilities and the alternatives for their recognition and measurement.
4. Measure warranty liabilities and warranty expense.
5. Analyze liquidity ratios using information contained in the current liabilities section.

Experience Financial Accounting

with Ruth's Chris Steak House

Ruth's Chris Steak House was founded in 1965 when Ruth Fertel mortgaged her home for $22,000 to purchase the "Chris Steak House," a 60-seat restaurant located near the New Orleans Fair Grounds racetrack. Today this brand is considered one of the top restaurants in the world with revenues of over $200 million and net income of approximately $11 million. Interestingly, over $36 million (approximately 13 percent) of its restaurant revenues comes from the sale of gift cards, which have become a popular holiday gift among business professionals. According to the National Retail Foundation, total holiday gift-card spending increased 34 percent in 2006 to $24.8 billion, with restaurants as the second most popular category.[1]

As you will learn in this chapter Ruth's Chris has a liability (unearned revenues) related to the sale of gift cards until the meal is provided. That is, gift-card revenue should not be recognized until the card is redeemed (for goods or services) or expires, and therefore, Ruth's Chris should not expect to see much of the revenue benefit from gift cards until the following year.

Ruth's Chris Steak House Revenues

■ Gift card sales

■ Restaurant sales

13%

87%

[1] Source: Jeff Omohundro, Katie H. Willett, and Jason Belcher, "Dining Less at the Mall," *Barron's Online*, October, 18, 2007: http://online.barrons.com/article/SB119265481714262454.html?mod=yahoobarrons&ru=yahoo. Accessed October 25, 2007.

Current and Contingent Liabilities

Chapters 4, 5, 6, and 7 explained accounting and reporting for assets. Now we want to move to the other side of the balance sheet and discuss liabilities and equity, which are the sources of cash and other financial resources used to acquire assets. We begin by examining liabilities.

Finding potential creditors, arranging attractive credit terms, structuring borrowings with lenders, and arranging to have enough cash coming in to pay the liabilities as they come due is one of the most important managerial functions. The result of liability management and the accounting recognition, measurement, and reporting issues for those activities appears in the liabilities portion of the balance sheet. The information provided by **Intel** in its 2007 balance sheet is typical:

Intel Corporation	
Consolidated Balance Sheets	
(in millions)	
December 30, 2007	
LIABILITIES	
Current liabilities:	
Short-term debt	$ 142
Accounts payable	2,361
Accrued compensation and benefits	2,417
Accrued advertising	749
Deferred income on shipments to distributors	625
Other accrued liabilities	1,938
Income taxes payable	339
Total current liabilities	$8,571
Long-term income taxes payable	785
Long-term debt	1,980
Other long-term liabilities	1553

Naturally, existing and potential creditors also find this information useful as they want to know about the obligations management has assumed.

In this chapter and the next we discuss the three kinds of business obligations: current liabilities, contingent liabilities, and long-term debt. Current liabilities are those obligations that are (1) expected to be retired with existing current assets or creation of new current liabilities, and (2) due within one year or one operating cycle, whichever is longer. All other liabilities are considered long-term. Contingent liabilities can be either current or long-term, but they are "iffy" in two ways. They may or may not turn into actual obligations and, for those contingencies that do become obligations, the timing and amount of the required payment is uncertain. In this chapter we focus on current and contingent liabilities and address the following questions:

- When are liabilities recognized?
- How are liabilities measured?
- What kind of activities produce current liabilities and how are they recorded in the accounting records?
- What are contingent liabilities and how are they recorded in the accounting records?
- How do you measure and record warranty liabilities?

OBJECTIVE ▶ 1

Explain liability recognition and measurement criteria.

Recognition and Measurement of Liabilities

Liabilities are probable future sacrifices of economic benefits. These commitments, which arise from activities that have already occurred, require the business to transfer assets or provide services to another entity sometime in the future. For example, an account payable arises from a past transaction in which the business received goods or services from a creditor and requires the business to pay cash to the creditor at some future time.

Within this general definition, liabilities have a wide variety of characteristics. Although liabilities frequently require the payment of cash, some may require the transfer of assets other than cash, or the performance of services. Although the exact amount and timing of future payments are usually known, for some liabilities they may not be. Further, though many liabilities are legally enforceable claims, some may represent merely *probable* claims. Finally, although liabilities usually identify the entity to be paid, the definition does not exclude payment to unknown recipients. Thus, the future outflow associated with a liability may or may not involve the payment of cash; may or may not be known with certainty; may or may not be legally enforceable; and may or may not be payable to a known recipient.

Recognition of Liabilities

Most liabilities are recognized when goods or services are received or money is borrowed (see Exhibit 8-1). When a liability depends on a future event (i.e., a contingent liability), such as the outcome of a lawsuit, recognition depends on how likely the occurrence of the event is and whether a good estimate of the payment amount can be made. If the future payment is judged to be less than likely to occur or the payment is not estimable, the obligation should not be recognized. Such obligations may require disclosure in footnotes to the financial statements, as explained later in this chapter.

Measurement of Liabilities

We all know that when you owe money you typically pay interest. That is, if you borrow $100 at 10 percent interest, then when you pay it back one year later you must repay $110 (the $100 principal and $10 [$100 × 10%] interest). Sometimes companies will appear to give you a zero percent interest loan. For example, furniture and electronics retailers frequently advertise "no interest, no money down for 12 months" or some such terms. Of course, we know this really means that the "interest" is included in the sales price because no business is going to truly provide zero percent interest.

In theory, the amount of the liability reported on the balance sheet should not include any interest that has not yet occurred. For example, on a balance sheet prepared six months after borrowing the $100 at 10 percent interest described above, you should report a liability of $105 (the $100 payable for the principal and $5 [$100 × 10% × 6/12] "interest payable" for the six months of interest that is currently owed).

However, many liabilities are more like your credit card or utilities bill. For example, you might owe your power company $150 for the use of electricity during September. You likely do not receive this bill until sometime during October and you do not have to pay it until near the end of November. Further, there appears to be no

Exhibit 8-1

Recognition of Current Liabilities

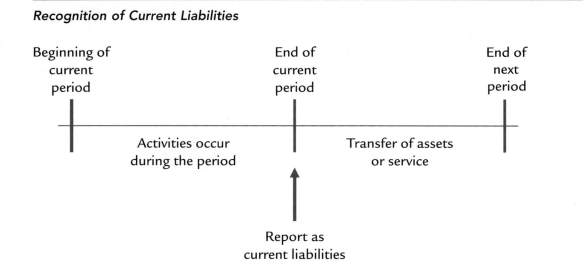

interest because you owe $150 whether you pay the bill when you receive it in October or wait until the November due date.

Despite the apparent lack of interest, we all know that theoretically interest exists. Consequently, in theory we should calculate the interest on such liabilities. For example, if we made a balance sheet at the end of September, then a liability for the power company should be calculated to exclude the theoretical interest included in the $150 payment at the end of November (i.e., two months interest at the market rate). Fortunately, we ignore the interest for most current liabilities because the amount of interest is relatively small. So most current liabilities are simply recorded and reported at the total amount owed as we will see in the next section.

Current Liabilities

OBJECTIVE ▸ 2

Identify and record the kinds of activities that produce current liabilities.

Current liabilities are obligations that require the firm to pay cash or another current asset, create a new current liability, or provide goods or services within the longer of one year or one operating cycle. Since most firms have operating cycles shorter than one year, the one-year rule usually applies.

Some firms combine their current liabilities into a very short list, while others provide considerable detail. Exhibit 8-2 compares the current liabilities sections of the balance sheets for two airlines—**Southwest** and **UAL (United Airlines)**. Although it's reasonable to assume that both airlines have similar types of current liabilities,

---

Exhibit 8-2

Current Liability Sections from Two Balance Sheets

Southwest Airlines Co.
Consolidated Balance Sheets
(in millions)

	December 31, 2007	December 31, 2006
Current liabilities:		
Accounts payable	$ 759	$ 643
Accrued liabilities	3,107	1,323
Air traffic liability	931	799
Current maturities of long-term debt	41	122
Total current liabilities	$4,838	$2,887

UAL Corporation
Statement of Consolidated Financial Position
(in millions)

	December 31	
	2007	2006
LIABILITIES AND SHAREHOLDERS' EQUITY		
Current liabilities:		
Advance ticket sales	$1,918	$1,669
Mileage Plus deferred revenue	1,268	1,111
Accrued salaries, wages and benefits	896	795
Accounts payable	877	667
Advanced purchase of miles	694	681
Long-term debt maturing within one year	678	1,687
Fuel purchase commitments	493	283
Distribution payable	257	—
Current obligations under capital leases	250	110
Accrued interest	141	241
Other	507	701
	$7,979	$7,945

Southwest combines theirs into a relatively short list while UAL provides more detail. Further, you will note that UAL orders its individual current liabilities from largest to smallest (with "other" at the end), while Southwest appears to order its current liabilities in alphabetical order, or perhaps the order in which the liabilities will be paid.

In the sections that follow we will briefly describe how various types of current liabilities arise, and the principles that underlie their recognition, measurement, and reporting.

Accounts Payable

An **account payable** arises when a business purchases goods or services on credit. It is really just the flip side of an account receivable—when you have a payable, the business you owe has a receivable. Credit terms generally require that the purchaser pay the amount due within 30 to 60 days and seldom require the payment of interest. Accounts payable do not require a formal agreement or contract. For example, your account with the power company usually does not require you to sign a formal contract.

You may recall from Chapter 5 that accounts receivable has some valuation issues related to estimating bad debts. Accounts payable, on the other hand, have no such issues. They are measured and reported at the total amount required to satisfy the account, which is the cost of the goods or services acquired. For example, if Game Time Sporting Goods buys and receives running shoes on May 15, 2009, for which it pays its supplier $2,000 on June 15, 2009, it would need to make the following journal entries:

Date	Account and Explanation	Debit	Credit
May 15	Inventory	2,000	
	Accounts Payable		2,000
	(Record purchase of inventory)		
June 15	Accounts Payable	2,000	
	Cash		2,000
	(Record payment to supplier)		

Notes Payable

A **note payable** typically arises when a business borrows money or purchases goods or services from a company that requires a formal agreement or contract (like when you signed a contract to lease your apartment or buy a car). In fact, this formal agreement or contract is what distinguishes the note payable from an account payable. This agreement typically states the timing of repayment and the amount (principal and/or interest) to be repaid. Notes payable typically mature in anywhere from three to 12 months, but it can be longer (of course, if it does not mature for over 12 months, it will be classified as a long-term liability). These longer maturities also explain why creditors are more likely to impose interest on notes payable than with accounts payable.

Notes payable normally specify the amount to be repaid indirectly, by stating the amount borrowed (the principal) and an interest rate. These notes are called *interest-bearing notes* because they explicitly state an **interest rate**. The maturity amount of an interest-bearing note is not stated explicitly but is determined from the interest rate, the principal amount, and the maturity date.

When a business borrows using a short-term, interest-bearing note, the transaction is recorded at the amount borrowed. For example, assume that Starcrest Cleaners borrows $600,000 cash from a bank with a six-month, 8 percent note payable. Starcrest borrows the money on March 1, 2011, to finance the acquisition of inventory for its spring selling season. Starcrest would recognize the note as follows:

Date	Account and Explanation	Debit	Credit
Mar. 1	Cash	600,000	
	Notes Payable		600,000
	(Record issuance of 6-month, 8% note)		
Aug. 31	Notes Payable	600,000	
	Interest Expense	24,000	
	Cash		624,000
	(Record payment of note)		

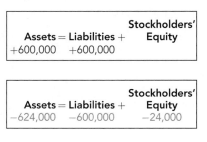

In addition to short-term borrowings, notes payable are often created when a borrower is unable to pay an account payable in a timely manner. In this case the borrower is typically granted a payment extension, but the creditor requires a formal note be signed to impose interest. You may recall from above that a current liability can be retired through creation of a new current liability. Rolling an account payable into a note payable would be an example of this. The accounting for such a transaction is straightforward as illustrated in Cornerstone 8-1.

CORNERSTONE 8-1

HOW TO Record Accounts and Notes Payable

Concept:

A liability must be recognized when a business is required to transfer assets (or provide services) to another entity at some point in the future for activities that have already occurred.

Information:

Gibson Shipping regularly orders packing materials from Ironman Enterprises. On March 8, 2010, Gibson orders $25,000 from Ironman on account. This amount is due on May 15, 2010. However, due to the unexpected loss of a large customer Gibson experiences a cash flow crunch. On May 15, Gibson approaches Ironman about a payment extension and Ironman grants the extension on the condition that Gibson sign a note that specifies 7 percent interest beginning on May 15, 2010, with a due date of November 15, 2010. Gibson pays the amount in full on November 15, 2010.

Required:

1. Provide the necessary journal entry for Gibson Shipping on March 8, 2010.
2. Provide the necessary journal entry for Gibson Shipping on May 15, 2010.
3. Provide the necessary journal entry for Gibson Shipping on November 15, 2010.

Solution:

1. Entry on March 8, 2010:

Date	Account and Explanation	Debit	Credit
Mar. 8	Supplies	25,000	
	Accounts Payable		25,000
	(Record purchase of packing materials)		

		Stockholders'
Assets =	Liabilities +	Equity
+25,000	+25,000	

2. Entry on May 15, 2010:

Date	Account and Explanation	Debit	Credit
May 15	Accounts Payable	25,000	
	Notes Payable		25,000
	(Record issuance of note payable)		

		Stockholders'
Assets =	Liabilities +	Equity
	+25,000	
	−25,000	

3. Entry on November 15, 2010:

Date	Account and Explanation	Debit	Credit
Nov. 15	Notes Payable	25,000	
	Interest Expense	875*	
	Cash		25,875
	(Record payment of note and interest)		

		Stockholders'
Assets =	Liabilities +	Equity
−25,875	−25,000	−875

*$25,000 × 7% × 6/12

Current Portion of Long-Term Debt

The current portion of long-term debt is the amount of long-term debt principal that is due within the next year. At the end of each accounting period, the long-term debt that is due during the next year is reclassified as a current liability (see Southwest Airlines and UAL in Exhibit 8-2). Since the reclassification of most long-term debt as current does not usually change the accounts or amounts involved, journal entries are not required. In some cases, long-term debt that is due within the next year will be paid with the proceeds of a new long-term debt issue. Remember current liabilities must be retired with existing current assets or creation of new current liabilities—a new long-term debt issue is creation of a new *long-term*, not current, liability. When such refinancing is expected, the maturing obligation is not transferred to current liabilities but is left as a long-term debt. We discuss long-term liabilities in more detail in Chapter 9.

Other Payables

Accounts payable are reserved for amounts owed to outside suppliers of goods and services, and notes payable reflect amounts owed in which formal agreements or contracts were signed. However, businesses will have other current liabilities that do not fall into these two categories. There are many situations that can give rise to these other payables, but we will restrict our discussion to some of the most common.

Accrued Payables   Unlike accounts and notes payable, which are recognized when goods or services change hands, **accrued payables** are recognized by adjusting entries. They usually represent the completed portion of activities that are in process at the end of the period. For example, Green's Landscaping pays wages of $10,000 (or $1,000 per work day) to its employees every other Friday. The standard entry is:

Date	Account and Explanation	Debit	Credit
Dec. 20	Wages Expense	10,000	
	Cash		10,000
	(Record payment of wages)		

Assets	=	Liabilities	+	Stockholders' Equity
−10,000				−10,000

What happens, however, when December 31 falls on the Tuesday before the Friday payday? In this case, the expense for the seven days that have already been worked (five days from last week and Monday and Tuesday of this week) must be matched to the proper period. Additionally, because the work has been performed, but the employees have not yet been paid, Green's Landscaping has a liability to its employees. As such, on December 31 Green's would make the following adjusting entry:

Date	Account and Explanation	Debit	Credit
Dec. 31	Wages Expense	7,000	
	Wages Payable		7,000
	(Record accrual of wages expense)		

Assets	=	Liabilities	+	Stockholders' Equity
		+7,000		−7,000

Further, when Green's pays $10,000 to its employees on January 3, three days' pay are an expense of the current year (Wednesday, January 1 through Friday, January 3) and seven days' pay retires the Wages Payable from December 31:

Date	Account and Explanation	Debit	Credit
Jan. 3	Wages Expense	3,000	
	Wages Payable	7,000	
	Cash		10,000
	(Record payment of wages)		

Assets	=	Liabilities	+	Stockholders' Equity
−10,000		−7,000		−3,000

This sort of process is used for a wide variety of activities that are completed over time. For example, taxes are paid on April 15 based on the previous year's net income. As such, on December 31 an adjusting entry will match the appropriate income tax expense to the current year and set up a liability (income taxes payable) that will be paid off by April 15. The same logic applies to other similar situations, such as property taxes and interest expense. Interest expense is illustrated in Cornerstone 8-2.

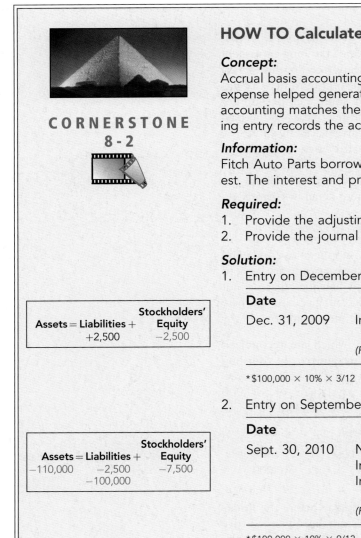

CORNERSTONE 8-2

HOW TO Calculate and Record Accrued Interest

Concept:
Accrual basis accounting requires us to match expenses to the period the expense helped generate revenues (the matching principle). When accrual accounting matches the expense to a period before it is actually paid, an adjusting entry records the accrued expense and corresponding payable amount.

Information:
Fitch Auto Parts borrowed $100,000 on October 1, 2009, at 10 percent interest. The interest and principal are due on September 30, 2010.

Required:
1. Provide the adjusting journal entry on December 31, 2009.
2. Provide the journal entry(ies) on September 30, 2010.

Solution:
1. Entry on December 31, 2009:

	Assets = Liabilities +	Stockholders' Equity
	+2,500	−2,500

Date	Account and Explanation	Debit	Credit
Dec. 31, 2009	Interest Expense	2,500*	
	Interest Payable		2,500
	(Record accrual of interest expense)		

*$100,000 × 10% × 3/12

2. Entry on September 30, 2010:

	Assets = Liabilities +	Stockholders' Equity
	−110,000 −2,500	−7,500
	−100,000	

Date	Account and Explanation	Debit	Credit
Sept. 30, 2010	Notes Payable	100,000	
	Interest Expense	7,500*	
	Interest Payable	2,500	
	Cash		110,000
	(Record payment of note and interest)		

*$100,000 × 10% × 9/12

Exhibit 8-3 illustrates the financial statement effects of the transactions recorded in Cornerstone 8-2. Notice that the interest payment of $10,000 is recorded as interest expense of $2,500 in 2009 and $7,500 in 2010.

Exhibit 8-3

Effect of Borrowing Money on the Annual Income Statement and Balance Sheet

10/1/09   12/31/09   9/30/10   12/31/10

	2009	2010
Annual income statement:		
Interest expense	$ 2,500	$ 7,500
Annual balance sheet:		
Note payable	$100,000	$ 0
Interest payable	2,500	0
Transactions:		
Cash borrowed	$100,000	
Principal payment		$100,000
Interest payment		10,000

Current Portion of Long-Term Debt

The current portion of long-term debt is the amount of long-term debt principal that is due within the next year. At the end of each accounting period, the long-term debt that is due during the next year is reclassified as a current liability (see Southwest Airlines and UAL in Exhibit 8-2). Since the reclassification of most long-term debt as current does not usually change the accounts or amounts involved, journal entries are not required. In some cases, long-term debt that is due within the next year will be paid with the proceeds of a new long-term debt issue. Remember current liabilities must be retired with existing current assets or creation of new current liabilities—a new long-term debt issue is creation of a new *long-term*, not current, liability. When such refinancing is expected, the maturing obligation is not transferred to current liabilities but is left as a long-term debt. We discuss long-term liabilities in more detail in Chapter 9.

Other Payables

Accounts payable are reserved for amounts owed to outside suppliers of goods and services, and notes payable reflect amounts owed in which formal agreements or contracts were signed. However, businesses will have other current liabilities that do not fall into these two categories. There are many situations that can give rise to these other payables, but we will restrict our discussion to some of the most common.

Accrued Payables   Unlike accounts and notes payable, which are recognized when goods or services change hands, **accrued payables** are recognized by adjusting entries. They usually represent the completed portion of activities that are in process at the end of the period. For example, Green's Landscaping pays wages of $10,000 (or $1,000 per work day) to its employees every other Friday. The standard entry is:

Date	Account and Explanation	Debit	Credit
Dec. 20	Wages Expense	10,000	
	Cash		10,000
	(Record payment of wages)		

Assets =	Liabilities +	Stockholders' Equity
−10,000		−10,000

What happens, however, when December 31 falls on the Tuesday before the Friday payday? In this case, the expense for the seven days that have already been worked (five days from last week and Monday and Tuesday of this week) must be matched to the proper period. Additionally, because the work has been performed, but the employees have not yet been paid, Green's Landscaping has a liability to its employees. As such, on December 31 Green's would make the following adjusting entry:

Date	Account and Explanation	Debit	Credit
Dec. 31	Wages Expense	7,000	
	Wages Payable		7,000
	(Record accrual of wages expense)		

Assets =	Liabilities +	Stockholders' Equity
	+7,000	−7,000

Further, when Green's pays $10,000 to its employees on January 3, three days' pay are an expense of the current year (Wednesday, January 1 through Friday, January 3) and seven days' pay retires the Wages Payable from December 31:

Date	Account and Explanation	Debit	Credit
Jan. 3	Wages Expense	3,000	
	Wages Payable	7,000	
	Cash		10,000
	(Record payment of wages)		

Assets =	Liabilities +	Stockholders' Equity
−10,000	−7,000	−3,000

This sort of process is used for a wide variety of activities that are completed over time. For example, taxes are paid on April 15 based on the previous year's net income. As such, on December 31 an adjusting entry will match the appropriate income tax expense to the current year and set up a liability (income taxes payable) that will be paid off by April 15. The same logic applies to other similar situations, such as property taxes and interest expense. Interest expense is illustrated in Cornerstone 8-2.

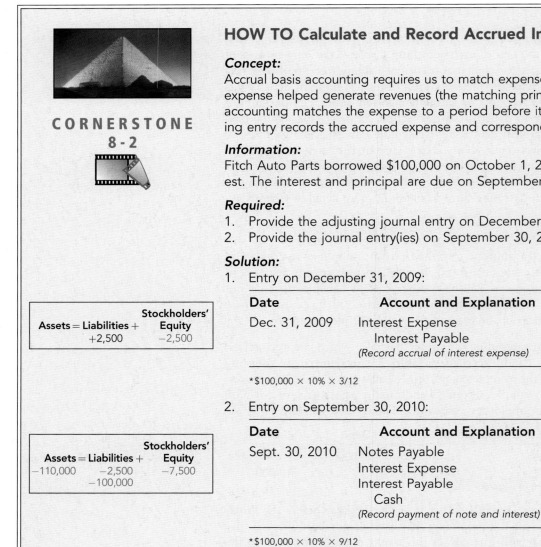

HOW TO Calculate and Record Accrued Interest

CORNERSTONE 8-2

Concept:
Accrual basis accounting requires us to match expenses to the period the expense helped generate revenues (the matching principle). When accrual accounting matches the expense to a period before it is actually paid, an adjusting entry records the accrued expense and corresponding payable amount.

Information:
Fitch Auto Parts borrowed $100,000 on October 1, 2009, at 10 percent interest. The interest and principal are due on September 30, 2010.

Required:
1. Provide the adjusting journal entry on December 31, 2009.
2. Provide the journal entry(ies) on September 30, 2010.

Solution:
1. Entry on December 31, 2009:

	Assets = Liabilities +	Stockholders' Equity
	+2,500	−2,500

Date	Account and Explanation	Debit	Credit
Dec. 31, 2009	Interest Expense	2,500*	
	Interest Payable		2,500
	(Record accrual of interest expense)		

*$100,000 × 10% × 3/12

2. Entry on September 30, 2010:

	Assets = Liabilities +	Stockholders' Equity
	−110,000 −2,500	−7,500
	−100,000	

Date	Account and Explanation	Debit	Credit
Sept. 30, 2010	Notes Payable	100,000	
	Interest Expense	7,500*	
	Interest Payable	2,500	
	Cash		110,000
	(Record payment of note and interest)		

*$100,000 × 10% × 9/12

Exhibit 8-3 illustrates the financial statement effects of the transactions recorded in Cornerstone 8-2. Notice that the interest payment of $10,000 is recorded as interest expense of $2,500 in 2009 and $7,500 in 2010.

Exhibit 8-3

Effect of Borrowing Money on the Annual Income Statement and Balance Sheet

10/1/09   12/31/09   9/30/10   12/31/10

	2009	2010
Annual income statement:		
Interest expense	$ 2,500	$ 7,500
Annual balance sheet:		
Note payable	$100,000	$ 0
Interest payable	2,500	0
Transactions:		
Cash borrowed	$100,000	
Principal payment		$100,000
Interest payment		10,000

Sales Tax   At the time of a sale, most retail businesses collect **sales taxes**, usage taxes, or excise taxes for various state, local, and federal taxing authorities. These taxes, although collected as part of the total selling price, are not additions to revenue. Instead, they are money collected from the customer for the governmental unit levying the tax. These tax collections are liabilities until they are paid to the taxing authority. For example, businesses typically must remit sales tax collected to the state every quarter. Cornerstone 8-3 illustrates the accounting for sales tax.

HOW TO Record the Liabilities for Sales Tax

**CORNERSTONE
8-3**

Concept:
By law, companies frequently collect sales tax from customers. However, the company has no rights to these monies; instead, the cash must be passed along to the taxing authority.

Information:
During the first quarter of 2009, McLean County Tire sold, on credit, 3,000 truck tires at $75 each plus State of Illinois sales tax of 5 percent. Included in the $75 price per tire was a $1.50/tire federal excise tax. Any taxes collected are paid to the appropriate taxing authority at the end of the quarter.

Required:
1. Provide the journal entry to record the first quarter sales.
2. Provide the journal entry to record the payment of the taxes to the appropriate taxing authority.

Solution:
1.

Date	Account and Explanation	Debit	Credit
Mar. 31	Accounts Receivable	236,250	
	Sales Revenue		220,500*
	Illinois Sales Tax Payable		11,250**
	Federal Excise Tax Payable		4,500***
	(Record sale of truck tires)		

	Assets =	Liabilities +	Stockholders' Equity
	+236,250	+11,250	+220,500
		+4,500	

*3,000 tires × ($75 − $1.50 per tire)
**3,000 tires × $75 × 5%
***3,000 tires × $1.50

Recognize that the receivable [(3,000 tires × $75 per tire) + (5% × 3,000 × $75)] is larger than the sales revenue. The difference is the amount of the taxes McLean County Tire collects for the state and federal government—liabilities to McLean County Tire until the governmental units are paid.

2. Entry to record payment of sales taxes:

Date	Account and Explanation	Debit	Credit
Apr. 10	Illinois Sales Tax Payable	11,250	
	Federal Excise Tax Payable	4,500	
	Cash		15,750
	(Record payment of first quarter sales tax)		

	Assets =	Liabilities +	Stockholders' Equity
	−15,750	−11,250	
		−4,500	

Withholding and Payroll Taxes   Businesses are required to withhold taxes from employees' earnings and to pay taxes based on wages and salaries paid to employees. These **withholding** and **payroll taxes** are liabilities until they are paid to the taxing authority. Note that there are really two sources for these taxes. First, you are well aware that employees must pay certain taxes that are "withheld" from their paycheck. This is the difference between your gross pay and your net pay. The business does not have any rights to this money; instead, as with sales tax, they must pay these amounts to the proper authority. The standard withholdings are federal, state, and possibly city or county income taxes, as well as Social Security and Medicare. Employees may also have amounts withheld for such things as retirement accounts (e.g., 401-K), parking, and health insurance, among other things, but these are not taxes.

Additionally, the business itself must pay certain taxes based on employee payrolls. You may be less aware of some of these taxes, but the dollar amounts are very real to any business. These amounts are not withheld from employee pay, rather they are additional amounts that must be paid over and above gross pay. For example, employers match your contribution to Social Security and Medicare (together these are called FICA). That is, if you have $400 withheld from your paycheck for Social Security, your employer pays the federal government $800 related to your employment. Employers also pay federal and state unemployment taxes (these are used to fund unemployment benefits) based on their history of firing employees (because fired employees are eligible to collect unemployment benefits). Finally, employers do have other costs—typically called fringe benefits—associated with employees, but these are not taxes. Examples of fringe benefits include employer contributions to retirement accounts and health insurance.

Most U.S. businesses have the following obligations to pay taxes or withhold them from employee earnings:

Tax	Business Payroll Tax	Withholding from Employee Pay
Old age, survivors, and disability (Social Security)*	6.20%	6.20%
Medicare tax	1.45	1.45
State unemployment tax	rate varies	
Federal unemployment tax	rate varies	
Federal income tax		rate varies
State income tax		rate varies

*Applies to the first $102,000 of wages in 2008. Maximum amount is increasing over time.

Cornerstone 8-4 illustrates the accounting for payroll withholding and payroll taxes.

CORNERSTONE 8-4

HOW TO Record Payroll Taxes

Concept:
Employers not only withhold taxes from the employees' gross pay and later pay these amount withheld to the taxing authority, but they also pay additional amounts over and above gross pay.

Information:
Assume that McLean County Tire's hourly employees earned $48,500 in the pay period ending July 31. Assume further that federal and state income taxes withheld are $8,245 and $1,940, respectively. The taxes noted above, plus a state unemployment tax rate of 3 percent and a federal unemployment tax rate of 5 percent, are applicable. We will recognize McLean County Tire's payroll activities in two steps.

Required:
1. Provide the journal entry related to the $48,500 gross pay earned by the employees.
2. Provide the journal entry related to the payroll taxes over and above gross pay.

Solution:

1. Entry to record wages expense and associated liabilities:

CORNERSTONE
8-4
(continued)

Date	Account and Explanation	Debit	Credit
July 31	Wages Expense	48,500.00*	
	Federal Income Tax Payable		8,245.00
	State Income Tax Payable		1,940.00
	Social Security Tax Payable		3,007.00*
	Medicare Tax Payable		703.25**
	Cash		34,604.75
	(Record wages and liabilities)		

Assets =	Liabilities +	Stockholders' Equity
−34,604.75	+8,245.00	−48,500.00
	+1,940.00	
	+3,007.00	
	+703.25	

* $48,500 × 6.2%
** $48,500 × 1.45%

2. Now we will recognize the employer tax expenses and the associated employer tax liabilities.

Date	Account and Explanation	Debit	Credit
July 31	Federal Unemployment Tax Expense	2,425.00	
	State Unemployment Tax Expense	1,455.00	
	Employer Social Security Tax Expense	3,007.00	
	Employer Medicare Tax Expense	703.25	
	Federal Unemployment Tax Payable		2,425.00*
	State Unemployment Tax Payable		1,455.00**
	Employer Social Security Tax Payable		3,007.00***
	Employer Medicare Tax Payable		703.25****
	(Record employer payroll taxes)		

Assets =	Liabilities +	Stockholders' Equity
	+2,425.00	−2,425.00
	+1,455.00	−1,455.00
	+3,007.00	−3,007.00
	+703.25	−703.25

* $48,500 × 5%
** $48,500 × 3%
*** $48,500 × 6.2%
*** $48,500 × 1.45%

Note that the $48,500.00 payroll is (1) smaller than the total expense of $56,090.25 (i.e., the sum of all expenses from both journal entries) and (2) larger than the $34,604.75 cash paid (i.e., net pay) to employees. As you can see from this discussion of payroll taxes, the actual cost of an employee is more than his or her gross pay.

DECISION-MAKING & ANALYSIS

The Cost of Fringe Benefits

The employer payroll taxes that were just discussed are only part of the costs above salary that a business pays when it brings a new employee onto the payroll. We will analyze this issue by assuming that you just accepted a new $52,000 per year staff job with VonZany Chocolates.

1. *What costs beyond salary might VonZany Chocolates incur by adding you to their payroll?*

   Most companies have some "fringe benefits" that they offer along with salary to full-time employees. These fringe benefits all come at some cost. Assume that VonZany offered you the fringe benefits identified below at the costs noted.

Fringe Benefit	Cost
Medical insurance	$ 8,400
Eye care, glasses, and contacts	500
Dental insurance	300
Disability insurance	750
Retirement (10% of salary)	5,200
Typical bonus (3 weeks' pay)	3,000
Total fringe benefits	$18,150

(Continued)

Now, add the employer payroll taxes using the rates identified above:

Employer Payroll Tax	Cost
OASDI (Social Security at 6.2%)	$3,224
Medicare (at 1.45%)	754
Federal and state unemployment (at 3.5%)	1,820
Total employer payroll taxes	$5,798

The total cost of bringing you on the payroll is $75,948. The fringe benefits and payroll taxes raise the cost of employing you to 46.1 percent more than your salary.

2. *How many more VonZany Chocolate bars have to be sold so that VonZany's income before taxes does not go down because you have been added to the payroll?*

VonZany would have to earn enough additional revenue to pay the $75,948 total cost of your employment plus the additional costs of producing and selling the additional chocolate bars. If we check a recent VonZany's income statement, we see that product costs plus selling, marketing, and administrative costs are approximately 87 percent of revenue. So VonZany's could use 13 percent of every sales dollar to pay for you.

Let's assume that VonZany sells VonZany Chocolate bars for $1 each. For each additional bar sold, the company will realize 13¢ toward the cost of your employment. So VonZany would have to sell 584,215 more VonZany bars each year to come out even after adding you to the payroll.

$$\frac{\$75,948}{\$0.13} = 584,215$$

Remember, your employer can afford to keep you employed *only* if you help make revenues go up (after subtracting the direct costs of producing the product) or expenses go down by at least enough to break even. Promotions will come to those who do better and termination to those who don't contribute enough.

Unearned Revenues   **Unearned revenue** is the liability created when customers pay for goods or services in advance. In such instances, the seller has a liability to the purchaser in the amount of the prepayment. This liability is discharged either by providing the goods or services purchased (at which time revenue is recognized) or by refunding the amount of the prepayment.[2]

Assume, for example, that Charter Air sold 30 roundtrip flights to Escape Travel for $990,000. The contract requires Charter to make one roundtrip flight with 150 seats each Saturday between New York and Miami for Escape's customers to meet cruise ships. The flights begin on January 15. Escape paid in advance for the flights, and Charter recognized the payment in its accounts as follows:

Date	Account and Explanation	Debit	Credit
Jan. 8	Cash	990,000	
	Unearned Sales Revenue		990,000
	(Record receipt of cash for service to be provided)		

Assets = Liabilities +	Stockholders' Equity
+990,000 +990,000	

Each time Charter provides one of the roundtrip flights, it should recognize the revenue that has been earned. The entry for each flight will look just like the entry for the first flight:

Date	Account and Explanation	Debit	Credit
Jan. 15	Unearned Sales Revenue	33,000	
	($990,000 ÷ 30 flights)		
	Sales Revenue		33,000
	(Record revenue earned)		

Assets = Liabilities +	Stockholders' Equity
−33,000	+33,000

Cornerstone 8-5 illustrates the accounting for unearned revenues.

[2] If the goods or services are not provided, the seller may also be liable for legal damages. The amount of such damages would be recorded as an expense.

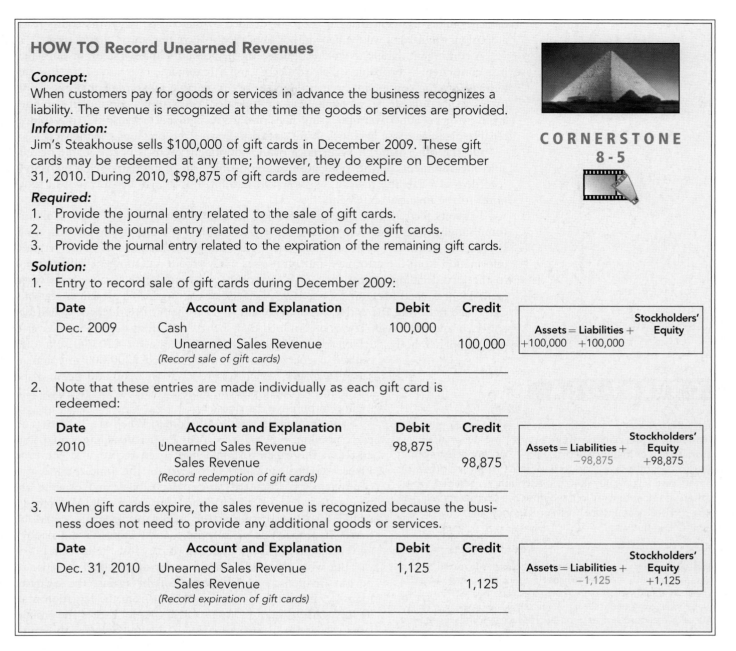

HOW TO Record Unearned Revenues

CORNERSTONE
8-5

Concept:
When customers pay for goods or services in advance the business recognizes a liability. The revenue is recognized at the time the goods or services are provided.

Information:
Jim's Steakhouse sells $100,000 of gift cards in December 2009. These gift cards may be redeemed at any time; however, they do expire on December 31, 2010. During 2010, $98,875 of gift cards are redeemed.

Required:
1. Provide the journal entry related to the sale of gift cards.
2. Provide the journal entry related to redemption of the gift cards.
3. Provide the journal entry related to the expiration of the remaining gift cards.

Solution:
1. Entry to record sale of gift cards during December 2009:

Date	Account and Explanation	Debit	Credit
Dec. 2009	Cash	100,000	
	Unearned Sales Revenue		100,000
	(Record sale of gift cards)		

Assets = Liabilities +	Stockholders' Equity
+100,000 +100,000	

2. Note that these entries are made individually as each gift card is redeemed:

Date	Account and Explanation	Debit	Credit
2010	Unearned Sales Revenue	98,875	
	Sales Revenue		98,875
	(Record redemption of gift cards)		

Assets = Liabilities +	Stockholders' Equity
−98,875	+98,875

3. When gift cards expire, the sales revenue is recognized because the business does not need to provide any additional goods or services.

Date	Account and Explanation	Debit	Credit
Dec. 31, 2010	Unearned Sales Revenue	1,125	
	Sales Revenue		1,125
	(Record expiration of gift cards)		

Assets = Liabilities +	Stockholders' Equity
−1,125	+1,125

A similar *long-term* liability, called *customer deposits*, is recorded when customers make advance payments or security deposits that are not expected to be earned or returned soon enough to qualify as current liabilities.

On a related point, this also demonstrates revenue recognition. Revenue will not be recognized until it is realized or realizable and earned. This amount is already realized, so the first criterion is met; however, it is not earned until the goods or services are provided.

Measurement of the liabilities described so far is not affected by uncertainties about the amount, timing, or recipient of future asset outflows. Such uncertainties are exhibited by the liabilities we examine next.

CONCEPT Q&A

Why is a liability recognized when a customer prepays for a good or service (i.e., an unearned revenue)?

Possible Answer:
Liabilities are probable future sacrifices of economic benefits which arise from activities that have already occurred. Because in this situation the business will provide the goods or services purchased by the customer at some future point, the prepayment meets the definition of a liability.

Contingent Liabilities

OBJECTIVE ▶ 3
Describe contingent liabilities and the alternatives for their recognition and measurement.

A contingency is defined as an "…existing condition, situation, or set of circumstances involving uncertainty as to a possible gain or loss that will be resolved when a future event occurs or fails to occur." A **contingent liability** (or, contingent loss) results when there is uncertainty about a possible loss. For example, a firm may be contingently liable for damages under a lawsuit that has yet to be decided by the courts. When the courts reach a decision, the liability will be known, but until then it is contingent on that decision.

A contingent liability is not recognized in the accounts unless the event on which it is contingent is probable (likely to occur) and a reasonable estimate of the loss can be made. If the contingent event is likely to occur, reliable measurement of the liability is usually possible, so recognition is appropriate. For example, contingent liabilities arising from product warranties and pensions are recognized, because it is possible to reliably measure those liabilities using statistics drawn from previous experiences.

On the other hand, if occurrence of the contingent event is not probable or reliable measurement of the obligation is impossible, the potential obligation is not recorded as a liability. Instead, as shown in Exhibit 8-4, it may be disclosed in footnotes to the financial statements.

Lawsuits filed against a business provide a classic example of contingent liabilities. Interestingly, most large companies are party to multiple lawsuits at any point in time. Estimating when a loss is probable and determining a reasonable estimate requires information from the attorneys, but businesses rarely record a contingent liability prior to the jury deciding against them. We've probably all heard of such lawsuits as when Stella Liebeck sued **McDonald's** in 1992. Liebeck was sitting in the passenger seat of a car. While removing the coffee cup's lid to add sugar to her coffee, Liebeck spilled her coffee, burning her legs. It was determined that she suffered third degree burns over 6 percent of her body. McDonald's could have settled the case for $20,000, but they refused. Liebeck ultimately was awarded $200,000 in compensatory damages, which was reduced to $160,000 because she was found to be 20 percent at fault. She also was awarded $2.7 million in punitive damages.

The accounting question becomes: When is a liability (and corresponding expense) recorded? Proper matching would suggest that the expense should have been recorded at the time Liebeck spilled the coffee. However, at this time the loss was contingent. As discussed above, the liability and expense are not recorded until it is deemed probable that McDonald's would lose the lawsuit and a reasonable estimate could be made. It probably is no surprise that McDonald's did not record a liability for this amount until they lost the lawsuit.

But what about lawsuits that most of us would consider to be less frivolous, such as those brought against the cigarette industry? Exhibit 8-5 shows an excerpt from the litigation note in **Reynolds American Inc.'s (RAI)** 10-K. RAI is the second largest cigarette manufacturer in the United States with brands including Camel and Winston. Of course, this is only a small excerpt consisting of approximately 500 words. The entire note contains over 24,000 words. This excerpt shows that RAI does not record contingent liabilities until final verdicts are reached.

CONCEPT Q&A

In financial accounting, a contingency is an "...existing condition, situation, or set of circumstances involving uncertainty" as to possible gain or loss (FAS No. 5, Par. 1). Accounts receivable have a contingent loss related to bad debts. That is, a group of customers owes us money (i.e., the accounts receivable), however, there is uncertainty about whether the customers will pay us. How do we account for this contingency and why do we account for it in this way?

Possible Answer:

As discussed in Chapter 5, companies typically use an estimate of uncollectible receivables to recognize "bad debt expense" and reduce the accounts receivable valuation through a credit to the "allowance for doubtful accounts." This is done because it is probable that amounts will be uncollectible and this amount is reasonably estimated (generally based on the companies' past experience). So, although bad debt expense does not produce a liability (instead it reduces an asset), the accounting for this contingency is consistent with accounting with contingent liabilities.

Exhibit 8-4

Recognition of Contingent Liabilities

	A Reasonable Estimate Can Be Made	No Reasonable Estimate Can Be Made
Probable	Make a journal entry to record the liability.	No journal entry is made: disclose information in footnote to the financial statements.
Reasonably Possible	No journal entry is made: disclose information in footnote to the financial statements.	No journal entry is made: disclose information in footnote to the financial statements.
Remote	Neither record as a liability nor disclose in a footnote to the financial statements.	Neither record as a liability nor disclose in a footnote to the financial statements.

Exhibit 8-5

Excerpts from Reynolds American Inc. Notes to Consolidated Financial Statements included in their 2007 10-K

Accounting for Tobacco-Related Litigation Contingencies

In accordance with GAAP, RAI and its subsidiaries, including RJR Tobacco and the Conwood companies, as applicable, record any loss concerning litigation at such time as an unfavorable outcome becomes probable and the amount can be reasonably estimated. In the third quarter of 2007, RJR Tobacco accrued $6 million related to unfavorable judgments in two individual plaintiff's cases tried in conjunction with the *Engle v. R. J. Reynolds Tobacco Co.* case. On February 8, 2008, RJR Tobacco paid $5.9 million relating to those judgments, which amount was determined using the total amount of verdicts together with accrued interest beginning November 7, 2000. Additional interest, if any, determined by the trial court will be immaterial to the Company. With the exception of two *Engle*-related verdicts, and for the reasons set forth below, RAI's management continues to conclude that the loss of any particular pending smoking and health tobacco litigation claim against RJR Tobacco or its affiliates or indemnitees, or the loss of any particular claim concerning the use of smokeless tobacco against the Conwood companies, when viewed on an individual basis, is not probable.

Subject to the foregoing paragraph, RJR Tobacco and its affiliates believe that they have valid defenses to the smoking and health tobacco litigation claims against them, as well as valid bases for appeal of adverse verdicts against them. RAI, RJR Tobacco and their affiliates and indemnitees have, through their counsel, filed pleadings and memoranda in pending smoking and health tobacco litigation that set forth and discuss a number of grounds and defenses that they and their counsel believe have a valid basis in law and fact. RJR Tobacco and its affiliates and indemnitees continue to win the majority of smoking and health tobacco litigation claims that reach trial, and a very high percentage of the tobacco-related litigation claims brought against them continue to be dismissed at or before trial. Based on their experience in the smoking and health tobacco litigation against them and the strength of the defenses available to them in such litigation, RJR Tobacco and its affiliates believe that their successful defense of smoking and health tobacco litigation in the past will continue in the future.

Except for verdicts in two individual smoking and health cases tried as part of the *Engle* class-action case mentioned above, no liability for pending smoking and health tobacco litigation was recorded in RAI's consolidated balance sheet as of December 31, 2007. RJR has liabilities totaling $94 million that were recorded in 1999 in connection with certain indemnification claims asserted by Japan Tobacco, Inc., referred to as JTI, against RJR and RJR Tobacco relating to certain activities of Northern Brands International, Inc., a now inactive, indirect subsidiary of RAI formerly involved in the international tobacco business, referred to as Northern Brands. For further information on Northern Brands and related litigation and the indemnification claims of JTI, see "—Litigation Affecting the Cigarette Industry—Other Litigation and Developments" and "—Other Contingencies and Guarantees" below.

Of course, the likelihood that a contingent event will occur may change over time. A contingent liability that should not be recorded or disclosed at one time may need to be recorded or disclosed at a later time because the facts and circumstances change. Contingent liabilities arising from litigation frequently have this character.

Warranties

OBJECTIVE ▶ 4
Measure warranty liabilities and warranty expense.

When goods are sold, the customer is often provided with a warranty against defects that might develop. A **warranty** usually guarantees the repair or replacement of defective goods during a period (ranging from a few days to several years) following the sale.

The use of parts and labor to satisfy warranty claims may occur in the accounting period in which the sale is made, but it is also likely to occur in some subsequent accounting period. The matching concept requires that all expenses required to produce sales revenue for a given period be recorded in that period. Since warranty costs are sales-related, they must be recorded in the sales period. And since all warranty costs probably have not been incurred by the end of the sales period, they must be estimated. Businesses are likely able to make reasonable estimates of their warranty costs based on past experience.

The recognition of warranty expense and estimated warranty liability is normally recorded by an adjustment at the end of the accounting period. As warranty claims are paid to customers or related expenditures are made, the estimated liability is reduced. Cornerstone 8-6 illustrates the accounting for warranties.

CONCEPT Q&A

Why are warranties expensed at the point of sale when a company often does not incur warranty costs until later periods?

Possible Answer:

This is a classic illustration of the matching principle. Remember, the matching principle says that expenses will be recognized in the periods they helped generate revenues. The presence of the warranty "helped" sell the item. Additionally, warranties are contingencies—if the product fails, then the company will experience a loss. As discussed above, when loss contingencies are probable and a reasonable estimate can be made, a journal entry is made to record the expense and recognize a liability.

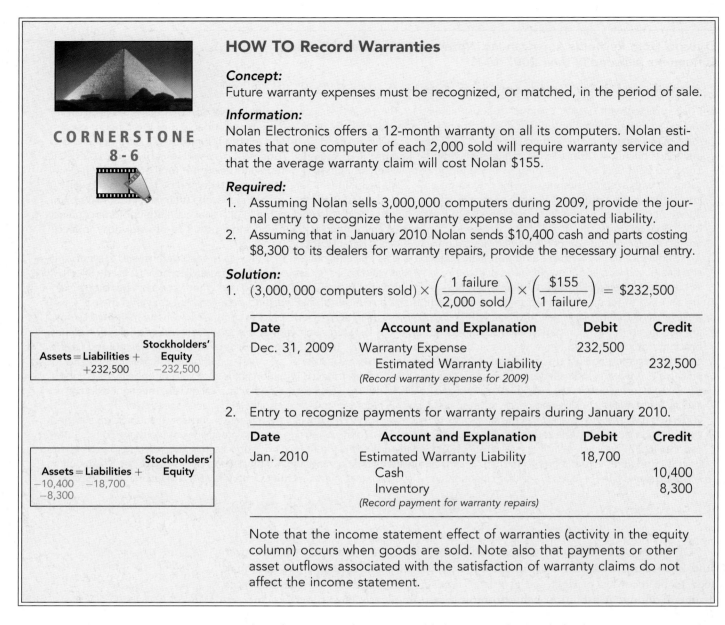

HOW TO Record Warranties

CORNERSTONE 8-6

Concept:
Future warranty expenses must be recognized, or matched, in the period of sale.

Information:
Nolan Electronics offers a 12-month warranty on all its computers. Nolan estimates that one computer of each 2,000 sold will require warranty service and that the average warranty claim will cost Nolan $155.

Required:
1. Assuming Nolan sells 3,000,000 computers during 2009, provide the journal entry to recognize the warranty expense and associated liability.
2. Assuming that in January 2010 Nolan sends $10,400 cash and parts costing $8,300 to its dealers for warranty repairs, provide the necessary journal entry.

Solution:
1. $(3,000,000 \text{ computers sold}) \times \left(\dfrac{1 \text{ failure}}{2,000 \text{ sold}}\right) \times \left(\dfrac{\$155}{1 \text{ failure}}\right) = \$232,500$

Assets =	Liabilities +	Stockholders' Equity
	+232,500	−232,500

Date	Account and Explanation	Debit	Credit
Dec. 31, 2009	Warranty Expense	232,500	
	Estimated Warranty Liability		232,500
	(Record warranty expense for 2009)		

2. Entry to recognize payments for warranty repairs during January 2010.

Assets =	Liabilities +	Stockholders' Equity
−10,400	−18,700	
−8,300		

Date	Account and Explanation	Debit	Credit
Jan. 2010	Estimated Warranty Liability	18,700	
	Cash		10,400
	Inventory		8,300
	(Record payment for warranty repairs)		

Note that the income statement effect of warranties (activity in the equity column) occurs when goods are sold. Note also that payments or other asset outflows associated with the satisfaction of warranty claims do not affect the income statement.

Actual warranty claims are unlikely to exactly equal the business' estimate. Any small overestimate or underestimate is usually combined with the next warranty estimate. However, large overestimates or underestimates must be recognized in the accounts and reported on the income statement as other income or other expenses as soon as they become apparent.

OBJECTIVE ▶ 5
Analyze liquidity ratios using information contained in the current liabilities section.

Analyzing Current Liabilities

Both investors and creditors are interested in a company's liquidity—that is, its ability to meet its short-term obligations. Failure to pay current liabilities can lead to suppliers refusing to sell to the company and employees leaving. As such, even companies with good business models can be forced into bankruptcy by their inability to pay current liabilities.

The following ratios are often used to analyze a company's ability to meet its current obligations:

$$\text{Current Ratio} = \frac{\text{Current Assets}}{\text{Current Liabilities}}$$

$$\text{Quick Ratio} = \frac{(\text{Cash} + \text{Marketable Securities} + \text{Accounts Receivable})}{\text{Current Liabilities}}$$

$$\text{Cash Ratio} = \frac{(\text{Cash} + \text{Marketable Securities})}{\text{Current Liabilities}}$$

$$\text{Operating Cash Flow Ratio} = \frac{\text{Cash flows from Operating Activities}}{\text{Current Liabilities}}$$

The first three ratios compare all or parts of current assets to current liabilities. The logic is that current liabilities need to be paid over approximately the same time frame that current assets are turned into cash. "Acceptable" current ratios vary from industry to industry, but the thought is that current assets must exceed current liabilities (which implies a current ratio > 1) to be able to meet current obligations. In fact, the general rule of thumb appears to be that a current ratio greater than two is appropriate. However, the second and third ratios recognize that some current assets are harder to liquidate. Both the quick and cash ratio exclude inventories because including inventories assumes that sales will be made. The quick ratio assumes that accounts receivable are liquid. This is true when customers have low credit risk and pay in relatively short amounts of time. Of course, such an assumption is not true for all industries. Consequently, the use of the cash ratio may be more appropriate in these cases. Operating cash flow, on the other hand, looks at the ability of cash generated from operating activities to meet current obligations. As with the current ratio, the operating cash flow ratio assumes that sales will continue into the future. Cornerstone 8-7 illustrates the analysis of current liabilities.

HOW TO Calculate Liquidity Ratios

Concept:
Investors and creditors are interested in a company's ability to meet its current obligations. Analysis of information contained in current liabilities provides such information.

CORNERSTONE
8-7

Information:
Consider the following information from **Standard Pacific**, a large builder of single-family homes, as of December 31, 2006 (in thousands).

Current liabilities	473,498	Receivables	77,725
Cash & equivalents	17,376	Inventories	3,472,285
Marketable securities	0	Cash flows from operating activities	(360,651)

Required:
Calculate the following:
1. current ratio
2. quick ratio
3. cash ratio
4. operating cash flow ratio

Solution:
Although the information to calculate these ratios is given, most of it can be found on the balance sheet (the exception is cash flows from operating activities, which is on the statement of cash flows).

1. current ratio: (17,376 + 0 + 77,725 + 3,472,285)/473,498 = 7.53
2. quick ratio: (17,376 + 0 + 77,725)/473,498 = 0.20
3. cash ratio: (17,376 + 0)/473,498 = 0.04
4. operating cash flow ratio: −360,651/473,498 = −0.76

In isolation, the current ratio discussed in Cornerstone 8-7 appears very strong. For most industries, a current ratio greater than seven is rare. However, closer examination reveals that a vast majority of the current assets is inventory (unsold homes). In strong real estate markets new homes can sell quite fast, but when a real estate slump hits, such homes can remain unsold for long periods of time. In fact, during 2007 such a slump hit the U.S. real estate market and Standard Pacific, and other home builders, experienced much slower sales (Standard Pacific's sales were down approximately 30 percent). In fact, a few home builders even resorted to selling homes at a loss to generate needed cash. The quick ratio and cash ratio also discussed in Cornerstone 8-7 show that Standard Pacific must sell homes to generate the necessary cash to meet its current obligations. The highly negative cash flows from operations were due to growing inventory in 2006. Although this growing inventory could be interpreted as expanding operations, it could also signal slowing sales.

DECISION-MAKING & ANALYSIS

A Decision for Short-Term Financing

Hydraulic Controls Company manufactures hydraulic clutch assemblies for compact foreign and domestic automobiles. The following data are available on Hydraulic's current liabilities, current assets, sales revenue, and net income (loss) for the past three years:

Item	2013	2012	2011
Accounts payable	$ 174,000	$ 146,000	$ 104,000
Short-term notes payable	332,000	291,000	229,000
Income taxes payable	-0-	43,000	50,000
Total current liabilities	$ 506,000	$ 480,000	$ 383,000
Total current assets	485,000	546,000	611,000
Sales revenue	5,047,000	5,293,000	5,538,000
Net income (loss)	(10,000)	89,000	130,000

Hydraulic Controls has asked its bank to increase its short-term notes payable by $100,000. Following are some questions the bank might ask Hydraulic's management:

1. *How will the short-term notes be repaid?*

The short-term notes would be repaid from current assets. But decline in the amount of current assets relative to current liabilities suggests that even the present amount of current liabilities may not be payable with the resources currently available.

2. *What might be causing the recent increases in current liabilities and decreases in current assets?*

Because profitability is declining, the firm may not be able to borrow from outside sources or secure cash from operations. Therefore, it may be drawing down current assets and increasing current liabilities to provide capital.

3. *Should the bank extend additional credit to Hydraulic?*

The decline in profitability, the trend in the ratio of current assets to current liabilities, and the present excess of current liabilities over current assets suggest that it would be unwise to extend additional credit at this time.

Summary

This chapter explains the measurement and reporting of current liabilities and contingent liabilities. Because current liabilities will be paid within a short time, they are measured at the value of what was received or at the amount of the payment to be made. Notes payable require adjustments when the note is outstanding at the end of the accounting period. Accrued payables—wages or rent, for example—are also recorded with adjustments. Payroll costs often include substantial amounts beyond the wages or salaries paid to employees; these, too, are current liabilities. When customers pay for goods or services in advance, the unearned revenues are treated in the same way.

Contingent liabilities arise when the firm has an obligation to outsiders for which the amount, timing, or recipient depends on future events. In such cases, the amount of the obligation must be estimated, and the required accounting depends on the likelihood of the future events or their measurability. A common example of contingent liabilities is warranties.

Summary of Learning Objectives

LO1.   Explain liability recognition and measurement criteria.
- Most liabilities are recognized in exchange for goods and services or the borrowing of money.
- In theory, the amount reported on the balance sheet should not include interest that has not yet accrued.
- However, for nearly all current liabilities, unaccrued interest is deemed immaterial, so most current liabilities are simply recorded and reported at the total amount due.

LO2.   Identify and record the kinds of activities that produce current liabilities.
- Current liabilities are obligations to outsiders that require the firm to pay cash or another current asset or provide goods or services within the longer of one year or one operating cycle.
- Such obligations are the result of many common transactions such as:
  - purchasing goods or services on credit (i.e., accounts payable)
  - the completed portion of activities that are in process at the end of the period such as wages or interest (i.e., accrued payables)
  - sales tax collected from customers
  - payroll taxes such as income taxes withheld from employees and Social Security
  - notes payable
  - goods or services paid for in advance by customers (i.e., unearned revenues)
  - the portion of long-term debt due within the year are all current liabilities

LO3.   Describe contingent liabilities and the alternatives for their recognition and measurement.
- A contingent liability is an obligation whose amount, timing, or recipient depends on future events.
- A contingent liability is not recognized in the accounts unless the event on which it is contingent is probable (likely to occur) and a reasonable estimate of the liability can be made.
- If occurrence of the contingent event is not probable or reliable measurement of the obligation is impossible, the potential obligation is not recorded as a liability, but may be disclosed in the footnotes.

LO4.   Measure warranty liabilities and warranty expense.
- Since warranties help generate sales, the estimated future cost of servicing the warranty must be recorded in the sales period (this is an example of the matching principle).
- This is done by expensing the estimate of the future cost of servicing the warranty and creating a liability.
- As warranty claims are paid to customers or related expenditures are made, the estimated liability is reduced.

LO5. **Analyze liquidity ratios using information contained in the current liabilities section.**

- Both investors and creditors are interested in a company's liquidity—that is, its ability to meet its short-term obligations.
- Failure to pay current liabilities can lead to suppliers refusing to sell needed inventory and employees leaving.
- As such, even companies with good business models can be forced into bankruptcy by their inability to pay current liabilities.
- Common ratios used to analyze a company's ability to meet its current obligations are:
  - current ratio
  - quick ratio
  - cash ratio
  - operating cash flow ratio

CORNERSTONES FOR CHAPTER 8

Key Terms

Review Problem

Recording Current Liabilities and Calculating the Current Ratio

ABC Co. has the following balances in its accounts as of the beginning of the day on December 31 (this is not all of the accounts):

Account	Debit	Credit
Accounts payable		$ 100,000
Accounts receivable	$150,000	
Cash	75,000	
Interest payable		0
Inventory	270,000	
Long-term notes payable		1,000,000
Other current assets	60,000	
Other current liabilities		45,000
Sales taxes payable		10,000
Short-term notes payable		0
Unearned revenues		30,000

The following information is *not* reflected in these balances:

a.   On December 31, ABC accepted delivery of $30,000 of inventory. ABC has not yet paid its suppliers.

b.   On December 1, ABC bought some equipment for $200,000 with a short-term note payable bearing 12 percent interest. ABC has not made any journal entries related to this transaction.

c.   Customers prepaid $10,600 related to services ABC will perform next year. This price included 6 percent sales tax.

d. $20,000 in gross salaries and wages are paid. Assume all employees are below the Social Security maximum; there is no state unemployment tax; and 1 percent federal unemployment tax, $2,000 of federal income tax, and $500 of state income tax are withheld.

Required:

1.   Prepare the necessary journal entries for *a–d*.
2.   Determine the current ratio before accounting for the additional information.
3.   Determine the current ratio after accounting for the additional information.
4.   Explain why ABC's current ratio deteriorated so badly.

Solution:

1.   The necessary journal entries for each part are as follows:

	Date	Account and Explanation	Debit	Credit
a.	Dec. 31	Inventory	30,000	
		Accounts Payable		30,000
		(Record purchase of inventory)		
b.	31	Equipment	200,000	
		Short-term Notes Payable		200,000
		(Record issue of note for equipment purchase)		
		ABC must also accrue interest on December 31.		
	31	Interest Expense (200,000 × 12% × 1/12)	2,000	
		Interest Payable		2,000
		(Record interest accrued on short-term note)		
c.	31	Cash	10,600	
		Unearned Revenue		10,000
		Sales Taxes Payable		600
		(Record unearned revenue and sales taxes)		
d.	31	Wages Expense	20,000	
		Social Security Tax Payable ($20,000 × 6.2%)		1,240
		Medicare Tax Payable ($20,000 × 1.45%)		290
		Federal Income Tax Payable		2,000
		State Income Tax Payable		500
		Cash		15,970
		(Record wages expense and related liabilities)		

a.

Assets	=	Liabilities	+	Stockholders' Equity
+30,000		+30,000		

b.

Assets	=	Liabilities	+	Stockholders' Equity
+200,000		+200,000		

Assets	=	Liabilities	+	Stockholders' Equity
		+2,000		−2,000

c.

Assets	=	Liabilities	+	Stockholders' Equity
+10,600		+10,000		
		+600		

d.

Assets	=	Liabilities	+	Stockholders' Equity
−15,970		+1,240		−20,000
		+290		
		+2,000		
		+500		

(Continued)

	Stockholders'	
Assets = Liabilities +	**Equity**	
+200	−200	
+1,240	−1,240	
+290	−290	

Date	Account and Explanation	Debit	Credit
31	Employer Social Security Tax Expense	1,240	
	Employer Medicare Tax Expense	290	
	Federal Unemployment Tax Expense ($20,000 × 1%)	200	
	Social Security Tax Payable		1,240
	Medicare Tax Payable		290
	Federal Unemployment Tax Payable		200
	(Record employer payroll taxes)		

2. Before accounting for the additional information:

Current assets:	
Cash	$ 75,000
Accounts receivable	150,000
Inventory	270,000
Other current assets	60,000
Total current assets	$555,000
Current liabilities:	
Accounts payable	$100,000
Interest payable	0
Sales taxes payable	10,000
Short-term notes payable	0
Unearned revenues	30,000
Other current liabilities	45,000
Total current liabilities	$185,000

Current Ratio = $555,000/$185,000 = 3.0

3. After accounting for the additional information:

	Debit	Credit	
Current assets:			
Cash	$10,600 (c)	$ 15,970 (d)	$ 69,630
Accounts receivable			150,000
Inventory	30,000 (a)		300,000
Other current assets			60,000
Total current assets			$579,630
Current liabilities:			
Accounts payable		30,000 (a)	$130,000
Interest payable		2,000 (b)	2,000
Sales taxes payable		600 (c)	10,600
Short-term notes payable		200,000 (b)	200,000
Unearned revenues		10,000 (c)	40,000
Other current liabilities		5,760 (d)*	50,760
Total current liabilities			$433,360

*1,240 + 290 + 2,000 + 500 + 200 + 1,240 + 290 = 5,760

Current Ratio = $579,630/$433,360 = 1.34

4. The primary cause of the deterioration of ABC's current ratio is the addition of the short-term note payable related to the equipment. This transaction almost doubled the current liabilities, but current assets were unaffected by the addition of equipment. Another way to think about this is that ABC financed long-term operational assets with short-term financing.

Discussion Questions

1. What are liabilities?
2. How is the amount of a liability measured?
3. When are most liabilities recognized?
4. What are current liabilities? Provide some common examples.
5. Describe two ways (the book mentions three, but you only need two) in which current liabilities are frequently ordered on the balance sheet.
6. What is the difference between an account payable and a note payable?
7. What sort of transaction typically creates an account payable?
8. What type of transaction typically creates a note payable?
9. Why is interest ignored when recording accounts payable?
10. How is interest computed on an interest-bearing short-term note?
11. When would debt that must be repaid within the next year be classified as long-term instead of current?
12. What do we mean by accrued liabilities? Provide some common examples.
13. Provide examples of payroll taxes that are paid by the employee through reduction of their gross pay. Provide some examples of payroll taxes that are paid by the employer.
14. Why do unearned revenues and customers' deposits qualify as liabilities?
15. What are contingent liabilities? Provide an example.
16. Why is the liability for warranties recognized when products are sold rather than when the warranty services are performed?
17. Describe the circumstances under which the current, quick, and cash ratios, respectively, are more appropriate measures of short-term liquidity than the other ratios?
18. Describe the differences between the current, quick, and cash ratios. Which one is the most conservative measure of short-term liquidity?
19. How does the rationale for the operating cash flow ratio differ from the rationale for the current, quick, and cash ratios?

Multiple-Choice Exercises

8-1 Liabilities are recognized:

a. in exchange for goods.
b. in exchange for services.
c. in exchange for borrowing money.
d. all of the above.

8-2 When reporting liabilities on a balance sheet, in theory, what measurement should be used?

a. future value of the present outflow
b. present value of the present outflow
c. future value of the future outflow
d. present value of the future outflow

8-3 Kinsella Seed borrowed $200,000 on October 1, 2008, at 10 percent interest. The interest and principal are due on September 30, 2009. What journal entry should be recorded on December 31, 2008?

a. Debit Interest Payable 5,000; credit Interest Expense 5,000.
b. Debit Interest Receivable 20,000; credit Interest Expense 20,000.
c. Debit Interest Expense 5,000; credit Interest Payable 5,000.
d. No entry is necessary.

8-4 Kinsella Seed borrowed $200,000 on October 1, 2008, at 10 percent interest. The interest and principal are due on September 30, 2009. What journal entry should be made with respect to the interest payment on September 30, 2009?

a. Debit Interest Expense 15,000; debit Interest Payable 5,000; credit Cash 20,000.
b. Debit Interest Expense 15,000; credit Cash 15,000.
c. Debit Interest Expense 20,000; credit Cash 20,000.
d. Debit Cash 20,000; credit Interest Expense 15,000; credit Interest Payable 5,000.

8-5 Which of the following is *not* a current liability?

a. bonds payable due in five years
b. unearned revenue
c. sales tax
d. accounts payable

8-6 Which of the following is *not* an example of an accrued payable?

a. wages payable
b. accounts payable
c. property taxes payable
d. interest payable

8-7 Kramerica, Inc., sold 200 oil drums to Thompson Manufacturing for $100 each. In addition to the $100 sale price per drum, there is a $2 per drum federal excise tax and a 10 percent state sales tax. What journal entry should be made to record this sale?

a. Debit Accounts Receivable 20,000; debit Tax Expense 2,400; credit Federal Excise Tax Payable $400; credit State Sales Tax Payable 2,000; credit Revenue 20,000.
b. Debit Accounts Receivable 22,400; credit Federal Excise Tax Payable $400; credit State Sales Tax Payable 2,000; credit Revenue 20,000.
c. Debit Accounts Receivable 22,400; credit Revenue 22,400.
d. Debit Accounts Receivable 20,000; credit Revenue 20,000.

8-8 All of the following represent taxes commonly collected by businesses from customers *except*:

a. State sales tax
b. Federal excise tax
c. Local sales tax
d. Unemployment tax

8-9 Payroll taxes typically include all of the following *except*:

a. Social Security tax
b. Federal excise tax
c. Medicare tax
d. Federal income tax

8-10 When a credit is made to the state income tax payable account, the corresponding debit is made to:

a. Tax Expense
b. Cash
c. Wages Expense
d. Tax Payable

8-11 When should a contingent liability be recognized?

a. when the contingent liability is probable
b. when a reasonable estimation can be made
c. A and B
d. neither A nor B

8-12 Which of the following is *true*?

a. A contingent liability should always be recorded in the footnotes to the financial statements.
b. A contingent liability should always be recorded within the financial statements.
c. A company can choose to record a contingent liability either within its financial statements or in the footnotes to the financial statements.
d. No journal entries or footnotes are necessary if the possibility of a contingent liability is remote.

8-13 Warranty expense is:

a. recorded in the period of sale.
b. recorded as it is incurred.
c. capitalized as a warranty asset.
d. none of the above.

8-14 To record warranties, the adjusting journal entry would be:

a. a debit to Warranty Expense and a credit to Estimated Warranty Liability.
b. a debit to Warranty Expense and a debit to Cash.
c. a debit to Estimated Warranty Liability and a credit to Warranty Expense.
d. a debit to Estimated Warranty Liability and a credit to Cash.

8-15 How is the current ratio calculated?

a. Current Assets/Current Liabilities
b. (Cash + Marketable Securities + Accounts Receivable)/Current Liabilities
c. (Cash + Marketable Securities)/Current Liabilities
d. Cash flows from Operating Activities/Current Liabilities

8-16 How is the cash ratio calculated?

a. Current Assets/Current Liabilities
b. (Cash + Marketable Securities + Accounts Receivable)/Current Liabilities
c. (Cash + Marketable Securities)/Current Liabilities
d. Cash Flows from Operating Activities/Current Liabilities

Cornerstone Exercises

Cornerstone Exercise 8-17 NOTES PAYABLE

On June 30, Carmean Inc. borrows $100,000 from 1st National Bank with a 10-month, 6 percent note.

Required:

What journal entry is made on June 30?

OBJECTIVE ➤ 2
CORNERSTONE 8-1

Cornerstone Exercise 8-18 NOTES PAYABLE

Rogers Machinery Company borrowed $240,000 on June 1, with a six-month, 8.5 percent, interest-bearing note.

OBJECTIVE ➤ 2
CORNERSTONE 8-1

Required:

1. Record the borrowing transaction.
2. Record the repayment transaction.

OBJECTIVE ▶ 2
CORNERSTONE 8-2

Cornerstone Exercise 8-19 ACCRUED INTEREST

On October 1, Wilshire Company borrowed $60,000 from People's National Bank on a one-year, 7 percent note.

Required:

What adjusting entry should Wilshire make at December 31?

OBJECTIVE ▶ 2
CORNERSTONE 8-2

Cornerstone Exercise 8-20 ACCRUED INTEREST

On May 1, the Garner Corporation borrowed $30,000 from the First Bank of Midlothian on a one-year, 6 percent note.

Required:

If the company keeps its records on a calendar year, what adjusting entry should Garner make on December 31?

OBJECTIVE ▶ 2
CORNERSTONE 8-2

Cornerstone Exercise 8-21 ACCRUED PROPERTY TAXES

Annual property taxes covering the preceding 12 months are always paid to the county on June 30. Elise, Inc., is always assessed a $2,500 property tax by the county.

Required:

Given this information, determine the adjusting journal entry that Elise, Inc., must make on December 31 (assuming that its fiscal year ends as of December 31).

OBJECTIVE ▶ 2
CORNERSTONE 8-3

Cornerstone Exercise 8-22 SALES TAX

Garner's Antique Hot Rods recently sold a 1957 Chevy for $13,000. The state sales tax is 7 percent, and there is a $100-per-car federal excise tax.

Required:

Provide the journal entry to record the sale.

OBJECTIVE ▶ 2
CORNERSTONE 8-3

Cornerstone Exercise 8-23 SALES TAX

Cobb Baseball Bats sold 150 bats for $50 each, plus an additional sales tax of 7 percent.

Required:

Provide the journal entry to record the sale.

OBJECTIVE ▶ 2
CORNERSTONE 8-4

Cornerstone Exercise 8-24 PAYROLL TAXES

Hernandez Builders has a gross payroll for June amounting to $400,000. The following amounts have been withheld:

Federal income tax	$70,000
State income tax	30,000
Social Security	9,000
Medicare	3,000
Charitable contributions	1% of gross pay
Union dues	2% of gross pay

Also, the unemployment tax rate is 3 percent, and applies to all but $50,000 of the gross payroll.

Required:

1. What is the amount of net pay recorded by Hernandez?
2. Make the journal entry to record the payroll.

Cornerstone Exercise 8-25 **PAYROLL TAXES**

Kinsella, Inc., has a gross payroll of $8,000 for the pay period. Social Security and Medicare for both the employees and Kinsella are 6.2% and 1.45%, respectively, of the entire payroll. Kinsella must also withhold $800 in federal income tax from the employees and pay state unemployment tax of $30.

Required:

Provide the necessary journal entries for Kinsella to record these payroll taxes.

Cornerstone Exercise 8-26 **PAYROLL ADJUSTING ENTRIES**

Employees earn $5,000 per day, work five days per week, Monday through Friday, and get paid every Friday. The previous payday was January 26 and the accounting period ends on January 31.

Required:

What is the ending balance in the wages payable account on January 31?

Cornerstone Exercise 8-27 **PAYROLL ADJUSTING ENTRIES**

A company's weekly payroll amounts to $50,000 and payday is every Friday. Employees work five days per week, Monday through Friday. The appropriate journal entry was recorded at the end of the accounting period, Tuesday, March 31, 2009.

Required:

What journal entry is made on Friday, April 3, 2009?

Cornerstone Exercise 8-28 **UNEARNED REVENUE**

Brand Landscaping offers a promotion where they will mow your lawn 15 times if the customer pays $600 in advance.

Required:

Make the journal entry to record:

1. The customers' prepayment of $600.
2. Brand's mowing of the lawn one time.

Cornerstone Exercise 8-29 **CONTINGENT LIABILITIES**

Contingent liabilities are existing conditions, situations, or sets of circumstances involving uncertainty as to possible loss.

Required:

Under what circumstances (if any) are contingent liabilities recognized on the balance sheet?

Cornerstone Exercise 8-30 **CONTINGENT LIABILITIES**

Many companies provide warranties with their products. Such warranties typically guarantee the repair or replacement of defective goods for some specified period of time following the sale.

Required:

Why do most warranties require companies to make a journal entry to record a liability for future warranty costs?

Cornerstone Exercise 8-31 **WARRANTIES**

In 2009, BMJ Plumbing Company sold 400 water heaters for $350 each. The water heaters carry a two-year warranty for repairs. BMJ Plumbing estimates that repair costs will average 2 percent of the total selling price.

Required:

How much is recorded in the warranty liability account as a result of selling the water heaters during 2009, assuming no warranty service has yet been performed?

OBJECTIVE ➤ 4
CORNERSTONE 8-6

Cornerstone Exercise 8-32 WARRANTIES

In 2009, Waldo Balloons sold 100 hot air balloons at $4,000 each. The balloons carry a five-year warranty for defects. Waldo estimates that repair costs will average 4 percent of the total selling price. The estimated warranty liability at the beginning of the year was $42,000. Claims of $11,000 were actually incurred during the year to honor their warranty.

Required:

What was the balance in the estimated warranty liability at the end of the year?

OBJECTIVE ➤ 5
CORNERSTONE 8-7

Cornerstone Exercise 8-33 CURRENT RATIO

A company has $200 in cash, $500 in accounts receivable, $700 in inventory, and $400 in current liabilities.

Required:

1. What is its current ratio?
2. What is its quick ratio?
3. What is its cash ratio?

OBJECTIVE ➤ 5
CORNERSTONE 8-7

Cornerstone Exercise 8-34 CURRENT RATIO

Assume cash is $150, short-term marketable securities are $50, accounts receivable are $350, inventories are $275, current liabilities are $65, and total liabilities are $100.

Required:

1. What is the current ratio?
2. What is the quick ratio?
3. What is the cash ratio?

Exercises

OBJECTIVE ➤ 2

Exercise 8-35 RECORDING VARIOUS LIABILITIES

Glenview Hardware had the following transactions that produced liabilities during 2009:

a. Purchased merchandise on credit for $20,000.
b. Year-end wages of $7,600 incurred, but not paid. Related federal income tax of $1,200, Medicare tax of $280, and state income tax of $195 are withheld.
c. Year-end estimated income taxes payable, but unpaid, for the year in the amount of $21,300.
d. Sold merchandise on account for $872, including sales tax of $32.
e. Employer's share of Social Security tax for the period was $1,154.
f. Borrowed cash under a 90-day, 9 percent, $9,000 interest-bearing note.

Required:

Prepare the entry to record each of these transactions (treat each transaction independently).

OBJECTIVE ➤ 1 2 4

Exercise 8-36 REPORTING LIABILITIES

Morton Electronics had the following obligations:

a. A legally enforceable claim against the business to be paid in three months.
b. A guarantee given by a seller to a purchaser to repair or replace defective goods during the first six months following a sale.
c. An amount payable to Bank One in 10 years.
d. An amount to be paid next year to Citibank on a long-term note payable.

Required:

Describe how each of these items should be reported in the balance sheet.

Exercise 8-37 ACCOUNTS PAYABLE

OBJECTIVE ➤ 2

For Hammerton Autos, a used-car dealer, the following transactions occurred during the first 10 days of August:

a.   Hammerton purchased, on credit, space for classified advertisements in the *Chicago Tribune* for $245. The advertising was run the day the space was purchased.

b.   Hammerton purchased office supplies from Office Depot on credit in the amount of $185.

c.   One of Hammerton's sales staff sold a car. The salesperson's commission is $100. The commission will be paid September 10. (Concern yourself only with the commission.)

d.   The electric bill for July was received. The bill is $239 and is due August 15.

e.   A $390 bill from Carey Alignment services was received. Carey had aligned 10 cars for Hammerton in late July. The payment is due August 20.

Required:

Prepare journal entries for the above transactions. Assume that Hammerton prepares annual financial statements on December 31.

Exercise 8-38 ACCRUED LIABILITIES

OBJECTIVE ➤ 2

Charger Electronics had the following items that require adjusting entries at the end of the year.

1.   Charger pays its employees $2,500 every Friday. This year December 31 falls on a Thursday.

2.   Charger earned income of $150,000 for the year for tax purposes. Its effective tax rate is 30 percent. These taxes must be paid by April 15 of next year.

3.   Charger borrowed $50,000 with a note payable dated October 1. This note specifies 8 percent. The interest and principal are due on March 31 of the following year.

4.   Charger's president earns a bonus equal to 10 percent of income in excess of $100,000. Income for the year was $150,000. This bonus is paid in May of the following year and any expense is charged to wages expense.

Required:

Prepare the adjusting journal entries to record these transactions at the end of the current year.

Exercise 8-39 ACCRUED LIABILITIES

OBJECTIVE ➤ 2

Thornwood Tile had the following items that require adjusting entries at the end of the year.

1.   Thornwood pays payroll of $30,000 every other Friday. This year December 31 falls on the Tuesday before payday.

2.   Thornwood purchased $100,000 of tile on March 1 with a note payable requiring 12 percent interest. The interest and principal on this note are due within one year. As of December 31, Thornwood had not made any principal or interest payments.

3.   Thornwood's earned income is $500,000 for the year for tax purposes. Its effective tax rate is 25 percent. These taxes must be paid by April 15 of next year.

Required:

Prepare the adjusting journal entries to record these transactions at the end of the current year.

OBJECTIVE ▶ 2

Exercise 8-40 SALES TAX

Weston Cellular provides wireless phone service. During April 2010, it billed customers a total of $75,000 before taxes. Weston also must pay the following taxes on these charges:

1. State of Illinois sales tax of 6 percent
2. Federal excise tax of 0.01 percent
3. State of Illinois use tax of 0.05 percent

Required:

Assuming Weston collects these taxes from the customer, what journal entry would Weston make when the customers pay their bills?

OBJECTIVE ▶ 2

Exercise 8-41 PAYROLL ACCOUNTING

Blitzen Marketing Research paid its weekly and monthly payroll on January 31. The following information is available about the payroll:

Item	Amount	Expense Classification
Monthly salaries	$25,400	Administrative expense
Hourly wages	79,600	Operating expense
FICA:		
Social Security (both employee & employer)	6.20%	
Medicare (both employee & employer)	1.45%	Administrative expense
Withholding for federal income tax	$21,240	
Withholding for state income tax	2,680	
Federal unemployment tax	1,200	Administrative expense
State unemployment tax	600	Administrative expense

Blitzen will pay both the employer's taxes and the taxes withheld on April 15.

Required:

Prepare the journal entry to record the payroll payment and the incurrence of the associated expenses and liabilities.

OBJECTIVE ▶ 2

Exercise 8-42 UNEARNED REVENUE

Irvine Pest Control signed a $2,100-per-month contract on November 1, 2009, to provide pest control services to rental units owned by Garden Grove Properties. Irvine received three months' service fees in advance, on signing the contract.

Required:

1. Prepare Irvine's journal entry to record the $6,300 cash receipt.
2. Prepare Irvine's adjusting entry at December 31, 2009.
3. How would the advance payment be reported in Irvine Pest Control's December 31, 2009, balance sheet? How would the advance payment be reported in Garden Grove Properties' December 31, 2009, balance sheet?

OBJECTIVE ▶ 3

Exercise 8-43 RECOGNITION AND REPORTING OF CONTINGENT LIABILITIES

A list of alternative accounting treatments is followed by a list of potential contingent liabilities.

Alternative Accounting Treatments
a. Estimate the amount of liability and record.
b. Do not record as a liability but disclose in a footnote to the financial statements.
c. Neither record as a liability nor disclose in a footnote to the financial statements.

Potential Contingent Liabilities
1. Income taxes related to revenue included in net income this year but taxable in a future year.

2. Income taxes related to cash collected, which will be included in both net income and taxable income in a future year.
3. Estimated cost of future services under a product warranty related to past sales.
4. Estimated cost of future services under a product warranty related to future sales.
5. Estimated cost of pension benefits related to past employee services that has yet to be funded.
6. Loss from out-of-court settlement of lawsuit that is likely to occur toward the end of next year.
7. Potential loss on environmental cleanup suit against company; a court judgment against the company is considered less than probable but more than remotely likely.
8. Potential loss under class-action suit by a group of customers; during the current year, the likelihood of a judgment against the company has increased from remote to possible but less than probable.
9. Potential loss under an affirmative action suit by a former employee; the likelihood of a judgment against the company is considered to be remote.
10. Potential loss from a downturn in future economic activity.

Required:

Match the appropriate accounting treatment with each of the potential liabilities listed below. Your answer should list the numbers 1 through 10 and, opposite each number, the letter of the appropriate accounting treatment.

Exercise 8-44 WARRANTIES

Moon Electronics sells television sets and other sound and video equipment. Sales and expected warranty claims for the year are as follows:

Item	Unit Sales	Expected Warranty Claims for Warranty Period	Cost per Claim
Television set	860	1 claim per 100 sold	$60
VCR	290	10 claims per 100 sold	38
Stereo	1,800	4 claims per 100 sold	42

Required:
Prepare the entry to record warranty expense for Moon Electronics for the year.

Exercise 8-45 RATIO ANALYSIS

Intel Corporation provided the following information on its 2006 balance sheet and statement of cash flows:

Current liabilities	$8,514,000,000	Inventories	$ 4,314,000,000
Cash and equivalents	6,598,000,000	Other current assets	2,146,000,000
Marketable securities	3,404,000,000	Cash flows from	
Receivables	2,709,000,000	operating activities	10,620,000,000

Required:
1. Calculate the following:
   a. current ratio
   b. quick ratio
   c. cash ratio
   d. operating cash flow ratio
2. Interpret these results.

Problem Set A

OBJECTIVE ➤ 2

Problem 8-46A ACCOUNTS PAYABLE WITH PURCHASE DISCOUNTS

Richmond Company engaged in the following transactions during 2009:

a. Purchased $16,000 of merchandise on February 16. The seller offered terms of 1/10, n/15.
b. Paid for the purchased merchandise (transaction *a*) on February 26.
c. Borrowed $140,000 on a 10-month, 9 percent interest-bearing note on April 30.
d. Purchased $28,000 of merchandise on June 4. The seller offered terms of 2/15, n/20.
e. Paid for the purchased merchandise (transaction d) on June 24.
f. Received from Haywood, Inc., on August 19 a $12,000 deposit against a total selling price of $120,000 for merchandise to be manufactured for Haywood.
g. Paid quarterly installments of Social Security and individual federal income tax withholdings, as shown below, on October 15. The Social Security was recorded as an expense during the quarter, and the amount paid represents both the employee and employer share (50% each).

Social Security tax	$116,000
Federal income tax withheld	419,000

Assume that Richmond records inventory using the gross method.

Required:

1. Prepare journal entries for these transactions.
2. Prepare any adjusting entries necessary at December 31, 2009.

OBJECTIVE ➤ 2

Problem 8-47A PAYROLL ACCOUNTING

Stadium Manufacturing has the following data available for its September 30, 2009, payroll:

Wages earned	$183,000*
Federal income tax withheld	45,900
State income tax withheld	4,300

*All subject to Social Security and Medicare matching and withholding of 6.2% and 1.45%, respectively.

Federal unemployment tax at 0.8 percent is payable on wages of $4,000, and state unemployment tax at 3.0 percent is payable on the same amount of wages.

Required:

Compute the amounts of taxes payable and the amount of wages that will be paid to employees. Then prepare the journal entries to record the wages earned and the payroll taxes.

OBJECTIVE ➤ 2

Problem 8-48A INTEREST-BEARING NOTE

Fairborne Company borrowed $240,000 on a five-month, 7 percent, interest-bearing note on November 1, 2008. Fairborne ends its fiscal year on December 31. The note was paid with interest on March 31, 2009.

Required:

1. Prepare the entry for this note on November 1, 2008.
2. Prepare the adjusting entry for this note on December 31, 2008.
3. Indicate how the note and the accrued interest would appear in the balance sheet at December 31, 2008.
4. Prepare the entry to record the repayment of the note on March 31, 2009.

Problem 8-49A INTEREST-BEARING NOTE REPLACING AN UNPAID ACCOUNT PAYABLE

OBJECTIVE ➤ 2

Conti Products owed $50,000 on account for inventory purchased on December 1, 2010. Conti's fiscal year ends on December 31. Conti was unable to pay the amount owed by the February 28 due date because of financial difficulties. On March 1, 2011, Conti signed a $50,000, 10 percent interest-bearing note. This note was repaid with interest on September 1, 2011.

Required:

1. Prepare the entry recorded on December 1, 2010.
2. Prepare the adjusting entry recorded on December 31, 2010.
3. Prepare the entry recorded on March 1, 2011.
4. Prepare the entry recorded on September 1, 2011.

Problem 8-50A SALES TAX

OBJECTIVE ➤ 2

Clinton Power provides electricity to a wide area of western Kentucky. During October 2011 it billed 1,000 of its residential customers located in the town of Heyworth a total of $131,000 for electricity. In addition Clinton Power is required to collect the following taxes:

a. Meter Charge: A flat rate of $4.50 per customer remitted to the local municipality (Heyworth) to maintain and read the customer's meter
b. Public Benefit Charge: A State of Kentucky mandated charge of $1.25 per customer for investing in energy efficiency, renewable energy, and low-income assistance programs
c. State Tax: A tax of 1 percent used to fund the Kentucky Energy Commission
d. Federal Excise Tax: A tax of 0.05 percent used to fund the Federal Energy Commission

Required:

1. Determine how much Clinton Power will bill these 1,000 customers in total for the month of October 2011.
2. Provide the entry to record the billing of these amounts.
3. Provide the entry to record the collection of these amounts.
4. Provide the entry to record the payment of the sales taxes to the appropriate governmental unit.

Problem 8-51A UNEARNED REVENUE AND CUSTOMER DEPOSITS

OBJECTIVE ➤ 2

On November 20, 2009, Green Bay Electronics agreed to manufacture and supply 500 electronic control units used by Wausau Heating Systems in large commercial and industrial installments. Wausau deposited $480 per unit upon signing the three-year purchase agreement, which set the selling price of each control unit at $1,500. Green Bay will record these units at $300 per unit in inventory. No units were delivered during 2009. In 2010, 100 units were delivered, 150 units were delivered during 2011, and the remaining units were delivered during 2012. Assume Green Bay uses a perpetual inventory system.

Required:

1. Prepare the entry by Green Bay to record receipt of the deposit during 2009. How would the deposit be reported in the financial statements at the end of 2009?
2. Prepare the entry by Green Bay to record the delivery of 100 units during 2010. How would the deposit be reported in the financial statements at the end of 2010?
3. Prepare the entry by Green Bay to record the delivery of 150 units during 2011. Wausau pays in cash upon delivery for units not covered by the deposit.

Problem 8-52A WARRANTIES

OBJECTIVE ➤ 4

Mason Auto Repair specializes in the repair of foreign car transmissions. To encourage business, Mason offers a six-month warranty on all repairs. The following data are available for 2009:

Transmissions repaired, 2009	2,430
Expected frequency of warranty claims	0.07 per repair
Actual warranty claims, 2009	181
Estimated warranty liability, 1/1/09	$1,100
Cost of each warranty claim	21

Assume that warranty claims are paid in cash.

Required:

1. Compute the warranty expense for 2009.
2. Prepare the entry to record the payment of the 2009 warranty claims.
3. What is the December 31, 2009, balance in the estimated warranty liability account? Why has the balance in the estimated warranty liability account changed from January 1, 2009?

OBJECTIVE ▶ 5   **Problem 8-53A RATIO ANALYSIS**

Consider the following information taken from Green Mountain Coffee Roaster's (GMCR's) financial statements:

	September 30 (in thousands)	
	2006	**2005**
Current assets:		
Cash and cash equivalents	$ 1,274	$ 6,450
Receivables	30,071	16,548
Inventories	31,796	14,072
Other current assets	4,818	2,620
Total current assets	$67,959	$39,690
Current liabilities:		
Current portion of long-term debt	$ 97	$ 3,530
Accounts payable	23,124	11,228
Accrued compensation costs	5,606	1,929
Accrued expenses	9,108	5,054
Other current liabilities	874	777
Total current liabilities	$38,809	$22,518

Also, Green Mountain Coffee Roaster's operating cash flows were $12,829 and $14,874 in 2006 and 2005, respectively.

Required:

1. Calculate GMCR's current ratio for 2006 and 2005.
2. Calculate GMCR's quick ratio for 2006 and 2005.
3. Calculate GMCR's cash ratio for 2006 and 2005.
4. Calculate GMCR's operating cash flow ratio for 2006 and 2005.
5. Provide some reasons why GMCR's liquidity may be considered to be improving and some reasons why it may be worsening.

Problem Set B

OBJECTIVE ▶ 2   **Problem 8-46B ACCOUNTS PAYABLE WITH PURCHASE DISCOUNTS**

Daniels Company engaged in the following transactions during 2010:

a. Purchased $48,000 of merchandise on January 26. The seller offered terms of 1/10, n/15.
b. Paid for the purchased merchandise (transaction a) on February 6.
c. Borrowed $420,000 on an eight-month, 7 percent interest-bearing note on May 31.

d. Purchased $84,000 of merchandise on June 2. The seller offered terms of 2/15, n/20.
e. Paid for the purchased merchandise (transaction *d*) on June 28.
f. Received from Haywood, Inc., on September 4 a $36,000 deposit against a total selling price of $360,000 for merchandise to be manufactured for Haywood.
g. Paid quarterly installments of Social Security and individual federal income tax withholdings, as shown below, on October 10. The Social Security was recorded as an expense during the quarter, and the amount paid represents both the employee and employer share (50% each).

Social Security tax	$ 348,000
Federal income tax withheld	1,257,000

Assume that Daniels records inventory using the gross method.

Required:

1. Prepare journal entries for these transactions.
2. Prepare any adjusting entries necessary at December 31, 2010.

Problem 8-47B PAYROLL ACCOUNTING

OBJECTIVE ➤ 2

McLaughlin Manufacturing has the following data available for its March 31, 2009, payroll:

Wages earned	$366,000*
Federal income tax withheld	91,800
State income tax withheld	8,600

*All subject to Social Security and Medicare matching and withholding at 6.2% and 1.45%, respectively.

Federal unemployment tax at 3.2 percent is payable on wages of $7,000, and state unemployment tax at 3.0 percent is payable on the same amount of wages.

Required:

Compute the taxes payable and wages that will be paid to employees. Then prepare the journal entries to record the wages earned and the payroll taxes.

Problem 8-48B INTEREST-BEARING NOTE

OBJECTIVE ➤ 2

Bordewick Company borrowed $120,000 on a seven-month, 9 percent, interest-bearing note on October 1, 2009. Bordewick ends its fiscal year on December 31. The note was paid with interest on April 30, 2010.

Required:

1. Prepare the entry for this note on October 1, 2009.
2. Prepare the adjusting entry for this note on December 31, 2009.
3. Indicate how the note and the accrued interest would appear on the balance sheet at December 31, 2009.
4. Prepare the entry to record the repayment of the note on April 30, 2010.

Problem 8-49B INTEREST-BEARING NOTE REPLACING AN UNPAID ACCOUNT PAYABLE

OBJECTIVE ➤ 2

Monte Cristo Products owed $100,000 on account for inventory purchased on November 1, 2010. Monte Cristo's fiscal year ends on December 31. Monte Cristo was unable to pay the amount owed by the January 31 due date because of financial difficulties. On February 1, 2011, Monte Cristo signed a $100,000, 12 percent interest-bearing note. This note was repaid with interest on August 31, 2011.

Required:

1. Prepare the entry recorded on November 1, 2010.
2. Prepare the adjusting entry recorded on December 31, 2010.
3. Prepare the entry recorded on February 1, 2011.
4. Prepare the entry recorded on August 31, 2011.

OBJECTIVE ▶ 2

Problem 8-50B SALES TAX

Yossarian Power Corporation provides electricity to a wide area of eastern Maine. During March 2009 it billed 3,000 of its residential customers located in the town of Maryville a total of $393,000 for electricity. In addition Yossarian Power is required to collect the following taxes:

a. Meter Charge: A flat rate of $3.50 per customer remitted to the local municipality (Maryville) to maintain and read the customer's meter
b. Public Benefit Charge: A State of Maine mandated charge of $1.05 per customer for investing in energy efficiency, renewable energy, and low-income assistance programs
c. State Tax: A tax of 2 percent used to fund the Maine Energy Commission
d. Federal Excise Tax: A tax of 0.15 percent used to fund the Federal Energy Commission

Required:

1. Determine how much Yossarian Power will bill these 3,000 customers in total for the month of March 2009.
2. Provide the entry to record the billing of these amounts.
3. Provide the entry to record the collection of these amounts.
4. Provide the entry to record the payment of the sales taxes to the appropriate governmental unit.

OBJECTIVE ▶ 2

Problem 8-51B UNEARNED REVENUE AND CUSTOMER DEPOSITS

On November 20, 2011, Billy Pilgrim Technology agreed to manufacture and supply 800 centrifuges used by Cathcart Systems to produce chemicals. Cathcart deposited $100 per unit upon signing the three-year purchase agreement, which set the selling price of each centrifuge at $500. Billy Pilgrim will record these units at $150 per unit in inventory. No units were delivered during 2011. During 2012, 125 units were delivered, 75 units were delivered during 2013, and the remaining units were delivered during 2014. Assume Billy Pilgrim uses a perpetual inventory system.

Required:

1. Prepare the entry by Billy Pilgrim to record receipt of the deposit during 2011. How would the deposit be reported in the financial statements at the end of 2011?
2. Prepare the entry by Billy Pilgrim to record the delivery of 125 units during 2012. How would the deposit be reported in the financial statements at the end of 2012?
3. Prepare the entry by Billy Pilgrim to record the delivery of 75 units during 2013. Cathcart pays in cash upon delivery for units not covered by the deposit.

OBJECTIVE ▶ 4

Problem 8-52B WARRANTIES

Montague Auto Repair specializes in the repair of foreign car transmissions. To encourage business, Montague offers a six-month warranty on all repairs. The following data are available for 2009:

Transmissions repaired, 2009	1,250
Expected frequency of warranty claims	0.12 per repair
Actual number of warranty claims, 2009	75
Estimated warranty liability, 1/1/09	$ 550
Cost of each warranty claim	$ 10

Assume that warranty claims are paid in cash.

Required:

1. Compute the warranty expense for 2009.
2. Prepare the entry to record the payment of the 2009 warranty claims.
3. What is the December 31, 2009, balance in the estimated warranty liability account? Why has the balance in the estimated warranty liability account changed from January 1, 2009?

Problem 8-53B **RATIO ANALYSIS**   OBJECTIVE  5

Consider the following information taken from Chicago Water Slide's (CWS's) financial statements:

| | September 30 (in thousands) | |
	2008	2007
Current assets:		
Cash and cash equivalents	$ 2,548	$12,900
Receivables	60,142	33,096
Inventories	63,592	28,144
Other current assets	9,636	5,240
Total current assets	$135,918	$79,380
Current liabilities:		
Current portion of long-term debt	$ 194	$ 7,060
Accounts payable	46,248	22,456
Accrued compensation costs	11,212	3,858
Accrued expenses	18,216	10,108
Other current liabilities	1,748	1,554
Total current liabilities	$ 77,618	$45,036

Also, Chicago Water Slide's Operating Cash Flows were $25,658 and $29,748 in 2008 and 2007, respectively.

Required:

1. Calculate CWS's current ratio for 2008 and 2007.
2. Calculate CWS's quick ratio for 2008 and 2007.
3. Calculate CWS's cash ratio for 2008 and 2007.
4. Calculate CWS's operating cash flow ratio for 2008 and 2007.
5. Provide some reasons why CWS's liquidity may be considered to be improving and some reasons why it may be worsening.

Cases

Case 8-54 **ETHICS AND CURRENT LIABILITIES**

Many long-term loans have contractual restrictions designed to protect the lender from deterioration of the borrower's liquidity or solvency in the future. These restrictions (typically called loan covenants) often take the form of financial-statement ratio values. For example, a lending agreement may state that the loan principal is immediately due and payable if the current ratio falls below 1.2. When borrowers are in danger of violating one or more of these loan covenants, pressure is put on management and the financial accountants to avoid such violations.

Jim is a second year accountant at a large publicly-traded corporation. His boss approaches him and says,

> "Jim, I know why we increased our warranty liability, but it puts our current ratio in violation of a loan covenant with our bank loan. I know the bank will pass on it this time, but it's a big hassle to get the waiver. I just don't want to deal with it. I need you to reduce our estimate of warranty liability as far as possible."

Required:

1. How would lowering the estimate of warranty liability affect the current ratio?
2. How should Jim respond to his boss?
3. Given that Jim's employer is a publicly-traded corporation, what safeguards should be at Jim's disposal?

Case 8-55 SHORT-TERM BORROWING WITH RESTRICTIONS

Rocky Mountain Products has a line-of-credit agreement with Norwest Bank that allows it to borrow up to $100,000 at any given time provided that Rocky Mountain's current assets always exceed its current liabilities by the principal amount of the out- standing loan. If this requirement is violated, the entire loan is payable immediately; thus Rocky Mountain is very careful to fulfill the requirement at all times. All loans under this line of credit are due in one month and bear interest at a rate of 1 percent per month. On January 1, 2009, Rocky Mountain has current assets of $150,000 and current liabilities of $92,000; hence, the excess of current assets over current liabilities is $58,000. Rocky Mountain's current liabilities at January 1, 2009, include a short-term loan under the line of credit of $35,000 due on February 1, 2009.

Required:

1. Prepare the journal entry to record the borrowing of $35,000 on January 1, 2009. By how much did this transaction increase or decrease the excess of current assets over current liabilities?
2. Assume that Rocky Mountain used the entire amount of the loan to purchase inventory. Prepare the journal entry to record the purchase. By how much did this purchase increase or decrease the excess of current assets over current liabilities?
3. Without violating the loan restriction, how much more could Rocky Mountain borrow under its line of credit on January 1, 2009, to invest in inventory? To invest in new equipment? Explain.

Case 8-56 RESEARCHING AND ANALYSIS USING THE ANNUAL 10-K

Obtain **Whole Foods'** 2007 annual report either through the "Investor Relations" portion of its website (do a web search for Whole Foods investor relations) or go to http://www.sec.gov and click "Search for company filings" under "Filings & Forms (EDGAR)."

Required:

1. What are Whole Foods' total current liabilities for 2007?
2. How much of their current liabilities is the current portion of long-term liabilities?
3. How much is the current portion of long-term debt (see Note 8)?
4. Look at Item 3 in the 10-K (this discusses Whole Foods' legal proceedings). Describe the major current legal proceedings involving Whole Foods. Based on the information in item 3, do you believe that Whole Foods has recognized a contin- gent liability related to these current legal proceedings?
5. Calculate Whole Foods' current ratio for 2007 and 2006.
6. Discuss Whole Foods' short-term liquidity based on the values and trends of the current ratio.
7. Calculate Whole Foods' quick ratio and cash ratio for 2007 and 2006.
8. Discuss the implications of these ratios when evaluating Whole Foods' short-term liquidity.
9. Calculate Whole Foods' operating cash flows ratio.
10. Discuss the implications of this ratio when evaluating Whole Foods' short-term li- quidity.

Case 8-57 COMPARATIVE ANALYSIS: ABERCROMBIE & FITCH vs. AEROPOSTALE

Refer to the financial statements of **Abercrombie & Fitch** and **Aeropostale** that are supplied with this text.

Required:

1. Both Abercrombie & Fitch (Note 14) and Aeropostale (Note 14) have notes that discuss contingencies. What contingencies do they disclose? Do you think any of these contingencies are included in the Income Statement or on the Balance Sheet? Why or why not?

2. Calculate Abercrombie & Fitch's and Aeropostale's current ratio for the years ended February 3, 2007, and January 28, 2006.
3. Compare Abercrombie & Fitch's and Aeropostale's short-term liquidity based on the values and trends of the current ratio.
4. Calculate Abercrombie & Fitch's and Aeropostale's quick ratio and cash ratio for the years ended February 3, 2007, and January 28, 2006.
5. Compare the values and trends of these ratios when evaluating Abercrombie & Fitch's and Aeropostale's short-term liquidity.
6. Calculate Abercrombie & Fitch's and Aeropostale's operating cash flows ratio for the years ended February 3, 2007, and January 28, 2006.
7. Compare Abercrombie & Fitch's and Aeropostale's short-term liquidity based on the values and trends of the operating cash flows ratio.

9

Long-Term Liabilities

After studying Chapter 9, you should be able to:

1. Describe debt securities and the markets in which they are issued.

2. Account for the issuance of long-term debt.

3. Use the straight-line method to account for premium/discount amortization.

4. Use the effective interest rate method to account for premium/discount amortization.

5. Determine the after-tax cost of financing with debt and explain financial leverage.

6. Contrast the terms and the accounting for operating and capital leases.

7. Analyze a company's long-term solvency using information related to long-term liabilities.

8. (Appendix 9A) Calculate the market price of long-term debt using present value techniques.

Experience Financial Accounting

with Marriott

Marriott International, Inc., is a worldwide operator and franchisor of approximately 3,000 hotels and related facilities. With 13 lodging brands ranging from the Ritz-Carlton to Fairfield Inn, Marriott has locations in 68 countries and territories. In 2007, Marriott's net income was almost $700 million with revenues of $12.90 billion. Further, the total value of their outstanding stock at the end of 2007 was approximately $12.2 billion, which was the highest in the industry. Marriott continues to expand with about 100,000 rooms under construction at the end of 2007, and their cash flows from operations are more than sufficient to finance their expansion and improvement plans.

However, Marriott's long-term debt continues to grow as it increased from approximately $1.8 billion at the end of 2006 to $2.8 billion at the end of 2007. Further, in the exhibit below, you will notice that the long-term debt appears to be increasing at a far greater rate than net income. Is the increasing long-term debt level a bad sign?

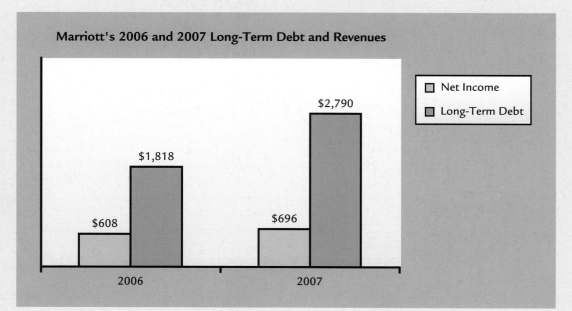

Marriott's 2006 and 2007 Long-Term Debt and Revenues

- Net Income
- Long-Term Debt

2006: $608, $1,818
2007: $696, $2,790

Industries that use property, plant, and equipment to generate revenues (e.g., hotels) typically have higher debt than industries that use intangible assets (e.g., software or pharmaceuticals). There are a number of reasons this is true, but one is that PP&E is readily transferable to creditors in the event of financial distress, so creditors are more receptive to lending at lower rates.

After reading the chapter, we will see that increasing long-term debt is not necessarily a bad sign. Although increasing long-term debt means increasing interest expense, interest expense has the advantage of being tax deductible unlike dividends paid to shareholders. Another advantage is that creditors do not share in the profits of the company, while shareholders do. Thus, if the borrowed money creates a return that is greater than the interest expense on the debt, the shareholders benefit. This is the concept of leverage. We will discuss this concept more in Chapter 12.

Long-term debt generally refers to obligations that extend beyond one year. Bonds, long-term notes, debentures, and capital leases belong in this category of liabilities. Exhibit 9-1 shows **Whirlpool**'s long-term debt obligations.[1]

On the balance sheet, long-term debt is typically reported as a single number. The more detailed list, like this one for Whirlpool, is usually included in the notes to the financial statements.

Notice that Whirlpool subtracted current maturities (just before the bottom line) from the rest of its long-term debt. The difference ($1,798 for 2006) is the amount included as long-term debt on the balance sheet. As we noted in Chapter 8, long-term debt that is due to mature over the next year is reported as a current liability. In the interest of simplifying our discussion of long-term debt, we will disregard the reclassification of long-term debt as current liabilities throughout this chapter.

Companies use long-term debt, along with issuing stock (see Chapter 10), as a way to finance and expand their operations. There is a long history of finance research investigating the optimal mix of debt and equity financing because there are advantages and disadvantages for both. Determining the optimal mix is beyond the scope of this book, but suffice it to say that factors affecting the optimal mix are difficult to quantify. One measure of this mix is the debt to equity ratio (see further discussion later in the chapter). Exhibit 9-2 shows the debt to equity ratio for select industries as taken from Google Finance. A debt to equity ratio above 1.0 indicates that liabilities are greater than stockholders' equity.

The cash flows or other economic sacrifices required to pay long-term debt obligations are clearly specified in debt contracts. They include repayment of principal

---

Exhibit 9-1

Excerpt from Whirlpool's 2006 10-K

	December 31,	
	2006	2005
	(in millions)	
Eurobonds (EUR 300 million)—5.875% due 2006	$ —	$ 357
Medium-term notes, from 5% to 9.03%, maturing from 2007 to 2015	314	—
Debentures—9.1%, maturing 2008	125	125
Variable rate notes, maturing through 2009	200	—
Senior notes, from 6.125% to 8.6%, maturing from 2010 to 2016	873	325
Debentures—7.75%, maturing 2016	243	243
Other (various maturing through 2013)	60	60
	$1,815	$1,110
Less current maturities	17	365
Total long-term debt, net of current maturities	$1,798	$ 745

---

[1] We use the term *debt* instead of *liabilities* in this chapter because this is the term used in real financial statements.

Exhibit 9-2

Debt to Equity Ratio Levels for Various Industries

Software and programming	0.16
Major drugs (pharmaceuticals)	0.35
Water utilities	1.13
Hotel and motels	1.44
Airlines	3.23

plus interest. Thus borrowing using long-term debt instruments creates interest expense. When an obligation extends over several interest periods, the amount of interest associated with each period must be determined. **Interest amortization** is the process used to determine the amount of interest to be recorded in each of the periods the liability is outstanding.[2]

There are two methods of interest amortization. The **effective interest rate method** is based on compound interest calculations. The **straight-line method**, on the other hand, represents a simple approximation of effective interest amortization. Although the effective interest rate method is the technically correct method, the straight-line method may be used if it produces approximately the same numerical results as the effective interest rate method. Frequently, the two methods do, in fact, produce quite similar results. In this book, the effective interest rate and straight-line methods are discussed separately.

Bonds Payable and Notes Payable

OBJECTIVE ▸1
Describe debt securities and the markets in which they are issued.

When a company borrows money from a bank, it typically signs a formal agreement or contract called a "note." Frequently, notes are also issued in exchange for a noncash asset such as equipment. Collectively, we refer to these notes as **notes payable**. Larger corporations typically elect to issue bonds instead of notes. A **bond** is a type of note which requires the issuing entity to pay the face value of the bond to the holder when it matures and usually to pay interest periodically at a specified rate. A bond issue essentially breaks down a large debt (large corporations frequently borrow hundreds of millions of dollars) into smaller chunks (usually $1,000) because the total amount borrowed is too large for a single lender. For example, rather than try to find a single bank willing (and able) to lend $800,000,000 at a reasonable interest rate, corporations typically find it easier and more economical to issue 800,000 bonds with a $1,000 face value. *However, the concept behind the way we account for notes and bonds is identical (the only difference is the account title—either "bonds payable" or "notes payable") and analysts typically do not distinguish between the two.* As such, the terms have come to be used somewhat interchangeably.

All such contracts require the borrower to repay the **face value** (also called **par value** or **principal**). Typically the face value is repaid at **maturity**, which is a specified date in the future. However, some contracts require the principal to be repaid in, for example, monthly installments. These contracts typically require equal payments to be made each period. A portion of each payment is interest and a portion is principal. Car and home loans are examples of installment loans. We illustrate installment debt later in the chapter.

Most debt contracts also require that the borrower make regular interest payments. Historically, interest payments were made when a bondholder detached a coupon from the debt contract and mailed it to the company on the interest payment date. These obligations are called *coupon notes, coupon debentures, or coupon bonds,*

[2] The same interest amortization procedures used by borrowers to account for liabilities are also used by lenders to account for the corresponding assets.

and the required interest payments are *coupon payments*. The terminology for coupons is still used today, but most often, the payments are automatically sent to the registered bondholder.

The amount of each interest payment can be calculated from the face amount, the interest rate, and the number of payments per year, all stated in the debt contract. (The interest rate identified in the contract goes by various names, including **stated rate**, **coupon rate**, and **contract rate**). Recall the formula for calculating interest:

$$\text{Face Value} \times \text{Interest Rate} \times \text{Time (in years)}$$

To illustrate, consider a contract with a face amount of $1,000, a stated interest rate of 8 percent, and semiannual interest payments. For this $1,000 note the amount of each semiannual interest payment is $40:

$$\$1,000 \times 8\% \times 6/12 = \$40$$

In practice, bonds also differ along a number of other dimensions. First, bonds are either **secured** or **unsecured**. A secured bond has some collateral pledged against the corporation's ability to pay. For example, **mortgage bonds** are secured by real estate. In this case, should the borrower fail to make the payments required by the bond, the lender can take possession of the real estate (i.e., repossess) that secures the bond. The real estate provides "security" for the lender in case the debt is not paid. Bonds are also frequently secured by the stocks or bonds of other corporations and, in theory, can be secured by anything of value.

Most bonds, however, are unsecured. These are typically called **debenture bonds**. In this case there is no collateral; instead, the lender is relying on the general credit of the corporation. What this really means is, should the borrower go bankrupt, any secured bondholders will get their collateral before the unsecured bondholders receive a single penny. That is, unsecured bondholders are the last lenders to be paid in bankruptcy (only the shareholders follow). You may have heard of the term **junk bonds**. These are unsecured bonds where the risk of the borrower failing to make the payments is relatively high. Why would anyone lend money under such circumstances? Because they receive a high enough rate of interest to compensate them for the risk.

Bonds also may be callable. **Callable bonds** give the borrower the right to pay off (or call) the bonds prior to their due date. The borrower typically "calls" debt when the interest rate being paid is much higher than the current market conditions. It is not unlike when homeowners refinance to obtain a lower interest rate on their home mortgage.

Finally, bonds also may be convertible. **Convertible bonds** allow the bondholder to convert the bond into another security—typically common stock. Convertible bonds will specify the conversion ratio. For example, each $1,000 bond may be convertible into 20 shares of common stock. In this case, bondholders will convert when the value of the 20 shares becomes more attractive than the interest payments and repayment of the $1,000 principal. Exhibit 9-3 summarizes long-term debt terms you will need to understand.

Selling New Debt Securities

Borrowing, through the use of notes or bonds, is attractive to businesses as a source of money because the relative cost of issuing debt (i.e., the interest payments) is often lower than the cost of issuing equity (i.e., giving up ownership shares). Businesses may sell bonds directly to institutions such as insurance companies or pension funds. However, bonds are frequently sold to the public through an underwriter. Underwriters generate a profit either by offering a price that is slightly less than the expected market price (thereby producing a profit on resale) or by charging the borrower a fee.

Underwriters examine the provisions of the instrument (i.e., secured or unsecured, callable or not callable, convertible or not convertible), the credit standing of the borrowing business, and the current conditions in the credit markets and

Exhibit 9-3

Long-Term Debt Terms

Notes/Bonds	Different names for debt instruments that require borrowers to pay the lender the face value and usually to make periodic interest payments.
Face Value/Par Value/Principal	The amount of money the borrower agrees to repay at maturity.
Maturity Date	The date on which the borrower agrees to pay the creditor the face (or par) value.
Stated/Coupon/Contract Rate	The rate of interest paid on the face (or par) value. The borrower pays the interest to the creditor each period until maturity.
Market/Yield Rate	The market rate of interest demanded by creditors. This is a function of economic factors and the creditworthiness of the borrower. It may differ from the stated rate.
Secured and Unsecured/ Debenture Bonds	Secured debt provides collateral (e.g., real estate or another asset) for the lender. That is, if the borrower fails to make the payments required by the debt, the lender can "repossess" the collateral. Debt that does not have collateral is unsecured. Unsecured bonds typically are called debenture bonds.
Junk Bonds	Junk bonds are unsecured bonds that are also very risky, and, therefore, pay a high rate of interest to compensate the lender for the added risk.
Callable Bonds	Callable bonds give the borrower the option to pay off the debt prior to maturity. Borrowers will typically exercise this option when the interest being paid on the debt is substantially greater than the current market rate of interest.
Convertible Bonds	Convertible bonds give the lender the option to convert the bond into other securities—typically shares of common stock. Lenders will typically exercise this option when the value of the shares of common stock is more attractive than the interest and principal payments supplied by the debt instrument.

the economy as a whole to determine the **market rate** of interest (or **yield**) for the bond. The yield may differ from the stated rate because the underwriter disagrees with the borrower as to the correct yield or because changes in the economy or creditworthiness of the borrower between the setting of the stated rate and the date of issue.

As shown in Exhibit 9-4, there are three possible relationships between the stated interest rate and yield: (1) they can be equal, (2) the yield can be less than the stated rate, or (3) the yield can be greater than the stated rate. If the yield is equal to the stated rate, the bonds sell for the face value, or par. If the yield is less than the stated rate, the bonds represent particularly good investments because the interest payments are higher than market. In this case, the demand for such bonds will bid the selling price up above face value. When this happens bonds are said to sell at a premium. On the other hand, if the yield is greater than the stated rate of interest, the below market interest payments will drive the selling price below the face value.

Exhibit 9-4

The Relationships between Stated Interest Rate and Yield

Bonds Sold at	Yield Compared to Stated Rate	Interest Over the Life of the Bonds
Premium (above Par)	Yield < Stated Rate	Interest Expense < Interest Paid
Par	Yield = Stated Rate	Interest Expense = Interest Paid
Discount (below Par)	Yield > Stated Rate	Interest Expense > Interest Paid

OBJECTIVE ▶ 2
Account for the issuance of long-term debt.

Accounting for Issuance of Long-Term Debt

As mentioned previously, the accounting for notes and bonds is conceptually identical. We will illustrate the accounting with some bond examples and some note examples, but remember that everything would stay the same in the examples if we substituted the word note for bond and vice versa.

There are three basic cash flows for which the issuing corporation must account: the cash received when the bonds are issued (the issue or selling price), the interest payments, and the repayment of the principal (or face value).

Assume that a corporation issues bonds with a total face value of $500,000, with a stated rate of 6.5 percent payable annually, and the principal is due in five years. Exhibit 9-5 depicts all three cash flows.

Recording Issuance

The market price for debt is typically quoted as a percentage of face value. For example, if $100,000 face value bonds are issued at 103, their selling price is 103 percent of face value, or $103,000. Any amount paid above the face value is called a premium. In this case, a $3,000 premium was paid. If the bond is issued below face value, this difference is called a discount. For example, if these $100,000 face value bonds were issued at 96, there would be a $4,000 discount.

At the time of issue, the borrower records the face value of the bonds in a bond payable account and records any premium or discount in a separate account called Premium on Bonds Payable or Discount on Bonds Payable (see Cornerstone 9-1). The premium and discount accounts are called "valuation" accounts because they affect the value at which the liability is shown on the balance sheet. That is, as you can see in Exhibit 9-6, both the premium and discount accounts are netted with bonds payable on the balance sheet, so on the date of issue the book value of the bonds payable is equal to the market value.

CONCEPT Q&A

Why is the market value of bonds not always equal to their face value?

Possible Answer:
If, for example, the stated rate of interest is higher than the market rate of interest, the bonds represent particularly good investments. As such, the demand for such bonds will bid up the price above face value. On the other hand, if the stated rate of interest is lower than the market rate of interest, the lack of demand for such bonds will bid the market price below face value.

Exhibit 9-5

Cash Flows for a Bond

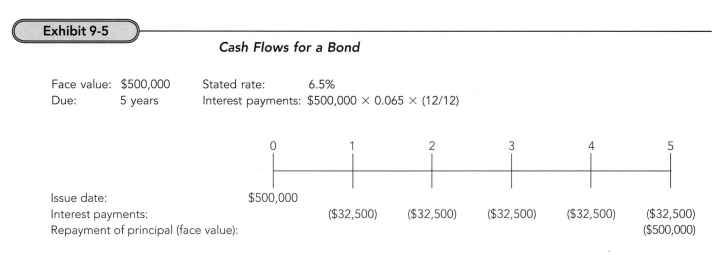

Face value:	$500,000	Stated rate:	6.5%
Due:	5 years	Interest payments:	$500,000 × 0.065 × (12/12)

	0	1	2	3	4	5
Issue date:	$500,000					
Interest payments:		($32,500)	($32,500)	($32,500)	($32,500)	($32,500)
Repayment of principal (face value):						($500,000)

Exhibit 9-6

Balance Sheet Presentation

Long-term liabilities:
Bonds payable	100,000	
Add: Premium on bonds payable	3,000	
Carrying value		103,000

Or

Long-term liabilities:
Bonds payable	100,000	
Less: Discount on bonds payable	4,000	
Carrying value		96,000

HOW TO Record the Issuance of Bonds

**CORNERSTONE
9 - 1**

Concept:
When bonds are issued, the Bonds Payable account is increased by the face amount of the bonds. As such, this represents the principal that must be repaid at maturity—regardless of the issue price of the bonds. Any premium or discount is recorded in a separate, valuation account. A premium exists when lenders pay more than face value for the bonds because the stated rate is greater than yield. A discount, on the other hand, exists when lenders pay less than face value for the bonds because the stated rate is less than yield.

Information:
On December 31, 2006, ABC Co. issued $100,000 face value of bonds, with a stated rate of 8 percent, due in five years with interest payable annually on December 31.

Required:
1. Provide the journal entry assuming the bonds sell for par.
2. Provide the journal entry assuming the bonds sell for 103.
3. Provide the journal entry assuming the bonds sell for 96.

Solution:
1. At par:

Date	Account and Explanation	Debit	Credit
Dec. 31, 2006	Cash	100,000	
	Bonds Payable		100,000
	(Record issuance of bonds at par)		

	Assets	=	Liabilities	+	Stockholders' Equity
	+100,000		+100,000		

2. At 103:

Date	Account and Explanation	Debit	Credit
Dec. 31, 2006	Cash (100,000 × 103%)	103,000	
	Bonds Payable		100,000
	Premium on Bonds Payable		3,000
	(Record issuance of bonds at premium)		

	Assets	=	Liabilities	+	Stockholders' Equity
	+103,000		+100,000		
			+3,000		

3. At 96:

Date	Account and Explanation	Debit	Credit
Dec. 31, 2006	Cash (100,000 × 96%)	96,000	
	Discount on Bonds Payable	4,000	
	Bonds Payable		100,000
	(Record issuance of bonds at discount)		

	Assets	=	Liabilities	+	Stockholders' Equity
	+96,000		+100,000		
			−4,000		

OBJECTIVE ▶ 3
Use the straight-line method to account for premium/discount amortization.

Recognizing Interest Expense and Repayment of Principal—The Straight-Line Method

Keep in mind that any amount paid to the lender in excess of the amount borrowed (i.e., face value less any discount or plus any premium) represents interest. Let's see why. When bonds mature, the face value is repaid to the lender, regardless of whether they were issued at face value, at a premium, or at a discount. In our examples above, when the bonds were issued at par (face value) the amount of cash received when issued was equal to the amount to be repaid at maturity. When the bonds were issued at a premium, the amount of cash received when issued was $103,000 ($3,000 greater than the face value), but only the face value ($100,000) is repaid at maturity. The $3,000 difference represents an effective reduction of the amount of interest paid to the borrower. In contrast, when the bonds were issued at a discount, the amount of cash received was $96,000 ($4,000 less than the face value), but the entire face value ($100,000) must be repaid at maturity. The additional $4,000 effectively represents additional interest. However, the accounting system must allocate this interest among the various accounting periods in which the debt is outstanding. This allocation has two parts: (1) the actual interest payment made to the lender during the period and (2) amortizing any premium or discount on the bond.

Although the interest payment made to the lender during the period is always a component of the period's interest expense, there are two methods for amortizing any premium or discount. In the effective interest rate method, interest expense for the period is always the yield (i.e., effective interest rate) times the carrying (or book) value of the bonds at the beginning of the period. The second method is the straight-line method. In this method equal amounts of premium or discount are amortized to interest expense each period. Although GAAP requires use of the effective interest rate method, the straight-line method may be used if the results are not materially different from the effective interest rate method.

Repayment of the principal at maturity is trivial. Recall that the principal amount repaid is equal to the face value. This is also the amount that was originally credited to the note or bond payable. As such, you merely need to debit the note or bond payable and credit the cash.

While it is possible for companies to sell an almost unlimited number of different kinds of debt instruments by varying parameters of the contract, we want to discuss three of the most frequently used forms:

1. Debt with regular interest payments sold at their face or par value.
2. Debt with no interest payments and a single payment of principal at maturity. Because no interest payments are made (i.e., a stated rate of zero percent), this debt is sold for a relatively large discount.
3. Debt with regular interest payments sold for more (a premium) or less (a discount) than the face or par value.

For each of these debt contracts, we will discuss how interest expense is allocated to the various accounting periods using the straight-line method.

Debt with Regular Interest Payments Sold at Par

When debt is sold at par there is no premium or discount to amortize. In this case, the interest expense reported on the income statement is equal to the interest payment(s) made to the creditor during the period (see Cornerstone 9-2). This situation typically happens when a business borrows from a single creditor. In this case, the two parties can easily agree on a stated rate that equals the appropriate yield. Cornerstone 9-2 illustrates how interest expense is recorded in this case.

Debt Requiring No Interest Payments

Some businesses want to avoid the necessity of making regular interest payments during the life of their long-term debt obligations so they can use the cash that would otherwise be paid in interest to invest in new assets. Fortunately, there are some

HOW TO Record Interest Expense for Bonds Sold at Par

**CORNERSTONE
9-2**

Concept:
When bonds are issued at par there is no discount or premium to amortize so the only component of interest expense is the interest paid to the lender for the period.

Information:
On December 31, 2006, ABC Co. issued $100,000 of 8 percent bonds at par. These bonds are due in five years with interest payable annually on December 31.

Required:
1. Calculate the interest payment made on December 31 of each year.
2. Provide the journal entry necessary to recognize the interest expense on December 31, 2007–2011.
3. Provide the journal entry to record the repayment of the loan principal on December 31, 2011.

Solution:
1. The interest payment on December 31 of each year will be:

$$\$100,000 \times 8\% = \$8,000$$

2. Recognition of interest expense on December 31, 2007–2011.

Date	Account and Explanation	Debit	Credit
Dec. 31	Interest Expense	8,000	
	Cash		8,000
	(Record interest payment)		

Assets	=	Liabilities	+	Stockholders' Equity
−8,000				−8,000

Note that the interest expense recorded is equal to the cash paid to the lender when the bond is issued at par.

3. Recognition of repayment of the bond principal on December 31, 2011.

Date	Account and Explanation	Debit	Credit
Dec. 31, 2011	Bonds Payable	100,000	
	Cash		100,000
	(Record repayment of principal)		

Assets	=	Liabilities	+	Stockholders' Equity
−100,000		−100,000		

investors who do not want to receive cash interest payments. The presence of these borrowers and lenders creates a market for *zero coupon* (no interest payment) debt.

A zero coupon debt instrument is sold at a substantial discount from face value because the stated rate (zero percent) is obviously below yield. For example, zero coupon bonds are also called *deep discount* bonds because of the substantial discount necessary to sell these bonds. Although no interest payments are made, a portion of the discount is amortized as interest expense each period. At maturity, the discount has been fully amortized (i.e., the discount balance is $0) and the borrower repays the lender the face value of the debt.

Exhibit 9-7 shows how the carrying value of the bond shown in Cornerstone 9-3 grows over time due to the discount amortization. Remember that carrying value is the bond payable balance (which is a credit) less the discount balance (which is a debit). It is also worth re-emphasizing three other points. First, as the discount is amortized, the carrying value increases. Second, at maturity the discount is fully amortized and the carrying value is equal to the face value. Third, zero-coupon bonds are issued at substantial discounts because 0 percent interest is substantially below market yield rates (in this case the yield would have been

CONCEPT Q&A

How can there be interest expense each period for zero-coupon bonds if there are no interest payments?

Possible Answer:
Zero-coupon bonds are sold at a deep discount. After all, who would lend $1 today to only receive $1 at some point in the future? The difference between the issue price (e.g., $24,000,000 in Cornerstone 9-3) and the face value repaid at maturity (e.g., $50,000,000 in Cornerstone 9-3) represents interest. This interest is allocated, or matched, to each of the accounting periods in which the loan is outstanding.

Exhibit 9-7

Carrying Value over the Life of a Zero-Coupon Bond

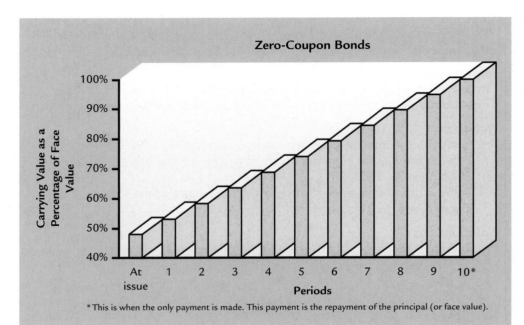

Zero-Coupon Bonds

* This is when the only payment is made. This payment is the repayment of the principal (or face value).

**CORNERSTONE
9-3**

HOW TO Record Interest Expense for Zero-Coupon Bonds

Concept:
When noninterest-bearing bonds are issued, the discount is amortized to interest expense each period. Under the straight-line method of amortization, an equal amount of discount is amortized each period.

Information:
On December 31, 2006, XYZ Co. issued $50,000,000 of 10-year, zero-coupon bonds at 48.

Required:
1. Provide the journal entry to record the issuance of the bonds on December 31, 2006.
2. Calculate the amount of discount that will be amortized each period.
3. Provide the journal entry necessary to recognize the interest expense on December 31, 2007–2016.
4. Provide the journal entry to record the repayment of the loan principal on December 31, 2016.
5. Complete the following amortization table:

Annual Period	Cash Payment (Credit)	Interest Expense (Debit)	Discount on Bonds Payable (Credit)	Discount on Bonds Payable Balance	Carrying Value*
At issue					
1					
2					
3					
4					
5					
6					
7					

Annual Period	Cash Payment (Credit)	Interest Expense (Debit)	Discount on Bonds Payable (Credit)	Discount on Bonds Payable Balance	Carrying Value*
8					
9					
10					

*Carrying Value = Face Value − Discount on Bonds Payable

Solution:

1. Entry to record the issuance of bonds:

Date	Account and Explanation	Debit	Credit
Dec. 31, 2006	Cash	24,000,000	
	Discount on Bonds Payable	26,000,000	
	Bonds Payable		50,000,000
	(Record issuance of zero-coupon bonds)		

	Stockholders'
Assets = Liabilities +	Equity
+24,000,000 −26,000,000	
+50,000,000	

2. The total discount is:

Face Value − Bond Issue Price = Discount

$50,000,000 − ($50,000,000 × 48\%) = $ Discount

$50,000,000 − $24,000,000 = $26,000,000$

The total discount will be amortized equally over the 10-year life of the bond:

$26,000,000/10 \text{ years} = $2,600,000$ per year

3. Recognition of interest expense on December 31, 2007–2016.

Date	Account and Explanation	Debit	Credit
Dec. 31	Interest Expense	2,600,000	
	Discount on Bonds Payable		2,600,000
	(Record interest expense on zero-coupon bonds)		

	Stockholders'
Assets = Liabilities +	Equity
+2,600,000	−2,600,000

4. Recognition of repayment of the bond principal on December 31, 2016.

Date	Account and Explanation	Debit	Credit
Dec. 31, 2016	Bonds Payable	50,000,000	
	Cash		50,000,000
	(Record repayment of principal)		

	Stockholders'
Assets = Liabilities +	Equity
−50,000,000 −50,000,000	

5.

Annual Period	Cash Payment (Credit)	Interest Expense (Debit)	Discount on Bonds Payable (Credit)	Discount on Bonds Payable Balance	Carrying Value
At issue				$26,000,000	$24,000,000
1	$0	$2,600,000	$2,600,000	23,400,000	26,600,000
2	0	2,600,000	2,600,000	20,800,000	29,200,000
3	0	2,600,000	2,600,000	18,200,000	31,800,000
4	0	2,600,000	2,600,000	15,600,000	34,400,000
5	0	2,600,000	2,600,000	13,000,000	37,000,000
6	0	2,600,000	2,600,000	10,400,000	39,600,000
7	0	2,600,000	2,600,000	7,800,000	42,200,000
8	0	2,600,000	2,600,000	5,200,000	44,800,000
9	0	2,600,000	2,600,000	2,600,000	47,400,000
10	0	2,600,000	2,600,000	0	50,000,000

Note that the discount on bonds payable is amortized to $0 at maturity.

approximately 7.63 percent). In this example notice that the beginning carrying value was less than 50 percent of the face value.

Debt with Regular Interest Payments Sold at a Premium or Discount

As mentioned above, the sale of a bond at a discount or premium affects the borrower's interest expense. This is because total interest expense is the difference between the payments to the lenders and the amount received by the borrowing business. Let us compare a $1,000,000, 10 percent, five-year bond contract with semiannual interest payments that are sold at a $10,000 discount (99 percent of par) with the same issue sold at a $20,000 premium (102 percent of par).

	Bond Sold at a Discount	Bond Sold at a Premium
Face amount payment at maturity	$1,000,000	$1,000,000
Interest payments (10 at $50,000 each)	500,000	500,000
Total payments to lenders	$1,500,000	$1,500,000
Less: Proceeds at issue	990,000	1,020,000
Total interest expense over life of bond	$ 510,000	$ 480,000

For the discounted bond, total interest expense ($510,000) exceeds interest payments ($500,000) by $10,000. For the bond issued at a premium, total interest expense ($480,000) is $20,000 less than the cash interest payments ($500,000).

This total interest expense is spread over the life of the bond. For the 10 percent, $1,000,000 bond sold at 99, interest expense would be $51,000 per six-month interest period:

$$\frac{\$510,000}{10} = \$51,000 \text{ per six-month interest period}$$

Another way of calculating this would be as follows:

Interest paid	$50,000
Amortization of discount (10,000/10 periods)	1,000
Total interest expense per period	$51,000

In fact, amortization tables like you see in Cornerstones 9-3, 9-4, and 9-5 are used to help calculate these amounts. Although such tables aren't really necessary when using the straight-line method for amortizing bond discount or premium, they are extremely helpful when the effective interest rate method is used, as is shown later in the chapter.

CORNERSTONE 9-4

HOW TO Record Interest Expense for Bonds Sold at a Discount

Concept:
When interest-bearing bonds are issued at a discount, the interest expense for the period is the amount of interest payment for the period *plus* the discount amortization for the period. Under the straight-line method of amortization, an equal amount of discount is amortized each period.

Information:
On December 31, 2006, ISU Inc. issues five-year, $100,000,000, 8 percent bonds at 99 ($99,000,000). The discount at the time of the sale is $1,000,000. Interest is paid semiannually on June 30 and December 31.

Required:
1. Provide the journal entry to record the issuance of the bonds on December 31, 2006.
2. Calculate the amount of discount that will be amortized each semiannual period.

3. Calculate the amount of interest expense for each semiannual period.
4. Complete the following amortization table:

CORNERSTONE
9-4
(continued)

Semiannual Period	Cash Payment (Credit)	Interest Expense (Debit)	Discount on Bonds Payable (Credit)	Discount on Bonds Payable Balance	Carrying Value
At issue					
1					
2					
3					
4					
5					
6					
7					
8					
9					
10					

5. Provide the journal entry necessary to recognize the interest expense on June 30 and December 31, 2007–2011.
6. Provide the journal entry to record the repayment of the loan principal on December 31, 2011.

Solution:

1. Entry to record the issuance of bonds at a discount:

Date	Account and Explanation	Debit	Credit
Dec. 31, 2006	Cash	99,000,000	
	Discount on Bonds Payable	1,000,000	
	Bonds Payable		100,000,000
	(Record issuance of bonds)		

	Assets = Liabilities + Stockholders' Equity
	+99,000,000 −1,000,000
	+100,000,000

2. Discount Amortization $= \dfrac{\$1,000,000}{10 \text{ periods}} = \$100,000$ per period

3. Interest Expense = Interest Payment + Discount Amortization
$$= (100,000,000 \times 8\% \times 6/12) + 100,000$$
$$= 4,000,000 + 100,000$$
$$= 4,100,000$$

4.

Semiannual Period	Cash Payment (Credit)	Interest Expense (Debit)	Discount on Bonds Payable (Credit)	Discount on Bonds Payable Balance	Carrying Value
At issue				$1,000,000	$ 99,000,000
1	$4,000,000	$4,100,000	$100,000	900,000	99,100,000
2	4,000,000	4,100,000	100,000	800,000	99,200,000
3	4,000,000	4,100,000	100,000	700,000	99,300,000
4	4,000,000	4,100,000	100,000	600,000	99,400,000
5	4,000,000	4,100,000	100,000	500,000	99,500,000
6	4,000,000	4,100,000	100,000	400,000	99,600,000
7	4,000,000	4,100,000	100,000	300,000	99,700,000
8	4,000,000	4,100,000	100,000	200,000	99,800,000
9	4,000,000	4,100,000	100,000	100,000	99,900,000
10	4,000,000	4,100,000	100,000	0	100,000,000

Note that the discount on bonds payable is amortized to $0 at maturity.

**CORNERSTONE
9-4
(continued)**

		Stockholders'
Assets =	Liabilities +	Equity
−4,000,000	+100,000	−4,100,000

5. The following entry would be made at all 10 interest payment dates:

Date	Account and Explanation	Debit	Credit
June 30/Dec. 31	Interest Expense	4,100,000	
	Cash		4,000,000
	Discount on Bonds Payable		100,000
	(Record interest payment on bonds)		

6. At maturity (December 31, 2011), the bond principal is paid off along with the final interest payment (the final interest payment was recorded in 4).

		Stockholders'
Assets =	Liabilities +	Equity
−100,000,000	−100,000,000	

Date	Account and Explanation	Debit	Credit
Dec. 31, 2011	Bonds Payable	100,000,000	
	Cash		100,000,000
	(Record repayment of principal)		

**CORNERSTONE
9-5**

HOW TO Record Interest Expense for Bonds Sold at a Premium

Concept:
When interest-bearing bonds are issued at a premium, the interest expense for the period is the amount of interest payment for the period *less* the premium amortization for the period. Under the straight-line method of amortization, an equal amount of premium is amortized each period.

Information:
On December 31, 2006, ISU Inc. issues five-year, $100,000,000, 8 percent bonds at 102 ($102,000,000). The premium at the time of the sale is $2,000,000. Interest is paid semiannually on June 30 and December 31.

Required:
1. Provide the journal entry to record the issuance of the bonds on December 31, 2006.
2. Calculate the amount of premium that will be amortized each semiannual period.
3. Calculate the amount of interest expense for each semiannual period.
4. Complete the following amortization table:

Semiannual Period	Cash Payment (Credit)	Interest Expense (Debit)	Premium on Bonds Payable (Debit)	Premium on Bonds Payable Balance	Carrying Value
At issue					
1					
2					
3					
4					
5					
6					
7					
8					
9					
10					

5. Provide the journal entry necessary to recognize the interest expense on June 30 and December 31, 2007–2011.
6. Provide the journal entry to record the repayment of the loan principal on December 31, 2011.

Solution:

1. Entry to record the issuance of bonds at a premium:

Date	Account and Explanation	Debit	Credit
Dec. 31, 2006	Cash	102,000,000	
	Bonds Payable		100,000,000
	Premium on Bonds Payable		2,000,000
	(Record issuance of bonds)		

	Stockholders'	
Assets =	**Liabilities** +	**Equity**
+102,000,000	+2,000,000	
	+100,000,000	

2. Premium Amortization = Total Premium/Number of Interest Periods
$$= 2,000,000/10$$
$$= 200,000$$

3. Interest Expense = Interest Payment − Premium Amortization
$$= (100,000,000 \times 8\% \times 6/12) - 200,000$$
$$= 4,000,000 - 200,000$$
$$= 3,800,000$$

4.

Semiannual Period	Cash Payment (Credit)	Interest Expense (Debit)	Premium on Bonds Payable (Debit)	Premium on Bonds Payable Balance	Carrying Value
At issue				$2,000,000	$102,000,000
1	$ 4,000,000	$3,800,000	$200,000	1,800,000	101,800,000
2	4,000,000	3,800,000	200,000	1,600,000	101,600,000
3	4,000,000	3,800,000	200,000	1,400,000	101,400,000
4	4,000,000	3,800,000	200,000	1,200,000	101,200,000
5	4,000,000	3,800,000	200,000	1,000,000	101,000,000
6	4,000,000	3,800,000	200,000	800,000	100,800,000
7	4,000,000	3,800,000	200,000	600,000	100,600,000
8	4,000,000	3,800,000	200,000	400,000	100,400,000
9	4,000,000	3,800,000	200,000	200,000	100,200,000
10	4,000,000	3,800,000	200,000	0	100,000,000

Note that the premium on bonds payable is amortized to $0 at maturity.

5. The following entry would be made at all 10 interest payment dates:

Date	Account and Explanation	Debit	Credit
June 30/Dec. 31	Interest Expense	3,800,000	
	Premium on Bonds Payable	200,000	
	Cash		4,000,000
	(Record interest payment on bonds)		

	Stockholders'	
Assets =	**Liabilities** +	**Equity**
−4,000,000	−200,000	−3,800,000

6. At maturity (December 31, 2011), the bond principal is paid off along with the final interest payment (the final interest payment was recorded in 4).

Date	Account and Explanation	Debit	Credit
Dec. 31, 2011	Bonds Payable	100,000,000	
	Cash		100,000,000
	(Record repayment of principal)		

	Stockholders'	
Assets =	**Liabilities** +	**Equity**
−100,000,000	−100,000,000	

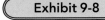

Exhibit 9-8

Carrying Value over the Life of a Bond Issued at a Discount

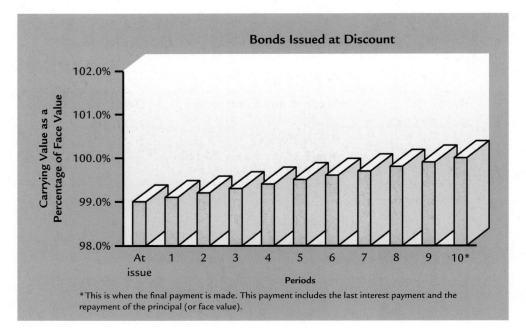

*This is when the final payment is made. This payment includes the last interest payment and the repayment of the principal (or face value).

Exhibit 9-8 illustrates how the carrying value of the bond shown in Cornerstone 9-4 grows over time due to the discount amortization. Notice that the beginning carrying value is 99 percent of the face value. This indicates that although the 8 percent stated rate is below market yield, it is only slightly below. (In fact, the yield would be approximately 8.25 percent.) Further, although the magnitude of the discount and the corresponding amortization is much smaller than it was on the zero-coupon bond, the discount amortization still increases the bond carrying value. In Cornerstone 9-5 we see how things change when the bond is issued at a premium.

Exhibit 9-9 illustrates how the carrying value of the bonds shown in Cornerstone 9-5 declines over time due to the premium amortization. Notice that the beginning carrying value is 102 percent of the face value. This indicates that the 8 percent stated rate is slightly above market yield. (In fact, the yield would be approximately 7.51 percent.) Notice that in this case, the carrying value is the face value of the bond plus the premium because both the bond payable and the premium have credit balances. Further, as the premium is amortized, the premium balance declines and the carrying value moves closer to face value.

CONCEPT Q&A

Why are premiums and discounts on bonds payable amortized to Interest Expense?

Possible Answer:

Discounts occur when the stated rate of interest is below the market rate of interest. In this, case lenders lend less than the face value to the borrower, but are repaid the entire face value at maturity. This difference between the amount lent and the amount repaid conceptually represents an additional interest payment to compensate the lender for accepting a below market interest rate. Similarly, premiums occur when the stated rate of interest is above the market rate of interest. In this case, lenders lend more than the face value to the borrower, but are only repaid the face value at maturity. This difference represents a prepayment of interest by the lender to compensate the borrower for providing above market interest payments.

Accruing Interest

In the previous discussion, interest payments were made on the last day of the period—December 31. This is frequently not the case in the real world. Assume that on September 1, 2007, Quark Communications borrows $120,000,000 with a three-year, 7 percent note. The note requires annual interest payments (each equal to 7 percent of $120,000,000) and repayment of the principal plus the final year's interest

Exhibit 9-9

Carrying Value over the Life of a Bond Issued at a Premium

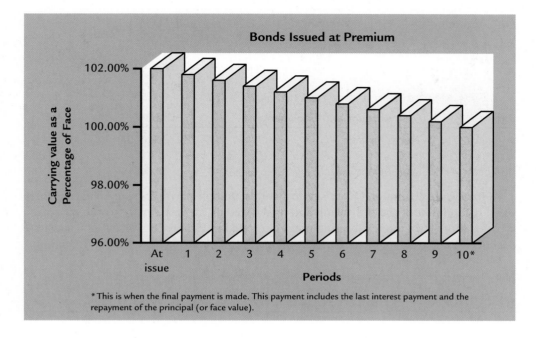

Bonds Issued at Premium

*This is when the final payment is made. This payment includes the last interest payment and the repayment of the principal (or face value).

at the end of the third year. This borrowing would be recognized in Quark's accounts as follows:

Date	Account and Explanation	Debit	Credit
Sept. 1, 2007	Cash	120,000,000	
	Notes Payable		120,000,000
	(Record issuance of note)		

	Stockholders'
Assets = Liabilities +	Equity
+120,000,000 +120,000,000	

The annual interest payment is $8,400,000 ($120,000,000 × 0.07), and is due on August 31 of 2007, 2008 and 2009. The total amount of cash paid over the life of the note is $145,200,000 [(3 × $8,400,000) + $120,000,000], and the total interest on the note is $25,200,000 ($145,200,000 − $120,000,000). Using straight-line procedures, the interest amortized to each interest period is $8,400,000 ($25,200,000/3)—exactly the same as the interest payment in each period.

Since no interest payment is made at Quark's year end (December 31), interest must be accrued for the period. Interest expense for the four-month period from September through December is $2,800,000 [(4/12) × $8,400,000]. That means interest expense for the eight-month period from January through August is $5,600,000 [(8/12) × $8,400,000]. Quark would recognize interest expense and the payment of interest on this note during 2007, 2008 and 2009 as follows:

9/1/07   12/31/07   8/31/08   12/31/08   8/31/09   12/31/09   8/31/10

| 4 months | 8 months | 4 months | 8 months | 4 months | 8 months |

accrue interest | $8,400,000 pay interest | accrue interest | $8,400,000 pay interest | accrue interest | $8,400,00 pay interest

1. *Adjustment to recognize interest expense and interest payable on 12/31/07, 12/31/08, and 12/31/09*

Date	Account and Explanation	Debit	Credit
Dec. 31	Interest Expense	2,800,000	
	Interest Payable		2,800,000
	(Record accrual of interest on note)		

	Stockholders'
Assets = Liabilities +	Equity
+2,800,000 −2,800,000	

2. *Recognition of interest expense (8 months) and payment of 12 months interest on 8/31/08, 8/31/09 and 8/31/10:*

Date	Account and Explanation	Debit	Credit
Aug. 31	Interest Expense	5,600,000	
	Interest Payable	2,800,000	
	Cash		8,400,000
	(Record payment of interest on note)		

3. *Recognition payment of note principal on 8/31/10:*

Date	Account and Explanation	Debit	Credit
Aug. 31, 2010	Notes Payable	120,000,000	
	Cash		120,000,000
	(Record repayment of principal on note)		

Observe that although Quark's note involves multiple payments extending over three years, recognition of the borrowing and its repayment are very similar to the procedure used for short-term interest-bearing notes illustrated in Chapter 8. We will now illustrate the effective interest rate method of accounting for premium and discount amortization.

OBJECTIVE ▶ 4
Use the effective interest rate method to account for premium/discount amortization.

Recognizing Interest Expense and Repayment of Principal—The Effective Interest Rate Method

The straight-line and effective interest rate methods are identical when a bond is issued at par because there are no premiums or discounts to amortize. Further, even when premiums or discounts exist, the *total* interest expense over the life of the bonds is identical. However, the interest expense allocated to the individual accounting periods differs because premiums and discounts are amortized in different manners.

Under the effective interest rate method, the amortization of premiums and discounts results in the interest expense for each accounting period being equal to a constant percentage of the bond book value (also called *carrying value*). That is, the interest expense changes every period, but the effective interest rate on the bond book value is constant. The straight-line method, on the other hand, has a constant interest expense each period, but the effective interest rate on the bond book value changes every period.

To use the effective interest method, you must distinguish between interest payments, which are calculated as follows:

$$\text{Face Value} \times \text{Stated Rate} \times \text{Time (in years)}$$

and effective interest expense, which is calculated as follows:

$$\text{Carrying Value} \times \text{Yield Rate} \times \text{Time (in years)}$$

This difference is so important it bears emphasis. Interest payments are calculated with face value and the stated rate of interest. These payments are the same each period. Interest expense, under the effective rate method, is calculated by using the Carrying Value (Face Value − Discount Balance or Face Value + Premium Balance) and the yield, or market rate, of interest.

Cornerstones 9-6 and 9-7 illustrate how discounts and premiums, respectively, are amortized under the effective interest rate method.

Note that the interest expense using the straight-line method is a constant amount. In contrast, the interest expense using the effective interest method results in a different amount each period. This is because the interest expense is based on a constant *rate*. This rate is applied to the remaining carrying value of the bonds each

HOW TO Record Interest Expense for Bonds Sold at a Discount using the Effective Interest Rate Method

CORNERSTONE 9-6

Concept:
When interest-bearing bonds are issued at a discount, the interest expense for the period is the amount of interest payment for the period *plus* the discount amortization for the period. Under the effective interest rate method of amortization, a constant (or effective) rate of interest on the bond book, or carrying, value is allocated to the period.

Information:
On December 31, 2006, ABC Co. issued $1,000,000 of 8 percent bonds, due in five years with interest payable annually on December 31. The market rate of interest is 9 percent. Assume the bond was issued at $961,103. This was calculated using time value of money concepts (see Cornerstone 9-10 in the appendix for calculation).

Required:

1. Complete the following amortization table:

Annual Period	Cash Payment (Credit)	Interest Expense (Debit)	Discount on Bonds Payable (Credit)	Discount on Bonds Payable Balance	Carrying Value
At issue					
12/31/07					
12/31/08					
12/31/09					
12/31/10					
12/31/11					

2. Provide the journal entry necessary to recognize the interest expense on December 31, 2007 and 2008.
3. Provide the journal entry to record the repayment of the loan principal on December 31, 2011.

Solution:

1.

Annual Period	Cash Payment* (Credit)	Interest Expense** (Debit)	Discount on Bonds Payable*** (Credit)	Discount on Bonds Payable Balance	Carrying Value****
At issue				$38,897	$ 961,103
12/31/07	$80,000	$86,499	$6,499	32,398	967,602
12/31/08	80,000	87,084	7,084	25,314	974,686
12/31/09	80,000	87,722	7,722	17,592	982,408
12/31/10	80,000	88,417	8,417	9,175	990,825
12/31/11	80,000	89,175	9,175	0	1,000,000

*Cash Payment = Face Value × 8% × 12/12 = $80,000
**Interest Expense = Carrying Value × 9% × 12/12
***Change in Discount Balance = Interest Expense − Cash Payment.
****New Carrying Value = Previous Carrying Value + Change in Discount on Bonds Payable Balance.

CORNERSTONE 9-6
(continued)

12/31/07

Assets =	Liabilities +	Stockholders' Equity
−80,000	+6,499	−86,499

12/31/08

Assets =	Liabilities +	Stockholders' Equity
−80,000	+7,084	−87,084

	Stockholders'
Assets = Liabilities +	Equity
−1,000,000 −1,000,000	

2. The following entries would be made on December 31, 2007 and 2008:

	12/31/07		12/31/08	
Account and Explanation	**Debit**	**Credit**	**Debit**	**Credit**
Interest Expense	86,499		87,084	
Cash		80,000		80,000
Discount on Bonds Payable		6,499		7,084
(Record interest payment on bonds)				

3. At maturity (December 31, 2011) the bond principal is paid off along with the final interest payment (assume the final interest payment was recorded in a separate entry as in 2).

Date	Account and Explanation	Debit	Credit
Dec. 31, 2011	Bonds Payable	1,000,000	
	Cash		1,000,000
	(Record repayment of principal)		

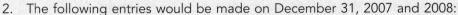

CORNERSTONE 9-7

HOW TO Record Interest Expense for Bonds Sold at a Premium using the Effective Interest Rate Method

Concept:
When interest-bearing bonds are issued at a premium, the interest expense for the period is the amount of interest payment for the period *minus* the premium amortization for the period. Under the effective interest rate method of amortization, a constant (or effective) rate of interest on the bond book, or carrying, value is allocated to the period.

Information:
On December 31, 2006, ABC Co. issued $1,000,000 of 8 percent bonds, due in five years with interest payable annually on December 31. The market rate of interest is 7 percent. Assume the bond was issued at $1,041,002 (see Cornerstone 9-10 for calculation).

Required:

1. Complete the following amortization table:

Annual Period	Cash Payment (Credit)	Interest Expense (Debit)	Premium on Bonds Payable (Debit)	Premium on Bonds Payable Balance	Carrying Value
At issue					
12/31/07					
12/31/08					
12/31/09					
12/31/10					
12/31/11					

2. Provide the journal entry necessary to recognize the interest expense on December 31, 2007 and 2008.
3. Provide the journal entry to record the repayment of the loan principal on December 31, 2001.

**CORNERSTONE
9-7**
(continued)

Solution:

1.

Annual Period	Cash Payment* (Credit)	Interest Expense** (Debit)	Premium on Bonds Payable*** (Debit)	Premium on Bonds Payable Balance	Carrying Value****
At issue				$41,002	$1,041,002
12/31/07	$80,000	$72,870	$7,130	33,872	1,033,872
12/31/08	80,000	72,371	7,629	26,243	1,026,243
12/31/09	80,000	71,837	8,163	18,080	1,018,080
12/31/10	80,000	71,266	8,734	9,346	1,009,346
12/31/11	80,000	70,654	9,346	0	1,000,000

* Cash Payment = Face Value × 8% × 12/12 = $80,000
** Interest Expense = Carrying Value × 7% × 12/12
*** Change in Premium Balance = Cash Payment − Interest Expense
**** New Carrying Value = Previous Carrying Value − Change in Premium on Bonds Payable Balance

2. The following entry would be made on December 31, 2007 and 2008:

Account and Explanation	12/31/07 Debit	12/31/07 Credit	12/31/08 Debit	12/31/08 Credit
Interest Expense	72,870		72,371	
Premium on Bonds Payable	7,130		7,629	
Cash		80,000		80,000
(Record interest payment on bonds)				

12/31/07

		Stockholders'
Assets =	**Liabilities** +	**Equity**
−80,000	−7,130	−72,870

12/31/08

		Stockholders'
Assets =	**Liabilities** +	**Equity**
−80,000	−7,629	−72,371

3. At maturity (December 31, 2011), the bond principal is paid off along with the final interest payment (assume the final interest payment was recorded in a separate entry as in 2).

Date	Account and Explanation	Debit	Credit
Dec. 31, 2011	Bonds Payable	1,000,000	
	Cash		1,000,000
	(Record repayment of principal)		

		Stockholders'
Assets =	**Liabilities** +	**Equity**
−1,000,000	−1,000,000	

period. Exhibit 9-10 illustrates how the carrying value of the bonds are different between the straight-line and effective interest methods for both a premium and a discount.

Installment Debt

Instead of paying off the principal at maturity, some debt requires a portion of the principal to be paid off each period (usually monthly), along with some interest. Classic installment debt payments are home mortgages or car payments. Installment debt payments are the same each period, but the portion that is considered interest changes because the outstanding principal balance is changing. To illustrate, consider buying a car for $20,000, at 6 percent annual interest, and 48 monthly payments. In this case, each monthly payment would be $469.70. After 48 payments you would have paid a total of $22,545.60 ($469.70 × 48). This means you would have paid $2,545.60 of interest and $20,000 of principal. However, the initial monthly

CONCEPT Q&A

Why is the effective interest rate method GAAP?

Possible Answer:

The effective interest rate method does a better job allocating, or matching, the time value of money to the proper period. Under the effective interest rate method, the interest expense is equal to market rate of interest (or yield) at issue on the bond book value. This makes sense because market forces will ensure that the creditor receives the market rate of return on the investment.

Exhibit 9-10

Long-Term Debt Carrying Value Using Straight-Line and Effective Interest Methods to Amortize Premium and Discount

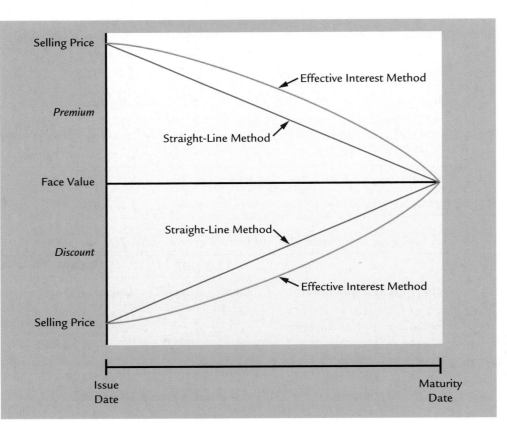

CONCEPT Q&A

How do credit cards calculate interest?

Possible Answer:

Although terms vary from card to card, they all charge some percentage of our average balance for the period. For example, if your card charges 1.5 percent of the average balance for the month and you have a $5,000 average balance, then interest would be $75. Interest of 1.5 percent may not sound that bad, but remember that this is per month. That equates to 18 percent per year (1.5 percent × 12 months). Further, if all you do is pay the interest, recognize that you are not lowering your outstanding balance at all.

payments would have a relatively high portion allocated to interest because your outstanding loan balance is relatively high. Your last few payments, on the other hand, would have a relatively low portion allocated to interest because your outstanding loan balance is relatively low. We use a home mortgage to illustrate installment debt in Cornerstone 9-8.

Exhibit 9-11 shows the installment note discussed in Cornerstone 9-8. Notice that interest is a decreasing portion of each payment. This is because the principal balance is decreasing with each payment. Although this exhibit doesn't provide the detail, with long-term installment loans (e.g., a home mortgage often requires monthly payments over 30 years—360 in total), a vast majority of the early payments will be interest expense.

**CORNERSTONE
9-8**

HOW TO Account for Installment Debt Using the Effective Interest Rate Method

Concept:

Installment debt has equal periodic payments with a portion of each payment being allocated to interest expense and the remainder paying down the principal balance. The interest expense portion is calculated as follows:

Outstanding Loan Balance at the Beginning of the Period × Interest Rate × Time (in years)

CORNERSTONE
9-8
(continued)

Accordingly, each payment reduces the outstanding loan balance, which in turn, reduces the interest expense in the subsequent period.

Information:
On December 31, 2009, Strand Ranch buys a John Deere combine for $190,000. Strand Ranch signs an installment note to pay off the debt with 10 semiannual payments (i.e., they'll pay it off over five years). The note specifies a 5 percent interest rate, which results in a $21,709.17 payment every six months for the next five years. (Note that the final payment is adjusted to be equal to the remaining balance. The difference occurs due to rounding.)

Required:
1. Provide the journal entry to record the purchase of the John Deere combine on December 31, 2009.
2. Complete the following amortization table:

Period	Cash Payment (Credit)	Interest Expense (Debit)	Reduction of Note Payable (Debit)	Note Payable Balance
At Issue				
1				
2				
3				
4				
5				
6				
7				
8				
9				
10				

3. Provide the journal entry to record the installment loan payment on June 30, 2011 (the third payment).
4. Provide the journal entry to record the installment loan payment on December 31, 2014 (the tenth, and final, payment).

Solution:
1. Entry to record the issuance of note for purchase of equipment:

Date	Account and Explanation	Debit	Credit
Dec. 31, 2009	Equipment	190,000	
	Notes Payable		190,000
	(Record note issued for equipment purchase)		

	Stockholders'
Assets = Liabilities + Equity	
+190,000 +190,000	

2.

Period	Cash Payment (Credit)	Interest Expense (Debit)	Reduction of Note Payable (Debit)	Note Payable Balance
At issue				$190,000.00
1	$21,709.17	$4,750.00	$16,959.17	173,040.83
2	21,709.17	4,326.02	17,383.15	155,657.68
3	21,709.17	3,891.44	17,817.73	137,839.95
4	21,709.17	3,446.00	18,263.17	119,576.78
5	21,709.17	2,989.42	18,719.75	100,857.03
6	21,709.17	2,521.43	19,187.74	81,669.29
7	21,709.17	2,041.73	19,667.44	62,001.85
8	21,709.17	1,550.05	20,159.12	41,842.73
9	21,709.17	1,046.07	20,663.10	21,179.63
10	21,709.12*	529.49	21,179.63	0.00

*Plug amount, slight difference due to rounding.

CORNERSTONE
9-8
(continued)

	Stockholders'
Assets = Liabilities +	Equity
−21,709.17 −17,817.73	−3,891.44

3. Recognize that the interest expense is declining each period because the outstanding loan balance (the column on the far right of the amortization table) is declining each period.

Date	Account and Explanation	Debit	Credit
June 30, 2011	Note Payable	17,817.73	
	Interest Expense	3,891.44	
	Cash		21,709.17
	(Record payment 3 on notes payable)		

4. Entry to record the final payment:

	Stockholders'
Assets = Liabilities +	Equity
−21,709.12 −21,179.63	−529.49

Date	Account and Explanation	Debit	Credit
Dec. 31, 2014	Note Payable	21,179.63	
	Interest Expense	529.49	
	Cash		21,709.12
	(Record payment 10 on notes payable)		

Exhibit 9-11

Amount of Interest and Principal Payment on an Installment Note

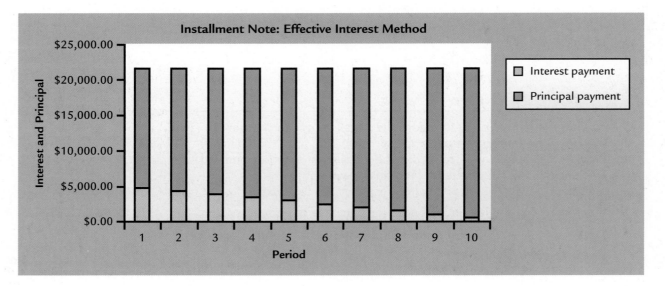

OBJECTIVE ▶ 5
Determine the after-tax cost of financing with debt and explain financial leverage.

Pros and Cons of Financing with Debt

A significant advantage of financing with debt rather than stock is the fact that the interest expense on debt is deductible for income tax purposes. Consider the case of Carmel Company which issued $1,000,000 of 8 percent bonds that resulted in interest expense of $80,000 per year. The net cash outflow for Carmel's bonds is significantly less than $80,000, however, because of the effect of interest deductibility.

Since interest expense is deductible, taxable income is $80,000 less than it is without the bond issue. At a rate of 30 percent ($80,000 × 30%), income taxes were reduced by $24,000, yielding a net cash outflow for the bonds of $56,000 ($80,000 − $24,000). In other words, the cost of financing with bonds (or any other form of debt with tax-deductible interest payments) is the interest *net of income taxes*, which is determined using the following formula:

$$\text{Interest Net of Income Taxes} = (1 - \text{Tax Rate})(\text{Interest})$$
$$= (1 - 0.30)(\$80,000)$$
$$= \$56,000$$

Another potential advantage of debt is that it fixes the amount of compensation to the lender. No matter how successful the firm is in using borrowed capital, its creditors receive only the return specified in the debt agreement (interest plus the face amount). Thus, if the borrowed capital generates income in excess of the interest on the debt, the firm's stockholders benefit. The use of borrowed capital to produce more income than needed to pay the interest on the debt is called **leverage.**

Under the right conditions, leverage has significant advantages. However, conditions also exist under which the use of leverage is disadvantageous. Exhibit 9-12 illustrates both conditions. Two companies—Carmel Company and Noblesville, Inc.—have identical financial circumstances except that Carmel finances its operations with debt as well as stock; Noblesville carries no debt. In 2008, favorable economic conditions allow Carmel to make the most of its leverage. Carmel's stockholders earn $3.64 per share, which includes an amount attributable to earnings in excess of the cost of borrowing. In contrast, Noblesville's stockholders earn only $2.80 per share in 2008. However, income from operations falls sharply in 2009. As a result, Carmel's stockholders earn only $0.84 per share compared with $0.93 per share for Noblesville's stockholders. Just as stockholders receive earnings in excess of the interest on debt, so they must bear the burden when the interest on debt exceeds earnings.

A third advantage of financing with debt is that in periods of inflation, debt permits the borrower to repay the lender in dollars that have declined in purchasing power. For instance, based on changes in the consumer price index (CPI), $1,000,000 borrowed in 1970 and repaid in 1990 provided the lender with only 30 percent of the purchasing power of the amount loaned in 1970.

The primary negative attribute of debt is the inflexibility of the payment schedule. Debt requires specified payments to creditors on specified dates. If a payment is not made as scheduled, the borrower can be forced into bankruptcy. This attribute of debt makes it a more risky source of capital than equity. The larger the proportion of debt an entity uses to finance its capital needs, the greater the risk of default. As risk increases (because of a higher proportion of debt), the cost of the debt increases. At a certain point, the risk becomes so great that additional debt cannot be issued at any cost. For firms whose operational and competitive circumstances produce substantial fluctuations in earnings, even low levels of debt may be considered too risky.

Exhibit 9-12

Effects of Financing with Debt

	2008		2009	
	Carmel Company	Noblesville, Inc.	Carmel Company	Noblesville, Inc.
Balance sheet:*				
Assets	$3,000,000	$3,000,000	$3,000,000	$3,000,000
Bonds payable	1,000,000	-0-	1,000,000	-0-
Stockholders' equity	2,000,000	3,000,000	2,000,000	3,000,000
Number of capital				
stock shares	100,000	150,000	100,000	150,000
Income statement:				
Income from				
operations	$ 600,000	$ 600,000	$ 200,000	$ 200,000
Interest expense (8%)	80,000	-0-	80,000	-0-
Income before taxes	$ 520,000	$ 600,000	$ 120,000	$ 200,000
Income taxes				
expense (30%)	156,000	180,000	36,000	60,000
Net income	$ 364,000	$ 420,000	$ 84,000	$ 140,000
Earnings per share	$ 3.64	$ 2.80	$ 0.84	$ 0.93

*Annual averages (assume that current liabilities are negligible).

In sum, a business must weigh both the negative and positive aspects of debt financing in deciding whether or not to take the risk. This extremely complex decision is treated more fully in finance courses.[3]

Occasionally, a business finds that it is unable to make the interest or principal payments required by its long-term debt. If there is reason to expect that the firm will eventually be able to secure enough cash to make part of or all the required payments, creditors may permit a restructuring of the cash payment schedule. The amount at which the firm's liabilities are measured may or may not be changed by such a restructuring. In such cases, creditors must analyze the situation to ensure that they are better off than they would be if they forced a bankruptcy.

We turn now to leases, which can serve as another means of financing asset acquisitions.

OBJECTIVE ➤ 6

Contrast the terms and the accounting for operating and capital leases.

Leases

During the past 30 years, leases have increasingly become an alternative to outright asset purchases for firms seeking to expand their operations. A **lease** enables a firm to use property without legally owning it. When firms first began to use leases as sources of capital, they generally omitted them from the liabilities sections of their balance sheets. In 1976, however, the Financial Accounting Standards Board identified two kinds of lease obligations, operating leases and capital leases, and required that capital leases be included among a firm's assets and liabilities.[4] We will discuss both types of leases and their accounting in the sections that follow.

Operating Leases

The most common form of lease is an **operating lease**, under which the lessor (the legal owner of the asset) retains the risks and obligations of ownership, while the lessee uses the asset during the term of the lease. Automobiles, apartments, retail space, and office space are usually rented with operating leases. All discussions of rental arrangements considered earlier in this book have been operating leases.

Under an operating lease, the leased asset does not appear in the records of the lessee, because the legal owner of the asset retains the risks and obligations of ownership. Rent paid in advance of the use of the asset is reported as prepaid rent, and rent expense is recognized in the period in which the leased asset is used. However, because many financial-statement users view leases as liabilities, the sum of all payments required by noncancelable operating leases for the next five years must be disclosed in a footnote to the lessee's financial statements. Exhibit 9-13 is taken from **Starbucks'** 2006 10-K.

Capital Leases

A **capital lease** is a noncancelable agreement that is in substance a purchase of the leased asset. If a lease has any of the following characteristics, it is essentially a purchase, and is therefore considered a capital lease:

1. A transfer of the leased asset to the lessee occurs at the end of the lease at no cost or at a "bargain price."
2. The term for the lease is at least 75 percent of the economic life of the leased asset.
3. The present value of the lease payments is at least 90 percent of the fair value of the leased asset.

Although the lessor remains the legal owner of the leased asset, a capital lease transfers virtually all the benefits of ownership to the lessee. Therefore, a capital lease

---

[3] The preceding discussion has explained the accounting concepts and procedures for debt used by borrowers. Although the concepts and procedures used by investors in debt securities are based on the same measurements and calculations, the reporting conventions are somewhat different. The most fundamental difference is that investors record debt acquired as assets rather than liabilities and record the interest as revenue rather than expense.

[4] Financial Accounting Standards Board, "Accounting for Leases," Statement of Financial Accounting Standards No. 13.

Exhibit 9-13

Excerpts from Starbucks' 2006 10-K

Note 13
Leases
Minimum future rental payments under noncancelable operating lease obligations as of October 1, 2006, are as follows (in thousands):

FISCAL YEAR ENDING	
2007	$ 531,634
2008	520,553
2009	492,759
2010	452,859
2011	408,412
Thereafter	1,486,721
Total minimum lease payments	$3,892,938

is appropriately shown among the lessee's assets and liabilities. At the beginning of such a lease, a capital lease liability is recorded at the present value of the future lease payments. At this time, an asset is recorded in the same amount. Over the life of the lease the asset is depreciated, using an appropriate depreciation method. The lease liability is reduced and interest expense recorded as lease payments are made.

To illustrate the computations and entries for capital leases, we will assume that on January 1, 2009, ABT Laboratories signed a five-year lease for data processing equipment. The current cash value (present value) of the future lease payments using a 9 percent interest rate—and the fair value of the data processing equipment—is $600,000. The equipment has an expected economic life of five years and no residual value. The terms of the lease require a payment of $154,255 at the end of each year.

On January 1, 2009, ABT would recognize the asset and the capital lease liability as follows:

Date	Account and Explanation	Debit	Credit
Jan. 1, 2009	Leased Asset	600,000	
	Capital Lease Liability		600,000
	(Record capital lease of equipment)		

		Stockholders'
Assets =	Liabilities +	Equity
+600,000	+600,000	

Interest expense on the lease for the first year is $54,000 ($600,000 × 9%). The lease payment ($154,255) is larger than the interest expense because the payment includes an amount to pay down the principal amount of the lease liability as well as the interest. At the end of the lease, the last lease payment will pay the last period's interest and will pay off the lease liability.

At the end of the first year, ABT would recognize the lease payment, interest expense, and reduction in the capital lease liability as follows:

Date	Account and Explanation	Debit	Credit
Dec. 31, 2009	Capital Lease Liability*	100,255	
	Interest Expense	54,000	
	Cash		154,255
	(Record capital lease payment)		

*The capital lease liability reduction is the cash payment minus the interest expense ($154,255 − $54,000 = $100,255).

		Stockholders'
Assets =	Liabilities +	Equity
−154,225	−100,255	−54,000

ABT would also recognize depreciation expense at the end of the first year with the following adjustment:

Date	Account and Explanation	Debit	Credit
Dec. 31, 2009	Depreciation Expense, Leased Asset	120,000*	
	Accumulated Depreciation, Leased Asset		120,000
	(Record depreciation on lease equipment)		

*(600,000/5 years)

		Stockholders'
Assets =	Liabilities +	Equity
−120,000		−120,000

Thus, the total first year expense for the property is the sum of the interest expense and the depreciation expense:

$$\$54,000 + \$120,000 = \$174,000$$

Disclosure rules for capital leases require that lease liabilities be reported with a business's long-term debt, and that future cash payments for capital leases be reported in a table like the one used for operating leases. The 2007 disclosure by **Federal Express Corporation** is typical, showing capital lease obligations as part of long-term debt (see Exhibit 9-14).

Depending on their terms, capital leases can be more or less attractive than borrowing as a means of financing asset acquisitions, as the following analysis demonstrates. Ives Corporation plans to acquire five new trucks. If purchased, the trucks will cost $12,000 each. One truck dealer will allow Ives to pay 10 percent down ($6,000) and will finance the remaining $54,000 on a five-year, 10 percent interest-bearing note requiring annual interest payments of $5,400 and a principal payment of $54,000 at maturity. Another dealer will lease trucks of the same make to Ives on a capital lease requiring annual payments of $15,828 for five years. The trucks would become Ives' property at the end of the lease.

The following tables show the interest expense under the two arrangements:

	Leasing	Borrowing
Cash payments:		
Year 1	$15,828	$11,400
Year 2	15,828	5,400
Year 3	15,828	5,400
Year 4	15,828	5,400
Year 5	15,828	59,400
Total for 5 years	$79,140	$87,000
Less: Principal	60,000	60,000
Interest expense for 5 years	$19,140	$27,000

Exhibit 9-14

Excerpts from Federal Express Corporation's 2007 10-K

		May 31	
in millions		2007	2006
Capital lease obligations		308	310

Our capital lease obligations include leases for aircraft and facilities. Our facility leases include leases that guarantee the repayment of certain special facility revenue bonds that have been issued by municipalities primarily to finance the acquisition and construction of various airport facilities and equipment. These bonds require interest payments at least annually, with principal payments due at the end of the related lease agreement.

A note on the firm's lease commitments contains the following disclosure:

A summary of future minimum lease payments under capital leases with an initial or remaining term of one year at May 31, 2007 is as follows (in millions):

2008	$103
2009	13
2010	97
2011	8
2012	8
Thereafter	137
	$366
Less amount representing interest	58
Present value of net minimum lease payments	$308

Although the leasing alternative promises a lower total cash outflow and lower total interest expense, its level payment schedule does not allow Ives to defer payment to the same extent as the borrowing option. The advantage of the deferred payment may more than offset the advantages offered by the lease.

In addition, the payment schedules shown above do not include the effects of the interest on income tax payments. Since the interest expense is greater under borrowing, the tax effects of borrowing will also be greater. Of course, the data presented here are insufficient to enable a final recommendation. A complete analysis of these alternatives would include an evaluation of the amounts and timing of the payments required by the two options and the income tax effects of both interest and depreciation. (Such analyses are explained in finance courses.)

Ratio Analysis

OBJECTIVE ➤ 7

Analyze a company's long-term solvency using information related to long-term liabilities.

Although long-term creditors are concerned with a company's short-term liquidity, they are primarily concerned with its long-term solvency. As such, long-term creditors focus on ratios that incorporate (1) long-term debt and (2) interest expense/payments.

The following ratios are often used to analyze a company's debt load:

$$\text{Debt to Equity} = \frac{\text{Total Liabilities}}{\text{Total Equity}}$$

$$\text{Debt to Total Assets} = \frac{\text{Total Liabilities}}{\text{Total Assets}}$$

$$\text{Long-Term Debt to Equity} = \frac{\text{Long-Term Debt}}{\text{Total Equity}}$$

The long-term debt to equity ratio is designed to look at the mix of debt and equity financing. For example, if the ratio is 1.00, then 50 percent of the company's financing comes from shareholders while the other 50 percent comes from creditors. However, over the last few decades borrowing arrangements have become much more varied. That is, historically when companies borrowed they locked themselves into long-term debt contracts. Now many companies use short-term borrowing, such as revolving credit, as part of their financing plan. This has the advantage of allowing companies to more frequently adjust their levels of borrowing based on current conditions. The downside is that short-term credit exposes them to greater risk of interest rate changes. For example, when interest rates increase, short-term borrowers may be forced to refinance at these higher rates while long-term borrowers will be locked in at the lower rates. Of course, short-term borrowers can, and do, hedge these interest rate risks, but that is a topic for advanced accounting and finance courses.

Because it is increasingly common to use short-term debt financing, the debt to equity and debt to total asset ratios contain all debt. Although the denominators for these two ratios differ, they both give a sense of the extent to which a company is financed with debt. You can see this more clearly by remembering that Total Assets = Total Liabilities + Total Equity. Both ratios therefore measure the relative size of Total Liabilities in the accounting equation.

Other ratios focus a company's ability to make interest payments. These ratios are often called coverage ratios because they provide information on the company's ability to meet or cover its interest payments. The most common ratios focus either on accrual basis interest expense or the cash basis interest payment and are typically measured pretax because interest expense is tax deductible.

Times Interest Earned (Accrual Basis)

$$= \frac{(\text{Net Income} + \text{Income Taxes} + \text{Interest Expense})}{\text{Interest Expense}}$$

Times Interest Earned (Cash Basis)

$$= \frac{(\text{Cash Flows from Operations} + \text{Taxes Paid} + \text{Interest Paid})}{\text{Interest Payments}}$$

CONCEPT Q&A

Is it always better to have lower debt to equity, debt to total assets, and long-term debt to equity ratios?

Possible Answer:

No. Debt provides opportunities for leverage. Think about it in this way—if you're guaranteed a return greater than your interest payments, it would not make sense to avoid borrowing. Of course, the reality is that while no returns are guaranteed, interest payments are unavoidable.

ETHICS When evaluating a company's solvency, a major concern is whether all debt was properly recorded. Companies have long engaged in transactions designed to hide debt. Such transactions are typically called *off-balance-sheet financing*. Interestingly, many such transactions are legal and considered to be ethical by most. For example, many companies structure their lease agreements to avoid meeting the criteria for capital leases that require recording an asset and liability related to the future lease obligation. Because these leases are then treated as operating leases, no asset or liability is recorded on the books (see the Lease Section on page 466).

Because many financial-statement users view operating leases as unavoidable obligations, FASB requires disclosure of operating lease obligations for each of the subsequent five years and in total (see Exhibit 9-13 on page 467). This disclosure allows users to adjust ratios. For example, in the footnotes of its 2006 10-K, American Airlines reports future minimum lease payments of $11.409 billion related to its operating leases. If we capitalize these amounts, their debt to equity ratio goes from 25.25 (see solution to Cornerstone 9-9) to 35.95 [(26,916 + 11,409)/ (1,066)].

**CORNERSTONE
9-9**

HOW TO Calculate and Analyze Long-Term Debt Ratios

Concept:
Investors and creditors are interested in a company's ability to meet its long-term obligations. Analysis of information about (1) long-term liabilities and (2) interest expense and payments provides such information.

Information:
Consider the following information from the 2006 10-Ks for **American Airlines** and **Southwest Airlines** (in millions).

American Airlines

Long-term debt	$ 8,799	Interest expense	$ 795
Total liabilities	26,916	Net income	164
Total assets	25,850	Interest payments	864
Total equity	(1,066)	Cash flows from operations	1,597
		Income tax expense	0
		Income taxes paid	0

Southwest Airlines

Long-term debt	$ 1,689	Interest expense	$ 128
Total liabilities	7,011	Net income	499
Total assets	13,460	Interest payments	90
Total equity	6,449	Cash flows from operations	1,406
		Income tax expense	291
		Income taxes paid	15

Required:
1. Calculate the following ratios for both companies:
   a. debt to equity
   b. debt to total assets
   c. long-term debt to equity
   d. times interest earned (accrual basis)
   e. times interest earned (cash basis)
2. Interpret these results.

Solution:

1.

	American Airlines	Southwest Airlines
a. debt to equity	$26,916/($1,066) = −25.25	$7,011/$6,449 = 1.09
b. debt to total assets	$26,916/$25,850 = 1.04	$7,011/$13,460 = 0.52
c. long-term debt to equity	$8,799/($1,066) = −8.25	$1,689/$6,449 = 0.26
d. times interest earned (accrual basis)	($164 + $0 + $795)/ $795 = 1.21	($499 + $291 + $128)/ $128 = 7.17
e. times interest earned (cash basis)	($1,597 + $0 + $864)/ $864 = 2.85	($1,406 + $15 + $90)/ $90 = 16.79

2. Southwest's solvency risk is clearly far lower than American's. Not only does American have an extremely high debt burden, but a huge portion of its earnings and cash flows are needed for interest. Southwest, on the other hand, has a relatively low debt load and can easily make its interest payments.

   Not surprisingly, American is well below industry averages on most ratios while Southwest is an industry leader. These ratios are also reflected in their credit ratings. American has fluctuated between B and B− while Southwest is typically an A or A−.

**CORNERSTONE
9-9**
(continued)

Many companies also create other legal entities (called "special purpose entities" or SPEs) to "hide" debt. As with leases, such transactions are legal when certain rules are met involving outside investors. Enron, however, created some SPEs in which the documentation appeared to meet the outside investor rules to keep the debt off Enron's balance sheet. In hindsight, however, either unwritten, side-agreements or complicated aspects of some of the contracts indicate that the debt should have been included on Enron's balance sheet. Keeping this debt off their balance sheet was important for Enron in maintaining its credit rating, but these unwritten, side-agreements and complicated aspects of the contracts were necessary to attract the outside investors. While virtually nobody considers structuring their leases to allow treatment as an operating lease to be unethical, the side-agreements and subterfuge used by Enron was not only unethical, but in many cases criminal.◆

Summary

Long-term debt arises from transactions supported by a variety of legal documents, including notes, bonds, and capital leases. This chapter explains the accounting procedures for calculating interest expense using both the straight-line and effective interest rate methods.

   Long-term debt accounting is complicated by the fact that debt is often sold at a premium or discount. A premium or discount affects the amount of interest expense associated with a debt instrument. There are advantages to financing asset acquisitions with long-term debt. For example, debt is frequently a less expensive source of capital than stock (equity) and interest payments are tax deductible.

   Leases represent an important alternative to notes, debentures, and equity as a means of acquiring assets. When a lease is, in substance, a purchase of leased facilities, it is known as a *capital lease*. An asset and a long-term liability are recorded for such leases. Since a firm's ability to borrow through debt or capital leases is usually limited, most firms are financed by a mixture of debt and equity. The use of equity as a source of long-term capital will be discussed in Chapter 10.

Summary of Learning Objectives

LO1. Describe debt securities and the markets in which they are issued.
- Debt securities are issued in exchange for borrowed cash.
- In return for the borrowed cash, the borrower typically makes periodic interest payments and repays the face, or par, value at maturity.
- These securities may be placed directly with a creditor such as a bank or pension fund or it may be more widely distributed with the help of an underwriter.

LO2. Account for the issuance of long-term debt.
- The issue price of long-term debt is typically quoted as a percentage of face value.
- At the time of issuance the borrower records the face value of the debt in bonds payable (or notes payable).
  - Any amount of cash received over the face value is credited to a premium
  - Any amount of cash received under the face value is debited to a discount
- The bonds payable (or notes payable) is netted with the premium or discount when reported on the balance sheet.

LO3. Use the straight-line method to account for premium/discount amortization.
- In the straight-line method, equal amounts of premium or discount are amortized to interest expense each period.
- This results in a constant interest expense each period.
- Although GAAP requires use of the effective interest rate method, the straight-line method may be used if the results are not materially different from the effective interest rate method.

LO4. Use the effective interest rate method to account for premium/discount amortization.
- GAAP requires the effective interest rate method to be used to amortize any premium or discount, unless the straight-line method is not materially different.
- Under this method, premiums and discounts are amortized in a manner that results in the interest expense for each accounting period being equal to a constant percentage of the bond book, or carrying, value.
- That is, the interest expense changes every period, but the effective interest rate on the bond book value is constant.
- This constant percentage is called the "yield" and represents the market rate of interest at the date of issue.

LO5. Determine the after-tax cost of financing with debt and explain financial leverage.
- Since interest expense is deductible for tax purposes, the presence of interest expense lowers the taxes owed.
- The formula for the after-tax effect of interest expense is $(1 - \text{Tax Rate}) \times \text{Interest Expense}$.

LO6. Contrast the terms and the accounting for operating and capital leases.
- A capital lease is a noncancelable agreement that is, in substance, a purchase of the leased asset.
- If a lease includes one of the following requirements it is considered a capital lease:
  - A transfer of the leased asset to the lessee occurs at the end of the lease at no cost or at a "bargain price," or
  - The term for the lease is at least 75 percent of the economic life of the leased asset, or
  - The present value of the lease payments is at least 90 percent of the fair value of the leased asset.

- If a lease qualifies as a capital lease an asset and liability must be recorded.
- If the lease does not meet requirements to be treated as a capital lease, then it is treated as an operating lease.
- Under an operating lease, the leased asset does not appear in the records of the lessee, because the legal owner of the asset retains the risks and obligations of ownership.
- Rent paid in advance of the use of the asset is reported as prepaid rent, and rent expense is recognized in the period in which the leased asset is used.

LO7. Analyze a company's long-term solvency using information related to long-term liabilities.
- Although long-term creditors are concerned with a company's short-term liquidity, they are primarily concerned with its long-term solvency.
- As such, long-term creditors focus on ratios that incorporate
  - long-term debt and
  - interest expense/payments.

CORNERSTONE 9-1	How to record the issuance of bonds, page 447	
CORNERSTONE 9-2	How to record interest expense for bonds sold at par, page 449	
CORNERSTONE 9-3	How to record interest expense for zero-coupon bonds, page 450	**CORNERSTONES FOR CHAPTER 9**
CORNERSTONE 9-4	How to record interest expense for bonds sold at a discount, page 452	
CORNERSTONE 9-5	How to record interest expense for bonds sold at a premium, page 454	
CORNERSTONE 9-6	How to record interest expense for bonds sold at a discount using the effective interest rate method, page 459	
CORNERSTONE 9-7	How to record interest expense for bonds sold at a premium using the effective interest rate method, page 460	
CORNERSTONE 9-8	How to account for installment debt using the effective interest rate method, page 462	
CORNERSTONE 9-9	How to calculate and analyze long-term debt ratios, page 470	

Key Terms

OBJECTIVE ▶ 8

Calculate the market price of long-term debt using present value techniques.

Appendix: Pricing Long-Term Debt

As stated in the chapter, debt agreements create contractually defined cash flows for the lender. Specifically, lenders typically receive (1) periodic interest payments and (2) repayment of the loan principal at some future date (i.e., loan maturity). To receive these cash flows, the lender must decide how much to lend. When you borrow from a bank or car dealer, this single lender will set the interest rate to reflect the desired market, or yield, rate. However, there are notable exceptions. For example, if you buy a car for $25,000 at 0.9 percent interest, does that mean the car dealer's yield is 0.9 percent? No, it really means that they would have been happy to sell you the car for something below $25,000, such as $24,250. In this case, the "extra" principal you repay ($750 = $25,000 − $24,250) represents interest.

Of course, similar situations happen to businesses, but by far the most common situation has to do with bonds because the stated rate of interest (e.g., 8 percent) on the bond does not provide the desired yield. The chapter discussed how if the yield is above the stated rate, the bond will sell at a discount (e.g., 98) and if the yield is below the stated rate, it will sell at a premium (e.g., 103). But, how are these prices determined?

Bonds are priced at the present value of the two future cash flows—the periodic interest payments provide an annuity, while the repayment of the principal is a lump sum. This calculation is shown in Cornerstone 9-10.

HOW TO Determine the Market Value of a Bond

Concept:
Bonds are issued at the present value of future cash flows. The interest payments and repayment of the bond principal (or face value) are the future cash flows. These amounts must be discounted at the market rate of interest (or yield).

CORNERSTONE 9-10

Information:
On December 31, 2006, ABC Co. issued $1,000,000 of 8 percent bonds, due in five years with interest payable annually on December 31.

Required:

1. Draw the cash flow diagram.
2. What is the market value of these bonds if sold to yield 8 percent?
3. What is the market value of these bonds if sold to yield 9 percent?
4. What is the market value of these bonds if sold to yield 7 percent?

Solution:

1. PV = ?

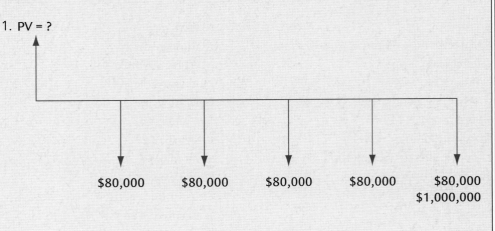

2. To calculate the present value of the future cash flows two calculations must be made. One recognizes that the interest payments represent an annuity, while the second recognizes that repayment of the principal is a single sum.

Using 8 percent yield:

PV of interest payments = (Interest payment)
   (PV of an annuity, 5 periods, 8%)
   = $80,000 × 3.992710* = $319,417

PV of principal payments = (Principal payment)
   (PV of a single sum, 5 periods, 8%)
   = $1,000,000 × 0.680583* = $680,583

Market price of bonds	$1,000,000

*Although present and future value tables provided at the end of Appendix 3 (Exhibits A3-7, A3-8, A3-9, and A3-10) only show five decimal places, we have used factors to six decimal places in these calculations (and those that follow). Use of six decimal places allows the market price of the bond when issued at par to be calculated with no rounding error.

3. Using 9 percent yield:

PV of interest payments = (Interest payment)
   (PV of an annuity, 5 periods, 9%)
   = $80,000 × 3.889651 = $311,172

PV of principal payments: = (Interest payment)
   (PV of a single sum, 5 periods, 9%)
   = $1,000,000 × 0.649931 = $649,931

Market price of bonds	$961,103

4. Using 7 percent yield:

PV of interest payments = (Interest payment)
   (PV of an annuity, 5 periods, 7%)
   = $80,000 × 4.100197 = $328,016

PV of principal payments = (Interest payment)
   (PV of a single sum, 5 periods, 7%)
   = $1,000,000 × 0.712986 = $712,986

Market price of bonds	$1,041,002

Appendix: Summary of Learning Objectives

LO8. **Calculate the market price of long-term debt using present value techniques.**
- Bonds are issued at the present value of future cash flows.
- The interest payments and repayment of the bond principal (or face value) are the future cash flows.
- These amounts must be discounted at the market rate of interest (or yield).

CORNERSTONES FOR APPENDIX 9

CORNERSTONE 9-10 How to determine the market value of a bond, page 474

Review Problem

I. Straight-Line Method

To finance a new hydroelectric plant, Midwest Electric issues $100,000,000 of 9 percent, 15-year bonds on December 31, 2005. The bonds pay interest semiannually on June 30 and December 31. Assume the market rate of interest on December 31, 2005, was above 9 percent.

Required:

1. Will the bonds be issued at par, a premium, or a discount? Why?
2. Describe the cash payments made by Midwest Electric.
3. Provide the journal entry to record the bond issue assuming the bonds were issued at 91.
4. What is the amount of discount amortization per six month interest period?
5. Complete the following amortization table through June 30, 2008.

Semiannual Period	Cash Payment (Credit)	Interest Expense (Debit)	Discount on Bonds Payable (Credit)	Discount on Bonds Payable Balance	Carrying Value
At issue					
6/30/06					
12/31/06					
6/30/07					
12/31/07					
6/30/08					

6. Provide the journal entries for December 31, 2007, and June 30, 2008.
7. How will the bonds be shown on the December 31, 2007, balance sheet?
8. Provide the journal entry to record the repayment of principal at maturity.

Solution:

1. The bonds will be issued at a discount (below par) because the stated rate is below the market rate. Thus, Midwest Electric will have to lower the price below face value to compensate creditors for accepting a below market interest payment.
2. The interest payments are made semiannually, so the interest payments are:

$$\$100,000,000 \times 9\% \times 6/12 = \$4,500,000$$

There are 30 interest payments over the 15-year life of the bonds, so total interest payments are:

$$\$4,500,000 \times 30 = \$135,000,000$$

At maturity, the face value of $100,000,000 is also repaid. Thus, total payments (interest plus principal) of $235,000,000 are made.

3.

Date	Account and Explanation	Debit	Credit
Dec. 31, 2005	Cash	91,000,000	
	Discount on Bonds Payable	9,000,000	
	Bonds Payable		100,000,000
	(Record issuance of bonds)		

	Stockholders'
Assets = Liabilities + Equity	
+91,000,000 −9,000,000	
+100,000,000	

4. Discount Amortization = Total Discount/Number of Interest Periods

$$= 9,000,000/30$$

$$= 300,000$$

5.

Semiannual Period	Cash Payment (Credit)	Interest Expense (Debit)	Discount on Bonds Payable (Credit)	Discount on Bonds Payable Balance	Carrying Value
At issue				$9,000,000	$91,000,000
6/30/06	$4,500,000	$4,800,000	$300,000	8,700,000	91,300,000
12/31/06	4,500,000	4,800,000	300,000	8,400,000	91,600,000
6/30/07	4,500,000	4,800,000	300,000	8,100,000	91,900,000
12/31/07	4,500,000	4,800,000	300,000	7,800,000	92,200,000
6/30/08	4,500,000	4,800,000	300,000	7,500,000	92,500,000

12/31/07

	Stockholders'
Assets = Liabilities + Equity	
−4,500,000 +300,000 −4,800,000	

6.

	12/31/07		6/30/08	
Account and Explanation	Debit	Credit	Debit	Credit
Interest Expense	4,800,000		4,800,000	
Cash		4,500,000		4,500,000
Discount on Bonds Payable		300,000		300,000
(Record interest payment on bonds)				

6/30/08

	Stockholders'
Assets = Liabilities + Equity	
−4,500,000 +300,000 −4,800,000	

7.

Long-term liabilities:		
Bonds payable	100,000,000	
Less: Discount on bonds payable	7,800,000	92,200,000

8.

Date	Account and Explanation	Debit	Credit
Dec. 31, 2021	Bonds Payable	100,000,000	
	Cash		100,000,000
	(Record repayment of bonds)		

	Stockholders'
Assets = Liabilities + Equity	
−100,000,000 −100,000,000	

II. Effective Interest Method

To finance a new hydroelectric plant, Midwest Electric issues $100,000,000 of 9 percent, 15-year bonds on December 31, 2005. The bonds pay interest semiannually on June 30 and December 31. Assume the market rate of interest on December 31, 2005, was 10 percent.

Required:

1. Will the bonds be issued at par, a premium, or a discount? Why?
2. Describe the cash flows.
3. Using present value techniques, verify the bond issue price of $92,309,730? (**This requires the appendix.**)
4. Provide the journal entry to record the bond issue.
5. Prepare an effective interest rate amortization table through June 30, 2008.

Semiannual Period	Cash Payment (Credit)	Interest Expense (Debit)	Discount on Bonds Payable (Credit)	Discount on Bonds Payable Balance	Carrying Value
At issue					
6/30/06					
12/31/06					
6/30/07					
12/31/07					
6/30/08					

6. Provide the journal entries for December 31, 2007, and June 30, 2008.
7. How will the bonds be shown on the December 31, 2007, balance sheet?
8. Provide the journal entry to record the repayment of principal at maturity.

Solution:

1. The bonds will be issued at a discount (below par) because the stated rate is below the market rate. Thus, Midwest Electric will have to lower the price below face value to compensate creditors for accepting a below market interest payment.

2. The interest payments are made semiannually, so the interest payments are:

$$\$100,000,000 \times 9\% \times 6/12 = \$4,500,000$$

There are 30 interest payments over the 15-year life of the bonds, so total interest payments are:

$$\$4,500,000 \times 30 = \$135,000,000$$

At maturity the face value of $100,000,000 is also repaid. Thus, total payments (interest plus principal) of $235,000,000 are made.

3. The issue price is the present value of the cash flows:

PV of interest payments = (*Interest payment*)

(*PV of an annuity, 30 semiannual periods, 5%*)

$$= \$4,500,000 \times 15.372451 = \$69,176,030$$

PV of principal payments = (*Principal payment*)

(*PV of a single sum, 30 semiannual periods, 5%*)

$$= \$100,000,000 \times 0.231337 = \$23,133,700$$

Market price of bonds	$92,309,730

4.

Assets =	Liabilities +	Stockholders' Equity
+92,309,730	−7,690,270	
	+100,000,000	

Date	Account and Explanation	Debit	Credit
Dec. 31, 2005	Cash	92,309,730	
	Discount on Bonds Payable	7,690,270	
	Bonds Payable		100,000,000
	(Record issuance of bonds)		

5.

Annual Period	Cash Payment (Credit)	Interest Expense (Debit)	Discount on Bonds Payable (Credit)	Discount on Bonds Payable Balance	Carrying Value
At issue				$7,690,270	$92,309,730
6/30/06	$4,500,000	$4,615,487	$115,487	7,574,783	92,425,217
12/31/06	$4,500,000	$4,621,261	$121,261	7,453,522	92,546,478
6/30/07	$4,500,000	$4,627,324	$127,324	7,326,198	92,673,802
12/31/07	$4,500,000	$4,633,690	$133,690	7,192,508	92,807,492
6/30/08	$4,500,000	$4,640,375	$140,375	7,052,133	92,947,867

12/31/07

Assets =	Liabilities +	Stockholders' Equity
−4,500,000	+133,690	−4,633,690

6/30/08

Assets =	Liabilities +	Stockholders' Equity
−4,500,000	+140,375	−4,640,375

6.

	12/31/07		6/30/08	
Account and Explanation	Debit	Credit	Debit	Credit
Interest Expense	4,633,690		4,640,375	
Cash		4,500,000		4,500,000
Discount on Bonds Payable		133,690		140,375
(Record interest payment on bonds)				

7. Long-term liabilities:

Bonds payable	$100,000,000	
Less: Discount on bonds payable	7,192,508	$92,807,492

8.

Assets =	Liabilities +	Stockholders' Equity
−100,000,000	−100,000,000	

Date	Account and Explanation	Debit	Credit
Dec. 31, 2021	Bonds Payable	100,000,000	
	Cash		100,000,000
	(Record repayment of bonds)		

Discussion Questions

1. What is long-term debt?
2. What is the difference between a bond and a note? How do the accounting treatments differ?
3. What does the face (or par) value of a bond represent?
4. What is the maturity date of a bond?
5. What is the stated or coupon rate of a bond?
6. How does a bond's stated rate differ from its yield rate? Which one is used to calculate the interest payment?
7. How does a secured bond differ from an unsecured bond?
8. What does it mean if a bond is "callable"?
9. What does it mean if a bond is "convertible"?
10. What is a junk bond?
11. How is total interest for long-term debt calculated?
12. Describe the process that businesses follow to sell new issues of long-term debt.
13. Describe how the relationship between the stated rate and yield rate affect the price at which bonds are sold.
14. How are premiums and discounts presented on the balance sheet?
15. How do premiums and discounts on long-term debt securities affect interest expense?
16. What is the difference between the straight-line and effective interest rate methods of amortizing premiums and discounts?
17. How can there be interest expense each period for zero-coupon bonds if there are no interest payments?
18. Under the effective interest rate method, describe the difference in calculating the (1) interest payment and (2) interest expense for the period.
19. How does a firm "leverage" its capital structure? When is leverage advantageous? When is it disadvantageous? Who receives the advantage or bears the disadvantage of leverage?
20. Name and describe two kinds of leases.
21. Which type of lease requires that a long-term debt and an asset be recorded at the inception of the lease?
22. Describe how the bond issue price is calculated.

Multiple-Choice Exercises

9-1 Which of the following statements regarding bonds payable is *true*?

a. Generally, bonds are issued in denominations of $100.
b. When an issuing company's bonds are traded in the "secondary" market, the company will receive part of the proceeds when the bonds are sold from the first purchaser to the second purchaser.
c. A debenture bond is backed by specific assets of the issuing company.
d. The entire principal amount of most bonds mature on a single date.

9-2 Bonds are sold at a premium if the

a. issuing company has a better reputation than other companies in the same business.
b. market rate of interest was less than the stated rate at the time of issue.
c. market rate of interest was more than the stated rate at the time of issue.
d. company will have to pay a premium to retire the bonds.

9-3 If bonds are issued at 101.25, this means that

a. a $1,000 bond sold for $101.25.
b. the bonds sold at a discount.
c. a $1,000 bond sold for $1,012.50.
d. the bond rate of interest is 10.13 percent of the market rate of interest.

9-4 What best describes the discount on bonds payable account?

a. An asset
b. An expense
c. A liability
d. A contra liability

9-5 The premium on bonds payable account is shown on the balance sheet as

a. a contra asset.
b. a reduction of an expense.
c. an addition to a long-term liability.
d. a subtraction from a long-term liability.

9-6 When bonds are issued by a company, the accounting entry typically shows an

a. increase in liabilities and a decrease in stockholders' equity.
b. increase in liabilities and an increase in stockholders' equity.
c. increase in assets and an increase in liabilities.
d. increase in assets and an increase in stockholders' equity.

9-7 The Bower Company sold $100,000 of 20-year bonds for $95,000. The stated rate on the bonds was 7 percent, and interest is paid annually on December 31. What entry would be made on December 31 when the interest is paid? (Numbers are omitted.)

a. Interest Expense
       Cash
b. Interest Expense
       Discount on Bonds Payable
       Cash
c. Interest Expense
   Discount on Bonds Payable
       Cash
d. Interest Expense
       Bonds Payable
       Cash

9-8 Bonds in the amount of $100,000 with a life of 10 years were issued by the Roundy Company. If the stated rate is 6 percent and interest is paid semiannually, what would be the total amount of interest paid over the life of the bonds?

a. $60,000
b. $120,000
c. $30,000
d. $6,000

9-9 Sean Corp. issued a $40,000, 10-year bond, with a stated rate of 8 percent, paid semiannually. How much cash will the bond investors receive at the end of the first interest period?

a. $800
b. $1,600
c. $3,200
d. $4,000

9-10 When noninterest-bearing bonds are issued, the discount is

a. disregarded for financial reporting purposes.
b. expensed immediately.
c. amortized to interest expense each period.
d. credited to revenue.

9-11 When interest-bearing bonds are issued at a discount, the interest expense for the period is

a. the amount of interest payment for the period plus the discount amortization for the period.
b. the amount of interest payment for the period minus the discount amortization for the period.
c. the amount of interest payment for the period plus the premium amortization for the period.
d. the amount of interest payment for the period minus the premium amortization for the period.

9-12 When interest-bearing bonds are issued at a premium, the interest expense for the period is

a. the amount of interest payment for the period plus the discount amortization for the period.
b. the amount of interest payment for the period minus the discount amortization for the period.
c. the amount of interest payment for the period plus the premium amortization for the period.
d. the amount of interest payment for the period minus the premium amortization for the period.

9-13 Installment bonds differ from typical bonds in what way?

a. Essentially they are the same.
b. Installment bonds do not have a stated rate.
c. A portion of each installment bond payment pays down the principal balance.
d. The entire principal balance is paid off at maturity for installment bonds.

9-14 In 2008, Drew Company issued $200,000 of bonds for $189,640. If the stated rate of interest was 8 percent and the yield was 6.73 percent, how would Drew calculate the interest expense for the first year on the bonds using the effective interest method?

a. $189,640 × 6.73%
b. $189,640 × 8%
c. $10,000 × 6.73%
d. $10,000 × 8%

9-15 The result of using the effective interest method of amortization of the discount on bonds is that the

a. interest expense for each amortization period is constant.
b. a constant interest rate is charged against the debt carrying value.
c. amount of interest expense decreases each period.
d. cash interest payment is greater than the interest expense.

9-16 Serenity Company issued $100,000 of 6 percent, 10-year bonds when the market rate of interest was 5 percent. The proceeds from this bond issue were $107,732. Using the effective interest method of amortization, which of the following statements is *true*? Assume interest is paid annually.

a. Interest payments to bondholders each period will be $6,464.
b. Interest payments to bondholders each period will be $5,000.
c. Amortization of the premium for the first interest period will be $613.
d. Amortization of the premium for the first interest period will be $1,464.

9-17 Bonds are a popular source of financing because:

a. bond interest expense is deductible for tax purposes, while dividends paid on stock are not.
b. financial analysts tend to downgrade a company that has raised large amounts of cash by frequent issues of stock.
c. a company having cash flow problems can postpone payment of interest to bond-holders.
d. the bondholders can always convert their bonds into stock if they choose.

9-18 Which of the following statements regarding leases is *false*?

a. Lease agreements are a popular form of financing the purchase of assets because leases do not require a large initial outlay of cash.
b. Accounting recognizes two types of leases—operating and capital leases.
c. If a lease is classified as an operating lease, the lessee records a lease liability on its balance sheet.
d. If a lease is classified as a capital lease, the lessee records a lease liability on its balance sheet.

9-19 Which of the following lease conditions would result in a capital lease to the lessee?

a. The lessee will return the property to the lessor at the end of the lease term.
b. The lessee can purchase the property for $1 at the end of the lease term.
c. The fair market value of the property at the inception of the lease is $18,000; the present value of the minimum lease payments is $15,977.
d. The lease term is 70 percent of the property's economic life.

9-20 On January 2, 2007, Sylvester Metals Co. leased a mining machine from EDH Leasing Corp. The lease qualifies as an operating lease. The annual payments are $4,000 paid at the end of each year, and the life of the lease is 10 years. What entry would Sylvester Metals Co. make when the machine is delivered by EDH Leasing Corp.?

a. Leased Asset   40,000
   Lease Liability   40,000
b. Prepaid Rent   40,000
   Lease Liability   40,000
c. Prepaid Rent   4,000
   Lease Liability   4,000
d. No entry is necessary.

9-21 WVA Mining Company has leased a machine from Franklin Machinery Company. The annual payments are $6,000, and the life of the lease is 8 years. It is estimated that the useful life of the machine is 9 years. How would WVA Mining record the acquisition of the machine?

a. The machine would be recorded as an asset with a cost of $48,000.
b. The company would not record the machine as an asset but would record rent expense of $6,000 per year.
c. The machine would be recorded as an asset, at the present value of the annual cash payments, $6,000 for eight years.
d. The machine would be recorded as an asset, at the present value of the annual cash payments, $6,000 for nine years.

9-22 Willow Corporation's balance sheet showed the following amounts: Current Liabilities, $5,000; Bonds Payable, $1,500; Lease Obligations, 2,300. Total stockholders' equity was $6,000. The debt-to-equity ratio is:

a. 0.63.
b. 0.83.
c. 1.42.
d. 1.47.

9-23 Kinsella Corporation's balance sheet showed the following amounts: Current Liabilities, $75,000; Total Liabilities, $100,000; Total Assets, $200,000. What is the long-term debt to equity ratio?

a. 0.75
b. 0.375
c. 0.25
d. 0.125

9-24 McLaughlin Corporation's balance sheet showed the following amounts: Current Liabilities, $75,000; Total Liabilities, $100,000; Total Assets, $200,000. What is the debt to total assets ratio?

a. 2
b. 1
c. 0.875
d. 0.5

9-25 (Appendix) The bond issue price is determined by calculating the:

a. present value of the stream of interest payments and the future value of the maturity amount.
b. future value of the stream of interest payments and the future value of the maturity amount.
c. future value of the stream of interest payments and the present value of the maturity amount.
d. present value of the stream of interest payments and the present value of the maturity amount.

Cornerstone Exercises

Cornerstone Exercise 9-26 REPORTING LONG-TERM DEBT ON THE BALANCE SHEET

OBJECTIVE ➤ 1
CORNERSTONE 9-1

Dennis Corp. has the following bonds:

a. $100,000 bond that has $2,000 of unamortized discount associated with it.
b. $100,000 bond that has $3,000 of unamortized premium associated with it.

Required:

Provide the balance sheet presentation for these two bonds.

Cornerstone Exercise 9-27 ISSUANCE OF LONG-TERM DEBT

OBJECTIVE ➤ 2
CORNERSTONE 9-1

Anne Corp. issued $400,000, 6 percent bonds.

Required:

Provide the necessary journal entry to record the issuance of these bonds assuming:

a. The bonds were issued at par.
b. The bonds were issued at 104.
c. The bonds were issued at 99.

OBJECTIVE ▶ 2
CORNERSTONE 9-1

Cornerstone Exercise 9-28 ISSUANCE OF LONG-TERM DEBT

EWO Enterprises issues $200,000 of bonds payable.

Required:

Provide the necessary journal entry to record the issuance of the bonds assuming:

a. The bonds were issued at par.
b. The bonds were issued at 102.
c. The bonds were issued at 97.

OBJECTIVE ▶ 2
CORNERSTONE 9-1

Cornerstone Exercise 9-29 ISSUANCE OF LONG-TERM DEBT

M. Nickles Company issued $500,000 of bonds for $498,351. Interest is paid semi-annually.

Required:

a. Provide the necessary journal entry to record the issuance of the bonds.
b. Is the yield greater or less than the stated rate? How do you know?

OBJECTIVE ▶ 3
CORNERSTONE 9-2

Cornerstone Exercise 9-30 DEBT ISSUED AT PAR

On December 31, 2008, Brock & Co. issued $250,000 of bonds payable at par. The bonds have a 10 percent stated rate, pay interest on June 30 and December 31, and mature on December 31, 2011.

Required:

Provide the journal entries to record the interest payment on June 30, 2010.

OBJECTIVE ▶ 3
CORNERSTONE 9-3

Cornerstone Exercise 9-31 ZERO COUPON BONDS (STRAIGHT LINE)

Dean Plumbing issues $1,000,000 face value, noninterest-bearing bonds on December 31, 2009. The bonds are issued at 65 and mature on December 31, 2013.

Required:

Assuming the straight-line amortization method is followed, provide the journal entry on December 31, 2012.

OBJECTIVE ▶ 3
CORNERSTONE 9-4

Cornerstone Exercise 9-32 DEBT ISSUED AT A DISCOUNT (STRAIGHT LINE)

On December 31, 2007, Drew Company issued $170,000, five-year bonds for $155,000. The stated rate of interest was 6 percent and interest is paid annually on December 31.

Required:

Provide the necessary journal entry on December 31, 2009, assuming the straight-line method is followed.

OBJECTIVE ▶ 3
CORNERSTONE 9-4

Cornerstone Exercise 9-33 DEBT ISSUED AT A DISCOUNT (STRAIGHT LINE)

Use the information from **Cornerstone Exercise 9-32**.

Required:

Prepare the amortization table for Drew Company's bonds.

OBJECTIVE ▶ 3
CORNERSTONE 9-5

Cornerstone Exercise 9-34 DEBT ISSUED AT A PREMIUM (STRAIGHT LINE)

On December 31, 2008, Ironman Steel issued $500,000, eight-year bonds for $508,000. The stated rate of interest was 9 percent and interest is paid annually on December 31.

Required:

Provide the necessary journal entry on December 31, 2012, assuming the straight-line method is followed.

Cornerstone Exercise 9-35 DEBT ISSUED AT A PREMIUM (STRAIGHT LINE)

OBJECTIVE ➤ 3
CORNERSTONE 9-5

Use the information from **Cornerstone Exercise 9-34**.

Required:

Prepare the amortization table for Ironman Steel's bonds.

Cornerstone Exercise 9-36 BONDS ISSUED AT A DISCOUNT (EFFECTIVE INTEREST)

OBJECTIVE ➤ 4
CORNERSTONE 9-6

Sicily Corporation issued $300,000 in 8 percent bonds (payable on December 31, 2018) on December 31, 2008, for $262,613. Interest is paid on June 30 and December 31. The market rate of interest is 10 percent.

Required:

Prepare the amortization table using the effective interest rate method.

Cornerstone Exercise 9-37 BONDS ISSUED AT A DISCOUNT (EFFECTIVE INTEREST)

OBJECTIVE ➤ 4
CORNERSTONE 9-6

Use the information from **Cornerstone Exercise 9-36**.

Required:

Record the journal entries for December 31, 2010 and 2011.

Cornerstone Exercise 9-38 BONDS ISSUED AT A DISCOUNT (EFFECTIVE INTEREST)

OBJECTIVE ➤ 4
CORNERSTONE 9-6

Crafty Corporation issued $650,000 of 10 percent, seven-year bonds on December 31, 2008, for $619,371. Interest is paid annually on December 31. The market rate of interest is 11 percent.

Required:

Prepare the amortization table using the effective interest rate method.

Cornerstone Exercise 9-39 BONDS ISSUED AT A DISCOUNT (EFFECTIVE INTEREST)

OBJECTIVE ➤ 4
CORNERSTONE 9-6

Use the information from **Cornerstone Exercise 9-38**.

Required:

Record the journal entry for December 31, 2009 and 2010.

Cornerstone Exercise 9-40 BONDS ISSUED AT A PREMIUM (EFFECTIVE INTEREST)

OBJECTIVE ➤ 4
CORNERSTONE 9-7

Cookie Dough Corporation issued $500,000 in 6 percent, 10-year bonds (payable on December 31, 2018) on December 31, 2008, for $581,757. Interest is paid on June 30 and December 31. The market rate of interest is 4 percent.

Required:

Prepare the amortization table using the effective interest rate method.

Cornerstone Exercise 9-41 BONDS ISSUED AT A PREMIUM (EFFECTIVE INTEREST)

OBJECTIVE ➤ 4
CORNERSTONE 9-7

Use the information from **Cornerstone Exercise 9-40**.

Required:

Record the journal entries for December 31, 2010 and 2011.

OBJECTIVE ▸ 4
CORNERSTONE 9-7

Cornerstone Exercise 9-42 BONDS ISSUED AT A PREMIUM (EFFECTIVE INTEREST)

Charger Battery issued $100,000 of 11 percent, seven-year bonds on December 31, 2008, for $104,868. Interest is paid annually on December 31. The market rate of interest is 10 percent.

Required:

Prepare the amortization table using the effective interest rate method.

OBJECTIVE ▸ 4
CORNERSTONE 9-7

Cornerstone Exercise 9-43 BONDS ISSUED AT A PREMIUM (EFFECTIVE INTEREST)

Use the information from **Cornerstone Exercise 9-42**.

Required:

Record the journal entries for December 31, 2010 and 2011.

OBJECTIVE ▸ 4
CORNERSTONE 9-8

Cornerstone Exercise 9-44 INSTALLMENT NOTES

Thornwood Lanes bought a service vehicle for $25,000 by issuing a 6 percent installment note on December 31, 2009. Thornwood will make 12 monthly payments of $2,151.66 at the end of each month.

Required:

Prepare the amortization table using the effective interest rate method.

OBJECTIVE ▸ 4
CORNERSTONE 9-8

Cornerstone Exercise 9-45 INSTALLMENT NOTES

Use the information from **Cornerstone Exercise 9-44**.

Required:

Record the journal entries for March 31, and April 30, 2010.

OBJECTIVE ▸ 4
CORNERSTONE 9-8

Cornerstone Exercise 9-46 INSTALLMENT NOTE

ABC bank loans $250,000 to Yossarian to purchase a new home. Yossarian will repay the note in equal monthly payments over a period of 30 years. The interest rate is 12 percent.

Required:

If the monthly payment is $2,571.53, how much of the first payment is interest expense and how much is principal repayment?

OBJECTIVE ▸ 5

Cornerstone Exercise 9-47 COST OF DEBT FINANCING

Barney Corporation's cost of debt financing is 8.5 percent. Its tax rate is 35 percent.

Required:

Calculate the after-tax interest rate to three decimal places.

OBJECTIVE ▸ 5

Cornerstone Exercise 9-48 COST OF DEBT FINANCING

Diamond Company's cost of debt financing is 9.5 percent. Its tax rate is 35 percent. Diamond has $2,000,000 of debt.

Required:

1. Calculate the after-tax cost amount of interest expense.
2. How does the tax effect of interest expense affect financial leverage?

OBJECTIVE ▸ 6

Cornerstone Exercise 9-49 LEASES

Southern Airlines has leased an aircraft from BAL Aircraft Company. The annual payments are $1,000,000, and the life of the lease is 18 years. It is estimated that the useful life of the aircraft is 20 years. The present value of the future lease payments is $8,755,630.

Required:

1. Would Southern Aircraft record the lease as an operating or capital lease? Why?
2. Provide the journal entry to record the acquisition.

Cornerstone Exercise 9-50 RATIO ANALYSIS

Watterson Corporation's balance sheet showed the following amounts: Current Liabilities, $70,000; Bonds Payable, $150,000; and Lease Obligations, $20,000. Total stockholders' equity was $90,000.

Required:

Calculate the debt-to-equity ratio.

Cornerstone Exercise 9-51 RATIO ANALYSIS

Blue Corporation had $2,000,000 in total liabilities and $3,500,000 in total assets as of December 31, 2009.

Required:

Calculate Blue's debt to equity ratio.

Cornerstone Exercise 9-52 RATIO ANALYSIS

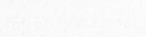

Red Corporation had $2,000,000 in total liabilities and $3,500,000 in total assets as of December 31, 2009. Of Red's total liabilities, $350,000 is long-term.

Required:

Calculate Red's debt to assets ratio and its long-term debt to equity ratio.

Cornerstone Exercise 9-53 (APPENDIX) BOND ISSUE PRICE

On December 31, 2009, Garner Hot Rods issued $2,000,000 of 6 percent, 10-year bonds. Interest is payable semiannually on June 30 and December 31.

Required:

What is the issue price if the bonds are sold to yield 8 percent?

Cornerstone Exercise 9-54 (APPENDIX) BOND ISSUE PRICE

On December 31, 2009, Callahan Auto issued $1,500,000 of 8 percent, 10-year bonds. Interest is payable semiannually on June 30 and December 31.

Required:

What is the issue price if the bonds are sold to yield 6 percent (round to nearest dollar)?

Exercises

Exercise 9-55 ISSUING AT PAR, A PREMIUM, OR A DISCOUNT

Kartel Company is planning to issue 500 bonds, each having a face amount of $1,000.

Required:

1. Prepare the journal entry to record the sale of the bonds at par.
2. Prepare the journal entry to record the sale of the bonds at a premium of $34,000.
3. Prepare the journal entry to record the sale of the bonds at a discount of $41,000.

Exercise 9-56 BOND PREMIUM AND DISCOUNT

Markway, Inc., is contemplating selling bonds. The issue is to be composed of 150 bonds, each with a face amount of $2,000.

OBJECTIVE ▸ ⟨3⟩

Required:

1. Calculate how much Markway is able to borrow if each bond is sold at a premium of $20.
2. Calculate how much Markway is able to borrow if each bond is sold at a discount of $30.
3. Calculate how much Markway is able to borrow if each bond is sold at 96 percent of par.
4. Calculate how much Markway is able to borrow if each bond is sold at 105 percent of par.
5. Assume that the bonds are sold for $1,975 each. Prepare the entry to recognize the sale of the 150 bonds.
6. Assume that the bonds are sold for $2,015 each. Prepare the entry to recognize the sale of the 150 bonds.

OBJECTIVE ▸ ⟨2⟩⟨3⟩

Exercise 9-57 INTEREST-BEARING BOND AT PAR WITH ANNUAL INTEREST PAYMENTS

Kiwi Corporation issued at par $200,000, 8 percent bonds on December 31, 2008. Interest is paid annually on December 31. The principal and the final interest payment are due on December 31, 2010.

Required:

1. Prepare the entry to recognize the issuance of the bonds.
2. Prepare the journal entry for December 31, 2009.
3. Prepare the journal entry for December 31, 2010.

OBJECTIVE ▸ ⟨2⟩⟨3⟩

Exercise 9-58 ISSUANCE AND INTEREST AMORTIZATION FOR ZERO COUPON NOTE (STRAIGHT LINE)

Kerwin Company borrowed $10,000 on a two-year, zero coupon note. The note was issued on December 31, 2008. The face amount of the note, $12,544, is to be paid at maturity on December 31, 2010.

Required:

1. Allocate the interest of $2,544 to the two one-year interest periods, using straight-line interest amortization.
2. Prepare the entries to recognize the borrowing, the first year's interest expense, and the second year's interest expense plus redemption of the note at maturity.

OBJECTIVE ▸ ⟨2⟩⟨3⟩

Exercise 9-59 INTEREST PAYMENTS AND INTEREST EXPENSE FOR BONDS (STRAIGHT LINE)

Klamath Manufacturing sold 10-year bonds with a total face amount of $400,000 and a stated rate of 8.4 percent. The bonds sold for $424,000 on December 31, 2008, and pay interest semiannually on June 30 and December 31.

Required:

1. Prepare the entry to recognize the sale of the bonds.
2. Determine the amount of the semiannual interest payment required by the bonds.
3. Prepare the journal entry made by Klamath at June 30, 2009, to recognize the interest expense and an interest payment.
4. Determine the amount of interest expense for 2009.

OBJECTIVE ▸ ⟨2⟩⟨3⟩

Exercise 9-60 INTEREST PAYMENTS AND INTEREST EXPENSE FOR BONDS (STRAIGHT LINE)

On December 31, 2009, Harrington Corporation sold $100,000 of 10-year, 9 percent bonds. The bonds sold for $96,000 and pay interest semiannually on June 30 and December 31.

Required:

1. Prepare the journal entry to record the sale of the bonds.
2. Calculate the amount of the semiannual interest payment.
3. Prepare the entry at June 30, 2010, to recognize the payment of interest and interest expense.
4. Calculate the annual interest expense for 2010.

Exercise 9-61 INTEREST PAYMENTS AND INTEREST EXPENSE FOR BONDS (STRAIGHT LINE)

On December 31, 2007, Philips Corporation issued bonds with a total face amount of $800,000 and a stated rate of 9 percent.

Required:

1. Calculate the interest expense for 2008 if the bonds were sold at par.
2. Calculate the interest expense for 2008 if the bonds were sold at a premium and the straight-line premium amortization for 2008 is $2,300.
3. Calculate the interest expense for 2008 if the bonds were sold at a discount and the straight-line discount amortization for 2008 is $1,700.

Exercise 9-62 COMPLETING A DEBT AMORTIZATION TABLE (STRAIGHT LINE)   OBJECTIVE ➤ 3

Cagney Company sold $200,000 of bonds on December 31, 2008. A portion of the amortization table appears below.

Period	Cash Payment (Credit)	Interest Expense (Debit)	Discount on Bonds Payable (Credit)	Discount on Bonds Payable Balance	Carrying Value
At issue				$6,000	$194,000
6/30/09	$11,000	$11,600	$600	5,400	194,600
12/31/09	11,000	11,600	600	4,800	195,200
6/30/10	?	?	?	?	?

Required:

1. Determine the stated interest rate on these bonds.
2. Calculate the interest expense and the discount amortization for the interest period ending June 30, 2010.
3. Calculate the liability balance shown on a balance sheet after the interest payment is recorded on June 30, 2010.

Exercise 9-63 USING A PREMIUM AMORTIZATION TABLE (STRAIGHT LINE)   OBJECTIVE ➤ 3

For Dingle Corporation, the following amortization table was prepared when $400,000 of five-year, 7 percent bonds were sold on December 31, 2008, for $420,000.

Period	Cash Payment (Credit)	Interest Expense (Debit)	Premium on Bonds Payable (Debit)	Premium on Bonds Payable Balance	Carrying Value
At issue				$20,000	$420,000
6/30/09	$14,000	$12,000	$2,000	18,000	418,000
12/31/09	14,000	12,000	2,000	16,000	416,000
6/30/10	14,000	12,000	2,000	14,000	414,000
12/31/10	14,000	12,000	2,000	12,000	412,000
6/30/11	14,000	12,000	2,000	10,000	410,000
12/31/11	14,000	12,000	2,000	8,000	408,000
6/30/12	14,000	12,000	2,000	6,000	406,000
12/31/12	14,000	12,000	2,000	4,000	404,000
6/30/13	14,000	12,000	2,000	2,000	402,000
12/31/13	14,000	12,000	2,000	0	400,000

Required:

1. Prepare the entry to recognize the issuance of the bonds on December 31, 2008.
2. Prepare the entry to recognize the first interest payment on June 30, 2009.
3. Determine what interest expense for this bond issue Dingle will report in its 2010 income statement.
4. Indicate how these bonds will appear in Dingle's December 31, 2012, balance sheet.

OBJECTIVE ▶ 3

Exercise 9-64 USING A DISCOUNT AMORTIZATION TABLE (STRAIGHT LINE)

Panamint Candy Company prepared the following amortization table for $500,000 of five-year, 9.2 percent bonds issued and sold by Panamint on December 31, 2009, for $472,000:

Period	Cash Payment (Credit)	Interest Expense (Debit)	Discount on Bonds Payable (Credit)	Discount on Bonds Payable Balance	Carrying Value
				$28,000	$472,000
6/30/10	$23,000	$25,800	$2,800	25,200	474,800
12/31/10	23,000	25,800	2,800	22,400	477,600
6/30/11	23,000	25,800	2,800	19,600	480,400
12/31/11	23,000	25,800	2,800	16,800	483,200
6/30/12	23,000	25,800	2,800	14,000	486,000
12/31/12	23,000	25,800	2,800	11,200	488,800
6/30/13	23,000	25,800	2,800	8,400	491,600
12/31/13	23,000	25,800	2,800	5,600	494,400
6/30/14	23,000	25,800	2,800	2,800	497,200
12/31/14	23,000	25,800	2,800	0	500,000

Required:

1. Prepare the entry to recognize the sale of the bonds on December 31, 2009.
2. Prepare the entry to recognize the first interest payment on June 30, 2010.
3. Determine the interest expense for these bonds that Panamint will report on its 2012 income statement.
4. Indicate how these bonds will appear in Panamint's December 31, 2013, balance sheet.

OBJECTIVE ▶ 3

Exercise 9-65 COMPLETING AN AMORTIZATION TABLE (STRAIGHT LINE)

Sondrini Corporation sold $200,000 face value of bonds at 102 on December 31, 2008. These bonds have a 6 percent stated rate and mature in four years. Interest is payable on June 30 and December 31 of each year.

Required:

1. Prepare a bond amortization table assuming straight-line amortization.
2. Provide the journal entry for December 31, 2010.
3. Indicate how these bonds will appear in Sondrini's balance sheet at December 31, 2010.

OBJECTIVE ▶ 3

Exercise 9-66 ZERO COUPON BOND

Johnson Company sold for $90,000 a $102,400, two-year zero coupon bond on December 31, 2008. The bond matures on December 31, 2010.

Required:

1. Prepare the entry to record the issuance of the bond.
2. Prepare the adjustment to recognize 2009 interest expense.
3. Prepare the entry to recognize the 2010 interest expense and the repayment of the bond on December 31, 2010.

OBJECTIVE ▶ 3

Exercise 9-67 ZERO COUPON NOTE

Dodge City Products borrowed $100,000 cash by issuing a 36-month, $120,880 zero coupon note on December 31, 2009. The note matures on December 31, 2012.

Required:

1. Prepare the entry to recognize issuance of the note.
2. Prepare the adjustments to recognize 2010 and 2011 interest.
3. Prepare the entry to recognize 2012 interest and repayment of the note at maturity.

Exercise 9-68 OPERATING LEASES AND CAPITAL LEASES

OBJECTIVE ▶ 6

On January 1, 2009, Moody Company leased a warehouse for $20,000 per year. The first annual payment is due December 31, 2009. The present value of the lease payments, which is also the fair value of the warehouse, is $113,000.

Required:

1. Assume that the lease is an *operating* lease. Prepare the journal entries made by Moody during 2009 and 2010 for the lease.
2. Assume that the lease is a *capital* lease with an effective interest rate of 12 percent per year. Depreciate the cost of the leased warehouse on a straight-line basis over 10 years with zero residual value. Prepare Moody's 2009 entries to recognize expenses and payments for the capital lease.

Exercise 9-69 NOTE INTEREST PAYMENT AND INTEREST EXPENSE (EFFECTIVE INTEREST)

OBJECTIVE ▶ 4

Cardinal Company sold $200,000 of 10-year, 8 percent notes for $175,075. The notes were sold December 31, 2007, and pay interest semiannually on June 30 and December 31. The effective interest rate was 10 percent. Assume Cardinal uses the effective interest rate method.

Required:

1. Prepare the entry to record the sale of the notes.
2. Determine the amount of the semiannual interest payments for the notes.
3. Prepare the amortization table through 2009.
4. Prepare the entry for Cardinal's journal at June 30, 2008 to record the payment of six months' interest and the related interest expense.
5. Determine interest expense for 2009.

Exercise 9-70 BOND INTEREST PAYMENTS AND INTEREST EXPENSE (EFFECTIVE INTEREST)

OBJECTIVE ▶ 4

On December 31, 2010, Hawthorne Corporation issued for $155,989, five-year bonds with a face amount of $150,000 and a stated (or coupon) rate of 9 percent. The bonds pay interest annually and have an effective interest rate of 8 percent. Assume Hawthorne uses the effective interest rate method.

Required:

1. Prepare the entry to record the sale of the bonds.
2. Calculate the amount of the interest payments for the bonds.
3. Prepare the amortization table through 2012.
4. Prepare the journal entry for December 31, 2011 to record the payment of interest and the related interest expense.
5. Calculate the annual interest expense for 2011 and 2012.

Exercise 9-71 COMPLETING A BOND AMORTIZATION TABLE (EFFECTIVE INTEREST RATE METHOD)

OBJECTIVE ▶ 4

Cagney Company sold $200,000 of bonds on June 30, 2010. A portion of the amortization table appears below.

Period	Cash Payment (Credit)	Interest Expense (Debit)	Discount on Bonds Payable (Credit)	Discount on Bonds Payable Balance	Carrying Value
12/31/11	$9,000	$9,277	$277	$2,340	$197,660
6/30/12	9,000	9,290	290	2,050	197,950
12/31/12	?	?	?	?	?

Required:

1. Indicate the stated interest rate on these bonds.
2. Calculate the effective annual interest rate on these bonds (rounded to the nearest 0.1 percent).

3. Determine the interest expense and discount amortization for the interest period ending December 31, 2012.
4. Determine the liability balance after the interest payment is recorded on December 31, 2012.

OBJECTIVE ▶ 4

Exercise 9-72 COMPLETING A BOND AMORTIZATION TABLE (EFFECTIVE INTEREST RATE METHOD)

MacBride Enterprises sold $200,000 of bonds on December 31, 2011. A portion of the amortization table appears below.

Period	Cash Payment (Credit)	Interest Expense (Debit)	Premium on Bonds Payable (Debit)	Premium on Bonds Payable Balance	Carrying Value
At issue				$6,457	$206,457
6/30/12	$9,000	$8,465	$535	5,922	205,922
12/31/12	9,000	8,443	557	5,365	205,365
6/30/13	9,000	8,420	580	4,784	204,785
12/31/13	?	?	?	?	?

Required:

1. Indicate the stated annual interest rate on these bonds.
2. Calculate the effective annual interest rate on these bonds (rounded to the nearest 0.1 percent).
3. Determine the interest expense and premium amortization for the interest period ending December 31, 2013.
4. Determine when the bonds will mature.

OBJECTIVE ▶ 7

Exercise 9-73 RATIO ANALYSIS

Rising Stars Academy provided the following information on its 2009 Balance Sheet and Statement of Cash Flows:

Long-term debt	$ 4,400	Interest expense	$ 398
Total liabilities	8,972	Net income	559
Total assets	38,775	Interest payments	432
Total equity	29,803	Cash flows from operations	1,015
		Income tax expense	266
		Income taxes paid	150

Required:

1. Calculate the following ratios for both companies:
   a. debt to equity
   b. debt to total assets
   c. long-term debt to equity
   d. times interest earned (accrual basis)
   e. times interest earned (cash basis)
2. Interpret these results.

OBJECTIVE ▶ 8

Exercise 9-74 (APPENDIX) CALCULATING BOND ISSUE PRICE

On December 31, 2008, University Theatres issued $500,000 face value of bonds. The stated rate is 6 percent, and interest is paid semiannually on June 30 and December 31. The bonds mature in 10 years.

a. Assuming the market rate of interest is 4 percent, calculate at what price the bonds are issued.
b. Assuming the market rate of interest is 8 percent, calculate at what price the bonds are issued.

Problem Set A

Problem 9-75A **REPORTING LONG-TERM DEBT**

OBJECTIVE ▶ 2

Fridley Manufacturing's accounting records reveal the following account balances after adjusting entries are made on December 31, 2012:

Accounts payable	$ 62,500
Bonds payable (9.4%, due in 2019)	800,000
Capital lease liability*	41,500
Bonds payable (8.7%, due in 2015)	50,000
Deferred tax liability*	133,400
Discount on bonds payable (9.4%, due in 2019)	12,600
Income taxes payable	26,900
Interest payable	38,700
Installment note payable (8% equal installments due 2013 to 2016)	120,000
Notes payable (7.8%, due in 2017)	400,000
Premium on notes payable (7.8%, due in 2017)	6,100
Zero coupon note payable, $50,000 face amount, due in 2018	31,900

*Long-term liability

Required:

Prepare the current liabilities and long-term debt portions of Fridley's balance sheet at December 31, 2012. Provide a separate line item for each issue (i.e., do not combine separate bonds or notes payable), but some items may need to be split into more than one item.

Problem 9-76A **ENTRIES FOR, AND FINANCIAL STATEMENT PRESENTATION OF A NOTE**

OBJECTIVE ▶ 2 3

Perez Company borrowed $60,000 from the First National Bank on April 1, 2008, on a three-year, 8.7 percent note. Interest is paid annually on March 31.

Required:

1. Record the borrowing transaction in Perez's journal.
2. Prepare the adjustments made at December 31, 2008 and 2009.
3. Prepare the necessary journal entry to recognize 2008 interest to date and the first interest payment on March 31, 2009.
4. Indicate how the note and associated interest would be presented in Perez's December 31, 2009, balance sheet.
5. Prepare the necessary journal entry to record the repayment of the note and the last year's interest on March 31, 2011.

Problem 9-77A **PREPARING A BOND AMORTIZATION TABLE (STRAIGHT LINE)**

OBJECTIVE ▶ 2 3

On December 31, 2012, Distel Company borrowed $25,900 by issuing three-year, 8.5 percent bonds with a face amount of $25,000. The bonds require annual interest payments (each equal to 8.5 percent of $25,000).

Required:

Prepare an amortization table using the following column headings:

Period	Cash Payment (Credit)	Interest Expense (Debit)	Premium on Bonds Payable (Debit)	Premium on Bonds Payable Balance	Carrying Value

OBJECTIVE ▸ 3   Problem 9-78A **NOTE COMPUTATIONS AND ENTRIES (STRAIGHT LINE)**

On December 31, 2008, Sisek Company borrowed $800,000 with a 10-year, 9.75 percent note, interest payable semiannually on June 30 and December 31. Cash in the amount of $792,800 was received when the note was issued.

Required:

1. Provide the necessary journal entry at December 31, 2008.
2. Provide the necessary journal entry at June 30, 2009.
3. Provide the necessary journal entry at December 31, 2009.
4. Determine the carrying amount of this note at the end of the fifth year (December 31, 2013).

OBJECTIVE ▸ 3   Problem 9-79A **PREPARING A BOND AMORTIZATION TABLE (STRAIGHT LINE)**

Edmonton-Alston Corporation issued five-year, 9.5 percent bonds with a total face value of $700,000 on December 31, 2011, for $726,000. The bonds pay interest on June 30 and December 31 of each year.

Required:

1. Prepare an amortization table.
2. Prepare the entries to recognize the bond issue and the interest payments made on June 30, 2012, and December 31, 2012.

OBJECTIVE ▸ 3   Problem 9-80A **PREPARING A BOND AMORTIZATION TABLE (STRAIGHT LINE)**

St. Cloud Manufacturing, Inc., issued five-year, 9.2 percent bonds with a total face value of $500,000 on December 31, 2008, for $484,000. The bonds pay interest on June 30 and December 31 of each year.

Required:

1. Prepare an amortization table.
2. Prepare the entries to recognize the bond issuance and the interest payments made on June 30, 2009, and December 31, 2009.

OBJECTIVE ▸ 3   Problem 9-81A **PREPARING AND USING AN AMORTIZATION TABLE (STRAIGHT LINE)**

Girves Development Corporation has agreed to construct a plant in a new industrial park. To finance the construction, the county government issued $5,000,000 of 10-year, 4.75 percent revenue bonds for $5,125,000 on December 31, 2008. Girves will pay the interest and principal on the bonds. When the bonds are repaid, Girves will receive title to the plant. In the interim, Girves will pay property taxes as if it owned the plant. This financing arrangement is attractive to Girves, as state and local government bonds are exempt from federal income taxation and thus carry a lower interest rate. The bonds are attractive to investors, as both Girves and the county are issuers. The bonds pay interest semiannually on June 30 and December 31.

Required:

1. Prepare an amortization table through December 31, 2010, for these revenue bonds assuming straight-line amortization.
2. Discuss whether or not Girves should record the plant as an asset after it is constructed.
3. Discuss whether or not Girves should record the liability for these revenue bonds.

OBJECTIVE ▸ 3   Problem 9-82A **ZERO COUPON NOTE (STRAIGHT LINE)**

On December 31, 2008, Felix Products borrowed $80,000 cash on a $105,800, 24-month zero coupon note. Felix uses the straight-line method of amortization.

Required:

1. Record the borrowing in Felix's journal.
2. Prepare the adjusting entries for December 31, 2009.
3. Prepare the entry to recognize the 2010 interest expense and repayment of the note on December 31, 2010.

Problem 9-83A PREPARING AN AMORTIZATION TABLE FOR A ZERO COUPON BOND (STRAIGHT LINE)

On December 31, 2009, Georgetown Distributors borrowed $2,180,000 by issuing four-year, zero coupon bonds. The face value of the bonds is $3,000,000. Georgetown uses the straight-line method to amortize any premium or discount.

Required:

Prepare an amortization table for these bonds, using the following column headings:

Period	Cash Payment (Credit)	Interest Expense (Debit)	Discount on Bonds Payable (Credit)	Discount on Bonds Payable Balance	Carrying Value

Problem 9-84A RECORDING CAPITAL AND OPERATING LEASES

OBJECTIVE ➤ 6

Trippler Company has decided to lease its new office building. The following information is available for the lease:

Lease:

Payments	$100,000 per year*
Length of lease	15 years
Economic life of building	16 years
Appropriate interest rate	8.4%
Cost of building if purchased	$875,000

*The first payment is due at the end of the first year of the lease.

Required:

1. Determine whether this is a capital lease or an operating lease.
2. Regardless of your answer to the preceding question, assume that this is a capital lease and that the present value of the lease payments is $829,500. Record the liability and corresponding asset for this acquisition.
3. Record the interest expense on the capital lease at the end of the first year. Also assume no residual value and a 15-year lease for the building. Record the first year's straight-line depreciation of the cost of the leased asset.

Problem Set B

Problem 9-75B REPORTING LONG-TERM DEBT

OBJECTIVE ➤ 2

Craig Corporation's accounting records reveal the following account balances after adjusting entries are made on December 31, 2008:

Accounts payable	$ 73,000
Bonds payable (9.4%, due in 2013)	900,000
Capital lease liability*	30,000
Bonds payable (8.3%, due in 2012)	60,000
Deferred tax liability*	127,600
Discount on bonds payable (9.4%, due in 2013)	11,900
Income taxes payable	28,100
Interest payable	33,400
Installment note payable (9%, equal installments due 2009 to 2015)	110,000
Notes payable (7.8%, due in 2017)	350,000
Premium on notes payable (7.8%, due in 2017)	5,000
Zero coupon note payable, $50,000 face amount, due in 2019	29,800

*Long-term liability

Required:

Prepare the current liabilities and long-term debt portions of Craig's balance sheet at December 31, 2008. Provide a separate line item for each issue (i.e., do not combine separate bonds or notes payable), but some items may need to be split into more than one item.

OBJECTIVE ► 2 3   **Problem 9-76B ENTRIES FOR, AND FINANCIAL STATEMENT PRESENTATION OF A NOTE**

Griddley Company borrowed $80,000 from the East Salvador Bank on February 1, 2008, on a three-year, 7.2 percent note. Interest is paid annually on January 31.

Required:

1. Record the borrowing transaction in Griddley's journal.
2. Prepare the adjustments made at December 31, 2008 and 2009.
3. Prepare the necessary journal entry to recognize 2009 interest to date and the first interest payment on January 31, 2009.
4. Indicate how the note and associated interest would be presented in Griddley's December 31, 2008, balance sheet.
5. Prepare the necessary journal entry to record the repayment of the note and the last year's interest on January 31, 2011.

OBJECTIVE ► 2 3   **Problem 9-77B PREPARING A BOND AMORTIZATION TABLE (STRAIGHT LINE)**

On December 31, 2008, The Rock Restaurant borrowed $36,000 by issuing three-year, 8.0 percent bonds with a face amount of $33,000. The bonds require annual interest payments (each equal to 8.0 percent of $33,000).

Required:

Prepare an amortization table using the following column headings:

Period	Cash Payment (Credit)	Interest Expense (Debit)	Premium on Bonds Payable (Debit)	Premium on Bonds Payable Balance	Carrying Value

OBJECTIVE ► 3   **Problem 9-78B NOTE COMPUTATIONS AND ENTRIES (STRAIGHT LINE)**

On December 31, 2009, Benton Corporation borrowed $1,000,000 with a 10-year, 8.75 percent note, interest payable semiannually on June 30 and December 31. Cash in the amount of $985,500 was received when the note was issued.

Required:

1. Provide the necessary journal entry at December 31, 2009.
2. Provide the necessary journal entry at June 30, 2010.
3. Provide the necessary journal entry at December 31, 2010.
4. Determine the carrying amount of this note at the end of the fifth year (December 31, 2014).

OBJECTIVE ► 3   **Problem 9-79B PREPARING A BOND AMORTIZATION TABLE (STRAIGHT LINE)**

Dalton Company issued five-year, 7.5 percent bonds with a total face value of $900,000 on December 31, 2008, for $950,000. The bonds pay interest on June 30 and December 31 of each year.

Required:

1. Prepare an amortization table.
2. Prepare the entries to recognize the bond issue and the interest payments made on June 30, 2009, and December 31, 2009.

OBJECTIVE ► 3   **Problem 9-80B PREPARING A BOND AMORTIZATION TABLE (STRAIGHT LINE)**

Pennington Corporation issued five-year, 8.6 percent bonds with a total face value of $700,000 on December 31, 2009, for $680,000. The bonds pay interest on June 30 and December 31 of each year.

10

Stockholders' Equity

After studying Chapter 10, you should be able to:

1. Describe the different elements of stockholders' equity and prepare the stockholders' equity section of the balance sheet.

2. Distinguish between the different forms of equity and describe their use in raising capital.

3. Record the issuance of capital stock.

4. Account for the distribution of assets to stockholders.

5. Describe the accounting issues related to retained earnings and accumulated other comprehensive income.

6. Analyze stockholder payout and profitability ratios using information contained in the stockholders' equity section.

Experience Financial Accounting

with Google

Although **Google** is only 10 years old, its name has become a verb. Millions of people everyday say, "I googled..." Founded in 1998 by Sergey Brin and Larry Page, two Ph.D. students at Stanford University, by 2006 Google had revenues in excess of $10.5 billion and net income of over $3 billion. This revenue figure is up over 300 percent from 2004, while the net income figure is up over 750 percent from 2004.

One way that stockholders earn a return on their investment is by receiving dividends. Despite their profitability, Google has never paid a dividend to stockholders. Why is this?

After reading the chapter, you will realize that instead of paying out dividends to stockholders, corporations may choose to pay down debt or invest in growth oppor-

tunities. A primary strategy fueling Google's growth is investment in growth opportunities. You are likely aware of Google's purchase of **YouTube** and its roll out of features such as Google Maps; however, Google's investments do not stop there. In fact, Google's 2006 statement of cash flows shows that Google spent more than $6 billion on investing activities. Past investment is responsible for Google's large growth in revenues and net income, and the hope is that the 2006 investments will fuel profitable growth in the coming years. Review the graph below and notice how Google's investing activities increased over the five-year period with very little increase in long-term debt. It is apparent that the investing dollars came from paid-in capital and retained earnings.

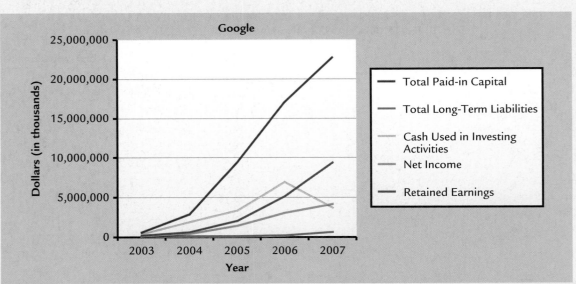

OBJECTIVE ▶ 1
Describe the different elements of
stockholders' equity and prepare the
stockholders' equity section of the
balance sheet.

Elements of Stockholders' Equity

Stockholders' equity, which also is called **equity**, represents the owners' claims against the assets of a corporation after all liabilities have been deducted. There are various elements of equity, and the stockholders' equity section of the balance sheet clearly classifies these elements according to their source: (1) capital stock—split between preferred and common stock and the associated paid-in capital in excess of par; (2) retained earnings or deficit; (3) accumulated other comprehensive income; and (4) treasury stock. Further, although it is not a required statement, a vast majority of corporations traded on U.S. stock exchanges also provide a statement of stockholders' equity. This latter statement reconciles the beginning and ending balances for each of the elements of stockholders' equity changes as is illustrated (see Exhibit 10-1) in the following excerpts from **Goldman Sachs'** balance sheet and statement of stockholders' equity.

Exhibit 10-1

Excerpts from Goldman Sachs' 2007 10-K

**THE GOLDMAN SACHS GROUP, INC. and SUBSIDIARIES
CONSOLIDATED BALANCE SHEET**

	Year Ended November	
	2007	**2006**
	(in millions, except per share amounts)	
Stockholders' Equity		
Preferred stock, par value $0.01 per share; 150,000,000 shares authorized, 124,000 shares issued and outstanding as of both November 2007 and November 2006, with liquidation preference of $25,000 per share	$ 3,100	$ 3,100
Common stock, par value $0.01 per share; 4,000,000,000 shares authorized, 618,707,032 and 599,697,200 shares issued as of November 2007 and November 2006, respectively, and 390,682,013 and 412,666,084 shares outstanding as of November 2007 and November 2006, respectively	6	6
Restricted stock units and employee stock options	9,302	6,290
Nonvoting common stock, par value $0.01 per share; 200,000,000 shares authorized, no shares issued and outstanding	—	—
Additional paid-in capital	22,027	19,731
Retained earnings	38,642	27,868
Accumulated other comprehensive income/(loss)	(118)	21
Common stock held in treasury, at cost, par value $0.01 per share; 228,025,019 and 187,031,116 shares as of November 2007 and November 2006, respectively	(30,159)	(21,230)
Total stockholders' equity	$ 42,800	$ 35,786

**THE GOLDMAN SACHS GROUP, INC. and SUBSIDIARIES CONDENSED CONSOLIDATED
STATEMENTS OF CHANGES IN SHAREHOLDERS' EQUITY**

	Year Ended November		
	2007	**2006**	**2005**
	(in millions, except per share amounts)		
Preferred stock			
Balance, beginning of year	$ 3,100	$ 1,750	$ —
Issued	—	1,350	1,750
Balance, end of year	$ 3,100	$ 3,100	$ 1,750
Common stock, par value $0.01 per share			
Balance, beginning of year	$ 6	$ 6	$ 6
Issued	—	—	—
Balance, end of year	$ 6	$ 6	$ 6

(Continued)

	Year Ended November		
	2007	**2006**	**2005**
	(in millions, except per share amounts)		
Restricted stock units and employee stock options			
Balance, beginning of year	$ 6,290	$ 3,415	$ 2,013
Issuance and amortization of restricted stock units and employee stock options	4,684	3,787	1,871
Delivery of common stock underlying restricted stock units	(1,548)	(781)	(423)
Forfeiture of restricted stock units and employee stock options	(113)	(129)	(37)
Exercise of employee stock options	(11)	(2)	(9)
Balance, end of year	$ 9,302	$ 6,290	$ 3,415
Additional paid-in capital			
Balance, beginning of year	$ 19,731	$ 17,159	$ 15,501
Issuance of common stock, including the delivery of common stock underlying restricted stock units and proceeds from the exercise of employee stock options	2,338	2,432	1,580
Cancellation of restricted stock units in satisfaction of withholding tax requirements	(929)	(375)	(163)
Stock purchase contract fee related to automatic preferred enhanced capital securities	(20)	—	—
Preferred stock issuance costs	—	(1)	(31)
Excess net tax benefit related to share-based compensation	908	653	272
Cash settlement of share-based compensation	(1)	(137)	—
Balance, end of year	$ 22,027	$ 19,731	$ 17,159
Retained earnings			
Balance, beginning of year, as previously reported	$ 27,868	$ 19,085	$ 13,970
Cumulative effect of adjustment from adoption of SFAS No. 157, net of tax	51	—	—
Cumulative effect of adjustment from adoption of SFAS No. 159, net of tax	(45)	—	—
Balance, beginning of year, after cumulative effect of adjustments	$ 27,874	$ 19,085	$ 13,970
Net earnings	11,599	9,537	5,626
Dividends and dividend equivalents declared on common stock and restricted stock units	(639)	(615)	(494)
Dividends declared on preferred stock	(192)	(139)	(17)
Balance, end of year	$ 38,642	$ 27,868	$ 19,085
Unearned compensation			
Balance, beginning of year	$ —	$ —	$ (117)
Amortization of restricted stock units	—	—	117
Balance, end of year	$ —	$ —	$ —
Accumulated other comprehensive income/(loss)			
Balance, beginning of year	$ 21	$ —	$ 11
Adjustment from adoption of SFAS No. 158, net of tax	(194)	—	—
Currency translation adjustment, net of tax	39	45	(27)
Minimum pension liability adjustment, net of tax	38	(27)	(11)
Net gains/(losses) on cash flow hedges, net of tax	(2)	(7)	9
Net unrealized gains/(losses) on available-for-sale securities, net of tax	(12)	10	18
Reclassification to retained earnings from adoption of SFAS No. 159, net of tax	(8)	—	—
Balance, end of year	$ (118)	$ 21	$ —
Common stock held in treasury, at cost			
Balance, beginning of year	$(21,230)	$(13,413)	$ (6,305)
Repurchased	(8,956)	(7,817)	(7,108)
Reissued	27	—	—
Balance, end of year	$(30,159)	$(21,230)	$(13,413)
Total shareholders' equity	$ 42,800	$ 35,786	$ 28,002

In this chapter, we will first describe the different forms of equity and how equity is used to raise capital for the corporation. This is followed by sections describing how corporations account for the various elements of stockholders' equity, including accounting for capital stock (preferred and common), dividends, stock splits, retained earnings, and accumulated other comprehensive income. The final section of the chapter analyzes stockholder payout and stockholder profitability using information contained in stockholders' equity.

Raising Equity Capital within a Corporation

OBJECTIVE ➤ 2
Distinguish between the different forms of equity and describe their use in raising capital.

Recall from Chapter 1, that most large businesses are organized as corporations because incorporation increases the company's ability to raise cash (or capital) by easing the transfer of ownership and limiting the liability of owners. Ownership of a corporation is divided into a large number of equal parts or *shares*. Shares are owned in varying numbers by the owners of the corporation called **stockholders** or **shareholders.**

New corporations are highly risky ventures; many more fail than succeed. Consequently, new corporations rarely have access to the major capital markets. Instead they must rely on *venture capital* provided by wealthy investors and institutions prepared to assume large risks. Businesses whose stock is held by a small group of private investors and are not offered to the general public are called *private* or *privately held corporations*.

Although the risk of loss is high, tremendous profits are possible from an investment in a new business that succeeds. Once a business becomes established, the owners can think about converting to a *public* or *publicly held corporation* that raises equity capital by selling stock to the general public. For example, when Google began active trading in August 2004, cofounders Larry Page and Sergey Brin retained stock worth approximately $3.85 billion each while raising about $1.67 billion in cash for the company.

Nonetheless, as an investment, the stock price performance of most initial public offerings (IPOs) are mediocre at best. Research for the years 1970 to 2006 shows that IPO stock bought on the first day of trading under performs similar-sized public companies by 3.7 percent over the subsequent five years. In another study published in the *Journal of Finance*, 34 percent[1] of all IPOs between 1980 and 2001 had earnings per share (EPS) less than zero.

Authorization to Issue Stock

Corporations are authorized, or *chartered,* in accordance with the provisions of state laws that govern the structure and operation of corporations. These laws differ from state to state and a corporation can charter in any state. For instance, although Google is headquartered in Mountain View, California, it is chartered in Delaware, as are many corporations due to Delaware's favorable laws.

Although the provisions of incorporation laws vary from state to state, all states require persons who wish to form a corporation to apply to a prescribed state official for the issuance of a charter. The **corporate charter,** which is sometimes called the **articles of incorporation,** is a document that authorizes the creation of the corporation, setting forth its name and purpose and the names of the incorporators.

The typical corporate charter contains provisions that describe how stock may be issued by the corporation. First, it authorizes the corporation to issue stock in a limited number of classes. It also sets an upper limit on the number of shares that the corporation may issue in each class. And finally, it sets a lower limit on the amount for which each share must be sold.

Shares of stock are sold, or issued, when a corporation is formed. Additional shares may be issued later. The maximum number of shares the business may issue in each class of stock is referred to as the number of **authorized shares.** This must be distinguished from the number of **issued shares,** which is the number of shares actually sold to stockholders. A corporation rarely issues all of its authorized shares.

[1] J. R. Ritter and I. Welch, "A Review of IPO Activity, Pricing, and Allocations," *The Journal of Finance* 62 (4) (2002), p. 1800.

Exhibit 10-2

Determination of Share Quantities

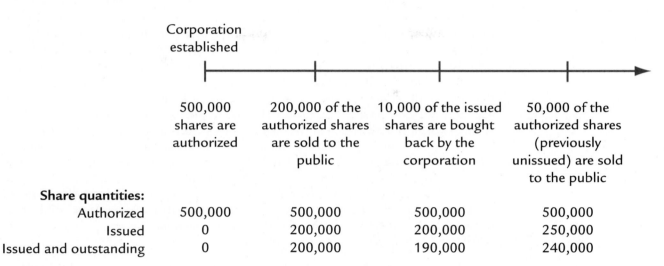

	Corporation established			
	500,000 shares are authorized	200,000 of the authorized shares are sold to the public	10,000 of the issued shares are bought back by the corporation	50,000 of the authorized shares (previously unissued) are sold to the public
Share quantities:				
Authorized	500,000	500,000	500,000	500,000
Issued	0	200,000	200,000	250,000
Issued and outstanding	0	200,000	190,000	240,000

Corporations can buy back their own stock for reasons explained later in this chapter. Thus, the number of shares issued is further distinguished from the number of **outstanding shares**—which is the number of issued shares actually in the hands of stockholders. When firms reacquire their own stock, the reacquired shares are not considered to be outstanding. Exhibit 10-2 illustrates how the share quantities are determined.

These three share quantities—the number of shares authorized, issued, and outstanding—are reported for each class of stock in the balance sheet or its accompanying notes (see Goldman Sachs' stockholders' equity section in Exhibit 10-1).

Common and Preferred Stock

All classes of stock are designated as either common stock or preferred stock. These come with different financial benefits and provide different rights regarding the governance of the corporation. The primary rights for owners of **common stock** are:

1. Voting in the election of the board of directors. You will recall that the board controls the operating and financial policies of the company.
2. Sharing in the profits and dividends of the company. We will talk more about this below.
3. Keeping the same percentage of ownership if new stock is issued (preemptive right).
4. Sharing in the assets in liquidation in proportion to their holdings. This is referred to as the "residual claim" because common stockholders are only paid after all creditors and preferred stockholders are paid in full (which is very rare in liquidation).

When you hear of someone who "made money by investing in stock" it is almost invariably through an investment in common stock. This is because, although the "residual claim" means common stockholders are only paid after the creditors and preferred stockholders are paid in full, it also means that common stockholders get *everything* that is left over after the creditors and preferred stockholders are paid in full. As such, the common stockholders receive the bulk of the financial gain from a profitable company through stock appreciation and dividends. Stock appreciation means that the value of the stock increases above the price initially paid (of course, it is also possible that the stock's value decreases if the company is unprofitable—this is a risk of owning stock).

Dividends are paid to a company's shareholders from earnings. These payments are usually in the form of cash, but noncash assets and stock can also be given as dividends. Payment of dividends to common shareholders, however, depends on a company's alternatives. The company may elect to pay down debt or, if the company has growth opportunities, they may elect to keep (or retain) earnings to fund these investment options rather than pay dividends. In fact, many companies do not pay dividends to common shareholders.

Preferred stock, on the other hand, generally pays a regular dividend. In this regard, preferred stock is similar to debt, with the preferred stock dividend equating to interest payments for debt. Additionally, the value of preferred stock, like the value of debt, is most closely tied to interest rate levels and the company's overall creditworthiness; the value of common stock, on the other hand, is most closely tied to the performance of the company. In this respect, preferred stock is a less risky investment than common stock. Preferred shareholders also receive priority over common shareholders in the payment of dividends and the distribution of assets in the event of liquidation.

As for corporate governance, common stock ownership allows shareholders to vote on the operating and financial policies of the company and elect the board of directors. In contrast, preferred stock usually does not give voting rights.

Some differences between preferred stock and common stock favor the preferred stockholder; other differences favor the common stockholder. Most differences between preferred and common stock are designated in the company's corporate charter and take one or more of the following forms:

1. *Dividend preferences:* Many preferred stock issues require that the issuing corporation pay dividends to preferred stockholders before paying dividends to common stockholders. This means that common stockholders may be obliged to miss a dividend in order that preferred dividends be paid. In addition, preferred dividends may be *cumulative and participating,* as explained on p. 521.

2. *Conversion privileges:* Some issues of preferred stock may be convertible into common shares if the preferred shareholder elects to do so and certain conditions are satisfied. For example, each share of preferred stock might be convertible into, say, 10 shares of common stock after a certain date.

3. *Liquidation preferences:* If and when a corporation is dissolved, liquidating distributions are made to stockholders. Corporate charters frequently require the claims of preferred stockholders to be satisfied before those of common stockholders. In addition, the charter may specify a liquidating amount for preferred shares.

4. *Call provisions (redeemable):* The corporate charter may authorize or even require the corporation to repurchase (or redeem) any preferred shares that are sold. In such cases, the charter usually fixes the *call price* (the amount to be paid to the preferred stockholders) and specifies a date on or after which the shares may or must be repurchased.

5. *Denial of voting rights:* Most preferred stock does not confer voting rights, which means that preferred stockholders, unlike common stockholders, cannot vote at stockholders' meetings.

Observe that the first three characteristics of preferred stock are advantageous for preferred stockholders. The last two characteristics usually work in the interest of common stockholders.

Because of the relative advantages of different forms of stock, corporations are typically authorized by their charters to issue several classes of preferred stock and several classes of common stock, each with a different set of terms and provisions. The 2007 edition of *Accounting Trends & Techniques* (an American Institute of Certified Public Accountants publication that surveys accounting practices followed in 600 sampled financial statements) indicates that only 49 of the 600 companies (about 8 percent) had outstanding preferred stock, but all corporations have outstanding common stock.[2]

CONCEPT Q&A

Describe some of the similarities between debt and preferred stock. If preferred stock is similar to debt, why not just issue debt?

Possible Answer:

Preferred dividends are conceptually similar to interest payments. Specifically, preferred dividends are a contractually defined amount (e.g., some percentage of par) and are typically paid each year. Further, both debt and preferred stock are paid off in full before common stockholders receive anything in liquidation. Finally, neither preferred stock nor debt provides voting rights.

Preferred stock is typically sold to other corporations because these corporations do not pay taxes on the full amount of the dividends (i.e., there is a big tax break relative to receiving interest payments). Further, preferred stock was historically always classified on the balance sheet as equity rather than debt, so if the issuer prefers to show lower debt totals, preferred stock will be advantageous. Securities that have both debt and equity characteristics are called "hybrid" securities. Some preferred stock issuances began to look so much like debt that in Accounting for Certain Financial Instruments with Characteristics of Both Liabilities and Equity, they are required to be classified as liabilities. For example, some preferred stock is "mandatorily redeemable" at a certain date. This requires the company to retire the preferred stock by paying the stockholders the face value of the share at a certain date. *This mandatory redemption date is conceptually identical to a maturity date on debt.*

---

[2] *Accounting Trends and Techniques for 2007, 61st edition, Table 2-36, p. 262.*

To illustrate, see the two classes of preferred stock and one class of common stock, as taken from **Procter & Gamble**'s 10-K.

(in millions)	2007	2006
Capital stock:		
Convertible Class A preferred stock, stated value $1 per share (600 shares authorized)	$1,406	$1,451
Nonvoting Class B preferred stock, stated value $1 per share (200 shares authorized)	—	—
Common stock, stated value $1 per share (10,000 shares authorized; issued: 2007—3,989.7, 2006—3,975.8)	3,990	3,976
Total capital stock	$5,396	$5,427

Accounting for Issuance of Capital Stock

OBJECTIVE ➤ 3
Record the issuance of capital stock.

In examples in previous chapters, we recorded the contributions of stockholders in exchange for stock in a single account. In practice, however, cash or other assets (i.e., capital) contributed by stockholders is usually divided between two accounts, on the basis of the par value of the stock. **Par value** is an arbitrary monetary amount printed on each share of stock that establishes a minimum price for the stock when issued, but does not determine its market value.[3] When a corporation receives more than par value for newly issued stock, as it usually does (stock rarely sells for exactly its par value), the par value and the excess over par are recorded in separate accounts. The par value multiplied by the number of shares sold is recorded in an account that describes the type of stock— for example, common stock or preferred stock. The amount received in excess of the par value is recorded in an account called **paid-in capital in excess of par.** These accounts are the first accounts shown in the stockholders' equity section of the balance sheet and taken together are known as **contributed capital.** Cornerstone 10-1 illustrates the accounting procedures for recording the sale of stock.

HOW TO Record the Sale of Capital Stock

**CORNERSTONE
10-1**

Concept:
Growing companies almost always need cash to fund expansion. Cash is obtained either by borrowing or by selling an ownership interest. However, the riskiness of new companies makes it relatively expensive to borrow large amounts of cash (i.e., the interest rates are high); instead, such companies often sell part of the company in the form of stock to raise cash. These ownership claims are recorded in the capital stock (including paid-in capital in excess of par) section of stockholders' equity.

Information:
Spectator Corporation is authorized by its charter from the state of Delaware to issue 1,000 shares of preferred stock with a 9 percent dividend rate and a par value of $20 per share and 50,000 shares of common stock with a par value of $2 per share. On January 2, 2009, Spectator Corporation issues 200 shares of preferred stock at $22 per share and 20,000 shares of common stock at $2.50 per share.

Required:
1. How much cash did Spectator raise through their stock issuance?
2. Prepare the journal entry necessary to record the sale of stock.
3. Provide the Stockholders' Equity section of Spectator's balance sheet assuming Spectator has yet to engage in any operations.

---

[3] The precise meaning of par value is established by securities laws that vary somewhat from state to state.

CORNERSTONE 10-1
(continued)

Solution:

1. The cash proceeds are calculated as follows:

Preferred stock ($22 × 200 shares)	$ 4,400
Common stock ($2.50 × 20,000 shares)	50,000
Total proceeds	**$54,400**

2. The journal entry required on January 2, 2009, is:

Date	Account and Explanation	Debit	Credit
Jan. 2	Cash	4,400	
	Preferred Stock (200 shares × $20 par)		4,000
	Paid-In Capital in Excess of Par—		400
	Preferred Stock [200 shares × ($22 − $20)]		
	(Record sale of preferred stock at $22 per share)		
2	Cash	50,000	
	Common Stock (20,000 shares × $2 par)		40,000
	Paid-In Capital in Excess of Par—Common		
	Stock [20,000 shares × ($2.50 − $2.00)]		10,000
	(Record sale of common stock at $2.50 per share)		

Assets =	Liabilities +	Stockholders' Equity
+4,400		+4,000
		+400

Assets =	Liabilities +	Stockholders' Equity
+50,000		+40,000
		+10,000

3. The balance sheet prepared by Spectator Corporation immediately after the issuance of shares on January 2, 2009, would contain the following stockholders' equity section:

Preferred stock, 9 percent, $20 par, 1,000 shares authorized, 200 shares issued and outstanding	$ 4,000	
Common stock, $2 par, 50,000 shares authorized, 20,000 shares issued and outstanding	40,000	
Paid-in capital in excess of par:		
Preferred stock	400	
Common stock	10,000	
Total capital stock		$54,400
Retained earnings*		—
Total stockholders' equity		$54,400

*Note that retained earnings displays a zero balance, because Spectator is a newly formed corporation.

CONCEPT Q&A

How do we account for stock issued in exchange for noncash assets or services (e.g., legal services in connection with incorporation)?

Possible Answer:

The amount recorded should be the fair market value of the stock or the fair market value of the asset/service, whichever is more clearly determinable. In the case of a newly organized corporation, the fair market value of the asset/service is usually more clearly determinable. But in the case of established corporations with widely traded stock, the fair market value of the stock is more clearly determinable than the fair market value of the asset/service.

Stated Capital and No-Par Stock

The stock issued by Spectator Corporation carried a par value that represents the stated capital of the corporation. **Stated capital (legal capital)** is the amount of capital that, under law, cannot be returned to the corporation's owners unless the corporation is liquidated. Even when state law permits the issuance of **no-par stock** (stock without a par value), it frequently requires that no-par stock have a stated (legal) value, set by the corporation, in order to establish the corporation's stated or legal capital. Further, this is a relatively infrequent occurrence.[4]

Stated value, like par value, is recorded in a separate equity account called *common* or *(preferred) stock, no-par.* Any

[4] *Accounting Trends & Techniques* for 2007 indicated that 63 of the 600 companies surveyed (just over 10 percent) had "no par value" common stock.

DECISION-MAKING & ANALYSIS

Going Public

Georgian Manufacturing, Inc., is a successful small manufacturer of electronic components for computer hardware. Georgian wishes to double its scale of operations in order to meet both existing and expected demand for its products. Georgian is a *privately held corporation*. High interest rates preclude Georgian from borrowing the necessary expansion capital from its current owners or financial institutions. Consequently, Georgian is forced to consider "going public" by selling common stock to the general public. A final decision has not been made, but the owners are discussing the following questions:

1. *What is the impact of going public on corporate control and profit?*

    The common stock issue required to double the size of operations would nearly double the number of shares outstanding. In addition, several of the original stockholders wish to sell their shares in the business; thus, the stock sale would be partly a *primary offering* of newly issued shares and partly a *secondary offering* of previously issued shares. Present stockholders would be unable to buy enough new shares to prevent new stockholders from ending up with more than 50 percent of the outstanding shares. If the new owners were sufficiently well-organized and cohesive, they could elect a majority of directors and control the company. On the other hand, if the new shares were purchased by a large number of investors with no organized interest in controlling Georgian, then effective control would remain in the hands of the original owners. Of course, the risk of losing control at some future time would still exist. Furthermore, Georgian expects its expansion to be immensely profitable. The new common stock would transfer more than half of the profit to the new shareholders.

2. *What is the impact of going public on the costs of financing the business?*

    The major capital markets are very efficient mechanisms for selling outstanding shares and issuing new ones. Thus, stock in public corporations is usually much easier to evaluate and sell than stock in private corporations. Further, capital obtained in a major capital market is likely to be less expensive than capital obtained in private or venture capital markets.

    Thus, the choice between operating as a private corporation or a public corporation depends on the current business environment and the circumstances of the firm. New businesses frequently are private corporations; established businesses, on the other hand, usually are public corporations. However, some large businesses operate as private corporations. Private corporations have the capacity to make major decisions quickly, without having to form a consensus among a large, diverse ownership. Further, private corporations need not issue the extensive financial reports and disclosures required of public corporations. The cost of financial reporting for public corporations has become even greater to comply with requirements of the Sarbanes-Oxley Act of 2002. This has lead to a record number of companies actually going private as ownership buys back stock from the public and stops having its stock publicly traded.

excess paid for the stock over its stated value is recorded in an equity account called *Paid-In Capital in Excess of Stated Value*.[5]

Warrants and Options

A **stock warrant** is the right granted by a corporation to purchase a specified number of shares of its capital stock at a stated price and within a stated time period. Corporations issue stock warrants in two situations. First, they may issue warrants along with bonds or preferred stock as an "equity kicker," to make the bonds or preferred stock more attractive. Such warrants often have a duration of five or more years. Second, they may issue warrants to existing stockholders who have a legal right to purchase a specified share of a new stock issue, in order to maintain their relative level of ownership in the corporation. Such warrants usually have a duration of less than six months.

Corporations also grant employees and executives the right to buy stock at a set price as compensation for their services. These "rights" are called *stock options*. Stock options are frequently given to employees and executives as compensation for their services. For example, the employer may give the executive the right to purchase in two years 5,000 shares of the company's stock at $50 per share, today's market price.

---

[5]In some states, stated value functions exactly as does the par value of stock to identify the legal capital portion of total paid-in or contributed capital. However, in other states, legal capital is defined as the entire paid-in or contributed capital associated with the no-par stock. In these states, the entire paid-in or contributed capital is recorded in a single common or preferred stock account.

If in two years the market price of the stock is higher than $50—say, $62—the executive will purchase the 5,000 shares for $50 each and receive effective compensation of $60,000 [($62 − $50) × 5,000 shares]. Of course, if the price is lower than $50, the executive will not exercise the option.

ETHICS The compensation expense recorded by a company when they grant stock options depends on many factors including the price at which employees can buy the stock (called the strike or exercise price) and the market value of the stock on the date of grant. As discussed above, the strike price of the options and the market value of the stock are generally the same on the date of grant. However, during 2006 many companies came under investigation for "back dating" stock options. That is, companies waited to announce the granting of options (this practice has been curtailed by the Sarbanes-Oxley Act) and then picked the date in the past when the stock price was lowest. This maximized the value of each individual option to the employee.

In and of itself, this is not illegal, but if, for example, on December 20 a company backdates options to May 1 (the lowest stock price of the year), the value of each option will be greater on December 20 than on May 1. As such, the company should calculate compensation expense using the market value of the stock on December 20. We will never know exactly how widespread the practice of backdating was, but approximately 80 firms were initially the subject of an SEC probe and research estimates that 29.2 percent of firms backdated grants to top executives between 1996 and 2005.◆

Corporations elect to grant stock options for two primary reasons. First, stock options allow cash-poor companies to compete for top talent in the employee market. For example, market salary for a manager of systems quality and assurance may be $200,000 per year—well beyond the means of many start-up companies. However, such a person may agree to work for $100,000 per year and a significant number of stock options. Second, stock options are believed to better align the incentives of the employee with those of the owners. This concept is easy to understand with a bit of exaggeration. Employees would like to be paid millions of dollars a year to do nothing, while owners would like the employees to work hundreds of hours a week for free. Stock options help align these incentives because now an employee's personal wealth is tied to the success of the company's stock price—just like the owners. Although knowledge of these uses of equity are important, further discussion of the complications of accounting for stock warrants and options must wait until later accounting courses.

OBJECTIVE ▶ 4

Account for the distribution of assets to stockholders.

Accounting for Distributions to Capital Stockholders

As discussed above, owners invest in corporations through the purchase of stock. Corporations can distribute cash to shareholders in two ways. First, the corporation can repurchase the shares from owners. Second, the corporation can issue dividends. Historically, dividends were the most common method of distributing cash. Over recent years, however, repurchasing shares has become a more frequent method of cash distribution because it has tax advantages for stockholders relative to dividends.[6] First, dividends are paid to *all* stockholders, thus creating tax consequences for everyone. Stock repurchases, on the other hand, only trigger tax consequences for those stockholders who elect to sell their stock back to the company. Thus, if a stockholder does not want to incur tax consequences in the current year, (s)he can elect not to sell the shares back to the company. Second, dividends have frequently been taxed at higher rates than capital gains, although at the current time this is not the case.[7] Dividends do have the advantage of allowing shareholders to receive assets from the corporation without reducing their ownership share.

---

[6] In fact, one study shows that the number of stock repurchases increased from 87 and $1.4 billion in 1988 to 1,570 and $222 billion in 1998 (Grullon, G. and D. Ikenberry. 2000. "What do we know about stock repurchases?" *Journal of Applied Corporate Finance.* Spring: 31–51.)

[7] However, at the time of this writing, the taxing of dividends at capital gains rates was set to expire at the end of 2010, unless Congress takes additional action.

Stock Repurchases (Treasury Stock)

When a corporation purchases its own previously issued stock, the stock that it buys is called **treasury stock.** Corporations purchase treasury stock for many reasons:

1. to buy out the ownership of one or more stockholders
2. to reduce the size of corporate operations
3. to reduce the number of outstanding shares of stock in an attempt to increase earnings per share and market value per share
4. to acquire shares to be transferred to employees under stock bonus, stock option, or stock purchase plans
5. to satisfy the terms of a business combination in which the corporation must give a quantity of shares of its stock as part of the acquisition of another business.
6. to reduce vulnerability to an unfriendly takeover.

The stock may be purchased on the open market, by a general offer to the stockholders (called a *tender offer*), or by direct negotiation with a major stockholder. If the objective of acquiring treasury stock is to reduce the size of corporate operations, the treasury shares may be retired after purchase. More frequently, however, repurchased stock is held in the corporation's treasury until circumstances favor its resale, or until it is needed to meet obligations of the corporation that must be satisfied with shares of its stock. Transactions in treasury stock, even very large ones, usually do not require stockholder approval.

The 2007 edition of *Accounting Trends & Techniques* indicates that 405 of the 600 companies surveyed hold treasury shares.[8] Interestingly, a few companies hold a relatively large portion of their issued shares in treasury. For example, at the end of 2007 Coca-Cola Company held approximately 34 percent of its shares in treasury at a repurchase cost of over $23 billion.

Purchase   At first thought, one might consider recording the acquisition of treasury stock as an exchange of cash for an investment in stock (an exchange of one asset for another). However, that approach fails to recognize that the treasury stock is already represented by amounts in the corporation's equity accounts. Although the shares would represent an asset to another entity if it acquired them, they cannot represent an asset to the entity that issued them. Thus, the purchase of treasury stock is a reduction of equity rather than the acquisition of an investment. Instead of requiring a debit to an investment account, the reacquisition of treasury stock requires a debit to a contra-equity account, treasury stock. This interpretation is consistent with the provisions of most state incorporation laws, which prohibit the payment of dividends on treasury stock.[9]

Resale   If the treasury shares are reissued at some point in the future, the original cost of the shares is removed from the treasury stock account. Any excess of proceeds over the cost of the shares is not considered a gain because a corporation cannot generate income by buying and selling its own stock (income is reserved for transactions with nonowners); instead, a credit is made to a special paid-in capital account—*paid-in capital from treasury stock transactions.* If the treasury shares are sold for less than their cost, a debit is first made to "Paid-in Capital from Treasury Stock Transactions." If the credit balance in Paid-in Capital from Treasury Stock Transactions is not large enough to absorb the shortfall, then the unabsorbed debit reduces retained earnings. Cornerstone 10-2 illustrates how to account for treasury stock.

CONCEPT Q&A

If a corporation buys the stock of another corporation and later sells that stock for a different price, a gain or loss is recorded on the income statement. However, when a corporation buys its own stock and later sells it for a different price, the income statement is not affected. Why is this?

Transactions with a corporation's owners cannot be included on the income statement.

Possible Answer:

---

[8] *Accounting Trends and Techniques for 2007, 61st edition,* Table 2-41, p. 272.

[9] The method of accounting for treasury stock demonstrated here is called the *cost method.* This method is used by approximately 95 percent of the companies engaging in treasury stock transactions. An alternative method, called the *par value method,* is demonstrated in intermediate accounting courses.

HOW TO Account for Treasury Stock

CORNERSTONE 10-2

Concept:
When purchasing its own previously issued stock, corporations record a reduction to stockholders' equity by debiting treasury stock. When purchasing the stock of another corporation, on the other hand, corporations record an investment, which increases assets.

Information:
On July 1, 2009, Spectator Corporation repurchases 1,000 shares of its outstanding common stock for $15 per share. On September 15, 2009, Spectator sells 500 shares of treasury stock for $18 per share and on December 1, 2009, Spectator sells 400 shares of treasury stock for $11 per share.

Required:
1. Provide the journal entry to record the purchase of treasury stock on July 1, 2009.
2. Provide the journal entry to record the sale of treasury stock on September 15, 2009.
3. Provide the journal entry to record the sale of treasury stock on December 1, 2009.

Solution:
1. The journal entry to required on July 1, 2009, is:

Assets = Liabilities +	Stockholders' Equity
−15,000	−15,000

Date	Account and Explanation	Debit	Credit
July 1, 2009	Treasury Stock (1,000 shares × $15)	15,000	
	Cash		15,000
	(Record purchase of treasury shares)		

2. The journal entry required on September 15, 2009, is:

Assets = Liabilities +	Stockholders' Equity
+9,000	+7,500
	+1,500

Date	Account and Explanation	Debit	Credit
Sept. 15, 2009	Cash (500 shares × $18)	9,000	
	Treasury Stock (500 × $15)		7,500
	Paid-In Capital from Treasury Stock		
	Transactions [500 × ($18 − $15)]		1,500
	(Record reissue of treasury shares)		

3. The journal entry required on December 1, 2009, is:

Assets = Liabilities +	Stockholders' Equity
+4,400	−1,500
	−100
	+6,000

Date	Account and Explanation	Debit	Credit
Dec. 1, 2009	Cash (400 shares × $11)	4,400	
	Paid-In Capital from Treasury Stock		
	Transactions	1,500*	
	Retained Earnings	100**	
	Treasury Stock (400 × $15)		6,000
	(Record reissue of treasury shares)		

*Paid-in capital from treasury stock transactions can be debited in a journal entry, but the result of the journal entry cannot be a debit *balance* to the account. Thus, there is a limit of $1,500 due to the credit in part 2.
**Retained earnings is debited if there is any remaining debit needed after paid-in capital from treasury stock transactions is zeroed out.

Transfers among Shareholders We have been considering the effects on the equity accounts when a corporation buys or sells its own stock. It should be remembered that treasury stock transactions constitute a special case. In general, the purchase or sale of stock after it is first issued does *not* alter the equity accounts of the issuing corporation, unless that corporation is itself the purchaser or seller. Although the issuing corporation's accounts do not change when shares are sold by one stockholder to another, the corporation's stockholder list must be updated. Large corporations usually retain an independent *stock transfer agent* to maintain their stockholder lists, which include the quantity and serial numbers of the shares held. Stock transfer agents also arrange for the transfer of certificates among stockholders and the issuance of new certificates to stockholders.[10]

Retirement of Treasury Shares   Occasionally, treasury shares are permanently retired. That is, these particular shares will no longer be traded. In this case the "common stock" account is debited for the par value of the stock and the "paid-in capital in excess of par" account is reduced for any excess of the purchase price of the treasury shares over par. In the Cornerstone example, if Spectator had retired the 1,000 shares it repurchased for $15/share, it would have made the following entry assuming the par value of the stock was $2:

Date	Account and Explanation	Debit	Credit
July 1, 2009	Common Stock (1,000 shares × $2)	2,000	
	Paid-In Capital in Excess of Par	13,000	
	Cash		15,000
	(Record purchase and retirement of shares)		

		Stockholders'
Assets =	Liabilities +	Equity
−15,000		−2,000
		−13,000

Dividends

A dividend is an amount paid periodically by a corporation to a stockholder as a return on invested capital. Dividends represent distributions of accumulated net income. They are usually paid in cash, but may also be paid in the form of noncash assets or even additional shares of a corporation's own stock. All dividends, whatever their form, reduce retained earnings.

Cash Dividends   Cash dividends are by far the most common form of dividend. The payment of a cash dividend is preceded by an official announcement or declaration by the board of directors of the company's intention to pay a dividend. The dividend declaration specifies:

1. the **declaration date**—the date on which a corporation announces its intention to pay a dividend on capital stock
2. the dollar amount of the dividend—usually stated as the number of dollars per share
3. the **date of record**—the date on which a stockholder must own one or more shares of stock in order to receive the dividend
4. the **payment date**—the date on which the dividend will actually be paid

Since the stock of most corporations is continually changing hands, it is necessary to set a date on which the ownership of shares is established as a basis for the payment of dividends. If a share of stock is sold between the date of record and the dividend payment date, the former owner of the share, rather than the new owner, receives the dividend. On the other hand, if a share of stock is sold between the declaration date and the date of record, the new owner, rather than the former owner, receives the dividend. As we have mentioned, when stock is widely traded, an independent stock transfer agent usually maintains the corporation's stockholder list. It is the agent's responsibility to determine who holds the outstanding shares on the date of record. The accounting for cash dividends is illustrated in Cornerstone 10-3.

CONCEPT Q&A

Why are dividends not an expense on the income statement?

Transactions with owners are not included on the income statement.

Possible Answer:

---

[10] Although the transfer of shares among stockholders does not affect the accounts of the issuing corporation, such transactions obviously require entries into the accounts of the buyers and sellers of the shares.

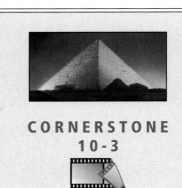

**CORNERSTONE
10-3**

HOW TO Record Cash Dividends

Concept:
Dividends are a common means of distributing cash to owners. State laws governing corporations generally require such payments to be made from current or undistributed past earnings (i.e., retained earnings).

Information:
The Kingsmill Corporation has issued 3,000 shares of common stock, all of the same class; 2,800 shares are outstanding and 200 shares are held as treasury stock. On November 15, 2009, Kingsmill's board of directors declares a cash dividend of $2.00 per share payable on December 15, 2009, to stockholders of record on December 1, 2009.

Required:
1. Provide the journal entry at the date of declaration (November 15, 2009).
2. Provide the journal entry at the date of record (December 1, 2009).
3. Provide the journal entry at the payment (December 15, 2009).

Solution:
1. Remember that dividends are not paid on treasury stock. Further, a liability is incurred on the date of declaration because the corporation has the legal obligation to pay after declaring the dividend. The journal entry to record the liability on November 15, 2009, is:

	Stockholders'
Assets = Liabilities +	**Equity**
+5,600	−5,600

Date	Account and Explanation	Debit	Credit
Nov. 15, 2009	Dividends (2,800 × $2)	5,600*	
	Dividends Payable		5,600
	(Record liability for dividends)		

*"Dividends" is closed to Retained Earnings at the end of the period.

2. No journal entry is made since the exact number of outstanding shares is generally known on the date of declaration.
3. The journal entry to record payment of the liability on December 15, 2009, is:

	Stockholders'
Assets = Liabilities +	**Equity**
−5,600 −5,600	

Date	Account and Explanation	Debit	Credit
Dec. 15, 2009	Dividends Payable	5,600	
	Cash		5,600
	(Record payment of dividends)		

Dividend Policy   The corporation's record of dividends and retained earnings provides useful information to boards of directors and managers who must formulate a dividend policy. In addition, it provides useful information to stockholders and potential investors who wish to evaluate past dividend policies and to assess prospects for future dividends. Historical records and long-term future projections of earnings and dividends are of particular interest to stockholders, because the dividend policies of most large corporations are characterized by long-term stability. In other words, they are designed to produce a smooth pattern of dividends over time. For this reason directors approach increases in the per-share dividend very cautiously, and avoid decreases at all costs—as the following Decision-Making & Analysis shown demonstrates.

Liquidating Dividends   When retained earnings has been reduced to zero, any additional dividends must come from paid-in capital. Such dividends are called **liquidating dividends,** and must be charged against capital stock accounts—first paid-in capital in excess of par, then par value. The payment of liquidating dividends usually accompanies the dissolution of the corporation, and is regulated by various laws

DECISION-MAKING & ANALYSIS

Dividend Policy

Edwardian Products, Inc., is a manufacturer of precision-engineered parts for high-performance engines. Edwardian was founded seven years ago. After several lean years, its net income began to grow at a rate of about 20 percent per year. Two years ago, the dividend was raised to $1.00 per share. The balance sheet for Edwardian has the following equity section:

Capital stock:

Preferred stock, 9 percent cumulative, $100 par, 5,000 shares authorized; 1,000 shares issued and outstanding	$100,000
Common stock, $20 par, 20,000 shares authorized; 10,000 shares issued and outstanding	200,000
Paid-in capital in excess of par, common stock	60,000
Retained earnings	120,000
Total equity	$480,000

Edwardian is required to pay a dividend of $9,000 to preferred stockholders if any dividend is paid to common stockholders. (If no dividends are paid to common stockholders, the amount of the preferred dividend is added to next year's preferred dividend requirement.) An agreement with bondholders requires at least $75,000 of retained earnings remain should a dividend be declared. Edwardian is in the process of formulating its cash dividend policy for the current year. The questions that follow bear on Edwardian's decision:

1. *How much cash is available for the payment of current dividends?*

   The board of directors has examined the firm's future cash needs and has determined that current cash dividends to holders of preferred and common shares cannot exceed $21,500. In determining this limitation, the board considered its plans for growth as well as cash needs arising from normal operations.

2. *What limitation is imposed on the current dividend by the restrictions on retained earnings?*

   The retained earnings balance is $120,000 but only $45,000 is available to support current dividends because of the $75,000 restriction imposed by bondholders. Edwardian's directors believe, however, that it would be imprudent to pay dividends up to the $45,000 limit. Moreover, the cash limitation prevents it.

3. *Should the dividend be increased to the limit of available cash?*

   After the preferred stock dividend is paid, $12,500 ($21,500 − $9,000) will be available for the payment of common stock dividends. This would permit Edwardian to increase the common stock dividend to $1.25 per share ($12,500/10,000 shares)—a 25 percent increase. However, the board decides to leave the dividend at $1.00 per share and to reconsider the matter next year. Several influential board members believe that there is a chance the firm's expansion plans could lead to several lean years, from a cash-flow standpoint. Although the chance of that occurring is small, being forced to cut the dividend could have disastrous effects on the way stockholders, customers and suppliers view the business. Thus a conservative strategy is deemed advisable.

   Scholars could debate the merits of Edwardian's decision. Some even argue that, as a matter of economic theory, the choice among alternative dividend policies makes little difference in the value of a business to stockholders.

designed to protect the interests of creditors and other holders of nonresidual equity. Thus, the presence of significant liabilities will usually prevent, or at least require close monitoring of, liquidating dividends. Since these dividends are a return of paid-in capital, they are not taxed as income to the recipients.

Stock Dividends   A cash dividend transfers cash from the corporation to its stockholders. In contrast, a **stock dividend** transfers shares of stock from the corporation to its stockholders—additional shares of the corporation's own stock. For each share outstanding, a fixed number of new shares is issued, and an amount of retained earnings is transferred to capital stock accounts in a process known as *capitalization of retained earnings*. While a cash dividend reduces both total assets and total equity, a stock dividend alters neither total assets nor total equity. A stock dividend merely notifies investors that the equity section of the balance sheet has been rearranged.

The amount of retained earnings capitalized for each new share depends on the size of the stock dividend. *Small stock dividends* increase the number of outstanding shares by less than 25 percent; they are capitalized using the stock's market value just before the dividend. *Large stock dividends* increase the number of outstanding shares by 25 percent or more; they are capitalized using the stock's par value, but this is discussed in more advanced accounting courses.

The following illustration demonstrates accounting for a small stock dividend. Arlington Corporation has 6,000 shares of outstanding common stock at a par value of $10 per share. Arlington's common stock is selling at $12 per share when the corporation declares and pays a 5 percent stock dividend. This means that 300 shares are issued through the stock dividend (6,000 × 0.05). In practice this means that one new share is issued for each 20 shares of outstanding common stock (6,000/300). Thus an investor holding 100 shares of Arlington's common stock would receive five additional shares [(0.05 × 100 shares) or (100 shares/20)] upon payment of the stock dividend. Declaration and payment of Arlington's stock dividend are summarized in the following journal entry:

Account and Explanation	Debit	Credit
Retained Earnings (300 shares × $12)	3,600	
Common Stock (300 shares × $10)		3,000
Paid-In Capital in Excess of Par—Common Stock		600
(Record stock dividend)		

Assets =	Liabilities +	Stockholders' Equity
		−3,600
		+ 3,000
		+ 600

Note that the stock dividend merely transfers $3,600 of equity from retained earnings to the capital stock accounts. Since this is a small stock dividend, the amount of equity transferred is based on the current market price of the stock.

Although a stock dividend increases the *number* of shares held by each stockholder, it does not alter the *proportion* of shares held. For example, if an investor held 1,500 out of 6,000 outstanding shares before a 10 percent stock dividend, that investor would hold 1,650 out of 6,600 outstanding shares after the dividend. Thus the investor would hold 25 percent of the outstanding shares both before and after the stock dividend [(1,500/6,000) = (1,650/6,600) = 0.25], and would have a 25 percent claim on earnings and stockholders' equity both before and after. Thus, stock dividends do not enhance a stockholder's proportionate ownership.

Further, despite the popular belief to the contrary among stockholders and even some financial managers, research shows that neither stock dividends nor stock splits, which we will consider next, enhance the total market value of a corporation's outstanding common stock. Stock dividends should be distinguished from dividend plans that allow stockholders to choose between receiving a cash dividend and a share of stock with equivalent current value. Such plans may enhance a stockholder's proportionate ownership and also avoid brokerage fees.

Stock Splits   A stock split, like a stock dividend, increases the number of outstanding shares without altering the proportionate ownership of a corporation. Unlike a stock dividend, however, a stock split involves a *decrease* in the per-share par value (or stated value), with no capitalization of retained earnings. In other words, a **stock split** is a stock issue that increases the number of outstanding shares of a corporation without changing the balances of its equity accounts.

Consider a corporation that has 10,000 common shares outstanding with a par value of $30 per share. In a two-for-one stock split, stockholders will exchange each of their 10,000 original shares for two new shares; the number of shares will rise from 10,000 to 20,000; and the par value of each share will be reduced to $15 per share. The total par value of all stock will remain $300,000 [($30 × 10,000 shares) = ($15 × 20,000 shares)]. The split has the effect of distributing the par value over a larger number of shares.

Stock splits are used to reduce the per-share price of a stock. If nothing else changes, a two-for-one split should cut the market price of a stock in half. A corporation may wish to reduce the per-share price to encourage trading of its stock. The assumption is that a higher per-share price is an obstacle to purchases and sales of stock, particularly for small investors.

Exhibit 10-3

Microsoft's Stock Price History

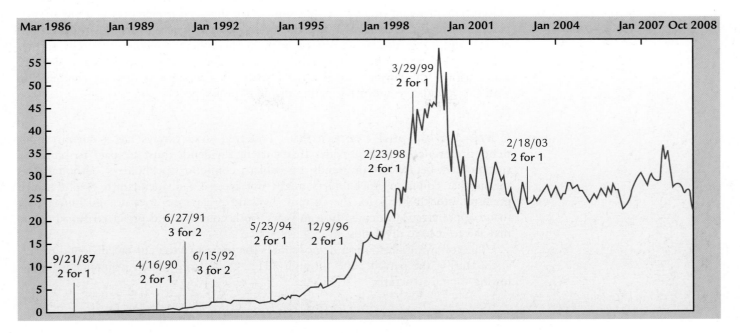

No entry is required to record a stock split, because no account balances change. The changes in the par value and the number of outstanding shares are merely noted in the corporation's records.

To illustrate how companies use stock splits, look at the **Microsoft** data in Exhibit 10-3. Note that Microsoft stock has split nine times in its history. That means if you had owned 1,000 shares of Microsoft stock prior to September 21, 1987 (and if you bought those 1,000 shares on September 20, 1987 they would have cost you approximately $115,000) and you never bought nor sold a single share, you would now have 288,000 shares (1,000 shares $\times$ 2 $\times$ 2 $\times$ (3/2) $\times$ (3/2) $\times$ 2 $\times$ 2 $\times$ 2 $\times$ 2 $\times$ 2). These shares would have been worth approximately $8,100,000 in June 2008. Further, if we assume that splits have no effect on price, the price of a share of Microsoft stock during June 2008, (which was trading slightly below $30 per share) would have been approximately $8,100 per share if there had been no stock splits.

Not many individual investors can pay $8,100 per share, but two notable companies—**Berkshire Hathaway** (Warren Buffet's company) and Google—do not issue stock splits. As a consequence, during August 2008, a share of Google stock was selling for approximately $500 per share (down from over $700 in late 2007) while Berkshire Hathaway Class B common was selling for approximately $3,900 per share and its Class A common was selling for approximately $116,000 per share (down from over $150,000 in late 2007). In fact, check to see what Berkshire Hathaway is selling for today, by going to Google Finance or Yahoo Finance and typing in "Berkshire Hathaway."

Preferred Dividend Preferences   While dividends on common stock are set by the corporation's board of directors, dividends on preferred stock are usually established as one of the terms of the issue. Most preferred stock issues fix their dividend rate as a percentage of the par value. For example, an 8 percent preferred share with a $100 par value has an annual dividend of $8 ($100 par $\times$ 8%). Of course, both preferred and common dividends are subject to various restrictions imposed by statute, by corporate charter, by the terms of preferred stock issues, and by contracts with bondholders and others.

Although preferred stockholders have no voting rights, they are "preferred" in the sense that corporations are required to pay dividends to them before paying dividends to common stockholders. Such dividend preferences can take three forms: (1) current dividend preference, (2) cumulative dividend preference, and (3) participating dividend preference. Most preferred stock issues grant a current dividend preference, and some also grant one or both of the other preferences, thereby further enhancing the likelihood of dividend payments. The following sections will describe and illustrate the current dividend preference, first alone and then in combination with the cumulative and participating dividend preferences.

Current Dividend Preference   Preferred stock always has a **current dividend preference**, which provides that current dividends must be paid to preferred stockholders before any dividends are paid to common stockholders. Although this means that common stockholders might not receive a dividend in a year in which preferred stockholders do, the current dividend preference does not guarantee payment of preferred dividends. In lean years, both common and preferred stockholders may fail to receive dividends.

The following illustration demonstrates the impact of the current dividend preference. During the period 2008 through 2011, Cook Corporation maintained the following capital structure:

Capital stock:

Preferred stock, 8 percent, $10 par, 5,000 shares authorized, 4,000 shares issued and outstanding	$ 40,000
Common stock, $5 par, 50,000 shares authorized, 30,000 shares issued and outstanding	150,000
Paid-in capital in excess of par, common stock	60,000
Total capital stock	$250,000

Cook's board of directors determined the total dollar amount available for preferred and common dividends in each year from 2008 through 2011 as shown in the second column of the following schedule:

Year	Amount Available for Dividends	Dividends to Preferred	Dividends to Common
2008	$12,200	$3,200*	$9,000**
2009	7,000	3,200	3,800
2010	2,000	2,000	-0-
2011	-0-	-0-	-0-

*0.08 × $40,000 = $3,200
**$12,200 − $3,200 = $9,000

This schedule shows that the common dividend is any positive amount remaining after the full preferred dividend has been paid. If the total amount available for dividends is less than the full preferred dividend, the entire amount is paid to preferred stockholders.

Cumulative Dividend Preference   Most preferred stock is cumulative. The **cumulative dividend preference** requires the eventual payment of all preferred dividends—both **dividends in arrears** and current dividends—before any dividends are paid to common stockholders. (Preferred stock dividends remaining unpaid for one or more years are considered to be in arrears.) In other words, no dividends can be paid to common stockholders until all prior and current preferred dividends have been paid. The cumulative dividend preference thus includes the current dividend preference. This is illustrated in Cornerstone 10-4.

Dividends do not become a liability of a corporation until they have been declared by the board of directors. If preferred dividends in arrears have not been declared, they are not recorded as liabilities, but are disclosed in a footnote to the financial statements.

Participating Dividend Preference   For some classes of preferred stock, dividends are not restricted to a fixed rate. Preferred stock that pays dividends in excess of its stated dividend rate is called *participating preferred stock*. (Preferred stock that cannot pay dividends in excess of the current dividend preference plus cumulative dividends in arrears, if any, is called *nonparticipating preferred stock*.)

The **participating dividend preference** provides that stockholders of participating preferred shares receive, in addition to the stated dividend, a share of amounts available for distribution as dividends to other classes of stock. Participating preferred

---

HOW TO Calculate Cumulative Preferred Dividends

CORNERSTONE 10-4

Concept:
Preferred stock has more in common with debt than with common stock. In fact, many preferred stockholders are "guaranteed" dividends through the cumulative feature. This feature requires corporations to pay all current and unpaid prior period dividends to preferred stockholders before paying any dividends to common shareholders.

Information:
Jefferson Manufacturing has a single class of common stock and a single class of cumulative preferred stock. The cumulative preferred stock requires the corporation to pay an annual dividend of $6,500 to preferred stockholders. On January 1, 2008, Jefferson's preferred dividends were one year in arrears, which means that Jefferson declared neither preferred nor common dividends in 2007. During the three years 2008–2010, Jefferson's board of directors determined they would be able to pay $9,000, $12,000, and $15,000, respectively.

Required:
Show how these anticipated payments will be split between preferred and common stockholders.

Solution:

Year	Amount Available for Dividends	Dividends to Preferred	Dividends to Common
2008	$ 9,000	$ 9,000*	$ -0-
2009	12,000	10,500**	1,500**
2010	15,000	6,500	8,500

*The $9,000 dividend paid to preferred stockholders in 2008 removes the $6,500 in arrears from 2007, but leaves dividends in arrears at January 1, 2009, of $4,000—the excess of preferred dividends for 2007 and 2008 over the amount paid in 2008 [(2 × $6,500) − $9,000 = $4,000].

**The $10,500 dividend to preferred stockholders in 2009 pays the current preferred dividend ($6,500), removes the $4,000 in arrears, and leaves $1,500 to be paid to common stockholders [$12,000 − $6,500 − $4,000 = $1,500].

stock may be either fully participating or partially participating. Fully participating preferred stock receives a share of *all* amounts available for dividends. Common stock is allocated a dividend at the same rate on par as the current dividend preference, and any remainder is divided between preferred and common stockholders—usually in proportion to the total par value of the two classes of stock. Partially participating preferred stock also receives a share of all amounts available for dividends, but the share is limited to a specified percentage of preferred par value.

OBJECTIVE ▶ 5

Describe the accounting issues related to retained earnings and accumulated other comprehensive income.

Accounting for Retained Earnings and Accumulated Other Comprehensive Income

Retained earnings (or deficit) is the accumulated earnings (or losses) over the entire life of the corporation that have not been paid out in dividends. Generally, ending retained earnings is calculated with a simple formula:

Beginning Retained Earnings
+ Net Income
− Dividends
= Ending Retained Earnings

Restrictions on Retained Earnings

Under most corporate charters, the balance of a corporation's retained earnings represents an upper limit on the entity's ability to pay dividends. (Dividends cannot reduce retained earnings below zero.) A corporation's capacity to pay dividends may be further restricted by agreements with lenders, by the corporation's board of directors, and by various provisions of state law, as follows:

1. An agreement between the corporation and bondholders may require that retained earnings never fall below a specified level so long as the bonds are outstanding.
2. The firm's board of directors may set aside a portion of retained earnings and declare it unavailable for the payment of dividends. Such an action may be used to communicate to stockholders changes in dividend policy made necessary by expansion programs or other decisions of the board.
3. State law may require that dividends not reduce retained earnings below the cost of treasury stock.

Restrictions of this sort are usually disclosed in footnotes to the financial statements to signify that the restricted amount is unavailable for dividends. In rare cases, a separate "reserve" account is established for the restricted portion of retained earnings. The reserve account is called either *restricted earnings* or *appropriation of retained earnings*. The account title frequently indicates, quite specifically, the nature of the restriction or the appropriation, as, for example, "restricted retained earnings under agreements with bondholders" or "appropriation of retained earnings for plant expansion." When reserve accounts are used, retained earnings is reported on two or more lines in the equity section of the balance sheet (see Exhibit 10-4). One line is devoted to each restriction, and to "unrestricted retained earnings" or "unappropriated retained earnings."

Error Corrections and Prior Period Adjustments
Errors in recording transactions can distort the financial statements. If errors are discovered and corrected before the closing process, then no great harm is done. However, if errors go undetected, then flawed financial statements are issued. No matter when they are discovered, errors should be corrected.

Exhibit 10-4

Information from Deere & Co. 2007 10-K

The following was included in Note 18 of Deere & Co.'s 2007 10-K:

The credit agreement also requires the Equipment Operations to maintain a ratio of total debt to total capital (total debt and stockholders' equity excluding accumulated other comprehensive income (loss)) of 65 percent or less at the end of each fiscal quarter according to accounting principles generally accepted in the U.S. in effect at October 31, 2006. Under this provision, the company's excess equity capacity and retained earnings balance free of restriction at October 31, 2007, was $6,661 million.

Although Deere & Co. did not choose to show this restriction in the Stockholders' Equity portion of their balance sheet, if they had it would have appeared as follows:

STOCKHOLDERS' EQUITY

		2007
Common stock, $1 par value (authorized – 1,200,000,000 shares; issued – 536,431,204 shares in 2007 and 2006), at stated value		2,777.0
Common stock in treasury, 96,795,090 shares in 2007 and 81,965,080 shares in 2006, at cost		(4,015.4)
Retained earnings:		
Restricted for credit agreement	2,370.7	
Unrestricted	6,661.0	9,031.7

If an error resulted in a misstatement of net income, then correction may require a direct adjustment to retained earnings, called a **prior period adjustment.** To illustrate, let us suppose that Byrnes Corporation uses a computer program to calculate depreciation expense. In 2008, a programming error caused the 2008 depreciation expense to be understated by $16,000. The error was not discovered until August 2009; consequently, 2008 net income after income taxes (which are paid at a rate of 25 percent) was overstated by $12,000 [$16,000(1 − 0.25)]. The error correction would be recorded in 2009 as follows:

Date	Account and Explanation	Debit	Credit
Aug. 31, 2009	Retained Earnings	12,000	
	Tax Refund Receivable	4,000	
	Accumulated Depreciation		16,000
	(Record prior period adjustment)		

Assets = Liabilities +	Stockholders' Equity
+ 4,000	−12,000
−16,000	

Byrnes Corporation's statement of changes in retained earnings for 2009 incorporates the $12,000 prior period adjustment as follows:

BYRNES CORPORATION
Statement of Changes in Retained Earnings
For the Year Ended December 31, 2009

Retained earnings, January 1, 2009		$157,000
Less: prior period adjustment:		
Correction of error in calculation of 2008 depreciation expense (net of tax)		12,000
Retained earnings as adjusted, December 31, 2008		$145,000
Add: Net income for 2009		65,000
Less: dividends declared in 2009:		
Cash dividend, preferred stock	$ 4,000	
Stock dividend, common stock	20,000	24,000
Retained earnings, December 31, 2009		$186,000

Notice that the adjustment is deducted from the beginning balance of retained earnings to produce an *adjusted* beginning balance.

Financial accounting standards define prior period adjustments in a way that specifically excludes adjustments arising from estimation errors and changes from one accounting principle to another. These changes are corrected by adjusting the related income accounts for the period in which they are discovered.

Accounting for Accumulated Other Comprehensive Income

The theory of financial accounting suggests that income represents the changes in the assets and liabilities of the corporation as a result of transactions with nonowners. This is why when a corporation sells treasury stock the "gain" or "loss" goes directly to stockholders' equity and not to the income statement (see Cornerstone 10-2). However, over time the FASB has allowed the effects of certain nonowner transactions to bypass the income statement and go directly to stockholders' equity. The FASB does, however, require separate disclosure of comprehensive income, which is net income plus/minus these other comprehensive income transactions. Corporations generally comply with this disclosure requirement in a Statement of Stockholders' Equity (see Exhibit 10-1 on p. 504).

OBJECTIVE ➤ 6

Analyze stockholder payout and profitability ratios using information contained in the stockholders' equity section.

Ratio Analysis

Stockholders want to understand (1) how the value of their shares of stock will change and (2) how the company will distribute any excess cash to stockholders. There is nothing particularly insightful about this statement because we all know that investors buy stock to increase their personal wealth. But how do stockholders use the financial statements to better understand these two dimensions?

Stockholder Profitability Ratios

A primary driver of an increase in stock price is profitability. Profitability refers to the return that the company earns (in other words, its net income). However, we care about more than the magnitude of the net income because it also matters how much we had to invest to earn the return. That is, would you rather earn $10 on a $100 investment or $20 on a $500 investment? Although the latter return is twice as large as the former, it also took an investment that was five times bigger. Assuming equal risk, etc., most investors would prefer to invest $100 to earn $10 because they then could use the extra $400 to invest somewhere else.

The two most common ratios used to evaluate stockholder profitability are (1) **return on common equity** and (2) **earnings per share (EPS)**. Return on common equity shows the growth in equity from operating activities. It is calculated as follows:

$$\text{Return on Common Equity} = \frac{\text{Net Income} - \text{Preferred Dividends}}{\text{Avg. Common Stockholders' Equity}}$$

Common stockholders' equity is calculated by taking total stockholders' equity and subtracting out preferred stock.

On the other hand, EPS measures the net income earned by each share of common stock. It is calculated as follows:

$$\text{EPS} = \frac{\text{Net Income} - \text{Preferred Dividends}}{\text{Avg. Common Shares Outstanding}}$$

Stockholder Payout

Stockholders, however, do not only experience an increase in wealth through an increasing stock price, they also may receive cash, or a payout, from the company. The most common stockholder payout ratios relate to dividends. Dividend yield considers the ratio of dividends paid to stock price. This ratio is conceptually similar to an interest rate for debt:

$$\text{Dividend Yield} = \frac{\text{Dividends per Common Share}}{\text{Common Stock Price}}$$

Another common dividend ratio calculates the proportion of dividends to earnings:

$$\text{Dividend Payout} = \frac{\text{Common Dividends}}{\text{Net Income (or Comprehensive Income)}}$$

However, as discussed earlier in the chapter, payouts to stockholders can also take the form of stock repurchases. As such, the total payout ratio is:

$$\text{Total Payout} = \frac{\text{Common Dividends} + \text{Common Stock Repurchases}}{\text{Net Income (or Comprehensive Income)}}$$

By using these two ratios, stockholders can easily calculate the proportion of earnings paid out in stock repurchases:

$$\text{Stock Repurchase Payout} = \text{Total Payout} - \text{Dividend Payout}$$

Cornerstones 10-5 and 10-6 illustrate how to calculate stockholder profitability and payout ratios, respectively.

HOW TO Calculate Stockholder Profitability Ratios

**CORNERSTONE
10-5**

Concept:
Stockholders are interested in a company's profitability and how such profits are paid out to them. Analysis of information contained in the statement of stockholders' equity allows stockholders to assess profitability and payout.

Information:
Consider the following information from Goldman Sachs' financial statements.

Stock price	$200/share	Avg. common shares	
Common dividends	$615 million	outstanding	449 million
Preferred dividends	$139 million	Dividends per	
2006 preferred stock	$3,100 million	common share	$1.30/share
2006 total stockholders'		Net income	$9,537 million
equity	$35,786 million	2005 preferred stock	$1,750 million
Purchases of treasury		2005 total stock-	
stock	$7,817 million	holders' equity	$28,002 million

Required:
Calculate the following stockholder profitability ratios:

1. Return on Common Equity
2. EPS

CORNERSTONE 10-5
(continued)

Solution:

Although the information to calculate these ratios is given, most of it can be found in the statement of stockholders' equity (and most all of it can be found within the financial statements and accompanying footnotes). Immediately following the calculations below, we discuss where in the financial statements this information can be found.

1. $$\text{Return on Common Equity} = \frac{\$9,537 - \$139}{[(\$35,786 - \$3,100) + (\$28,002 - \$1,750)]/2}$$
$$= 31.89\%$$

The numerator is net income less preferred dividends. Both of these totals are found in the retained earnings section of the statement of changes in stockholders' equity. Average common stockholders' equity (denominator) is the average of total stockholders' equity less preferred stock at the end and the beginning of the year. Total stockholders' equity for both 2006 and 2005 is found at the bottom of the statement of changes in stockholders' equity. Total preferred stock for both years is found in the preferred stock section near the top of the statement of changes in stockholders' equity.

2. $$\text{EPS} = \frac{\$9,537 - \$139}{449} = \$20.93 \text{ per share}$$

Both net income and preferred dividends (numerator) are found in the retained earnings section of the statement of changes in stockholders' equity. The number of average common shares outstanding (denominator) is given in the information section of this Cornerstone. This figure is often difficult to calculate in real world settings. You will learn how to do this in intermediate financial accounting.

CORNERSTONE 10-6

HOW TO Calculate Stockholder Payout Ratios

Concept:

Stockholders are interested in a company's profitability and how such profits are paid out to them. Analysis of information contained in the statement of stockholders' equity allows stockholders to assess profitability and payout.

Information:

Consider the following information from Goldman Sachs' financial statements.

Stock price	$200/share	Avg. common shares	
Common dividends	$615 million	outstanding	449 million
Preferred dividends	$139 million	Dividends per	
2006 preferred stock	$3,100 million	common share	$1.30/share
2006 total stock-holders' equity	$35,786 million	Net income	$9,537 million
		2005 preferred stock	$1,750 million
Purchases of treasury stock	$7,817 million	2005 total stock-holders' equity	$28,002 million

Required:

Calculate the following stockholder payout ratios:

1. Dividend yield
2. Dividend payout

3. Total payout
4. Stock repurchase payout

Solution:

Although the information to calculate these ratios is given, most of it can be found in the statement of stockholders' equity (and most all of it can be found within the financial statements and accompanying footnotes). Immediately following the calculations below, we discuss where in the financial statements this information can be found.

1. Dividend Yield $= \dfrac{\$1.30}{\$200} = 0.65\%$

   The dividends per common share (numerator) is disclosed in the footnotes and can be found in the financial press (e.g., Google finance, ticker symbol GS). The common stock price is found at any website quoting stock prices.

2. Dividend Payout $= \dfrac{\$615}{\$9,537} = 6.45\%$

   Both the common dividends (numerator) and net income (denominator) can be found in the retained earnings section of the statement of changes in stockholders' equity.

3. Total Payout $= \dfrac{\$615 + \$7,817}{\$9,537} = 88.41\%$

   This is the same as 2 except we add stock repurchases to the numerator. This figure can be found in the "Common stock held in treasury, at cost" near the bottom of the statement of changes in stockholders' equity.

4. Stock Repurchase Payout $= 88.41\% - 6.45\% = 81.96\%$

   Or $\dfrac{\$7,817}{\$9,537} = 81.96\%$

   This can be calculated directly as stock repurchases divided by net income. But if you have already calculated dividend and total payout, you can simply take the difference because dividend payout + stock repurchase payout = total payout.

Summary

Stockholders' equity represents the claims of owners against the net assets of a business entity. Equity takes many different forms but most can be characterized as a type of either common or preferred stock. Common stockholders control the corporation; preferred stockholders have the right to receive dividends before dividends are paid to common stockholders. Accounting reports present useful information about equity to both managers and stock market investors. Both groups use accounting information about equity transactions to evaluate the effects of past decisions and to project the effects of future decisions.

Although common stock usually has a par value, no-par stock is permitted in some states. When stock is issued at amounts in excess of par or stated value, the excess is recorded in a separate capital stock account. In addition to issuing shares of stock, corporations can also issue warrants and options—rights to acquire stock in the future. They may also

CONCEPT Q&A

What do the stockholder profitability and payout ratios mean?

Possible Answer:

The results of these ratios are usually used in two ways. First, they are compared over time to evaluate trends. For example, in 2006 Goldman Sachs' EPS was $20.93. This might be great news if EPS in 2005 were $11.00 or bad news if it were $28.00. In fact, EPS for 2004 and 2005 were $9.30 and $11.73, respectively, so EPS has more than doubled in two years. This is exceptionally good news. Second, the ratios can be compared to results for other companies in the industry. For example, the 2006 return on common equity for Morgan Stanley was 23.57 percent and for Merrill Lynch it was 21.25 percent, which makes Goldman Sachs' 31.89 percent look very good.

repurchase their own stock after issuance. Repurchased stock is called *treasury stock* and is recorded in a contra-equity account that is subtracted from the total of stockholders' equity.

Dividends reduce retained earnings. Cash dividends distribute cash to stockholders. Stock dividends distribute additional shares to stockholders, which results in the reclassification of a portion of retained earnings as paid-in capital. Stock splits also transfer additional shares to stockholders but do not produce changes in equity.

Recent changes in equity are summarized in a financial statement called the *statement of changes in stockholders' equity,* which appears in most annual reports. The statement shows changes to all elements of stockholders' equity. The information contained in this statement is useful for assessing stockholder profitability and payout.

Summary of Learning Objectives

LO1. **Describe the different elements of stockholders' equity and prepare the stockholders' equity section of the balance sheet.**
- There are various elements of equity and the stockholders' equity section of the balance sheet clearly classifies these elements according to their source:
  - capital stock—split between preferred and common stock and associated paid-in capital in excess of par;
  - retained earnings or deficit;
  - accumulated other comprehensive income; and
  - treasury stock.
- Corporations split their stockholders' equity into these sections, although most corporations do not have all of these elements.

LO2. **Distinguish between the different forms of equity and describe their use in raising capital.**
- Corporations sell both common stock and preferred stock to raise capital.
- Preferred stock generally guarantees a regular dividend and receives priority over common stock in the payment of dividends and distribution of assets in liquidation.
- Common stock has voting rights and receives all benefits not assigned to the preferred stockholders or creditors.
- Selling different classes of stock (with different features) attracts shareholders with diverse risk preferences and tax situations.

LO3. **Record the issuance of capital stock.**
- Both preferred and common stock are generally recorded at par or stated value.
- Any extra consideration received is recorded as "paid-in capital in excess of par."

LO4. **Account for the distribution of assets to stockholders.**
- Assets are distributed to stockholders by:
  - repurchasing their shares of stock, or
  - paying dividends.
- Generally the cost of stock repurchases are recorded as a reduction in stockholders' equity (a debit to "treasury stock").
- Typically the corporation pays dividends with cash.
- Stock dividends and stock splits do not represent a payout to stockholders. These transactions have no effect on total stockholders' equity.
- Preferred stock generally has dividend preferences such as being cumulative or participating.

**CORNERSTONE
10-6**
(continued)

LO5. Describe the accounting issues related to retained earnings and accumulated other comprehensive income.

- Retained earnings represents the earnings that the corporation elects not to pay out in dividends.
- Ending retained earnings is calculated by adding net income and subtracting dividends to beginning retained earnings.
- Retained earnings can be restricted, which communicates to stockholders that this portion of retained earnings is not eligible for dividend payout.

LO6. Analyze stockholder payout and profitability ratios using information contained in the stockholders' equity section.

- Stockholders are primarily interested in two things:
  - the creation of value, and
  - the distribution of value.
- Analysis of the stockholders' equity section of the balance sheet in conjunction with the statement of stockholders' equity allows stockholders to separate these concepts.

CORNERSTONES FOR CHAPTER 10

Key Terms

Review Problem

Stockholders' Equity

Grace Industries, a privately held corporation, has decided to go public. The current ownership group has 10,000,000 common shares (purchased at an average price of $0.50 per share) and the articles of incorporation authorize 50,000,000, $0.10 par, common shares and 1,000,000, 10%, $30 par, cumulative, preferred shares. On January 1, 2008, the public offering issues 8,000,000 common shares at $14 per share and 100,000 preferred shares at $33 per share.

On October 3, 2009, Grace Industries repurchases 750,000 common shares at $12 per share. After the repurchase Grace's board of directors decides to declare dividends totaling $4,050,000 (no dividends were declared or paid in 2008). This dividend will be declared on November 15, 2009, to all shareholders of record on December 8, 2009. This dividend will be paid on December 23, 2009. On December 28, 2009, 100,000 of the treasury shares are reissued for $15 per share.

At December 31, 2009, Grace Industries has $12,000,000 of retained earnings and accumulated other comprehensive income of ($250,000).

Required:

1. Provide the journal entry to record the January 1, 2008, issuance of the common and preferred stock.
2. Provide the journal entry to record the October 3, 2009, stock repurchase.
3. Determine how much of the dividend will go to preferred shareholders.
4. Calculate what the dividends per common share will be.
5. Provide the journal entry for the dividend declaration on November 15, 2009.
6. Provide the journal entry on the date of record (December 8, 2009).
7. Provide the journal entry on the dividend payment date (December 23, 2009).
8. Provide the journal entry for the reissuance of treasury shares on December 28, 2009.
9. Prepare the stockholders' equity section of the balance sheet at December 31, 2009.

Solution:

1.

Date	Account and Explanation	Debit	Credit
Jan. 1, 2008	Cash (100,000 × $33)	3,300,000	
	Preferred Stock (100,000 × $30 par)		3,000,000
	Paid-in Capital in Excess of Par—Preferred Stock [100,000 × ($33 − $30)]		300,000
	(Record issuance of preferred stock)		
	Cash (8,000,000 × $14)	112,000,000	
	Common Stock (8,000,000 × $0.10 par)		800,000
	Paid-in Capital in Excess of Par—Common Stock [8,000,000 × ($14 − $0.10)]		111,200,000
	(Record issuance of common stock)		

	Stockholders'
Assets = Liabilities +	**Equity**
+3,300,000	+3,000,000
+112,000,000	+300,000
	+800,000
	+111,200,000

2.

Date	Account and Explanation	Debit	Credit
Oct. 3, 2009	Treasury Stock (750,000 × $12)	9,000,000	
	Cash		9,000,000
	(Record repurchase of common stock)		

	Stockholders'
Assets = Liabilities +	**Equity**
−9,000,000	−9,000,000

3. The preferred stock is cumulative, so the preferred shareholders must be paid their annual dividend for 2009 (the current year) and for 2008 (dividends in arrears).

Preferred Dividends
[($30 par × 10% × 2 years) × 100,000 shares] $600,000

4. The common stockholders receive any dividend remaining after the preferred dividend has been paid (because the preferred is not participating). Because common dividends are only paid to outstanding stock, the treasury shares must be subtracted from the issued shares. Remember that the ownership group owned 10,000,000 shares then issued 8,000,000 shares in the initial public offering.

Common Dividends $\dfrac{\$4,050,000 - \$600,000}{18,000,000 \text{ issued shares} - 750,000 \text{ treasury shares}}$ $0.20 per share

5.

Date	Account and Explanation	Debit	Credit
Nov. 15, 2009	Dividends*	4,050,000	
	Cash Dividends Payable		4,050,000
	(Record declaration of cash dividends)		

Assets =	Liabilities +	Stockholders' Equity
	+4,050,000	−4,050,000

*Dividends is closed to retained earnings

6.   No entry is necessary on the date of record.

7.

Date	Account and Explanation	Debit	Credit
Dec. 23, 2009	Cash Dividends Payable	4,050,000	
	Cash		4,050,000
	(Record payment of cash dividends)		

Assets =	Liabilities +	Stockholders' Equity
−4,050,000	−4,050,000	

8.

Date	Account and Explanation	Debit	Credit
Dec. 28, 2009	Cash (100,000 × $15)	1,500,000	
	Treasury Stock (100,000 × $12)		1,200,000
	Paid-in Capital from Treasury Stock		
	Transactions		300,000
	(Record reissuance of treasury shares)		

Assets =	Liabilities +	Stockholders' Equity
+1,500,000		+1,200,000
		+300,000

9.   **Stockholders' equity:**

Capital stock:

Preferred stock, 10 percent, $30 par,
  1,000,000 shares authorized, 100,000
   shares issued and outstanding $ 3,000,000*

Common stock, $0.10 par, 50,000,000
  shares authorized, 18,000,000 shares
   issued and 17,350,000 outstanding   1,800,000**

Paid-in capital in excess of par:

  Preferred stock   300,000***

  Common stock   115,200,000[†]

  Treasury stock   300,000[††]

    Total capital stock $120,600,000

Retained earnings   12,000,000[†††]

Less:

  Accumulated other comprehensive income   (250,000)[‡]

  Treasury stock (650,000 shares at cost)   (7,800,000)[‡‡]

    Total stockholders' equity $124,550,000

*100,000 shares issued at $30 par (see journal entry from 1).
**18,000,000 shares issued at $0.10 par.
***100,000 shares issued at $3 more than par ($33 selling price less $30 par) See journal entry from 1.

Discussion Questions

1.   What does stockholders' equity represent?
2.   What does a share of stock represent?
3.   Why do corporations issue stock?
4.   What are the benefits which common stockholders may receive?
5.   How do common stock and preferred stock differ?
6.   Why would the number of shares issued be different from the number of shares outstanding?
7.   Why is preferred stock sometimes regarded as being similar to debt?
8.   How is a preferred stock dividend calculated?
9.   Why do corporations utilize different forms of equity?
10.   On what balance sheet accounts does the issuance of common stock have an effect?
11.   What is treasury stock?
12.   How would the purchase of treasury stock affect a corporation's balance sheet?
13.   What is a stock dividend? How does it differ from a stock split?
14.   Compare and contrast cash dividends and liquidating dividends.

15. What are retained earnings?
16. How may a corporation's retained earnings be restricted?
17. Distinguish between retained earnings and accumulated other comprehensive income.
18. How are dividend payout and profitability ratios useful to investors?
19. What is the difference between par value and stated value?
20. What is the difference between a privately- and publicly-held corporation?
21. What is a stock warrant? How are they used by corporations?
22. Give four reasons why a company might purchase treasury stock.
23. What entries are made (if any) at the declaration date, date of record, and date of payment for cash dividends?
24. What is the effect of a stock split on stockholders' equity account balances?
25. Describe the statement of changes in stockholders' equity.
26. When are prior period adjustments used?
27. Describe two ways corporations make payouts to stockholders.
28. Explain each of the following preferred stock dividend preferences: (1) current dividend preference, (2) cumulative dividend preference, and (3) participating dividend preference.
29. Are dividends in arrears reported among the liabilities of the dividend-paying firm? If not, how are they reported, and why?

Multiple-Choice Exercises

10-1 Which of the following is not a direct nor indirect component of stock-holders' equity?

a. dividends payable
b. loss on sale of equipment
c. retained earnings
d. net income

10-2 Which of the following statements is *true* with regard to contributed capital?

a. Preferred stock is stock that has been retired.
b. It is very unlikely corporations may have more than one class of stock outstanding.
c. The outstanding number of shares is the maximum number of shares that can be issued by a corporation.
d. The shares that are in the hands of the stockholders are said to be outstanding.

10-3 Authorized stock represents the:

a. maximum number of shares that can be issued.
b. number of shares that have been sold.
c. number of shares that are currently held by stockholders.
d. number of shares that have been repurchased by the corporation.

10-4 Harvey Corporation shows the following in the stockholders' equity section of its balance sheet: The par value of its common stock is $0.50 and the total balance in the common stock account is $37,500. Also noted is that 5,000 shares are currently designated as treasury stock. The number of shares *outstanding* is:

a. 80,000.
b. 75,000.
c. 72,500.
d. 70,000.

10-5 With regard to preferred stock,

a. its issuance provides no flexibility to the issuing company because its terms always require mandatory dividend payments.
b. no dividends are expected by the stockholders.
c. its stockholders may have the right to participate, along with common stockholders, if an extra dividend is declared.
d. there is a legal requirement for a corporation to declare a dividend on preferred stock.

10-6 Murphy Parts Shop began business on January 1, 2007. The corporate charter authorized issuance of 10,000 shares of $2 par value common stock and 4,000 shares of $8 par value, 6 percent cumulative preferred stock. Murphy issued 2,400 shares of common stock for cash at $20 per share on January 2, 2007. What effect does the entry to record the issuance of stock have on total stockholders' equity?

a. increase of $4,800
b. decrease of $4,800
c. decrease of $48,000
d. increase of $48,000

10-7 Marx Company began business on January 1, 2007. The corporate charter authorized issuance of 5,000 shares of $1 par value common stock, and 4,000 shares of $8 par value, 6 percent cumulative preferred stock, of which none were issued. On July 1, Marx issued 1,000 shares of common stock in exchange for two years rent on a retail location. The cash rental price is $2,400 per month and the rental period begins on July 1. What is the correct entry to record the July 1 transaction?

a. Debit to Cash, $57,600; Credit to Prepaid Rent, $57,600
b. Debit to Prepaid Rent, $57,600; Credit to Common Stock, $57,600
c. Debit to Prepaid Rent, $57,600; Credit to Common Stock, $1,000; Credit to Additional Paid-In Capital—Common, $56,600
d. Debit to Prepaid Rent, $57,600; Credit to Common Stock, $5,000; Credit to Additional Paid-In Capital—Common, $52,600

10-8 A company would repurchase its own stock for all of the following reasons *except*:

a. it needs the stock for employee bonuses.
b. it wishes to make an investment in its own stock.
c. it wishes to prevent unwanted takeover attempts.
d. it wishes to improve the company's financial ratios.

10-9 When a company purchases treasury stock, which of the following statements is *true*?

a. Treasury stock is considered to be an asset because cash is paid for the stock.
b. The cost of the treasury stock reduces stockholders' equity.
c. Dividends continue to be paid on the treasury stock because it is still issued.
d. Since treasury stock is held by the original issuer, it is no longer considered to be issued.

10-10 If a company purchases treasury stock for $6,000 and then reissues it for $5,000, the difference of $1,000 is:

a. treated as a gain on the sale.
b. treated as a loss on the sale.
c. an increase in stockholders' equity.
d. a decrease in stockholders' equity.

10-11 **When a company wishes to purchase and retire its own stock, the company must:**

a. decrease the stock account balances by the original issue price.
b. record a gain or loss depending on the difference between original selling price and repurchase cost.
c. get the approval of the state to do so.
d. issue a different class of stock to the former stockholders.

10-12 **Which of the following should be considered when a company decides to declare a cash dividend on common stock?**

a. the retained earnings balance only
b. the amount of authorized shares of common stock
c. the book value of the company's stock
d. the cash available and the retained earnings balance

10-13 **When a company declares a cash dividend, which of the following is *true*?**

a. Stockholders' equity is increased.
b. Liabilities are increased.
c. Assets are decreased.
d. Assets are increased.

10-14 **What is the effect of a stock dividend on stockholders' equity?**

a. Stockholders' equity is decreased.
b. Retained earnings is increased.
c. Additional paid-in capital is decreased.
d. Total stockholders' equity stays the same.

10-15 **As a result of a stock split,**

a. an entry must be made showing the effect on stockholders' equity.
b. the market price of the outstanding stock is increasing because a split is evidence of a profitable company.
c. the par value of the stock is changed in the reverse proportion as the stock split.
d. the stockholders have a higher proportionate ownership of the company.

10-16 **The balance of the $0.50 par value common stock account for Patriot Company was $60,000 before its recent 3-for-1 stock split. The market price of the stock was $30 per share before the stock split. What occurred as a result of the stock split?**

a. The balance in the retained earnings account decreased.
b. The balance in the common stock account was reduced to $20,000.
c. The market price of the stock was not affected.
d. The market price of the stock dropped to approximately $10 per share.

10-17 **When a company declares a 3-for-1 stock split, the number of outstanding shares:**

a. is tripled compared to the number of shares that were outstanding prior to the split.
b. stays the same, but the number of issued shares triples.
c. is tripled, while the number of issued shares is reduced to one-third of the original issued shares.
d. is reduced, and the number of issued shares is tripled.

10-18 Shea Company has 20,000 shares of 5 percent, $40 par value, cumulative preferred stock. In 2008, no dividends were declared on preferred stock. In 2009, Shea had a profitable year and decided to pay dividends to stockholders of both preferred and common stock. If they have $150,000 available for dividends in 2009, how much could it pay to the common stockholders?

a. $70,000
b. $110,000
c. $130,000
d. $150,000

10-19 Comprehensive income is:

a. considered an appropriation of retained earnings when reported in the stockholders' equity section of the balance sheet.
b. the result of all events and transactions that affect income during the accounting period that are reported on the income statement.
c. reporting all items that are not under management's control on the statement of retained earnings.
d. an all-inclusive approach to income that includes transactions that affect stockholders' equity with the exception of those transactions that affect owners.

10-20 FASB's concept of comprehensive income:

a. excludes transactions that involve the payment of dividends.
b. requires that all transactions must be shown on the income statement.
c. has a primary drawback because it allows management to manipulate the income figure to a certain extent.
d. allows items that are not necessarily under management's control, such as natural disasters, to be shown as an adjustment of retained earnings.

10-21 Garner Corporation issued $100,000 in common stock dividends in 2008. Its net income for 2008 was $200,000. What is Garner's dividend payout ratio?

a. 0.5
b. 2
c. 1
d. 5

Cornerstone Exercises

Cornerstone Exercise 10-22 ISSUANCE OF STOCK

OBJECTIVE ➤ 1

Ramsden Corporation shows the following information in the stockholders' equity section of its balance sheet: The par value of common stock is $2.00 and the total balance in the common stock account is $150,000. The 8,000 shares are currently designated as treasury stock.

Required:

What is the number of shares outstanding?

Cornerstone Exercise 10-23 CONTRIBUTED CAPITAL

OBJECTIVE ➤ 1

Stahl Company was incorporated as a new business on January 1, 2007. The company is authorized to issue 20,000 shares of $5 par value common stock and 10,000 shares of 6 percent, $10 par value, cumulative, participating preferred stock. On January 1, 2007, the company issued 8,000 shares of common stock for $15 per share and 2,000 shares of preferred stock for $30 per share. Net income for the year ended December 31, 2007, was $375,000.

Required:

What is the amount of Stahl's total contributed capital at December 31, 2007?

OBJECTIVE ▶ 1 2   Cornerstone Exercise 10-24 **PREPARATION OF STOCKHOLDERS' EQUITY SECTION**

Refer to the information provided in **Cornerstone Exercise 10-23**.

Required:

Prepare the stockholders' equity section of the balance sheet for Stahl Company.

OBJECTIVE ▶ 2   Cornerstone Exercise 10-25 **COMMON STOCK vs. PREFERRED STOCK**

Corporations issue two general types of capital stock—common and preferred.

Required:

Describe the major differences between common and preferred stock.

OBJECTIVE ▶ 3
CORNERSTONE 10-1   Cornerstone Exercise 10-26 **RECORDING THE SALE OF COMMON AND PREFERRED STOCK**

Donahue Corporation is authorized by its charter from the state of Illinois to issue 750 shares of preferred stock with a 7 percent dividend rate and a par value of $50 per share and 22,000 shares of common stock with a par value of $0.01 per share. On January 1, 2009, Donahue Corporation issues 250 shares of preferred stock at $55 per share and 12,000 shares of common stock at $13 per share.

Required:

Record the necessary journal entry for January 1, 2009.

OBJECTIVE ▶ 3
CORNERSTONE 10-1   Cornerstone Exercise 10-27 **RECORDING THE SALE OF COMMON STOCK**

Des Peres Company issues 450 shares of common stock (par value $0.01) for $32 per share on June 30, 2009.

Required:

Provide the necessary journal entry to record this transaction.

OBJECTIVE ▶ 4   Cornerstone Exercise 10-28 **DISTRIBUTION TO STOCKHOLDERS**

Owners invest in corporations through the purchase of stock.

Required:

Describe two ways that corporations distribute assets to stockholders. Discuss their relative advantages and disadvantages.

OBJECTIVE ▶ 4
CORNERSTONE 10-2   Cornerstone Exercise 10-29 **ACCOUNTING FOR TREASURY STOCK**

On February 1, 2009, Wild Bill Corporation repurchases 650 shares of its outstanding common stock for $9 per share. On March 1, 2009, Wild Bill sells 150 shares of treasury stock for $12 per share. On May 10, 2009, Wild Bill sells the remaining 500 shares of its treasury stock for $6 per share.

Required:

Provide the necessary journal entries to record these transactions.

OBJECTIVE ▶ 4
CORNERSTONE 10-2   Cornerstone Exercise 10-30 **ACCOUNTING FOR TREASURY STOCK**

On January 1, 2009, Tommyboy Corporation repurchases 12,000 shares of its outstanding common stock for $26 per share. On May 1, 2009, Tommyboy sells 9,500 shares of treasury stock for $17 per share. On October 1, 2009, Tommyboy sells 1,500 shares of its treasury stock for $44 per share.

Required:

Provide the necessary journal entries to record these transactions.

Cornerstone Exercise 10-31 TREASURY STOCK

A company purchases 2,000 shares of treasury stock for $5 per share.

Required:

How will this transaction affect stockholders' equity?

Cornerstone Exercise 10-32 TREASURY STOCK

Refer to the information in **Cornerstone Exercise 10-31**.

Required:

What is the appropriate journal entry to record the transaction?

Cornerstone Exercise 10-33 CASH DIVIDENDS

King Tut Corporation has issued 7,000 shares of common stock, all of the same class; 3,800 shares are outstanding and 3,200 shares are held as treasury stock. On December 1, 2009, King Tut's board of directors declares a cash dividend of $1.75 per share payable on December 15, 2009, to stockholders of record on December 10, 2009.

Required:

Provide the appropriate journal entries for the date of declaration, date of record, and date of payment.

Cornerstone Exercise 10-34 DECLARATION OF CASH DIVIDEND

A corporation declared a cash dividend of $50,000 on December 31, 2009.

Required:

What is the appropriate journal entry to record this declaration?

Cornerstone Exercise 10-35 STOCK SPLIT

Toy World reported the following information:

> Common stock, $1 par, 200,000 shares authorized, 100,000 shares issued and outstanding.

Required:

What is the typical effect of a 2-for-1 stock split on the information Toy World's reports above? If the market value of the common stock is $20 per share when the stock split is declared, what would you expect the approximate market value per share to be immediate after the split?

Cornerstone Exercise 10-36 STOCK DIVIDEND

Bowman Corporation reported the following information:

> Common stock, $3 par, 10,000 shares authorized, 5,000 shares issued and outstanding.

Required:

What is the appropriate journal entry to record a 10 percent stock dividend, if the market price of the common stock is $30 per share when the dividend is declared?

OBJECTIVE ▶ 4

CORNERSTONE 10-4

Cornerstone Exercise 10-37 PREFERRED AND COMMON STOCK DIVIDENDS

Yossarian Corporation has a single class of common stock and a single class of cumulative preferred stock. The cumulative preferred stock requires the corporation to pay an annual dividend of $3,750 to preferred stockholders. On January 1, 2009, Yossarian's preferred dividends were one year in arrears, which means that Yossarian declared neither preferred nor common dividends in 2008. During the three years (2009–2011), Yossarian's board of directors determined they would be able to pay $5,000, $7,000, and $13,000, respectively.

Required:

Show how these anticipated payments will be split between preferred and common stockholders.

OBJECTIVE ▶ 4

CORNERSTONE 10-4

Cornerstone Exercise 10-38 PREFERRED STOCK DIVIDENDS

Seashell Corporation has 10,000 shares outstanding of 10 percent, $20 par value, cumulative preferred stock. In 2007 and 2008, no dividends were declared on preferred stock. In 2009, Seashell had a profitable year and decided to pay dividends to stockholders of both preferred and common stock.

Required:

If the company has $200,000 available for dividends in 2009, how much could it pay to the common stockholders?

OBJECTIVE ▶ 5

Cornerstone Exercise 10-39 RETAINED EARNINGS

Titanic Corporation's net income for the year ended December 31, 2007, is $235,000. On June 30, 2007, a cash dividend was declared for all common stockholders in the amount of $0.50 per share. Common stock in the amount of 22,000 shares was outstanding at the time. The market price of Titanic's stock at year-end (12/31/07) is $27 per share. Titanic had a $1,250,000 credit balance in retained earnings at December 31, 2006.

Required:

Calculate the ending balance (12/31/07) of retained earnings.

OBJECTIVE ▶ 5

Cornerstone Exercise 10-40 RETAINED EARNINGS

Refer to the information provided in **Cornerstone Exercise 10-39**. Assume that on July 31, 2007, Titanic discovered that 2006 depreciation was overstated by $50,000.

Required:

Provide Titanic's statement of changes in retained earnings for the year ended December 31, 2007, assuming the 2006 tax rate was 30%.

OBJECTIVE ▶ 6

CORNERSTONE 10-6

Cornerstone Exercise 10-41 STOCKHOLDER PAYOUT RATIOS

The following information pertains to Milo Minderbender Corporation:

Net income	$46,000
Dividends per common share	$1.50
Common shares	1,000
Purchases of treasury stock	$3,700
Common share price	$37

Required:

Calculate the dividend yield, dividend payout, and total payout.

Cornerstone Exercise 10-42 STOCKHOLDER PROFITABILITY RATIOS

OBJECTIVE ▸ 6
CORNERSTONE 10-5

The following information pertains to Montague Corporation:

Net income	$55,000
Average common equity	$1,500,000
Preferred dividends	$7,500
Average common shares outstanding	100,000

Required:

Calculate the return on common equity and the earnings per share.

Exercises

Exercise 10-43 ISSUING COMMON STOCK

OBJECTIVE ▸ 3

Thoman Products, Inc., sold 21,250 shares of common stock to stockholders at the time of its incorporation. Thoman received $24.40 per share for the stock.

Required:

1. Assume that the stock has a $20 par value per share. Prepare the journal entry to record the sale and issue of the stock.
2. Assume that the stock has a $15 stated value per share. Prepare the journal entry to record the sale and issue of the stock.
3. Assume that the stock has no par value and no stated value. Prepare the journal entry to record the sale and issue of the stock.

Exercise 10-44 ISSUING AND REPURCHASING STOCK

OBJECTIVE ▸ 3

Redbird, Inc., had the following transactions related to its common and preferred stock:

January 15   Sold 50,000 shares of $0.50 par common stock for $12 per share. Sold 2,000 shares of $10 par preferred stock at $14 per share.

October 1   Repurchased 4,000 shares of the common stock at $20 per share.

Required:

Prepare the journal entries for the above transactions.

Exercise 10-45 PREPARE THE STOCKHOLDERS' EQUITY SECTION

OBJECTIVE ▸ 1

Renee Corporation has the following stockholders' equity information:

	$10 Par Common	$50 Par Preferred
Paid-in capital in excess of par	$ 750,000	$ 30,000
Shares:		
Authorized	1,000,000	100,000
Issued	250,000	15,000
Outstanding	246,500	15,000

Retained earnings is $109,400, and the cost of treasury shares is $42,000.

Required:

Prepare the stockholders' equity portion of Renee's balance sheet.

OBJECTIVE ▸ 1   ### Exercise 10-46 PREPARE THE STOCKHOLDERS' EQUITY SECTION

Wildcat Drilling has the following accounts on its trial balance.

	Debit	Credit
Retained earnings		1,500,000
Cash	125,000	
Paid-in capital in excess of par—common		10,000,000
Paid-in capital in excess of par—preferred		2,000,000
Accounts payable		75,000
Accounts receivable	150,000	
Common stock, $2 par		800,000
Preferred stock, $10 par		600,000
Inventory	500,000	
Treasury stock—common (40,000 shares)	250,000	
Accumulated other comprehensive income		50,000

Required:

Prepare the stockholders' equity portion of Wildcat's balance sheet.

OBJECTIVE ▸ 2   ### Exercise 10-47 ACCOUNTING FOR SHARES

Kress Products' corporate charter authorizes the firm to sell 800,000 shares of $10 par common stock. At the beginning of 2009, Kress had sold 243,000 shares and had reacquired 1,650 of those shares. The reacquired shares were held as treasury stock. During 2009 Kress sold an additional 16,300 shares and purchased 3,100 more treasury shares.

Required:

Determine the number of authorized, issued, and outstanding shares at December 31, 2009.

OBJECTIVE ▸ 4   ### Exercise 10-48 TREASURY STOCK TRANSACTIONS

Dennison Service Corporation had no treasury stock at the beginning of 2009. During January 2009, Dennison purchased 7,600 shares of treasury stock at $21 per share. In April 2009, Dennison sold 4,100 of the treasury shares for $25 per share. In August 2009, Dennison sold the remaining treasury shares for $20 per share.

Required:

Prepare journal entries for the January, April, and August treasury stock transactions.

OBJECTIVE ▸ 4   ### Exercise 10-49 CASH DIVIDENDS ON COMMON STOCK

Berkwild Company is authorized to issue 1,000,000 shares of common stock. At the beginning of 2009, Berkwild had 338,000 issued and outstanding shares. On July 2, 2009, Berkwild purchased 1,310 shares of common stock for its treasury. On March 1 and September 1, Berkwild declared a cash dividend of $1.10 per share. The dividends were paid on April 1 and October 1.

Required:

1. Prepare the entries to record the declaration of the two cash dividends.
2. Prepare the entries to record the payment of the two dividends.
3. Explain why the amounts of the two dividends are different.

Exercise 10-50 STOCK DIVIDENDS

OBJECTIVE ▸ 4

Crystal Corporation has the following information regarding its common stock:

> Its common stock is $20 par, with 300,000 shares authorized, 132,000 shares issued, and 130,600 shares outstanding.

In August 2009, Crystal declared and paid a 15 percent stock dividend when the market price of the common stock was $28 per share.

Required:

Prepare the journal entry to record declaration and payment of this stock dividend.

Exercise 10-51 STOCK DIVIDENDS AND STOCK SPLITS

OBJECTIVE ▸ 4

The balance sheet of Castle Corporation includes the following equity section:

Capital stock:	
Common stock, $2 par, 50,000 shares authorized,	
30,000 shares issued and outstanding	$ 60,000
Paid-in capital in excess of par	71,800
Total capital stock	$131,800
Retained earnings	73,000
Total equity	$204,800

Required:

1. Assume that Castle issued 30,000 shares for cash at the inception of the corporation and that no new shares have been issued since. Determine how much cash was received for the shares issued at inception.
2. Assume that Castle issued 15,000 shares for cash at the inception of the corporation and subsequently declared a 2-for-1 stock split. Determine how much cash was received for the shares issued at inception.
3. Assume that Castle issued 25,000 shares for cash at the inception of the corporation and that the remaining 5,000 shares issued are the result of stock dividends that capitalized retained earnings of $21,600. Determine how much cash was received for the shares issued at inception.

Exercise 10-52 PREFERRED DIVIDENDS

OBJECTIVE ▸ 4

Nathan Products' equity includes 10.8 percent, $100 par preferred stock. There are 100,000 shares authorized and 20,000 shares outstanding. Assume that Nathan Products declares and pays preferred dividends quarterly.

Required:

1. Prepare the journal entry to record declaration of one quarterly dividend.
2. Prepare the journal entry to record payment of the one quarterly dividend.

Exercise 10-53 CUMULATIVE PREFERRED DIVIDENDS

OBJECTIVE ▸ 4

Capital stock of Barr Company includes:

Capital stock:	
Common stock, $10 par, 150,000 shares outstanding	$1,500,000
Preferred stock, 12 percent cumulative, $100 par,	
5,000 shares outstanding	500,000

As of December 31, 2009, three years' dividends are in arrears on the preferred stock. During 2009, Barr plans to pay dividends that total $460,000.

Required:

1. Determine the amount of dividends that will be paid to Barr's common and preferred stockholders in 2010.
2. If Barr paid $280,000 of dividends, determine how much each group of stockholders would receive.

OBJECTIVE ▸ 5   **Exercise 10-54 RETAINED EARNINGS**

Gibson Products had beginning retained earnings of $1,000,000. During the year Gibson paid $50,000 of cash dividends to preferred shareholders and $25,000 of cash dividends to common shareholders. Net income for the year was $385,000.

Required:

1. Reproduce the retained earnings T-account for the year starting with the beginning balance.
2. Determine what Gibson's ending retained earnings is assuming that during the year they discover that net income was overstated by $15,000 in prior years due to an error. The error was corrected and the current year's net income is correct.

OBJECTIVE ▸ 1 5   **Exercise 10-55 RESTRICTIONS ON RETAINED EARNINGS**

At December 31, 2008, Longfellow Clothing had $107,300 of retained earnings, all unrestricted. During 2009, Longfellow earned net income of $39,500 and declared and paid cash dividends on common stock of $12,400. During 2009, Longfellow sold a bond issue with a covenant that required Longfellow to transfer from retained earnings to restricted retained earnings an amount equal to the principal of the bond issue, $40,000. At December 31, 2009, Longfellow has 10,000 shares of $10 par common stock issued and outstanding. Paid-in capital in excess of par on the common stock is $142,500.

Required:

Prepare the stockholders' equity portion of Longfellow's December 31, 2009, balance sheet.

OBJECTIVE ▸ 6   **Exercise 10-56 RATIO ANALYSIS**

Consider the following information from **Priceline.com**.

Stock price	$43.61/share	Avg. common shares	
Common dividends	$0	outstanding	38,650,000
Preferred dividends	$1,927,000	Dividends per common	
2006 preferred stock	$13,470,000	share	$0/share
2006 total stockholders'		Net income	$74,466,000
equity	$1,105,648,000	2005 preferred stock	$13,470,000
Purchases of treasury stock		2005 total stockholders'	
	$135,840,000	equity	$754,028,000

Required:

1. Calculate the stockholder payout ratios.
2. Calculate the stockholder profitability ratios.

OBJECTIVE ▸ 1 2   **Exercise 10-57 STOCKHOLDERS' EQUITY TERMINOLOGY**

A list of terms and a list of definitions or examples are presented below. Make a list of the numbers 1 through 12 and match the letter of the most directly related definition or example with each number.

Terms

1. stock warrant
2. date of record
3. par value
4. stock split
5. treasury stock
6. stock dividend
7. preferred stock
8. outstanding shares
9. authorized shares
10. declaration date
11. comprehensive income
12. retained earnings

Definitions and Examples

a. The state of Louisiana set an upper limit of 1,000,000 on the number of shares that Gump's Catch, Inc., can issue.
b. Shares that never earn dividends
c. On October 15, 2008, General Electric announced its intention to pay a dividend on common stock.
d. Shares issued minus treasury shares
e. Common stock divided by the number of shares issued
f. A stock issue that requires no journal entry
g. Shares that may earn guaranteed dividends
h. Capitalizes retained earnings.
i. A right to purchase stock at a specified future time and specified price
j. Emerson Electric will pay a dividend to all persons holding shares of its common stock on December 15, 2008, even if they just bought the shares and sell them a few days later.
k. Any changes to stockholders' equity from transactions with nonowners
l. The accumulated earnings over the entire life of the corporation that have not been paid out in dividends

Problem Set A

Problem 10-58A PRESENTATION OF STOCKHOLDERS' EQUITY

Yeager Corporation was organized in January 2009. During 2009, Yeager engaged in the following stockholders' equity activities:

a. Secured approval for a corporate charter that authorizes Yeager to sell 500,000, $10 par common shares and 40,000, $100 par preferred shares
b. Sold 60,000 of the common shares for $16 per share
c. Sold 2,000 of the preferred shares for $102 per share
d. Purchased 550 of the common shares for the treasury at a cost of $18 each
e. Earned net income of $31,300
f. Paid dividends of $6,000

Required:

Prepare the stockholders' equity portion of Yeager's balance sheet.

Problem 10-59A ISSUING COMMON AND PREFERRED STOCK

OBJECTIVE ▶ 3

Klaus Herrmann, a biochemistry professor, organized Bioproducts, Inc., early this year. The firm will manufacture antibiotics using gene splicing technology. Bioproducts' charter authorizes the firm to issue 5,000 shares of 12 percent, $50 par preferred stock and 100,000 shares of $10 par common stock. During the year, the firm engaged in the following transactions:

a. Issued 25,000 common shares to Klaus Herrmann in exchange for $275,000 cash.
b. Sold 10,000 common shares to a potential customer for $11 per share.
c. Issued 3,000 shares of preferred stock to a venture capital firm for $52 per share.
d. Gave 75 shares of common stock to Margaret Robb, a local attorney, in exchange for Margaret's work in arranging for the firm's incorporation. Margaret usually charges $900 for an incorporation.

Required:

Prepare a journal entry for each of these transactions.

Problem 10-60A TREASURY STOCK TRANSACTIONS

OBJECTIVE ▶ 4

Hansen, Inc., engaged in the following transactions during the current year:

a. Purchased 4,000 shares of its own $20 par common stock for $26 per share on January 14.
b. Sold 2,400 treasury shares to employees for $20 per share on January 31.
c. Purchased 2,000 common shares for the treasury at a cost of $27 each on July 24.
d. Sold the remaining 1,600 shares from the January 14 purchase and 1,500 of the shares from the July 24 purchase to employees for $22 per share on August 1.

Required:

1. Prepare journal entries for each of these transactions.
2. Determine what the effect on total stockholders' equity is for each of the four transactions.

OBJECTIVE ➤ 1 3

Problem 10-61A STATEMENT OF STOCKHOLDERS' EQUITY

At the end of 2009, Jeffco, Inc., had the following equity accounts and balances:

Common stock, $20 par	$410,000
Paid-in capital in excess of par, common stock	381,400
Retained earnings	102,470

During 2010, Jeffco engaged in the following transactions involving its equity accounts:

a. Sold 2,900 shares of common stock for $41 per share.
b. Sold 1,500 shares of 12 percent, $100 par preferred stock at $102 per share.
c. Declared and paid cash dividends of $11,500.
d. Purchased 1,000 shares of treasury stock (common) for $45 per share.
e. Sold 600 of the treasury shares for $43 per share.

Required:

1. Provide the journal entries for *a* through *e*.
2. Assume that 2010 net income was $51,300. Prepare a statement of stockholders' equity at December 31, 2010.

OBJECTIVE ➤ 4

Problem 10-62A COMMON DIVIDENDS

Papke Payroll Service began 2009 with 1,000,000 authorized and 225,000 issued and outstanding $10 par common shares. During 2009, Papke entered into the following transactions:

a. Declared a $0.40 per share cash dividend on March 10.
b. Paid the $0.40 per share dividend on April 10.
c. Purchased 8,000 common shares for the treasury at a cost of $24 each on May 2.
d. Sold 3,000 unissued common shares for $26 per share on June 9.
e. Declared a $0.55 per share cash dividend on August 10.
f. Paid the $0.55 per share dividend on September 10.
g. Declared and paid a 10 percent stock dividend on October 15 when the market price of the common stock was $28 per share.
h. Declared a $0.60 per share cash dividend on November 10.
i. Paid the $0.60 per share dividend on December 10.

Required:

1. Prepare journal entries for each of these transactions.
2. Determine the total amount of dividends (cash and stock) for the year.
3. Determine the effect on total assets and total stockholders' equity of these dividend transactions.

OBJECTIVE ➤ 4

Problem 10-63A STOCK DIVIDENDS AND STOCK SPLITS

Lance Products' balance sheet includes total assets of $320,000 and the following equity account balances at December 31, 2009:

Capital stock:
Common stock, $5 par, 20,000 shares issued and
  outstanding $100,000
Paid-in capital in excess of par   44,000
    Total capital stock $144,000
Retained earnings   53,600
    Total stockholders' equity $197,600

Lance's common stock is selling for $24 per share on December 31, 2009.

Required:

1. How much would Lance Products have reported for total assets and retained earnings on December 31, 2009, if the firm had declared and paid a $10,000 cash dividend on December 31, 2009? Provide the journal entry for this cash dividend.
2. How much would Lance have reported for total assets and retained earnings on December 31, 2009, if the firm had issued a 10 percent stock dividend on December 31, 2009? Provide the journal entry for this stock dividend.
3. How much would Lance have reported for total assets and retained earnings on December 31, 2009, if the firm had effected a 2-for-1 stock split on December 31, 2009? Is a journal entry needed to record the stock split? Why or why not?

Problem 10-64A **PREFERRED DIVIDENDS**

OBJECTIVE  4

Magic Conglomerates had the following preferred stock outstanding at the end of a recent year:

$25 par, 10 percent	6,000 shares
$40 par, 8 percent, cumulative	11,000 shares
$50 par, 12 percent, cumulative, convertible	2,000 shares
$80 par, 11 percent, nonparticipating	15,000 shares

Required:

1. Determine the amount of annual dividends on each issue of preferred stock and the total annual dividend on all four issues.
2. Calculate what the amount of dividends in arrears would be if the dividends were omitted for one year.

Problem 10-65A **RATIO ANALYSIS**

OBJECTIVE 6

Consider the following information taken from the stockholders' equity section:

	(dollar amount in thousands)	
	2010	**2009**
Preferred stock	$ 1,000	$ 1,000
Common stock, 334,328,193 and 330,961,869 shares issued in 2010 and 2009, respectively	3,343	3,310
Paid-in capital in excess of par	766,382	596,239
Retained earnings	5,460,629	4,630,390
Accumulated other comprehensive (loss) income	(206,662)	58,653
Treasury stock (76,275,837 and 56,960,213 shares in 2010 and 2009, respectively) at cost	(3,267,955)	(2,205,987)
Total stockholders' equity	$ 2,756,737	$ 3,083,605

Additional Information (all numbers in thousands
other than per share information):

Weighted average common shares outstanding	264,453
Price per share	$ 70.47
Net income	1,123,153
Preferred dividends	80,000
Common dividends	212,914
Common dividends per share	0.81
Stock repurchases	1,061,968

Required:

1. Calculate the following:

Stockholder Payout	**Stockholder Profitability**
Dividend yield	Return on common equity
Dividend payout	EPS
Total payout	
Stock repurchase payout	

2. Assume last year's ratios were:

Stockholder Payout	**Stockholder Profitability**
Dividend yield: 1.05%	Return on common equity: 34.26%
Dividend payout: 15.80%	EPS: $3.51
Total payout: 75.00%	
Stock repurchase payout: 59.20%	

and the current year industry averages are:

Stockholder Payout	**Stockholder Profitability**
Dividend yield: 0.76%%	Return on common equity: 23.81%
Dividend payout: 42.35%	EPS: $1.23
Total payout: 88.37%%	
Stock repurchase payout: 46.02%	

How do you interpret the company's payout and profitability performance?

Problem Set B

OBJECTIVE ▶ 1 **Problem 10-58B PRESENTATION OF STOCKHOLDERS' EQUITY**

Steven's Restorations was organized in January 2008. During 2008, Steven's engaged in the following stockholders' equity activities:

a. Secured approval for a corporate charter that authorizes Steven's to sell 1,000,000 $5 par common shares and 50,000, $100 par preferred shares.
b. Sold 80,000 of the common shares for $7 per share.
c. Sold 15,000 of the preferred shares for $104 per share.
d. Purchased 700 of the common shares for the treasury at a cost of $10 each.
e. Earned net income of $49,000.
f. Paid dividends of $9,000.

Required:

Prepare the stockholders' equity portion of Steven's balance sheet.

OBJECTIVE ▶ 3 **Problem 10-59B ISSUING COMMON AND PREFERRED STOCK**

Tom Smith, a biochemistry professor, organized Biointernational, Inc., earlier this year. The firm will manufacture antibiotics using gene splicing technology. Biointernational's charter authorizes the firm to issue 50,000 shares of 10 percent, $60 par preferred stock and 75,000 shares of $12 par common stock. During the year, the firm engaged in the following transactions:

a. Issued 15,000 common shares to Tom Smith in exchange for $250,000 cash.
b. Sold 20,000 common shares to a potential customer for $13 per share.
c. Issued 2,000 shares of preferred stock to a venture capital firm for $65 per share.
d. Gave 75 shares of common stock to Susie Thomas, a local attorney, in exchange for Susie's work in arranging for the firm's incorporation. Susie usually charges $1,000 for an incorporation.

Required:

Prepare a journal entry for each of these transactions.

Problem 10-60B TREASURY STOCK TRANSACTIONS

Bentonite Adhesives, Inc., engaged in the following transactions during the current year:

a. Purchased 5,000 shares of its own $15 par common stock for $17 per share on January 14.
b. Sold 2,100 of the treasury shares to employees for $15 per share on January 31.
c. Purchased 1,500 common shares for the treasury at a cost of $25 each on July 24.
d. Sold the remaining 2,900 shares from the January 14 purchase and 1,000 of the shares from the July 24 purchase to employees for $18 per share on August 1.

Required:

1. Prepare journal entries for each of these transactions.
2. Determine the effect on total stockholders' equity for each of the four transactions.

Problem 10-61B STATEMENT OF STOCKHOLDERS' EQUITY

At the end of 2009, Stanley Utilities, Inc., had the following equity accounts and balances:

Common stock, $10 par	$200,000
Paid-in capital in excess of par, common stock	168,100
Retained earnings	53,500

During 2010, Stanley Utilities engaged in the following transactions involving its equity accounts:

a. Sold 2,900 shares of common stock for $20 per share.
b. Sold 1,500 shares of 12 percent, $50 par preferred stock at $75 per share.
c. Declared and paid cash dividends of $4,500.
d. Purchased 1,000 shares of treasury stock (common) for $22 per share.
e. Sold 600 of the treasury shares for $24 per share.

Required:

1. Provide the journal entries for a through e.
2. Assume that 2010 net income was $36,850. Prepare a statement of stockholders' equity at December 31, 2010.

Problem 10-62B COMMON DIVIDENDS

Thompson Payroll Service began in 2008 with 2,000,000 authorized and 450,000 issued and outstanding $7 par common shares. During 2008, Thompson entered into the following transactions:

a. Declared a $0.25 per share cash dividend on March 24.
b. Paid the $0.25 per share dividend on April 6.
c. Purchased 13,000 common shares for the treasury at a cost of $17 each on May 9.

d. Sold 4,600 unissued common shares for $29 per share on June 19.
e. Declared a $0.30 per share cash dividend on August 1.
f. Paid the $0.30 per share dividend on September 14.
g. Declared and paid a 20 percent stock dividend on October 25 when the market price of the common stock was $26 per share.
h. Declared a $0.50 per share cash dividend on November 20.
i. Paid the $0.50 per share dividend on December 20.

Required:

1. Prepare journal entries for each of these transactions.
2. What is the total amount of dividends (cash and stock) for the year?
3. Determine the effect on total assets and total stockholders' equity of these dividend transactions.

OBJECTIVE ▶ 4

Problem 10-63B STOCK DIVIDENDS AND STOCK SPLITS

Murphy's Products balance sheet includes total assets of $620,000 and the following equity account balances at December 31, 2008:

Capital stock:	
Common stock, $8 par, 10,000 shares issued and outstanding	$ 80,000
Paid-in capital in excess of par	44,000
Total capital stock	$124,000
Retained earnings	53,600
Total stockholders' equity	$177,600

Murphy's common stock is selling for $24 per share on December 31, 2008.

Required:

1. Determine how much Murphy's Products would have reported for total assets and retained earnings on December 31, 2008, if the firm had declared and paid a $10,000 cash dividend on December 31, 2008. Provide the journal entry for this cash dividend.
2. Determine how much Murphy would have reported for total assets and retained earnings on December 31, 2008, if the firm had issued a 10 percent stock dividend on December 31, 2008. Provide the journal entry for this stock dividend.
3. How much would Murphy have reported for total assets and retained earnings on December 31, 2008, if the firm had effected a 2-for-1 stock split on December 31, 2008? Is a journal entry needed to record the stock split? Why or why not?

OBJECTIVE ▶ 4

Problem 10-64B PREFERRED DIVIDENDS

Steel Corporation had the following preferred stock outstanding at the end of a recent year:

$20 par, 12 percent	10,000 shares
$40 par, 6 percent, cumulative	13,000 shares
$50 par, 10 percent, cumulative, convertible	12,000 shares
$100 par, 11 percent, nonparticipating	5,000 shares

Required:

1. Determine the amount of annual dividends on each issue of preferred stock and the total annual dividend on all four issues.
2. Calculate what the amount of dividends in arrears would be if the dividends were omitted for one year.

OBJECTIVE ▶ 6

Problem 10-65B RATIO ANALYSIS

Consider the following information taken from the stockholders' equity section:

	(dollar amount in thousands)	
	2009	2008
Preferred stock	$ 1,000	$ 2,000
Common stock, 230,000,000 and 176,000,000 shares issued in 2009 and 2008, respectively	2,300	1,760
Paid-in capital in excess of par	567,000	432,000
Retained earnings	4,604,600	3,700,000
Accumulated other comprehensive (loss) income	(454,600)	147,000
Treasury stock (37,000,000 and 19,000,000 shares in 2009 and 2008, respectively) at cost	(1,750,000)	(975,000)
Total stockholders' equity	$ 2,970,300	$3,307,760

Additional Information (all numbers in thousands other than per share information):

Weighted average common shares outstanding	204,000
Price per share	$ 65.31
Net income	1,224,600
Preferred dividends	65,000
Common dividends	255,000
Common dividends per share	1.25
Stock repurchases	775,000

Required:

1. Calculate the following:

Stockholder Payout	**Stockholder Profitability**
Dividend yield	Return on common equity
Dividend payout	EPS
Total payout	
Stock repurchase payout	

2. Assume last year's ratios were:

Stockholder Payout	**Stockholder Profitability**
Dividend yield: 2.31%	Return on common equity: 37.41%
Dividend payout: 23.65%	EPS: $6.12
Total payout: 88.59%	
Stock repurchase payout: 64.94%	

and the current year industry averages are:

Stockholder Payout	**Stockholder Profitability**
Dividend yield: 2.50%	Return on common equity: 44.44%
Dividend payout: 25.83%	EPS: $6.48
Total payout: 95.10%	
Stock repurchase payout: 69.27%	

How do you interpret the company's payout and profitability performance?

Cases

Case 10-66 ETHICS AND EQUITY

Roger and Gordon are middle managers at a large, publicly traded corporation. Roger tells Gordon that the company is about to sign an exclusive product distribution agreement with a small, publicly traded manufacturer. This contract will quadruple the manufacturer's revenue.

Roger mentions to Gordon that the manufacturer's stock price will likely go "through the roof." Gordon says, "Maybe we should buy some stock or, better yet, some call options."

Required:

1. Are Roger and Gordon being smart, being unethical but not breaking the law, or breaking the law?
2. How does the SEC monitor such activity?

Case 10-67 CAPITAL STOCK TRANSACTIONS AND ETHICS

Charlene Jones is the office manager for MK Corporation. MK constructs, owns, and manages apartment complexes. Charlene has been involved in negotiations between MK and prospective lenders as MK attempts to raise $425 million that it plans to use to build apartments in a growing area of Kansas City. Based on her experience with past negotiations Charlene knows that lenders are concerned about MK's debt-to-equity ratio. When the negotiations began, MK had debt of $80 million and equity of $50 million. Charlene believes that MK's debt-to-equity ratio of 1.6 is probably the minimum that lenders will accept.

Charlene is also aware that MK Corporation issued $10 million of common stock to a long-time friend of the corporation's president in exchange for some land just before the negotiations with lenders began. The president's friend constructs and sells single family homes. The land is in an area zoned only for single family housing and would be an attractive site for single family homes. Thus, the land is worth at least $10 million. However, MK does not intend to build any single family homes.

Required:

1. What would have been MK's debt-to-equity ratio if the $10 million of stock had not been issued for the land?
2. If Charlene believes that the $10 million stock issue was undertaken only to improve MK's debt-to-equity ratio and that it will be reversed whenever the president's friend wants the land back or when MK's debt-to-equity position improves, what should she do?

Case 10-68 COMMON AND PREFERRED STOCK

Expansion Company now has $2,500,000 of equity (100,000 common shares). Current income is $400,000 and Expansion Company needs $500,000 of additional capital. The firm's bankers insist that this capital be acquired by selling either common or preferred stock. If Expansion sells common stock, the ownership share of the current stockholders will be diluted by 16.7 percent (20,000 more shares will be sold). If preferred stock is sold, the dividend rate will be 15 percent of the $500,000. Furthermore, the preferred stock will have to be cumulative, participating, and convertible into 20,000 shares of common stock.

Required:

Indicate whether Expansion should sell additional common or preferred stock, and explain the reasons for your choice.

Case 10-69 LEVERAGE

Enrietto Aquatic Products' offer to acquire Fiberglass Products for $2,000,000 cash has been accepted. Enrietto has $1,000,000 of liquid assets that can be converted into cash and plans to either sell common stock or issue bonds to raise the remaining $1,000,000. Before this acquisition, Enrietto's condensed balance sheet and condensed income statement were as follows:

ENRIETTO AQUATIC PRODUCTS
Preacquisition Condensed Balance Sheet

Assets		Liabilities and Equity	
Assets	$20,000,000	Liabilities	$ 8,000,000
		Common stock, $10 par	6,000,000
		Retained earnings	6,000,000
		Total liabilities & stock-holders' equity	$20,000,000

ENRIETTO AQUATIC PRODUCTS
Preacquisition Condensed Income Statement

Income from operations	$6,000,000
Less: Interest expense	1,000,000
Income before taxes	$5,000,000
Less: Income taxes expense (0.34)	1,700,000
Net income	$3,300,000

Enrietto's policy is to pay 60 percent of net income to stockholders as dividends. Enrietto expects to be able to raise the $1,000,000 it needs for the acquisition by selling 50,000 shares of common stock at $20 each or by issuing $1,000,000 of 20-year, 12 percent bonds. Enrietto expects income from operations to grow by $700,000 after Fiberglass Products has been acquired. (Interest expense will increase if debt is used to finance the acquisition.)

Required:

1. Determine the return on equity (net income/total equity) before the acquisition and for both financing alternatives.
2. If Enrietto sells additional stock, what will be the cash outflow for dividends?
3. If Enrietto sells bonds, what will be the net cash outflows for new interest and for all dividends? (Remember that interest is tax-deductible.)
4. Assume that Enrietto sells stock and that none of the preacquisition stockholders buy any of the 50,000 new shares. What total amount of dividends will the preacquisition stockholders receive after the acquisition? How does this amount compare with the dividends they receive before the acquisition?
5. Which alternative is better for Enrietto's preacquisition stockholders?

Case 10-70 RESEARCHING AND ANALYSIS USING THE ANNUAL REPORT

Obtain **Priceline.com**'s 2006 10-K through the "Investor Relations" portion of their website (do a web search for investor relations), or go to http://www.sec.gov and click "Search for company filings" under "Filings & Forms (EDGAR)."

Required:

1. How many shares of common stock are authorized, issued, and outstanding?
2. Why didn't Priceline.com pay dividends to common stockholders in any of the three years shown?
3. What is the common stockholders' equity for 2006?
4. How many shares of treasury stock were held at the end of 2006?
5. Calculate the dividend and stock repurchase payouts.
6. Taking the weighted average number of basic common shares outstanding from the EPS information at the bottom of the income statement, calculate the stockholder profitability ratios.

Case 10-71 COMPARATIVE ANALYSIS: ABERCROMBIE & FITCH vs. AEROPOSTALE

Refer to the financial statements of **Abercrombie & Fitch** and **Aeropostale** that are supplied with this text.

Common Stock Price	January 28, 2006	February 3, 2007
Abercrombie & Fitch	$64.06	$80.77
Aeropostale	20.32	24.05

Required:

1. Both Abercrombie & Fitch (Note 13) and Aeropostale (Note 15) have notes that discuss contingencies. What contingencies do they disclose? Do you think any of these contingencies are included in the income statement or on the balance sheet? Why or why not?
2. Calculate Abercrombie & Fitch's and Aeropostale's dividend yield and dividend payout for the years ended February 3, 2007 and January 28, 2006.
3. Calculate Abercrombie & Fitch's and Aeropostale's total payout and stock repurchase payout for the years ended February 3, 2007 and January 28, 2006.
4. Compare Abercrombie & Fitch's and Aeropostale's stockholder payouts based on the values and trends identified in these stockholder payout ratios.
5. Calculate Abercrombie & Fitch's and Aeropostale's return on common equity and earnings per share for the years ended February 3, 2007 and January 28, 2006.
6. Compare the values and trends of these stockholder profitability ratios for Abercrombie & Fitch and Aeropostale.

11

The Statement of Cash Flows

After studying this chapter, you should be able to:

1. Explain the purpose of a statement of cash flows.

2. Identify and classify business activities that produce cash inflows and outflows.

3. Understand the relationship between changes in cash and the changes in the balance sheet accounts.

4. Prepare the cash flows from operating activities section of a statement of cash flows using the indirect method.

5. Prepare the cash flows from investing activities section of a statement of cash flows.

6. Prepare the cash flows from financing activities section of a statement of cash flows.

7. Analyze information contained in the statement of cash flows.

8. (Appendix 11A) Prepare the cash flows from operating activities section of a statement of cash flows using the direct method.

9. (Appendix 11B) Use a spreadsheet to prepare the statement of cash flows.

Experience Financial Accounting
with Deere & Company

Founded in 1837, **Deere & Company** (collectively known as John Deere), is an American success story. From humble beginnings as a blacksmith shop in Illinois, John Deere has grown into one of the world's largest corporations, currently standing at 98 in the Fortune 500 ranking of the world's largest corporations. Not only is John Deere the world's leading manufacturer of farm and forestry equipment, John Deere also sells a broad line of lawn tractors and other outdoor consumer products and is one of the world's largest equipment finance companies. Despite its growth, John Deere is still guided by four core values: integrity, quality, commitment, and innovation.

In addition to the income statement, the balance sheet, and the statement of retained earnings, companies are also required to provide a statement of cash flows. The statement of cash flows measures a company's inflows (sources) and outflows (uses) of cash during a period of time. While various insights can be gained from the statement of cash flows, many financial statement users look to cash flow as a means to assess the quality of

earnings—that is, the degree to which a company's reported earnings reflects what the company actually earned. Because the recognition of revenues and expenses can occur at different times than the related cash inflow or outflow, a company's net income does not always equal the amount of cash that it received and spent. When the cash generated from operations is greater than net income, many analysts will consider the earnings to be of high quality.

With operating cash flow more than $900 million greater than net income, John Deere is considered to have high quality earnings. From this perspective, it is easy to see why some think the color of money is John Deere green!

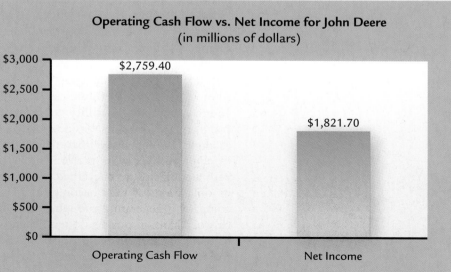

Operating Cash Flow vs. Net Income for John Deere
(in millions of dollars)

Operating Cash Flow: $2,759.40
Net Income: $1,821.70

In addition to being interested in the information in the accrual-basis financial statements, most financial statement users also want to know about the amount, timing, and uncertainties of cash flows. Investors want to know whether a company can pay cash dividends and whether it can continue to expand its productive capacity. Lenders are interested in the company's ability to pay interest and borrowed principal. Employees want to assess the company's ability to pay larger salaries and fringe benefits. Suppliers want to know if the company can pay for goods purchased on credit. The statement of cash flows helps meet these information needs.

The statement of cash flows is one of the primary financial statements. Because the other financial statements—the income statement, the balance sheet, and the statement of retained earnings—provide only limited information about a company's cash flows, the statement of cash flows can be viewed as a complement to these other financial statements. That is, while the income statement provides information about the company's performance on an accrual basis, it does not tell how much cash was generated or used as a result of the company's operations. Similarly, the balance sheet provides information on the changes in net assets, but it doesn't provide information on how much cash was used or received in relation to these changes. The statement of cash flows fills this void by explaining the sources from which a company has acquired cash (inflows of cash) and the uses to which the business has applied cash (outflows of cash).

In this chapter, we will explain how a statement of cash flows is prepared from the information contained in the balance sheet and the income statement. We will explore the measurement, presentation, and analysis of cash flow information and address the following questions:

- How is the information in the statement of cash flows used by investors, creditors, and others?
- What are the principal sources and uses of cash?
- How is the statement of cash flows prepared and reported to external users?
- How is the statement of cash flows used in financial analysis?

Role of the Statement of Cash Flows

OBJECTIVE ▶ 1
Explain the purpose of a statement of cash flows.

The purpose of the **statement of cash flows** is to provide relevant information about a company's cash receipts (inflows of cash) and cash payments (outflows of cash) during an accounting period. The information in a statement of cash flows helps investors, creditors, and others:

1. **Assess a company's ability to produce future net cash inflows**. You may have heard the age-old business expression "cash is king." Cash is certainly the lifeblood of a company and is critical to a company's success. One goal of financial reporting is to provide information that is helpful in predicting the amounts, timing, and uncertainty of a company's future cash flows. While accrual-basis net income is generally viewed to be the best single predictor of future cash flows, information about cash receipts and cash payments can, along with net income, allow users to predict future cash flows better than net income alone.

2. **Judge a company's ability to meet its obligations and pay dividends**. As a company performs its business activities, it will incur various obligations. For example, a company will have to pay its suppliers for merchandise purchased and its employees for work performed. Suppliers, employees, and others who interact with a company are concerned about whether a company has enough cash to pay its obligations as they become due. Similarly, investors often wish to know if a company is generating enough cash to be able to pay dividends. In addition, success or failure in business often depends on whether a company has enough cash to meet unexpected obligations and take advantage of unexpected opportunities. Information about cash receipts and cash payments helps financial statement users make these important judgments.

3. **Estimate the company's needs for external financing**. As companies operate, the various expenditures can be financed through either internally generated funds or by external financing (debt or equity). Knowing the amount of cash that a company generates internally helps financial statement users assess whether a company will have to borrow additional funds from creditors or seek additional cash from investors.

4. **Understand the reasons for the differences between net income and related cash receipts and cash payments**. As you have already noticed, the amount of a company's net income and the amount of cash generated from operations are often different amounts due to the application of accrual accounting concepts. Because of the judgments and estimates involved in accrual accounting, many financial statement users question the usefulness of reported income. However, when provided with cash flow information, these users can gain insights into the quality and reliability of the reported income amounts.

5. **Evaluate the balance sheet effects of both cash and noncash investing and financing transactions**. Not all changes in cash are directly related to a company's operations (e.g., manufacturing a product or selling a good or service). Instead a company may make investments in productive assets as it expands its operations or upgrades its facilities. In addition, a company may seek sources of cash by issuing debt or equity. These activities can be just as crucial to a company's long-term success as its current operations.

In summary, information about a company's cash receipts and cash payments, along with information contained in the balance sheet and the income statement, is critical to understanding and analyzing a company's operations.

Cash Flow Classifications

OBJECTIVE ▸2
Identify and classify business activities that produce cash inflows and outflows.

Because a statement of cash flows describes the cash payments and cash receipts for a period of time, it is important to have a clear understanding of what is included in the term *cash*. For purposes of the statement of cash flows, cash includes both funds on hand (coins and currency) and cash equivalents. **Cash equivalents** are short-term, highly liquid investments that are readily convertible to cash and have original maturities of three months or less. Examples of cash equivalents include money market funds and investments in U.S. government securities (e.g., treasury bills) or commercial paper (a short-term note payable issued by a corporation). Because of their high liquidity or nearness to cash, cash equivalents are treated as cash for the purpose of the statement of cash flows.

During an accounting period, a company engages in many activities that can be categorized as operating activities, investing activities, or financing activities. These three categories represent the fundamental business activities as discussed in Chapter 1. Each of these activities can contribute to (a cash inflow) or reduce (a cash outflow) a company's cash balance. Therefore, the statement of cash flows reconciles the beginning and ending balances of cash by describing the effects of business activities on a company's cash balance. This relationship is shown in Exhibit 11-1.

Cash Flows from Operating Activities

Cash flows from operating activities (or operating cash flows) encompass the cash inflows and outflows that relate to acquiring (purchasing or manufacturing), selling, and delivering goods or services. Cash inflows from operating activities include cash sales and collection of accounts receivable that arise from credit sales. They also include cash dividends or interest received on investments in equity and debt securities. Cash outflows from operating activities include payments for goods and services purchased from suppliers, payments for wages and salaries, payments for property and income taxes, and payments of interest on debt.

Operating cash flows correspond to the *types* of items that determine net income (revenues and expenses). However, the *amounts* are different because the income

Exhibit 11-1

How the Statement of Cash Flows Links the Two Balance Sheets

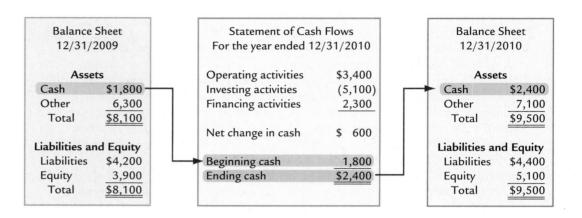

statement is accrual-based while the statement of cash flows is cash-based. Therefore, to isolate the current period operating cash flow, companies must adjust the current period income statement items for any related noncash items, which can be determined by examining the changes in the related current assets and current liabilities. (The procedure to compute cash flows from operating activities is discussed in a later section of this chapter.) In general, operating cash flows relate to income statement items adjusted by any increases or decreases in current assets or liabilities.

Cash Flows from Investing Activities

Cash flows from investing activities (or investing cash flows) are the cash inflows and outflows that relate to:

- acquiring and disposing of operating assets
- acquiring and selling investments (current and long-term)
- lending money and collecting loans

Cash inflows from investing activities include cash received from the sale of property, plant, and equipment, the collection of the principal amount of loans from borrowers, the issuance of loans made by the company, and the sale of investments in other companies. (Remember that the cash inflows from interest or dividends go into the determination of income and, therefore, are treated as operating cash flows.) Cash outflows from investing activities include payments made to acquire property, plant, and equipment, to purchase the debt or equity securities of another company as an investment, and to make loans to borrowers. In general, investing cash flows relate to increases or decreases of long-term assets and investments.

Cash Flows from Financing Activities

Cash flows from financing activities (or financing cash flows) include obtaining resources from creditors and owners. Cash inflows from financing activities include cash received from the issuance of stock and the issuance of debt (bonds or notes payable). Cash outflows from financing activities include cash payments to repay the principal amount borrowed, to repurchase a company's own stock, and to pay dividends. (Remember that cash outflows related to the payment of interest go into the determination of income and, therefore, are treated as operating cash flows.) In general, financing cash flows involve cash receipts and payments that affect long-term liabilities and stockholders' equity.

Noncash Investing and Financing Activities

Occasionally, investing and financing activities take place without affecting cash. For example, a company may choose to acquire an operating asset (e.g., building) by issuing long-term debt. Alternatively, a company may acquire one asset by exchanging it for another. These types of activities are referred to as **noncash investing and financing activities**. Because these activities do not involve cash, they are not reported on the statement of cash flows. However, these transactions still provide useful information about a company's overall investing and financing activities. Any significant noncash investing and financing activities are required to be reported in a supplementary schedule that is shown either at the bottom of the statement of cash flows or in the notes to the financial statements. This requirement to disclose any significant noncash investing and financing activities is consistent with the full-disclosure principle—any information that would make a difference to financial statement users should be made known.

Cornerstone 11-1 shows how business activities can be classified as either operating, investing, financing, or noncash activities.

CONCEPT Q&A

If we already have the balance sheet and income statement, why is a statement of cash flows so important?

Possible Answer:

The statement of cash flows provides information about a company's cash inflows and cash outflows separated into three categories (operating, investing, and financing activities) that correspond to a company's business activities. Knowing the sources of cash—especially from operating activities—provides users with a good idea of a company's financial strength and its long-term viability. The decision to invest in a company is much safer if a potential investor—be it a bank or stockholder—knows how much cash is being produced and where it is coming from.

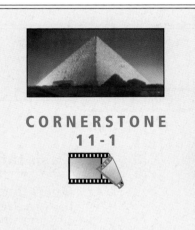

HOW TO Classify Business Activities

CORNERSTONE 11-1

Concept:
Cash flows from operating activities correspond to the cash effects of items that determine net income. Cash flows from investing activities relate to increases or decreases in long-term assets and investments. Cash flows from financing activities involve cash receipts and payments that affect long-term liabilities and stockholders' equity.

Information:
Moore Inc. engaged in the following activities during the current year:

a. Payment of wages to employees
b. Issuance of common stock
c. Purchase of property, plant, and equipment
d. Collection of cash from customers
e. Issuance of bonds
f. Retirement of debt by issuing stock
g. Purchase of inventory
h. Sale of property, plant, and equipment
i. Payment of dividends
j. Payment of interest

Required:
Classify each of the above activities as an operating, investing, or financing activity and indicate whether the activity involved a cash receipt or cash payment. If the transaction does not involve cash, classify it as a noncash investing and financing activity.

Solution:
a. Wages are an expense on the income statement. Therefore, the payment of wages is classified as a cash payment from an operating activity.
b. The issuance of common stock results in an increase of stockholders' equity and cash. Therefore, it is classified as a cash receipt from a financing activity.

**CORNERSTONE
11-1**
(continued)

c. The purchase of property, plant, and equipment results in an increase to a long-term asset and a decrease of cash. Therefore, it is classified as a cash payment from an investing activity.

d. The collection of cash from customers relates to sales revenue on the income statement. Therefore, it is classified as a cash receipt from an operating activity.

e. Issuing bonds results in an increase to long-term liabilities and cash. Therefore, it is classified as a cash receipt from a financing activity.

f. The retirement of debt by issuing stock is a financing activity that does not involve cash. It is classified as a noncash investing and financing activity.

g. Because inventory is a component of cost of goods sold on the income statement, the purchase of inventory is classified as a cash payment from an operating activity.

h. The sale of property, plant, and equipment results in a decrease in a long-term asset and an increase in cash. Therefore, it is classified as a cash receipt from an investing activity.

i. The payment of dividends is a reduction in retained earnings, which is a part of stockholders' equity. Therefore, the payment of dividends is classified as a cash outflow from a financing activity.

j. Interest is an expense on the income statement. Therefore, the payment of interest is classified as a cash outflow from an operating activity.

Exhibit 11-2 summarizes the classification of business activities as either operating, investing, or financing activities.

Exhibit 11-2

Classification of Cash Flows

Cash Inflows

Operating Activities
Cash received from:
- Customers for cash sales
- Collections of accounts receivable
- Dividends
- Interest

Investing Activities
Cash received from:
- The sale of property, plant, and equipment
- The collection of principal on a loan
- The sale or maturity of investments

Financing Activities
Cash received from:
- Issuing stock to owners
- Issuing notes or bonds (debt) to creditors
- Selling treasury stock

Cash Outflows

Operating Activities
Cash paid to:
- Suppliers of goods and services
- Employees for salaries and wages
- Governments for taxes
- Lenders for interest

Investing Activities
Cash paid to:
- Purchase property, plant, and equipment
- Make loans to other companies
- Purchase investments

Financing Activities
Cash paid to:
- Repayment of principal of long-term debt
- Dividends to owners
- Purchase of treasury stock

DECISION-MAKING & ANALYSIS

Cash Flows and Income

Five years ago, Jester Corporation was a very successful regional clothing retailer. Begun in a single location, Jester had added nineteen additional stores over a period of 40 years. About five years ago, a new management team undertook an aggressive program of expansion financed by the issuance of long-term, high-interest debt. The number of stores increased to 70. The firm acquired several other regional clothing chains and a large national in-store and catalog retailer.

At first, Jester had difficulty meeting its interest payments, but the retail clothing market was growing, and Jester was able to hold its share of the total market. Competition among domestic clothing manufacturers, the tremendous growth in Pacific Rim clothing manufacturing, and a strong U.S. dollar held down Jester's cost of goods sold. After a few years, Jester was able to retire 20 percent of its debt, but interest expense was still 40 percent of gross margin.

Recently, the U.S. dollar has weakened, raising the cost of merchandise from Pacific Rim clothing manufacturers. Further, an economic downturn has depressed the retail clothing market and intensified price competition among retailers. Thus retailers' gross margins have fallen. Jester, however, has been able to maintain approximately the same level of net income as in preceding years.

1. *What questions might an investor or creditor raise concerning Jester's cash flows from operating activities?*

   Does the statement of cash flows indicate impending problems for Jester, despite its level net income? Did company operations generate enough cash last year to pay the interest on the firm's debt and provide a dividend? If cash flow from operating activities was not sufficient to pay interest and dividends, how did the company make up the difference? Did it reduce dividends, increase liabilities, or dispose of assets? Does the company's cash position appear to be stable?

2. *What questions might an investor or creditor raise concerning Jester's cash flows from investing activities?*

   Did the company sell any investments during the period to cover a cash shortage? If not, is it likely to do so in the future? How much cash could Jester produce if it sold all of its investments?

3. *What questions might an investor or creditor raise concerning Jester's cash flows from financing activities?*

   Has the company been retiring its debt at the same rate as in prior years? If debt retirement has slowed, has the company been able to refinance its outstanding debt? Did the company borrow additional amounts to cover a cash shortage? If not, is the company likely to be able to borrow additional amounts in the future?

Format of the Statement of Cash Flows

Once a company has properly classified its cash inflows and outflows as operating, investing, or financing activities, it reports each of these three categories as shown in Exhibit 11-3.

Note that the three cash flow categories are summed to obtain the net increase or decrease in cash. This change in cash reconciles the beginning and ending balances of cash as noted in Exhibit 11-1.

Analyzing the Accounts for Cash Flow Data

OBJECTIVE ▶ 3
Understand the relationship between changes in cash and the changes in the balance sheet accounts.

Accrual-basis accounting requires the recognition of business activities when they occur instead of when cash is received or paid. Therefore, unlike the balance sheet and the income statement, the statement of cash flows cannot be prepared by simply using information obtained from an adjusted trial balance. Instead, each item on the balance sheet and the income statement must be analyzed to *explain* why cash changed by the amount that it did. In other words, the accrual-basis numbers in the balance sheet and the income statement must be adjusted to a cash basis. Notice that our concern is not with determining the change in cash but the *reasons why* cash changed.

The recording of any business activity creates two types of financial measures— *balances and changes*. Balances measure the dollar amount of an asset, liability, or

Exhibit 11-3

Format of the Statement of Cash Flows

Brooke Sportswear Inc.
Statement of Cash Flows
For the Year Ended December 31, 2009

Cash flows from operating activities		
Cash inflows	$ xxx	
Cash outflows	(xxx)	
Net cash provided (used) by operating activities		$ xxx
Cash flows from investing activities		
Cash inflows	$ xxx	
Cash outflows	(xxx)	
Net cash provided (used) by investing activities		xxx
Cash flows from financing activities		
Cash inflows	$ xxx	
Cash outflows	(xxx)	
Net cash provided (used) by financing activities		xxx
Net increase (decrease) in cash and cash equivalents		$ xxx
Cash and cash equivalents at beginning of year		xxx
Cash and cash equivalents at end of year		$ xxx

Schedule or note disclosure of noncash investing and financing activities

equity at a given time. Changes measure the increases or decreases in account balances over a period of time. For example, consider the following T-account:

Accounts Receivable			
Balance, 12/31/2009	11,000		
2010 credit sales	90,000	92,000	Cash collections for 2010
Balance, 12/31/2010	9,000		

This T-account shows two balances and two changes. The beginning and ending balances ($11,000 and $9,000) measure accounts receivable at December 31, 2009 and 2010, respectively. The credit sales ($90,000) and cash collections ($92,000) are changes that measure the effects of selling goods and collecting cash. Like accounts receivable, every balance sheet account can be described in terms of balances and changes.

To understand a company's cash flows, the relationships between the *changes* in balance sheet accounts and the company's cash flows need to be analyzed. We will begin our analysis with the fundamental accounting equation:

$$\text{Assets} = \text{Liabilities} + \text{Stockholders' Equity}$$

Next, we will restate this equation in terms of changes (Δ):

$$\Delta \text{ Assets} = \Delta \text{ Liabilities} + \Delta \text{ Stockholders' Equity}$$

Separating assets into cash and noncash accounts:

$$\Delta \text{ Cash} + \Delta \text{ Noncash Assets} = \Delta \text{ Liabilities} + \Delta \text{ Stockholders' Equity}$$

Finally, moving the changes in noncash assets to the right-hand side:

$$\Delta \text{ Cash} = \Delta \text{ Liabilities} + \Delta \text{ Stockholders' Equity} - \Delta \text{ Noncash Assets}$$

Where:

Increases in Cash = Increases in Liabilities + Increases in Stockholders' Equity + Decreases in Noncash Assets

Decreases in Cash = Decreases in Liabilities + Decreases in Stockholders' Equity + Increases in Noncash Assets

This analysis reveals that **all cash receipts or cash payments are reflected by changes in the balance sheet accounts.** Cornerstone 11-2 illustrates how to classify specific balance sheet accounts as increases in cash or decreases in cash.

HOW TO Classify Changes in Balance Sheet Accounts

Concept:
Increases in cash result from increases in liabilities, increases in stockholders' equity, and decreases in noncash assets. Decreases in cash result from decreases in liabilities, decreases in stockholders' equity, and increases in non-cash assets.

Information:
The following changes in the balance sheet accounts have been observed for the current period:

Account	1/1/2009	12/31/2009	Change
a. Accounts receivable	$ 25,000	$ 18,000	$ (7,000)
b. Bonds payable	400,000	300,000	(100,000)
c. Equipment	145,000	175,000	30,000
d. Inventory	15,000	18,000	3,000
e. Common stock	150,000	175,000	25,000
f. Retained earnings	75,000	95,000	20,000
g. Accounts payable	12,000	10,000	(2,000)
h. Unearned revenue	17,000	19,000	2,000

Required:
Classify each change as either an increase in cash or a decrease in cash.

Solution:
a. Increase in cash
b. Decrease in cash
c. Decrease in cash
d. Decrease in cash
e. Increase in cash
f. Increase in cash
g. Decrease in cash
h. Increase in cash

**CORNERSTONE
11-2**

Exhibit 11-4 integrates the analysis of the relationships between the *changes* in balance sheet accounts and the company's cash flows with the cash flow classifications discussed in the previous section.

Examining Exhibit 11-4, several items are of interest:

- Cash flows from operating activities generally involve income statement items (which are reflected in retained earnings) and changes in current assets or liabilities.
- Investing activities are related to changes in long-term assets.
- Financing activities are related to changes in long-term liabilities and stockholders' equity.

CONCEPT Q&A

Why do we analyze changes in the balance sheets accounts to determine the inflows and outflows of cash? Wouldn't it be easier to simply look at the cash account in the general ledger?

Possible Answer:
It is correct that the cash account in the general ledger will contain all cash inflows and cash outflows and a statement of cash flows can be prepared by analyzing this account. However, preparing a statement of cash flows in this manner would require individuals to identify, understand, and classify every single cash receipt or cash payment. With the large volume of cash transactions, this would an extremely time-consuming and inefficient task. It is much easier to determine cash flows by analyzing the changes in the balance sheet accounts.

Exhibit 11-4

Cash Flow Classifications and Changes in Balance Sheet Accounts

Classification	Cash Effect	Balance Sheet Items Affected	Example
Operating	Inflow (+)	Decreases in current assets Increases in current liabilities Increases in retained earnings	Collecting an accounts receivable Receipt of revenue in advance Making a cash sale
	Outflow (−)	Increases in current assets Decreases in current liabilities Decreases in retained earnings	Purchasing inventory Paying an accounts payable Paying interest
Investing	Inflow (+)	Decreases in long-term assets	Selling equipment
	Outflow (−)	Increases in long-term assets	Buying equipment
Financing	Inflow (+)	Increases in long-term liabilities Increases in stockholders' equity	Issuing long-term debt Issuing stock
	Outflow (−)	Decreases in long-term liabilities Decreases in stockholders' equity	Retiring long-term debt Paying dividends

- Retained earnings affects both cash flows from operating activities (e.g., revenues, expenses, net income, or a net loss) and cash flows from financing activities (e.g., payment of dividends).
- Each item on the balance sheet and the income statement is analyzed to explain the change in cash.

Now that we have seen how the accounts are analyzed to identify cash inflows and outflows, we turn to the preparation and reporting of a statement of cash flows.

Preparing a Statement of Cash Flows

To prepare a statement of cash flows, you need:

- **Comparative balance sheets** used to determine the changes in assets, liabilities, and stockholders' equity during a period.
- A **current income statement** that is used in the determination of cash flows from operating activities.
- **Additional information** about selected accounts that will be useful in determining the reason why cash was received or paid (generally used to explain investing and financing activities).

Using this information, there are five basic steps in preparing the statement of cash flows.

Step 1: Compute the net cash flow from operating activities. This involves adjusting the amounts on the income statement for noncash changes reflected in the balance sheet. Two methods, the indirect or direct method (explained below), may be used to determine this amount.

Step 2: Compute the net cash flow from investing activities. Information from the balance sheet as well as any additional information provided will need to be analyzed to identify the cash inflows and outflows associated with long-term assets.

Step 3: Compute the net cash flow from financing activities. Information from the balance sheet as well as any additional information provided will need to be analyzed to identify the cash inflows and outflows associated with long-term liabilities and stockholders' equity.

Step 4: Combine the net cash flows from operating, investing, and financing activities to obtain the net change in cash for the period.

Step 5: Compute the change in cash for the period and compare this with the change in cash from Step 4. The change in cash, computed from the beginning balance of cash and the ending balance of cash as shown on the balance sheet, should reconcile with the net cash flow computed in Step 4.

The statement of cash flows for John Deere is shown in Exhibit 11-5.

Preparing Cash Flows from Operating Activities

OBJECTIVE ➤ 4

Prepare the cash flows from operating activities section of a statement of cash flows using the indirect method.

The cash flows from operating activities section of the statement of cash flows may be prepared using either of two methods: the indirect method or the direct method. Both methods arrive at an identical amount—the net cash provided (used) by operating activities. The two methods differ only in how this amount is computed.

The **indirect method** begins with net income and then adjusts it for noncash items to produce net cash flow from operating activities. These adjustments to net income are necessary to (1) eliminate income statement items that do not

Exhibit 11-5

Statement of Cash Flows for John Deere

Deere and Company
Statement of Consolidated Cash Flows*
For the Year Ended October 31, 2007
(in millions of dollars)

Cash flows from operating activities		
Net income	$ 1,821.7	
Adjustments to reconcile net income to net cash provided by operating activities:		
Bad debt expense	71.0	
Depreciation and amortization	744.4	
Other noncash items	60.7	
Changes in assets and liabilities:		
Decrease in receivables related to sales	131.1	
Increase in inventories	(357.2)	
Increase in accounts payable and accrued expenses	418.6	
Net change in accrued income taxes payable/receivable	10.5	
Net change in retirement benefit accruals/ prepaid pension costs	(163.2)	
Other	21.8	
Net cash provided by operating activities		$ 2,759.4
Cash flows from investing activities		
Collections of notes receivable	$ 10,335.3	
Proceeds from sales of financing receivables	141.4	
Proceeds from maturities and sales of marketable securities	2,458.5	
Proceeds from sales of equipment on operating leases	355.2	
Cost of notes receivable acquired	(11,388.3)	
Purchases of marketable securities	(2,251.6)	
Purchases of property, plant, and equipment	(1,022.5)	
Cost of equipment on operating leases acquired	(461.7)	
Other	(99.6)	
Net cash used by investing activities		(1,933.3)
Cash flows from financing activities		
Increase in short-term borrowings	$ 99.4	
Proceeds from long-term borrowings	4,283.9	
Payments of long-term borrowings	(3,136.5)	
Proceeds from issuance of common stock	285.7	
Repurchases of common stock	(1,517.8)	
Dividends paid	(386.7)	
Other	91.0	
Net cash provided by (used for) financing activities		(281.0)
Effect of exchange rate changes on cash and cash equivalents		46.0
Net increase (decrease) in cash and cash equivalents		$ 591.1
Cash and cash equivalents at beginning of year		1,687.5
Cash and cash equivalents at end of year		$ 2,278.6

* The statement of cash flow information was taken from the annual report of Deere and Company and has been summarized and reformatted by the authors.

affect cash (e.g., depreciation and gains/losses on sales of assets) and (2) adjust accrual-basis revenues and expenses to cash receipts and cash payments. The changes in the related current asset and current liability accounts contain the information necessary to make the adjustments to revenue and expense accounts. Approximately 99 percent of U.S. companies use the indirect method as shown in Exhibit 11-6.

Generally, companies prefer the indirect method because it is easier and less costly to prepare and focuses on the *differences* between net income and net cash flow from operating activities rather than the individual cash flows.

ETHICS By highlighting the differences between cash flows and net income, financial statement users may be able to more easily see attempts at earnings management. If managers try to manage earnings by manipulating the accrual accounting process (e.g., increase revenues or decrease expenses on the income statement to increase income), these actions will often have no cash flow effect but instead reveal themselves by changes in the accrual-basis accounts. When there are growing differences between cash flow from operations and net income, the indirect method allows users to examine the changes in the accrual accounts to judge the cause of these differences.◆

In the **direct method**, cash inflows and cash outflows are listed for each type of operating activity that a company performs. These cash flows are generally computed by adjusting *each item* on the income statement by the changes in the related current asset or liability accounts. Typical cash flow categories reported are cash collected from customers, cash paid to suppliers, cash paid to employees, cash paid for interest, and cash paid for taxes. The cash inflows are then subtracted from the cash outflows to determine the net cash flow from operating activities. If the direct method is used, companies must also provide a supplementary schedule that shows the reconciliation of net income with net cash flow from operating activities. The FASB prefers the use of the direct method because it is more consistent with the purpose of the statement of cash flows, but it is not widely used.

We will illustrate the preparation of cash flows from operating activities for Brooke Sportswear using the more popular indirect method. The direct method is illustrated in Appendix 11A. However, remember two important points.

- Cash flow from operating activities is the same under either method.
- The indirect and direct methods only apply to the operating activities section of the statement of cash flows. The investing and financing sections will be prepared the same way regardless of which method is used to prepare the operating activities section.

The income statement and comparative balance sheets for Brooke Sportswear are shown in Exhibit 11-7.

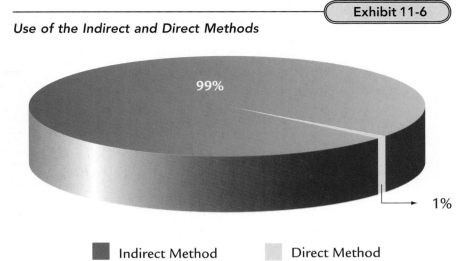

Exhibit 11-6

Use of the Indirect and Direct Methods

99%

1%

■ Indirect Method   ■ Direct Method

Source: Accounting Trends and Techniques, 2007.

Indirect Method

Because income statements are prepared on an accrual basis, the revenues and expenses recognized on the income statement are not necessarily the same as the cash receipts and cash payments for a period. For example, revenues may include credit sales for which the company has not collected cash and exclude collections of cash from credit sales made in a previous period. Similarly, expenses may have been incurred for which no cash has been paid or cash may have been paid related to

Exhibit 11-7

Financial Statements for Brooke Sportswear

Brooke Sportswear
Balance Sheets
December 31, 2009 and 2008

ASSETS	2009	2008
Current assets:		
Cash	$ 15,000	$ 13,000
Accounts receivable	53,000	46,000
Prepaid insurance	1,000	2,000
Inventory	63,000	51,000
Total current assets	$ 132,000	$ 112,000
Property, plant, and equipment:		
Land	325,000	325,000
Equipment	243,000	210,000
Accumulated depreciation	(178,000)	(150,000)
Investments	53,000	41,000
Total assets	$ 575,000	$ 538,000

LIABILITIES AND EQUITY		
Current liabilities:		
Accounts payable	$ 13,000	$ 17,000
Wages payable	3,500	2,000
Interest payable	1,500	1,000
Income taxes payable	3,000	6,000
Total current liabilities	$ 21,000	$ 26,000
Long-term liabilities:		
Notes payable	109,000	115,000
Total liabilities	$ 130,000	$ 141,000
Equity:		
Common stock	$ 165,000	$ 151,000
Retained earnings	280,000	246,000
Total stockholders' equity	$ 445,000	$ 397,000
Total liabilities and equity	$ 575,000	$ 538,000

Brooke Sportswear
Income Statement
For the Year Ended December 31, 2009

Sales revenue	$ 472,000
Less: Cost of goods sold	232,000
Gross margin	$ 240,000
Less operating expenses:	
Wages expense	(142,000)
Insurance expense	(15,000)
Depreciation expense	(40,000)
Income from operations	$ 43,000
Other income and expenses:	
Loss on sale of equipment	(6,000)
Gain on sale of investment	15,000
Interest expense	(5,000)
Income before taxes	$ 47,000
Less: Income tax expense	8,000
Net income	$ 39,000

Additional Information:

1. Equipment with a cost of $20,000 and accumulated depreciation of $12,000 was sold for $2,000 cash. Equipment was purchased for $53,000 cash.
2. Long-term investments with a cost of $16,000 were sold for $31,000 cash. Additional investments were purchased for $28,000 cash.
3. Notes payable in the amount of $35,000 were repaid, and new notes payable in the amount of $29,000 were issued for cash.
4. Common stock was issued for $14,000 cash.
5. Cash dividends of $5,000 were paid (obtained from the statement of retained earnings).

expenses incurred in a previous period. Therefore, net income must be adjusted for these timing differences between the recognition of net income and the receipt or payment of cash.

Under the indirect method, four types of adjustments must be made to net income to adjust it to net cash flow from operating activities. These adjustments and the computation of net cash flow from operating activities are illustrated in Cornerstone 11-3.

HOW TO Calculate Net Cash Flow from Operating Activities: Indirect Method

**CORNERSTONE
11-3**

Concept:

Four types of adjustments are needed to calculate net cash flow from operating activities:

1. Add to net income any noncash expenses and subtract from net income any noncash revenues.
2. Add to net income any losses and subtract from net income any gains.
3. Add to net income any decreases in current assets or increases in current liabilities that are related to operating activities.
4. Subtract from net income any increases in current assets and decreases in current liabilities that are related to operating activities.

Information:

Refer to the income statement and the current assets and current liabilities sections of Brooke Sportswear's balance sheets found in Exhibit 11-7 (page 568).

Required:

Compute the net cash flow from operating activities using the indirect method.

Solution:

Net income		$39,000
Adjustments to reconcile net income to net cash		
flow from operating activities:*		
Depreciation expense	$ 40,000	
Loss of sale of equipment	6,000	
Gain on sale of long-term investment	(15,000)	
Increase in accounts receivable	(7,000)	
Decrease in prepaid insurance	1,000	
Increase in inventory	(12,000)	
Decrease in accounts payable	(4,000)	
Increase in wages payable	1,500	
Increase in interest payable	500	
Decrease in income taxes payable	(3,000)	8,000
Net cash provided by operating activities		$47,000

* The explanation of these adjustments is given in the text of this section.

The adjustments made in Cornerstone 11-3 are explained below.

Adjustment of Noncash Revenues and Expenses   The income statement often includes various noncash items such as depreciation expense, amortization expense, and bad debt expense. Noncash expenses reduce net income but they do not reduce cash. Therefore, under the indirect method **noncash expenses are added back to net income**. Similarly, noncash revenues increase income but do not increase cash. Under the indirect method, **noncash revenues are subtracted from net income.**

Adjustment of Gains and Losses   The sale of a long-term asset or the extinguishment of a long-term liability often produces either a gain or loss that is reported on the income statement. However, the gain or loss does not affect cash flow and should, therefore, not be included as an operating activity. Furthermore, the gain or loss does not reveal the total amount of cash received or paid. Instead, it only gives the amount received or paid in excess of the book value of the asset or liability. The correct procedure is to eliminate the gain or loss from net income and record the full amount of the cash flow as either an investing activity or a financing activity. Because gains increase net income, under the indirect method, **gains are subtracted from net income.**

Because losses decrease net income, under the indirect method, **losses are added back to net income**.

Adjustments for Changes in Current Assets and Current Liabilities

As discussed earlier in the chapter, all cash receipts or cash payments are reflected by changes in the balance sheet accounts. Generally, current assets and liabilities are related to the operating activities of a company, and changes in these accounts cause a difference between net income and cash flows from operating activities. Based on the earlier analysis of the balance sheet accounts, two general rules emerge:

- **Increases in current assets and decreases in current liabilities are subtracted from net income.**
- **Decreases in current assets and increases in current liabilities are added to net income.**

To see the logic of these two rules, we will examine the specific changes experienced by Brooke Sportswear.

Accounts Receivable

The accounts receivable account increases when credit sales are recorded and decreases when cash is collected from customers.

Accounts Receivable			
Beginning balance	46,000		
Credit sales	xxx	xxx	Cash collections
Balance, 12/31/2009	53,000		

The increase of accounts receivable implies that credit sales were $7,000 greater than the cash collected from customers. Notice that this is consistent with the results of our earlier analysis indicating that increases in noncash assets are related to decreases in cash. Because cash collections were less than the sales reported on in the income statement, the company would need to subtract the increase in accounts receivable from net income when computing net cash flow from operating activities. (A decrease in accounts receivable would be added to net income when computing net cash flow from operating activities).

Prepaid Insurance

The prepaid insurance account increases when cash prepayments are made and decreases when expenses are incurred.

Prepaid Insurance			
Balance, 1/1/2009	2,000		
Cash prepayments	xxx	xxx	Expense incurred
Balance, 12/31/2009	1,000		

The decrease in prepaid insurance indicates that expenses recorded on the income statement were $1,000 higher than the cash payments. Because more expenses were incurred than were paid in cash, the company actually has more cash available at the end of the period than at the beginning of the period (because less cash was paid). This is consistent with the results of our earlier analysis indicating that decreases in noncash assets are related to increases in cash. Therefore, the decrease in the prepaid insurance account needs to be added to net income when computing net cash flow from operating activities. (Increases in prepaid insurance would be subtracted from net income.)

Inventory

The inventory account increases when inventory is purchased and decreases as inventory is sold.

Inventory			
Balance, 1/1/2009	51,000		
Purchases	xxx	xxx	Cost of goods sold
Balance, 12/31/2009	63,000		

The increase in inventory implies that purchases of inventory exceeded the cost of the inventory sold reported on the income statement by $12,000. Therefore, the company made "extra" cash purchases that were not included in cost of goods sold and subtracted from revenue in determining net income. To adjust net income to net cash flow from operating activities, the increase in the inventory account, which represents the extra cash purchases, needs to be subtracted from net income. (Decreases in inventory would be added to net income)

Accounts Payable The accounts payable account increases when purchases are made on credit and decreases when cash payments are made to suppliers.

The decrease in accounts payable indicates that the cash payments to suppliers exceeded the purchases of inventory by $4,000. Because the purchase of inventory is part of cost of goods sold, this implies that more cash was paid than was reflected in expenses. This is consistent with the results of our earlier analysis indicating that decreases in liabilities are related to decreases in cash. Therefore, the decrease in accounts payable needs to be subtracted from net income when computing the net cash flow from operating activities. (Increases of accounts payable are added to net income.)

Accounts Payable			
		17,000	Balance, 1/1/2009
Cash payments	xxx	xxx	Credit purchases
		13,000	Balance, 12/31/2009

Wages Payable The wages payable account increases when wages are accrued (incurred but not yet paid) and decreases when wages are paid.

The increase in wages payable indicates that wages expense recorded on the income statement was greater than the cash paid for wages by $1,500. Because less cash was paid than expensed, the company actually has more cash available. This is consistent with the results of our earlier analysis indicating that increases in liabilities are related to increases in cash. Therefore, the increase in wages payable is added to net income when computing the net cash flow from operating activities. (Decreases in wages payable are subtracted from net income.)

Wages Payable			
		2,000	Balance, 1/1/2009
Cash payments	xxx	xxx	Wages expense
		3,500	Balance, 12/31/2009

Interest Payable Interest payable increases when interest expense is recorded and decreases when interest is paid.

The increase in interest payable implies that interest expense recorded on the income statement was $500 greater than the cash paid for interest. Therefore, the increase in interest payable is added to net income when computing the net cash flow from operating activities. (Decreases in interest payable are subtracted from net income)

Interest Payable			
		1,000	Balance, 1/1/2009
Cash payments	xxx	xxx	Interest expense
		1,500	Balance, 12/31/2009

Income Taxes Payable			
		6,000	Balance, 1/1/2009
Cash payments	xxx	xxx	Income tax expense
		3,000	Balance, 12/31/2009

Income Taxes Payable The income tax payable account increases when income tax expense is incurred and decreases when income taxes are paid.

The decrease in income taxes payable implies that the cash payments for income taxes were $3,000 greater than the income tax expense reported on the income statement. Therefore, less cash is available at the end of the period and the decrease in income taxes payable is subtracted from net income when computing the net cash flow from operating activities. (Increases in income taxes payable are added to net income.)

CONCEPT Q&A

Why are there differences between net income and net cash flow from operating activities?

Possible Answer:
Net income is prepared under the accrual basis of accounting which records business activities when they occur instead of when cash is received or paid. Therefore, all of the adjustments that are made to net income reflect timing differences between the reporting of revenues and expenses and the related inflow or outflow of cash.

OBJECTIVE ▸ 5

Prepare the cash flows from investing activities section of a statement of cash flows.

Preparing Cash Flows from Investing Activities

The second major section of the statement of cash flows reports the net cash flow from investing activities. Investing activities include buying and selling property, plant, and equipment or other operating assets and purchasing and selling investments in other companies. Investing activities also include lending and collecting the principal amount of loans from borrowers.

Information for preparing the investing activities portion of the statement of cash flows is obtained from the investment and long-term asset accounts. Because all of these accounts are assets, increases that were financed by cash would be treated as outflows of cash. Decreases in the assets that produced cash receipts would be treated as inflows of cash.

Although the beginning and ending balance sheets are useful sources for identifying changes in these accounts, you must refer to any additional data provided to determine the actual amount of investing cash inflows and outflows. For example, a company might purchase land at a cost of $200,000 and, during the same accounting period, sell land that had a cost of $145,000. If only the beginning and ending amounts for land are examined, one would erroneously conclude that there had been a single cash outflow of $55,000 for land, instead of two separate cash flows—a cash outflow of $200,000 and a cash inflow of $145,000. The analysis of the general types of investing activities is shown below.

Analyzing Investing Activities

To analyze investing activities, follow these three basic steps:

Step 1: Recreate the journal entries to describe the activities that took place during the period.

Step 2: Record the cash flows as inflows or outflows of cash in the investing activities section of the statement of cash flows.

Step 3: Enter the information obtained from the financial statements, the additional information, and the recreation of the journal entries into the T-account (or accounts) being analyzed to make sure the account activity has been completely explained.

To illustrate the analysis of the relevant accounts and the recreation of the journal entries, consider the information in Brooke Sportswear's financial statements found in Exhibit 11-7 (page 568).

Land   Notice that no change occurred in the land account, nor was any additional information given concerning this account. Therefore, there was no cash flow associated with land for the year.

Property, Plant, and Equipment   The equipment account is analyzed by examining both the equipment and the related accumulated depreciation account. (For any operating asset that depreciates, you will need to analyze the two related accounts together.) Using the information obtained from the financial statements and the additional information in Exhibit 11-7, you can recreate the activity in the accounts by making the following journal entries.

Assets = Liabilities +	Stockholders' Equity
+2,000	−6,000
−12,000	
−20,000	

Assets = Liabilities +	Stockholders' Equity
+53,000	
−53,000	

Sale of Equipment	Cash	2,000	
	Accumulated Depreciation	12,000	
	Loss on Sale of Equipment	6,000	
	Equipment		20,000
Purchase of Equipment	Equipment	53,000	
	Cash		53,000

Notice that the there are only two cash flows related to investing activities—a $2,000 cash flow associated with the disposal of equipment and a $53,000 cash flow associated with the purchase of equipment. The loss on the sale of equipment does not involve cash and is included as an adjustment in the operating section of the statement of cash flows. The analysis performed above is used to reconcile the change in the equipment and accumulated depreciation accounts as shown in the following T-accounts.

Equipment

Beg. bal.	$210,000		
Purchase	53,000	20,000	Disposal
End. bal.	243,000		

Accumulated Depreciation

		150,000	Beg. bal.
Disposal	$12,000	40,000	Dep. exp.
		178,000	End. bal.
		178,000	End. bal.

Investments   The investment account is analyzed by recreating the activity in the investment account. Using the information obtained from the financial statements and the additional information in Exhibit 11-7, you can recreate the activity in the investment account by making the following journal entries.

Sale of Investment	Cash	31,000	
	Investment		16,000
	Gain on Sale of Investment		15,000
Purchase of Investment	Investment	28,000	
	Cash		28,000

Assets =	Liabilities +	Stockholders' Equity
+31,000		+15,000
−16,000		

Assets =	Liabilities +	Stockholders' Equity
+28,000		+15,000
−28,000		

Again, notice that two cash flows were related to investing activities—a $31,000 inflow of cash related to the sale of an investment and a $28,000 outflow of cash related to the purchase of an investment. The gain is on the sale of the investment does not involve cash and is included as an adjustment in the operating section of the statement of cash flows. The analysis performed above is used to reconcile the change in the investment account as shown in the following T-account.

Investment

Beg. bal.	41,000		
Purchase	28,000	16,000	Disposal
	53,000		End. bal.

Cornerstone 11-4 shows how to compute the investing activities section of the statement of cash flows for Brooke Sportswear.

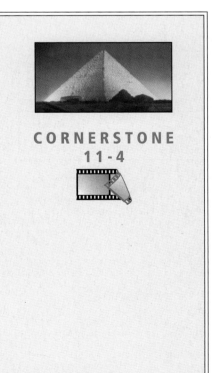

HOW TO Calculate Net Cash Flow from Investing Activities

Concept:
The cash flow effects of changes in long-term assets and investments are reported as investing cash flows.

Information:
Refer to the income statement, the long-term assets sections of Brooke Sportswear's balance sheets, and the first two items of additional information found in Exhibit 11-7 (page 568).

Required:
Compute the net cash flow from investing activities.

CORNERSTONE
11-4

Solution:

Cash flows from investing activities:	
Cash received from sale of equipment	$ 2,000
Purchase of equipment	(53,000)
Cash received from sale of investments	31,000
Purchase of investments	(28,000)
Net cash used for investing activities	$(48,000)

OBJECTIVE ▸ 6

Prepare the cash flows from financing activities section of a statement of cash flows.

Preparing Cash Flows from Financing Activities

The intent of the financing activities section of the statement of cash flows is to identify cash inflows and outflows of cash arising from business activities that either produced capital (long-term debt or equity) for the company or repaid capital supplied to the company. Financing activities include borrowing and repayment of the principal amount of the borrowing (remember that interest expense is classified as an operating cash flow), sale of common or preferred stock, payment of cash dividends, and the purchase and sale of treasury stock.

Information for preparing the financing activities portion of the statement of cash flows is obtained from the long-term debt and equity accounts. Because all of these accounts are liabilities and equity, increases in these accounts suggest that cash has been received and decreases suggest that cash has been paid. (Because treasury stock is a contra-equity account, increases indicate cash outflows and decreases indicate cash inflows).

Analyzing Financing Activities

To analyze financing activities, the same basic steps used to analyze investing activities are followed:

Step 1: Recreate the journal entries to describe the activities that took place during the period.

Step 2: Record the cash flows as inflows or outflows of cash in the financing activities section of the statement of cash flows.

Step 3: Enter the information obtained from the financial statements, the additional information, and the recreation of the journal entries into the T-account (or accounts) being analyzed to make sure the account activity has been completely explained.

To illustrate the analysis of the relevant accounts and the recreation of the journal entries, consider the information in Brooke Sportswear's balance sheet found in Exhibit 11-7 (page 568).

Notes Payable   The notes payable account is analyzed by recreating the activity in the notes payable account. Using information obtained from the financial statements and the additional information in Exhibit 11-7, you can recreate the activity in the investment account by making the following journal entries.

Assets =	Liabilities +	Stockholders' Equity
−35,000	−35,000	

Assets =	Liabilities +	Stockholders' Equity
+29,000	+29,000	

Repayment of Principal	Note Payable	35,000	
	Cash		35,000
Issuance of Note	Cash	29,000	
	Note Payable		29,000

Notice that there are two cash flows related to investing activities—a $35,000 cash outflow associated with the repayment of principal and a $29,000 cash inflow associated with issuing the note. The payment of interest is considered an operating activity and is not relevant to this analysis. The analysis performed above is used to reconcile the change in the note payable account as shown in the following T-account.

	Notes Payable	
	115,000	Beg. bal.
Repaid principal 35,000	29,000	Issued note
	109,000	End. bal.

Common Stock   The common stock account is analyzed by recreating the activity in the common stock account. Using information obtained from the financial statements and the additional information in Exhibit 11-7, you can recreate activity in the common stock account by making the following journal entry:

| Issuance of stock | Cash | 14,000 | |
| | Common Stock | | 14,000 |

	Assets = Liabilities +	Stockholders' Equity
	+14,000	+14,000

One cash inflow ($14,000) has caused the change in common stock. The credit entry to the common stock account is used to reconcile the change in the common stock account as shown in the following T-account.

Common Stock

		151,000	Beg. bal.
Retired stock	0	14,000	Issued stock
		165,000	End. bal.

Retained Earnings   Retained earnings must be analyzed by recreating the activity in the retained earnings account. Retained earnings increases with net income (decreases with a net loss) and decreases due to the payment of cash dividends[1] as follows:

| Payment of dividends | Retained Earnings | 5,000 | |
| | Cash | | 5,000 |

	Assets = Liabilities +	Stockholders' Equity
	−5,000	−5,000

One cash flow, the payment of dividends, is a financing activity. Net income does not affect net cash flow from financing activities because it is considered an operating activity (See Cornerstone 11-3). The following T-account summarizes the activity in the retained earnings account.

Retained Earnings

		246,000	Beg. bal.
Dividends	5,000	39,000	Net income
		280,000	End. bal.

Cornerstone 11-5 shows how to compute the financing activities section of the statement of cash flows for Brooke Sportswear.

HOW TO Calculate Net Cash Flow from Financing Activities

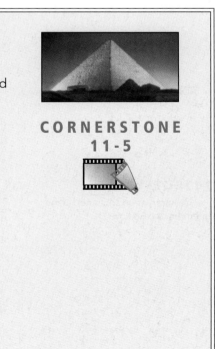

CORNERSTONE 11-5

Concept:
The cash flow effects of changes in long-term liabilities and equity are reported as financing cash flows.

Information:
Refer to the income statement, long-term assets, liabilities and equity sections of Brooke Sportswear's balance sheet, and items three through five of additional information found in Exhibit 11-7 (page 568).

Required:
Compute the net cash flow from financing activities.

Solution:

Cash flows from financing activities:	
Cash paid to retire principal on note payable	$(35,000)
Cash received from issuing note payable	29,000
Cash received from issuance of common stock	14,000
Cash paid for dividends	(5,000)
Net cash provided by financing activities	$ 3,000

---

[1] Dividends declared but not paid also reduce retained earnings but are classified as a noncash activity.

Combining Cornerstones 11-3 through 11-5, a complete statement of cash flows is presented in Exhibit 11-8. This exhibit presents cash flows from operating activities using the indirect method. Notice that the statement of cash flows explains the change in cash shown on the balance sheet of Brooke Sportswear in Exhibit 11-7 (page 568).

Exhibit 11-8

Statement of Cash Flows for Brooke Sportswear

Brooke Sportswear
Statement of Cash Flows
For the Year Ended December 31, 2009

Cash flows from operating activities		
Net income		$ 39,000
Adjustments to reconcile net income to net cash flow from operating activities:		
Depreciation expense	40,000	
Loss of sale of equipment	6,000	
Gain on sale of long-term investment	(15,000)	
Increase in accounts receivable	(7,000)	
Decrease in prepaid insurance	1,000	
Increase in inventory	(12,000)	
Decrease in accounts payable	(4,000)	
Increase in wages payable	1,500	
Increase in interest payable	500	
Decrease in income taxes payable	(3,000)	
Net cash provided by operating activities		$ 47,000
Cash flows from investing activities		
Cash received from sale of equipment	$ 2,000	
Purchase of equipment	(53,000)	
Cash received from sale of investments	31,000	
Purchase of investments	(28,000)	
Net cash used for investing activities		(48,000)
Cash flows from financing activities		
Cash paid to retire principal on note payable	$(35,000)	
Cash received from issuing note payable	29,000	
Cash received from issuance of common stock	14,000	
Cash paid for dividends	(5,000)	
Net cash provided by financing activities		3,000
Net change in cash		$ 2,000
Cash and cash equivalents, 1/1/2009		13,000
Cash and cash equivalents, 12/31/2009		$ 15,000

OBJECTIVE ▶ 7
Analyze information contained in the statement of cash flows.

Using the Statement of Cash Flows

Effective analysis of the statement of cash flows requires (1) an examination of the statement of cash flows itself, (2) a comparison of the information on the current statement of cash flows with earlier statements, and (3) a comparison of the information in the current statement of cash flows with information from other companies' statements of cash flow. In this section, we will discuss each of these analyses, beginning with the examination of the statement of cash flows itself.

A number of insights can be gained by inspecting the current period's statement of cash flows. One of the most important is an estimate of how long it will take to recover the cash outflow associated with long-term uses of cash (e.g., purchase of property, plant, and equipment) or permanent uses of cash (e.g., payment of dividends or repayment of debt). Investments in property, plant, and equipment are likely to require several years of successful operation by the company before the investment is completely recovered through the sale of goods or services. Therefore, prudent managers will seek long-term or permanent sources of cash, such as long-term debt or equity, which will not need to be repaid before the original investment has been recovered through profitable operations.

The sources most frequently used to provide permanent or long-term cash inflows are operations, the sale of long-term debt, and the sale of stock. Of these three, operations is generally considered the least risky, or the most controllable. The sale of debt or equity requires that investors or creditors make sizable commitments to the firm. Although cash inflows from operations also require that an outsider (the customer) make a commitment, the size and timing of a customer's cash commitments are more flexible. Thus, it is more likely that the company can produce cash inflows from customers on a regular basis. For this reason, most companies attempt to secure a sizable portion of their total cash inflows from operations. Generally, analysts view cash flows from operations as the most important section of the statement of cash flows because, in the long-run, this will be a company's source of cash used to provide a return to investors and creditors.

Because the cost of selling large debt or equity issues in the public capital markets is high, most large companies sell debt or equity in relatively large amounts. They also make smaller long-term or short-term borrowings directly from banks, insurance companies, and other financial intermediaries. Many businesses arrange a "preapproved" line of credit that can be used, up to some limit, for borrowing whenever cash is needed. Sales of small amounts of stock to employees through stock option and stock bonus plans also help increase cash inflows.

An analysis of the statement of cash flows also requires a comparison of the company's current statement of cash flows with earlier statements of cash flow. When a series of statements are examined, the analysis should focus on a period of several consecutive years in order to determine trends in cash inflows and cash outflows. The following questions may be helpful in beginning the analysis of a series of cash flow statements:

1. What proportions of cash have come from operating, financing, and investing activities?
2. Are there discernible trends in these proportions?
3. What proportions of long-term uses of cash are financed by long-term sources of cash?
4. How has the company financed any permanent increases in current assets?
5. Has the company begun any investment programs that are likely to require significant cash outflows in the future?
6. What are the probable sources for the cash inflows the company will need in the near future?
7. Are these sources likely to be both able and willing to provide the cash that is needed?
8. If the company is unable to secure all the cash it needs, could cash outflows be restricted to the available supply of cash without seriously affecting operations?

Financial statement users will rely on summary cash flow measures to help them make these assessments. Two such measures are a company's free cash flow and its cash flow adequacy ratio. A company's **free cash flow** represents the cash flow that a company is able to generate after considering the maintenance or expansion of its assets (capital expenditures) and the payment of dividends. Free cash flow is computed as:

$$\begin{array}{cccc} \text{Free Cash} = \text{Net Cash Flow from} & - & \text{Capital} & - & \text{Cash} \\ \text{Flow} & \text{Operating Activities} & \text{Expenditures} & \text{Dividends} \end{array}$$

Having positive free cash flow allows a company to pursue profit-generating opportunities. However, negative free cash flow is not necessarily a bad thing. For example, a company making large investments in productive assets (large capital expenditures) may show negative free cash flow. If these investments provide a high rate of return, this strategy will be good for the company in the long run.

A second useful measure is the **cash flow adequacy ratio**. The cash flow adequacy ratio provides a measure of the company's ability to meet its debt obligations and is calculated as:

$$\text{Cash Flow Adequacy} = \frac{\text{Free Cash Flow}}{\text{Average Amount of Debt Maturing over the Next Five Years}}$$

Cornerstone 11-6 illustrates how to compute these ratios for John Deere.

CORNERSTONE 11-6

HOW TO Compute Free Cash Flow and Cash Flow Adequacy

Concept:
Cash flow measures can be used to help assess a company's ability to expand its operations, meet its obligations, obtain financing, and pay dividends.

Information:
In its October 31, 2007, annual report, John Deere reported net cash provided by operating activities of $2,759,400,000, capital expenditures of $1,022,500,000, dividends of $386,700,000, and average maturities of long-term debt over the next five years of $2,663,600,000.

Required:
1. Compute John Deere's free cash flow for 2007.
2. Compute John Deere's cash flow adequacy ratio for 2007.

Solution:
1. John Deere's free cash flow of $1,350,200,000 is computed as:

$$\begin{array}{c}\text{Free Cash} \\ \text{Flow}\end{array} = \begin{array}{c}\text{Net Cash Flow from} \\ \text{Operating Activities}\end{array} - \begin{array}{c}\text{Capital} \\ \text{Expenditures}\end{array} - \begin{array}{c}\text{Cash} \\ \text{Dividends}\end{array}$$

$$= \$2,759,400,000 - \$1,022,500,000 - \$386,700,000$$
$$= \underline{\mathbf{\$1,350,200,000}}$$

Having approximately $1.3 billion in free cash flow indicates that John Deere has the financial flexibility necessary to take advantage of profit-generating opportunities and internally finance its expansion needs.
2. With a cash flow adequacy ratio of 0.51 (computed below), John Deere appears to be able to meet its debt obligations over the next five years.

$$\begin{array}{c}\text{Cash Flow} \\ \text{Adequacy}\end{array} = \frac{\text{Free Cash Flow}}{\text{Average Amount of Debt Maturing over the Next Five Years}}$$

$$= \frac{\$1,350,200,000}{\$2,663,600,000}$$
$$= \underline{\mathbf{0.51}}$$

Finally, the analysis of the statement of cash flows requires comparing information from similar companies. Such comparisons provide good reference points, because similar companies generally secure cash from similar sources and are likely to spend cash for similar activities. Comparative analysis can reveal significant deviations in (1) the amounts of cash inflows, (2) the source of those inflows, and (3) the types of activities to which cash is applied. When significant differences are found among similar companies, an explanation should be sought in the other financial statements, in the notes accompanying the statements, or from management.

DECISION-MAKING & ANALYSIS

Analyzing Cash Flows over Time

Slater Toy Company operates retail toy stores in major metropolitan areas in the United States, Canada, and Europe. Summarized cash flow information for the six-year period, 2004–2009 is as follows:

Slater Toy Company
Summarized Cash Flow Data
For the Years Ended (in thousands)

	12/31/09	12/31/08	12/31/07	12/31/06	12/31/05	12/31/04
Cash flows from operating activities						
Net earnings	$ 437,524	$ 339,529	$ 325,988	$ 321,080	$ 268,024	$ 203,922
Adjustments:						
Depreciation	119,034	100,701	79,093	65,839	54,564	43,716
Receivables	(5,307)	9,092	(20,072)	14,932	(5,886)	(24,642)
Inventory	(108,066)	(115,436)	(44,775)	(299,274)	(158,287)	(243,894)
Payables	112,232	462,152	(40,130)	92,316	158,802	144,364
Other	9,149	45,090	(21,622)	6,181	11,097	10,206
Net cash from operations	$ 564,566	$ 841,128	$ 278,482	$ 201,074	$ 328,314	$ 133,672
Cash flows from investing activities						
Capital expenditures, net	$(421,564)	$(548,538)	$(485,269)	$(371,851)	$(327,010)	$(314,827)
Other	(22,175)	(17,110)	—	(5,114)	4,463	15,137
Cash used for investment	$(443,739)	$(565,648)	$(485,269)	$(376,965)	$(322,547)	$(299,690)
Cash flows from financing activities						
Short-term borrowing, net	$(170,887)	$ (94,811)	$ 180,957	$ 129,380	$ 58,476	$ 17,663
Long-term borrowing	318,035	197,802	33,152	-0-	693	96,611
Repayment of debt	(7,926)	(1,590)	(10,864)	(1,199)	(3,899)	(1,860)
Sale of stock	86,323	32,707	30,344	19,861	52,429	15,221
Purchase of treasury stock	(27,244)	—	(32,692)	(54,168)	(36,550)	-0-
Cash flow from financing	$ 198,301	$ 134,108	$ 200,897	$ 93,874	$ 71,149	$ 127,635
Increase (decrease) in cash	$ 319,128	$ 409,588	$ (5,890)	$ (82,017)	$ 76,916	$ (38,383)
Beginning of year	444,593	35,005	40,895	122,912	45,996	84,379
End of year	$ 763,721	$ 444,593	$ 35,005	$ 40,895	$ 122,912	$ 45,996

This annual information on cash flows may be further summarized as inflows and outflows. Over the six-year period, Slater secured cash and applied cash in the amounts and proportions that follow:

	Total Six-Year Amount*	Percentage of Total Inflows or Outflows
Inflows of cash:		
Operations	$2,347,236	64.6
Long-term and short-term borrowing	1,032,769	28.4
Sale of stock	236,885	6.5
Other inflows	19,600	0.5
Total inflows	$3,636,490	100.0
Outflows of cash:		
Repayment of short and long-term borrowing	$ 293,036	9.9
Investment in property	2,469,059	83.5
Purchase of treasury stock	150,654	5.1
Other outflows	44,399	1.5
Total outflows	$2,957,148	100.0
Excess of outflows over inflows	$ 679,342	

* Amounts in thousands.

Using this six-year summary and the annual statements of cash flows, we examine the following issues:

1. *What cash sources has Slater employed?*

Operating activities have been the most significant source of cash over this six-year period. Operating activities account for 64.6 percent of total cash inflows. Long-term borrowing and the sale of equity have also produced sizable cash inflows.

2. *What have been the major uses of cash?*

Investment in property has been by far the largest use of cash. Cash has also been used to repay short and long-term borrowings and to purchase treasury stock.

3. *Has Slater matched the time commitments of its cash inflows and outflows?*

The company appears to have matched the time commitment of inflows and outflows adequately. Nearly all the outflows have been for investments in property, a long-term use of cash. Inflows (primarily from operations, long-term borrowing, and the sale of stock) are sources of cash that will be invested in the firm permanently or for the long-term.

4. *Are debt and equity likely to be available as sources of cash in the near future?*

During the six-year period, operations have provided 64.6 percent of the cash inflows. Although Slater has borrowed and sold equity, those two sources have not been overused, and should continue to provide 30 percent or more of the firm's total cash needs. Another important factor in a firm's ability to secure cash from creditors is profitability. Slater has been highly profitable, so one would expect that potential investors and creditors would continue to invest cash in the firm.

5. *What are the trends in inflows and outflows?*

The annual cash inflow from operating activities has grown over the six-year period, although not in every year. In several years, the cash flow from operating activities has been less than the year before due to an increase in inventories. The proportion of cash provided by financing activities has also varied from year to year, generally rising when cash flows from operations have fallen. The investment in property has increased every year until the most recent year, indicating a strong commitment to growth.

6. *What projections would you make regarding inflows and outflows in the near future?*

So long as operations continue to provide a substantial portion of the cash needed for investment in property, Slater is likely to continue to grow. Should profitability decline, however, the company may find it difficult to secure cash from creditors and investors. If cash should become scarce, Slater may have to postpone its expansion into new markets. However, it does appear that Slater has invested wisely and has operated efficiently. Therefore, one would expect that it will continue to be profitable.

Summary of Learning Objectives

LO1. **Explain the purpose of a statement of cash flows.**
- The statement of cash flows is one of the primary financial statements whose purpose is to provide information about a company's cash receipts (inflows of cash) and cash payments (outflows of cash) during an accounting period.
- The statement of cash flows is complementary to the information contained in the income statement and the balance sheet and is critical to understanding and analyzing a company's operations.

LO2. **Identify and classify business activities that produce cash inflows and outflows.**
- The statement of cash flows is divided into three main sections based on the fundamental business activities that a company engages in during a period:
  - cash flows from operating activities which encompass the cash inflows and outflows that relate to the determination of net income;
  - cash flows from investing activities which are related to acquisitions and disposals of long-term assets and investments; and
  - cash flows from financing activities which are related to the external financing of the company (debt or equity).

- Some business activities take place without affecting cash and are referred to as noncash investing and financing activities.

LO3. **Understand the relationship between changes in cash and the changes in the balance sheet accounts.**
- Because of timing issues between the recognition of revenues and expenses and the inflows and outflows of cash, information about a company's cash flows can be obtained by examining the changes in the balance sheet account balances over a period.
- Increases in cash result from increases in liabilities, increases in stockholders' equity, and decreases in noncash assets.
- Decreases in cash result from decreases in liabilities, decreases in stockholders' equity, and increases in noncash assets.

LO4. **Prepare the cash flows from operating activities section of a statement of cash flows using the indirect method.**
- The indirect method for reporting cash flows from operating activities begins with net income and adjusts it for noncash items to produce net cash flow from operating activities.
- The adjustments to net income are necessary to eliminate income statement items that do not affect cash and to adjust accrual-basis revenues and expenses to cash receipts and cash payments.
- Four types of adjustments are necessary:
  - add to net income any noncash expenses and subtract from net income any noncash revenues;
  - add to net income any losses and subtract from net income any gains;
  - add to net income any decreases in current assets or increases in current liabilities that are related to operating activities; and
  - subtract from net income any increases in current assets and decreases in current liabilities that are related to operating activities.

LO5. **Prepare the cash flows from investing activities section of a statement of cash flows.**
- The cash flows from the investing activities section report the net cash flow related to buying and selling property, plant, and equipment or other operating assets, purchasing and selling investments in other companies and lending and collecting the principal amount of loans from borrowers.
- The preparation of the investing activities section of a statement of cash flows involves a careful analysis of the information in the financial statements as well as a recreation of the journal entries that describe the activities that took place during a period.

LO6. **Prepare the cash flows from financing activities section of a statement of cash flows.**
- The cash flows from the financing activities section report the net cash flow related to the borrowing and repayment of the principal amount of long-term debt, the sale of common or preferred stock, the payment of dividends, and the purchase and sale of treasury stock.
- The preparation of the financing activities section of a statement of cash flows involves a careful analysis of the information in the financial statements as well as a recreation of the journal entries that describe the activities that took place during a period.

LO7. **Analyze information contained in the statement of cash flows.**
- Effective analysis of the statement of cash flows requires an examination of the statement of cash flows itself, a comparison of the information on the current statement of cash flows with earlier statements, and a comparison of the information in the current statement of cash flows with information from other companies' statements of cash flow.

- Financial statement users may also rely on summary cash flow measures such as free cash flow (the cash flow that a company is able to generate after considering the maintenance or expansion of its assets) and the cash flow adequacy ratio (a measure of a company's ability to meet its debt obligations).

CORNERSTONES FOR CHAPTER 11

Key Terms

OBJECTIVE ▶ 8

Prepare the cash flows from operating activities section of a statement of cash flows using the direct method.

Appendix 11A: The Direct Method

In the direct method of computing net cash flow from operating activities, inflows and outflows of cash are listed for each type of operating activity that a company performs. This involves adjusting *each item* on the income statement by the changes in the related current asset or liability accounts. Typical operating cash flows and the adjustments necessary to compute them are given below.

Cash Collected from Customers Sales revenue includes both cash sales and credit sales. When all sales are for cash, the cash collected from customers equals sales. However, when credit sales are made, the amount of cash that was collected during a period must be determined by analyzing the sales and accounts receivable accounts. The accounts receivable account increases when credit sales are recorded and decreases when cash is collected from customers.

Accounts Receivable	
Beg. balance	
Credit sales	Cash collections from customers
End. balance	

Therefore, to compute cash collections from customers, sales must be adjusted as follows:

$$\text{Cash Collected from Customers} = \text{Sales} \begin{cases} + \text{ Decrease in Accounts Receivable} \\ - \text{ Increase in Accounts Receivable} \end{cases}$$

Other Cash Collections   If other revenues exist (e.g., interest or rent), similar adjustments are made to determine the cash collections. For example, interest revenue is adjusted for any change in interest receivable as follows:

$$\text{Cash Collected for Interest} = \text{Interest Revenue} \begin{cases} + \text{Decrease in Interest Receivable} \\ - \text{Increase in Interest Receivable} \end{cases}$$

Cash Paid to Suppliers   A company pays its suppliers for inventory which it later sells to customers, as represented by cost of goods sold. These purchases of inventory from suppliers may be either cash purchases or credit purchases, reflected as accounts payable. To compute cash paid to suppliers it is necessary to analyze two accounts—inventory and accounts payable—and make two adjustments.

Inventory	
Beg. balance	
Purchases	Cost of goods sold
End. balance	

Accounts Payable	
	Beg. balance
Cash payments	Credit purchases
	End. balance

When inventory increases, purchases are greater than cost of goods sold; a decrease in inventory means purchases are less than cost of goods sold. The first adjustment is to compute the cost of purchases by adjusting cost of goods sold as follows:

$$\text{Cost of Purchases} = \text{Cost of Goods Sold} \begin{cases} + \text{Increases in Inventory} \\ - \text{Decreases in Inventory} \end{cases}$$

Next, we adjust the cost of purchases by the change in accounts payable to compute the cash paid to suppliers. An increase in accounts payable means that cash payments were less than the cost purchase; a decrease in accounts payable means that cash payments were less than the cost of purchases. The second adjustment is:

$$\text{Cash Paid to Suppliers} = \text{Cost of Purchases} \begin{cases} + \text{Decreases in Accounts Payable} \\ - \text{Increases in Accounts Payable} \end{cases}$$

Combining this adjustment with the first adjustment, cost paid to suppliers is computed as follows:

$$\text{Cash Paid to Suppliers} = \begin{cases} + \text{Increases in Inventory} \\ - \text{Decreases in Inventory} \end{cases} \begin{cases} + \text{Decrease in Accounts Payable} \\ - \text{Increase in Accounts Payable} \end{cases}$$

Cash Paid for Operating Expenses   Recall that operating expenses are the expenses the business incurs in selling goods or providing services and managing the company. These are usually divided into selling and administrative expenses and include items such as advertising expense, salaries and wages, insurance expense, utilities expense, property tax expense, and depreciation. These expenses are recognized when goods and services are used, not when cash is paid. Therefore, the expense amounts reported on the income statement will probably not equal the amount of cash actually paid during the period. Some expenses are paid before they are actually recognized (e.g., prepaid insurance); other expenses are paid for after they are recognized, creating a payable account at the time of the cash payment (e.g., salaries payable).

   To determine the amount of cash payments for operating expenses, it is necessary to analyze the changes in the balance sheet accounts that are related to operating expenses— prepaid expenses and accrued liabilities. A prepaid expense increases when cash prepayments are made and decreases when expenses are incurred. An accrued liability increases when expenses are accrued (incurred but not yet paid) and decreases when cash payments are made.

Prepaid Expenses	
Beg. balance	
Cash prepayments	Expense incurred
End. balance	

Accrued Liabilities	
	Beg. balance
Cash payments	Expense accrued
	End. balance

An increase in prepaid expenses means that cash payments were higher than the expenses recognized on the income statement; a decrease in prepaid expenses indicates that expenses recorded on the income statement were higher than the cash payments. Therefore, increases in prepaid expenses must be added to operating expenses and decreases in prepaid expenses must be subtracted from operating expenses to compute cash paid for operating expenses.

In addition, an increase in accrued liabilities indicates that operating expenses recorded on the income statement were greater than the cash payments. A decrease in accrued liabilities implies that cash payments were greater than the expense recorded on the income statement. Therefore, an increase in accrued liabilities is subtracted from operating expenses and an increase in accrued liabilities is added to operating expenses to compute cash paid for operating expenses.

Combining these two adjustments, the formula to compute cash paid for operating expenses is:

$$\text{Cash Paid for Operating Expenses} = \text{Operating Expenses} \begin{cases} + \text{ Increases in Prepaid Expenses} \\ - \text{ Decreases in Prepaid Expenses} \\ \begin{cases} + \text{ Decrease in Accrued Liabilities} \\ - \text{ Increase in Accrued Liabilities} \end{cases} \end{cases}$$

Cash Paid for Interest and Income Taxes

Computing cash paid for interest and income taxes is similar to that for operating expenses. Interest payable increases when interest expense is recorded and decreases when interest is paid.

Interest Payable	
	Beg. balance
Cash payments	Interest expense
	End. balance

An increase in interest payable implies that interest expense recorded on the income statement was greater than the cash paid for interest; a decrease in interest expense indicates that the cash paid for interest is greater than the interest expense recorded on the income statement. Therefore, the adjustment required to compute cash paid for interest is:

$$\text{Cash Paid for Interest} = \text{Interest Expense} \begin{cases} + \text{ Decreases in Interest Payable} \\ - \text{ Increases in Interest Payable} \end{cases}$$

The income tax payable account increases when income tax expense is incurred and decreases when income taxes are paid.

Income Taxes Payable	
	Beg. balance
Cash payments	Income tax expense
	End. balance

A decrease in income taxes payable implies that the cash payments for income taxes were greater than the income tax expense reported on the income statement; an increase implies that income tax expense reported on the income statement is greater than the cash paid for income taxes. Therefore, the adjustment required to compute cash paid for income taxes is:

$$\text{Cash Paid for Income Taxes} = \text{Income Tax Expense} \begin{cases} + \text{ Decrease in Income Taxes Payable} \\ - \text{ Increase in Income Taxes Payable} \end{cases}$$

Other Items *Noncash Revenues and Expenses* The income statement often includes various noncash items such as depreciation expense, amortization expense, and bad debt expense. Noncash items do not affect cash flow. Therefore, under the direct method, *noncash items are not reported on the statement of cash flows*. Sometimes, depreciation expense (or some other noncash expense) is included as part of operating expenses. In this case, depreciation expense must be subtracted from operating expenses to compute the cash paid for operating expenses.

Gains and Losses The sale of a long-term asset or the extinguishment of a long-term liability often produces either a gain or loss that is reported on the income statement. However, the gain or loss does not affect cash flow and should not be included as an operating activity. Furthermore, the gain or loss does not reveal the total amount of cash received or paid. Instead, it only gives the amount received or paid in excess of the book value of the asset or liability. *Therefore, gains and losses are not reported on the statement of cash flows under the direct method.*

Application of the Direct Method Cornerstone 11-7 illustrates how to compute the net cash flow from operating activities using the direct method. We will base this illustration on the financial statements of Brooke Sportswear given in Exhibit 11-7 (page 568). Because each item on the income statement is adjusted under the direct method, we will begin our analysis with the first item on the income statement (sales) and proceed down the income statement in the order that the accounts are listed.

It is important to note that both the indirect and direct methods arrive at the identical amount for the net cash provided (used) by operating activities. Therefore,

---

HOW TO Calculate Net Cash Flows from Operating Activities: Direct Method

Concept:
To compute net cash flow from operating activities under the direct method, each item on the income statement must be adjusted for changes in the related asset and liability accounts.

Information:
Refer to the financial statements for Brooke Sportswear in Exhibit 11-7.

Required:
Compute the net cash flow from operating activities using the direct method.

CORNERSTONE 11-7

**CORNERSTONE
11-7**
(continued)

Solution:

Cash flows from operating activities

Cash collected from customers ($472,000 sales − $7,000 change in accounts receivable)		$ 465,000
Cash paid:		
To suppliers of merchandise ($232,000 cost of goods sold + $12,000 change in inventory + $4,000 change in accounts payable)	$(248,000)	
For wages ($142,000 wages expense − $1,500 change in wages payable)	(140,500)	
For insurance ($15,000 insurance expense − $1,000 change in prepaid insurance)	(14,000)	
For interest ($5,000 interest expense − $500 change in interest payable)	(4,500)	
For income taxes ($8,000 income tax expense + $3,000 change in income taxes payable)	(11,000)	(418,000)
Net cash provided by operating activities		$ 47,000

the net cash provided by operating activities of $47,000 computed above are the same as the net cash flow from operating activities computed under the indirect method shown in Cornerstone 11-3. The two methods differ only in how this amount is computed and the presentation of the details on the statement of cash flows. In addition, if the direct method is used, companies must also provide a supplementary schedule that shows the reconciliation of net income with net cash flow from operating activities. This supplementary schedule is, in effect, the presentation shown under the indirect method in Cornerstone 11-3 (on page 569).

Appendix 11A: Summary of Learning Objectives

LO8. Prepare the cash flows from operating activities section of a statement of cash flows using the direct method.

- The direct method for reporting cash flows from operating activities lists cash inflows and cash outflows for each type of operating activity that a company performs.
- Cash flows from operating activities are generally computed by adjusting each item on the income statement by the changes in the related current asset or current liability accounts.
- Typical cash flow categories reported under the direct method include cash collected from customers, cash paid to suppliers, cash paid to employees, cash paid for interest, and cash paid for taxes.

CORNERSTONE 11-7 How to calculate net cash flows from operating activities: direct method, page 585

**CORNERSTONES
FOR APPENDIX 11A**

Appendix 11B: Using a Spreadsheet to Prepare the Statement of Cash Flows

OBJECTIVE ➤ 9
Use a spreadsheet to prepare the statement of cash flows.

The spreadsheet approach provides a means of systematically analyzing changes in the balance sheet amounts, along with the information from the income statement and any additional information, to produce a statement of cash flows. This approach produces spreadsheet entries (made only on the spreadsheet and not in the general ledger) that simultaneously reconstruct and explain the changes in the balance sheet account balances and identify the cash inflows and outflows. The spreadsheet is based on the same underlying principles as discussed in the chapter. Its primary advantage is that it provides a systematic approach to analyze the data, which is helpful in more complex situations.

To construct the spreadsheet:

Step 1: Construct five columns. The first column will contain the balance sheet account titles. Immediately beneath the balance sheet accounts, set up the three sections of the statement of cash flows. The second column will contain the beginning balances of the balance sheet accounts (enter the amounts at this time). The third and fourth column will contain the debit and credit adjustments, respectively. The fifth column will contain the ending balances of the balance sheet accounts (enter the amounts at this time).

Step 2: Analyze each change in the balance sheet accounts in terms of debits and credits. Enter the effects in the adjustments column. Note that each entry will adjust both the balance sheet account being considered and either a statement of cash flows section of the spreadsheet or another balance sheet account (other than cash). Note that all inflows of cash are recorded as debits and all outflows of cash are recorded as credits.

Step 3: Prepare the statement of cash flows from the information contained in the statement of cash flows section of the spreadsheet.

Exhibit 11-9 illustrates the spreadsheet approach to preparing the statement of cash flows for Brooke Sportswear. You should note that the logic behind the analysis of the changes in the spreadsheet accounts was given earlier in the chapter. You may want to refer to this reasoning as you analyze the items below.

The spreadsheet should begin with net income.

a. Net income is listed as a cash inflow in the operating activities section. Because net income flows into retained earnings during the closing process, a credit to retained earnings reflects the effect of the closing entry.

Next any noncash items are adjusted.

b. For Brooke Sportswear, the only noncash item was depreciation expense which is added back to net income in the operating activities section and is reflected as a credit to accumulated depreciation.

The next four entries adjust for gains and/or losses due to investing and financing activities.

c. The actual proceeds from the sale of equipment are shown as a cash inflow in the investing activities section. The loss on the sale of equipment is added back to net income in the operating activities section. In addition, both equipment and accumulated depreciation should be adjusted to reflect the sale.

d. The actual proceeds from the sale of equipment are shown as a cash inflow in the investing activities section. At this point, note that the beginning and ending balances of the equipment and accumulated depreciation accounts are reconciled.

e. The actual proceeds from the sale of an investment are shown as a cash inflow in the investing activities section. The gain on the sale of the investment is subtracted from net income in the operating activities section. In addition, the investment account should be adjusted to reflect the sale.

Exhibit 11-9

Spreadsheet to Prepare Statement of Cash Flows

	A	B	C	D	E	F	G
1		Brooke Sportswear					
2		Spreadsheet to Prepare the Statement of Cash Flows					
3		For the Year Ended December 31, 2009					
4							
5		Beginning		Adjustments			Ending
6		Balance		Debit	Credit		Balance
7	**Balance Sheet Accounts**						
8	Cash	13,000	(r)	2,000			15,000
9	Accounts receivable	46,000	(g)	7,000			53,000
10	Prepaid insurance	2,000			1,000	(h)	1,000
11	Inventory	51,000	(i)	12,000			63,000
12	Land	325,000					325,000
13	Equipment	210,000	(d)	53,000	20,000	(c)	243,000
14	Accumulated depreciation	150,000	(c)	12,000	40,000	(b)	178,000
15	Investments	41,000	(f)	28,000	16,000	(e)	53,000
16							
17	Accounts payable	17,000	(j)	4,000			13,000
18	Wages payable	2,000			1,500	(k)	3,500
19	Interest payable	1,000			500	(l)	1,500
20	Income taxes payable	6,000	(m)	3,000			3,000
21	Notes payable	115,000	(n)	35,000	29,000	(o)	109,000
22	Common stock	151,000			14,000	(p)	165,000
23	Retained earnings	246,000	(q)	5,000	39,000	(a)	280,000
24							
25	**Statement of Cash Flows**						
26	Cash flow from opeating activities						
27	Net income		(a)	39,000			
28	Adjustments to reconcile net						
29	income to net cash flow from						
30	operating activities						
31	Depreciation expense		(b)	40,000			
32	Loss on sale of equipment		(c)	6,000			
33	Gain on sale of investments				15,000	(e)	
34	Increase in accounts receivable				7,000	(g)	
35	Decrease in prepaid insurance		(h)	1,000			
36	Increase in inventory				12,000	(i)	
37	Decrease in accounts payable				4,000	(j)	
38	Increase in wages payable		(k)	1,500			
39	Increase in interest payable		(l)	500			
40	Decrease in income taxes payable				3,000	(m)	
41							
42	Cash flows from investing activities						
43	Sale of equipment		(c)	2,000			
44	Purchase equipment				53,000	(d)	
45	Sale of investments		(e)	31,000			
46	Purchase of investment				28,000	(f)	
47							
48	Cash flows from financing activities						
49	Repaid note payable				35,000	(n)	
50	Issued note payable		(o)	29,000			
51	Issued common stock		(p)	14,000			
52	Paid dividend				5,000	(q)	
53							
54	Net change in cash				2,000	(r)	
55							
56				325,000	325,000		
57							
58							

f. The actual proceeds from the sale of the investment are shown as a cash inflow in the investing activities section. At this point, note that the beginning and ending balances of the investment account are reconciled.

The next seven items represent adjustment for changes in current assets and current liabilities.

g. The increase in accounts receivable is subtracted from net income and reconciles the change in the accounts receivable account.
h. The decrease in prepaid insurance is added to net income and reconciles the change in the prepaid insurance account.
i. The increase in inventory is subtracted from net income and reconciles the change in the inventory account.
j. The decrease in accounts payable is subtracted from net income and reconciles the change in the accounts payable account.
k. The increase in wages payable is added to net income and reconciles the change in the wages payable account.
l. The increase in interest payable is added to net income and reconciles the change in the interest payable account.
m. The decrease in income taxes payable is subtracted from net income and reconciles the change in the income taxes payable account.

The next four items represent the cash inflows and outflows associated with financing activities.

n. The repayment of the notes payable is a cash outflow from a financing activity and adjusts the notes payable account.
o. The issuance of a notes payable is a cash inflow from a financing activity and reconciles the change in the notes payable account.
p. The issuance of common stock is a cash inflow from a financing activity and reconciles the change in the common stock account.
q. The payment of dividends is a cash outflow from a financing activity and, together with the first entry, item (a), reconciles the change in retained earnings. The final entry reconciles the cash balance.
r. The summation of the three sections of the statement of cash flows equals the change in cash for the period. This amount can be checked by summing the net cash flows from operating, investing, and financing activities computed in the previous steps.

The statement of cash flows can now be prepared from the information developed in the statement of cash flows portion of the spreadsheet. The statement of cash flows for Brooke Sportswear is shown in Exhibit 11-8 (page 576).

Appendix 11B: Summary of Learning Objectives

LO9.   Use a spreadsheet to prepare the statement of cash flows.
- A spreadsheet provides a means of systematically analyzing changes in the balance sheet amounts, along with the information from the income statement and any additional information, to produce a statement of cash flows.

Review Problem

The Statement of Cash Flows

Concept:

The statement of cash flows measures a company's inflows (sources) and outflows (uses) of cash during a period of time. These cash inflows and cash outflows are classified as operating, investing, and financing activities.

Information:

The income statement and comparative balance sheet for Solar System Company are shown below.

Solar System Company
Balance Sheets
December 31, 2009 and 2008

ASSETS	2009	2008
Current assets:		
Cash	$ 56,000	$ 47,000
Accounts receivable	123,000	107,000
Prepaid expenses	10,000	9,000
Inventory	52,000	46,000
Total current assets	$ 241,000	$ 209,000
Property, plant, and equipment:		
Equipment	270,000	262,000
Accumulated depreciation	(118,000)	(109,000)
Total assets	$ 393,000	$ 362,000

LIABILITIES AND EQUITY		
Current liabilities:		
Accounts payable	$ 18,000	$ 11,000
Salaries payable	5,000	9,000
Income taxes payable	7,000	5,000
Total current liabilities	$ 30,000	$ 25,000
Long-term liabilities:		
Notes payable	120,000	130,000
Total liabilities	$ 150,000	$ 155,000
Equity:		
Common stock	$ 213,000	$ 200,000
Retained earnings	30,000	7,000
Total stockholders' equity	$ 243,000	$ 207,000
Total liabilities and equity	$ 393,000	$ 362,000

Solar Systems Company
Income Statement
For the Year Ended December 31, 2009

Sales revenue	$1,339,000
Less: Cost of goods sold	908,000
Gross margin	$ 431,000
Less operating expenses:	
Salaries expense	(230,000)
Depreciation	(24,000)
Other operating expenses	(116,000)
Income from operations	$ 61,000
Other income and expenses:	
Gain on sale of equipment	3,000
Interest expense	(14,000)
Income before taxes	$ 50,000
Less: Income tax expense	12,000
Net income	$ 38,000

Additional Information:

1. Equipment with a cost of $24,000 and accumulated depreciation of $15,000 was sold for $12,000 cash. Equipment was purchased for $32,000 cash.
2. Notes payable in the amount of $10,000 were repaid.
3. Common stock was issued for $13,000 cash during 2009.
4. Cash dividends of $15,000 were paid during 2009.

Required:

Prepare a statement of cash flows for Solar Systems Company using the indirect method.

Solution:

Statement of Cash Flows
Solar Systems Company
For the Year Ended December 31, 2009

Cash flows from operating activities

Net income	$ 38,000	
Adjustments to reconcile net income to net cash flow from operating activities:		
Depreciation expense	24,000	
Gain on sale of equipment	(3,000)	
Increase in accounts receivable	(16,000)	
Increase in prepaid expenses	(1,000)	
Increase in inventory	(6,000)	
Increase in accounts payable	7,000	
Decrease in salaries payable	(4,000)	
Increase in income taxes payable	2,000	
Net cash provided by operating activities		$ 41,000
Cash flows from investing activities		
Cash received from sale of equipment	$ 12,000	
Purchase of equipment	(32,000)	
Net cash used by investing activities		(20,000)
Cash flows from financing activities		
Cash paid to retire note payable	$(10,000)	
Cash received from issuance of common stock	13,000	
Cash paid for dividends	(15,000)	
Net cash used by financing activities		(12,000)
Net change in cash		$ 9,000
Cash and cash equivalents, 1/1/2009		47,000
Cash and cash equivalents, 12/31/2009		$ 56,000

Discussion Questions

1. What is a statement of cash flows?
2. How do investors, creditors, and others typically use the information in the statement of cash flows?
3. How is a statement of cash flows different from an income statement?
4. What are cash equivalents? How are cash equivalents reported on the statement of cash flows?
5. What are the three categories into which inflows and outflows of cash are divided? Be sure to describe what is included in each of these three categories.
6. Why are companies required to report noncash investing and financing activities? How are these activities reported?
7. Why are direct exchanges of long-term debt for items of property, plant, and equipment included in supplementary information for the statement of cash flows even though the exchanges do not affect cash?
8. Describe the relationship between changes in cash and changes in noncash assets, liabilities, and stockholders' equity.
9. What are two ways to report a company's net cash flow from operating activities? Briefly describe the advantages and disadvantages of each method.
10. Why are depreciation, depletion, and amortization added to net income when the indirect method is used to report net cash flows from operating activities?
11. Where do the components of the changes in retained earnings appear in the statement of cash flows? Assume the indirect method is used to prepare the statement of cash flows.

12. How is the sale of equipment at a loss reported on the statement of cash flows? Assume the indirect method is used to prepare the statement of cash flows.
13. What does an increase in inventory imply? How would this increase in inventory be reported under the indirect method?
14. What does an increase in accounts payable imply? How would this increase in accounts payable be reported under the indirect method?
15. Does the fact that the cash flow from operating activities is normally positive imply that cash and cash equivalents usually increase each year?
16. What are the most common sources of cash inflows from financing and investing activities?
17. What are the most common cash outflows related to investing and financing activities?
18. What balance sheet account changes might you expect to find for a company that must rely on sources other than operations to fund its cash outflows?
19. From what source(s) should most companies secure the majority of cash inflows? Why?
20. Why should companies attempt to secure cash for investment in property, plant, and equipment from long-term or permanent sources?
21. When using the direct method, which items usually constitute the largest components of cash inflows from operating activities?
22. Describe how to compute each of the cash inflows and cash outflows from operating activities under the direct method.
23. Why is depreciation expense not generally reported on the statement of cash flows when using the direct method?
24. Why do companies often use a spreadsheet to prepare the statement of cash flows?

Multiple-Choice Exercises

11-1 Which of the following is *not* a use of the statement of cash flows?

a. Aids in the prediction of future cash flow
b. Helps estimate the amount of funds that will be needed from creditors or stock-holders
c. Provides insights into the quality and reliability of reported income
d. Provides a measure of the future obligations of the company

11-2 Which of the following would be classified as a cash outflow from an operating activity?

a. Purchase of an investment
b. Payment of goods purchased from suppliers
c. Payment of dividends
d. Purchase of equipment

11-3 Which of the following is an example of a cash inflow from an operating activity?

a. Collection of an account receivable from a credit sale
b. Collection of cash relating to a note receivable
c. Sale of property, plant, and equipment
d. None of the above

11-4 Which of the following is an example of a cash outflow from a financing activity?

a. Payment of interest on a note payable
b. Payment of cash dividends to stockholders
c. Payment of wages to employees
d. Issuance of common stock for cash

11-5 Which of the following is *true*?

a. A decrease in cash may result from an increase in liabilities
b. An increase in cash may result from a decrease in stockholders' equity
c. An increase in cash may result from an increase in noncash assets
d. An increase in cash may result from an increase in liabilities

11-6 Which of the following statements is *true*?

a. Many companies prefer the indirect method because it is easier and less costly to prepare.
b. Cash flow from operating activities must be prepared using the indirect method.
c. The indirect method adjusts sales for changes in noncash items to produce net cash flow from operating activities.
d. The FASB prefers the indirect method.

11-7 Mullinix Inc. reported the following information: net income, $45,000; increase in accounts receivable, $10,000; increase in accounts payable $8,000; and depreciation expense, $3,000. What amount did Mullinix report as cash flow from operating activities on its statement of cash flows?

a. $24,000
b. $30,000
c. $40,000
d. $46,000

11-8 Which item is added to net income when computing cash flows from operating activities?

a. Gain on the sale of property, plant, and equipment
b. Increase in wages payable
c. Increase in inventory
d. Increase in prepaid rent

11-9 Cornett Company reported the following information: cash received from the issuance of common stock, $125,400; cash received from the sale of equipment, $23,700; cash paid to purchase an investment, $13,500; cash paid to retire a note payable, $50,000; cash collected from sales to customers, $248,000. What amount should Cornett report on its statement of cash flows as net cash flows from investing activities?

a. $10,200
b. $75,400
c. $85,600
d. None of the above

11-10 Use the same information as in Multiple-Choice Exercise 11-9. What amount should Cornett report on its statement of cash flows as net cash flows from financing activities?

a. $10,200
b. $75,400
c. $85,600
d. None of the above

11-11 Chasse Building Supply Inc. reported net cash provided by operating activities of $256,000, capital expenditures of $124,900, cash dividends of $33,200, and average maturities of long-term debt over the next five years of $134,300. What is Chasse's free cash flow and cash flow adequacy ratio?

a. $97,900 and 0.73, respectively
b. $97,900 and 1.91, respectively
c. $131,100 and 0.98, respectively
d. $164,300 and 1.22, respectively

11-12 Smoltz Company reported the following information for the current year: cost of goods sold, $347,000; increase in inventory, $14,700; and increase in accounts payable, $8,200. What is the amount of cash paid to suppliers that Smoltz would report on its statement of cash flows under the direct method?

a. $324,100
b. $340,500
c. $353,500
d. $369,900

11-13 Romo Inc. reported the following information for the current year: operating expenses, $210,000; decrease in prepaid expenses, $4,900; and increase in accrued liabilities, $6,100. What is the amount of cash paid for operating expenses that Romo would report on its statement of cash flows under the direct method?

a. $199,000
b. $208,800
c. $211,200
d. $221,000

Cornerstone Exercises

OBJECTIVE ▶ 2
CORNERSTONE 11-1

Cornerstone Exercise 11-14 CLASSIFICATION OF CASH FLOWS

Stanfield Inc. reported the following items in its statement of cash flows presented using the indirect method.

a. Purchased equipment for cash
b. Depreciation expense
c. Declared and paid a cash dividend to stockholders
d. Decrease in inventory
e. Issued long-term debt
f. Sold a building for cash

Required:

Indicate whether each item should be classified as a cash flow from operating activities, a cash flow from investing activities, or a cash flow from financing activities.

OBJECTIVE ▶ 2
CORNERSTONE 11-1

Cornerstone Exercise 11-15 CLASSIFICATION OF CASH FLOWS

Patel Company reported the following items in its statement of cash flows presented using the indirect method.

a. Sold equipment for cash
b. Issuance of common stock
c. Cash paid for interest
d. Repayment of principal on long-term debt
e. Loss on sale of equipment.
f. Receipt of cash dividend on investment

Required:

Indicate whether each item should be classified as a cash flow from operating activities, a cash flow from investing activities, or a cash flow from financing activities.

OBJECTIVE ▶ 3
CORNERSTONE 11-2

Cornerstone Exercise 11-16 ANALYZING THE ACCOUNTS

A review of the balance sheet of Peterson Inc. revealed the following changes in the account balances:

a. Decrease in long-term investment
b. Decrease in accounts receivable
c. Increase in common stock
d. Increase in long-term debt

e. Decrease in accounts payable
f. Decrease in supplies inventory
g. Increase in prepaid insurance
h. Decrease in retained earnings

Required:

Indicate whether each of the changes above produces a cash inflow, a cash outflow, or is a noncash activity.

Cornerstone Exercise 11-17 CLASSIFICATION OF CASH FLOWS

Refer to the information in **Cornerstone Exercise 11-16.**

Required:

Classify each change in the balance sheet account as a cash flow from operating activities (indirect method), a cash flow from investing activities, a cash flow from financing activities, or a noncash investing and financing activity.

Cornerstone Exercise 11-18 COMPUTING NET CASH FLOW FROM OPERATING ACTIVITIES

An analysis of the balance sheet and income statement of Sanchez Company revealed the following: net income, $15,400; depreciation expense, $45,000: decrease in accounts receivable, $32,500: increase in inventory, $12,100: increase in accounts payable, $15,200: and a decrease in interest payable of $800.

Required:

Compute the net cash flows from operating activities using the indirect method.

Cornerstone Exercise 11-19 COMPUTING NET CASH FLOW FROM OPERATING ACTIVITIES

Brandon Inc. reported the following items in its balance sheet and income statement: net income, $85,600; gain on sale of equipment, $12,800; increase in accounts receivable, $15,400; decrease in accounts payable, $25,900, and increase in common stock, $40,000.

Required:

Compute the net cash flows from operating activities using the indirect method.

Cornerstone Exercise 11-20 COMPUTING NET CASH FLOW FROM INVESTING ACTIVITIES

Davis Inc. reported the following information for equipment:

	12/31/2009	12/31/2008
Equipment	$160,000	$115,000
Accumulated depreciation	(85,000)	(59,000)
Long-term investment	10,000	14,600

In addition, Davis sold equipment costing $10,000 with accumulated depreciation of $8,000 for $2,200 cash, producing a $200 gain. Davis reported net income for 2009 of $110,000.

Required:

Compute net cash flow from investing activities.

Cornerstone Exercise 11-21 COMPUTING NET CASH FLOW FROM FINANCING ACTIVITIES

Hebert Company reported the following information for 2009:

Repaid long-term debt	$30,000
Paid interest on note payable	1,200
Issued common stock	50,000
Paid dividends	5,000

Required:

Compute net cash flow from financing activities.

OBJECTIVE ▸ 2
CORNERSTONE 11-1

OBJECTIVE ▸ 4
CORNERSTONE 11-3

OBJECTIVE ▸ 4
CORNERSTONE 11-3

OBJECTIVE ▸ 5
CORNERSTONE 11-4

OBJECTIVE ▸ 6
CORNERSTONE 11-5

OBJECTIVE ▶ 7
CORNERSTONE 11-6

Cornerstone Exercise 11-22 ANALYZING THE STATEMENT OF CASH FLOWS

Rollins Inc. is considering expanding its operations into different regions of the country; however this expansion will require significant cash flow as well as additional financing. Rollins reported the following information for 2009: cash provided by operating activities, $425,000; cash provided by investing activities, $115,000; average debt maturing over the next five years, $380,000; capital expenditures, $240,000; dividends, $40,000.

Required:

Compute free cash flow and the cash flow adequacy ratio. Comment on Rollins' ability to expand its operations.

OBJECTIVE ▶ 8
CORNERSTONE 11-7

Cornerstone Exercise 11-23 (APPENDIX 11A) CASH RECEIPTS FROM CUSTOMERS

Singleton Inc. had accounts receivable of $365,000 at January 1, 2009, and $410,000 at December 31, 2009. Net income for 2009 was $550,000 and sales revenue was $925,000.

Required:

Compute the amount of cash collected from customers.

OBJECTIVE ▶ 8
CORNERSTONE 11-7

Cornerstone Exercise 11-24 (APPENDIX 11A) CASH PAYMENTS TO SUPPLIERS

Blackmon Company reported net income of $805,000 and cost of goods sold of $1,525,000 on its 2009 income statement. In addition, Blackmon reported an increase in inventory of $65,000, a decrease in prepaid insurance of $12,000, and a decrease in accounts payable of $51,000.

Required:

Compute the amount of cash payments to suppliers.

OBJECTIVE ▶ 8
CORNERSTONE 11-7

Cornerstone Exercise 11-25 (APPENDIX 11A) CASH PAYMENTS FOR OPERATING EXPENSES

Luna Inc. reported operating expenses of $130,000, excluding depreciation expense of $36,000 for 2009. During 2009, Luna reported a decrease in prepaid expenses of $12,500 and a decrease in accrued liabilities of $18,200.

Required:

Compute the amount of cash payments for operating expenses.

Exercises

OBJECTIVE ▶ 2

Exercise 11-26 CLASSIFICATION OF CASH FLOWS

A review of the financial records for Rogers, Inc., uncovered the following items:

a. Received cash from the issuance of bonds
b. Collected accounts receivable
c. Paid cash to purchase equipment
d. Paid rent on building for the current period
e. Issued common stock for land
f. Paid interest on long-term debt
g. Depreciation on equipment
h. Declared and paid dividends to stockholders
i. Sold equipment at book value
j. Paid cash to settle an accounts payable
k. Received cash dividend on investment
l. Amortization of a copyright
m. Repaid the principal amount of long-term debt
n. Sold a long-term investment at a gain

Rogers, Inc., uses the indirect method to prepare the operating activities of its statement of cash flows.

Required:

Indicate whether each item should be classified as a cash flow from operating activities, a cash flow from investing activities, a cash flow from financing activities, or a noncash investing and financing activity.

Exercise 11-27 CLASSIFICATION OF CASH FLOWS

The following are several items that might be disclosed on a company's statement of cash flows presented using the indirect method.

a. Depreciation expense
b. Issuance of common stock
c. Net income
d. Loss on sale of equipment
e. Converted bonds into common stock
f. Purchase of a building
g. Decrease in accounts payable
h. Increase in inventory
i. Sale of long-term investment
j. Payment of interest

Required:

Indicate whether each item should be classified as a cash flow from operating activities, a cash flow from investing activities, a cash flow from financing activities, or a noncash investing and financing activity.

Exercise 11-28 ANALYZING THE ACCOUNTS

A review of the balance sheet of Mathews Company revealed the following changes in the account balances:

a. Increase in accounts receivable
b. Increase in retained earnings
c. Decrease in salaries payable
d. Increase in common stock
e. Decrease in inventory
f. Increase in accounts payable
g. Decrease in long-term debt
h. Increase in property, plant, and equipment

Required:

1. For each of the above items, indicate whether it produces a cash inflow or a cash outflow.
2. Classify each change as a cash flow from operating activities (indirect method), a cash flow from investing activities, or a cash flow from financing activities.

Exercise 11-29 ANALYZING THE ACCOUNTS

OBJECTIVE ▶ 3

Casey Company engaged in the following transactions:

a. Made credit sales of $600,000. The cost of the merchandise sold was $410,000
b. Collected accounts receivable in the amount of $580,000
c. Purchased goods on credit in the amount of $425,000
d. Paid accounts payable in the amount of $392,000

Required:

Recreate the journal entries necessary to record the transactions. Indicate whether each transaction increased cash, decreased cash, or had no effect on cash.

OBJECTIVE ▶ 3

Exercise 11-30 ANALYZING THE ACCOUNTS

The controller for Summit Sales, Inc., provides the following information on transactions that occurred during the year:

a. Purchased supplies on credit, $30,000
b. Paid $22,600 cash toward the purchase in transaction *a*
c. Provided services to customers on credit, $37,800
d. Collected $47,000 cash from accounts receivable
e. Recorded depreciation expense, $7,350
f. Employees earned salaries, $9,200
g. Paid $9,200 cash to employees for salaries earned
h. Accrued interest expense on long-term debt, $2,400
i. Paid a total of $15,000 on long-term debt, that includes $2,400 interest from transaction *h*
j. Paid $1,850 cash for one-year's insurance coverage in advance
k. Recognized insurance expense, $925, that was paid in a previous period
l. Sold old equipment with a book value of $3,900 for $3,900 cash
m. Declared cash dividend, $5,000
n. Paid cash dividend declared in transaction *m*
o. Purchased new equipment for $14,300 cash
p. Issued common stock for $20,000 cash
q. Used $28,100 of supplies to produce revenues

Summit Sales, Inc., uses the indirect method to prepare its statement of cash flows.

Required:

1. Construct a table similar to the one shown. Analyze each transaction and indicate its effect on the fundamental accounting equation. If the transaction increases a financial statement element, write the amount of the increase preceded by a plus sign (+) in the appropriate column. If the transaction decreases a financial statement element, write the amount of the decrease preceded by a minus sign (−) in the appropriate column.
2. Indicate whether each transaction results in a cash inflow or a cash outflow in the "Effect on Cash Flows" column. If the transaction has no effect on cash flow, then indicate this by placing "none" in the "Effect on Cash Flows" column.
3. For each transaction that affected cash flows, indicate whether the cash flow would be classified as a cash flow from operating activities, a cash flow from investing activities, or a cash flow from financing activities. If there is no effect on cash flows, indicate this as a noncash activity.

| | Effect on Accounting Equation | | | | | |
| | Assets | | Liabilities and Equity | | | |
Transaction	Current	Noncurrent	Current Liabilities	Noncurrent Liabilities	Equity	Effect on Cash Flows

OBJECTIVE ▶ 4

Exercise 11-31 REPORTING NET CASH FLOW FROM OPERATING ACTIVITIES

The following information is available for Cornelius Inc.:

Selected Income Statement Information	Amount
Depreciation expense	$11,000
Net income	38,000

Selected Balance Sheet Information	Beginning Balance	Ending Balance
Accounts receivable	$21,000	$27,000
Inventory	47,000	43,000
Accounts payable	24,000	32,000

Required:

1. Prepare the net cash flows from operating activities using the indirect method.
2. Explain why Cornelius was able to report net cash flow from operating activities that was higher than net income. Explain why this is important to financial statement users.

Exercise 11-32 REPORTING NET CASH FLOW FROM OPERATING ACTIVITIES

OBJECTIVE ➤ 4

The following information is available for Bernard Corporation:

Net income	$206,000
Decrease in accounts receivable	4,900
Increase in inventory	15,300
Decrease in prepaid rent	2,100
Increase in salaries payable	14,400
Increase in income taxes payable	11,200
Increase in notes payable	20,000
Depreciation expense	42,000
Loss on sale of equipment	5,000

Required:

1. Prepare the net cash flows from operating activities using the indirect method.
2. What are the causes of the major differences between net income and net cash flow from operating activities?

Exercise 11-33 DETERMINING CASH FLOWS FROM INVESTING ACTIVITIES

OBJECTIVE ➤ 5

Burns Company's 2009 and 2008 balance sheets presented the following data for equipment:

	12/31/2009	12/31/2008
Equipment	$260,000	$225,000
Accumulated depreciation	115,000	92,000
Book value	$145,000	$133,000

During 2009, equipment costing $35,000 with accumulated depreciation of $30,000 was sold for cash, producing a $4,400 gain.

Required:

1. Calculate the amount of depreciation expense for 2009.
2. Calculate the amount of cash spent for equipment during 2009.
3. Calculate the amount that should be included as a cash inflow from the sale of equipment.

Exercise 11-34 DETERMINING CASH FLOWS FROM INVESTING ACTIVITIES

OBJECTIVE ➤ 5

Airco owns several aircraft and its balance sheet indicated the following amounts for its aircraft accounts at the end of 2009 and 2008:

	12/31/2009	12/31/2008
Equipment, aircraft	$28,500,000	$21,750,000
Accumulated depreciation	11,900,000	10,100,000
Book value	$16,600,000	$11,650,000

Required:

1. Assume that Airco did not sell any aircraft during 2009. Determine the amount of depreciation expense for 2009 and the cash spent for aircraft purchases in 2009.
2. If Airco sold for cash aircraft that cost $4,100,000 with accumulated depreciation of $3,500,000, producing a gain of $300,000, determine (a) the amount of depreciation expense, (b) the cash paid for aircraft purchases in 2009 and (c) the cash inflow from the sale of aircraft.

OBJECTIVE ▶ 6

Exercise 11-35 DETERMINING CASH FLOWS FROM FINANCING ACTIVITIES

Solomon Construction Company reported the following amount on its balance sheet at the end of 2009 and 2008 for notes payable:

	12/31/2009	12/31/2008
Notes payable	$180,000	$150,000

Required:

1. If Solomon did not repay any notes payable during 2009, determine how much cash Solomon received from the issuance of notes payable.
2. If Solomon repaid $60,000 of notes payable during 2009, determine what amounts Solomon would report in the financing activities section of the statement of cash flows.

OBJECTIVE ▶ 6

Exercise 11-36 DETERMINING CASH FLOWS FROM FINANCING ACTIVITIES

Nichols Inc. reported the following amounts on its balance sheet at the end of 2009 and 2008 for equity:

	12/31/2009	12/31/2008
Common stock	$130,000	$110,000
Retained earnings	458,000	385,000

Required:

Assume that Nichols did not retire any stock during 2009, it reported $94,000 of net income for 2009, and any dividends declared were paid in cash. Determine the amounts Nichols would report in the financing section of the statement of cash flows.

OBJECTIVE ▶ 4 5 6

Exercise 11-37 PARTIAL STATEMENT OF CASH FLOWS

Service Company had net income during the current year of $111,000. The following information was obtained from the balance sheet of Service Company:

Accounts receivable	$20,000 increase
Inventory	25,000 increase
Accounts payable	16,000 decrease
Interest payable	9,000 increase
Accumulated depreciation, equipment*	27,000 increase
Accumulated depreciation, building	12,000 increase
Retained earnings**	

* Equipment with accumulated depreciation of $15,000 was sold during the year.
** Includes net income of $111,000 and cash dividends paid of $36,000

Required:

1. Prepare the net cash flows from operating activities using the indirect method.
2. How would the cash proceeds from the sale of equipment be reported on the statement of cash flows?
3. How would the cash dividends be reported on the statement of cash flows?

OBJECTIVE ▶ 7

Exercise 11-38 ANALYZING THE STATEMENT OF CASH FLOWS

Information for Ditka Inc. and McMahon Company is given below:

	Ditka Inc	McMahon Company
Cash provided by operating activities	$2,475,000	$1,639,000
Capital expenditures	1,157,000	748,000
Dividends	285,000	189,000
Average debt maturity over next 5 years	1,988,000	1,212,000

Required:

Compare Ditka Inc. and McMahon Company by computing and analyzing the following cash-based performance measures for each company: (a) free cash flow and (b) cash flow adequacy ratio.

Exercise 11-39 PREPARING THE STATEMENT OF CASH FLOWS

OBJECTIVE ▸ 4 5 6 7

The comparative balance sheets for Beckwith Products Company are presented below.

	2009	2008
Assets:		
Cash	$ 36,400	$ 25,000
Accounts receivable	63,000	78,000
Inventory	45,300	36,000
Property, plant, and equipment	221,000	153,000
Accumulated depreciation	(30,000)	(20,000)
Total assets	$335,700	$272,000
Liabilities and Equity:		
Accounts payable	$ 13,100	$ 11,000
Interest payable	13,500	8,000
Wages payable	4,100	9,000
Notes payable	75,000	90,000
Common stock	90,000	50,000
Retained earnings	140,000	104,000
Total liabilities and equity	$335,700	$272,000

Additional information:

1. Net income for 2009 was $52,000.
2. Cash dividends of $16,000 were declared and paid during 2009.
3. During 2009, Beckwith issued $20,000 of notes payable and repaid $35,000 principal relating to notes payable.
4. Common stock was issued for $40,000 cash.
5. Depreciation expense was $10,000, and there were no disposals of equipment.

Required:

1. Prepare a statement of cash flows (indirect method) for Beckwith Products for 2009.
2. Compute the following cash-based performance measures:
   a. Free cash flow
   b. Cash flow adequacy (assume that the average amount of debt maturing over the next five years is $85,000).
3. List the major reasons for the difference between net income and net cash flow from operating activities.

Exercise 11-40 (APPENDIX 11A) PREPARING NET CASH FLOWS FROM OPERATING ACTIVITIES—DIRECT METHOD

OBJECTIVE ▸ 8

Colassard Industries has the following data available for preparation of its statement of cash flows:

Sales revenue	$345,000	Inventory, increase	$ 9,700
Cost of goods sold	182,500	Prepaid insurance, increase	6,100
Wages expense	34,400	Accounts payable, increase	11,600
Insurance expense	12,000	Notes payable, increase	32,000
Interest expense	20,800	Interest payable, increase	5,000
Income taxes expense	16,200	Wages payable, decrease	5,400
Accounts receivable, decrease	14,300		

Required:

Prepare the cash flows from operating activities section of the statement of cash flows, using the direct method.

OBJECTIVE ➤ 8

Exercise 11-41 (APPENDIX 11A) PREPARING A STATEMENT OF CASH FLOWS—DIRECT METHOD

The controller of Newstrom Software, Inc., provides the following information as the basis for a statement of cash flows:

Cash collected from customers	$794,000
Cash paid for interest	22,100
Cash paid to employees and other suppliers of goods and services	215,000
Cash paid to suppliers of merchandise	388,000
Cash received from the issuance of long-term debt	12,700
Cash received from sale of equipment	44,000
Cash received from sale of long-term investments	71,400
Income taxes paid	58,300
Payment of dividends	24,000
Principal payments on mortgage payable	50,000
Principal payments on long-term debt	15,000
Proceeds from the issuance of common stock	85,000
Purchase of equipment	120,000
Purchase of long-term investments	83,000

Required:

1. Using the information provided above, calculate the net cash provided (used) by operating activities.
2. Using the information provided above, calculate the net cash provided (used) by investing activities.
3. Using the information provided above, calculate the net cash provided (used) by financing activities.

OBJECTIVE ➤ 8

Exercise 11-42 (APPENDIX 11A) PREPARING A STATEMENT OF CASH FLOWS—DIRECT METHOD

Financial statements for Rowe Publishing Company are presented below.

Rowe Publishing Company
Balance Sheets
December 31, 2009 and 2008

ASSETS	2009		2008	
Current assets:				
Cash		$ 85,000		$ 66,000
Accounts receivable		240,000		231,000
Inventory		190,000		170,000
Total current assets		$515,000		$467,000
Property, plant, and equipment:				
Building	$ 400,000		$ 400,000	
Equipment	155,000		130,000	
	$ 555,000		$ 530,000	
Accumulated depreciation	(375,000)		(350,000)	
Net property, plant, and equipment		180,000		180,000
Total assets		$695,000		$647,000

LIABILITIES AND EQUITY	2009		2008	
Current liabilities:				
Accounts payable	$ 133,000		$ 121,000	
Salaries payable	15,000		11,000	
Income taxes payable	10,000		17,000	
Total current liabilities		$158,000		$149,000
Long-term liabilities:				
Notes payable	$ 115,000		$ 150,000	
Bonds payable	50,000		0	
Total long-term liabilities		165,000		$150,000
Total liabilities		$323,000		$299,000
Equity:				
Common stock	$ 300,000		$ 300,000	
Retained earnings	72,000		48,000	
Total equity		372,000		348,000
Total liabilities and equity		$695,000		$647,000

Rowe Publishing Company
Income Statement
For the Year Ended December 31, 2009

Sales		$1,051,000
Less: Cost of goods sold		578,000
Gross margin		$ 473,000
Less operating expenses:		
Salaries	$351,000	
Depreciation	25,000	376,000
Income from operations		$ 97,000
Less: Interest expense		16,000
Income before taxes		$ 81,000
Less: Income tax expense		22,000
Net income		$ 59,000

Additional information:

a. No buildings nor equipment were sold during 2009. Equipment was purchased for $25,000 cash.

b. Notes payable in the amount of $35,000 were repaid during 2009.

c. Bonds payable of $50,000 were issued for cash during 2009.

d. Rowe Publishing declared and paid dividends of $35,000 during 2009.

Required:

Prepare a statement of cash flows for 2009, using the direct method to determine net cash flow from operating activities.

Exercise 11-43 (APPENDIX 11B) USING A SPREADSHEET TO PREPARE A STATEMENT OF CASH FLOWS

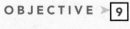

Comparative balance sheets for Cincinnati Health Club are presented below.

Cincinnati Health Club
Balance Sheets
December 31, 2009 and 2008

ASSETS	2009	2008
Current assets:		
Cash	$ 5,300	$ 9,200
Accounts receivable	10,500	8,900
Inventory	19,800	18,600
Total current assets	$ 35,600	$ 36,700
Property, plant, and equipment:		
Building	$ 490,000	$ 490,000
Equipment	280,000	270,000
	$ 770,000	$ 760,000
Accumulated depreciation	(148,000)	(120,000)
Net property, plant, and equipment	622,000	640,000
Total assets	$657,600	$676,700

LIABILITIES AND EQUITY		
Current liabilities:		
Accounts payable	$ 55,300	$ 36,100
Salaries payable	9,500	11,700
Income taxes payable	1,100	9,900
Total current liabilities	$ 65,900	$ 57,700
Long-term liabilities:		
Bonds payable	350,000	400,000
Total liabilities	$415,900	$457,700
Equity:		
Common stock	$ 180,000	$ 150,000
Retained earnings	61,700	69,000
Total equity	241,700	219,000
Total liabilities and equity	$657,600	$676,700

Additional information:

a. Cincinnati Health Club reported net income of $2,700 for 2009.
b. No buildings nor equipment were sold during 2009. Equipment was purchased for $10,000 cash.
c. Depreciation expense for 2009 was $28,000.
d. Bonds payable of $50,000 were issued for cash during 2009.
e. Common stock of $30,000 was issued during 2009.
f. Cash dividends of $10,000 were declared and paid during 2009.

Required:

Using a spreadsheet, prepare a statement of cash flows for 2009. Assume Cincinnati Health Club uses the indirect method.

Problem Set A

OBJECTIVE ▶ 2 3

Problem 11-44A CLASSIFYING AND ANALYZING BUSINESS ACTIVITIES

CTT Inc. reported the following business activities during 2009:

a. Purchased merchandise inventory for cash
b. Recorded depreciation on property, plant, and equipment
c. Purchased merchandise inventory on credit

d. Collected cash sales from customers
e. Purchased a two-year insurance policy for cash
f. Paid salaries of employees
g. Borrowed cash by issuing a note payable
h. Sold property, plant, and equipment for cash
i. Paid cash dividends
j. Purchased property, plant, and equipment for cash
k. Issued common stock
l. Paid cash for principal amount of mortgage
m. Paid interest on mortgage

Required:

1. Indicate whether each activity should be classified as a cash flow from operating activities, a cash flow from investing activities, a cash flow from financing activities, or a noncash investing and financing activity. Assume that CTT Inc. uses the indirect method.
2. For each activity that is reported on the statement of cash flows, indicate whether each activity produces a cash inflow, a cash outflow, or has no cash effect.

Problem 11-45A REPORTING NET CASH FLOW FROM OPERATING ACTIVITIES

OBJECTIVE ➤ 4

The income statement for Granville Manufacturing Company is presented below.

Granville Manufacturing Company
Income Statement
For the Year Ended December 31, 2009

Sales		$4,200,000
Cost of goods sold		1,720,000
Gross margin		$2,480,000
Operating expenses:		
Salaries expense	$720,000	
Administrative expense	131,000	
Bad debt expense	156,000	
Depreciation expense	610,000	
Other expenses	255,000	1,872,000
Net income		$ 608,000

The following balance sheet changes occurred during the year:

- Accounts receivable increased by $900,000.
- Inventory decreased by $110,000.
- Prepaid expenses increased by $49,000.
- Accounts payable increased by $132,000.
- Salaries payable decreased by $58,000.

Required:

1. Prepare the net cash flows from operating activities using the indirect method.
2. What are the causes of the major differences between net income and net cash flow from operating activities.

Problem 11-46A CLASSIFICATION OF CASH FLOWS

OBJECTIVE ➤ 2 3 4

Rolling Meadows Country Club, Inc., is a privately owned corporation that operates a golf club. Rolling Meadows reported the following inflows and outflows of cash during 2009:

Net income	$106,000
Decrease in accounts receivable, dues	4,000
Increase in pro shop inventory	28,600

Increase in prepaid insurance	$ 15,800
Increase in accounts payable	11,400
Decrease in wages payable	10,400
Increase in income taxes payable	7,500
Cash paid for new golf carts	123,000
Cash received from sale of used golf carts	7,000
Depreciation expense, buildings	49,000
Depreciation expense, golf carts	23,000
Proceeds from issuance of note payable	35,000
Payment on mortgage payable	45,000
Cash received from issuance of common stock	38,500
Payment of cash dividends	40,000

Rolling Meadows had cash on hand at 1/1/09 of $10,300.

Required:

Prepare a properly formatted statement of cash flows using the indirect method.

OBJECTIVE  **Problem 11-47A PREPARING A STATEMENT OF CASH FLOWS**

Erie Company reported the following comparative balance sheets for 2009:

	2009	2008
Assets:		
Cash	$ 33,200	$ 12,000
Accounts receivable	53,000	45,000
Inventory	29,500	27,500
Prepaid rent	2,200	6,200
Long-term investments	17,600	31,800
Property, plant, and equipment	162,000	150,000
Accumulated depreciation	(61,600)	(56,200)
Total assets	$235,900	$216,300
Liabilities and Equity:		
Accounts payable	$ 16,900	$ 18,000
Interest payable	3,500	4,800
Wages payable	9,600	7,100
Income taxes payable	5,500	3,600
Notes payable	28,000	53,000
Common stock	100,000	70,000
Retained earnings	72,400	59,800
Total liabilities and equity	$235,900	$216,300

Additional information:
a. Net income for 2009 was $20,500.
b. Cash dividends of $7,900 were declared and paid during 2009.
c. Long-term investments with a cost of $35,000 were sold for cash at a gain of $4,100. Additional long-term investments were purchased for $20,800 cash.
d. Equipment with a cost of $15,000 and accumulated depreciation of $13,500 was sold for $3,800 cash. New equipment was purchased for $27,000 cash.
e. Depreciation expense was $18,900.
f. A principal payment of $25,000 was made on long-term notes.
g. Common stock was sold for $30,000 cash.

Required:

Prepare a statement of cash flows for Erie, using the indirect method to compute net cash flow from operating activities.

Problem 11-48A **PREPARING A STATEMENT OF CASH FLOWS**

Monon Cable Television Company reported the following financial statements for 2009:

OBJECTIVE ▷ 4 5 6

Monon Cable Television Company
Income Statement
For the Year Ended December 31, 2009

Sales		$519,000
Less operating expenses:		
Royalty expense	$240,000	
Salaries expense	26,000	
Utilities expense	83,000	
Supplies expense	13,000	
Rent expense	79,000	
Depreciation expense	28,000	469,000
Income from operations		$ 50,000
Other income (expenses):		
Gain on sale of antenna	$ 800	
Interest expense	(1,800)	(1,000)
Income before taxes		$ 49,000
Less: Income taxes expense		9,000
Net income		$ 40,000

Monon Cable Television Company
Balance Sheets
December 31, 2009 and 2008

ASSETS	2009		2008	
Current assets:				
Cash		$ 2,000		$ 3,000
Accounts receivable		11,300		11,000
Supplies inventory		1,200		1,700
Total current assets		$ 14,500		$ 15,700
Property, plant, and equipment:				
Antenna	$ 60,000		$ 35,000	
Equipment	210,000		190,000	
Cable system	81,000		75,000	
	$ 351,000		$ 300,000	
Accumulated depreciation	(125,000)		(131,000)	
Net property, plant, and equipment		226,000		169,000
Total assets		$240,500		$184,700

LIABILITIES AND EQUITY				
Current liabilities:				
Accounts payable	$ 6,500		$ 8,000	
Rent payable	4,900		13,600	
Royalties payable	3,300		3,100	
Total current liabilities		$ 14,700		$ 24,700
Long-term liabilities:				
Long-term notes payable		40,000		0
Total liabilities		$ 54,700		$ 24,700
Equity:				
Common stock	$ 100,000		$ 100,000	
Retained earnings	85,800		60,000	
Total equity		185,800		160,000
Total liabilities and equity		$240,500		$184,700

Additional information:

a.   The old antenna with a cost of $35,000 and accumulated depreciation of $34,000 was taken down and sold as scrap for $1,800 cash during 2009. A new antenna was purchased for cash at an installed cost of $60,000.

b.   Additional equipment was purchased for $20,000 cash.

c.   Wiring for 300 additional homes was purchased for $6,000 cash.

d.   Depreciation expense for 2009 was $28,000.

e.   A long-term note payable was issued for $40,000 cash.

f.   Dividends of $14,200 were paid during 2009.

Required:

Prepare a statement of cash flows, using the indirect method to compute net cash flow from operating activities.

OBJECTIVE ➤ 8   Problem 11-49A **(APPENDIX 11A) PREPARING NET CASH FLOWS FROM OPERATING ACTIVITIES—DIRECT METHOD**

Yogurt Plus, a restaurant, collected the following information on inflows and outflows for 2009:

Inflows	
Sales (all for cash)	$379,000
Cash received from sale of common stock	50,000
Proceeds from issuance of long-term notes payable	40,000
Proceeds from sale of used restaurant fixtures	13,000
Proceeds from issuance of short-term note payable	35,000
Notes payable issued in exchange for kitchen equipment	30,000
Outflows	
Cash payments made for merchandise sold	$203,000
Cash payments for operating expenses	125,000
Cash payments for interest	22,000
Cash payments for income taxes	8,000
Purchase of restaurant fixtures for cash	105,000
Principal payment on mortgage	35,000
Payment of dividends	6,000
Cost of kitchen equipment acquired in exchange for note payable	30,000

Yogurt Plus had a cash balance of $21,800 at 1/1/09.

Required:

Prepare a statement of cash flows, using the direct method to determine net cash flow from operating activities.

OBJECTIVE ➤ 8   Problem 11-50A **(APPENDIX 11A) PREPARING NET CASH FLOWS FROM OPERATING ACTIVITIES—DIRECT METHOD**

Refer to the information for Granville Manufacturing Company in Problem 11-45A.

Required:

Prepare the cash flows from operating activities section of the statement of cash flows, using the direct method.

OBJECTIVE ➤ 9   Problem 11-51A **(APPENDIX 11B) USING A SPREADSHEET TO PREPARE A STATEMENT OF CASH FLOWS**

Jane Bahr, a controller of Endicott & Thurston, prepared the following balance sheets at the end of 2009 and 2008:

Endicott & Thurston Associates
Balance Sheets
December 31, 2009 and 2008

ASSETS	2009		2008	
Current assets:				
Cash		$ 2,000		$ 17,000
Accounts receivable		78,000		219,000
Prepaid rent		29,000		104,000
Total current assets		$109,000		$340,000
Long-term investments		51,000		40,000
Property, plant, and equipment:				
Equipment, computing	$ 488,000		$ 362,000	
Equipment, office furniture	400,000		365,000	
	$ 888,000		$ 727,000	
Accumulated depreciation	(366,000)		(554,000)	
Net property, plant, and equipment		522,000		173,000
Total assets		$682,000		$553,000

LIABILITIES AND EQUITY				
Current liabilities:				
Accounts payable	$ 56,000		$ 58,000	
Salaries payable	89,000		105,000	
Total current liabilities		$145,000		$163,000
Long-term liabilities:				
Long-term notes payable		80,000		105,000
Bonds payable		140,000		0
Total liabilities		$365,000		$268,000
Equity:				
Common stock	$ 225,000		$ 225,000	
Retained earnings	92,000		60,000	
Total equity		317,000		285,000
Total liabilities and equity		$682,000		$553,000

Additional information:

a. Computing equipment with a cost of $250,000 and accumulated depreciation of $230,000 was sold for $5,000. New computing equipment was purchased for $376,000.

b. New office furniture was purchased at a cost of $35,000.

c. Depreciation expense for 2009 was $42,000.

d. Investments costing $20,000 were sold for cash at a loss of $2,000. Additional investments were purchased for $31,000 cash.

e. A $25,000 principal payment on the long-term note was made during 2009.

f. A portion of the cash needed to purchase computing equipment was secured by issuing bonds payable for $140,000 cash.

g. Net income was $70,000 and dividends were $38,000.

Required:

1. Using a spreadsheet, prepare a statement of cash flows for 2009. Assume Endicott & Thurston use the indirect method.

2. Discuss whether Endicott & Thurston appear to have matched the timing of inflows and outflows of cash.

Problem Set B

OBJECTIVE ▶ 2 3

Problem 11-44B CLASSIFYING AND ANALYZING BUSINESS ACTIVITIES

Cowell Company had the following business activities during 2009:

a. Paid cash for inventory
b. Paid cash dividend to shareholders
c. Issued common stock for cash
d. Purchased equipment for cash
e. Paid interest on long-term debt
f. Acquired land in exchange for common stock
g. Received cash from the sale of merchandise
h. Issued bonds payable in exchange for cash
i. Paid salaries to employees
j. Sold equipment for cash
k. Purchased inventory on account
l. Recorded amortization related to an intangible asset

Cowell Company uses the indirect method to prepare its statement of cash flows.

Required:

1. Indicate whether each activity should be classified as a cash flow from operating activities, a cash flow from investing activities, a cash flow from financing activities, or a noncash investing and financing activity. Assume that Cowell Company uses the indirect method.
2. For each activity that is reported on the statement of cash flows, indicate whether each activity produces a cash inflow, a cash outflow, or has no cash effect.

OBJECTIVE ▶ 4

Problem 11-45B REPORTING NET CASH FLOW FROM OPERATING ACTIVITIES

The income statement for Dunn Products Inc. is presented below.

Dunn Products Inc.
Income Statement
For the Year Ended December 31, 2009

Sales		$3,700,000
Cost of goods sold		2,157,000
Gross margin		$1,543,000
Operating expenses:		
Salaries expense	$358,000	
Administrative expense	147,000	
Bad debt expense	37,000	
Depreciation expense	485,000	
Other expenses	328,000	1,355,000
Net income		$ 188,000

The following balance sheet changes occurred during the year:

- Accounts receivable decreased by $80,000
- Inventory increased by $150,000
- Prepaid expenses increased by $99,000
- Accounts payable decreased by $54,000
- Salaries payable increased by $21,000

Required:

1. Prepare the net cash flows from operating activities using the indirect method.
2. What are the causes of the major differences between net income and net cash flow from operating activities.

Problem 11-46B CLASSIFICATION OF CASH FLOWS

Fannin Company is a manufacturer of premium athletic equipment. Fannin reported the following inflows and outflows of cash during 2009.

Net income	$589,000
Increase in accounts receivable	32,000
Decrease in inventory	59,400
Decrease in prepaid insurance	45,800
Decrease in accounts payable	59,600
Decrease in income taxes payable	11,200
Increase in wages payable	21,600
Cash received from sale of investment	9,000
Cash paid for property, plant, and equipment	102,000
Depreciation expense	103,300
Proceeds from issuance of note payable	55,000
Payment on bonds payable	50,000
Cash received from issuance of common stock	25,000
Payment of cash dividends	55,000

Fannin had cash on hand at 1/1/09 of $218,500.

Required:

Prepare a properly formatted statement of cash flows using the indirect method.

Problem 11-47B PREPARING A STATEMENT OF CASH FLOWS

Volusia Company reported the following comparative balance sheets for 2009:

	2009	2008
Assets:		
Cash	$ 28,100	$ 18,000
Accounts receivable	26,500	32,000
Inventory	24,100	28,200
Prepaid rent	3,900	1,800
Long-term investments	37,200	25,500
Property, plant, and equipment	115,000	102,000
Accumulated depreciation	(47,100)	(38,600)
Total assets	$187,700	$168,900
Liabilities and Equity:		
Accounts payable	$ 24,900	$ 21,200
Interest payable	4,700	3,300
Wages payable	4,600	6,900
Income taxes payable	3,500	5,200
Notes payable	35,000	30,000
Common stock	72,900	65,000
Retained earnings	42,100	37,300
Total liabilities and equity	$187,700	$168,900

Additional information:

1. Net income for 2009 was $15,300.
2. Cash dividends of $10,500 were declared and paid during 2009.
3. Long-term investments with a cost of $18,000 were sold for cash at a loss of $1,500. Additional long-term investments were purchased for $29,700 cash.
4. Equipment with a cost of $20,000 and accumulated depreciation of $16,300 was sold for $4,500 cash. New equipment was purchased for $33,000 cash.
5. Depreciation expense was $24,800.
6. A principal payment of $8,000 was made on long-term notes. Volusia issued notes payable for $13,000 cash.
7. Common stock was sold for $7,900 cash.

Required:

Prepare a statement of cash flows for Volusia, using the indirect method to compute net cash flow from operating activities.

OBJECTIVE ▷ 4 5 6   **Problem 11-48B** **PREPARING A STATEMENT OF CASH FLOWS**

SDPS, Inc., provides airport transportation services in southern California. An income statement for 2009 and balance sheets for 2009 and 2008 appear below.

SDPS, Inc.
Income Statement
For the Year Ended December 31, 2009

Sales		$937,000
Less operating expenses:		
Wages expense	$278,000	
Rent expense	229,000	
Fuel expense	83,000	
Maintenance expense	138,000	
Depreciation expense	215,000	943,000
Income (loss) from operations		$ (6,000)
Other income (expenses):		
Loss on sale of vehicles	$ (3,000)	
Interest expense	(14,000)	(17,000)
Net loss		$ (23,000)

SDPS, Inc.
Balance Sheets
December 31, 2009 and 2008

ASSETS	2009		2008	
Current assets:				
Cash		$ 40,000		$ 82,000
Accounts receivable		126,000		109,000
Inventory, fuel		11,000		25,000
Total current assets		$177,000		$216,000
Property, plant, and equipment:				
Equipment, vehicles	$ 524,000		$ 409,000	
Accumulated depreciation	(174,000)		(136,000)	
Net property, plant, and equipment		350,000		273,000
Total assets		$527,000		$489,000

LIABILITIES AND EQUITY				
Current liabilities:				
Accounts payable	$ 103,000		$ 58,000	
Wages payable	22,000		29,000	
Maintenance service payable	41,000		34,000	
Rent payable	92,000		51,000	
Total current liabilities		$258,000		$172,000
Long-term liabilities:				
Long-term notes payable		100,000		125,000
Total liabilities		$358,000		$297,000
Equity:				
Common stock	$ 150,000		$ 150,000	
Retained earnings	19,000		42,000	
Total equity		169,000		192,000
Total liabilities and equity		$527,000		$489,000

Additional information:

a. Vehicles with a cost of $310,000 and accumulated depreciation of $177,000 were sold for $130,000 cash. New vehicles were purchased for $425,000 cash.

b. A $25,000 principal payment on the long-term note was made during 2009.

c. No dividends were paid during 2009.

Required:

1. Prepare a statement of cash flows, using the indirect method to compute net cash flow from operating activities.

2. Explain what has been responsible for the decrease in cash.

3. Determine whether an examination of the changes in the current liability accounts suggest how SDPS financed its increase in net property, plant, and equipment during a period in which it had a substantial net loss.

Problem 11-49B (APPENDIX 11A) PREPARING NET CASH FLOWS FROM OPERATING ACTIVITIES—DIRECT METHOD

OBJECTIVE ➤ 8

Befuddled Corporation collected the following information on inflows and outflows for 2009:

Inflows	
Cash collections from sales	$941,500
Proceeds from sale of equipment	7,000
Proceeds received from issuance of notes payable	50,000
Outflows	
Cash payments for cost of goods sold	$523,900
Cash payments for operating expenses	173,200
Cash payments for interest	38,600
Cash payments for income taxes	41,300
Cash payments for purchases of equipment	209,000
Repayment of short-term notes payable	15,000
Payment of cash dividends	48,000

Befuddled had a cash balance of $89,200 on 1/1/09.

Required:

Prepare a statement of cash flows, using the direct method to determine net cash flow from operating activities.

Problem 11-50B (APPENDIX 11A) PREPARING NET CASH FLOWS FROM OPERATING ACTIVITIES—DIRECT METHOD

OBJECTIVE ➤ 8

Refer to the information for Dunn Products Inc. in **Problem 11-45B**.

Required:

Prepare the cash flows from operating activities section of the statement of cash flows, using the direct method.

Problem 11-51B (APPENDIX 11B) USING A SPREADSHEET TO PREPARE A STATEMENT OF CASH FLOWS

OBJECTIVE ➤ 9

Fleet Limousine Service Inc. began operations in late March 2009. At the end of 2009, the following balance sheet was prepared for Fleet.

Fleet Limousine Service Inc.
Balance Sheets
December 31, 2009

ASSETS

Current assets:		
Cash	$ 7,200	
Accounts receivable	15,900	
Supplies inventory	3,100	
Total current assets		$ 26,200
Long-term investments		15,000
Property, plant, and equipment:		
Land	$ 11,000	
Building	175,000	
Equipment	233,400	
	$419,400	
Accumulated depreciation	(35,500)	
Net property, plant, and equipment		383,900
Total assets		$425,100

LIABILITIES AND EQUITY

Current liabilities:		
Accounts payable	$ 12,700	
Unearned revenue	21,800	
Salaries payable	4,600	
Rent payable	8,200	
Total current liabilities		$ 47,300
Long-term liabilities:		
Long-term notes payable		95,000
Total liabilities		$142,300
Equity:		
Common stock	$300,000	
Retained earnings	(17,200)	
Total equity		282,800
Total liabilities and equity		$425,100

Additional information:

a. During 2009, land was purchased for $11,000, a building was purchased for $175,000, and equipment was purchased for $233,400.

b. Depreciation expense for 2009 was $35,500.

c. The long-term note was issued for $100,000, and a principal payment of $5,000 was made during 2009.

d. Common stock was issued for $300,000 cash during 2009.

e. During 2009, there was a net loss of 17,200 and no dividends were paid.

Required:

1. Using a spreadsheet, prepare a statement of cash flows for 2009. Assume Fleet Limousine uses the indirect method.

2. Discuss whether Fleet Limousine appears to have matched the timing of inflows and outflows of cash.

Cases

Case 11-52 THE STATEMENT OF CASH FLOWS AND CREDIT ANALYSIS

June's Camera Shop sells cameras and photographic supplies of all types to retail customers. June's also repairs cameras and provides color prints. To compete with other camera departments, June's offers fast, efficient, and effective repairs and photographic processing. For fiscal 2009 and 2008, June's accountant prepared the following statements of cash flows:

June's Camera Shop
Statements of Cash Flows
For the Years Ended January 31, 2009 and 2008

	2009		2008	
Cash flows from operating activities				
Net income		$ 87,000		$ 63,000
Adjustments to reconcile net income to net cash provided by operating activities:				
Increase in accounts receivable	$(17,000)		$(12,000)	
Increase in inventory	(19,000)		(11,000)	
Increase in accounts payable	15,000		14,000	
Increase in wages payable	11,000		5,000	
Increase in income taxes payable	6,000		3,000	
Depreciation expense	41,000		37,000	
Total adjustments		37,000		36,000
Net cash provided by operating activities		$124,000		$ 99,000
Cash flows from investing activities				
Purchase of long-term investments	$(15,000)		$(10,000)	
Purchase of equipment	(45,000)		(40,000)	
Net cash used by investing activities		(60,000)		(50,000)
Cash flows from financing activities				
Principal payments on mortgage	$(15,000)		$(15,000)	
Payment of dividends	(12,000)		(10,000)	
Net cash used by financing activities		(27,000)		(25,000)
Net increase in cash and cash equivalents		$ 37,000		$ 24,000
Cash and cash equivalents at beginning of year		158,000		134,000
Cash and cash equivalents at end of year		$195,000		$158,000

Required:

1. Does June's Camera Shop appear to have grown in size during the past two years?
2. June's president, June Smith, would like to open a second store. Smith believes that $225,000 is needed to equip the facility properly. The business has $100,000 of cash and liquid investments to apply toward the $225,000 required. Do the data in the 2009 and 2008 statements of cash flow suggest whether or not June's Camera Shop is likely to be able to secure a loan for the remaining $125,000 needed for the expansion?
3. How long should it take June's Camera Shop to pay back the $125,000?

Case 11-53 PROFITABILITY DECLINES AND THE STATEMENT OF CASH FLOWS

The Bookbarn, Inc., is a retail seller of new books in a moderate-sized city. Although initially very successful, The Bookbarn's sales volume has declined since the opening of two competing bookstores two years ago. The accountant for The Bookbarn prepared the following statement of cash flows at the end of the current year:

The Bookbarn, Inc.
Statement of Cash Flows
For the Year Ended December 31, 2009

Cash flows from operating activities		
Net income		$ 26,500
Adjustments to reconcile net income to net		
cash provided by operating activities:		
Depreciation expense	$ 38,500	
Loss on sale of equipment	2,100	
Increase in accounts receivable	(1,200)	
Increase in inventory	(3,800)	
Increase in accounts payable	6,700	
Decrease in wages payable	(1,200)	
Total adjustments		41,100
Net cash provided by operating activities		$ 67,600
Cash flows from investing activities		
Equipment purchase	$(12,000)	
Proceeds from sale of equipment	2,300	
Net cash used by investing activities		$ (9,700)
Cash flows from financing activities		
Payment of dividends	$ (4,000)	
Repayment of mortgage	(10,000)	
Net cash used by financing activities		(14,000)
Net increase in cash		$ 43,900

Your analysis suggests that The Bookbarn's net income will continue to decline by $8,000 per year to $18,500 as sales continue to fall. Thereafter, you expect sales to stabilize.

Required:

1. What will happen to the amount of cash provided by operations as net income decreases?
2. Assume that equipment is nearly fully depreciated but that it will be fully serviceable for several years. What will happen to cash flows from operations as depreciation declines?
3. Do the operations of businesses experiencing declining sales volumes always consume cash? Explain your answer.
4. Can current assets and current liabilities buffer operating cash flows against the impact of declines in sales volume in the short run? In the long run? Explain your answer.

Case 11-54 PREPARING A PROSPECTIVE STATEMENT OF CASH FLOWS

Jane and Harvey Wentland have decided to open a retail athletic supply store, Fitness Outfitters, Inc. They will stock clothing, shoes, and supplies used in running, swimming, bicycling, weight lifting, and other exercise and athletic activities. During their first year of operations, 2009, they expect the following results. (Subsequent years are expected to be more successful.)

Sales revenue	$629,000
Less: Cost of goods sold	291,000
Gross margin	$338,000
Less: Operating expenses	355,000
Net loss	$ (17,000)

By the end of 2009, Fitness Outfitters needs to have a cash balance of $5,000 and is expected to have the following partial balance sheet:

ASSETS		
Inventory		$ 53,000
Store equipment	$97,000	
Accumulated depreciation, store equipment	15,000	82,000
LIABILITIES AND EQUITY		
Accounts payable		$ 37,000
Common stock		100,000
Retained earnings		(17,000)

Assume that all sales will be for cash and that store equipment will be acquired for cash.

Required:

1. Prepare as much of the statement of cash flows for 2009 as you can. Use the direct method to determine cash flows from operations.
2. In the statement that you prepared for requirement 1, by how much does the prospective cash balance exceed or fall short of the desired cash balance? If a shortfall occurs, where would you suggest that Jane and Harvey seek additional cash?
3. Does the preparation of a prospective statement of cash flows seem worthwhile for an ongoing business? Why?

Case 11-55 INCOME, CASH FLOW, AND FUTURE LOSSES

On January 1, 2007, Cermack National Bank loaned $5,000,000 under a two-year, zero coupon note to a real estate developer. The bank recognized interest revenue on this note of approximately $400,000 per year. Due to an economic downturn, the developer was unable to pay the $5,800,000 maturity amount on December 31, 2008. The bank convinced the developer to pay $800,000 on December 31, 2008, and agreed to extend $5,000,000 credit to the developer despite the gloomy economic outlook for the next several years. Thus, on December 31, 2008, the bank issued a new two-year, zero coupon note to the developer to mature on December 31, 2010 for $6,000,000. The bank recognized interest revenue on this note of approximately $500,000 per year.

The bank's external auditor insisted that the riskiness of the new loan be recognized by increasing the allowance for uncollectible notes by $1,500,000 on December 31, 2008, and $2,000,000 on December 31, 2009. On December 31, 2010, the bank received $1,200,000 from the developer and learned that the developer is in bankruptcy and that no additional amounts would be recovered.

Required:

1. Prepare a schedule showing annual cash flows for the two notes in each of the four years.
2. Prepare a schedule showing the effect of the notes on net income in each of the four years.
3. Which figure, net income or net cash flow, does the better job of telling the bank's stockholders about the effect of these notes on the bank? Explain by reference to the schedules prepared in requirements 1 and 2.
4. A commonly used method for predicting future cash flows is to predict future income and adjust it for anticipated differences between net income and net cash flow. Does the Cermack National Bank case shed any light on the justification for using net income in this way rather than simply predicting future cash flows by reference to past cash flows?

Case 11-56 RESEARCHING ACCOUNTING STANDARDS: DISSENTING VIEWS AND THE STATEMENT OF CASH FLOWS

The preparation of cash flow statements is required by Statement of Financial Accounting Standards No. 95, "The Statement of Cash Flows," adopted by a four-to-three vote of the FASB. Several members of the Board took exception to various aspects of the statement, including (1) the classification of interest and dividends received and interest paid as cash flows from operations and (2) the use of the indirect method.

Required:

Obtain a copy of Statement of Financial Accounting Standards No. 95 (FAS 95) from the FASB website. This can be obtained by:

a. Entering the following web address in your browser: http://www.fasb.org
b. Selecting "Pronouncements and EITF Abstracts" from the menu at the left.
c. Selecting "Statement of Accounting Standards No. 95"

Answer the following questions:

1. How did dissenting members of the FASB prefer that interest and dividends received and interest paid be classified? (See the section following paragraph 34 of the full text of Statement No. 95.) How did the FASB justify classifying these items as cash flows from operations? (See paragraph 90 of Statement No. 95.)
2. Why did dissenting members of the FASB take exception to the indirect method? (See the section following paragraph 34 of the full text of Statement No. 95.) How did the FASB justify permitting use of the indirect method? (See paragraphs 108, 109, and 119 of Statement No. 95.)

Case 11-57 RESEARCH AND ANALYSIS USING THE ANNUAL REPORT

Obtain John Deere's 2007 annual report either through the "Investor Relations" portion of their website (do a web search for John Deere investor relations) or go to http://www.sec.gov and click "Search for company filings" under "Filings & Forms (EDGAR)."

Required:

Answer the following questions:

1. What method of computing net cash flow from operating activities did John Deere use?
2. What was the amount of net cash provided by operating activities for the two most current years? What were the most significant adjustments that caused a difference between net income and net cash provided by operating activities?
3. What amount did the company pay for interest during the most current year? For taxes during the most current year? (Hint: You may need to refer to the notes to the financial statements.)
4. Why was the provision for depreciation and amortization added to net income to compute the net cash provided by operating activities?
5. Refer to John Deere's investing and financing activities. What were some of John Deere's significant uses of cash? What were some of John Deere's significant sources of cash?
6. What was the amount of cash dividends paid by John Deere for the most current year?
7. Are the time commitments of inflows and outflows well matched by John Deere?
8. Are debt and equity likely to be available as inflows of cash in the near future?

Case 11-58 COMPARATIVE ANALYSIS: ABERCROMBIE & FITCH vs. AEROPOSTALE

Refer to the financial statements of **Abercrombie & Fitch** and **Aeropostale** that are supplied with this text.

Required:

Answer the following questions:

1. What method of computing net cash flow from operating activities did Abercrombie & Fitch use? What method of computing net cash flow from operating activities did Aeropostale use? Would you expect these to be the same? Why or why not?
2. Find net cash provided by operating activities for each company:
   a. What was the amount of cash provided by operating activities for the year ending February 3, 2007 (fiscal 2006) for Abercrombie & Fitch? What was the amount of cash provided by operating activities for the year ending February 3, 2007, for Aeropostale?
   b. What was the most significant adjustment that caused a difference between net income and net cash provided by operating activities?
   c. Comparing net income to net cash provided by operating activities, can you draw any conclusions as to the quality of each company's earnings?
3. Refer to each company's investing and financing activities. What were some of the more significant uses of cash? What were some of the more significant sources of cash?
4. Refer Does each company match the time commitments of inflows and outflows of cash well?
5. Refer Are debt and equity likely to be available as inflows of cash in the near future?

12

Financial Statement Analysis

After studying Chapter 12, you should be able to:

1. Explain how creditors, investors, and others use financial statements in their decisions.

2. Become familiar with the most important SEC filings.

3. Understand the difference between cross sectional and time series analysis.

4. Analyze financial statements using horizontal and vertical analysis.

5. Calculate and use financial statement ratios to evaluate a company.

6. Understand the effect accounting policies may have on financial statement analysis.

Experience Financial Accounting
with Abercrombie & Fitch

The **Abercrombie & Fitch** brand was established in 1892. Originally an outdoor store, it became well known for supplying Admiral Byrd's expeditions to the North and South Poles and safaris for Teddy Roosevelt and Ernest Hemingway. As such, A&F products gained a reputation for being rugged, high-quality outdoor gear.

One hundred years later, in 1992, Abercrombie & Fitch was repositioned as a fashion-oriented, casual apparel brand. Marketing was aimed at both male and female college students to reflect East Coast/Ivy League traditions.

Since 1992, the target market has been expanded down to teens and children and now also includes the abercrombie, Hollister, and RUEHL brands. Certainly most of us have seen these brands being worn around our campuses and towns. Yet, how do we know whether Abercrombie & Fitch would be a good company in which to invest? In reading this chapter, you will learn about a number of tools used by investors and creditors to analyze the financial status of Abercrombie & Fitch and other companies.

UNITED STATES SECURITIES AND EXCHANGE COMMISSION
Washington, D. C. 20549

FORM 10-K

(Mark One)

☑ **ANNUAL REPORT PURSUANT TO SECTION 13 OR 15(d) OF THE SECURITIES EXCHANGE ACT OF 1934**

For the fiscal year ended February 3, 2007

OR

☐ **TRANSITION REPORT PURSUANT TO SECTION 13 OR 15(d) OF THE SECURITIES EXCHANGE ACT OF 1934**

For the transition period from _____ to _____

Commission file number 1-12107

ABERCROMBIE & FITCH CO.
(Exact name of registrant as specified in its charter)

Throughout this book, you have learned how to record (i.e., the debits and the credits) many of the most common transactions in which a company engages. You have also studied how these debits and credits are summarized in the financial statements and how this information is useful to those interested in the company.

In this chapter, we review, extend, and summarize the role of financial statements in business decision-making. The types of decisions facing customers, suppliers, employees, creditors, and investors are discussed. However, we concentrate primarily on investment and credit decisions.

Potential investors and creditors typically restate financial statements into percentage terms to facilitate comparison to other companies and previous years. Techniques such as horizontal analysis, vertical analysis, and ratio analysis use percentages for comparison purposes. A comparison of a company's performance in one time period with its performance in different time periods is called time series, or trend analysis. When the performance of a company is compared with similar companies, in either current or past periods, it is referred to as cross sectional analysis. These comparisons are useful because very few analysis techniques involve comparison with an absolute standard that can be applied to a large variety of companies for multiple periods.

In this chapter, we will examine these various techniques in detail. We will begin with a discussion of the various groups of decision makers who use financial statements as well as a discussion of the SEC filings required for all publicly traded corporations. Then, after exploring various financial-statement analysis techniques, the chapter closes with a discussion of the impact that different accounting methods can have on the analysis of financial statements.

Reading this chapter will help you answer the following questions:

- What decision-making groups use financial statements and what questions are they able to answer by analyzing the financial statements?
- What information can be found in SEC filings?
- Where can various information be found in the Form 10-K?
- How are financial statements analyzed?

OBJECTIVE ▸ 1

Explain how creditors, investors, and others use financial statements in their decisions.

Use of Financial Statements in Decisions

The role of financial statements is to provide information that will help creditors, investors, and others make judgments which serve as the foundation for various decisions. While customers, suppliers, employees, creditors, and investors all use financial statement data to make decisions, as shown in Exhibit 12-1, each group uses the

Exhibit 12-1

Users of Financial Statements and Typical Questions

Suppliers
Will the company be able to continue to buy and pay for goods and services?

Customers
Will the company be around to service any repairs?

Employees
Will I get a raise this year?

Accounting Information

Should I lend money to this business?

Creditors

Investors

Will the company earn enough income to provide a satisfactory return?

accounting information to answer different questions. In this section, we briefly examine the decisions made by each group and the financial statement data that are used. We will then concentrate on how investors and creditors analyze a company.

Customer Decisions

Customers want to buy from companies that will (1) continue to produce goods or provide services in the future, and (2) provide repair or warranty service if required. The financial statements contain data describing the profitability and efficiency of a company's operations. These data can be used by customers to estimate the likelihood that a potential supplier will be able to deliver goods or services now and in the future.

Supplier Decisions

A company that is considering selling goods or providing services to another company wants to know whether its customer will (1) pay for the purchase as agreed and (2) be able to continue to purchase and pay for goods and services. In the short term, a supplier is actually a short-term creditor. Suppliers, therefore, are concerned about the resources available to pay for items purchased, as well as other claims against those resources. In the long term, a supplier is much like a long-term creditor or investor, in that the long-term supplier must invest in the resources necessary to produce goods for or provide services to customers.

Suppliers use balance sheet data to estimate the likelihood that a customer will be able to pay for current purchases. They use income statement data to analyze whether a customer will be able to continue purchasing and paying for goods or services in the future.

Employment Decisions

When you select an employer, you want to be sure that the company will provide (1) competitive salary and benefits, (2) experiences that will prepare you to assume increased responsibility, and (3) a secure position for the foreseeable future. Employees invest their time, energy, and expertise in an organization. In the short term, they realize returns from the same resources used to satisfy the claims of short-term creditors—the excess of the company's current assets over the claims against those assets. In the long term, salary and advancement will come from the profit and growth of the company—the same factors considered by creditors, investors, customers, and suppliers. Income statement data can help a prospective employee assess the likelihood that a company will provide the growth and profits necessary to support a successful career.

In related decisions, unions representing employees use the financial statements. For example, when the employer's income statement suggests the employer is performing very well, the union will seek greater wages and benefits. Conversely, when the income statement suggests the employer is performing poorly (e.g., the airline industry), unions may accept lower wages and benefits to help the employer stay in operation.

Credit Decisions

An individual or an organization that is considering making a loan needs to know whether the borrower will be able to repay the loan and its interest. For short-term loans (those of one year or less), the principal and interest will be repaid from current assets—cash on hand and cash that can be secured by selling inventory and collecting accounts receivable. A short-term lender, then, is most interested in the composition and amounts of a borrowing company's current assets and current liabilities. The excess of the current assets over current liabilities, an amount called *working capital*, is particularly important.

For a long-term loan, the principal and interest will be repaid from cash provided by profits earned over the period of the loan. A long-term lender, then, is most interested in estimating (1) the future profits of the enterprise and (2) the amount of other claims against those profits, such as dividends to stockholders, payments to other lenders, and future investments by the firm.

Information from three different statements is useful in making credit decisions. An analysis of the balance sheet can provide information about the borrower's current liquidity. Profitability data developed from current and previous income statements are often helpful in forecasting future profitability. And sources and uses of cash presented in the statement of cash flows are helpful in forecasting the amount and timing of future claims against profits.

Investment Decisions

Investors who buy stock in a corporation expect to earn returns on their investment from (1) dividends and (2) an increase in the value of the stock (a capital gain). Both dividends and increases in the value of the stock depend on the future profitability of the company. The larger the profits, the more resources the company has available for payment of dividends and for investment in new assets to use in creating additional profits.

Although detailed analysis of the corporation is where you find the best information for predicting (or forecasting) future profits, this cannot be done in a vacuum. You must also understand economic and industry factors. For example, if you ignore how economic factors such as rising interest rates affect home construction (it slows it down), then forecasts of corporations whose performances are tied to this industry, such as **Lowe's** or **Home Depot**, may be overly optimistic. As such, most analysts take a top-down approach when trying to predict future profits. This approach starts with gathering economic and industry data. In fact, professional analysts typically specialize in certain industries so that their knowledge of how the economy and industry interact will be applicable to all the corporations they analyze (or "follow"). Yet, at some point, you must begin to analyze the corporation itself.

OBJECTIVE ▶ 2
Become familiar with the most important SEC filings.

SEC Filings

Publicly traded corporations must file a variety of financial information, including audited financial statements, with the Securities and Exchange Commission (SEC) on an ongoing basis. For example, annual reports on **Form 10-K**, quarterly reports on **Form 10-Q**, and current reports for numerous specified events on **Form 8-K**, as well as many other disclosure requirements must be submitted to the SEC in a timely manner. These filings are the most important and complete source of financial information about the corporation and are the major source of information about the business for most investors (and creditors). A summary of the most important SEC filings is provided in Exhibit 12-2. A complete list of mandatory filings with more detailed descriptions is provided at http://www.sec.gov/about/forms/secforms.htm.

Format and Content of Form 10-K

The most useful filing is Form 10-K, which is filed after each fiscal year end. We provide excerpts from Abercrombie & Fitch's and **Aeropostale**'s 10-Ks at the end of the book in Appendices 1 and 2, respectively. The 10-K includes audited financial statements, but there is also a wealth of additional information. As seen in Appendices 1 and 2, 10-Ks are quite long (frequently well over 100 pages, remember these are just excerpts); however, all 10-Ks must follow a format mandated by the SEC. If you familiarize yourself with the mandated format, you will be able to find information of interest more efficiently.

Item 1 outlines the history of the company, discusses recent developments, and provides an overview of its industry and competitors. There is a detailed discussion of such things as major products, major suppliers and sources of raw materials, key customers, seasonalities, government regulations, and risk factors. A thorough read of this section is a good way to better understand the business and determine whether the company has a good strategy for creating profits.

Typically there is little important information in Items 2, 3, and 4. However, you should scan these items for anything of interest. Item 2 describes the property holdings of the company; Item 3 discusses lawsuits in which the company is involved;

Exhibit 12-2

The Most Important SEC Filings

Filing	Description
Form 10-K	The annual report on Form 10-K provides a comprehensive overview of the corporation's business and financial condition and includes <u>audited</u> financial statements. Although similarly named, the annual report on Form 10-K is distinct from the "annual report to shareholders," which a corporation must send to its shareholders when it holds an annual meeting to elect directors. For larger filers the 10-K must be filed within 60 days of their fiscal year end.
Form 10-Q	The Form 10-Q includes <u>unaudited</u> financial statements and provides a continuing view of the corporation's financial position during the year. The report must be filed for each of the first three fiscal quarters of the corporation's fiscal year. For larger filers this must be done within 40 days of the end of the quarter.
Form 8-K	In addition to filing Forms 10-K and 10-Q, public corporations must report material corporate events on a more current basis. Form 8-K is the "current report" companies must file with the SEC to announce major events that are important to investors and creditors.
Form DEF 14A (Proxy Statement)	The Proxy Statement notifies shareholders of issues that will be voted on at the annual shareholders' meeting. For example, shareholders commonly vote on the audit firm, executive compensation issues, and representation on the Board of Directors.
Forms 3, 4, and 5	Corporate officers, directors, and 10+ percent shareholders are collectively known as "insiders." Form 3 must be filed upon becoming an officer, director, or 10+ percent shareholder. Insiders must file Form 4 within two days of buying or selling the corporation's stock. Form 5 is a special annual filing.
Forms S-1 and S-2 (Registration Statements)	Corporations must file these forms to "register" their securities with the SEC prior to offering them to investors.
Rule 424 (Prospectus)	Contains information for potential investors related to the sale of stock by the corporation. When the corporation sells stock to the public for the first time it is called an "Initial Public Offering" or IPO. Subsequent offerings are referred to as Secondary Offerings.

*Descriptions taken from the SEC website

Item 4 discusses anything brought to a shareholder vote in the fourth quarter (the 10-Qs handle this matter for the first three quarters). Item 3 is likely the most important of these items, as you will want to be aware of any serious litigation facing the company. However, most companies are parties to multiple lawsuits at any point in time, and a vast majority of these lawsuits will not materially affect the company. For example, if you look at Note 14 of Abercrombie & Fitch's 10-K (p. 727), you will see that Abercrombie & Fitch is aware of 20 lawsuits filed against it.

Item 5 provides a summary of recent stock price and dividend activity, while Item 6 summarizes financial data for the last five years. There is not much detail to these sections, but they do provide a nice overview. Further, Item 6 often provides information about key performance indicators, such as sales per square foot in the retail industry or revenues per passenger mile in the airline industry, which are not included in the financial statements.

Item 7 is Management's Discussion and Analysis, more frequently referred to as **MD&A**. This is one of the key parts of the 10-K. In this section, management discusses their views of the financial condition and performance of the company. Management is required to disclose trends, events, or known uncertainties that would materially affect the company. Included in this section are many statements about what will likely happen in the future. Although there is obviously uncertainty about whether these future events will happen, this information is designed to provide investors with information management believes necessary to understand the company and predict, or forecast, future performance. Item 7A is where the effect of market risk factors, such as fluctuating interest rates or currency exchange rates, on the company's financial performance is discussed. It is important to read the MD&A.

Item 8 contains the corporation's balance sheets for the last two years and income statements and statements of cash flows for the last three years. These three financial statements are the primary sources of information for analysts. Specifically, as discussed in other chapters and later in this chapter, financial statement ratio analysis provides analysts with a wealth of information to evaluate such things as the corporation's profitability, asset and debt management, and short-term liquidity. One part of Item 8 that should not be ignored is the footnotes provided as a supplement to the financial statements. This is where you will find information about the corporation's accounting policies (e.g., does the company use LIFO or FIFO?), as well as disclosures providing additional detail about various accounts listed on the financial statements. Unfortunately, a detailed analysis of the footnotes is beyond the scope of this course, but much information can be gained through a careful reading of this section.

Finally, Item 8 also includes the auditor's opinions on (1) the effectiveness of the corporation's system of internal controls over financial reporting and (2) the appropriateness of the financial statements and accompanying footnotes. Although these opinions are typically "unqualified" indicating no major problems, you should definitely look at these opinions to ensure this is true. Auditing financial statements is one of the primary services provided by CPAs and is the focus of multiple courses for accounting majors.

Item 9 is reserved for changes in or disagreements with the auditors. This item also rarely indicates a problem, but you should look at it just in case. Item 9A is a recent addition to 10-K's in response to requirements made by the passage of the Sarbanes-Oxley Act. Here management acknowledges their responsibility for establishing and maintaining a system of internal controls over financial reporting, their testing of this system's effectiveness, and their opinion of its effectiveness. It is this system of internal controls on which the auditors provide an opinion, although as discussed in the previous paragraph, the opinion is frequently included in Item 8.

Items 10 through 14 provide information that is usually provided in the proxy statement (see Form DEF 14A in Exhibit 12-2) because shareholders typically vote on whether to retain directors, officers, and auditors (i.e., principal accountants). Of course, the names of the parties are disclosed, as are their business experience or any family relationships with other directors or officers. Finally, Item 15 is a listing of the financial statements (discussed as part of Item 8) and other required filings.

OBJECTIVE ▶ 3
Understand the difference between cross sectional and time series analysis.

Analyzing Financial Statements with Cross Sectional and Time Series Analysis

As with many things in life, context is all important in financial statement analysis. For example, how well do you believe a corporation with $3.3 billion in net sales is performing? Your answer should be that it depends. That is, if net sales for the previous two years were $4.5 billion and $3.9 billion, respectively, you would say the trend is quite negative. However, if net sales for the previous two years were $2.0 billion and $2.8 billion, respectively, then you would conclude the trend is quite positive. Or, you could see how this corporation's sales growth stacks up against a major competitor's.

The context with which we placed our hypothetical corporation's net sales and sales growth demonstrates the two general comparisons we make when analyzing financial statements—cross sectional analysis and time series (or trend) analysis.

Cross sectional analysis compares one corporation to another corporation and to industry averages. Although this method is useful, it is often difficult to find a good comparison corporation, and even corporations classified in the same industry frequently have different aspects to their operations. For example, the Retail (Apparel) Industry in which Abercrombie & Fitch and Aeropostale are placed also includes The Shoe Carnival. Nonetheless, it is useful to highlight similarities, differences, strengths, and weaknesses of the corporation as compared to the competition and the industry as a whole. For example, for the year ended February 3, 2007, A&F's sales and net income grew by 19.2 percent and 26.4 percent, respectively. This sounds good, but we would be less impressed if Aeropostale's growth rates were far better than A&F's. In fact, over the same period, Aeropostale's sales and net income grew by 17.3 percent and 27.0 percent, respectively. So, these corporations' performance—at least along these two dimensions—are quite comparable. We will discuss more comparisons between A&F and Aeropostale later in the chapter.

Time series (or trend) analysis compares a single corporation across time. For example, if you look at Abercrombie & Fitch's Income Statement (p. 704), you see that its net sales were $2.02 billion in fiscal 2004, $2.78 billion in fiscal 2005, and $3.32 billion in fiscal 2006 (fiscal years end around the end of January of the following year), which shows a positive trend. Year-to-year comparisons of important accounts and account groups help to identify the causes of changes in a company's income or financial position. Knowing the causes of these changes is helpful in forecasting a company's future profitability and financial position. In fact, the SEC requires comparative financial statements (two years for the balance sheet and three years for both the income statement and statement of cash flows) in the 10-K, which facilitates trend analysis. Cross sectional and time series analysis are demonstrated in Cornerstone 12-1.

HOW TO Interpret Cross Sectional and Time Series (or Trend) Analysis

CORNERSTONE 12-1

Concept:
Two common ways to analyze a corporation's financial statements are (1) cross sectional analysis and (2) time series (or trend) analysis. In cross sectional analysis, you compare the corporation's financial statements to a competitor or industry averages. In time series analysis, you compare specific line items of the financial statements over multiple years to see if the trends are positive or negative.

Information:
Below is some information taken from Abercrombie & Fitch's and Aeropostale's financial statements.

Abercrombie & Fitch (in thousands)

	Fiscal Year Ended		
	2/3/07	1/28/06	1/29/05
Net sales	$3,318,158	$2,784,711	$2,021,253
Cost of goods sold	1,109,152	933,295	680,029
Gross profit	$2,209,006	$1,851,416	$1,341,224

Aeropostale (in thousands)

	Fiscal Year Ended		
	2/3/07	1/28/06	1/29/05
Net sales	$1,413,208	$1,204,347	$964,212
Cost of goods sold	957,791	841,872	644,305
Gross profit	$ 455,417	$ 362,475	$319,907

Required:
1. Using time series analysis, comment on the trend of A&F's cost of goods sold and gross profit.
2. What are some weaknesses of using time series analysis alone?
3. What is the primary weakness of using raw financial statement numbers in cross sectional analysis? What can you do about it?
4. Using cross sectional analysis, compare A&F's gross profit to that of Aeropostale's.

Solution:
1. A&F's cost of goods sold increased by $253,266 ($933,295 − $680,029) from 2005 to 2006 and by $175,857 between 2006 and 2007. In isolation this may seem bad, but of course, the primary reason for this increase is that sales were also increasing. In fact, A&F has a positive trend in gross profit, which increased by $510,192 and $357,590 between 2005 and 2006 and 2006 and 2007, respectively.

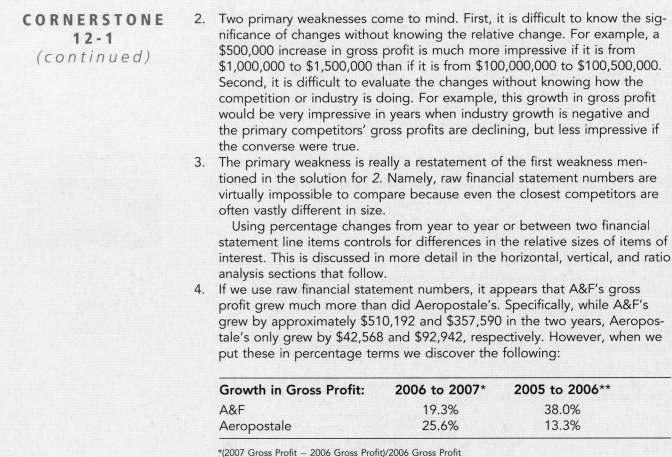

CORNERSTONE 12-1 *(continued)*

2. Two primary weaknesses come to mind. First, it is difficult to know the significance of changes without knowing the relative change. For example, a $500,000 increase in gross profit is much more impressive if it is from $1,000,000 to $1,500,000 than if it is from $100,000,000 to $100,500,000. Second, it is difficult to evaluate the changes without knowing how the competition or industry is doing. For example, this growth in gross profit would be very impressive in years when industry growth is negative and the primary competitors' gross profits are declining, but less impressive if the converse were true.

3. The primary weakness is really a restatement of the first weakness mentioned in the solution for *2*. Namely, raw financial statement numbers are virtually impossible to compare because even the closest competitors are often vastly different in size.

   Using percentage changes from year to year or between two financial statement line items controls for differences in the relative sizes of items of interest. This is discussed in more detail in the horizontal, vertical, and ratio analysis sections that follow.

4. If we use raw financial statement numbers, it appears that A&F's gross profit grew much more than did Aeropostale's. Specifically, while A&F's grew by approximately $510,192 and $357,590 in the two years, Aeropostale's only grew by $42,568 and $92,942, respectively. However, when we put these in percentage terms we discover the following:

Growth in Gross Profit:	2006 to 2007*	2005 to 2006**
A&F	19.3%	38.0%
Aeropostale	25.6%	13.3%

*(2007 Gross Profit − 2006 Gross Profit)/2006 Gross Profit
**(2006 Gross Profit − 2005 Gross Profit)/2005 Gross Profit

This analysis suggests that A&F had a far better 2006, while Aeropostale had a better 2007—at least with respect to gross profit.

The comparative financial statements included in the 10-K report the results in dollar amounts. This makes it easy to detect large changes between years in accounts or groups of accounts. These changes may indicate that the corporation is changing or that the conditions under which the corporation operates are changing. However, while comparative financial statements show changes in the amounts of financial statement items, analysts often prefer to restate the financial statements in percentages. Typically, this is done with horizontal analysis, vertical analysis, and ratio analysis.

Analyzing the Financial Statements with Horizontal and Vertical Analysis

OBJECTIVE 4
Analyze financial statements using horizontal and vertical analysis.

As mentioned previously, size differences (in dollars) from year to year or between companies can make time series and cross sectional analysis difficult. To combat this problem, many analysts use common size statements. **Common size statements** express each financial statement line item in percentage terms, which highlights differences.

In **horizontal analysis** each financial statement line item is expressed as a percent of the base year (typically the first year shown). Cornerstone 12-2 shows how to prepare a common size income statement for horizontal analysis, while Cornerstone 12-3 shows how to prepare a common size income statement and balance sheet for vertical analysis.

HOW TO Prepare Common Size Statements for Horizontal Analysis

CORNERSTONE
12-2

Concept:
Horizontal analysis expresses each financial statement line item as a percent of the base year.

Information:
Below is Aeropostale's income statement from its 2007 10-K.

Aeropostale, Inc.
Consolidated Statements of Income
(In thousands)

	Fiscal Year Ended		
	Feb. 3, 2007	Jan. 28, 2006	Jan. 29, 2005
Net sales	$1,413,208	$1,204,347	$ 964,212
Cost of goods sold	957,791	841,872	644,305
Gross profit	$ 455,417	$ 362,475	$ 319,907
Selling, general, and administrative expenses	(289,736)	(227,044)	(183,977)
Other income, net	2,085	—	—
Income from operations	$ 167,766	$ 135,431	$ 135,930
Interest income	7,064	3,670	1,438
Income before taxes	$ 174,830	$ 139,101	$ 137,368
Income taxes	68,183	55,147	53,256
Net income	$ 106,647	$ 83,954	$ 84,112

Required:
Prepare a common size income statement to be used in horizontal analysis for Aeropostale.

Solution:

Aeropostale, Inc.
Consolidated Statements of Income

	Fiscal Year Ended		
	Feb. 3, 2007	Jan. 28, 2006	Jan. 29, 2005
Net sales	146.6%	124.9%	100.0%
Cost of goods sold	148.7%	130.7%	100.0%
Gross profit	142.4%	113.3%	100.0%
Selling, general, and administrative expenses	(157.5%)	(123.4%)	(100.0%)
Other income, net	—*	—	—
Income from operations	123.4%	99.6%	100.0%
Interest Income	491.2%	255.2%	100.0%
Income before taxes	127.3%	101.3%	100.0%
Income taxes	128.0%	103.6%	100.0%
Net Income	126.8%	99.8%	100.0%

*Because the base year value for other income is $0, the common-size value is technically infinite. In this case you should consider what created this unusual item. In the MD&A section of the 10-K (p. 18), Aeropostale states, "Other income of $2.1 million in fiscal 2006 was the result of the resolution of a dispute with a vendor regarding the enforcement of our intellectual property rights."

**CORNERSTONE
12-3**

HOW TO Prepare Common Size Statements for Vertical Analysis

Concept:
Vertical analysis expresses each financial statement line item as a percent of the largest amount on the statement.

Information:
Below are Aeropostale's income statements and balance sheets taken from its 2007 10-K.

Aeropostale, Inc.
Consolidated Statements of Income
(In thousands)

	Fiscal Year Ended		
	Feb. 3, 2007	Jan. 28, 2006	Jan. 29, 2005
Net sales	$1,413,208	$1,204,347	$ 964,212
Cost of goods sold	957,791	841,872	644,305
Gross profit	$ 455,417	$ 362,475	$ 319,907
Selling, general, and administrative expenses	(289,736)	(227,044)	(183,977)
Other income, net	2,085	—	—
Income from operations	$ 167,766	$ 135,431	$ 135,930
Interest income	7,064	3,670	1,438
Income before taxes	$ 174,830	$ 139,101	$ 137,368
Income taxes	68,183	55,147	53,256
Net income	$ 106,647	$ 83,954	$ 84,112

Aeropostale, Inc.
Consolidated Balance Sheet
(In thousands)

	Feb. 3, 2007	Jan. 28, 2006
ASSETS		
Current assets:		
Cash and cash equivalents	$ 200,064	$ 205,235
Short-term investments	76,223	20,037
Merchandise inventory	101,476	91,908
Prepaid expenses	12,175	12,314
Deferred income taxes	1,185	—
Other current assets	7,670	9,845
Total current assets	$ 398,793	$ 339,339
Fixtures, equipment and improvements (net)	175,591	160,229
Intangible assets	1,400	2,455
Deferred income taxes	3,784	—
Other assets	1,596	1,928
Total assets	$ 581,164	$ 503,951

	Feb. 3, 2007	Jan. 28, 2006
LIABILITIES & STOCKHOLDERS' EQUITY		
Current liabilities:		
Accounts payable	$ 63,918	$ 57,165
Deferred income taxes		5,195
Accrued expenses	100,880	63,993
Total current liabilities	$ 164,798	$ 126,353
Deferred rent and tenant allowances	88,344	81,499
Retirement benefit plan liabilities	15,906	8,654
Deferred income taxes	—	2,655
Commitments and contingent liabilities	—	—
Total liabilities	$ 269,048	$ 219,161
Stockholders' equity:		
Common stock	$ 593	$ 586
Preferred stock	—	—
Additional paid-in capital	101,429	88,213
Other comprehensive income	(5,274)	(1,557)
Deferred compensation	—	(2,577)
Retained earnings	414,916	308,269
Treasury stock	(199,548)	(108,144)
Total stockholders' equity	$ 312,116	$ 284,790
Total liabilities and stockholders' equity	$ 581,164	$ 503,951

Required:

Prepare common size income statements and balance sheets to be used in vertical analysis for Aeropostale.

Solution:

Aeropostale, Inc.
Consolidated Statements of Income
(In thousands)

	Fiscal Year Ended		
	Feb. 3, 2007	Jan. 28, 2006	Jan. 29, 2005
Net sales	100.0%	100.0%	100.0%
Cost of goods sold	67.8%	69.9%	66.8%
Gross profit	32.2%	30.1%	33.2%
Selling, general, and administrative	(20.5%)	(18.9%)	(19.1%)
Other income, net	0.1%	0.0%	0.0%
Income from operations	11.9%	11.2%	14.1%
Interest income	0.5%	0.3%	0.1%
Income before taxes	12.4%	11.5%	14.2%
Income taxes	4.8%	4.6%	5.5%
Net income	7.5%*	7.0%*	8.7%

*The sum of the percentages in this column may be off slightly due to rounding.

CORNERSTONE 12-3
(continued)

Aeropostale, Inc.
Consolidated Balance Sheet
(In thousands)

	Feb. 3, 2007	Jan. 28, 2006
ASSETS		
Current assets:		
Cash and cash equivalents	34.4%	40.7%
Short-term investments	13.1%	4.0%
Merchandise inventory	17.5%	18.2%
Prepaid expenses	2.1%	2.4%
Deferred income taxes	0.2%	0.0%
Other current assets	1.3%	2.0%
Total current assets	68.6%	67.3%
Fixtures, equipment and improvements (net)	30.2%	31.8%
Intangible assets	0.2%	0.5%
Deferred income taxes	0.7%	0.0%
Other assets	0.3%	0.4%
Total assets	100.0%	100.0%
LIABILITIES & STOCKHOLDERS' EQUITY		
Current liabilities:		
Accounts payable	11.0%	11.3%
Deferred income taxes	0.0%	1.0%
Accrued expenses	17.4%	12.7%
Total current liabilities	28.4%	25.1%*
Deferred rent and tenant allowances	15.2%	16.2%
Retirement benefit plan liabilities	2.7%	1.7%
Deferred income taxes	0.0%	0.5%
Commitments and contingent liabilities	0.0%	0.0%
Total liabilities	46.3%	43.5%
Stockholders' equity:		
Common stock	0.1%	0.1%
Preferred stock	0.0%	0.0%
Additional paid-in capital	17.5%	17.5%
Other comprehensive income	(0.9%)	(0.3%)
Deferred compensation	0.0%	(0.5%)
Retained earnings	71.4%	61.2%
Treasury stock	(34.3%)	(21.5%)
Total stockholders' equity	53.7%*	56.5%
Total liabilities and stockholders' equity	100.0%	100.0%

*The sum of the percentages in this column may be off slightly due to rounding.

Horizontal analysis is good for highlighting the growth (or shrinkage) in financial statement line items from year to year and is particularly useful for trend analysis. For example, looking at Aeropostale's common-size income statement in Cornerstone 12-3, we see that cost of goods sold has grown slightly faster than sales when comparing 2007 to 2005. This has resulted in the gross profit growth trailing the sales growth and raises the question of why the gross profit margin is shrinking.

Vertical analysis, on the other hand, expresses each financial statement line item as a percent of the largest amount on the statement. On the income statement, this is net sales and on the balance sheet it is total assets. Vertical analysis helps distinguish between changes in account balances that result from growth and changes that are likely to have arisen from other causes.

Identifying nongrowth changes and their causes can help forecast a company's future profitability or its future financial position. For example, we see that selling, general and administrative expenses (SG&A) have grown from approximately 19 percent of net sales in 2005 and 2006 to 20.5 percent of net sales in 2007. Because much of SG&A is essentially fixed (e.g., salaries and store costs), we might expect SG&A to decrease as a percentage of net sales in a period when net sales increased by almost 50 percent. Further, vertical analysis of the balance sheet reveals an essentially stable condition; a vast majority of the accounts, and all of the large dollar accounts, are about the same percentage of total assets in each year.

Of course, you can, and should, get much more in depth with such analysis. A careful horizontal and vertical analysis serves as a starting point for an inquiry into the causes of these changes, with the objective of forecasting the corporation's future financial statements.

Analyzing the Financial Statements with Ratio Analysis

OBJECTIVE ➤ 5
Calculate and use financial statement ratios to evaluate a company.

Ratio analysis is an examination of financial statements conducted by preparing and evaluating a series of ratios. **Ratios** (or **financial ratios**), like other financial analysis data, normally provide meaningful information only when compared with ratios from previous periods for the same firm (i.e., time series/trend analysis) or similar firms (i.e., cross sectional analysis). As discussed previously, ratios help by removing most of the effects of size differences. When dollar amounts are used, size differences between firms may make a meaningful comparison impossible. However, properly constructed financial ratios permit the comparison of firms regardless of size.

We discuss six categories of ratio analysis: *Short-term liquidity ratios* are particularly helpful to short-term creditors, but all investors and creditors have an interest in these ratios. *Debt management ratios* and *profitability ratios* provide information for long-term creditors and stockholders. *Asset efficiency (or operating) ratios* help management operate the firm and indicate to outsiders the efficiency with which certain of the company's activities are performed. *Stockholder ratios* are of interest to a corporation's stockholders. Finally, *Dupont analysis* decomposes return on equity into margin, turnover, and leverage. All these ratios are shown and defined in Exhibit 12-4 on page 654.

We will use data from Abercrombie & Fitch's financial statements (pp. 704-708) to illustrate each of these types of financial statement ratios. We turn first to an examination of the ratios used to judge short-term liquidity.

Short-Term Liquidity Ratios

Analysts want to know the likelihood that a company will be able to pay its current obligations as they come due. Failure to pay current liabilities can lead to suppliers refusing to sell needed inventory and employees leaving. As such, even companies with good business models can be forced into bankruptcy by their inability to pay current liabilities.

The cash necessary to pay current liabilities will come from existing cash or from receivables and inventory, which should turn into cash approximately at the same time the current liabilities become due. Property, plant, and equipment and other long-lived assets are much more difficult to turn into cash in time to meet current obligations without harming future operations. Accordingly, the **short-term liquidity ratios** compare some combination of current assets or operations to current liabilities.

Current Ratio   Since a company must meet its current obligations primarily by using its current assets, the current ratio is especially useful to short-term creditors. The **current ratio** is computed by dividing current assets by current liabilities. Expressed as an equation, this ratio is:

$$\text{Current Ratio} = \frac{\text{Current Assets}}{\text{Current Liabilities}}$$

Looking at Abercrombie & Fitch's 2007 balance sheet we find current assets and current liabilities and calculate the current ratio as follows:

	2007	2006
Total current assets	$1,092,078	$947,084
Total current liabilities	510,627	491,554
Current ratio	**2.14**	**1.93**

A&F's current ratio increased because current assets increased more rapidly than current liabilities. In fact, if you look at the details of A&F's current assets you see that although receivables were about the same in 2007 as in 2006, cash, marketable securities, and inventories all increased. On the current liabilities side, increases in accounts payable and accrued expenses were essentially offset by decreases in outstanding checks, deferred lease credits, and income taxes payable.

There are no absolute standards for ratios, so a company's ratios are typically compared to the industry averages and/or competitors. The average for the Retail - Apparel & Accessories is 2.07. By these standards, A&F's current ratio was somewhat weak in 2006. Does this mean that there is short-term liquidity risk? No, but it does mean that you should investigate further (perhaps looking harder at the more conservative short-term liquidity ratios discussed below).

Quick Ratio   Some analysts believe that the current ratio overstates short-term liquidity. They argue that prepaid expenses (expenses for which payments are made before consumption) often cannot be converted into cash. Further, inventories must be sold and receivables collected from those sales before cash is obtained to pay maturing current liabilities. Both the sale of inventory and collection of receivables can require a lengthy period. Conservative analysts argue that only those current assets that can be turned into cash almost immediately should be used to measure short-term liquidity.

A more conservative measure of short-term liquidity is based on *quick assets* (usually cash, receivables, and short-term investments) and current liabilities. Expressed in equation form, the **quick ratio** (or *acid test ratio*, as it is sometimes called) is calculated as shown:

$$\text{Quick Ratio} = \frac{\text{Cash} + \text{Short-Term Investments} + \text{Receivables}}{\text{Current Liabilities}}$$

Looking at the detail of Abercrombie & Fitch's current assets, we can find the quick assets and liabilities and calculate the quick ratio as follows:

	2007	2006
Current assets:		
Cash and equivalents	$ 81,959	$ 50,687
Marketable securities	447,793	411,167
Receivables	43,240	41,855
Inventories	427,447	362,536
Deferred income taxes	33,170	29,654
Other current assets	58,469	51,185
Total current assets	$1,092,078	$947,084
Quick assets	572,992	503,709
Total current liabilities	$ 510,627	$491,554
Quick ratio	**1.12**	**1.02**

Generally, a quick ratio above 1.0 is considered adequate because there are enough liquid assets available to meet current obligations. Using this guideline, we see that A&F had little difficulty meeting its current obligations in 2006 or 2007. Further, A&F is well above the industry average of 0.92.

Cash Ratio   An even more conservative short-term liquidity ratio is the **cash ratio**. Specifically, while the current and quick ratios assume that receivables will be collected, the cash ratio does not make this assumption. This ratio may be more appropriate for industries in which collectibility is uncertain or for corporations with high credit risk receivables. Expressed in equation form, the cash ratio is:

$$\text{Cash Ratio} = \frac{\text{Cash} + \text{Short-Term Investments}}{\text{Current Liabilities}}$$

Although Abercrombie & Fitch does not have high credit risk receivables, we can calculate the cash ratio as follows:

	2007	2006
Current assets:		
Cash and equivalents	$ 81,959	$ 50,687
Marketable securities	447,793	411,167
Receivables	43,240	41,855
Inventories	427,447	362,536
Deferred income taxes	33,170	29,654
Other current assets	58,469	51,185
Total current assets	$1,092,078	$947,084
Cash and marketable securities	529,752	461,854
Total current liabilities	$ 510,627	$491,554
Cash ratio	**1.04**	**0.94**

If you questioned the collectability of A&F's receivables, you may have been slightly concerned with its short-term liquidity in 2006 because there was not enough cash and marketable securities to pay off the current liabilities. Fortunately, this condition improved in 2007. Obviously, a cash ratio above 1.0 clearly indicates the ability to meet short-term obligations.

Operating Cash Flow Ratio   The **operating cash flow ratio** takes a slightly different approach than the other three ratios. This ratio looks at the ability of operations to generate cash, which recognizes the more general concept that current obligations will be paid through operations (after all, selling inventory and collecting receivables is a big part of operations). This ratio is calculated as:

$$\text{Operating Cash Flow Ratio} = \frac{\text{Cash Flows from Operating Activities}}{\text{Current Liabilities}}$$

Looking at A&F's statement of cash flows and balance sheet we can obtain the necessary information and calculate the operating cash flow ratio as follows:

	2007	2006
Cash flows from operating activities	$582,171	$453,590
Total current liabilities	510,627	491,554
Operating cash flow ratio	**1.14**	**0.92**

In this case, we see similar results to what was calculated for the quick ratio (of course, they are not always similar). However, the conclusions are a bit more definitive. In 2006, A&F's operations did not generate enough cash to meet the current obligations due at the end of the year. That means that A&F's operations were going to have to improve in 2007 (obviously they did) or A&F would need to obtain cash through additional borrowing or selling of stock.

All the ratios increased in 2007, which indicates an improvement in A&F's short-term liquidity. For creditors, this is clearly good news. Creditors typically prefer all these measures of short-term liquidity be as high as possible. However, because investments in current assets (especially cash, receivables, and inventory) earn very small returns compared with the returns on investments in noncurrent assets, management must minimize the proportion of capital invested in current assets if it is to maximize profit. Cornerstone 12-4 illustrates how to calculate and interpret short-term liquidity ratios for Aeropostale.

Debt Management Ratios

Debt management ratios provide information on two aspects of debt. First, they provide information on the relative mix of debt and equity financing (often referred to as its capital structure). The primary advantages of debt over equity are (1) interest payments are tax-deductible and (2) creditors do not share in profits. Debt, however, is riskier than equity, because unless the interest and principal payments are made when due, the firm may fall into bankruptcy. In most corporations, management attempts to achieve an appropriate balance between the cost advantage of debt and its extra risk.

Second, debt management ratios also try to show the corporation's ability to meet, or cover, its debt obligations through operations because interest and principal payments must be made as scheduled, or a company can be declared bankrupt. The times interest earned ratio is an example of the latter type of measurement.

**CORNERSTONE
12-4**

HOW TO Calculate and Interpret Short-Term Liquidity Ratios

Concept:
Short-term liquidity ratios compare some or all of current assets, as well as cash flows from operations, to current liabilities in order to assess the corporation's ability to meet its current obligations. The logic of the current ratio is that current liabilities need to be paid over approximately the same time frame that current assets are turned into cash. Both the quick and cash ratios recognize that some current assets are harder to liquidate. The quick ratio excludes inventories because including inventories assumes that sales will be made; however, the quick ratio assumes that accounts receivable are easily turned into cash (i.e., liquid). This is true when customers have low credit risk and pay in relatively short amounts of time. Of course, such an assumption is not true for all industries. Consequently, the use of the cash ratio may be more appropriate in these cases because it excludes receivables in addition to inventories. In fact, the only current assets included are cash and marketable securities. The operating cash flow ratio, on the other hand, looks at the ability of cash generated from operating activities to meet current obligations. As with the current ratio, the operating cash flow ratio assumes that sales will continue into the future.

Information:
Use Aeropostale's income statement and balance sheet in Exhibit 12-3 (on page 638) to calculate short-term liquidity ratios. You will also need to know that Aeropostale's cash flows from operations were (in thousands) $144,384 and $177,445 in 2006 and 2007, respectively.

Required:
1. Calculate Aeropostale's current ratio for 2006 and 2007.
2. Calculate Aeropostale's quick ratio for 2006 and 2007.
3. Calculate Aeropostale's cash ratio for 2006 and 2007.
4. Calculate Aeropostale's operating cash flow ratio for 2006 and 2007 (operating cash flows are provided in the Information section above).
5. Comment on Aeropostale's short-term liquidity compared to the Abercrombie & Fitch ratios shown in the body of the text.

Solution:

1. Current Ratio $= \dfrac{\text{Current Assets}}{\text{Current Liabilities}}$

	2007	2006
Current Ratio	$\dfrac{\$398{,}793}{\$164{,}798} = 2.42$	$\dfrac{\$339{,}339}{\$126{,}353} = 2.69$

2. Quick Ratio $= \dfrac{\text{Cash} + \text{Short-Term Investments} + \text{Accounts Receivable}}{\text{Current Liabilities}}$

	2007	2006
Quick Ratio	$\dfrac{\$200{,}064 + \$76{,}223 + 0}{\$164{,}798} = 1.68$	$\dfrac{\$205{,}235 + 20{,}037 + 0}{\$126{,}353} = 1.78$

3. Cash Ratio $= \dfrac{\text{Cash} + \text{Short-Term Investments}}{\text{Current Liabilities}}$

	2007	2006
Cash Ratio	$\dfrac{\$200{,}064 + \$76{,}223}{\$164{,}798} = 1.68$	$\dfrac{\$205{,}235 + 20{,}037}{\$126{,}353} = 1.78$

4. Operating Cash Flow Ratio $= \dfrac{\text{Cash Flows from Operating Activities}}{\text{Current Liabilities}}$

	2007	2006
Operating Cash Flow Ratio	$\dfrac{\$177{,}445^*}{\$164{,}798} = 1.08$	$\dfrac{\$144{,}384^*}{\$126{,}353} = 1.14$

*Taken from the statement of cash flows. The numbers were provided in the Information Section of this Cornerstone.

5. Aeropostale's current ratio is well above the industry average of 2.07. Further, its quick and cash ratios are far above the 1.0 threshold considered adequate and its operating cash flow ratio, although weaker than the others, is adequate.

   Aeropostale's short-term liquidity ratios are stronger than Abercrombie & Fitch's. This suggests that Aeropostale's risk of short-term insolvency is lower, although neither corporation is in much danger. Nonetheless, while A&F's ratios were all stronger in 2007 than in 2006, Aeropostale's ratios have all weakened. Investigation of Aeropostale's balance sheet indicates that the primary reason for the weakening ratios is the large increase in accrued expenses. Investigation of Note 7 shows that accrued expenses are made up of items such as wages and salaries payable, rent payable, outstanding gift cards, income taxes payable, etc. These items can fluctuate depending on the timing of year end. For example, if year end falls on a pay day, then wages and salaries payable will be much lower than if it does not. Obviously, Aeropostale must still pay these amounts, but given the strength of their ratios, their ability to pay is not the concern—rather it is the negative trend. Thus, concern about the negative trend is minimized because of the nature of the items that appear to drive the weakening ratios.

Exhibit 12-3

Aeropostale, Inc. Income Statement and Balance Sheet

Aeropostale, Inc.
Consolidated Statements of Income
(In thousands)

	Fiscal Year Ended		
	Feb. 3, 2007	Jan. 28, 2006	Jan. 29, 2005
Net sales	$1,413,208	$1,204,347	$ 964,212
Cost of goods sold	957,791	841,872	644,305
Gross profit	$ 455,417	362,475	319,907
Selling, general, and administrative expenses	(289,736)	(227,044)	(183,977)
Other income, net	2,085	—	—
Income from operations	$ 167,766	$ 135,431	$ 135,930
Interest income	7,064	3,670	1,438
Income before taxes	$ 174,830	$ 139,101	$ 137,368
Income taxes	68,183	55,147	53,256
Net income	$ 106,647	$ 83,954	$ 84,112

Aeropostale, Inc.
Consolidated Balance Sheets
(In thousands)

	Feb. 3, 2007	Jan. 28, 2006	Jan. 29, 2005
ASSETS			
Current assets:			
Cash and cash equivalents	$200,064	$205,235	$106,128
Short-term investments	76,223	20,037	76,224
Merchandise inventory	101,476	91,908	81,238
Prepaid expenses	12,175	12,314	10,138
Deferred income taxes	1,185	—	—
Other current assets	7,670	9,845	5,759
Total current assets	$398,793	$339,339	$279,487
Fixtures, equipment and improvements (net)	175,591	160,229	122,651
Intangible assets	1,400	2,455	2,529
Deferred income taxes	3,784	—	—
Other assets	1,596	1,928	1,152
Total assets	$581,164	$503,951	$405,819
LIABILITIES & STOCKHOLDERS' EQUITY			
Current liabilities:			
Accounts payable	$ 63,918	$ 57,165	$ 44,858
Deferred income taxes	—	5,195	893
Accrued expenses	100,880	63,993	51,243
Total current liabilities	$ 164,798	$ 126,353	$ 96,994
Deferred rent and tenant allowances	88,344	81,499	63,065
Retirement benefit plan liabilities	15,906	8,654	6,158
Deferred income taxes	—	2,655	1,351
Total liabilities	$ 269,048	$ 219,161	$167,568
Stockholders' equity:			
Common stock	$ 593	$ 586	$ 581
Preferred stock	—	—	—
Additional paid-in capital	101,429	88,213	79,069
Other comprehensive income	(5,274)	(1,557)	(1,271)
Deferred compensation	—	(2,577)	(817)
Retained earnings	414,916	308,269	224,315
Treasury stock	(199,548)	(108,144)	(63,626)
Total stockholders' equity	$ 312,116	$ 284,790	$238,251
Total liabilities and stockholders' equity	$ 581,164	$ 503,951	$405,819

Times Interest Earned Ratio Some liabilities, like accounts payable, have flexible payment schedules that can be modified when necessary. Other liabilities—primarily short-term and long-term debt—have specific payment schedules that must be met. The cash used to make these payments must come from operations. Analysts use the **times interest earned ratio**, which measures the excess of net income over interest to gauge a firm's ability to repay its debt. The larger the excess of net income over interest, the greater the probability that a firm will be able to meet the interest payments on current or contemplated obligations. The concept is similar to when you hear statements about how much of the government's tax revenues are used to pay off debt.

In the times interest earned ratio, interest expense and income tax expense are added back to net income. The use of this subtotal is so common that it is known by its own acronym EBIT (earnings before interest and taxes). Taxes are excluded because they are paid after interest payments. In other words, if income were just large enough to cover interest payments, taxes would be zero. The equation used to calculate the ratio is:

$$\text{Times Interest Earned Ratio} = \frac{\text{EBIT}}{\text{Interest Expense}}$$

Note that you often have to go to the financial-statement footnotes to find interest expense because many corporations net interest income with interest expense on the face of the income statement. Nonetheless, Abercrombie & Fitch does not have any interest expense (or if they do it is so insignificant they do not disclose it separately), thus their times interest earned ratio is infinite. The industry average is 4.97; obviously, Abercrombie & Fitch compares very well to the industry average on this dimension.

Now let us turn to the second type of debt-management ratio. We will consider four different ways of measuring the proportion of debt within a corporation's capital structure.

Long-Term Debt-to-Equity Ratio Despite its apparent misnomer, we prefer to define long-term debt as the sum of long-term debt and the debt-like obligations in current liabilities (notes or short-term loans). It is called the long-term debt-to-equity ratio because historically when corporations borrowed money, they locked themselves into long-term debt contracts. The **long-term debt-to-equity ratio** provides information on the proportion of capital provided by this type of debt and by stockholders. Of course, this type of debt also includes any current portion (i.e., long-term debt principal that must be repaid within the next 12 months). Additionally, it includes more flexible borrowing arrangements, such as lines of credit, that may be classified as current liabilities. The equation used in calculating this ratio is:

$$\text{Long-Term Debt-to-Equity Ratio} = \frac{\text{Long-Term Debt (including current portion)}}{\text{Total Equity}}$$

Debt-to-Equity Ratio Debt is also occasionally defined as the sum of long-term debt and all current liabilities. This is a more inclusive view of debt recognizing that if corporations did not have current liabilities such as accounts payable, they would have to take out other borrowings or sell stock to finance its assets. The equation used in calculating the **debt-to-equity ratio** is:

$$\text{Debt-to-Equity Ratio} = \frac{\text{Total Liabilities}}{\text{Total Equity}}$$

Long-Term Debt or Debt-to-Total Assets The proportion of total capital provided by creditors is also shown by the **long-term debt-to-total assets ratio** and the **debt-to-total assets ratio**. These measures are more useful when equity is small or subject to substantial changes. The ratio is computed as the sum of long-term and short-term debt divided by total assets (or by total liabilities plus equity):

$$\text{Long-Term Debt-to-Total Assets Ratio} = \frac{\text{Long-Term Debt (including current portion)}}{\text{Total Assets}}$$

$$\text{Debt-to-Total Assets Ratio} = \frac{\text{Total Liabilities}}{\text{Total Assets}}$$

Cornerstone 12-5 demonstrates how to calculate and interpret debt management ratios.

CORNERSTONE 12-5

HOW TO Calculate and Interpret Debt Management Ratios

Concept:
Debt management ratios provide information on two aspects of debt. First, they provide information on the relative mix of debt and equity financing (often referred to as its capital structure). Second, debt management ratios also try to show the corporation's ability to meet its debt obligations through operations because interest and principal payments must be made as scheduled, or a company can be forced into bankruptcy.

Information:
The following information is taken from **American Airlines'** 2007 10-K:

	2007	2006
Current liabilities:		
Accounts payable	$ 1,083	$ 987
Accrued salaries and wages	520	516
Accrued liabilities	1,608	1,648
Air traffic liability	3,986	3,782
Payable to affiliates	1,610	1,071
Current maturities of long-term debt	382	1,012
Other current liabilities	147	101
Total current liabilities	**$ 9,336**	**$ 9,117**
Long-term debt, less current maturities	6,600	7,787
Other long-term debt	8,005	10,012
Total long-term liabilities	**$14,605**	**$17,799**
Total liabilities	**$23,941**	**$26,916**
Total stockholders' equity	$ 1,444	$ (1,066)
Total assets	25,385	25,850
Interest expense	708	795
Net income	356	164
Income tax expense	0	0

Required:
1. Calculate American Airlines' times interest earned ratio for 2006 and 2007.
2. Calculate American Airlines' long-term debt-to-equity ratio for 2006 and 2007.
3. Calculate American Airlines' debt-to-equity ratio for 2006 and 2007.
4. Calculate American Airlines' long-term debt-to-total assets ratio for 2006 and 2007.
5. Calculate American Airlines' debt-to-total assets ratio for 2006 and 2007.
6. Comment on American Airlines' debt management.

Solution:
1.
$$\text{Times Interest Earned Ratio} = \frac{\text{EBIT}}{\text{Interest Expense}}$$

	2007	2006
Times Interest Earned Ratio	$\frac{(\$356 + \$0 + \$708)}{\$708} = 1.50$	$\frac{(\$164 + \$0 + \$795)}{\$795} = 1.21$

2. Long-Term Debt-to-Equity Ratio $= \dfrac{\text{Long-Term Debt (including current portion)}}{\text{Total Equity}}$

CORNERSTONE 12-5 *(continued)*

	2007	2006
Long-Term Debt to Equity	$\dfrac{\$6,600 + \$382}{\$1,444} = 4.84$	$\dfrac{\$7,787 + \$1,012}{\$(1,066)} = (8.25)$

3. Debt-to-Equity Ratio $= \dfrac{\text{Total Liabilities}}{\text{Total Equity}}$

	2007	2006
Debt-to-Equity	$\dfrac{\$23,941}{\$1,444} = 16.58$	$\dfrac{\$26,916}{\$(1,066)} = (25.25)$

4. Long-Term Debt-to-Total Assets Ratio $= \dfrac{\text{Long-Term Debt (including current portion)}}{\text{Total Assets}}$

	2007	2006
Long-Term Debt-to-Total Assets	$\dfrac{\$6,600 + \$382}{\$25,385} = 0.28$	$\dfrac{\$7,787 + \$1,012}{\$25,850} = 0.34$

5. Debt-to-Total Assets Ratio $=$ Total Liabilities/Total Assets

	2007	2006
Debt-to-Total Assets	$\dfrac{\$23,941}{\$25,385} = 0.94$	$\dfrac{\$26,916}{\$25,850} = 1.04$

6. From the times interest earned ratio, you can see that the bulk of American Airlines' net income is necessary to cover its interest expense in 2006 and 2007. Of course, this is a risky situation that must be investigated further. For example, now you may want to consider recurring income that is not in income from operations (e.g., interest income) and look at cash flows from operations and interest payments.

The long-term debt-to-equity and debt-to-equity ratios paint a similar picture. Specifically, American Airlines has a lot more debt financing than equity financing. The debt-to-equity ratio reveals that there is over 16 times more debt than equity in 2007.

Although the debt-to-equity ratios are improving, the negative equity in 2006 makes it more difficult to evaluate. In this case, a good option is to look at the debt-to-total asset ratios. The long-term debt-to-total asset ratio shows that approximately 28 percent of total assets are financed with long-term debt in 2007. The debt-to-total asset ratio shows that liabilities are 94 percent of total assets in 2007 and the ratio of above 1.0 in 2006 indicates negative equity. These ratios also suggest improvement and the percentage improvement is more meaningful. Namely, the long-term debt-to-total assets improved by about 18 percent and the debt-to-total assets improved by approximately 10 percent.

Asset Efficiency Ratios

Asset efficiency ratios (or **operating ratios**) are measures of how efficiently a company uses its assets. The principal operating ratios are measures of **turnover**, that is, the average length of time required for assets to be consumed or replaced. The faster an asset is turned over, the more efficiently it is being used. These ratios provide managers and other users of a corporation's financial statements with easily interpreted measures of the time required to turn receivables into cash, inventory into cost of goods sold, or total assets into sales.

But managers are not the only people interested in asset efficiency ratios. Since well-managed, efficiently operated companies are usually among the most profitable, and since profits are the sources of cash from which long-term creditors receive their interest and principal payments, creditors seek information about the corporation's profit prospects from operating ratios. And stockholders find that larger profits are usually followed by increased dividends and higher stock prices, so they, too, are concerned with indicators of efficiency.

Accounts Receivable Turnover Ratio

The length of time required to collect the receivable from a credit sale is the time required to turn over accounts receivable. The **accounts receivable turnover ratio** indicates how many times accounts receivable is turned over each year. The more times accounts receivable turns over each year, the more efficient are the firm's credit-granting and credit-collection activities.

Receivables turnover is computed by dividing net credit sales (credit sales less sales returns and allowances) by the average receivables balance. While some firms make all their sales on credit, many also make a substantial proportion of their sales for cash (or on credit cards which are essentially cash sales). It is unusual for a company making cash and credit sales to report the proportion that is credit sales. For that reason, the accounts receivable turnover ratio is often computed using whatever number the firm reports for sales.

$$\text{Accounts Receivable Turnover Ratio} = \frac{\text{Net Credit Sales or Net Sales}}{\text{Average Accounts Receivable}}$$

To find the average balance for any financial statement account, divide the sum of the beginning and ending balances by two.

Careful analysts examine quarterly or monthly financial statements, when available, to determine whether the amount of receivables recorded in the annual statements is representative of the receivables carried during the year. For example, retailers often have much larger receivables after the Christmas selling season than during other parts of the year. Using net sales, Abercrombie & Fitch's receivables turnover ratios were 69.95 and 77.99 for 2006 and 2007, respectively, so they are very efficient at collecting cash from their sales. This is far better than the industry average of 46.93. This superior ratio probably means that a vast majority of their sales are for cash (or third party credit cards that are collected very quickly). Although their 10-K does not discuss it in detail, A&F also has an in-store credit card, which, as discussed in Chapter 9, will increase receivables balances and reduce third-party credit card fees.

Inventory Turnover Ratio

Inventory turnover is the length of time required to sell inventory to customers. The more efficient a firm, the more times inventory will be turned over. The **inventory turnover ratio** indicates the number of times inventory is sold during the year. It is computed by dividing the cost of goods sold by the average inventory. (Average inventory is beginning inventory plus ending inventory divided by 2.)

$$\text{Inventory Turnover Ratio} = \frac{\text{Cost of Goods Sold}}{\text{Average Inventory}}$$

Abercrombie & Fitch's inventory turnover ratios were 3.25 and 2.81 for 2006 and 2007, respectively. This means that A&F turns over its inventory about three times per year or once every four months. Remember that inventory sitting in the warehouse or on the shelf is not earning a return. The weakening inventory turnover deserves some attention. For example, does the slower moving inventory indicate weakening sales? Further, the industry average is 4.68, so Abercrombie & Fitch is relatively inefficient with its inventory.

Now that we have examined both receivables and inventory turnover, let us combine these measurements to approximate the length of the operating cycle (the length of time required for an investment in inventory to produce cash). Abercrombie & Fitch's 2007 operating cycle can be estimated by adding the number of days needed to turn over both receivables and inventory. The inventory turns over in approximately 130 days (365 days/2.81 inventory turnover ratio) and the receivables turn over in approximately 4.7 days (365 days/77.99 receivables turnover ratio), which gives an operating cycle of approximately 135 days.

The longer the operating cycle, the larger the investment necessary in receivables and inventory. When assets are larger, more liabilities and equity are required to finance them. Large amounts of capital negatively affect net income and cash flows for dividends. Therefore, firms attempt to maintain as short an operating cycle as possible. A&F's operating cycle is relatively long.

Asset Turnover Ratio Another measure of the efficiency of a corporation's operations is the **asset turnover ratio**. This ratio measures the efficiency with which a corporation's assets are used to produce sales revenues. The more sales dollars produced by each dollar invested in assets, the more efficiently a firm is considered to be operating. The ratio is computed by dividing net sales by average total assets (beginning total assets plus ending total assets divided by 2):

$$\text{Asset Turnover Ratio} = \frac{\text{Net Sales}}{\text{Average Total Assets}}$$

It is important to note that turnover ratios must be interpreted carefully. A company's ability to increase its receivables turnover is limited by competitive considerations. If competitors allow customers a lengthy period before payment is expected, then the firm must offer similar credit terms or lose customers. In periods of high interest rates, the cost of carrying customers' receivables should not be underestimated. For example, a firm with credit sales of $10,000 per day that collects in 30 rather than 90 days would save $72,000 per year at a 12 percent interest rate [(60 days)($10,000 sales per day)(12%)].

However, a corporation's ability to increase its inventory turnover is also affected by its strategy and what the competition is doing. For example, if its strategy is to offer a wide selection or if its competitors stock large quantities of inventory, a corporation will be forced to keep more inventory on hand. This, of course, leads to lower inventory turnover.

Care must be exercised when evaluating the asset turnover ratio. Some industries (such as electric utilities and capital intensive manufacturers) require a substantially larger investment in assets to produce a sales dollar than do other industries (such as fast-food restaurants or footwear and catalog merchants). And obviously, a company's total assets turn over much more slowly than its inventories and receivables. Abercrombie & Fitch's asset turnover ratios were 1.75 and 1.64 in 2006 and 2007, respectively, which means about every 223 days (365/1.64) in 2007. The asset turnover average for the industry is 1.96, so Abercrombie & Fitch is well below the average. But, it is not as far below on asset turnover as it is on accounts receivable turnover. Cornerstone 12-6 illustrates how to calculate and interpret asset efficiency ratios.

Operating ratios measure the efficiency of a corporation's operations—a factor ultimately related to the corporation's profits. Let us now examine some direct measures of a corporation's profitability.

**CORNERSTONE
12-6**

HOW TO Calculate and Interpret Asset Efficiency Ratios

Concept:
Asset efficiency ratios are measures of how efficiently a corporation uses its assets. The principal operating ratios are measures of the average length of time required for assets to be consumed or replaced, or what the ratio calls turnover. The faster an asset is turned over, the more efficiently it is being used. These ratios provide managers and other users of a corporation's financial statements with easily interpreted measures of the time required to turn receivables into cash, inventory into cost of goods sold, or total assets into sales.

Information:
Use Aeropostale's income statement and balance sheet in Exhibit 12-3 to calculate asset efficiency ratios.

Required:
1. Calculate Aeropostale's accounts receivable turnover ratio for 2006 and 2007.
2. Calculate Aeropostale's inventory turnover ratio for 2006 and 2007.
3. Calculate Aeropostale's asset turnover ratio for 2006 and 2007.
4. Comment on Aeropostale's asset efficiency ratios comparing them to the Abercrombie & Fitch ratios shown in the body of the text.

Solution:
Note: Average Balance = $\dfrac{\text{Beginning Balance} + \text{Ending Balance}}{2}$

1. Accounts Receivable Turnover Ratio = Net Sales/Average Accounts Receivable

	2007		2006	
Accounts Receivable Turnover Ratio	$\dfrac{\$1,413,208}{\$0}$	= Infinite	$\dfrac{\$1,204,347}{\$0}$	= Infinite

2. Inventory Turnover Ratio = Cost of Good Sold/Average Inventories

	2007		2006	
Inventory Turnover Ratio	$\dfrac{\$957,791}{(\$101,476 + \$91,908)/2}$	= 9.91	$\dfrac{\$841,872}{(\$91,908 + \$81,238)/2}$	= 9.72

3. Asset Turnover Ratio = Net Sales/Average Total Assets

	2007		2006	
Asset Turnover Ratio	$\dfrac{\$1,413,208}{(\$581,164 + \$503,951)/2}$	= 2.60	$\dfrac{\$1,204,347}{(\$503,951 + \$405,819)/2}$	= 2.65

4. Aeropostale does not have significant receivables. This is because all its sales are made with cash or third-party credit cards. Although its accounts receivable turnover is obviously stronger than A&F's, A&F does have a strong accounts receivable turnover ratio. Aeropostale's inventory turnover ratios of 9.72 and 9.91 are much stronger than A&F's ratios of 3.25 and 2.81 (and well above the industry averages). These two ratios imply an operating cycle of approximately 36 days for Aeropostale compared to 135 days for A&F. All this information is also consistent with the asset turnover ratio, which is much stronger for Aeropostale.

   Does this mean that Aeropostale is a much better run corporation? Perhaps it does, but we will discuss alternative explanations for these differences in the Dupont Analysis section.

Profitability Ratios

Profitability ratios measure two aspects of a corporation's profits: (1) those elements of operations that contribute to profit and (2) the relationship of profit to total investment and investment by stockholders. The first group of profitability ratios [gross profit (or gross margin) percentage, operating margin percentage, and net profit margin percentage] expresses income statement elements as percentages of net sales. The second group of profitability ratios (return on assets and return on equity) divides measures of income by measures of investment. The gross profit percentage is explained first.

Gross Profit (or Gross Margin) Percentage

Gross profit percentage is a measurement of the proportion of each sales dollar that is available to pay other expenses and provide profit for owners. The gross profit percentage indicates the effectiveness of pricing, marketing, purchasing, and production decisions. It is computed by dividing gross margin by net sales:

$$\text{Gross Profit Percentage} = \frac{\text{Gross Profit}}{\text{Net Sales}}$$

Abercrombie & Fitch's gross profit percentage was 66.5 percent in 2006 and 66.6 percent in 2007. This means that for every dollar in sales the merchandise cost approximately 33 cents, which results in approximately 67 cents in gross profit. This is far above the industry average of 37.7 percent.

In evaluating the gross profit, operating margin, and net profit margin percentage, it is important to recognize that there is substantial variation in profit margins from industry to industry. For example, retail grocery stores earn a relatively small amount of gross profit, operating margin, and net income per sales dollar. Pharmaceutical manufacturers, on the other hand, earn much more per sales dollar. Since the magnitude of these percentages is affected by many factors, changes from period to period must be investigated to determine the cause.

Operating Margin Percentage

The **operating margin percentage** measures the profitability of a company's operations in relation to its sales. All operating revenues and expenses are included in income from operations, but expenses, revenues, gains, and losses that are unrelated to operations are excluded. For example, a retailer would exclude interest revenues produced by its credit activities from income from operations. The operating margin percentage is expressed as follows:

$$\text{Operating Margin Percentage} = \frac{\text{Income from Operations}}{\text{Net Sales}}$$

Abercrombie & Fitch's operating margin percentage was 19.5 percent in 2006 and 19.8 percent in 2007. The difference between the gross profit and operating margin percentage of approximately 47 percent (66.6 percent gross margin percentage − 19.8 percent operating margin percentage) means that approximately 47 cents on every dollar of sales are spent on operating expenses. Abercrombie & Fitch's operating margin percentage is well above the industry average of 10.0 percent.

Net Profit Margin Percentage

The **net profit margin percentage** measures the proportion of each sales dollar that is profit. The ratio is determined by dividing net income by net sales:

$$\text{Net Profit Margin Percentage} = \frac{\text{Net Income}}{\text{Net Sales}}$$

Abercrombie & Fitch's net profit margin percentage was 12.0 percent in 2006 and 12.7 percent in 2007, which exceeds the industry average of 6.4 percent. Unlike the previous two percentages, which were essentially unchanged, there is slight improvement in the net profit margin percentage. Now let us examine two profitability measures that are based on income per dollar of investment.

Return on Assets   The **return on assets** ratio measures the profit earned by a corporation through use of all its capital, or the total of the investment by both creditors and owners. Profit, or return, is determined by adding interest expense net of tax to net income. Interest expense net of tax is calculated as follows:

$$\text{Interest Net of Tax} = \text{Interest Expense} \times (1 - \text{Tax Rate})$$

Interest expense is added to net income because it is a return to creditors for their capital contributions. Because the actual capital contribution made by creditors is included in the denominator (average total assets), the numerator must be computed on a comparable basis. The equation is:

$$\text{Return on Assets} = \frac{\text{Net Income} + [\text{Interest Expense} \times (1 - \text{Tax Rate})]}{\text{Average Total Assets}}$$

Abercrombie & Fitch's return on assets was 21.03 percent in 2006 and 20.86 percent in 2007. As with the percentages discussed above, appropriate values for this ratio vary from industry to industry because of differences in risk. Over a several-year period, the average return on assets for an electric utility ought to be smaller than the average return on assets for a company that makes and sells home appliances. Companies in the home appliance industry have a much larger variability of net income because their operations are more sensitive to economic conditions. The average for the Retail—Apparel industry is 12.0 percent, so Abercrombie & Fitch is also well above the mean for this ratio.

Return on Equity   The **return on equity** ratio measures the profit earned by a firm through the use of capital supplied by stockholders. Return on equity is similar to return on assets, except that the payments to creditors are removed from the numerator and the creditors' capital contributions are removed from the denominator. Therefore, return on equity is simply net income divided by average equity:

$$\text{Return on Equity} = \frac{\text{Net Income}}{\text{Average Equity}}$$

One of the primary objectives of the management of a firm is to maximize returns for its stockholders. Although the link between a corporation's net income and increases in dividends and share price return is not perfect, the return on equity ratio is still an effective measure of management's performance for the stockholders. As is the case with return on assets, firms often differ in return on equity because of differences in risk. For example, the average several-year return on equity for a grocery store should be lower than the average return on equity for a retail department store because of the lower sensitivity to economic conditions. The return on equity for Abercrombie & Fitch was 40.1 percent and 35.2 percent in 2006 and 2007, respectively, which is substantially above the industry average of 26.2 percent. Cornerstone 12-7 demonstrates how to calculate and interpret profitability ratios.

**CORNERSTONE
12-7**

HOW TO Calculate and Interpret Profitability Ratios

Concept:
Profitability ratios measure two aspects of a corporation's profits: (1) those elements of operations that contribute to profit and (2) the relationship of profit to total investment and investment by stockholders. The first group of profitability ratios [gross profit (or gross margin) percentage, operating margin percentage, and net profit margin percentage] express income statement elements as percentages of net sales. The second group of profitability ratios (return on assets and return on equity) divide measures of income by measures of investment.

Information:
Use Aeropostale's income statement and balance sheet in Exhibit 12-3 to calculate profitability ratios. In Aeropostale's Income Statement, interest expense is netted with interest income.

Required:
1. Calculate Aeropostale's gross profit percentage for 2006 and 2007.
2. Calculate Aeropostale's operating margin percentage for 2006 and 2007.
3. Calculate Aeropostale's net profit margin percentage for 2006 and 2007.
4. Calculate Aeropostale's return on assets for 2006 and 2007. Assume that Aeropostale's interest expense is $1,560 and $1,813 in 2006 and 2007, respectively.
5. Calculate Aeropostale's return on equity for 2006 and 2007.
6. Comment on Aeropostale's profitability ratios comparing them to the Abercrombie & Fitch ratios shown in the body of the text.

Solution:

Note: Average Balance $= \dfrac{\text{Beginning Balance} + \text{Ending Balance}}{2}$

1. Gross Profit Percentage = Gross Profit/Net sales

	2007	2006
Gross Profit Percentage	$\dfrac{\$455,417}{\$1,413,208} = 32.2\%$	$\dfrac{\$362,475}{\$1,204,347} = 30.1\%$

2. Operating Margin Percentage = Income from Operations/Net Sales

	2007	2006
Operating Margin Percentage	$\dfrac{\$167,766}{\$1,413,208} = 11.9\%$	$\dfrac{\$135,431}{\$1,204,347} = 11.2\%$

3. Net Profit Margin Percentage = Net Income/Net Sales

	2007	2006
Net Profit Margin Percentage	$\dfrac{\$106,647}{\$1,413,208} = 7.5\%$	$\dfrac{\$83,954}{\$1,204,347} = 7.0\%$

4. Return on Assets $= \dfrac{\text{Net Income} + [\text{Interest Expense} \times (1 - \text{Tax Rate})]}{\text{Average Total Assets}}$

	2007	2006
Return on Assets	$\dfrac{\$106,647 + [1,813^* \times (1 - 0.39)]}{(\$581,164 + \$503,951)/2} = 19.9\%$	$\dfrac{\$83,594 + [1,560^* \times (1 - 0.396)]}{(\$503,951 + \$405,819)/2} = 18.6\%$

Note: (Tax Rate = Income Taxes/Income before Taxes)

* Provided in the part 4 of the Required section of this cornerstone.

5. Return on Equity = Net Income/Average Equity

	2007	2006
Return on Equity	$\dfrac{\$106,647}{(\$312,116 + \$284,790)/2} = 35.7\%$	$\dfrac{\$83,954}{(\$284,790 + \$238,251)/2} = 32.1\%$

6. Abercrombie & Fitch's gross profit percentage is more than twice as high as Aeropostale's. Specifically, A&F makes over 30 cents more in gross profit on every sales dollar than does Aeropostale [(66.6% × $1) − (32.2% × $1)]. However, much of this advantage is wiped out by the time we reach operating margin, as A&F's operating margin and net income are only about eight cents and five cents better, respectively, than Aeropostale's on every sales dollar. The return ratios, on the other hand, are virtually identical as both corporations earn a return of about 19 percent on assets and about 35 percent on equity.

We now turn to the stockholder ratios.

Stockholder Ratios

Stockholders are primarily interested in two things: (1) the creation of value, and (2) the distribution of value. **Stockholder ratios** such as earnings per share and return on common equity provide information about the creation of value for shareholders. As discussed in Chapter 10, value is distributed to shareholders in one of two ways. Either the corporation issues dividends or repurchases stock. The remainder of the stockholder ratios—dividend yield, dividend payout, stock repurchase payout, and total payout—address this distribution of value.

Earnings per Share (EPS)

Earnings per share ratio, or **EPS**, measures the income available for common stockholders on a per-share basis. EPS is one item that is examined by nearly all statement users. Conceptually, it is very simple: net income less preferred dividends divided by the average number of common shares outstanding. (Remember that treasury shares are not considered to be outstanding.) Preferred dividends are subtracted from net income because those payments are a return to holders of shares other than common stock. In fact, the numerator, net income less preferred dividends, is often called *income available for common shareholders*. The equation for the earnings per share ratio is:

$$\text{Earnings per Share Ratio} = \frac{\text{Net Income} - \text{Preferred Dividends}}{\text{Average Number of Common Shares Outstanding}}$$

Although this formula allows you to calculate EPS on your own, corporations are also required to disclose EPS on the income statement. For example, Abercrombie & Fitch's EPS was $3.83 in 2006 and $4.79 in 2007, which represents 25 percent growth.

Return on Common Equity

The **return on common equity ratio** is basically the same as the return on equity discussed in the profitability ratio section. We place this ratio here because it is arguably the most important ratio for investors. Plus, it gives us the opportunity to modify the ratio slightly by calculating the return on *common* equity rather than equity. To calculate common equity you subtract any contributed capital from preferred stock from total stockholders' equity (Total Equity − Preferred Stock − Paid-in Capital–Preferred Stock).

$$\text{Return on Common Equity} = \frac{\text{Net Income}}{\text{Average Common Equity}}$$

Dividend Yield Ratio

The **dividend yield ratio** measures the rate at which dividends provide a return to stockholders, by comparing dividends with the market price of a share of stock. This ratio is conceptually similar to an interest rate on debt where the dividend is like the interest payment and the cost of the share of stock is the principal.

This ratio is affected by both the corporation's dividend policy and the behavior of its stock price. Because stock prices often change by substantial amounts over short periods, the dividend yield ratio is not stable. In fact, when a stock is traded regularly, the market price is likely to change many times each day. For this reason, some analysts compute dividend yield based on the average stock price for a given period. Others use the highest and the lowest prices for a period and present the dividend yield as a range. For ease, we calculate dividend yield using the closing market price for the year.

$$\text{Dividend Yield Ratio} = \frac{\text{Dividends per Common Share}}{\text{Closing Market Price per Share for the Year}}$$

For the year ended February 3, 2007, Abercrombie & Fitch paid dividends of $0.70 per share and the closing market value of their common shares was $80.77. This gives a dividend yield ratio of 0.9 percent, which is below the industry average of 1.8 percent.

Dividend Payout Ratio

The **dividend payout ratio** measures the proportion of a corporation's profits that are returned to the stockholders immediately as dividends. To calculate this ratio, we will look at common dividends and net income.

$$\text{Dividend Payout Ratio} = \frac{\text{Common Dividends}}{\text{Net Income}}$$

You could calculate dividend payout using per share amounts (i.e., dividends per share/EPS), but this makes it more difficult to combine with the stock repurchases, so we use the total dollar amounts. You can find the dividends paid in the retained earnings column of the statement of stockholders' equity. For A&F, the common dividends paid were $52,218 in 2006 and $61,623 in 2007. With net income of $333,986 in 2006 and $422,186 in 2007, this produces dividend payout ratios of 15.6 percent and 14.6 percent in 2006 and 2007, respectively.

The dividend payout ratio varies from corporation to corporation, even within a given industry. Most corporations attempt to pay some stable proportion of earnings as dividends. Corporations are reluctant to reduce dividends unless absolutely necessary. The result of these two tendencies is that dividends per share are usually increased only when management is confident that higher earnings per share can be sustained. An increase in the dividend payout ratio is usually a signal that management expects future net income to be larger and sustainable.

Total Payout Ratio

The **total payout ratio** adds stock repurchases to common dividends and compares this to net income. You can find stock repurchases by looking at the treasury stock column of the statement of stockholders' equity.

$$\text{Total Payout Ratio} = \frac{\text{Common Dividends} + \text{Common Stock Repurchases}}{\text{Net Income}}$$

Abercrombie & Fitch had $103,296 in stock repurchases during 2006 and none in 2007. When coupled with the dividends and net income of $333,986 in 2006 and $422,186 in 2007, this produces total payout ratios of 46.6 percent and 14.6 percent in 2006 and 2007, respectively.

Stock Repurchase Payout Ratio

The **stock repurchase payout ratio** can be calculated directly by taking:

$$\text{Stock Repurchase Payout Ratio} = \frac{\text{Common Stock Repurchases}}{\text{Net Income}}$$

or, indirectly by taking:

$$\text{Stock Repurchase Payout Ratio} = \text{Total Payout Ratio} - \text{Dividend Payout Ratio}$$

Using this latter formula, we see that A&F had a stock repurchase payout ratio of 31 percent in 2006 and 0 percent in 2007. Cornerstone 12-8 demonstrates how to calculate and interpret the stockholder ratios.

Dupont Analysis

Return on equity/return on common equity (hereafter, ROE) is the most important measure of profitability for investors. It represents the amount of income generated per dollar of book value of equity or common equity. In that way it is conceptually similar to an interest rate. Recall that ROE is calculated as:

$$ROE = \frac{\text{Net Income}}{\text{Average Equity}}$$

In earlier sections of this chapter, we learned that Abercrombie & Fitch and Aeropostale had very similar ROEs in 2007 (both return on equity and return on common equity because neither corporation had preferred stock), although A&F's ROE was down from 2006 while Aeropostale's was up:

	2007 ROE	2006 ROE
Abercrombie & Fitch	35.2%	40.1%
Aeropostale	35.7%	32.1%

Dupont analysis recognizes that ROE can be broken down into three important aspects of return—net profit margin, asset turnover, and leverage.

$$= \frac{\text{Net Income}}{\text{Sales}} \times \frac{\text{Sales}}{\text{Average Total Assets}} \times \frac{\text{Average Total Assets}}{\text{Average Equity}}$$
$$= \text{Net Profit Margin} \times \text{Asset Turnover} \times \text{Total Leverage}$$

The logic of this breakdown is compelling. First, profitability requires that the corporation is able to earn an adequate gross profit margin. That is, Abercrombie & Fitch and Aeropostale must be able to sell their products for more than it costs to buy them. Net profit margin carries this idea down the income statement from gross profit to net income. As we learned earlier in the chapter, the net profit margin represents how many cents of profit there are on every sales dollar.

Second, how efficient is the corporation with its net assets? The desire for asset efficiency is obvious. Everyone knows that you would rather earn $1,000,000 on an investment of $5,000,000 than an investment of $50,000,000. Before discussing leverage, we will focus a little more closely on net profit margin and asset turnover, which taken together give us return on assets (Net Income/Average Total Assets), albeit ignoring the after tax effect of interest expense in the numerator (see p. 646). To illustrate, consider Abercrombie & Fitch and Aeropostale for 2007. Their net profit margins and asset turnovers were:

	Net Profit Margin	Asset Turnover	Return on Assets
Abercrombie & Fitch	12.72%	1.64	20.86%
Aeropostale	7.55%	2.60	19.63%*

*This differs from the return on assets shown in part 4 of Cornerstone 12-7 because Dupont analysis does not add back the after tax effect of interest expense to net income (see discussion on p. 646).

Remember, although Abercrombie & Fitch and Aeropostale have quite different net profit margins and asset turnovers, their ROEs were very similar for 2007. This highlights different strategies for achieving profitability. Aeropostale is more efficient with their assets. This is consistent with a corporation that is seeking to compete on price because to keep costs down you must be efficient with net assets. Abercrombie & Fitch, on the other hand, is a product differentiator. A successful product differentiator can earn higher margins on their products because customers view their products as sufficiently different from the competition's to warrant paying higher prices. Although not specifically part of the Dupont analysis, this is illustrated by Abercrombie & Fitch's gross profit margin percentage (66.6 percent) being more than double Aeropostale's (32.2 percent).

Most product differentiators experience lower asset turnover. You can probably think of these distinctions within and between industries. For example, **Wal-Mart** is a cost leader. They have very low margins, but make up for it by being extremely efficient with their assets. **Nordstrom**'s, on the other hand, has much higher margins, but this is offset by lower turnover. Grocery stores have low margins and high turnover; auto dealers and jewelry stores have high margins and low turnover. Further, the trade-off between margins and turnover is evident in a number of decisions. For example, if a store puts an item on sale, it sacrifices margins and hopes to make up for it with higher turnover.

Although Abercrombie & Fitch has a higher return on assets than Aeropostale, as we can see in Cornerstone 12-9, Aeropostale ends up with a slightly higher ROE because of its higher leverage (1.82 for Aeropostale and 1.68 for Abercrombie & Fitch). Return on *equity* can be made larger than return on *assets* by leveraging these assets through the use of debt. The idea of leverage is simple. For example, if you can borrow at 8 percent and earn 10 percent (assuming the same tax rates on the interest and return), then you win. If you could guarantee these two figures after taxes, you should borrow all you can because you are netting 2 percent on every dollar. That is, if you borrow $1,000,000 you will make $20,000 (a $100,000 return less $80,000 in interest); of course, if you can borrow $1,000,000,000, then you will make $20,000,000.

HOW TO Calculate and Interpret Stockholder Ratios

**CORNERSTONE
12-8**

Concept:
Stockholder ratios measure (1) the creation of value and (2) the distribution of value to shareholders. Earnings per share and return on common equity provide information about the creation of value for shareholders. Value is distributed to shareholders in two ways; either the corporation issues dividends or repurchases stock. Dividend yield, dividend payout, stock repurchase payout, and total payout address the distribution of value.

Information:
Use Aeropostale's income statement and balance sheet in Exhibit 12-3 to calculate stockholder ratios. Aeropostale's average common shares for 2007 and 2006 were 53,285 and 54,994, respectively. They paid no dividends in 2007 or 2006. Aeropostale repurchased $91,404 of common shares in 2007 and $44,518 of common shares in 2006. (Average common shares are typically disclosed on the income statement. Information regarding dividends and stock repurchases can be found in the statement of stockholders' equity.)

Required:
1. Calculate Aeropostale's earnings per share for 2006 and 2007.
2. Calculate Aeropostale's return on common equity for 2006 and 2007.
3. Calculate Aeropostale's dividend yield for 2006 and 2007.
4. Calculate Aeropostale's dividend payout for 2006 and 2007.
5. Calculate Aeropostale's total payout for 2006 and 2007.
6. Calculate Aeropostale's share repurchase payout for 2006 and 2007.
7. Comment on Aeropostale's shareholder ratios comparing them to the Abercrombie & Fitch ratios shown in the body of the text.

Solution:
1.
$$\text{Earnings per Share Ratio} = \frac{\text{Net Income} - \text{Preferred Dividends}}{\text{Average Number of Common Shares Outstanding}}$$

	2007	2006
EPS	$\frac{\$106,647}{53,285} = \$2.00$	$\frac{\$83,954}{54,994} = \$1.53$

2.
$$\text{Return on Common Equity} = \frac{\text{Net Income}}{\text{Average Common Equity*}}$$

*Common Equity = Total Equity − Preferred Stock − Paid-in capital from Preferred Stock

	2007	2006
Return on Common Equity	$\frac{\$106,647}{[(\$312,116-\$0-\$0)+(\$284,790-\$0-\$0)]/2} = 35.7\%$	$\frac{\$83,954}{[(\$284,790-\$0-\$0)+(\$238,251-\$0-\$0)]/2} = 32.1\%$

**CORNERSTONE
12-8**
(continued)

3. $$\text{Dividend Yield Ratio} = \frac{\text{Dividends per Common Share*}}{\text{Closing Market Price per Share for the Year}}$$

*Dividends per share are taken from the Statement of Stockholders' Equity

	2007	2006
Dividend Yield Ratio	$\dfrac{\$0}{\$24.03} = 0.0\%$	$\dfrac{\$0}{\$20.31} = 0.0\%$

4. Dividend Payout Ratio = Common Dividends/Net Income

	2007	2006
Dividend Payout Ratio	$\dfrac{\$0}{\$106,647} = 0.0\%$	$\dfrac{\$0}{\$83,954} = 0.0\%$

5. $$\text{Total Payout Ratio} = \frac{\text{Common Dividends} + \text{Common Stock Repurchases}}{\text{Net Income}}$$

	2007	2006
Total Payout Ratio	$\dfrac{\$0 + \$91,404}{\$106,647} = 85.7\%$	$\dfrac{\$0 + \$44,518}{\$83,954} = 53.0\%$

6. Stock Repurchase Payout Ratio = Total Payout Ratio − Dividend Payout Ratio

	2007	2006
Stock Repurchase Payout Ratio	85.7% − 0.0% = 85.7%	53.0% − 0.0% = 53.0%

7. Aeropostale's 2007 EPS of $2.00 is much lower than A&F's EPS of $4.79. However, its growth in EPS of 30.7 percent was quite a bit better than A&F's growth of 25 percent. Both corporations' return on common equity was approximately 35 percent in 2007, but Aeropostale's 2007 ROE was up by about 11 percent, whereas A&F's was down by about 12 percent from 2006.

   As for shareholder payout, the firms pursued quite different strategies. Aeropostale did not pay any dividends, but spent 85 percent of net income in 2007 and 53 percent of net income in 2006 on share repurchases. A&F, on the other hand, paid dividends of approximately 15 percent of net income in 2006 and 2007. Additionally, in 2007 they spent 31 percent of net income on share repurchases, which resulted in a total payout ratio of approximately 47 percent.

This effect is captured by the total leverage component of the Dupont analysis. Recall that a company can raise money to finance its business by either selling stock or borrowing. If they choose to sell stock, then shareholders are entitled to their share of the returns. If they borrow the money, on the other hand, the creditors do not share in the returns. So why don't all corporations use debt instead of equity? First, they may not be able to find a low enough interest rate. Second, while interest is guaranteed, returns are not. That is, while the returns may seem better than the interest right now, in a few years it may not be so. For evidence of this, consider stories of people who borrowed money at 15+ percent on credit cards to invest in the stock market in the late 1990s. Cornerstone 12-9 illustrates how to perform and interpret Dupont Analysis.

HOW TO Perform and Interpret Dupont Analysis

Concept:
Dupont analysis decomposes a corporation's ROE into net profit margin, asset turnover, and total leverage.

CORNERSTONE
12-9

Information:
Use Aeropostale's income statement and balance sheet in Exhibit 12-3 and the following information for Abercrombie & Fitch:

Net income	$ 422,186
Sales	3,318,158
Beginning total assets	1,789,718
Ending total assets	2,248,067
Beginning stockholders' equity	995,117
Ending stockholders' equity	1,405,297

Required:
1. Perform Dupont analysis for both corporations for 2007.
2. What do you learn about the two corporations' ROE from this analysis?

Solution:
1. **Aeropostale**

$$\text{Dupont Analysis: ROE} = \frac{\text{Net Income}}{\text{Sales}} \times \frac{\text{Sales}}{\text{Average Total Assets}} \times \frac{\text{Average Total Assets}}{\text{Average Equity}}$$

$$= (\$106,647/\$1,413,208) \times$$
$$\{(\$1,413,208/\{[(\$503,951 + \$581,164)/2]\} \times$$
$$\{[(\$503,951 + \$581,164)/2]/[(\$284,790 + \$312,116)/2]\}$$
$$= 7.55\% \times 2.60 \times 1.82$$
$$= 35.7\%^*$$

*Note that this equals the ROE of 35.7% calculated in Cornerstone 12-6.

Abercrombie & Fitch

$$= (\$422,186/\$3,318,158) \times$$
$$\{(\$3,318,158/[(\$1,789,718 + \$2,248,067)/2]\} \times$$
$$\{[(\$1,789,718 + \$2,248,067)/2]/[(\$995,117 + \$1,405,297)/2]\}$$
$$= 12.72\% \times 1.64 \times 1.68$$
$$= 35.0\%^*$$

*Does not equal ROE of 35.2% (shown on p. 650) because of rounding in the individual components.

2. The Dupont analysis shows that Abercrombie & Fitch has a far better net profit margin (12.72 percent versus 7.55 percent), but Aeropostale has far better asset turnover (2.60 versus 1.64). This suggests that Abercrombie & Fitch has done a better job differentiating its products from the competition because its customers are willing to pay prices that support higher margins. Aeropostale, on the other hand, is much more efficient with its assets, as shown by its superior asset turnover. This is consistent with a cost leader (i.e., offering the lower prices) because asset efficiency helps contain costs and cost containment is necessary to compete on price.

   Multiplying the net profit margin by asset turnover gives return on assets, which is 20.86 percent for Abercrombie & Fitch and 19.63 percent for Aeropostale. However, Aeropostale has slightly higher leverage (1.82 versus 1.68), which means Aeropostale has a higher proportion of debt financing. This higher proportion of debt financing "leverages" its return on assets to produce a higher ROE than Abercrombie & Fitch despite its lower return on assets.

Exhibit 12-4

Summary of Financial Ratios

Short-Term Liquidity Ratios

1. Current Ratio $= \dfrac{\text{Current Assets}}{\text{Current Liabilities}}$

2. Quick Ratio $= \dfrac{\text{Cash} + \text{Short-Term Investments} + \text{Receivables}}{\text{Current Liabilities}}$

3. Cash Ratio $= \dfrac{\text{Cash} + \text{Short-Term Investments}}{\text{Current Liabilities}}$

4. Operating Cash Flow Ratio $= \dfrac{\text{Cash Flows from Operating Activities}}{\text{Current Liabilities}}$

Debt-Management Ratios

5. Times Interest Earned Ratio $= \dfrac{\text{EBIT}}{\text{Interest Expense}}$

6. Long-Term Debt-to-Equity Ratio $= \dfrac{\text{Long-Term Debt (including current portion)}}{\text{Total Equity}}$

7. Debt-to-Equity Ratio $= \dfrac{\text{Total Liabilities}}{\text{Total Equity}}$

8. Long-Term Debt-to-Total Assets Ratio $= \dfrac{\text{Long-Term Debt (including current portion)}}{\text{Total Assets}}$

9. Debt-to-Total Assets Ratio $= \dfrac{\text{Total Liabilities}}{\text{Total Assets}}$

Asset Efficiency Ratios

10. Accounts Receivable Turnover Ratio $= \dfrac{\text{Net Credit Sales or Net Sales}}{\text{Average Accounts Receivable}}$

11. Inventory Turnover Ratio $= \dfrac{\text{Cost of Goods Sold}}{\text{Average Inventory}}$

12. Asset Turnover Ratio $= \dfrac{\text{Net Sales}}{\text{Average Total Assets}}$

Profitability Ratios

13. Gross Profit Percentage $= \dfrac{\text{Gross Profit}}{\text{Net Sales}}$

14. Operating Margin Percentage $= \dfrac{\text{Income from Operations}}{\text{Net Sales}}$

15. Net Profit Margin Percentage $= \dfrac{\text{Net Income}}{\text{Net Sales}}$

16. Return on Assets $= \dfrac{\text{Net Income} + [\text{Interest Expense} \times (1 - \text{Tax Rate})]}{\text{Average Total Assets}}$

17. Return on Equity $= \dfrac{\text{Net Income}}{\text{Average Equity}}$

Stockholder Ratios

18. Earnings per Share (EPS) $= \dfrac{(\text{Net Income} - \text{Preferred Dividends})}{\text{Average Number of Common Shares Outstanding}}$

19. Return on Common Equity $= \dfrac{\text{Net Income}}{\text{Average Common Equity}}$

20. Dividend Yield Ratio $= \dfrac{\text{Dividends per Common Share}}{\text{Closing Market Price per Share for the Year}}$

21. Dividend Payout Ratio $= \dfrac{\text{Common Dividends Paid}}{\text{Net Income}}$

22. Total Payout Ratio $= \dfrac{(\text{Common Dividends} + \text{Common Stock Repurchases})}{\text{Net Income}}$

23. Stock Repurchase Payout = Total Payout Ratio − Dividend Payout Ratio

Dupont Analysis

24. Return on Equity $= \left(\dfrac{\text{Net Income}}{\text{Sales}}\right) \times \left(\dfrac{\text{Sales}}{\text{Average Total Assets}}\right) \times \left(\dfrac{\text{Average Total Assets}}{\text{Average Equity}}\right)$

Exhibit 12-4 summarizes the financial ratios presented in this chapter.

More advanced accounting texts may present additional ratios; however, those introduced here are among the most widely used. Two important steps in ratio analysis are developing data for comparisons and interpreting the effect of accounting alternatives on the data (and thereby the ratios). We will discuss these topics in the next section.

Data for Ratio Comparisons

As we pointed out earlier in the chapter, developing information from financial ratios requires that comparisons be made among the ratios of (1) the same corporation over time, (2) similar corporations over time, and (3) similar corporations at the present time. Analysts rely on several sources to fulfill their need for a broad range of data for individual corporations as well as for industries and the economy.

We believe the best source of information about the corporation starts with the investor relations section of their website. This part of the website should contain links to the corporation's 10-K (and other SEC filings), analyst conference calls, and press releases. However, you can also gain information through the financial press (e.g., *The Wall Street Journal*, etc.) and investor discussion boards, although the latter must be evaluated with a critical eye.

Information on the industry can be obtained from industry guides such as Standard & Poor's and IBIS World. These are often available through your university library website or in hard copy at the library. We also like websites like Google Finance, Yahoo! Finance, BizStats, and MSN.

Accounting Policy and Financial Statement Analysis

OBJECTIVE ▶ 6
Understand the effect accounting policies may have on financial statement analysis.

We indicated early in the text that accounting amounts are often not precise statements of a company's assets, liabilities, equity, revenues, and expenses. In many cases, the amounts are estimates. In other cases, amounts are determined largely by the accounting policies adopted by management. Certain portions of the financial statements can be substantially affected by accounting policy choices or estimates. Careful analysts examine the items in these sections closely, noting the particular accounting policies and estimates that underlie the data. Following is a list of the questions analysts are most likely to ask about accounting policies and the treatment of specific items in the financial statements.

Revenues
1. *The policy employed for recognizing revenues on installment sales*: Are revenues recognized at the time of the sale, or are they recognized over the collection period?
2. *The tax component of sales revenue*: Are sales, value-added, excise, or producers' taxes included in revenues?
3. *Interest revenues*: Are customers' finance charges included as a revenue, or are they treated as an offset against interest expense or some other expense?

Expenses
1. *Inventory accounting policy*: Is inventory valued on a FIFO, LIFO, or weighted-average basis?
2. *Depreciation*: What estimates are used for expected life and residual value? What depreciation method is used?
3. *Depletion:* Are the estimates of recoverable reserves reasonable?
4. *Uncollectible accounts:* What method is used to estimate uncollectibles? Are the estimates appropriate?
5. *Warranties:* Do warranty provisions cover actual expenditures?
6. *Pensions:* Does the firm expense the minimum or maximum amount for pensions?
7. *Postretirement benefits:* How does the company estimate the cost of postretirement benefits?

Balance Sheet

1. *Receivables:* Is the allowance for uncollectible accounts large enough?
2. *Inventories:* What inventory method is used? Are obsolete or unmarketable items written off as soon as the decline in value is apparent?
3. *Property, plant, and equipment:* Will these assets provide future services that are sufficient to recover the undepreciated cost?
4. *Intangibles:* Do intangible assets represent real economic advantages that justify their unamortized cost?
5. *Liabilities:* Are all liabilities reported? Are they properly classified? Are estimated liabilities large enough?

Most firms assist statement users in identifying items that are affected by accounting policy choices by including a list of the company's important choices in the first note to the financial statements.

Summary

Customers, suppliers, potential employees, creditors, and investors use financial statements to make decisions. However, the principal users are investors and creditors. To analyze a corporation you must understand how economic conditions will affect the industry and corporation itself, but at some point you must begin to understand the corporation.

The primary sources of information about the corporation are its SEC filings, and the most important of these filings is the 10-K. The 10-K includes the audited financial statements as well as a wealth of other information and is often hundreds of pages long. However, you can find information of interest more efficiently if you learn the required format of the 10-K.

Analyzing a corporation's financial statements involves comparison to its primary competitors and industry averages. This is called cross sectional analysis. Analysis also involves comparisons of the current year to previous years. This is called time series, or trend, analysis. Often, differences exist in the size of two corporations or even in the same corporation from year to year (perhaps due to the acquisition of another corporation). Analysts address this problem by restating the financial statements in percentage terms.

This restatement is typically done with horizontal analysis, vertical analysis, and ratio analysis. In horizontal analysis each financial statement line item is expressed as a percent of the base year (typically the least recent year shown). In vertical analysis, on the other hand, each financial statement line item is expressed as a percent of the largest statement amount—net sales on the income statement and total assets on the balance sheet.

Ratio analysis is an examination of financial statements conducted by preparing and evaluating a series of ratios. We classify ratios as follows: *Short-term liquidity ratios* are particularly helpful to short-term creditors, but all investors and creditors have an interest in these ratios. *Debt management ratios* and *profitability ratios* provide information for long-term creditors and stockholders. *Asset efficiency (or operating) ratios* help management operate the firm and indicate to outsiders the efficiency with which certain of the company's activities are performed. *Stockholder ratios* are of interest to a corporation's stockholders. Finally, *Dupont analysis* decomposes return on equity into margin, turnover, and leverage. However, when performing ratio analysis, or any financial statement analysis, you must understand how the corporation's accounting policies affect the financial statement. For example, inventory on the balance sheet and cost of goods sold on the income statement are affected by the corporation's decision to use LIFO instead of FIFO.

Summary of Learning Objectives

LO1. Explain how creditors, investors, and others use financial statements in their decisions.
- The role of financial statements is to provide information for
  - creditors
  - investors
  - customers
  - suppliers
  - employees

  This information will help these groups form judgments, which will serve as the foundation for various decisions.

LO2. Become familiar with the most important SEC filings.
- Publicly traded corporations must file a variety of financial information, including audited financial statements, with the Securities and Exchange Commission (SEC) on an ongoing basis. For example,
  - annual reports on Form 10-K
  - quarterly reports on Form 10-Q
  - current reports for numerous specified events on Form 8-K
- The annual report on Form 10-K provides a comprehensive overview of the corporation's business and financial condition and includes *audited* financial statements.
- Although similarly named, the annual report on Form 10-K is distinct from the "annual report to shareholders," which a corporation must send to its shareholders when it holds an annual meeting to elect directors.
- For larger filers, the 10-K must be filed within 60 days of their fiscal year end.

LO3. Understand the difference between cross sectional and time series analysis.
- Cross sectional analysis entails comparing a corporation's financial statements to its primary competitors and industry averages.
- Time series (or trend) analysis involves comparisons of the current year to previous years.
- Differences may exist in the size of two corporations or even in the same corporation from year to year (perhaps due to the acquisition of another corporation). Analysts address this problem by restating the financial statements in percentage terms.

LO4. Analyze financial statements using horizontal and vertical analysis.
- In horizontal analysis, each financial statement line item is expressed as a percent of the base year (typically the least recent year shown).
- In vertical analysis, each financial statement line item is expressed as a percent of the largest statement amount—net sales on the income statement and total assets on the balance sheet.

LO5. Calculate and use financial statement ratios to evaluate a company.
- Ratios help remove the effects of size differences (as measured in dollars).
- Six categories of ratios are discussed:
  - short-term liquidity
  - debt management
  - profitability
  - asset efficiency (or operating)
  - stockholder
  - Dupont
- More advanced accounting and finance texts may present additional ratios; however, those introduced here are among the most widely used.

LO6. Understand the effect accounting policies may have on financial statement analysis.

- Financial statement ratios are affected by the accounting policies selected by the corporation. For example, all else held equal, a corporation that uses LIFO will have different inventory turnover and gross margin ratios than a corporation that uses FIFO.

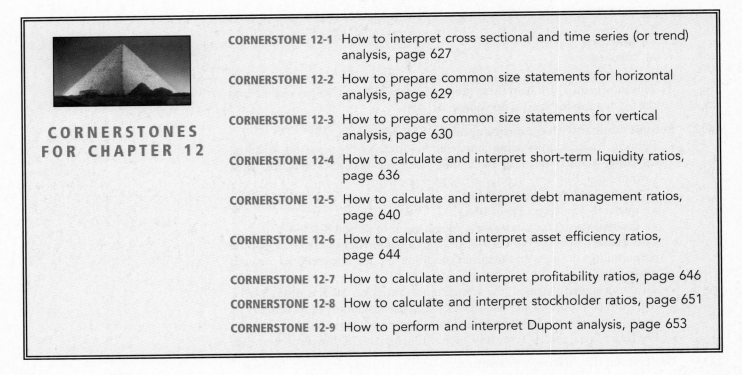

CORNERSTONES FOR CHAPTER 12

Key Terms

Review Problem

Ratio Analysis

Following are comparative balance sheets and income statements for **Under Armour**:

Under Armour, Inc. and Subsidiaries
Consolidated Balance Sheets
(In thousands)

	December 31,		
	2007	**2006**	**2005**
ASSETS			
Current assets:			
Cash and cash equivalents	$ 40,588	$ 70,655	$ 62,977
Accounts receivable, net	93,515	71,867	53,132
Inventories	166,082	81,031	53,607
Income taxes receivable	614	4,310	—
Other current assets	11,028	8,944	5,252
Deferred income taxes	10,418	8,145	6,822
Total current assets	**$322,245**	**$244,952**	**$181,790**
Property and equipment, net	52,332	29,923	20,865
Intangible assets, net	6,470	7,875	—
Deferred income taxes	8,173	5,180	—
Other noncurrent assets	1,393	1,438	1,032
Total assets	**$390,613**	**$289,368**	**$203,687**
LIABILITIES AND STOCKHOLDERS' EQUITY			
Current liabilities:			
Accounts payable	$ 55,012	$ 42,718	$ 31,699
Accrued expenses	36,111	25,403	11,449
Income taxes payable	—	—	716
Current maturities of long-term debt	4,111	2,648	1,967
Current maturities of capital lease obligations	465	794	1,841
Total current liabilities	**$ 95,699**	**$ 71,563**	**$ 47,672**
Long-term debt, net of current maturities	9,298	1,893	2,868
Capital lease obligations, net of current maturities	458	922	1,715
Deferred income taxes	—	—	330
Other long-term liabilities	4,673	602	272
Total liabilities	**$ 110,128**	**$ 74,980**	**$ 52,857**
Stockholders' equity:			
Class A common stock	$ 12	$ 12	$ 10
Class B common stock	4	4	5
Additional paid-in capital	162,362	148,562	124,803
Retained earnings	117,782	66,376	28,067
Unearned compensation	(182)	(463)	(1,889)
Notes receivable from stockholders	—	—	(163)
Accumulated other comprehensive income	507	(103)	(3)
Total stockholders' equity	**$280,485**	**$214,388**	**$150,830**
Total liabilities and stockholders' equity	**$390,613**	**$289,368**	**$203,687**

Under Armour, Inc. and Subsidiaries
Consolidated Statements of Income
(In thousands)

	December 31,		
	2007	2006	2005
Net sales	$ 606,561	$ 430,689	$ 281,053
Cost of goods sold	301,517	215,089	145,203
Gross profit	**$305,044**	**$215,600**	**$135,850**
Operating expenses			
Selling, general and administrative expenses	218,779	158,682	100,040
Income from operations	**$ 86,265**	**$ 56,918**	**$ 35,810**
Interest income	1,549	2,231	273
Interest expense	(800)	(774)	(3,188)
Other income, net	2,029	712	79
Income before income taxes	**$ 89,043**	**$ 59,087**	**$ 32,974**
Income tax expense	36,485	20,108	13,255
Net income	**$ 52,558**	**$ 38,979**	**$ 19,719**
Cumulative preferred dividends on preferred stock	—	—	5,307
Net income available to common shareholders	**$ 52,558**	**$ 38,979**	**$ 14,412**

Additionally, you will need the following information:

Weighted average common shares outstanding	48,021	46,983	37,199
Cash flows from operating activities	(14,628)	10,701	15,795
Dividends per share	0	0	0
Dividends	0	0	0
Stock repurchases	0	0	0
Market price per share at year end	$43.67	$50.45	$38.31

Required:

1. Calculate the short-term liquidity ratios for Under Armour for 2006 and 2007.
2. Calculate the debt management ratios for Under Armour for 2006 and 2007.
3. Calculate the asset efficiency ratios for Under Armour for 2006 and 2007.
4. Calculate the profitability ratios for Under Armour for 2006 and 2007.
5. Calculate the stockholder ratios for Under Armour for 2006 and 2007.

Solution:

1. Short-term liquidity ratios

Current Ratio = Current Assets/Current Liabilities

	2007	2006
Current assets	$322,245	$244,952
Current liabilities	95,699	71,563
Current ratio	**3.37**	**3.42**

$$\text{Quick Ratio} = \frac{\text{Cash} + \text{Short-Term Investments} + \text{Accounts Receivable}}{\text{Current Liabilities}}$$

	2007	2006
Cash	$40,588	$70,655
Short-Term investments	—	—
Accounts receivable	93,515	71,867
Current liabilities	95,699	71,563
Quick ratio	**1.40**	**1.99**

$$\text{Cash Ratio} = \frac{\text{Cash + Short-Term Investments}}{\text{Current Liabilities}}$$

	2007	2006
Cash	$40,588	$70,655
Short-term investments	—	—
Current liabilities	95,699	71,563
Cash ratio	**0.42**	**0.99**

$$\text{Operating Cash Flow Ratio} = \frac{\text{Cash Flows from Operating Activities}}{\text{Current Liabilities}}$$

	2007	2006
Cash flows from operating activities	$(14,628)*	$10,701*
Current liabilities	95,699	71,563
Operating cash flow ratio	**(0.15)**	**0.15**

*Provided in the Information section

2. Debt management ratios

Times Interest Earned = EBIT/Interest Expense

	2007	2006
Net income	$52,558	$38,979
Income tax expense	36,485	20,108
Interest expense	800	774
Times interest earned	**112.30**	**77.34**

$$\text{Long-Term Debt-to-Equity Ratio} = \frac{\text{Long-Term Debt (including current portion)}}{\text{Total Equity}}$$

	2007	2006
Long-term debt	$ 9,298	$ 1,893
Current portion of long-term debt	4,111	2,648
Total equity	280,485	214,388
Long-term debt-to-equity	**0.05**	**0.02**

Debt to Equity Ratio = Total Liabilities/Total Equity

	2007	2006
Total liabilities	$110,128	$ 74,980
Total equity	280,485	214,388
Debt-to-equity	**0.39**	**0.35**

$$\text{Long-Term Debt-to-Total Assets Ratio} = \frac{\text{Long-Term Debt (including current portion)}}{\text{Total Assets}}$$

	2007	2006
Long-term debt	$ 9,298	$ 1,893
Current portion of long-term debt	4,111	2,648
Total assets	390,613	289,368
Long-term debt-to-total assets	**0.03**	**0.02**

Debt-to-Total Assets Ratio = Total Liabilities/Total Assets

	2007	2006
Total liabilities	$110,128	$ 74,980
Total assets	390,613	289,368
Debt-to-total assets	**0.28**	**0.26**

3. Asset efficiency ratios

    Note: Average Balance = (Beginning Balance + Ending Balance)/2

    Accounts Receivable Turnover Ratio = Net Sales/Average Accounts Receivable

	2007	2006	2005
Net sales	$606,561	$430,689	$281,053
Receivables	93,515	71,867	53,132
Accounts receivable turnover ratio	**7.34**	**6.89**	

    Inventory Turnover Ratio = Cost of Goods Sold/Average Inventories

	2007	2006	2005
Cost of goods sold	$301,517	$215,089	$145,203
Inventories	166,082	81,031	53,607
Inventory turnover ratio	**2.44**	**3.20**	

    Asset Turnover Ratio = Net Sales/Average Total Assets

	2007	2006	2005
Net sales	$606,561	$430,689	$281,053
Total assets	390,613	289,368	203,687
Asset turnover ratio	**1.78**	**1.75**	

4. Profitability ratios

    Note: Average Balance = (Beginning Balance + Ending Balance)/2

    Gross Profit Percentage = Gross Profit/Net Sales

	2007	2006
Net sales	$606,561	$430,689
Gross profit	305,044	215,600
Gross profit percentage	**50.29%**	**50.06%**

    Operating Margin Percentage = Income from Operations/Net Sales

	2007	2006
Net sales	$606,561	$430,689
Income from operations	86,265	56,918
Operating margin percentage	**14.22%**	**13.22%**

    Net Profit Margin Percentage = Net Income/Net Sales

	2007	2006
Net sales	$606,561	$430,689
Net income	52,558	38,979
Net profit margin percentage	**8.67%**	**9.05%**

    $$\text{Return on Assets} = \frac{\text{Net Income} + [\text{Interest Expense} \times (1 - \text{Tax Rate})]}{\text{Average Total Assets}}$$

	2007	2006	2005
Total assets	$390,613	$289,368	$203,687
Income taxes	36,485	20,108	
Net Income	52,558	38,979	
Interest Expense	800	774	
Income before taxes	89,043	59,087	
Tax rate*	40.97%	34.03%	
Return on assets	**15.60%**	**16.02%**	

    *Income Taxes/Income before Taxes

Return on Equity = Net Income/Average Equity

	2007	2006	2005
Net income	$ 52,558	$ 38,979	
Stockholders' equity	280,485	214,388	$150,830
Return on equity	**21.24%**	**21.35%**	

5.   Stockholder ratios

$$\text{Earnings per Share Ratio} = \frac{\text{Net Income} - \text{Preferred Dividends}}{\text{Average Number of Common Shares Outstanding}}$$

	2007	2006
Net income	$52,558	$38,979
Preferred dividends	0	0
Average common shares*	48,021	46,983
EPS	**$1.09**	**$0.83**

*Provided in the information section.

Return on Common Equity = Net Income/Average Common Equity*

*Common Equity = Total Equity − Preferred Stock − Paid-in capital from preferred stock

	2007	2006	2005
Net income	$ 52,558	$ 38,979	
Stockholders' equity	280,485	214,388	$150,830
Preferred stock	0	0	0
Paid-in capital—preferred stock	0	0	0
Return on common equity	**21.24%**	**21.35%**	

$$\text{Dividend Yield Ratio} = \frac{\text{Dividends per Common Share}}{\text{Closing Market Price per Share for the Year}}$$

	2007	2006
Dividends per share*	$ 0	$ 0
Closing market price for year*	43.67	50.45
Dividend yield ratio	**0.0%**	**0.0%**

*Provided in the information section.

Dividend Payout Ratio = Common Dividends/Net Income

	2007	2006
Common dividends*	$ 0	$ 0
Net income	52,558	38,979
Dividend yield ratio	**0.0%**	**0.0%**

*Provided in the information section.

$$\text{Total Payout Ratio} = \frac{\text{Common Dividends} + \text{Common Stock Repurchases}}{\text{Net Income}}$$

	2007	2006
Common dividends*	$ 0	$ 0
Common stock repurchases*	0	0
Net income	52,558	38,979
Total payout ratio	**0%**	**0%**

*Provided in the information section.

Discussion Questions

1. Describe how some of the primary groups of users use financial statements.
2. What is a 10-K?
3. How does the 10-K differ from the 10-Q?
4. Describe the information provided in Item 1 of the 10-K.
5. Describe the information provided in Item 7 of the 10-K.
6. Describe the information provided in Item 8 of the 10-K.
7. What is the difference between time series and cross sectional analysis?
8. What is the difference between horizontal and vertical analysis?
9. How do the current and quick ratios differ? Which is a more conservative measure of short-term liquidity? Support your answer.
10. How does the operating cash flow ratio differ from the current, quick, and cash ratios?
11. What are you trying to learn by calculating debt-management ratios?
12. Why are higher asset turnover ratios considered to be better than lower turnover ratios?
13. What two aspects of a company's profitability are measured by profitability ratios?
14. What are the two major categories of stockholder ratios?
15. Dupont analysis breaks down return on equity into what three components?
16. Why must you analyze the accounting policies of a company when performing financial-statement analysis? Provide an example of how knowledge of accounting policies would affect your analysis of inventory.

Multiple-Choice Exercises

12-1 Which of the following use financial statement data to make decisions?

a. customers
b. investors
c. suppliers
d. all of the above

12-2 Which statement would best provide information about a company's current liquidity?

a. balance sheet
b. income statement
c. statement of cash flows
d. none of the above

12-3 A banker is analyzing a company that operates in the petroleum industry. Which of the following might be a major consideration in determining whether the company should receive a loan?

a. The petroleum industry suffers from political pressures concerning the selling price of its products.
b. Inflation has been high for several years in a row.
c. All companies in the petroleum industry use the same accounting principles.
d. The company has a large amount of interest payments related to many outstanding loans.

12-4 Which of the following filings includes unaudited financial statements, provides a continuing view of the corporation's financial position during the year, and must be filed for each of the first three fiscal quarters of the corporation's fiscal year?

a. 8-K
b. 10-K
c. 10-Q
d. Form 13F

12-5 Which of the following filings is known as the "current report" that companies must file with the SEC to announce major events that are important to investors and creditors?

a. 8-K
b. 10-K
c. 10-Q
d. Form 13F

12-6 Which section of the Form 10-K includes an analysis of the company's financial condition and performance of the company?

a. Item 4—Submission of Matters to Vote
b. Item 5—Market for Common Stock
c. Item 6—Selected Financial Data
d. Item 7—Management Discussion and Analysis

12-7 Which of the following are required to be included in the Form 10-K?

a. a list of all financial statements and exhibits required to be filed
b. the name of every person or group who owns more than 5 percent of a class of stock
c. information on the salary and other forms of compensation paid to executive officers and directors
d. all of the above

12-8 Which type of analysis compares a single corporation across time?

a. cross sectional analysis
b. time series analysis
c. timetable analysis
d. company analysis

12-9 Which of the following types of analysis compares one corporation to another corporation and to industry averages?

a. cross sectional analysis
b. time series analysis
c. timetable analysis
d. company analysis

12-10 Which of the following types of analysis is particularly useful for trend analysis?

a. vertical analysis
b. timetable analysis
c. trend-setting analysis
d. horizontal analysis

12-11 Vertical analysis expresses each financial statement line item as a percent of:

a. the average statement amount
b. the smallest statement amount
c. the largest statement amount
d. the mean statement amount

12-12 Horizontal analysis expresses each financial statement line item as a percent of:

a. net income
b. total assets
c. base year
d. stockholders' equity

12-13 How is the current ratio calculated?

a. Current Assets/Current Liabilities
b. (Cash + Marketable Securities + Accounts Receivable)/Current Liabilities
c. (Cash + Marketable Securities)/Current Liabilities
d. Cash Flows from Operating Activities/Current Liabilities

12-14 Partial information from Blain Company's balance sheet is as follows:

Current Assets:	
Cash	$ 1,200,000
Marketable securities	3,750,000
Accounts receivable	28,800,000
Inventories	33,150,000
Prepaid expenses	600,000
Total current assets	$67,500,000
Current Liabilities:	
Notes payable	$ 750,000
Accounts payable	9,750,000
Accrued expenses	6,250,000
Income taxes payable	250,000
Total current liabilities	$17,000,000

What is Blain's current ratio?

a. 0.25
b. 3.0
c. 1.8
d. 3.97

12-15 Hilton Inc. has $30,000 in current assets and $15,000 in current liabilities. What is Hilton Inc.'s current ratio?

a. 0.5
b. 1
c. 2
d. 3

12-16 How is the cash ratio calculated?

a. Current Assets/Current Liabilities
b. (Cash + Marketable Securities + Accounts Receivable)/Current Liabilities
c. (Cash + Marketable Securities)/Current Liabilities
d. Cash Flows from Operating Activities/Current Liabilities

12-17 A firm's quick ratio is typically computed as follows:

a. Total Liabilities/Total Assets
b. (Cash + Short-Term Investments + Receivables)/Current Liabilities
c. Current Liabilities/Current Assets
d. Current Assets/Current Liabilities

12-18 ABC Company has $40,000 in current liabilities, $20,000 in cash, and $25,000 in marketable securities. What is the cash ratio for ABC Company?

a. 1.125
b. 0.889
c. 1.6
d. 0.625

12-19 What ratio is used to measure a firm's liquidity?

a. debt ratio
b. asset turnover
c. current ratio
d. return on equity

12-20 Which of the following transactions could increase a firm's current ratio?

a. purchase of inventory for cash
b. payment of accounts payable
c. collection of accounts receivable
d. purchase of temporary investments for cash

12-21 Total Liabilities/Total Equity equals:

a. Times Interest Earned Ratio
b. Accounts Payable Turnover Ratio
c. Debt-to-Equity Ratio
d. Receivables Turnover Ratio

12-22 Which of the following ratios is not a debt management ratio?

a. times interest earned
b. debt-to-equity ratio
c. long-term debt-to-equity ratio
d. return on equity ratio

12-23 The balance sheet for Parker Inc. at the end of the first year of operations indicates the following:

	2009
Total current assets	$600,000
Total investments	85,000
Total property, plant, and equipment	900,000
Current portion of long-term debt	250,000
Total long-term liabilities	350,000
Common stock, $10 par	600,000
Paid-in capital in excess of par—common stock	60,000
Retained earnings	325,000

What is the long-term debt to total assets ratio for 2009 (rounded to one decimal place)?

a. 37.9%
b. 40.0%
c. 22.1%
d. 41.7%

12-24 When analyzing a company's debt-to-equity ratio, if the ratio has a value that is greater than one, then the company has:

a. less debt than equity
b. more debt than equity
c. equal amounts of debt and equity
d. none of these are correct

12-25 Cost of goods sold divided by average inventory is the formula to compute:

a. accounts receivable turnover
b. inventory turnover
c. gross profit percentage
d. return on sales percentage

12-26 A firm's asset turnover ratio is typically computed as follows:

a. Net Sales/Average Total Assets
b. Gross Profit/Net Sales
c. Operating Income/Net Sales
d. Net Income + [Interest Expense × (1 − Tax Rate)]/Average Total Assets

12-27 Which of the following ratios is used to measure a firm's efficiency at using its assets?

a. current ratio
b. asset turnover ratio
c. return on sales ratio
d. return on equity

12-28 Which of the following ratios is used to measure a firm's efficiency?

a. Net Income/Equity
b. Sales/Assets
c. Assets/Equity
d. Net Income/Sales

12-29 United Corporation has $65,000 of cost of goods sold and average inventory of $30,000. What is United Corporation's inventory turnover ratio?

a. 0.46
b. 1.17
c. 1.46
d. 2.17

12-30 If a company has an inventory turnover of 7.3 and a receivables turnover of 9.6, approximately how long is its operating cycle?

a. 72 days
b. 88 days
c. 95 days
d. There is not enough information to calculate the operating cycle.

12-31 Which of the following ratios is used to measure the profit earned on each dollar invested in a firm?

a. current ratio
b. asset turnover ratio
c. return on sales ratio
d. return on equity

12-32 Which of the following is the formula to compute the net profit margin percentage?

a. Net Income/Net Sales
b. Operating Income/Net Sales
c. Net Income/Average Equity
d. Net Income + [Interest Expense × (1 − Tax Rate)]/Average Total Assets

12-33 Selected information for Henry Company is as follows:

Average common stock	$600,000
Average additional paid-in capital	250,000
Average retained earnings	370,000
Sales revenue for year	915,000
Net income for year	240,000

Henry's return on equity, rounded to the nearest percentage point, is

a. 20 percent
b. 21 percent
c. 28 percent
d. 40 percent

12-34 Which of the following ratios is used to measure a firm's profitability?

a. Liabilities/Equity
b. Sales/Assets
c. Assets/Equity
d. Net Income/Sales

12-35 Why might an industry group have higher five-year average returns on equity than do other industries?

a. It is a higher-risk industry.
b. It is a lower-risk industry.
c. It is a high-growth industry.
d. None of the above.

12-36 The dividend yield ratio measures:

a. the income available for common stockholders on a per-share basis
b. the rate at which dividends provide a return to stockholders
c. the proportion of a corporation's profits that are returned to the stockholders immediately as dividends
d. the profit earned by a firm through the use of capital supplied by stockholders

12-37 Corporations are required to disclose earnings per share on which of the following statements?

a. balance sheet
b. income statement
c. statement of cash flows
d. all of the above

12-38 Jackson Company has preferred dividends of $15,000, a net income of $40,000, and average common shares outstanding of 8,000. What is Jackson Company's earnings per share?

a. $2.67
b. $5.00
c. $3.13
d. $2.13

12-39 Which of the following are NOT part of common equity?

a. common stock
b. treasury stock
c. retained earnings
d. preferred stock

12-40 Dupont analysis recognizes that return on equity can be broken down into three important aspects of return, which are:

a. net profit margin, asset turnover, and leverage
b. net profit margin, asset turnover, and average assets
c. sales, income, and leverage
d. sales, income, and equity

12-41 If a company has a higher net profit margin than most of its competitors, this means that:

a. the company is more efficient with its assets
b. the company has more loyal customers
c. the company has a lower proportion of debt financing
d. the company has a higher proportion of each sales dollar that is profit

12-42 Which of the following ratios is decomposed using the Dupont framework?

a. return on equity
b. asset turnover
c. assets-to-equity ratio
d. return on sales

12-43 Which of the following is NOT included in the Dupont framework?

a. a measure of profitability
b. a measure of efficiency
c. a measure of market share
d. a measure of leverage

12-44 When Dupont analysis reveals that a company has much higher than average asset turnover and much lower than average profit margin, what can be concluded about the company's strategy?

a. It is a product differentiator.
b. It is a low-cost provider.
c. It has no strategy.
d. It needs to concentrate on improving its profit margins.

12-45 Which of the following questions would be appropriate for an analyst to investigate regarding a company's liabilities?

a. Are all liabilities reported?
b. Are the liabilities properly classified?
c. Are estimated liabilities large enough?
d. all of the above

Cornerstone Exercises

OBJECTIVE ▶ 3
CORNERSTONE 12-1

Cornerstone Exercise 12-46 **CROSS SECTIONAL ANALYSIS**

Cross sectional analysis entails comparing a company to its competitors.

Required:

Indicate one of the biggest weaknesses of using cross sectional analysis when analyzing a company.

OBJECTIVE ▶ 3
CORNERSTONE 12-1

Cornerstone Exercise 12-47 **TIME SERIES ANALYSIS**

Time series analysis involves comparing a company's income statement and balance sheet for the current year to the its previous years' income statements and balance sheets.

Required:

Explain whether it is always bad if a company's cost of goods sold is increasing from year to year.

OBJECTIVE ▶ 4
CORNERSTONE 12-2
CORNERSTONE 12-3

Cornerstone Exercise 12-48 **HORIZONTAL AND VERTICAL ANALYSIS**

Use the following selected data from the financial statements of Harry's Hardware Company to answer the questions that follow.

	2009	2008
Accounts receivable	$ 60,000	$ 38,000
Merchandise inventory	12,000	16,000
Total assets	450,000	380,000
Net sales	380,000	270,000
Cost of goods sold	160,000	210,000

Required:

1. Calculate how much accounts receivable, merchandise inventory, total assets, net sales, and cost of goods sold increased or decreased from 2008 to 2009.
2. Indicate what happened from 2008 to 2009 to accounts receivable and merchandise inventory as a percentage of total assets. Indicate what happened from 2008 to 2009 to cost of goods sold as a percentage of net sales.

Cornerstone Exercise 12-49 SHORT-TERM LIQUIDITY RATIOS

Below are three ratios calculated for Huey, Louie, and Dewey Companies for 2008 and 2009.

(In millions)		Huey	Louie	Dewey
Current ratio	12/31/09	2.8 to 1	2.3 to 1	1.8 to 1
	12/31/08	2.0 to 1	1.5 to 1	2.2 to 1
Inventory turnover ratio	12/31/09	6.9 times	5.8 times	8.0 times
	12/31/08	7.6 times	5.8 times	9.6 times
Quick ratio	12/31/09	2.5 to 1	2.1 to 1	0.5 to 1
	12/31/08	1.0 to 1	1.4 to 1	1.2 to 1

Required:

Explain which company appears to be the most liquid.

Cornerstone Exercise 12-50 DEBT MANAGEMENT RATIOS

Below are selected data from the financial statements of Jewell Company for 2008 and 2009.

	2009	2008
Total liabilities	$1,205,000	$952,000
Common stock ($30 par)	250,000	225,000
Paid-in capital in excess of par—common stock	150,000	135,000
Retained earnings	155,000	145,000

Required:

Determine whether the debt-to-equity ratio is increasing or decreasing and whether the company should be concerned.

Cornerstone Exercise 12-51 DEBT MANAGEMENT AND SHORT-TERM LIQUIDITY RATIOS

The following items appear on the balance sheet of Lawless Company at the end of 2008 and 2009:

	2009	2008
Current assets	$6,000	$3,000
Long-term assets	7,000	4,000
Current liabilities	2,000	3,000
Long-term liabilities	7,000	0
Stockholders' equity	4,000	4,000

Required:

Between 2008 and 2009, indicate whether Lawless Company's debt-to-equity ratio increased or decreased. Also, indicate whether the company's current ratio increased or decreased. Interpret these ratios.

OBJECTIVE ➤ 5
CORNERSTONE 12-4

OBJECTIVE ➤ 5
CORNERSTONE 12-5

OBJECTIVE ➤ 5
CORNERSTONE 12-4
CORNERSTONE 12-5

OBJECTIVE ➤ 5
CORNERSTONE 12-6

Cornerstone Exercise 12-52 ASSET EFFICIENCY RATIOS

Selected financial statement numbers for Frederick Company are given below.

Net sales	$277,480
Cost of goods sold	179,000
Average accounts receivable	20,730
Average inventory	4,145
Average property, plant, and equipment	75,705
Average total assets	126,127

Required:

1. Using this information, calculate Frederick's receivable turnover ratio (round to two decimal places).
2. Using this information, calculate Frederick's asset turnover ratio and also convert the ratio into days.

OBJECTIVE ➤ 5
CORNERSTONE 12-7

Cornerstone Exercise 12-53 PROFITABILITY RATIOS

The following data came from the financial statements of the Bradshaw Company:

Revenue	$900,000
Expenses	600,000
Net income	300,000
Assets	600,000
Liabilities	100,000
Average Equity	500,000

Required:

Compute the return on equity.

OBJECTIVE ➤ 5
CORNERSTONE 12-7

Cornerstone Exercise 12-54 PROFITABILITY RATIOS

Brimfield Corporation's balance sheet indicates the following balances as of December 31, 2009.

Cash	$ 70,000
Accounts receivable	80,000
Inventory	55,000
Property, plant, and equipment	500,000
Accounts payable	75,000
Bonds payable (due in 2015)	100,000
Common stock (12/31/2008)	275,000
Common stock (12/31/2009)	325,000
Retained earnings (12/31/2008)	200,000
Retained earnings (12/31/2009)	260,000

Required:

If Brimfield's 2009 net income is $80,000, determine its return on equity.

OBJECTIVE ➤ 5
CORNERSTONE 12-7

Cornerstone Exercise 12-55 PROFITABILITY RATIOS

Presented below are selected data from the financial statements of Eagle's Nest Corp. for 2009 and 2008.

	2009	2008
Net income	$150,000	$120,000
Cash dividends paid on preferred stock	15,000	15,000
Cash dividends paid on common stock	42,000	38,000
Weighted average number of preferred shares outstanding	20,000	20,000
Weighted average number of common shares outstanding	105,000	95,000

Required:

Calculate the earnings per share as it would be reported on the 2009 income statement.

Cornerstone Exercise 12-56 STOCKHOLDER RATIOS

OBJECTIVE ➤ 5
CORNERSTONE 12-8

Presented below are selected data from the financial statements of Debonair Corp. for 2009 and 2008.

	2009	2008
Net income	$110,000	$123,000
Cash dividends paid on common stock	42,000	38,000
Market price per share of common stock at the end of the year	16.00	13.00
Shares of common stock outstanding	140,000	140,000

Required:

Calculate the dividend payout ratio for 2009.

Exercises

Exercise 12-57 FINANCIAL STATEMENT USERS

OBJECTIVE ➤ 1

Many groups analyze financial statements to make decisions.

Required:

1. Explain why a person who is selecting an employer should be sure to view and analyze the company's financial statements.
2. Explain why a business that is considering selling goods or providing services to another business should review the company's financial statements.

Exercise 12-58 SEC FILINGS

OBJECTIVE ➤ 2

The SEC requires publicly-traded companies to file many different forms.

Required:

Describe the Form 10-Q.

Exercise 12-59 FORM 10-K

OBJECTIVE ➤ 2

Form 10-K has many different items.

Required:

1. Indicate what is included in the Management's Discussion and Analysis section of the 10-K.
2. List five important things that are included in the Form 10-K.

Exercise 12-60 GETTING FAMILIAR WITH THE FORMAT OF THE 10-K

OBJECTIVE ➤ 2

Use Aeropostale's 10-K for the year ended February 3, 2007 (filed April 2, 2007), to answer the following questions. You should look up the 10-K online (which allows you to search and reference the entire 10-K) by searching for "Aeropostale investor relations." Once at that site, click on "SEC Filings," move the "Groupings Filter (View SEC Groupings descriptions)" pull down menu to "Annual Filings," and click the "Search" button.

Required:

Answer the following questions and include in which item number of the 10-K the information was found:

1. Who does Aeropostale principally target with their merchandise?
2. How many stores did Aeropostale plan to open during fiscal 2007 (which will end in February 2008)? How many of these stores will be in Canada?
3. Describe the seasonality of Aeropostale's business.

4. Is Aeropostale involved in any litigation that may materially affect its financial position?
5. What are some "key indicators" of financial condition and operational performance that Aeropostale uses to analyze its business?
6. What are three of Aeropostale's most critical accounting estimates?
7. Who audits Aeropostale?

OBJECTIVE ▶ 3 4

Exercise 12-61 HORIZONTAL ANALYSIS OF INCOME STATEMENTS

Consolidated income statements for Peach Computer appear below:

PEACH COMPUTER, INC.
Consolidated Statements of Income
(In thousands except per share amounts)

Three fiscal years ended December 31	2009	2008	2007
Sales	$9,188,748	$7,976,954	$7,086,542
Costs and expenses:			
Cost of goods sold	$6,844,915	$5,248,834	$3,991,337
Research and development	564,303	664,564	602,135
Selling, general, and administrative	1,384,111	1,632,362	1,687,262
Restructuring costs and other	(126,855)	320,856	—
	$8,666,474	$7,866,616	$6,280,734
Operating income	$ 522,274	$ 110,338	$ 805,808
Interest and other income, net	(21,988)	29,321	49,634
Income before income taxes	$ 500,286	$ 139,659	$ 855,442
Provision for income taxes	190,108	53,070	325,069
Net income	$ 310,178	$ 86,589	$ 530,373
Earnings per common and common equivalent share	$2.61	$0.73	$4.33
Common and common equivalent shares used in the calculations of earnings per share	118,735	119,125	122,490

Required:

1. Prepare common size income statements for horizontal analysis.
2. Explain why net income decreased in 2008 and increased in 2009.

OBJECTIVE ▶ 3 4

Exercise 12-62 HORIZONTAL ANALYSIS OF BALANCE SHEETS

Consolidated balance sheets for Peach Computer appear below:

Peach Computer, Inc.
Consolidated Balance Sheets
December 31, 2009 and 2008
(Dollars in thousands)

ASSETS	2009	2008
Current assets:		
Cash and cash equivalents	$1,203,488	$ 676,413
Short-term investments	54,368	215,890
Accounts receivable, net of allowance for doubtful accounts of $90,992 ($83,776 in 2008)	1,581,347	1,381,946
Inventories	1,088,434	1,506,638
Deferred tax assets	293,048	268,085
Other current assets	255,767	289,383
Total current assets	$4,476,452	$4,338,355
Property, plant, and equipment:		
Land and buildings	$ 484,592	$ 404,688
Machinery and equipment	572,728	578,272
Office furniture and equipment	158,160	167,905

ASSETS	2009	2008
Leasehold improvements	236,708	261,792
	$1,452,188	$1,412,657
Accumulated depreciation and amortization	(785,088)	(753,111)
Net property, plant, and equipment	$ 667,100	$ 659,546
Other assets	$ 159,194	$ 173,511
Total assets	$5,302,746	$5,171,412

LIABILITIES AND SHAREHOLDERS' EQUITY		
Current liabilities:		
Short-term borrowings	$ 292,200	$ 823,182
Accounts payable	881,717	742,622
Accrued compensation and employee benefits	136,895	144,779
Accrued marketing and distribution	178,294	174,547
Accrued restructuring costs	58,238	307,932
Other current liabilities	396,961	315,023
Total current liabilities	$1,944,305	$2,508,085
Long-term debt	304,472	7,117
Deferred tax liabilities	670,668	629,832
Total liabilities	$2,919,445	$3,145,034
Shareholders' equity:		
Common stock, no par value: 320,000,000 shares authorized; 119,542,527 shares issued and outstanding in 2009 (116,147,035 shares in 2008)	$ 297,929	$ 203,613
Retained earnings	2,096,206	1,842,600
Accumulated translation adjustment	(10,834)	(19,835)
Total shareholders' equity	$2,383,301	$2,026,378
Total liabilities and shareholders' equity	$5,302,746	$5,171,412

Required:

1. Prepare common size balance sheets for horizontal analysis.
2. Indicate from what sources Peach appears to have secured the resources for its asset increase.

Exercise 12-63 HORIZONTAL ANALYSIS USING INCOME STATEMENTS

OBJECTIVE ▶ 3 4

The consolidated 2009, 2008, and 2007 income statements for Cola, Inc., and Subsidiaries appear below.

Cola, Inc., and Subsidiaries
Consolidated Statement of Income
(In millions except per share amounts)

	December 31,		
	2009	2008	2007
Net sales	$ 25,020.7	$ 21,970.0	$19,292.2
Costs and expenses:			
Cost of goods sold	(11,946.1)	(10,611.7)	(9,366.2)
Selling, general, and administrative expenses	(9,864.4)	(8,721.2)	(7,605.9)
Amortization of intangible assets	(303.7)	(265.9)	(208.3)
Operating profit	$ 2,906.5	$ 2,371.2	$ 2,111.8
Interest expense	(572.7)	(586.1)	(613.7)
Interest income	88.7	113.7	161.6
Income before income taxes	$ 2,422.5	$ 1,898.8	$ 1,659.7
Provision for income taxes	834.6	597.1	597.5
Net income	$ 1,587.9	$ 1,301.7	$ 1,062.2

Required:

1. Prepare common size income statements for horizontal analysis.
2. Indicate what Cola's 2009, 2008, and 2007 tax rates were on its income before taxes.
3. Explain why net income increased by a larger percentage than sales in 2009 and 2008.

OBJECTIVE ▶ ③ ④   **Exercise 12-64 HORIZONTAL ANALYSIS USING BALANCE SHEETS**

The consolidated 2009 and 2008 balance sheets for Cola, Inc., and Subsidiaries appear below.

Cola, Inc., and Subsidiaries
Consolidated Balance Sheet
(In millions except per share amounts)

ASSETS	December 31,	
	2009	**2008**
Current assets:		
Cash and cash equivalents	$ 226.9	$ 169.9
Short-term investments at cost which approximates market	1,629.3	1,888.5
Accounts and notes receivable, less allowance: $128.3 in 2009 and $112.0 in 2008	1,883.4	1,588.5
Inventories	924.7	768.8
Prepaid expenses, taxes, and other current assets	499.8	426.6
Total current assets	$ 5,164.1	$ 4,842.3
Investments in affiliates and other assets	1,756.6	1,707.9
Property, plant, and equipment, net	8,855.6	7,442.0
Intangible assets, net	7,929.5	6,959.0
Total assets	$23,705.8	$20,951.2

LIABILITIES AND SHAREHOLDERS' EQUITY		
Current liabilities:		
Short-term borrowings	$ 2,191.2	$ 706.8
Accounts payable	1,390.0	1,164.8
Income taxes payable	823.7	621.1
Accrued compensation and benefits	726.0	638.9
Accrued marketing	400.9	327.0
Other current liabilities	1,043.1	1,099.0
Total current liabilities	$ 6,574.9	$ 4,557.6
Long-term debt	7,442.6	7,964.8
Other liabilities	1,342.0	1,390.8
Deferred income taxes	2,007.6	1,682.3
Total liabilities	$17,367.1	$15,595.5
Shareholders' equity:		
Capital stock, par value $1\frac{2}{3}$ ¢ per share: authorized 1,800.0 shares, issued 863.1 shares	14.4	14.4
Capital in excess of par value	879.5	667.6
Retained earnings	6,541.9	5,439.7
Currency translation adjustment and other	(183.9)	(99.0)
Less: Treasury stock, at cost: 64.3 shares in 2009 and 2008	(913.2)	(667.0)
Total shareholders' equity	6,338.7	5,355.7
Total liabilities and shareholders' equity	$23,705.8	$20,951.2

Required:

1. Calculate the percentage that Cola's total assets increased by during 2009.
2. Determine whether any of the asset categories experienced larger increases than others.
3. Indicate where Cola acquired the capital to finance its asset growth.
4. Indicate whether any of the individual liability or equity items increased at a rate different from the rate at which total liabilities and equity increased.

Exercise 12-65 PREPARATION OF COMMON SIZE STATEMENTS FOR VERTICAL ANALYSIS

OBJECTIVE ▶ 3 4

Financial statements for Apparel, Inc., appear below.

Apparel, Inc.
Consolidated Statements of Income
(In thousands except per share amounts)

	2009	2008	2007
Net sales	$ 7,245,088	$ 6,944,296	$ 6,149,218
Cost of goods sold	(5,286,253)	(4,953,556)	(4,355,675)
Gross income	$ 1,958,835	$ 1,990,740	$ 1,793,543
General and administrative expenses	(1,259,896)	(1,202,042)	(1,080,843)
Special and nonrecurring items	2,617	—	—
Operating income	$ 701,556	$ 788,698	$ 712,700
Interest expense	(63,685)	(62,398)	(63,927)
Other income	7,308	10,080	11,529
Gain on sale of investments	—	9,117	—
Income before income taxes	$ 645,179	$ 745,497	$ 660,302
Provision for income taxes	254,000	290,000	257,000
Net income	$ 391,179	$ 455,497	$ 403,302
Net income per share	$1.08	$1.25	$1.11

Apparel, Inc.
Consolidated Balance Sheets
(In thousands)

ASSETS	Dec. 31, 2009	Dec. 31, 2008
Current assets:		
Cash and equivalents	$ 320,558	$ 41,235
Accounts receivable	1,056,911	837,377
Inventories	733,700	803,707
Other	109,456	101,811
Total current assets	$2,220,625	$1,784,130
Property and equipment, net	1,666,588	1,813,948
Other assets	247,892	248,372
Total assets	$4,135,105	$3,846,450

LIABILITIES AND SHAREHOLDERS' EQUITY		
Current liabilities		
Accounts payable	$ 250,363	$ 309,092
Accrued expenses	347,892	274,220
Certificates of deposit	15,700	—
Income taxes	93,489	137,466
Total current liabilities	$ 707,444	$ 720,778
Long-term debt	$ 650,000	$ 541,639
Deferred income taxes	275,101	274,844
Other long-term liabilities	61,267	41,572
Total liabilities	$1,693,812	$1,578,833

LIABILITIES AND SHAREHOLDERS' EQUITY		
Shareholders' equity:		
Common stock	$ 189,727	$ 189,727
Paid-in capital	128,906	127,776
Retained earnings	2,397,112	2,136,794
	$2,715,745	$2,454,297
Less: Treasury stock, at cost	(274,452)	(186,680)
Total shareholders' equity	$2,441,293	$2,267,617
Total liabilities and shareholders' equity	$4,135,105	$3,846,450

Required:

1. Prepare common size income statements and balance sheets for Apparel to be used in vertical analysis.
2. Indicate whether gross margin grew as much as sales between 2007 and 2008 and between 2008 and 2009 and if so why it grew.
3. Indicate whether the relative proportion of Apparel's assets changed between 2008 and 2009 and if so, explain the change.
4. Indicate whether the relative proportion of Apparel's liabilities and equity changed between 2008 and 2009 and if so, explain the change.
5. Explain how Apparel appears to have financed the 7.5 percent increase in assets that occurred between 2008 and 2009.

OBJECTIVE ▶ 3 4   **Exercise 12-66 COMMON SIZE STATEMENTS FOR VERTICAL ANALYSIS**

The following comparative percentage income statements and balance sheets are available for Charger Products:

Charger Products
Statements of Income

	Year Ended December 31,					
	2009		**2008**		**2007**	
	Amount	%	Amount	%	Amount	%
Revenues	$901,170	100.0	$728,035	100.0	$661,850	100.0
Costs and expenses:						
Cost of good sold	$539,801	59.9	$439,005	60.3	$401,743	60.7
Selling and administrative	318,113	35.3	206,034	28.3	176,052	26.6
Interest	17,122	1.9	18,201	2.5	17,208	2.6
Other expenses (income)	9,913	1.1	2,912	0.4	(1,324)	(0.2)
Total costs and expenses	$884,949	98.2	$666,152	91.5	$593,679	89.7
Income before provision for income taxes	16,221	1.8	61,883	8.5	68,171	10.3
Provision for income taxes	4,506	0.5	22,569	3.1	23,827	3.6
Net income	$ 11,715	1.3	$ 39,314	5.4	$ 44,344	6.7

Element	Usefulness	Suggestion for Improvement
Chapter Opener (pg 57)		
Cornerstone 2-1 (pg 64)		
Summary of Learning Objectives (pg 82)		
Concept Q & A (pg 60)		
Decision-Making & Analysis (pg 76)		
Review Problem (pg 84)		

Competition

16. Comparing the Cornerstones book to competing texts, which Canadian textbook or Canadian Editions most directly compete with this textbook?

17. What would you say is the competitive advantage of this textbook over the books currently competing in the market?

Supplements

18. Which supplements that accompany the textbook you are currently using, are you making use of? Which supplements are absolutely critical in making your textbook selection?

19. Are there any types of supplements that you wish you had access to but are not available with your current textbook?

20. Are you currently making use of any on-line homework management system that accompanies your textbook? If so, what is your level of satisfaction with it and how could it be improved?

Adoption Potential

21. Based on your review of the current US textbook, the Table of Contents and assuming a thorough Canadianization of this book, do you think this textbook will be successful in the marketplace? Why or why not?

Overall Questions

Please select 3 chapters and review the contents of those chapters.

8. Is the writing and conceptual level of the presentation in the chapters that you selected, at the appropriate level for the course that you teach?

> [ ]

9. Did the presentation in the chapters have an appropriate teaching emphasis compared to how you present these topics? Did you find the balance between the procedures/technical detail of accounting and the conceptual emphasis appropriate?

> [ ]

10. What is your reaction to the end-of-chapter assignments (Discussion Questions, Multiple Choice Exercises, Exercises, Problems, and Cases)? Are they at the appropriate level and challenge for your students?

> [ ]

11. Was there an appropriate balance between the service and manufacturing sectors in the examples and end-of-chapter assignments?

> [ ]

Cornerstones

12. One of the major differentiating features of this textbook are what the authors refer to as "Cornerstones". Do you agree with the Cornerstones that they have identified? Would you add or delete any key procedures?

> [ ]

13. Each Cornerstones has a worked out example and a parallel exercise (for example, see Pages 64/93) that reinforce the topic/procedure, are these effective?

> [ ]

14. Please go to www.cengage.com/community/cornerstones, please review a few of the parallel Cornerstone videos, do these look to be effective? Would your students use these and find them useful? How difficult do you think it would be to Canadianize these videos?

> [ ]

Pedagogy

Please review the pedagogical elements of the textbook and give us your impressions:

15. How useful do you find each of these features? Would you like to see any pedagogical elements added? Deleted?

Element	Usefulness	Suggestion for Improvement

Charger Products
Comparative Balance Sheets

ASSETS	December 31,					
	2009		**2008**		**2007**	
	Amount	%	Amount	%	Amount	%
Current assets	$147,129	31.4	$ 62,417	14.3	$ 66,927	16.1
Investment	30,925	6.6	95,589	21.9	91,453	22.0
Property, plant, and equipment (net)	270,831	57.8	261,015	59.8	241,519	58.1
Other assets	19,680	4.2	17,459	4.0	15,796	3.8
Total assets	$468,565	100.0	$436,480	100.0	$415,695	100.0

LIABILITIES AND STOCKHOLDERS' EQUITY

Current liabilities	$ 68,410	14.6	$ 29,244	6.7	$ 28,683	6.9
Long-term debt	152,284	32.5	162,807	37.3	152,976	36.8
Total liabilities	$220,694	47.1	$192,051	44.0	$181,659	43.7
Common stock	$183,209	39.1	$182,332	41.8	$171,266	41.2
Retained earnings	64,662	13.8	62,097	14.2	62,770	15.1
Total stockholders' equity	$247,871	52.9	$244,429	56.0	$234,036	56.3
Total liabilities and stockholders' equity	$468,565	100.0	$436,480	100.0	$415,695	100.0

Required:

1. Explain why income from operations decreased in 2008 and 2009 while sales increased.
2. Determine whether the proportion of resources invested in the various asset categories changed.
3. Determine whether the proportion of capital supplied by creditors changed.
4. Indicate from what sources Charger secured the capital to finance its increase in current assets in 2009.

Exercise 12-67 SHORT-TERM LIQUIDITY RATIOS

OBJECTIVE ▶ 5

The financial statements for Retail Corporation appear below.

Retail Corporation
Consolidated Results of Operations

(Millions of dollars, except per share data)	December 31		
	2009	**2008**	**2007**
Revenues	$19,233	$17,927	$16,115
Costs and expenses:			
Cost of retail sales, buying, and occupancy	$14,164	$13,129	$11,751
Selling, publicity, and administration	3,175	2,978	2,801
Depreciation	498	459	410
Interest expense, net	446	437	398
Taxes other than income taxes	343	313	283
Total costs and expenses	$18,626	$17,316	$15,643
Earnings before income taxes	$ 607	$ 611	$ 472
Provision for income taxes	232	228	171
Net earnings	$ 375	$ 383	$ 301

Retail Corporation
Consolidated Statements of Financial Position
(Millions of dollars)

ASSETS	December 31, 2009	December 31, 2008
Current assets:		
Cash and cash equivalents	$ 321	$ 117
Accounts receivable	1,536	1,514
Merchandise inventories	2,497	2,618
Other	157	165
Total current assets	$ 4,511	$ 4,414
Property and equipment:		
Land	$ 1,120	$ 998
Buildings and improvements	4,753	4,342
Fixtures and equipment	2,162	2,197
Construction-in-progress	248	223
Accumulated depreciation	(2,336)	(2,197)
Net property and equipment	$ 5,947	$ 5,563
Other	320	360
Total assets	$10,778	$10,337

LIABILITIES AND STOCKHOLDERS' EQUITY		
Current liabilities:		
Notes payable	$ 200	$ 23
Accounts payable	1,654	1,596
Accrued liabilities	903	849
Income taxes payable	145	125
Current portion of long-term debt	173	371
Total current liabilities	$ 3,075	$ 2,964
Long-term debt	4,279	4,330
Deferred income taxes and other	536	450
Loan to ESOP	(217)	(267)
Total liabilities	$ 7,673	$ 7,477
Stockholders' equity:		
Preferred stock	$ 368	$ 374
Common stock	72	71
Additional paid-in capital (common)	73	58
Retained earnings	2,592	2,357
Total stockholders' equity	$ 3,105	$ 2,860
Total liabilities and stockholders' equity	$10,778	$10,337

Required:

1. Compute the four short-term liquidity ratios for 2008 and 2009 assuming operating cash flows are $281 million and $483 million, respectively.
2. Indicate which ratios appear to be most appropriate for a retail organization. Indicate what other information you would like to know to comment on Retail's short-term liquidity.

OBJECTIVE ▶ 5

Exercise 12-68 DEBT MANAGEMENT RATIOS

Use Apparel's financial statements in **Exercise 12-65** to respond to the following requirements.

Required:

1. Compute the five debt-management ratios for 2008 and 2009.
2. Indicate whether the ratios have changed and whether the ratios suggest that Apparel is more or less risky for long-term creditors at December 31, 2009 than at December 31, 2008.

Exercise 12-69 ASSET EFFICIENCY RATIOS

OBJECTIVE ▶ 5

Use Apparel's financial statements in **Exercise 12-65** and the information below to respond to the following requirements.

Statement Item	January 1, 2008 (In Thousands)
Accounts receivable	$ 752,945
Inventories	698,604
Total assets	3,485,233

Required:

1. Compute the three asset efficiency ratios for 2008 and 2009.
2. Indicate Apparel's operating cycle for the years ended December 31, 2009, and December 31, 2008.

Exercise 12-70 PROFITABILITY RATIOS

OBJECTIVE ▶ 5

Use Apparel's financial statements in **Exercise 12-65** and the information below to respond to the following requirements.

Statement Item	January 1, 2008 (In Thousands)
Total assets	$3,485,233
Total stockholders' equity	2,083,122

Required:

1. Compute the five profitability ratios for 2008 and 2009.
2. Explain what these ratios suggest about Apparel's profitability. Indicate what other information you would like to know to further access Apparel's profitability.

Exercise 12-71 STOCKHOLDER RATIOS

OBJECTIVE ▶ 5

Use Apparel's financial statements in **Exercise 12-65** and the information below to respond to the following requirements.

Item	Year Ended December 31, 2009	Year Ended December 31, 2008
Average number of common shares outstanding (thousands)	362,202	364,398
Preferred dividends (thousands)	$ 24,000	$ 24,000
Dividends per common share	$ 0.36	$ 1.54
Dividends (thousands)	130,861.00	561,172.30
Common stock repurchases	0	0
Market price per share:		
High	$ 83.25	$ 79.10
Low	63.25	59.00
Close	78.42	66.36
At January 1, 2008, total stockholders' equity was $2,083,122 and there was no preferred stock.		

Required:

1. Compute the four stockholder ratios for 2008 and 2009.
2. Indicate whether there were significant changes in these ratios between the years ended December 31, 2009, and December 31, 2008. Determine whether the stockholder ratios suggest that Apparel was a better investment at December 31, 2009, or December 31, 2008.

OBJECTIVE ▶ 5

Exercise 12-72 DUPONT ANALYSIS

Use Apparel's financial statements in **Exercise 12-65** to respond to the following requirements.

Statement Item	January 1, 2008 (In Thousands)
Total assets	$3,485,233
Total stockholders' equity	2,083,122

Industry Averages	Year Ended December 31,	
	2009	2008
Return on equity	5.31%	12.54%
Profit margin	4.00%	6.21%
Asset turnover	0.83	1.96
Leverage	1.60	1.03

Required:

1. Perform Dupont analysis for 2008 and 2009.
2. Explain what you learn about Apparel's trends from 2008 to 2009 by comparing its performance to the industry averages.

OBJECTIVE ▶ 6

Exercise 12-73 ACCOUNTING ALTERNATIVES AND FINANCIAL RATIOS

The 2008 annual report for Zimmer Cable included the following information on a change in the procedure for amortizing its investment in pay-TV programming:

> *In the first quarter of 2008, the Company changed the rate of amortization of its pay-TV programming costs to more closely reflect audience viewing patterns. The effect of this change was to reduce programming costs by $58 million and $57 million, resulting in increased net income of $35 million and $31 million, or $0.58 per share and $0.49 per share, during 2008 and 2007, respectively.*

Required:

1. Indicate which financial ratios would be affected by this change.
2. Explain whether you would expect this change in amortization policy to affect the accounts by a larger or smaller amount in future years and why.

OBJECTIVE ▶ 6

Exercise 12-74 ACCOUNTING POLICY CHOICE

Accounting policies can affect financial statement analysis.

Required:

1. Name a few accounting policies concerning the balance sheet that could affect financial statement analysis.
2. Name a few accounting policies related to expenses that could affect financial statement analysis.

Problem Set A

Problem 12-75A USING COMMON SIZE DATA FOR CREDIT ANALYSIS

OBJECTIVE ➤ 3 4

You are the credit manager for Materials Supply Company. One of your sales staff has made a $50,000 credit sale to Stewart Electronics, a manufacturer of small computers. Your responsibility is to decide whether to approve the sale. You have the following data for the computer industry and Stewart Electronics:

For the Years 2005–2009	Industry	Stewart Electronics
Average annual sales growth	13.4%	17.6%
Average annual operating income growth	10.8%	9.7%
Average annual net income growth	14.4%	9.9%
Average annual asset growth	10.3%	14.2%
Average debt to equity ratio	0.32	0.26
Average current ratio	4.04	3.71
Average inventory turnover ratio	2.53	2.06
Average accounts receivable turnover ratio	3.95	4.18

For Stewart Electronics, you have the following data for the year ended December 31, 2009:

Sales revenue	$3,908,000
Net income	359,000
Total assets	3,626,000
Current ratio	1.82
Debt to equity ratio	0.37
Inventory turnover ratio	1.79
Accounts receivable turnover ratio	3.62

The salesperson believes that Stewart Electronics would order about $200,000 per year of materials that would provide a gross margin of $35,000 to Materials Supply if reasonable credit terms could be arranged.

Required:

State whether or not you would grant authorization for Stewart to purchase on credit and support your decision.

Problem 12-76A USING COMMON SIZE DATA FOR INVESTMENT ANALYSIS

OBJECTIVE ➤ 3 4

Assume that you are a trust officer for the West Side Bank. You are attempting to select a pharmaceutical manufacturer's stock for a client's portfolio. You have secured the following data:

	Five-Year Averages				
	Industry Average	Firm A	Firm B	Firm C	Firm D
Sales growth	8.3%	9.8%	7.9%	7.2%	10.1%
Net income growth	13.0	12.0	10.7	4.2	16.1
Asset growth	5.0	6.1	4.6	4.4	6.2
	Current Year				
Return on equity	16.2%	17.5%	17.5%	19.4%	21.6%
Return on assets	8.5	7.8	12.7	8.4	11.4
Dividend payout	43.0	40.0	23.0	31.0	31.0

Required:

Comment on the relative performance of these firms.

Problem 12-77A USING COMMON SIZE INCOME STATEMENT DATA

OBJECTIVE ➤ 3 4

The 2009, 2008, and 2007 income statements for Entertainment Enterprises appear on the following page.

**Entertainment Enterprises
Income Statement**

| | Year Ended December 31, | | |
	2009	2008	2007
Revenues			
Theme parks and resorts	$3,440.7	$3,306.9	$2,794.3
Filmed entertainment	3,673.4	3,115.2	2,593.7
Consumer products	1,415.1	1,081.9	724.0
	$8,529.2	$7,504.0	$6,112.0
Costs and Expenses			
Theme parks and resorts	$2,693.8	$2,662.9	$2,247.7
Filmed entertainment	3,051.2	2,606.9	2,275.6
Consumer products	1,059.7	798.9	494.2
	$6,804.7	$6,068.7	$5,017.5
Operating Income			
Theme parks and resorts	$ 746.9	$ 644.0	$ 546.6
Filmed entertainment	622.2	508.3	318.1
Consumer products	355.4	283.0	229.8
	$1,724.5	$1,435.3	$1,094.5
Corporate Activities			
General and administrative expenses	$ 164.2	$ 148.2	$ 160.8
Interest expense	157.7	126.8	105.0
Investment and interest income	(186.1)	(130.3)	(119.4)
	$ 135.8	$ 144.7	$ 146.4
Income (loss) on investment in Asian theme park	$ (514.7)	$ 11.2	$ 63.8
Income before income taxes	$1,074.0	$1,301.8	$1,011.9
Income taxes	402.7	485.1	375.3
Net income	$ 671.3	$ 816.7	$ 636.6

Required:

1. Calculate how much each of the revenues and expenses changed from 2007 through 2009.
2. Explain what were the primary causes of Entertainment Enterprises' increase in net income in 2008 and the decrease in 2009.

OBJECTIVE ▶ 3 4

Problem 12-78A USING COMMON SIZE STATEMENTS

The following income statement and vertical analysis data are available for Robbins Audio Products:

**Robbins Audio Products
Comparative Statements of Income**

| | Year Ended June 30, | | | | | |
| | 2009 | | 2008 | | 2007 | |
(in thousands)	Amount	%	Amount	%	Amount	%
Sales	$2,970.0	100.0	$3,465.0	100.0	$3,960.0	100.0
Other income, net	23.7	0.8	34.6	1.0	39.6	1.0
Total revenues	$2,993.7	100.8	$3,499.6	101.0	$3,999.6	101.0
Costs and expenses:						
Cost of goods sold	$1,303.8	43.9	$1,566.2	45.2	$1,920.6	48.5
Selling and administrative	1,571.1	52.9	1,593.9	46.0	1,564.2	39.5
Interest	62.4	2.1	65.8	1.9	59.4	1.5

| (in thousands) | Year Ended June 30, | | | | | |
	2009		2008		2007	
	Amount	%	Amount	%	Amount	%
Total costs and expenses	$2,937.3	98.9	$3,225.9	93.1	$3,544.2	89.5
Income before income taxes	$ 56.4	1.9	$ 273.7	7.9	$ 455.4	11.5
Income taxes expense	14.8	0.5	107.4	3.1	182.2	4.6
Net income	$ 41.6	1.4	$ 166.3	4.8	$ 273.2	6.9

Required:

1. Suggest why net income declined from $273,200 to $41,600 while the cost of goods sold percentage decreased each year and selling and administrative expenses remained nearly constant.
2. Determine what could cause sales to decline while the gross margin percentage increases.

Problem 12-79A USING COMMON SIZE STATEMENTS

OBJECTIVE ▸ 3 4

Logo, Inc., owns and operates a small chain of sportswear stores located near colleges and universities. Logo has experienced significant growth in recent years. The following data are available for Logo:

Logo, Inc.
Comparative Statements of Income

| (In thousands) | Year Ended December 31, | | |
	2009	2008	2007
Sales	$51,638	$41,310	$34,425
Cost of goods sold	31,050	24,840	20,700
Gross margin	$20,588	$16,470	$13,725
Other income, net	383	426	405
	$20,971	$16,896	$14,130
Costs and expenses:			
Selling and administrative	$16,570	$13,465	$11,350
Interest	1,237	765	554
Total costs and expenses	$17,807	$14,230	$11,904
Income before income taxes	$ 3,164	$ 2,666	$ 2,226
Provision for income taxes	885	746	623
Net income	$ 2,279	$ 1,920	$ 1,603

Logo, Inc.
Comparative Balance Sheets
(In thousands)

| ASSETS | December 31, | | |
	2009	2008	2007
Current assets:			
Cash	$ 360	$ 293	$ 236
Accounts receivable	4,658	3,690	3,285
Inventories	6,064	4,478	3,442
Total current assets	$11,082	$ 8,461	$ 6,963
Property, plant, and equipment (net)	4,860	3,600	2,756
Other assets	574	585	562
Total assets	$16,516	$12,646	$10,281

LIABILITIES AND STOCKHOLDERS' EQUITY			
Current liabilities:			
Short-term notes payable	$ 4,230	$ 1,620	$ 450
Accounts payable	1,147	1,013	720
Total current liabilities	$ 5,377	$ 2,633	$ 1,170
Long-term debt	3,150	3,150	3,150
Total liabilities	$ 8,527	$ 5,783	$ 4,320
Paid-in capital	$ 4,725	$ 4,725	$ 4,725
Retained earnings	3,264	2,138	1,236
Total stockholders' equity	$ 7,989	$ 6,863	$ 5,961
Total liabilities and stockholders' equity	$16,516	$12,646	$10,281

Required:

1. Determine how much Logo's sales, net income, and assets have grown during these three years.
2. Explain how Logo has financed the increase in assets.
3. Determine whether Logo's liquidity is adequate.
4. Explain why interest expense is growing.
5. If Logo's sales grow by 25 percent in 2010, what would you expect net income to be?
6. If Logo's assets must grow by 25 percent to support the 25 percent sales increase and if 50 percent of net income is paid in dividends, how much capital must Logo raise?

OBJECTIVE ▸ 3 4

Problem 12-80A PREPARING COMMON SIZE STATEMENTS

The financial statements for Jane's Shoes, Inc., appear below and on the next page:

Jane's Shoes, Inc.
Income Statement

(In thousands, except per share data)	Year Ended December 31,		
	2009	2008	2007
Revenues	$3,930,984	$3,405,211	$3,003,610
Costs and expenses:			
Cost of goods sold	$2,386,993	$2,089,089	$1,850,530
Selling and administrative	922,261	761,498	664,061
Interest	25,739	30,665	27,316
Other expenses (income)	1,475	2,141	(43)
Total costs and expenses	$3,336,468	$2,883,393	$2,541,864
Income before income taxes	$ 594,516	$ 521,818	$ 461,746
Income taxes	229,500	192,600	174,700
Net income	$ 365,016	$ 329,218	$ 287,046

Jane's Shoes, Inc.
Balance Sheets
(In thousands)

ASSETS	December 31,	
	2009	2008
Current assets:		
Cash and equivalents	$ 291,284	$ 260,050
Accounts receivable, less allowance for doubtful accounts of $19,447 and $20,046	667,547	596,018
Inventories	592,986	471,202
Deferred income taxes	26,378	27,511
Prepaid expenses	42,452	32,977
Total current assets	$1,620,647	$1,387,758

ASSETS	December 31,	
	2009	2008
Property, plant, and equipment	$ 571,032	$ 497,795
Less accumulated depreciation	193,037	151,758
Net property, plant, and equipment	$ 377,995	$ 346,037
Goodwill	157,894	110,363
Other assets	30,927	28,703
Total assets	$2,187,463	$1,872,861

LIABILITIES AND SHAREHOLDERS' EQUITY		
Current liabilities:		
Current portion of long-term debt	$ 52,985	$ 3,652
Notes payable	108,165	105,696
Accounts payable	135,701	134,729
Accrued liabilities	138,563	134,089
Income taxes payable	17,150	42,422
Total current liabilities	$ 452,564	$ 420,588
Long-term debt	15,033	77,022
Noncurrent deferred income taxes	29,965	27,074
Other noncurrent liabilities	43,575	23,728
Commitments and contingencies	—	—
Redeemable preferred stock	300	300
Total liabilities	$ 541,437	$ 548,712
Shareholders' equity:		
Common stock at stated value:		
Class A convertible—26,691 and 26,919		
shares outstanding	$ 159	$ 161
Class B—49,161 and 48,591 shares		
outstanding	2,720	2,716
Capital in excess of stated value	108,451	93,799
Treasury stock (common at cost)	(7,790)	(6,860)
Retained earnings	1,542,486	1,234,333
Total shareholders' equity	$1,646,026	$1,324,149
Total liabilities and shareholders' equity	$2,187,463	$1,872,861

Required:

1. Prepare common income statements to be used for horizontal analysis for Jane's Shoes for 2007 to 2009.
2. Indicate why Jane's net income increased between 2007 and 2009.
3. Prepare common size balance sheets to be used for vertical analysis for 2009 and 2008.
4. Indicate whether the proportion of dollars invested in the various categories of assets has changed significantly between 2008 and 2009.
5. Indicate whether the proportion of capital raised from the various liability categories and common shareholders' equity has changed significantly between 2008 and 2009.
6. Describe Jane's performance and financial position.

Problem 12-81A PREPARATION OF RATIOS

 OBJECTIVE 5

Use the Logo, Inc., financial statements in **Problem 12-79A** to respond to the following requirements.

Required:

1. Compute asset efficiency ratios for Logo for 2009 and 2008. Indicate whether efficiency has changed.
2. Determine whether Logo's profitability changed for the two-year period 2008–2009.
3. Compute the debt-management ratios for 2008 and 2009. Discuss whether creditors are as secure in 2009 as they were in 2008.

OBJECTIVE ▶ 5

Problem 12-82A COMPARING FINANCIAL RATIOS

Presented below are selected ratios for four firms: Firm A is a heavy equipment manufacturer, Firm B is a newspaper publisher, Firm C is a food manufacturer, and Firm D is a grocery chain.

	Firm A	Firm B	Firm C	Firm D
Short-term liquidity				
Current ratio	1.3	1.7	1.0	1.6
Debt-management ratio				
Long-term debt-to-equity	1.81	.45	.30	.09
Asset efficiency ratios				
Accounts receivable turnover	4.66	8.28	11.92	116.15
Inventory turnover	6.26	40.26	7.29	8.43
Profitability ratios				
Operating income	12.6%	25.4%	21.2%	3.8%
Net income	5.9	10.9	10.8	1.9
Return on assets	4.7	10.6	16.8	10.3
Return on equity	36.0	22.6	38.0	21.2

Required:

1. Which firm has the weakest current ratio?
2. Explain why the turnover ratios vary so much among the four firms.
3. Explain why the return on equity ratio is larger than the return on asset ratio for all four firms.
4. Discuss whether the large differences in the return on equity ratios can exist over long periods of time.

OBJECTIVE ▶ 5

Problem 12-83A PREPARATION OF RATIOS

Use Jane's Shoes' financial statements in **Problem 12-80A** and the following data to respond to the requirements below.

	2009	2008	2007
Average number of common shares outstanding	77,063	76,602	76,067
Accounts receivable	$ 667,547	$ 596,018	$ 521,588
Inventories	592,986	471,202	586,594
Total assets	2,187,463	1,872,861	1,708,430
Shareholders' equity	1,646,026	1,324,149	1,032,789
Stock repurchases	930,111	581,134	288,320
Cash flows from operating activities	190,000	150,000	137,000
Common dividends paid	57,797	45,195	39,555
Dividends per common share	0.75	0.59	0.52
Market price per share:			
High	90.25	77.45	54.50
Low	55.00	35.12	26.00
Close	86.33	71.65	43.22

	Year Ended December 31,	
Industry Averages	2009	2008
Return on equity	25.98%	23.04%
Profit margin	0.05	0.04
Asset turnover	2.24	2.56
Leverage	2.32	2.25

Required:

1. Prepare all the financial ratios for Jane's Shoes for 2009 and 2008.
2. Explain whether Jane's Shoes' short-term liquidity is adequate.

3. Discuss whether Jane's Shoes uses their assets efficiently.
4. Determine whether Jane's Shoes is profitable.
5. Discuss whether long-term creditors should regard Jane's Shoes as a high-risk or a low-risk firm.
6. Perform Dupont analysis for 2008 and 2009.

Problem 12-84A ACCOUNTING ALTERNATIVES AND FINANCIAL ANALYSIS

OBJECTIVE ➤ 6

Shady Deal Automobile Sales Company has asked your bank for a $100,000 loan to expand its sales facility. Shady Deal provides you with the following data:

	2009	2008	2007
Sales revenue	$6,100,000	$5,800,000	$5,400,000
Net income	119,000	112,000	106,000
Ending inventory (FIFO)*	665,000	600,000	500,000
Purchases	5,370,000	5,105,000	4,860,000
Depreciable assets	1,240,000	1,150,000	1,090,000

*The 2006 ending inventory was $470,000 (FIFO).

Your inspection of the financial statements of other automobiles sales firms indicates that most of these firms adopted the LIFO method in the late 1970s. You further note that Shady Deal has used 5 percent of depreciable asset cost when computing depreciation expense and that other automobile dealers use 10 percent. Assume that Shady Deal's effective tax rate is 25 percent of income before tax. Also assume the following:

	2009	2008	2007
Ending inventory (LIFO)*	$508,000	$495,000	$480,000

*The 2006 ending inventory was $470,000 (LIFO).

Required:

1. Compute cost of goods sold for 2007–2009, using both the FIFO and the LIFO methods.
2. Compute depreciation expense for Shady Deal for 2007–2009, using both 5 percent and 10 percent of the cost of depreciable assets.
3. Recompute Shady Deal's net income for 2007–2009, using LIFO and 10 percent depreciation. (Don't forget the tax impact of the increases in cost of goods sold and depreciation expense.)
4. Explain whether Shady Deal appears to have materially changed its financial statements by the selection of FIFO (rather than LIFO) and 5 percent (rather than 10 percent) depreciation.

Problem Set B

Problem 12-75B USING COMMON SIZE DATA FOR CREDIT ANALYSIS

OBJECTIVE ➤ 3 4

You are the credit manager for Super Supply, Inc. One of your sales staff has made a $60,000 credit sale to Tim's Technology, a manufacturer of small computers. Your responsibility is to decide whether to approve the sale. You have the following data for the computer industry and Tim's Technology:

For the Years 2005–2009	Industry	Tim's Technology
Average annual sales growth	12.6%	16.8%
Average annual operating income growth	11.2%	10.2%
Average annual net income growth	15.3%	10.6%
Average annual asset growth	9.9%	13.9%
Average debt to equity ratio	0.36	0.29
Average current ratio	4.12	3.88
Average inventory turnover ratio	2.61	2.19
Average accounts receivable turnover ratio	3.89	4.11

For Tim's Technology, you have the following data for the year ended December 31, 2009:

Sales revenue	$4,120,000
Net income	367,000
Total assets	3,752,000
Current ratio	1.79
Debt-to-equity ratio	0.42
Inventory turnover ratio	1.83
Accounts receivable turnover ratio	3.71

The salesperson believes that Tim's Technology would order about $240,000 per year of materials that would provide a gross margin of $40,000 to Super Supply if reasonable credit terms could be arranged.

Required:

State whether or not you would grant authorization for Tim's Technology to purchase on credit and support your decision.

OBJECTIVE ▶ 3 4   **Problem 12-76B USING COMMON SIZE DATA FOR INVESTMENT ANALYSIS**

Assume that you are a trust officer for the Bank of New York. You are attempting to select a pharmaceutical manufacturer's stock for a client's portfolio. You have secured the following data:

	Five-Year Averages				
	Industry Average	Firm A	Firm B	Firm C	Firm D
Sales growth	9.3%	8.8%	10.2%	10.0%	7.9%
Net income growth	16.0	15.3	18.9	17.4	15.6
Asset growth	7.0	6.6	8.3	8.9	6.3

	Current Year				
Return on equity	19.5%	18.4%	22.7%	20.8%	17.3%
Return on assets	11.7	10.4	13.7	12.8	11.1
Dividend payout	31.0	30.0	39.0	37.0	29.0

Required:

Comment on the relative performance of these firms.

OBJECTIVE ▶ 3 4   **Problem 12-77B USING COMMON SIZE INCOME STATEMENT DATA**

The 2009, 2008, and 2007 income statements for Electronics Unlimited appear below.

Electronics Unlimited
Income Statement

	Year Ended December 31,		
	2009	**2008**	**2007**
Revenues			
Theme parks and resorts	$2,723.8	$3,299.9	$3,502.7
Filmed entertainment	2,601.4	3,127.3	3,682.4
Consumer products	752.3	1,121.6	1,493.5
	$6,077.5	$7,548.8	$8,678.6
Costs and expenses			
Theme parks and resorts	$2,263.9	$2,723.4	$2,703.7
Filmed entertainment	2,300.2	2,566.3	3,104.9
Consumer products	503.7	804.5	1,120.6
	$5,067.8	$6,094.2	$6,929.2

	Year Ended December 31,		
	2009	**2008**	**2007**
Operating income			
Theme parks and resorts	$ 459.9	$ 576.5	$ 799.0
Filmed entertainment	301.2	561.0	577.5
Consumer products	248.6	317.1	372.9
	$1,009.7	$1,454.6	$1,749.4
Corporate activities			
General and administrative expenses	$ 161.2	$ 150.2	$ 165.3
Interest expense	103.7	130.8	158.9
Investment and interest income	(121.1)	(127.4)	(193.6)
	$ 143.8	$ 153.6	$ 130.6
Income (loss) on investment in Asian theme park	$ 62.1	$ 13.6	$ (520.8)
Income before income taxes	$ 928.0	$1,314.6	$1,098.0
Income taxes	376.2	492.3	410.4
Net income	$ 551.8	$ 822.3	$ 687.6

Required:

1. Calculate how much each of the revenues and expenses changed from 2007 through 2009.
2. Discuss the primary causes of Electronics Unlimited's increase in net income in 2008 and the decrease in 2009.

Problem 12-78B USING COMMON SIZE STATEMENTS

OBJECTIVE ▸ 3 4

The following income statement and vertical analysis data are available for Willis Audio Products:

Willis Audio Products
Comparative Statements of Income

	Year Ended June 30,					
	2009		**2008**		**2007**	
(in thousands)	**Amount**	**%**	**Amount**	**%**	**Amount**	**%**
Sales	$4,122.0	100.0	$3,566.0	100.0	$2,965.0	100.0
Other income, net	39.7	1.0	36.7	1.0	21.3	0.7
Total revenues	$4,161.7	101.0	$3,602.7	101.0	$2,986.3	100.7
Costs and expenses:						
Cost of goods sold	$1,893.6	45.9	$1,610.3	45.2	$1,310.8	44.2
Selling and administrative	1,610.3	39.1	1,603.6	45.0	1,505.3	50.8
Interest	61.4	1.5	69.7	2.0	63.2	2.1
Total costs and expenses	$3,565.3	86.5	$3,283.6	92.2	$2,879.3	97.1
Income before income taxes	$ 596.4	14.5	$ 319.1	8.9	$ 107.0	3.6
Income taxes expense	181.5	4.4	109.6	3.1	14.5	.5
Net income	$ 414.9	10.1	$ 209.5	5.9	$ 92.5	3.1

Required:

1. Suggest why net income increased from $92,500 to $414,900 while the cost of goods sold percentage increased each year and selling and administrative expenses remained nearly constant.
2. Explain what could cause sales to increase while the gross margin percentage decreases.

OBJECTIVE ▶ 3 4   **Problem 12-79B USING COMMON SIZE STATEMENTS**

Greg's Graphics Company owns and operates a small chain of sportswear stores located near colleges and universities. Greg's Graphics has experienced significant growth in recent years. The following data are available for Greg's Graphics:

Greg's Graphics Company
Comparative Statements of Income

(In thousands)	Year Ended December 31, 2009	2008	2007
Sales	$54,922	$42,893	$35,526
Cost of goods sold	32,936	25,682	21,721
Gross margin	$21,986	$17,211	$13,805
Other income, net	397	439	421
	$22,383	$17,650	$14,226
Costs and expenses:			
Selling and administrative	$17,857	$14,665	$12,754
Interest	1,356	863	622
	$19,213	$15,528	$13,376
Income before income taxes	$ 3,170	$ 2,122	$ 850
Provision for income taxes	885	746	623
Net income	$ 2,285	$ 1,376	$ 227

Greg's Graphics Company
Comparative Balance Sheets
(In thousands)

ASSETS	December 31, 2009	2008	2007
Current assets:			
Cash	$ 372	$ 301	$ 245
Accounts receivable	4,798	3,546	3,369
Inventories	5,673	4,521	3,389
Total current assets	$10,843	$ 8,368	$ 7,003
Property, plant, and equipment (net)	4,912	3,541	2,937
Other assets	592	592	552
Total assets	$16,347	$12,501	$10,492

LIABILITIES AND STOCKHOLDERS' EQUITY			
Current liabilities:			
Short-term notes payable	$ 4,314	$ 1,731	$ 463
Accounts payable	1,256	987	783
Total current liabilities	$ 5,570	$ 2,718	$ 1,246
Long-term debt	3,241	3,234	3,266
Total liabilities	$ 8,811	$ 5,952	$ 4,512
Paid-in capital	$ 4,367	$ 4,598	$ 4,725
Retained earnings	3,169	1,951	1,255
Total stockholders' equity	$ 7,536	$ 6,549	$ 5,980
Total liabilities and stockholders' equity	$16,347	$12,501	$10,492

Required:

1. Calculate how much Greg's Graphics' sales, net income, and assets have grown during these three years.
2. Explain how Greg's Graphics has financed the increase in assets.
3. Discuss whether Greg's Graphics' liquidity is adequate.
4. Explain why interest expense is growing.
5. If Greg's Graphics' sales grow by 25 percent in 2010, what would you expect net income to be?
6. If Greg's Graphics' assets must grow by 25 percent to support the 25 percent sales increase and if 50 percent of net income is paid in dividends, how much capital must Greg's Graphics raise?

Problem 12-80B PREPARING COMMON SIZE STATEMENTS

OBJECTIVE ▶ 3 4

The financial statements for Matt's Hats, Inc., appear below and on the next page.

Matt's Hats, Inc.
Income Statement

(In thousands, except per share data)	Year Ended December 31,		
	2009	2008	2007
Revenues	$4,102,721	$3,652,412	$3,178,569
Costs and expenses:			
Cost of goods sold	$2,256,236	$2,234,985	$1,952,123
Selling and administrative	927,412	653,986	598,236
Interest	23,974	32,596	31,853
Other expenses (income)	1,925	2,254	(102)
Total costs and expenses	$3,209,547	$2,923,821	$2,582,110
Income before income taxes	$ 893,174	$ 728,591	$ 596,459
Income taxes	247,692	183,456	163,524
Net income	$ 645,482	$ 545,135	$ 432,935

Matt's Hats, Inc.
Balance Sheets
(In thousands)

ASSETS	December 31,	
	2009	2008
Current assets:		
Cash and equivalents	$ 301,695	$ 269,648
Accounts receivable, less allowance for doubtful accounts of $20,568 and $18,322	670,469	604,236
Inventories	601,396	469,582
Deferred income taxes	23,415	24,397
Prepaid expenses	43,624	36,478
Total current assets	$1,640,599	$1,404,341
Property, plant, and equipment	$ 583,152	$ 501,239
Less accumulated depreciation	206,452	148,231
Net property, plant, and equipment	$ 376,700	$ 353,008
Goodwill	162,325	127,695
Other assets	29,158	23,598
Total assets	$2,208,782	$1,908,642

LIABILITIES AND STOCKHOLDERS' EQUITY		
Current liabilities:		
Current portion of long-term debt	$ 63,169	$ 5,665
Notes payable	112,596	110,423
Accounts payable	128,696	139,364
Accrued liabilities	143,874	133,569
Income taxes payable	23,541	38,972
Total current liabilities	$ 471,876	$ 427,993
Long-term debt	16,254	83,456
Noncurrent deferred income taxes	33,489	31,238
Other noncurrent liabilities	46,685	27,434
Commitments and contingencies	—	—
Redeemable preferred stock	200	200
Total liabilities	$ 568,504	$ 570,321
Shareholders' equity:		
Common stock at stated value:		
Class A convertible—27,723 and		
25,832 shares outstanding	$ 164	$ 175
Class B—49,756 and 47,652		
shares outstanding	3,152	3,120
Capital in excess of stated value	110,596	96,546
Treasury stock (common at cost)	(8,741)	(7,859)
Retained earnings	1,535,107	1,246,339
Total stockholders' equity	$1,640,278	$1,338,321
Total liabilities and stockholders' equity	$2,208,782	$1,908,642

Required:

1. Prepare common income statements to be used for horizontal analysis for Matt's Hats for 2007 to 2009.
2. Indicate why Matt's net income increased between 2007 and 2009.
3. Prepare common size balance sheets to be used for vertical analysis for 2009 and 2008.
4. Determine whether the proportion of dollars invested in the various categories of assets has changed significantly between 2008 and 2009.
5. Determine whether the proportion of capital raised from the various liability categories and common shareholders' equity has changed significantly between 2008 and 2009.
6. Indicate how you would describe Matt's performance and financial position?

OBJECTIVE ▶ 5   **Problem 12-81B PREPARATION OF RATIOS**

Use the Greg's Graphics financial statements in **Problem 12-79B** to respond to the following requirements.

Required:

1. Compute asset efficiency ratios for Greg's Graphics for 2009 and 2008 and determine whether their asset efficiency has changed.
2. Determine whether Greg's Graphics' profitability has changed during the two-year period 2008–2009.
3. Compute the debt-management ratios for 2008 and 2009. Discuss whether creditors are as secure in 2009 as they were in 2008.

Problem 12-82B COMPARING FINANCIAL RATIOS

OBJECTIVE ➤ 5

Presented below are selected ratios for four firms: Firm A is a distiller, Firm B is a jewelry retailer, Firm C is an airline, and Firm D is a hotel chain.

	Firm A	Firm B	Firm C	Firm D
Short-term liquidity				
Current ratio	1.5	3.5	0.9	1.4
Debt-management ratio				
Long-term debt to equity	0.24	0.20	562.11	209.48
Asset efficiency ratios				
Accounts receivable turnover	7.66	17.07	19.72	11.09
Inventory turnover	2.30	0.95	31.43	7.24
Profitability ratios				
Operating income	17.7%	15.5%	4.2%	9.2%
Net income	13.1	9.6	2.2	5.4
Return on assets	11.9	8.6	1.8	7.9
Return on equity	23.7	14.9	49.2	34.5

Required:

1. Explain why the long-term debt-to-equity ratio is so much higher for the airline and hotel chain than it is for the distiller and jewelry retailer.
2. Explain why the turnover ratios vary so much among the four firms.
3. Explain why the return on equity for the airline and hotel chain is higher than for the distiller and jewelry retailer when their operating income and net income percentages are considerably smaller.

Problem 12-83B PREPARATION OF RATIOS

OBJECTIVE ➤ 5

Use Matt's Hats' financial statements in **Problem 12-80B** and the following data to respond to the requirements below.

	2009	2008	2007
Average number of common shares outstanding	78,273	77,325	77,021
Accounts receivable	$ 672,139	$ 598,243	$ 545,556
Inventories	596,468	469,327	592,524
Total assets	2,190,254	1,925,632	1,699,432
Shareholders' equity	1,852,695	1,410,723	1,075,952
Stock repurchases	990,521	623,259	310,132
Cash flows from operating activities	495,000	380,000	265,000
Common dividends paid	61,836	49,488	37,740
Dividends per common share	0.79	0.64	0.49
Market price per share:			
High	92.17	79.13	56.22
Low	56.59	37.23	27.10
Close	88.47	73.83	44.26

	Year Ended December 31,	
Industry Averages	2009	2008
Return on equity	32.71%	27.86%
Profit margin	0.06	0.05
Asset turnover	2.31	2.51
Leverage	2.36	2.22

Required:

1. Prepare all the financial ratios for Matt's Hats for 2009 and 2008.
2. Indicate whether Matt's Hats' short-term liquidity is adequate.
3. Discuss whether Matt's Hats' uses their assets efficiently.
4. Determine whether Matt's Hats is profitable.
5. Discuss whether long-term creditors should regard Matt's Hats as a high-risk or a low-risk firm.
6. Perform Dupont analysis for 2009 and 2008.

OBJECTIVE ▸ 6   Problem 12-84B **ACCOUNTING ALTERNATIVES AND FINANCIAL ANALYSIS**

Cheap Auto, Inc., has asked your bank for a $100,000 loan to expand its sales facility. Cheap Auto provides you with the following data:

	2009	2008	2007
Sales revenue	$6,900,000	$6,400,000	$6,100,000
Net income	120,000	113,000	109,000
Ending inventory (FIFO)*	675,000	620,000	510,000
Purchases	5,410,000	5,200,000	4,990,000
Depreciable assets	1,320,000	1,230,000	1,120,000

*The 2006 ending inventory was $420,000 (FIFO).

Your inspection of the financial statements of other auto sales firms indicates that most of these firms adopted the LIFO method in the late 1970s. You further note that Cheap Auto has used 10 percent of depreciable asset cost when computing depreciation expense and that other automobile dealers use 20 percent. Assume that Cheap Auto's effective tax rate is 30 percent of income before tax. Also assume the following:

	2009	2008	2007
Ending inventory (LIFO)*	$518,000	$512,000	$500,000

*The 2006 ending inventory was $420,000 (LIFO).

Required:

1. Compute cost of goods sold for 2007–2009, using both the FIFO and the LIFO methods.
2. Compute depreciation expense for Cheap Auto for 2007–2009, using both 10 percent and 20 percent of the cost of depreciable assets.
3. Recompute Cheap Auto's net income for 2007–2009, using LIFO and 20 percent depreciation. (Don't forget the tax impact of the increases in cost of goods sold and depreciation expense.)
4. Does Cheap Auto appear to have materially changed its financial statements by the selection of FIFO (rather than LIFO) and 10 percent (rather than 20 percent) depreciation?

Cases

Case 12-85 **ETHICS AND EQUITY**

Anne Yates is employed as a financial analyst at a large brokerage house. Her job is to follow companies in the computer hardware sector and issue reports that will be used by her firm's brokers in making recommendations to the brokerage house's clients. Her reports are summarized by her ratings of the company—strong buy, buy, hold, sell, or strong sell. She is in frequent contact with the top management of the companies she follows.

After a thorough investigation, she believes she should downgrade Dreamware from a "strong buy" to a "hold." However, when she informs Dreamware's CFO, the CFO threatens to call her boss. Later that week, her boss calls her to request that she reconsider her downgrade and states that her cooperation will be "greatly appreciated."

Required:

How should Anne respond to her boss? Are there any other steps she should consider taking?

Case 12-86 ASSESSING THE EFFECTS OF THE "CLEAN AIR" LEGISLATION

In late 1990, Congress passed and the President signed into law legislation that required significant reductions over a several-year period in the quantity of sulfur dioxide that electric utilities will be allowed to discharge into the air. Electric utilities that generate their electricity by burning inexpensive, but relatively high-sulfur, coal were most affected by this legislation. Some utilities complied with this legislation by changing to coal with a lower sulfur content. Other utilities complied with this legislation by installing devices on power plant smokestacks that would remove sulfur dioxide before it is discharged into the air.

Required:

1. In what places on the financial statements of coal-dependent electric utilities do you expect to observe the effects of this legislation?
2. In what places on the financial statements of companies that mine coal do you expect to observe the effects of this legislation?

Case 12-87 CHANGES IN THE PRICE OF FUEL FOR AIRCRAFT

The cost of fuel is reported to be about 20 percent of the total operating cost for a major airline. Events in the Middle East caused jet fuel costs to nearly double from 2006 to 2009.

Required:

1. If you were the CEO of a major airline, how would you suggest that the airline respond to the fuel price increase?
2. How would you expect the financial statements of major airlines to be affected by the fuel price increase and the actions that the airlines would take in response?

Case 12-88 ANALYZING GROWTH

Comparative financial statements for Initech Corporation follow:

Initech Corporation
Consolidated Statements of Income

(In millions except per share amounts)	Three Years Ended December 31,		
	2009	2008	2007
Net revenues	$8,782	$5,844	$4,779
Cost of goods sold	$3,252	$2,557	$2,316
Research and development	970	780	618
Marketing, general and administrative	1,168	1,017	765
Operating costs and expenses	$5,390	$4,354	$3,699
Operating income	$3,392	$1,490	$1,080
Interest expense	(50)	(54)	(82)
Interest income and other, net	188	133	197
Income before taxes	$3,530	$1,569	$1,195
Provision for taxes	1,235	502	376
Net income	$2,295	$1,067	$ 819

Initech Corporation
Consolidated Balance Sheets

(In millions except per share amounts)	December 31,	
ASSETS	2009	2008
Current assets:		
Cash and cash equivalents	$ 1,659	$1,843
Short-term investments	1,477	993
Accounts and notes receivable, net of allowance for doubtful accounts of $22 ($26 in 2008)	1,448	1,069
Inventories	838	535
Deferred tax assets	310	205
Other current assets	70	46
Total current assets	5,802	4,691
Property, plant, and equipment:		
Land and buildings	1,848	1,463
Machinery and equipment	4,148	2,874
Construction in progress	317	311
	6,313	4,648
Less accumulated depreciation	2,317	1,832
Property, plant, and equipment, net	3,996	2,816
Long-term investments	1,416	496
Other assets	130	86
Total assets	$11,344	$8,089

LIABILITIES AND STOCKHOLDERS' EQUITY		
Current liabilities:		
Short-term debt	$ 399	$ 202
Long-term debt redeemable within one year	98	110
Accounts payable	427	281
Deferred income on shipments to distributors	200	149
Accrued compensation and benefits	544	435
Other accrued liabilities	374	306
Income taxes payable	391	359
Total current liabilities	$ 2,433	$1,842
Long-term debt	426	249
Deferred tax liabilities	297	180
Other long-term liabilities	688	373
Total liabilities	$ 3,844	$2,644
Stockholders' equity:		
Preferred stock, $0.001 par value, 50 shares authorized; none issued	—	—
Common stock, $0.001 par value, 1,400 shares authorized; 1,000 issued and outstanding in 2009 and 2008	1	1
Capital in excess of par value	2,193	1,775
Retained earnings	5,306	3,669
Total stockholders' equity	7,500	5,445
Total liabilities and stockholders' equity	$11,344	$8,089

Required:

1. Prepare common size income statements to be used for both vertical and horizontal analysis for 2007–2009.
2. Using the common size income statements for both vertical and horizontal analysis prepared in part (1), indicate why Initech's profits increased more rapidly than sales for 2008 and 2009.
3. Prepare common size balance sheets for vertical analysis for 2008 and 2009.
4. Did the proportion of assets invested in the various classes of assets change significantly from 2008 to 2009?
5. How has Initech financed its growth in assets?
6. Did the income statement change as much between 2008 and 2009 as the balance sheet?

Case 12-89 IDENTIFYING THE CAUSES OF PROFITABILITY CHANGES

The consolidated financial statements for Carmody Shipping Corporation and Subsidiaries appear below and on the following pages.

Carmody Shipping Corporation and Subsidiaries
Consolidated Statements of Operations

In thousands, except per share amounts	Years Ended May 31,		
	2009	2008	2007
Revenues	$7,808,043	$7,550,060	$7,688,296
Operating expenses:			
Salaries and employee benefits	$3,807,493	$3,637,080	$3,438,391
Rentals and landing fees	658,138	672,341	650,001
Depreciation and amortization	579,896	577,157	562,207
Fuel	495,384	508,386	663,327
Maintenance and repairs	404,639	404,311	449,394
Restructuring charges	(12,500)	254,000	121,000
Other	1,497,820	1,473,818	1,551,850
	$7,430,870	$7,527,093	$7,436,170
Operating income	$ 377,173	$ 22,967	$ 252,126
Other income (expenses):			
Interest, net	$ (160,923)	$ (164,315)	$ (181,880)
Gain on disposition of aircraft and related equipment	4,633	2,832	11,375
Other, net	(17,307)	(8,312)	(8,679)
Payroll tax loss	—	—	(32,000)
Other income (expenses), net	$ (173,597)	$ (169,795)	$ (211,184)
Income (loss) before Income taxes and extraordinary loss	$ (203,576)	$ (146,828)	$ 40,942
Provision (credit) for income taxes	93,767	(33,046)	35,044
Income (loss) before Extraordinary loss	$ 109,809	$ (113,782)	$ 5,898
Extraordinary loss, net of tax benefit of $34,287	(55,943)	—	—
Net income (loss)	$ 53,866	$ (113,782)	$ 5,898

Carmody Shipping Corporation and Subsidiaries
Consolidated Balance Sheets
(In thousands)

ASSETS	May 31,	
	2009	2008
Current assets:		
Cash and cash equivalents	$ 155,456	$ 78,177
Receivable, less allowance for doubtful accounts of $31,308 and $32,074	922,727	899,773
Spare parts, supplies and fuel	164,087	158,062
Prepaid expenses and other	63,573	69,994
Deferred income taxes	133,875	—
Total current assets	$1,439,718	$1,206,006
Property and equipment, at cost		
Flight equipment	$2,843,253	$2,540,350
Package handling and ground support equipment	1,413,793	1,352,659
Computer and electronic equipment	947,913	851,686
Other	1,501,250	1,433,212
	$6,706,209	$6,177,907
Less accumulated depreciation and amortization	3,229,941	2,766,610
Net property and equipment	$3,476,268	$3,411,297
Other assets:		
Goodwill	$ 432,215	$ 487,780
Equipment deposits and other assets	444,863	358,103
Total other assets	$ 877,078	$ 845,883
Total assets	$5,793,064	$5,463,186

LIABILITIES AND STOCKHOLDERS' EQUITY		
Current liabilities:		
Current portion of long-term debt	$ 133,797	$ 155,257
Accounts payable	554,111	430,130
Accrued expenses	761,357	799,468
Total current liabilities	$1,449,265	$1,384,855
Long-term debt, less current portion	1,882,279	1,797,844
Deferred income taxes	72,479	123,715
Other liabilities	717,660	577,050
Total liabilities	$4,121,683	$3,883,464
Common stockholders' equity:		
Common stock, $0.10 par value, 100,000 shares authorized, 54,743 and 54,100 shares issued	$ 5,474	$ 5,410
Additional paid-in capital	699,385	672,727
Retained earnings	969,515	906,555
	$1,674,374	$1,584,692
Less treasury stock and deferred compensation related to stock plans	$ 2,993	$ 4,970
Total common stockholders' equity	1,671,381	1,579,722
Total liabilities and stockholders' equity	$5,793,064	$5,463,186

Required:

1. Evaluate Carmody Shipping's performance in 2009.
2. What were the primary factors responsible for Carmody Shipping's loss in 2008 and return to profitability in 2009?
3. How did Carmody Shipping finance the $329,878,000 increase in assets in 2009?

UNITED STATES SECURITIES AND EXCHANGE COMMISSION
Washington, D. C. 20549

FORM 10-K

(Mark One)

☑ **ANNUAL REPORT PURSUANT TO SECTION 13 OR 15(d) OF THE SECURITIES EXCHANGE ACT OF 1934**

For the fiscal year ended February 3, 2007

OR

☐ **TRANSITION REPORT PURSUANT TO SECTION 13 OR 15(d) OF THE SECURITIES EXCHANGE ACT OF 1934**

For the transition period from _____ to _____

Commission file number 1-12107

ABERCROMBIE & FITCH CO.

(Exact name of registrant as specified in its charter)

ITEM 8. FINANCIAL STATEMENTS AND SUPPLEMENTARY DATA.

ABERCROMBIE & FITCH

CONSOLIDATED STATEMENTS OF NET INCOME AND COMPREHENSIVE INCOME

(Thousands, except per share amounts)

	2006 *	2005	2004
NET SALES	$3,318,158	$2,784,711	$2,021,253
Cost of Goods Sold	1,109,152	933,295	680,029
GROSS PROFIT	2,209,006	1,851,416	1,341,224
Stores and Distribution Expense	1,187,071	1,000,755	738,244
Marketing, General & Administrative Expense	373,828	313,457	259,835
Other Operating Income, Net	(9,983)	(5,534)	(4,490)
OPERATING INCOME	658,090	542,738	347,635
Interest Income, Net	(13,896)	(6,674)	(5,218)
INCOME BEFORE INCOME TAXES	671,986	549,412	352,853
Provision for Income Taxes	249,800	215,426	136,477
NET INCOME	$ 422,186	$ 333,986	$ 216,376
NET INCOME PER SHARE:			
BASIC	$ 4.79	$ 3.83	$ 2.33
DILUTED	$ 4.59	$ 3.66	$ 2.28
WEIGHTED-AVERAGE SHARES OUTSTANDING:			
BASIC	88,052	87,161	92,777
DILUTED	92,010	91,221	95,110
DIVIDENDS DECLARED PER SHARE	$ 0.70	$ 0.60	$ 0.50
OTHER COMPREHENSIVE INCOME			
Cumulative Foreign Currency Translation Adjustments	$ (239)	$ (78)	—
Unrealized Gains (Losses) on Marketable Securities, net of taxes of $20 and $0 for Fiscal 2006 and Fiscal 2005, respectively	41	(718)	—
Other Comprehensive Loss	$ (198)	$ (796)	—
COMPREHENSIVE INCOME	$ 421,988	$ 333,190	$ 216,376

---

*   Fiscal 2006 is a fifty-three week year.

The accompanying Notes are an integral part of these Consolidated Financial Statements.

ABERCROMBIE & FITCH CO. 10-K

ABERCROMBIE & FITCH

CONSOLIDATED BALANCE SHEETS
(Thousands, except share amounts)

	February 3, 2007	January 28, 2006
ASSETS		
CURRENT ASSETS:		
Cash and Equivalents	$ 81,959	$ 50,687
Marketable Securities	447,793	411,167
Receivables	43,240	41,855
Inventories	427,447	362,536
Deferred Income Taxes	33,170	29,654
Other Current Assets	58,469	51,185
TOTAL CURRENT ASSETS	1,092,078	947,084
PROPERTY AND EQUIPMENT, NET	1,092,282	813,603
OTHER ASSETS	63,707	29,031
TOTAL ASSETS	$2,248,067	$1,789,718
LIABILITIES AND SHAREHOLDERS' EQUITY		
CURRENT LIABILITIES:		
Accounts Payable	$ 100,919	$ 86,572
Outstanding Checks	27,391	58,741
Accrued Expenses	260,219	215,034
Deferred Lease Credits	35,423	31,727
Income Taxes Payable	86,675	99,480
TOTAL CURRENT LIABILITIES	510,627	491,554
LONG TERM LIABILITIES:		
Deferred Income Taxes	30,394	38,496
Deferred Lease Credits	203,943	191,225
Commitments	—	—
Other Liabilities	97,806	73,326
TOTAL LONG TERM LIABILITIES		
SHAREHOLDERS' EQUITY:		
Class A Common Stock — $.01 par value: 150,000,000 shares authorized and 103,300,000 shares issued at February 3, 2007 and January 28, 2006, respectively	1,033	1,033
Paid-In Capital	289,732	229,261
Retained Earnings	1,646,290	1,290,208
Accumulated Other Comprehensive Income	(994)	(796)
Deferred Compensation	—	26,206
Treasury Stock, at Average Cost 14,999,945 and 15,573,789 shares at February 3, 2007 and January 28, 2006, respectively	(530,764)	(550,795)
TOTAL SHAREHOLDERS' EQUITY	1,405,297	995,117
TOTAL LIABILITIES AND SHAREHOLDERS' EQUITY	$2,248,067	$1,789,718

The accompanying Notes are an integral part of these Consolidated Financial Statements.

54

ABERCROMBIE & FITCH CO. 10-K

ABERCROMBIE & FITCH

CONSOLIDATED STATEMENTS OF SHAREHOLDERS' EQUITY

(Thousands)

	Common Stock		Paid-In Capital	Retained Earnings	Deferred Compensation	Other Comprehensive Income	Treasury Stock		Total Shareholders' Equity
	Shares Outstanding	Par Value					Shares	At Average Cost	
Balance, January 31, 2004	94,607	$ 1,033	$159,244	$ 885,980	$ 6,265	$ —	8,692	$(194,758)	$ 857,764
Purchase of Treasury Stock	(11,151)	—	—	—	—	—	11,151	(434,658)	(434,658)
Net Income	—	—	—	216,376	—	—	—	—	216,376
Restricted Stock Unit Issuance	24	—	—	108	(1,578)	—	(24)	542	(928)
Restricted Stock Unit Expense	—	—	—	—	10,361	—	—	—	10,361
Stock Option Exercises	2,556	—	—	(16,304)	—	—	(2,556)	65,845	49,541
Dividends ($0.50 per share)	—	—	—	(46,438)	—	—	—	—	(46,438)
Tax Benefit from Exercise of Stock Options and Issuance of Restricted Stock Units	—	—	17,308	—	—	—	—	—	17,308
Balance, January 29, 2005	86,036	$ 1,033	$176,552	$1,039,722	$ 15,048	$ —	17,263	$(563,029)	$ 669,326
Purchase of Treasury Stock	(1,765)	—	—	—	—	—	1,765	(103,296)	(103,296)
Net Income	—	—	—	333,986	—	—	—	—	333,986
Restricted Stock Unit Issuance	166	—	—	(4,297)	(12,966)	—	(166)	5,650	(11,613)
Restricted Stock Unit Expense	—	—	—	—	24,124	—	—	—	24,124
Stock Option Exercises	3,289	—	—	(26,985)	—	—	(3,289)	109,880	82,895
Dividends ($0.60 per share)	—	—	—	(52,218)	—	—	—	—	(52,218)
Unrealized Gains (Losses) on Marketable Securities	—	—	—	—	—	(718)	—	—	(718)
Cumulative Foreign Currency Translation Adjustments	—	—	—	—	—	(78)	—	—	(78)
Tax Benefit from Exercise of Stock Options and Issuance of Restricted Stock Units	—	—	52,709	—	—	—	—	—	52,709

ABERCROMBIE & FITCH CO. 10-K

Balance, January 28, 2006	87,726	$ 1,033	$229,261	$1,290,208	$ 26,206	$ (796)	15,574	$(550,795)	$ 995,117
Deferred Compensation Reclassification	—	—	26,206	—	(26,206)	—	—	—	—
Net Income	—	—	—	422,186	—	—	—	—	422,186
Restricted Stock Unit Issuance	145	—	(7,710)	(1,011)	—	—	(145)	4,302	(4,419)
Restricted Stock Unit Expense	—	—	19,964	—	—	—	—	—	19,964
Stock Option Exercises	429	—	1,384	(3,470)	—	—	(429)	15,729	13,643
Stock Option Expense	—	—	15,155	—	—	—	—	—	15,155
Dividends ($0.70 per share)	—	—	—	(61,623)	—	—	—	—	(61,623)
Unrealized Gains (Losses) on Marketable Securities	—	—	—	—	—	41	—	—	41
Cumulative Foreign Currency Translation Adjustments	—	—	$ —	—	—	(239)	—	—	(239)
Tax Benefit from Exercise of Stock Options and Issuance of Restricted Stock Units	—	—	5,472	—	—	—	—	—	5,472
Balance, February 3, 2007	88,300	$1,033	$289,732	$1,646,290	$ —	$ (994)	15,000	$(530,764)	$1,405,297

The accompanying Notes are an integral part of these Consolidated Financial Statements.

ABERCROMBIE & FITCH CO. 10-K

ABERCROMBIE & FITCH

CONSOLIDATED STATEMENTS OF CASH FLOWS

	2006*	(Thousands) 2005	2004
OPERATING ACTIVITIES:			
Net Income	$ 422,186	$ 333,986	$ 216,376
Impact of Other Operating Activities on Cash Flows:			
Depreciation and Amortization	146,156	124,206	105,814
Amortization of Deferred Lease Credits	(34,485)	(32,527)	(32,794)
Share-Based Compensation	35,119	24,124	10,372
Tax Benefit from Share-Based Compensation	5,472	52,709	17,308
Excess Tax Benefit from Share-Based Compensation	(3,382)	—	—
Deferred Taxes	(11,638)	(2,099)	3,942
Non-Cash Charge for Asset Impairment	298	272	1,190
Loss on Disposal of Assets	6,261	7,386	4,664
Lessor Construction Allowances	49,387	42,336	55,009
Changes in Assets and Liabilities:			
Inventories	(61,940)	(146,314)	(34,445)
Accounts Payable and Accrued Expenses	24,579	(2,912)	99,388
Income Taxes	(12,805)	43,893	1,659
Other Assets and Liabilities	16,963	8,530	(24,699)
NET CASH PROVIDED BY OPERATING ACTIVITIES	582,171	453,590	423,784
INVESTING ACTIVITIES:			
Capital Expenditures	(403,476)	(256,422)	(185,065)
Purchases of Trust Owned Life Insurance Policies	(15,258)	—	—
Purchases of Marketable Securities	(1,459,835)	(1,016,986)	(4,314,070)
Proceeds from Sales of Marketable Securities	1,404,805	605,101	4,778,770
NET CASH (USED FOR) PROVIDED BY INVESTING ACTIVITIES	(473,764)	(668,307)	(668,307)
FINANCING ACTIVITIES:			
Dividends Paid	(61,623)	(52,218)	(46,438)
Change in Outstanding Checks and Other	(31,770)	8,467	19,383
Proceeds from Share-Based Compensation	12,876	73,716	49,948
Excess Tax Benefit from Share-Based Compensation	3,382	—	—
Purchase of Treasury Stock	—	(103,296)	(434,658)
NET CASH USED FOR FINANCING ACTIVITIES	(77,135)	(73,331)	(411,765)
NET INCREASE (DECREASE) IN CASH AND EQUIVALENTS	31,272	(288,048)	291,654
Cash and Equivalents, Beginning of Year	50,687	338,735	47,081
CASH AND EQUIVALENTS, END OF YEAR	$ 81,959	$ 50,687	$ 338,735
SIGNIFICANT NON-CASH INVESTING ACTIVITIES:			
Change in Accrual for Construction in Progress	$ 28,455	$ 3,754	($15,513)

---

*   Fiscal 2006 is a fifty-three week year.

The accompanying Notes are an integral part of these Consolidated Financial Statements.

ABERCROMBIE & FITCH

NOTES TO CONSOLIDATED FINANCIAL STATEMENTS

1. BASIS OF PRESENTATION

Abercrombie & Fitch Co. ("A&F"), through its wholly-owned subsidiaries (collectively, A&F and its wholly-owned subsidiaries are referred to as "Abercrombie & Fitch" or the "Company"), is a specialty retailer of high-quality, casual apparel for men, women and kids with an active, youthful lifestyle. The business was established in 1892.

The accompanying consolidated financial statements include the historical financial statements of, and transactions applicable to, A&F and its wholly-owned subsidiaries and reflect the assets, liabilities, results of operations and cash flows on a historical cost basis.

FISCAL YEAR

The Company's fiscal year ends on the Saturday closest to January 31, typically resulting in a fifty-two week year, but occasionally giving rise to an additional week, resulting in a fifty-three week year. Fiscal years are designated in the financial statements and notes by the calendar year in which the fiscal year commences. All references herein to "Fiscal 2006" represent the results of the 53-week fiscal year ended February 3, 2007; to "Fiscal 2005" represent the 52-week fiscal year ended January 28, 2006; and to "Fiscal 2004" represent the 52-week fiscal year ended January 29, 2005. In addition, all references herein to "Fiscal 2007" represent the 52-week fiscal year that will end on February 2, 2008.

RECLASSIFICATIONS

Certain amounts have been reclassified to conform with the current year presentation. The Company periodically acquires shares of its Class A Common Stock, par value $0.01 per share ("Common Stock") under various Board of Directors authorized share buy-back plans. The shares acquired are held as treasury stock and are not retired. The Company utilizes the treasury stock when issuing shares for stock option exercises and restricted stock unit vestings. In accordance with the Accounting Principles Board ("APB") Opinion No. 6, "*Status of Accounting Research Bulletins*," "gains" on sales of treasury stock not previously accounted for as constructively retired should be credited to paid-in capital; "losses" may be charged to paid-in capital to the extent of previous net "gains" from sales or retirements of the same class of stock, otherwise to retained earnings. On the Consolidated Balance Sheet for the year ended January 28, 2006, the Company reclassified cumulative treasury stock "losses" of $67.6 million to retained earnings that were previously netted against paid-in capital. On the Consolidated Statements of Shareholders' Equity for the year ended January 31, 2004, the Company reclassified cumulative treasury stock "losses" of $20.1 million to retained earnings that were previously netted against paid-in capital. In addition, on the Consolidated Statements of Shareholders' Equity for the years ended January 29, 2005 and January 28, 2006, the Company reclassified treasury stock "losses" of $16.2 million and $31.3 million, respectively, to retained earnings that were previously netted against paid-in capital. Amounts reclassified did not have an effect on the Company's results of operations or Consolidated Statements of Cash Flows.

ABERCROMBIE & FITCH CO. 10-K

SEGMENT REPORTING

In accordance with Statement of Financial Accounting Standards ("SFAS") No. 131, *"Disclosures about Segments of an Enterprise and Related Information,"* the Company determined its operating segments on the same basis that it uses to evaluate performance internally. The operating segments identified by the Company, Abercrombie & Fitch, abercrombie, Hollister and RUEHL, have been aggregated and are reported as one reportable financial segment. The Company aggregates its operating segments because they meet the aggregation criteria set forth in paragraph 17 of SFAS No. 131. The Company believes its operating segments may be aggregated for financial reporting purposes because they are similar in each of the following areas: class of consumer, economic characteristics, nature of products, nature of production processes and distribution methods. Revenues relating to the Company's international sales in Fiscal 2006 were not material and are not reported separately from domestic revenues.

2. SUMMARY OF SIGNIFICANT ACCOUNTING POLICIES

PRINCIPLES OF CONSOLIDATION

The consolidated financial statements include the accounts of A&F and its subsidiaries. All intercompany balances and transactions have been eliminated in consolidation.

CASH AND EQUIVALENTS

Cash and equivalents include amounts on deposit with financial institutions and investments with original maturities of less than 90 days. Outstanding checks at year-end are reclassified in the balance sheet from cash to be reflected as liabilities.

INVESTMENTS

Investments with original maturities greater than 90 days are accounted for in accordance with SFAS No. 115, *"Accounting for Certain Investments in Debt and Equity Securities,"* and are classified accordingly by the Company at the time of purchase. At February 3, 2007, the Company's investments in marketable securities consisted primarily of investment grade municipal notes and bonds and investment grade auction rate securities, all classified as available-for-sale and reported at fair value based on the market, with maturities that could range from one month to 40 years.

The Company began investing in municipal notes and bonds during Fiscal 2005. These investments have early redemption provisions at predetermined prices. For the fiscal years ended February 3, 2007 and January 28, 2006, there were no realized gains or losses. Net unrealized holding losses were approximately $0.7 million for both the fiscal years ended February 3, 2007 and January 28, 2006.

For the Company's investments in auction rate securities, the interest rates reset through an auction process at predetermined periods ranging from seven to 49 days. Due to the frequent nature of the reset feature, the investment's market price approximates its fair value; therefore, there are no realized or unrealized gains or losses associated with these marketable securities.

ABERCROMBIE & FITCH CO. 10-K

The Company held approximately $447.8 million and $411.2 million in marketable securities as of February 3, 2007 and January 28, 2006, respectively.

As of February 3, 2007 and January 28, 2006, approximately $346.1 million and $285.4 million, respectively, of marketable securities were invested in auction rate securities. As of February 3, 2007 and January 28, 2006, approximately $97.1 million and $120.8 million, respectively, of marketable securities were invested in municipal notes and bonds. As of February 3, 2007 and January 28, 2006, approximately $4.6 millions and $5.0 million, respectively, of the marketable securities were invested in dividend received deduction.

The Company established an irrevocable rabbi trust during the third quarter of Fiscal 2006, the purpose is to be a source of funds to match respective funding obligations to participants in the Abercrombie & Fitch Nonqualified Savings and Supplemental Retirement Plan and the Chief Executive Officer Supplemental Executive Retirement Plan. As of February 3, 2007, total assets related to the Rabbi Trust were $33.5 million, which included $18.3 million of available-for-sale securities and $15.3 million related to the cash surrender value of trust owned life insurance policies. The Rabbi Trust assets are consolidated in accordance with Emerging Issues Task Force 97-14 ("EITF 97-14") and recorded at fair value in other assets on the Consolidated Balance Sheet and were restricted as to their use as noted above.

CREDIT CARD RECEIVABLES

As part of the normal course of business, the Company has approximately two to three days of sales transactions outstanding with its third-party credit card vendors at any point. The Company classifies these outstanding balances as receivables.

INVENTORIES

Inventories are principally valued at the lower of average cost or market utilizing the retail method. The Company determines market value as the anticipated future selling price of the merchandise less a normal margin. Therefore, an initial markup is applied to inventory at cost in order to establish a cost-to-retail ratio. Permanent markdowns, when taken, reduce both the retail and cost components of inventory on hand so as to maintain the already established cost-to-retail relationship.

The fiscal year is comprised of two principal selling seasons: Spring (the first and second quarters) and Fall (the third and fourth quarters). The Company classifies its inventory into three categories: spring fashion, fall fashion and basic. The Company reduces inventory valuation at the end of the first and third quarters to reserve for projected inventory markdowns required to sell through the current season inventory prior to the beginning of the following season. Additionally, the Company reduces inventory at season end by recording a markdown reserve that represents the estimated future anticipated selling price decreases necessary to sell through the remaining carryover fashion inventory for the season just passed. Further, as part of inventory valuation, inventory shrinkage estimates, based on historical trends from actual physical inventories, are made that reduce the inventory value for lost or stolen items. The Company performs physical inventories throughout the year and adjusts the shrink reserve accordingly.

The markdown reserve was $6.8 million, $10.0 million and $6.6 million at February 3, 2007, January 28, 2006 and January 29, 2005, respectively. The shrink reserve was $7.7 million, $3.8 million and $2.9 million at February 3, 2007, January 28, 2006 and January 29, 2005, respectively.

ABERCROMBIE & FITCH CO. 10-K

STORE SUPPLIES

The initial inventory of supplies for new stores including, but not limited to, hangers, signage, security tags and point-of-sale supplies are capitalized at the store opening date. In lieu of amortizing the initial balances over their estimated useful lives, the Company expenses all subsequent replacements and adjusts the initial balance, as appropriate, for changes in store quantities or replacement cost. This policy approximates the expense that would have been recognized under generally accepted accounting principles ("GAAP"). Store supply categories are classified as current or non-current based on their estimated useful lives. Packaging is expensed as used. Current store supplies were $20.0 million and $16.1 million at February 3, 2007 and January 28, 2006, respectively. Non-current store supplies were $20.6 million at both February 3, 2007 and January 28, 2006.

PROPERTY AND EQUIPMENT

Depreciation and amortization of property and equipment are computed for financial reporting purposes on a straight-line basis, using service lives ranging principally from 30 years for buildings, the lesser of ten years or the life of the lease for leasehold improvements and three to ten years for other property and equipment. The cost of assets sold or retired and the related accumulated depreciation or amortization are removed from the accounts with any resulting gain or loss included in net income. Maintenance and repairs are charged to expense as incurred. Major renewals and betterments that extend service lives are capitalized.

Long-lived assets are reviewed at the store level periodically for impairment or whenever events or changes in circumstances indicate that full recoverability of net assets through future cash flows is in question. Factors used in the evaluation include, but are not limited to, management's plans for future operations, recent operating results and projected cash flows. The Company incurred impairment charges of approximately $0.3 million for both Fiscal 2006 and Fiscal 2005.

INCOME TAXES

Income taxes are calculated in accordance with SFAS No. 109, *"Accounting for Income Taxes,"* which requires the use of the asset and liability method. Deferred tax assets and liabilities are recognized based on the difference between the financial statement carrying amounts of existing assets and liabilities and their respective tax bases. Deferred tax assets and liabilities are measured using current enacted tax rates in effect in the years in which those temporary differences are expected to reverse. Inherent in the measurement of deferred balances are certain judgments and interpretations of enacted tax law and published guidance with respect to applicability to the Company's operations. A valuation allowance has been provided for losses related to the start-up costs associated with operations in foreign countries. No other valuation allowances have been provided for deferred tax assets because management believes that it is more likely than not that the full amount of the net deferred tax assets will be realized in the future. The effective tax rate utilized by the Company reflects management's judgment of the expected tax liabilities within the various taxing jurisdictions.

ABERCROMBIE & FITCH CO. 10-K

FOREIGN CURRENCY TRANSLATION

Some of the Company 's international operations use local currencies as the functional currency. In accordance with SFAS No. 52, *"Foreign Currency Translation "*, assets and liabilities denominated in foreign currencies were translated into U.S. dollars (the reporting currency) at the exchange rate prevailing at the balance sheet date. Revenues and expenses denominated in foreign currencies were translated into U.S. dollars at the monthly average exchange rate for the period. Gains and losses resulting from foreign currency transactions are included in the results of operations, whereas related translation adjustments are reported as an element of other comprehensive income in accordance with SFAS No. 130, *"Reporting Comprehensive Income "*.

CONTINGENCIES

In the normal course of business, the Company must make continuing estimates of potential future legal obligations and liabilities, which require management 's judgment on the outcome of various issues. Management may also use outside legal advice to assist in the estimating process. However, the ultimate outcome of various legal issues could be different than management estimates, and adjustments may be required. The Company accrues for its legal obligations for outstanding bills, expected defense costs and, if appropriate, settlements. Accruals are made for personnel, general litigation and intellectual property.

SHAREHOLDERS ' EQUITY

At February 3, 2007 and January 28, 2006, there were 150 million shares of $.01 par value Class A Common Stock authorized, of which 88.3 million and 87.7 million shares were outstanding at February 3, 2007 and January 28, 2006, respectively, and 106.4 million shares of $.01 par value Class B Common Stock authorized, none of which were outstanding at February 3, 2007 or January 28, 2006. In addition, 15 million shares of $.01 par value Preferred Stock were authorized, none of which have been issued. See Note 15 of the Notes to Consolidated Financial Statements for information about Preferred Stock Purchase Rights.

Holders of Class A Common Stock generally have identical rights to holders of Class B Common Stock, except that holders of Class A Common Stock are entitled to one vote per share while holders of Class B Common Stock are entitled to three votes per share on all matters submitted to a vote of shareholders.

REVENUE RECOGNITION

The Company recognizes retail sales at the time the customer takes possession of the merchandise and purchases are paid for, primarily with either cash or credit card. Direct-to-consumer sales are recorded upon customer receipt of merchandise. Amounts relating to shipping and handling billed to customers in a sale transaction are classified as revenue and the related direct shipping and handling costs are classified as stores and distribution expense. Associate discounts are classified as a reduction of revenue. The Company reserves for sales returns through estimates based on historical experience and various other assumptions that management believes to be reasonable. The sales return reserve was $8.9 million, $8.2 million and $6.7 million of February 3, 2007, January 28, 2006 and January 29, 2005, respectively.

ABERCROMBIE & FITCH CO. 10-K

The Company's gift cards do not expire or lose value over periods of inactivity. The Company accounts for gift cards by recognizing a liability at the time a gift card is sold. The liability remains on the Company's books until the earlier of redemption (recognized as revenue) or when the Company determines the likelihood of redemption is remote (recognized as other operating income). The Company determines the probability of the gift card being redeemed to be remote based on historical redemption patterns and at these times recognizes the remaining balance as other operating income. At February 3, 2007 and January 28, 2006, the gift card liability on the Company's Consolidated Balance Sheet was $65.0 million and $53.2 million, respectively.

The Company is not required by law to escheat the value of unredeemed gift cards to the states in which it operates. During Fiscal 2006, Fiscal 2005 and Fiscal 2004, the Company recognized other operating income for adjustments to the gift card liability of $5.2 million, $2.4 million and $4.3 million, respectively.

The Company does not include tax amounts collected as part of the sales transaction in its net sales results.

COST OF GOODS SOLD

Cost of goods sold includes among others, cost of merchandise, markdowns, inventory shrink and valuation reserves and freight expenses.

STORES AND DISTRIBUTION EXPENSE

Stores and distribution expense includes store payroll, store management, rent, utilities and other landlord expenses, depreciation and amortization, repairs and maintenance and other store support functions and direct-to-consumer and DC expenses.

MARKETING, GENERAL & ADMINISTRATIVE EXPENSE

Marketing, general and administrative expense includes photography and media ads, store marketing, home office payroll, except for those departments included in stores and distribution expense, information technology, outside services such as legal and consulting, relocation and employment and travel expenses.

OTHER OPERATING INCOME, NET

Other operating income consists primarily of gift card balances whose likelihood of redemption has been determined to be remote and are therefore recognized as income. Other operating income in Fiscal 2006 also included non-recurring benefits from insurance reimbursements received for fire and Hurricane Katrina damage.

ABERCROMBIE & FITCH CO. 10-K

CATALOGUE AND ADVERTISING COSTS

Catalogue costs consist primarily of catalogue production and mailing costs and are expensed as incurred as a component of "Stores and Distribution Expense." Advertising costs consist of in-store photographs and advertising in selected national publications and billboards and are expensed as part of "Marketing, General and Administrative Expense" when the photographs or publications first appear. Catalogue and advertising costs, which include photo shoot costs, amounted to $39.3 million in Fiscal 2006, $36.8 million in Fiscal 2005 and $33.8 million in Fiscal 2004.

OPERATING LEASES

The Company leases property for its stores under operating leases. Most lease agreements contain construction allowances, rent escalation clauses and/or contingent rent provisions.

For construction allowances, the Company records a deferred lease credit on the consolidated balance sheet and amortizes the deferred lease credit as a reduction of rent expense on the consolidated statement of net income and comprehensive income over the terms of the leases. For scheduled rent escalation clauses during the lease terms, the Company records minimum rental expenses on a straight-line basis over the terms of the leases on the consolidated statement of net income and comprehensive income. The term of the lease over which the Company amortizes construction allowances and minimum rental expenses on a straight-line basis begins on the date of initial possession, which is generally when the Company enters the space and begins to make improvements in preparation for intended use.

Certain leases provide for contingent rents, which are determined as a percentage of gross sales in excess of specified levels. The Company records a contingent rent liability in accrued expenses on the Consolidated Balance Sheet and the corresponding rent expense when management determines that achieving the specified levels during the fiscal year is probable.

STORE PRE-OPENING EXPENSES

Pre-opening expenses related to new store openings are charged to operations as incurred.

DESIGN AND DEVELOPMENT COSTS

Costs to design and develop the Company's merchandise are expensed as incurred and are reflected as a component of "Marketing, General and Administrative Expense."

FAIR VALUE OF FINANCIAL INSTRUMENTS

The recorded values of current assets and current liabilities, including receivables, marketable securities, other assets and accounts payable, approximate fair value due to the short maturity and because the average interest rate approximates current market origination rates.

ABERCROMBIE & FITCH CO. 10-K

EARNINGS PER SHARE

Net income per share is computed in accordance with SFAS No. 128, *"Earnings Per Share."* Net income per basic share is computed based on the weighted-average number of outstanding shares of common stock. Net income per diluted share includes the weighted-average effect of dilutive stock options and restricted stock units.

Weighted-Average Shares Outstanding (in thousands):

	2006	2005	2004
Shares of Class A Common Stock issued	103,300	103,300	103,300
Treasury shares outstanding	(15,248)	(16,139)	(10,523)
Basic shares outstanding	88,052	87,161	92,777
Dilutive effect of options and restricted shares	3,958	4,060	2,333
Diluted shares outstanding	92,010	91,221	95,110

Options to purchase 0.1 million, 0.2 million and 5.2 million shares of Class A Common Stock were outstanding for Fiscal 2006, Fiscal 2005 and Fiscal 2004, respectively, but were not included in the computation of net income per diluted share because the options' exercise prices were greater than the average market price of the underlying shares.

SHARE-BASED COMPENSATION

See Note 4 of the Notes to Consolidated Financial Statements.

USE OF ESTIMATES IN THE PREPARATION OF FINANCIAL STATEMENTS

The preparation of financial statements in conformity with GAAP requires management to make estimates and assumptions that affect the reported amounts of assets and liabilities as of the date of the financial statements and the reported amounts of revenues and expenses during the reporting period. Since actual results may differ from those estimates, the Company revises its estimates and assumptions as new information becomes available.

3. RECENTLY ISSUED ACCOUNTING PRONOUNCEMENTS

In July 2006, the FASB released Interpretation No. 48, *"Accounting for Uncertainty in Income Taxes – an Interpretation of FASB Statement 109, Accounting for Income Taxes"* ("FIN 48"). FIN 48 provides a comprehensive model for how a company should recognize, measure, present and disclose in its financial statements uncertain tax positions that the company has taken or expects to take on a tax return. FIN 48 defines the threshold for recognizing tax return positions in the financial statements as "more likely than not" that the position is sustainable, based on its merits. FIN 48 also provides guidance on the measurement, classification and disclosure of tax return positions in the financial statements. FIN 48 is effective for the first reporting period beginning after December 15, 2006, with the cumulative effect of the change in accounting principle recorded as an adjustment to the beginning balance of retained earnings in the period of adoption. An analysis of the impact of this interpretation is not yet complete; however, the Company expects to record an adjustment to reduce opening retained earnings in the first quarter of Fiscal 2007 by an amount which is not material to its financial statements.

ABERCROMBIE & FITCH CO. 10-K

In September 2006, the Securities and Exchange Commission issued Staff Accounting Bulletin ("SAB") No. 108, "*Considering the Effects of Prior Year Misstatements when Quantifying Misstatements in Current Year Financial Statements.*" SAB No. 108 requires a "dual approach" for quantifications of errors using both a method that focuses on the income statement impact, including the cumulative effect of prior years' misstatements, and a method that focuses on the period-end balance sheet. SAB No. 108 was effective for the Company for Fiscal 2006. The adoption of SAB No. 108 did not have any impact on the Company's consolidated financial statements.

In September 2006, the FASB released FASB Statement No. 157, "*Fair Value Measurements*" ("SFAS 157"). SFAS 157 establishes a common definition for fair value under GAAP, establishes a framework for measuring fair value and expands disclosure requirements about such fair value measurements. SFAS 157 will be effective for the Company on February 3, 2008. The Company is currently evaluating the potential impact on the consolidated financial statements of adopting SFAS 157.

In February 2007, the FASB released FASB Statement No. 159, "*The Fair Value Option for Financial Assets and Financial Liabilities*" ("SFAS 159"). SFAS 159 permits companies to measure many financial instruments and certain other assets and liabilities at fair value on an instrument by instrument basis. SFAS 159 also establishes presentation and disclosure requirements to facilitate comparisons between companies that select different measurement attributes for similar types of assets and liabilities. SFAS 159 will be effective for the Company on February 3, 2008. The Company is currently evaluating the potential impact on the consolidated financial statements of adopting SFAS 159.

4. SHARE-BASED COMPENSATION

Background

On January 29, 2006, the Company adopted SFAS No. 123 (Revised 2004), "*Share-Based Payment*" ("SFAS No. 123(R)"), which requires share-based compensation to be measured based on estimated fair values at the date of grant using an option-pricing model. Previously, the Company accounted for share-based compensation using the intrinsic value method in accordance with APB Opinion No. 25, "*Accounting for Stock Issued to Employees,*" and related interpretations, for which no expense was recognized for stock options if the exercise price was equal to the market value of the underlying Common Stock on the date of grant, and if the Company provided the required pro forma disclosures in accordance with SFAS No. 123, "*Accounting for Stock-Based Compensation*" ("SFAS No. 123"), as amended.

The Company adopted SFAS No. 123(R) using the modified prospective transition method, which requires share-based compensation to be recognized for all unvested share-based awards beginning in the first quarter of adoption. Accordingly, prior period information presented in these financial statements has not been restated to reflect the fair value method of expensing stock options. Under the modified prospective method, compensation expense recognized for the fifty-three weeks ended February 3, 2007 includes compensation expense for: a) all share-based awards granted prior to, but not yet vested as of, January 29, 2006, based on the grant-date fair value estimated in accordance with the original provisions of SFAS No. 123 and b) all share-based awards granted subsequent to January 29, 2006, based on the grant-date fair value estimated in accordance with the provisions of SFAS No. 123(R).

ABERCROMBIE & FITCH CO. 10-K

Financial Statement Impact

Total share-based compensation expense recognized under SFAS No. 123(R) was $35.1 million for the fifty-three week period ended February 3, 2007. Share-based compensation expense of $24.1 million and $10.4 million was recognized for the fifty-two week periods ended January 28, 2006 and January 29, 2005, under APB 25.

The Company also realized $5.5 million, $52.7 million and $17.3 million in cash tax benefits for the fifty-three week period ended February 3, 2007 and the fifty-two week periods ended January 28, 2006 and January 29, 2005, respectively, related to stock option exercises and restricted stock issuances.

The following table summarizes the incremental effect of the adoption of SFAS No. 123(R) to the Company's consolidated financial statements for the fifty-three weeks ended February 3, 2007:

(Thousands, except per share amounts)	Fifty-Three Weeks Ended February 3, 2007
Stores and distribution expense	$ 463
Marketing, general and administrative expense	13,627
Operating income	14,090
Provision for income taxes	(4,210)
Net income	$ 9,880
Net income per basic share	$ 0.11
Net income per diluted share	$ 0.11
Net cash used for operating activities	$ (3,382)
Net cash provided by financing activities	$ 3,382

The following table is presented for comparative purposes and illustrates the pro forma effect on net income and net income per share for the fifty-two weeks ended January 28, 2006 and January 29, 2005, as if the Company had applied the fair value recognition provisions of SFAS No. 123 to stock options granted under the Company's share-based compensation plans prior to January 29, 2006:

(Thousands, except per share amounts)	Fifty-Two Weeks Ended January 28, 2006	Fifty-Two Weeks Ended January 29, 2005
Net income:		
As reported	$ 333,986	$ 216,376
Share-based compensation expense included in reported net income, net of tax(1)	14,716	6,358
Share-based compensation expense determined under fair value based method, net of tax	(36,689)	(27,720)
Pro forma	$ 312,013	$ 195,014
Net income per basic share:		
As reported	$ 3.83	$ 2.33
Pro forma	$ 3.58	$ 2.10
Net income per diluted share:		
As reported	$ 3.66	$ 2.28
Pro forma	$ 3.38	$ 2.05

(1)   Includes share-based compensation expense related to restricted stock unit awards actually recognized in net income in each period presented using the intrinsic value method.

ABERCROMBIE & FITCH CO. 10-K

Share-based compensation expense is recognized, net of estimated forfeitures, over the requisite service period on a straight line basis. The Company adjusts share-based compensation on a quarterly basis for actual forfeitures and on a periodic basis for changes to the estimate of expected forfeitures based on actual forfeiture experience. The effect of adjusting the forfeiture rate is recognized in the period the forfeiture estimate is changed. The effect of forfeiture adjustments during the fifty-three week period ended February 3, 2007 was immaterial.

Upon adoption of SFAS No. 123(R), the Company began presenting the deferred compensation for share-based compensation in the Condensed Consolidated Balance Sheet as part of paid-in capital and the related tax benefit in paid-in capital. Additionally, the Company began presenting the excess tax benefit in the Consolidated Statement of Cash Flows as part of the financing activities. Prior to adoption of SFAS No. 123(R), the deferred compensation was presented in the Condensed Consolidated Balance Sheet as deferred compensation and the related tax benefit was presented in the Condensed Consolidated Statement of Cash Flows in operating activities.

Plans

As of February 3, 2007, the Company had two primary share-based compensation plans, the 2002 Stock Plan for Associates (the "2002 Plan") and the 2005 Long-Term Incentive Plan (the "2005 LTIP"), under which it grants stock options and restricted stock units to its associates and non-associate board members. The Company also has three other share-based compensation plans under which it granted stock options and restricted stock units to its associates and non-associate Board members in prior years.

The 2005 LTIP, which is a shareholder approved plan, permits the Company to grant up to approximately 2.0 million shares of A&F's Common Stock to the majority of associates who are subject to Section 16 of the Securities Exchange Act of 1934, as amended, and any non-associate directors of the Company. The 2002 Plan, which is not a shareholder approved plan, permits the Company to grant up to 7.0 million shares of A&F's Common Stock to any associate. Under both plans, stock options and restricted stock units vest primarily over four years for associates. Under the 2005 LTIP, stock options and restricted stock units vest over one year for non-associate directors. Stock options have a ten year contractual term and the plans provide for accelerated vesting if there is a change of control as defined in the plans.

The Company issues shares for stock option exercises and restricted stock unit vestings from treasury stock. As of February 3, 2007, the Company had enough treasury stock available to cover stock options and restricted stock units outstanding without having to repurchase additional stock.

Fair Value Estimates

The Company estimates the fair value of stock options granted using the Black-Scholes option-pricing model, which requires the Company to estimate the expected term of the stock option grants and expected future stock price volatility over the term. The term represents the expected period of time the Company believes the options will be outstanding based on historical experience. Estimates of expected future stock price volatility are based on the historic volatility of the Company's stock for the period equal to the expected term of the stock option. The Company calculates the volatility as the annualized standard deviation of the differences in the natural logarithms of the weekly stock closing price, adjusted for stock splits.

ABERCROMBIE & FITCH CO. 10-K

The weighted-average estimated fair values of stock options granted during the fifty-three week period ended February 3, 2007 and the fifty-two week periods ended January 28, 2006 and January 29, 2005, as well as the weighted-average assumptions used in calculating such values, on the date of grant, were as follows:

	Fifty-Three Weeks Ended		Fifty-Two Weeks Ended	Fifty-Two Weeks Ended
	February 3, 2007		January 28, 2006	January 29, 2005
	Executive Officers	Other Associates	Executive Officers and Other Associates	Executive Officers and Other Associates
Exercise price	$58.22	$58.12	$ 60.10	$ 36.49
Fair value	$24.92	$20.69	$ 23.01	$ 14.56
Assumptions:				
Price volatility	47%	42%	47%	56%
Expected term (Years)	5	4	4	4
Risk-free interest rate	4.9%	4.9%	4.0%	3.2%
Dividend yield	1.2%	1.2%	1.1%	1.3%

In the case of restricted stock units, the Company calculates the fair value of the restricted stock units granted as the market price of the underlying Common Stock on the date of issuance adjusted for anticipated dividend payments during the vesting period.

Stock Option Activity

Below is the summary of stock option activity for Fiscal 2006:

Stock Options	Fifty-Three Weeks Ended February 3, 2007			
	Number of Shares	Weighted-Average Exercise Price	Aggregate Intrinsic Value	Weighted-Average Remaining Contractual Life
Outstanding at January 29, 2006	9,060,831	$ 37.18		
Granted	411,300	58.16		
Exercised	(440,457)	31.74		
Forfeited or expired	(226,950)	53.18		
Outstanding at February 3, 2007	8,804,724	$ 38.07	$ 375,970,520	3.7
Options expected to vest at February 3, 2007	625,242	$ 54.92	$ 16,162,506	8.4
Options exercisable at February 3, 2007	8,136,922	$ 36.67	$ 358,856,161	3.4

ABERCROMBIE & FITCH CO. 10-K

7. LEASED FACILITIES AND COMMITMENTS

Annual store rent is comprised of a fixed minimum amount, plus contingent rent based on a percentage of sales exceeding a stipulated amount. Store lease terms generally require additional payments covering taxes, common area costs and certain other expenses.

A summary of rent expense follows (thousands):

	2006*	2005	2004
Store rent:			
Fixed minimum	$ 196,690	$ 170,009	$ 141,450
Contingent	20,192	16,178	6,932
Total store rent	216,882	186,187	148,382
Buildings, equipment and other	5,646	3,241	1,663
Total rent expense	$ 222,528	$ 189,428	$ 150,045

*   Fiscal 2006 is a fifty-three week year.

At February 3, 2007, the Company was committed to non-cancelable leases with remaining terms of one to 15 years. A summary of operating lease commitments under non-cancelable leases follows (thousands):

Fiscal 2007	$215,499
Fiscal 2008	$215,670
Fiscal 2009	$206,830
Fiscal 2010	$195,007
Fiscal 2011	$178,448
Thereafter	$660,227

8. ACCRUED EXPENSES

Accrued expenses included gift card liabilities of $65.0 million and construction in progress of $48.0 million at February 3, 2007. Accrued expenses included gift card liabilities of $53.2 million and construction in progress of $19.5 million at January 28, 2006.

9. OTHER LIABILITIES

Other liabilities included straight-line rent of $45.8 million and $38.8 million at February 3, 2007 and January 28, 2006, respectively.

ABERCROMBIE & FITCH CO. 10-K

10. INCOME TAXES

The provision for income taxes consisted of (thousands):

	2006*	2005	2004
Currently Payable:			
Federal	$ 236,553	$ 184,884	$ 112,537
State	24,885	32,641	19,998
	$ 261,438	$ 217,525	$ 132,535
Deferred:			
Federal	$ (10,271)	$ (5,980)	$ 2,684
State	(1,367)	3,881	1,258
	$ (11,638)	$ (2,099)	$ 3,942
Total provision	$ 249,800	$ 215,426	$ 136,477

*   Fiscal 2006 is a fifty-three week year.

A reconciliation between the statutory federal income tax rate and the effective income tax rate follows:

	2006	2005	2004
Federal income tax rate	35.0%	35.0%	35.0%
State income tax, net of federal income tax effect	2.3	4.3	3.9
Other items, net	(0.1)	(0.1)	(0.2)
Total	37.2%	39.2%	38.7%

Amounts paid directly to taxing authorities were $272.0 million, $122.0 million and $114.0 million in Fiscal 2006, Fiscal 2005, and Fiscal 2004, respectively.

ABERCROMBIE & FITCH CO. 10-K

The effect of temporary differences which give rise to deferred income tax assets (liabilities) were as follows (thousands):

	2006*	2005
Deferred tax assets:		
Deferred compensation	$ 37,725	$ 24,046
Rent	76,890	88,399
Accrued expenses	15,003	14,317
Inventory	5,642	3,982
Foreign net operation losses	2,709	—
Valuation allowance on foreign net operation losses	(2,709)	—
Total deferred tax assets	$ 135,260	$ 130,744
Deferred tax liabilities:		
Store supplies	$ (11,578)	$ (10,851)
Property and equipment	(120,906)	(128,735)
Total deferred tax liabilities	$ (132,484)	$ (139,586)
Net deferred income tax liabilities	$ 2,776	$ (8,842)

---

*   Fiscal 2006 is a fifty-three week year.

At February 3, 2007, the Company had foreign net operating loss carryovers that could be utilized to reduce future years' tax liabilities. A portion of these net operating losses begin expiring in the year 2012, and some have an indefinite carryforward period. The Company has established a valuation allowance to reflect the uncertainty of realizing the benefits of these net operating losses in foreign jurisdictions. No other valuation allowance has been provided for deferred tax assets because management believes that it is more likely than not that the full amount of the net deferred tax assets will be realized in the future.

11. LONG-TERM DEBT

On December 15, 2004, the Company entered into an amended and restated $250 million syndicated unsecured credit agreement (the "Amended Credit Agreement"). The primary purposes of the Amended Credit Agreement are for trade and stand-by letters of credit and working capital. The Amended Credit Agreement has several borrowing options, including an option where interest rates are based on the agent bank's "Alternate Base Rate," and another using the London Interbank Offered Rate. The facility fees payable under the Amended Credit Agreement are based on the ratio of the Company's leveraged total debt plus 600% of forward minimum rent commitments to consolidated earnings before interest, taxes, depreciation, amortization and rent for the trailing four fiscal quarter periods. The facility fees are projected to accrue at either 0.15% or 0.175% on the committed amounts per annum. The Amended Credit Agreement contains limitations on indebtedness, liens, sale-leaseback transactions, significant corporate changes including mergers and acquisitions with third parties, investments, restricted payments (including dividends and stock repurchases) and transactions with affiliates. The Amended Credit Agreement will mature on December 15, 2009. Letters of credit totaling approximately $53.7 million and $45.1 million were outstanding under the Amended Credit Agreement on February 3, 2007 and January 28, 2006, respectively. No borrowings were outstanding under the Amended Credit Agreement on February 3, 2007 or on January 28, 2006.

12. RELATED PARTY TRANSACTIONS

There were no material related party transactions in Fiscal 2006. Shahid & Company, Inc. has provided advertising and design services for the Company since 1995. Sam N. Shahid, Jr., who served on A&F's Board of Directors until June 15, 2005, has been President and Creative Director of Shahid & Company, Inc. since 1993. Fees paid to Shahid & Company, Inc. for services provided during his tenure as a Director in Fiscal 2005 and Fiscal 2004 were approximately $0.9 million and $2.1 million respectively. These amounts do not include reimbursements to Shahid & Company, Inc. for expenses incurred while performing these services.

13. RETIREMENT BENEFITS

The Company maintains the Abercombie & Fitch Co. Savings & Retirement Plan, a qualified plan. All associates are eligible to participate in this plan if they are at least 21 years of age and have completed a year of employment with a 1,000 or more hours of service. In addition, the Company maintains the Abercrombie & Fitch Co. Nonqualified Savings and Supplemental Retirement Plan. Participation in this plan is based on service and compensation. The Company's contributions are based on a percentage of associates' eligible annual compensation. The cost of these plans was $15.0 million in Fiscal 2006, $10.5 million in Fiscal 2005 and $9.9 million in Fiscal 2004.

Effective February 2, 2003, the Company established a Chief Executive Officer Supplemental Executive Retirement Plan (the "SERP") to provide additional retirement income to its Chairman and Chief Executive Officer ("CEO"). Subject to service requirements, the CEO will receive a monthly benefit equal to 50% of his final average compensation (as defined in the SERP) for life. The SERP has been actuarially valued by an independent third party and the expense associated with the SERP is being accrued over the stated term of the Amended and Restated Employment Agreement, dated as of August 15, 2005, between the Company and its CEO. The cost of this plan was $6.6 million in Fiscal 2006, $2.5 million in Fiscal 2005 and $1.9 million in Fiscal 2004.

The Company established the rabbi trust during the third quarter of Fiscal 2006, the purpose is to be a source of funds to match respective funding obligations to participants in the Abercrombie & Fitch Nonqualified Savings and Supplemental Retirement Plan and the Chief Executive Officer Supplemental Executive Retirement Plan. As of February 3, 2007, total assets related to the Rabbi Trust were $33.5 million, which included $18.3 million of available-for-sale securities and $15.3 million related to the cash surrender value of trust owned life insurance policies.

ABERCROMBIE & FITCH CO. 10-K

14. CONTINGENCIES

A&F is a defendant in lawsuits arising in the ordinary course of business.

The Company previously reported that it was aware of 20 actions that had been filed against it and certain of its current and former officers and directors on behalf of a purported class of shareholders who purchased A&F's Common Stock between October 8, 1999 and October 13, 1999. These actions originally were filed in the United States District Courts for the Southern District of New York and the Southern District of Ohio, Eastern Division, alleging violations of the federal securities laws and seeking unspecified damages, and were later transferred to the Southern District of New York for consolidated pretrial proceedings under the caption In re Abercrombie & Fitch Securities Litigation. The parties have reached a settlement of these matters. According to the terms of the settlement, the Company's insurance company, on behalf of the defendants, has paid $6.1 million into a settlement fund in full consideration for the settlement and release of all claims that were asserted or could have been asserted in the action by the plaintiffs and the other members of the settlement class. The settlement will not have a material effect on the Company's financial statements. The judge who was presiding over the cases, after notice to the settlement class and a hearing held on January 31, 2007, determined that the proposed settlement was fair, reasonable and adequate and approved the settlement as final and binding.

The Company has been named as a defendant in five class action lawsuits (as described in more detail below) regarding overtime compensation. Four of the cases were previously reported. Of these four, one was dismissed and not appealed, another was dismissed and unsuccessfully appealed, the parties have tentatively agreed to a settlement of a third and a fourth remains pending. In addition, a fifth class action has been filed against the Company involving overtime compensation. In each overtime compensation action, the plaintiffs, on behalf of their respective purported class, seek injunctive relief and unspecified amounts of economic and liquidated damages.

In Melissa Mitchell, et al. v. Abercrombie & Fitch Co. and Abercrombie & Fitch Stores, Inc., which was filed on June 13, 2003 in the United States District Court for the Southern District of Ohio, the plaintiffs allege that assistant managers and store managers were not paid overtime compensation in violation of the Fair Labor Standards Act ("FLSA") and Ohio law. On March 31, 2006, the Court issued an order granting defendants' motions for summary judgment on all of the claims of each of the three plaintiffs. All three plaintiffs filed a Notice of Appeal to the Sixth Circuit Court of Appeals on April 28, 2006. The matter was fully briefed on October 26, 2006. Oral arguments before the Sixth Circuit Court of Appeals were held on March 15, 2007, and on March 29, 2007, that court affirmed the summary judgment in favor of the Company.

In Eltrich v. Abercrombie & Fitch Stores, Inc., which was filed on November 22, 2005 in the Washington Superior Court of King County, the plaintiff alleges that store managers, assistant managers and managers in training were misclassified as exempt from the overtime compensation requirements of the State of Washington, and improperly denied overtime compensation. The complaint seeks relief on a class-wide basis for unpaid overtime compensation, liquidated damages, attorneys' fees and costs and injunctive relief. The defendant filed an answer to the complaint on or about January 27, 2006. The defendant filed a motion for summary judgment as to all of Eltrich's claims on July 5, 2006. The court granted the motion for summary judgment to Eltrich's individual claims on October 6, 2006, dismissing Eltrich's individual claims with prejudice. On October 31, 2006, the court dismissed the claims of putative class members without prejudice. Eltrich did not appeal and, accordingly, this case is terminated.

ABERCROMBIE & FITCH CO. 10-K

Lisa Hashimoto, et al. v. Abercrombie & Fitch Co. and Abercrombie & Fitch Stores, Inc., was filed in the Superior Court of the State of California for the County of Los Angeles on June 23, 2006. Three plaintiffs allege, on behalf of a putative class of California store managers employed in Hollister and abercrombie stores, that they were entitled to receive overtime pay as "non-exempt" employees under California wage and hour laws. The complaint seeks injunctive relief, equitable relief, unpaid overtime compensation, unpaid benefits, penalties, interest and attorneys' fees and costs. The defendants filed an answer to the complaint on August 21, 2006. The parties are engaging in discovery.

Mitchell Green, et al. v. Abercrombie & Fitch Co., Abercrombie & Fitch Stores, Inc. and Abercrombie & Fitch Trading Co., was filed in the United States District Court for the Southern District of New York on November 2, 2006. Five plaintiffs allege, on behalf of a putative class of nation-wide loss prevention agents employed by the Company, that they were entitled to receive overtime pay as "non-exempt" employees under the FLSA and New York wage and hour laws. The complaint seeks injunctive relief, unpaid overtime compensation, liquidated damages, interest, and attorneys' fees and costs. The parties have tentatively agreed to a settlement which will not have a material effect on the financial statements.

Edrik Diaz v. Abercrombie & Fitch Stores, Inc. was filed in the United States District Court for the Southern District of Florida on February 8, 2007. Diaz alleges, on behalf of a putative class of managers in training and assistant managers, that the Company did not properly pay overtime compensation. The complaint seeks liquidated damages, interest, and attorneys' fees and costs.

On September 2, 2005, a purported class action, styled Robert Ross v. Abercrombie & Fitch Company, et al., was filed against A&F and certain of its officers in the United States District Court for the Southern District of Ohio on behalf of a purported class of all persons who purchased or acquired shares of A&F's Common Stock between June 2, 2005 and August 16, 2005. In September and October of 2005, five other purported class actions were subsequently filed against A&F and other defendants in the same Court. All six securities cases allege claims under the federal securities laws, and seek unspecified monetary damages, as a result of a decline in the price of A&F's Common Stock during the summer of 2005. On November 1, 2005, a motion to consolidate all of these purported class actions into the first-filed case was filed by some of the plaintiffs. A&F joined in that motion. On March 22, 2006, the motions to consolidate were granted, and these actions (together with the federal court derivative cases described in the following paragraph) were consolidated for purposes of motion practice, discovery and pretrial proceedings. A consolidated amended securities class action complaint was filed on August 14, 2006. On October 13, 2006, all defendants moved to dismiss that complaint. The motion has been fully briefed and is pending.

ABERCROMBIE & FITCH CO. 10-K

On September 16, 2005, a derivative action, styled The Booth Family Trust v. Michael S. Jeffries, et al., was filed in the United States District Court for the Southern District of Ohio, naming A&F as a nominal defendant and seeking to assert claims for unspecified damages against nine of A&F's present and former directors, alleging various breaches of the directors' fiduciary duty and seeking equitable and monetary relief. In the following three months (October, November and December of 2005), four similar derivative actions were filed (three in the United States District Court for the Southern District of Ohio and one in the Court of Common Pleas for Franklin County, Ohio) against present and former directors of A&F alleging various breaches of the directors' fiduciary duty and seeking equitable and monetary relief. A&F is also a nominal defendant in each of the four later derivative actions. On November 4, 2005, a motion to consolidate all of the federal court derivative actions with the purported securities law class actions described in the preceding paragraph was filed. On March 22, 2006, the motion to consolidate was granted, and the federal court derivative actions have been consolidated with the aforesaid purported securities law class actions for purposes of motion practice, discovery and pretrial proceedings. A consolidated amended derivative complaint was filed in the federal proceeding on July 10, 2006. A&F has filed a motion to stay the consolidated federal derivative case and that motion has been granted. The state court action has also been stayed. On February 16, 2007, A&F announced its Board of Directors received a report of its Special Litigation Committee established by the Board to investigate and act with respect to claims asserted in certain previously disclosed derivative lawsuits brought against current and former directors and management, including Chairman and Chief Executive Officer Michael S. Jeffries. The Special Litigation Committee has concluded that there is no evidence to support the asserted claims and directed the Company to seek dismissal of the derivative actions. A&F has advised both the federal and state courts in which the derivative actions are pending, that it believes the derivative cases should be stayed until the pending motion to dismiss the related consolidated securities cases has been finally decided, as described in the preceding paragraph.

In December 2005, the Company received a formal order of investigation from the SEC concerning trading in shares of A&F's Common Stock. The SEC has requested information from A&F and certain of its current and former officers and directors. The Company and its personnel are cooperating fully with the SEC.

Management intends to defend the aforesaid matters vigorously, as appropriate. Management is unable to assess the potential exposure of the aforesaid matters. However, management's assessment of the Company's current exposure could change in the event of the discovery of additional facts with respect to legal matters pending against the Company or determinations by judges, juries or other finders of fact that are not in accord with management's evaluation of the claims.

15. PREFERRED STOCK PURCHASE RIGHTS

On July 16, 1998, A&F's Board of Directors declared a dividend of one Series A Participating Cumulative Preferred Stock Purchase Right (the "Rights") for each outstanding share of Class A Common Stock, par value $.01 per share (the "Common Stock"), of A&F. The dividend was paid on July 28, 1998 to shareholders of record on that date. Shares of Common Stock issued after July 28, 1998 and prior to May 25, 1999 were issued with one Right attached. A&F's Board of Directors declared a two-for-one stock split (the "Stock Split") on A&F's Common Stock, payable on June 15, 1999 to the holders of record at the close of business on May 25, 1999. In connection with the Stock Split, the number of Rights associated with each share of Common Stock outstanding as of the close of business on May 25, 1999, or issued or delivered after May 25, 1999 and prior to the "Distribution Date" (as defined below), was proportionately adjusted from one Right to 0.50 Right. Each share of Common Stock issued after May 25, 1999 and prior to the Distribution Date has been and will be issued with 0.50 Right attached so that all shares of Common Stock outstanding prior to the Distribution Date will have 0.50 Right attached.

The Rights initially will be attached to the shares of Common Stock. The Rights will separate from the Common Stock after a Distribution Date occurs. The "Distribution Date" generally means the earlier of (i) the close of business on the 10th day after the date (the "Share Acquisition Date") of the first public announcement that a person or group (other than A&F or any of A&F's subsidiaries or any employee benefit plan of A&F or of any of A&F's subsidiaries) has acquired beneficial ownership of 20% or more of A&F's outstanding shares of Common Stock (an "Acquiring Person") or (ii) the close of business on the 10th business day (or such later date as A&F's Board of Directors may designate before any person has become an Acquiring Person) after the date of the commencement of a tender or exchange offer by any person which would, if consummated, result in such person becoming an Acquiring Person. The Rights are not exercisable until the Distribution Date. After the Distribution Date, each whole Right may be exercised to purchase, at an initial exercise price of $250, one one-thousandth of a share of Series A Participating Cumulative Preferred Stock.

At any time after any person becomes an Acquiring Person (but before the occurrence of any of the events described in the immediately following paragraph), each holder of a Right (other than the Acquiring Person and certain affiliated persons) will be entitled to purchase, upon exercise of the Right, shares of Common Stock having a market value of twice the exercise price of the Right. At any time after any person becomes an Acquiring Person (but before any person becomes the beneficial owner of 50% or more of the outstanding shares of Common Stock or the occurrence of any of the events described in the immediately following paragraph), A&F's Board of Directors may exchange all or part of the Rights (other than Rights beneficially owned by an Acquiring Person and certain affiliated persons) for shares of Common Stock at an exchange ratio of one share of Common Stock per 0.50 Right.

If, after any person has become an Acquiring Person, (i) A&F is involved in a merger or other business combination transaction in which A&F is not the surviving corporation or A&F's Common Stock is exchanged for other securities or assets or (ii) A&F and/or one or more of A&F's subsidiaries sell or otherwise transfer 50% or more of the assets or earning power of A&F and its subsidiaries, taken as a whole, each holder of a Right (other than the Acquiring Person and certain affiliated persons) will be entitled to buy, for the exercise price of the Rights, the number of shares of common stock of the other party to the business combination or sale (or in certain circumstances, an affiliate) which at the time of such transaction will have a market value of twice the exercise price of the Right.

The Rights will expire on July 16, 2008, unless earlier exchanged or redeemed. A&F may redeem all of the Rights at a price of $.01 per whole Right at any time before any person becomes an Acquiring Person.

Rights holders have no rights as a shareholder of A&F, including the right to vote and to receive dividends.

ABERCROMBIE & FITCH CO. 10-K

16. QUARTERLY FINANCIAL DATA (UNAUDITED)

Summarized unaudited quarterly financial results for Fiscal 2006 and Fiscal 2005 follow (thousands, except per share amounts):

Fiscal 2006 Quarter	First	Second	Third	Fourth*
Net sales	$657,271	$658,696	$863,448	$1,138,743
Gross profit	$429,915	$455,258	$568,198	$ 755,635
Operating income	$ 83,985	$102,429	$162,841	$ 308,834
Net income	$ 56,240	$ 65,722	$102,031	$ 198,192
Net income per basic share	$ 0.64	$ 0.75	$ 1.16	$ 2.25
Net income per diluted share	$ 0.62	$ 0.72	$ 1.11	$ 2.14

* Fourth Quarter Fiscal 2006 is a fourteen week quarter.

Fiscal 2005 Quarter	First	Second	Third	Fourth
Net sales	$546,810	$571,591	$704,918	$961,392
Gross profit	$357,252	$389,660	$465,086	$639,418
Operating income	$ 68,289	$ 91,087	$115,874	$267,488
Net income	$ 40,359	$ 57,401	$ 71,600	$164,626
Net income per basic share	$ 0.47	$ 0.66	$ 0.81	$ 1.88
Net income per diluted share	$ 0.45	$ 0.63	$ 0.79	$ 1.80

17. SUBSEQUENT EVENT

As of March 29, 2007, the Company repurchased approximately 1.0 million shares of its outstanding Common Stock having a value of approximately $79.0 million pursuant to the Board of Directors authorization.

ABERCROMBIE & FITCH CO. 10-K

Report of Independent Registered Public Accounting Firm

To the Board of Directors and Shareholders
of Abercrombie & Fitch Co.:

We have completed integrated audits of Abercrombie & Fitch Co.'s consolidated financial statements and of its internal control over financial reporting as of February 3, 2007, in accordance with the standards of the Public Company Accounting Oversight Board (United States). Our opinions, based on our audits, are presented below.

<u>Consolidated financial statements</u>

In our opinion, the consolidated financial statements listed in the index appearing under Item 15(1) present fairly, in all material respects, the financial position of Abercrombie & Fitch Co. and its subsidiaries at February 3, 2007 and January 28, 2006, and the results of their operations and their cash flows for the years ended February 3, 2007, January 28, 2006 and January 29, 2005 in conformity with accounting principles generally accepted in the United States of America. These financial statements are the responsibility of the Company's management. Our responsibility is to express an opinion on these financial statements based on our audits. We conducted our audits of these statements in accordance with the standards of the Public Company Accounting Oversight Board (United States). Those standards require that we plan and perform the audit to obtain reasonable assurance about whether the financial statements are free of material misstatement. An audit of financial statements includes examining, on a test basis, evidence supporting the amounts and disclosures in the financial statements, assessing the accounting principles used and significant estimates made by management, and evaluating the overall financial statement presentation. We believe that our audits provide a reasonable basis for our opinion.

As discussed in Note 4 to the consolidated financial statements, effective January 29, 2006, the Company changed the manner in which it accounts for share-based compensation.

<u>Internal control over financial reporting</u>

Also, in our opinion, management's assessment, included in Management's Report on Internal Control over Financial Reporting appearing under Item 9A, that the Company maintained effective internal control over financial reporting as of February 3, 2007 based on criteria established in *Internal Control — Integrated Framework* issued by the Committee of Sponsoring Organizations of the Treadway Commission (COSO), is fairly stated, in all material respects, based on those criteria. Furthermore, in our opinion, the Company maintained, in all material respects, effective internal control over financial reporting as of February 3, 2007, based on criteria established in *Internal Control — Integrated Framework* issued by the COSO. The Company's management is responsible for maintaining effective internal control over financial reporting and for its assessment of the effectiveness of internal control over financial reporting. Our responsibility is to express opinions on management's assessment and on the effectiveness of the Company's internal control over financial reporting based on our audit. We conducted our audit of internal control over financial reporting in accordance with the standards of the Public Company Accounting Oversight Board (United States). Those standards require that we plan and perform the audit to obtain reasonable assurance about whether effective internal control over financial reporting was maintained in all material respects. An audit of internal control over financial reporting includes obtaining an understanding of internal control over financial reporting, evaluating management's assessment, testing and evaluating the design and operating effectiveness of internal control, and performing such other procedures as we consider necessary in the circumstances. We believe that our audit provides a reasonable basis for our opinions.

ABERCROMBIE & FITCH CO. 10-K

A company's internal control over financial reporting is a process designed to provide reasonable assurance regarding the reliability of financial reporting and the preparation of financial statements for external purposes in accordance with generally accepted accounting principles. A company's internal control over financial reporting includes those policies and procedures that (i) pertain to the maintenance of records that, in reasonable detail, accurately and fairly reflect the transactions and dispositions of the assets of the company; (ii) provide reasonable assurance that transactions are recorded as necessary to permit preparation of financial statements in accordance with generally accepted accounting principles, and that receipts and expenditures of the company are being made only in accordance with authorizations of management and directors of the company; and (iii) provide reasonable assurance regarding prevention or timely detection of unauthorized acquisition, use, or disposition of the company's assets that could have a material effect on the financial statements.

Because of its inherent limitations, internal control over financial reporting may not prevent or detect misstatements. Also, projections of any evaluation of effectiveness to future periods are subject to the risk that controls may become inadequate because of changes in conditions, or that the degree of compliance with the policies or procedures may deteriorate.

/s/ PricewaterhouseCoopers LLP
Columbus, Ohio
March 30, 2007

UNITED STATES SECURITIES AND EXCHANGE COMMISSION
Washington, D.C. 20549

Form 10-K

(Mark One)

☑ ANNUAL REPORT PURSUANT TO SECTION 13 OR 15(d) OF THE
SECURITIES EXCHANGE ACT OF 1934

For the Fiscal Year Ended February 3, 2007

or

☐ TRANSITION REPORT PURSUANT TO SECTION 13 OR 15(d) OF THE
SECURITIES EXCHANGE ACT OF 1934

Commission File Number: 001-31314

AÉROPOSTALE, INC.

(Exact name of registrant as specified in its charter)

REPORT OF INDEPENDENT REGISTERED PUBLIC ACCOUNTING FIRM

To the Board of Directors and Shareholders of Aéropostale, Inc.:

We have audited the accompanying consolidated balance sheets of Aéropostale, Inc. and its subsidiaries (the "Company") as of February 3, 2007 and January 28, 2006, and the related consolidated statements of income and comprehensive income, stockholders' equity, and cash flows for each of the three years in the period ended February 3, 2007. Our audits also included the financial statement schedule listed in the Index at Item 15. These financial statements and financial statement schedule are the responsibility of the Company's management. Our responsibility is to express an opinion on these financial statements and the financial statement schedule based on our audits.

We conducted our audits in accordance with the standards of the Public Company Accounting Oversight Board (United States). Those standards require that we plan and perform the audit to obtain reasonable assurance about whether the financial statements are free of material misstatement. An audit includes examining, on a test basis, evidence supporting the amounts and disclosures in the financial statements. An audit also includes assessing the accounting principles used and significant estimates made by management, as well as evaluating the overall financial statement presentation. We believe that our audits provide a reasonable basis for our opinion.

In our opinion, such consolidated financial statements present fairly, in all material respects, the financial position of the Company as of February 3, 2007 and January 28, 2006, and the results of its operations and its cash flows for each of the three years in the period ended February 3, 2007, in conformity with accounting principles generally accepted in the United States of America. Also, in our opinion, such consolidated financial statement schedule, when considered in relation to the basic consolidated financial statements taken as a whole, presents fairly, in all material respects, the information set forth therein.

As discussed in Note 1 to the Notes to Consolidated Financial Statements the Company adopted Statement of Financial Accounting Standards No. 123(R), *Share-Based Payment*, as revised, effective January 29, 2006. Also, as discussed in Note 1 to the Notes to Consolidated Financial Statements the Company adopted Statement of Financial Accounting Standards No. 158, *Employers' Accounting for Defined Benefit Pension and Other Postretirement Plans*, relating to the recognition and related disclosure provisions, effective February 3, 2007.

We have also audited, in accordance with the standards of the Public Company Accounting Oversight Board (United States), the effectiveness of the Company's internal control over financial reporting as of February 3, 2007, based on the criteria established in Internal Control — Integrated Framework issued by the Committee of Sponsoring Organizations of the Treadway Commission and our report dated April 2, 2007 expressed an unqualified opinion on management's assessment of the effectiveness of the Company's internal control over financial reporting and an unqualified opinion on the effectiveness of the Company's internal control over financial reporting.

/s/ Deloitte & Touche LLP

New York, New York
April 2, 2007

REPORT OF INDEPENDENT REGISTERED PUBLIC ACCOUNTING FIRM

To the Board of Directors and Shareholders of Aéropostale, Inc.:

We have audited management's assessment, included in the accompanying *Management's Report on Internal Control over Financial Reporting*, that Aéropostale and its subsidiaries (the "Company") maintained effective internal control over financial reporting as of February 3, 2007, based on criteria established in Internal Control — Integrated Framework issued by the Committee of Sponsoring Organizations of the Treadway Commission. The Company's management is responsible for maintaining effective internal control over financial reporting and for its assessment of the effectiveness of internal control over financial reporting. Our responsibility is to express an opinion on management's assessment and an opinion on the effectiveness of the Company's internal control over financial reporting based on our audit.

We conducted our audit in accordance with the standards of the Public Company Accounting Oversight Board (United States). Those standards require that we plan and perform the audit to obtain reasonable assurance about whether effective internal control over financial reporting was maintained in all material respects. Our audit included obtaining an understanding of internal control over financial reporting, evaluating management's assessment, testing and evaluating the design and operating effectiveness of internal control, and performing such other procedures as we considered necessary in the circumstances. We believe that our audit provides a reasonable basis for our opinions.

A company's internal control over financial reporting is a process designed by, or under the supervision of, the company's principal executive and principal financial officers, or persons performing similar functions, and effected by the Company's board of directors, management, and other personnel to provide reasonable assurance regarding the reliability of financial reporting and the preparation of financial statements for external purposes in accordance with generally accepted accounting principles. A company's internal control over financial reporting includes those policies and procedures that (1) pertain to the maintenance of records that, in reasonable detail, accurately and fairly reflect the transactions and dispositions of the assets of the company; (2) provide reasonable assurance that transactions are recorded as necessary to permit preparation of financial statements in accordance with generally accepted accounting principles, and that receipts and expenditures of the company are being made only in accordance with authorizations of management and directors of the company; and (3) provide reasonable assurance regarding prevention or timely detection of unauthorized acquisition, use or disposition of the company's assets that could have a material effect on the financial statements.

Because of the inherent limitations of internal control over financial reporting, including the possibility of collusion or improper management override of controls, material misstatements due to error or fraud may not be prevented or detected on a timely basis. Also, projections of any evaluation of the effectiveness of the internal control over financial reporting to future periods are subject to the risk that the controls may become inadequate because of changes in conditions, or that the degree of compliance with the policies or procedures may deteriorate.

In our opinion, management's assessment that the Company maintained effective internal control over financial reporting as of February 3, 2007, is fairly stated, in all material respects, based on the criteria established in Internal Control — Integrated Framework issued by the Committee of Sponsoring Organizations of the Treadway Commission. Also in our opinion, the Company maintained, in all material respects, effective internal control over financial reporting as of February 3, 2007, based on the criteria established in Internal Control — Integrated Framework issued by the Committee of Sponsoring Organizations of the Treadway Commission.

We have also audited, in accordance with the standards of the Public Company Accounting Oversight Board (United States), the consolidated financial statements and financial statement schedule as of and for the year ended February 3, 2007, of the Company and our report dated April 2, 2007, expressed an unqualified opinion on those financial statements and the financial statement schedule and includes an explanatory paragraph relating to the Company's adoption of Statement of Financial Accounting Standards No. 123(R), *Share-Based Payment*, as revised, effective January 29, 2006, and the Company's adoption of Statement of Financial Accounting Standards No. 158, *Employers' Accounting for Defined Benefit Pension and Other Postretirement Plans*, relating to the recognition and related disclosure provisions, effective February 3, 2007.

/s/ Deloitte & Touche LLP

New York, New York
April 2, 2007

28

AÉROPOSTALE, INC.

CONSOLIDATED BALANCE SHEETS

	February 3, 2007	January 28, 2006
	(In thousands)	
ASSETS		
Current assets:		
Cash and cash equivalents	$ 200,064	$ 205,235
Short-term investments	76,223	20,037
Merchandise inventory	101,476	91,908
Prepaid expenses	12,175	12,314
Deferred income taxes	1,185	—
Other current assets	7,670	9,845
Total current assets	398,793	339,339
Fixtures, equipment and improvements — net	175,591	160,229
Intangible assets	1,400	2,455
Deferred income taxes	3,784	—
Other assets	1,596	1,928
Total assets	$ 581,164	$ 503,951
LIABILITIES AND STOCKHOLDERS' EQUITY		
Current liabilities:		
Accounts payable	$ 63,918	$ 57,165
Deferred income taxes	—	5,195
Accrued expenses	100,880	63,993
Total current liabilities	164,798	126,353
Deferred rent and tenant allowances	88,344	81,499
Retirement benefit plan liabilities	15,906	8,654
Deferred income taxes	—	2,655
Commitments and contingent liabilities		
Stockholders' equity		
Common stock — par value, $0.01 per share; 200,000 shares authorized, 59,332 and 58,598 shares issued	593	586
Preferred stock — par value, $0.01 per share; 5,000 shares authorized, no shares issued or outstanding	—	—
Additional paid-in capital	101,429	88,213
Other comprehensive loss	(5,274)	(1,557)
Deferred compensation	—	(2,577)
Retained earnings	414,916	308,269
Treasury stock at cost (7,687 and 4,548 shares)	(199,548)	(108,144)
Total stockholders' equity	312,116	284,790
Total liabilities and stockholders' equity	$ 581,164	$ 503,951

See Notes to Consolidated Financial Statements.

AÉROPOSTALE, INC.

CONSOLIDATED STATEMENTS OF INCOME

	Fiscal Year Ended		
	February 3, 2007	January 28, 2006	January 29, 2005
	(In thousands, except per share data)		
Net sales	$1,413,208	$1,204,347	$ 964,212
Cost of sales (includes certain buying, occupancy and warehousing expenses)	957,791	841,872	644,305
Gross profit	455,417	362,475	319,907
Selling, general and administrative expenses	289,736	227,044	183,977
Other income	2,085	—	—
Income from operations	167,766	135,431	135,930
Interest income	7,064	3,670	1,438
Income before income taxes	174,830	139,101	137,368
Income taxes	68,183	55,147	53,256
Net income	$ 106,647	$ 83,954	$ 84,112
Basic earnings per common share	$ 2.00	$ 1.53	$ 1.51
Diluted earnings per common share	$ 1.98	$ 1.50	$ 1.47
Weighted average basic shares	53,285	54,994	55,735
Weighted average diluted shares	53,758	55,937	57,255

CONSOLIDATED STATEMENTS OF COMPREHENSIVE INCOME

	Fiscal Year Ended		
	February 3, 2007	January 28, 2006	January 29, 2005
	(In thousands)		
Net income	$ 106,647	$ 83,954	$ 84,112
Minimum pension liability (net of tax of $69, $494, and $92)	110	(740)	(145)
Comprehensive income	$ 106,757	$ 83,214	$ 83,967

See Notes to Consolidated Financial Statements.

30

AÉROPOSTALE, INC.

CONSOLIDATED STATEMENTS OF STOCKHOLDERS' EQUITY

	Common Stock Shares	Amount	Additional Paid-in Capital	Deferred Compensation	Treasury Stock, at Cost Shares	Amount	Accumulated Other Comprehensive Loss	Retained Earnings	Total
					(In thousands)				
BALANCE, JANUARY 31, 2004	56,795	$ 568	$ 63,289	$ —	(945)	$ (17,695)	$ (672)	$140,203	$185,693
Net income	—	—	—	—	—	—	—	84,112	84,112
Stock options exercised	1,320	13	1,016	—	—	—	—	—	1,029
Excess tax benefit from Stock-based compensation	—	—	12,893	—	—	—	—	—	12,893
Repurchase of common stock	—	—	—	—	(1,804)	(45,931)	—	—	(45,931)
Issuance of non-vested stock	—	—	1,871	(1,871)	—	—	—	—	—
Stock-based compensation	—	—	—	600	—	—	—	—	600
Minimum pension liability (net of tax of $92)	—	—	—	—	—	—	(145)	—	(145)
BALANCE, JANUARY 29, 2005	58,115	581	79,069	(1,271)	(2,749)	(63,626)	(817)	224,315	238,251
Net income	—	—	—	—	—	—	—	83,954	83,954
Stock options exercised	477	5	1,338	—	—	—	—	—	1,343
Excess tax benefit from Stock-based compensation	—	—	4,759	—	—	—	—	—	4,759
Repurchase of common stock	—	—	—	—	(1,799)	(44,518)	—	—	(44,518)
Net issuance of non-vested stock	—	—	3,047	(3,047)	—	—	—	—	—
Stock-based compensation	—	—	—	1,741	—	—	—	—	1,741
Vesting of stock	6	—	—	—	—	—	—	—	
Minimum pension liability (net of tax of $494)	—	—	—	—	—	—	(740)	—	(740)
BALANCE, JANUARY 28, 2006	58,598	586	88,213	(2,577)	(4,548)	(108,144)	(1,557)	308,269	284,790
Net income	—	—	—	—	—	—	—	106,647	106,647
Stock options exercised	719	7	2,347	—	—	—	—	—	2,354
Minimum pension liability (net of tax of $69)	—	—	—	—	—	—	110	—	110
Adoption of SFAS No. 123 (R)	—	—	(2,577)	2577	—	—	—	—	—
Excess tax benefit from Stock-based compensation	—	—	7,568	—	—	—	—	—	7,568
Adoption of SFAS No. 158 (net of tax of $2,413)	—	—	—	—	—	—	(3,827)	—	(3,827)
Repurchase of common stock	—	—	—	—	(3,139)	(91,404)	—	—	(91,404)
Stock-based compensation	—	—	5,878	—	—	—	—	—	5,878
Vesting of stock	15	—	—	—	—	—	—	—	
BALANCE, FEBRUARY 3, 2007	59,332	$ 593	$ 101,429	$ —	(7,687)	$(199,548)	$ (5,274)	$414,916	$312,116

See Notes to Consolidated Financial Statements.

AÉROPOSTALE, INC.

CONSOLIDATED STATEMENTS OF CASH FLOWS

	Fiscal Year Ended		
	February 3, 2007	January 28, 2006	January 29, 2005
	(In thousands)		
Cash Flows Provided By Operating Activities			
Net income	$ 106,647	$ 83,954	$ 84,112
Adjustments to reconcile net income to net cash from operating activities:			
Depreciation and amortization	30,029	22,347	16,635
Stock-based compensation	5,878	1,741	600
Amortization of tenant allowances and above market leases	(9,195)	(7,756)	(6,717)
Amortization of deferred rent expense	2,333	3,716	7,474
Pension expense	2,246	1,672	3,008
Deferred income taxes	(10,474)	6,100	2,409
Excess tax benefits from stock-based compensation	(7,568)	—	—
Other	—	—	(1,197)
Changes in operating assets and liabilities:			
Merchandise inventory	(9,568)	(10,670)	(19,431)
Prepaid expenses and other assets	2,646	(7,059)	(3,741)
Accounts payable	6,753	12,307	14,381
Accrued expenses and other liabilities	57,718	38,032	39,442
Net cash provided by operating activities	177,445	144,384	136,975
Cash Flows Used For Investing Activities			
Purchase of fixtures, equipment and improvements	(44,949)	(58,289)	(46,677)
Purchase of short-term investments	(513,909)	(310,901)	(441,386)
Sale of short-term investments	457,723	367,088	365,162
Purchase of intangible assets	—	—	(1,400)
Net cash used for investing activities	(101,135)	(2,102)	(124,301)
Cash Flows Used For Financing Activities			
Purchase of treasury stock	(91,403)	(44,518)	(45,931)
Proceeds from stock options exercised	2,354	1,343	1,029
Excess tax benefits from stock-based compensation	7,568	—	—
Net cash used for financing activities	(81,481)	(43,175)	(44,902)
Net (Decrease) Increase In Cash And Cash Equivalents	(5,171)	99,107	(32,228)
Cash And Cash Equivalents, Beginning Of Year	205,235	106,128	138,356
Cash And Cash Equivalents, End Of Year	$ 200,064	$ 205,235	$ 106,128
Supplemental Disclosures Of Cash Flow Information			
Income taxes paid	$ 48,352	$ 37,274	$ 36,456
Excess tax benefit from stock-based compensation included in change in accrued expenses and other liabilities	$ —	$ 4,759	$ 12,893
Non-cash operating and investing activities	$ 1,984	$ 1,541	$ —

See Notes to Consolidated Financial Statements.

32

AÉROPOSTALE, INC.

NOTES TO CONSOLIDATED FINANCIAL STATEMENTS

1. Summary of Significant Accounting Policies

Organization

References to the "Company," "we," "us," or "our" means Aéropostale, Inc. and its subsidiaries, except as expressly indicated or unless the context otherwise requires. We are a mall-based specialty retailer of casual apparel and accessories for young women and men. As of February 3, 2007, we operated 742 stores, consisting of 728 Aéropostale stores in 47 states and 14 Jimmy'Z stores in 11 states.

Fiscal Year

Our fiscal year ends on the Saturday nearest to January 31. Fiscal 2006 was the 53-week period ended February 3, 2007, fiscal 2005 was the 52-week period ended January 28, 2006, and fiscal 2004 was the 52-week period ended January 29, 2005. Fiscal 2007 will be the 52-week period ending February 2, 2008.

Use of Estimates

The preparation of the consolidated financial statements in conformity with accounting principles generally accepted in the United States requires us to make estimates and assumptions that affect the amounts reported in our consolidated financial statements and accompanying notes. Actual results could differ from those estimated.

The most significant estimates made by management include those made in the areas of merchandise inventory, defined benefit retirement plans, long-lived assets, and income taxes. Management periodically evaluates estimates used in the preparation of the consolidated financial statements for continued reasonableness. Appropriate adjustments, if any, to the estimates used are made prospectively based on such periodic evaluations.

Seasonality

Our business is highly seasonal, and historically we have realized a significant portion of our sales, net income, and cash flow in the second half of the fiscal year, attributable to the impact of the back-to-school selling season in the third quarter and the holiday selling season in the fourth quarter. Additionally, working capital requirements fluctuate during the year, increasing in mid-summer in anticipation of the third and fourth quarters.

Cash Equivalents

We consider credit card receivables and all short-term investments with an original maturity of three months or less to be cash equivalents.

Fair Value of Financial Instruments

The fair value of cash and cash equivalents, short-term investments, receivables, and accounts payable approximates their carrying value due to their short-term maturities.

Merchandise Inventory

Merchandise inventory consists of finished goods and is valued utilizing the cost method at the lower of cost or market determined on a weighted-average basis. Merchandise inventory includes warehousing, freight, merchandise and design costs as an inventory product cost. We make certain assumptions regarding future demand and net realizable selling price in order to assess that our inventory is recorded properly at the lower of cost or market. These assumptions are based on both historical experience and current information. We recorded an adjustment to inventory and cost of sales for lower of cost or market of $8.0 million as of February 3, 2007, $7.4 million as of January 28, 2006, and $4.9 million as of January 29, 2005.

AÉROPOSTALE, INC.

NOTES TO CONSOLIDATED FINANCIAL STATEMENTS — (Continued)

Fixtures, Equipment and Improvements

Fixtures, equipment and improvements are stated at cost. Depreciation and amortization are provided for by the straight-line method over the following estimated useful lives:

Fixtures and equipment	10 years
Leasehold improvements	Lesser of life of the asset or lease term
Computer equipment and software	5 years

Evaluation for Long-Lived Asset Impairment

We periodically evaluate the need to recognize impairment losses relating to long-lived assets in accordance with Statement of Financial Accounting Standards, or SFAS No. 144, *Accounting for the Impairment or Disposal of Long-lived Assets.* Long-lived assets are evaluated for recoverability whenever events or changes in circumstances indicate that an asset may have been impaired. In evaluating an asset for recoverability, we estimate the future cash flows expected to result from the use of the asset and eventual disposition. If the sum of the expected future cash flows is less than the carrying amount of the asset, we would write the asset down to fair value and we would record an impairment charge, accordingly. We recorded impairment charges of $0.1 million in fiscal 2006, $0.4 million in fiscal 2005, and none in fiscal 2004.

Pre-Opening Expenses

New store pre-opening costs are expensed as they are incurred.

Leases

Rent expense under our operating leases typically provide for fixed non-contingent rent escalations. Rent payments under our store leases typically commence when the store opens, and these leases include a pre-opening period that allows us to take possession of the property to construct the store. We recognize rent expense on a straight-line basis over the non-cancelable term of each individual underlying lease, commencing when we take possession of the property (see below).

In addition, our store leases require us to pay additional rent based on specified percentages of sales, after we achieve specified annual sales thresholds. We use store sales trends to estimate and record liabilities for these additional rent obligations during interim periods. Most of our store leases entitle us to receive tenant allowances from our landlords. We record these tenant allowances as a deferred rent liability, which we amortize as a reduction of rent expense over the non-cancelable term of each underlying lease.

In the fourth quarter of fiscal 2004, we corrected an error and recorded a one-time, non-cash rent charge of $4.7 million ($2.8 million, after tax) related to the timing of rent expense for store leases during the pre-opening period. Previously, we had followed a prevailing retail industry practice in which we began recording rent expense at the earlier of the time a store opened or when rent payments commenced. The charge was cumulative, and $0.5 million after tax was related to fiscal 2004, and $2.3 million after tax was related to prior periods. Our financial statements for prior periods were not restated due to the immateriality of this issue to our results of operations, statements of financial position, and cash flows for fiscal 2004 or any individual prior year. This correction did not impact cash flows or timing of payments under related leases and did not have a material impact on our consolidated financial statements.

Revenue Recognition

Sales revenue is recognized at the "point of sale" in our stores, and at the time our e-commerce customers take possession of merchandise. Sales revenue related to gift cards and the issuance of store credits are recognized when

AÉROPOSTALE, INC.

NOTES TO CONSOLIDATED FINANCIAL STATEMENTS — (Continued)

they are redeemed. Allowances for sales returns are recorded as a reduction of net sales in the periods in which the related sales are recognized.

Cost of Sales

Cost of sales includes costs related to merchandise sold, including inventory valuation adjustments, distribution and warehousing, freight from the distribution center and warehouse to the stores, payroll for our design, buying and merchandising departments, and occupancy costs. Occupancy costs include rent, contingent rents, common area maintenance, real estate taxes, utilities, repairs, maintenance and all depreciation.

Selling, General and Administrative Expenses

Selling, general and administrative expenses, or SG&A, include costs related to selling expenses, store management and corporate expenses such as payroll and employee benefits, marketing expenses, employment taxes, information technology maintenance costs and expenses, insurance and legal expenses, and store pre-opening and other corporate level expenses. Store pre-opening expenses include store level payroll, grand opening event marketing, travel, supplies and other store pre-opening expenses.

Self-Insurance

We self-insure our workers compensation risk and a portion of our employee medical benefits. The recorded liabilities for these risks are calculated primarily using historical experience and current information. The liabilities include amounts for actual claims and claims incurred but not yet reported.

Retirement Benefit Plans

Our retirement benefit plan costs are accounted for using actuarial valuations required by SFAS No. 87, *Employers' Accounting for Pensions* and SFAS No. 106, *Employers' Accounting for Postretirement Benefits Other Than Pensions.*

We adopted SFAS No. 158, *Employer's Accounting for Defined Benefit Pension and Other Postretirement Plans — an amendment of FASB Statements No. 87, 88, 106, and 132(R)*, or FAS 158, as of February 3, 2007. SFAS 158 requires an entity to recognize the funded status of its defined pension plans on the balance sheet and to recognize changes in the funded status, that arise during the period but are not recognized as components of net periodic benefit cost, within other comprehensive income, net of income taxes. See the section Recent Accounting Developments and note 11 for additional information regarding the adoption of SFAS 158.

Marketing Costs

Marketing costs, which includes internet, television, print, radio and other media advertising and collegiate athlete conference sponsorships, are expensed as incurred and were $11.3 million in fiscal 2006, $6.8 million in fiscal 2005, and $5.3 million in fiscal 2004.

Stock-Based Compensation

On January 29, 2006, the first day of our 2006 fiscal year, we adopted the provisions of Statement of Financial Accounting Standards No. 123(R), *Share-Based Payment, a revision of SFAS No. 123, Accounting for Stock-Based Compensation*, or SFAS No. 123(R), as interpreted by SEC Staff Accounting Bulletin No. 107. Under SFAS No. 123(R), all forms of share-based payment to employees and directors, including stock options, must be treated as compensation and recognized in the income statement. Previous to the adoption of SFAS No. 123(R), we accounted for stock options under the provisions of Accounting Principles Board Opinion No. 25, *Accounting for Stock Issued to Employees*, and, accordingly, did not recognize compensation expense in our consolidated financial statements.

AÉROPOSTALE, INC.

NOTES TO CONSOLIDATED FINANCIAL STATEMENTS — (Continued)

Segment Reporting

SFAS No. 131, *Disclosures about Segments of an Enterprise and Related Information,* establishes standards for reporting information about a company's operating segments. It also establishes standards for related disclosures about products and services, geographic areas and major customers. We operate in a single aggregated operating segment, which includes the operation of our Aéropostale and Jimmy'Z specialty retail stores and our Aéropostale e-commerce site. Revenues from external customers are derived from merchandise sales and we do not rely on any major customers as a source of revenue. Our consolidated net sales mix by merchandise category was as follows:

Merchandise Categories	Fiscal		
	2006	**2005**	**2004**
Young Women's	60%	61%	60%
Young Men's	25	25	26
Accessories	15	14	14
Total Merchandise Sales	100%	100%	100%

Recent Accounting Developments

In February 2007, The Financial Accounting Standards Board, or "FASB," issued SFAS No. 159, *The Fair Value Option for Financial Assets and Financial Liabilities — Including an amendment of FASB Statement No. 115*. This statement permits entities to choose to measure many financial instruments and certain other items at fair value. SFAS No. 159 is effective at the beginning of an entity's first fiscal year that begins after November 15, 2007. We expect that the adoption of SFAS No. 159 will not have a material impact on our consolidated financial statements.

In September 2006, The FASB issued SFAS No. 158, *Employer's Accounting for Defined Benefit Pension and Other Postretirement Plans — an amendment of FASB Statements No. 87, 88, 106, and 132(R)*. This statement requires an employer to recognize the over-funded or under-funded status of a defined benefit postretirement plan as an asset or in its statement of financial position and to recognize through accumulated other comprehensive income changes in that funded status in the year in which they occur.. This statement also requires an employer to measure the funded status of a plan as of the date of its year-end statement of financial position, with limited exceptions. SFAS No. 158 is effective for fiscal years ending after December 15, 2006. The adoption of SFAS No. 158 on February 3, 2007 did not have a material impact on our financial statements. See note 11 for a further discussion.

In September 2006, the FASB issued SFAS No. 157, *Fair Value Measurements*. This statement defines fair value, establishes a framework for measuring fair value in generally accepted accounting principles, and expands disclosures about fair value measurements. This statement applies under other accounting pronouncements that require or permit fair value measurements, the Board having concluded in those other accounting pronouncements that fair value is the relevant measurement attribute. This statement is effective for financial statements issued for fiscal years beginning after November 15, 2007, and interim periods within those fiscal years. We expect that the adoption of SFAS No. 157 will not have a material impact on our consolidated financial statements.

In September 2006, the Securities and Exchange Commission issued Staff Accounting Bulletin No. 108, or "SAB 108," *Considering the Effects of Prior Year Misstatements when Quantifying Misstatements in Current Year Financial Statements*. SAB 108 provides guidance on the consideration of effects of prior year misstatements in quantifying current year misstatements for the purpose of a materiality assessment. SAB No. 108 is effective for the first annual period ending after November 15, 2006. We adopted SAB No. 108 in the fourth quarter of 2006 and the adoption of SAB No. 108 did not have a material impact on our consolidated financial statements.

In July 2006, The FASB issued Interpretation No. 48, or "FIN 48," *Accounting for Uncertainty in Income Taxes*, which clarifies the accounting for uncertainty in income taxes recognized in the financial statements in accordance with SFAS No. 109, *Accounting for Income Taxes*. FIN 48 provides guidance on the financial statement

AÉROPOSTALE, INC.

NOTES TO CONSOLIDATED FINANCIAL STATEMENTS — (Continued)

recognition and measurement of a tax position taken or expected to be taken in a tax return. FIN 48 also provides guidance on de-recognition, classification interest and penalties, accounting in interim periods, disclosures and transition. FIN 48 was effective for fiscal years beginning after December 15, 2006. We are currently evaluating the impact that the adoption of FIN 48 will have on our consolidated financial statements.

In March 2005, the FASB issued Interpretation No. 47, *"Accounting for Conditional Asset Retirement Obligations"*, or "FIN 47," which clarifies that the term "conditional asset retirement obligation" as used in FASB statement No. 143, *"Accounting for Asset Retirement Obligations"*. Conditional asset retirement obligation refers to a legal obligation to perform an asset retirement activity in which the timing and/or method of settlement are conditional on a future event that may or may not be within the control of the entity. An entity is required to recognize a liability for the fair value of a conditional asset retirement obligation if the fair value of the liability can be reasonably estimated. FIN 47 is effective for fiscal years ending after December 15, 2005. The adoption of FIN 47 unfavorably impacted net earnings by $0.2 million for the year ended January 28, 2006. We were uncertain of the timing of payment for the asset retirement obligations, therefore a liability was not previously recognized in the consolidated financial statements. The adoption of FIN 47 did not have a material impact on our consolidated financial statements.

2. Common Stock Split

In April 2004, we completed a three-for-two stock split on all shares of our common stock that was affected in the form of a stock dividend. All prior period share and per share amounts presented in this report have been restated to give retroactive recognition to the common stock split.

3. Short-Term Investments

Short-term investments consist of auction rate debt and preferred stock securities. Auction rate securities are term securities earning income at a rate that is periodically reset, typically within 35 days, to reflect current market conditions through an auction process. These securities are classified as "available-for-sale" securities under the provisions of SFAS No. 115, *Accounting for Certain Investments in Debt and Equity Securities*. Accordingly, these short-term investments are recorded at fair-value, with any related unrealized gains and losses included as a separate component of stockholders' equity, net of tax. Realized gains and losses and investment income are included in earnings. As of February 3, 2007, the auction rate debt securities had contractual ultimate maturities ranging from 2022 through 2040.

4. Supplier Risk Concentration

Three suppliers in the aggregate constituted approximately 30% of our purchases in fiscal 2006, approximately 33% in fiscal 2005 and approximately 35% in fiscal 2004. In addition, in fiscal 2006, approximately 64% of our merchandise was directly sourced from our top 10 suppliers, and one agent sourced approximately 19% of our merchandise. The loss of any of these sources could adversely impact our ability to operate our business. We will cease doing business with South Bay Apparel Inc., one of our largest suppliers of graphic T-shirts and fleece, in July 2007 (see note 5 for a further discussion). We are in the process of replacing this business with new vendors and through our existing vendor base.

5. Other Matters

On November 8, 2006, we announced that Christopher L. Finazzo, who had been our Executive Vice President and Chief Merchandising Officer, had been terminated for cause, effective immediately, based upon information uncovered by management and after an independent investigation was conducted at the direction, and under the

AÉROPOSTALE, INC.

NOTES TO CONSOLIDATED FINANCIAL STATEMENTS — (Continued)

supervision, of a special committee of our Board of Directors. The investigation, being carried out by our outside legal counsel and a third-party investigation firm, revealed that Mr. Finazzo:

- concealed from management and our Board of Directors, and failed to disclose in corporate disclosure documents, his personal ownership interests in, and officer positions of, certain corporate entities affiliated with one of our primary vendors at the time, South Bay Apparel, Inc.,

- without the knowledge or authorization of our management, executed a corporate Guaranty Agreement in March 1999, that, had it been enforceable, would have obligated us to guarantee any payments due from South Bay Apparel, Inc. to Tricot Richelieu, Inc., an apparel manufacturer and vendor to South Bay Apparel, Inc., and

- failed to disclose unauthorized business relationships and transactions between immediate and extended family members of Mr. Finazzo and certain other of our vendors.

These activities, and their concealment, constituted numerous instances of conflicts of interest that were in breach of, among other things, our Code of Business Conduct and Ethics, as well as numerous violations of Mr. Finazzo's employment agreement.

South Bay Apparel, Inc. had been a vendor to us since 1996, providing apparel products including women's and men's graphic tee shirts, fleece and other tops. At least one affiliate of South Bay Apparel, Inc. involved in this matter has received orders from us aggregating approximately $0.6 million during fiscal 2006, approximately $1.0 million during fiscal 2005 and approximately $2.4 million during fiscal 2004.

Our management and our Board of Directors had no prior knowledge of any of these unauthorized activities by Mr. Finazzo, including the unauthorized Guaranty Agreement discussed above. On December 5, 2006, we entered into a Confirmatory Termination and Revocation Agreement with South Bay Apparel, Inc. and Tricot Richelieu, Inc., whereby all parties agreed that the Guaranty Agreement was thereby and has been permanently, irrevocably and absolutely terminated, revoked and expired in all respects. Therefore, the Guaranty Agreement was not recorded in the accompanying consolidated financial statements.

Also on December 5, 2006, we entered into an agreement with South Bay Apparel, Inc. and Douglas Dey, South Bay Apparel, Inc.'s President, whereby the parties agreed to resolve certain outstanding matters between them. As such, South Bay Apparel, Inc. agreed to pay us $8.0 million, representing (i) a concession of $7.1 million by South Bay Apparel, Inc. and Mr. Dey concerning prior purchases of merchandise by us, which was reflected as a reduction in the cost of merchandise in fiscal 2006, and (ii) reimbursement by South Bay Apparel, Inc. of $0.9 million, which offset professional fees that we incurred associated with the negotiation of the Agreement and the investigation of the underlying facts surrounding this Agreement. In addition, South Bay Apparel, Inc. and Mr. Dey agreed to a reduction in the price of merchandise sold to us to a price that we believe represents fair value, based on costs of comparable merchandise. We have agreed to continue purchasing merchandise from South Bay Apparel, Inc. through July 2, 2007, the date this agreement terminates. As of February 3, 2007, there was approximately $16.2 million in Aeropostale inventory remaining at South Bay Apparel, Inc.

Due to the numerous undisclosed conflicts of interests discussed above, we determined that transactions initiated or authorized by Mr. Finazzo, during his employment with us, with the above mentioned related parties cannot be presumed to have been carried out on an arm's-length basis, as the requisite conditions of competitive, free-market dealings may not have existed. However, we believe that our historical consolidated financial statements were fairly stated in all material respects. In addition, we believe that our historical trend of earnings would not have been materially impacted by any of these items.

AÉROPOSTALE, INC.

NOTES TO CONSOLIDATED FINANCIAL STATEMENTS — (Continued)

6. Fixtures, Equipment and Improvements

Fixtures, equipment and improvements consist of the following (in thousands):

	February 3, 2007	January 28, 2006
Leasehold improvements	$ 160,428	$ 135,619
Store fixtures and equipment	77,739	68,073
Computer equipment and software	23,226	18,178
Construction in progress	1,915	1,687
	263,308	223,557
Less accumulated depreciation and amortization	87,717	63,328
	$ 175,591	$ 160,229

Depreciation and amortization expense was $30.0 million in fiscal 2006, $22.3 million in fiscal 2005, and $16.6 million in fiscal 2004.

7. Accrued Expenses

Accrued expenses consist of the following (in thousands):

	February 3, 2007	January 28, 2006
Accrued compensation	$ 15,553	$ 10,714
Sales and use tax	4,369	2,868
Accrued rent	11,030	9,933
Accrued gift cards and credits	19,290	16,327
Income tax payable	37,802	14,159
Sales return liability	630	654
Payroll tax liabilities	1,549	1,033
Other	10,657	8,305
	$ 100,880	$ 63,993

8. Revolving Credit Facility

We have a revolving credit facility (the "credit facility") with Bank of America, N.A., which allows us to borrow or obtain letters of credit up to an aggregate of $50.0 million, with letters of credit having a sub-limit of $15.0 million. The amount of available credit can be increased to an aggregate of $75.0 million if we so request. The credit facility matures in April 2010, and our assets collateralize indebtedness under the credit facility. Borrowings under the credit facility bear interest at our option, either at (a) the lender's prime rate or (b) the Euro Dollar Rate plus 0.75% to 1.25%, dependent upon our financial performance. We are required to pay an annual credit facility fee of $25,000. There are no covenants in the credit facility requiring us to achieve certain earnings levels and there are no capital spending limitations. There are certain negative covenants under the credit facility including, but not limited to, limitations on our ability to incur other indebtedness, encumber our assets, or undergo a change of control. Additionally, we are required to maintain a ratio of 2:1 for the value of our inventory to the amount of the loans under the credit facility. As of February 3, 2007, we were in compliance with all covenants under the credit facility. Events of default under the credit facility include, subject to grace periods and notice provisions in certain circumstances, failure to pay principal amounts when due, breaches of covenants, misrepresentation, default of leases or other indebtedness, excess uninsured casualty loss, excess uninsured judgment or restraint of business, business failure or application for bankruptcy, indictment of us or institution of any legal process or proceeding

AÉROPOSTALE, INC.

NOTES TO CONSOLIDATED FINANCIAL STATEMENTS — (Continued)

under federal, state, municipal or civil statutes, legal challenges to loan documents, and a change in control. If an event of default occurs, the lenders under the credit facility will be entitled to take various actions, including the acceleration of amounts due thereunder and requiring that all such amounts be immediately paid in full as well as possession and sale of all assets that have been used as collateral. At February 3, 2007, we had no amount outstanding under the credit facility, and no stand-by or commercial letters of credit issued under the credit facility. In addition, we have not had outstanding borrowings under the credit facility since November 2002.

9. Earnings Per Share

In accordance with SFAS No. 128, *Earnings Per Share*, basic earnings per share has been computed based upon the weighted average of common shares, after deducting preferred dividend requirements. Diluted earnings per share gives effect to outstanding stock options.

Earnings per common share has been computed as follows (in thousands, except per share data):

	Fiscal		
	2006	**2005**	**2004**
Net income	$106,647	$83,954	$84,112
Weighted average basic shares	53,285	54,994	55,735
Impact of dilutive securities	473	943	1,520
Weighted average diluted shares	53,758	55,937	57,255
Per common share:			
Basic earnings per share	$ 2.00	$ 1.53	$ 1.51
Diluted earnings per share	$ 1.98	$ 1.50	$ 1.47

Options to purchase 419,000 shares in fiscal 2006, 387,000 shares in fiscal 2005, and 74,000 in fiscal 2004 were excluded from the computation of diluted earnings per share because the exercise prices of the options were greater than the average market price of the common shares.

10. Stock-Based Compensation

On January 29, 2006, the first day of our 2006 fiscal year, we adopted the provisions of Statement of Financial Accounting Standards No. 123(R), *Share-Based Payment, a revision of SFAS No. 123, Accounting for Stock-Based Compensation*, or SFAS No. 123(R), as interpreted by SEC Staff Accounting Bulletin No. 107. Under SFAS No. 123(R), all forms of share-based payment to employees and directors, including stock options, must be treated as compensation and recognized in the income statement. We recognized $3.7 million ($2.2 million after-tax, or $0.04 per diluted share) in compensation expense related to stock options during fiscal 2006. Previous to the adoption of SFAS No. 123(R), we accounted for stock options under the provisions of Accounting Principles Board Opinion No. 25, *Accounting for Stock Issued to Employees*, and, accordingly, did not recognize compensation expense in our consolidated financial statements. We adopted the modified prospective transition method provided under SFAS No. 123(R), and consequently, have not retroactively adjusted results from prior periods. Under this transition method, compensation cost associated with stock options recognized in fiscal 2006 includes: 1) quarterly amortization related to the remaining unvested portion of all stock option awards granted prior to January 29, 2006, based on the grant-date fair value estimated in accordance with the original provisions of SFAS No. 123; and 2) quarterly amortization related to all stock option awards granted subsequent to January 29, 2006, based on the grant-date fair value estimated in accordance with the provisions of SFAS No. 123(R).

Under SFAS No. 123(R), we are required to select a valuation technique or option-pricing model that meets the criteria as stated in the standard, which include a binomial model and the Black-Scholes model. At the present time,

AÉROPOSTALE, INC.

NOTES TO CONSOLIDATED FINANCIAL STATEMENTS — (Continued)

we will continue to use the Black-Scholes model, which requires the input of subjective assumptions. These assumptions include estimating the length of time employees will retain their vested stock options before exercising them ("expected term"), the estimated volatility of our common stock price over the expected term and the number of options that will ultimately not complete their vesting requirements ("forfeitures"). Changes in the subjective assumptions can materially affect the estimate of fair value of stock — based compensation and consequently, the related amount recognized in the consolidated statements of income.

In November 2005, the FASB issued FASB Staff Position No. FAS 123R-3 *"Transition Election Related to Accounting for Tax Effects of Share-Based Payment Awards. "* We have elected to adopt the alternative transition method provided in the FASB Staff Position for calculating the tax effects of stock-based compensation pursuant to SFAS No. 123(R). The alternative transition method includes simplified methods to establish the beginning balance of the additional paid-in capital pool ("APIC pool") related to the tax effects of employee stock-based compensation, and to determine the subsequent impact on the APIC pool and Consolidated Statements of Cash Flows of the tax effects of employee stock-based compensation awards that are outstanding upon adoption of SFAS No. 123(R).

Prior to the adoption of SFAS No. 123(R), we presented all tax benefits resulting from the exercise of stock options as operating cash flows in the Condensed Consolidated Statement of Cash Flows. SFAS No. 123(R) requires that cash flows resulting from tax deductions in excess of the cumulative compensation cost recognized for options exercised be classified as financing cash flows. Previously, all tax benefits from stock options had been reported as an operating activity. For fiscal 2006, net cash provided by operating activities, and net cash used for financing activities, was decreased by $7.6 million related to excess tax benefits realized from the exercise of stock options.

We have stock option plans under which we may grant qualified and non-qualified stock options to purchase shares of our common stock to executives, consultants, directors, or other key employees. As of February 3, 2007, a total of 857,733 shares were available for future grant under our plans. Stock options may not be granted at less than the fair market value at the date of grant. Stock options generally vest over four years on a pro rata basis and expire after eight years. All outstanding stock options immediately vest upon change in control.

The following tables summarize stock option transactions for common stock for fiscal 2006:

	Shares (In thousands)	Weighted Average Exercise Price	Weighted-Average Remaining Contractual Term (In years)	Aggregate Intrinsic Value (In millions)
Outstanding as of January 29, 2006	2,041	$ 12.63		
Granted	320	$ 28.90		
Exercised	(721)	$ 3.27		
Cancelled	(265)	$ 14.53		
Outstanding as of February 3, 2007	1,375	$ 20.96	5.28	$ 15.3
Exercisable as of February 3, 2007	564	$ 13.80	4.17	$ 10.3

AÉROPOSTALE, INC.

NOTES TO CONSOLIDATED FINANCIAL STATEMENTS — (Continued)

The following table summarizes stock option transactions for common stock for fiscal 2005 and fiscal 2004 (shares in thousands):

| | Fiscal 2005 | | Fiscal 2004 | |
	Shares	Weighted Average Exercise Price	Shares	Weighted Average Exercise Price
Outstanding, beginning of period	2,258	$ 7.93	3,092	$ 2.23
Granted	321	32.33	528	23.79
Exercised	(477)	2.82	(1,320)	0.78
Cancelled	(61)	18.81	(42)	12.88
Outstanding, end of period	2,041	$ 12.63	2,258	$ 7.93
Options exercisable at end of period	1,106	$ 4.27	1,314	$ 1.36
Weighted average fair value of options granted during the year		$ 13.34		$ 13.99

The weighted-average grant-date fair value of options granted was $14.59 during fiscal 2006, $13.34 during fiscal 2005, and $13.99 during fiscal 2004. The intrinsic value of options exercised was $19.3 million in fiscal 2006, $12.0 million in fiscal 2005, and $34.7 million in fiscal 2004.

The following tables summarize information regarding currently outstanding options as of February 3, 2007:

| | Options Outstanding | | | Options Exercisable | |
Range of Exercise Prices	Number Outstanding at February 3, 2007 (In thousands)	Weighted-Average Remaining Contractual Life (In years)	Weighted-Average Exercise Price	Number Exercisable at February 3, 2007 (In thousands)	Weighted-Average Exercise Price
0.26 to 0.57	143	2.2	$ 0.44	143	$ 0.44
7.63 to 11.80	287	4.1	$ 8.88	186	$ 8.86
18.57 to 23.32	352	5.2	$ 23.07	159	$ 22.84
23.91 to 33.65	593	6.7	$ 30.50	76	$ 32.14
	1,375			564	

	Shares (In thousands)	Weighted Average Grant-Date Fair Value
Non-vested as of January 29, 2006	935	$ 12.11
Granted	320	$ 14.37
Vested	(322)	$ 11.44
Cancelled	(122)	$ 12.56
Non-vested as of February 3, 2007	811	$ 13.20

Based on our forfeiture experience, we expect that approximately 648 of the above non-vested options will vest.

As of February 3, 2007, there was $6.5 million of total unrecognized compensation cost related to non-vested options that we expect to be recognized over the remaining weighted-average vesting period of 2.4 years. We expect

AÉROPOSTALE, INC.

NOTES TO CONSOLIDATED FINANCIAL STATEMENTS — (Continued)

to recognize $3.3 million of this cost in fiscal 2007, $2.0 million in fiscal 2008, $1.0 million in fiscal 2009, and $0.2 million in fiscal 2010.

Certain of our employees and all of our directors have been awarded non-vested stock, pursuant to non-vested stock agreements. The non-vested stock awarded to employees vests at the end of three years of continuous service with us. Initial grants of non-vested stock awarded to directors vest, pro-rata, over a three-year period, based upon continuous service. Subsequent grants of non-vested stock awarded to directors vest in full one year after the grant-date. Total compensation expense is being amortized over the vesting period. Amortization expense was $2.2 million for fiscal 2006, $1.7 million for fiscal 2005 and $0.6 million for fiscal 2004. As of February 3, 2007, there was $4.8 million of unrecognized compensation cost related to non-vested stock awards that is expected to be recognized over the weighted average period of 1.6 years. In the fourth quarter of 2006, we recorded a reduction of a previously recorded compensation expense of $0.3 million, resulting from the termination for cause of Christopher L. Finazzo, our then Executive Vice President and Chief Merchandising Officer on November 8, 2006 (see note 5 for a further discussion).

The following table summarizes non-vested shares of stock outstanding at February 3, 2007:

	Shares (In thousands)	Weighted-Average Grant-Date Fair Value
Outstanding as of January 29, 2006	168	$ 28.48
Granted	190	$ 29.94
Vested	(14)	$ 30.66
Cancelled	(40)	$ 28.52
Outstanding as of February 3, 2007	304	$ 29.29

Prior to fiscal 2006, no compensation expense was recognized for stock options. Had compensation cost for our stock option plans been determined consistent with SFAS No. 123(R), our net income and earnings per share for fiscal 2005 and fiscal 2004 would have been reduced to the following pro forma amounts (in thousands, except per share data):

	Fiscal	
	2005	2004
	(In thousands, except per share data)	
Net income:		
As reported	$83,954	$84,112
Add: non-vested stock amortization, net of taxes	1,050	366
Less: total stock-based compensation expense determined under fair value method, net of taxes	(2,756)	(1,525)
Pro-forma	$82,248	$82,953
Basic earnings per common share:		
As reported	$ 1.53	$ 1.51
Pro-forma	$ 1.50	$ 1.49
Diluted earnings per common share:		
As reported	$ 1.50	$ 1.47
Pro-forma	$ 1.47	$ 1.45

AÉROPOSTALE, INC.

NOTES TO CONSOLIDATED FINANCIAL STATEMENTS — (Continued)

In accordance with SFAS No. 123(R), the fair value of each option grant is estimated on the date of grant using the Black-Scholes option-pricing model based on the following assumptions for grants in the respective periods:

| | Fiscal | | |
	2006	2005	2004
Expected volatility	50%	40%	69%
Expected life	5.25 years	5 years	5 years
Risk-free interest rate	4.86%	4.11%	2.80%
Expected dividend yield	0%	0%	0%
Expected forfeiture rate	20%	20%	20%

The effects of applying SFAS No. 123(R) and the results obtained through the use of the Black-Scholes option-pricing model are not necessarily indicative of future values.

11.   Retirement Benefit Plans

We maintain a qualified, defined contribution retirement plan with a 401(k) salary deferral feature that covers substantially all of our employees who meet certain requirements. Under the terms of the plan, employees may contribute up to 14% of gross earnings and we will provide a matching contribution of 50% of the first 5% of gross earnings contributed by the participants. We also have the option to make additional contributions. The terms of the plan provide for vesting in our matching contributions to the plan over a five-year service period with 20% vesting after two years and 50% vesting after year three. Vesting increases thereafter at a rate of 25% per year so that participants will be fully vested after year five. Contribution expense was $0.8 million in fiscal 2006 and $0.5 million in both fiscal 2005 and fiscal 2004.

We adopted SFAS No. 158 on February 3, 2007, which impacted our Supplemental Executive Retirement Plan, or SERP, and our postretirement benefit plan. Since the full recognition of the funded status of an entity's defined benefit pension plan is recorded on the balance sheet, an additional minimum liability ("AML") is no longer recorded under SFAS No. 158. However, because the recognition provisions of SFAS No. 158 were adopted as of February 3, 2007, we first measured and recorded changes to our previously recognized AML through other comprehensive income and then applied the recognition provisions of SFAS No. 158 through accumulated other comprehensive income to fully recognize the funded status of our defined benefit pension plans. See the section Recent Accounting Developments in Note 1 for a further discussion regarding SFAS No. 158.

The following table summarizes the impact of adopting SFAS No. 158 (in thousands):

	Before Adopting SFAS No. 158	Adjustments	After Adopting SFAS No. 158
Other intangible assets	$ 2,381	$ (981)	$ 1,400
Deferred income tax assets (non-current)	1,371	2,413	3,784
Total assets	579,732	1,432	581,164
Retirement benefit plan liabilities	10,647	5,259	15,906
Total liabilities	263,789	5,259	269,048
Accumulated other comprehensive loss	(1,447)	(3,827)	(5,274)
Total stockholders' equity	315,943	(3,827)	312,116

Our SERP is a non-qualified defined benefit plan for certain officers. The plan is non-contributory and not funded and provides benefits based on years of service and compensation during employment. Participants are fully vested upon entrance in the plan. Pension expense is determined using various actuarial cost methods to estimate the total benefits ultimately payable to officers and this cost is allocated to service periods. The actuarial assumptions used to calculate pension costs are reviewed annually.

AÉROPOSTALE, INC.

NOTES TO CONSOLIDATED FINANCIAL STATEMENTS — (Continued)

The following information about the SERP is provided below (in thousands):

	February 3, 2007	January 28, 2006
CHANGE IN BENEFIT OBLIGATION:		
Net benefit obligation at beginning of period	$ 15,004	$ 10,884
Service cost	492	421
Interest cost	932	732
Plan amendments	—	—
Actuarial (gain)/ loss	(1,281)	3,303
Settlements	—	—
Gross benefits paid	—	(336)
Net benefit obligation at end of period	$ 15,147	$ 15,004
Accumulated benefit obligation	N/A	$ 8,446
CHANGE IN PLAN ASSETS:		
Fair value of plan assets at beginning of period	$ —	$ —
Employer contributions	—	336
Gross benefits paid	—	(336)
Actual return on plan assets	—	—
Fair value of plan assets at end of period	$ —	$ —
Funded status at end of period	$ (15,147)	$ (15,004)
Unrecognized net actuarial loss	N/A	9,130
Unrecognized prior service and cost	N/A	1,055
Net amount recognized	$ (15,147)	$ (4,819)
Intangible assets	N/A	$ 1,055
Accrued benefit cost	(15,147)	(8,446)
Accumulated other comprehensive income	N/A	2,572
Net amount recognized	$ (15,147)	$ (4,819)

AÉROPOSTALE, INC.

NOTES TO CONSOLIDATED FINANCIAL STATEMENTS — (Continued)

Pension expense includes the following components (in thousands):

	Fiscal		
	2006	2005	2004
COMPONENTS OF NET PERIODIC BENEFIT COST:			
Service cost	$ 492	$ 421	$ 278
Interest cost	932	732	626
Prior service cost	74	74	74
Amortization of prior experience loss	568	550	321
Loss recognized due to settlement	—	—	1,396
Net periodic benefit cost	$2,066	$1,777	$2,695
WEIGHTED-AVERAGE ASSUMPTIONS USED:			
Discount rate to determine benefit obligations	5.75%	5.50%	5.25%
Discount rate to determine net periodic pension cost	5.50%	5.25%	6.00%
Rate of compensation increase	4.50%	4.50%	4.50%

The discount rate was determined by matching a published set of zero coupon yields and associated durations to expected plan benefit payment streams to obtain an implicit internal rate of return. The loss recognized due to settlement in fiscal 2004 resulted from the early retirement of our former President and Chief Operating Officer. We made a contribution of $2.4 million in fiscal 2004 in connection with this early retirement.

We currently do not expect to make any contributions to the SERP in fiscal 2007. We project making a benefit payment of approximately $13.3 million in 2010, which reflects expected future service, and assumes retirement at age 65.

We have a long-term incentive deferred compensation plan established for the purpose of providing long-term incentives to a select group of management, with a liability of $0.2 million as of February 3, 2007 and $0.1 million at January 28, 2006 for this plan. The plan is a non-qualified, defined contribution plan and is not funded. Participants in this plan include all employees designated by us as Vice President, or other higher-ranking positions that are not participants in the SERP. We will record annual monetary credits to each participant's account based on compensation levels and years as a participant in the plan. Annual interest credits will be applied to the balance of each participant's account based upon established benchmarks. Each annual credit is subject to a three-year cliff-vesting schedule, and participants' accounts will be fully vested upon retirement after completing five years of service and attaining age 55.

We have a postretirement benefit plan for certain officers with a liability of $0.5 million as of February 3, 2007 and $0.1 million at January 28, 2006 for this plan.

12.   Stock Repurchase Program

We repurchase our common stock from time to time under a stock repurchase program. On March 14, 2007, our Board of Directors approved a $100.0 million increase in repurchase availability under the program, bringing total repurchase authorization, since inception of the program, to $350.0 million. The repurchase program may be modified or terminated by the Board of Directors at any time, and there is no expiration date for the program. The extent and timing of repurchases will depend upon general business and market conditions, stock prices, opening and closing of our stock trading window, and liquidity and capital resource requirements going forward. We repurchased 3.1 million shares of our common stock for $91.4 million during fiscal 2006, 1.8 million shares for $44.5 million during fiscal 2005, and 1.8 million shares for $45.9 million during fiscal 2004. We repurchased 7.7 million shares for $199.5 million since the inception of the repurchase program through February 3, 2007, with

AÉROPOSTALE, INC.

NOTES TO CONSOLIDATED FINANCIAL STATEMENTS — (Continued)

$150.5 million of repurchase availability remaining under the program as of February 3, 2007, including the additional $100.0 million of availability that was approved on March 14, 2007.

13. Income Taxes

The provision for income taxes consists of the following (in thousands):

	Fiscal		
	2006	2005	2004
Current:			
Federal	$ 63,561	$39,360	$42,728
State and local	15,096	9,687	8,119
	78,657	49,047	50,847
Deferred:			
Federal	(8,253)	5,026	2,035
State and local	(2,221)	1,074	374
	(10,474)	6,100	2,409
	$ 68,183	$55,147	$53,256

Reconciliation of the U.S. statutory tax rate with our effective tax rate is summarized as follows:

	Fiscal		
	2006	2005	2004
Federal statutory rate	35.0%	35.0%	35.0%
Increase (decrease) in tax resulting from:			
State income taxes, net of federal tax benefits	4.8	4.9	4.0
Other	(0.8)	(0.3)	(0.2)
Effective rate	39.0%	39.6%	38.8%

47

AÉROPOSTALE, INC.

NOTES TO CONSOLIDATED FINANCIAL STATEMENTS — (Continued)

The components of the net deferred income tax assets/ (liabilities) are as follows (in thousands):

	February 3, 2007	January 28, 2006
Current:		
Inventory	$ 1,094	$ (5,417)
Other	91	222
Total current assets/ (liabilities)	$ 1,185	$ (5,195)
Non-current:		
Furniture, equipment and improvements	$ (11,537)	$ (13,886)
Retirement benefit plan liabilities	6,124	2,847
Deferred rent and tenant allowances	6,151	7,636
Stock-based compensation	2,394	520
Jimmy'Z state net operating loss carry-forwards	1,303	457
Valuation allowances for Jimmy'Z state net operating loss carry-forwards	(651)	(229)
Total non-current liabilities	3,784	(2,655)
Net deferred income tax assets/(liabilities)	$ 4,969	$ (7,850)

We have recorded valuation allowances against state net operating loss carry-forwards, or "NOL's", generated by our Jimmy'Z subsidiary. Subsequent recognition of these deferred tax assets would result in an income tax benefit in the year of such recognition. The NOL's expire between 2020 and 2026.

We record liabilities for tax contingencies when it is probable that a liability to a taxing authority has been incurred and the amount of the contingency can be reasonably estimated. Tax contingency liabilities are adjusted for changes in circumstances and additional uncertainties, such as significant amendments to existing tax law. We had tax contingency liabilities of $2.6 million as of February 3, 2007 and $1.7 million as of January 28, 2006. We will adopt the provisions of FIN 48, *"Accounting for Uncertainty in Income Taxes,"* which clarifies the accounting for uncertainty in income taxes recognized in the financial statements, at the beginning of our 2007 fiscal year. See the section Recent Accounting Developments in Note 1 for a further discussion.

14.   Commitments and Contingencies

We are committed under non-cancelable leases for our entire store and office space locations, which generally provide for minimum rent plus additional increases in real estate taxes, certain operating expenses, etc. Certain leases also require contingent rent based on sales.

The aggregate minimum annual rent commitments as of February 3, 2007 are as follows (in thousands):

Due in Fiscal Year	Total
2007	$ 76,163
2008	76,457
2009	74,782
2010	70,386
2011	65,027
Thereafter	189,335
Total	$552,150

AÉROPOSTALE, INC.

NOTES TO CONSOLIDATED FINANCIAL STATEMENTS — (Continued)

Rental expense consists of the following (in thousands):

| | Fiscal | | |
	2006	2005	2004
Minimum rentals	$71,272	$61,681	$49,481
Contingent rentals	12,164	10,376	8,704
Office space rentals	2,255	1,207	1,159

Employment Agreements — As of February 3, 2007, we had outstanding employment agreements with certain members of our senior management totaling $4.8 million. These employment agreements expire at the end of fiscal 2009, except for the employment agreement with our Chief Executive Officer, which expires at the end of fiscal 2007. In addition, we executed a three-year employment agreement with our new President and Chief Merchandising Officer effective March 16, 2007 which provides for a minimum of $2.9 million, comprised of base salary and guaranteed bonus over the three-year period.

Legal Proceedings — We are party to various litigation matters and proceedings in the ordinary course of business. In the opinion of our management, dispositions of these matters are not expected to have a material adverse effect on our financial position, results from operations or cash flows.

Event Sponsorship and Advertising Agreements — We are a party to event sponsorship and advertising agreements with remaining payment obligations of $1.5 million in fiscal 2007, $1.3 million in fiscal 2008, and $0.7 million in fiscal 2009.

Guarantees — There were no financial guarantees outstanding at February 3, 2007. We have not provided any financial guarantees, other than the unauthorized guaranty that was executed by Christopher L. Finazzo, our then Executive Vice President and Chief Merchandising Officer, that was revoked and terminated on December 5, 2006 (see note 5 for a further discussion). We had no commercial commitments outstanding as of February 3, 2007.

15. Selected Quarterly Financial Data (Unaudited)

The following table sets forth certain unaudited quarterly financial information (in thousands, except per share amounts):

| | 13 Weeks Ended | | | 14 Weeks Ended |
| | April 29, 2006 | July 29, 2006 | October 28, 2006 | February 3, 2007 |
		(1)		(2)
Fiscal 2006				
Net sales	$246,292	$274,624	$ 385,455	$ 506,837
Gross profit	70,478	72,576	123,599	188,764
Net income	8,363	8,423	32,570	57,291
Basic earnings per share	0.15	0.16	0.62	1.09
Diluted earnings per share	0.15	0.16	0.61	1.08

AÉROPOSTALE, INC.

NOTES TO CONSOLIDATED FINANCIAL STATEMENTS — (Continued)

| | 13 Weeks Ended | | | |
	April 30, 2005	July 30, 2005	October 29, 2005	January 28, 2006
Fiscal 2005				
Net sales	$211,674	$232,770	$ 324,657	$ 435,246
Gross profit	59,771	62,027	94,719	145,958
Net income	8,614	7,449	26,085	41,806
Basic earnings per share	0.16	0.13	0.48	0.77
Diluted earnings per share	0.15	0.13	0.47	0.76

---

(1) — Includes other income of $2.1 million ($1.3 million, after tax, or $0.03 per diluted share) from the resolution of a dispute with a vendor regarding the enforcement of our intellectual property rights.

(2) — Includes $7.4 million ($4.5 million, after tax, or $0.08 per diluted share), net of professional fees, representing concessions, primarily from South Bay Apparel Inc., to us for prior purchases of merchandise (see note 5 for a further discussion).

Appendix

Time Value of Money

After studying Appendix 3, you should be able to:

➤ **1** Explain how compound interest works.

➤ **2** Use future value and present value tables to apply compound interest to accounting transactions.

This appendix explains the time value of money. Time value of money is widely used in business to measure today's value of future cash outflows or inflows and the amount to which liabilities (or assets) will grow when compound interest accumulates.

In transactions involving the borrowing and lending of money, it is customary for the borrower to pay *interest*. In effect, interest is the **time value of money**. The amount of interest paid is determined by the length of the loan and the interest rate.

Interest is not restricted to loans made to borrowers by financial institutions. It also arises on investments (particularly, investments in debt securities and savings accounts), on installment sales, and on a variety of other contractual arrangements. In all cases, the arrangement between the two parties—the note, security, or purchase agreement—creates an asset in the accounting records of one party and a corresponding liability in the accounting records of the other. All such assets and liabilities increase as interest is earned by the asset holder and decrease as payments are made by the liability holder.

Our purpose here is to explain the basic time-value-of-money calculations using compound interest procedures. We will do that using several simple financial arrangements.

Compound Interest Calculations

OBJECTIVE ▶ 1
Explain how compound interest works.

Compound interest is a method of calculating the time value of money in which interest is earned on the previous periods' interest. That is, interest for the period is added to the account balance and interest is earned on this new balance in the next period. Compound interest calculations require careful specification of the interest period and the interest rate. The **interest period** is the time interval between interest calculations. The **interest rate** is the percentage that is multiplied by the beginning-of-period balance to yield the amount of interest for that period. The interest rate must agree with the interest period. For example, if the interest period is one month, then the interest rate used to calculate interest must be stated as a percentage "per month."

When an interest rate is stated in terms of a time period that differs from the interest period, the rate must be adjusted before interest can be calculated. Suppose, for example, that a bank advertises interest at a rate of 12 percent per year compounded monthly. The words *compounded monthly* indicate that the interest period is one month. Since there are 12 interest periods in one year, the interest rate for one month is one-twelfth the annual rate, or 1 percent. In general, if the *rate statement period* differs from the *interest period*, the stated rate must be divided by the number of interest periods included in the rate statement period.

Consider the following examples of stated rates and the corresponding adjusted rates required for interest computations:

Stated Rate	Adjusted Rate for Computations
12% per year compounded semiannually	6% per six-month period (12%/2)
12% per year compounded quarterly	3% per quarter (12%/4)
12% per year compounded monthly	1% per month (12%/12)

Whenever an interest rate is stated without reference to a rate statement period or an interest period, assume that the unmentioned period is one year. For example, both "12 percent" and "12 percent per year" should be interpreted as 12 percent per year compounded annually.

The term compound interest refers to the fact that interest is computed on the original amount plus undistributed interest earned in previous periods. The simplest compound interest calculation involves putting a single amount into an account and adding interest to it at the end of each period.

Students new to compound interest often see a calculation like the one shown in Cornerstone A3-1 and wonder why compounding is so important if it only amounts to 25¢. One of the reasons is time. If the investment period is sufficiently long, the amount of compound interest grows large even at relatively small interest rates. For example, suppose your parents invested $1,000 at ½ percent per month when you were born with the objective of giving you a college graduation present at age 21. How much would that investment be worth after 21 years? The answer is $3,514. In 21 years the compound interest is $2,514—more than 2½ times the original principal. Without compounding, interest over the same period would have been only $1,260.

**CORNERSTONE
A3-1**

HOW TO Compute Future Values Using Compound Interest

Concept:
When deposits earn compound interest, interest is earned on the interest.

Information:
An investor deposits $20,000 in a savings account on January 1, 2009. The bank pays interest of 6 percent per year compounded monthly.

Required:
Assuming that the only activity to the account is the deposit of interest at the end of each month, how much money will be in the account after the interest payment on March 31, 2009?

Solution:
Monthly interest will be ½% (6% per year/12 months)

Account balance, 1/1/09	$20,000.00
January interest ($20,000.00 × ½%)	100.00
Account balance, 1/31/09	$20,100.00
February interest ($20,100.00 × ½%)	100.50
Account balance, 2/28/09	$20,200.50
March interest ($20,200.50 × ½%)	101.00
Account balance, 3/31/09	$20,301.50

As long as the investor does not withdraw money from the account, its balance continues to grow each month by an increasing amount of interest. The amount of monthly interest increases because interest is *compounded*; that is, interest is computed on accumulated interest as well as on principal. For example, February interest of $100.50 consists of $100 interest on the $20,000 principal and 50¢ interest on the $100 January interest ($100 × 0.005 = 50¢).

In Cornerstone 3-1, interest was the only factor that altered the account balance after the initial deposit. In more complex situations, the account balance is changed by subsequent deposits and withdrawals as well as by interest. Withdrawals reduce the balance and therefore, the amount of interest in subsequent periods. Additional deposits have the opposite effect, increasing the balance and the amount of interest earned.

The amount to which an account will grow when interest is compounded is the **future value** of the account. (Later in this appendix, we will explain how to use mathematical tables as a shortcut for the calculation of future values.) Compound interest calculations can assume two fundamentally different forms: (1) calculations of future values and (2) calculations of present values. As we have just seen, calculations of future values are projections of future balances based on past and future cash flows and interest payments. In contrast, calculations of present values, to which we now turn, are determinations of present amounts based on expected future cash flows.

Present Value of Future Cash Flows

Whenever a contract establishes a relationship between an initial amount borrowed or loaned and one or more future cash flows, the initial amount borrowed or loaned is the **present value** of those future cash flows. The present value can be interpreted in two ways. From the borrower's viewpoint, it is the liability that will be exactly paid by the future payments. From the lender's viewpoint, it is the receivable balance that will be exactly satisfied by the future receipts.

To illustrate, suppose that the Hilliard Corporation borrows $100,000 from Citizens Bank of New Hope on January 1, 2010. The note requires three $38,803.35 payments, one each at the end of 2010, 2011, and 2012, and includes interest at 8 percent per year. The cash flows for Hilliard are shown in Exhibit A3-1.

Cash flow diagrams that display both the amounts and the times of the cash flows specified by a contract are extremely helpful in the solution of time-value-of-money exercises and problems. It is customary in these diagrams to use a time line that runs from left to right. Inflows are represented as arrows pointing upward and outflows as arrows pointing downward.

The calculation that follows shows, from the borrower's perspective, the relationship between the amount borrowed (*the present value*) and the future payments (*future cash flows*) required by Hilliard's note. Observe that this *reverse* compound interest calculation results in a zero balance after the last payment. The three payments of $38,803.35 exactly pay off the liability created by the note.

Amount borrowed, 1/1/10	$100,000.00
Add: 2010 interest ($100,000.00 × 0.08)	8,000.00
Subtract payment on 12/31/10	(38,803.35)
Liability at 12/31/10	$ 69,196.65
Add: 2011 interest ($69,196.65 × 0.08)	5,535.73
Subtract payment on 12/31/11	(38,803.35)
Liability at 12/31/11	$ 35,929.03
Add: 2012 interest ($35,929.03 × 0.08)	2,874.32
Subtract payment on 12/31/12	(38,803.35)
Liability at 12/31/12	$ 0.00

Present value calculations like this one, are future value calculations in reverse. Since the reversal of future value calculations can present a burdensome and sometimes difficult algebraic problem, shortcut methods using tables have been developed. In the next section, we will examine the application of tables to the calculation of both present values and future values.

Interest and the Frequency of Compounding

Before we end our discussion of the mechanics of compound interest calculations, there is one more point we need to make. The number of interest periods into which

---

Exhibit A3-1

Cash Flow Diagram

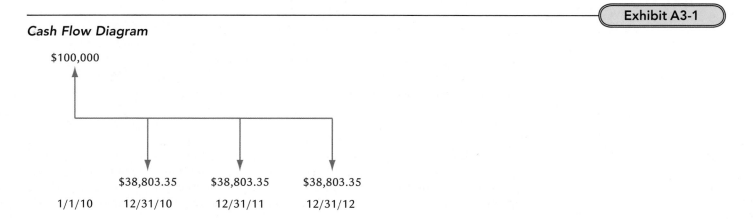

Exhibit A3-2

Effect of Interest Periods on Compound Interest

Investment	Interest Period	I	N	Calculation of Future Amount In One Year*
A	1 year	12%	1	($10,000 × 1.12000) = $11,200
B	6 months	6%	2	($10,000 × 1.12360) = 11,236
C	1 quarter	3%	4	($10,000 × 1.12551) = 11,255
D	1 month	1%	12	($10,000 × 1.12683) = 11,268

*The multipliers (1.12 for Investment A, 1.12360 for investment B, and so on) are taken from the present and future value tables that are discussed below.

a compound interest problem is divided can make a significant difference in the amount of compound interest.

To illustrate, assume that you are evaluating four 1-year investments, each of which requires an initial $10,000 deposit. All four investments earn interest at a rate of 12 percent per year, but they have different compounding periods. The data in Exhibit A3-2 demonstrate the impact of compounding frequency on future value. Observe that investment D, which offers monthly compounding, accumulates $68 more interest by the end of the year than investment A, which offers only annual compounding.

OBJECTIVE ▶ 2

Use future value and present value tables to apply compound interest to accounting transactions.

Four Basic Compound Interest Problems

The four problems presented here are called basic because any present value or future value problem can be broken down into one or more of these four problems. The basic problems can be solved with the aid of the present value and future value tables provided at the end of this appendix (pages 780-783). Solutions to the basic problems then can be combined to derive the solution to more complex problems.

Future Value of a Single Amount

The first basic problem is determining the future value of a single amount. The problem has four symbolic elements.

- f represents the cash flow
- FV the future value
- n the number of periods between the cash flow and the future value
- i the interest rate per period

The future value of a single amount can be found simply by establishing an account for f dollars and adding compound interest at i percent to that account for n periods. The balance of the account after n periods is the future value and can be found with the following formula:

$$FV = (f)(1 + i)^n$$

An alternative and easier solution technique makes use of the Future Value of a Single Amount table (see p. 780) where M_1 is the multiple from Exhibit A3-7 that corresponds to the appropriate values of n and i.

$$FV = (f)(M_1)$$

The following example illustrates a different solution technique. Suppose **General Motors Acceptance Corporation (GMAC)** loans $200,000 at a rate of 6 percent per year compounded annually to a Pontiac dealer for four years. The basic problem of finding the future value (FV) at the end of the four years—the amount that will

Future Value of a Single Amount: An Example

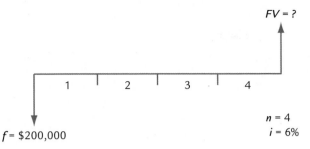

FV = ?

1   2   3   4

$n = 4$
$i = 6\%$

$f = \$200,000$

be repaid—is diagrammed in Exhibit A3-3. We assume GMAC's viewpoint (the lender's). Using a compound interest calculation, the unknown future value (FV) is found as follows:

Amount loaned	$200,000.00
First year's interest ($200,000.00 × 0.06)	12,000.00
Loan receivable at end of first year	$212,000.00
Second year's interest ($212,000.00 × 0.06)	12,720.00
Loan receivable at end of second year	$224,720.00
Third year's interest ($224,720.00 × 0.06)	13,483.20
Loan receivable at end of third year	$238,203.20
Fourth year's interest ($238,203.20 × 0.06)	14,292.19
Loan receivable at end of the fourth year	$252,495.39

Observe that the amount of interest increases each year. This growth is the effect of computing interest for each year based on an amount that includes the interest earned in prior years.

The shortcut calculation, using the table in Exhibit A3-7, is made as follows:

$$FV = (F)(M_1)$$
$$= (\$200,000)(1.26248)$$
$$= \$252,496$$

The multiple 1.26248 is found at the intersection of the 6 percent column ($i = 6\%$) and the fourth row ($n = 4$) or by calculating 1.06^4. The multiple can be interpreted as the future value of the single amount after having been borrowed (or invested) for four years at 6 percent interest. The future value of $200,000 is 200,000 times the multiple.

Note, the difference between the answer of $252,495.39 developed in the compound interest calculation and the $252,496 determined using the multiple from the table. The discrepancy is due to the fact that the figures in the table are rounded off to five decimal places. If they were taken to eight digits ($1.06^4 = 1.26247696$), then the two answers would be equal. Cornerstone A3-2 provides another illustration of how to compute the future value of a single amount.

HOW TO Compute the Future Value of a Single Amount

Concept:
The future value of a single amount is the original cash flow plus compound interest as of a specific future date.

Information:
The Kitchner Company sells an unneeded factory site for $200,000 on July 1, 2009. Kitchner expects to purchase a different site in 18 months so that it can expand into a new market. Meanwhile, Kitchner decides to invest the $200,000

CORNERSTONE
A3-2

**CORNERSTONE
A3-2**
(continued)

in a money market fund that is guaranteed to earn 6 percent per year compounded semiannually (3 percent per six-month period).

Required:

1. Draw a cash flow diagram for this investment from Kitchner's perspective.
2. Calculate the amount of money in the money market fund on December 31, 2009, and provide the journal entry to recognize interest revenue.
3. Calculate the amount of money in the money market fund on December 31, 2010, and provide the journal entry to recognize interest revenue.

Solution:

1.

$FV = ?$

$n = 3$
$i = 3\%$

| | 1 | | 2 | | 3 |

$f = \$200,000$

7/1/09   12/31/09   7/1/10   12/31/10

2. Because we are calculating the value at 12/31/09, we only have one period.

$FV = (f)$ (*FV of a Single Amount, 1 period, 3%*)
$= (\$200,000)(1.03)$
$= \$206,000$

The excess of the amount of money over the original deposit is the interest earned from July 1 through December 31, 2009.

	Stockholders'
Assets = Liabilities +	**Equity**
+6,000	+6,000

Cash	6,000	
Interest Revenue		6,000

3. To calculate the amount of money in the money market fund at December 31, 2009, perform the following calculation:

$FV = (f)$(*FV of a Single Amount, 3 periods, 3%*)
$= (\$200,000)(1.09273)$
$= \$218,546$

The interest revenue for the year is the increase in the amount of money during 2009, which is $12,546 ($218,546 − $206,000). This leads to the following journal entry:

	Stockholders'
Assets = Liabilities +	**Equity**
+12,546	+12,546

Cash	12,546	
Interest Revenue		12,546

Present Value of a Single Amount

The second basic problem is to find the present value of a single amount. This problem also has four symbolic elements.

- f represents the future cash flow
- PV the present value
- n the number of periods between the present time and the future cash flow
- i the interest rate per period

In present value problems, the interest rate is sometimes called the *discount rate*. Problems of this form can be solved with the following formula:

$$PV = \frac{f}{(1 + i)^n}$$

You can also use the Present Value of a Single Amount table (see p. 78) where M_2 is the multiple from Exhibit A3-8 that corresponds to the appropriate values of n and i.

$$PV = (f)(M_2)$$

We will use this solution technique to determine the present value of a single cash flow from the borrower's viewpoint. Suppose **Marathon Oil** has purchased property on which it plans to develop oil wells. The seller has agreed to accept a single $150,000,000 payment three years from now when Marathon expects to be selling oil from the field. Also assume that the appropriate interest rate is 7 percent per year. This basic problem is diagrammed in Exhibit A3-4. The present value can be calculated using the table in Exhibit A3-8:

$$
\begin{aligned}
PV &= (f)(M_2) \\
&= (\$150,000,000)(.81630) \\
&= \$122,445,000
\end{aligned}
$$

The multiple 0.81630 is found at the intersection of the 7 percent column ($i = 7\%$) and the third row ($n = 3$) in Exhibit A3-8 or by calculating $[1/(1.07)^3]$. The multiple can be interpreted as the present value of a \$1 cash inflow or outflow in three years at 7 percent. Thus the present value of \$150,000,000 is 150,000,000 times as much as the multiple.

Although the future value calculation cannot be used to determine the present value, it can be used to verify that the present value calculated by using the table is correct. The following calculation is proof for the present value problem at hand:

Calculated present value (*PV*)	$122,445,000
First year's interest ($122,445,000 × 0.07)	8,571,150
Loan payable at end of first year	$131,016,150
Second year's interest ($131,016,150 × 0.07)	9,171,131
Loan payable at end of second year	$140,187,281
Third year's interest ($140,187,281 × 0.07)	9,813,110
Loan payable at end of the third year (*f*)	$150,000,391

Exhibit A3-4

Present Value of a Single Amount: An Example

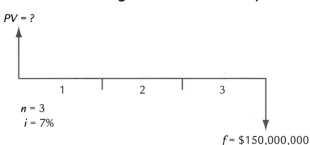

PV = ?

1   2   3

n = 3
i = 7%

f = $150,000,000

Note the $391 difference between the amount developed in this calculation and the assumed $150,000,000 cash flow. The discrepancy is due to the fact that the multiples in the table are rounded off to five decimal places. We can therefore ignore the difference.

When interest is compounded on the calculated present value of $122,445,000, then the present value calculation is reversed and we return to the future cash flow of $150,000,000. This reversal proves that $122,445,000 is the correct present value. Cornerstone A3-3 provides another illustration of how to compute the present value of a single amount.

CORNERSTONE A3-3

HOW TO Compute Present Value of a Single Amount

Concept:
The present value of a single cash flow is the original cash flow that must be invested to produce a known value at a specific future date.

Information:
On October 1, 2009, Adelsman Manufacturing Company sold a new machine to Randell, Inc. The machine represented a new design that Randell was eager to place in service. Since Randell was unable to pay for the machine on the date of purchase, Adelsman agreed to defer the $60,000 payment for 15 months. The appropriate rate of interest in such transactions is 8 percent per year compounded quarterly (2 percent per three-month period).

Required:

1. Draw the cash flow diagram for this deferred-payment purchase from Randell's (the borrower's) perspective.
2. Calculate the present value of this deferred-payment purchase.
3. Provide the journal entry to record the acquisition of the machine.

Solution:

1.

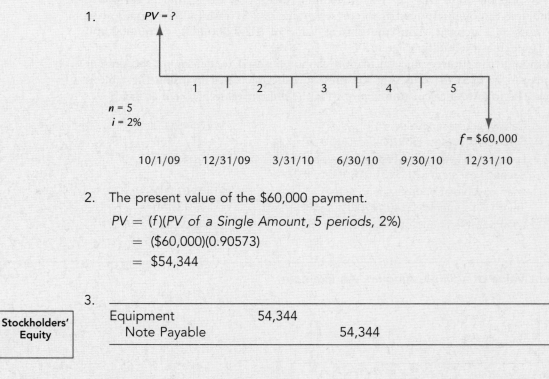

2. The present value of the $60,000 payment.

$$PV = (f)(PV \text{ of a Single Amount, 5 periods, 2\%})$$
$$= (\$60,000)(0.90573)$$
$$= \$54,344$$

3.

Equipment	54,344	
Note Payable		54,344

Assets = Liabilities +	Stockholders' Equity
+54,344	+54,344

Both the first and the second basic problems involve a single cash flow. We turn now to problems involving multiple cash flows one period apart.

Future Value of an Annuity

The third and fourth basic problems involve series of cash flows called *annuities*. An **annuity** is a number of equal cash flows; one to each interest period. For example, an investment in a security that pays $1,000 to an investor every December 31 for 10 consecutive years is an annuity. A loan repayment schedule that calls for a payment of $367.29 on the first day of each month can also be considered an annuity. (Although the number of days in a month varies from 28 to 31, the interest period is defined as one month without regard to the number of days in each month.)

The third problem is to find the future value of an annuity. In this problem.

- f represents the amount of each repeating cash flow
- FV the future value after the last (nth) cash flow
- n is the number of cash flows
- i the interest rate per period

Problems of this kind can be solved by the following formula:

$$FV = (f)\left[\frac{(1 + i)^n - 1}{i}\right]$$

You can also use the Future Value of an Annuity table (see p. 782) where M_3 is the multiple from Exhibit A3-9 that corresponds to the appropriate values of n and i compound interest calculations:

$$FV = (f)(M_3)$$

The following example demonstrates the computation of the future value of an annuity. Assume that **Bank One** wants to advertise a new savings program to its customers. The savings program requires the customers to make four annual payments of $5,000 each, with the first payment due three years before the program ends. Bank One advertises a 6 percent interest rate compounded annually. Find the future value of this annuity immediately after the fourth cash payment. This problem is diagrammed in Exhibit A3-5 from the investor's perspective.

Note that the first period in Exhibit A3-5 is drawn with a dotted line. When using annuities, the time-value-of-money model assumes that all cash flows occur at the end of a period. Therefore, the first cash flow in the future value of an annuity occurs at the end of the first period. However, since interest cannot be earned until the first deposit has been made, the first period is identified as a no-interest period.

Exhibit A3-5

Future Value of An Annuity: An Example

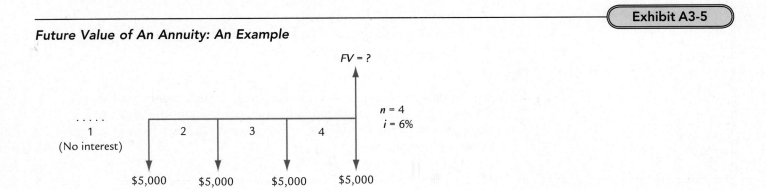

Let us find the future value (FV) using a detailed compound interest calculation:

Interest for first period ($0 × 6%)	$ 0.00
First deposit	5,000.00
Investment balance at end of first year	$ 5,000.00
Second year's interest ($5,000.00 × 0.06)	300.00
Second deposit	5,000.00
Investment balance at end of second year	$10,300.00
Third year's interest ($10,300.00 × 0.06)	618.00
Third deposit	5,000.00
Investment balance at end of third year	$15,918.00
Fourth year's interest ($15,918.00 × 0.06)	955.08
Fourth deposit	5,000.00
Investment at end of the fourth year	$21,873.08

This calculation shows that the lender has accumulated a future value (*FV*) of $21,873.08 by the end of the fourth period, immediately after the fourth cash investment.

An easier way of computing the future value is to use the table shown in Exhibit A3-9, as follows:

$$FV = (f)(M_3)$$
$$= (\$5,000)(4.37462)$$
$$= \$21,873$$

The multiple 4.3746 is found at the intersection of the 6 percent column ($i = 6\%$) and the fourth row ($n = 4$) in the Future Value of an Annuity table or by calculating $(1.06^4 - 1)/0.06$. The multiple can be interpreted as the future value of an annuity of four cash flows of $1 each at 6 percent. The future value of an annuity of $5,000 cash flows is 5,000 times the multiple. Thus, the table enables us to calculate the future value of an annuity by a single multiplication, no matter how many cash flows are involved. Cornerstone A3-4 provides another illustration of how to compute the future value of an annuity.

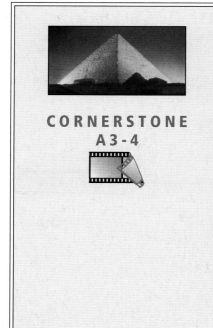

CORNERSTONE
A 3 - 4

HOW TO Compute Future Value of an Annuity

Concept:
The future value of an annuity is the value of a series of equal cash flows made at regular intervals with compound interest at some specific future date.

Information:
Greg Smith is a lawyer and CPA specializing in retirement and estate planning. One of Greg's clients, the owner of a large farm, wants to retire in five years. To provide funds to purchase a retirement annuity from New York Life at the date of retirement, Greg asks the client to give him annual payments of $170,000 which Greg will deposit in a special fund that will earn 7 percent per year.

Required:

1. Draw the cash flow diagram for the fund from Greg's client's perspective.
2. Calculate the future value of the fund immediately after the fifth deposit.
3. If Greg's client needs $1,000,000 to purchase the annuity, how much must be deposited every year?

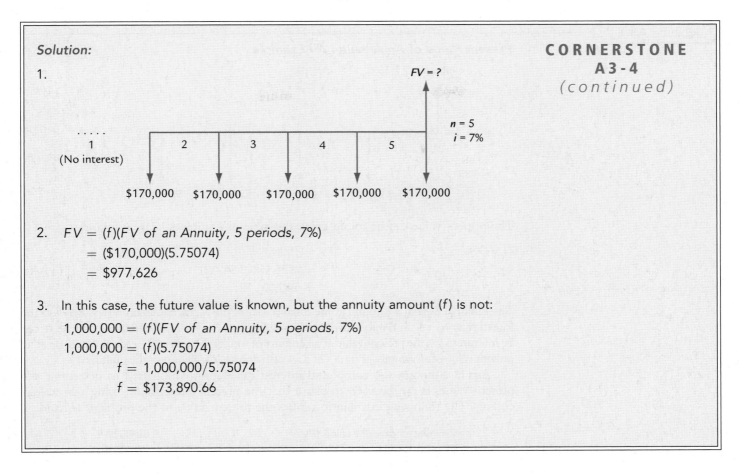

Solution:

1.

2.   FV = (f)(FV of an Annuity, 5 periods, 7%)

   = ($170,000)(5.75074)

   = $977,626

3.   In this case, the future value is known, but the annuity amount (f) is not:

   1,000,000 = (f)(FV of an Annuity, 5 periods, 7%)

   1,000,000 = (f)(5.75074)

   f = 1,000,000/5.75074

   f = $173,890.66

**CORNERSTONE
A3-4**
(continued)

Present Value of an Annuity

The fourth and final basic problem is to find the present value of an annuity. In this problem.

* f represents the amount of each repeating cash flow
* PV the present value of the n future cash flows
* n the number of cash flows and periods
* i the interest (or discount) rate per period

   Problems of this form can be solved by using the following formula:

$$PV = (f)\frac{1 - \dfrac{1}{(1+i)^n}}{i}$$

You can also use the Present Value of an Annuity table (see p. 783) where M_4 is the multiple from Exhibit A3-10 that corresponds to the appropriate values of n and i.

$$PV = (f)(M_4)$$

   The following example illustrates this type of problem and its solution. Assume that **Xerox Corporation** purchased a new machine for its manufacturing operations. The purchase agreement requires Xerox to make four equally-spaced payments of $24,154 each. The interest rate is 8 percent compounded annually and the first cash flow occurs one year after the purchase. Determine the present value of this annuity. This problem, as diagrammed in Exhibit A3-6, assumes Xerox's (the borrower's) perspective. Bear in mind that the same solution techniques are applicable to both the lender's and borrower's perspectives.

Exhibit A3-6

Present Value of An Annuity: An Example

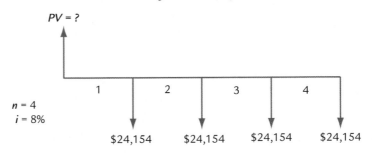

$PV = ?$

$n = 4$
$i = 8\%$

| | 1 | 2 | 3 | 4 |

$24,154 $24,154 $24,154 $24,154

The present value can be found using the table in Exhibit A3-10, as follows:

$$PV = (f)(M_4)$$
$$= (\$24,154)(3.31213)$$
$$= \$80,001.19$$

The multiple 3.31213 is found at the intersection of the 8 percent column ($i = 8\%$) and the fourth row ($n = 4$) in Exhibit A3-10 or by solving for $[1 - (1/1.08^4)]/0.08$. The multiple can be interpreted as the present value of an annuity of four cash flows of $1 each at 8 percent. The present value of an annuity of four $24,154 cash flows is 24,154 times the multiple.

Again, although the compound interest calculation is not used to determine the present value, it can be used to prove that the present value found using the table is correct. The following calculation verifies the present value in the problem at hand:

Calculated present value (PV)	$ 80,001.19
Interest for first year ($80,001.19 × 0.08)	6,400.10
Less: First cash flow	(24,154.00)
Balance at end of first year	$ 62,247.29
Interest for second year ($62,247.29 × 0.08)	4,979.78
Less: Second cash flow	(24,154.00)
Balance at end of second year	$ 43,073.07
Interest for third year ($43,073.07 × 0.08)	3,445.85
Less: Third cash flow	(24,154.00)
Balance at end of third year	$ 22,364.92
Interest for fourth year ($22,364.92 × 0.08)	1,789.19
Less: Fourth cash flow	(24,154.00)
Balance at end of fourth year	$ 0.11

This proof uses a compound interest calculation that is the reverse of the present value formula. If the present value (*PV*) calculated with the formula is correct, then the proof should end with a balance of zero immediately after the last cash flow. This proof ends with a balance of $.11 because of rounding in the proof itself and in the table in Exhibit A3-10. Cornerstone A3-5 provides another illustration of how to compute the present value of an annuity.

CORNERSTONE
A3-5

HOW TO Compute Present Value of an Annuity

Concept:
The present value of an annuity is the value of a series of equal future cash flows made at regular intervals with compound interest discounted back to today.

Information:
Bates Builders purchased a subdivision site from the Second National Bank and Trust Co. on January 1, 2009. Bates gave the bank an installment note. The note

requires Bates to make four annual payments of $600,000 each on December 31 of each year, beginning in 2009. Interest is computed at 9 percent.

CORNERSTONE
A3-5
(continued)

Required:

1. Draw the cash flow diagram for this purchase from Bates' perspective.
2. Calculate the cost of the land as recorded by Bates on January 1, 2009.
3. Provide the journal entry that Bates will make to record the purchase of the land.

Solution:

1.

2. $PV = (f)(PV \text{ of an Annuity, 4 periods, 9\%})$
   $= (\$600,000)(3.23972)$
   $= \$1,943,832$

3.

Land	1,943,832	
Notes Payable		1,943,832

	Stockholders'
Assets = Liabilities +	**Equity**
+1,943,832 +1,943,832	

Summary

This appendix covers the elements of compound interest (time value of money), a measurement technique used to account for cash flows that extend over more than one period. The time value of money is based on a simple idea: A cash flow in the future is less valuable than a cash flow at present. We explained four basic compound interest problems: (1) the future value of a single amount, (2) the present value of a single amount, (3) the future value of an annuity, and (4) the present value of an annuity. We also demonstrated how to use tables to solve these basic problems. We strongly recommend the use of cash flow diagrams for analyzing time-value-of-money problems.

Summary of Learning Objectives

LO1. Explain how compound interest works.
- In transactions involving the borrowing and lending of money, it is customary for the borrower to pay interest.
- With compound interest, interest for the period is added to the account and interest is earned on the total balance in the next period.
- Compound interest calculations require careful specification of the interest period and the interest rate.

LO2. Use future value and present value tables to apply compound interest to accounting transactions.

- Cash flows are described as either
  - single cash flows, or
  - annuities.
- An annuity is a number of equal cash flows made at regular intervals.
- All other cash flows are a series of one or more single cash flows.
- Accounting for such cash flows may require
  - calculation of the amount to which a series of cash flows will grow when interest is compounded (i.e., the future value) or
  - the amount a series of future cash flows is worth today after taking into account compound interest (i.e., the present value).

CORNERSTONE A3-1	How to compute future values using compound interest, page 762
CORNERSTONE A3-2	How to compute future value of a single amount, page 765
CORNERSTONE A3-3	How to compute present value of a single amount, page 768
CORNERSTONE A3-4	How to compute future value of an annuity, page 770
CORNERSTONE A3-5	How to compute present value of an annuity, page 772

CORNERSTONES FOR APPENDIX 3

Key Terms

Annuity, 769

Compound interest, 761

Future value, 762

Interest period, 761

Interest rate, 761

Present value, 763

Time value of money, 761

Discussion Questions

1. Why does money have a time value?
2. Describe the four basic time-value-of-money problems.
3. How is compound interest computed? What is a future value? What is a present value?
4. Define an annuity in general terms. Describe the cash flows related to an annuity from the viewpoint of the lender in terms of receipts and payments.
5. Explain how to use time-value-of-money calculations to measure an installment note liability.

Cornerstone Exercises

OBJECTIVE ➤ 1
CORNERSTONE A3-1

Cornerstone Exercise A3-1 EXPLAIN HOW COMPOUND INTEREST WORKS

Assume you have $6,000.

Required:

Calculate the future value of the $6,000 at 12 percent compounded quarterly for five years.

OBJECTIVE ➤ 2
CORNERSTONE A3-4

Cornerstone Exercise A3-2 USE FUTURE VALUE TABLES TO APPLY COMPOUND INTEREST TO ACCOUNTING TRANSACTIONS

Effingham Lumber makes annual deposits of $500 at 6 percent compounded annually for three years.

Required:

What is the future value of these deposits?

Cornerstone Exercise A3-3 USE FUTURE VALUE AND PRESENT VALUE TABLES TO APPLY COMPOUND INTEREST TO ACCOUNTING TRANSACTIONS

OBJECTIVE ▸ 2
CORNERSTONE A3-2

Lisa inherited $140,000 from an aunt.

Required:

If Lisa decides not to spend her inheritance but to leave the money in her savings account until she retires in 15 years, how much money will she have assuming an annual interest rate of 8 percent, compounded semiannually?

Cornerstone Exercise A3-4 USE FUTURE VALUE AND PRESENT VALUE TABLES TO APPLY COMPOUND INTEREST TO ACCOUNTING TRANSACTIONS

OBJECTIVE ▸ 2
CORNERSTONE A3-4

Tim wants to save some money so that he can make a down payment of $3,000 on a car when he graduates from college in four years.

Required:

If he opens a savings account and earns 3 percent on his money, compounded annually, how much will he have to invest now?

Cornerstone Exercise A3-5 USE FUTURE VALUE AND PRESENT VALUE TABLES TO APPLY COMPOUND INTEREST TO ACCOUNTING TRANSACTIONS

OBJECTIVE ▸ 2
CORNERSTONE A3-4

Joe makes equal deposits of $500 semiannually for four years.

Required:

What is the future value at 8 percent?

Cornerstone Exercise A3-6 USE FUTURE VALUE AND PRESENT VALUE TABLES TO APPLY COMPOUND INTEREST TO ACCOUNTING TRANSACTIONS

OBJECTIVE ▸ 2
CORNERSTONE A3-4

Curtis, a high school math teacher, wants to set up an IRA account into which he will deposit $2,000 per year. He plans to teach for 20 more years and then retire.

Required:

If the interest on his account is 7 percent compounded annually, how much will be in his account when he retires?

Cornerstone Exercise A3-7 USE FUTURE VALUE AND PRESENT VALUE TABLES TO APPLY COMPOUND INTEREST TO ACCOUNTING TRANSACTIONS

OBJECTIVE ▸ 2
CORNERSTONE A3-3

Joan will receive $7,000 in seven years.

Required:

What is the present value at 7 percent compounded annually?

Cornerstone Exercise A3-8 USE FUTURE VALUE AND PRESENT VALUE TABLES TO APPLY COMPOUND INTEREST TO ACCOUNTING TRANSACTIONS

OBJECTIVE ▸ 2
CORNERSTONE A3-3

A bank is willing to lend money at 6 percent interest, compounded annually.

Required:

How much would the bank be willing to loan you in exchange for a payment of $600 four years from now?

OBJECTIVE ▸ 2
CORNERSTONE A3-5

Cornerstone Exercise A3-9 USE FUTURE VALUE AND PRESENT VALUE TABLES TO APPLY COMPOUND INTEREST TO ACCOUNTING TRANSACTIONS

Bill can earn 6 percent.

Required:

How much would have to be deposited in a savings account in order for Bill to be able to make equal annual withdrawals of $200 at the end of each of 10 years? The balance at the end of the last year would be zero.

OBJECTIVE ▸ 2
CORNERSTONE A3-5

Cornerstone Exercise A3-10 USE FUTURE VALUE AND PRESENT VALUE TABLES TO APPLY COMPOUND INTEREST TO ACCOUNTING TRANSACTIONS

Justice wins the lottery. He wins $20,000 per year to be paid to him for 10 years. The state offers him the choice of a cash settlement now instead of the annual payments for 10 years.

Required:

If the interest rate is 6 percent, what is the amount the state will offer for a settlement today?

Exercises

OBJECTIVE ▸ 2

Exercise A3-11 PRACTICE WITH TABLES

Using the appropriate tables in the text,

Required:

Determine:

a. the future value of a single cash flow of $5,000 that earns 7 percent interest compounded annually for 10 years.
b. the future value of an annual annuity of 10 cash flows of $500 each that earns 7 percent compounded annually.
c. The present value of $5,000 to be received 10 years from now, assuming that the interest (discount) rate is 7 percent per year.
d. The present value of an annuity of $500 per year for 10 years for which the interest (discount) rate is 7 percent per year and the first cash flow occurs one year from now.

OBJECTIVE ▸ 2

Exercise A3-12 PRACTICE WITH TABLES

Using the appropriate tables in the text,

Required:

Determine:

a. the present value of $1,200 to be received in seven years, assuming that the interest (discount) rate is 8 percent per year.
b. the present value of an annuity of seven cash flows of $1,200 each (one at the end of each of the next seven years) for which the interest (discount) rate is 8 percent per year.
c. the future value of a single cash flow of $1,200 that earns 8 percent per year for seven years.
d. the future value of an annuity of seven cash flows of $1,200 each (one at the end of each of the next seven years), assuming that the interest rate is 8 percent per year.

OBJECTIVE ▸ 2

Exercise A3-13 FUTURE VALUES

Using the appropriate tables in the text,

Required:

Determine:

a. the future value of a single deposit of $15,000 that earns compound interest for four years at an interest rate of 10 percent per year.

b. the annual interest rate that will produce a future value of $13,416.80 in six years from a single deposit of $8,000.

c. the size of annual cash flows for an annuity of nine cash flows that will produce a future value of $79,428.10 at an interest rate of 9 percent per year.

d. the number of periods required to produce a future value of $17,755.50 from an initial deposit of $7,500 if the annual interest rate is 9 percent.

Exercise A3-14 FUTURE VALUES AND LONG-TERM INVESTMENTS

Pueblo Pottery, Inc., engaged in the following transactions during 2009:

a. On January 1, 2009, Pueblo deposited $12,000 in a certificate of deposit paying 6 percent interest compounded semiannually (3 percent per six-month period). The certificate will mature on December 31, 2012.

b. On January 1, 2009, Pueblo established an account with Durango Investment Management. Pueblo will make quarterly payments of $2,500 to Durango beginning on March 31, 2009, and ending on December 31, 2010. Durango guarantees an interest rate of 8 percent compounded quarterly (2 percent per three-month period).

Required:

1. Prepare the cash flow diagram for each of these two investments.
2. Calculate the amount to which each of these investments will accumulate at maturity.

Exercise A3-15 FUTURE VALUES

On January 1, you make a single deposit of $8,000 in an investment account that earns 8 percent interest.

Required:

1. Calculate the balance in the account in five years assuming the interest is compounded annually.
2. Determine how much interest will be earned on the account in seven years if interest is compounded annually.
3. Calculate the balance in the account in five years assuming the 8 percent interest is compounded quarterly.

Exercise A3-16 FUTURE VALUES

OBJECTIVE ▸ 2

Fargo Transit Company invested $70,000 in a tax-anticipation note on June 30, 2009. The note earns 12 percent interest compounded monthly (1 percent per month) and matures on March 31, 2010.

Required:

1. Prepare the cash flow diagram for this investment.
2. Determine the amount Fargo will receive when the note matures.
3. Determine how much interest Fargo will earn on this investment from June 30, 2009, through December 31, 2009.

Exercise A3-17 PRESENT VALUES

Using the appropriate tables in the text,

Required:

Determine:

a. the present value of a single $14,000 cash flow in seven years if the interest (discount) rate is 8 percent per year.

b. the number of periods for which $5,820 must be invested at an annual interest (discount) rate of 7 percent to produce an investment balance of $10,000.

c. the size of the annual cash flow for a 25-year annuity with a present value of $49,113 and an annual interest rate of 9 percent. One payment is made at the end of each year.

d. the annual interest rate at which an investment of $2,542 will provide for a single $4,000 cash flow in four years.

e. the annual interest rate earned by an annuity that costs $17,119 and provides 15 payments of $2,000 each, one at the end of each of the next 15 years.

OBJECTIVE ▶ 2   ## Exercise A3-18 PRESENT VALUES

Ramon Company signed notes to make the following two purchases on January 1, 2009:

a. a new truck for $60,000, with payment deferred until December 31, 2010. The appropriate interest rate is 9 percent compounded annually.
b. a small building from Wandrow Builders. The terms of the purchase require a $75,000 payment at the end of each quarter, beginning March 31, 2009, and ending June 30, 2011. The appropriate interest rate is 2 percent per quarter.

Required:

1. Prepare the cash flow diagrams for these two purchases.
2. Prepare the entries to record these purchases in Ramon's journal.
3. Prepare the cash payment and interest expense entries for purchase *b* at March 31, 2009, and June 30, 2009.
4. Prepare the adjusting entry for purchase *a* at December 31, 2009.

OBJECTIVE ▶ 2   ## Exercise A3-19 PRESENT VALUES

You have an opportunity to purchase a government security that will pay $200,000 in five years.

Required:

1. Calculate what you would pay for the security if the appropriate interest (discount) rate is 6 percent compounded annually.
2. Calculate what you would pay for the security if the appropriate interest (discount) rate is 10 percent compounded annually.
3. Calculate what you would pay for the security if the appropriate interest (discount) rate is 6 percent compounded semiannually.

OBJECTIVE ▶ 2   ## Exercise A3-20 FUTURE VALUES OF AN ANNUITY

On December 31, 2009, you sign a contract to make annual deposits of $4,200 in an investment account that earns 10 percent. The first deposit is made on December 31, 2009.

Required:

1. Calculate what the balance in this investment account will be just after the seventh deposit has been made if interest is compounded annually.
2. Determine how much interest will have been earned on this investment account just after the seventh deposit has been made if interest is compounded annually.

OBJECTIVE ▶ 2   ## Exercise A3-21 FUTURE VALUES OF AN ANNUITY

Purdue Savings Bank pays 8 percent interest compounded weekly (0.154 percent per week) on savings accounts. The bank has asked your help in preparing a table to show potential customers the number of dollars that will be available at the end of 10-, 20-, 30-, and 40-week periods during which there are weekly deposits of $1, $5, $10, or $50. The following data are available:

Length of Annuity	Future Value of Annuity at an Interest Rate of 0.154% per Week
10 weeks	10.0696
20 weeks	20.2953
30 weeks	30.6796
40 weeks	41.2250

Required:

Prepare and complete a table similar to the one below.

	Amount of Each Deposit			
Number of Deposits	$1	$5	$10	$50
10				
20				
30				
40				

Exercise A3-22 FUTURE VALUE OF A SINGLE CASH FLOW

OBJECTIVE ➤ 2

Shubert Products has just been paid $25,000 by Apex Enterprises, which has owed Shubert this amount for 30 months but been unable to pay because of financial difficulties. Had it been able to invest this cash, Shubert assumes that it would have earned an interest rate of 12 percent compounded monthly (1 percent per month).

Required:

1. Prepare a cash flow diagram for the investment that could have been made if Apex had paid 30 months ago.
2. Determine how much Shubert has lost by not receiving the $25,000 when it was due 30 months ago.
3. Indicate whether Shubert would make an entry to account for this loss. Why, or why not?

Exercise A3-23 INSTALLMENT SALE

OBJECTIVE ➤ 2

Johnson Properties owns land on which natural gas wells are located. Columbus Gas Company signs a note to buy this land from Johnson on January 1, 2009. The note requires Columbus to pay Johnson $775,000 per year for 25 years. The first payment is to be made on December 31, 2009. The appropriate interest rate is 9 percent compounded annually.

Required:

1. Prepare a diagram of the appropriate cash flows from Columbus Gas Company's perspective.
2. Determine the present value of the payments.
3. Indicate what entry Columbus Gas should make at January 1, 2009.

Exercise A3-24 INSTALLMENT SALE

OBJECTIVE ➤ 2

Jeffrey's Billiards sold a pool table to C. Cobbs on October 31, 2009. The terms of the sale are no money down and payments of $50 per month for 30 months, with the first payment due on November 30, 2009. The table they sold to Cobbs cost Jeffrey's $800. Jeffrey's uses an interest rate of 12 percent compounded monthly (1 percent per month).

Required:

1. Prepare the cash flow diagram for this sale.
2. Calculate the amount of revenue Jeffrey's should record on October 31, 2009.
3. Prepare the entry to record the sale on October 31. Assume that Jeffrey's records cost of goods sold at the time of the sale (perpetual inventory accounting).
4. Determine how much interest revenue Jeffrey's will record from October 31, 2009, through December 31, 2009.
5. Determine how much Jeffrey's 2009 income before taxes increased by this sale.

Exhibit A3-7

Future Value of a Single Amount

$$FV = 1 \,(1 + i)^n$$

n/i	1%	2%	3%	4%	5%	6%	7%	8%	9%	10%	12%	14%	16%	18%	20%	25%	30%
1	1.01000	1.02000	1.03000	1.04000	1.05000	1.06000	1.07000	1.08000	1.09000	1.10000	1.12000	1.14000	1.16000	1.18000	1.20000	1.25000	1.30000
2	1.02010	1.04040	1.06090	1.08160	1.10250	1.12360	1.14490	1.16640	1.18810	1.21000	1.25440	1.29960	1.34560	1.39240	1.44000	1.56250	1.69000
3	1.03030	1.06121	1.09273	1.12486	1.15763	1.19102	1.22504	1.25971	1.29503	1.33100	1.40493	1.48154	1.56090	1.64303	1.72800	1.95313	2.19700
4	1.04060	1.08243	1.12551	1.16986	1.21551	1.26248	1.31080	1.36049	1.41158	1.46410	1.57352	1.68896	1.81064	1.93878	2.07360	2.44141	2.85610
5	1.05101	1.10408	1.15927	1.21665	1.27628	1.33823	1.40255	1.46933	1.53862	1.61051	1.76234	1.92541	2.10034	2.28776	2.48832	3.05176	3.71293
6	1.06152	1.12616	1.19405	1.26532	1.34010	1.41852	1.50073	1.58687	1.67710	1.77156	1.97382	2.19497	2.43640	2.69955	2.98598	3.81470	4.82681
7	1.07214	1.14869	1.22987	1.31593	1.40710	1.50363	1.60578	1.71382	1.82804	1.94872	2.21068	2.50227	2.82622	3.18547	3.58318	4.76837	6.27485
8	1.08286	1.17166	1.26677	1.36857	1.47746	1.59385	1.71819	1.85093	1.99256	2.14359	2.47596	2.85259	3.27841	3.75886	4.29982	5.96046	8.15731
9	1.09369	1.19509	1.30477	1.42331	1.55133	1.68948	1.83846	1.99900	2.17189	2.35795	2.77308	3.25195	3.80296	4.43545	5.15978	7.45058	10.60450
10	1.10462	1.21899	1.34392	1.48024	1.62889	1.79085	1.96715	2.15892	2.36736	2.59374	3.10585	3.70722	4.41144	5.23384	6.19174	9.31323	13.78585
11	1.11567	1.24337	1.38423	1.53945	1.71034	1.89830	2.10485	2.33164	2.58043	2.85312	3.47855	4.22623	5.11726	6.17593	7.43008	11.64153	17.92160
12	1.12683	1.26824	1.42576	1.60103	1.79586	2.01220	2.25219	2.51817	2.81266	3.13843	3.89598	4.81790	5.93603	7.28759	8.91610	14.55192	23.29809
13	1.13809	1.29361	1.46853	1.66507	1.88565	2.13293	2.40985	2.71962	3.06580	3.45227	4.36349	5.49241	6.88579	8.59936	10.69932	18.18989	30.28751
14	1.14947	1.31948	1.51259	1.73168	1.97993	2.26090	2.57853	2.93719	3.34173	3.79750	4.88711	6.26135	7.98752	10.14724	12.83918	22.73737	39.37376
15	1.16097	1.34587	1.55797	1.80094	2.07893	2.39656	2.75903	3.17217	3.64248	4.17725	5.47357	7.13794	9.26552	11.97375	15.40702	28.42171	51.18589
16	1.17258	1.37279	1.60471	1.87298	2.18287	2.54035	2.95216	3.42594	3.97031	4.59497	6.13039	8.13725	10.74800	14.12902	18.48843	35.52714	66.54166
17	1.18430	1.40024	1.65285	1.94790	2.29202	2.69277	3.15882	3.70002	4.32763	5.05447	6.86604	9.27646	12.46768	16.67225	22.18611	44.40892	86.50416
18	1.19615	1.42825	1.70243	2.02582	2.40662	2.85434	3.37993	3.99602	4.71712	5.55992	7.68997	10.57517	14.46251	19.67325	26.62333	55.51115	112.45541
19	1.20811	1.45681	1.75351	2.10685	2.52695	3.02560	3.61653	4.31570	5.14166	6.11591	8.61276	12.05569	16.77652	23.21444	31.94800	69.38894	146.19203
20	1.22019	1.48595	1.80611	2.19112	2.65330	3.20714	3.86968	4.66096	5.60441	6.72750	9.64629	13.74349	19.46076	27.39303	38.33760	86.73617	190.04964
21	1.23239	1.51567	1.86029	2.27877	2.78596	3.39956	4.14056	5.03383	6.10881	7.40025	10.80385	15.66758	22.57448	32.32378	46.00512	108.42022	247.06453
22	1.24472	1.54598	1.91610	2.36992	2.92526	3.60354	4.43040	5.43654	6.65860	8.14027	12.10031	17.86104	26.18640	38.14206	55.20614	135.52527	321.18389
23	1.25716	1.57690	1.97359	2.46472	3.07152	3.81975	4.74053	5.87146	7.25787	8.95430	13.55235	20.36158	30.37622	45.00763	66.24737	169.40659	417.53905
24	1.26973	1.60844	2.03279	2.56330	3.22510	4.04893	5.07237	6.34118	7.91108	9.84973	15.17863	23.21221	35.23642	53.10901	79.49685	211.75824	542.80077
25	1.28243	1.64061	2.09378	2.66584	3.38635	4.29187	5.42743	6.84848	8.62308	10.83471	17.00006	26.46192	40.87424	62.66863	95.39622	264.69780	705.64100
26	1.29526	1.67342	2.15659	2.77247	3.55567	4.54938	5.80735	7.39635	9.39916	11.91818	19.04007	30.16658	47.41412	73.94898	114.47546	330.87225	917.33330
27	1.30821	1.70689	2.22129	2.88337	3.73346	4.82235	6.21387	7.98806	10.24508	13.10999	21.32488	34.38991	55.00038	87.25980	137.37055	413.59031	1192.53329
28	1.32129	1.74102	2.28793	2.99870	3.92013	5.11169	6.64884	8.62711	11.16714	14.42099	23.88387	39.20449	63.80044	102.96656	164.84466	516.98788	1550.29328
29	1.33450	1.77584	2.35657	3.11865	4.11614	5.41839	7.11426	9.31727	12.17218	15.86309	26.74993	44.69312	74.00851	121.50054	197.81359	646.23485	2015.38126
30	1.34785	1.81136	2.42726	3.24340	4.32194	5.74349	7.61226	10.06266	13.26768	17.44940	29.95992	50.95016	85.84988	143.37064	237.37631	807.79357	2619.99564

Exhibit A3-8

Present Value of a Single Amount

$$PV = \frac{1}{(1+i)^n}$$

n/i	1%	2%	3%	4%	5%	6%	7%	8%	9%	10%	12%	14%	16%	18%	20%	25%	30%
1	0.99010	0.98039	0.97087	0.96154	0.95238	0.94340	0.93458	0.92593	0.91743	0.90909	0.89286	0.87719	0.86207	0.84746	0.83333	0.80000	0.76923
2	0.98030	0.96117	0.94260	0.92456	0.90703	0.89000	0.87344	0.85734	0.84168	0.82645	0.79719	0.76947	0.74316	0.71818	0.69444	0.64000	0.59172
3	0.97059	0.94232	0.91514	0.88900	0.86384	0.83962	0.81630	0.79383	0.77218	0.75131	0.71178	0.67497	0.64066	0.60863	0.57870	0.51200	0.45517
4	0.96098	0.92385	0.88849	0.85480	0.82270	0.79209	0.76290	0.73503	0.70843	0.68301	0.63552	0.59208	0.55229	0.51579	0.48225	0.40960	0.35013
5	0.95147	0.90573	0.86261	0.82193	0.78353	0.74726	0.71299	0.68058	0.64993	0.62092	0.56743	0.51937	0.47611	0.43711	0.40188	0.32768	0.26933
6	0.94205	0.88797	0.83748	0.79031	0.74622	0.70496	0.66634	0.63017	0.59627	0.56447	0.50663	0.45559	0.41044	0.37043	0.33490	0.26214	0.20718
7	0.93272	0.87056	0.81309	0.75992	0.71068	0.66506	0.62275	0.58349	0.54703	0.51316	0.45235	0.39964	0.35383	0.31393	0.27908	0.20972	0.15937
8	0.92348	0.85349	0.78941	0.73069	0.67684	0.62741	0.58201	0.54027	0.50187	0.46651	0.40388	0.35056	0.30503	0.26604	0.23257	0.16777	0.12259
9	0.91434	0.83676	0.76642	0.70259	0.64461	0.59190	0.54393	0.50025	0.46043	0.42410	0.36061	0.30751	0.26295	0.22546	0.19381	0.13422	0.09430
10	0.90529	0.82035	0.74409	0.67556	0.61391	0.55839	0.50835	0.46319	0.42241	0.38554	0.32197	0.26974	0.22668	0.19106	0.16151	0.10737	0.07254
11	0.89632	0.80426	0.72242	0.64958	0.58468	0.52679	0.47509	0.42888	0.38753	0.35049	0.28748	0.23662	0.19542	0.16192	0.13459	0.08590	0.05580
12	0.88745	0.78849	0.70138	0.62460	0.55684	0.49697	0.44401	0.39711	0.35553	0.31863	0.25668	0.20756	0.16846	0.13722	0.11216	0.06872	0.04292
13	0.87866	0.77303	0.68095	0.60057	0.53032	0.46884	0.41496	0.36770	0.32618	0.28966	0.22917	0.18207	0.14523	0.11629	0.09346	0.05498	0.03302
14	0.86996	0.75788	0.66112	0.57748	0.50507	0.44230	0.38782	0.34046	0.29925	0.26333	0.20462	0.15971	0.12520	0.09855	0.07789	0.04398	0.02540
15	0.86135	0.74301	0.64186	0.55526	0.48102	0.41727	0.36245	0.31524	0.27454	0.23939	0.18270	0.14010	0.10793	0.08352	0.06491	0.03518	0.01954
16	0.85282	0.72845	0.62317	0.53391	0.45811	0.39365	0.33873	0.29189	0.25187	0.21763	0.16312	0.12289	0.09304	0.07078	0.05409	0.02815	0.01503
17	0.84438	0.71416	0.60502	0.51337	0.43630	0.37136	0.31657	0.27027	0.23107	0.19784	0.14564	0.10780	0.08021	0.05998	0.04507	0.02252	0.01156
18	0.83602	0.70016	0.58739	0.49363	0.41552	0.35034	0.29586	0.25025	0.21199	0.17986	0.13004	0.09456	0.06914	0.05083	0.03756	0.01801	0.00889
19	0.82774	0.68643	0.57029	0.47464	0.39573	0.33051	0.27651	0.23171	0.19449	0.16351	0.11611	0.08295	0.05961	0.04308	0.03130	0.01441	0.00684
20	0.81954	0.67297	0.55368	0.45639	0.37689	0.31180	0.25842	0.21455	0.17843	0.14864	0.10367	0.07276	0.05139	0.03651	0.02608	0.01153	0.00526
21	0.81143	0.65978	0.53755	0.43883	0.35894	0.29416	0.24151	0.19866	0.16370	0.13513	0.09256	0.06383	0.04430	0.03094	0.02174	0.00922	0.00405
22	0.80340	0.64684	0.52189	0.42196	0.34185	0.27751	0.22571	0.18394	0.15018	0.12285	0.08264	0.05599	0.03819	0.02622	0.01811	0.00738	0.00311
23	0.79544	0.63416	0.50669	0.40573	0.32557	0.26180	0.21095	0.17032	0.13778	0.11168	0.07379	0.04911	0.03292	0.02222	0.01509	0.00590	0.00239
24	0.78757	0.62172	0.49193	0.39012	0.31007	0.24698	0.19715	0.15770	0.12640	0.10153	0.06588	0.04308	0.02838	0.01883	0.01258	0.00472	0.00184
25	0.77977	0.60953	0.47761	0.37512	0.29530	0.23300	0.18425	0.14602	0.11597	0.09230	0.05882	0.03779	0.02447	0.01596	0.01048	0.00378	0.00142
26	0.77205	0.59758	0.46369	0.36069	0.28124	0.21981	0.17220	0.13520	0.10639	0.08391	0.05252	0.03315	0.02109	0.01352	0.00874	0.00302	0.00109
27	0.76440	0.58586	0.45019	0.34682	0.26785	0.20737	0.16093	0.12519	0.09761	0.07628	0.04689	0.02908	0.01818	0.01146	0.00728	0.00242	0.00084
28	0.75684	0.57437	0.43708	0.33348	0.25509	0.19563	0.15040	0.11591	0.08955	0.06934	0.04187	0.02551	0.01567	0.00971	0.00607	0.00193	0.00065
29	0.74934	0.56311	0.42435	0.32065	0.24295	0.18456	0.14056	0.10733	0.08215	0.06304	0.03738	0.02237	0.01351	0.00823	0.00506	0.00155	0.00050
30	0.74192	0.55207	0.41199	0.30832	0.23138	0.17411	0.13137	0.09938	0.07537	0.05731	0.03338	0.01963	0.01165	0.00697	0.00421	0.00124	0.00038

Future Value of an Annuity

$$FVA = \frac{(1 + i)^n - 1}{i}$$

n/i	1%	2%	3%	4%	5%	6%	7%	8%	9%	10%	12%	14%	16%	18%	20%	25%	30%
1	1.00000	1.00000	1.00000	1.00000	1.00000	1.00000	1.00000	1.00000	1.00000	1.00000	1.00000	1.00000	1.00000	1.00000	1.00000	1.00000	1.00000
2	2.01000	2.02000	2.03000	2.04000	2.05000	2.06000	2.07000	2.08000	2.09000	2.10000	2.12000	2.14000	2.16000	2.18000	2.20000	2.25000	2.30000
3	3.03010	3.06040	3.09090	3.12160	3.15250	3.18360	3.21490	3.24640	3.27810	3.31000	3.37440	3.43960	3.50560	3.57240	3.64000	3.81250	3.99000
4	4.06040	4.12161	4.18363	4.24646	4.31013	4.37462	4.43994	4.50611	4.57313	4.64100	4.77933	4.92114	5.06650	5.21543	5.36800	5.76563	6.18700
5	5.10101	5.20404	5.30914	5.41632	5.52563	5.63709	5.75074	5.86660	5.98471	6.10510	6.35285	6.61010	6.87714	7.15421	7.44160	8.20703	9.04310
6	6.15202	6.30812	6.46841	6.63298	6.80191	6.97532	7.15329	7.33593	7.52333	7.71561	8.11519	8.53552	8.97748	9.44197	9.92992	11.25879	12.75603
7	7.21354	7.43428	7.66246	7.89829	8.14201	8.39384	8.65402	8.92280	9.20043	9.48717	10.08901	10.73049	11.41387	12.14152	12.91590	15.07349	17.58284
8	8.28567	8.58297	8.89234	9.21423	9.54911	9.89747	10.25980	10.63663	11.02847	11.43589	12.29969	13.23276	14.24009	15.32700	16.49908	19.84186	23.85769
9	9.36853	9.75463	10.15911	10.58280	11.02656	11.49132	11.97799	12.48756	13.02104	13.57948	14.77566	16.08535	17.51851	19.08585	20.79890	25.80232	32.01500
10	10.46221	10.94972	11.46388	12.00611	12.57789	13.18079	13.81645	14.48656	15.19293	15.93742	17.54874	19.33730	21.32147	23.52131	25.95868	33.25290	42.61950
11	11.56683	12.16872	12.80780	13.48635	14.20679	14.97164	15.78360	16.64549	17.56029	18.53117	20.65458	23.04452	25.73290	28.75514	32.15042	42.56613	56.40535
12	12.68250	13.41209	14.19203	15.02581	15.91713	16.86994	17.88845	18.97713	20.14072	21.38428	24.13313	27.27075	30.85017	34.93107	39.58050	54.20766	74.32695
13	13.80933	14.68033	15.61779	16.62684	17.71298	18.88214	20.14064	21.49530	22.95338	24.52271	28.02911	32.08865	36.78620	42.21866	48.49660	68.75958	97.62504
14	14.94742	15.97394	17.08632	18.29191	19.59863	21.01507	22.55049	24.21492	26.01919	27.97498	32.39260	37.58107	43.67199	50.81802	59.19592	86.94947	127.91255
15	16.09690	17.29342	18.59891	20.02359	21.57856	23.27597	25.12902	27.15211	29.36092	31.77248	37.27971	43.84241	51.65951	60.96527	72.03511	109.68684	167.28631
16	17.25786	18.63929	20.15688	21.82453	23.65749	25.67253	27.88805	30.32428	33.00340	35.94973	42.75328	50.98035	60.92503	72.93901	87.44213	138.10855	218.47220
17	18.43044	20.01207	21.76159	23.69751	25.84037	28.21288	30.84022	33.75023	36.97370	40.54470	48.88367	59.11760	71.67303	87.06804	105.93056	173.63568	285.01386
18	19.61475	21.41231	23.41444	25.64541	28.13238	30.90565	33.99903	37.45024	41.30134	45.59917	55.74971	68.39407	84.14072	103.74028	128.11667	218.04460	371.51802
19	20.81090	22.84056	25.11687	27.67123	30.53900	33.75999	37.37896	41.44626	46.01846	51.15909	63.43968	78.96923	98.60323	123.41353	154.74000	273.55576	483.97343
20	22.01900	24.29737	26.87037	29.77808	33.06595	36.78559	40.99549	45.76196	51.16012	57.27500	72.05244	91.02493	115.37975	146.62797	186.68800	342.94470	630.16546
21	23.23919	25.78332	28.67649	31.96920	35.71925	39.99273	44.86518	50.42292	56.76453	64.00250	81.69874	104.76842	134.84051	174.02100	225.02560	429.68087	820.21510
22	24.47159	27.29898	30.53678	34.24797	38.50521	43.39229	49.00574	55.45676	62.87334	71.40275	92.50258	120.43600	157.41499	206.34479	271.03072	538.10109	1067.27963
23	25.71630	28.84496	32.45288	36.61789	41.43048	46.99583	53.43614	60.89330	69.53194	79.54302	104.60289	138.29704	183.60138	244.48685	326.23686	673.62636	1388.46351
24	26.97346	30.42186	34.42647	39.08260	44.50200	50.81558	58.17667	66.76476	76.78981	88.49733	118.15524	158.65862	213.97761	289.49448	392.48424	843.03295	1806.00257
25	28.24320	32.03030	36.45926	41.64591	47.72710	54.86451	63.24904	73.10594	84.70090	98.34706	133.33387	181.87083	249.21402	342.60349	471.98108	1054.79118	2348.80334
26	29.52563	33.67091	38.55304	44.31174	51.11345	59.15638	68.67647	79.95442	93.32398	109.18177	150.33393	208.33274	290.08827	405.27211	567.37730	1319.48898	3054.44434
27	30.82089	35.34432	40.70963	47.08421	54.66913	63.70577	74.48382	87.35077	102.72313	121.09994	169.37401	238.49933	337.50239	479.22109	681.85276	1650.36123	3971.77764
28	32.12910	37.05121	42.93092	49.96758	58.40258	68.52811	80.69769	95.33883	112.96822	134.20994	190.69889	272.88923	392.50277	566.48089	819.22331	2063.95153	5164.31093
29	33.45039	38.79223	45.21885	52.96629	62.32271	73.63980	87.34653	103.96594	124.13536	148.63093	214.58275	312.09373	456.30322	669.44745	984.06797	2580.93941	6714.60421
30	34.78489	40.56808	47.57542	56.08494	66.43885	79.05819	94.46079	113.28321	136.30754	164.49402	241.33268	356.78685	530.31173	790.94799	1181.88157	3227.17427	8729.98548

Exhibit A3-10

Present Value of an Annuity

$$PVA = \frac{1 - \frac{1}{(1+i)^n}}{i}$$

n/i	1%	2%	3%	4%	5%	6%	7%	8%	9%	10%	12%	14%	16%	18%	20%	25%	30%
1	0.99010	0.98039	0.97087	0.96154	0.95238	0.94340	0.93458	0.92593	0.91743	0.90909	0.89286	0.87719	0.86207	0.84746	0.83333	0.80000	0.76923
2	1.97040	1.94156	1.91347	1.88609	1.85941	1.83339	1.80802	1.78326	1.75911	1.73554	1.69005	1.64666	1.60523	1.56564	1.52778	1.44000	1.36095
3	2.94099	2.88388	2.82861	2.77509	2.72325	2.67301	2.62432	2.57710	2.53129	2.48685	2.40183	2.32163	2.24589	2.17427	2.10648	1.95200	1.81611
4	3.90197	3.80773	3.71710	3.62990	3.54595	3.46511	3.38721	3.31213	3.23972	3.16987	3.03735	2.91371	2.79818	2.69006	2.58873	2.36160	2.16624
5	4.85343	4.71346	4.57971	4.45182	4.32948	4.21236	4.10020	3.99271	3.88965	3.79079	3.60478	3.43308	3.27429	3.12717	2.99061	2.68928	2.43557
6	5.79548	5.60143	5.41719	5.24214	5.07569	4.91732	4.76654	4.62288	4.48592	4.35526	4.11141	3.88867	3.68474	3.49760	3.32551	2.95142	2.64275
7	6.72819	6.47199	6.23028	6.00205	5.78637	5.58238	5.38929	5.20637	5.03295	4.86842	4.56376	4.28830	4.03857	3.81153	3.60459	3.16114	2.80211
8	7.65168	7.32548	7.01969	6.73274	6.46321	6.20979	5.97130	5.74664	5.53482	5.33493	4.96764	4.63886	4.34359	4.07757	3.83716	3.32891	2.92470
9	8.56602	8.16224	7.78611	7.43533	7.10782	6.80169	6.51523	6.24689	5.99525	5.75902	5.32825	4.94637	4.60654	4.30302	4.03097	3.46313	3.01900
10	9.47130	8.98259	8.53020	8.11090	7.72173	7.36009	7.02358	6.71008	6.41766	6.14457	5.65022	5.21612	4.83323	4.49409	4.19247	3.57050	3.09154
11	10.36763	9.78685	9.25262	8.76048	8.30641	7.88687	7.49867	7.13896	6.80519	6.49506	5.93770	5.45273	5.02864	4.65601	4.32706	3.65640	3.14734
12	11.25508	10.57534	9.95400	9.38507	8.86325	8.38384	7.94269	7.53608	7.16073	6.81369	6.19437	5.66029	5.19711	4.79322	4.43922	3.72512	3.19026
13	12.13374	11.34837	10.63496	9.98565	9.39357	8.85268	8.35765	7.90378	7.48690	7.10336	6.42355	5.84236	5.34233	4.90951	4.53268	3.78010	3.22328
14	13.00370	12.10625	11.29607	10.56312	9.89864	9.29498	8.74547	8.24424	7.78615	7.36669	6.62817	6.00207	5.46753	5.00806	4.61057	3.82408	3.24867
15	13.86505	12.84926	11.93794	11.11839	10.37966	9.71225	9.10791	8.55948	8.06069	7.60608	6.81086	6.14217	5.57546	5.09158	4.67547	3.85926	3.26821
16	14.71787	13.57771	12.56110	11.65230	10.83777	10.10590	9.44665	8.85137	8.31256	7.82371	6.97399	6.26506	5.66850	5.16235	4.72956	3.88741	3.28324
17	15.56225	14.29187	13.16612	12.16567	11.27407	10.47726	9.76322	9.12164	8.54363	8.02155	7.11963	6.37286	5.74870	5.22233	4.77463	3.90993	3.29480
18	16.39827	14.99203	13.75351	12.65930	11.68959	10.82760	10.05909	9.37189	8.75563	8.20141	7.24967	6.46742	5.81785	5.27316	4.81219	3.92794	3.30369
19	17.22601	15.67846	14.32380	13.13394	12.08532	11.15812	10.33560	9.60360	8.95011	8.36492	7.36578	6.55037	5.87746	5.31624	4.84350	3.94235	3.31053
20	18.04555	16.35143	14.87747	13.59033	12.46221	11.46992	10.59401	9.81815	9.12855	8.51356	7.46944	6.62313	5.92884	5.35275	4.86958	3.95388	3.31579
21	18.85698	17.01121	15.41502	14.02916	12.82115	11.76408	10.83553	10.01680	9.29224	8.64869	7.56200	6.68696	5.97314	5.38368	4.89132	3.96311	3.31984
22	19.66038	17.65805	15.93692	14.45112	13.16300	12.04158	11.06124	10.20074	9.44243	8.77154	7.64465	6.74294	6.01133	5.40990	4.90943	3.97049	3.32296
23	20.45582	18.29220	16.44361	14.85684	13.48857	12.30338	11.27219	10.37106	9.58021	8.88322	7.71843	6.79206	6.04425	5.43212	4.92453	3.97639	3.32535
24	21.24339	18.91393	16.93554	15.24696	13.79864	12.55036	11.46933	10.52876	9.70661	8.98474	7.78432	6.83514	6.07263	5.45095	4.93710	3.98111	3.32719
25	22.02316	19.52346	17.41315	15.62208	14.09394	12.78336	11.65358	10.67478	9.82258	9.07704	7.84314	6.87293	6.09709	5.46691	4.94759	3.98489	3.32861
26	22.79520	20.12104	17.87684	15.98277	14.37519	13.00317	11.82578	10.80998	9.92897	9.16095	7.89566	6.90608	6.11818	5.48043	4.95632	3.98791	3.32970
27	23.55961	20.70690	18.32703	16.32959	14.64303	13.21053	11.98671	10.93516	10.02658	9.23722	7.94255	6.93515	6.13636	5.49189	4.96360	3.99033	3.33054
28	24.31644	21.28127	18.76411	16.66306	14.89813	13.40616	12.13711	11.05108	10.11613	9.30657	7.98442	6.96066	6.15204	5.50160	4.96967	3.99226	3.33118
29	25.06579	21.84438	19.18845	16.98371	15.14107	13.59072	12.27767	11.15841	10.19828	9.36961	8.02181	6.98304	6.16555	5.50983	4.97472	3.99381	3.33168
30	25.80771	22.39646	19.60044	17.29203	15.37245	13.76483	12.40904	11.25778	10.27365	9.42691	8.05518	7.00266	6.17720	5.51681	4.97894	3.99505	3.33206

Appendix

4

International Financial Reporting Standards

After studying Appendix 4, you should be able to:

1 Understand and describe some of the important aspects of international financial reporting standards.

International Financial Reporting

Business is becoming an increasingly global activity as companies conduct operations across national boundaries. Not only are companies engaging in international transactions, companies are increasingly seeking capital from foreign stock exchanges. Due to a variety of factors (e.g., cultural differences, differences in legal systems, differences in business environments), the historical development of accounting standards on a country-by-country basis has led to considerable diversity in financial accounting practices. To facilitate the conduct of business in an international environment, there has been increasing interest in the development of international accounting standards. The purpose of this appendix is to address some of the more frequently asked questions with regard to *international financial reporting standards (IFRS)*.

What Are IFRS?

IFRS is a general term that describes an international set of generally accepted accounting standards. IFRS encompasses both international accounting standards (IAS) issued prior to 2001 and international financial reporting standards issued after 2001. In addition, IFRS includes interpretations of these standards. IFRS are generally considered less detailed and more concept-based than U.S. GAAP. These international financial reporting standards are quickly gaining global acceptance. IFRS are currently used by over 100 countries, including European Union countries and Australia. Countries such as Israel, Chile, Korea, Brazil, and Canada are expected to transition to IFRS by 2011. Over the last several years, IFRS have assumed the role as the common language of financial reporting in much of the world.

When Are IFRS Expected to Be Used in the United States?

The United States currently allows foreign companies who trade on U.S. stock exchanges to use IFRS without a reconciliation to U.S. GAAP. The Securities and Exchange Commission (SEC) has proposed a "roadmap" for the mandatory adoption of IFRS by U.S. companies. Under this roadmap, adoption of IFRS in the United States is targeted to begin in 2014; however, several milestones (e.g., continued improvement in IFRS accounting standards and progress in IFRS education and training in the United States) would have to be achieved prior to the SEC mandating the use of IFRS for all U.S. companies. Early adoption of IFRS will be allowed for a small number of U.S. companies (about 110 companies) beginning in December 2009. Clearly, the use of IFRS for U.S. companies is not a matter of "if" it will occur but "when" it will occur.

Who Develops IFRS?

IFRS are developed by the *International Accounting Standards Board (IASB)*. The IASB is an independent, privately-funded accounting standard-setting body which consists of 14 members from nine countries.[1] The goal of the IASB is to develop a single set of high-quality accounting standards that result in transparent and comparable information reported in general purpose financial statements. The IASB is overseen by the International Accounting Standards Committee (IASC) Foundation. The IASC Foundation funds, appoints the members of, and oversees the IASB. In addition to the IASB, the International Financial Reporting Interpretations Committee (IFRIC) reviews and interprets IFRS that are developed by the IASB. Finally, the Standards Advisory Council (SAC) advises the IASB on a number of issues, such as items which should be on the IASB agenda, input on the timetable of the various IASB projects, and advice on various aspects of these projects.

---

[1] The IASB is considering increasing the number of members from 14 to 16. If this is approved, the change is not expected to take plus until 2012.

How Long Has the IASB Been Issuing Standards?

International standard setting actually began in 1973 with the formation of the IASC. Between 1973 and 1988, the IASC completed a set of core standards, which began to gain global acceptance. In all, the IASC issued 41 International Accounting Standards (IAS). In 2001, the IASB was established as the successor organization of the IASC and assumed the standard-setting responsibilities from the IASC. The IASB endorsed the standards of the IASC and began issuing its own standards, which are called International Financial Reporting Standards (IFRS). At this point, with support from the Securities and Exchange Commission (SEC), the Financial Accounting Standards Board (FASB), the European Union (EU), and others, the movement to a single set of high-quality international accounting standards began to pick up considerable momentum. Therefore, IFRS represent a relatively young body of accounting literature.

What Organizations Have Played a Role in the Development of IFRS?

In 2002, the FASB and the IASB reached an agreement, known as the Norwalk Agreement, in which both standard setters formalized their commitment to develop "as quickly as practicable" a common set of accounting standards. This process, commonly referred to as *convergence* or *harmonization* of U.S. GAAP and IFRS, involves removing existing differences between the two sets of accounting standards and working together on future accounting standards. The FASB and the IASB are currently involved in several joint standard setting projects aimed at reducing the differences between U.S. GAAP and IFRS. The FASB chairman has publicly stated that convergence may take until 2013 to 2018.

The SEC has long supported (as long ago as 1988) the development of an internationally acceptable set of accounting standards, and it publicly supported the Norwalk Agreement. In 2005, SEC Chief Accountant Don Nicolaison established a plan for the use of IFRS in the United States. In 2007, the SEC allowed foreign companies who trade on U.S. stock exchanges to use IFRS without a reconciliation to U.S. GAAP. The SEC is currently considering allowing domestic companies to use IFRS.

The EU has been instrumental to the global acceptance of IFRS. In 2002, the EU decided to require its member countries to use IFRS by 2005. With the EU adoption of IFRS, the number of countries using IFRS more than doubled between 2003 and 2006. The EU adoption of IFRS was a pivotal event in the use of IFRS.

Why Do We Need IFRS? What Are the Advantages of IFRS?

Proponents of IFRS cite four major advantages. First, the use of IFRS should increase the comparability and transparency of financial information between companies that operate in different countries. Second, IFRS will allow companies and investors to more easily access foreign capital markets. This ease of access is expected to be a stimulus for economic growth. Third, IFRS should allow for a more efficient use of company resources as companies streamline their financial reporting processes. Finally, IFRS generally require more judgments than the strict application of rules. The use of judgment is seen as a means of preventing the financial abuses that have occurred under U.S. GAAP. Overall, the reduction in complexities from the use of a single, high-quality standard is expected to have major benefits for investors, companies, and the capital markets in general.

Are There Potential Problems with Adopting IFRS?

The movement toward IFRS presents many challenges as well as opportunities. First, many view U.S. GAAP as the best accounting standards in the world that have stood the test of time. Adopting the relatively new IFRS could be viewed as adopting a lower quality standard. Second, integrating world-wide cultural differences to ensure that

IFRS are applied and interpreted consistently is sure to be a difficult task. Third, companies will incur significant costs in creating new accounting policies, modifying their accounting systems, and training their employees with regard to IFRS. Fourth, IFRS generally require more judgment and less reliance on rules than U.S. GAAP. While this exercise of judgment can be a positive aspect of IFRS, many see the potential abuses of judgment as a key problem with IFRS. Finally, not all countries will use the same version of IFRS. Many countries that currently use IFRS have selectively modified (or carved out) certain standards with which they did not agree. Such modification will reduce comparability and increase complexity in financial reporting.

How Will IFRS Impact My Study of Accounting?

To aid in understanding the impact of IFRS on the cornerstones of financial accounting, review Exhibit A4-1. As you can see, while IFRS is expected to have far-reaching impacts on financial accounting, the cornerstones of accounting covered in this text will still provide you with a solid foundation for your study of accounting.

Exhibit A4-1

Effect of IFRS on Cornerstones of Financial Accounting

Chapter	Cornerstones Affected	Comments
1	Cornerstone 1-2: How to Prepare a Classified Balance Sheet Cornerstone 1-3: How to Prepare an Income Statement Cornerstone 1-4: How to Prepare a Statement of Retained Earnings	• The fundamental accounting equation (Assets = Liabilities + Stockholders' Equity) is the same under IFRS as under U.S. GAAP. • Terminology differences do exist. For example, on the balance sheet, stockholders' equity may be called "capital and reserves," and retained earnings may be called "accumulated profits and losses." On the income statement, sales may be referred to as "turnover." • The elements of the balance sheet are the same as under U.S. GAAP; however, IFRS do not specify a particular format. Therefore, the balance sheet classifications are often listed in the reverse order as compared to U.S. GAAP. For example, IFRS classify assets as either noncurrent or current. Noncurrent assets are typically presented first, followed by current assets. Additionally, stockholders' equity is often presented, followed by noncurrent liabilities and, then, current liabilities. • With regard to the income statement, IFRS do not prescribe a specific format (e.g., single-step or multiple-step). In addition, IFRS allow income statement items to be classified either by their nature or their function. U.S. GAAP classifies income statement items by their function (e.g., cost of goods sold). • IFRS do not specify the statement of retained earnings as a required financial statement. Instead, IFRS require the change in retained earnings be shown on the statement of changes in equity.
2	No Cornerstones Affected	• The IASB and the FASB are currently working on a joint conceptual framework that can serve to guide standard setters and help determine GAAP when more specific standards are not available. The outcome of this project is likely to change the existing conceptual framework found in U.S. GAAP. • Under IFRS, transactions are analyzed, journalized, and posted in the same manner as under U.S. GAAP.

(Continued)

Chapter	Cornerstones Affected	Comments
3	No Cornerstones Affected	• The adjustment process under IFRS is the same as the adjustment process under U.S. GAAP. • While revenue recognition concepts under IFRS are similar to U.S. GAAP, U.S. GAAP contains much more specific rules and guidance.
4	No Cornerstones Affected	• Internal control issues are company and financial accounting system-specific, and the issues would be similar in an international environment. However, the documentation and assessment requirements of Section 404 of the Sarbanes-Oxley Act (SOX) impose a much greater burden on U.S. companies compared to international companies. • The management, control, and accounting for cash are the same under IFRS as under U.S. GAAP.
5	No Cornerstones Affected	• The recognition of sales revenue under IFRS is generally similar to U.S. GAAP. However, the amount of guidance provided by IFRS as to when revenue should be recognized is considerably less and more principles-based than the amount of guidance provided by U.S. GAAP.
6	Cornerstone 6-6: How to Apply the LIFO Inventory Costing Method Cornerstone 6-8: How to Value Inventory at Lower of Cost or Market	• The purchase and sale of inventory is generally the same under IFRS as under U.S. GAAP. • IFRS do not allow the use of LIFO for determining the cost of inventory. • IFRS require the use of the lower of cost or market method, but it defines market value as net realizable value (the estimated selling price less costs of completion and disposal) instead of replacement cost.
7	Cornerstone 7-5: How to Record an Impairment of Property, Plant, and Equipment	• The impairment model under IFRS is a single-step process rather than the two-step process that is used in U.S. GAAP. • IFRS allow for companies to increase the value of their property, plant, equipment, and intangible assets up to fair value. This is not permitted under U.S. GAAP. • Under IFRS, research costs are expensed while development costs are capitalized if it is probable that the asset will generate future benefits.
8	No Cornerstones Affected	• IFRS refer to loss contingencies that are recognized in the financial statements as "provisions." Loss contingencies that are not recognized in the financial statements are referred to as "contingencies." • Similar to U.S. GAAP, IFRS recognize provisions when the contingent event is probable. However, IFRS define probable as "more likely than not" while U.S. GAAP defines probable as "likely." Therefore, more events will be recognized as provisions under IFRS.
9	No Cornerstones Affected	• The accounting for bonds payable is generally the same under IFRS as under U.S. GAAP.
10	No Cornerstones Affected	• Under IFRS, stockholders' equity is typically called "capital and reserves." The use of the term "reserves" has generally been discouraged under U.S. GAAP.
11	Cornerstone 11-1: How to Classify Business Activities	• The classification of certain business activities does differ under IFRS relative to U.S. GAAP. For example, IFRS allow companies to report the payment of dividends and interest as either an operating cash outflow or a financing cash outflow. In addition, the payment of income taxes can be reported as an investing or financing transaction if it can be identified with an investing or financing activity.
12	No Cornerstones Affected	• The analysis of financial statements is the same under IFRS as it is under U.S. GAAP.

Where Can I Go to Find Out More About IFRS?

IASB website:
www.iasb.org

American Institute of Certified Public Accountants' (AICPA) website for IFRS Resources:
www.IFRS.com

Ernst & Young IFRS page:
http://www.ey.com/GLOBAL/content.nsf/International/Assurance_-_IAS_Overview

Deloitte & Touch IFRS page:
http://www.iasplus.com

International Association for Accounting Education and Research:
http://www.iaaer.org/resources

PricewaterhouseCoopers IFRS page:
http://www.pwc.com/Extweb/service.nsf/docid/8E714A79E0DD6C9980256BBC00382351

KPMG IFRS page:
http://www.kpmgifrg.com

Multiple-Choice Exercises

A4-1 Which of the following best describes international financial reporting standards?

a. IFRS describes the generally accepted accounting principles that are currently used by all companies in the United States.
b. IFRS consist only of standards that have been issued since the IASB was formed in 2001.
c. IFRS are considered to be more concept-based than U.S. GAAP.
d. IFRS will be required to be used in the United States beginning in 2014.

A4-2 Which of the following statements is *true*?

a. The FASB has consistently resisted the adoption of IFRS in the United States for fear that it will lose its standard-setting authority.
b. The requirement to use IFRS by the European Union led to a significant increase in the global acceptance of IFRS.
c. IFRS has existed for nearly as long as U.S. GAAP; however, it only recently began to gain acceptance as a body of high-quality accounting standards.
d. The SEC is considering allowing foreign companies who trade stock on the U.S. stock exchanges to use IFRS.

A4-3 Convergence of U.S. GAAP and IFRS is best described as:

a. The replacement of U.S. GAAP by IFRS.
b. The replacement of IFRS by U.S. GAAP.
c. Changing existing U.S. GAAP so that any differences in IFRS will be insignificant.
d. Changing both existing U.S. GAAP and IFRS to reduce differences and developing new GAAP through a joint standard-setting process.

A4-4 Which of the following organizations has the responsibility to create IFRS?

a. Financial Accounting Standards Board
b. International Accounting Standards Committee
c. International Accounting Standards Board
d. Securities and Exchange Commission

A4-5 Which of the following is *not* an advantage of IFRS?

a. The use of IFRS should increase the comparability and transparency of financial information.
b. The use of IFRS will make it easier to access foreign capital markets.
c. IFRS requires more judgments than U.S. GAAP.
d. IFRS is less conservative than U.S. GAAP so net income under IFRS will generally be higher than net income under U.S. GAAP.

A4-6 Which of the following is *not* a disadvantage of IFRS?

a. IFRS will require significantly more training and education than required for U.S. GAAP.
b. The use of IFRS could be viewed as adopting a lower quality standard.
c. Due to cultural differences among countries, it will be difficult to ensure consistent application and interpretation of IFRS.
d. Different versions of IFRS exist that may cause confusion for users of financial statements.

A4-7 With regard to the presentation of financial information under IFRS, which of the following is *true*?

a. The terminology on the balance sheet and the income statement is the same under IFRS and U.S. GAAP.
b. Under IFRS, the element of the balance sheet are often presented in reverse order relative to U.S. GAAP, with noncurrent assets presented before current assets and stockholders' equity presented before liabilities.
c. Under IFRS, the elements of the income statement are often presented in reverse order, with expenses presented first followed by revenues.
d. IFRS do not require the presentation of a statement of cash flows.

A4-8 Which of the following inventory costing methods is *not* allowed under IFRS?

a. FIFO
b. Specific Identification
c. Average Cost
d. LIFO

A4-9 Which of the following is *true*?

a. IFRS allows property, plant, and equipment to be revalued upward if fair value is higher than historical cost.
b. IFRS contains more extensive guidance on revenue recognition than U.S. GAAP.
c. IFRS has a much more broad definition of cash than U.S. GAAP.
d. The accounting for research and development costs is identical under IFRS and U.S. GAAP.

A4-10 Which of the following is *true* with regard to contingent liabilities?

a. IFRS and U.S. GAAP use the same terminology to refers to contingent liabilities.
b. A contingent liability is recognized under IFRS when it is more likely than not that the contingent event will occur.
c. Fewer events will be recognized as contingent liabilities under IFRS than under U.S. GAAP.
d. Provisions are contingent liabilities that are not recognized in the financial statements.

Current Trends in Accounting

Accounting, like all of business, operates in a rapidly changing environment. As a student of accounting and a future business leader, you have a professional responsibility to be aware of these changes and their potential impact on your company. To assist you in this process, we have supplied a brief summary of four "current trends" in accounting that may greatly impact not only the accounting profession, but also the general business environment. We encourage you to follow developments in these areas through your own research in the financial media.

The Codification

Generally accepted accounting principles (GAAP) are the common set of rules and conventions that have been developed by several different organizations over many years to guide the preparation of financial statements. As an accountant, it is critical that you have a good understanding of and the ability to research GAAP to determine an appropriate solution to an accounting issue. However, the documents that comprise GAAP vary in format, completeness, structure and, in some cases, are inconsistent with each other. Because of the lack of a consistent and logical structure for GAAP, determining the "right" answer to an accounting issue is often a difficult and time-consuming task. In response to these concerns, the Financial Accounting Standards Board (FASB) developed the Accounting Standards Codification (or simply, the *Codification*).

The Codification is an electronic database that integrates and topically organizes the more than 2,000 documents that comprise GAAP. For the first time, all of the authoritative literature that makes up GAAP will be located in one place. The Codification does not change GAAP; instead, it restructures GAAP and changes the way that it is documented, presented, and updated. As you study accounting and attempt to learn the intricacies of GAAP, the Codification will prove an invaluable resource. The Codification is expected to become authoritative in July 2009 and can be accessed at http://asc.fasb.org/home.

Conceptual Framework

GAAP rests on a conceptual framework that provides a logical structure and direction to financial accounting and reporting and supports the development of a consistent set of accounting standards. However, the conceptual framework has often been criticized as being internally inconsistent and as providing incomplete recognition and measurement guidance. Given these criticisms, the FASB and the International Accounting Standards Board (IASB) have decided to revisit the framework. Their goal is to refine and update the conceptual framework so that it can serve as a fundamental basis for future accounting standards. In addition, these efforts should also promote the convergence or harmonization of U.S. GAAP and international financial reporting standards (IFRS). A final document relating to the first phase of this conceptual framework project is expected to be issued in the second half of 2009.

In the revised conceptual framework, the FASB and the IASB have identified two fundamental characteristics that useful information should possess—relevance and faithful representation. The application of these criteria determines which economic events should be shown in the financial statements and how best to record these events. *Relevant* accounting information is capable of making a difference in user decisions by helping the user predict future events (predictive value) or by providing feedback about prior expectations (confirmatory value). Accounting information should also be a *faithful representation* of the real-world economic event that it represents. While faithful representation encompasses many of the qualities that the previous conceptual framework included as aspects of reliability (e.g., neutrality), the importance of accounting in faithfully representing real-world phenomena, regardless of its form, has been elevated. (This is often referred to as "substance over form.") It should be noted that the increased emphasis on relevance and faithful representation is viewed by some as opening the door to the increased use of fair value measurements in accounting.

In addition to the fundamental characteristics, four enhancing characteristics—comparability, verifiability, timeliness, and understandability—have been identified. These enhancing characteristics are considered complementary to the fundamental characteristics, and their presence should help determine the degree of the information's usefulness. The first enhancing characteristic is *comparability,* which includes consistency. Comparability is normally achieved when different companies use the same accounting methods; it is considered to be a goal of useful information. Consistency—the application of the same accounting principles by a single company over time—is seen as a means of achieving comparability. Second, *verifiability* (when independent parties agree that the information is free from error or bias) enhances the fundamental characteristic of faithful representation. That is, when multiple independent observers can reach a general consensus, there is an implication that the information faithfully represents the economic event being measured. A third enhancing characteristic is *timeliness.* Information is timely if it is available to users before it loses its ability to influence decisions. Finally, *understandability* presumes that users have a reasonable knowledge of accounting and business activities.

Two constraints to these qualitative characteristics help to further clarify what accounting information should be disclosed in the financial statements. First, the benefit received from accounting information should be greater than the cost of providing that information. This is known as the *cost constraint* or the *cost vs. benefit constraint.* Second, useful information should be **material**; that is, the information should be capable of influencing a decision. Exhibit A5-1 illustrates this revised conceptual framework.

Use of Fair Values

A fundamental principle used in the measurement and recording of business activities is the historical cost principle (see Chapter 2). It should be noted that the financial statements contain various other measurement bases as well (e.g., fair value, net realizable value, and amortized cost). The advantage of historical cost over these alternative measurement methods was that historical cost produces relatively more objective and verifiable measurements. While fair value measurements have existed in GAAP for quite some time, the use of fair value measurements has received increasing emphasis over the last several years. In many areas (e.g., the accounting for investments as discussed in Chapter 4), fair values have become the primary means by which to measure and report certain assets and liabilities as users seek a more relevant and faithful representation of economic events. With the recent economic troubles, considerable media attention has been focused on how the use of fair value (often

Qualitative Characteristics of Accounting Information

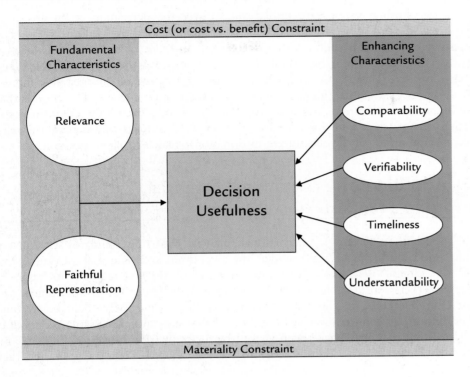

referred to as *mark-to-market accounting*) exacerbated the problems in the credit markets. Therefore, a fundamental understanding of fair value is important in both the current economic debate as well as the future development of accounting standards.

Fair value accounting is a way to measure assets and liabilities using current market prices (which are generally considered to be more relevant) instead of historical transaction prices. The objective of fair value accounting for assets and liabilities is to determine a price that would be received if an asset were sold or paid if a liability was settled (commonly referred to as an *exit price*). However, the determination of fair value is not always straightforward and can rest on various assumptions, or inputs. To increase consistency and comparability in these various fair value measurements, the FASB developed a "fair value hierarchy" that encourages the use of quoted market prices in *active* markets for *identical* assets or liabilities (referred to as *Level 1* inputs). In the absence of Level 1 inputs, the fair value hierarchy permits the application of valuation techniques that use either quoted prices in *active* or *inactive* markets for *identical* or *similar* assets and liabilities or observable inputs other than quoted prices (Level 2 inputs). Finally, if Level 1 and Level 2 inputs are both unavailable, unobservable inputs, such as the company's own economic analysis of the asset or liability, may be used (Level 3 inputs). Notice that the subjectivity of the fair value measurement increases (and the objectivity decreases) as one progresses through the fair value hierarchy.

With the high profile failure of Lehman Brothers and the large bank bailouts around the world, media attention has focused on fair value accounting as a reason for the severity of this credit crisis. Many have even called for the suspension of fair value accounting! So, what is the proper role of fair value in the credit crisis? In short, with the depressed stock market, many financial institutions have been left with assets (securities) that have declined sharply in value. In many cases, the most recent market price for these assets was not from an "orderly" transaction but from a forced "fire-sale" at greatly reduced prices. However, using Level 1 inputs, these financial institutions have been forced to write down these assets and take large losses based on information that they believe is not truly representative of the assets' fair values. Because of such write-downs, financial institutions have less capital available to lend, which leads to more business failures and further write-downs. Therefore, fair value measurements are blamed for causing a downward spiral in the credit markets and the overall economy.

The accounting response to public outcry over the deepening credit crisis has been to allow more subjective fair value measurements based on Level 3 inputs. The underlying basis for this action is that the market for many of these assets is inactive and, therefore, the current observable transaction price was not indicative of a true transaction price. This action opens the door for greater use of unobservable inputs, and, all things being equal, higher fair value measurements of assets. The hope is that these higher asset valuations will help stop the downward spiral in the credit markets. Whether or not the use of these unobservable (Level 3) inputs will increase the relevance and usefulness of the accounting information remains an open question.

U.S. Adoption of International Financial Reporting Standards

As discussed in Appendix 4, international financial reporting standards are quickly gaining global acceptance, and under the Securities and Exchange Commission (SEC) "roadmap" issued in 2008, U.S. adoption of IFRS is targeted to begin in 2014. However, considerable uncertainty exists as to whether the United States will adopt IFRS according to this plan. For example, SEC Chair Mary Schapiro's comments during her confirmation hearings that she would "not necessarily feel bound by the existing roadmap" have been viewed by many that the move to IFRS may be slower than expected. In addition, FASB Chairman Robert Herz has indicated that convergence of U.S. GAAP with IFRS would not occur for 10 to 15 years, which considerably lengthens the timeframe initially set by the SEC. However, Chairman Herz has indicated that full convergence should not delay the United States from adopting IFRS in the next three to five years. Clearly, U.S. progress toward adoption of IFRS will certainly be a major issue worth tracking for some time to come.

Glossary

A

Accelerated depreciation A generic term to describe depreciation computed using one of several depreciation methods (e.g., declining balance depreciation method) that allocate a larger amount of an asset's cost to the early years of its life.

Account A record of increases and decreases in each of the basic elements of the financial statements (each of the company's asset, liability, stockholders' equity, revenue, expense, gain, and loss items).

Account payable An obligation that arises when a business purchases goods or services on credit.

Account receivable Money due from another business or individual as payment for services performed or goods delivered. Payment is typically due in 30 to 60 days and does not involve a formal note between the parties nor does it include interest.

Accounting The process of identifying, measuring, recording, and communicating financial information about a company's activities so decision makers can make informed decisions.

Accounting cycle The procedures that a company uses to transform the results of its business activities into financial statements.

Accounting entity An organization that has an identity separate and apart from that of its owners and managers and for which accounting records are kept and financial statements are issued.

Accounting system The methods and records used to identify, measure, record, and communicate financial information about a business.

Accrual accounting See *accrual-basis accounting*

Accrual-basis accounting A method of accounting in which revenues are generally recorded when earned (rather than when cash is received) and expenses are matched to the periods in which they help produce revenues (rather than when cash is paid).

Accrued expenses Previously unrecorded expenses that have been incurred, but not yet paid in cash.

Accrued payables A type of payable that represents the completed portion of activities that are in process at the end of a period and that is recognized by an adjusting entry rather than when goods or services change hands.

Accrued revenues Previously unrecorded revenues that have been earned but for which no cash has yet been received.

Accumulated depreciation The total amount of depreciation expense that has been recorded for an asset since the asset was acquired. It is reported on the balance sheet as a contra-asset.

Acquisition cost Any expenditure necessary to acquire a fixed asset and to prepare the asset for use.

Adjusted trial balance An updated trial balance that reflects the changes to account balances as the result of adjusting entries.

Adjusting entries Journal entries that are made at the end of an accounting period to record the completed portion of partially completed transactions.

Aging method A method in which bad debt expense is estimated indirectly by determining the ending balance desired in the allowance for doubtful accounts and then computing the necessary adjusting entry to achieve this balance; the amount of this adjusting entry is also the amount of bad debt expense.

Allowance for Doubtful Accounts A contra-asset account that is established to "store" the estimate of uncollectible accounts until specific accounts are identified as uncollectible.

Amortization The process whereby companies systematically allocate the cost of their intangible operating assets as an expense among the accounting periods in which the asset is used and the benefits are received.

Annuity A series of equal cash flows at regular intervals.

Articles of incorporation A document that authorizes the creation of the corporation, setting forth its name, purpose, and the names of the incorporators.

Asset efficiency ratios (operating ratios) Ratios that measure how efficiently a company uses its assets.

Asset turnover ratio A ratio that measures the efficiency with which a corporation's assets (usually accounts receivable or inventory) are used to produce sales revenues.

Assets Economic resources representing expected future economic benefits controlled by the business (e.g., cash, accounts receivable, inventory, land, buildings, equipment, and intangible assets).

Audit report The auditor's opinion as to whether the company's financial statements are fairly stated in accordance with generally accepted accounting principles (GAAP).

Authorized shares The maximum number of shares a company may issue in each class of stock.

Available-for-sale securities Investments in equity and debt securities of other companies that management intends to sell in the future, but not necessarily in the near term.

Average age of fixed assets A rough estimate of the age of fixed assets that can be computed by dividing accumulated depreciation by depreciation expense.

Average cost method An inventory costing method that allocates the cost of goods available for sale between ending inventory and cost of goods sold based on a weighted average cost per unit.

Average days to sell inventory An estimate of the number of days it takes a company to sell its inventory. It is found by dividing 365 days by the inventory turnover ratio.

B

Bad debt expense The expense that results from receivables that are not paid.

Balance sheet A financial statement that reports the resources (assets) owned by a company and the claims against those resources (liabilities and stockholders' equity) at a specific point in time.

Bank reconciliation The process of reconciling any differences between a company's accounting records and the bank's accounting records.

Bond A type of note that requires the issuing entity to pay the face value of the bond to the holder when it matures and, usually, periodic interest at a specified rate.

Book value (carrying value) The value of an asset or liability as it appears on the balance sheet. Book value is calculated as the cost of the asset or liability minus the balance in its related contra-account (e.g., cost of equipment less accumulated depreciation; notes payable less discount on notes payable).

Business process risks Threats to the internal processes of a company.

C

Callable bonds Bonds that give the borrower the right to pay off (or call) the bonds prior to their due date. The borrower typically "calls" debt when the interest rate being paid is much higher than the current market conditions.

Capital A company's assets less its liabilities. Capital is also known as stockholders' equity.

Capital expenditures Expenditures to acquire long-term assets or extend the life, expand the productive capacity, increase the efficiency, or improve the quality of existing long-term assets.

Capital lease A noncancelable agreement that is in substance a purchase of the leased asset.

Cash equivalents Short-term, highly liquid investments that are readily convertible to cash and have original maturities of three months or less.

Cash flow adequacy ratio The cash flow adequacy ratio provides a measure of the company's ability to meet its debt obligations and is calculated as: Cash Flow Adequacy = Free Cash Flow ÷ Average Amount of Debt Maturing over the Next Five Years.

Cash flows from financing activities Any cash flow related to obtaining resources from creditors or owners, which includes the issuance and repayment of debt, common and preferred stock transactions, and the payment of dividends.

Cash flows from investing activities The cash inflows and outflows that relate to acquiring and disposing of operating assets, acquiring and selling investments (current and long-term), and lending money and collecting loans.

Cash flows from operating activities Any cash flows directly related to earning income, including cash sales and collections of accounts receivable as well as cash payments for goods, services, salaries, and interest.

Cash ratio A short-term liquidity ratio that is calculated as: (Cash + Short-Term Investments) ÷ Current Liabilities.

Cash over and short An account that records the discrepancies between deposited amounts of actual cash received and the total of the cash register tape.

Cash-basis accounting A method of accounting in which revenue is recorded when cash is received, regardless of when it is actually earned. Similarly, an expense is recorded when cash is paid, regardless of when it is actually incurred. Cash-basis accounting does not tie recognition of revenues and expenses to the actual business activity but rather to the exchange of cash.

Chart of accounts The list of accounts used by a company.

Closing entries The final step of the accounting cycle that transfers the effects of revenues, expenses, and dividends to the stockholders' equity account, Retained Earnings. Closing entries also serve to reduce the balances in revenues, expenses, and dividends to zero so that these accounts are ready to accumulate the business activities of the next accounting period.

Common-size statements Financial statements that express each financial statement line item in percentage terms.

Common stock The basic ownership interest in a corporation. Owners of common stock have the right to vote in the election of the board of directors, share in the profits and dividends of the company, keep the same percentage of ownership if new stock is issued (preemptive right), and share in the assets in liquidation in proportion to their holdings.

Comparability One of the four qualitative characteristics that useful information should possess. Information has comparability if it allows comparisons to be made between companies.

Compound interest A method of calculating the time value of money in which interest is earned on the previous periods' interest.

Conservatism principle A principle which states that when more than one equally acceptable accounting method exists, the method that results in the lower assets and revenues or higher liabilities and expenses should be selected.

Consistency One of the four qualitative characteristics that useful information should possess. Consistency refers to the application of the same accounting principles by a single company over time.

Contingent liability An obligation whose amount or timing is uncertain and depends on future events. For example, a firm may be contingently liable for damages under a lawsuit that has yet to be decided by the courts.

Continuity (or going concern) assumption One of the four basic assumptions that underlie accounting that assumes a company will continue to operate long enough to carry out its existing commitments.

Contra accounts Accounts that have a balance that is opposite of the balance in the related account.

Contract rate See *interest rate*

Control activities The policies and procedures that top management establishes to help insure that its objectives are met.

Control environment The collection of environmental factors that influence the effectiveness of control procedures such as the philosophy and operating style of management, the personnel policies and practices of the business, and the overall integrity, attitude, awareness, and actions of everyone in the business concerning the importance of control.

Convertible bonds Bonds that allow the bondholder to convert the bond into another security—typically common stock.

Copyright An intangible asset that grants the holder the right to publish, sell, or control a literary or artistic work. The legal life is the life of author plus 70 years.

Corporate charter See *articles of incorporation*

Corporation A company chartered by the state to conduct business as an "artificial person" and owned by one or more stockholders.

Cost of goods available for sale The sum of the cost of beginning inventory and the cost of purchases.

Cost of goods sold An expense that represents the outflow of resources caused by the sale of inventory. This is often computed as the cost of goods available for sale less the cost of ending inventory.

Cost vs. benefit A constraint on the qualities that useful information should possess which encompasses the idea that the benefit received from accounting information should be greater than the costs of providing the information.

Coupon rate See *interest rate*

Credit cards A card that authorizes the holder to make purchases up to some limit from specified retailers. Credits cards are a special form of factoring in which the issuer of the credit card pays the seller the amount of each sale less a service charge and then collects the full amount of the sale from the buyer at some later date.

Credit sales method A method for determining bad debt expense directly by multiplying credit sales by an estimate of the percentage of the current period's credit sales that will eventually become uncollectible.

Credit The right side of a T account; alternatively, credit may refer to the act of entering an amount on the right side of an account.

Creditor The person to whom money is owed.

Cross sectional analysis A type of analysis that compares one corporation to another corporation and to industry averages.

Cumulative dividend preference A provision that requires the eventual payment of all preferred dividends—both dividends in arrears and current dividends—to preferred stockholders before any dividends are paid to common stockholders.

Current assets Cash and other assets that are reasonably expected to be converted into cash within one year or one operating cycle, whichever is longer.

Current dividend preference A provision that requires that current dividends must be paid to preferred stockholders before any dividends are paid to common stockholders.

Current liabilities Obligations that require a firm to pay cash or another current asset, create a new current liability, or provide goods or services within one year or one operating cycle, whichever is longer.

Current ratio A measure of liquidity that is computed as: Current Assets ÷ Current Liabilities.

D

Date of record The date on which a stockholder must own one or more shares of stock in order to receive the dividend.

Debenture bonds Another name for unsecured bonds.

Debit The left side of a T account; alternatively, debit may refer to the act of entering an amount on the left side of an account.

Debit card A card that authorizes a bank to make an immediate electronic withdrawal (debit) from the holder's bank account and a corresponding deposit to another party's account.

Debt management ratios A type of ratio that provides information on two aspects of debt: (1) the relative mix of debt and equity financing (often referred to as its capital structure) and (2) the corporation's ability to meet its debt obligations through operations because interest and principal payments must be made as scheduled, or a company can be declared bankrupt.

Debt-to-equity ratio A measure of the proportion of capital provided by creditors relative to that provided by stockholders. This ratio is calculated as: Total Liabilities ÷ Total Equity.

Debt-to-total assets ratio A measure of the proportion of capital provided by creditors. This ratio is calculated as: Total Liabilities ÷ Total Assets.

Declaration date The date on which a corporation announces its intention to pay a dividend on common stock.

Declining balance depreciation method An accelerated depreciation method that produces a declining amount of depreciation expense each period by multiplying the declining book value of an asset by a constant depreciation rate. Declining balance depreciation expense for each period of an asset's useful life equals the declining balance rate times the asset's book value (cost less accumulated depreciation) at the beginning of the period.

Deferred (or prepaid) expenses Asset arising from the payment of cash which has not been used or consumed by the end of the period.

Deferred (or unearned) revenues Liability arising from the receipt of cash for which revenue has not yet been earned.

Depletion The process of allocating the cost of a natural resource to each period in which the resource is removed from the earth.

Deposit in transit An amount received and recorded by a company, but which has not been recorded by the bank in time to appear on the current bank statement.

Depreciable cost Depreciable cost is calculated as the cost of the asset less its residual (or salvage) value. This amount will be depreciated (expensed) over the asset's useful life.

Depreciation The process whereby companies systematically allocate the cost of their tangible operating assets (other than land) as an expense in each period in which the asset is used.

Depreciation expense The amount of depreciation recorded on the income statement.

Depreciation method A standardized calculation for determining periodic depreciation expense.

Direct method A method of computing net cash flow from operating activities by adjusting each item on the income statement by the changes in the related current asset or liability accounts. Typical cash flow categories reported are cash collected from customers, cash paid to suppliers, cash paid to employees, cash paid for interest, and cash paid for taxes.

Discount period The reduced payment period associated with purchase discounts.

Dividend Amounts paid periodically by a corporation to its stockholders as a return of their invested capital. Dividends represent a distribution of retained earnings, not an expense.

Dividend payout ratio A ratio that measures the proportion of a corporation's profits that are returned to the stockholders immediately as dividends. It is calculated as: Common Dividends ÷ Net Income.

Dividend yield ratio A ratio that measures the rate at which dividends provide a return to stockholders, by comparing dividends with the market price of a share of stock. It is calculated as: Dividends per Common Share ÷ Closing Market Price per Share for the Year.

Dividends in arrears Cumulative preferred stock dividends remaining unpaid for one or more years are considered to be in arrears.

Double-entry accounting A type of accounting in which the two-sided effect that every transaction has on the accounting equation is recorded in the accounting system.

Dupont analysis A type of analysis that recognizes that ROE can be broken down into three important components—net profit margin, asset turnover, and leverage.

E

Earned One of two requirements for the recognition of revenue. Revenues are considered "earned" when the earnings process is substantially complete. This typically happens when the goods are delivered or the service is provided.

Earnings per share (EPS) A ratio that measures the income available for common stockholders on a per-share basis. EPS is calculated as net income less preferred dividends divided by the average number of common shares outstanding.

Economic entity assumption One of the four basic assumptions that underlie accounting that assumes each company is accounted for separately from its owners.

Effective interest rate See *market rate*

Effective interest rate method A method of interest amortization that is based on compound interest calculations.

Equity See *stockholders' equity*

Events Events make up the multitude of activities in which companies engage. External events result from exchange between the company and another outside entity, and internal events result from a company's own actions that do not involve other companies.

Expenses The cost of assets used, or the liabilities created, in the operation of the business.

F

Face value The amount of money that a borrower must repay at maturity; also called par value or principal.

Factor A method of handling receivables in which the seller receives an immediate cash payment reduced by the factor's fees. The factor, the buyer of the receivables, acquires the right to collect the receivables and the risk of uncollectibility. In a typical factoring arrangement, the sellers of the receivables have no continuing responsibility for their collection.

Financial accounting Accounting and reporting to satisfy the outside demand (primarily investors and creditors) for accounting information.

Financial Accounting Standards Board (FASB) The primary accounting standard-setter in the United States which has been granted this power to set standards by the Securities and Exchange Commission.

Financial statements A set of standardized reports in which the detailed transactions of a company's activities are reported and summarized so they can be communicated to decision-makers.

Financing cycle The elapsed time between the receipt of financial resources from owners and creditors and the repayment of the original amounts received.

First-in, first-out (FIFO) method An inventory costing system in which the earliest (oldest) purchases (the first in) are assumed to be the first sold (the first out) and the more recent purchases are in ending inventory.

Fiscal year An accounting period that runs for one year.

Fixed asset turnover ratio A ratio that indicates how efficiently a company uses its fixed assets. This ratio is calculated by dividing net sales by average fixed assets.

F.O.B. destination A shipping arrangement in which ownership of inventory passes when the goods are delivered to the buyer.

F.O.B. shipping point A shipping arrangement in which ownership of inventory passes from the seller to the buyer at the shipping point.

Form 10-K The annual report on Form 10-K provides a comprehensive overview of the corporation's business and financial condition and includes *audited* financial statements. Although similarly named, the annual report on Form 10-K is distinct from the "annual report to shareholders," which a corporation must send to its shareholders when it holds an annual meeting to elect directors. For larger filers the 10-K must be filed within 60 days of their fiscal year end.

Form 10-Q The Form 10-Q includes *unaudited* financial statements and provides a continuing view of the corporation's financial position during the year. The report must be filed for each of the first three fiscal quarters of the corporation's fiscal year. For larger filers this must be done within 40 days of the end of the quarter.

Form 8-K The "current report" companies must file with the SEC to announce major events that are important to investors and creditors.

Franchise An exclusive right to conduct a certain type of business in some particular geographic area.

Free cash flow The cash flow that a company is able to generate after considering the maintenance or expansion of its assets (capital expenditures) and the payment of dividends. Free cash flow is calculated as Net Cash Flow from Operating Activities – Capital Expenditures – Cash Dividends.

Freight-in The transportation costs that are normally paid by the buyer under F.O.B. shipping point terms.

Freight-out The transportation costs that the seller is usually responsible for paying under F.O.B. destination shipping terms.

Full disclosure A policy that requires any information that would make a difference to financial statement users to be revealed.

Fundamental accounting equation Assets = Liabilities + Stockholders' Equity. The left side of the accounting equation shows the assets, or economic resources of a company. The right side of the accounting equation indicates who has a claim on the company's assets.

Future value Projections of future balances based on past and future cash flows and interest payments.

G

GAAP See *generally accepted accounting principles*

General ledger A collection of all the individual financial statement accounts that a company uses in its financial statements.

Generally accepted accounting principles (GAAP) A common set of rules and conventions that have been developed to guide the preparation of financial statements.

Goodwill An unidentifiable intangible asset that arises from factors such as customer satisfaction, quality products, skilled employees, and business location.

Gross margin (gross profit) A key performance measure that is computed as sales revenue less cost of goods sold.

Gross profit ratio A measurement of the proportion of each sales dollar that is available to pay other expenses and provide profit for owners; it is computed by dividing gross margin by net sales.

H

Historical cost principle A principle that requires the activities of a company to be initially measured at their cost—the exchange price at the time the activity occurs.

Horizontal analysis A type of analysis in which each financial statement line item is expressed as a percent of the base year (typically the first year shown).

I

Impairment A permanent decline in the future benefits or service potential of an asset.

Income before taxes Income from operations plus the amount of other revenues and gains less the amount of other expenses and losses.

Income from operations Gross margin less operating expenses. This represents the results of the core operations of the business.

Income statement A financial statement that reports the profitability of a business over a specific period of time.

Income summary A temporary account to which all revenues and expenses are closed and which is itself closed to retained earnings.

Indirect method A method that computes operating cash flows by adjusting net income for items that do not affect cash flows.

Intangible assets Assets that provide a benefit to a company over a number of years but lack physical substance. Examples of intangible assets include patents, copyrights, trademarks, and goodwill.

Interest The excess of the total amount of money paid to a lender over the amount borrowed.

Interest amortization The process used to determine the amount of interest to be recorded in each of the periods a liability is outstanding.

Interest period is the time interval between interest calculations.

Interest rate A percentage of the principal that must be paid in order to have use of the principal. It is multiplied by the beginning-of-period balance to yield the amount of interest for the period.

Internal control system The policies and procedures established by top management and the board of directors to provide reasonable assurance that the company's objectives are being met in three areas: (1) effectiveness and efficiency of operations, (2) reliability of financial reporting, and (3) compliance with applicable laws and regulations.

International Accounting Standards Board (IASB) An independent, privately-funded accounting standard-setting body with the goal of developing a single set of high-quality accounting standards that result in transparent and comparable information reported in general purpose financial statements.

International Financial Reporting Standards (IFRS) A general term that describes an international set of generally accepted accounting standards.

Inventory Products held for resale that are classified as current assets on the balance sheet.

Inventory costing methods Various systematic methods of determining the cost of ending inventory, each based on a different assumption about the composition of the ending inventory in terms of the different prices paid for goods over time.

Inventory turnover ratio A ratio that describes how quickly inventory is purchased (or produced) and sold. It is calculated as cost of goods sold divided by average inventory.

Involuntary disposal A type of disposal that occurs when assets are lost or destroyed through theft, acts of nature, or by accident.

Issued shares The number of shares actually sold to stockholders.

J

Journal A chronological record showing the debit and credit effects of transactions on a company.

Journal entry A record of a transaction that is made in a journal so that the entire effect of the transaction is contained in one place.

Junk bonds Unsecured bonds where the risk of the borrower failing to make the payments is relatively high.

L

Last-in, first-out (LIFO) method An inventory costing system that allocates the cost of goods available for sale between ending inventory and cost of goods sold based on the assumption that the most recent purchases (the last in) are the first to be sold (the first out).

Lease An agreement that enables a company to use property without legally owning it.

Ledger See *general ledger*

Leverage The use of borrowed capital to produce more income than needed to pay the interest on a debt.

Liabilities Probable future sacrifices of economic benefits; liabilities usually require the payment of cash, the transfer of assets other than cash, or the performance of services.

LIFO reserve The amount that inventory would increase (or decrease) if the company had used FIFO.

Liquidating dividends Dividends that return paid-in capital to stockholders; liquidating dividends occur when retained earnings has been reduced to zero.

Liquidity A company's ability to pay obligations as they become due.

Long-term debt-to-equity ratio A ratio that provides information on the proportion of capital provided by this type of debt and by stockholders. It is calculated as: Long-Term Debt (including current portion) ÷ Total Equity.

Long-term debt-to-total assets ratio A measure of the proportion of capital provided by long-term creditors which is calculated as: Long-Term Debt (including current portion) ÷ Total Assets.

Long-term investments Investments that the company expects to hold for longer than one year. This includes land or buildings that a company is not currently using in operations, as well as debt and equity securities.

Long-term liabilities The obligations of the company that will require payment beyond one year or the operating cycle, whichever is longer.

Lower of cost or market (LCM) rule A rule that requires a company to reduce the carrying value of its inventory to its market value if the market value is lower than its cost.

M

Management's Discussion and Analysis (MD&A) A section of the annual report that provides a discussion and explanation of various items reported in the financial statements. Management uses this section to highlight favorable and unfavorable trends and significant risks facing the company.

Market rate The market rate of interest demanded by creditors.

Matching principle A principle that requires an expense to be recorded and reported in the same period as the revenue that it helped generate.

Material The idea that accounting information included in financial statements should be capable of influencing a decision.

Maturity The date on which a borrower agrees to pay the creditor the face (or par) value.

Merchandise inventory The inventory held by merchandisers.

Monetary unit assumption One of the four basic assumptions that underlie accounting that requires that a company account for and report its financial results in monetary terms (e.g., U.S. dollar, euro, Japanese yen).

Mortgage bonds Bonds that are secured by real estate.

N

Natural resources Resources, such as coal deposits, oil reserves, and mineral deposits, that are physically consumed as they are used by a company and that can generally be replaced or restored only by an act of nature.

Net income The excess of a company's revenue over its expenses during a period of time.

Net loss The excess of a company's expenses over its revenues during a period of time.

Net profit margin percentage A measure of the proportion of each sales dollar that is profit, determined by dividing net income by net sales.

Net sales revenue Computed as gross sales revenue minus sales returns and allowances, as well as sales discounts.

Noncash investing and financing activities Investing and financing activities that take place without affecting cash. For example, a company may choose to acquire an operating asset (e.g., building) by issuing long-term debt.

Non-Sufficient Funds (NSF) check A check that has been returned to the depositor because funds in the issuer's account are not sufficient to pay the check (also called a "bounced" check).

Nontrade receivables Receivables that arise from transactions not involving inventory (e.g., interest receivable or cash advances to employees).

No-par stock Stock without a par value.

Normal balance The type of balance expected of an account based on its effect on the fundamental accounting equation. Assets, expenses and dividends have normal debit balances while liabilities, stockholders' equity, and revenues have normal credit balances.

Note(s) payable A payable that arises when a business borrows money or purchases goods or services from a company that requires a formal agreement or contract.

Notes receivable Receivables that generally specify an interest rate and a maturity date at which any interest and principal must be repaid.

Notes to the financial statements (or footnotes) Notes that clarify and expand upon the information presented in the financial statements.

O

Operating assets The long-lived assets that are used by the company in the normal course of operations.

Operating cash flow ratio A ratio that looks at the ability of operations to generate cash, which recognizes the more general concept that current obligations will be paid through operations (after all, selling inventory and collecting receivables is a big part of operations). This ratio is calculated as Cash Flows from Operating Activities ÷ Current Liabilities.

Operating cycle The average time that it takes a company to purchase goods, resell the goods, and collect the cash from customers.

Operating expenses The expenses a company incurs in selling goods or providing services and in managing the business.

Operating lease The most common form of lease in which the lessor (the legal owner of the asset) retains the risks and obligations of ownership, while the lessee uses the asset during the term of the lease.

Operating margin percentage A measure of the profitability of a company's operations in relation to its sales that is calculated as Income from Operations ÷ Net Sales.

Organizational costs Significant costs such as legal fees, stock issue costs, accounting fees, and promotional fees that a company may incur when it is formed.

Outstanding check A check that has been issued and recorded by the business but that has not been "cashed" by the recipient of the check.

Outstanding shares The number of issued shares actually in the hands of stockholders.

P

Paid-in capital in excess of par The excess of the total amount paid for common or preferred stock over its par value.

Par value For stock, it is an arbitrary monetary amount printed on each share of stock that establishes a minimum price for the stock when issued, but does not determine its market value. For debt, par value is the amount of money the borrower agrees to repay at maturity.

Participating dividend preference A provision that stockholders of participating preferred shares receive, in addition to the stated dividend, a share of amounts available for distribution as dividends to other classes of stock.

Partnership A business owned jointly by two or more individuals.

Patent A type of intangible asset that grants the holder the right to manufacture, sell, or use a product. The legal life is 20 years from the date of the grant.

Payment date The date on which the dividend will actually be paid.

Payroll taxes Taxes that businesses must pay based on employee payrolls; these amounts are not withheld from employee pay, rather they are additional amounts that must be paid over and above gross pay.

Periodic inventory system An inventory system that records the cost of purchases as they occur (in an account separate from the inventory account), takes a physical count of inventory at the end of the period, and applies the cost of goods sold model to determine the balances of ending inventory and cost of goods sold. The inventory account reflects the correct inventory balance only at the end of each accounting period.

Permanent accounts Accounts of asset, liability, and stockholders' equity items whose balances are carried forward from the current accounting period to future accounting periods.

Perpetual inventory system An inventory system in which balances for inventory and cost of goods sold are continually (perpetually) updated with each sale or purchase of inventory. The accounts reflect the correct inventory and cost of goods sold balances throughout the period.

Petty cash A fund used to pay for small dollar amounts.

Posting The process of transferring information from journalized transactions to the general ledger.

Preferred stock A class of stock that generally does not give voting rights, but grants specific guarantees and dividend preferences.

Present value Determinations of present amounts based on expected future cash flows.

Principal The amount of money borrowed and promised to be repaid (usually with interest).

Prior period adjustment The correction of an error made in the financial statements of a prior period. The adjustment is entered as a direct adjustment to retained earnings.

Profitability ratios Ratios that measure two aspects of a corporation's profits: (1) those elements of operations that contribute to profit and (2) the relationship of profit to total investment and investment by stockholders.

Property, plant, and equipment The tangible, long-lived, productive assets used by a company in its operations to produce revenue. This includes land, buildings, machinery, manufacturing equipment, office equipment, and furniture.

Purchase allowance A situation in which the purchaser chooses to keep the merchandise if the seller is willing to grant a deduction (allowance) from the purchase price.

Purchase discounts Price reductions (usually expressed as a percentage of the purchase price) that companies offer their customers to encourage prompt payment.

Purchase returns The cost of merchandise returned to suppliers.

Purchases The cost of merchandise acquired for resale during the accounting period.

Q

Quick ratio A measure of a company's short-term liquidity that is calculated as follows: (Cash + Short-Term Investments + Receivables) ÷ Current Liabilities.

R

Ratio analysis An examination of financial statements conducted by preparing and evaluating a series of ratios.

Realized/realizable One of two requirements for revenue to be recognized. An item is realized, or realizable, if noncash resources (i.e., inventory) have been exchanged for cash or near cash (e.g., accounts receivable).

Receivable turnover ratio A ratio that indicates how many times accounts receivable is turned over each year. It is calculated as: Net Sales ÷ Average Accounts Receivable.

Recognition The act of recording transactions in the accounting system which involves determination of which events qualify to be recorded and, if they do, when they should be recorded.

Relevant One of the four qualitative characteristics that useful information should possess. Accounting information is said to be relevant if it is capable of making a difference in a business decision by helping users users predict future events or by providing feedback about prior expectations. Relevant information must also be provided in a timely manner.

Reliable One of the four qualitative characteristics that useful information should possess. To be reliable, information should be verifiable (independent parties agree that the information is free from error or bias), representationally faithful (the information accurately portrays what it is intended to portray), and neutral (free from bias).

Research and development (R&D) expense The cost of internal development of intangible assets that is expensed as incurred.

Residual value (salvage value) The amount of cash or trade-in consideration that the company expects to receive when an asset is retired from service.

Retained earnings (or deficit) The accumulated earnings (or losses) over the entire life of the corporation that have not been paid out in dividends.

Return on assets A ratio that measures the profit earned by a corporation through use of all its capital, or the total of the investment by both creditors and owners. Return on assets is calculated as: [Net Income + Interest (1 – Tax Rate)]/Average Total Assets.

Return on common equity ratio A ratio that is basically the same as the return on equity ratio. It is calculated as: Net Income/(Total Equity + Preferred Stock + Paid-In Capital − Preferred Stock).

Return on equity A ratio that measures the profit earned by a firm through the use of capital supplied by stockholders. Return on equity is computed as net income divided by average equity.

Revenue The increase in assets that results from the sale of products or services.

Revenue expenditures Expenditures that do not increase the future economic benefits of the asset. These expenditures are expensed as they are incurred.

Revenue recognition principle A principle that requires revenue to be recognized or recorded in the period in which it is earned and the collection of cash is reasonably assured.

S

Safeguarding The physical protection of assets through, for example, fireproof vaults, locked storage facilities, keycard access, and anti-theft tags on merchandise.

Sales allowance A price reduction offered by the seller to induce the buyer to keep the goods when the goods are only slightly defective, are shipped late, or in some other way are rendered less valuable.

Sales discount A price reduction (usually expressed as a percentage of the selling price) that companies may offer to encourage prompt payment.

Sales returns Merchandise or goods returned by the customer to the seller.

Sales revenue Revenue resulting from the sale of goods or services.

Sales taxes Money collected from the customer for the governmental unit levying the tax.

Salvage value See *residual value*

Secured A term used for a bond that has some collateral pledged against the corporation's ability to pay.

Securities and Exchange Commission (SEC) The federal agency established by Congress to regulate securities markets and ensure effective public disclosure of accounting information. The SEC has the power to set accounting rules for publicly traded companies.

Securitization A process in which large businesses and financial institutions frequently package factored receivables as financial instruments or securities and sell them to investors.

Segregation of duties The idea that accounting and administrative duties should be performed by different individuals, so that no one person has access to the asset and prepares all the documents and records for an activity.

Service charges Fees charged by the bank for checking account services.

Shareholders See *stockholders*

Short-term liquidity ratios A type of ratio that compares some combination of current assets or operations to current liabilities.

Sole proprietorship A business owned by one person.

Specific identification method An inventory costing method that determines the cost of ending inventory and the cost of goods sold based on the identification of the actual units sold and in inventory. This method does not require an assumption about the flow of costs but actually assigns cost based on the specific flow of inventory.

Stated capital (legal capital) The amount of capital that, under law, cannot be returned to the corporation's owners unless the corporation is liquidated.

Stated rate See *interest rate*

Statement of cash flows A financial statement that provides relevant information about a company's cash receipts (inflows of cash) and cash payments (outflows of cash) during an accounting period.

Statement of retained earnings A financial statement that reports how much of the company's income was retained in the business and how much was distributed to owners for a period of time.

Stock dividend A dividend paid to stockholders in the form of additional shares of stock (instead of cash).

Stock repurchase payout ratio A ratio that addresses the distribution of company value and can be calculated directly as Common Stock Repurchase ÷ Net Income, or indirectly as Stock Repurchase Payout Ratio = Total Payout Ratio – Dividend Payout Ratio.

Stock split A stock issue that increases the number of outstanding shares of a corporation without changing the balances of its equity accounts.

Stock warrant The right granted by a corporation to purchase a specified number of shares of its capital stock at a stated price and within a stated time period.

Stockholder ratios Ratios such as earnings per share and return on common equity that provide information about the creation of value for shareholders.

Stockholders The owners of a corporation who own its shares in varying numbers.

Stockholders' equity The owners' claims against the assets of a corporation after all liabilities have been deducted.

Straight-line depreciation A depreciation method that allocates an equal amount of an asset's cost to depreciation expense for each year of the asset's useful life. Straight-line depreciation expense for each period is calculated by dividing the depreciable cost of an asset by the asset's useful life.

Strategic risks Possible threats to the organization's success in accomplishing its objectives that are external to the organization.

T

T-account A graphical representation of an account that gets its name because it resembles the capital letter T. A T-account is a two-column record that consists of an account title and two sides divided by a vertical line—the left side is called the debit side and the right side is called the credit side.

Temporary accounts The accounts of revenue, expense, and dividend items that are used to collect the activities of only one period.

Time period assumption One of the four basic assumptions that underlie accounting that allows the life of a company to be divided into artificial time periods so net income can be measured for a specific period of time (e.g., monthly, quarterly, annually).

Time series (or trend) analysis A type of analysis that compares a single corporation across time.

Time value of money The idea that a cash flow in the future is less valuable than a cash flow at present.

Times interest earned ratio A ratio that measures the excess of net income over interest to gauge a firm's ability to repay its debt. It is calculated as: Income from Operations ÷ Interest Expense.

Total payout ratio A ratio that adds stock repurchases to common dividends and compares this to net income. It is calculated as: Total Payout Ratio = (Common Dividends + Common Stock Repurchases)/Net Income.

Trade receivable An account receivable that is due from a customer purchasing inventory in the ordinary course of business.

Trademark An intangible asset that grants the holder the right to the exclusive use of a distinctive name, phrase, or symbol. The legal life is 20 years but it can be renewed indefinitely.

Trading securities Investments in equity or debt securities of other companies that management intends to sell in the near term. Trading securities are bought and sold frequently and typically are owned for under one month.

Transaction Any event, external or internal, that is recognized in the financial statements.

Transaction analysis The process of determining the economic effects of a transaction on the elements of the accounting equation.

Transportation-in See *freight-in*

Treasury stock Previously issued stock that is repurchased by the issuing corporation.

Trial balance A list of all active accounts and each account's debit or credit balance.

Turnover The average length of time required for assets to be consumed or replaced.

U

Unearned revenue A liability that occurs when a company receives payment for goods that will be delivered or services that will be performed in the future.

Units-of-production method A depreciation method that allocates the cost of an asset over its expected life in direct proportion to the actual use of the asset; depreciation expense is computed by multiplying an asset's depreciable cost by a usage ratio.

Unsecured A term used for bonds in which the lender is relying on the general credit of the borrowing corporation rather than on collateral.

Useful life The period of time over which the company anticipates deriving benefit from the use of the asset.

V

Vertical analysis A type of analysis that expresses each financial statement line item as a percent of the largest amount on the statement.

Voluntary disposal A type of disposal that occurs when a company determines that the asset is no longer useful; the disposal may occur at the end of the asset's useful life or at some other time.

W

Warranty A warranty is a guarantee to repair or replace defective goods during a period (ranging from a few days to several years) following the sale.

Weighted average cost method See *average cost method*

Withholding Businesses are required to withhold taxes from employees' earnings; standard withholdings include federal, state, and possibly city or county income taxes, as well as Social Security and Medicare. Employees may also have amounts withheld for such things as retirement accounts and health insurance.

Working capital A measure of liquidity computed as: Current Assets – Current Liabilities.

Worksheet An informal schedule that accountants use to assist them in organizing and preparing the information necessary to perform the end-of-period steps in the accounting cycle—namely the preparation of adjusting entries, financial statements, and closing entries.

Y

Yield The market rate of interest demanded by creditors; yield may differ from stated rate because the underwriter disagrees with the borrower as to the correct yield or because of changes in the economy or creditworthiness of the borrower between the setting of the stated rate and the date of issue.

Decision-Making & Analysis

Cornerstones